June 1989.

EIGH COLLEGE
The E

D1380925

Thankyou to you all and
wishing you continued success
in the future.

With love,
Belinda

86 0046885 9

WIGAN AND LEIGH COLLEGE

•BLOOMSBURY THEMATIC DICTIONARY OF QUOTATIONS

BLOOMSBURY

All rights reserved; no part of this publication may be
reproduced, stored in a retrieval system, or transmitted
in any form or by any means, electronic, mechanical,
photocopying or otherwise, without the prior
written permission of the Publishers.

First published 1988

Copyright © 1988 by Bloomsbury Publishing Limited
Bloomsbury Publishing Limited, 2 Soho Square,
London W1V 5DE

British Library Cataloguing in Publication Data

Bloomsbury thematic dictionary of quotations.
    1. Quotations, English
    080   PN6081

ISBN 0 7475 0045 2

Compiled and typeset by
Market House Books, Ltd., Aylesbury
Printed in Great Britain by
Butler & Tanner Limited, Frome and London

• Contents

• Acknowledgments

Editors

John Daintith
Rosalind Fergusson
Edmund Wright
Alan Isaacs
Elizabeth Martin
David Pickering

Contributors

Elizabeth Bonham
Deborah Chapman
Sue Cope
Eve Daintith
Hazel Egerton
Joanna Gosling
Jock Graham
Lawrence Holden
Amanda Isaacs
Valerie Illingworth
Stephen Jones
Jennifer Monk
Ruth Salomon
Jessica Scholes
Gwynneth Shaw
Mary Shields
Kate Smith
Anne Stibbs

• Introduction

This book is a companion volume to the *Bloomsbury Dictionary of Quotations* (first published in 1987), which is arranged alphabetically by author. The present volume contains quotations listed in that work but many other quotations have been added.

Here we have classified over 10,000 quotations under about 800 thematic headings. These are arranged alphabetically. Many of them are subjects that one might expect – 'big issues' such as *love, marriage, youth, age, death*, etc. But we have also included current topics such as *pollution, feminism*, and *healthy living*. At the beginning of each entry there is a list of cross references to related themes. For example, those interested in *adultery* are also advised to read about *sex, unfaithfulness*, and *marriage*.

In general, the quotations under a theme are things said **about** the subject, but we have also used quotations that are **examples** of a theme. For instance, under the heading *epitaphs* will be found quotations that are epitaphs as well as things said about epitaphs.

The entry on *last words* contains examples of last words, *Goldwynisms* gives a selection of Goldwyn's supposed sayings, *insults* provides the reader with a number of possibilities, and so on. Some of the themes have been sub-classified, for example sayings in favour of *feminism* and sayings against. This has not always been possible – thus, it proved too difficult to find much to be said in favour of *critics*. And in most cases sub-classifying is not desirable. One of the interesting features of this method of organization is the juxtaposition of different viewpoints on the same subject.

Within a thematic entry itself, the quotations are arranged alphabetically by author; for the first appearance of an author within an entry, the author's dates and brief biographical note are given. This is followed by any explanatory note that may be required and the source, if it is known. Anonymous quotations come at the beginning of a thematic entry and biblical quotations will be found alphabetized under **Bible** within the entry.

The thematic arrangement is ideal for seeking an apt quotation on a particular theme. But it is also an interesting and amusing book through which to browse. For example, under the entry *politicians* a wide variety of quotations appear, from Shakespeare, through Curzon and Churchill, to Kinnock and Thatcher.

In addition, an author index provides the user with the opportunity of seeking *bon mots* from their favourite personalities. This index lists the themes under which each author is represented, thus providing an entirely different way of making use of the thematic arrangement.

The other index provided, is based on the *keyword* or *-words* in a quotation, directing the user to the theme under which a particular quotation is listed. So users who remember only one or two words of a quotation can complete it correctly and find the source. As Dorothy Parker once said

'I might repeat to myself ... a list of quotations beautiful from minds profound – If I can remember any of the damn things.'

We hope that this book will help jog the memory as well as providing an informative and enjoyable selection.

The Editors

A

ABSENCE

See also presence, separation

1   Long absent, soon forgotten.
Proverb

2   Out of sight, out of mind.
Proverb

3   When the cat's away, the mice will play.
Proverb

4   Absence makes the heart grow fonder,
Isle of Beauty, Fare thee well!
Thomas Haynes Bayly (1797–1839) British writer.
Isle of Beauty

5   What's become of Waring
Since he gave us all the slip?
Robert Browning (1812–89) British poet.
Waring

6   Absence is to love what wind is to fire; it
extinguishes the small, it inflames the great.
Bussy-Rabutin (Roger de Rabutin, Comte de Bussy;
1618–93) French soldier and writer.
Histoire amoureuse des Gaules

7   What's the good of a home, if you are never
in it?
George Grossmith (1847–1912) British singer and
comedian.
The Diary of a Nobody, Ch. 1

8   Has anybody here seen Kelly?
Kelly from the Isle of Man?
C. W. Murphy (19th century) British songwriter.
Has Anybody Here Seen Kelly?

9   We seek him here, we seek him there,
Those Frenchies seek him everywhere.
Is he in heaven? – Is he in hell?
That damned elusive Pimpernel?
Baroness Orczy (1865–1947) British novelist.
The Scarlet Pimpernel, Ch. 12

10 Why art thou silent! Is thy love a plant
Of such weak fibre that the treacherous air
Of absence withers what was once so fair?
William Wordsworth (1770–1850) British poet.
Miscellaneous Sonnets, III

ABSTINENCE

See also alcohol, self-denial, sex, smoking

1   He neither drank, smoked, nor rode a
bicycle. Living frugally, saving his money, he
died early, surrounded by greedy relatives. It
was a great lesson to me.
John Barrymore (1882–1942) US actor.
The Stage, Jan 1941 (J. P. McEvoy)

2   Teetotallers lack the sympathy and
generosity of men that drink.
W. H. Davies (1871–1940) British poet.
Shorter Lyrics of the 20th Century, Introduction

3   It was a brilliant affair; water flowed like
champagne.
William M. Evarts (1818–1901) US lawyer and
statesman.
Describing a dinner given by US President Rutherford B.
Hayes (1877–81), an advocate of temperance
Attrib.

4   If you resolve to give up smoking, drinking
and loving, you don't actually live longer; it
just seems longer.
Clement Freud (1924–) British Liberal politician and
broadcaster.
The Observer, 27 Dec 1964

5   Mr Mercaptan went on to preach a brilliant
sermon on that melancholy sexual perversion
known as continence.
Aldous Huxley (1894–1964) British novelist.
Antic Hay, Ch. 18

6   The few bad poems which occasionally are
created during abstinence are of no great
interest.
Wilhelm Reich (1897–1957) Austrian-born US
psychiatrist.
The Sexual Revolution

7   The people who are regarded as moral
luminaries are those who forego ordinary
pleasures themselves and find compensation
in interfering with the pleasures of others.
Bertrand Russell (1872–1970) British philosopher.
Sceptical Essays

8   Lastly (and this is, perhaps, the golden rule),
no woman should marry a teetotaller, or a
man who does not smoke.
Robert Louis Stevenson (1850–94) Scottish writer.
Virginibus Puerisque

9   Though in silence, with blighted affection, I
pine,
Yet the lips that touch liquor must never touch
mine!
G. W. Young (19th century) British writer.
The Lips That Touch Liquor

ACADEMICS

See also education, intellectuals

1   A professor is one who talks in someone
else's sleep.
W. H. Auden (1907–73) British poet.
Attrib.

2   First come I; my name is Jowett.
There's no knowledge but I know it.
I am Master of this college:

What I don't know isn't knowledge.

H. C. Beeching (1859–1919) British academic.
Referring to Benjamin Jowett, master of Balliol College, Oxford
The Masque of Balliol

3 It's no use trying to be *clever* – we are all clever here; just try to be *kind* – a little kind.

F. J. Foakes Jackson (1855–1941) British academic.
Advice given to a new don at Jesus College, Cambridge
Noted in A. C. Benson's Commonplace Book

4 Like so many ageing college people, Pnin had long ceased to notice the existence of students on the campus.

Vladimir Nabokov (1899–1977) Russian-born US novelist.
Pnin, Ch. 3

5 I am the Dean of Christ Church, Sir:
There's my wife; look well at her.
She's the Broad and I'm the High;
We are the University.

Cecil Arthur Spring-Rice (1859–1918) British diplomat.
The Masque of Balliol

ACCIDENTS

See also chance, disaster, misfortune

1 The Act of God designation on all insurance policies; which means, roughly, that you cannot be insured for the accidents that are most likely to happen to you.

Alan Coren (1938–) British humorist and writer.
The Lady from Stalingrad Mansions, 'A Short History of Insurance'

2 Accidents will occur in the best-regulated families.

Charles Dickens (1812–70) British novelist.
David Copperfield, Ch. 28

3 My good man, I'm not a strawberry.

Edward VII (1841–1910) King of the United Kingdom.
Rebuking a footman who had spilt cream on him
The Last Country Houses (C. Aslat)

4 Heard there was a party. Came.

Beatrice Lillie (Constance Sylvia Munston, Lady Peel; 1898–) Canadian-born British actress.
On arriving breathlessly at a friend's house seeking help after a car crash
Attrib.

5 O Diamond! Diamond! thou little knowest the mischief done!

Isaac Newton (1642–1727) British scientist.
Said to a dog that set fire to some papers, representing several years' work, by knocking over a candle
Wensley-Dale . . . a Poem (Thomas Maude)

6 Knocked down a doctor? With an ambulance? How could she? It's a contradiction in terms.

N. F. Simpson (1919–) British dramatist.
One-Way Pendulum, I

7 The chapter of accidents is the longest chapter in the book.

John Wilkes (1725–97) British politician.
Attrib. in *The Doctor* (Southey), Vol. IV

ACCUSATION

See also responsibility

1 I do not know the method of drawing up an indictment against an whole people.

Edmund Burke (1729–97) British politician.
Speech on Conciliation with America (House of Commons, 22 Mar 1775)

2 Never make a defence or apology before you be accused.

Charles I (1600–49) King of England.
Letter to Lord Wentworth, 3 Sept 1636

3 *J'accuse.*
I accuse.

Émile Zola (1840–1902) French novelist.
Title of an open letter to the French President, denouncing the French army's conduct in the Dreyfus affair
L'Aurore, 13 Jan 1898

ACHIEVEMENT

See also effort, success

1 Ye shall know them by their fruits. Do men gather grapes of thorns, or figs of thistles? Even so every good tree bringeth forth good fruit; but a corrupt tree bringeth forth evil fruit.
A good tree cannot bring forth evil fruit, neither can a corrupt tree bring forth good fruit.
Every tree that bringeth not forth good fruit is hewn down, and cast into the fire.
Wherefore by their fruits ye shall know them.

Bible: Matthew
7:16–20

2 One never notices what has been done; one can only see what remains to be done. . . .

Marie Curie (1867–1934) Polish chemist.
Letter to her brother, 18 Mar 1894

3 We never do anything well till we cease to think about the manner of doing it.

William Hazlitt (1778–1830) British essayist.
On Prejudice

4 I do not want to die . . . until I have faithfully made the most of my talent and cultivated the seed that was placed in me until the last small twig has grown.

Käthe Kollwitz (1867–1945) German sculptor and graphic artist.
Diaries and Letters, 15 Feb 1915

5 For, as I suppose, no man in this world hath lived better than I have done, to achieve that I have done.

Thomas Malory (1400–71) English writer.
Morte d'Arthur, Bk. XVII, Ch. 16

6 Log-cabin to White House.

W. M. Thayer (1820–98) US writer.
The title of his biography of James Garfield, US president

7 To achieve great things we must live as though we were never going to die.

Marquis de Vauvenargues (1715–47) French soldier and writer.
Réflexions et maximes

ACTING

See also action, actors, cinema, criticism, plays, theatre

1 Theatre director: a person engaged by the management to conceal the fact that the players cannot act.

James Agate (1877–1947) British theatre critic.
Attrib.

2 For the theatre one needs long arms; it is better to have them too long than too short. An *artiste* with short arms can never, never make a fine gesture.

Sarah Bernhardt (Sarah Henriette Rosine Bernard; 1844–1923) French actress.
Memories of My Life, Ch. 6

3 Pray to God and say the lines.

Bette Davis (Ruth Elizabeth Davis; 1908–) US film star.
Advice to the actress Celeste Holm
Attrib.

4 It is easier to get an actor to be a cowboy than to get a cowboy to be an actor.

John Ford (Sean O'Feeney; 1895–1973) US film director.
Attrib.

5 Acting is therefore the lowest of the arts, if it is an art at all.

George Moore (1852–1933) Irish writer and art critic.
Mummer-Worship

6 The art of acting consists in keeping people from coughing.

Ralph Richardson (1902–83) British actor.
The Observer

7 In music, the punctuation is absolutely strict, the bars and the rests are absolutely defined. But our punctuation cannot be quite strict, because we have to relate it to the audience. In other words, we are continually changing the score.

Ralph Richardson
The Observer Magazine, 'Tynan on Richardson', 18 Dec 1977

8 Imagination! imagination! I put it first years ago, when I was asked what qualities I thought necessary for success upon the stage.

Ellen Terry (1847–1928) British actress.
The Story of My Life, Ch. 2

9 Ladies, just a little more virginity, if you don't mind.

Herbert Beerbohm Tree (1853–1917) British actor and theatre manager.
Directing a group of sophisticated actresses
Smart Aleck (H. Teichmann)

ACTION

See also acting

1 Barking dogs seldom bite.
Proverb

2 Doing is better than saying.
Proverb

3 Easier said than done.
Proverb

4 Footprints on the sands of time are not made by sitting down.
Proverb

5 Saying is one thing, and doing another.
Proverb

6 Let's meet, and either do, or die.
Francis Beaumont (1584–1616) English dramatist.
The Island Princess, II:2

7 He who desires but acts not, breeds pestilence.
William Blake (1757–1827) British poet.
The Marriage of Heaven and Hell, 'Proverbs of Hell'

8 Liberty's in every blow!
Let us do or die!
Robert Burns (1759–96) Scottish poet.
Scots, Wha Hae

9 Deliberation is the work of many men. Action, of one alone.
Charles De Gaulle (1890–1970) French general and statesman.
War Memoirs, Vol. 2

10 Suit the action to the word, the word to the action; with this special observance, that you o'erstep not the modesty of nature.
William Shakespeare (1564–1616) English dramatist.
Hamlet, III:2

11 If to do were as easy as to know what were good to do, chapels had been churches, and poor men's cottages princes' palaces.
William Shakespeare
The Merchant of Venice, I:2

12 So many worlds, so much to do,
So little done, such things to be.
Alfred, Lord Tennyson (1809–92) British poet.
In Memoriam A.H.H., LXXIII

13 It's dogged as does it. It ain't thinking about it.
Anthony Trollope (1815–82) British novelist.
Last Chronicle of Barset, Ch. 61

ACTORS

See also acting, cinema, criticism, plays, theatre

1 John Wayne is dead

The hell I am

Anonymous
Inscription on a wall in Bermondsey Antique Market, together
with a ghostly denial
Evening Standard, 1980

2 An actor's a guy who, if you ain't talking
about him, ain't listening.
Marlon Brando (1924–) US film star.
The Observer, 'Sayings of the Year', Jan 1956

3 Never meddle with play-actors, for they're a
favoured race.
Miguel de Cervantes (1547–1616) Spanish novelist.
Don Quixote, Pt. II, Ch. 11

4 Chaplin is no business man – all he knows is
that he can't take anything less.
Samuel Goldwyn (Samuel Goldfish; 1882–1974) Polish-
born US film producer.
Attrib.

5 Actors should be treated like cattle.
Alfred Hitchcock (1889–1980) British film director.
Said in clarification of a remark attributed to him, 'Actors are
like cattle'
Quote, Unquote (N. Rees)

6 At one time I thought he wanted to be an
actor. He had certain qualifications, including
no money and a total lack of responsibility.
Hedda Hopper (1890–1966) US writer.
From Under My Hat

7 She looked as though butter wouldn't melt in
her mouth – or anywhere else.
Elsa Lanchester (1902–86) British-born US actress.
Referring to Maureen O'Hara
Attrib.

8 They didn't act like people and they didn't act
like actors. It's hard to explain. They acted
more like they knew they were celebrities
and all. I mean they were good, but they
were *too* good.
J. D. Salinger (1919–) US novelist.
The Catcher in the Rye, Ch. 17

9 Goodbye Norma Jean
Though I never knew you at all
You had the grace to hold yourself
While those around you crawled.
They crawled out of the woodwork
And they whispered into your brain
Set you on the treadmill
And made you change your name.
Bernie Taupin (1913–) British songwriter.
Lyrics for a song by Elton John
Candle in the Wind (song)

10 Ah, every day dear Herbert becomes *de plus
en plus Oscarié*. It is a wonderful case of
nature imitating art.
Oscar Wilde (1854–1900) Irish-born British dramatist.
Referring to Beerbohm Tree's unconscious adoption of some
of the mannerisms of a character he was playing in one of
Wilde's plays
Great Theatrical Disasters (G. Brandreth)

ADAPTABILITY

1 Remember that to change your mind and
follow him who sets you right is to be none
the less free than you were before.
Marcus Aurelius (121–180 AD) Roman emperor.
Meditations, Bk. VIII, Ch. 16

2 Mahomet made the people believe that he
would call a hill to him . . . when the hill
stood still, he was never a whit abashed, but
said, 'If the hill will not come to Mahomet,
Mahomet will go to the hill.'
Francis Bacon (1561–1626) English philosopher.
Often misquoted as 'If the mountain will not come to Mohammed' . . .
Essays, 'Of Boldness'

3 President Robbins was so well adjusted to his
environment that sometimes you could not
tell which was the environment and which
was President Robbins.
Randall Jarrell (1914–65) US author.
Pictures from an Institution, Pt. I, Ch. 4

4 As time requireth, a man of marvellous mirth
and pastimes, and sometimes of as sad
gravity, as who say: a man for all seasons.
Robert Whittington (16th century) English writer.
Referring to Sir Thomas More; after Erasmus
Vulgaria, Pt. II, 'De constructione nominum'

ADDICTION

1 Cocaine isn't habit-forming. I should know –
I've been using it for years.
Tallulah Bankhead (1903–68) US actress.
Pentimento (Lillian Hellman), 'Theatre'

2 Every form of addiction is bad, no matter
whether the narcotic be alcohol or morphine
or idealism.
Carl Gustav Jung (1875–1961) Swiss psychoanalyst.
Memories, Dreams, Reflections, Ch. 12

ADDRESSES

1 Addresses are given to us to conceal our
whereabouts.
Saki (Hector Hugh Munro; 1870–1916) British writer.
Cross Currents

2 Three addresses always inspire confidence,
even in tradesmen.
Oscar Wilde (1854–1900) Irish-born British dramatist.
The Importance of Being Earnest, III

ADMIRATION

See also compliments, love, respect, praise, wonder

1 Miss J. Hunter Dunn, Miss J. Hunter Dunn,
Furnish'd and burnish'd by Aldershot sun.
John Betjeman (1906–84) British poet.
A Subaltern's Love Song

2 Here's looking at you, kid.
Humphrey Bogart (1899–1957) US film star.
Casablanca

3 A fool always finds a greater fool to admire him.
Nicolas Boileau (1636–1711) French writer.
L'Art poétique, I

4 There is a garden in her face,
Where roses and white lilies grow;
A heav'nly paradise is that place,
Wherein all pleasant fruits do flow.
There cherries grow, which none may buy
Till 'Cherry ripe' themselves do cry.
Thomas Campion (1567–1620) English poet.
Fourth Book of Airs

5 I do think better of womankind than to suppose they care whether Mister John Keats five feet high likes them or not.
John Keats (1795–1821) British poet.
Letter to Benjamin Bailey, 18 July 1818

6 'There is a report that Piso is dead; it is a great loss; he was an honest man, who deserved to live longer; he was intelligent and agreeable, resolute and courageous, to be depended upon, generous and faithful.'
Add: 'provided he is really dead'.
Jean de La Bruyère (1645–96) French satirist.
Les Caractères

7 On Richmond Hill there lives a lass,
More sweet than May day morn,
Whose charms all other maids surpass,
A rose without a thorn.
Leonard MacNally (1752–1820) Irish dramatist and poet.
The Lass of Richmond Hill

8 Many a man has been a wonder to the world, whose wife and valet have seen nothing in him that was even remarkable. Few men have been admired by their servants.
Michel de Montaigne (1533–92) French essayist.
Essais, III

9 Charlie is my darling, my darling, my darling,
Charlie is my darling, the young Chevalier.
Baroness Nairne (1766–1845) Scottish songwriter.
Referring to Bonnie Prince Charlie
Charlie is my Darling

10 Not to admire, is all the art I know
To make men happy, and to keep them so.
Alexander Pope (1688–1744) British poet.
Imitations of Horace, 'To Mr. Murray'

11 Where'er you walk, cool gales shall fan the glade,
Trees, where you sit, shall crowd into a shade:
Where'er you tread, the blushing flow'rs shall rise,
And all things flourish where you turn your eyes.
Alexander Pope
Pastorals, 'Summer'

12 But search the land of living men,
Where wilt thou find their like agen?
Walter Scott (1771–1832) Scottish novelist.
Marmion, I

13 The barge she sat in, like a burnish'd throne,
Burn'd on the water. The poop was beaten gold;
Purple the sails, and so perfumed that
The winds were love-sick with them; the oars were silver,
Which to the tune of flutes kept stroke and made
The water which they beat to follow faster,
As amorous of their strokes. For her own person,
It beggar'd all description.
William Shakespeare (1564–1616) English dramatist.
Antony and Cleopatra, II:2

14 Age cannot wither her, nor custom stale
Her infinite variety. Other women cloy
The appetites they feed, but she makes hungry
Where most she satisfies.
William Shakespeare
Antony and Cleopatra, II:2

15 'A was a man, take him for all in all,
I shall not look upon his like again.
William Shakespeare
Hamlet, I:2

16 Who is Silvia? What is she,
That all our swains commend her?
Holy, fair, and wise is she.
William Shakespeare
The Two Gentlemen of Verona, IV:2

17 He was a great patriot, a humanitarian, a loyal friend – provided, of course, that he really is dead.
Voltaire (François-Marie Arouet; 1694–1778) French writer.
Giving a funeral oration
Attrib.

18 The sweetest thing that ever grew
Beside a human door!
William Wordsworth (1770–1850) British poet.
Lucy Gray

ADULTERY

See also marriage, sex, unfaithfulness

1 What men call gallantry, and gods adultery,
Is much more common where the climate's sultry.
Lord Byron (1788–1824) British poet.
Don Juan, I

2 I have looked on a lot of women with lust. I've committed adultery in my heart many times. God recognises I will do this and forgives me.
Jimmy Carter (1924–) US statesman and president.
Remark

3 Sara could commit adultery at one end and

weep for her sins at the other, and enjoy both operations at once.
Joyce Cary (1888–1957) British novelist.
The Horse's Mouth, Ch. 8

4 You know, of course, that the Tasmanians, who never committed adultery, are now extinct.
W. Somerset Maugham (1874–1965) British novelist.
The Bread-Winner

5 Madame, you must really be more careful. Suppose it had been someone else who found you like this.
Duc de Richelieu (1766–1822) French statesman.
Discovering his wife with her lover
The Book of Lists (D. Wallechinsky)

6 With all my heart. Whose wife shall it be?
John Horne Tooke (1736–1812) British clergyman, politician, and etymologist.
Replying to the suggestion that he take a wife
Attrib.

ADVICE

1 A good scare is worth more than good advice.
Proverb

2 Don't teach your grandmother to suck eggs.
Proverb

3 He that has no children brings them up well.
Proverb

4 He that has no wife, beats her oft.
Proverb

5 Advice is seldom welcome; and those who want it the most always like it the least.
Earl of Chesterfield (1694–1773) English statesman.
Letter to his son, 29 Jan 1748

6 Your business is to put me out of business.
Dwight D. Eisenhower (1890–1969) US general and statesman.
Addressing a graduating class at a university
Procession (J. Gunther)

7 I intended to give you some advice but now I remember how much is left over from last year unused.
George Harris (1844–1922) US congressman.
Said when addressing students at the start of a new academic year
Braude's Second Encyclopedia (J. Braude)

8 On my twenty-first birthday my father said, 'Son, here's a million dollars. Don't lose it.'
Larry Niven (1938–) US science-fiction writer.
When asked 'What is the best advice you have ever been given?'
Attrib.

9 One gives nothing so freely as advice.
Duc de la Rochefoucauld (1613–80) French writer.
Maximes, 110

10 Don't tell your friends their social faults, they will cure the fault and never forgive you.
Logan Pearsall Smith (1865–1946) US writer.
Afterthoughts

11 No one wants advice – only corroboration.
John Steinbeck (1902–68) US novelist.

12 It's queer how ready people always are with advice in any real or imaginary emergency, and no matter how many times experience has shown them to be wrong, they continue to set forth their opinions, as if they had received them from the Almighty!
Annie Sullivan (1866–1936) US teacher of the handicapped.
Letter, 12 June 1887

13 I have lived some thirty years on this planet, and I have yet to hear the first syllable of valuable or even earnest advice from my seniors.
Henry David Thoreau (1817–62) US writer.
Walden, 'Economy'

14 Are you in trouble? Do you need advice? Write to Miss Lonelyhearts and she will help.
Nathaniel West (Nathan Weinstein; 1903–40) US novelist.
Miss Lonelyhearts

AFFECTATION

See also ostentation

1 Don't you sit there and sigh gal like you was Lady Nevershit.
Arnold Wesker (1932–) British dramatist.
Roots, III

2 She keeps on being Queenly in her own room with the door shut.
Edith Wharton (1862–1937) US novelist.
The House of Mirth, Bk. II, Ch. 1

AFTERLIFE

See also heaven

1 CLOV. Do you believe in the life to come?
HAMM. Mine was always that.
Samuel Beckett (1906–) Irish novelist and dramatist.
Endgame

2 That which is the foundation of all our hopes and of all our fears; all our hopes and fears which are of any consideration: I mean a Future Life.
Joseph Butler (1692–1752) British churchman.
The Analogy of Religion, Introduction

3 We have no reliable guarantee that the afterlife will be any less exasperating than this one, have we?
Noël Coward (1899–1973) British dramatist.
Blithe Spirit, I

4 We sometimes congratulate ourselves at the

moment of waking from a troubled dream; it may be so the moment after death.
Nathaniel Hawthorne (1804–64) US novelist and writer.
American Notebooks

5 Is there another life? Shall I awake and find all this a dream? There must be, we cannot be created for this sort of suffering.
John Keats (1795–1821) British poet.
Letter, 1820

6 My doctrine is: Live that thou mayest desire to live again – that is thy duty – for in any case thou wilt live again!
Friedrich Wilhelm Nietzsche (1844–1900) German philosopher.
Eternal Recurrence

7 After your death you will be what you were before your birth.
Arthur Schopenhauer (1788–1860) German philosopher.
Parerga and Paralipomena

8 The dread of something after death –
The undiscover'd country, from whose bourn
No traveller returns.
William Shakespeare (1564–1616) English dramatist.
Hamlet, III:1

9 I am going a long way
With these thou seest – if indeed I go
(For all my mind is clouded with a doubt) –
To the island-valley of Avilion;
Where falls not hail, or rain, or any snow,
Nor ever wind blows loudly; but it lies
Deep-meadow'd, happy, fair with orchard lawns
And bowery hollows crown'd with summer sea,
Where I will heal me of my grievous wound.
Alfred, Lord Tennyson (1809–92) British poet.
Idylls of the King, 'The Passing of Arthur'

10 One world at a time.
Henry David Thoreau (1817–62) US writer.
On being asked his opinion of the hereafter
Attrib.

AGE

See also longevity, old age, youth

1 Never too late to learn.
Proverb

2 There's many a good tune played on an old fiddle.
Proverb

3 All evil comes from the old. They grow fat on ideas and young men die of them.
Jean Anouilh (1910–87) French dramatist.
Catch as Catch Can

4 I am past thirty, and three parts iced over.
Matthew Arnold (1822–88) British poet and critic.
Letter to A. H. Clough, 12 Feb 1853

5 Age will not be defied.
Francis Bacon (1561–1626) English philosopher.
Essays, 'Of Regiment of Health'

6 A man that is young in years may be old in hours, if he have lost no time.
Francis Bacon
Essays, 'Of Youth and Age'

7 The only thing I regret about my past life is the length of it. If I had my past life over again I'd make all the same mistakes – only sooner.
Tallulah Bankhead (1903–68) US actress.
The Times, 28 July 1981

8 What is an adult? A child blown up by age.
Simone de Beauvoir (1908–86) French writer.
La Femme rompue

9 If thou hast gathered nothing in thy youth, how canst thou find any thing in thine age?
Bible: Ecclesiasticus
25:3

10 No man also having drunk old wine straightway desireth new: for he saith, The old is better.
Bible: Luke
5:39

11 Old age is . . . a lot of crossed off names in an address book.
Ronald Blythe (1922–) British author.
The View in Winter

12 Being now come to the years of discretion.
The Book of Common Prayer
Order of Confirmation

13 Therefore I summon age
To grant youth's heritage.
Robert Browning (1812–89) British poet.
Rabbi ben Ezra, XIII

14 Ah well, perhaps one has to be very old before one learns how to be amused rather than shocked.
Pearl Buck (1892–1973) US novelist.
China, Past and Present, Ch. 6

15 A lady of a 'certain age', which means Certainly aged.
Lord Byron (1788–1824) British poet.
Don Juan, VI

16 A man is as old as he's feeling,
A woman as old as she looks.
Mortimer Collins (1827–76) British writer.
The Unknown Quantity

17 Youth is a blunder; manhood a struggle; old age a regret.
Benjamin Disraeli (1804–81) British statesman.
Coningsby, Bk. III, Ch. 1

18 I am resolved to grow fat and look young till forty, and then slip out of the world with the

first wrinkle and the reputation of five-and-twenty.
John Dryden (1631–1700) British poet and dramatist.
The Maiden Queen, III

19 Men are but children of a larger growth;
Our appetites as apt to change as theirs,
And full as craving too, and full as vain.
John Dryden
All for Love, IV

20 The years between fifty and seventy are the hardest. You are always being asked to do things, and you are not yet decrepit enough to turn them down.
T. S. Eliot (1888–1965) US-born British poet and dramatist.
Time, 23 Oct 1950

21 Here I am, an old man in a dry month,
Being read to by a boy, waiting for rain.
T. S. Eliot
Gerontion

22 *Si jeunesse savait; si vieillesse pouvait.*
If only youth knew, if only age could.
Henri Estienne (1528–98) French scholar.
Les Prémices

23 At sixteen I was stupid, confused, insecure and indecisive. At twenty-five I was wise, self-confident, prepossessing and assertive. At forty-five I am stupid, confused, insecure and indecisive. Who would have supposed that maturity is only a short break in adolescence?
Jules Feiffer (1929–) US writer, cartoonist, and humorist.
The Observer, 3 Feb 1974

24 Though the Jazz Age continued, it became less and less an affair of youth. The sequel was like a children's party taken over by the elders.
F. Scott Fitzgerald (1896–1940) US novelist.
The Crack-Up

25 At twenty years of age, the will reigns; at thirty, the wit; and at forty, the judgement.
Benjamin Franklin (1706–90) US scientist and statesman.
Poor Richard's Almanack

26 A diplomat is a man who always remembers a woman's birthday but never remembers her age.
Robert Frost (1875–1963) US poet.
Attrib.

27 She may very well pass for forty-three
In the dusk, with a light behind her!
W. S. Gilbert (1836–1911) British dramatist.
Trial by Jury

28 'Old Cary Grant fine. How you?'
Cary Grant (Archibald Leach; 1904–86) British-born US film star.
Replying to a telegram sent to his agent inquiring: 'How old Cary Grant?'
The Filmgoer's Book of Quotes (Leslie Halliwell)

29 You will recognize, my boy, the first sign of old age: it is when you go out into the streets of London and realize for the first time how young the policemen look.
Seymour Hicks (1871–1949) British actor-manager.
They Were Singing (C. Pulling)

30 What do the ravages of time not injure? Our parents' age (worse than our grandparents') has produced us, more worthless still, who will soon give rise to a yet more vicious generation.
Horace (Quintus Horatius Flaccus; 65–8 BC) Roman poet.
Odes, III

31 Whenever a man's friends begin to compliment him about looking young, he may be sure that they think he is growing old.
Washington Irving (1783–1859) US writer.
Bracebridge Hall, 'Bachelors'

32 It is sobering to consider that when Mozart was my age he had already been dead for a year.
Tom Lehrer (1928–) US university teacher and songwriter.
An Encyclopedia of Quotations about Music (N. Shapiro)

33 I am just turning forty and taking my time about it.
Harold Lloyd (1893–1971) US silent-film comedian.
Reply when, aged 77, he was asked his age
The Times, 23 Sept 1970

34 Growth is a greater mystery than death. All of us can understand failure, we all contain failure and death within us, but not even the successful man can begin to describe the impalpable elations and apprehensions of growth.
Norman Mailer (1923–) US writer.
Advertisements for Myself

35 But at my back I always hear
Time's winged chariot hurrying near;
And yonder all before us lie
Deserts of vast eternity.
Andrew Marvell (1621–78) English poet.
To His Coy Mistress

36 A man is only as old as the woman he feels.
Groucho Marx (Julius Marx; 1895–1977) US comedian.
Attrib.

37 I am old enough to be – in fact am – your mother.
A. A. Milne (1882–1956) British writer.
Belinda

38 How soon hath Time, the subtle thief of youth,
Stolen on his wing my three-and-twentieth year!
John Milton (1608–74) English poet.
Sonnet: 'On Being Arrived at the Age of Twenty-three'

39 Do you think my mind is maturing late,

Or simply rotted early?
Ogden Nash (1902–71) US poet.
Lines on Facing Forty

40 At. 50, everyone has the face he deserves.
George Orwell (Eric Blair; 1903–50) British novelist.
Last words in his manuscript notebook, 17 Apr 1949

41 Each generation imagines itself to be more intelligent than the one that went before it, and wiser than the one that comes after it.
George Orwell
Book Review

42 From forty to fifty a man is at heart either a stoic or a satyr.
Arthur Pinero (1855–1934) British dramatist.
The Second Mrs Tanqueray, I

43 One of the pleasures of middle age is to *find out* that one WAS right, and that one was much righter than one knew at say 17 or 23.
Ezra Pound (1885–1972) US poet.
ABC of Reading, Ch. 1

44 You know, by the time you reach my age, you've made plenty of mistakes if you've lived your life properly
Ronald Reagan (1911–) US politician and president.
The Observer, 'Sayings of the Week', 8 Mar 1987

45 It is fun to be in the same decade with you.
Franklin D. Roosevelt (1882–1945) US Democratic president.
After Churchill had congratulated him on his 60th birthday
The Hinge of Fate (Winston S. Churchill), Ch. 4

46 I have always felt that a woman has the right to treat the subject of her age with ambiguity until, perhaps, she passes into the realm of over ninety. Then it is better she be candid with herself and with the world.
Helena Rubinstein (1882–1965) Polish-born US cosmetics manufacturer.
My Life for Beauty, Pt. I, Ch. 1

47 The young have aspirations that never come to pass, the old have reminiscences of what never happened.
Saki (Hector Hugh Munro; 1870–1916) British writer.
Reginald at the Carlton

48 The young man who has not wept is a savage, and the old man who will not laugh is a fool.
George Santayana (1863–1952) US philosopher.
Dialogues in Limbo, Ch. 3

49 When I was young, I was told: 'You'll see, when you're fifty. I am fifty and I haven't seen a thing.
Erik Satie (1866–1925) French composer.
From a letter to his brother
Erik Satie (Pierre-Daniel Templier), Ch. 1

50 Thou hast nor youth nor age;
But, as it were, an after-dinner's sleep,
Dreaming on both.
William Shakespeare (1564–1616) English dramatist.
Measure for Measure, III:1

51 Doth not the appetite alter? A man loves the meat in his youth that he cannot endure in his age.
William Shakespeare
Much Ado About Nothing, II:3

52 Crabbed age and youth cannot live together:
Youth is full of pleasure, age is full of care;
Youth like summer morn, age like winter weather;
Youth like summer brave, age like winter bare.
William Shakespeare
The Passionate Pilgrim, XII

53 All that the young can do for the old is to shock them and keep them up to date.
George Bernard Shaw (1856–1950) Irish dramatist and critic.
Fannie's First Play

54 It's a funny thing about that bust. As time goes on it seems to get younger and younger.
George Bernard Shaw
Referring to a portrait bust sculpted for him by Rodin
More Things I Wish I'd Said (K. Edwards)

55 One's prime is elusive. You little girls, when you grow up, must be on the alert to recognize your prime at whatever time of your life it may occur. You must then live it to the full.
Muriel Spark (1918–) British novelist.
The Prime of Miss Jean Brodie, Ch. 1

56 The mark of the immature man is that he wants to die nobly for a cause, while the mark of the mature man is that he wants to live humbly for one.
Wilhelm Stekel (1868–1940) Viennese psychiatrist.
The Catcher in the Rye (J. D. Salinger), Ch. 24

57 Men come of age at sixty, women at fifteen.
James Stephens (1882–1950) Irish novelist.
The Observer, 'Sayings of the Week', 1 Oct 1944

58 I was born old and get younger every day. At present I am sixty years young.
Herbert Beerbohm Tree (1853–1917) British actor and theatre manager.
Beerbohm Tree (Hesketh Pearson)

59 Life begins at forty.
Sophie Tucker (Sophia Abuza; 1884–1966) Russian-born US singer.
Attrib.

60 From birth to age eighteen, a girl needs good parents. From eighteen to thirty-five, she needs good looks. From thirty-five to fifty-five, she needs a good personality. From fifty-five on, she needs good cash.
Sophie Tucker
Attrib.

61 There are no old men any more. *Playboy* and *Penthouse* have between them made an ideal

of eternal adolescence, sunburnt and saunaed,
with the grey dorianed out of it.
Peter Ustinov (1921–) British actor.
Dear Me, Ch. 18

62 It is charming to totter into vogue.
Horace Walpole (1717–97) British writer.
Letter to G. A. Selwyn, 1765

63 No woman should ever be quite accurate
about her age. It looks so calculating.
Oscar Wilde (1854–1900) Irish-born British dramatist.
The Importance of Being Earnest, III

64 One should never trust a woman who tells
one her real age. A woman who would tell
one that, would tell one anything.
Oscar Wilde
A Woman of No Importance, I

65 The older one grows the more one likes
indecency.
Virginia Woolf (1882–1941) British novelist.
Monday or Tuesday

66 My heart leaps up when I behold
A rainbow in the sky:
So was it when my life began;
So is it now I am a man;
So be it when I shall grow old,
Or let me die!
The Child is Father of the Man;
And I could wish my days to be
Bound each to each by natural piety.
William Wordsworth (1770–1850) British poet.
My Heart Leaps Up

67 One that is ever kind said yesterday:
'Your well-belovèd's hair has threads of grey,
And little shadows come about her eyes.'
W. B. Yeats (1865–1939) Irish poet.
The Folly of Being Comforted

68 Where, where but here have Pride and
Truth,
That long to give themselves for wage,
To shake their wicked sides at youth
Restraining reckless middle age?
W. B. Yeats
*On hearing that the Students of our New University have joined
the Agitation against Immoral Literature*

69 Though leaves are many, the root is one;
Through all the lying days of my youth
I swayed my leaves and flowers in the sun;
Now I may wither into the truth.
W. B. Yeats
The Coming of Wisdom with Time

70 Wine comes in at the mouth
And love comes in at the eye;
That's all we shall know for truth
Before we grow old and die.
W. B. Yeats
A Drinking Song

71 Be wise with speed,

A fool at forty is a fool indeed.
Edward Young (1683–1765) British poet.
Love of Fame, II

AGGRAVATION

1 This is adding insult to injuries.
Edward Moore (1712–57) British dramatist.
The Foundling, V

2 The point is that nobody likes having salt
rubbed into their wounds, even if it is the
salt of the earth.
Rebecca West (Cicely Isabel Fairfield; 1892–1983) British
novelist and journalist.
The Salt of the Earth, Ch. 2

AGREEMENT

1 My cousin Francis and I are in perfect accord
– he wants Milan, and so do I.
Charles V (1500–58) Holy Roman Emperor.
Referring to his dispute with Francis I of France over Italian
territory
The Story of Civilization (W. Durant), Vol. 5

2 I am always of the opinion with the learned,
if they speak first.
William Congreve (1670–1729) British Restoration
dramatist.
Incognita

3 'My idea of an agreeable person,' said Hugo
Bohun, 'is a person who agrees with me.'
Benjamin Disraeli (1804–81) British statesman.
Lothair, Ch. 35

4 We seldom attribute common sense except to
those who agree with us.
Duc de la Rochefoucauld (1613–80) French writer.
Maximes, 347

5 Very like a whale.
William Shakespeare (1564–1616) English dramatist.
Hamlet, III:2

6 Our agenda is now exhausted. The secretary
general is exhausted. All of you are
exhausted. I find it comforting that, beginning
with our very first day, we find ourselves in
such complete unanimity.
Paul Henri Spaak (1899–1972) Belgian statesman.
Concluding the first General Assembly meeting of the United
Nations

7 Ah! don't say you agree with me. When
people agree with me I always feel that I
must be wrong.
Oscar Wilde (1854–1900) Irish-born British dramatist.
The Critic as Artist, Pt. 2

8 If two men on the same job agree all the
time, then one is useless. If they disagree all
the time, then both are useless.
Darryl F. Zanuck (1902–79) US film producer.
The Observer, 'Sayings of the Week', 23 Oct 1949

AGRICULTURE

See also countryside

1 We plough the fields, and scatter
The good seed on the land,
But it is fed and watered
By God's Almighty Hand.
He sends the snow in winter,
The warmth to swell the grain,
The breezes and the sunshine,
And soft refreshing rain.
Jane Montgomery Campbell (1817–78) British hymn
writer.
Hymn

2 Three acres and a cow.
Jesse Collings (1831–1920) British politician.
Slogan used in his land-reform propaganda

3 Is my team ploughing,
That I was used to drive?
A. E. Housman (1859–1936) British scholar and poet.
A Shropshire Lad, 'Bredon Hill'

4 'O Mary, go and call the cattle home,
And call the cattle home,
And call the cattle home,
Across the sands of Dee.'
The western wind was wild and dank with
foam,
And all alone went she.
Charles Kingsley (1819–75) British writer.
The Sands of Dee

5 This bread I break was once the oat,
This wine upon a foreign tree
Plunged in its fruit;
Man in the day or wind at night
Laid the crops low, broke the grape's joy.
Dylan Thomas (1914–53) Welsh poet.
This bread I break

ALCOHOL

See also abstinence, drinks, drunkenness, public houses

1 A cask of wine works more miracles than a
church full of saints.
Italian proverb
Proverb

2 Adam's ale is the best brew.
Proverb

3 A good drink makes the old young.
Proverb

4 He who drinks a little too much drinks much
too much.
Proverb

5 Take a hair of the dog that bit you.
Proverb

6 There's many a slip 'twixt the cup and the
lip.
Proverb

7 When the wine is in, the wit is out.
Proverb

8 If all be true that I do think,
There are five reasons we should drink;
Good wine – a friend – or being dry –
Or lest we should be by and by –
Or any other reason why.
Dean Aldrich (1647–1710) English poet.
Reasons for Drinking

9 I feel no pain, dear mother, now
But oh, I am so dry!
O take me to a brewery
And leave me there to die.
Anonymous
Shanty

10 So who's in a hurry?
Robert Benchley (1889–1945) US humorist.
When asked whether he knew that drinking was a slow death
Attrib.

11 He is believed to have liked port, but to have
said of claret that 'it would be port if it
could'.
Richard Bentley (1662–1742) English academic.
Bentley (R. C. Jebb)

12 Woe unto them that rise up early in the
morning, that they may follow strong drink;
that continue until night, till wine inflame
them!
Bible: Isaiah
5:11

13 Drink no longer water, but use a little wine
for thy stomach's sake and thine often
infirmities.
Bible: I Timothy
5:23

14 When the ruler of the feast had tasted the
water that was made wine, and knew not
whence it was: (but the servants which drew
the water knew;) the governor of the feast
called the bridegroom,
And saith unto him, Every man at the beginning doth set forth good wine; and when
men have well drunk, then that which is
worse: but thou hast kept the good wine until
now.
Bible: John
2:9–10

15 No man also having drunk old wine
straightway desireth new: for he saith, The
old is better.
Bible: Luke
5:39

16 Look not thou upon the wine when it is red,
when it giveth his colour in the cup, when it
moveth itself aright.
At the last it biteth like a serpent, and stingeth
like an adder.
Bible: Proverbs
23:31–32

17 The heart which grief hath cankered
Hath one unfailing remedy – the Tankard.
C. S. Calverley (1831–84) British poet.
Beer

18 Alcohol is like love: the first kiss is magic,
the second is intimate, the third is routine.
After that you just take the girl's clothes off.
Raymond Chandler (1888–1959) US novelist.
The Long Good-bye

19 So was hir joly whistle wel y-wet.
Geoffrey Chaucer (c. 1342–1400) English poet.
The Canterbury Tales, 'The Reve's Tale'

20 I must point out that my rule of life
prescribed as an absolutely sacred rite
smoking cigars and also the drinking of
alcohol before, after, and if need be during all
meals and in the intervals between them.
Winston Churchill (1874–1965) British statesman.
Said during a lunch with the Arab leader Ibn Saud, when he
heard that the king's religion forbade smoking and alcohol
The Second World War

21 Apart from cheese and tulips, the main
product of the country is advocaat, a drink
made from lawyers.
Alan Coren (1938–) British humorist and writer.
Referring to Holland
The Sanity Inspector, 'All You Need to Know about Europe'

22 Then trust me, there's nothing like drinking
So pleasant on this side the grave;
It keeps the unhappy from thinking,
And makes e'en the valiant more brave.
Charles Dibdin (1745–1814) British actor and dramatist.
Nothing like Grog

23 'Did you ever taste beer?' 'I had a sip of it
once,' said the small servant. 'Here's a state
of things!' cried Mr Swiveller . . . . 'She *never*
tasted it – it can't be tasted in a sip!'
Charles Dickens (1812–70) British novelist.
The Old Curiosity Shop, Ch. 57

24 First you take a drink, then the drink takes a
drink, then the drink takes you.
F. Scott Fitzgerald (1896–1940) US novelist.
Ackroyd (Jules Feiffer), '1964, May 7'

25 Best while you have it use your breath,
There is no drinking after death.
John Fletcher (1579–1625) English dramatist.
With Jonson and others
The Bloody Brother, II:2

26 And he that will go to bed sober,
Falls with the leaf still in October.
John Fletcher
The Bloody Brother, II:2

27 A taste for drink, combined with gout,
Had doubled him up for ever.
W. S. Gilbert (1836–1911) British dramatist.
The Gondoliers, I

28 Let schoolmasters puzzle their brain,
With grammar, and nonsense, and learning,

Good liquor, I stoutly maintain,
Gives genius a better discerning.
Oliver Goldsmith (1728–74) Irish-born British writer.
She Stoops to Conquer, I

29 Malt does more than Milton can
To justify God's ways to man.
A. E. Housman (1859–1936) British scholar and poet.
A Shropshire Lad, 'The Welsh Marches'

30 Claret is the liquor for boys; port for men;
but he who aspires to be a hero must drink
brandy.
Samuel Johnson (1709–84) British lexicographer.
Life of Johnson (J. Boswell), Vol. III

31 No, Sir; there were people who died of
dropsies, which they contracted in trying to
get drunk.
Samuel Johnson
Scornfully criticizing the strength of the wine in Scotland
before the Act of Union in response to Boswell's claim that
there had been a lot of drunkenness
Tour to the Hebrides (J. Boswell)

32 Come, let me know what it is that makes a
Scotchman happy!
Samuel Johnson
Ordering for himself a glass of whisky
Tour to the Hebrides (J. Boswell)

33 My friends should drink a dozen of Claret on
my Tomb.
John Keats (1795–1821) British poet.
Letter to Benjamin Bailey, 14 Aug 1819

34 O, for a draught of vintage! that hath been
Cool'd a long age in the deep-delved earth.
John Keats
Ode to a Nightingale

35 O for a beaker full of the warm South,
Full of the true, the blushful Hippocrene,
With beaded bubbles winking at the brim,
And purple-stained mouth.
John Keats
Ode to a Nightingale

36 Even though a number of people have tried,
no one has yet found a way to drink for a
living.
Jean Kerr (1923–) US dramatist.
Poor Richard

37 If we heard it said of Orientals that they
habitually drank a liquor which went to their
heads, deprived them of reason and made
them vomit, we should say: 'How very
barbarous!'
Jean de La Bruyère (1645–96) French satirist.
Les Caractères

38 Frenchmen drink wine just like we used to
drink water before Prohibition.
Ring Lardner Jnr (1885–1933) American humorist.
Wit's End (R. E. Drennan)

39 It takes a good deal of physical courage to
ride a horse. This, however, I have. I get it

at about forty cents a flask, and take it as required.

Stephen Leacock (1869–1944) English-born Canadian economist and humorist.
Literary Lapses, 'Reflections on Riding'

40 If die I must, let me die drinking in an inn.

Walter Map (c. 1140–c. 1209) Welsh clergyman and writer.
De Nugis Curialium

41 I've made it a rule never to drink by daylight and never to refuse a drink after dark.

H. L. Mencken (1880–1956) US journalist.
New York Post, 18 Sept 1945

42 No man is genuinely happy, married, who has to drink worse gin than he used to drink when he was single.

H. L. Mencken
Prejudices, 'Reflections on Monogamy'

43 Then to the spicy nut-brown ale.

John Milton (1608–74) English poet.
L'Allegro

44 A torchlight procession marching down your throat.

John L. O'Sullivan (1813–95) US writer.
Referring to whisky
Collections and Recollections (G. W. E. Russell), Ch. 19

45 *In vino veritas.*
Truth comes out in wine.

Pliny the Elder (Gaius Plinius Secundus; 23–79 AD) Roman scholar.
Natural History, XIV

46 It is WRONG to do what everyone else does – namely, to hold the wine list just out of sight, look for the second cheapest claret on the list, and say, 'Number 22, please'.

Stephen Potter (1900–69) British writer.
One-Upmanship, Ch. 14

47 A good general rule is to state that the bouquet is better than the taste, and vice versa.

Stephen Potter
One-Upmanship, Ch. 14

48 It is the unbroken testimony of all history that alcoholic liquors have been used by the strongest, wisest, handsomest, and in every way best races of all times.

George Edward Bateman Saintsbury (1845–1933) British writer and critic.
Notes on a Cellar-Book

49 People may say what they like about the decay of Christianity; the religious system that produced green Chartreuse can never really die.

Saki (Hector Hugh Munro; 1870–1916) British writer.
Reginald on Christmas Presents

50 By insisting on having your bottle pointing to the north when the cork is being drawn, and calling the waiter Max, you may induce an impression on your guests which hours of laboured boasting might be powerless to achieve. For this purpose, however, the guests must be chosen as carefully as the wine.

Saki
The Chaplet

51 It provokes the desire, but it takes away the performance. Therefore much drink may be said to be an equivocator with lechery.

William Shakespeare (1564–1616) English dramatist.
Macbeth, II:3

52 I am only a beer teetotaller, not a champagne teetotaller.

George Bernard Shaw (1856–1950) Irish dramatist and critic.
Candida

53 Alcohol is a very necessary article . . . It enables Parliament to do things at eleven at night that no sane person would do at eleven in the morning.

George Bernard Shaw
Major Barbara, II

54 Gin was mother's milk to her.

George Bernard Shaw
Pygmalion, III

55 Well, then, my stomach must just digest in its waistcoat.

Richard Brinsley Sheridan (1751–1816) British dramatist.
On being warned that his drinking would destroy the coat of his stomach
The Fine Art of Political Wit (L. Harris)

56 Selwyn Macgregor, the nicest boy who ever committed the sin of whisky.

Muriel Spark (1918–   ) British novelist.
The Go-Away Bird, 'A Sad Tale's Best for Winter'

57 Fifteen men on the dead man's chest
Yo-ho-ho, and a bottle of rum!
Drink and the devil had done for the rest –
Yo-ho-ho, and a bottle of rum!

Robert Louis Stevenson (1850–94) Scottish writer.
Treasure Island, Ch. 1

58 There are two things that will be believed of any man whatsoever, and one of them is that he has taken to drink.

Booth Tarkington (1869–1946) US novelist.
Penrod, Ch. 10

59 It's a Naive Domestic Burgundy, Without Any Breeding. But I think you'll be Amused by its Presumption.

James Thurber (1894–1961) US humorist.
Men, Women and Dogs

60 'Joe,' I said, 'was perhaps the first great nonstop literary drinker of the American nineteenth century. He made the indulgences of Coleridge and De Quincey seem like a bit

of mischief in the kitchen with the cooking sherry.'
James Thurber
Alarms and Diversions, 'The Moribundant Life . . .'

61 I prefer temperance hotels – although they sell worse kinds of liquor than any other kind of hotels.
Artemus Ward (Charles Farrar Browne; 1834–67) US humorous writer.
Artemus Ward's Lecture

62 I hadn't the heart to touch my breakfast. I told Jeeves to drink it himself.
P. G. Wodehouse (1881–1975) British humorous novelist.
My Man Jeeves

63 It was my Uncle George who discovered that alcohol was a food well in advance of modern medical thought.
P. G. Wodehouse
The Inimitable Jeeves, Ch. 16

64 I must get out of these wet clothes and into a dry Martini.
Alexander Woollcott (1887–1943) US journalist.
Reader's Digest

65 Father, dear father, come home with me now,
The clock in the steeple strikes one.
Henry Clay Work (1832–84) US songwriter.
A temperance song
Come Home, Father

AMBITION

See also desire

1 He who rides a tiger is afraid to dismount.
Proverb

2 *Per ardua ad astra.*
Hard and high to the stars!
Anonymous
Motto of the Royal Air Force

3 Ah, but a man's reach should exceed his grasp,
Or what's a heaven for?
Robert Browning (1812–89) British poet.
Andrea del Sarto

4 Man partly is and wholly hopes to be.
Robert Browning
A Death in the Desert

5 You seem to have no real purpose in life and won't realize at the age of twenty-two that for a man life means work, and hard work if you mean to succeed. . . .
Jennie Jerome Churchill (1854–1921) US-born British hostess and writer.
Letter to Winston Churchill, 26 Feb 1897
Jennie (Ralph G. Martin), Vol. II

6 I have found some of the best reasons I ever had for remaining at the bottom simply by looking at the men at the top.
Frank More Colby (1865–1925) US editor.
Essays, II

7 If thy heart fails thee, climb not at all.
Elizabeth I (1533–1603) Queen of England.
Written on a window in reply to Walter RALEIGH's line.
Worthies of England (Fuller), Vol. I

8 Hitch your wagon to a star.
Ralph Waldo Emerson (1803–82) US poet and essayist.
Society and Solitude, 'Civilization'

9 I would like to throw an egg into an electric fan.
Oliver Herford (1863–1935) British-born US humorist.
When asked if he really had no ambition beyond making people laugh
Attrib.

10 I am going to build the kind of nation that President Roosevelt hoped for, President Truman worked for and President Kennedy died for.
Lyndon B. Johnson (1908–73) US statesman.
The Sunday Times, 27 Dec 1964

11 A slave has but one master; an ambitious man has as many masters as there are people who may be useful in bettering his position.
Jean de La Bruyère (1645–96) French satirist.
Les Caractères

12 The shades of night were falling fast,
As through an Alpine village passed
A youth, who bore, 'mid snow and ice,
A banner with the strange device,
Excelsior!
Henry Wadsworth Longfellow (1807–82) US poet.
Opening of a poem best known as a Victorian drawing-room ballad, and the butt of many music-hall jokes. Excelsior means 'higher' (Latin)
Excelsior

13 If you would hit the mark, you must aim a little above it;
Every arrow that flies feels the attraction of earth.
Henry Wadsworth Longfellow
Elegiac Verse

14 Fain would I climb, yet fear I to fall.
Walter Raleigh (1554–1618) English explorer.
Written on a window pane. For the reply *see* ELIZABETH I
Attrib.

15 Ambition should be made of sterner stuff.
William Shakespeare (1564–1616) English dramatist.
Julius Caesar, III:2

16 I have no spur
To prick the sides of my intent, but only
Vaulting ambition, which o'er-leaps itself,
And falls on th' other.
William Shakespeare
Macbeth, I:7

17 And he that strives to touch the stars,

Oft stumbles at a straw.
Edmund Spenser (1552–99) English poet.
The Shepherd's Calendar, 'July'

18 There is always room at the top.
Daniel Webster (1782–1852) US statesman.
When advised not to become a lawyer because the profession was overcrowded
Attrib.

19 Well, good luck to you, kid! I'm going to write the Great Australian Novel.
Patrick White (1912–   ) British-born Australian novelist.
The Vivisector, 112

AMERICA

See also Americans

1 Our society distributes itself into Barbarians, Philistines, and Populace; and America is just ourselves, with the Barbarians quite left out, and the Populace nearly.
Matthew Arnold (1822–88) British poet and critic.
Culture and Anarchy, Preface

2 God bless the USA, so large,
So friendly, and so rich.
W. H. Auden (1907–73) British poet.
On the Circuit

3 Yankee Doodle came to town
Riding on a pony;
Stuck a feather in his cap
And called it Macaroni.
Edward Bangs (fl. 1775) US songwriter.
Yankee Doodle; or Father's Return to Camp

4 O beautiful for spacious skies,
For amber waves of grain,
For purple mountain majesties
Above the fruited plain!
America! America!
God shed His grace on thee
And crown thy good with brotherhood
From sea to shining sea!
Katharine Lee Bates (1859–1929) US writer and poet.
America the Beautiful

5 I called the New World into existence to redress the balance of the Old.
George Canning (1770–1827) British statesman.
Speech, 12 Dec 1826

6 This is virgin territory for whorehouses.
Al Capone (1899–1947) Italian-born US gangster.
Talking about suburban Chicago
The Bootleggers (Kenneth Allsop), Ch. 16

7 How beautiful it would be for someone who could not read.
G. K. Chesterton (1874–1936) British writer.
Referring to the lights on Broadway
Attrib.

8 America is the only nation in history which miraculously has gone directly from barbarism to degeneration without the usual interval of civilization.
Georges Clemenceau (1841–1929) French statesman.
Attrib.

9 Patriotism is easy to understand in America; it means looking out for yourself while looking out for your country.
Calvin Coolidge (1872–1833) US president.
Attrib.

10 The business of America is business.
Calvin Coolidge
Speech, Washington, 17 Jan 1925

11 Poor Mexico, so far from God and so near to the United States!
Porfirio Díaz (1830–1915) Mexican general and statesman.
Attrib.

12 Whatever America hopes to bring to pass in this world must first come to pass in the heart of America.
Dwight D. Eisenhower (1890–1969) US general and statesman.
Inaugural address, 1953

13 America is a country of young men.
Ralph Waldo Emerson (1803–82) US poet and essayist.
Society and Solitude, 'Old Age'

14 Our country is the world – our countrymen are all mankind.
William Lloyd Garrison (1805–79) US abolitionist.
The Liberator, 15 Dec 1837

15 . . . New York . . . that unnatural city where every one is an exile, none more so than the American.
Charlotte Perkins Gilman (1860–1935) US writer.
The Living of Charlotte Perkins Gilman

16 The United States is like a gigantic boiler. Once the fire is lighted under it there is no limit to the power it can generate.
Lord Grey (1862–1933) British statesman.
Their Finest Hour (Winston S. Churchill), Ch. 32

17 The United States, I believe, are under the impression that they are twenty years in advance of this country; whilst, as a matter of actual verifiable fact, of course, they are just about six hours behind it.
Harold Hobson (1904–   ) British theatre critic and writer.
The Devil in Woodford Wells, Ch. 8

18 The American system of rugged individualism.
Herbert Clark Hoover (1874–1964) US statesman.
Speech, New York, 22 Oct 1928

19 The United States has to move very fast to even stand still.
John Fitzgerald Kennedy (1917–63) US statesman.
The Observer, 'Sayings of the Week', 21 July 1963

20 'Tis the star-spangled banner; O long may it wave

O'er the land of the free, and the home of the brave!

Francis Scott Key (1779–1843) US lawyer.
The Star-Spangled Banner

21 Give me your tired, your poor,
Your huddled masses yearning to breathe free,
The wretched refuse of your teeming shore,
Send these, the homeless, tempest-tossed to me,
I lift my lamp beside the golden door!

Emma Lazarus (1849–87) US poet and philanthropist.
Used as an inscription on the Statue of Liberty
The New Colossus

22 In other countries, art and literature are left to a lot of shabby bums living in attics and feeding on booze and spaghetti, but in America the successful writer or picture-painter is indistinguishable from any other decent business man.

Sinclair Lewis (1885–1951) US novelist.
Babbitt, Ch. 14

23 In an English ship, they say, it is poor grub, poor pay, and easy work; in an American ship, good grub, good pay, and hard work. And this is applicable to the working populations of both countries.

Jack London (1876–1916) US novelist.
The People of the Abyss, Ch. 20

24 First the sweetheart of the nation, then the aunt, woman governs America because America is a land of boys who refuse to grow up.

Salvador de Madariaga y Rogo (1886–1978) Spanish diplomat and writer.
The Perpetual Pessimist (Sagitarius and George)

25 If there is any country on earth where the course of true love may be expected to run smooth, it is America.

Harriet Martineau (1802–76) British writer.
Society in America, Vol. III, 'Marriage'

26 The immense popularity of American movies abroad demonstrates that Europe is the unfinished negative of which America is the proof.

Mary McCarthy (1912–) US novelist.
On the Contrary

27 The national dish of America is menus.

Robert Robinson (1927–) British writer and broadcaster.
BBC TV programme, *Robinson's Travels*, Aug 1977

28 I pledge you, I pledge myself, to a new deal for the American people.

Franklin D. Roosevelt (1882–1945) US Democratic president.
Speech accepting nomination for presidency, Chicago, 2 July 1932

29 America . . . where law and customs alike are based on the dreams of spinsters.

Bertrand Russell (1872–1970) British philosopher.
Marriage and Morals

30 In the United States there is more space where nobody is than where anybody is. That is what makes America what it is.

Gertrude Stein (1874–1946) US writer.
The Geographical History of America

31 I like to walk around Manhattan, catching glimpses of its wild life, the pigeons and cats and girls.

Rex Todhunter Stout (1886–1975) US writer.
Three Witnesses, 'When a Man Murders'

32 I found there a country with thirty-two religions and only one sauce.

Talleyrand (Charles Maurice de Talleyrand-Périgord; 1754–1838) French politician.
Autant en apportent les mots (Pedrazzini)

33 America is a large, friendly dog in a very small room. Every time it wags its tail it knocks over a chair.

Arnold Toynbee (1889–1975) British historian.
Broadcast news summary, 14 July 1954

34 By the waters of Babylon we sit down and weep, when we think of thee, O America!

Horace Walpole (1717–97) British writer.
On the eve of the American Revolution
Letter to Mason, 12 June 1775

35 Up from the meadows rich with corn,
Clear in the cool September morn,

The clustered spires of Frederick stand
Green-walled by the hills of Maryland.

John Greenleaf Whittier (1807–92) US poet.
Barbara Frietchie

36 There exists in the world today a gigantic reservoir of good will toward us, the American people.

Wendell Lewis Willkie (1892–1944) US lawyer and businessman.
One World, Ch. 10

37 Sometimes people call me an idealist. Well, that is the way I know I am an American. America is the only idealistic nation in the world.

Woodrow Wilson (1856–1925) US statesman.
Speech, Sioux Falls, 8 Sept 1919

38 America . . . is the prize amateur nation of the world. Germany is the prize professional nation.

Woodrow Wilson
Speech, Aug 1917
Mr Wilson's War (John Dos Passos), Pt. III, Ch. 13

39 New York is a small place when it comes to the part of it that wakes up just as the rest is going to bed.

P. G. Wodehouse (1881–1975) British humorous novelist.
My Man Jeeves, 'The Aunt and the Sluggard'

40 America is God's Crucible, the great Melting-

Pot where all the races of Europe are melting and re-forming!
Israel Zangwill (1864–1926) British writer.
The Melting Pot, I

AMERICANS

1 Good Americans, when they die, go to Paris.
Thomas Gold Appleton (1812–84) US writer.
Autocrat of the Breakfast Table (O. W. Holmes), Ch. 6

2 A Boston man is the east wind made flesh.
Thomas Gold Appleton
Attrib.

3 There is nothing the matter with Americans except their ideals. The real American is all right; it is the ideal American who is all wrong.
G. K. Chesterton (1874–1936) British writer.
New York Times, 1 Feb 1931

4 Scratch an American and you get a Seventh Day Adventist every time.
Lord Hailsham (1907–) British Conservative politician.
The Observer, 'Sayings of the Week', 1 June 1969

5 I am willing to love all mankind, *except an American.*
Samuel Johnson (1709–84) British lexicographer.
Life of Johnson (J. Boswell), Vol. III

6 Does that mean that because Americans won't listen to sense, you intend to talk nonsense to them?
John Maynard Keynes (1883–1946) British economist.
Said before a monetary conference, 1944 or 1945

7 'There won't be any revolution in America . . . The people are too clean. They spend all their time changing their shirts and washing themselves. You can't feel fierce and revolutionary in a bathroom.
Eric Linklater (1899–1974) Scottish novelist.
Juan in America, Pt. V, Ch. 3

8 No one can kill Americans and brag about it. No one.
Ronald Reagan (1911–) US politician and president.
The Observer, 'Sayings of the Week', 27 Apr 1986

9 An American is either a Jew, or an anti-Semite, unless he is both at the same time.
Jean-Paul Sartre (1905–80) French writer.
Altona

10 That strange blend of the commercial traveller, the missionary, and the barbarian conqueror, which was the American abroad.
Olaf Stapledon (1886–1950) British philosopher and science-fiction writer.
Last and First Men, Ch. 3

11 Americans have been conditioned to respect newness, whatever it costs them.
John Updike (1932–) US novelist.
A Month of Sundays, Ch. 18

12 American writers want to be not good but great; and so are neither.
Gore Vidal (1925–) US novelist.
Two Sisters

13 MRS ALLONBY. They say, Lady Hunstanton, that when good Americans die they go to Paris.
LADY HUNSTANTON. Indeed? And when bad Americans die, where do they go to?
LORD ILLINGWORTH. Oh, they go to America.
Oscar Wilde (1854–1900) Irish-born British dramatist.
See Thomas Gold APPLETON
A Woman of No Importance, I

14 Like so many substantial Americans, he had married young and kept on marrying, springing from blonde to blonde like the chamois of the Alps leaping from crag to crag.
P. G. Wodehouse (1881–1975) British humorous novelist.
Wodehouse at Work to the End (Richard Usborne), Ch. 2

ANALOGY

See also similarity

1 Though analogy is often misleading, it is the least misleading thing we have.
Samuel Butler (1835–1902) British writer.
Notebooks

2 She, and comparisons are odious.
John Donne (1573–1631) English poet.
Elegies, 8, 'The Comparison'

3 My mistress' eyes are nothing like the sun; Coral is far more red than her lips' red.
William Shakespeare (1564–1616) English dramatist.
Sonnet 130

4 And yet, by heaven, I think my love as rare As any she belied with false compare.
William Shakespeare
Sonnet 130

5 Jeeves coughed one soft, low, gentle cough like a sheep with a blade of grass stuck in its throat.
P. G. Wodehouse (1881–1975) British humorous novelist.
The Inimitable Jeeves, Ch. 13

ANCESTRY

See also aristocracy, family

1 I am my own ancestor.
Duc d'Abrantes (1771–1813) French general.
Said on being made a duke
Attrib.

2 I can trace my ancestry back to a protoplasmal primordial atomic globule. Consequently, my family pride is something in-conceivable. I can't help it. I was born sneering.
W. S. Gilbert (1836–1911) British dramatist.
The Mikado, I

3 The difference between us is that my family begins with me, whereas yours ends with you.
Iphicrates (d. 353 BC) Athenian general.
Reply to a descendant of Harmodius (an Athenian hero), who had derided Iphicrates for being the son of a cobbler
Attrib.

4 Being Southerners, it was a source of shame to some members of the family that we had no recorded ancestors on either side of the Battle of Hastings.
Harper Lee (1926–) US writer.
To Kill a Mockingbird, Pt. I, Ch. 1

5 I don't know who my grandfather was; I am much more concerned to know what his grandson will be.
Abraham Lincoln (1809–65) US statesman.
Taking part in a discussion on ancestry
Attrib.

ANGER

1 The man who gets angry at the right things and with the right people, and in the right way and at the right time and for the right length of time, is commended.
Aristotle (384–322 BC) Greek philosopher.
Nicomachean Ethics, Bk. IV

2 When they heard these things, they were cut to the heart, and they gnashed on him with their teeth.
Bible: Acts
7:54

3 Never go to bed mad. Stay up and fight.
Phyllis Diller (1917–) US writer and comedienne.
Phyllis Diller's Housekeeping Hints

4 Anger is one of the sinews of the soul.
Thomas Fuller (1608–61) English historian.
The Holy State and the Profane State

5 Spleen can subsist on any kind of food.
William Hazlitt (1778–1830) British essayist.
On Wit and Humour

6 Anger has overpowered him, and driven him to a revenge which was rather a stupid one, I must acknowledge, but anger makes us all stupid.
Johanna Spyri (1827–1901) Swiss writer.
Heidi, Ch. 23

7 Anger supplies the arms.
Virgil (Publius Vergilius Maro; 70–19 BC) Roman poet.
Aeneid, Bk. I

ANIMALISM

See also evolution, lust, mankind, sex

1 My brain: it's my second favourite organ.
Woody Allen (Allen Stewart Konigsberg; 1935–) US film actor.
Sleeper

2 But oh, the farmyard world of sex!
Harley Granville-Barker (1877–1946) British actor and dramatist.
The Madras House, IV

3 Be a good animal, true to your animal instincts.
D. H. Lawrence (1885–1930) British novelist.
The White Peacock, Pt. II, Ch. 2

4 It's all this cold-hearted fucking that is death and idiocy.
D. H. Lawrence
Lady Chatterley's Lover, Ch. 14

5 The soul started at the knee-cap and ended at the navel.
Wyndham Lewis (1882–1957) British novelist.
The Apes of God, Pt. XII

6 – 'Do you come here often?'
'Only in the mating season.'
Spike Milligan (1918–) British comic actor and author.
The Goon Show

7 The wren goes to't, and the small gilded fly
Does lecher in my sight.
William Shakespeare (1564–1616) English dramatist.
King Lear, IV:6

ANIMALS

See also cats, dogs, horses, rabbits

1 There was a young lady of Riga,
Who went for a ride on a tiger;
They returned from the ride
With the lady inside,
And a smile on the face of the tiger.
Anonymous

2 The fox knows many things – the hedgehog one *big* one.
Archilochus (c. 680–c. 640 BC) Greek poet.
Attrib.

3 And God said, Let the earth bring forth the living creature after his kind, cattle, and creeping thing, and beast of the earth after his kind: and it was so.
Bible: Genesis
1:24

4 Tiger! Tiger! burning bright
In the forests of the night,
What immortal hand or eye
Could frame thy fearful symmetry?
William Blake (1757–1827) British poet.
Songs of Experience, 'The Tiger'

5 Rats!
They fought the dogs and killed the cats,
And bit the babies in the cradles.
Robert Browning (1812–89) British poet.
The Pied Piper of Hamelin

6 And the muttering grew to a grumbling;
And the grumbling grew to a mighty rumbling;

And out of the houses the rats came tumbling.
Robert Browning
The Pied Piper of Hamelin

7 Wee, sleekit, cow'rin', tim'rous beastie,
O what a panic's in thy breastie!
Robert Burns (1759–96) Scottish poet.
To a Mouse

8 Whenever you observe an animal closely, you
feel as if a human being sitting inside were
making fun of you.
Elias Canetti (1905–   ) Bulgarian-born novelist.
The Human Province

9 The devil's walking parody
On all four-footed things.
G. K. Chesterton (1874–1936) British writer.
The Donkey

10 Animals are such agreeable friends – they
ask no questions, they pass no criticisms.
George Eliot (Mary Ann Evans; 1819–80) British
novelist.
Scenes of Clerical Life, 'Mr Gilfil's Love Story', Ch. 7

11 Mary had a little lamb,
Its fleece was white as snow,
And everywhere that Mary went
The lamb was sure to go.
Sarah Josepha Hale (1788–1879) US writer.
Poems for Our Children, 'Mary's Little Lamb'

12 'Twould ring the bells of Heaven
The wildest peal for years,
If Parson lost his senses
And people came to theirs,
And he and they together
Knelt down with angry prayers
For tamed and shabby tigers
And dancing dogs and bears,
And wretched, blind, pit ponies,
And little hunted hares.
Ralph Hodgson (1871–1962) British poet.
The Bells of Heaven

13 The stars grew bright in the winter sky,
The wind came keen with a tang of frost,
The brook was troubled for new things lost,
The copse was happy for old things found,
The fox came home and he went to ground.
John Masefield (1878–1967) British poet.
Reynard the Fox

14 I never nurs'd a dear gazelle,
To glad me with its soft black eye
But when it came to know me well,
And love me, it was sure to die!
Thomas Moore (1779–1852) Irish poet.
Lalla Rookh

15 Dogs, like horses, are quadrupeds. That is to
say, they have four rupeds, one at each
corner, on which they walk.
Frank Muir (1920–   ) British writer and broadcaster.
You Can't Have Your Kayak and Heat It (Frank Muir and Denis Norden), 'Ta-ra-ra-boom-de-ay!'

16 The cow is of the bovine ilk;

One end is moo, the other, milk.
Ogden Nash (1902–71) US poet.
The Cow

17 Nothing can be more obvious than that all
animals were created solely and exclusively
for the use of man.
Thomas Love Peacock (1785–1866) British novelist.
Headlong Hall, Ch. 2

18 *Exit, pursued by a bear.*
William Shakespeare (1564–1616) English dramatist.
Stage direction
The Winter's Tale, III:3

19 There are two things for which animals are
to be envied: they know nothing of future
evils, or of what people say about them.
Voltaire (François-Marie Arouet; 1694–1778) French
writer.
Letter, 1739

20 Let dogs delight to bark and bite,
For God hath made them so;
Let bears and lions growl and fight,
For 'tis their nature too.
Isaac Watts (1674–1748) English theologian and hymn
writer.
Divine Songs for Children, 'Against Quarrelling'

21 Feather-footed through the plashy fen passes
the questing vole.
Evelyn Waugh (1903–66) British novelist.
Scoop, Bk. I, Ch. 1

22 I think I could turn and live with animals,
they're so placid and self-contained,
I stand and look at them long and long.
Walt Whitman (1819–92) US poet.
Song of Myself, 32

ANTHROPOMORPHISM

1 The Romans and Greeks found everything
human. Everything had a face, and a human
voice. Men spoke, and their fountains piped
an answer.
D. H. Lawrence (1885–1930) British novelist.
Fantasia of the Unconscious, Ch. 4

ANTICIPATION

See also expectation

1 A stitch in time saves nine.
Proverb

2 Don't cross the bridge till you get to it.
Proverb

3 The early bird catches the worm.
Proverb

4 Don't count your chickens before they are
hatched.
Aesop (6th century BC) Reputed Greek writer of fables.
Fables, 'The Milkmaid and her Pail'

5 To swallow gudgeons ere they're catched,

And count their chickens ere they're hatched.
Samuel Butler (1612–80) English satirist.
Hudibras, Pt. II

6 He told me never to sell the bear's skin
before one has killed the beast.
Jean de La Fontaine (1621–95) French poet.
Fables, V, 'L'Ours et les deux Compagnons'

7 To travel hopefully is a better thing than to
arrive, and the true success is to labour.
Robert Louis Stevenson (1850–94) Scottish writer.
Virginibus Puerisque

APOLOGIES

See also regret

1 Very sorry can't come. Lie follows by post.
Charles Beresford (1846–1919) British naval officer.
Reply, by telegram, to a dinner invitation at short notice from
Edward, Prince of Wales
The World of Fashion 1837–1922 (R. Nevill), Ch. 5

2 Miss Otis regrets she's unable to lunch
today.
Cole Porter (1893–1964) US songwriter.
Hi Diddle Diddle, Miss Otis Regrets

3 Love means never having to say you're
sorry.
Erich Segal (1937–   ) US writer.
Love Story

4 Mr. Speaker, I said the honorable member
was a liar it is true and I am sorry for it.
The honourable member may place the
punctuation where he pleases.
Richard Brinsley Sheridan (1751–1816) British
dramatist.
On being asked to apologize for calling a fellow MP a liar
Attrib.

5 It is a good rule in life never to apologize.
The right sort of people do not want
apologies, and the wrong sort take a mean
advantage of them.
P. G. Wodehouse (1881–1975) British humorous
novelist.
The Man Upstairs and Other Stories

APPEARANCE

See also appearances, beauty, clothes, cosmetics, eyes

1 Fine feathers make fine birds.
Proverb

2 Handsome is as handsome does.
Proverb

3 A homely face and no figure have aided many
women heavenward.
Minna Antrim (1861–?) US writer.
Naked Truth and Veiled Allusions

4 Take a close-up of a woman past sixty! You
might as well use a picture of a relief map of
Ireland!
Nancy Astor (1879–1964) American-born British politician.
When asked for a close-up photograph
Attrib.

5 But if a woman have long hair, it is a glory
to her: for her hair is given her for a
covering.
Bible: I Corinthians
11:15

6 Alas, after a certain age every man is
responsible for his face.
Albert Camus (1913–60) French existentialist writer.
The Fall

7 Ears like bombs and teeth like splinters:
A blitz of a boy is Timothy Winters.
Charles Causley (1917–   ) British poet and broadcaster.
Timothy Winters

8 It was a blonde. A blonde to make a bishop
kick a hole in a stained-glass window.
Raymond Chandler (1888–1959) US novelist.
Farewell, My Lovely, Ch. 13

9 Sunburn is very becoming – but only when it
is even – one must be careful not to look
like a mixed grill.
Noël Coward (1899–1973) British dramatist.
The Lido Beach

10 The ring so worn, as you behold,
So thin, so pale, is yet of gold.
George Crabbe (1754–1832) British poet.
His Mother's Wedding Ring

11 The most delightful advantage of being bald –
one can hear snowflakes.
R. G. Daniels (1916–   ) British magistrate.
The Observer, 'Sayings of the Week', 11 July 1976

12 He had but one eye, and the popular
prejudice runs in favour of two.
Charles Dickens (1812–70) British novelist.
Said by Mr Squeers
Nicholas Nickleby, Ch. 4

13 It was not a bosom to repose upon, but it
was a capital bosom to hang jewels upon.
Charles Dickens
Describing Mrs Merdle
Little Dorrit, Bk. I, Ch. 21

14 I am so changed that my oldest creditors
would hardly know me.
Henry Stephen Fox (1791–1846) British diplomat.
Remark after an illness
Letter from Byron to John Murray, 8 May 1817

15 There is a great difference between painting
a face and not washing it.
Thomas Fuller (1608–61) English historian.
Church History, Bk. VII

16 The flowers that bloom in the spring,
Tra la,
Have nothing to do with the case.
I've got to take under my wing,

Tra la,
A most unattractive old thing,
Tra la,
With a caricature of a face.
W. S. Gilbert (1836–1911) British dramatist.
The Mikado, II

17 Where's the cheek that doth not fade,
Too much gaz'd at? Where's the maid
Whose lip mature is ever new?
John Keats (1795–1821) British poet.
Fancy, I

18 It always seemed to me that men wore their
beards, like they wear their neckties, for
show. I shall always remember Lewis for
saying his beard was part of him.
D. H. Lawrence (1885–1930) British novelist.
St Mawr

19 There was an Old Man with a beard,
Who said, 'It is just as I feared! –
Two Owls and a Hen,
Four Larks and a Wren,
Have all built their nests in my beard!'
Edward Lear (1812–88) British artist and writer.
Book of Nonsense

20 The Lord prefers common-looking people.
That is why he makes so many of them.
Abraham Lincoln (1809–65) US statesman.
Our President (James Morgan), Ch. 6

21 He looks as if he had been weaned on a
pickle.
Alice Roosevelt Longworth (1884–1980) US hostess.
Referring to John Calvin Coolidge, US president 1923–29
Crowded Hours

22 Gentlemen always seem to remember
blondes.
Anita Loos (1891–1981) US novelist.
Gentlemen Prefer Blondes, Ch. 1

23 In high school and college my sister Mary
was very popular with the boys, but I had
braces on my teeth and got high marks.
Betty MacDonald (1908–58) US writer.
The Egg and I, Ch. 2

24 There's a man outside with a big black
moustache.
– Tell him I've got one.
Groucho Marx (Julius Marx; 1895–1977) US comedian.
Horse Feathers

25 To Crystal, hair was the most important
thing on earth. She would never get married
because you couldn't wear curlers in bed.
Edna O'Brien (1936–) Irish novelist.
Winter's Tales, 8, 'Come into the Drawing Room, Doris'

26 Men seldom make passes
At girls who wear glasses.
Dorothy Parker (1893–1967) US writer.
Attrib.

27 All I say is, nobody has any business to go

around looking like a horse and behaving as if
it were all right. You don't catch horses
going around looking like people, do you?
Dorothy Parker
Horsie

28 Had Cleopatra's nose been shorter, the
whole face of the world would have changed.
Blaise Pascal (1623–62) French philosopher and
mathematician.
Pensées, II

29 To church; and with my mourning, very
handsome, and new periwig, make a great
show.
Samuel Pepys (1633–1703) English diarist.
Diary, 31 Mar 1667

30 My nose is huge! Vile snub-nose, flat-nosed
ass, flat-head, let me inform you that I am
proud of such an appendage, since a big nose
is the proper sign of a friendly, good,
courteous, witty, liberal, and brave man,
such as I am.
Edmond Rostand (1868–1918) French poet and
dramatist.
Cyrano de Bergerac, I:1

31 In the spring . . . your lovely Chloë lightly
turns to one mass of spots.
Ronald Searle (1920–) British cartoonist.
The Terror of St Trinian's, Ch. 7

32 LORD NORTHCLIFFE. The trouble with you, Shaw,
is that you look as if there were famine in
the land.
G.B.S. The trouble with you, Northcliffe, is that
you look as if you were the cause of it.
George Bernard Shaw (1856–1950) Irish dramatist and
critic.
Attrib.

33 A short neck denotes a good mind . . . You
see, the messages go quicker to the brain
because they've shorter to go.
Muriel Spark (1918–) British novelist.
The Ballad of Peckham Rye, Ch. 7

34 But Shelley had a hyper-thyroid face.
John Collings Squire (1884–1958) British journalist.
Ballade of the Glandular Hypothesis

35 . . . his nicotine eggyellow weeping walrus
Victorian moustache worn thick and long in
memory of Doctor Crippen.
Dylan Thomas (1914–53) Welsh poet.
Under Milk Wood

36 Very hard for a man with a wig to keep
order.
Evelyn Waugh (1903–66) British novelist.
Decline and Fall, Pt. I, Ch. 3

37 Enclosing every thin man, there's a fat man
demanding elbow-room.
Evelyn Waugh
Officers and Gentlemen, Interlude

38 But there are other things than dissipation that thicken the features. Tears, for example.
Rebecca West (Cicely Isabel Fairfield; 1892–1983) British novelist and journalist.
Black Lamb and Grey Falcon, 'Serbia'

39 Grief has turned her fair.
Oscar Wilde (1854–1900) Irish-born British dramatist.
Referring to the fact that a recently-bereaved lady friend had dyed her hair blonde
Attrib.

40 Big chap with a small moustache and the sort of eye that can open an oyster at sixty paces.
P. G. Wodehouse (1881–1975) British humorous novelist.
The Code of the Woosters

41 The stationmaster's whiskers are of a Victorian bushiness and give the impression of having been grown under glass.
P. G. Wodehouse
Wodehouse at Work to the End (Richard Usborne), Ch. 2

APPEARANCES

See also appearance, deception, hypocrisy

1 All that glitters is not gold.
Proverb

2 Appearances are deceptive.
Proverb

3 Never judge from appearances.
Proverb

4 Still waters run deep.
Proverb

5 Things are not always what they seem.
Proverb

6 Vice is often clothed in virtue's habit.
Proverb

7 You can't tell a book by its cover.
Proverb

8 The lamb that belonged to the sheep whose skin the wolf was wearing began to follow the wolf in the sheep's clothing.
Aesop (6th century BC) Reputed Greek writer of fables.
Fables, 'The Wolf in Sheep's Clothing'

9 The French are wiser than they seem, and the Spaniards seem wiser than they are.
Francis Bacon (1561–1626) English philosopher.
Essays, 'Of Seeming Wise'

10 No-wher so bisy a man as he ther nas,
And yet he semed bisier than he was.
Geoffrey Chaucer (c. 1342–1400) English poet.
Referring to the man of law
The Canterbury Tales, Prologue

11 Keep up appearances; there lies the test
The world will give thee credit for the rest.
Charles Churchill (1731–64) British poet.
Night

12 I may not hope from outward forms to win
The passion and the life, whose fountains are within.
Samuel Taylor Coleridge (1772–1834) British poet.
Dejection: An Ode

13 Appearances are not held to be a clue to the truth. But we seem to have no other.
Ivy Compton-Burnett (1892–1969) British novelist.
Manservant and Maidservant

14 No man could be so wise as Thurlow looked.
Charles James Fox (1749–1806) British Whig politician.
Lives of the Lord Chancellors (Campbell), Vol. V

15 Ah, pray make no mistake,
We are not shy;
We're very wide awake,
The moon and I.
W. S. Gilbert (1836–1911) British dramatist.
The Mikado, II

16 An' for all 'is dirty 'ide
'E was white, clear white, inside
When 'e went to tend the wounded under fire!
Rudyard Kipling (1865–1936) Indian-born British writer.
Gunga Din

17 And you cannot tell by the way a party looks or how he lives in this town, if he has any scratch, because many a party who is around in automobiles, and wearing good clothes, and chucking quite a swell is nothing but a phonus bolonus and does not have any real scratch whatever.
Damon Runyon (1884–1946) US writer.
More than Somewhat, 'The Snatching of Bookie Bob'

18 Things are entirely what they appear to be and *behind them* . . . there is nothing.
Jean-Paul Sartre (1905–80) French writer.
Nausea

19 Care I for the limb, the thews, the stature, bulk, and big assemblance of a man! Give me the spirit.
William Shakespeare (1564–1616) English dramatist.
Henry IV, Part Two, III:2

20 Through tatter'd clothes small vices do appear;
Robes and furr'd gowns hide all.
William Shakespeare
King Lear, IV:6

21 Our purses shall be proud, our garments poor;
For 'tis the mind that makes the body rich;
And as the sun breaks through the darkest clouds,
So honour peereth in the meanest habit.
William Shakespeare
The Taming of the Shrew, IV:3

22 It is only shallow people who do not judge by appearances.
Oscar Wilde (1854–1900) Irish-born British dramatist.
The Picture of Dorian Gray, Ch. 2

ARCHITECTURE

See also houses, stately homes

1 Sir Christopher Wren
Said, 'I am going to dine with some men.
If anybody calls
Say I am designing St Paul's.'
Edmund Clerihew Bentley (1875–1956) British writer.
Biography for Beginners

2 A very stately palace before him, the name
of which was Beautiful.
John Bunyan (1628–88) English writer.
The Pilgrim's Progress, Pt. I

3 You have to give this much to the Luftwaffe
– when it knocked down our buildings it did
not replace them with anything more
offensive than rubble. We did that.
Charles, Prince of Wales (1948–) Eldest son of
Elizabeth II.
The Observer, 'Sayings of the Week', 6 Dec 1987

4 Like a carbuncle on the face of an old and
valued friend.
Charles, Prince of Wales
Referring to a proposed modern extension to the National
Gallery
Speech, 1986

5 'Fan vaulting' . . . an architectural device
which arouses enormous enthusiasm on
account of the difficulties it has all too
obviously involved but which from an
aesthetic standpoint frequently belongs to the
'Last-supper-carved-on-a-peach-stone' class of
masterpiece.
Osbert Lancaster (1908–86) British cartoonist.
Pillar to Post, 'Perpendicular'

6 What has happened to architecture since the
second world war that the only passers-by
who can contemplate it without pain are
those equipped with a white stick and a dog?
Bernard Levin (1928–) British journalist.
The Times, 1983

7 I declare this thing open – whatever it is.
Prince Philip (1921–) The consort of Queen Elizabeth
II.
Opening a new annex at Vancouver City Hall
Attrib.

8 No person who is not a great sculptor or
painter can be an architect. If he is not a
sculptor or painter, he can only be a *builder*.
John Ruskin (1819–1900) British art critic and writer.
Lectures on Architecture and Painting

9 When we build let us think that we build for
ever.
John Ruskin
The Seven Lamps of Architecture, Ch. 6, 'The Lamp of Memory'

10 Architecture in general is frozen music.
Friedrich Wilhelm Joseph von Schelling (1775–1854)
German philosopher.
Philosophie der Kunst

11 Many of my buildings are condemned now in
advance.
Richard Seifert (1910–) British architect.
He designed Centre Point, London and other office block
schemes
The Observer, 'Sayings of the Week', 6 Aug 1972

12 It's beige! My color!
Elsie De Wolfe (1865–1950) US designer.
On first sighting the Acropolis
Elsie de Wolfe (J. Smith)

13 In *Architecture* as in all other *Operative* Arts,
the *end* must direct the *Operation*. The *end*
is to build well. Well building hath three
Conditions. *Commodity, Firmness,* and
Delight.
Henry Wotton (1568–1639) English poet and diplomat.
Elements of Architecture, Pt. I

ARGUMENTS

1 It takes two to make a quarrel.
Proverb

2 Least said soonest mended.
Proverb

3 For every why he had a wherefore.
Samuel Butler (1612–80) English satirist.
Hudibras, Pt. I

4 Many a long dispute among divines may be
thus abridged: It is so. It is not so. It is so.
It is not so.
Benjamin Franklin (1706–90) US scientist and statesman.
Poor Richard's Almanack

5 In every age and clime we see,
Two of a trade can ne'er agree.
John Gay (1685–1732) English poet and dramatist.
Fables

6 Scholars dispute, and the case is still before
the courts.
Horace (Quintus Horatius Flaccus; 65–8 BC) Roman poet.
Ars Poetica c. 8 BC

7 'It's like the question of the authorship of the
Iliad,' said Mr Cardan. 'The author of that
poem is either Homer or, if not Homer,
somebody else of the same name.'
Aldous Huxley (1894–1964) British novelist.
Those Barren Leaves, Pt. V, Ch. 4

8 It takes in reality only one to make a quarrel.
It is useless for the sheep to pass resolutions
in favour of vegetarianism while the wolf
remains of a different opinion.
Dean Inge (1860–1954) British churchman.
Outspoken Essays

9 Sir, I have found you an argument; but I am
not obliged to find you an understanding.
Samuel Johnson (1709–84) British lexicographer.
Life of Johnson (J. Boswell), Vol. IV

10 Though a quarrel in the streets is a thing to
be hated, the energies displayed in it are

fine; the commonest man shows a grace in his quarrel.
John Keats (1795–1821) British poet.
Letter

11 When men understand what each other mean, they see, for the most part, that controversy is either superfluous or hopeless.
Cardinal Newman (1801–90) British theologian.
Sermon, Oxford, Epiphany 1839

12 Quarrels would not last so long if the fault were on only one side.
Duc de la Rochefoucauld (1613–80) French writer.
Maximes, 496

13 The most savage controversies are those about matters as to which there is no good evidence either way.
Bertrand Russell (1872–1970) British philosopher.
Unpopular Essays

14 I love argument, I love debate. I don't expect anyone just to sit there and agree with me, that's not their job.
Margaret Thatcher (1925–   ) British politician and prime minister.
The Times, 1980

15 I did not know that we had ever quarrelled.
Henry David Thoreau (1817–62) US writer.
On being urged to make his peace with God
Attrib.

16 I am, sir for the last time in my life, Your Humble Servant Horace Walpole.
Horace Walpole (1717–97) British writer.
Ending a letter written to an uncle with whom he had recently quarrelled
Horace Walpole (R. Ketton-Cremes)

17 I am not arguing with you – I am telling you.
James Whistler (1834–1903) US painter.
The Gentle Art of Making Enemies

18 No question is ever settled
Until it is settled right.
Ella Wheeler Wilcox (1850–1919) US poet.
Settle the Question Right

ARISTOCRACY

See also ancestry, class, Houses of Parliament, nobility, stately homes, titles

1 One has often wondered whether upon the whole earth there is anything so unintelligent, so unapt to perceive how the world is really going, as an ordinary young Englishman of our upper class.
Matthew Arnold (1822–88) British poet and critic.
Culture and Anarchy, Ch. 2

2 Like many of the upper class
He liked the sound of broken glass.
Hilaire Belloc (1870–1953) French-born British poet.
See also Evelyn WAUGH.
New Cautionary Tales, 'About John'

3 The nobility of England, my lord, would have snored through the Sermon on the Mount.
Robert Bolt (1924–   ) British playwright.
A Man for All Seasons

4 We, my lords, may thank heaven that we have something better than our brains to depend upon.
Earl of Chesterfield (1694–1773) English statesman.
Speech, House of Lords
The Story of Civilization (W. Durant), Vol. 9

5 Democracy means government by the uneducated, while aristocracy means government by the badly educated.
G. K. Chesterton (1874–1936) British writer.
New York Times, 1 Feb 1931

6 The Stately Homes of England
How beautiful they stand,
To prove the upper classes
Have still the upper hand.
Noël Coward (1899–1973) British dramatist.
Operette, 'The Stately Homes of England'

7 If human beings could be propagated by cutting, like apple trees, aristocracy would be biologically sound.
J. B. S. Haldane (1892–1964) British geneticist.
The Inequality of Man, title essay

8 There are no credentials They do not even need a medical certificate. They need not be sound either in body or mind. They only require a certificate of birth – just to prove that they are first of the litter. You would not choose a spaniel on these principles.
David Lloyd George (1863–1945) British Liberal statesman.
Budget Speech, 1909

9 A fully equipped Duke costs as much to keep up as two Dreadnoughts, and Dukes are just as great a terror, and they last longer.
David Lloyd George
Speech, Limehouse, 30 July 1909

10 An aristocracy in a republic is like a chicken whose head has been cut off: it may run about in a lively way, but in fact it is dead.
Nancy Mitford (1904–73) British writer.
Noblesse Oblige

11 He is without strict doubt a Hoorah Henry, and he is generally figured as nothing but a lob as far as doing anything useful in this world is concerned.
Damon Runyon (1884–1946) US writer.
Short Takes, 'Tight Shoes'

12 Kind hearts are more than coronets,
And simple faith than Norman blood.
Alfred, Lord Tennyson (1809–92) British poet.
Lady Clara Vere de Vere, VI

13 My Lord Bath, you and I are now two as insignificant men as any in England.
Robert Walpole (1676–1745) British statesman.
Said to William Pulteney, Earl of Bath, when they were promoted to the peerage (1742)
Political & Literary Anecdotes (W. King)

14 The sound of the English county families baying for broken glass.
Evelyn Waugh (1903–66) British novelist.
See also Hilaire BELLOC.
Decline and Fall, Prelude

15 Unlike the male codfish which, suddenly finding itself the parent of three million five hundred thousand little codfish, cheerfully resolves to love them all, the British aristocracy is apt to look with a somewhat jaundiced eye on its younger sons.
P. G. Wodehouse (1881–1975) British humorous novelist.
Wodehouse at Work to the End (Richard Usborne), Ch. 5

ARMY

See also officers, soldiers, war, weapons

1 Oh! the grand old Duke of York
He had ten thousand men;
He marched them up to the top of the hill,
And he marched them down again.
And when they were up they were up,
And when they were down they were down,
And when they were only half way up,
They were neither up nor down.
Anonymous

2 Conduct . . . to the prejudice of good order and military discipline.
Anonymous
Army Act, 40

3 The chief attraction of military service has consisted and will consist in this compulsory and irreproachable idleness.
Leo Tolstoy (1828–1910) Russian writer.
War and Peace, Bk. VII, Ch. 1

4 An army is a nation within a nation; it is one of the vices of our age.
Alfred de Vigny (1797–1863) French writer.
Servitude et grandeur militaire, 1

5 Ours is composed of the scum of the earth.
Duke of Wellington (1769–1852) British general.
Of the British army
Remark, 4 Nov 1831

6 The army ages men sooner than the law and philosophy; it exposes them more freely to germs, which undermine and destroy, and it shelters them more completely from thought, which stimulates and preserves.
H. G. Wells (1866–1946) British writer.
Bealby, Pt. VIII, Ch. 1

ARROGANCE

See also conceit, egotism, pride

1 The need to be right – the sign of a vulgar mind.
Albert Camus (1913–60) French existentialist writer.
Notebooks, 1935–42.

2 I am sure no man in England will take away my life to make you King.
Charles II (1630–85) King of England.
To his brother James following revelation of Popish Plot fabricated by Titus Oates
Attrib.

3 He was like a cock who thought the sun had risen to hear him crow.
George Eliot (Mary Ann Evans; 1819–80) British novelist.
Adam Bede

4 If this young man expresses himself in terms too deep for *me*,
Why, what a very singularly deep young man this deep young man must be!
W. S. Gilbert (1836–1911) British dramatist.
Patience, I

5 There, but for the Grace of God, goes God.
Herman J. Mankiewicz (1897–1953) US journalist and screenwriter.
Said of Orson Welles in the making of *Citizen Kane*. Also attributed to others
The Citizen Kane Book

6 The bullet that is to kill me has not yet been moulded.
Napoleon I (Napoleon Bonaparte; 1769–1821) French emperor.
In reply to his brother Joseph, King of Spain, who had asked whether he had ever been hit by a cannonball
Attrib.

7 What His Royal Highness most particularly prides himself upon, is the excellent harvest.
Richard Brinsley Sheridan (1751–1816) British dramatist.
Lampooning George IV's habit of taking credit for everything good in England
The Fine Art of Political Wit (L. Harris)

8 A LADY. This landscape reminds me of your work.
WHISTLER. Yes madam, Nature is creeping up.
James Whistler (1834–1903) US painter.
Whistler Stories (D. Seitz)

9 Well, not bad, but there are decidedly too many of them, and they are not very well arranged. I would have done it differently.
James Whistler
His reply when asked if he agreed that the stars were especially beautiful one night
Attrib.

10 The Admiral of the Atlantic salutes the Admiral of the Pacific.
Wilhelm II (1859–1941) King of Prussia and Emperor of Germany.
Telegram sent to Czar Nicholas II during a naval exercise
The Shadow of the Winter Palace (E. Crankshaw)

11 All men think all men mortal, but themselves.
Edward Young (1683–1765) British poet.
Night Thoughts

ART

See also artists, arts, painting, sculpture

1 The works of art, by being publicly exhibited and offered for sale, are becoming articles of trade, following as such the unreasoning laws of markets and fashion; and public and even private patronage is swayed by their tyrannical influence.
Prince Albert (1819–61) The consort of Queen Victoria.
Referring to the Great Exhibition
Speech, Royal Academy Dinner, 3 May 1851

2 The object of art is to give life a shape.
Jean Anouilh (1910–87) French dramatist.
The Rehearsal

3 The lower one's vitality, the more sensitive one is to great art.
Max Beerbohm (1872–1956) British writer.
Seven Men, 'Enoch Soames'

4 It would follow that 'significant form' was form behind which we catch a sense of ultimate reality.
Clive Bell (1881–1964) British art critic.
Art, Pt. I, Ch. 3

5 Art is the only thing that can go on mattering once it has stopped hurting.
Elizabeth Bowen (1899–1973) Irish novelist.
The Heat of the Day, Ch. 16

6 Art for art's sake.
Victor Cousin (1792–1867) French philosopher.
Lecture, Sorbonne, 1818

7 Art is a jealous mistress.
Ralph Waldo Emerson (1803–82) US poet and essayist.
Conduct of Life, 'Wealth'

8 Works of art, in my opinion, are the only objects in the material universe to possess internal order, and that is why, though I don't believe that only art matters, I do believe in Art for Art's sake.
E. M. Forster (1879–1970) British novelist.
Art for Art's Sake

9 . . . I rarely draw what I see. I draw what I feel in my body.
Barbara Hepworth (1903–75) British sculptor.
World of Art Series (A. M. Hammersmith)

10 In free society art is not a weapon . . . Artists are not engineers of the soul.
John Fitzgerald Kennedy (1917–63) US statesman.
Address at Dedication of the Robert Frost Library, 26 Oct 1963

11 But the Devil whoops, as he whooped of old: 'It's clever, but is it art?'
Rudyard Kipling (1865–1936) Indian-born British writer.
The Conundrum of the Workshops

12 Art is not a special sauce applied to ordinary cooking; it is the cooking itself if it is good.
W. R. Lethaby (1857–1931) British architect.
Form in Civilization, 'Art and Workmanship'

13 I do not know whether he draws a line himself. But I assume that his is the direction . . . It makes Disney the most significant figure in graphic art since Leonardo.
David Low (1871–1963) New-Zealand-born newspaper cartoonist.
Walt Disney (R. Schickel), Ch. 20

14 In England, pop art and fine art stand resolutely back to back.
Colin MacInnes (1914–76) British novelist.
England, Half English, 'Pop Songs and Teenagers'

15 Art is not a mirror to reflect the world, but a hammer with which to shape it.
Vladimir Mayakovsky (1893–1930) Soviet poet.
The Guardian, 11 Dec 1974

16 Nothing unites the English like war. Nothing divides them like Picasso.
Hugh Mills (1913–71) British screenwriter.
Prudence and the Pill

17 To be aristocratic in Art one must avoid polite society.
George Moore (1852–1933) Irish writer and art critic.
Enemies of Promise (Cyril Connolly), Ch. 15

18 All art deals with the absurd and aims at the simple. Good art speaks truth, indeed *is* truth, perhaps the only truth.
Iris Murdoch (1919–) Irish-born British novelist.
The Black Prince, 'Bradley Pearson's Foreword'

19 All art constantly aspires towards the condition of music.
Walter Pater (1839–94) British critic.
The Renaissance, 'The School of Giorgione'

20 When I was their age, I could draw like Raphael, but it took me a lifetime to learn to draw like them.
Pablo Picasso (1881–1973) Spanish painter.
Visiting an exhibition of drawings by children
Picasso: His Life and Work (Ronald Penrose)

21 Burnings of people and (what was more valuable) works of art.
A. L. Rowse (1903–) British historian and critic.
Historical Essays (H. R. Trevor-Roper)

22 Life without industry is guilt, and industry without art is brutality.
John Ruskin (1819–1900) British art critic and writer.
Lectures on Art, 3, 'The Relation of Art to Morals', 23 Feb 1870

23 Fine art is that in which the hand, the head, and the heart of man go together.
John Ruskin
The Two Paths, Lecture II

24 The trouble, Mr Goldwyn is that you are

only interested in art and I am only
interested in money.
George Bernard Shaw (1856–1950) Irish dramatist and
critic.
Turning down Goldwyn's offer to buy the screen rights of his
plays
The Movie Moguls (Philip French), Ch. 4

25 Skill without imagination is craftsmanship and
gives us many useful objects such as
wickerwork picnic baskets. Imagination
without skill gives us modern art.
Tom Stoppard (1937–) Czech-born British dramatist.
Artist Descending a Staircase

26 Art is not a handicraft, it is the transmission
of feeling the artist has experienced.
Leo Tolstoy (1828–1910) Russian writer.
What is Art?, Ch. 19

27 What a delightful thing this perspective is!
Paolo Uccello (1397–1475) Italian painter.
Men of Art (T. Craven)

28 . . . any authentic work of art must start an
argument between the artist and his
audience.
Rebecca West (Cicely Isabel Fairfield; 1892–1983) British
novelist and journalist.
The Court and the Castle, Pt. I, Ch. 1

29 Art is the imposing of a pattern on
experience, and our aesthetic enjoyment is
recognition of the pattern.
A. N. Whitehead (1861–1947) British philosopher.
Dialogues, 228

30 Art never expresses anything but itself.
Oscar Wilde (1854–1900) Irish-born British dramatist.
The Decay of Lying

31 All Art is quite useless.
Oscar Wilde
The Picture of Dorian Gray, Preface

32 Art is the most intense mode of individualism
that the world has known.
Oscar Wilde
The Soul of Man Under Socialism

ARTHURIAN LEGEND

1 What were they going to do with the Grail
when they found it, Mr Rossetti?
Max Beerbohm (1872–1956) British writer.
Caption to a cartoon

2 On either side the river lie
Long fields of barley and of rye,
That clothe the wold and meet the sky;
And thro' the field the road runs by
To many-tower'd Camelot.
Alfred, Lord Tennyson (1809–92) British poet.
The Lady of Shalott, Pt. I

3 An arm
Rose up from out the bosom of the lake,

Clothed in white samite, mystic, wonderful.
Alfred, Lord Tennyson
Idylls of the King, 'The Passing of Arthur'

ARTISTS

See also art, painting

1 When Sir Joshua Reynolds died
All Nature was degraded;
The King dropped a tear in the Queen's ear,
And all his pictures faded.
William Blake (1757–1827) British poet.
On Art and Artists

2 Poets and painters are outside the class
system, or rather they constitute a special
class of their own, like the circus people and
the gipsies.
Gerald Brenan (Edward Fitzgerald Brenan; 1894–1987)
British writer.
Thoughts in a Dry Season, 'Writing'

3 Remember I'm an artist. And you know what
that means in a court of law. Next worst to
an actress.
Joyce Cary (1888–1957) British novelist.
The Horse's Mouth, Ch. 14

4 Beware of the artist who's an intellectual
also. The artist who doesn't fit.
F. Scott Fitzgerald (1896–1940) US novelist.
This Side of Paradise, Bk. II, Ch. 5

5 I don't advise any one to take it up as a
business proposition, unless they really have
talent, and are crippled so as to deprive them
of physical labor.
Grandma Moses (Anna Mary Robertson Moses; 1860–
1961) US primitive painter.
Referring to painting
The New York Times, 'How Do I Paint?', 11 May 1947

6 I should desire that the last words which I
should pronounce in this Academy, and from
this place, might be the name of – Michael
Angelo.
Joshua Reynolds (1723–92) British portrait painter.
Discourse to Students of the Royal Academy, 10 Dec 1790

7 Nobody cares much at heart about Titian,
only there is a strange undercurrent of
everlasting murmur about his name, which
means the deep consent of all great men that
he is greater than they.
John Ruskin (1819–1900) British art critic and writer.
The Two Paths, Lecture II

8 An amateur is an artist who supports himself
with outside jobs which enable him to paint.
A professional is someone whose wife works
to enable him to paint.
Ben Shahn (1898–1969) US artist.
Attrib.

9 What is an artist? For every thousand people
there's nine hundred doing the work, ninety

doing well, nine doing good, and one lucky bastard who's the artist.
Tom Stoppard (1937–) Czech-born British dramatist.
Travesties, I

10 If Botticelli were alive today he'd be working for *Vogue*.
Peter Ustinov (1921–) British actor.
The Observer, 'Sayings of the Week', 21 Oct 1962

11 An artist is someone who produces things that people don't need to have but that he – for *some reason* – thinks it would be a good idea to give them.
Andy Warhol (Andrew Warhola; 1926–87) US pop artist.
From A to B and Back Again, 'Atmosphere'

12 No, I ask it for the knowledge of a lifetime.
James Whistler (1834–1903) US painter.
Replying to the taunt, during the Ruskin trial, that he was asking a fee of 200 guineas for two days' painting
Lives of the Wits (H. Pearson)

13 A living is made, Mr Kemper, by selling something that everybody needs at least once a year. Yes, sir! And a million is made by producing something that everybody needs every day. You artists produce something that nobody needs at any time.
Thornton Wilder (1897–1975) US novelist and dramatist.
The Matchmaker, II

ARTS

1 Every man's work, whether it be literature or music or pictures or architecture or anything else, is always a portrait of himself.
Samuel Butler (1835–1902) British writer.
The Way of All Flesh, Ch. 14

2 The artistic temperament is a disease that afflicts amateurs.
G. K. Chesterton (1874–1936) British writer.
Heretics, Ch. 17

3 No poet, no artist of any sort, has his complete meaning alone. His significance, his appreciation is the appreciation of his relation to the dead poets and artists.
T. S. Eliot (1888–1965) US-born British poet and dramatist.
Tradition and the Individual Talent

4 Yes, the work comes out more beautiful from a material that resists the process, verse, marble, onyx, or enamel.
Théophile Gautier (1811–72) French poet and critic.
L'Art

5 The excellence of every art is its intensity, capable of making all disagreeables evaporate, from their being in close relationship with beauty and truth.
John Keats (1795–1821) British poet.
Letter to G. and T. Keats, 21 Dec 1817

6 The whole of art is an appeal to a reality which is not without us but in our minds.
Desmond MacCarthy (1877–1952) British writer and theatre critic.
Theatre, 'Modern Drama'

7 Music begins to atrophy when it departs too far from the dance; . . . poetry begins to atrophy when it gets too far from music.
Ezra Pound (1885–1972) US poet.
ABC of Reading, 'Warning'

8 The secret of the arts is to correct nature.
Voltaire (François-Marie Arouet; 1694–1778) French writer.
Épîtres, 'À M. de Verrière'

ASSASSINATION

See also killing, murder

1 Assassination has never changed the history of the world.
Benjamin Disraeli (1804–81) British statesman.
Speech, House of Commons, 1 May 1865

2 My fellow citizens, the President is dead, but the Government lives and God Omnipotent reigns.
James A. Garfield (1831–81) US statesman.
Speech following the assassination of Lincoln

3 They really are bad shots.
Charles De Gaulle (1890–1970) French general and statesman.
Remark after narrowly escaping death in an assassination attempt
Ten First Ladies of the World (Pauline Frederick)

4 Will no one rid me of this turbulent priest?
Henry II (1133–89) King of England.
Referring to Thomas Becket, Archbishop of Canterbury; four of Henry's household knights took these words literally, hurried to Canterbury, and killed Becket in the cathedral (Dec 1170)
Attrib.

5 Assassination is the extreme form of censorship.
George Bernard Shaw (1856–1950) Irish dramatist and critic.
The Shewing-Up of Blanco Posnet, 'The Limits of Toleration'

ASTRONOMY

See also moon, space, stars, sun, universe

1 There is one glory of the sun, and another glory of the moon, and another glory of the stars: for one star differeth from another star in glory.
Bible: I Corinthians
15:41–42

2 *Eppur si muove.*
Yet it moves.
Galileo Galilei (1564–1642) Italian scientist.
Referring to the Earth. Remark supposedly made after his recantation (1632) of belief in the Copernican system
Attrib.

3 Astronomy teaches the correct use of the sun and the planets.
Stephen Leacock (1869–1944) English-born Canadian economist and humorist.
Literary Lapses, 'A Manual of Education'

ATHEISM

See also God, religion

1 An atheist is one point beyond the devil.
Proverb

2 God never wrought miracle to convince atheism, because his ordinary works convince it.
Francis Bacon (1561–1626) English philosopher.
Essays, 'Of Atheism'

3 For none deny there is a God, but those for whom it maketh that there were no God.
Francis Bacon
Essays, 'Of Atheism'

4 I am an atheist still, thank God.
Luis Buñuel (1900–83) Spanish film director.
Luis Buñuel: an Introduction (Ado Kyrou)

5 An atheist is a man who has no invisible means of support.
Harry Emerson Fosdick (1878–1969) US baptist minister.
Attrib.

6 Perhaps if I wanted to be understood or to understand I would bamboozle myself into belief, but I am a reporter; God exists only for leader-writers.
Graham Greene (1904–) British novelist.
The Quiet American

7 If you don't find a God by five o'clock this afternoon you must leave the college.
Benjamin Jowett (1817–93) British theologian.
Responding to a conceited young student's assertion that he could find no evidence for a God
Attrib.

8 He was an embittered atheist (the sort of atheist who does not so much disbelieve in God as personally dislike Him).
George Orwell (Eric Blair; 1903–50) British novelist.
Down and Out in Paris and London, Ch. 30

9 It has been said that the highest praise of God consists in the denial of Him by the atheist, who finds creation so perfect that he can dispense with a creator.
Marcel Proust (1871–1922) French novelist.
À la recherche du temps perdu: Le Côté de Guermantes

AUDIENCES

1 Long experience has taught me that in England nobody goes to the theatre unless he or she has bronchitis.
James Agate (1877–1947) British theatre critic.
See also Artur SCHNABEL
Ego, 6

2 Ladies and gentlemen, unless the play is stopped, the child cannot possibly go on.
John Philip Kemble (1757–1823) British tragic actor.
Announcement to the audience when the play he was in was continually interrupted by a child crying
A Book of Anecdotes (D. George)

3 Those people on the stage are making such a noise I can't hear a word you're saying.
Henry Taylor Parker (1867–1934) US music critic.
Rebuking some talkative members of an audience, near whom he was sitting
The Humor of Music (L. Humphrey)

4 A nice respectable, middle-class, middle-aged maiden lady, with time on her hands and the money to help her pass it . . . Let us call her Aunt Edna . . . Aunt Edna is universal, and to those who feel that all the problems of the modern theatre might be saved by her liquidation, let me add that . . . She is also immortal.
Terence Rattigan (1911–77) British dramatist.
Collected Plays, Vol II, Preface

5 I know two kinds of audience only – one coughing and one not coughing.
Artur Schnabel (1882–1951) Austrian concert pianist.
See also James AGATE
My Life and Music, Pt. II, Ch. 10

6 I quite agree with you, sir, but what can two do against so many?
George Bernard Shaw (1856–1950) Irish dramatist and critic.
Responding to a solitary hiss heard amongst the applause at the first performance of *Arms and the Man* in 1894
Oxford Book of Literary Anecdotes

AUTHORITARIANISM

See also tyranny

1 *Roma locuta est; causa finita est.*
Rome has spoken; the case is concluded.
St Augustine of Hippo (354–430) Bishop of Hippo.
Sermons, Bk. I

2 Then cometh the end, when he shall have delivered up the kingdom to God, even the Father; when he shall have put down all rule and all authority and power.
For he must reign, till he hath put down all enemies under his feet.
The last enemy that shall be destroyed is death.
Bible: I Corinthians
15:24–26

3 Dictators ride to and fro upon tigers which they dare not dismount. And the tigers are getting hungry.
Winston Churchill (1874–1965) British statesman.
While England Slept

4 I will have this done, so I order it done; let my will replace reasoned judgement.
Juvenal (Decimus Junius Juvenalis; 60–130 AD) Roman satirist.
Satires, VI

5 Big Brother is watching you.
George Orwell (Eric Blair; 1903–50) British novelist.
Nineteen Eighty-Four

6 I am painted as the greatest little dictator, which is ridiculous – you always take some consultations.
Margaret Thatcher (1925–) British politician and prime minister.
The Times, 1983

7 I don't mind how much my ministers talk – as long as they do what I say.
Margaret Thatcher
The Times, 1987

8 As for being a General, well, at the age of four with paper hats and wooden swords we're all Generals. Only some of us never grow out of it.
Peter Ustinov (1921–) British actor.
Romanoff and Juliet, I

AUTUMN

See also months, seasons

1 Season of mists and mellow fruitfulness,
Close bosom-friend of the maturing sun;
Conspiring with him how to load and bless
With fruit the vines that round the thatch-eaves run.
John Keats (1795–1821) British poet.
To Autumn

B

BABIES

See also birth, children

1 There is no more sombre enemy of good art than the pram in the hall.
Cyril Connolly (1903–74) British journalist.
Enemies of Promise, Ch. 3

2 Every baby born into the world is a finer one than the last.
Charles Dickens (1812–70) British novelist.
Nicholas Nickleby, Ch. 36

3 Other people's babies –
That's my life!
Mother to dozens,
And nobody's wife.
A. P. Herbert (1890–1971) British writer and politician.
A Book of Ballads, 'Other People's Babies'

4 A loud noise at one end and no sense of responsibility at the other.
Ronald Knox (1888–1957) British Roman Catholic priest.
Attrib.

5 Sweetes' li'l' feller,
Everybody knows;
Dunno what to call 'im,
But he's mighty lak' a rose!
Frank L. Stanton (1857–1927) US journalist and poet.
Sweetes' Li'l' Feller

BEAUTY

See also admiration, appearance, compliments

1 A good face is a letter of recommendation.
Proverb

2 Beauty is only skin-deep.
Proverb

3 Beauty is potent but money is omnipotent.
Proverb

4 Small is beautiful.
Proverb

5 My Love in her attire doth show her wit,
It doth so well become her:
For every season she hath dressings fit,
For winter, spring, and summer.
No beauty she doth miss,
When all her robes are on;
But beauty's self she is,
When all her robes are gone.
Anonymous
Madrigal

6 There is no excellent beauty that hath not some strangeness in the proportion.
Francis Bacon (1561–1626) English philosopher.
Essays, 'Of Beauty'

7 Beauty and the lust for learning have yet to be allied.
Max Beerbohm (1872–1956) British writer.
Zuleika Dobson, Ch. 7

8 Exuberance is Beauty.
William Blake (1757–1827) British poet.
The Marriage of Heaven and Hell, 'Proverbs of Hell'

9 For beauty being the best of all we know
Sums up the unsearchable and secret aims
Of nature.
Robert Bridges (1844–1930) British poet.
The Growth of Love

10 Beauty sat with me all the summer day,
Awaiting the sure triumph of her eye;
Nor mark'd I till we parted, how, hard by,
Love in her train stood ready for his prey.
Robert Bridges
The Growth of Love

11 It is better to be first with an ugly woman than the hundredth with a beauty.
Pearl Buck (1892–1973) US novelist.
The Good Earth, Ch. 1

12 Beauty in distress is much the most affecting beauty.
Edmund Burke (1729–97) British politician.
On the Sublime and Beautiful, Pt. III

13 She walks in beauty, like the night
Of cloudless climes and starry skies;
And all that's best of dark and bright
Meet in her aspect and her eyes.
Lord Byron (1788–1824) British poet.
She Walks in Beauty

14 SONYA. I'm not beautiful.
HELEN. You have lovely hair.
SONYA. No, when a woman isn't beautiful, people always say, 'You have lovely eyes, you have lovely hair.'
Anton Chekhov (1860–1904) Russian dramatist.
Uncle Vanya, III

15 There is nothing ugly; *I never saw an ugly thing in my life:* for let the form of an object be what it may, – light, shade, and perspective will always make it beautiful.
John Constable (1776–1837) British landscape painter.
Letter to John Fisher, 23 Oct 1821

16 Love built on beauty, soon as beauty, dies.
John Donne (1573–1631) English poet.
Elegies, 2, 'The Anagram'

17 One girl can be pretty – but a dozen are only a chorus.
F. Scott Fitzgerald (1896–1940) US novelist.
The Last Tycoon

18 Against the beautiful and the clever and the successful, one can wage a pitiless war, but not against the unattractive.
Graham Greene (1904–   ) British novelist.
The Heart of the Matter

19 Glory be to God for dappled things –
For skies of couple-colour as a brinded cow;
For rose-moles all in stipple upon trout that swim.
Gerard Manley Hopkins (1844–99) British Jesuit and poet.
Pied Beauty

20 Beauty in things exists in the mind which contemplates them.
David Hume (1711–76) Scottish philosopher.
Essays, 'Of Tragedy'

21 Beauty is altogether in the eye of the beholder.
Margaret Wolfe Hungerford (c. 1855–97) Irish novelist.
Also attributed to the US soldier and writer Lew Wallace (1827–1905)
Molly Bawn

22 A thing of beauty is a joy for ever:
Its loveliness increases; it will never

Pass into nothingness; but still will keep
A bower quiet for us, and a sleep
Full of sweet dreams, and health, and quiet breathing.
John Keats (1795–1821) British poet.
Endymion, I

23 'Beauty is truth, truth beauty,' – that is all
Ye know on earth, and all ye need to know.
John Keats
Ode on a Grecian Urn

24 Was this the face that launch'd a thousand ships
And burnt the topless towers of Ilium?
Sweet Helen, make me immortal with a kiss.
Christopher Marlowe (1564–93) English dramatist.
Doctor Faustus, V:1

25 Oh, thou art fairer than the evening air
Clad in the beauty of a thousand stars.
Christopher Marlowe
Doctor Faustus, V:1

26 You're the most beautiful woman I've ever seen, which doesn't say much for you.
Groucho Marx (Julius Marx; 1895–1977) US comedian.
Animal Crackers

27 Beauty stands
In the admiration only of weak minds
Led captive.
John Milton (1608–74) English poet.
Paradise Regained, Bk. II

28 I hate that aesthetic game of the eye and the mind, played by these connoisseurs, these mandarins who 'appreciate' beauty. What *is* beauty, anyway? There's no such thing. I never 'appreciate', any more than I 'like'. I love or I hate.
Pablo Picasso (1881–1973) Spanish painter.
Life with Picasso (Françoise Gilot and Carlton Lake), Ch. 2

29 And when I told them how beautiful you are
They didn't believe me! They didn't believe me!
M. E. Rourke (20th century) US songwriter and lyricist.
They Didn't Believe Me (song)

30 There are no ugly women, only lazy ones.
Helena Rubinstein (1882–1965) Polish-born US cosmetics manufacturer.
My Life for Beauty, Pt. II, Ch. 1

31 All she has to do is to walk around and about Georgie White's stage with only a few light bandages on, and everybody considers her very beautiful, especially from the neck down.
Damon Runyon (1884–1946) US writer.
Furthermore, 'A Very Honourable Guy'

32 Remember that the most beautiful things in the world are the most useless, peacocks and lilies for instance.
John Ruskin (1819–1900) British art critic and writer.
The Stones of Venice, Vol. I, Ch. 2

33 I always say beauty is only sin deep.
Saki (Hector Hugh Munro; 1870–1916) British writer.
Reginald's Choir Treat

34 Beauty itself doth of itself persuade
The eyes of men without an orator.
William Shakespeare (1564–1616) English dramatist.
The Rape of Lucrece, I

35 From fairest creatures we desire increase,
That thereby beauty's rose might never die.
William Shakespeare
Sonnet 1

36 For she was beautiful – her beauty made
The bright world dim, and everything beside
Seemed like the fleeting image of a shade.
Percy Bysshe Shelley (1792–1822) British poet.
The Witch of Atlas, XII

37 Half light, half shade,
She stood, a sight to make an old man young.
Alfred, Lord Tennyson (1809–92) British poet.
The Gardener's Daughter

38 But Lancelot mused a little space;
He said, 'She has a lovely face;
God in his mercy lend her grace,
The Lady of Shalott.'
Alfred, Lord Tennyson
The Lady of Shalott, Pt. IV

39 A woman of so shining loveliness
That men threshed corn at midnight by a
tress,
A little stolen tress.
W. B. Yeats (1865–1939) Irish poet.
The Secret Rose

40 All changed, changed utterly:
A terrible beauty is born.
W. B. Yeats
Easter 1916

BED

See also idleness, rest, sleep

1 Early to bed and early to rise, makes a man
healthy, wealthy and wise.
Proverb

2 Go to bed with the lamb, and rise with the
lark.
Proverb

3 I'm Burlington Bertie:
I rise at ten-thirty.
W. F. Hargreaves (1846–1919) British songwriter.
Burlington Bertie

4 I have, all my life long, been lying till noon;
yet I tell all young men, and tell them with
great sincerity, that nobody who does not
rise early will ever do any good.
Samuel Johnson (1709–84) British lexicographer.
Tour to the Hebrides (J. Boswell)

5 O! it's nice to get up in the mornin',

But it's nicer to stay in bed.
Harry Lauder (Hugh MacLennon; 1870–1950) Scottish
music-hall artist.
Song

6 It was such a lovely day I thought it was a
pity to get up.
W. Somerset Maugham (1874–1965) British novelist.
Our Betters, II

7 And so to bed.
Samuel Pepys (1633–1703) English diarist.
Diary, 6 May 1660 and *passim*

8 Not to be abed after midnight is to be up
betimes.
William Shakespeare (1564–1616) English dramatist.
Twelfth Night, II:3

9 Early to rise and early to bed makes a male
healthy and wealthy and dead.
James Thurber (1894–1961) US humorist.
Fables for Our Time, 'The Shrike and the Chipmunks'

BEGINNING

See also prophecy

1 Fingers were made before forks, and hands
before knives.
Proverb

2 From small beginnings come great things.
Proverb

3 Great oaks from little acorns grow.
Proverb

4 The first step is the hardest.
Proverb

5 No task is a long one but the task on which
one dare not start. It becomes a nightmare.
Charles Baudelaire (1821–67) French poet.
My Heart Laid Bare

6 She looked at him, as one who awakes:
The past was a sleep, and her life began.
Robert Browning (1812–89) British poet.
The Statue and the Bust

7 The distance doesn't matter; it is only the
first step that is difficult.
Marquise du Deffand (Marie de Vichy-Chamrond; 1697–
1780) French noblewoman.
Referring to the legend of St Denis, who is traditionally believed to have carried his severed head for six miles after his
execution
Letter to d'Alembert, 7 July 1763

8 From today and from this place there begins
a new epoch in the history of the world.
Goethe (1749–1832) German poet and dramatist.
On witnessing the victory of the French at the battle of Valmy
The Story of Civilization (W. Durant), Vol. II

9 'Tis always morning somewhere in the world.
Richard Henry Horne (1803–84) English writer.
Orion, Bk III, Ch. 2

10 There is an old saying 'well begun is half

done' – 'tis a bad one. I would use instead –
Not begun at all until half done.
John Keats (1795 – 1821) British poet.
Letter, 1817

11 We stand today on the edge of a new
frontier.
John Fitzgerald Kennedy (1917 – 63) US statesman.
Said on his nomination as Presidential candidate
Speech, Democratic Party Convention, 15 July 1960

12 Are you sitting comfortably? Then I'll begin.
Julia S. Lang (1921 –   ) British broadcaster.
Introduction to the story in *Listen with Mother*

BELIEF

See also faith

1 Believe nothing of what you hear, and only
half of what you see.
Proverb

2 Seeing is believing.
Proverb

3 Vain are the thousand creeds
That move men's hearts: unutterably vain;
Worthless as wither'd weeds.
Emily Brontë (1818 – 48) British novelist.
Last Lines

4 If Jesus Christ were to come to-day, people
would not even crucify him. They would ask
him to dinner, and hear what he had to say,
and make fun of it.
Thomas Carlyle (1795 – 1881) Scottish historian and
essayist.
Carlyle at his Zenith (D. A. Wilson)

5 *Action will furnish belief,* – but will that
belief be the true one?
This is the point, you know.
Arthur Hugh Clough (1819 – 61) British poet.
Amours de voyage, V

6 Believe it or not.
R. L. Ripley (1893 – 1949) US writer.
Title of newspaper column

7 I believe because it is impossible.
Tertullian (c. 160 – 225 AD) Carthaginian father of the
church.
The usual misquotation of 'It is certain because it is
impossible.'
De Carne Christi, V

8 If there were a verb meaning 'to believe
falsely', it would not have any significant first
person, present indicative.
Ludwig Wittgenstein (1889 – 1951) Austrian philosopher.
A Certain World (W. H. Auden)

BEQUESTS

1 When you have told anyone you have left him

a legacy the only decent thing to do is to die
at once.
Samuel Butler (1835 – 1902) British writer.
Samuel Butler: A Memoir (Festing Jones), Vol. 2

2 I'm sorry to hear that, sir, you don't happen
to have the shilling about you now, do you?
Tom Sheridan (1775 – 1817) Son of the dramatist Richard
Brinsley Sheridan.
To his father, on learning that he was to be cut off in his will
with a shilling
The Fine Art of Political Wit (L. Harris)

3 The man who leaves money to charity in his
will is only giving away what no longer
belongs to him.
Voltaire (François-Marie Arouet; 1694 – 1778) French
writer.
Letter, 1769

BETRAYAL

See also treason

1 And forthwith he came to Jesus, and said,
Hail, master; and kissed him.
And Jesus said unto him, Friend, wherefore art
thou come? Then came they, and laid hands
on Jesus, and took him.
Bible: Matthew
26:49 – 50

2 Just for a handful of silver he left us,
Just for a riband to stick in his coat.
Robert Browning (1812 – 89) British poet.
The Lost Leader

3 I hate the idea of causes, and if I had to
choose between betraying my country and
betraying my friend, I hope I should have the
guts to betray my country.
E. M. Forster (1879 – 1970) British novelist.
Two Cheers for Democracy, 'What I Believe'.

4 I'm waiting for the cock to crow.
William Morris Hughes (1864 – 1952) Australian
statesman.
Said in parliament, after being viciously critized by a member
of his own party
The Fine Art of Political Wit (L. Harris)

5 He . . . felt towards those whom he had
deserted that peculiar malignity which has, in
all ages, been characteristic of apostates.
Lord Macaulay (1800 – 59) British historian.
History of England, Vol. I, Ch. 1

6 I let down my friends, I let down my
country. I let down our system of
government.
Richard Milhous Nixon (1913 –   ) US president.
The Observer, 'Sayings of the Week', 8 May 1977

7 *Et tu, Brute?*
You too, Brutus?
William Shakespeare (1564 – 1616)
English dramatist.
Julius Caesar, III:1

BIBLE

See also religion

1 He will find one English book and one only,
where, as in the *Iliad* itself, perfect plainness
of speech is allied with perfect nobleness;
and that book is the Bible.
Matthew Arnold (1822–88) British poet and critic.
On Translating Homer

2 Candidates should not attempt more than six
of these.
Hilaire Belloc (1870–1953) French-born British poet.
Suggested addition to the Ten Commandments
Attrib.

3 There's a great text in Galatians,
Once you trip on it, entails
Twenty-nine distinct damnations,
One sure, if another fails.
Robert Browning (1812–89) British poet.
Soliloquy of the Spanish Cloister

4 We have used the Bible as if it was a
constable's handbook – an opium-dose for
keeping beasts of burden patient while they
are being overloaded.
Charles Kingsley (1819–75) British writer.
Letters to the Chartists, 2

5 The English Bible, a book which, if
everything else in our language should perish,
would alone suffice to show the whole extent
of its beauty and power.
Lord Macaulay (1800–59) British historian.
Essays and Biographies, 'John Dryden'. *Edinburgh Review*

6 The number one book of the ages was
written by a committee, and it was called
The Bible.
Louis B. Mayer (1885–1957) Russian-born US film
producer.
Comment to writers who had objected to changes in their work
The Filmgoer's Book of Quotes (Leslie Halliwell)

7 There's a Bible on that shelf there. But I
keep it next to Voltaire – poison and
antidote.
Bertrand Russell (1872–1970) British philosopher.
Kenneth Harris Talking To: 'Bertrand Russell' (Kenneth Harris)

8 The Bible is literature, not dogma.
George Santayana (1863–1952) US philosopher.
Introduction to the Ethics of Spinoza

9 LORD ILLINGWORTH. The Book of Life begins with
a man and a woman in a garden.
MRS ALLONBY. It ends with Revelations.
Oscar Wilde (1854–1900) Irish-born British dramatist.
A Woman of No Importance, I

BIOGRAPHY

1 The Art of Biography
Is different from Geography.
Geography is about Maps,
But Biography is about Chaps.
Edmund Clerihew Bentley (1875–1956) British writer.
Biography for Beginners

2 A well-written Life is almost as rare as a
well-spent one.
Thomas Carlyle (1795–1881) Scottish historian and
essayist.
Critical and Miscellaneous Essays, 'Richter'

3 History is the essence of innumerable
biographies.
Thomas Carlyle
Critical and Miscellaneous Essays, 'History'

4 Campbell has added another terror to death.
John Singleton Copley (1772–1863) US-born British
lawyer.
Referring to Lord Campbell's controversial *Lives of the Lord
Chancellors* (1845–47), from which Lyndhurst was excluded
because he was still alive

5 There is properly no history; only biography.
Ralph Waldo Emerson (1803–82) US poet and essayist.
Essays, 'History'

6 Just how difficult it is to write biography can
be reckoned by anybody who sits down and
considers just how many people know the
real truth about his or her love affairs.
Rebecca West (Cicely Isabel Fairfield; 1892–1983) British
novelist and journalist.
Vogue magazine

BIRDS

1 That's the wise thrush; he sings each song
twice over,
Lest you should think he never could recapture
The first fine careless rapture!
Robert Browning (1812–89) British poet.
Home Thoughts from Abroad

2 With my cross-bow
I shot the albatross.
Samuel Taylor Coleridge (1772–1834) British poet.
The Rime of the Ancient Mariner, I

3 It was the Rainbow gave thee birth,
And left thee all her lovely hues.
W. H. Davies (1871–1940) British poet.
The Kingfisher

4 On a tree by a river a little tom-tit
Sang 'Willow, titwillow, titwillow!'
W. S. Gilbert (1836–1911) British dramatist.
The Mikado, II

5 Thou wast not born for death, immortal Bird!
No hungry generations tread thee down;
The voice I hear this passing night was heard
In ancient days by emperor and clown:
Perhaps the self-same song that found a path
Through the sad heart of Ruth, when sick for
home,
She stood in tears amid the alien corn;
The same that oft-times hath
Charm'd magic casements, opening on the
foam

Of perilous seas, in faery lands forlorn.
John Keats (1795–1821) British poet.
Ode to a Nightingale

6 Ye living lamps, by whose dear light
The nightingale does sit so late,
And studying all the summer night,
Her matchless songs does meditate.
Andrew Marvell (1621–78) English poet.
The Mower to the Glow-worms

7 A Nightingale Sang in Berkeley Square.
Eric Maschwitz (20th century) British songwriter.
Song title

8 To hear the lark begin his flight,
And singing startle the dull night,
From his watch-tower in the skies,
Till the dappled dawn doth rise.
John Milton (1608–74) English poet.
L'Allegro

9 Sweet bird, that shunn'st the noise of folly,
Most musical, most melancholy!
John Milton
Referring to the nightingale
Il Penseroso

10 Hail to thee, blithe Spirit!
Bird thou never wert,
That from Heaven, or near it,
Pourest thy full heart
In profuse strains of unpremeditated art.
Percy Bysshe Shelley (1792–1822) British poet.
To a Skylark

11 Ethereal minstrel! pilgrim of the sky!
Dost thou despise the earth where cares
abound?
William Wordsworth (1770–1850) British poet.
To a Skylark

12 O Nightingale, thou surely art
A creature of a 'fiery heart'.
William Wordsworth
O Nightingale

13 The pious bird with the scarlet breast,
Our little English robin.
William Wordsworth
The Redbreast chasing the Butterfly

14 Thrice welcome, darling of the spring!
Even yet thou art to me
No bird, but an invisible thing,
A voice, a mystery.
William Wordsworth
To the Cuckoo

BIRTH

See also babies, life and death

1 A woman when she is in travail hath sorrow,
because her hour is come: but as soon as
she is delivered of the child, she
remembereth no more the anguish, for joy
that a man is born into the world.
Bible: John
16:21

2 For all men have one entrance into life, and
the like going out.
Bible: Wisdom
7:6

3 My mother groan'd, my father wept,
Into the dangerous world I leapt;
Helpless, naked, piping loud,
Like a fiend hid in a cloud.
William Blake (1757–1827) British poet.
Songs of Experience, 'Infant Sorrow'

4 For man's greatest crime is to have been
born.
Pedro Calderón de la Barca (1600–81) Spanish
dramatist.
La Vida es Sueño, I

5 If men had to have babies they would only
ever have one each.
Diana, Princess of Wales (1961–) Wife of Prince
Charles.
The Observer, 'Sayings of the Week', 29 July 1984

6 I'll simply say here that I was born Beatrice
Gladys Lillie at an extremely tender age
because my mother needed a fourth at
meals.
Beatrice Lillie (Constance Sylvia Munston, Lady Peel;
1898–) Canadian-born British actress.
Every Other Inch a Lady, Ch. 1

7 MACBETH. I bear a charmed life, which must not
yield
To one of woman born.
MACDUFF. Despair thy charm;
And let the angel whom thou still hast serv'd
Tell thee Macduff was from his mother's womb
Untimely ripp'd.
William Shakespeare (1564–1616) English dramatist.
Macbeth, V:8

8 The explanation is quite simple. I wished to
be near my mother.
James Whistler (1834–1903) US painter.
Explaining to a snobbish lady why he had been born in such an
unfashionable place as Lowell, Massachusetts
Attrib.

BITTERNESS

1 The dupe of friendship, and the fool of love;
have I not reason to hate and to despise
myself? Indeed I do; and chiefly for not
having hated and despised the world enough.
William Hazlitt (1778–1830) British essayist.
On the Pleasure of Hating

2 It is very difficult to get up resentment
towards persons whom one has never seen.
Cardinal Newman (1801–90) British theologian.
Apologia pro Vita Sua (1864), 'Mr Kingsley's Method of Dispu-
tation'

3 He gave a deep sigh – I saw the iron enter
into his soul!
Laurence Sterne (1713–68) Irish-born British writer.
A Sentimental Journey, 'The Captive. Paris'

BLESSING

See also prayer

1 Matthew, Mark, Luke and John,
The bed be blest that I lie on.
Thomas Ady (17th century) British poet.
A Candle in the Dark

2 I see the moon,
And the moon sees me;
God bless the moon,
And God bless me.
Anonymous
Gammer Gurton's Garland

3 Thank you, sister. May you be the mother of
a bishop!
Brendan Behan (1923–64) Irish playwright.
Said to a nun nursing him on his deathbed
Attrib.

4 The Lord bless thee, and keep thee:
The Lord make his face shine upon thee, and
be gracious unto thee:
The Lord lift up his countenance upon thee,
and give thee peace.
Bible: Numbers
6:24–26

5 And the peace of God, which passeth all
understanding, shall keep your hearts and
minds through Christ Jesus.
Bible: Philippians
4:7

6 'God bless us every one!' said Tiny Tim, the
last of all.
Charles Dickens (1812–70) British novelist.
A Christmas Carol

BLINDNESS

See also disability

1 A nod is as good as a wink to a blind horse.
Proverb

2 How reconcile this world of fact with the
bright world of my imagining? My darkness
has been filled with the light of intelligence,
and behold, the outer day-light world was
stumbling and groping in social blindness.
Helen Keller (1880–1968) US writer and lecturer.
The Cry for Justice (ed. Upton Sinclair)

3 Ask for this great deliverer now, and find
him
Eyeless in Gaza at the mill with slaves.
John Milton (1608–74) English poet.
Samson Agonistes

4 O dark, dark, dark, amid the blaze of noon,
Irrecoverably dark, total eclipse,

Without all hope of day!
John Milton
Samson Agonistes

5 When I consider how my light is spent
Ere half my days in this dark world and wide,
And that one talent which is death to hide
Lodged with me useless.
John Milton
Sonnet: 'On his Blindness'

6 He clapped the glass to his sightless eye,
And 'I'm damned if I see it', he said.
Henry John Newbolt (1862–1938) British poet.
Referring to Lord Nelson at the Battle of Copenhagen
Admirals All

7 And so I betake myself to that course, which
is almost as much as to see myself go into
my grave – for which, and all the
discomforts that will accompany my being
blind, the good God prepare me!
Samuel Pepys (1633–1703) English diarist.
The closing words of Pepys's *Diary*; he lived another 34 years
and did not go blind
Diary, 31 May 1669

BOASTS

1 I have done almost every human activity
inside a taxi which does not require main
drainage.
Alan Brien (1925–) British critic.
Punch, 5 July 1972

2 CAPTAIN. I'm never, never sick at sea!
ALL. What never?
CAPTAIN. No, never!
ALL. What, *never*?
CAPTAIN. Hardly ever!
W. S. Gilbert (1836–1911) British dramatist.
HMS Pinafore, I

3 All my shows are great. Some of them are
bad. But they are all great.
Lew Grade (1906–) British impressario.
Attrib.

4 If, drunk with sight of power, we loose
Wild tongues that have not Thee in awe,
Such boastings as the Gentiles use,
Or lesser breeds without the Law.
Rudyard Kipling (1865–1936) Indian-born British writer.
Recessional

5 I can piss the old boy in the snow.
Max Liebermann (1847–1935) German painter.
Remark to an artist who said he could not draw General Paul
von Hindenburg's face
Conversations with Stravinsky (Igor Stravinsky and Robert
Craft)

6 And when we open our dykes, the waters
are ten feet deep.
Wilhelmina (1880–1962) Queen of the Netherlands.
Replying to a boast by Wilhelm II that his guardsmen were all
seven feet tall
Attrib.

BOATS

See also navy, sea

1 There's something wrong with our bloody
ships today.
Earl Beatty (1871–1936) British admiral.
Remark during Battle of Jutland, 30 May 1916
Attrib.

2 All rowed fast but none so fast as stroke.
Desmond Coke (1879–1931) British writer.
Popular misquotation, derived from the passage: 'His blade
struck the water a full second before any other . . . until . . . as
the boats began to near the winning post, his own was dipping into the water *twice* as often as any other.')
Sandford of Merton

3 As idle as a painted ship
Upon a painted ocean.
Samuel Taylor Coleridge (1772–1834) British poet.
The Rime of the Ancient Mariner, I

4 Jolly boating weather,
And a hay harvest breeze,
Blade on the feather,
Shade off the trees
Swing, swing together
With your body between your knees.
William Johnson Cory (1823–92) British schoolmaster
and poet.
Eton Boating Song

5 Fair stood the wind for France
When we our sails advance.
Michael Drayton (1563–1631) English poet.
Agincourt

6 For you dream you are crossing the Channel,
and tossing about in a steamer from Harwich
Which is something between a large bathing
machine and a very small second-class
carriage.
W. S. Gilbert (1836–1911) British dramatist.
Iolanthe, II

7 There is nothing – absolutely nothing – half
so much worth doing as simply messing
about in boats.
Kenneth Grahame (1859–1932) Scottish writer.
The Wind in the Willows, Ch. 1

8 The little ships, the unforgotten Homeric
catalogue of *Mary Jane* and *Peggy IV*, of
Folkestone Belle, *Boy Billy*, and *Ethel Maud*,
of *Lady Haig* and *Skylark* . . . the little ships
of England brought the Army home.
Philip Guedalla (1889–1944) British writer.
Referring to the evacuation of Dunkirk
Mr. Churchill

9 No man will be a sailor who has contrivance
enough to get himself into a jail; for being in
a ship is being in a jail, with the chance of
being drowned . . . A man in a jail has more

room, better food, and commonly better
company.
Samuel Johnson (1709–84) British lexicographer.
Life of Johnson (J. Boswell), Vol. I

10 I'd like to get you
On a slow boat to China.
Frank Loesser (1910–69) US songwriter.
Slow Boat to China

11 It was the schooner Hesperus,
That sailed the wintry sea;
And the skipper had taken his little daughter,
To bear him company.
Henry Wadsworth Longfellow (1807–82) US poet.
The Wreck of the Hesperus

12 Quinquireme of Nineveh from distant Ophir
Rowing home to haven in sunny Palestine,
With a cargo of ivory,
And apes and peacocks,
Sandalwood, cedarwood, and sweet white
wine.
John Masefield (1878–1967) British poet.
Cargoes

13 Dirty British coaster with a salt-caked smoke
stack,
Butting through the Channel in the mad March
days,
With a cargo of Tyne coal,
Road-rail, pig-lead,
Firewood, iron-ware, and cheap tin trays.
John Masefield
Cargoes

14 Now the sunset breezes shiver,
And she's fading down the river,
But in England's song for ever
She's the Fighting Téméraire.
Henry John Newbolt (1862–1938) British poet.
The Fighting Téméraire

15 Only fools and passengers drink at sea.
Alan John Villiers (1903–) Australian naval commander.
The Observer, 'Sayings of the Week', 28 Apr 1957

BOLDNESS

See also courage, danger, frankness, impertinence

1 Boldness, and again boldness, and always
boldness!
Georges Jacques Danton (1759–94) French political
activist.
Speech, French Legislative Committee, 2 Sept 1792

2 Oliver Twist has asked for more.
Charles Dickens (1812–70) British novelist.
Oliver Twist, Ch. 2

3 If the creator had a purpose in equipping us
with a neck, he surely meant us to stick it
out.
Arthur Koestler (1905–83) Hungarian-born British writer.
Encounter, May 1970

BOOKS

See also criticism, fiction, literature, novels, publishing, reading, writing

1 Books and friends should be few but good.
Proverb

2 Some books are undeservedly forgotten; none are undeservedly remembered.
W. H. Auden (1907–73) British poet.
The Dyer's Hand, 'Reading'

3 Some books are to be tasted, others to be swallowed, and some few to be chewed and digested.
Francis Bacon (1561–1626) English philosopher.
Essays, 'Of Studies'

4 Books must follow sciences, and not sciences books.
Francis Bacon
Proposition touching Amendment of Laws

5 When I am dead, I hope it may be said:
'His sins were scarlet, but his books were read.'
Hilaire Belloc (1870–1953) French-born British poet.
Epigrams, 'On His Books'

6 Child! do not throw this book about;
Refrain from all the unholy pleasure
Of cutting all the pictures out!
Preserve it as your chiefest treasure.
Hilaire Belloc
The Bad Child's Book of Beasts, 'Dedication'

7 And further, by these, my son, be admonished: of making many books there is no end; and much study is a weariness of the flesh.
Bible: Ecclesiastes
12:12

8 I keep my books at the British Museum and at Mudie's.
Samuel Butler (1835–1902) British writer.
The Humour of Homer, 'Ramblings in Cheapside'

9 'Tis pleasant, sure, to see one's name in print;
A book's a book, although there's nothing in't.
Lord Byron (1788–1824) British poet.
English Bards and Scotch Reviewers

10 A good book is the purest essence of a human soul.
Thomas Carlyle (1795–1881) Scottish historian and essayist.
Speech made in support of the London Library
Carlyle and the London Library (F. Harrison)

11 'What is the use of a book,' thought Alice, 'without pictures or conversation?'
Lewis Carroll (Charles Lutwidge Dodgson; 1832–98) British writer.
Alice's Adventures in Wonderland, Ch. 1

12 Go, litel book, go litel myn tragedie.

O moral Gower, this book I directe To thee.
Geoffrey Chaucer (c. 1342–1400) English poet.
Troilus and Criseyde, 5

13 Due attention to the inside of books, and due contempt for the outside, is the proper relation between a man of sense and his books.
Earl of Chesterfield (1694–1773) English statesman.
Letter to his son, 10 Jan 1749

14 Books cannot always please, however good;
Minds are not ever craving for their food.
George Crabbe (1754–1832) British poet.
The Borough, 'Schools'

15 Books, we are told, propose to *instruct* or to *amuse*. Indeed! . . . The true antithesis to knowledge, in this case, is not *pleasure*, but *power*. All that is literature seeks to communicate power; all that is not literature, to communicate knowledge.
Thomas De Quincey (1785–1859) British writer.
Letters to a Young Man

16 Books are made not like children but like pyramids . . . and they're just as useless! and they stay in the desert! . . . Jackals piss at their foot and the bourgeois climb up on them.
Gustave Flaubert (1821–80) French novelist.
Letter to Ernest Feydeau, 1857

17 Learning hath gained most by those books by which the printers have lost.
Thomas Fuller (1608–61) English historian.
The Holy State and the Profane State

18 A book may be amusing with numerous errors, or it may be very dull without a single absurdity.
Oliver Goldsmith (1728–74) Irish-born British writer.
The Vicar of Wakefield, Advertisement

19 Few books today are forgivable.
R. D. Laing (1927–) British psychiatrist.
The Politics of Experience, Introduction

20 Get stewed:
Books are a load of crap.
Philip Larkin (1922–85) British poet.
A Study of Reading Habits

21 To every man who struggles with his own soul in mystery, a book that is a book flowers once, and seeds, and is gone.
D. H. Lawrence (1885–1930) British novelist.
Phoenix, 'A Bibliography of D.H.L.'

22 Never judge a cover by its book.
Fran Lebowitz (1950–) US writer.
Metropolitan Life

23 There can hardly be a stranger commodity in the world than books. Printed by people who don't understand them; sold by people who don't understand them; bound, criticized and read by people who don't understand them;

and now even written by people who don't understand them.
Georg Christoph Lichtenberg (1742-99) German physicist and writer.
Aphorisms

24 Who kills a man kills a reasonable creature, God's image; but he who destroys a good book, kills reason itself, kills the image of God, as it were in the eye.
John Milton (1608-74) English poet.
Areopagitica

25 A good book is the precious life-blood of a master spirit, embalmed and treasured up on purpose to a life beyond life.
John Milton
Areopagitica

26 The books one reads in childhood, and perhaps most of all the bad and good bad books, create in one's mind a sort of false map of the world, a series of fabulous countries into which one can retreat at odd moments throughout the rest of life, and which in some cases can even survive a visit to the real countries which they are supposed to represent.
George Orwell (Eric Blair; 1903-50) British novelist.
Riding Down from Bangor

27 At last, an unprintable book that is readable.
Ezra Pound (1885-1972) US poet.
Referring to *Tropic of Cancer* by Henry Miller

28 An anthology is like all the plums and orange peel picked out of a cake.
Walter Raleigh (1861-1922) British scholar.
Letter to Mrs Robert Bridges, 15 Jan 1915

29 I have known her pass the whole evening without mentioning a single book, or *in fact anything unpleasant* at all.
Henry Reed (1914-) British poet and dramatist.
A Very Great Man Indeed

30 When a new book is published, read an old one.
Samuel Rogers (1763-1855) British poet.
Attrib.

31 We all know that books burn – yet we have the greater knowledge that books cannot be killed by fire. People die, but books never die. No man and no force can abolish memory... In this war, we know, books are weapons.
Franklin D. Roosevelt (1882-1945) US Democratic president.
Message to American Booksellers Association, 23 Apr 1942

32 If a book is worth reading, it is worth buying.
John Ruskin (1819-1900) British art critic and writer.
Sesame and Lilies, 'Of Kings' Treasuries'

33 All books are divisible into two classes, the books of the hour, and the books of all time.
John Ruskin
Sesame and Lilies, 'Of Kings' Treasuries'

34 How long most people would look at the best book before they would give the price of a large turbot for it!
John Ruskin
Sesame and Lilies, 'Of Kings' Treasuries'

35 A library is thought in cold storage.
Herbert Samuel (1870-1963) British Liberal statesman.
A Book of Quotations

36 Children... have no use for psychology. They detest sociology. They still believe in God, the family, angels, devils, witches, goblins, logic, clarity, punctuation, and other such obsolete stuff... When a book is boring, they yawn openly. They don't expect their writer to redeem humanity, but leave to adults such childish illusions.
Isaac Bashevis Singer (1904-) Polish-born US writer.
Speech on receiving the Nobel Prize for Literature
The Observer, 17 Dec 1978

37 A best-seller is the gilded tomb of a mediocre talent.
Logan Pearsall Smith (1865-1946) US writer.
Afterthoughts, 'Art and Letters'

38 No furniture so charming as books.
Sydney Smith (1771-1845) British clergyman and essayist.
Memoir (Lady Holland)

39 Books are good enough in their own way, but they are a mighty bloodless substitute for life.
Robert Louis Stevenson (1850-94) Scottish writer.
Virginibus Puerisque

40 My brother-in-law wrote an unusal murder story. The victim got killed by a man from another book.
Robert Sylvester (1907-75) US writer.

41 A good book is the best of friends, the same to-day and for ever.
Martin Farquhar Tupper (1810-89) British writer.
Proverbial Philosophy, 'Of Reading'

42 Books, I don't know what you see in them ... I can understand a person reading them, but I can't for the life of me see why people have to write them.
Peter Ustinov (1921-) British actor.
Photo-Finish

43 There is no such thing as a moral or an immoral book. Books are well written, or badly written.
Oscar Wilde (1854-1900) Irish-born British dramatist.
The Picture of Dorian Gray, Preface

BOREDOM

See also bores

1 Nothing happens, nobody comes, nobody goes, it's awful!
Samuel Beckett (1906–) Irish novelist and dramatist.
Waiting for Godot, I

2 I wanted to be bored to death, as good a way to go as any.
Peter De Vries (1910–) US novelist.
Comfort me with Apples, Ch. 17

3 You ought not to be ashamed of being bored. What you ought to be ashamed of is being boring.
Lord Hailsham (1907–) British Conservative politician.
The Observer, 'Sayings of the Week', 12 Oct 1975

4 Symmetry is tedious, and tedium is the very basis of mourning. Despair yawns.
Victor Hugo (1802–85) French writer.
Les Misérables, Vol. II, Bk. IV, Ch. 1

5 The effect of boredom on a large scale in history is underestimated. It is a main cause of revolutions, and would soon bring to an end all the static Utopias and the farmyard civilization of the Fabians.
Dean Inge (1860–1954) British churchman.
The End of an Age, Ch. 6

6 Is not life a hundred times too short for us to bore ourselves?
Friedrich Wilhelm Nietzsche (1844–1900) German philosopher.
Jenseits von Gut und Böse

7 When you're bored with yourself, marry and be bored with someone else.
David Pryce-Jones (1936–) British author and critic.
Owls and Satyrs

BORES

See also boredom

1 *Bore*, n. A person who talks when you wish him to listen.
Ambrose Bierce (1842–?1914) US writer and journalist.
The Devil's Dictionary

2 Society is now one polish'd horde,
Form'd of two mighty tribes, the *Bores* and *Bored*.
Lord Byron (1788–1824) British poet.
Don Juan, XIII

3 Sir, you are like a pin, but without either its head or its point.
Douglas William Jerrold (1803–57) British dramatist.
Speaking to a small thin man who was boring him
Attrib.

4 He is not only a bore but he bores for England.
Malcolm Muggeridge (1903–) British writer.
Referring to Sir Anthony Eden
In *Newstatesmanship* (E. Hyams), 'Boring for England'

5 A bore is a man who, when you ask him how he is, tells you.
Bert Leston Taylor (1866–1921) US journalist.
Attrib.

6 Somebody's boring me, I think it's me.
Dylan Thomas (1914–53) Welsh poet.
Remark made after he had been talking continuously for some time
Four Absentees (Rayner Heppenstall)

7 He is an old bore; even the grave yawns for him.
Herbert Beerbohm Tree (1853–1917) British actor and theatre manager.
Referring to Israel Zangwill
Beerbohm Tree (Hesketh Pearson)

8 A healthy male adult bore consumes each year one and a half times his own weight in other people's patience.
John Updike (1932–) US novelist.
Assorted Prose, 'Confessions of a Wild Bore'

9 Dear Frank, we believe you; you have dined in every house in London – *once*.
Oscar Wilde (1854–1900) Irish-born British dramatist.
Interrupting Frank Harris's interminable account of the houses he had dined at
Attrib.

BORROWING

1 Borrowed garments never fit well.
Proverb

2 I don't trust a bank that would lend money to such a poor risk.
Robert Benchley (1889–1945) US humorist.
To a bank that granted his request for a loan
Attrib.

3 Be not made a beggar by banqueting upon borrowing, when thou hast nothing in thy purse: for thou shalt lie in wait for thine own life, and be talked on.
Bible: Ecclesiasticus
18:33

4 One of the mysteries of human conduct is why adult men and women all over England are ready to sign documents which they do not read, at the behest of canvassers whom they do not know, binding them to pay for articles which they do not want, with money which they have not got.
Gerald Hurst (1877–1957) British writer and judge.
Closed Chapters

5 The human species, according to the best theory I can form of it, is composed of two distinct races, the men who borrow, and the men who lend.
Charles Lamb (1775–1834) British essayist.
Essays of Elia, 'The Two Races of Men'

6 Borrowers of books – those mutilators of

collections, spoilers of the symmetry of shelves, and creators of odd volumes.
Charles Lamb
Essays of Elia, 'The Two Races of Men'

7 Not everyone is a debtor who wishes to be; not everyone who wishes makes creditors.
François Rabelais (1483–1553) French satirist.
Pantagruel, Bk. III, Ch. 3

8 Neither a borrower nor a lender be;
For loan oft loses both itself and friend,
And borrowing dulls the edge of husbandry.
This above all: to thine own self be true,
And it must follow, as the night the day,
Thou canst not then be false to any man.
William Shakespeare (1564–1616) English dramatist.
Hamlet, I:3

9 Thank God, that's settled.
Richard Brinsley Sheridan (1751–1816) British dramatist.
Handing one of his creditors an IOU
Wit, Wisdom, and Foibles of the Great (C. Shriner)

10 It is not my interest to pay the principal, nor my principle to pay the interest.
Richard Brinsley Sheridan
To his tailor when he requested the payment of a debt, or of the interest on it at least
Attrib.

11 My dear fellow, be reasonable; the sum you ask me for is a very considerable one, whereas I only ask you for twenty-five pounds.
Richard Brinsley Sheridan
On being refused a further loan of £25 from a friend to whom he already owed £500
Literary and Scientific Anecdotes (W. Keddie)

12 Let us all be happy, and live within our means, even if we have to borrer the money to do it with.
Artemus Ward (Charles Farrar Browne; 1834–67) US humorous writer.
Science and Natural History

13 I don't owe a penny to a single soul – not counting tradesmen, of course.
P. G. Wodehouse (1881–1975) British humorous novelist.
My Man Jeeves, 'Jeeves and the Hard-Boiled Egg'

BOUNDARIES

See also neighbours

1 When you think about the defence of England you no longer think of the chalk cliffs of Dover. You think of the Rhine. That is where our frontier lies to-day.
Stanley Baldwin (1867–1947) British statesman.
Speech, House of Commons, 30 July 1934

2 Something there is that doesn't love a wall.
Robert Frost (1875–1963) US poet.
North of Boston, 'Mending Wall'

BREVITY

See also sermons, speeches, verbosity

1 Good things, when short, are twice as good.
Baltasar Gracián (1601–58) Spanish writer.
The Art of Worldly Wisdom

2 I strive to be brief, and I become obscure.
Horace (Quintus Horatius Flaccus; 65–8 BC) Roman poet.
Ars Poetica

3 ?
Victor Hugo (1802–85) French writer.
The entire contents of a telegram sent to his publishers asking how *Les Misérables* was selling; the reply was '!'
The Literary Life (R. Hendrickson)

4 But the shortest works are always the best.
Jean de La Fontaine (1621–95) French poet.
Fables, X, 'Les Lapins'

5 Brevity is the soul of lingerie.
Dorothy Parker (1893–1967) US writer.
While Rome Burns (Alexander Woollcott)

6 Trust the man who hesitates in his speech and is quick and steady in action, but beware of long arguments and long beards.
George Santayana (1863–1952) US philosopher.
Soliloquies in England, 'The British Character'

7 Brevity is the soul of wit.
William Shakespeare (1564–1616) English dramatist.
Hamlet, II:2

8 Men of few words are the best men.
William Shakespeare
Henry V, III:2

9 Nurse unupblown.
Evelyn Waugh (1903–66) British novelist.
Cable sent after he had failed, while a journalist serving in Ethiopia, to substantiate a rumour that an English nurse had been blown up in an Italian air raid
Our Marvelous Native Tongue (R. Claiborne)

BRIBERY

See also corruption

1 When their lordships asked Bacon
How many bribes he had taken
He had at least the grace
To get very red in the face.
Edmund Clerihew Bentley (1875–1956) British writer.
Baseless Biography

2 To a shower of gold most things are penetrable.
Thomas Carlyle (1795–1881) Scottish historian and essayist.
History of the French Revolution, Pt. I, Bk. III, Ch. 7

3 I have often noticed that a bribe . . . has that effect – it changes a relation. The man who offers a bribe gives away a little of his own importance; the bribe once accepted, he

becomes the inferior, like a man who has paid for a woman.
Graham Greene (1904–) British novelist.
The Comedians, Pt. I, Ch. 4

4 Though authority be a stubborn bear, yet he is oft led by the nose with gold.
William Shakespeare (1564–1616) English dramatist.
The Winter's Tale, IV:3

BRITAIN

See also British, British Empire, England, Ireland, patriotism, Scotland, Wales

1 Great Britain has lost an Empire and has not yet found a role.
Dean Acheson (1893–1971) US lawyer and statesman.
Speech, Military Academy, West Point, 5 Dec 1962

2 A nation of shop-keepers are very seldom so disinterested.
Samuel Adams (1722–1803) US revolutionary leader.
Referring to Britain, following the Declaration of Independence, 4 July 1776
Speech, Philadelphia, 1 Aug 1776

3 Land of Hope and Glory, Mother of the Free,
How shall we extol thee, who are born of thee?
Wider still and wider shall thy bounds be set;
God who made thee mighty, make thee mightier yet.
A. C. Benson (1862–1925) British writer.
Land of Hope and Glory

4 Britain has lived for too long on borrowed time, borrowed money and even borrowed ideas.
James Callaghan (1912–) British politician and prime minister.
The Observer, 'Sayings of the Week', 3 Oct 1976

5 God save our Gracious King,
Long live our noble King,
God save the King.
Send him victorious,
Happy and glorious.
Henry Carey (c. 1690–1743) English poet and musician.
God Save the King

6 When the British warrior queen,
Bleeding from the Roman rods,
Sought, with an indignant mien,
Counsel of her country's gods.
William Cowper (1731–1800) British poet.
Boadicea

7 Britain is not a country that is easily rocked by revolution . . . In Britain our institutions evolve. We are a Fabian Society writ large.
William Hamilton (1917–) Scottish MP.
My Queen and I, Ch. 9

8 We may be a small island, but we are not a small people.
Edward Heath (1916–) British politician.
The Observer, 'Sayings of the Week', 21 June 1970

9 Sir, it is not so much to be lamented that Old England is lost, as that the Scotch have found it.
Samuel Johnson (1709–84) British lexicographer.
Life of Johnson (J. Boswell), Vol. III

10 This is a very fine country to be acutely ill or injured in, but take my advice and do not be old and frail or mentally ill here – at least not for a few years. This is definitely not a good country to be deaf or blind in either.
Keith Joseph (1918–) British politician.
The Observer, 'Sayings of the Week', 1 July 1973

11 Once, when a British Prime Minister sneezed, men half a world away would blow their noses. Now when a British Prime Minister sneezes nobody else will even say 'Bless You'.
Bernard Levin (1928–) British journalist.
The Times, 1976

12 When Britain first, at heaven's command,
Arose from out the azure main,
This was the charter of the land,
And guardian angels sung this strain:
'Rule, Britannia, rule the waves;
Britons never will be slaves.'
James Thomson (1700–48) British poet.
Alfred: a Masque, Act II

13 I should like to help Britain to become a Third Programme country.
Ellen Cicely Wilkinson (1891–1947) British feminist and politician.
The Observer, 'Sayings of the Week', 2 Feb 1947

BRITISH

See also Britain, English, Irish, Scots, Welsh

1 A young Scotsman of your ability let loose upon the world with £300, what could he not do? It's almost appalling to think of; especially if he went among the English.
J. M. Barrie (1860–1937) British novelist and dramatist.
What Every Woman Knows, I

2 There are no countries in the world less known by the British than these selfsame British Islands.
George Henry Borrow (1803–81) British writer.
Lavengro, Preface

3 The British love permanence more than they love beauty.
Hugh Casson (1910–) British architect.
The Observer, 'Sayings of the Week', 14 June 1964

4 It must be owned, that the Graces do not seem to be natives of Great Britain; and I doubt, the best of us here have more of rough than polished diamond.
Earl of Chesterfield (1694–1773) English statesman.
Letter to his son, 18 Nov 1748

5 The maxim of the British people is 'Business as usual'.
Winston Churchill (1874–1965) British statesman.
Speech, Guildhall, 9 Nov 1914

6 They are the only people who like to be told how bad things are – who like to be told the worst.
Winston Churchill
Speech, 1921

7 Of all noxious animals, too, the most noxious is a tourist. And of all tourists the most vulgar, ill-bred, offensive and loathsome is the British tourist.
Francis Kilvert (1840–79) British diarist and clergyman.
Diary, 5 Apr 1870

8 It is beginning to be hinted that we are a nation of amateurs.
Earl of Rosebery (1847–1929) British statesman.
Rectorial Address, Glasgow, 16 Nov 1900

9 Other nations use 'force'; we Britons alone use 'Might'.
Evelyn Waugh (1903–66) British novelist.
Scoop, Bk. II, Ch. 5

BRITISH EMPIRE

1 I have not become the King's First Minister in order to preside over the liquidation of the British Empire.
Winston Churchill (1874–1965) British statesman.
Speech, Mansion House, 10 Nov 1942

2 How is the Empire?
George V (1865–1936) King of the United Kingdom.
Last words
The Times, 21 Jan 1936

3 'Can't' will be the epitaph of the British Empire – unless we wake up in time.
Oswald Mosley (1896–1980) British politician.
Speech, Manchester, 9 Dec 1937

4 His Majesty's dominions, on which the sun never sets.
Christopher North (John Wilson; 1785–1854) Scottish writer.
Noctes Ambrosianae, 20 Apr 1829

5 The Empire is a Commonwealth of Nations.
Earl of Rosebery (1847–1929) British statesman.
Speech, Adelaide, 18 Jan 1884

6 We the English seem, as it were, to have conquered and peopled half the world in a fit of absence of mind.
John Robert Seeley (1834–95) British historian.
The Expansion of England, I

BUREAUCRACY

1 A memorandum is written not to inform the reader but to protect the writer.
Dean Acheson (1893–1971) US lawyer and statesman.
Attrib.

2 I'm surprised that a government organization could do it that quickly.
Jimmy Carter (1924–) US statesman.
Visiting Egypt, when told that it took twenty years to build the Great Pyramid
Presidential Anecdotes (P. Boller)

3 A committee is a cul-de-sac down which ideas are lured and then quietly strangled.
Barnett Cocks (1907–) British political writer.
New Scientist, 1973

4 Whatever was required to be done, the Circumlocution Office was beforehand with all the public departments in the art of perceiving – HOW NOT TO DO IT.
Charles Dickens (1812–70) British novelist.
Little Dorrit, Bk. I, Ch. 10

5 A Royal Commission is a broody hen sitting on a china egg.
Michael Foot (1913–) British Labour politician and journalist.
Speech, House of Commons, 1964

6 A difficulty for every solution.
Herbert Samuel (1870–1963) British Liberal statesman.
Referring to the Civil Service
Attrib.

7 The working of great institutions is mainly the result of a vast mass of routine, petty malice, self interest, carelessness, and sheer mistake. Only a residual fraction is thought.
George Santayana (1863–1952) US philosopher.
The Crime of Galileo

8 My life's been a meeting, Dad, one long meeting. Even on the few committees I don't yet belong to, the agenda winks at me when I pass.
Gwyn Thomas (1913–81) British writer.
The Keep, I

BUSINESS

See also capitalism

1 In Dublin's fair city, where the girls are so pretty,
I first set my eyes on sweet Molly Malone,
As she wheeled her wheelbarrow, through streets broad and narrow,
Crying, Cockles and mussels! alive, alive, O!

She was a fishmonger, but sure 'twas no wonder,
For so were her father and mother before.
Anonymous
Cockles and Mussels

2 Who will change old lamps for new ones? . . . new lamps for old ones?
The Arabian Nights (c. 1500) A collection of tales from the East.
The History of Aladdin

3 You ask me what it is I do. Well actually, you know,

I'm partly a liaison man and partly P.R.O.
Essentially I integrate the current export drive
And basically I'm viable from ten o'clock till
five.
John Betjeman (1906–84) British poet.
Executive

4 Here's the rule for bargains: 'Do other men,
for they would do you.' That's the true
business precept.
Charles Dickens (1812–70) British novelist.
Martin Chuzzlewit, Ch. 11

5 No nation was ever ruined by trade.
Benjamin Franklin (1706–90) US scientist and statesman.
Essays, 'Thoughts on Commercial Subjects'

6 Remember that time is money.
Benjamin Franklin
Advice to a Young Tradesman

7 The salary of the chief executive of the large
corporation is not a market award for
achievement. It is frequently in the nature of
a warm personal gesture by the individual to
himself.
John Kenneth Galbraith (1908–   ) US economist.
Annals of an Abiding Liberal

8 Where wealth and freedom reign,
contentment fails,
And honour sinks where commerce long
prevails.
Oliver Goldsmith (1728–74) Irish-born British writer.
The Traveller

9 Cherry ripe, ripe, ripe, I cry.
Full and fair ones; come and buy.
Robert Herrick (1591–1674) English poet.
Hesperides, 'Cherry Ripe'

10 When you are skinning your customers, you
should leave some skin on to grow so that
you can skin them again.
Nikita Khrushchev (1894–1971) Soviet statesman.
Said to British businessmen
The Observer, 'Sayings of the Week', 28 May 1961

11 He is the only man who is for ever
apologizing for his occupation.
H. L. Mencken (1880–1956) US journalist.
Referring to the businessman
Prejudices, 'Types of Men'

12 A dinner lubricates business.
William Scott (1745–1836) British jurist.
Life of Johnson (J. Boswell), 1791

13 The customer is always right.
H. Gordon Selfridge (1857–1947) US-born businessman.
Slogan adopted at his shops

14 A snapper-up of unconsidered trifles.
William Shakespeare (1564–1616) English dramatist.
The Winter's Tale, IV:2

15 The big print giveth and the fine print taketh
away.
J. Fulton Sheen (1895–1979) US Roman Catholic
archbishop.
Referring to his contract for a television appearance
Attrib.

16 People of the same trade seldom meet
together but the conversation ends in a
conspiracy against the public, or in some
diversion to raise prices.
Adam Smith (1723–90) Scottish economist.
The Wealth of Nations

17 You never expected justice from a company,
did you? They have neither a soul to lose nor
a body to kick.
Sydney Smith (1771–1845) British clergyman and
essayist.
Memoir (Lady Holland)

18 I have heard of a man who had a mind to sell
his house, and therefore carried a piece of
brick in his pocket, which he shewed as a
pattern to encourage purchasers.
Jonathan Swift (1667–1745) Irish-born Anglican priest and
writer.
The Drapier's Letters, 2 (4 Aug 1724)

19 It's just like having a licence to print your
own money.
Lord Thomson of Fleet (1894–1976) Canadian-born
British newspaper proprietor.
Speaking about commercial television
Attrib.

20 All business sagacity reduces itself in the last
analysis to a judicious use of sabotage.
Thorstein Bunde Veblen (1857–1929) US social
scientist.
The Nature of Peace

21 If Max gets to Heaven he won't last long. He
will be chucked out for trying to pull off a
merger between Heaven and Hell . . . after
having secured a controlling interest in key
subsidiary companies in both places, of
course.
H. G. Wells (1866–1946) British writer.
Referring to Lord Beaverbrook
Beaverbrook (A. J. P. Taylor)

22 For many years I thought what was good for
our country was good for General Motors,
and vice versa.
Charles Erwin Wilson (1890–1961) US engineer.
Said in testimony to the Senate Armed Services Committee,
Jan 1953
Attrib.

23 Business underlies everything in our national
life, including our spiritual life. Witness the
fact that in the Lord's Prayer the first
petition is for daily bread. No one can
worship God or love his neighbour on an
empty stomach.
Woodrow Wilson (1856–1925) US statesman.
Speech, New York, 1912

BYRON

See also poets

1 When Byron's eyes were shut in death,
We bow'd our head and held our breath.
He taught us little: but our soul
Had *felt* him like the thunder's roll.
Matthew Arnold (1822–88) British poet and critic.
Memorial Verses

2 If they had said the sun and the moon was
gone out of the heavens it could not have
struck me with the idea of a more awful and
dreary blank in the creation than the words:
Byron is dead.
Jane Welsh Carlyle (1801–66) The wife of Thomas
Carlyle.
Letter to Thomas Carlyle, 1824

3 Mad, bad, and dangerous to know.
Lady Caroline Lamb (1785–1828) The wife of William
Lamb.
Said of Byron in her journal
Journal

C

CAMBRIDGE

See also England, Oxford

1 Oxford is on the whole more attractive than
Cambridge to the ordinary visitor; and the
traveller is therefore recommended to visit
Cambridge first, or to omit it altogether if he
cannot visit both.
Karl Baedeker (1801–59) German publisher.
Baedeker's Great Britain, 'From London to Oxford'

2 The King to Oxford sent a troop of horse,
For Tories own no argument but force:
With equal skill to Cambridge books he sent,
For Whigs admit no force but argument.
William Browne (1692–1774) English physician.
A reply to TRAPP
Literary Anecdotes (Nichols), Vol. III

3 Spring and summer did happen in Cambridge
almost every year.
Vladimir Nabokov (1899–1977) Russian-born US novelist.
The Real Life of Sebastian Knight, Ch. 5

4 This is the city of perspiring dreams.
Frederic Raphael (1931–) British author.
The Glittering Prizes: An Early Life, III

5 The King, observing with judicious eyes
The state of both his universities,
To Oxford sent a troop of horse, and why?
That learned body wanted loyalty;
To Cambridge books, as very well discerning
How much that loyal body wanted learning.
Joseph Trapp (1679–1747) English churchman and
academic.
Written after George I donated the Bishop of Ely's library to
Cambridge; for a reply see BROWNE
Literary Anecdotes (Nichols), Vol. III

CAMPING

1 Those who have never dwelt in tents have
no idea either of the charm or of the
discomfort of a nomadic existence. The
charm is purely romantic, and consequently
very soon proves to be fallacious.
Vita Sackville-West (Victoria Sackville-West; 1892–1962)
British poet and novelist.
Twelve Days, Ch. 6

CANNIBALISM

1 Eating people is wrong.
Michael Flanders (1922–75) British comedian and
songwriter.
The Reluctant Cannibal

2 The better sort of Ishmaelites have been
Christian for many centuries and will not
publicly eat human flesh uncooked in Lent,
without special and costly dispensation from
their bishop.
Evelyn Waugh (1903–66) British novelist.
Scoop, Bk. II, Ch. 1

CANT

See also hypocrisy, insincerity

1 Ancient sculpture is the true school of
modesty. But where the Greeks had
modesty, we have cant; where they had
poetry, we have cant; where they had
patriotism, we have cant; where they had
anything that exalts, delights, or adorns
humanity, we have nothing but cant, cant,
cant.
Thomas Love Peacock (1785–1866) British novelist.
Crotchet Castle, Ch. 7

CAPITALISM

See also business

1 It is closing time in the gardens of the West.
Cyril Connolly (1903–74) British journalist.
The Condemned Playground

2 Property has its duties as well as its rights.
Thomas Drummond (1797–1840) British engineer and
statesman.
Letter to the Earl of Donoughmore, 22 May 1838

3 If I had to give a definition of capitalism I
would say: the process whereby American
girls turn into American women.
Christopher Hampton (1946–) British writer and
dramatist.
Savages, Sc. 16

4 It is the unpleasant and unacceptable face of
capitalism but one should not suggest that

the whole of British industry consists of practices of this kind.
Edward Heath (1916–) British politician and prime minister.
Referring to the Lonrho Affair
Speech, House of Commons, 15 May 1973

5 ... militarism ... is one of the chief bulwarks of capitalism, and the day that militarism is undermined, capitalism will fail.
Helen Keller (1880–1968) US writer and lecturer.
The Story of My Life

6 We cannot remove the evils of capitalism without taking its source of power: ownership.
Neil Kinnock (1942–) British politician.
Tribune, 1975

7 Under capitalism we have a state in the proper sense of the word, that is, a special machine for the suppression of one class by another.
Lenin (Vladimir Ilich Ulyanov; 1870–1924) Russian revolutionary leader.
The State and Revolution, Ch. 5

8 Not every problem someone has with his girlfriend is necessarily due to the capitalist mode of production.
Herbert Marcuse (1898–1979) German-born US philosopher.
The Listener

9 Capitalist production begets, with the inexorability of a law of nature, its own negation.
Karl Marx (1818–83) German philosopher and revolutionary.
Das Kapital, Ch. 15

10 Man is the only creature that consumes without producing.
George Orwell (Eric Blair; 1903–50) British novelist.
Animal Farm, Ch. 1

11 I have gone to war too ... I am going to fight capitalism even if it kills me. It is wrong that people like you should be comfortable and well fed while all around you people are starving.
Sylvia Pankhurst (1882–1960) British suffragette.
The Fighting Pankhursts (David Mitchell)

12 Property is theft.
Pierre Joseph Proudhon (1809–65) French socialist.
Qu'est-ce que la Propriété?, Ch. 1

13 Property is organised robbery.
George Bernard Shaw (1856–1950) Irish dramatist and critic.
Major Barbara, Preface

14 Lenin was the first to discover that capitalism 'inevitably' caused war; and he discovered this only when the First World War was already being fought. Of course he was right. Since every great state was capitalist in

1914, capitalism obviously 'caused' the First World War; but just as obviously it had 'caused' the previous generation of Peace.
A. J. P. Taylor (1906–) British historian.
The Origins of the Second World War, Ch. 6

15 The public be damned. I am working for my stockholders.
William Henry Vanderbilt (1821–85) US railway chief.
Refusing to speak to a reporter, who was seeking to find out his views on behalf of the public

CATHOLICISM

See also Christianity, Protestantism, religion

1 A priest is a man who is called Father by everyone except his own children who are obliged to call him Uncle.
Italian proverb

2 *Ad majorem Dei gloriam.*
To the greater glory of God.
Anonymous
Motto of the Jesuits

3 I expect you know my friend Evelyn Waugh, who, like you, your Holiness, is a Roman Catholic.
Randolph Churchill (1911–68) British political journalist.
Remark made during an audience with the Pope

4 I have a Catholic soul, but a Lutheran stomach.
Erasmus (1466–1536) Dutch humanist, scholar, and writer.
Replying to criticism of his failure to fast during Lent
Dictionnaire Encyclopédique

5 The Papacy is not other than the Ghost of the deceased Roman Empire, sitting crowned upon the grave thereof.
Thomas Hobbes (1588–1679) English philosopher.
Leviathan, Pt. IV, Ch. 37

6 There is no idolatry in the Mass. They believe God to be there, and they adore him.
Samuel Johnson (1709–84) British lexicographer.
Life of Johnson (J. Boswell), Vol. II

7 We know these new English Catholics. They are the last words in Protest. They are Protestants protesting against Protestantism.
D. H. Lawrence (1885–1930) British novelist.
Phoenix, 'Review of Eric Gill, *Art Nonsense*'

8 Since God has given us the papacy, let us enjoy it.
Leo X (Giovanni de' Medici; 1475–1521) Pope (1513–21).
Men of Art (T. Craven)

9 I was fired from there, finally, for a lot of things, among them my insistence that the Immaculate Conception was spontaneous combustion.
Dorothy Parker (1893–1967) US writer.
Writers at Work, First Series (Malcolm Cowley)

10 The Pope! How many divisions has *he* got?

Joseph Stalin (J. Dzhugashvili; 1879–1953) Soviet statesman.
When urged by Pierre Laval to tolerate Catholicism in the USSR to appease the Pope, 13 May 1935
The Second World War (W. S. Churchill), Vol. I, Ch. 8

11 Becoming an Anglo-Catholic must surely be a sad business – rather like becoming an amateur conjurer.

John St Loe Strachey (1901–63) British politician.
The Coming Struggle for Power, Pt. III, Ch. 11

12 'God knows how you Protestants can be expected to have any sense of direction,' she said. 'It's different with us. I haven't been to mass for years, I've got every mortal sin on my conscience, but I know when I'm doing wrong. I'm still a Catholic.

Angus Wilson (1913–) British novelist.
The Wrong Set, 'Significant Experience'

CATS

See also animals

1 Cruel, but composed and bland,
Dumb, inscrutable and grand,
So Tiberius might have sat,
Had Tiberius been a cat.

Matthew Arnold (1822–88) British poet and critic.
Poor Matthias

2 Macavity, Macavity, there's no one like Macavity,
There never was a Cat of such deceitfulness and suavity.
He always has an alibi, and one or two to spare:
At whatever time the deed took place – MACAVITY WASN'T THERE!

T. S. Eliot (1888–1965) US-born British poet and dramatist.
Macavity: The Mystery Cat

3 I have noticed that what cats most appreciate in a human being is not the ability to produce food which they take for granted – but his or her entertainment value.

Geoffrey Household (1900–) British writer.
Rogue Male

4 When I observed he was a fine cat, saying, 'why yes, Sir, but I have had cats whom I liked better than this'; and then as if perceiving Hodge to be out of countenance, adding, 'but he is a very fine cat, a very fine cat indeed.'

Samuel Johnson (1709–84) British lexicographer.
Life of Johnson (J. Boswell), Vol. IV

5 If a fish is the movement of water embodied, given shape, then cat is a diagram and pattern of subtle air.

Doris Lessing (1919–) British novelist.
Particularly Cats, Ch. 2

6 When I play with my cat, who knows whether she is not amusing herself with me more than I with her?

Michel de Montaigne (1533–92) French essayist.
Essais, II

7 If a dog jumps onto your lap it is because he is fond of you; but if a cat does the same thing it is because your lap is warmer.

A. N. Whitehead (1861–1947) British philosopher and mathematician.
Dialogues

CAUTION

See also prudence

1 Better be safe than sorry.

Proverb

2 Don't put all your eggs in one basket.

Proverb

3 He that fights and runs away, may live to fight another day.

Proverb

4 He who sups with the devil should have a long spoon.

Proverb

5 If you trust before you try, you may repent before you die.

Proverb

6 Keep your mouth shut and your eyes open.

Proverb

7 Keep your weather-eye open.

Proverb

8 Look before you leap.

Proverb

9 And all should cry, Beware! Beware!
His flashing eyes, his floating hair!
Weave a circle round him thrice,
And close your eyes with holy dread,
For he on honey-dew hath fed,
And drunk the milk of Paradise.

Samuel Taylor Coleridge (1772–1834) British poet.
Kubla Khan

10 Chi Wen Tzu always thought three times before taking action. Twice would have been quite enough.

Confucius (K'ung Fu-tzu; 551–479 BC) Chinese philosopher.
Analects

11 Take example by your father, my boy, and be very careful o' vidders all your life.

Charles Dickens (1812–70) British novelist.
Pickwick Papers, Ch. 13

12 Don't go into Mr McGregor's garden: your Father had an accident there; he was put in a pie by Mrs McGregor.

Beatrix Potter (1866–1943) British children's writer.
The Tale of Peter Rabbit

CENSORSHIP

See also pornography, prudery

1 Whenever books are burned men also in the end are burned.
Heinrich Heine (1797–1856) German poet and writer.
Almansor

2 Censorship is more depraving and corrupting than anything pornography can produce.
Tony Smythe (1938–) Chairman of the National Council for Civil Liberties, Great Britain.
The Observer, 'Sayings of the Week', 18 Sept 1972

3 God forbid that any book should be banned. The practice is as indefensible as infanticide.
Rebecca West (Cicely Isabel Fairfield; 1892–1983) British novelist and journalist.
The Strange Necessity, 'The Tosh Horse'

CERTAINTY

See also self-confidence

1 If a man will begin with certainties, he shall end in doubts, but if he will be content to begin with doubts, he shall end in certainties.
Francis Bacon (1561–1626) English philosopher.
The Advancement of Learning, Bk. I, Ch. 5

2 Of that there is no manner of doubt –
No probable, possible shadow of doubt –
No possible doubt whatever.
W. S. Gilbert (1836–1911) British dramatist.
The Gondoliers, I

CHANCE

See also luck, opportunity

1 Throw out a sprat to catch a mackerel.
Proverb

2 I returned, and saw under the sun, that the race is not to the swift, nor the battle to the strong, neither yet bread to the wise, nor yet riches to men of understanding, nor yet favour to men of skill; but time and chance happeneth to them all.
For man also knoweth not his time: as the fishes that are taken in an evil net, and as the birds that are caught in the snare; so are the sons of men snared in an evil time, when it falleth suddenly upon them.
Bible: Ecclesiastes
9:11–12

3 I shot an arrow into the air,
It fell to earth, I knew not where.
Henry Wadsworth Longfellow (1807–82) US poet.
The Arrow and the Song

4 Accidental and fortuitous concurrence of atoms.
Lord Palmerston (1784–1865) British statesman.
Speech, House of Commons, 1857

5 When you take the bull by the horns . . .
what happens is a toss up.
William Pett Ridge (1860–1930) British novelist.
Love at Paddington Green, Ch. 4

CHANGE

See also conservatism, constancy, progress, transience

1 Can the Ethiopian change his skin, or the leopard his spots? then may ye also do good, that are accustomed to do evil.
Bible: Jeremiah
13:23

2 All reform except a moral one will prove unavailing.
Thomas Carlyle (1795–1881) Scottish historian and essayist.
Critical and Miscellaneous Essays, 'Corn Law Rhymes'

3 The time's come: there's a terrific thunder-cloud advancing upon us, a mighty storm is coming to freshen us up. . . . It's going to blow away all this idleness and indifference, and prejudice against work. . . . I'm going to work, and in twenty-five or thirty years' time every man and woman will be working.
Anton Chekhov (1860–1904) Russian dramatist.
Three Sisters, I

4 Variety's the very spice of life
That gives it all its flavour.
William Cowper (1731–1800) British poet.
The Task

5 Most women set out to try to change a man, and when they have changed him they do not like him.
Marlene Dietrich (Maria Magdalene von Losch; 1904–) German-born film star.
Attrib.

6 Come mothers and fathers
Throughout the land
And don't criticize
What you can't understand.
Bob Dylan (Robert Allen Zimmerman; 1941–) US popular singer.
The Times They Are A-Changin'

7 Man is so made that he can only find relaxation from one kind of labour by taking up another.
Anatole France (Jacques Anatole François Thibault; 1844–1924) French writer.
The Crime of Sylvestre Bonnard

8 Everything flows and nothing stays.
Heraclitus (c. 535–c. 475 BC) Greek philosopher.
Cratylus (Plato), 402a

9 You can't step into the same river twice.
Heraclitus
Cratylus (Plato), 402a

10 Change is not made without inconvenience, even from worse to better.
Richard Hooker (c. 1554–1600) English theologian.
English Dictionary (Johnson), Preface

11 There is a certain relief in change, even though it be from bad to worse; as I have found in travelling in a stage-coach, that it is often a comfort to shift one's position and be bruised in a new place.
Washington Irving (1783–1859) US writer.
Tales of a Traveller, 'To the Reader'

12 An old Dutch farmer, who remarked to a companion once that it was not best to swap horses in mid-stream.
Abraham Lincoln (1809–65) US statesman.
Speech, 9 June 1864

13 Well, I find that a change of nuisances is as good as a vacation.
David Lloyd George (1863–1945) British Liberal statesman.
On being asked how he maintained his cheerfulness when beset by numerous political obstacles
Attrib.

14 The wind of change is blowing through the continent. Whether we like it or not, this growth of national consciousness is a political fact.
Harold Macmillan (1894–1986) British politician and prime minister.
Speech, South African Parliament, 3 Feb 1960

15 At last he rose, and twitched his mantle blue: To-morrow to fresh woods, and pastures new.
John Milton (1608–74) English poet.
Lycidas

16 Poor old Daddy – just one of those sturdy old plants left over from the Edwardian Wilderness, that can't understand why the sun isn't shining any more.
John Osborne (1929–) British dramatist.
Look Back in Anger, II.2

17 Through all the changing scenes of life.
Nahum Tate (1652–1715) Irish-born English poet.
New Version of the Psalms, 'Through all the Changing'

18 And slowly answer'd Arthur from the barge: 'The old order changeth, yielding place to new, And God fulfils himself in many ways.'
Alfred, Lord Tennyson (1809–92) British poet.
Idylls of the King, 'The Passing of Arthur'

CHARACTER

1 Monday's child is fair of face, Tuesday's child is full of grace; Wednesday's child is full of woe, Thursday's child has far to go; Friday's child is loving and giving, Saturday's child works hard for its living; and the child that's born on the Sabbath day, is fair and wise and good and gay.
Proverb

2 Every man is as Heaven made him, and sometimes a great deal worse.
Miguel de Cervantes (1547–1616) Spanish novelist.
Don Quixote, Pt. II, Ch. 4

3 He was as fresh as is the month of May.
Geoffrey Chaucer (c. 1342–1400) English poet.
Referring to the squire
The Canterbury Tales, Prologue

4 Souninge in moral vertu was his speche, And gladly wolde he lerne, and gladly teche.
Geoffrey Chaucer
Referring to the clerk
The Canterbury Tales, Prologue

5 From a timid, shy girl I had become a woman of resolute character, who could not longer be frightened by the struggle with troubles.
Anna Dostoevsky (1846–1918) Russian diarist and writer.
Dostoevsky Portrayed by His Wife

6 What e'r he did was done with so much ease, In him alone, 'twas Natural to please.
John Dryden (1631–1700) British poet and dramatist.
Absalom and Achitophel, I

7 A patronizing disposition always has its meaner side.
George Eliot (Mary Ann Evans; 1819–80) British novelist.
Adam Bede

8 I am a man for whom the outside world exists.
Théophile Gautier (1811–72) French poet and critic.
Journal des Goncourt, 1 May 1857

9 Talent develops in quiet places, character in the full current of human life.
Goethe (1749–1832) German poet and dramatist.
Torquato Tasso, I

10 Strong enough to answer back to desires, to despise distinctions, and a whole man in himself, polished and well-rounded.
Horace (Quintus Horatius Flaccus; 65–8 BC) Roman poet.
Satires, II

11 A tart temper never mellows with age, and a sharp tongue is the only edged tool that grows keener with constant use.
Washington Irving (1783–1859) US writer.
The Sketch Book, 'Rip Van Winkle'

12 What is character but the determination of incident? What is incident but the illustration of character?
Henry James (1843–1916) US novelist.
Partial Portraits, 'The Art of Fiction'

13 He was a vicious man, but very kind to me. If you call a dog *Hervey*, I shall love him.
Samuel Johnson (1709–84) British lexicographer.
Life of Johnson (J. Boswell), Vol. I

14 A very unclubable man.
Samuel Johnson
Referring to Sir John Hawkins
Life of Johnson (J. Boswell), Vol. I

15 I recognize that I am made up of several

persons and that the person that at the moment has the upper hand will inevitably give place to another. But which is the real one? All of them or none?
W. Somerset Maugham (1874–1965) British novelist.
A Writer's Notebook

16 It is with narrow-souled people as with narrow-necked bottles: the less they have in them, the more noise they make in pouring it out.
Alexander Pope (1688–1744) British poet.
Thoughts on Various Subjects

17 Children with Hyacinth's temperament don't know better as they grow older; they merely know more.
Saki (Hector Hugh Munro; 1870–1916) British writer.
Hyacinth

18 There is no such thing as psychological. Let us say that one can improve the biography of the person.
Jean-Paul Sartre (1905–80) French writer.
The Divided Self (R. D. Laing), Ch. 8

19 A certain person may have, as you say, a wonderful presence: I do not know. What I do know is that he has a perfectly delightful absence.
Idries Shah (1924–) British author.
Reflections, 'Presence and Absence'

20 His life was gentle; and the elements
So mix'd in him that Nature might stand up
And say to all the world 'This was a man!'
William Shakespeare (1564–1616) English dramatist.
Referring to Brutus
Julius Caesar, V:5

21 A man of great common sense and good taste, – meaning thereby a man without originality or moral courage.
George Bernard Shaw (1856–1950) Irish dramatist and critic.
Referring to Julius Caesar
Caesar and Cleopatra, Notes

22 I'm not hard – I'm frightfully soft. But I will not be hounded.
Margaret Thatcher (1925–) British politician and prime minister.
Daily Mail, 1972

23 He is a man of brick. As if he was born as a baby literally of clay and decades of exposure have baked him to the colour and hardness of brick.
John Updike (1932–) US novelist.
Rabbit, Run

24 There aren't many left like him nowadays, what with education and whisky the price it is.
Evelyn Waugh (1903–66) British novelist.
Decline and Fall, Pt. I, Ch. 7

25 I've met a lot of hardboiled eggs in my time, but you're twenty minutes.
Billy Wilder (Samuel Wilder; 1906–) Austrian-born US film director.
Ace in the Hole

CHARITY

See also generosity, help, parasites, philanthropy

1 Charity begins at home.
Proverb

2 The living need charity more than the dead.
George Arnold (1834–65) US poet and humorist.
The Jolly Old Pedagogue

3 In charity there is no excess.
Francis Bacon (1561–1626) English philosopher.
Essays, 'Of Goodness, and Goodness of Nature'

4 Don't bother to thank me. I know what a perfectly ghastly season it's been for you Spanish dancers.
Tallulah Bankhead (1903–68) US actress.
Said on dropping fifty dollars into a tambourine held out by a Salvation Army collector
With Malice Toward All (D. Hermann)

5 Though I speak with the tongues of men and of angels, and have not charity, I am become as sounding brass, or a tinkling cymbal.
And though I have the gift of prophecy, and understand all mysteries, and all knowledge; and though I have all faith, so that I could remove mountains, and have not charity, I am nothing.
And though I bestow all my goods to feed the poor, and though I give my body to be burned, and have not charity, it profiteth me nothing.
Charity suffereth long, and is kind; charity envieth not; charity vaunteth not itself, is not puffed up,
Doth not behave itself unseemly, seeketh not her own, is not easily provoked, thinketh no evil;
Rejoiceth not in iniquity, but rejoiceth in the truth;
Beareth all things, believeth all things, hopeth all things, endureth all things.
Charity never faileth: but whether there be prophecies, they shall fail; whether there be tongues, they shall cease; whether there be knowledge, it shall vanish away.
For we know in part, and we prophesy in part.
But when that which is perfect is come, then that which is in part shall be done away.
When I was a child, I spake as a child, I understood as a child, I thought as a child: but when I became a man, I put away childish things.
For now we see through a glass, darkly; but then face to face: now I know in part; but then shall I know even as also I am known.

And now abideth faith, hope, charity, these three; but the greatest of these is charity.
Bible: I Corinthians
13:1–13

6 Now as touching things offered unto idols, we know that we all have knowledge. Knowledge puffeth up, but charity edifieth.
Bible: I Corinthians
8:1

7 But a certain Samaritan, as he journeyed, came where he was: and when he saw him, he had compassion on him,
And went to him, and bound up his wounds, pouring in oil and wine, and set him on his own beast, and brought him to an inn, and took care of him.
And on the morrow when he departed, he took out two pence, and gave them to the host, and said unto him, Take care of him; and whatsoever thou spendest more, when I come again, I will repay thee.
Bible: Luke
10:33–35

8 All our doings without charity are nothing worth.
The Book of Common Prayer
Collect, Quinquagesima Sunday

9 Charity begins at home, is the voice of the world.
Thomas Browne (1605–82) English physician and writer.
Religio Medici, Pt. II

10 I have always heard, Sancho, that doing good to base fellows is like throwing water into the sea.
Miguel de Cervantes (1547–1616) Spanish novelist.
Don Quixote, Pt. I, Ch. 23

11 Charity is the power of defending that which we know to be indefensible. Hope is the power of being cheerful in circumstances which we know to be desperate.
G. K. Chesterton (1874–1936) British writer.
Heretics, Ch. 12

12 No people do so much harm as those who go about doing good.
Mandell Creighton (1843–1901) British churchman.
Life

13 I'm not interested in the bloody system! Why has he no food? Why is he starving to death?
Bob Geldof (1952–) Irish rock musician.
The Observer, 'Sayings of the Week', 27 Oct 1985

14 She's the sort of woman who lives for others – you can always tell the others by their hunted expression.
C. S. Lewis (1898–1963) British academic and writer.
The Screwtape Letters

15 In the field of world policy; I would dedicate this nation to the policy of the good neighbor.
Franklin D. Roosevelt (1882–1945) US Democratic president.
First Inaugural Address, 4 Mar 1933

16 When they will not give a doit to relieve a lame beggar, they will lay out ten to see a dead Indian.
William Shakespeare (1564–1616) English dramatist.
The Tempest, II:2

17 If you see anybody fallen by the wayside and lying in the ditch, it isn't much good climbing into the ditch and lying by his side.
H. R. L. Sheppard (1880–1937) British clergyman.
Dick Sheppard (Carolyn Scott)

18 The white man knows how to make everything, but he does not know how to distribute it.
Sitting Bull (c. 1834–90) US Sioux Indian chief.
Attrib.

19 You find people ready enough to do the Samaritan, without the oil and twopence.
Sydney Smith (1771–1845) British clergyman and essayist.
Memoir (Lady Holland)

20 To keep a lamp burning we have to keep putting oil in it.
Mother Teresa (Agnes Gonxha Bojaxhui; 1910–) Yugoslavian missionary in Calcutta.
Time, 'Saints Among Us', 29 Dec 1975

21 As for doing good, that is one of the professions which are full.
Henry David Thoreau (1817–62) US writer.
Walden, 'Economy'

22 I have always depended on the kindness of strangers.
Tennessee Williams (1911–83) US dramatist.
A Streetcar Named Desire, II:3

CHARM

1 It's a sort of bloom on a woman. If you have it, you don't need to have anything else; and if you don't have it, it doesn't much matter what else you have.
J. M. Barrie (1860–1937) British novelist and dramatist.
What Every Woman Knows, I

2 All charming people have something to conceal, usually their total dependence on the appreciation of others.
Cyril Connolly (1903–74) British journalist.
Enemies of Promise, Ch. 16

3 Oozing charm from every pore,
He oiled his way around the floor.
Alan Jay Lerner (1918–86) US songwriter.
My Fair Lady, II:1

4 It is absurd to divide people into good and bad. People are either charming or tedious.
Oscar Wilde (1854–1900) Irish-born British dramatist.
Lady Windermere's Fan, I

CHILDREN

See also babies, family, innocence of childhood, youth

1 Spare the rod and spoil the child.
Proverb

2 There's only one pretty child in the world, and every mother has it.
Proverb

3 It was no wonder that people were so horrible when they started life as children.
Kingsley Amis (1922–) British novelist.
One Fat Englishman, Ch. 14

4 Only those in the last stage of disease could believe that children are true judges of character.
W. H. Auden (1907–73) British poet.
The Orators, 'Journal of an Airman'

5 Children sweeten labours, but they make misfortunes more bitter.
Francis Bacon (1561–1626) English philosopher.
Essays, 'Of Parents and Children'

6 Children have never been very good at listening to their elders, but they have never failed to imitate them.
James Baldwin (1924–87) US writer.
Esquire, 1960

7 I am married to Beatrice Salkeld, a painter. We have no children, except me.
Brendan Behan (1923–64) Irish playwright.
Attrib.

8 I wish I'd been a mixed infant.
Brendan Behan
The Hostage, II

9 Alas! That such affected tricks
Should flourish in a child of six!
Hilaire Belloc (1870–1953) French-born British poet.
Cautionary Tales, 'Godolphin Horne'

10 A trick that everyone abhors
In little girls is slamming doors.
Hilaire Belloc
Cautionary Tales, 'Rebecca'

11 Desire not a multitude of unprofitable children, neither delight in ungodly sons.
Bible: Ecclesiasticus
16:1

12 But when Jesus saw it, he was much displeased, and said unto them. Suffer the little children to come unto me, and forbid them not: for of such is the kingdom of God.
Bible: Mark
10:14

13 And there came a certain poor widow, and she threw in two mites, which make a farthing. And he called unto him his disciples, and saith unto them, Verily I say unto you, That this poor widow hath cast more in, than all they which have cast into the treasury:
For all they did cast in of their abundance; but she of her want did cast in all that she had, even all her living.
Bible: Mark
12:42–44

14 Verily I say unto you, Except ye be converted, and become as little children, ye shall not enter into the kingdom of heaven.
Bible: Matthew
18:3

15 And whoso shall receive one such little child in my name receiveth me.
But whoso shall offend one of these little ones which believe in me, it were better for him that a millstone were hanged about his neck, and that he were drowned in the depth of the sea.
Bible: Matthew
18:5–6

16 He that spareth his rod hateth his son: but he that loveth him chasteneth him betimes.
Bible: Proverbs
13:24

17 'Twas on a Holy Thursday, their innocent faces clean,
The children walking two and two, in red and blue and green.
William Blake (1757–1827) British poet.
Songs of Innocence, 'Holy Thursday'

18 There is no finer investment for any community than putting milk into babies.
Winston Churchill (1874–1965) British statesman.
Radio Broadcast, 21 Mar 1943

19 Boys do not grow up gradually. They move forward in spurts like the hands of clocks in railway stations.
Cyril Connolly (1903–74) British journalist.
Enemies of Promise, Ch. 18

20 It is only rarely that one can see in a little boy the promise of a man, but one can almost always see in a little girl the threat of a woman.
Alexandre Dumas, fils (1824–95) French writer.
Attrib.

21 Anybody who hates children and dogs can't be all bad.
W. C. Fields (1880–1946) US actor.
Attrib.

22 To bear many children is considered not only a religious blessing but also an investment. The greater their number, some Indians reason, the more alms they can beg.
Indira Gandhi (1917–84) Indian stateswoman.
New York Review of Books, 'Indira's Coup' (Oriana Fallaci)

23 Three little maids from school are we,
Pert as a school-girl well can be,
Filled to the brim with girlish glee.
W. S. Gilbert (1836–1911) British dramatist.
The Mikado, I

24 Look at little Johnny there,
Little Johnny Head-in-Air.
Heinrich Hoffman (1809–74) German writer.
Struwwelpeter, 'Johnny Head-in-Air'

25 Anything to me is sweeter
Than to see Shock-headed Peter.
Heinrich Hoffman
Struwwelpeter, 'Shock-headed Peter'

26 The business of being a child interests a child
not at all. Children very rarely play at being
other children.
David Holloway (1924–) Literary editor.
The Daily Telegraph, 15 December 1966

27 A child deserves the maximum respect; if
you ever have something disgraceful in mind,
don't ignore your son's tender years.
Juvenal (Decimus Junius Juvenalis; 60–130 AD) Roman
satirist.
Satires, XIV

28 The real menace in dealing with a five-year-
old is that in no time at all you begin to
sound like a five-year-old.
Jean Kerr (1923–) US dramatist.
Please Don't Eat the Daisies

29 At every step the child should be allowed to
meet the real experiences of life; the thorns
should never be plucked from his roses.
Ellen Key (Karolina Sofia Key; 1849–1926) Swedish
writer.
The Century of the Child, Ch. 3

30 Boys are capital fellows in their own way,
among their mates; but they are
unwholesome companions for grown people.
Charles Lamb (1775–1834) British essayist.
Essays of Elia, 'The Old and the New Schoolmaster'

31 A child's a plaything for an hour.
Mary Lamb (1764–1847) Sister of Charles Lamb.
Parental Recollections

32 Where are the children I might have had?
You suppose I might have wanted them.
Drowned to the accompaniment of the
rattling of a thousand douche bags.
Malcolm Lowry (1909–57) British novelist.
Under the Volcano, Ch. 10

33 Part of the reason for the ugliness of adults,
in a child's eyes, is that the child is usually
looking upwards, and few faces are at their
best when seen from below.
George Orwell (Eric Blair; 1903–50) British novelist.
Essays

34 Parents learn a lot from their children about
coping with life.
Muriel Spark (1918–) British novelist.
The Comforters, Ch. 6

35 I have a big house – and I hide a lot.
Mary Ure (1933–75) British actress.
Explaining how she coped with her large family of children
Attrib.

36 Never have children, only grandchildren.
Gore Vidal (1925–) US novelist.
Two Sisters

37 A food is not necessarily essential just
because your child hates it.
Katherine Whitehorn (1926–) British journalist.
How to Survive Children

CHIVALRY

See also courtesy

1 A gentleman is any man who wouldn't hit a
woman with his hat on.
Fred Allen (1894–1956) US comedian.
Attrib.

2 Even nowadays a man can't step up and kill a
woman without feeling just a bit unchivalrous.
Robert Benchley (1889–1945) US humorist.
Chips off the Old Benchley, 'Down in Front'

3 Somebody has said, that a king may make a
nobleman, but he cannot make a gentleman.
Edmund Burke (1729–97) British politician.
Letter to William Smith, 29 Jan 1795

4 He was a verray parfit gentil knight.
Geoffrey Chaucer (c. 1342–1400) English poet.
Referring to the knight
The Canterbury Tales, Prologue

5 Madame, I would have given you another!
Alfred Jarry (1873–1907) French surrealist dramatist.
On being reprimanded by a woman for firing his pistol in the
vicinity of her child, who might have been killed
Recollections of a Picture Dealer (A. Vollard)

6 Some say that the age of chivalry is past,
that the spirit of romance is dead. The age of
chivalry is never past, so long as there is a
wrong left unredressed on earth.
Charles Kingsley (1819–75) British writer.
Life (Mrs C. Kingsley), Vol. II, Ch. 28

7 For he's one of Nature's Gentlemen, the best
of every time.
W. J. Linton (1812–97) British writer.
Nature's Gentleman

8 It is almost a definition of a gentleman to say
that he is one who never inflicts pain.
Cardinal Newman (1801–90) British theologian.
The Idea of a University, 'Knowledge and Religious Duty'

9 O, young Lochinvar is come out of the west,
Through all the wide Border his steed was the
best.
Walter Scott (1771–1832) Scottish novelist.
Marmion, V

10 So faithful in love, and so dauntless in war,

There never was knight like the young
Lochinvar.
Walter Scott
Marmion, V

11 A bow-shot from her bower-eaves,
He rode between the barley-sheaves,
The sun came dazzling thro' the leaves
And flamed upon the brazen graves
Of bold Sir Lancelot.
Alfred, Lord Tennyson (1809–92) British poet.
The Lady of Shalott, Pt. III

CHOICE

1 Any colour, so long as it's black.
Henry Ford (1863–1947) US car manufacturer.
Referring to the colour options offered for the Model-T Ford
car
Attrib.

2 Two roads diverged in a wood, and I –
I took the one less traveled by,
And that has made all the difference.
Robert Frost (1875–1963) US poet.
The Road Not Taken

3 More ways of killing a cat than choking her
with cream.
Charles Kingsley (1819–75) British writer.
Westward Ho!, Ch. 20

4 We have to believe in free will. We've got no
choice.
Isaac Bashevis Singer (1904–) Polish-born US writer.
The Times, 21 June 1982

CHRISTIANITY

See also Catholicism, Protestantism, religion

1 There is a green hill far away,
Without a city wall,
Where the dear Lord was crucified,
Who died to save us all.
C. F. Alexander (1818–95) British hymn writer.
There is a Green Hill Far Away

2 'Christianity, of course but why journalism?'
Arthur Balfour (1848–1930) British statesman.
In reply to Frank Harris's remark, '. . . all the faults of the age
come from Christianity and journalism'
Autobiography (Margot Asquith), Ch. 10

3 Onward, Christian soldiers,
Marching as to war,
With the Cross of Jesus
Going on before.
Sabine Baring-Gould (1834–1924) British author and
hymn writer.
Onward Christian Soldiers

4 Beware lest any man spoil you through
philosophy and vain deceit, after the tradition
of men, after the rudiments of the world, and
not after Christ.
Bible: Colossians
2:8

5 Where there is neither Greek nor Jew,
circumcision nor uncircumcision, Barbarian,
Scythian, bond nor free; but Christ is all, and
in all.
Bible: Colossians
3:11

6 Take heed to yourselves, that your heart be
not deceived, and ye turn aside, and serve
other gods, and worship them.
Bible: Deuteronomy
11:16

7 There is neither Jew nor Greek, there is
neither bond nor free, there is neither male
nor female: for ye are all one in Christ Jesus.
Bible: Galatians
3:28

8 But the fruit of the Spirit is love, joy, peace,
longsuffering, gentleness, goodness, faith,
Meekness, temperance: against such there is
no law.
Bible: Galatians
5:22–23

9 Therefore the Lord himself shall give you a
sign; Behold, a virgin shall conceive, and
bear a son, and shall call his name Immanuel.
Butter and honey shall he eat, that he may
know to refuse the evil, and choose the good.
Bible: Isaiah
7:14–15

10 He shall feed his flock like a shepherd: he
shall gather the lambs with his arm, and
carry them in his bosom, and shall gently
lead those that are with young.
Bible: Isaiah
40:11

11 He it is, who coming after me is preferred
before me, whose shoe's latchet I am not
worthy to unloose.
Bible: John
1:27

12 The next day John seeth Jesus coming unto
him, and saith, Behold the Lamb of God,
which taketh away the sin of the world.
Bible: John
1:29

13 For God so loved the world, that he gave his
only begotten Son, that whosoever believeth
in him should not perish, but have everlasting
life.
Bible: John
3:16

14 Then spake Jesus again unto them, saying, I
am the light of the world: he that followeth
me shall not walk in darkness, but shall have
the light of life.
Bible: John
8:12

15 I am the good shepherd: the good shepherd giveth his life for the sheep.
Bible: John
10:11

16 Jesus said unto her, I am the resurrection, and the life: he that believeth in me, though he were dead, yet shall he live.
Bible: John
11:25

17 Jesus saith unto him, I am the way, the truth, and the life: no man cometh unto the Father, but by me.
Bible: John
14:6

18 Come unto me, all ye that labour and are heavy laden, and I will give you rest.
Take my yoke upon you, and learn of me; for I am meek and lowly in heart: and ye shall find rest unto your souls.
For my yoke is easy, and my burden is light.
Bible: Matthew
11:28–30

19 Then said Jesus unto his disciples, If any man will come after me, let him deny himself, and take up his cross, and follow me.
Bible: Matthew
16:24

20 How very hard it is
To be a Christian!
Robert Browning (1812–89) British poet.
Easter-Day, I

21 It was just one of those parties which got out of hand.
Lenny Bruce (1925–66) US comedian.
Referring to the Crucifixion
The Guardian, 10 May 1979

22 He who begins by loving Christianity better than Truth will proceed by loving his own sect or church better than Christianity, and end by loving himself better than all.
Samuel Taylor Coleridge (1772–1834) British poet.
Aids to Reflection: Moral and Religious Aphorisms,

23 His Christianity was muscular.
Benjamin Disraeli (1804–81) British statesman.
Endymion, Bk. 1, Ch. 14

24 Christianity has done a great deal for love by making a sin of it.
Anatole France (Jacques Anatole François Thibault; 1844–1924) French writer.
The Garden of Epicurus

25 What about it? Do you want to crucify the boy?
Lew Grade (Lewis Winogradsky; 1906–) British film and TV producer.
Referring to the revelation that an actor portraying Christ on television was living with a woman to whom he was not married
Attrib.

26 Christianity is part of the Common Law of England.
Matthew Hale (1609–76) English judge.
Historia Placitorum Coronae (ed. Sollom Emlyn)

27 Tell me the old, old story
Of unseen things above,
Of Jesus and His glory
Of Jesus and His love.
Katherine Hankey (1834–1911) British hymn writer.
Tell Me the Old, Old Story

28 A local cult called Christianity.
Thomas Hardy (1840–1928) British novelist.
The Dynasts, I:6

29 The Christian religion not only was at first attended with miracles, but even at this day cannot be believed by any reasonable person without one. Mere reason is insufficient to convince us of its veracity: and whoever is moved by faith to assent to it, is conscious of a continued miracle in his own person, which subverts all the principles of his understanding, and gives him a determination to believe what is most contrary to custom and experience.
David Hume (1711–76) Scottish philosopher.
Essays, 'Of Miracles'

30 Christianity accepted as given a metaphysical system derived from several already existing and mutually incompatible systems.
Aldous Huxley (1894–1964) British novelist.
Grey Eminence, Ch. 3

31 There must be several young women who would render the Christian life intensely difficult to him if only you could persuade him to marry one of them.
C. S. Lewis (1898–1963) British academic and writer.
The Screwtape Letters

32 Ride on! ride on in majesty!
In lowly pomp ride on to die.
Henry Hart Milman (1791–1868) British poet and historian.
Ride On

33 Fight the good fight with all thy might,
Christ is thy strength and Christ thy right,
Lay hold on life, and it shall be
Thy joy and crown eternally.
John Monsell (1811–75) British hymn writer.
Hymn

34 No kingdom has ever had as many civil wars as the kingdom of Christ.
Baron de Montesquieu (1688–1755) French writer.
Lettres persanes

35 I call Christianity the one great curse, the one enormous and innermost perversion, the one great instinct of revenge, for which no means are too venomous, too underhand, too

underground and too petty – I call it the one immortal blemish of mankind.
Friedrich Wilhelm Nietzsche (1844–1900) German philosopher.
The Antichrist

36 Christianity has made of death a terror which was unknown to the gay calmness of the Pagan.
Ouida (Marie Louise de la Ramée; 1839–1908) British novelist.
The Failure of Christianity

37 All hail, the power of Jesus' name!
Let angels prostrate fall.
Edward Perronet (1726–92) British hymn writer.
Hymn

38 Whether you think Jesus was God or not, you must admit that he was a first-rate political economist.
George Bernard Shaw (1856–1950) Irish dramatist and critic.
Androcles and the Lion, Preface, 'Jesus as Economist'

39 Who dreamed that Christ has died in vain?
He walks again on the Seas of Blood,
He comes in the terrible Rain.
Edith Sitwell (1887–1964) British poet and writer.
The Shadow of Cain

40 The Church's one foundation
Is Jesus Christ her Lord;
She is His new creation
By water and the Word.
Samuel. J. Stone (1839–1901) US hymn writer.
Hymn

41 Well, you might try getting crucified and rising again on the third day.
Talleyrand (Charles Maurice de Talleyrand-Périgord; 1754–1838) French politician.
Giving his opinion upon what action might impress the French peasantry
Attrib.

42 Christianity is the most materialistic of all great religions.
William Temple (1881–1944) British churchman.
Reading in St John's Gospel, Vol. I, Introduction

43 And so the Word had breath, and wrought
With human hands the creed of creeds
In loveliness of perfect deeds,
More strong than all poetic thought.
Alfred, Lord Tennyson (1809–92) British poet.
In Memoriam A.H.H., XXXVI

44 The blood of the martyrs is the seed of the Church.
Tertullian (c. 160–225 AD) Carthaginian father of the church.
Traditional misquotation: more accurately, 'Our numbers increase as often as you cut us down: the blood of Christians is the seed.'
Apologeticus, L

45 See how these Christians love one another.
Tertullian
Apologeticus, XXXIX

46 Fraser . . . left his children unbaptized – his wife did it secretly in the washing basin.
Virginia Woolf (1882–1941) British novelist.
Jacob's Room, Ch. 9

CHRISTMAS

See also Christianity

1 I have often thought, says Sir Roger, it happens very well that Christmas should fall out in the Middle of Winter.
Joseph Addison (1672–1719) British essayist.
The Spectator, 269

2 Once in royal David's city
Stood a lowly cattle shed,
Where a Mother laid her Baby
In a manger for His bed:
Mary was that Mother mild,
Jesus Christ her little Child.
C. F. Alexander (1818–95) British hymn writer.
Once in Royal David's City

3 As I sat on a sunny bank,
On Christmas Day in the morning,
I spied three ships come sailing by.
Anonymous
As I sat on a Sunny Bank

4 God rest you merry, gentlemen,
Let nothing you dismay.
Anonymous
God Rest you Merry

5 The holly and the ivy,
When they are both full grown,
Of all the trees that are in the wood,
The holly bears the crown.
The rising of the sun
And the running of the deer,
The playing of the merry organ,
Sweet singing in the choir.
Anonymous
The Holly and the Ivy

6 For unto us a child is born, unto us a son is given: and the government shall be upon his shoulder: and his name shall be called Wonderful, Counsellor, The mighty God, The everlasting Father, The Prince of Peace.
Of the increase of his government and peace there shall be no end, upon the throne of David, and upon his kingdom, to order it, and to establish it with judgment and with justice from henceforth even for ever. The zeal of the Lord of hosts will perform this.
Bible: Isaiah
9:6–7

7 And she brought forth her firstborn son, and wrapped him in swaddling clothes, and laid him in a manger; because there was no room for them in the inn.
Bible: Luke
2:7

8 And there were in the same country

shepherds abiding in the field, keeping watch over their flock by night.

And, lo, the angel of the Lord came upon them, and the glory of the Lord shone round about them: and they were sore afraid.

And the angel said unto them, Fear not: for, behold, I bring you good tidings of great joy, which shall be to all people.

Bible: Luke
2:8–10

9 Now when Jesus was born in Bethlehem of Judaea in the days of Herod the king, behold, there came wise men from the east to Jerusalem,

Saying, Where is he that is born King of the Jews? for we have seen his star in the east, and are come to worship him.

When Herod the king had heard these things, he was troubled, and all Jerusalem with him.

Bible: Matthew
2:1–3

10 And when they were come into the house, they saw the young child with Mary his mother, and fell down, and worshipped him: and when they had opened their treasures, they presented unto him gifts; gold, and frankincense, and myrrh.

And being warned of God in a dream that they should not return to Herod, they departed into their own country another way.

Bible: Matthew
2:11–12

11 O little town of Bethlehem,
How still we see thee lie;
Above thy deep and dreamless sleep
The silent stars go by.

Phillips Brooks (1835–93) US Episcopal bishop.
O Little Town of Bethlehem

12 Christians awake, salute the happy morn,
Whereon the Saviour of the world was born.

John Byrom (1692–1763) British poet and hymn writer.
Hymn for Christmas Day

13 'Twas the night before Christmas, when all through the house
Not a creature was stirring, not even a mouse;
The stockings were hung by the chimney with care,
In hopes that St Nicholas soon would be there.

Clement Clarke Moore (1779–1863) US writer.
In *Troy Sentinel*, 23 Dec 1823, 'A Visit from St. Nicholas'

14 Good King Wenceslas looked out,
On the Feast of Stephen;
When the snow lay round about,
Deep and crisp and even.

John Mason Neale (1818–66) British churchman.
Good King Wenceslas

15 O come all ye faithful,
Joyful and triumphant,

O come ye, O come ye to Bethlehem.

Frederick Oakeley (1802–80) British churchman.
Translated from the Latin hymn, *Adeste Fideles*
O Come All Ye Faithful

16 It came upon the midnight clear,
That glorious song of old,
From Angels bending near the earth
To touch their harps of gold;
'Peace on the earth; good will to man
From Heaven's all gracious King.'
The world in solemn stillness lay
To hear the angels sing.

E. H. Sears (1810–76) US clergyman.
That Glorious Song of Old

17 While shepherds watch'd their flocks by night,
All seated on the ground,
The Angel of the Lord came down,
And Glory shone around.

Nahum Tate (1652–1715) Irish-born English poet.
Supplement to the New Version of the Psalms, 'While Shepherds Watched'

18 At Christmas play and make good cheer,
For Christmas comes but once a year.

Thomas Tusser (1524–80) English farmer.
Five Hundred Points of Good Husbandry, 'The Farmer's Daily Diet'

19 To perceive Christmas through its wrapping becomes more difficult with every year.

Elwyn Brooks White (1899–1985) US journalist and humorist.
The Second Tree from the Corner

CHURCH

See also clergy, religion

1 And I say also unto thee, That thou art Peter, and upon this rock I will build my church; and the gates of hell shall not prevail against it.

And I will give unto thee the keys of the kingdom of heaven: and whatsoever thou shalt bind on earth shall be bound in heaven: and whatsoever thou shalt loose on earth shall be loosed in heaven.

Bible: Matthew
16:18–19

2 For where two or three are gathered together in my name, there am I in the midst of them.

Bible: Matthew
18:20

3 And of all plagues with which mankind are curst,
Ecclesiastic tyranny's the worst.

Daniel Defoe (1660–1731) British journalist and writer.
The True-Born Englishman, Pt. II

4 It is hard to tell where MCC ends and the Church of England begins.

J. B. Priestley (1894–1984) British novelist.
New Statesman, 20 July 1962, 'Topside Schools'

5 The Church exists for the sake of those
outside it.
William Temple (1881–1944) British churchman.
Attrib.

CHURCHILL

See also politicians, World War II

1 It hasn't taken Winston long to get used to
American ways. He hadn't been an American
citizen for three minutes before attacking an
ex-secretary of state!
Dean Acheson (1893–1971) US lawyer and statesman.
At a ceremony in 1963 to make Churchill an honorary American citizen, Churchill obliquely attacked Acheson's reference
to Britain losing an empire
Randolph Churchill (K. Halle)

2 Then comes Winston with his hundred-horse-
power mind and what can I do?
Stanley Baldwin (1867–1947) British statesman.
Stanley Baldwin (G. M. Young), Ch. 11

3 I thought he was a young man of promise;
but it appears he was a young man of
promises.
Arthur Balfour (1848–1930) British statesman.
Said of Winston Churchill on his entry into politics, 1899
Winston Churchill (Randolph Churchill), Vol. I

4 He is a man suffering from petrified
adolescence.
Aneurin Bevan (1897–1960) British Labour politician.
Aneurin Bevan (Vincent Brome), Ch. 11

5 The nation had the lion's heart. I had the
luck to give the roar.
Winston Churchill (1874–1965) British statesman.
Said on his 80th birthday

6 The first time you meet Winston you see all
his faults and the rest of your life you spend
in discovering his virtues.
Lady Constance Lytton (1869–1923) British suffragette.
Edward Marsh (Christopher Hassall), Ch. 7

7 Simply a radio personality who outlived his
prime.
Evelyn Waugh (1903–66) British novelist.
Evelyn Waugh (Christopher Sykes)

CINEMA

See also Goldwynisms

1 If my books had been any worse I should not
have been invited to Hollywood, and if they
had been any better I should not have come.
Raymond Chandler (1888–1959) US novelist.
The Life of Raymond Chandler (F. MacShane)

2 I was born at the age of twelve on a Metro-
Goldwyn-Mayer lot.
Judy Garland (Frances Gumm; 1922–69) US film star.
The Observer, 'Sayings of the Week', 18 Feb 1951

3 I like a film to have a beginning, a middle and
an end, but not necessarily in that order.
Jean-Luc Godard (1930–) French film director.
Attrib.

4 Photography is truth. And cinema is truth
twenty-four times a second.
Jean-Luc Godard
Le Petit Soldat

5 Why should people go out and pay money to
see bad films when they can stay at home
and see bad television for nothing?
Samuel Goldwyn (Samuel Goldfish; 1882–1974) Polish-
born US film producer.
The Observer, 'Sayings of the Week', 9 Sept 1956

6 A wide screen just makes a bad film twice as
bad.
Samuel Goldwyn
Attrib.

7 In Hollywood, if you don't have happiness
you send out for it.
Rex Reed (1938–) US columnist and actor.
Colombo's Hollywood, 'Hollywood the Bad' (J. R. Colombo)

8 Take that black box away. I can't act in front
of it.
Herbert Beerbohm Tree (1853–1917) British actor and
theatre manager.
Objecting to the presence of the camera while performing in a
silent film
Hollywood: The Pioneers (K. Brownlow)

9 Thanks to the movies, gunfire has always
sounded unreal to me, even when being fired
at.
Peter Ustinov (1921–) British actor.
Dear Me, Ch. 7

10 Me? Tarzan?
Johnny Weissmuller (1904–84) US swimmer and film
actor.
Reacting to an invitation to play Tarzan
Attrib.

11 When you get the personality, you don't need
the nudity.
Mae West (1892–1980) US actress.
The Observer, 'Sayings of the Week', 4 Aug 1968

CIVILIZATION

See also culture

1 Civilization is a method of living, an attitude
of equal respect for all men.
Jane Addams (1860–1935) US social worker.
Speech, Honolulu, 1933

2 I wish I could bring Stonehenge to Nyasaland
to show there was a time when Britain had a
savage culture.
Hastings Banda (1906–) Malawi statesman.
The Observer, 'Sayings of the Week', 10 Mar 1963

3 The three great elements of modern

civilization, Gunpowder, Printing, and the
Protestant Religion.
Thomas Carlyle (1795–1881) Scottish historian and
essayist.
Critical and Miscellaneous Essays, 'The State of German Literature'

4 The modern world . . . has no notion except
that of simplifying something by destroying
nearly everything.
G. K. Chesterton (1874–1936) British writer.
All I Survey

5 In essence the Renaissance was simply the
green end of one of civilization's hardest
winters.
John Fowles (1926–) British novelist.
The French Lieutenant's Woman, Ch. 10

6 I think it would be a good idea.
Mahatma Gandhi (Mohandas Karamchand Gandhi; 1869–
1948) Indian national leader.
On being asked for his view on Western civilization
Attrib.

7 There is precious little in civilization to appeal
to a Yeti.
Edmund Hillary (1919–) New Zealand mountaineer.
The Observer, 'Sayings of the Week', 3 June 1960

8 As civilization advances, poetry almost
necessarily declines.
Lord Macaulay (1800–59) British historian.
Literary Essays Contributed to the 'Edinburgh Review', 'Milton'

9 The degree of a nation's civilization is marked
by its disregard for the necessities of
existence.
W. Somerset Maugham (1874–1965) British novelist.
Our Betters, I

CLARITY

See also communication, confusion

1 Oh! rather give me commentators plain,
Who with no deep researches vex the brain;
Who from the dark and doubtful love to run,
And hold their glimmering tapers to the sun.
George Crabbe (1754–1832) British poet.
The Parish Register, 'Baptisms'

2 It's odd how people waiting for you stand out
far less clearly than people you are waiting
for.
Jean Giraudoux (1882–1944) French dramatist.
Tiger at the Gates, I

3 When man's whole frame is obvious to a flea.
Alexander Pope (1688–1744) British poet.
The Dunciad, IV

CLASS

See also aristocracy, equality, public, snobbery

1 There's one law for the rich, and another for
the poor.
Proverb

2 You can measure the social caste of a person
by the distance between the husband's and
wife's apartments.
Alfonso XIII (1886–1941) Spanish monarch.
Attrib.

3 I often, therefore, when I want to distinguish
clearly the aristocratic class from the
Philistines proper, or middle class, name the
former, in my own mind *the Barbarians*.
Matthew Arnold (1822–88) British poet and critic.
Culture and Anarchy, Ch. 3

4 When Adam delved and Eve span,
Who was then the gentleman?
John Ball (d. 1381) English priest.
Text of sermon

5 Yet it is better to drop thy friends, O my
daughter, than to drop thy 'H's'.
C. S. Calverley (1831–84) British poet.
Proverbial Philosophy, 'Of Friendship'

6 One of those refined people who go out to
sew for the rich because they cannot bear
contact with the poor.
Colette (1873–1954) French novelist.
The Other One

7 Servants should not be ill. We have quite
enough illnesses of our own without them
adding to the symptoms.
Lady Diana Cooper (1892–1986) Actress and writer.
Diana Cooper (Philip Ziegler)

8 He bade me observe it, and I should always
find, that the calamities of life were shared
among the upper and lower part of mankind;
but that the middle station had the fewest
disasters.
Daniel Defoe (1660–1731) British journalist and writer.
Robinson Crusoe, Pt. I

9 O let us love our occupations,
Bless the squire and his relations,
Live upon our daily rations,
And always know our proper stations.
Charles Dickens (1812–70) British novelist.
The Chimes, '2nd Quarter'

10 He differed from the healthy type that was
essentially middle-class – he never seemed
to perspire.
F. Scott Fitzgerald (1896–1940) US novelist.
This Side of Paradise, Bk. I, Ch. 2

11 All shall equal be.
The Earl, the Marquis, and the Dook,
The Groom, the Butler, and the Cook,
The Aristocrat who banks with Coutts,
The Aristocrat who cleans the boots.
W. S. Gilbert (1836–1911) British dramatist.
The Gondoliers, I

12 He combines the manners of a Marquis with
the morals of a Methodist.
W. S. Gilbert
Ruddigore, I

13 Bow, bow, ye lower middle classes!
Bow, bow, ye tradesmen, bow, ye masses!
W. S. Gilbert
Iolanthe, I

14 All the world over, I will back the masses
against the classes.
William Ewart Gladstone (1809–98) British statesman.
Speech, Liverpool, 28 June 1886

15 Dialect words – those terrible marks of the
beast to the truly genteel.
Thomas Hardy (1840–1928) British novelist.
The Mayor of Casterbridge, Ch. 20

16 'Bourgeois,' I observed, 'is an epithet which
the riff-raff apply to what is respectable, and
the aristocracy to what is decent'.
Anthony Hope (Sir Anthony Hope Hawkins; 1863–1933)
British novelist.
The Dolly Dialogues

17 You may be the most liberal Liberal
Englishman, and yet you cannot fail to see
the categorical difference between the
responsible and the irresponsible classes.
D. H. Lawrence (1885–1930) British novelist.
Kangaroo, Ch. 1

18 A Social-Democrat must never forget that the
proletariat will inevitably have to wage a class
struggle for Socialism even against the most
democratic and republican bourgeoisie and
petty bourgeoisie.
Lenin (Vladimir Ilich Ulyanov; 1870–1924) Russian
revolutionary leader.
The State and Revolution, Ch. 10

19 An Englishman's way of speaking absolutely
classifies him
The moment he talks he makes some other
Englishman despise him.
Alan Jay Lerner (1918–86) US songwriter.
My Fair Lady, I:1

20 I'm not interested in classes . . . Far be it
from me to foster inferiority complexes
among the workers by trying to make them
think they belong to some special class. That
has happened in Europe but it hasn't
happened here yet.
John Llewellyn Lewis (1880–1969) US labour leader.
The Coming of the New Deal (A. M. Schlesinger, Jnr), Pt. 7,
Ch. 25

21 Said Marx: 'Don't be snobbish, we seek to
abolish
The 3rd Class, not the 1st.'
Christopher Logue (1926–) British poet and dramatist.
Christopher Logue's ABC, 'M'

22 The history of all hitherto existing society is
the history of class struggles.
Karl Marx (1818–83) German philosopher and
revolutionary.
The Communist Manifesto, 1

23 The one class you do *not* belong to and are

not proud of at all is the lower-middle class.
No one ever describes himself as belonging
to the lower-middle class.
George Mikes (1912–87) Hungarian-born British writer.
How to be Inimitable

24 We have nothing to lose but our aitches.
George Orwell (Eric Blair; 1903–50) British novelist.
Referring to the middle classes
The Road to Wigan Pier, Ch. 13

25 I don't think one 'comes down' from Jimmy's
university. According to him, it's not even
red brick, but white tile.
John Osborne (1929–) British dramatist.
Look Back in Anger, II:1

26 You can be in the Horse Guards and still be
common, dear.
Terence Rattigan (1911–77) British dramatist.
Separate Tables: 'Table Number Seven'

27 U and Non-U, An Essay in Sociological
Linguistics.
Alan Strode Campbell Ross (1907–78) British professor
of linguistics.
Essay title, *Noblesse Oblige*, 1956

28 There are two classes in good society in
England. The equestrian classes and the
neurotic classes.
George Bernard Shaw (1856–1950) Irish dramatist and
critic.
Heartbreak House

29 I am a gentleman. I live by robbing the poor.
George Bernard Shaw
Man and Superman

30 I have to live for others and not for myself;
that's middle class morality.
George Bernard Shaw
Pygmalion

31 It is impossible for one class to appreciate
the wrongs of another.
Elizabeth Stanton (1815–1902) US suffragette.
History of Woman Suffrage (with Susan B. Anthony and Mathilda Gage), Vol. I

32 The charm of Britain has always been the
ease with which one can move into the
middle class.
Margaret Thatcher (1925–) British politician and prime
minister.
The Observer, 'Sayings of the Week', 27 Oct 1974

33 The ship follows Soviet custom: it is riddled
with class distinctions so subtle, it takes a
trained Marxist to appreciate them.
Paul Theroux (1941–) US-born writer.
The Great Railway Bazaar, Ch. 30

34 For generations the British bourgeoisie have
spoken of themselves as gentlemen, and by
that they have meant, among other things, a
self-respecting scorn of irregular perquisites.
It is the quality that distinguishes the

gentleman from both the artist and the aristocrat.

Evelyn Waugh (1903–66) British novelist.
Decline and Fall, Pt. I, Ch. 6

35 No writer before the middle of the 19th century wrote about the working classes other than as grotesque or as pastoral decoration. Then when they were given the vote certain writers started to suck up to them.

Evelyn Waugh
Interview
Paris Review, 1963

36 Bricklayers kick their wives to death, and dukes betray theirs; but it is among the small clerks and shopkeepers nowadays that it comes most often to the cutting of throats.

H. G. Wells (1866–1946) British writer.
Short Stories, 'The Purple Pileus'

37 Margaret Thatcher's great strength seems to be the better people know her, the better they like her. But, of course, she has one great disadvantage – she is a daughter of the people and looks trim, as the daughters of the people desire to be. Shirley Williams has such an advantage over her because she's a member of the upper-middle class and can achieve that kitchen-sink-revolutionary look that one cannot get unless one has been to a really good school.

Rebecca West (Cicely Isabel Fairfield; 1892–1983) British novelist and journalist.
Said in an interview with Jilly Cooper
The Sunday Times, 25 July 1976

38 Really, if the lower orders don't set us a good example, what on earth is the use of them?

Oscar Wilde (1854–1900) Irish-born British dramatist.
The Importance of Being Earnest, I

39 The constitution does not provide for first and second class citizens.

Wendell Lewis Willkie (1892–1944) US lawyer and businessman.
An American Programme, Ch. 2

CLASSICS

1 They were a tense and peculiar family, the Oedipuses, weren't they?

Max Beerbohm (1872–1956) British writer.
Max: A Biography (D. Cecil)

2 So they told me how Mr Gladstone read Homer for fun, which I thought served him right.

Winston Churchill (1874–1965) British statesman.
My Early Life, Ch. 2

3 Nor can I do better, in conclusion, than impress upon you the study of Greek literature which not only elevates above the

vulgar herd, but leads not infrequently to positions of considerable emolument.

Thomas Gaisford (1799–1855) British classicist.
Christmas Day Sermon at Oxford
Reminiscences of Oxford (Revd W. Tuckwell)

4 To the Greeks the Muse gave native wit, to the Greeks the gift of graceful eloquence.

Horace (Quintus Horatius Flaccus; 65–8 BC) Roman poet.
Ars Poetica

5 Thou hadst small Latin, and less Greek.

Ben Jonson (1573–1637) English dramatist.
To the Memory of William Shakespeare

6 The classics are only primitive literature. They belong in the same class as primitive machinery and primitive music and primitive medicine.

Stephen Leacock (1869–1944) English-born Canadian economist and humorist.
Homer and Humbug

7 Every man with a belly full of the classics is an enemy of the human race.

Henry Miller (1891–1980) US novelist.
Tropic of Cancer, 'Dijon'

8 Nobody can say a word against Greek: it stamps a man at once as an educated gentleman.

George Bernard Shaw (1856–1950) Irish dramatist and critic.
Major Barbara, I

9 We were taught as the chief subjects of instruction Latin and Greek. We were taught very badly because the men who taught us did not habitually use either of these languages.

H. G. Wells (1866–1946) British writer.
The New Machiavelli, Bk. I., Ch. 3

CLASSIFICATION

See also generalizations

1 One of the unpardonable sins, in the eyes of most people, is for a man to go about unlabelled. The world regards such a person as the police do an unmuzzled dog, not under proper control.

T. H. Huxley (1825–95) British biologist.
Evolution and Ethics

2 The young Cambridge group, the group that stood for 'freedom' and flannel trousers and flannel shirts open at the neck, and a well-bred sort of emotional anarchy, and a whispering, murmuring sort of voice, and an ultra-sensitive sort of manner.

D. H. Lawrence (1885–1930) British novelist.
Lady Chatterley's Lover, Ch. 1

3 Decades have a delusive edge to them. They are not, of course, really periods at all, except as any other ten years would be. But we, looking at them, are caught by the different name each bears, and give them

different attributes, and tie labels on them, as if they were flowers in a border.

Rose Macaulay (1889–1958) British writer.
Told by an Idiot, Pt. II, Ch. 1

CLEANNESS

1 Bath twice a day to be really clean, once a day to be passably clean, once a week to avoid being a public menace.

Anthony Burgess (John Burgess Wilson; 1917–) British novelist.
Mr Enderby, Pt. I, Ch. 2

2 MR PRITCHARD. I must dust the blinds and then I must raise them.

MRS OGMORE-PRITCHARD. And before you let the sun in, mind it wipes its shoes.

Dylan Thomas (1914–53) Welsh poet.
Under Milk Wood

3 Have you ever taken anything out of the clothes basket because it had become, relatively, the cleaner thing?

Katherine Whitehorn (1926–) British journalist.
The Observer, 'On Shirts', 1964

CLERGY

See also Church, religion

1 I always like to associate with a lot of priests because it makes me understand anti-clerical things so well.

Hilaire Belloc (1870–1953) French-born British poet.
Letter to E. S. P. Haynes, 9 Nov 1909

2 This is a true saying, If a man desire the office of a bishop, he desireth a good work. A bishop then must be blameless, the husband of one wife, vigilant, sober, of good behaviour, given to hospitality, apt to teach;
Not given to wine, no striker, not greedy of filthy lucre; but patient, not a brawler, not covetous.

Bible: I Timothy
3:1–3

3 Make him a bishop, and you will silence him at once.

Earl of Chesterfield (1694–1773) English statesman.
When asked what steps might be taken to control the evangelical preacher George Whitefield
Attrib.

4 It is no accident that the symbol of a bishop is a crook, and the sign of an archbishop is a double-cross.

Dom Gregory Dix (1901–52) British monk.
Letter to *The Times*, 3 Dec 1977 (Francis Bown)

5 For clergy are men as well as other folks.

Henry Fielding (1707–54) British novelist.
Joseph Andrews, Bk II, Ch. 6

6 That whisky priest, I wish we had never had him in the house.

Graham Greene (1904–) British novelist.
The Power and the Glory, Pt. I

7 In old time we had treen chalices and golden priests, but now we have treen priests and golden chalices.

John Jewel (1522–71) English bishop.
Certain Sermons Preached Before the Queen's Majesty

8 A man who is good enough to go to heaven, is good enough to be a clergyman.

Samuel Johnson (1709–84) British lexicographer.
Life of Johnson (J. Boswell), Vol. II

9 Damn it all, another Bishop dead, – I verily believe they die to vex me.

Lord Melbourne (1779–1848) British statesman.
Attrib.

10 How can a bishop marry? How can he flirt? The most he can say is, 'I will see you in the vestry after service.'

Sydney Smith (1771–1845) British clergyman and essayist.
Memoir (Lady Holland)

11 I never saw, heard, nor read, that the clergy were beloved in any nation where Christianity was the religion of the country. Nothing can render them popular, but some degree of persecution.

Jonathan Swift (1667–1745) Irish-born Anglican priest and writer.
Thoughts on Religion

12 There is a certain class of clergyman whose mendicity is only equalled by their mendacity.

Frederick Temple (1821–1902) British churchman.
Remark at a meeting of the Ecclesiastical Commissioners
Years of Endeavour (Sir George Leveson Gower)

13 But the churchmen fain would kill their church,
As the churches have kill'd their Christ.

Alfred, Lord Tennyson (1809–92) British poet.
Maud, V

14 If I were a cassowary
On the plains of Timbuctoo,
I would eat a missionary,
Cassock, band, and hymn-book too.

Samuel Wilberforce (1805–73) British churchman.
Also attrib. to W. M. Thackeray
Attrib.

CLOCKS

1 My poor fellow, why not carry a watch?

Herbert Beerbohm Tree (1853–1917) British actor and theatre manager.
Remark made to a man carrying a grandfather clock
Beerbohm Tree (Hesketh Pearson)

2 My grandfather's clock was too large for the shelf.

So it stood ninety years on the floor.
Henry Clay Work (1832–84) US songwriter.
Grandfather's Clock

3 But it stopped short – never to go again –
When the old man died.
Henry Clay Work
Grandfather's Clock

CLOTHES

See also appearance, beauty, fashion, nakedness

1 It is not only fine feathers that make fine birds.
Aesop (6th century BC) Reputed Greek writer of fables.
Fables, 'The Jay and the Peacock'

2 She just wore
Enough for modesty – no more.
Robert Williams Buchanan (1841–1901) British poet and writer.
White Rose and Red, I

3 I go to a better tailor than any of you and pay more for my clothes. The only difference is that you probably don't sleep in yours.
Clarence Seward Darrow (1857–1938) US lawyer.
Reply when teased by reporters about his appearance
2500 Anecdotes (E. Fuller)

4 'Good heavens!' said he, 'if it be our clothes alone which fit us for society, how highly we should esteem those who make them.'
Marie Ebner von Eschenbach (1830–1916) Austrian writer.
The Two Countesses

5 The sense of being well-dressed gives a feeling of inward tranquillity which religion is powerless to bestow.
C. F. Forbes (1817–1911) British writer.
Social Aims (Emerson)

6 Those who make their dress a principal part of themselves, will, in general, become of no more value than their dress.
William Hazlitt (1778–1830) British essayist.
On the Clerical Character

7 A sweet disorder in the dress
Kindles in clothes a wantonness.
Robert Herrick (1591–1674) English poet.
Hesperides, 'Delight in Disorder'

8 Whenas in silks my Julia goes
Then, then (methinks) how sweetly flows
That liquefaction of her clothes.
Robert Herrick
Hesperides, 'Upon Julia's Clothes'

9 Fine clothes are good only as they supply the want of other means of procuring respect.
Samuel Johnson (1709–84) British lexicographer.
Life of Johnson (J. Boswell), Vol. II

10 The uniform 'e wore
Was nothin' much before,

An' rather less than 'arf o' that be'ind.
Rudyard Kipling (1865–1936) Indian-born British writer.
Gunga Din

11 How do you look when I'm sober?
Ring Lardner Jnr (1885–1933) American humorist.
Speaking to a flamboyantly dressed stranger who walked into the club where he was drinking
Ring (J. Yardley)

12 Brevity is the soul of lingerie.
Dorothy Parker (1893–1967) US writer.
While Rome Burns (Alexander Woollcott)

13 Where did you get that hat?
Where did you get that tile?
James Rolmaz (19th century) British songwriter.
Where Did You Get That Hat?

14 Not a gentleman; dresses too well.
Bertrand Russell (1872–1970) British philosopher.
Referring to Anthony Eden
Six Men (A. Cooke)

15 His socks compelled one's attention without losing one's respect.
Saki (Hector Hugh Munro; 1870–1916) British writer.
Ministers of Grace

16 Costly thy habit as thy purse can buy,
But not express'd in fancy; rich, not gaudy;
For the apparel oft proclaims the man.
William Shakespeare (1564–1616) English dramatist.
Hamlet, I:3

17 The only man who really needs a tail coat is a man with a hole in his trousers.
John Taylor (20th century) The editor of the *Tailor and Cutter*.
The Observer, 'Shouts and Murmurs'

18 You can say what you like about long dresses, but they cover a multitude of shins.
Mae West (1892–1980) US actress.
Peel Me a Grape (J. Weintraub)

19 Hats divide generally into three classes: offensive hats, defensive hats, and shrapnel.
Katherine Whitehorn (1926–) British journalist.
Shouts and Murmurs, 'Hats'

20 Then the little man wears a shocking bad hat.
Duke of York and Albany (1763–1827) The second son of George III.
Referring to Horace Walpole
Attrib.

CLOWNS

See also humour

1 I remain just one thing, and one thing only – and that is a clown.
It places me on a far higher plane than any politician.
Charlie Chaplin (Sir Charles Spencer C.; 1889–1977) British film actor.
The Observer, 'Sayings of the Week', 17 June 1960

2 Send in the Clowns.

Stephen Sondheim (1930–) US composer and lyricist.
Song title

COLD WAR

1 Let us not be deceived – we are today in the midst of a cold war.

Bernard Baruch (1870–1965) US financier and presidential adviser.
Speech, South Carolina Legislature, 16 Apr 1947

2 An iron curtain has descended across the Continent.

Winston Churchill (1874–1965) British statesman.
The phrase 'iron curtain' was originally coined by Joseph Goebbels
Address, Westminster College, Fulton, USA, 5 Mar 1946

3 Now we are in a period which I can characterize as a period of cold peace.

Trygve Lie (1896–1968) Norwegian lawyer.
The Observer, 'Sayings of the Week', 21 Aug 1949

COMFORT

See also endurance, sympathy

1 The crash of the whole solar and stellar systems could only kill you once.

Thomas Carlyle (1795–1881) Scottish historian and essayist.
Letter to John Carlyle, 1831

2 For this relief much thanks. 'Tis bitter cold, And I am sick at heart.

William Shakespeare (1564–1616) English dramatist.
Hamlet, I:1

3 I beg cold comfort.

William Shakespeare
King John, V:7

4 Like a bridge over troubled water, I will ease your mind.

Paul Simon (1941–) US singer.
Bridge Over Troubled Water

COMMITMENT

1 In for a penny, in for a pound.

Proverb

2 Never do things by halves.

Proverb

3 One cannot be a part-time nihilist.

Albert Camus (1913–60) French existentialist writer.
The Rebel

4 Catholics and Communists have committed great crimes, but at least they have not stood aside, like an established society, and been indifferent. I would rather have blood on my hands than water like Pilate.

Graham Greene (1904–) British novelist.
The Comedians, Pt. III, Ch. 4

5 I love being at the centre of things.

Margaret Thatcher (1925–) British politician and prime minister.
Reader's Digest, 1984

6 Miss Madeleine Philips was making it very manifest to Captain Douglas that she herself was a career; that a lover with any other career in view need not – as the advertisements say – apply.

H. G. Wells (1866–1946) British writer.
Bealby, Pt. V, Ch. 5

COMMUNICATION

See also clarity, conversation, language, letter-writing, speech

1 Only connect!

E. M. Forster (1879–1970) British novelist.
Howards End, Epigraph

2 Unless one is a genius, it is best to aim at being intelligible.

Anthony Hope (Sir Anthony Hope Hawkins; 1863–1933) British novelist.
The Dolly Dialogues

3 The medium is the message. This is merely to say that the personal and social consequences of any medium . . . result from the new scale that is introduced into our affairs by each extension of ourselves or by any new technology.

Marshall McLuhan (1911–81) Canadian sociologist.
Understanding Media, Ch. 1

4 What have we to say to India?

John Ruskin (1819–1900) British art critic and writer.
Referring to the completion of the British-Indian cable
Attrib.

COMMUNISM

See also Marxism, Russia, socialism

1 Its relationship to democratic institutions is that of the death watch beetle – it is not a Party, it is a conspiracy.

Aneurin Bevan (1897–1960) British Labour politician.
Referring to the Communist Party
Tribune

2 Communism with a human face.

Alexander Dubček (1921–) Czech statesman.
A resolution by the party group in the Ministry of Foreign Affairs, in 1968, referred to Czechoslovak foreign policy acquiring 'its own defined face'
Attrib.

3 Every year humanity takes a step towards Communism. Maybe not you, but at all events your grandson will surely be a Communist.

Nikita Khrushchev (1894–1971) Soviet statesman.
Said to Sir William Hayter, June 1956

4 Communism is Soviet power plus the electrification of the whole country.
Lenin (Vladimir Ilich Ulyanov; 1870–1924) Russian revolutionary leader.
Political slogan of 1920, promoting the programme of electrification

5 There's no such thing in Communist countries as a load of old cod's wallop, the cod's wallop is always fresh made.
Robert Morley (1908–) British actor.
Punch, 20 Feb 1974

6 Communism is like prohibition, it's a good idea but it won't work.
Will Rogers (1879–1935) US actor and humorist.
Autobiography, Nov 1927

7 For us in Russia communism is a dead dog, while, for many people in the West, it is still a living lion.
Alexander Solzhenitsyn (1918–) Soviet novelist.
The Listener, 15 Feb 1979

8 Every communist has a fascist frown, every fascist a communist smile.
Muriel Spark (1918–) British novelist.
The Girls of Slender Means, Ch. 4

9 The party is the rallying-point for the best elements of the working class.
Joseph Stalin (J. Dzhugashvili; 1879–1953) Soviet statesman.
Attrib.

10 Communism continued to haunt Europe as a spectre – a name men gave to their own fears and blunders. But the crusade against Communism was even more imaginary than the spectre of Communism.
A. J. P. Taylor (1906–) British historian.
The Origins of the Second World War, Ch. 2

11 Lenin's method leads to this: the party organization at first substitutes itself for the party as a whole. Then the central committee substitutes itself for the party organization, and finally a single dictator substitutes himself for the central committee.
Leon Trotsky (Lev Davidovich Bronstein; 1879–1940) Russian revolutionary.
The Communist Parties of Western Europe (N. McInnes), Ch. 3

COMPLAINTS

1 We have first raised a dust and then complain we cannot see.
Bishop Berkeley (1685–1753) Irish churchman and philosopher.
Principles of Human Knowledge, Introduction

2 The world is disgracefully managed, one hardly knows to whom to complain.
Ronald Firbank (1886–1926) British novelist.
Vainglory

3 If you are foolish enough to be contented, don't show it, but grumble with the rest.
Jerome K. Jerome (1859–1927) British humorist.
Idle Thoughts of an Idle Fellow

4 Nay, Madam, when you are declaiming, declaim; and when you are calculating, calculate.
Samuel Johnson (1709–84) British lexicographer.
Commenting on Mrs Thrales's discourse on the price of children's clothes
Life of Johnson (J. Boswell), Vol. III

5 I want to register a complaint. Do you know who sneaked into my room at three o'clock this morning? . . .
– Who? . . .
Nobody, and that's my complaint.
Groucho Marx (Julius Marx; 1895–1977) US comedian.
Monkey Business

COMPLIMENTS

See also admiration, beauty, flattery, love, praise

1 She isn't a bad bit of goods, the Queen! I wish all the fleas in my bed were as good.
Miguel de Cervantes (1547–1616) Spanish novelist.
Don Quixote, Pt. I, Ch. 30

2 She is Venus when she smiles;
But she's Juno when she walks,
And Minerva when she talks.
Ben Jonson (1573–1637) English dramatist.
The Underwood, 'Celebration of Charis, V. His Discourse with Cupid'

3 Your eyes shine like the pants of my blue serge suit.
Groucho Marx (Julius Marx; 1895–1977) US comedian.
The Cocoanuts

4 Shall I compare thee to a summer's day?
Thou art more lovely and more temperate.
Rough winds do shake the darling buds of May,
And summer's lease hath all too short a date.
William Shakespeare (1564–1616) English dramatist.
Sonnet 18

5 Won't you come into the garden? I would like my roses to see you.
Richard Brinsley Sheridan (1751–1816) British dramatist.
Said to a young lady
Attrib. in *The Perfect Hostess*

6 She would rather light candles than curse the darkness, and her glow has warmed the world.
Adlai Stevenson (1900–65) US statesman.
Referring to Eleanor Roosevelt
Address, United Nations General Assembly, 9 Nov 1962

7 What, when drunk, one sees in other women, one sees in Garbo sober.
Kenneth Tynan (1927–80) British theatre critic.
The Sunday Times, 25 Aug 1963

8 Of this blest man, let his just praise be
given,
Heaven was in him, before he was in heaven.
Izaak Walton (1593–1683) English writer.
Referring to Dr Richard Sibbes
Written in a copy of *Returning Backslider* by Richard Sibbes

9 Roses are flowering in Picardy,
But there's never a rose like you.
Frederic Edward Weatherly (1848–1929) British lawyer
and songwriter.
Roses of Picardy

COMPOSERS

See also criticism, music, musicians

1 Off with you! You're a happy fellow, for you'll
give happiness and joy to many other people.
There is nothing better or greater than that!
Ludwig van Beethoven (1770–1827) German composer.
Said to Franz Liszt when Liszt, aged 11, had visited Beetho-
ven and played for him
Beethoven: Letters, Journals and Conversations (M.
Hamburger)

2 A master is dead. Today we sing no more.
Johannes Brahms (1833–97) German composer.
Stopping a choral rehearsal on hearing of the death of Wagner
Brahms (P. Latham)

3 The public doesn't want new music: the main
thing it demands of a composer is that he be
dead.
Arthur Honegger (1892–1955) French composer.
Attrib.

4 Wagner is the Puccini of music.
J. B. Morton (1893–1979) British journalist.
Attrib.

5 Rachmaninov's immortalizing totality was his
scowl. He was a six-and-a-half-foot-tall scowl.
Igor Stravinsky (1882–1971) Russian-born US composer.
Conversations with Igor Stravinsky (Igor Stravinsky and Robert
Craft)

6 A good composer does not imitate; he steals.
Igor Stravinsky
Twentieth Century Music (Peter Yates)

7 Ah, a German and a genius! a prodigy, admit
him!
Jonathan Swift (1667–1745) Irish-born Anglican priest and
writer.
Learning of the arrival of Handel: Swift's last words
Attrib.

COMPROMISE

1 It takes two to tango.
Proverb

2 For the flesh lusteth against the Spirit, and
the Spirit against the flesh: and these are
contrary the one to the other: so that ye
cannot do the things that ye would.
Bible: Galatians
5:17

3 All government, indeed every human benefit
and enjoyment, every virtue, and every
prudent act, is founded on compromise and
barter.
Edmund Burke (1729–97) British politician.
Speech on Conciliation with America (House of Commons, 22
Mar 1775)

4 Compromise used to mean that half a loaf
was better than no bread. Among modern
statesmen it really seems to mean that half a
loaf is better than a whole loaf.
G. K. Chesterton (1874–1936) British writer.
What's Wrong with the World

CONCEIT

See also arrogance, boasts, egotism, pride

1 I'm the greatest!
Muhammad Ali (Cassius Clay; 1942–   ) US boxer.
Remark, often said after his fights

2 A man . . . must have a very good opinion of
himself when he asks people to leave their
own fireside, and encounter such a day as
this, for the sake of coming to see him. He
must think himself a most agreeable fellow.
Jane Austen (1775–1817) British novelist.
Emma, Ch. 13

3 It was prettily devised of Aesop, 'The fly sat
upon the axletree of the chariot-wheel and
said, what a dust do I raise.'
Francis Bacon (1561–1626) English philosopher.
Essays, 'Of Vain-Glory'

4 To give an accurate and exhaustive account
of that period would need a far less brilliant
pen than mine.
Max Beerbohm (1872–1956) British writer.
1880

5 If ever he went to school without any boots
it was because he was too big for them.
Ivor Bulmer-Thomas (1905–   ) British writer and
politician.
Referring to Harold Wilson
Remark, Conservative Party Conference, 1949

6 Vanity plays lurid tricks with our memory.
Joseph Conrad (Teodor Josef Konrad Korzeniowski;
1857–1924) Polish-born British novelist.
Lord Jim

7 I know he is, and he adores his maker.
Benjamin Disraeli (1804–81) British statesman.
Replying to a remark made in defence of John Bright that he
was a self-made man; often also attrib. to Bright referring to
Disraeli
The Fine Art of Political Wit (L. Harris)

8 We are so vain that we even care for the
opinion of those we don't care for.
Marie Ebner von Eschenbach (1830–1916) Austrian
writer.
Aphorism

9 I am the Captain of the *Pinafore*;

And a right good captain too!

W. S. Gilbert (1836–1911) British dramatist.
HMS Pinafore, I

10 I have a left shoulder-blade that is a miracle of loveliness. People come miles to see it. My right elbow has a fascination that few can resist.

W. S. Gilbert
The Mikado, II

11 All my shows are great. Some of them are bad. But they are all great.

Lew Grade (Lewis Winogradsky; 1906–) British film and TV producer.
The Observer, 'Sayings of the Week', 14 Sept 1975

12 Conceit is the finest armour a man can wear.

Jerome K. Jerome (1859–1927) British humorist.
Idle Thoughts of an Idle Fellow

13 He fell in love with himself at first sight and it is a passion to which he has always remained faithful. Self-love seems so often unrequited.

Anthony Powell (1905–) British novelist.
A Dance to the Music of Time: The Acceptance World, Ch. 1

14 Self-love is the greatest of all flatterers.

Duc de la Rochefoucauld (1613–80) French writer.
Maximes, 2

15 Besides Shakespeare and me, who do you think there is?

Gertrude Stein (1874–1946) US writer.
Speaking to a friend she considered knew little about literature
Charmed Circle (J. Mellow)

16 The Jews have produced only three originative geniuses: Christ, Spinoza, and myself.

Gertrude Stein
Charmed Circle (J. Mellow)

17 Vanity dies hard; in some obstinate cases it outlives the man.

Robert Louis Stevenson (1850–94) Scottish writer.
Prince Otto

18 He would like to destroy his old diaries and to appear before his children and the public only in his patriarchal robes. His vanity is immense!

Sophie Tolstoy (1844–1919) Russian writer.
A Diary of Tolstoy's Wife, 1860–1891

19 Isn't it? I know in my case I would grow intolerably conceited.

James Whistler (1834–1903) US painter.
Replying to the pointed observaton that it was as well that we do not not see ourselves as others see us
The Man Whistler (H. Pearson)

20 A LADY. I only know of two painters in the world: yourself and Velasquez.
WHISTLER. Why drag in Velasquez?

James Whistler
Whistler Stories (D. Seitz)

21 No, no, Oscar, you forget. When you and I are together we never talk about anything except me.

James Whistler
Cable replying to Oscar Wilde's message: 'When you and I are together we never talk about anything except ourselves'
The Gentle Art of Making Enemies

22 I cannot tell you that, madam. Heaven has granted me no offspring.

James Whistler
Replying to a lady who had inquired whether he thought genius hereditary
Whistler Stories (D. Seitz)

23 Nothing, except my genius.

Oscar Wilde (1854–1900) Irish-born British dramatist.
Replying to a US customs official on being asked if he had anything to declare
Attrib.

24 To love oneself is the beginning of a lifelong romance.

Oscar Wilde
An Ideal Husband, III

25 Who am I to tamper with a masterpiece?

Oscar Wilde
Refusing to make alterations to one of his own plays
Attrib.

CONFLICT

See also doublethink, opposites

1 Attack is the best form of defence.

Proverb

2 Fight fire with fire.

Proverb

3 He who lives by the sword dies by the sword.

Proverb

4 Without Contraries is no progression. Attraction and Repulsion, Reason and Energy, Love and Hate, are necessary to Human existence.

William Blake (1757–1827) British poet.
The Marriage of Heaven and Hell, 'The Argument'

5 No, when the fight begins within himself, A man's worth something.

Robert Browning (1812–89) British poet.
Bishop Blougram's Apology

6 Two souls dwell, alas! in my breast.

Goethe (1749–1832) German poet and dramatist.
Faust, Pt. I

7 Two loves I have, of comfort and despair, Which like two spirits do suggest me still; The better angel is a man right fair, The worser spirit a woman colour'd ill.

William Shakespeare (1564–1616) English dramatist.
Sonnet 144

CONFORMITY

See also orthodoxy

1 Who spits against the wind, it falls in his face.

Proverb

2 When in Rome, live as the Romans do: when elsewhere, live as they live elsewhere.

St Ambrose (c. 339–97) Bishop of Milan.
Advice to St Augustine

3 Take the tone of the company you are in.

Earl of Chesterfield (1694–1773) English statesman.
Letter to his son, 9 Oct 1747

4 Whoso would be a man must be a nonconformist.

Ralph Waldo Emerson (1803–82) US poet and essayist.
Essays, 'Self-Reliance'

5 Why do you have to be a nonconformist like everybody else?

James Thurber (1894–1961) US humorist.
Attrib. Actually a cartoon caption by Stan Hunt in the *New Yorker*

CONFUSION

1 Well, my deliberate opinion is – it's a jolly strange world.

Arnold Bennett (1867–1931) British novelist.
The Title, I

2 I can't say I was ever lost, but I was bewildered once for three days.

Daniel Boone (1734–1820) US pioneeer.
Reply when asked if he had ever been lost
Attrib.

3 'Curiouser and curiouser!' cried Alice.

Lewis Carroll (Charles Lutwidge Dodgson; 1832–98) British writer.
Alice's Adventures in Wonderland, Ch. 2

4 This world is very odd we see,
We do not comprehend it;
But in one fact we all agree,
God won't, and we can't mend it.

Arthur Hugh Clough (1819–61) British poet.
Dipsychus, Bk. II

5 Bewitched, Bothered and Bewildered.

Lorenz Hart (1895–1943) US songwriter.
From the musical *Babes in Arms*
Song title

6 I had nothing to offer anybody except my own confusion.

Jack Kerouac (1922–69) US novelist.
On the Road, Pt. II

7 I don't want you to think I'm not incoherent.

Harold W. Ross (1892–1951) US journalist.
The Years with Ross (James Thurber)

8 For mine own part, it was Greek to me.

William Shakespeare (1564–1616) English dramatist.
Julius Caesar, I:2

9 That blessed mood,
In which the burthen of the mystery,
In which the heavy and the weary weight

Of all this unintelligible world,
Is lightened.

William Wordsworth (1770–1850) British poet.
Lines composed a few miles above Tintern Abbey

CONSCIENCE

See also integrity

1 Conscience, I say, not thine own, but of the other: for why is my liberty judged of another man's conscience?

Bible: I Corinthians
10:29

2 Conscience is the internal perception of the rejection of a particular wish operating within us.

Sigmund Freud (1856–1939) Austrian psychoanalyst.
Totem and Taboo

3 Conscience is a coward, and those faults it has not strength enough to prevent it seldom has justice enough to accuse.

Oliver Goldsmith (1728–74) Irish-born British writer.
The Vicar of Wakefield, Ch. 13

4 Conscience is the inner voice that warns us somebody may be looking.

H. L. Mencken (1880–1956) US journalist.
A Mencken Chrestomathy

5 Thus conscience does make cowards of us all;
And thus the native hue of resolution
Is sicklied o'er with the pale cast of thought.

William Shakespeare (1564–1616) English dramatist.
Hamlet, III:1

CONSERVATION

1 The biggest waste of water in the country by far is when you spend half a pint and flush two gallons.

Prince Philip (1921–) The consort of Queen Elizabeth II.
Speech, 1965

CONSERVATISM

See also change

1 All conservatism is based upon the idea that if you leave things alone you leave them as they are. But you do not. If you leave a thing alone you leave it to a torrent of change.

G. K. Chesterton (1874–1936) British writer.
Orthodoxy, Ch. 7

2 I love everything that's old: old friends, old times, old manners, old books, old wine.

Oliver Goldsmith (1728–74) Irish-born British writer.
She Stoops to Conquer, I

3 You can't teach the old maestro a new tune.

Jack Kerouac (1922–69) US novelist.
On the Road, Pt. I

4 I do not know which makes a man more conservative – to know nothing but the present, or nothing but the past.
John Maynard Keynes (1883–1946) British economist.
The End of Laisser-Faire, I

5 What is conservatism? Is it not adherence to the old and tried, against the new and untried?
Abraham Lincoln (1809–65) US statesman.
Speech, 27 Feb 1860

6 You can't teach an old dogma new tricks.
Dorothy Parker (1893–1967) US writer.
Wit's End (R. E. Drennan)

7 The radical invents the views. When he has worn them out, the conservative adopts them.
Mark Twain (Samuel Langhorne Clemens; 1835–1910) US writer.
Notebooks

CONSTANCY

See also change, conservatism

1 A foolish consistency is the hobgoblin of little minds, adored by little statesmen and philosophers and divines. With consistency a great soul has simply nothing to do.
Ralph Waldo Emerson (1803–82) US poet and essayist.
Essays, 'Self-reliance'

2 Consistency is contrary to nature, contrary to life. The only completely consistent people are the dead.
Aldous Huxley (1894–1964) British novelist.
Do What you Will

3 *Plus ça change, plus c'est la même chose.*
The more things change, the more they stay the same.
Alphonse Karr (1808–90) French writer.
Les Guêpes, Jan 1849

4 For men may come and men may go
But I go on for ever.
Alfred, Lord Tennyson (1809–92) British poet.
The Brook

5 Still glides the Stream, and shall for ever glide;
The Form remains, the Function never dies.
William Wordsworth (1770–1850) British poet.
The River Duddon, 'After-Thought'

CONTEMPT

See also ridicule

1 She was nothing more than a mere good-tempered, civil and obliging young woman; as such we could scarcely dislike her – she was only an Object of Contempt.
Jane Austen (1775–1817) British novelist.
Love and Friendship

2 'You threaten us, fellow? Do your worst,
Blow your pipe there till you burst!'
Robert Browning (1812–89) British poet.
The Pied Piper of Hamelin

3 He looked at me as if I was a side dish he hadn't ordered.
Ring Lardner Jnr (1885–1933) American humorist.
Referring to W. H. Taft, US president (1909–13)
The Home Book of Humorous Quotations (A. K. Adams)

CONTENTMENT

See also happiness, satisfaction

1 Live with the gods. And he does so who constantly shows them that his soul is satisfied with what is assigned to him.
Marcus Aurelius (121–180 AD) Roman emperor.
Meditations, Bk. V, Ch. 27

2 Sweet Stay-at-Home, sweet Well-content.
W. H. Davies (1871–1940) British poet.
Sweet Stay-at-Home

3 Here with a Loaf of Bread beneath the Bough,
A Flask of Wine, a Book of Verse – and Thou
Beside me singing in the Wilderness –
And Wilderness is Paradise enow.
Edward Fitzgerald (1809–83) British poet.
The Rubáiyát of Omar Khayyám

4 Notwithstanding the poverty of my outside experience, I have always had a significance for myself, and every chance to stumble along my straight and narrow little path, and to worship at the feet of my Deity, and what more can a human soul ask for?
Alice James (1848–92) US diarist.
The Diary of Alice James (ed. Leon Edel)

5 If I had not been born Perón, I would have liked to be Perón.
Juan Perón (1895–1974) Argentine statesman.
The Observer, 'Sayings of the Week', 21 Feb 1960

6 Nought's had, all's spent,
Where our desire is got without content.
'Tis safer to be that which we destroy,
Than by destruction dwell in doubtful joy.
William Shakespeare (1564–1616) English dramatist.
Macbeth, III:2

7 O, this life
Is nobler than attending for a check,
Richer than doing nothing for a bribe,
Prouder than rustling in unpaid-for silk.
William Shakespeare
Cymbeline, III:3

CONTRACEPTION

See also sex

1 I want to tell you a terrific story about oral

contraception. I asked this girl to sleep with me and she said 'no'.
Woody Allen (Allen Stewart Konigsberg; 1935–) US film actor.
Woody Allen: Clown Prince of American Humor (Adler and Feinman), Ch. 2

2 The command 'Be fruitful and multiply was promulgated according to our authorities, when the population of the world consisted of two people.
Dean Inge (1860–1954) British churchman; Dean of St Pauls.
More Lay Thoughts of a Dean

3 It is now quite lawful for a Catholic woman to avoid pregnancy by a resort to mathematics, though she is still forbidden to resort to physics and chemistry.
H. L. Mencken (1880–1956) US journalist.
Notebooks, 'Minority Report'

4 Contraceptives should be used on every conceivable occasion.
Spike Milligan (1918–) British comic actor and author.
The Last Goon Show of All

5 Skullion had little use for contraceptives at the best of times. Unnatural, he called them, and placed them in the lower social category of things along with elastic-sided boots and made-up bow ties. Not the sort of attire for a gentleman.
Tom Sharpe (1928–) British novelist.
Porterhouse Blue, Ch. 9

6 Protestant women may take the Pill. Roman Catholic women must keep taking the *Tablet*.
Irene Thomas (1920–) British writer.
The Tablet is a British Roman Catholic newspaper.
Attrib.

CONVERSATION

See also speech

1 Although there exist many thousand subjects for elegant conversation, there are persons who cannot meet a cripple without talking about feet.
Chinese proverb
Proverb

2 I have but ninepence in ready money, but I can draw for a thousand pounds.
Joseph Addison (1672–1719) British essayist.
Comparing his ability to make conversation and to write
Life of Johnson (Boswell)

3 JOHNSON. Well, we had a good talk.
BOSWELL. Yes, Sir; you tossed and gored several persons.
James Boswell (1740–95) Scottish lawyer and writer.
Life of Johnson, Vol. II

4 Questioning is not the mode of conversation among gentlemen.
Samuel Johnson (1709–84) British lexicographer.
Life of Johnson (J. Boswell), Vol. II

5 Beware of the conversationalist who adds 'in other words'. He is merely starting afresh.
Robert Morley (1908–) British actor.
The Observer, 'Sayings of the Week', 6 Dec 1964

6 Ideal conversation must be an exchange of thought, and not, as many of those who worry most about their shortcomings believe, an eloquent exhibition of wit or oratory.
Emily Post (1873–1960) US writer.
Etiquette, Ch. 6

7 Conversation has a kind of charm about it, an insinuating and insidious something that elicits secrets from us just like love or liquor.
Seneca (c. 4 BC–65 AD) Roman author.
Epistles

8 Teas,
Where small talk dies in agonies.
Percy Bysshe Shelley (1792–1822) British poet.
Peter Bell the Third

9 There is no such thing as conversation. It is an illusion. There are intersecting monologues, that is all.
Rebecca West (Cicely Isabel Fairfield; 1892–1983) British novelist and journalist.
There Is No Conversation, Ch. 1

10 A good listener is not someone who has nothing to say. A good listener is a good talker with a sore throat.
Katherine Whitehorn (1926–) British journalist.
Attrib.

CORRUPTION

See also bribery, decline

1 Among a people generally corrupt, liberty cannot long exist.
Edmund Burke (1729–97) British politician.
Letter to the Sheriffs of Bristol, 1777

2 Corruption, the most infallible symptom of constitutional liberty.
Edward Gibbon (1737–94) British historian.
Decline and Fall of the Roman Empire, Ch. 21

3 The hungry sheep look up, and are not fed,
But, swoln with wind and the rank mist they draw,
Rot inwardly, and foul contagion spread.
John Milton (1608–74) English poet.
Lycidas

4 As killing as the canker to the rose.
John Milton
Lycidas

5 Any institution which does not suppose the people good, and the magistrate corruptible is evil.
Robespierre (1758–94) French lawyer and revolutionary.
Déclaration des Droits de l'homme, 24 Apr 1793

6 Something is rotten in the state of Denmark.
William Shakespeare (1564–1616) English dramatist.
Hamlet, I:4

7 For sweetest things turn sourest by their deeds:
Lilies that fester smell far worse than weeds.
William Shakespeare
Sonnet 94

8 All those men have their price.
Robert Walpole (1676–1745) British statesman.
Memoirs of Sir Robert Walpole (W. Coxe)

COSMETICS

See also appearance

1 Most women are not so young as they are painted.
Max Beerbohm (1872–1956) British writer.
A Defence of Cosmetics

2 Wherever one wants to be kissed.
Coco Chanel (1883–1971) French dress designer.
When asked where one should wear perfume
Coco Chanel, Her Life, Her Secrets (Marcel Haedrich)

3 In the factory we make cosmetics. In the store we sell hope.
Charles Revson (1906–75) US business tycoon.
Fire and Ice (A. Tobias)

COUNTRYSIDE

See also agriculture, ecology, flowers, Nature, trees

1 I nauseate walking; 'tis a country diversion, I loathe the country and everything that relates to it.
William Congreve (1670–1729) British Restoration dramatist.
The Way of the World, IV:4

2 God made the country, and man made the town.
William Cowper (1731–1800) British poet.
The Task

3 Ever charming, ever new,
When will the landscape tire the view?
John Dyer (1700–58) British poet.
Grongar Hill

4 There is nothing good to be had in the country, or, if there is, they will not let you have it.
William Hazlitt (1778–1830) British essayist.
Observations on Wordsworth's 'Excursion'

5 When I am in the country I wish to vegetate like the country.
William Hazlitt
On Going a Journey

6 Here of a Sunday morning
My love and I would lie,
And see the coloured counties,
And hear the larks so high

About us in the sky.
A. E. Housman (1859–1936) British scholar and poet.
A Shropshire Lad, 'Bredon Hill'

7 It must be generations since anyone but highbrows lived in this cottage . . . I imagine most of the agricultural labourers round here commute from London.
Anthony Powell (1905–) British novelist.
A Dance to the Music of Time: The Kindly Ones, Ch. 2

8 O, Brignal banks are wild and fair,
And Gretna woods are green,
And you may gather garlands there
Would grace a summer queen.
Walter Scott (1771–1832) Scottish novelist.
Rokeby, III

9 Under the greenwood tree
Who loves to lie with me,
And turn his merry note
Unto the sweet bird's throat,
Come hither, come hither, come hither.
Here shall he see
No enemy
But winter and rough weather.
William Shakespeare (1564–1616) English dramatist.
As You Like It, II:5

10 Anybody can be good in the country.
Oscar Wilde (1854–1900) Irish-born British dramatist.
The Picture of Dorian Gray, Ch. 19

COURAGE

See also endurance, heroism, patriotism

1 The sons of the prophet were brave men and bold,
And quite unaccustomed to fear,
But the bravest by far in the ranks of the Shah
Was Abdul the Bulbul Amir.
Anonymous
Abdul the Bulbul Amir

2 No coward soul is mine,
No trembler in the world's storm-troubled sphere:
I see Heaven's glories shine,
And faith shines equal, arming me from fear.
Emily Brontë (1818–48) British novelist.
Last Lines

3 Perhaps your fear in passing judgement is greater than mine in receiving it.
Giordano Bruno (1548–1600) Italian philosopher.
Said to the cardinals who excommunicated him, 8 Feb 1600
Attrib.

4 And though hard be the task,
'Keep a stiff upper lip.'
Phoebe Cary (1824–71) US poet.
Keep a Stiff Upper Lip

5 Down these mean streets a man must go who is not himself mean; who is neither tarnished nor afraid.
Raymond Chandler (1888–1959) US novelist.
The Simple Art of Murder

6 The Red Badge of Courage.
Stephen Crane (1871–1900) US writer.
Title of novel

7 Because of my title, I was the first to enter here. I shall be the last to go out.
Duchesse d'Alençon (d. 1897) Bavarian-born duchess.
Refusing help during a fire, 4 May 1897, at a charity bazaar in Paris. She died along with 120 others.
Attrib.

8 I'll bell the cat.
Archibald Douglas (1449–1514) Scottish nobleman.
Of his proposed capture of Robert Cochrane (executed 1482); the phrase 'bell the cat' was earlier used by Eustache Deschamps in his *Ballade: Le Chat et les souris*

9 None but the Brave deserves the Fair.
John Dryden (1631–1700) British poet and dramatist.
Alexander's Feast

10 Courage is the price that Life exacts for granting peace.
Amelia Earhart (1898–1937) US flyer.
Courage

11 Come cheer up, my lads! 'tis to glory we steer,
To add something more to this wonderful year;
To honour we call you, not press you like slaves,
For who are so free as the sons of the waves?
Heart of oak are our ships,
Heart of oak are our men:
We always are ready;
Steady, boys, steady;
We'll fight and we'll conquer again and again.
David Garrick (1717–79) British actor and manager.
Heart of Oak

12 The boy stood on the burning deck
Whence all but he had fled;
The flame that lit the battle's wreck
Shone round him o'er the dead.
Felicia Dorothea Hemans (1793–1835) British poet.
Casabianca

13 It is better to be the widow of a hero than the wife of a coward.
Dolores Ibarruri (1895–) Spanish politician.
Speech, Valencia, 1936

14 Then out spake brave Horatius,
The Captain of the Gate:
'To every man upon this earth
Death cometh soon or late.
And how can man die better
Than facing fearful odds,
For the ashes of his fathers,
And the temples of his Gods?'
Lord Macaulay (1800–59) British historian.
Lays of Ancient Rome, 'Horatius', 27

15 The stubborn spear-men still made good
Their dark impenetrable wood,
Each stepping where his comrade stood,
The instant that he fell.
Walter Scott (1771–1832) Scottish novelist.
Marmion, VI

16 Once more unto the breach, dear friends, once more;
Or close the wall up with our English dead.
William Shakespeare (1564–1616) English dramatist.
Henry V, III:1

17 He was a bold man that first eat an oyster.
Jonathan Swift (1667–1745) Irish-born Anglican priest and writer.
Polite Conversation, Dialogue 2

18 Half a league, half a league,
Half a league onward,
All in the valley of Death
Rode the six hundred.
Alfred, Lord Tennyson (1809–92) British poet.
The Charge of the Light Brigade

19 Into the jaws of Death,
Into the mouth of Hell.
Alfred, Lord Tennyson
The Charge of the Light Brigade

20 Fortune favours the brave.
Terence (Publius Terentius Afer; c. 190–159 BC) Roman poet.
Phormio

21 The three-o'-clock in the morning courage, which Bonaparte thought was the rarest.
Henry David Thoreau (1817–62) US writer.
Walden, 'Sounds'

COURTESY

See also chivalry, etiquette, manners, respect

1 Civility costs nothing.
Proverb

2 If a man be gracious and courteous to strangers, it shews he is a citizen of the world.
Francis Bacon (1561–1626) English philosopher.
Essays, 'Of Goodness and Goodness of Nature'

3 The English are polite by telling lies. The Americans are polite by telling the truth.
Malcolm Bradbury (1932–) British academic and novelist.
Stepping Westward, Bk. II, Ch. 5

4 Courtesy is not dead – it has merely taken refuge in Great Britain.
Georges Duhamel (1884–1966) French writer.
The Observer, 'Sayings of Our Times', 31 May 1953

COWARDICE

See also self-preservation

1 Probably a fear we have of facing up to the real issues. Could you say we were guilty of Noël Cowardice?
Peter De Vries (1910–) US novelist.
Comfort me with Apples, Ch. 8

2 None but a coward dares to boast that he
has never known fear.
Marshal Foch (1851–1929) French soldier.
Attrib.

3 He led his regiment from behind
He found it less exciting.
W. S. Gilbert (1836–1911) British dramatist.
The Gondoliers, I

4 When the foeman bares his steel,
Tarantara! tarantara!
We uncomfortable feel.
W. S. Gilbert
The Pirates of Penzance, II

5 To a surprising extent the war-lords in
shining armour, the apostles of the martial
virtues, tend not to die fighting when the
time comes. History is full of ignominious
getaways by the great and famous.
George Orwell (Eric Blair; 1903–50) British novelist.
Who Are the War Criminals?

6 The summer soldier and the sunshine patriot
will, in this crisis, shrink from the service of
their country.
Thomas Paine (1737–1809) British writer.
Pennsylvania Journal, 'The American Crisis'

7 Some craven scruple
Of thinking too precisely on th' event.
William Shakespeare (1564–1616) English dramatist.
Hamlet, IV:4

8 I dare not fight; but I will wink and hold out
mine iron.
William Shakespeare
Henry V, II:1

9 Cowards die many times before their deaths:
The valiant never taste of death but once.
William Shakespeare
Julius Caesar, II:2

CREATION

1 The Hand that made us is divine.
Joseph Addison (1672–1719) British essayist.
The Spectator, 465

2 In the beginning God created the heaven and
the earth.
And the earth was without form, and void; and
darkness was upon the face of the deep. And
the Spirit of God moved upon the face of the
waters.
And God said, Let there be light: and there
was light.
And God saw the light, that it was good: and
God divided the light from the darkness.
And God called the light Day, and the darkness
he called Night. And the evening and the
morning were the first day.
Bible: Genesis
1:1–5

3 And God called the dry land Earth; and the
gathering together of the waters called he
Seas: and God saw that it was good.
And God said, Let the earth bring forth grass,
the herb yielding seed, and the fruit tree
yielding fruit after his kind, whose seed is in
itself, upon the earth: and it was so.
Bible: Genesis
1:10–11

4 And God made two great lights: the greater
light to rule the day, and the lesser light to
rule the night: he made the stars also.
Bible: Genesis
1:16

5 And God said, Let the earth bring forth the
living creature after his kind, cattle, and
creeping thing, and beast of the earth after
his kind: and it was so.
Bible: Genesis
1:24

6 And God said, Let us make man in our
image, after our likeness: and let them have
dominion over the fish of the sea, and over
the fowl of the air, and over the cattle, and
over all the earth, and over every creeping
thing that creepeth upon the earth.
So God created man in his own image, in the
image of God created he him; male and female created he them.
And God blessed them, and God said unto
them, Be fruitful, and multiply, and replenish
the earth, and subdue it: and have dominion
over the fish of the sea, and over the fowl of
the air, and over every living thing that
moveth upon the earth.
Bible: Genesis
1:26–28

7 When the stars threw down their spears,
And watered heaven with their tears,
Did he smile his work to see?
Did he who made the Lamb make thee?
William Blake (1757–1827) British poet.
Songs of Experience, 'The Tiger'

8 Little Lamb, who made thee?
Dost thou know who made thee?
William Blake
Songs of Innocence, 'The Lamb'

9 Whan that the month in which the world
bigan,
That highte March, whan God first maked
man.
Geoffrey Chaucer (c. 1342–1400) English poet.
The Canterbury Tales, 'The Nun's Priest's Tale'

10 'Who *is* the Potter, pray, and who the Pot?'
Edward Fitzgerald (1809–83) British poet.
The Rubáiyát of Omar Khayyám

11 I cannot forgive Descartes; in all his
philosophy he did his best to dispense with
God. But he could not avoid making Him set

the world in motion with a flip of His thumb;
after that he had no more use for God.
Blaise Pascal (1623–62) French philosopher and
mathematician.
Pensées, II

12 'Do you know who made you?' 'Nobody, as I
knows on,' said the child, with a short laugh
... 'I 'spect I grow'd.'
Harriet Beecher Stowe (1811–96) US novelist.
Uncle Tom's Cabin, Ch. 20

13 God made everything out of nothing. But the
nothingness shows through.
Paul Valéry (1871–1945) French poet and writer.
Mauvaises Pensées et autres

14 The art of creation
is older than the art of killing.
Andrei Voznesensky (1933–) Soviet poet.
Poem with a Footnote

CRICKET

See also sport

1 It's not in support of cricket but as an
earnest protest against golf.
Max Beerbohm (1872–1956) British writer.
Said when giving a shilling towards W. G. Grace's testimonial
Carr's Dictionary of Extraordinary English Cricketers

2 I do love cricket – it's so very English.
Sarah Bernhardt (Sarah Henriette Rosine Bernard; 1844–
1923) French actress.
On seeing a game of football
Nijinsky (R. Buckle)

3 They came to see me bat not to see you
bowl.
W. G. Grace (1848–1915) British doctor and cricketer.
Refusing to leave the crease after being bowled first ball in
front of a large crowd
Attrib.

4 It's more than a game. It's an institution.
Thomas Hughes (1822–96) British novelist.
Referring to cricket
Tom Brown's Schooldays, Pt. II, Ch. 7

5 There's a breathless hush in the Close
tonight –
Ten to make and the match to win –
A bumping pitch and a blinding light,
An hour to play and the last man in.
Henry John Newbolt (1862–1938) British poet.
Vitaï Lampada

6 I have always looked upon cricket as
organised loafing.
William Temple (1881–1944) British churchman.
Address to parents when headmaster of Repton School

7 It requires one to assume such indecent
postures.
Oscar Wilde (1854–1900) Irish-born British dramatist.
Explaining why he did not play cricket
Attrib.

CRIME

See also theft, murder

1 And surely your blood of your lives will I
require; at the hand of every beast will I
require it, and at the hand of man; at the
hand of every man's brother will I require
the life of man.
Whoso sheddeth man's blood, by man shall his
blood be shed: for in the image of God made
he man.
Bible: Genesis
9:5–6

2 How many crimes committed merely because
their authors could not endure being wrong!
Albert Camus (1913–60) French existentialist writer.
The Fall

3 He is the Napoleon of crime.
Arthur Conan Doyle (1856–1930) British writer.
Referring to Professor Moriarty
The Final Problem

4 If poverty is the mother of crime, stupidity is
its father.
Jean de La Bruyère (1645–96) French satirist.
Les Caractères

5 Crime, like virtue, has its degrees.
Jean Racine (1639–99) French dramatist.
Phèdre, IV:2

6 I came to the conclusion many years ago that
almost all crime is due to the repressed
desire for aesthetic expression.
Evelyn Waugh (1903–66) British novelist.
Decline and Fall, Pt. III, Ch. 1

CRITICISM

See also actors, compliments, insults, poets, writers

1 I am bound by my own definition of criticism:
a disinterested endeavour to learn and
propagate the best that is known and thought
in the world.
Matthew Arnold (1822–88) British poet and critic.
Essays in Criticism, First Series, 'Functions of Criticism at the
Present Time'

2 There is less in this than meets the eye.
Tallulah Bankhead (1903–68) US actress.
Referring to a revival of a play by Maeterlinck
Shouts and Murmurs (A. Woollcott), 'Capsule Criticism'

3 Too much counterpoint; what is worse,
Protestant counterpoint.
Thomas Beecham (1879–1961) British conductor.
Said of J. S. Bach
The Guardian, 8 Mar 1971

4 Of all fatiguing, futile, empty trades, the
worst, I suppose, is writing about writing.
Hilaire Belloc (1870–1953) French-born British poet.
The Silence of the Sea

5 And why beholdest thou the mote that is in

thy brother's eye, but considerest not the beam that is in thine own eye?
Bible: Matthew
7:3

6 He who discommendeth others obliquely commendeth himself.
Thomas Browne (1605–82) English physician and writer.
Christian Morals, Pt. I

7 A great deal of contemporary criticism reads to me like a man saying: 'Of course I do not like green cheese: I am very fond of brown sherry.'
G. K. Chesterton (1874–1936) British writer.
All I Survey

8 To see him act, is like reading Shakespeare by flashes of lightning.
Samuel Taylor Coleridge (1772–1834) British poet.
Referring to Kean
Table Talk

9 I never realized before that Albert married beneath him.
Noël Coward (1899–1973) British dramatist.
After seeing a certain actress in the role of Queen Victoria
Tynan on Theatre (K. Tynan)

10 This paper will no doubt be found interesting by those who take an interest in it.
John Dalton (1766–1844) British scientist.
Said on many occasions when chairing scientific meetings
Attrib.

11 If you hear that someone is speaking ill of you, instead of trying to defend yourself you should say: 'He obviously does not know me very well, since there are so many other faults he could have mentioned'.
Epictetus (c. 60–110 AD) Stoic philosopher.
Enchiridion

12 He played the King as though under momentary apprehension that someone else was about to play the ace.
Eugene Field (1850–95) US poet and journalist.
Referring to Creston Clarke's performance in the role of King Lear
Attrib.

13 Funny without being vulgar.
W. S. Gilbert (1836–1911) British dramatist.
Referring to Sir Henry Irving's *Hamlet*
Attrib.

14 My dear chap! Good isn't the word!
W. S. Gilbert
Speaking to an actor after he had given a poor performance
Attrib.

15 We were as nearly bored as enthusiasm would permit.
Edmund Gosse (1849–1928) British writer and critic.
Referring to a play by Swinburne
Biography of Edward Marsh (C. Hassall)

16 There are two things which I am confident I can do very well: one is an introduction to any literary work, stating what it is to contain, and how it should be executed in the most perfect manner; the other is a conclusion, shewing from various causes why the execution has not been equal to what the author promised to himself and to the public.
Samuel Johnson (1709–84) British lexicographer.
Life of Johnson (J. Boswell), Vol. I

17 It is burning a farthing candle at Dover, to shew light at Calais.
Samuel Johnson
Referring to the impact of Sheridan's works upon the English language
Life of Johnson (J. Boswell), Vol. I

18 You *may* abuse a tragedy, though you cannot write one. You may scold a carpenter who has made you a bad table, though you cannot make a table. It is not your trade to make tables.
Samuel Johnson
Referring to the qualifications needed to indulge in literary criticism
Life of Johnson (J. Boswell), Vol. I

19 This man I thought had been a Lord among wits; but, I find, he is only a wit among Lords.
Samuel Johnson
Referring to Lord Chesterfield
Life of Johnson (J. Boswell), Vol. I

20 They teach the morals of a whore, and the manners of a dancing master.
Samuel Johnson
Referring to Lord Chesterfield's *Letters*
Life of Johnson (J. Boswell), Vol. I

21 Yes, Sir, many men, many women, and many children.
Samuel Johnson
When asked by Dr Blair whether any man of their own time could have written the poems of Ossian
Life of Johnson (J. Boswell), Vol. I

22 Difficult do you call it, Sir? I wish it were impossible.
Samuel Johnson
On hearing a famous violinist
Johnsonian Miscellanies (ed. G. B. Hill), Vol. II

23 They are forced plants, raised in a hot-bed; and they are poor plants; they are but cucumbers after all.
Samuel Johnson
Referring to Gray's *Odes*
Life of Johnson (J. Boswell), Vol. IV

24 The pleasure of criticizing robs us of the pleasure of being moved by some very fine things.
Jean de La Bruyère (1645–96) French satirist.
Les Caractères

25 They are great parables, the novels, but false art. They are only parables. All the people are *fallen angels* – even the dirtiest scrubs.

This I cannot stomach. People are not fallen angels, they are merely people.
D. H. Lawrence (1885–1930) British novelist.
Referring to the novels of Dostoyevsky
Letter to J. Middleton Murray and Katherine Mansfield, 17 Feb 1916

26 His verse exhibits . . . something that is rather like Keats's vulgarity with a Public School accent.
F. R. Leavis (1895–1978) British literary critic.
Referring to Rupert Brooke
New Bearings in English Poetry, Ch. 2

27 I cried all the way to the bank.
Liberace (Wladzin Valentino Liberace; 1919–87) US pianist and showman.
Said when asked whether he minded being criticized
Liberace: An Autobiography, Ch. 2

28 People who like this sort of thing will find this is the sort of thing they like.
Abraham Lincoln (1809–65) US statesman.
A comment on a book
Attrib.

29 His writing bears the same relation to poetry which a Turkey carpet bears to a picture. There are colours in the Turkey carpet out of which a picture might be made. There are words in Mr Montgomery's writing which, when disposed in certain orders and combinations, have made, and will make again, good poetry. But, as they now stand, they seem to be put together on principle in such a manner as to give no image of anything 'in the heavens above, or in the earth beneath, or in the waters under the earth'.
Lord Macaulay (1800–59) British historian.
Literary Essays Contributed to the 'Edinburgh Review', 'Mr. Robert Montgomery's Poems'

30 It was a book to kill time for those who like it better dead.
Rose Macaulay (1889–1958) British writer.
Attrib.

31 I was so long writing my review that I never got around to reading the book.
Groucho Marx (Julius Marx; 1895–1977) US comedian.
Attrib.

32 People ask you for criticism, but they only want praise.
W. Somerset Maugham (1874–1965) British novelist.
Of Human Bondage, Ch. 50

33 Yea, marry, now it is somewhat, for now it is rhyme; before, it was neither rhyme nor reason.
Thomas More (1478–1535) English lawyer and scholar.
On reading an unremarkable book recently rendered into verse by a friend of his
Apophthegms (Bacon), 287

34 Prolonged, indiscriminate reviewing of books involves constantly *inventing* reactions towards books about which one has no spontaneous feelings whatever.
George Orwell (Eric Blair; 1903–50) British novelist.
Confessions of a Book Reviewer

35 She ran the whole gamut of the emotions from A to B.
Dorothy Parker (1893–1967) US writer.
Referring to a performance by Katharine Hepburn on Broadway
Attrib.

36 This is not a novel to be tossed aside lightly. It should be thrown with great force.
Dorothy Parker
Book review
Wit's End (R. E. Dremman)

37 'Tis hard to say, if greater want of skill Appear in writing or in judging ill.
Alexander Pope (1688–1744) British poet.
An Essay on Criticism

38 Damn with faint praise, assent with civil leer, And, without sneering, teach the rest to sneer.
Alexander Pope
Epistle to Dr. Arbuthnot

39 I never read anything concerning my work. I feel that criticism is a letter to the public which the author, since it is not directed to him, does not have to open and read.
Rainer Maria Rilke (1875–1926) Austrian poet.
Letters

40 Very good, but it has its *longueurs*.
Antoine de Rivarol (1753–1801) French writer and wit.
Giving his opinion of a couplet by a mediocre poet
Das Buch des Lachens (W. Scholz)

41 The Stealthy School of Criticism.
Dante Gabriel Rossetti (1828–82) British painter and poet.
Letter to the *Athenaeum*, 1871

42 Wagner has lovely moments but awful quarters of an hour.
Gioacchino Rossini (1792–1868) Italian operatic composer.
Remark made to Emile Naumann, April 1867
Italienische Tondichter (Naumann)

43 I have seen, and heard, much of Cockney impudence before now; but never expected to hear a coxcomb ask two hundred guineas for flinging a pot of paint in the public's face.
John Ruskin (1819–1900) British art critic and writer.
On Whistler's painting 'Nocturne in Black and Gold'
Letter, 18 June 1877

44 For I am nothing if not critical.
William Shakespeare (1564–1616) English dramatist.
Othello, II:1

45 It does not follow . . . that the right to criticize Shakespeare involves the power of writing better plays. And in fact . . . I do not profess to write better plays.
George Bernard Shaw (1856–1950) Irish dramatist and critic.
Three Plays for Puritans, Preface

46 It is disappointing to report that George Bernard Shaw appearing as George Bernard Shaw is sadly miscast in the part. Satirists should be heard and not seen.
Robert E. Sherwood (1896–1955) US writer and dramatist.
Reviewing a Shaw play

47 It had only one fault. It was kind of lousy.
James Thurber (1894–1961) US humorist.
Remark made about a play
Attrib.

48 A strange, horrible business, but I suppose good enough for Shakespeare's day.
Victoria (1819–1901) Queen of the United Kingdom.
Giving her opinion of *King Lear*
Living Biographies of Famous Rulers (H. Thomas)

49 I do not think this poem will reach its destination.
Voltaire (François-Marie Arouet; 1694–1778) French writer.
Reviewing Rousseau's poem 'Ode to Posterity'
Attrib.

50 As far as criticism is concerned, we don't resent that unless it is absolutely biased, as it is in most cases.
John Vorster (Balthazar Johannes Vorster; 1915–83) South African politician.
The Observer, 'Sayings of the Week', 9 Nov 1969

51 My dear fellow a unique evening! I wouldn't have left a turn unstoned.
Arthur Wimperis (1874–1953) British screenwriter.
Replying when asked his opinion of a vaudeville show
Fifty Years of Vaudeville (E. Short)

52 I saw it at a disadvantage – the curtain was up.
Walter Winchell (1879–1972) US journalist.
Referring to a show starring Earl Carroll
Come to Judgment (A. Whiteman)

53 Trivial personalities decomposing in the eternity of print.
Virginia Woolf (1882–1941) British novelist.
The Common Reader, 'Jane Eyre'

54 *Middlemarch*, the magnificent book which with all its imperfections is one of the few English novels for grown up people.
Virginia Woolf
The Common Reader, 'George Eliot'

55 He is all blood, dirt and sucked sugar stick.
W. B. Yeats (1865–1939) Irish poet.
Referring to Wilfred Owen
Letters on Poetry to Dorothy Wellesley, Letter, 21 Dec 1936

CRITICS

1 I will try to account for the degree of my aesthetic emotion. That, I conceive, is the function of the critic.
Clive Bell (1881–1964) British art critic.
Art, Pt. II, Ch. 3

2 A man must serve his time to every trade Save censure – critics all are ready made.
Lord Byron (1788–1824) British poet.
English Bards and Scotch Reviewers

3 Reviewers are usually people who would have been poets, historians, biographers, . . . if they could; they have tried their talents at one or at the other, and have failed; therefore they turn critics.
Samuel Taylor Coleridge (1772–1834) British poet.
Lectures on Shakespeare and Milton, I

4 A good critic is one who narrates the adventures of his mind among masterpieces.
Anatole France (Jacques Anatole François Thibault; 1844–1924) French writer.
The Literary Life, Preface

5 I sometimes think
His critical judgement is so exquisite
It leaves us nothing to admire except his opinion.
Christopher Fry (1907–) British dramatist.
The Dark is Light Enough, II

6 Asking a working writer what he thinks about critics is like asking a lamp-post how it feels about dogs.
Christopher Hampton (1946–) British writer and dramatist.
The Sunday Times Magazine, 16 Oct 1977

7 What is a modern poet's fate?
To write his thoughts upon a slate;
The critic spits on what is done,
Gives it a wipe – and all is gone.
Thomas Hood (1799–1845) British poet.
Alfred Lord Tennyson, A Memoir (Hallam Tennyson), Vol. II, Ch. 3

8 There is a certain race of men that either imagine it their duty, or make it their amusement, to hinder the reception of every work of learning or genius, who stand as sentinels in the avenues of fame, and value themselves upon giving Ignorance and Envy the first notice of a prey.
Samuel Johnson (1709–84) British lexicographer.
The Rambler

9 A fly, Sir, may sting a stately horse and make him wince; but one is but an insect, and the other is a horse still.
Samuel Johnson
Life of Johnson (J. Boswell), Vol. I

10 Dear Roger Fry whom I love as a man but detest as a movement.
Edward Howard Marsh (1872–1953) British civil servant and writer.
Roger Fry (1866–1934) was an artist and art critic, who championed the postimpressionists
Edward Marsh (Christopher Hassall), Ch. 11

11 Insects sting, not from malice, but because they want to live. It is the same with critics – they desire our blood, not our pain.
Friedrich Wilhelm Nietzsche (1844–1900) German philosopher.
Miscellaneous Maxims and Reflections

12 Nor in the critic let the man be lost.
Alexander Pope (1688–1744) British poet.
An Essay on Criticism

13 They will review a book by a writer much older than themselves as if it were an over-ambitious essay by a second-year student . . . It is the little dons I complain about, like so many corgis trotting up, hoping to nip your ankles.
J. B. Priestley (1894–1984) British novelist.
Outcries and Asides

14 I doubt that art needed Ruskin any more than a moving train needs one of its passengers to shove it.
Tom Stoppard (1937–) Czech-born British dramatist.
Times Literary Supplement, 3 June 1977

15 I had another dream the other day about music critics. They were small and rodent-like with padlocked ears, as if they had stepped out of a painting by Goya.
Igor Stravinsky (1882–1971) Russian-born US composer.
The Evening Standard, 29 Oct 1969

16 A whipper-snapper of criticism who quoted dead languages to hide his ignorance of life.
Herbert Beerbohm Tree (1853–1917) British actor and theatre manager.
Referring to A. B. Walkley
Beerbohm Tree (Hesketh Pearson)

17 A critic is a man who knows the way but can't drive the car.
Kenneth Tynan (1927–80) British theatre critic.
New York Times Magazine, 9 Jan 1966

18 A good drama critic is one who perceives what is happening in the theatre of his time. A great drama critic also perceives what is not happening.
Kenneth Tynan
Tynan Right and Left, Foreword

CRUELTY

See also hurt, nastiness, violence

1 The wish to hurt, the momentary intoxication with pain, is the loophole through which the pervert climbs into the minds of ordinary men.
Jacob Bronowski (1908–74) British scientist and writer.
The Face of Violence, Ch. 5

2 Man's inhumanity to man
Makes countless thousands mourn!
Robert Burns (1759–96) Scottish poet.
Man was Made to Mourn

3 Fear is the parent of cruelty.
J. A. Froude (1818–94) British historian.
Short Studies on Great Subjects, 'Party Politics'

4 A cruel story runs on wheels, and every hand oils the wheels as they run.
Ouida (Marie Louise de la Ramée; 1839–1908) British novelist.
Wisdom, Wit and Pathos, 'Moths'

5 Whipping and abuse are like laudanum: You have to double the dose as the sensibilities decline.
Harriet Beecher Stowe (1811–96) US novelist.
Uncle Tom's Cabin, Ch. 20

CULTURE

See also civilization, philistinism

1 Culture, the acquainting ourselves with the best that has been known and said in the world, and thus with the history of the human spirit.
Matthew Arnold (1822–88) British poet and critic.
Literature and Dogma, Preface

2 Culture is the passion for sweetness and light, and (what is more) the passion for making them prevail.
Matthew Arnold
Literature and Dogma, Preface

3 Culture is an instrument wielded by professors to manufacture professors, who when their turn comes will manufacture professors.
Simone Weil (1909–43) French philosopher.
The Need for Roots

4 Mrs Ballinger is one of the ladies who pursue Culture in bands, as though it were dangerous to meet it alone.
Edith Wharton (1862–1937) US novelist.
Xingu, Ch. 1

CURIOSITY

See also interfering, wonder

1 Ask no questions and hear no lies.
Proverb

2 Curiosity killed the cat.
Proverb

3 Be not curious in unnecessary matters: for more things are shewed unto thee than men understand
Bible: Ecclesiasticus
3:23

4 There is no such thing on earth as an uninteresting subject; the only thing that can exist is an uninterested person.
G. K. Chesterton (1874–1936) British writer.
Heretics, Ch. 1

5 The world is but a school of inquiry.
Michel de Montaigne (1533–92) French essayist.
Essais, III

6 I ofen looked up at the sky an' assed meself

the question – what is the stars, what is the stars?
Sean O'Casey (1884–1964) Irish dramatist.
Juno and the Paycock, I

7 Curiosity will conquer fear even more than bravery will.
James Stephens (1882–1950) Irish novelist.
The Crock of Gold

8 Disinterested intellectual curiosity is the life blood of real civilisation.
George Macaulay Trevelyan (1876–1962) British historian
English Social History, Preface

CURSES

1 A plague o' both your houses!
They have made worms' meat of me.
William Shakespeare (1564–1616) English dramatist.
Romeo and Juliet, III:1

2 Curses are like young chickens, they always come home to roost.
Robert Southey (1774–1843) British poet.
The Curse of Kehama, Motto

3 'The curse is come upon me,' cried
The Lady of Shalott.
Alfred, Lord Tennyson (1809–92) British poet.
The Lady of Shalott, Pt. III

4 She has heard a whisper say,
A curse is on her if she stay
To look down to Camelot.
Alfred, Lord Tennyson
The Lady of Shalott, Pt. II

CUSTOM

See also habit

1 *O tempora! O mores!*
What times! What customs!
Cicero (106–43 BC) Roman orator and statesman.
In Catilinam, I

2 Custom, then, is the great guide of human life.
David Hume (1711–76) Scottish philosopher.
An Enquiry Concerning Human Understanding

3 But to my mind, though I am native here
And to the manner born, it is a custom
More honour'd in the breach than the observance.
William Shakespeare (1564–1616) English dramatist.
Hamlet, I:4

4 Custom calls me to't.
What custom wills, in all things should we do't,
The dust on antique time would lie unswept,
And mountainous error be too highly heap'd
For truth to o'erpeer.
William Shakespeare
Coriolanus, II:3

CYNICISM

1 One is not superior merely because one sees the world in an odious light.
Vicomte de Chateaubriand (1768–1848) French diplomat and writer.
Attrib.

2 Cynicism is an unpleasant way of saying the truth.
Lillian Hellman (1905–84) US dramatist.
The Little Foxes, I

3 Cynicism is humour in ill-health.
H. G. Wells (1866–1946) British writer.
Short Stories, 'The Last Trump'

4 A man who knows the price of everything and the value of nothing.
Oscar Wilde (1854–1900) Irish-born British dramatist.
A cynic
Lady Windermere's Fan, III

D

DAMNATION

See also devil, hell

1 Blot out his name, then, record one lost soul more,
One task more declined, one more footpath untrod,
One more devils'-triumph and sorrow for angels,
One wrong more to man, one more insult to God!
Robert Browning (1812–89) British poet.
The Lost Leader

2 You will be damned if you do – And you will be damned if you don't.
Lorenzo Dow (1777–1834) British churchman.
Speaking of Calvinism
Reflections on the Love of God

3 Now hast thou but one bare hour to live,
And then thou must be damn'd perpetually!
Stand still, you ever-moving spheres of heaven,
That time may cease, and midnight never come.
Christopher Marlowe (1564–93) English dramatist.
Doctor Faustus, V:2

4 Ugly hell, gape not! come not, Lucifer!

I'll burn my books!
Christopher Marlowe
Doctor Faustus, V:2

DANCING

1 On with the dance! let joy be unconfined;
No sleep till morn, when Youth and Pleasure meet
To chase the glowing Hours with flying feet.
Lord Byron (1788–1824) British poet.
Childe Harold's Pilgrimage, III

2 Will you, won't you, will you, won't you, will you join the dance?
Lewis Carroll (Charles Lutwidge Dodgson; 1832–98) British writer.
Alice's Adventures in Wonderland, Ch. 10

3 Dance, dance, dance little lady.
Noël Coward (1899–1973) British dramatist.
Title of song

4 I have discovered the dance. I have discovered the art which has been lost for two thousand years.
Isadora Duncan (1878–1927) US dancer.
My Life

5 Any time you're Lambeth way,
Any evening, any day,
You'll find us all doin' the Lambeth walk.
Douglas Furber (1885–1961) British songwriter.
Doin' the Lambeth Walk

6 My men, like satyrs grazing on the lawns,
Shall with their goat-feet dance an antic hay.
Christopher Marlowe (1564–93) English dramatist.
Edward the Second, I:1

7 Come, and trip it as you go
On the light fantastic toe.
John Milton (1608–74) English poet.
L'Allegro

8 . . . although one may fail to find happiness in theatrical life, one never wishes to give it up after having once tasted its fruits. To enter the School of the Imperial Ballet is to enter a convent whence frivolity is banned, and where merciless discipline reigns.
Anna Pavlova (1881–1931) Russian ballet dancer.
Pavlova: A Biography (ed. A. H. Franks), 'Pages of My Life'

DANGER

1 Any port in a storm.
Proverb

2 If you play with fire you get burnt.
Proverb

3 Defend us from all perils and dangers of this night.
The Book of Common Prayer
Morning Prayer, Prayer of St Chrysostom

4 Dangers by being despised grow great.
Edmund Burke (1729–97) British politician.
Speech, House of Commons, 11 May 1792

5 Of course I realized there was a measure of danger. Obviously I faced the possibility of not returning when first I considered going. Once faced and settled there really wasn't any good reason to refer to it.
Amelia Earhart (1898–1937) US flyer.
Referring to her flight in the 'Friendship'
20 Hours: 40 Minutes – Our Flight in the Friendship, Ch. 5

6 Believe me! The secret of reaping the greatest fruitfulness and the greatest enjoyment from life is to *live dangerously!*
Friedrich Wilhelm Nietzsche (1844–1900) German philosopher.
Die Fröhliche Wissenschaft, Bk. IV

7 There's a snake hidden in the grass.
Virgil (Publius Vergilius Maro; 70–19 BC) Roman poet.
Eclogue, Bk. III

DAY

1 Now the day is over,
Night is drawing nigh,
Shadows of the evening
Steal across the sky.
Sabine Baring-Gould (1834–1924) British author and hymn writer.
The Evening Hymn

2 The day begins to droop, –
Its course is done:
But nothing tells the place
Of the setting sun.
Robert Bridges (1844–1930) British poet.
Winter Nightfall

3 Where the quiet-coloured end of evening smiles,
Miles and miles.
Robert Browning (1812–89) British poet.
Love among the Ruins, I

4 The day Thou gavest, Lord, is ended,
The darkness falls at Thy behest.
John Ellerton (1826–93) British churchman.
A Liturgy for Missionary Meetings

5 Awake! for Morning in the Bowl of Night
Has flung the Stone that puts the Stars to Flight:
And Lo! the Hunter of the East has caught
The Sultan's Turret in a Noose of Light.
Edward Fitzgerald (1809–83) British poet.
The Rubáiyát of Omar Khayyám

6 The Curfew tolls the knell of parting day,
The lowing herd winds slowly o'er the lea,
The plowman homeward plods his weary way,
And leaves the world to darkness and to me.
Thomas Gray (1716–71) British poet.
Elegy Written in a Country Churchyard

7 Oh, what a beautiful morning!

Oh, what a beautiful day!
Oscar Hammerstein (1895–1960) US lyricist.
From the musical *Oklahoma*
Oh, What a Beautiful Morning

8 Sweet day, so cool, so calm, so bright,
The bridal of the earth and sky.
George Herbert (1593–1633) English poet.
Virtue

9 The candles burn their sockets,
The blinds let through the day,
The young man feels his pockets
And wonders what's to pay.
A. E. Housman (1859–1936) British scholar and poet.
Last Poems, 'Eight O'Clock'

10 Under the opening eye-lids of the morn.
John Milton (1608–74) English poet.
Lycidas

11 Now came still Evening on, and Twilight grey
Had in her sober livery all things clad.
John Milton
Paradise Lost, Bk. IV

12 Midnight brought on the dusky hour
Friendliest to sleep and silence.
John Milton
Paradise Lost, Bk. V

13 Three o'clock is always too late or too early
for anything you want to do.
Jean-Paul Sartre (1905–80) French writer.
Nausea

DEATH

See also afterlife, assassination, drowning, epitaphs, equality in
death, execution, funerals, killing, last words, life and death,
love and death, memorials, mortality, mourning, murder,
obituaries, posterity, suicide

1 A man can die but once.
Proverb

2 A piece of churchyard fits everybody.
Proverb

3 As soon as man is born he begins to die.
Proverb

4 Dead men tell no tales.
Proverb

5 Death defies the doctor.
Proverb

6 Death is the great leveller.
Proverb

7 Fear of death is worse than death itself.
Proverb

8 Never speak ill of the dead.
Proverb

9 Nothing is certain but death and taxes.
Proverb

10 The good die young.
Proverb

11 The old man has his death before his eyes;
the young man behind his back.
Proverb

12 There will be sleeping enough in the grave.
Proverb

13 It's not that I'm afraid to die. I just don't
want to be there when it happens.
Woody Allen (Allen Stewart Konigsberg; 1935–) US
film actor.
Without Feathers, 'Death (A Play)'

14 God grants an easy death only to the just.
Svetlana Alliluyeva (1926–) Russian writer; daughter
of Joseph Stalin.
Twenty Letters to a Friend

15 O Death, where is thy sting-a-ling-a-ling,
O Grave, thy victoree?
The bells of hell go ting-a-ling-a-ling
For you but not for me.
Anonymous
Song of World War I

16 Swing low sweet chariot,
Comin' for to carry me home,
I looked over Jordan an' what did I see?
A band of Angels coming after me,
Comin' for to carry me home.
Anonymous
Swing Low, Sweet Chariot

17 He's gone to join the majority.
Petronius Arbiter (1st century AD) Roman satirist.
Referring to a dead man
Satyricon: Cena Trimalchionis, 42

18 Now he is dead! Far hence he lies
In the lorn Syrian town;
And on his grave, with shining eyes,
The Syrian stars look down.
Matthew Arnold (1822–88) British poet and critic.
Obermann Once More

19 I have often thought upon death, and I find it
the least of all evils.
Francis Bacon (1561–1626) English philosopher.
An Essay on Death

20 I do not believe that any man fears to be
dead, but only the stroke of death.
Francis Bacon
An Essay on Death

21 Men fear death, as children fear to go in the
dark; and as that natural fear in children is
increased with tales, so is the other.
Francis Bacon
Essays, 'Of Death'

22 It is natural to die as to be born; and to a
little infant, perhaps, the one is as painful as
the other.
Francis Bacon
Essays, 'Of Death'

23 To die will be an awfully big adventure.
J. M. Barrie (1860–1937) British novelist and dramatist.
Peter Pan, III

24 What I like about Clive
Is that he is no longer alive.
There is a great deal to be said
For being dead.
Edmund Clerihew Bentley (1875–1956) British writer.
Biography for Beginners

25 The physician cutteth off a long disease; and
he that is today a king tomorrow shall die.
Bible: Ecclesiasticus
10:10

26 Behold, I shew you a mystery; We shall not
all sleep, but we shall all be changed,
In a moment, in the twinkling of an eye, at the
last trump: for the trumpet shall sound, and
the dead shall be raised incorruptible, and we
shall be changed.
For this corruptible must put on incorruption,
and this mortal must put on immortality.
So when this corruptible shall have put on incorruption, and this mortal shall have put on
immortality, then shall be brought to pass
the saying that is written, Death is swallowed
up in victory.
O death, where is thy sting? O grave, where is
thy victory?
Bible: I Corinthians
15:51–55

27 For all flesh is as grass, and all the glory of
man as the flower of grass. The grass
withereth, and the flower thereof falleth
away.
Bible: I Peter
1:23–24

28 Lord, now lettest thou thy servant depart in
peace, according to thy word:
For mine eyes have seen thy salvation,
Which thou hast prepared before the face of all
people;
A light to lighten the Gentiles, and the glory of
thy people Israel.
Bible: Luke
2:29–32

29 And I looked, and behold a pale horse: and
his name that sat on him was Death, and
Hell followed with him. And power was given
unto them over the fourth part of the earth,
to kill with sword, and with hunger, and with
death, and with the beasts of the earth.
Bible: Revelations
6:8

30 Its visits,
Like those of angels, short, and far between.
Robert Blair (1699–1746) Scottish poet.
The Grave

31 In the hour of death, and in the day of
judgement.
The Book of Common Prayer
Morning Prayer, Prayer of St Chrysostom

32 Any amusing deaths lately?
Maurice Bowra (1898–1971) British scholar.
Attrib.

33 For I say, this is death, and the sole death,
When a man's loss comes to him from his gain,
Darkness from light, from knowledge
ignorance,
And lack of love from love made manifest.
Robert Browning (1812–89) British poet.
A Death in the Desert

34 It is important what a man still plans at the
end. It shows the measure of injustice in his
death.
Elias Canetti (1905–   ) Bulgarian-born novelist.
The Human Province

35 Days and moments quickly flying,
Blend the living with the dead;
Soon will you and I be lying
Each within our narrow bed.
Edward Caswall (1814–78) British hymn writer.
Hymn

36 He had been, he said, a most unconscionable
time dying; but he hoped that they would
excuse it.
Charles II (1630–85) King of England.
History of England (Macaulay), Vol. I, Ch. 4

37 Alack he's gone the way of all flesh.
William Congreve (1670–1729) British Restoration
dramatist.
Squire Bickerstaff Detected, attrib.

38 We perish'd, each alone:
But I beneath a rougher sea,
And whelm'd in deeper gulphs than he.
William Cowper (1731–1800) British poet.
The Castaway

39 He'd make a lovely corpse.
Charles Dickens (1812–70) British novelist.
Martin Chuzzlewit, Ch. 25

40 Because I could not stop for Death,
He kindly stopped for me;
The carriage held but just ourselves
And Immortality.
Emily Dickinson (1830–86) US poet.
The Chariot

41 Our journey had advanced;
Our feet were almost come
To that odd fork in Being's road,
Eternity by term.
Emily Dickinson
Our Journey had Advanced

42 Death be not proud, though some have called
thee

Mighty and dreadful, for, thou art not so.
John Donne (1573–1631) English poet.
Holy Sonnets, 10

43 Any man's death diminishes me, because I
am involved in Mankind; And therefore never
send to know for whom the bell tolls; it tolls
for thee.
John Donne
Devotions, 17

44 Sin brought death, and death will disappear
with the disappearance of sin.
Mary Baker Eddy (1821–1910) US religious leader.
Science and Health, with Key to the Scriptures

45 Death is my neighbour now.
Edith Evans (1888–1976) British actress.
Said a week before her death
BBC radio interview, 14 Oct 1976

46 It hath been often said, that it is not death,
but dying, which is terrible.
Henry Fielding (1707–54) British novelist.
Amelia, Bk. III, Ch. 4

47 Strange, is it not? that of the myriads who
Before us pass'd the door of Darkness
through,
Not one returns to tell us of the Road,
Which to discover we must travel too.
Edward Fitzgerald (1809–83) British poet.
The Rubáiyát of Omar Khayyám

48 He hath shook hands with time.
John Ford (c. 1586–c. 1640) English dramatist.
The Broken Heart, V:2

49 Death destroys a man, the idea of Death
saves him.
E. M. Forster (1879–1970) British novelist.
Howards End, Ch. 27

50 Dere's no more work for poor old Ned,
He's gone whar de good niggers go.
Stephen Foster (1826–64) US composer of popular
songs.
Uncle Ned

51 If Mr Selwyn calls again, shew him up: if I
am alive I shall be delighted to see him; and
if I am dead he would like to see me.
Henry Fox (1705–74) British politician.
Said during his last illness. George Selwyn was known for his
morbid fascination for dead bodies.
George Selwyn and his Contemporaries (J. H. Jesse), Vol. III

52 Something lingering, with boiling oil in it, I
fancy.
W. S. Gilbert (1836–1911) British dramatist.
The Mikado, II

53 I am told he makes a very handsome corpse,
and becomes his coffin prodigiously.
Oliver Goldsmith (1728–74) Irish-born British writer.
The Good-Natured Man, I

54 Can storied urn or animated bust
Back to its mansion call the fleeting breath?
Can honour's voice provoke the silent dust,

Or flatt'ry soothe the dull cold ear of death?
Thomas Gray (1716–71) British poet.
Elegy Written in a Country Churchyard

55 Here rests his head upon the lap of Earth
A youth to fortune and to fame unknown.
Fair Science frown'd not on his humble birth,
And Melancholy mark'd him for her own.
Thomas Gray
Elegy Written in a Country Churchyard

56 Grieve not that I die young. Is it not well
To pass away ere life hath lost its brightness?
Lady Flora Hastings (1806–39) British poet.
Swan Song

57 Death is still working like a mole,
And digs my grave at each remove.
George Herbert (1593–1633) English poet.
Grace

58 Anno domini – that's the most fatal complaint
of all in the end.
James Hilton (1900–54) British novelist.
Good-bye, Mr Chips, Ch. 1

59 Death . . . It's the only thing we haven't
succeeded in completely vulgarizing.
Aldous Huxley (1894–1964) British novelist.
Eyeless in Gaza, Ch. 31

60 Our civilization is founded on the shambles,
and every individual existence goes out in a
lonely spasm of helpless agony.
William James (1842–1910) US psychologist and
philosopher.
Varieties of Religious Experience

61 I die because I do not die.
St John of the Cross (Juan de Yepes y Alvarez; 1542–
91) Spanish churchman and poet.
Coplas del alma que pena por ver a dios

62 It matters not how a man dies, but how he
lives. The act of dying is not of importance,
it lasts so short a time.
Samuel Johnson (1709–84) British lexicographer.
Life of Johnson (J. Boswell), Vol. II

63 I am able to follow my own death step by
step. Now I move softly towards the end.
Pope John XXIII (Angelo Roncalli; 1881–1963) Italian
churchman.
Remark made two days before he died
The Guardian, 3 June 1963

64 Above ground I shall be food for kites; below
I shall be food for mole-crickets and ants.
Why rob one to feed the other?
Juang-zu (4th century BC) Chinese Taoist philosopher.
When asked on his deathbed what his wishes were regarding
the disposal of his body
Famous Last Words (B. Conrad)

65 All right, my lord creator, Don Miguel, you
too will die and return to the nothing whence
you came. God will cease to dream you!
Miguel de Unamuno y Jugo (1864–1936) Spanish
writer.
Mist

66 Darkling I listen; and, for many a time
I have been half in love with easeful Death,
Call'd him soft names in many a mused rhyme,
To take into the air my quiet breath;
Now more than ever seems it rich to die,
To cease upon the midnight with no pain,
While thou art pouring forth thy soul abroad
In such an ecstasy!
John Keats (1795–1821) British poet.
Ode to a Nightingale

67 I shall soon be laid in the quiet grave –
thank God for the quiet grave – O! I can
feel the cold earth upon me – the daisies
growing over me – O for this quiet – it will
be my first.
John Keats
In a letter to John Taylor by Joseph Severn, 6 Mar 1821

68 Teach me to live, that I may dread
The grave as little as my bed.
Thomas Ken (1637–1711) English bishop.
An Evening Hymn

69 In the long run we are all dead.
John Maynard Keynes (1883–1946) British economist.
Collected Writings, 'A Tract on Monetary Reform'

70 That is the road we all have to take – over
the Bridge of Sighs into eternity.
Soren Kierkegaard (1813–55) Danish philosopher.
Kierkegaard Anthology (Auden)

71 O pity the dead that are dead, but cannot
make
the journey, still they moan and beat
against the silvery adamant walls of life's exclusive city.
D. H. Lawrence (1885–1930) British novelist.
The Houseless Dead

72 The dead don't die. They look on and help.
D. H. Lawrence
Letter

73 I detest life-insurance agents. They always
argue that I shall some day die, which is not
so.
Stephen Leacock (1869–1944) English-born Canadian
economist and humorist.
Literary Lapses

74 There is a Reaper whose name is Death,
And, with his sickle keen,
He reaps the bearded grain at a breath,
And the flowers that grow between.
Henry Wadsworth Longfellow (1807–82) US poet.
The Reaper and the Flowers

75 It is the only disease you don't look forward
to being cured of.
Herman J. Mankiewicz (1897–1953) US journalist and
screenwriter.
Referring to death
Citizen Kane

76 Cut is the branch that might have grown full
straight,
And burned is Apollo's laurel-bough,

That sometime grew within this learned man.
Christopher Marlowe (1564–93) English dramatist.
Doctor Faustus, Epilogue

77 The grave's a fine and private place,
But none, I think, do there embrace.
Andrew Marvell (1621–78) English poet.
To His Coy Mistress

78 Either he's dead or my watch has stopped.
Groucho Marx (Julius Marx; 1895–1977) US comedian.
A Day at the Races

79 My husband is dead.
– I'll bet he's just using that as an excuse.
I was with him to the end.
– No wonder he passed away.
I held him in my arms and kissed him.
– So it was murder!
Groucho Marx
Duck Soup

80 Dying is a very dull, dreary affair. And my
advice to you is to have nothing whatever to
do with it.
W. Somerset Maugham (1874–1965) British novelist.
Escape from the Shadows (Robin Maugham)

81 Alas! Lord and Lady Dalhousie are dead, and
buried at last,
Which causes many people to feel a little
downcast.
William McGonagall (1830–1902) Scottish poet.
The Death of Lord and Lady Dalhousie

82 Whom the gods love dies young.
Menander (c. 341–c. 290 BC) Greek dramatist.
Dis Exapaton

83 One dies only once, and it's for such a long
time!
Molière (Jean Baptiste Poquelin; 1622–73) French
dramatist.
Le Dépit amoureux, V:3

84 Oh well, no matter what happens, there's
always death.
Napoleon I (Napoleon Bonaparte; 1769–1821) French
emperor.
Attrib.

85 And in the happy no-time of his sleeping
Death took him by the heart.
Wilfred Owen (1893–1918) British poet.
Asleep

86 It costs me never a stab nor squirm
To tread by chance upon a worm.
'Aha, my little dear,' I say,
'Your clan will pay me back one day.'
Dorothy Parker (1893–1967) US writer.
Sunset Gun, 'Thought for a Sunshiny Morning'

87 I mount! I fly!
O grave! where is thy victory?
O death! where is thy sting?
Alexander Pope (1688–1744) British poet.
The Dying Christian to his Soul

88 Here am I, dying of a hundred good symptoms.
Alexander Pope
Anecdotes by and about Alexander Pope (Joseph Spence)

89 How often are we to die before we go quite off this stage? In every friend we lose a part of ourselves, and the best part.
Alexander Pope
Letter to Jonathan Swift, 5 Dec 1732

90 The hero is strangely akin to those who die young.
Rainer Maria Rilke (1875–1926) Austrian poet.
Duineser Elegien, VI

91 I shall have more to say when I am dead.
Edwin Arlington Robinson (1869–1935) US poet.
John Brown

92 When I am dead, my dearest,
Sing no sad songs for me;
Plant thou no roses at my head,
Nor shady cypress tree:
Be the green grass above me
With showers and dewdrops wet;
And if thou wilt, remember,
And if thou wilt, forget.
Christina Rossetti (1830–74) British poet.
When I am Dead

93 To that dark inn, the grave!
Walter Scott (1771–1832) Scottish novelist.
The Lord of the Isles, VI

94 His morning walk was beneath the elms in the churchyard; 'for death,' he said, 'had been his next-door neighbour for so many years, that he had no apology for dropping the acquaintance.'
Walter Scott
The Legend of Montrose, Introduction

95 I have a rendezvous with Death
At some disputed barricade.
Alan Seeger (1888–1916) US poet.
I Have a Rendezvous with Death

96 The rest is silence.
William Shakespeare (1564–1616) English dramatist.
Hamlet, V:2

97 Why, he that cuts off twenty years of life
Cuts off so many years of fearing death.
William Shakespeare
Julius Caesar, III:1

98 O mighty Caesar! dost thou lie so low?
Are all thy conquests, glories, triumphs, spoils,
Shrunk to this little measure?
William Shakespeare
Julius Caesar, III:1

99 Ay, but to die, and go we know not where;
To lie in cold obstruction, and to rot;
This sensible warm motion to become
A kneaded clod; and the delighted spirit
To bathe in fiery floods or to reside

In thrilling region of thick-ribbed ice.
William Shakespeare
Measure for Measure, III:1

100 Full fathom five thy father lies;
Of his bones are coral made;
Those are pearls that were his eyes;
Nothing of him that doth fade
But doth suffer a sea-change
Into something rich and strange.
William Shakespeare
The Tempest, I:2

101 He that dies pays all debts.
William Shakespeare
The Tempest, III:2

102 Nothing in his life
Became him like the leaving it: he died
As one that had been studied in his death
To throw away the dearest thing he ow'd
As 'twere a careless trifle.
William Shakespeare
Macbeth, I:4

103 But thoughts, the slaves of life, and life, time's fool,
And time, that takes survey of all the world,
Must have a stop.
William Shakespeare
Henry IV, Part One, V:4

104 His nose was as sharp as a pen, and 'a babbl'd of green fields.
William Shakespeare
Referring to Falstaff on his deathbed
Henry V, II:3

105 I care not; a man can die but once; we owe God a death.
William Shakespeare
Henry IV, Part Two, III:2

106 Death is the veil which those who live call life:
They sleep, and it is lifted.
Percy Bysshe Shelley (1792–1822) British poet.
Prometheus Unbound, III

107 It is a modest creed, and yet
Pleasant if one considers it,
To own that death itself must be,
Like all the rest, a mockery.
Percy Bysshe Shelley
The Sensitive Plant, III

108 I cannot forgive my friends for dying: I do not find these vanishing acts of theirs at all amusing.
Logan Pearsall Smith (1865–1946) US writer.
Trivia

109 I do really think that death will be marvellous ... If there wasn't death, I think you couldn't go on.
Stevie Smith (Florence Margaret Smith; 1902–71) British poet.
The Observer, 9 Nov 1969

110 The whole of his life had prepared Podduyev for living, not for dying.
Alexander Solzhenitsyn (1918–) Soviet novelist.
Cancer Ward, Pt. I, Ch. 8

111 Sleep after toil, port after stormy seas,
Ease after war, death after life does greatly please.
Edmund Spenser (1552–99) English poet.
The Faerie Queene, I:9

112 Under the wide and starry sky
Dig the grave and let me lie.
Glad did I live and gladly die,
– And I laid me down with a will.
This is the verse you grave for me:
'Here he lies where he longed to be;
Home is the sailor, home from sea,
And the hunter home from the hill.'
Robert Louis Stevenson (1850–94) Scottish writer.
Underwoods, Bk. I, 'Requiem'

113 Row upon row with strict impunity
The headstones yield their names to the element.
Allen Tate (1899–) US poet.
Ode to the Confederate Dead

114 A day less or more
At sea or ashore,
We die – does it matter when?
Alfred, Lord Tennyson (1809–92) British poet.
The Revenge, XI

115 I, born of flesh and ghost, was neither
A ghost nor man, but mortal ghost.
And I was struck down by death's feather.
Dylan Thomas (1914–53) Welsh poet.
Before I knocked

116 After the first death, there is no other.
Dylan Thomas
A Refusal to Mourn the Death, by Fire, of a Child in London

117 Do not go gentle into that good night,
Old age should burn and rave at close of day;
Rage, rage, against the dying of the light.
Dylan Thomas
Do not go gentle into that good night

118 There is not any book
Or face of dearest look
That I would not turn from now
To go into the unknown
I must enter, and leave, alone,
I know not how.
Edward Thomas (1878–1917) British poet.
Lights Out

119 Go and try to disprove death. Death will disprove you, and that's all!
Ivan Turgenev (1818–83) Russian novelist.
Fathers and Sons, Ch. 27

120 While I thought that I was learning how to live, I have been learning how to die.
Leonardo da Vinci (1452–1519) Italian artist.
Notebooks

121 There's no repentance in the grave.
Isaac Watts (1674–1748) English theologian and hymn writer.
Divine Songs for Children, 'Solemn Thoughts of God and Death'

122 For he who lives more lives than one
More deaths than one must die.
Oscar Wilde (1854–1900) Irish-born British dramatist.
The Ballad of Reading Gaol, III:37

123 Dead! and . . . never called me mother.
Mrs Henry Wood (1814–87) British novelist.
East Lynne (dramatized version; the words do not occur in the novel)

124 Three years she grew in sun and shower,
Then Nature said, 'A lovelier flower
On earth was never sown;
This child I to myself will take;
She shall be mine, and I will make
A Lady of my own.
William Wordsworth (1770–1850) British poet.
Three Years she Grew

125 We are laid asleep
In body, and become a living soul:
While with an eye made quiet by the power
Of harmony, and the deep power of joy,
We see into the life of things.
William Wordsworth
Lines composed a few miles above Tintern Abbey

DEBAUCHERY

See also animalism, lust, pleasure, sex

1 A fool bolts pleasure, then complains of moral indigestion.
Minna Antrim (1861–?) US writer.
Naked Truth and Veiled Allusions

2 A great many people have come up to me and asked how I manage to get so much work done and still keep looking so dissipated.
Robert Benchley (1889–1945) US humorist.
Chips off the Old Benchley, 'How to Get Things Done'

3 *Debauchee*, n. One who has so earnestly pursued pleasure that he has had the misfortune to overtake it.
Ambrose Bierce (1842–?1914) US writer and journalist.
The Devil's Dictionary

4 So, we'll go no more a roving
So late into the night,
Though the heart be still as loving,
And the moon be still as bright.
Lord Byron (1788–1824) British poet.
So, we'll go no more a roving

5 I've over-educated myself in all the things I shouldn't have known at all.
Noël Coward (1899–1973) British dramatist.
Wild Oats

6 No one ever suddenly became depraved.
Juvenal (Decimus Junius Juvenalis; 60–130 AD) Roman satirist.
Satires, II

7 We're poor little lambs who've lost our way,
Baa! Baa! Baa!
We're little black sheep who've gone astray,
Baa-aa-aa!
Gentleman-rankers out on the spree,
Damned from here to Eternity,
God ha' mercy on such as we,
Baa! Yah! Bah!
Rudyard Kipling (1865–1936) Indian-born British writer.
Gentleman-Rankers

8 Home is heaven and orgies are vile
But you need an orgy, once in a while.
Ogden Nash (1902–71) US poet.
Home, 99.44100% Sweet Home

9 Once: a philosopher; twice: a pervert!
Voltaire (François-Marie Arouet; 1694–1778) French writer.
Turning down an invitation to an orgy, having attended one the previous night for the first time
Attrib.

DECEPTION

See also appearances, hypocrisy, insincerity, lying

1 To deceive oneself is very easy.
Proverb

2 Beware of false prophets, which come to you in sheep's clothing, but inwardly they are ravening wolves.
Bible: Matthew
7:15

3 Almost every man wastes part of his life in attempts to display qualities which he does not possess, and to gain applause which he cannot keep.
Samuel Johnson (1709–84) British lexicographer.
The Rambler

4 You can fool some of the people all the time and all the people some of the time; but you can't fool all the people all the time.
Abraham Lincoln (1809–65) US statesman.
Attrib.

5 False face must hide what the false heart doth know.
William Shakespeare (1564–1616) English dramatist.
Macbeth, I:7

6 You can fool too many of the people too much of the time.
James Thurber (1894–1961) US humorist.
Fables for Our Time, 'The Owl Who Was God'

7 I have invented an invaluable permanent invalid called Bunbury, in order that I may be able to go down into the country whenever I choose.
Oscar Wilde (1854–1900) Irish-born British dramatist.
The Importance of Being Earnest, I

DECISION

See also determination

1 Tender-handed stroke a nettle,
And it stings you for your pains;
Grasp it like a man of mettle,
And it soft as silk remains.
Aaron Hill (1685–1750) British poet and dramatist.
Verses Written on Window

2 Like all weak men he laid an exaggerated stress on not changing one's mind.
W. Somerset Maugham (1874–1965) British novelist.
Of Human Bondage, Ch. 37

3 If someone tells you he is going to make 'a realistic decision', you immediately understand that he has resolved to do something bad.
Mary McCarthy (1912–) US novelist.
On the Contrary

DECLINE

1 And though the Van Dycks have to go
And we pawn the Bechstein grand,
We'll stand by the Stately Homes of England.
Noël Coward (1899–1973) British dramatist.
Operette, The Stately Homes of England

2 That's Why the Lady Is a Tramp.
Lorenz Hart (1895–1943) US songwriter.
From the musical *Babes in Arms*
Song title

3 It is the logic of our times,
No subject for immortal verse –
That we who lived by honest dreams
Defend the bad against the worse.
C. Day Lewis (1904–72) British poet.
Where are the War Poets?

4 From morn
To noon he fell, from noon to dewy eve,
A summer's day, and with the setting sun
Dropped from the zenith, like a falling star.
John Milton (1608–74) English poet.
Paradise Lost, Bk. I

5 Macmillan seemed, in his very person, to embody the national decay he supposed himself to be confuting. He exuded a flavour of moth-balls.
Malcolm Muggeridge (1903–) British writer.
Tread Softly For You Tread on My Jokes, 'England, whose England'

6 It is only a step from the sublime to the ridiculous.
Napoleon I (Napoleon Bonaparte; 1769–1821) French emperor.
Remark following the retreat from Moscow, 1812
Attrib.

7 We have on our hands a sick man – a very sick man.
Nicholas I (1796–1855) Tsar of Russia.
Referring to Turkey, the 'sick man of Europe'; said to Sir G. H. Seymour, British envoy to St Petersburg, Jan 1853
Attrib.

8 Now there are fields where Troy once was.
Ovid (Publius Ovidius Naso; 43 BC–17 AD) Roman poet.
Heroides, Bk. I

9 There may have been disillusionments in the lives of the medieval saints, but they would scarcely have been better pleased if they could have foreseen that their names would be associated nowadays chiefly with racehorses and the cheaper clarets.
Saki (Hector Hugh Munro; 1870–1916) British writer.
Reginald at the Carlton

10 I shall be like that tree; I shall die from the top.
Jonathan Swift (1667–1745) Irish-born Anglican priest and writer.
Predicting his own mental decline on seeing a tree with a withered crown
Lives of the Wits (H. Pearson)

11 I dreamed there would be Spring no more,
That Nature's ancient power was lost.
Alfred, Lord Tennyson (1809–92) British poet.
In Memoriam A.H.H., LXIX

12 The difference between our decadence and the Russians' is that while theirs is brutal, ours is apathetic.
James Thurber (1894–1961) US humorist.
The Observer, 'Sayings of the Week', 5 Feb 1961

13 I started at the top and worked my way down.
Orson Welles (1915–85) US film actor.
The Filmgoer's Book of Quotes (Leslie Halliwell)

14 Plain living and high thinking are no more.
William Wordsworth (1770–1850) British poet.
Sonnets, 'O friend! I know not'

15 Milton! thou shouldst be living at this hour:
England hath need of thee; she is a fen
Of stagnant waters: altar, sword, and pen,
Fireside, the heroic wealth of hall and bower,
Have forfeited their ancient English dower
Of inward happiness.
William Wordsworth
Sonnets, 'Milton! thou shouldst'

DEFEAT

See also loss

1 'Tis better to have fought and lost,
Than never to have fought at all.
Arthur Hugh Clough (1819–61) British poet.
Peschiera

2 Of all I had, only honour and life have been spared.
Francis I (1494–1547) King of France.
Referring to his defeat at the Battle of Pavia, 24 Feb 1525; usually misquoted as 'All is lost save honour.'
Letter to Louise of Savoy (his mother), 1525

3 A man can be destroyed but not defeated.
Ernest Hemingway (1899–1961) US novelist.
The Old Man and the Sea

4 Woe to the vanquished.
Livy (Titus Livius; 59 BC–17 AD) Roman historian.
History, V:48

5 When I am dead and opened, you shall find 'Calais' lying in my heart.
Mary I (1516–58) Queen of England.
Chronicles (Holinshed), III

6 Every man meets his Waterloo at last.
Wendell Phillips (1811–84) US reformer.
Speech, Brooklyn, 1 Nov 1859

7 Well, I have one consolation, No candidate was ever elected ex-president by such a large majority!
William Howard Taft (1857–1930) US statesman.
Referring to his disastrous defeat in the 1912 presidential election
Attrib.

8 It is the beginning of the end.
Talleyrand (Charles Maurice de Talleyrand-Périgord; 1754–1838) French politician.
Referring to Napoleon's defeat at Borodino, 1813
Attrib.

9 Another year! – another deadly blow!
Another mighty empire overthrown!
And we are left, or shall be left, alone.
William Wordsworth (1770–1850) British poet.
Napoleon defeated Prussia at the Battles of Jena and Anerstädt, 14 Oct 1806
Sonnets, 'Another year!'

DELUSION

1 But yet the light that led astray
Was light from Heaven.
Robert Burns (1759–96) Scottish poet.
The Vision

2 Take care, your worship, those things over there are not giants but windmills.
Miguel de Cervantes (1547–1616) Spanish novelist.
Don Quixote, Pt. I, Ch. 8

3 Didn't I tell you, Don Quixote, sir, to turn back, for they were not armies you were going to attack, but flocks of sheep?
Miguel de Cervantes
Don Quixote, Pt. I, Ch. 18

4 Take the life-lie away from the average man and straight away you take away his happiness.
Henrik Ibsen (1828–1906) Norwegian dramatist.
The Wild Duck, V

5 Many people have delusions of grandeur but you're deluded by triviality.
Eugène Ionesco (1912–) French dramatist.
Exit the King

DEMOCRACY

See also class, government, majority, public, republic

1 Democracy means government by discussion but it is only effective if you can stop people talking.
Clement Attlee (1883–1967) British statesman and Labour prime minister.
Anatomy of Britain (Anthony Sampson)

2 One man shall have one vote.
John Cartwright (1740–1824) British writer.
People's Barrier Against Undue Influence

3 Democracy means government by the uneducated, while aristocracy means government by the badly educated.
G. K. Chesterton (1874–1936) British writer.
New York Times, 1 Feb 1931

4 Some comrades apparently find it hard to understand that democracy is just a slogan.
Mikhail Gorbachov (1931–) Soviet statesman.
The Observer, 'Sayings of the Week', 1 Feb 1987

5 Democracy is only an experiment in government, and it has the obvious disadvantage of merely counting votes instead of weighing them.
Dean Inge (1860–1954) British churchman.
Possible Recovery?

6 No man is good enough to govern another man without that other's consent.
Abraham Lincoln (1809–65) US statesman.
Speech, 1854

7 The ballot is stronger than the bullet.
Abraham Lincoln
Speech, 19 May 1856

8 This country, with its institutions, belongs to the people who inhabit it. Whenever they shall grow weary of the existing government, they can exercise their constitutional right of amending it, or their revolutionary right to dismember or overthrow it.
Abraham Lincoln
First Inaugural Address, 4 Mar 1861

9 . . . that government of the people, by the people, and for the people, shall not perish from the earth.
Abraham Lincoln
Speech, 19 Nov 1863, dedicating the national cemetery on the site of the Battle of Gettesburg

10 Man's capacity for evil makes democracy necessary and man's capacity for good makes democracy possible.
Reinhold Niebuhr (1892–) US churchman.
Quoted by Anthony Wedgwood Benn in *The Times*, 18 Jul 1977

11 Democracy passes into despotism.
Plato (429–347 BC) Greek philosopher.
Republic, Bk. 8

12 I think if the people of this country can be reached with the truth, their judgment will be in favor of the many, as against the privileged few.
Eleanor Roosevelt (1884–1962) US writer and lecturer.
Ladies' Home Journal

13 We must be the great arsenal of democracy.
Franklin D. Roosevelt (1882–1945) US Democratic president.
Broadcast address to Forum on Current Problems, 29 Dec 1940

14 We must be thoroughly democratic and patronise everybody without distinction of class.
George Bernard Shaw (1856–1950) Irish dramatist and critic.
John Bull's Other Island

15 It's not the voting that's democracy; it's the counting.
Tom Stoppard (1937–) Czech-born British dramatist.
Jumpers

16 I shall not vote because I do not aspire to advise my sovereign on the choice of her servants.
Evelyn Waugh (1903–66) British novelist.
A Little Order

17 Democracy means simply the bludgeoning of the people by the people for the people.
Oscar Wilde (1854–1900) Irish-born British dramatist.
The Soul of Man under Socialism

18 The world must be made safe for democracy.
Woodrow Wilson (1856–1925) US statesman.
Address to Congress, asking for a declaration of war 2 Apr 1917

DENIAL

1 I am the spirit that always denies.
Goethe (1749–1832) German poet and dramatist.
Faust, Pt. I

2 No, I am no one's contemporary – ever. That would have been above my station . . . How I loathe that other with my name. He certainly never was me.
Osip Mandelstam (1891–1938) Russian poet.
Poems, No. 141

3 I am not a crook.
Richard Milhous Nixon (1913–) US president.
Attrib., 17 Nov 1973

4 He would, wouldn't he?
Mandy Rice-Davies (1944–) British call girl.
Of Lord Astor, when told that he had repudiated her evidence at the trial of Stephen Ward, 29 June 1963

DEPARTURE

See also dismissal, parting

1 Come, dear children, let us away;
Down and away below.
Matthew Arnold (1822–88) British poet and critic.
The Forsaken Merman

2 She left lonely for ever
The kings of the sea.
Matthew Arnold
The Forsaken Merman

3 Adieu, adieu! my native shore
Fades o'er the waters blue.
Lord Byron (1788–1824) British poet.
Childe Harold's Pilgrimage, I

4 My native Land – Good Night!
Lord Byron
Childe Harold's Pilgrimage, I

5 Let us go then, you and I,
When the evening is spread out against the sky
Like a patient etherized upon a table.
T. S. Eliot (1888–1965) US-born British poet and
dramatist.
The Love Song of J. Alfred Prufrock

6 And they are gone: aye, ages long ago
These lovers fled away into the storm.
John Keats (1795–1821) British poet.
The Eve of Saint Agnes, XLII

7 She's leaving home after living alone for so
many years.
John Lennon (1940–80) British rock musician.
She's Leaving Home (with Paul McCartney)

DESIRE

See also hunger, lust, thirst

1 Those who restrain Desire, do so because
theirs is weak enough to be restrained.
William Blake (1757–1827) British poet.
The Marriage of Heaven and Hell, 'Those who restrain Desire
. . .'

2 Sooner murder an infant in its cradle than
nurse unacted desires.
William Blake
The Marriage of Heaven and Hell, 'Proverbs of Hell'

3 Man's Desires are limited by his Perceptions;
none can desire what he has not perceived.
William Blake
There is no Natural Religion

4 A sight to dream of, not to tell!
Samuel Taylor Coleridge (1772–1834) British poet.
Christabel, I

5 O, she is the antidote to desire.
William Congreve (1670–1729) British Restoration
dramatist.
The Way of the World, IV:14

6 Someday I'll wish upon a star.
E. Y. Harburg (1896–1981) US songwriter.
From the musical *The Wizard of Oz*
Over the Rainbow

7 Somewhere over the rainbow,

Way up high:
There's a land that I heard of
Once in a lullaby.
E. Y. Harburg
From the musical *The Wizard of Oz*
Over the Rainbow

8 Ship me somewheres east of Suez, where
the best is like the worst,
Where there aren't no Ten Commandments,
an' a man can raise a thirst:
For the temple-bells are callin', an' it's there
that I would be –
By the old Moulmein Pagoda, looking lazy at
the sea.
Rudyard Kipling (1865–1936) Indian-born British writer.
The Road to Mandalay

9 All I want is a room somewhere,
Far away from the cold night air;
With one enormous chair . . .
Oh, wouldn't it be loverly?
Alan Jay Lerner (1918–86) US songwriter.
My Fair Lady, I:1

10 There is wishful thinking in Hell as well as on
earth.
C. S. Lewis (1898–1963) British academic and writer.
The Screwtape Letters, Preface

11 There is nothing like desire for preventing
the thing one says from bearing any
resemblance to what one has in mind.
Marcel Proust (1871–1922) French novelist.
À la recherche du temps perdu: Le Côté de Guermantes

12 Appetite comes with eating.
François Rabelais (1483–1553) French satirist.
Gargantua, Bk. I, Ch. 5

13 That she belov'd knows nought that knows
not this:
Men prize the thing ungain'd more than it is.
William Shakespeare (1564–1616) English dramatist.
Troilus and Cressida, I:2

14 There are two tragedies in life. One is to
lose your heart's desire. The other is to gain
it.
George Bernard Shaw (1856–1950) Irish dramatist and
critic.
Man and Superman, IV

15 Desire is the very essence of man.
Benedict Spinoza (Baruch de Spinoza; 1632–77) Dutch
philosopher.
Ethics

16 And pluck till time and times are done
The silver apples of the moon
The golden apples of the sun.
W. B. Yeats (1865–1939) Irish poet.
The Song of Wandering Aengus

DESPAIR

See also sorrow

1 And about the ninth hour Jesus cried with a

loud voice, saying, Eli, Eli, lama sabachthani?
that is to say, My God, my God, why hast
thou forsaken me?
Bible: Matthew
27:46

2 The name of the slough was Despond.
John Bunyan (1628–88) English writer.
The Pilgrim's Progress, Pt. I

3 A castle called Doubting Castle, the owner
whereof was Giant Despair.
John Bunyan
The Pilgrim's Progress, Pt. I

4 Not, I'll not, carrion comfort, Despair, not
feast on thee;
Not untwist – slack they may be – these last
strands of man
In me or, most weary, cry *I can no more.* I
can;
Can something, hope, wish day come, not
choose not to be.
Gerard Manley Hopkins (1844–99) British Jesuit and
poet.
Carrion Comfort

5 Don't despair, not even over the fact that
you don't despair.
Franz Kafka (1883–1924) Czech novelist.
Diary

6 The mass of men lead lives of quiet
desperation.
Henry David Thoreau (1817–62) US writer.
Walden, 'Economy'

DESTINY

See also purpose

1 What must be, must be.
Proverb

2 Whatever may happen to you was prepared
for you from all eternity; and the implication
of causes was from eternity spinning the
thread of your being.
Marcus Aurelius (121–180 AD) Roman emperor.
Meditations, Bk. X, Ch. 5

3 Everything that happens happens as it
should, and if you observe carefully, you will
find this to be so.
Marcus Aurelius
Meditations, Bk. IV, Ch. 10

4 I felt as if I were walking with destiny, and
that all my past life had been but a
preparation for this hour and this trial.
Winston Churchill (1874–1965) British statesman.
The Gathering Storm, Ch. 38

5 Which brings me to my conclusion upon Free
Will and Predestination, namely – let the
reader mark it – that they are identical.
Winston Churchill
My Early Life, Ch. 3

6 'Tis all a Chequer-board of Nights and Days
Where Destiny with Men for Pieces plays:
Hither and thither moves, and mates, and
slays,
And one by one back in the Closet lays.
Edward Fitzgerald (1809–83) British poet.
The Rubáiyát of Omar Khayyám, XLIX

7 The Moving Finger writes; and, having writ,
Moves on: nor all thy Piety nor Wit
Shall lure it back to cancel half a Line,
Nor all thy Tears wash out a Word of it.
Edward Fitzgerald
The Rubáiyát of Omar Khayyám, LI

8 And that inverted Bowl we call The Sky,
Whereunder crawling coop't we live and die,
Lift not thy hands to *It* for help – for It
Rolls impotently on as Thou or I.
Edward Fitzgerald
The Rubáiyát of Omar Khayyám, LII

9 Drink! for you know not whence you came,
nor why:
Drink! for you know not why you go, nor
where.
Edward Fitzgerald
The Rubáiyát of Omar Khayyám, LXXIV

10 Tempt not the stars, young man, thou canst
not play
With the severity of fate.
John Ford (c. 1586–c. 1640) English dramatist.
The Broken Heart, I:3

11 I go the way that Providence dictates with
the assurance of a sleepwalker.
Adolf Hitler (1889–1945) German dictator.
Referring to his successful re-occupation of the Rhineland, de-
spite advice against the attempt
Speech, Munich, 15 Mar 1936

12 Do not try to find out – we're forbidden to
know – what end the gods have in store for
me, or for you.
Horace (Quintus Horatius Flaccus; 65–8 BC) Roman poet.
Odes, I

13 Who can foretell for what high cause
This darling of the Gods was born?
Andrew Marvell (1621–78) English poet.
The Picture of Little T.C. in a Prospect of Flowers

14 And yet the order of the acts is planned,
The way's end destinate and unconcealed.
Alone. Now is the time of Pharisees.
To live is not like walking through a field.
Boris Pasternak (1890–1960) Russian Jewish poet and
novelist.
Hamlet (trans. Henry Kamen)

15 We may become the makers of our fate
when we have ceased to pose as its
prophets.
Karl Popper (1902–) Austrian-born British philosopher.
The Observer, 28 Dec 1975

16 Man never found the deities so kindly

As to assure him that he'd live tomorrow.
François Rabelais (1483–1553) French satirist.
Pantagruel, Bk. III, Ch. 2

17 There's a divinity that shapes our ends,
Rough-hew them how we will.
William Shakespeare (1564–1616) English dramatist.
Hamlet, V:2

18 As flies to wanton boys are we to th' gods –
They kill us for their sport.
William Shakespeare
King Lear, IV:1

19 The ancient saying is no heresy:
Hanging and wiving goes by destiny.
William Shakespeare
The Merchant of Venice, II:9

20 One God, one law, one element,
And one far-off divine event,
To which the whole creation moves.
Alfred, Lord Tennyson (1809–92) British poet.
In Memoriam A.H.H., CXXXI

21 I embrace the purpose of God and the doom assigned.
Alfred, Lord Tennyson
Maud, III

22 We are merely the stars' tennis-balls, struck and bandied
Which way please them.
John Webster (1580–1625) English dramatist.
The Duchess of Malfi, V:4

23 Every bullet has its billet.
William III (1650–1702) King of England.
Journal (John Wesley), 6 June 1765

DETERMINATION

See also endurance, inflexibility, persistence, stubbornness

1 He who hesitates is lost.
Proverb

2 Where there's a will there's a way.
Proverb

3 There is no such thing as a great talent without great will-power.
Honoré de Balzac (1799–1850) French novelist.
La Muse du département

4 Let us determine to die here, and we will conquer.
There is Jackson standing like a stone wall.
Rally behind the Virginians.
Barnard Elliot Bee (1824–61) US soldier.
Said at the First Battle of Bull Run, 1861; hence Gen Thomas Jackson's nickname, 'Stonewall Jackson'
Reminiscences of Metropolis (Poore), II

5 We will not go to Canossa.
Bismarck (1815–98) German statesman.
A declaration of his anti-Roman Catholic policy; the Emperor Henry IV had submitted to Pope Gregory VII at Canossa, N. Italy, in 1077
Speech, Reichstag, 14 May 1872

6 The spirit burning but unbent,
May writhe, rebel – the weak alone repent!
Lord Byron (1788–1824) British poet.
The Corsair, II

7 I purpose to fight it out on this line, if it takes all summer.
Ulysses Simpson Grant (1822–85) US general.
Dispatch to Washington, 11 May 1864

8 I will be conquered; I will not capitulate.
Samuel Johnson (1709–84) British lexicographer.
Referring to his illness
Life of Johnson (J. Boswell), Vol. IV

9 I have not yet begun to fight.
John Paul Jones (1747–92) Scottish-born US naval commander.
Retort when informed his ship was sinking
Life and Letters of J. P. Jones (De Koven), Vol. I

10 I shall return.
Douglas Macarthur (1880–1964) US general.
Message (11 Mar 1942) on leaving Corregidor in the Philippines after being dismissed by Truman

11 What though the field be lost?
All is not lost – the unconquerable will,
And study of revenge, immortal hate,
And courage never to submit or yield:
And what is else not to be overcome?
John Milton (1608–74) English poet.
Paradise Lost, Bk. I

12 Look for me by moonlight;
Watch for me by moonlight;
I'll come to thee by moonlight, though hell should bar the way!
Alfred Noyes (1880–1958) British poet.
The Highwayman

13 *Ils ne passeront pas.*
They shall not pass.
Marshal Pétain (1856–1951) French marshal.
Attrib; probably derived from General R.-G. Nivelle's Order of the Day, '*Vous ne les laissérez pas passer*' (June 1916). It is also attributed to the Spanish politician Dolores Ibarruri.

14 We are not now that strength which in old days
Moved earth and heaven; that which we are, we are;
One equal temper of heroic hearts,
Made weak by time and fate, but strong in will
To strive, to seek, to find, and not to yield.
Alfred, Lord Tennyson (1809–92) British poet.
Ulysses

DEVIL

See also damnation, hell

1 The devil is not so black as he is painted.
Proverb

2 And he said unto them, I beheld Satan as lightning fall from heaven.
Bible: Luke
10:18

3 And he asked him, What is thy name? And
he answered, saying. My name is Legion: for
we are many.
Bible: Mark
5:9

4 And there was war in heaven: Michael and
his angels fought against the dragon; and the
dragon fought and his angels,
And prevailed not; neither was their place
found any more in heaven.
And the great dragon was cast out, that old
serpent, called the Devil, and Satan, which
deceiveth the whole world: he was cast out into the earth, and his angels were cast out
with him.
Bible: Revelations
12:7-9

5 And that no man might buy or sell, save he
that had the mark, or the name of the beast,
or the number of his name.
Here is wisdom. Let him that hath understanding count the number of the beast: for it is
the number of a man; and his number is Six
hundred threescore and six.
Bible: Revelations
13:17-18

6 O Thou! Whatever title suit thee –
Auld Hornie, Satan, Nick, or Clootie.
Robert Burns (1759-96) Scottish poet.
Address to the Devil

7 Wherever God erects a house of prayer,
The Devil always builds a chapel there;
And 'twill be found, upon examination,
The latter has the largest congregation.
Daniel Defoe (1660-1731) British journalist and writer.
The True-Born Englishman, Pt. I

8 It is so stupid of modern civilization to have
given up believing in the devil when he is the
only explanation of it.
Ronald Knox (1888-1957) British Roman Catholic priest.
Let Dons Delight

9 It is no good casting out devils. They belong
to us, we must accept them and be at peace
with them.
D. H. Lawrence (1885-1930) British novelist.
Phoenix, 'The Reality of Peace'

10 High on a throne of royal state, which far
Outshone the wealth of Ormus and of Ind,
Or where the gorgeous East with richest hand
Showers on her kings barbaric pearl and gold,
Satan exalted sat, by merit raised
To that bad eminence.
John Milton (1608-74) English poet.
Paradise Lost, Bk. II

11 Sometimes
The Devil is a gentleman.
Percy Bysshe Shelley (1792-1822) British poet.
Peter Bell the Third

DIARIES

1 Let diaries, therefore, be brought in use.
Francis Bacon (1561-1626) English philosopher.
Essays, 'Of Travel'

2 Only good girls keep diaries. Bad girls don't
have the time.
Tallulah Bankhead (1903-68) US actress.
Attrib.

3 With the publication of his Private Papers in
1952, he committed suicide 25 years after his
death.
Lord Beaverbrook (1879-1964) British newspaper owner
and politician.
Referring to Earl Haig
Men and Power

4 I do not keep a diary. Never have. To write
a diary every day is like returning to one's
own vomit.
Enoch Powell (1912-) British politician.
Sunday Times, 6 Nov 1977

5 What is a diary as a rule? A document useful
to the person who keeps it, dull to the
contemporary who reads it, invaluable to the
student, centuries afterwards, who treasures
it!
Ellen Terry (1847-1928) British actress.
The Story of My Life, Ch. 14

6 I never travel without my diary. One should
always have something sensational to read in
the train.
Oscar Wilde (1854-1900) Irish-born British dramatist.
The Importance of Being Earnest, II

DICKENS

See also criticism, writers

1 We were put to Dickens as children but it
never quite took. That unremitting humanity
soon had me cheesed off.
Alan Bennett (1934-) British playwright.
The Old Country, II

2 It does not matter that Dickens' world is not
life-like; it is alive.
Lord Cecil (1902-86) British writer and critic.
Early Victorian Novelists

3 One would have to have a heart of stone to
read the death of Little Nell without laughing.
Oscar Wilde (1854-1900) Irish-born British dramatist.
Lecturing upon Dickens
Lives of the Wits (H. Pearson)

DIFFERENCE

See also individuality, opposites, similarity, taste

1 Every man after his fashion.
Proverb

2 Every one to his taste.
Proverb

3 One man's meat is another man's poison.
Proverb

4 There is more than one way to skin a cat.
Proverb

5 There is no accounting for tastes.
Proverb

6 There's nowt so queer as folk.
Proverb

7 All colours will agree in the dark.
Francis Bacon (1561–1626) English philosopher.
Essays, 'Of Unity in Religion'

8 If we cannot now end our differences, at least we can help make the world safe for diversity.
John Fitzgerald Kennedy (1917–63) US statesman.
Speech, American University (Washington, DC), 10 June 1963

DIPLOMACY

See also tact

1 It is better for aged diplomats to be bored than for young men to die.
Warren Austin (1877–1962) US politician and diplomat.
When asked if he got tired during long debates at the UN
Attrib.

2 There are three groups that no British Prime Minister should provoke: the Vatican, the Treasury and the miners.
Stanley Baldwin (1867–1947) British statesman.
A similar remark is often attributed to Harold Macmillan
Attrib.

3 An honest broker.
Bismarck (1815–98) German statesman.
His professed role in the diplomacy of 1878, including the Congress of Berlin
Speech, Reichstag, 19 Feb 1878

4 The healthy bones of a single Pomeranian grenadier.
Bismarck
A price too high for Germany to pay regarding the Eastern Question
Speech, Reichstag, 5 Dec 1876

5 To jaw-jaw is better than to war-war.
Winston Churchill (1874–1965) British statesman.
Speech, Washington, 26 June 1954

6 An appeaser is one who feeds a crocodile – hoping that it will eat him last.
Winston Churchill
Attrib.

7 When you have to kill a man it costs nothing to be polite.
Winston Churchill
Justifying the fact that the declaration of war against Japan was made in the usual diplomatic language
The Grand Alliance

8 America has all that Russia has not. Russia has things America has not. Why will America not reach out a hand to Russia, as I have given my hand?
Isadora Duncan (1878–1927) US dancer.
Speaking in support of Russia following the 1917 Revolution
Speech, Symphony Hall, Boston, 1922

9 REPORTER: If Mr Stalin dies, what will be the effect on international affairs?
EDEN: That is a good question for you to ask, not a wise question for me to answer.
Anthony Eden (1897–1977) British statesman.
Interview on board the *Queen Elizabeth*, 4 Mar 1953

10 Treaties are like roses and young girls – they last while they last.
Charles De Gaulle (1890–1970) French general and statesman.
Attrib.

11 I met the great little man, the man who can be silent in several languages.
James Guthrie Harbord (1866–1947) US general.
Referring to Colonel House
Mr Wilson's War (John Dos Passos), Ch. 3

12 Official dignity tends to increase in inverse ratio to the importance of the country in which the office is held.
Aldous Huxley (1894–1964) British novelist.
Beyond the Mexique Bay

13 The great nations have always acted like gangsters, and the small nations like prostitutes.
Stanley Kubrick (1928–) US film director.
The Guardian, 5 June 1963

14 All diplomacy is a continuation of war by other means.
Chou En Lai (1898–1976) Chinese statesman.

15 *La cordiale entente qui existe entre mon gouvernement et le sien.*
The friendly understanding that exists between my government and hers.
Louis Philippe (1773–1850) King of France.
Referring to an informal understanding reached between Britain and France in 1843. The more familiar phrase, 'entente cordiale', was first used in 1844.
Speech, 27 Dec 1843

16 The reluctant obedience of distant provinces generally costs more than it is worth.
Lord Macaulay (1800–59) British historian.
Historical Essays Contributed to the 'Edinburgh Review', 'Lord Mahon's War of the Succession'

17 Let them especially put their demands in such a way that Great Britain could say that she supported both sides.
Ramsey MacDonald (1866–1937) British statesman and prime minister.
Referring to France and Germany
The Origins of the Second World War (A. J. P. Taylor), Ch. 3

18 Austria will astound the world with the magnitude of her ingratitude.

Prince Schwarzenberg (1800–52) Austrian statesman.
On being asked whether Austria was under any obligation to Russia for help received previously
The Fall of the House of Habsburg (E. Crankshaw)

19 A diplomat these days is nothing but a head-waiter who's allowed to sit down occasionally.

Peter Ustinov (1921–) British actor and dramatist.
Romanoff and Juliet, I

20 No nation is fit to sit in judgement upon any other nation.

Woodrow Wilson (1856–1925) US statesman.
Address, Apr 1915

21 An ambassador is an honest man sent to lie abroad for the good of his country.

Henry Wotton (1568–1639) English poet and diplomat.
Life (Izaak Walton)

DISABILITY

See also blindness

1 If there are any of you at the back who do not hear me, please don't raise your hands because I am also nearsighted.

W. H. Auden (1907–73) British poet.
Starting a lecture in a large hall
In *Book of the Month Club News*, Dec 1946

2 I'm a coloured, one-eyed Jew.

Sammy Davis Jnr (1925–) Black US singer.
When asked what his handicap was during a game of golf
Attrib.

DISAPPOINTMENT

See also disillusion, expectation

1 Unhappiness is best defined as the difference between our talents and our expectations.

Edward de Bono (1933–) British physician and writer.
The Observer, 'Sayings of the Week', 12 June 1977

2 The best laid schemes o' mice an' men
Gang aft a-gley,
An' lea'e us nought but grief an' pain
For promis'd joy.

Robert Burns (1759–96) Scottish poet.
To a Mouse

3 Mountains will heave in childbirth, and a silly little mouse will be born.

Horace (Quintus Horatius Flaccus; 65–8 BC) Roman poet.
Ars Poetica

4 A mountain in labour shouted so loud that everyone, summoned by the noise, ran up expecting that she would be delivered of a city bigger than Paris; she brought forth a mouse.

Jean de La Fontaine (1621–95) French poet.
Fables, V, 'La Montagne qui accouche'

5 Levin wanted friendship and got friendliness; he wanted steak and they offered spam.

Bernard Malamud (1914–) US novelist.
A New Life, VI

6 Look in my face; my name is Might-have-been.
I am also called No-more, Too-late, Farewell.

Dante Gabriel Rossetti (1828–82) British painter and poet.
The House of Life, 'A Superscription'

7 Oh, I wish that God had not given me what I prayed for! It was not so good as I thought.

Johanna Spyri (1827–1901) Swiss writer.
Heidi, Ch. 11

8 He said that he was too old to cry, but it hurt too much to laugh.

Adlai Stevenson (1900–65) US statesman.
Said after losing an election, quoting a story told by Abraham Lincoln
Speech, 5 Nov 1952

DISASTER

See also accidents

1 Bad news travels fast.
Proverb

2 Let us hope . . . that a kind of Providence will put a speedy end to the acts of God under which we have been labouring.

Peter De Vries (1910–) US novelist.
The Mackerel Plaza, Ch. 3

3 An Act of God was defined as *something which no reasonable man could have expected.*

A. P. Herbert (1890–1971) British writer and politician.
Uncommon Law

4 Beautiful Railway Bridge of the Silv'ry Tay!
Alas, I am very sorry to say
That ninety lives have been taken away
On the last Sabbath day of 1879,
Which will be remember'd for a very long time.

William McGonagall (1830–1902) Scottish poet.
The Tay Bridge Disaster

DISCONTENT

See also envy

1 And sigh that one thing only has been lent
To youth and age in common – discontent.

Matthew Arnold (1822–88) British poet and critic.
Youth's Agitations

2 The idiot who praises, with enthusiastic tone,
All centuries but this, and every country but his own.

W. S. Gilbert (1836–1911) British dramatist.
The Mikado, I

3 So have I loitered my life away, reading books, looking at pictures, going to plays, hearing, thinking, writing on what pleased me best. I have wanted only one thing to make me happy, but wanting that have wanted everything.

William Hazlitt (1778–1830) British essayist.
English Literature, Ch. XVII, 'My First Acquaintance with Poets'

4 How is it, Maecenas, that no one lives contented with his lot, whether he has planned it for himself or fate has flung him into it, but yet he praises those who follow different paths?

Horace (Quintus Horatius Flaccus; 65–8 BC) Roman poet.
Satires, I

5 Ever let the fancy roam,
Pleasure never is at home.

John Keats (1795–1821) British poet.
Fancy, I

6 I am sick o' wastin' leather on these gritty pavin'-stones,
An' the blasted English drizzle wakes the fever in my bones;
Tho' I walks with fifty 'ousemaids outer Chelsea to the Strand,
An' they talks a lot o' lovin', but wot do they understand?
Beefy face an' grubby 'and –
Law! Wot do they understand?
I've a neater, sweeter maiden in a cleaner, greener land!

Rudyard Kipling (1865–1936) Indian-born British writer.
The Road to Mandalay

7 He disdains all things above his reach, and preferreth all countries before his own.

Thomas Overbury (1581–1613) English poet.
Miscellaneous Works, 'An Affectate Traveller'

8 When in disgrace with fortune and men's eyes
I all alone beweep my outcast state,
And trouble deaf heaven with my bootless cries,
And look upon myself, and curse my fate,
Wishing me like to one more rich in hope
Featur'd like him, like him with friends possess'd,
Desiring this man's art, and that man's scope,
With what I most enjoy contented least.

William Shakespeare (1564–1616) English dramatist.
Sonnet 29

9 While not exactly disgruntled, he was far from feeling gruntled.

P. G. Wodehouse (1881–1975) British humorous novelist.
The Code of the Woosters

10 I'd rather be
A Pagan suckled in a creed outworn;
So might I, standing on this pleasant lea,
Have glimpses that would make me less forlorn;
Have sight of Proteus rising from the sea;
Or hear Old Triton blow his wreathed horn.

William Wordsworth (1770–1850) British poet.
Sonnets, 'The world is too much with us'

DISCOVERY

See also exploration, science, space

1 *Eureka!*
I have found it!

Archimedes (c. 287–212 BC) Greek mathematician.
An exclamation of joy supposedly uttered as, stepping into a bath and noticing the water overflowing, he saw the answer to a problem and began the train of thought that led to his principle of buoyancy
Attrib.

2 Look, stranger, at this island now
The leaping light for your delight discovers.

W. H. Auden (1907–73) British poet.
Look, Stranger

3 They are ill discoverers that think there is no land, when they can see nothing but sea.

Francis Bacon (1561–1626) English philosopher.
The Advancement of Learning, Bk. II, Ch. 7

4 God could cause us considerable embarrassment by revealing all the secrets of nature to us: we should not know what to do for sheer apathy and boredom.

Goethe (1749–1832) German poet and dramatist.
Memoirs (Riemer)

5 Then felt I like some watcher of the skies
When a new planet swims into his ken;
Or like stout Cortez when with eagle eyes
He star'd at the Pacific – and all his men
Look'd at each other with a wild surmise –
Silent, upon a peak in Darien.

John Keats (1795–1821) British poet.
On first looking into Chapman's Homer

6 I do not know what I may appear to the world, but to myself I seem to have been only like a boy playing on the sea-shore, and diverting myself in now and then finding a smoother pebble or a prettier shell than ordinary, whilst the great ocean of truth lay all undiscovered before me.

Isaac Newton (1642–1727) British scientist.
Isaac Newton (L. T. More)

7 The people – could you patent the sun?

Jonas E. Salk (1914–) US virologist.
On being asked who owned the patent on his polio vaccine
Famous Men of Science (S. Bolton)

8 Discovery consists of seeing what everybody has seen and thinking what nobody has thought.

Albert Szent-Györgyi (1893–) Hungarian-born US biochemist.
The Scientist Speculates (I. J. Good)

DISILLUSION

See also disappointment, innocence of childhood

1 The price one pays for pursuing any

profession or calling is an intimate knowledge of its ugly side.
James Baldwin (1924–87) US writer.
Nobody Knows My Name

2   If you live long enough, you'll see that every victory turns into a defeat.
Simone de Beauvoir (1908–86) French writer.
Tous les hommes sont mortels

3   The coach has turned into a pumpkin and the mice have all run away.
Ladybird Johnson (1912–   ) Wife of Lyndon B. Johnson.
Said after Lyndon Johnson gave up the presidency
The Vantage Point (Lyndon B. Johnson)

4   I have protracted my work till most of those whom I wished to please have sunk into the grave; and success and miscarriage are empty sounds.
Samuel Johnson (1709–84) British lexicographer.
Dictionary of the English Language

5   One stops being a child when one realizes that telling one's trouble does not make it better.
Cesare Pavese (1908–50) Italian novelist and poet.
The Business of Living: Diaries 1935–50

DISMISSAL

See also departure

1   You have sat too long here for any good you have been doing. Depart, I say, and let us have done with you. In the name of God, *go!*
Leopold Amery (1873–1955) British statesman.
Said to Neville Chamberlain using Cromwell's words
Speech, House of Commons, May 1940

2   You have delighted us long enough.
Jane Austen (1775–1817) British novelist.
Pride and Prejudice, Ch. 18

3   It is not fit that you should sit here any longer! . . . you shall now give place to better men.
Oliver Cromwell (1599–1658) English soldier and statesman.
Speech to the Rump Parliament, 22 Jan 1655

4   Take away that fool's bauble, the mace.
Oliver Cromwell
Speech dismissing Parliament, 20 Apr 1653

5   Go, and never darken my towels again!
Groucho Marx (Julius Marx; 1895–1977) US comedian.
Duck Soup

6   There comes a time in every man's life when he must make way for an older man.
Reginald Maudling (1917–77) British politician.
Remark made on being replaced in the shadow cabinet by John Davies, his elder by four years
The Guardian, 20 Nov 1976

7   We Don't Want To Lose You But We Think You Ought To Go.
Paul Alfred Rubens (1875–1917) British dramatist and songwriter.
Title of song

8   Stand not upon the order of your going,
But go at once.
William Shakespeare (1564–1616) English dramatist.
Macbeth, III:4

9   Dropping the pilot.
John Tenniel (1820–1914) British illustrator and cartoonist.
Caption of a cartoon. The cartoon refers to Bismarck's resignation portraying him as a ship's pilot walking down the gangway of the ship while Wilhelm II watches from the deck.
Punch, 29 Mar 1890

DOCTORS

See also health, illness, medicine, remedies

1   I am dying with the help of too many physicians.
Alexander the Great (356–323 BC) King of Macedon.
Attrib.

2   And he said unto them, Ye will surely say unto me this proverb, Physician, heal thyself: whatsoever we have heard done in Capernaum, do also here in thy country.
Bible: Luke
4:23

3   The doctor found, when she was dead,
Her last disorder mortal.
Oliver Goldsmith (1728–74) Irish-born British writer.
Elegy on Mrs. Mary Blaize

4   I suppose one has a greater sense of intellectual degradation after an interview with a doctor than from any human experience.
Alice James (1848–92) US diarist.
The Diary of Alice James (ed. Leon Edel), 27 Sept 1890

5   It is incident to physicians, I am afraid, beyond all other men, to mistake subsequence for consequence.
Samuel Johnson (1709–84) British lexicographer.
Life of Johnson (J. Boswell), Vol. I

6   Who shall decide when doctors disagree?
Alexander Pope (1688–1744) British poet.
Moral Essays, III

7   Cur'd yesterday of my disease,
I died last night of my physician.
Matthew Prior (1664–1721) British poet.
The Remedy Worse than the Disease

8   First they get *on*, then they get *honour*, then they get *honest*.
Humphrey Rolleston (1862–1944) British physician.
Referring to physicians
Confessions of an Advertising Man (David Ogilvy)

9 Physicians are like kings, – they brook no contradiction.
John Webster (1580–1625) English dramatist.
The Duchess of Malfi, V:2

DOGS

See also animals

1 A huge dog, tied by a chain, was painted on the wall and over it was written in capital letters 'Beware of the dog.'
Petronius Arbiter (1st century AD) Roman satirist.
Latin, *Cave canem*
Satyricon: Cena Trimalchionis, 29

2 The woman who is really kind to dogs is always one who has failed to inspire sympathy in men.
Max Beerbohm (1872–1956) British writer.
Zuleika Dobson

3 It's the one species I wouldn't mind seeing vanish from the face of the earth. I wish they were like the White Rhino – six of them left in the Serengeti National Park, and all males.
Alan Bennett (1934–) British playwright.
Referring to dogs
Getting On, I

4 The great pleasure of a dog is that you may make a fool of yourself with him and not only will he not scold you, he will make a fool of himself too.
Samuel Butler (1835–1902) British writer.
Notebooks

5 'Tis sweet to hear the watch-dog's honest bark
Bay deep-mouthed welcome as we draw near home;
'Tis sweet to know there is an eye will mark
Our coming, and look brighter when we come.
Lord Byron (1788–1824) British poet.
Don Juan, I

6 Anybody who hates children and dogs can't be all bad.
W. C. Fields (1880–1946) US actor.
Attrib.

7 The dog, to gain some private ends,
Went mad and bit the man.
Oliver Goldsmith (1728–74) Irish-born British writer.
Elegy on the Death of a Mad Dog

8 The man recovered of the bite,
The dog it was that died.
Oliver Goldsmith
Elegy on the Death of a Mad Dog

9 Stop running those dogs on your page. I wouldn't have them peeing on my cheapest rug.
William Randolph Hearst (1863–1951) US newspaper owner.
Referring to the publication of Thurber's drawings by one of his editors
The Years with Ross (James Thurber)

10 A door is what a dog is perpetually on the wrong side of.
Ogden Nash (1902–71) US poet.
A Dog's Best Friend Is His Illiteracy

11 I am His Highness' dog at Kew;
Pray tell me sir, whose dog are you?
Alexander Pope (1688–1744) British poet.
On the collar of a dog given to Frederick, Prince of Wales

12 That indefatigable and unsavoury engine of pollution, the dog.
John Sparrow (1906–) British lawyer and academic.
Letter to *The Times*, 30 Sep 1975

13 I loathe people who keep dogs. They are cowards who haven't got the guts to bite people themselves.
August Strindberg (1849–1912) Swedish dramatist.
A Madman's Diary

14 Daddy wouldn't buy me a bow-wow, bow-wow.
I've got a little cat
And I'm very fond of that.
Joseph Tabrar (20th century) US songwriter.
Daddy Wouldn't Buy Me A Bow-wow (song)

DOOMSDAY

1 That at what time ye hear the sound of the cornet, flute, harp, sackbut, psaltery, dulcimer, and all kinds of musick, ye fall down and worship the golden image that Nebuchadnezzar the king hath set up:
And whoso falleth not down and worshippeth shall the same hour be cast into the midst of a burning fiery furnace.
Bible: Daniel
3:5–6

2 Immediately after the tribulation of those days shall the sun be darkened, and the moon shall not give her light, and the stars shall fall from heaven, and the powers of the heavens shall be shaken:
And then shall appear the sign of the Son of man in heaven: and then shall all the tribes of the earth mourn, and they shall see the Son of man coming in the clouds of heaven with power and great glory.
And he shall send his angels with a great sound of a trumpet, and they shall gather together his elect from the four winds, from one end of heaven to the other.
Bible: Matthew
24:29–31

3 'Tis the Last Judgment's fire must cure this place,
Calcine its clods and set my prisoners free.
Robert Browning (1812–89) British poet.
Childe Roland to the Dark Tower Came, XI

4 Don't wait for the Last Judgement. It takes place every day.
Albert Camus (1913–60) French existentialist writer.
The Fall

5 When all the world dissolves,
And every creature shall be purified,
All place shall be hell that is not heaven.
Christopher Marlowe (1564–93) English dramatist.
Doctor Faustus, II:1

DOUBLETHINK

See also conflict, opposites

1 War is Peace, Freedom is Slavery, Ignorance is Strength.
George Orwell (Eric Blair; 1903–50) British novelist.
Nineteen Eighty-Four

2 Doublethink means the power of holding two contradictory beliefs in one's mind simultaneously, and accepting both of them.
George Orwell
Nineteen Eighty-Four

DOUBT

See also scepticism, uncertainty

1 If a man will begin with certainties, he shall end in doubts, but if he will be content to begin with doubts, he shall end in certainties.
Francis Bacon (1561–1626) English philosopher.
The Advancement of Learning, Bk. I, Ch. 5

2 And immediately Jesus stretched forth his hand, and caught him, and said unto him, O thou of little faith, wherefore didst thou doubt?
Bible: Matthew
14:31

3 He who shall teach the child to doubt
The rotting grave shall ne'er get out.
William Blake (1757–1827) British poet.
Auguries of Innocence

4 All we have gained then by our unbelief
Is a life of doubt diversified by faith,
For one of faith diversified by doubt:
We called the chess-board white, – we call it black.
Robert Browning (1812–89) British poet.
Bishop Blougram's Apology

5 His doubts are better than most people's certainties.
Lord Hardwicke (1690–1764) English judge.
Referring to Dirleton's *Doubts*
Life of Johnson (J. Boswell)

6 Negative Capability, that is, when a man is capable of being in uncertainties, mysteries, doubts, without any irritable reaching after fact and reason.
John Keats (1795–1821) British poet.
Letter to G. and T. Keats, 21 Dec 1817

7 The trouble with the world is that the stupid are cocksure and the intelligent full of doubt.
Bertrand Russell (1872–1970) British philosopher.
Autobiography

8 Those obstinate questionings
Of sense and outward things,
Fallings from us, vanishings;
Blank misgivings of a Creature
Moving about in worlds not realised,
High instincts before which our mortal nature
Did tremble like a guilty thing surprised.
William Wordsworth (1770–1850) British poet.
Ode. Intimations of Immortality, IX

DREAMS

1 Dreams and predictions ought to serve but for winter talk by the fireside.
Francis Bacon (1561–1626) English philosopher.
Essays, 'Of Prophecies'

2 It was a dream of perfect bliss,
Too beautiful to last.
Thomas Haynes Bayly (1797–1839) British writer.
It was a Dream

3 So I awoke, and behold it was a dream.
John Bunyan (1628–88) English writer.
The Pilgrim's Progress, Pt. I

4 I do not know whether I was then a man dreaming I was a butterfly, or whether I am now a butterfly dreaming I am a man.
Chuang Tse (*or* Zhuangzi; c. 369–286 BC) Chinese philosopher.
Chuang Tse (H. A. Giles), Ch. 2

5 The people's prayer, the glad diviner's theme,
The young men's vision, and the old men's dream!
John Dryden (1631–1700) British poet and dramatist.
Absalom and Achitophel, I

6 Last night I dreamt I went to Manderley again.
Daphne Du Maurier (1907–) British novelist.
Rebecca, Ch. 1

7 Underneath the arches
We dream our dreams away.
Bud Flanagan (Robert Winthrop; 1896–1968) British comedian.
Underneath the Arches

8 Castles in the air – they're so easy to take refuge in. So easy to build, too.
Henrik Ibsen (1828–1906) Norwegian dramatist.
The Master Builder, III

9 Alas, all the castles I have, are built with air, thou know'st.
Ben Jonson (1573–1637) English dramatist.
Eastward Ho, II:2

10 All men dream: but not equally. Those who dream by night in the dusty recesses of their minds wake in the day to find that it was vanity: but the dreamers of the day are dangerous men, for they may act their dream with open eyes, to make it possible.

T. E. Lawrence (1888–1935) British soldier and writer.
Seven Pillars of Wisdom, Ch. 1

11 Abou Ben Adhem (may his tribe increase!)
Awoke one night from a deep dream of peace,
And saw, within the moonlight in his room,
Making it rich, and like a lily in bloom,
An angel writing in a book of gold: – . . .

Leigh Hunt (1784–1859) British poet.
Abou Ben Adhem and the Angel

12 Many's the long night I've dreamed of cheese
– toasted, mostly.

Robert Louis Stevenson (1850–94) Scottish writer.
Treasure Island, Ch. 15

13 Dreams are true while they last, and do we not live in dreams?

Alfred, Lord Tennyson (1809–92) British poet.
The Higher Pantheism

14 I have spread my dreams under your feet.
Tread softly because you tread on my dreams.

W. B. Yeats (1865–1939) Irish poet.
He wishes For The Cloths of Heaven

DRINKS

See also alcohol, drunkenness, water

1 The infusion of a China plant sweetened with the pith of an Indian cane.

Joseph Addison (1672–1719) British essayist.
The Spectator, 69

2 I the Trinity illustrate,
Drinking watered orange-pulp –
In three sips the Arian frustrate;
While he drains his at one gulp.

Robert Browning (1812–89) British poet.
Soliloquy of the Spanish Cloister

3 I am willing to taste any drink once.

James Cabell (1879–1958) US novelist and journalist.
Jurgen, Ch. 1

4 While the bubbling and loud-hissing urn
Throws up a steamy column, and the cups,
That cheer but not inebriate, wait on each,
So let us welcome peaceful evening in.

William Cowper (1731–1800) British poet.
The Task

5 Tea for Two, and Two for Tea.

Otto Harback (1873–1963) US dramatist.
From the musical *No! No! Nanette*
Song title

6 Coffee which makes the politician wise,
And see through all things with his half-shut eyes.

Alexander Pope (1688–1744) British poet.
The Rape of the Lock, III

7 Here thou great Anna! whom three realms obey,

Dost sometimes counsel take – and sometimes Tea.

Alexander Pope
The Rape of the Lock, III

8 Our trouble is that we drink too much tea. I see in this the slow revenge of the Orient, which has diverted the Yellow River down our throats.

J. B. Priestley (1894–1984) British novelist.
The Observer, 'Sayings of the Week', 15 May 1949

9 I think it must be so, for I have been drinking it for sixty-five years and I am not dead yet.

Voltaire (François-Marie Arouet; 1694–1778) French writer.
On learning that coffee was considered a slow poison
Attrib.

DROWNING

See also death

1 The western tide crept up along the sand,
And o'er and o'er the sand,
And round and round the sand,
As far as eye could see.
The rolling mist came down and hid the land:
And never home came she.

Charles Kingsley (1819–75) British writer.
The Sands of Dee

2 O Lord, methought what pain it was to drown,
What dreadful noise of waters in my ears,
What sights of ugly death within my eyes!

William Shakespeare (1564–1616) English dramatist.
Richard III, I:4

3 Nobody heard him, the dead man,
But still he lay moaning:
I was much further out than you thought
And not waving but drowning.

Stevie Smith (Florence Margaret Smith; 1902–71) British poet.
Not Waving But Drowning

DRUNKENNESS

See also alcohol

1 There are more old drunkards than old doctors.

Proverb

2 His mouth has been used as a latrine by some small animal of the night.

Kingsley Amis (1922–) British novelist.
Describing a hangover
Lucky Jim

3 Come landlord, fill the flowing bowl,
Until it doth run over . . .
For tonight we'll merry, merry be,
Tomorrow we'll be sober.

Anonymous
Come, Landlord, Fill the Flowing Bowl

4 What shall we do with the drunken sailor
Early in the morning?
Hoo-ray and up she rises
Early in the morning.
Anonymous
What shall we do with the Drunken Sailor?

5 Ha, ha, ha, you and me,
Little brown jug, don't I love thee!
Anonymous
The Little Brown Jug

6 One reason I don't drink is that I want to
know when I am having a good time.
Nancy Astor (1879–1964) American-born British politician.
Attrib.

7 For when the wine is in, the wit is out.
Thomas Becon (1512–67) English Protestant churchman.
Catechism, 375

8 Others mocking said, These men are full of
new wine.
Bible: Acts
2:13

9 Wine is a mocker, strong drink is raging: and
whosoever is deceived thereby is not wise.
Bible: Proverbs
20:1

10 Man, being reasonable, must get drunk;
The best of life is but intoxication.
Lord Byron (1788–1824) British poet.
Don Juan, II

11 It's my opinion, sir, that this meeting is
drunk.
Charles Dickens (1812–70) British novelist.
Pickwick Papers, Ch. 33

12 I am as sober as a Judge.
Henry Fielding (1707–54) British novelist.
Don Quixote in England, III:14

13 If merely 'feeling good' could decide,
drunkenness would be the supremely valid
human experience.
William James (1842–1910) US psychologist and
philosopher.
Varieties of Religious Experience

14 A branch of the sin of drunkenness, which is
the root of all sins.
James I (1566–1625) King of England.
A Counterblast to Tobacco

15 A man who exposes himself when he is
intoxicated, has not the art of getting drunk.
Samuel Johnson (1709–84) British lexicographer.
Life of Johnson (J. Boswell), Vol. III

16 Better sleep with a sober cannibal than a
drunken Christian.
Herman Melville (1819–91) US novelist.
Moby Dick, Ch. 3

17 I am as drunk as a lord, but then, I am one,
so what does it matter?
Bertrand Russell (1872–1970) British philosopher.
Bertrand Russell, Philosopher of the Century (Ralph
Schoenman)

18 No, thank you, I was born intoxicated.
George William Russell (1867–1935) Irish poet and
dramatist.
Refusing a drink that was offered him
10,000 Jokes, Toasts, and Stories (L. Copeland)

19 But I'm not so think as you drunk I am.
John Collings Squire (1884–1958) British journalist.
Ballade of Soporific Absorption

20 Come, Robert, you shall drink twice while I
drink once, for I cannot permit the son in his
sober senses to witness the intoxication of
his father.
Horace Walpole (1717–97) British writer.
Explaining why he filled his son's glass twice for every glass he
drank himself
Attrib.

DULLNESS

See also boredom, stupidity

1 He'd be sharper than a serpent's tooth, if he
wasn't as dull as ditch water.
Charles Dickens (1812–70) British novelist.
Our Mutual Friend, Bk. III, Ch. 10

2 He is not only dull in himself, but the cause
of dullness in others.
Samuel Foote (1720–77) British actor and dramatist.
Parody of a line from Shakespeare's *Henry IV, Part 2*
Life of Johnson (J. Boswell)

DUTY

See also obligation

1 From a very early age, I had imbibed the
opinion, that it was every man's duty to do
all that lay in his power to leave his country
as good as he had found it.
William Cobbett (1763–1835) British journalist and writer.
Political Register, 22 Dec 1832

2 Do your duty and leave the rest to the Gods.
Pierre Corneille (1606–84) French dramatist.
Horace, II:8

3 England expects every man will do his duty.
Lord Nelson (1758–1805) British admiral.
Signal hoisted prior to the Battle of Trafalgar, 1805

4 When a stupid man is doing something he is
ashamed of, he always declares that it is his
duty.
George Bernard Shaw (1856–1950) Irish dramatist and
critic.
Caesar and Cleopatra, III

5 Sunset and evening star,
And one clear call for me!
And may there be no moaning of the bar

When I put out to sea.
Alfred, Lord Tennyson (1809–92) British poet.
Crossing the Bar

E

ECOLOGY

See also environment

1 Over increasingly large areas of the United States, spring now comes unheralded by the return of the birds, and the early mornings are strangely silent where once they were filled with the beauty of bird song.
Rachel Carson (1907–64) US biologist.
The Silent Spring

2 As cruel a weapon as the cave man's club, the chemical barrage has been hurled against the fabric of life.
Rachel Carson
The Silent Spring

3 Man has been endowed with reason, with the power to create, so that he can add to what he's been given. But up to now he hasn't been a creator, only a destroyer. Forests keep disappearing, rivers dry up, wild life's become extinct, the climate's ruined and the land grows poorer and uglier every day.
Anton Chekhov (1860–1904) Russian dramatist.
Uncle Vanya, I

4 It will be said of this generation that it found England a land of beauty and left it a land of beauty spots.
Cyril Joad (1891–1953) British writer and broadcaster.
The Observer, 'Sayings of Our Times', 31 May 1953

5 We are living beyond our means. As a people we have developed a life-style that is draining the earth of its priceless and irreplaceable resources without regard for the future of our children and people all around the world.
Margaret Mead (1901–78) US anthropologist.
Redbook, 'The Energy Crisis – Why Our World Will Never Again Be the Same.'

6 We are wealthy and wasteful but this can't go on. If we don't eat dog biscuits, we could end up eating our dog instead.
Magnus Pyke (1908–) British scientist, television personality, and writer.
The Observer, 'Sayings of the Week', 12 Jan 1975

ECONOMICS

1 Don't spoil the ship for a ha'porth of tar.
Proverb

2 John Stuart Mill
By a mighty effort of will
Overcame his natural bonhomie
And wrote 'Principles of Political Economy'.
Edmund Clerihew Bentley (1875–1956) British writer.
Biography for Beginners

3 Respectable Professors of the Dismal Science.
Thomas Carlyle (1795–1881) Scottish historian and essayist.
Referring to economists
Latter-Day Pamphlets, 1

4 Provided that the City of London remains as at present, the Clearing-house of the World.
Joseph Chamberlain (1836–1914) British politician.
Speech, Guildhall, London, 19 Jan 1904

5 Annual income twenty pounds, annual expenditure nineteen nineteen six, result happiness. Annual income twenty pounds, annual expenditure twenty pounds ought and six, result misery.
Charles Dickens (1812–70) British novelist.
David Copperfield, Ch. 12

6 When every blessed thing you hold
Is made of silver, or of gold,
You long for simple pewter.
When you have nothing else to wear
But cloth of gold and satins rare,
For cloth of gold you cease to care –
Up goes the price of shoddy.
W. S. Gilbert (1836–1911) British dramatist.
The Gondoliers, 1

7 I will not be a party to debasing the currency.
John Maynard Keynes (1883–1946) British economist.
On refusing to pay more than a small tip on having his shoes polished, whilst on a visit to Africa
John Maynard Keynes (C. Hession)

8 Inflation in the Sixties was a nuisance to be endured, like varicose veins or French foreign policy.
Bernard Levin (1928–) British journalist.
The Pendulum Years, 'Epilogue'

9 Population, when unchecked, increases in a geometrical ratio. Subsistence only increases in an arithmetical ratio.
Thomas Robert Malthus (1766–1834) British clergyman and economist.
Essays on the Principle of Population

10 A nation is not in danger of financial disaster merely because it owes itself money.
Andrew William Mellon (1855–1937) US financier.
Attrib.

11 Recession is when a neighbour loses his job; depression is when you lose yours.
Ronald Reagan (1911–) US politician and president.
The Observer, 'Sayings of the Week', 26 Oct 1980

12 If all economists were laid end to end, they would not reach a conclusion.
George Bernard Shaw (1856–1950) Irish dramatist and critic.
Attrib.

13 Give me a one-handed economist! All my economists say, 'on the one hand . . . on the other.
Harry S. Truman (1884–1972) US statesman.
Presidential Anecdotes (P. Boller)

14 From now, the pound is worth 14 per cent or so less in terms of other currencies. It does not mean, of course, that the pound here in Britain, in your pocket or purse or in your bank, has been devalued.
Harold Wilson (1916–) British politician and prime minister.
Speech after devaluation of the pound, 20 Nov 1967

15 One man's wage rise is another man's price increase.
Harold Wilson
The Observer, 'Sayings of the Week', 11 Jan 1970

EDITORS

See also books, journalism, newspapers, publishing

1 Where were you fellows when the paper was blank?
Fred Allen (1894–1956) US comedian.
Said to writers who heavily edited one of his scripts
Attrib.

2 He made righteousness readable.
James Bone (1872–1962) British journalist.
Referring to C. P. Scott, former editor of *The Manchester Guardian*
Attrib.

3 An editor is one who separates the wheat from the chaff and prints the chaff.
Adlai Stevenson (1900–65) US statesman.
The Stevenson Wit

EDUCATION

See also academics, classics, examinations, indoctrination, learning, punishment

1 Soon learnt, soon forgotten.
Proverb

2 What we must look for here is, first, religious and moral principles; secondly, gentlemanly conduct; thirdly, intellectual ability.
Thomas Arnold (1795–1842) British educator.
Address to the Scholars at Rugby

3 My object will be, if possible to form Christian men, for Christian boys I can scarcely hope to make.
Thomas Arnold
Letter on appointment as Headmaster of Rugby, 1828

4 Universities incline wits to sophistry and affectation.
Francis Bacon (1561–1626) English philosopher.
Valerius Terminus of the Interpretation of Nature, Ch. 26

5 Studies serve for delight, for ornament, and for ability.
Francis Bacon
Essays, 'Of Studies'

6 It is Oxford that has made me insufferable.
Max Beerbohm (1872–1956) British writer.
More, 'Going back to School'

7 The dread of beatings,
Dread of Being Late
And greatest dread of all, the dread of games.
John Betjeman (1906–84) British poet.
Summoned by Bells

8 The true University of these days is a collection of books.
Thomas Carlyle (1795–1881) Scottish historian and essayist.
Heroes and Hero-Worship, 'The Hero as Man of Letters'

9 'Reeling and Writhing, of course, to begin with,' the Mock Turtle replied; 'and then the different branches of Arithmetic – Ambition, Distraction, Uglification, and Derision.'
Lewis Carroll (Charles Lutwidge Dodgson; 1832–98) British writer.
Alice's Adventures in Wonderland, Ch. 9

10 His English education at one of the great public schools had preserved his intellect perfectly and permanently at the stage of boyhood.
G. K. Chesterton (1874–1936) British writer.
The Man Who Knew Too Much

11 Education is simply the soul of a society as it passes from one generation to another.
G. K. Chesterton
The Observer, 'Sayings of the Week', 6 July 1924

12 Headmasters have powers at their disposal with which Prime Ministers have never yet been invested.
Winston Churchill (1874–1965) British statesman.
My Early Life, Ch. 2

13 The ape-like virtues without which no one can enjoy a public school.
Cyril Connolly (1903–74) British journalist.
Enemies of Promise, Ch. 1

14 When he has learnt that bottinney means a knowledge of plants, he goes and knows 'em. That's our system, Nickleby; what do you think of it?
Charles Dickens (1812–70) British novelist.
Said by Mr Squeers
Nicholas Nickleby, Ch. 8

15 I pay the schoolmaster, but 'tis the schoolboys that educate my son.
Ralph Waldo Emerson (1803–82) US poet and essayist.
Journal

16 Public schools are the nurseries of all vice and immorality.
Henry Fielding (1707–54) British novelist.
Joseph Andrews, Bk. III, Ch. 5

17 It is not that the Englishman can't feel – it is that he is afraid to feel. He has been taught at his public school that feeling is bad form. He must not express great joy or sorrow, or even open his mouth too wide when he talks – his pipe might fall out if he did.
E. M. Forster (1879–1970) British novelist.
Abinger Harvest, 'Notes on the English character'

18 They go forth into it with well-developed bodies, fairly developed minds, and undeveloped hearts.
E. M. Forster
Referring to public schoolboys going into the world
Abinger Harvest, 'Notes on the English Character'

19 Spoon feeding in the long run teaches us nothing but the shape of the spoon.
E. M. Forster
The Observer, 'Sayings of the Week', 7 Oct 1951

20 To the University of Oxford I acknowledge no obligation; and she will as cheerfully renounce me for a son, as I am willing to disclaim her for a mother. I spent fourteen months at Magdalen College: they proved the fourteen months the most idle and unprofitable of my whole life.
Edward Gibbon (1737–94) British historian.
Autobiography

21 Education made us what we are.
Claude-Adrien Helvétius (1715–71) French philosopher.
Discours XXX, Ch. 30

22 And seek for truth in the groves of Academe.
Horace (Quintus Horatius Flaccus; 65–8 BC) Roman poet.
Epistles, II

23 You sought the last resort of feeble minds with classical educations. You became a schoolmaster.
Aldous Huxley (1894–1964) British novelist and essayist.
Antic Hay

24 Some experience of popular lecturing had convinced me that the necessity of making things plain to uninstructed people was one of the very best means of clearing up the obscure corners in one's own mind.
T. H. Huxley (1825–95) British biologist.
Man's Place in Nature, Preface

25 Any attempt to reform the university without attending to the system of which it is an integral part is like trying to do urban renewal in New York City from the twelfth storey up.
Ivan Illich (1926–) Austrian sociologist.
Deschooling Society, Ch. 3

26 It is no matter what you teach them first, any more than what leg you shall put into your breeches first.
Samuel Johnson (1709–84) British lexicographer.
Life of Johnson (J. Boswell), Vol. I

27 There is now less flogging in our great schools than formerly, but then less is learned there; so that what the boys get at one end they lose at the other.
Samuel Johnson
Life of Johnson (J. Boswell), Vol. II

28 I find the three major administrative problems on a campus are sex for the students, athletics for the alumni and parking for the faculty.
Clark Kerr (1911–) US educator.
Time, 17 Nov 1958

29 Nothing would more effectively further the development of education than for all flogging pedagogues to learn to educate with the head instead of with the hand.
Ellen Key (Karolina Sofia Key; 1849–1926) Swedish writer.
The Century of the Child, Ch. 3

30 If every day in the life of a school could be the last day but one, there would be little fault to find with it.
Stephen Leacock (1869–1944) English-born Canadian economist and humorist.
College Days, 'Memories and Miseries of a Schoolmaster'

31 Four times, under our educational rules, the human pack is shuffled and cut – at eleven-plus, sixteen-plus, eighteen-plus and twenty-plus – and happy is he who comes top of the deck on each occasion, but especially the last. This is called Finals, the very name of which implies that nothing of importance can happen after it. The British postgraduate student is a lonely forlorn soul . . . for whom nothing has been real since the Big Push.
David Lodge (1935–) British author.
Changing Places, Ch. 1

32 If you educate a man you educate a person, but if you educate a woman you educate a family.
Ruby Manikan (20th century) Indian Church leader.
The Observer, 'Sayings of the Week', 30 Mar 1947

33 A gentleman need not know Latin, but he should at least have forgotten it.
Brander Matthews (1852–1929) US writer.
Attrib.

34 A whale ship was my Yale College and my Harvard.
Herman Melville (1819–91) US novelist.
Moby Dick, Ch. 24

35 One tongue is sufficient for a woman.
John Milton (1608–74) English poet.
On being asked whether he would allow his daughters to learn foreign languages
Attrib.

36 And if education is always to be conceived along the same antiquated lines of a mere transmission of knowledge, there is little to be hoped from it in the bettering of man's future. For what is the use of transmitting knowledge if the individual's total development lags behind?
Maria Montessori (1870–1952) Italian doctor and educationalist.
The Absorbent Mind

37 We teachers can only help the work going on, as servants wait upon a master.
Maria Montessori
The Absorbent Mind

38 Discussion in class, which means letting twenty young blockheads and two cocky neurotics discuss something that neither their teacher nor they know.
Vladimir Nabokov (1899–1977) Russian-born US novelist.
Pnin, Ch. 6

39 Every schoolmaster after the age of 49 is inclined to flatulence, is apt to swallow frequently, and to puff.
Harold Nicolson (1886–1968) British writer.
The Old School

40 The schoolteacher is certainly underpaid as a childminder, but ludicrously overpaid as an educator.
John Osborne (1929–) British dramatist.
The Observer, 'Sayings of the Week', 21 July 1985

41 He was sent, as usual, to a public school, where a little learning was painfully beaten into him, and from thence to the university, where it was carefully taken out of him.
Thomas Love Peacock (1785–1866) British novelist.
Nightmare Abbey, Ch. 1

42 'Tis education forms the common mind, Just as the twig is bent, the tree's inclined.
Alexander Pope (1688–1744) British poet.
Moral Essays, I

43 A man who has never gone to school may steal from a freight car, but if he has a university education he may steal the whole railroad.
Franklin D. Roosevelt (1882–1945) US Democratic president.
Attrib.

44 But, good gracious, you've got to educate him first.
You can't expect a boy to be vicious till he's been to a good school.
Saki (Hector Hugh Munro; 1870–1916) British writer.
Reginald in Russia

45 For every person wishing to teach there are thirty not wanting to be taught.
W. C. Sellar (1898–1951) British humorous writer.
And Now All This

46 No profit grows where is no pleasure ta'en;

In brief, sir, study what you most affect.
William Shakespeare (1564–1616) English dramatist.
The Taming of the Shrew, I:1

47 A learned man is an idler who kills time by study.
George Bernard Shaw (1856–1950) Irish dramatist and critic.
Man and Superman

48 There is nothing on earth intended for innocent people so horrible as a school. It is in some respects more cruel than a prison. In a prison, for example, you are not forced to read books written by the warders and the governor.
George Bernard Shaw
Parents and Children

49 He who can, does. He who cannot, teaches.
George Bernard Shaw
Man and Superman, 'Maxims for Revolutionists'

50 Indeed one of the ultimate advantages of an education is simply coming to the end of it.
B. F. Skinner (1904–) US psychologist.
The Technology of Teaching

51 Education is what survives when what has been learnt has been forgotten.
B. F. Skinner
New Scientist, 21 May 1964, 'Education in 1984'

52 To me education is a leading out of what is already there in the pupil's soul. To Miss Mackay it is a putting in of something that is not there, and that is not what I call education, I call it intrusion. . . .
Muriel Spark (1918–) British novelist.
The Prime of Miss Jean Brodie, Ch. 2

53 Soap and education are not as sudden as a massacre, but they are more deadly in the long run.
Mark Twain (Samuel Langhorne Clemens; 1835–1910) US writer.
The Facts concerning the Recent Resignation

54 People at the top of the tree are those without qualifications to detain them at the bottom.
Peter Ustinov (1921–) British actor.
Attrib.

55 I expect you'll be becoming a schoolmaster sir. That's what most of the gentlemen does sir, that gets sent down for indecent behaviour.
Evelyn Waugh (1903–66) British novelist.
Decline and Fall, Prelude

56 We class schools you see, into four grades: Leading School, First-rate School, Good School, and School.
Evelyn Waugh
Decline and Fall, Pt. I, Ch. 1

57 We schoolmasters must temper discretion with deceit.
Evelyn Waugh
Decline and Fall, Pt. I, Ch. 1

58 That's the public-school system all over. They may kick you out, but they never let you down.
Evelyn Waugh
Decline and Fall, Pt. I, Ch. 3

59 Anyone who has been to an English public school will always feel comparatively at home in prison.
Evelyn Waugh
Decline and Fall, Pt. III, Ch. 4

60 Assistant masters came and went . . . . Some liked little boys too little and some too much.
Evelyn Waugh
A Little Learning

61 The battle of Waterloo was won on the playing fields of Eton.
Duke of Wellington (1769–1852) British general.
Attrib.

62 A very large part of English middle-class education is devoted to the training of servants . . . In so far as it is, by definition, the training of upper servants, it includes, of course, the instilling of that kind of confidence which will enable the upper servants to supervise and direct the lower servants.
Raymond Henry Williams (1921–   ) British academic and writer.
Culture and Society, Ch. 3

EFFORT

See also work

1 If a job's worth doing, it's worth doing well.
Proverb

2 Energy is Eternal Delight.
William Blake (1757–1827) British poet.
The Marriage of Heaven and Hell, 'The Voice of the Devil'

3 I have nothing to offer but blood, toil, tears and sweat.
Winston Churchill (1874–1965) British statesman.
On becoming prime minister
Speech, House of Commons, 13 May 1940

4 A world where nothing is had for nothing.
Arthur Hugh Clough (1819–61) British poet.
The Bothie of Tober-na-Vuolich, Bk. VIII, Ch. 5

5 As is the case in all branches of art, success depends in a very large measure upon individual initiative and exertion, and cannot be achieved except by dint of hard work.
Anna Pavlova (1881–1931) Russian ballet dancer.
Pavlova: A Biography (ed. A. H. Franks), 'Pages of My Life'

6 And here is the lesson I learned in the army.

If you want to do a thing badly, you have to work at it as though you want to do it well.
Peter Ustinov (1921–   ) British actor.
Dear Me, Ch. 8

7 Please do not shoot the pianist. He is doing his best.
Oscar Wilde (1854–1900) Irish-born British dramatist.
Impressions of America, 'Leadville'

EGOTISM

See also arrogance, conceit, pride, selfishness

1 Against whom?
Alfred Adler (1870–1937) Austrian psychiatrist.
Said when he heard that an egocentric had fallen in love
Some of My Best Friends (J. Bishop), 'Exponent of the Soul'

2 No poet or novelist wishes he were the only one who ever lived, but most of them wish they were the only one alive, and quite a number fondly believe their wish has been granted.
W. H. Auden (1907–73) British poet.
The Dyer's Hand, 'Writing'

3 *Egotist*, n. A person of low taste, more interested in himself than in me.
Ambrose Bierce (1842–?1914) US writer and journalist.
The Devil's Dictionary

4 Someone said of a very great egotist: 'He would burn your house down to cook himself a couple of eggs.
Nicolas Chamfort (1741–94) French writer.
Caractères et anecdotes

5 An author who speaks about his own books is almost as bad as a mother who talks about her own children.
Benjamin Disraeli (1804–81) British statesman.
Speech in Glasgow, 19 Nov 1873

6 If the Almighty himself played the violin, the credits would still read 'Rubinstein, God, and Piatigorsky', in that order.
Jascha Heifetz (1901–87) Russian-born US violinist.
Whenever Heifetz played in trios with Arthur Rubinstein (piano) and Gregor Piatigorsky (cello), Rubinstein always got top billing
Los Angeles Times, 29 Aug 1982

7 One had rather malign oneself than not speak of oneself at all.
Duc de la Rochefoucauld (1613–80) French writer.
Maximes, 138

8 As who should say 'I am Sir Oracle,
And when I ope my lips let no dog bark'.
William Shakespeare (1564–1616) English dramatist.
The Merchant of Venice, I:1

9 A pompous woman of his acquaintance, complaining that the head-waiter of a restaurant had not shown her and her husband immediately to a table, said, 'We had

to tell him who we were.' Gerald, interested, enquired, 'And who were you?'
Edith Sitwell (1887–1964) British poet and writer.
Taken Care Of, Ch. 15

10 No man thinks there is much ado about nothing when the ado is about himself.
Anthony Trollope (1815–82) British novelist.
The Bertrams, Ch. 27

11 I am the only person in the world I should like to know thoroughly.
Oscar Wilde (1854–1900) Irish-born British dramatist.
Lady Windermere's Fan, II

EMBARRASSMENT

1 The question about everything was, would it bring a blush to the cheek of a young person?
Charles Dickens (1812–70) British novelist.
Pondered by Mr Podsnap
Our Mutual Friend, Bk. I, Ch. 11

2 Man is the only animal that blushes. Or needs to.
Mark Twain (Samuel Langhorne Clemens; 1835–1910) US writer.
Following the Equator, heading of Ch. 27

EMOTION

See also passion, sentimentality

1 There is a road from the eye to the heart that does not go through the intellect.
G. K. Chesterton (1874–1936) British writer.
The Defendant

2 'There are strings', said Mr Tappertit, 'in the human heart that had better not be wibrated.'
Charles Dickens (1812–70) British novelist.
Barnaby Rudge, Ch. 22

3 Grief and disappointment give rise to anger, anger to envy, envy to malice, and malice to grief again, till the whole circle be completed.
David Hume (1711–76) Scottish philosopher.
A Treatise of Human Nature

4 The intellect is always fooled by the heart.
Duc de la Rochefoucauld (1613–80) French writer.
Maximes, 102

5 Light breaks where no sun shines;
Where no sea runs, the waters of the heart
Push in their tides.
Dylan Thomas (1914–53) Welsh poet.
Light breaks where no sun shines

6 Pure and complete sorrow is as impossible as pure and complete joy.
Leo Tolstoy (1828–1910) Russian writer.
War and Peace, Bk. XV, Ch. 1

ENDING

1 All good things must come to an end.
Proverb

2 All's well that ends well.
Proverb

3 This is the way the world ends
Not with a bang but a whimper.
T. S. Eliot (1888–1965) US-born British poet and dramatist.
The Hollow Men

4 We'll to the woods no more,
The laurels all are cut.
A. E. Housman (1859–1936) British scholar and poet.
Last Poems, Introductory

5 That but this blow
Might be the be-all and the end-all here –
But here upon this bank and shoal of time –
We'd jump the life to come.
William Shakespeare (1564–1616) English dramatist.
Macbeth, I:7

6 The bright day is done,
And we are for the dark.
William Shakespeare
Antony and Cleopatra, V:2

7 Ring out, wild bells, to the wild sky,
The flying cloud, the frosty light:
The year is dying in the night;
Ring out, wild bells, and let him die.
Alfred, Lord Tennyson (1809–92) British poet.
In Memoriam A.H.H., CVI

ENDURANCE

See also comfort, courage, determination, misfortune, suffering

1 Even a worm will turn.
Proverb

2 The last straw breaks the camel's back.
Proverb

3 What can't be cured, must be endured.
Proverb

4 Nothing happens to any man that he is not formed by nature to bear.
Marcus Aurelius (121–180 AD) Roman emperor.
Meditations, Bk. V, Ch. 18

5 Through the night of doubt and sorrow
Onward goes the pilgrim band,
Singing songs of expectation,
Marching to the Promised Land.
Sabine Baring-Gould (1834–1924) British author and hymn writer.
Through the Night of Doubt and Sorrow

6 In the fell clutch of circumstance,
I have not winced nor cried aloud;
Under the bludgeonings of chance
My head is bloody, but unbowed.
William Ernest Henley (1849–1903) British writer.
Echoes, IV, 'Invictus. In Mem. R.T.H.B.'

7 . . . we could never learn to be brave and patient, if there were only joy in the world.
Helen Keller (1880–1968) US writer and lecturer.
Atlantic Monthly (May 1890)

8 Job endured everything – until his friends came to comfort him, then he grew impatient.
Soren Kierkegaard (1813–55) Danish philosopher.
Journal

9 Sorrow and silence are strong, and patient endurance is godlike.
Henry Wadsworth Longfellow (1807–82) US poet.
Evangeline

10 Know how sublime a thing it is
To suffer and be strong.
Henry Wadsworth Longfellow
The Light of Stars

11 The weariest nights, the longest days, sooner or later must perforce come to an end.
Baroness Orczy (1865–1947) British novelist.
The Scarlet Pimpernel, Ch. 22

12 No pain, no palm; no thorns, no throne; no gall, no glory; no cross, no crown.
William Penn (1644–1718) English preacher.
No Cross, No Crown

13 The Muse but serv'd to ease some friend, not Wife,
To help me through this long disease, my life.
Alexander Pope (1688–1744) British poet.
Epistle to Dr. Arbuthnot

14 The pain passes, but the beauty remains.
Pierre Auguste Renoir (1841–1919) French impressionist painter.
Explaining why he still painted when his hands were twisted with arthritis
Attrib.

15 Does the road wind up-hill all the way?
Yes, to the very end.
Will the day's journey take the whole long day?
From morn to night, my friend.
Christina Rossetti (1830–74) British poet.
Up-Hill

16 Had we lived, I should have had a tale to tell of the hardihood, endurance, and courage of my companions which would have stirred the heart of every Englishman. These rough notes and our dead bodies must tell the tale.
Captain Robert Falcon Scott (1868–1912) British explorer.
Message to the Public

17 Men must endure
Their going hence, even as their coming hither:
Ripeness is all.
William Shakespeare (1564–1616) English dramatist.
King Lear, V:2

18 For there was never yet philosopher
That could endure the toothache patiently.
William Shakespeare
Much Ado About Nothing, V:1

19 Let's talk sense to the American people.

Let's tell them the truth, that there are no gains without pains.
Adlai Stevenson (1900–65) US statesman.
Speech, Chicago, 26 July 1952

20 If you can't stand the heat, get out of the kitchen.
Harry S. Truman (1884–1972) US statesman.
Perhaps proverbial in origin, possibly echoes the expression 'kitchen cabinet'
Mr Citizen, Ch. 15

21 O you who have borne even heavier things, God will grant an end to these too.
Virgil (Publius Vergilius Maro; 70–19 BC) Roman poet.
Aeneid, Bk. I

22 Maybe one day we shall be glad to remember even these hardships.
Virgil
Aeneid, Bk. I

23 I sing of arms and the man who first from the shores
of Troy came destined an exile to Italy and the Lavinian beaches, much buffeted he on land and on
the deep by force of the gods because of fierce Juno's never-forgetting anger.
Virgil
Referring to Aeneas
Aeneid, Bk. I

24 Much in sorrow, oft in woe,
Onward, Christians, onward go.
Henry Kirke White (1785–1806) British poet.
A hymn, better known in its later form, 'Oft in danger, oft in woe'

ENEMIES

1 Better a thousand enemies outside the house than one inside.
Arabic proverb
Proverb

2 But I say unto you, That ye resist not evil: but whosoever shall smite thee on thy right cheek, turn to him the other also.
And if any man will sue thee at the law, and take away thy coat, let him have thy cloke also.
And whosoever shall compel thee to go a mile, go with him twain.
Bible: Matthew
5:39–41

3 But I say unto you, Love your enemies, bless them that curse you, do good to them that hate you, and pray for them which despitefully use you, and persecute you;
That ye may be the children of your Father which is in heaven: for he maketh his sun to rise on the evil and on the good, and sendeth rain on the just and on the unjust.
For if ye love them which love you, what re-

ward have ye? do not even the publicans the same?
Bible: Matthew
5:44–46

4 Even a paranoid can have enemies.
Henry Kissinger (1923–) German-born US politician and diplomat.
Time, 24 Jan 1977

5 They made peace between us; we embraced, and we have been mortal enemies ever since.
Alain-René Lesage (1668–1747) French writer.
Le Diable boiteux, Ch. 3

6 You must hate a Frenchman as you hate the devil.
Lord Nelson (1758–1805) British admiral.
Life of Nelson (Southey), Ch. 3

7 The only good Indians I ever saw were dead.
Philip H. Sheridan (1831–88) US general.
The People's Almanac 2 (D. Wallechinsky)

8 He makes no friend who never made a foe.
Alfred, Lord Tennyson (1809–92) British poet.
Idylls of the King, 'Lancelot and Elaine'

9 I should be like a lion in a cave of savage Daniels.
Oscar Wilde (1854–1900) Irish-born British dramatist.
Explaining why he would not be attending a function at a club whose members were hostile to him
Attrib.

ENGLAND

See also Britain, Cambridge, English, London, Oxford, patriotism

1 Oh! who can ever be tired of Bath?
Jane Austen (1775–1817) British novelist.
Northanger Abbey, Ch. 10

2 One has no great hopes from Birmingham. I always say there is something direful in the sound.
Jane Austen
Emma, Ch. 36

3 Come, friendly bombs, and fall on Slough
It isn't fit for humans now.
There isn't grass to graze a cow
Swarm over, Death!
. . .
Come, friendly bombs, and fall on Slough
To get it ready for the plough.
The cabbages are coming now:
The earth exhales.
John Betjeman (1906–84) British poet.
Slough

4 And did those feet in ancient time
Walk upon England's mountains green?
And was the holy lamb of God
On England's pleasant pastures seen?
. . .
I will not cease from mental fight,

Nor shall my sword sleep in my hand,
Till we have built Jerusalem
In England's green and pleasant land.
William Blake (1757–1827) British poet.
Better known as the hymn 'Jerusalem', with music by Sir Hubert Parry; not to be confused with Blake's longer poem *Jerusalem*.
Milton, Preface

5 England is the mother of parliaments.
John Bright (1811–89) British radical politician.
Speech, Birmingham, 18 Jan 1865

6 For England's the one land, I know,
Where men with Splendid Hearts may go;
And Cambridgeshire, of all England,
The shire for Men who Understand.
Rupert Brooke (1887–1915) British poet.
The Old Vicarage, Grantchester

7 Oh, to be in England
Now that April's there.
Robert Browning (1812–89) British poet.
Home Thoughts from Abroad

8 Without class differences, England would cease to be the living theatre it is.
Anthony Burgess (John Burgess Wilson; 1917–) British novelist.
The Observer, 'Sayings of the Week', 26 May 1985

9 In England there are sixty different religions, and only one sauce.
Domenico Caracciolo (1715–89) Governor of Sicily.
Attrib.

10 This could have occurred nowhere but in England, where men and sea interpenetrate, so to speak.
Joseph Conrad (Teodor Josef Konrad Korzeniowski; 1857–1924) Polish-born British novelist.
Youth

11 Very flat, Norfolk.
Noël Coward (1899–1973) British dramatist.
Private Lives

12 Regions Caesar never knew
Thy posterity shall sway,
Where his eagles never flew,
None invincible as they.
William Cowper (1731–1800) British poet.
Boadicea

13 There are many things in life more worthwhile than money. One is to be brought up in this our England which is still the envy of less happy lands.
Lord Denning (1899–) British judge.
The Observer, 'Sayings of the Week', 4 Aug 1968

14 Kent, sir – everybody knows Kent – apples, cherries, hops and women.
Charles Dickens (1812–70) British novelist.
Pickwick Papers, Ch. 2

15 The Continent will not suffer England to be the workshop of the world.
Benjamin Disraeli (1804–81) British statesman.
Speech, House of Commons, 15 Mar 1838

16 England is the paradise of women, the purgatory of men, and the hell of horses.
John Florio (c. 1553–1625) English lexicographer.
Second Fruits

17 Living in England, provincial England, must be like being married to a stupid but exquisitely beautiful wife.
Margaret Halsey (1910–) US writer.
With Malice Toward Some

18 All of Stratford, in fact, suggests powdered history –add hot water and stir and you have a delicious, nourishing Shakespeare.
Margaret Halsey
With Malice Toward Some

19 Dr Johnson's morality was as English an article as a beefsteak.
Nathaniel Hawthorne (1804–64) US novelist and writer.
Our Old Home, 'Lichfield and Uttoxeter'

20 Pass a law to give every single wingeing bloody Pommie his fare home to England. Back to the smoke and the sun shining ten days a year and shit in the streets. Yer can have it.
Thomas Keneally (1935–) Australian novelist.
The Chant of Jimmy Blacksmith

21 Winds of the World, give answer! They are whimpering to and fro –
And what should they know of England who only England know?
Rudyard Kipling (1865–1936) Indian-born British writer.
The English Flag

22 It was one of those places where the spirit of aboriginal England still lingers, the old savage England, whose last blood flows still in a few Englishmen, Welshmen, Cornishmen.
D. H. Lawrence (1885–1930) British novelist.
St Mawr

23 And suddenly she craved again for the more absolute silence of America. English stillness was so soft, like an inaudible murmur of voices, of presences.
D. H. Lawrence
St Mawr

24 In an English ship, they say, it is poor grub, poor pay, and easy work; in an American ship, good grub, good pay, and hard work. And this is applicable to the working populations of both countries.
Jack London (1876–1916) US novelist.
The People of the Abyss, Ch. 20

25 In no country, I believe, are the marriage laws so iniquitous as in England, and the conjugal relation, in consequence, so impaired.
Harriet Martineau (1802–76) British writer.
Society in America, Vol. III, 'Marriage'

26 In England there is only silence or scandal.
André Maurois (Émile Herzog; 1885–1967) French writer.
Attrib.

27 When people say England, they sometimes mean Great Britain, sometimes the United Kingdom, sometimes the British Isles, – but never England.
George Mikes (1912–87) Hungarian-born British writer.
How to be an Alien

28 It was twenty-one years ago that England and I first set foot on each other. I came for a fortnight; I have stayed ever since.
George Mikes
How to be Inimitable

29 A family with the wrong members in control – that, perhaps, is as near as one can come to describing England in a phrase.
George Orwell (Eric Blair; 1903–50) British novelist.
The Lion and the Unicorn, 'The Ruling Class'

30 There can hardly be a town in the South of England where you could throw a brick without hitting the niece of a bishop.
George Orwell
The Road to Wigan Pier, Ch. 7

31 There'll always be an England
While there's a country lane,
Wherever there's a cottage small
Beside a field of grain.
Clarke Ross Parker (1914–74) British songwriter.
There'll Always Be an England

32 The real fact is that I could no longer stand their eternal cold mutton.
Cecil Rhodes (1853–1902) South African statesman.
Explaining why he had left his friends in England and come to South Africa
Cecil Rhodes (G. le Sueur)

33 England is the paradise of individuality, eccentricity, heresy, anomalies, hobbies, and humours.
George Santayana (1863–1952) US philosopher.
Soliloquies in England, 'The British Character'

34 This royal throne of kings, this sceptred isle,
This earth of majesty, this seat of Mars,
This other Eden, demi-paradise,
This fortress built by Nature for herself
Against infection and the hand of war,
This happy breed of men, this little world,
This precious stone set in the silver sea,
Which serves it in the office of a wall,
Or as a moat defensive to a house,
Against the envy of less happier lands;
This blessed plot, this earth, this realm, this England,
This nurse, this teeming womb of royal kings,
Fear'd by their breed, and famous by their birth.
William Shakespeare (1564–1616) English dramatist.
Richard II, II:1

35 Well, I cannot last ever; but it was always

yet the trick of our English nation, if they have a good thing, to make it too common.
William Shakespeare
Henry IV, Part Two, I:2

36 The English take their pleasures sadly after the fashion of their country.
Duc de Sully (1560–1641) French statesman.
Memoirs

37 They say that men become attached even to Widnes.
A. J. P. Taylor (1906–) British historian.
The Observer, 15 Sept 1963

38 Yes. I remember Adlestrop –
The name, because one afternoon
Of heat the express train drew up there
Unwontedly. It was late June.
Edward Thomas (1878–1917) British poet.
Adlestrop

39 You never find an Englishman among the underdogs – except in England of course.
Evelyn Waugh (1903–66) British novelist.
The Loved One

ENGLISH

See also British, nationality

1 An Englishman's home is his castle.
Proverb

2 An Englishman's word is his bond.
Proverb

3 That typically English characteristic for which there is no English name – *esprit de corps*.
Frank Ezra Adcock (1886–1968) British classicist.
Presidential address

4 The English instinctively admire any man who has no talent and is modest about it.
James Agate (1877–1947) British theatre critic.
Attrib.

5 But of all nations in the world the English are perhaps the least a nation of pure philosophers.
Walter Bagehot (1826–77) British economist and journalist.
The English Constitution, 'The Monarchy'

6 I like the English. They have the most rigid code of immorality in the world.
Malcolm Bradbury (1932–) British academic and novelist.
Eating People is Wrong, Ch. 5

7 The wish to spread those opinions that we hold conducive to our own welfare is so deeply rooted in the English character that few of us can escape its influence.
Samuel Butler (1835–1902) British writer.
Erewhon, Ch. 20

8 The most dangerous thing in the world is to make a friend of an Englishman, because he'll

come sleep in your closet rather than spend 10s on a hotel.
Truman Capote (1924–84) US novelist.
The Observer, 'Sayings of the Week', 24 Mar 1968

9 Thirty millions, mostly fools.
Thomas Carlyle (1795–1881) Scottish historian and essayist.
When asked what the population of England was
Attrib.

10 He's an Anglo-Saxon Messenger – and those are Anglo-Saxon attitudes.
Lewis Carroll (Charles Lutwidge Dodgson; 1832–98) British writer.
Through the Looking-Glass, Ch. 7

11 All the faces here this evening seem to be bloody Poms.
Charles, Prince of Wales (1948–) Eldest son of Elizabeth II.
Remark at Australia Day dinner, 1973

12 Smile at us, pay us, pass us; but do not quite forget.
For we are the people of England, that never have spoken yet.
G. K. Chesterton (1874–1936) British writer.
The Secret People

13 It is said, I believe, that to behold the Englishman at his *best* one should watch him play tip-and-run.
Ronald Firbank (1886–1926) British novelist.
The Flower Beneath the Foot, Ch. 14

14 *Non Angli sed Angeli*
Not Angles, but angels.
Gregory I (540–604) Pope and saint.
Attrib.

15 . . . it takes a great deal to produce ennui in an Englishman and if you do, he only takes it as convincing proof that you are well-bred.
Margaret Halsey (1910–) US writer.
With Malice Toward Some

16 The attitude of the English . . . toward English history reminds one a good deal of the attitude of a Hollywood director toward love.
Margaret Halsey
With Malice Toward Some

17 . . . the English think of an opinion as something which a decent person, if he has the misfortune to have one, does all he can to hide.
Margaret Halsey
With Malice Toward Some

18 The English (it must be owned) are rather a foul-mouthed nation.
William Hazlitt (1778–1830) British essayist.
On Criticism

19 The Englishman never enjoys himself except for a noble purpose.
A. P. Herbert (1890–1971) British writer and politician.
Uncommon Law

20 When two Englishmen meet, their first talk is of the weather.
Samuel Johnson (1709–84) British lexicographer.
The Idler

21 The English people on the whole are surely the *nicest* people in the world, and everyone makes everything so easy for everybody else, that there is almost nothing to resist at all.
D. H. Lawrence (1885–1930) British novelist.
Dull London

22 England is . . . a country infested with people who love to tell us what to do, but who very rarely seem to know what's going on.
Colin MacInnes (1914–76) British novelist.
England, Half English, 'Pop Songs and Teenagers'

23 An Englishman, even if he is alone, forms an orderly queue of one.
George Mikes (1912–87) Hungarian-born British writer.
How to be an Alien

24 Continental people have sex life; the English have hot-water bottles.
George Mikes
How to be an Alien

25 English women are elegant until they are ten years old, and perfect on grand occasions.
Nancy Mitford (1904–73) British writer.
The Wit of Women (L. and M. Cowan)

26 The English are busy; they don't have time to be polite.
Baron de Montesquieu (1688–1755) French writer.
Pensées diverses

27 It has to be admitted that we English have sex on the brain, which is a very unsatisfactory place to have it.
Malcolm Muggeridge (1903–) British writer.
The Observer, 'Sayings of the Decade', 1964

28 England is a nation of shopkeepers.
Napoleon I (Napoleon Bonaparte; 1769–1821) French emperor.
Attrib.

29 To be an Englishman is to belong to the most exclusive club there is.
Ogden Nash (1902–71) US poet.
England Expects

30 But Lord! to see the absurd nature of Englishmen, that cannot forbear laughing and jeering at everything that looks strange.
Samuel Pepys (1633–1703) English diarist.
Diary, 27 Nov 1662

31 Remember that you are an Englishman, and have consequently won first prize in the lottery of life.
Cecil Rhodes (1853–1902) South African statesman.
Dear Me (Peter Ustinov), Ch. 4

32 The English have no respect for their language, and will not teach their children to speak it . . . It is impossible for an Englishman to open his mouth, without making some other Englishman despise him.
George Bernard Shaw (1856–1950) Irish dramatist and critic.
Pygmalion, Preface

33 I think for my part one half of the nation is mad – and the other not very sound.
Tobias Smollett (1721–71) British novelist.
The Adventures of Sir Launcelot Greaves, Ch. 6

34 I cannot but conclude the bulk of your natives to be the most pernicious race of little odious vermin that nature ever suffered to crawl upon the surface of the earth.
Jonathan Swift (1667–1745) Irish-born Anglican priest and writer.
Gulliver's Travels, 'Voyage to Brobdingnag', Ch. 6

35 The national sport of England is obstacle-racing. People fill their rooms with useless and cumbersome furniture, and spend the rest of their lives in trying to dodge it.
Herbert Beerbohm Tree (1853–1917) British actor and theatre manager.
Beerbohm Tree (Hesketh Pearson)

ENTHUSIASM

1 How can I take an interest in my work when I don't like it?
Francis Bacon (1909–) British painter.
Francis Bacon (Sir John Rothenstein)

2 It is unfortunate, considering that enthusiasm moves the world, that so few enthusiasts can be trusted to speak the truth.
Arthur Balfour (1848–1930) British statesman.
Letter to Mrs Drew, 1918

3 Nothing great was ever achieved without enthusiasm.
Ralph Waldo Emerson (1803–82) US poet and essayist.
Essays, 'Circles'

4 The love of life is necessary to the vigorous prosecution of any undertaking.
Samuel Johnson (1709–84) British lexicographer.
The Rambler

5 Don't clap too hard – it's a very old building.
John Osborne (1929–) British dramatist.
The Entertainer

6 Every man loves what he is good at.
Thomas Shadwell (1642–92) English dramatist.
A True Widow, V:1

7 To business that we love we rise betime,
And go to't with delight.
William Shakespeare (1564–1616) English dramatist.
Antony and Cleopatra, IV:4

ENVIRONMENT

See also ecology

1 One cannot assess in terms of cash or exports and imports an imponderable thing like the turn of a lane or an inn or a church tower or a familiar skyline.

John Betjeman (1906–84) British poet.
On siting a new London airport at Wing.
The Observer, 'Sayings of the Week', 20 July 1969

2 They improvidentially piped growing volumes of sewage into the sea, the healing virtues of which were advertised on every railway station.

Robert Cecil (1913–) British writer.
Referring to seaside resorts
Life in Edwardian England

3 If sunbeams were weapons of war, we would have had solar energy long ago.

George Porter (1920–) British chemist.
The Observer, 'Sayings of the Week', 26 Aug 1973

4 The emergence of intelligence, I am convinced, tends to unbalance the ecology. In other words, intelligence is the great polluter. It is not until a creature begins to manage its environment that nature is thrown into disorder.

Clifford D. Simak (1904–) US journalist.
Shakespeare's Planet

ENVY

See also discontent, jealousy

1 Better be envied than pitied.
Proverb

2 The rich man has his motor car,
His country and his town estate.
He smokes a fifty-cent cigar
And jeers at Fate.

F. P. Adams (1881–1960) US journalist.
The Rich Man

3 Yet though my lamp burns low and dim,
Though I must slave for livelihood –
Think you that I would change with him?
You bet I would!

F. P. Adams
The Rich Man

4 I am sure the grapes are sour.

Aesop (6th century BC) Reputed Greek writer of fables.
Fables, 'The Fox and the Grapes'

5 Fools may our scorn, not envy raise,
For envy is a kind of praise.

John Gay (1685–1732) English poet and dramatist.
Fables

6 The man with toothache thinks everyone happy whose teeth are sound.

George Bernard Shaw (1856–1950) Irish dramatist and critic.
Man and Superman

7 Whenever a friend succeeds, a little something in me dies.

Gore Vidal (1925–) US novelist.
The Sunday Times Magazine, 16 Sept 1973

8 Never having been able to succeed in the world, he took his revenge by speaking ill of it.

Voltaire (François-Marie Arouet; 1694–1778) French writer.
Zadig, Ch. 4

EPITAPHS

1 Their name, their year, spelt by the unlettered muse,
The place of fame and elegy supply:
On many a holy text around she strews,
That teach the rustic moralist to die.

Thomas Gray (1716–71) British poet.
Elegy Written in a Country Churchyard

2 In lapidary inscriptions a man is not upon oath.

Samuel Johnson (1709–84) British lexicographer
Life of Johnson (J. Boswell), Vol. II

3 Nowhere probably is there more true feeling, and nowhere worse taste, than in a churchyard – both as regards the monuments and the inscriptions. Scarcely a word of true poetry anywhere.

Benjamin Jowett (1817–93) British theologian.
Letters of B. Jowett (Abbott and Campbell)

Some actual and literary examples

4 Hereabouts died a very gallant gentleman, Captain L. E. G. Oates of the Inniskilling Dragoons. In March 1912, returning from the Pole, he walked willingly to his death in a blizzard, to try and save his comrades, beset by hardships.

E. L. Atkinson (1882–1929) British naval officer.
Epitaph on memorial in the Antarctic

5 I've played everything but the harp.
When asked what words he would like engraved on his tombstone
Lionel Barrymore (1848–1954) US actor.
Attrib.

6 When Sir Joshua Reynolds died
All Nature was degraded;
The King dropped a tear in the Queen's ear,
And all his pictures faded.

William Blake (1757–1827) British poet.
On Art and Artists

7 With death doomed to grapple,
Beneath this cold slab, he
Who lied in the chapel
Now lies in the Abbey.

Byron, George Gordon, 6th Baron (1788–1824) British poet.
Epitaph for William Pitt

8 Here Skugg
Lies snug
As a bug
In a rug.

Benjamin Franklin (1706–90) US scientist.

Letter to Georgiana Shipley, 26 Sept 1772
An epitaph for a squirrel, 'skugg' being a dialect name for the animal

9 The body of
Benjamin Franklin, printer,
(Like the cover of an old book,
Its contents worn out,
And stript of its lettering and gilding)
Lies here, food for worms!
Yet the work itself shall not be lost,
For it will, as he believed, appear once more
In a new
And more beautiful edition,
Corrected and amended
By its Author!
Benjamin Franklin
Suggestion for his own epitaph

10 Here rests his head upon the lap of Earth
A youth to fortune and to fame unknown.
Fair Science frown'd not on his humble birth,
And Melancholy mark'd him for her own.
Thomas Gray (1716–71) British poet
Elegy Written in a Country Churchyard

11 He gave to Mis'ry all he had, a tear,
He gain'd from Heav'n ('twas all he wish'd) a friend.
Thomas Gray
Elegy Written in a Country Churchyard

12 John Brown's body lies a-mouldering in the grave,
His soul is marching on!
Charles Sprague Hall (19th century) US songwriter.
John Brown's Body
The song commemorates the American hero who died in the cause of abolishing slavery

13 To Oliver Goldsmith, A Poet, Naturalist, and Historian, who left scarcely any style of writing untouched, and touched none that he did not adorn.
Samuel Johnson (1709–84) British lexicographer.
Life of Johnson (J. Boswell), Vol. III
Epitaph on Goldsmith

14 Over my dead body!
George S. Kaufman (1889–1961) US dramatist.
The Algonquin Wits (R. Drennan)
On being asked to suggest his own epitaph

15 Here lies one whose name was writ in water.
John Keats (1795–1821) British poet.
Life of Keats (Lord Houghton), Ch. 2
Suggesting his own epitaph (recalling a line from *Philaster* by Beaumont and Fletcher)

16 'There is a report that Piso is dead; it is a great loss; he was an honest man, who deserved to live longer; he was intelligent and agreeable, resolute and courageous, to be depended upon, generous and faithful.'
Add: 'provided he is really dead'.
Jean de La Bruyère (1645–96) French satirist.
Les Caractères

17 Go, stranger, and tell the Lacedaemonians that here we lie, obedient to their commands.

Leonidas (died 480 BC) King of Sparta.
Epitaph over the tomb in which he and his followers were buried after their defeat at Thermopylae

18 Beneath this slab
John Brown is stowed.
He watched the ads
And not the road.
Ogden Nash (1902–71) US poet.
Lather as You Go

19 For all the Brothers were valiant, and all the Sisters virtuous.
Margaret, Duchess of Newcastle (1624–74) Second wife of William Cavendish.
Epitaph, in Westminster Abbey

20 He lies below, correct in cypress wood,
And entertains the most exclusive worms.
Dorothy Parker (1893–1967) US writer.
Epitaph for a Very Rich Man

21 The poor son-of-a-bitch!
Dorothy Parker
Thalberg: Life and Legend (B. Thomas)
Quoting from *The Great Gatsby* on paying her last respects to F. Scott Fitzgerald

22 In wit a man; simplicity a child.
Alexander Pope (1688–1744) British poet.
Epitaph on Mr. Gay

23 At last God caught his eye.
Suggested epitaph for a head waiter
Harry Secombe (1921–) Welsh comedian.
In *Punch*, May 1962

24 Alas, poor Yorick! I knew him, Horatio: a fellow of infinite jest, of most excellent fancy.
William Shakespeare (1564–1616) English dramatist.
Hamlet, V:1

25 *Si monumentum requiris, circumspice.*
If you seek my monument, look around you.
Sir Christopher Wren (1632–1723) English architect.
Inscription in St Paul's Cathedral, London

26 Under bare Ben Bulben's head
In Drumcliff churchyard Yeats is laid . . .
On limestone quarried near the spot
By his command these words are cut:
W. B. Yeats (1865–1939) Irish poet.
Under Ben Bulben, VI

Some anonymous examples

27 All who come my grave to see
Avoid damp beds and think of me.
Epitaph of Lydia Eason, St Michael's, Stoke

28 Beneath this stone, in hope of Zion,
Doth lie the landlord of the 'Lion'.
His son keeps on the business still,
Resign'd unto the Heavenly will.
Epitaph, Upton-on-Severn churchyard

29 Here lie I and my four daughters,
Killed by drinking Cheltenham waters.
Had we but stick to Epsom salts,

We wouldn't have been in these here vaults.
Cheltenham Waters

30 Here lie I by the chancel door;
They put me here because I was poor.
The further in, the more you pay,
But here lie I as snug as they.
Epitaph, Devon churchyard

31 Here lies a man who was killed by lightning;
He died when his prospects seemed to be brightening.
He might have cut a flash in this world of trouble,
But the flash cut him, and he lies in the stubble.
Epitaph, Torrington, Devon

32 Here lies a valiant warrior
Who never drew a sword;
Here lies a noble courtier
Who never kept his word;
Here lies the Earl of Leicester
Who governed the estates
Whom the earth could never living love,
And the just heaven now hates.
Attrib. to Ben Jonson in *Collection of Epitaphs* (Tissington), 1857

33 Here lies father and mother and sister and I,
We all died within the space of one short year;
They all be buried at Wimble, except I,
And I be buried here.
Epitaph, Staffordshire churchyard

34 Here lies Fred,
Who was alive and is dead:
Had it been his father,
I had much rather;
Had it been his brother,
Still better than another;
Had it been his sister,
No one would have missed her;
Had it been the whole generation,
Still better for the nation:
But since 'tis only Fred,
Who was alive and is dead, –
There's no more to be said.
Referring to Frederick, Prince of Wales (d. 1751), eldest son of George II and father of George III.
Memoirs of George II (Horace Walpole)

35 Here lies my wife,
Here lies she;
Hallelujah!
Hallelujee!
Epitaph, Leeds churchyard

36 Here lies the body of Mary Ann Lowder,
She burst while drinking a seidlitz powder.
Called from the world to her heavenly rest,
She should have waited till it effervesced.
Epitaph

37 Here lies the body of Richard Hind,
Who was neither ingenious, sober, nor kind.
Epitaph

38 Here lies Will Smith – and, what's something rarish,
He was born, bred, and hanged, all in the same parish.
Epitaph

39 Mary Ann has gone to rest,
Safe at last on Abraham's breast,
Which may be nuts for Mary Ann,
But is certainly rough on Abraham.
Epitaph

40 My sledge and anvil lie declined
My bellows too have lost their wind
My fire's extinct, my forge decayed,
And in the Dust my Vice is laid
My coals are spent, my iron's gone
My Nails are Drove, My Work is done.
An epitaph to William Strange, blacksmith, died 6 June 1746 and buried in Nettlebed churchyard

41 Sacred to the memory of
Captain Anthony Wedgwood
Accidentally shot by his gamekeeper
Whilst out shooting
"Well done thou good and faithful servant"
Epitaph

42 Stranger! Approach this spot with gravity!
John Brown is filling his last cavity.
Epitaph of a dentist

43 This the grave of Mike O'Day
Who died maintaining his right of way.
His right was clear, his will was strong.
But he's just as dead as if he'd been wrong.
Epitaph

44 Warm summer sun shine kindly here:
Warm summer wind blow softly here:
Green sod above lie light, lie light:
Good-night, Dear Heart: good-night, good-night.
Memorial to Clorinda Haywood, St Bartholomew's, Edgbaston

EQUALITY

See also class, feminism, human rights

1 A cat may look at a king.
Proverb

2 All cats are grey in the dark.
Proverb

3 Equality may perhaps be a right, but no power on earth can ever turn it into a fact.
Honoré de Balzac (1799–1850) French novelist.
La Duchesse de Langeais

4 From the point of view of sexual morality the aeroplane is valuable in war in that it destroys men and women in equal numbers.
Ernest William Barnes (1874–1953) British clergyman and mathematician.
Rise of Christianity

5 What makes equality such a difficult business is that we only want it with our superiors.
Henry Becque (1837–99) French dramatist.
Querelles littéraires

6 All service ranks the same with God –
With God, whose puppets, best and worst,
Are we: there is no last or first.
Robert Browning (1812–89) British poet.
Pippa Passes, Pt. I

7 The terrorist and the policeman both come from the same basket.
Joseph Conrad (Teodor Josef Konrad Korzeniowski; 1857–1924) Polish-born British novelist.
The Secret Agent, Ch. 4

8 The majestic egalitarianism of the law, which forbids rich and poor alike to sleep under bridges, to beg in the streets, and to steal bread.
Anatole France (Jacques Anatole François Thibault; 1844–1924) French writer.
The Red Lily, Ch. 7

9 Men are made by nature unequal. It is vain, therefore, to treat them as if they were equal.
J. A. Froude (1818–94) British historian.
Short Studies on Great Subjects, 'Party Politics'

10 That all men are equal is a proposition to which, at ordinary times, no sane individual has ever given his assent.
Aldous Huxley (1894–1964) British novelist.
Proper Studies

11 Your levellers wish to level *down* as far as themselves; but they cannot bear levelling *up* to themselves.
Samuel Johnson (1709–84) British lexicographer.
Life of Johnson (J. Boswell), Vol. I

12 It is better that some should be unhappy than that none should be happy, which would be the case in a general state of equality.
Samuel Johnson
Life of Johnson (J. Boswell), Vol. III

13 I have a dream that one day this nation will rise up, live out the true meaning of its creed: we hold these truths to be self-evident, that all men are created equal.
Martin Luther King (1929–68) US Black civil-rights leader.
He used the words 'I have a dream' in a number of speeches
Speech, Washington, 27 Aug 1963

14 Never descend to the ways of those above you.
George Mallaby (1902–78) British diplomat and writer.
From My Level

15 All animals are equal but some animals are more equal than others.
George Orwell (Eric Blair; 1903–50) British novelist.
Animal Farm, Ch. 10

16 In America everybody is of the opinion that he has no social superiors, since all men are equal, but he does not admit that he has no social inferiors.
Bertrand Russell (1872–1970) British philosopher.
Unpopular Essays

17 I think the King is but a man as I am: the violet smells to him as it doth to me.
William Shakespeare (1564–1616) English dramatist.
Henry V, IV:1

18 Hath not a Jew eyes? Hath not a Jew hands, organs, dimensions, senses, affections, passions, fed with the same food, hurt with the same weapons, subject to the same diseases, healed by the same means, warmed and cooled by the same winter and summer, as a Christian is? If you prick us, do we not bleed? If you tickle us, do we not laugh? If you poison us, do we not die? And if you wrong us, shall we not revenge?
William Shakespeare
The Merchant of Venice, III:1

19 This is a movie, not a lifeboat.
Spencer Tracy (1900–67) US film star.
Defending his demand for equal billing with Katherine Hepburn
Attrib.

20 Everybody should have an equal chance – but they shouldn't have a flying start.
Harold Wilson (1916–) British politician and prime minister.
The Observer, 'Sayings of the Year', 1963

Equality in death

See also death, equality

21 It comes equally to us all, and makes us all equal when it comes. The ashes of an Oak in the Chimney, are no epitaph of that Oak, to tell me how high or how large that was; It tells me not what flocks it sheltered while it stood, nor what men it hurt when it fell. The dust of great persons' graves is speechless too, it says nothing, it distinguishes nothing.
John Donne (1573–1631) English poet.
Sermons, XV

22 Now at last our child is just like all children.
Charles De Gaulle (1890–1970) French general and statesman.
On the death of his retarded daughter Anne
Ten First Ladies of the World (Pauline Frederick)

23 Pale Death kicks his way equally into the cottages of the poor and the castles of kings.
Horace (Quintus Horatius Flaccus; 65–8 BC) Roman poet.
Odes, I

24 A heap of dust alone remains of thee;
'Tis all thou art, and all the proud shall be!
Alexander Pope (1688–1744) British poet.
Elegy to the Memory of an Unfortunate Lady

ESCAPE

1 I bet you a hundred bucks he ain't in here.
Charles Bancroft Dillingham (1868–1934) US theatrical manager.
Referring to the escapologist Harry Houdini; said at his funeral, while carrying his coffin
Attrib.

2 He can run, but he can't hide.
Joe Louis (Joseph Louis Barrow; 1914–81) US boxer.
Referring to the speed for which his coming opponent, Billy Conn, was renowned
Attrib.

ETERNITY

See also immortality, time

1 Kiss till the cow comes home.
Francis Beaumont (1584–1616) English dramatist.
Scornful Lady, II:2

2 As it was in the beginning, is now, and ever shall be: world without end.
The Book of Common Prayer
Morning Prayer, Gloria

3 Thou, silent form, dost tease us out of thought
As doth eternity: Cold Pastoral!
John Keats (1795–1821) British poet.
Ode on a Grecian Urn

4 Eternity's a terrible thought. I mean, where's it going to end?
Tom Stoppard (1937–) Czech-born British dramatist.
Rosencrantz and Guildenstern Are Dead, II

ETIQUETTE

See also manners

1 Phone for the fish knives Norman,
As Cook is a little unnerved;
You kiddies have crumpled the serviettes
And I must have things daintily served.
John Betjeman (1906–84) British poet.
How to get on in Society

2 'It is very pleasant dining with a bachelor,' said Miss Matty, softly, as we settled ourselves in the counting-house. 'I only hope it is not improper; so many pleasant things are!'
Elizabeth Gaskell (1810–65) British novelist.
Cranford, Ch. 4

3 We could not lead a pleasant life,
And 'twould be finished soon,
If peas were eaten with the knife,
And gravy with the spoon.
Eat slowly: only men in rags
And gluttons old in sin
Mistake themselves for carpet bags
And tumble victals in.
Walter Alexander Raleigh (1861–1922) British scholar.
Laughter from a Cloud, 'Stans puer ad mensam'

4 'How did you think I managed at dinner, Clarence?' 'Capitally!' 'I had a knife and two forks left at the end,' she said regretfully.
William Pett Ridge (1860–1930) British novelist.
Love at Paddington Green, Ch. 6

5 I think she must have been very strictly brought up, she's so desperately anxious to do the wrong thing correctly.
Saki (Hector Hugh Munro; 1870–1916) British writer.
Reginald on Worries

EUROPE

See also Britain, England, France, Germany, Ireland, Russia, Scotland, Switzerland, Venice, Wales

1 Rome's just a city like anywhere else. A vastly overrated city, I'd say. It trades on belief just as Stratford trades on Shakespeare.
Anthony Burgess (John Burgess Wilson; 1917–) British novelist.
Mr Enderby, Pt. II, Ch. 2

2 But the age of chivalry is gone. That of sophisters, economists, and calculators, has succeeded; and the glory of Europe is extinguished for ever.
Edmund Burke (1729–97) British politician.
Reflections on the Revolution in France

3 The isles of Greece, the isles of Greece!
Where burning Sappho loved and sung,
Where grew the arts of war and peace,
Where Delos rose, and Phoebus sprung!
Eternal summer gilds them yet,
But all, except their sun, is set.
Lord Byron (1788–1824) British poet.
Don Juan, III

4 The mountains look on Marathon –
And Marathon looks on the sea:
And musing there an hour alone,
I dream'd that Greece might still be free.
Lord Byron
Don Juan, III

5 While stands the Coliseum, Rome shall stand;
When falls the Coliseum, Rome shall fall;
And when Rome falls – the World.
Lord Byron
Childe Harold's Pilgrimage, IV

6 We must build a kind of United States of Europe.
Winston Churchill (1874–1965) British statesman.
Speech, Zurich, 19 Sept 1946

7 Apart from cheese and tulips, the main product of the country is advocaat, a drink made from lawyers.
Alan Coren (1938–) British humorist and writer.
Referring to Holland
The Sanity Inspector, 'All You Need to Know about Europe'

8 Holland . . . lies so low they're only saved by being dammed.
Thomas Hood (1799–1845) British poet.
Up the Rhine

9 It's not enough to be Hungarian, you must have talent too.
Alexander Korda (Sandor Kellner; 1893–1956) Hungarian-born British film director.
Alexander Korda (K. Kulik)

10 In Western Europe there are now only small countries – those that know it and those that don't know it yet.
Théo Lefèvre (1914–73) Belgian prime minister.
The Observer, 'Sayings of the Year', 1963

11 I am inclined to notice the ruin in things, perhaps because I was born in Italy.
Arthur Miller (1915–) US dramatist.
A View from the Bridge, I

12 Austria is Switzerland speaking pure German and with history added.
J. E. Morpurgo (1918–) British writer and academic.
The Road to Athens

13 Providence has given to the French the empire of the land, to the English that of the sea, and to the Germans that of the air.
Jean Paul Richter (Johann Paul Friedrich Richter; 1763–1825) German novelist.
Quoted by Thomas Carlyle

14 The people of Crete unfortunately make more history than they can consume locally.
Saki (Hector Hugh Munro; 1870–1916) British writer.
The Jesting of Arlington Stringham

15 We are part of the community of Europe and we must do our duty as such.
Marquess of Salisbury (1830–1903) British statesman.
Speech, Caernarvon, 11 Apr 1888

16 We're from Madeira, but perfectly respectable, so far.
George Bernard Shaw (1856–1950) Irish dramatist and critic.
You Never Can Tell, I

17 Let there be light! said Liberty,
And like sunrise from the sea,
Athens arose!
Percy Bysshe Shelley (1792–1822) British poet.
Hellas, I

18 This going into Europe will not turn out to be the thrilling mutual exchange supposed. It is more like nine middle-aged couples with failing marriages meeting in a darkened bedroom in a Brussels hotel for a Group Grope.
E. P. Thompson (1924–) British historian.
On the Europe debate, *Sunday Times*, 27 Apr 1975

19 Every place I look at I work out the cubic feet, and I say it will make a good warehouse or it won't. Can't help myself. One of the best warehouses I ever see was the Vatican in Rome.
Arnold Wesker (1932–) British dramatist.
Chips with Everything, I:6

20 That Europe's nothin' on earth but a great big auction, that's all it is.
Tennessee Williams (1911–83) US dramatist.
Cat on a Hot Tin Roof, I

EVIL

See also good and evil, sin, vice

1 *Honi soit qui mal y pense.*
Evil be to him who evil thinks.
Anonymous
Motto for the Order of the Garter

2 It takes a certain courage and a certain greatness even to be truly base.
Jean Anouilh (1910–87) French dramatist.
Ardele

3 Wherefore I praised the dead which are already dead more than the living which are yet alive.
Yea, better is he than both they, which hath not yet been, who hath not seen the evil work that is done under the sun.
Bible: Ecclesiastes
4:2–3

4 But evil men and seducers shall wax worse and worse, deceiving, and being deceived.
Bible: II Timothy
3:13

5 And this is the condemnation, that light is come into the world, and men loved darkness rather than light, because their deeds were evil.
Bible: John
3:19

6 I never saw a brute I hated so;
He must be wicked to deserve such pain.
Robert Browning (1812–89) British poet.
Childe Roland to the Dark Tower Came, XIV

7 The belief in a supernatural source of evil is not necessary; men alone are quite capable of every wickedness.
Joseph Conrad (Teodor Josef Konrad Korzeniowski; 1857–1924) Polish-born British novelist.
Under Western Eyes, Part 2

8 There's a young man hid with me, in comparison with which young man I am a Angel. That young man hears the words I speak. That young man has a secret way pecooliar to himself, of getting at a boy, and at his heart, and at his liver.
Charles Dickens (1812–70) British novelist.
Said by Magwitch
Great Expectations, Ch. 1

9 Something nasty in the woodshed.

Stella Gibbons (1902–) British poet and novelist.
Cold Comfort Farm

10 But evil is wrought by want of thought,
As well as want of heart!

Thomas Hood (1799–1845) British poet.
The Lady's Dream

11 Farewell remorse! All good to me is lost;
Evil, be thou my Good.

John Milton (1608–74) English poet.
Paradise Lost, Bk. IV

12 Take thy beak from out my heart, and take
thy form from off my door!
Quoth the Raven, 'Nevermore.'

Edgar Allan Poe (1809–49) US poet and writer.
The Raven

13 There is scarcely a single man sufficiently
aware to know all the evil he does.

Duc de la Rochefoucauld (1613–80) French writer.
Maximes, 269

14 She is a smart old broad. It is a pity she is
so nefarious.

Damon Runyon (1884–1946) US writer.
Runyon à la carte, 'Broadway Incident'

15 Friends, Romans, countrymen, lend me your
ears
I come to bury Caesar, not to praise him.
The evil that men do lives after them;
The good is oft interred with their bones.

William Shakespeare (1564–1616) English dramatist.
Julius Caesar, III:2

EVOLUTION

See also survival

1 Descended from the apes? My dear, we will
hope it is not true. But if it is, let us pray
that it may not become generally known.

Anonymous
Remark by the wife of a canon of Worcester Cathedral
Man's Most Dangerous Myth, The Fallacy of Race (F. Ashley
Montagu)

2 From an evolutionary point of view, man has
stopped moving, if he ever did move.

Pierre Teilhard de Chardin (1881–1955) French Jesuit
and palaeontologist.
The Phenomenon of Man, Postscript

3 We must, however, acknowledge, as it
seems to me, that man with all his noble
qualities, still bears in his bodily frame the
indelible stamp of his lowly origin.

Charles Darwin (1809–82) British life scientist.
Closing words
Descent of Man, Ch. 21

4 We will now discuss in a little more detail the
struggle for existence.

Charles Darwin
Origin of Species, Ch. 3

5 I have called this principle, by which each

slight variation, if useful, is preserved, by the
term of Natural Selection.

Charles Darwin
Origin of Species, Ch. 3

6 The expression often used by Mr Herbert
Spencer of the Survival of the Fittest is more
accurate, and is sometimes equally
convenient.

Charles Darwin
Origin of Species, Ch. 3

7 The question is this: Is man an ape or an
angel? I, my lord, am on the side of the
angels.

Benjamin Disraeli (1804–81) British statesman.
Speech, 25 Nov 1864

8 Philip is a living example of natural selection.
He was as fitted to survive in this modern
world as a tapeworm in an intestine.

William Golding (1911–) British novelist.
Free Fall, Ch. 2

9 I asserted – and I repeat – that a man has
no reason to be ashamed of having an ape for
his grandfather. If there were an ancestor
whom I should feel shame in recalling it
would rather be a *man* – a man of restless
and versatile intellect – who, not content
with an equivocal success in his own sphere
of activity, plunges into scientific questions
with which he has no real acquaintance, only
to obscure them by an aimless rhetoric, and
distract the attention of his hearers from the
real point at issue by eloquent digressions
and skilled appeals to religious prejudice.

T. H. Huxley (1825–95) British biologist.
Replying to Bishop WILBERFORCE in the debate on Darwin's
theory of evolution at the meeting of the British Association at
Oxford. No transcript was taken at the time; the version
above is commonly quoted. After hearing Wilberforce's
speech, and before rising himself, Huxley is said to have remarked, 'The Lord has delivered him into my hands!'
Speech, 30 June 1860

10 And, in conclusion, I would like to ask the
gentleman . . . whether the ape from which he
is descended was on his grandmother's or his
grandfather's side of the family.

Samuel Wilberforce (1805–73) British churchman.
See T. H. HUXLEY
Speech, 30 June 1860

EXAMINATIONS

See also education

1 Examinations are formidable even to the best
prepared, for the greatest fool may ask more
than the wisest man can answer.

Charles Caleb Colton (?1780–1832) British clergyman
and writer.
Lacon, Vol. II

2 Do not on any account attempt to write on
both sides of the paper at once.

W. C. Sellar (1898–1951) British humorous writer.
1066 And All That, Test Paper 5

3 If silicon had been a gas I should have been a major-general.
James Whistler (1834–1903) US painter.
Referring to his failure in a West Point chemistry examination
English Wits (L. Russell)

EXAMPLE

1 Practise what you preach.
Proverb

2 Example is the school of mankind, and they will learn at no other.
Edmund Burke (1729–97) British politician.
Letters on a Regicide Peace, letter 1

3 Do as you would be done by is the surest method that I know of pleasing.
Earl of Chesterfield (1694–1773) English statesman.
Letter to his son, 16 Oct 1747

4 What you do not want done to yourself, do not do to others.
Confucius (K'ung Fu-tzu; 551–479 BC) Chinese philosopher.
Analects

5 Men are not hanged for stealing horses, but that horses may not be stolen.
George Saville (1633–95) English statesman.
Political, Moral and Miscellaneous Thoughts and Reflections

6 A precedent embalms a principle.
William Scott (1745–1836) British jurist.
An opinion given while Advocate-General
Attrib.; also quoted by Benjamin Disraeli (1848)

7 Preachers say, Do as I say, not as I do. But if the physician had the same disease upon him that I have, and he should bid me do one thing, and himself do quite another, could I believe him?
John Selden (1584–1654) English historian.
Table Talk

8 Do not, as some ungracious pastors do,
Show me the steep and thorny way to heaven,
Whiles, like a puff'd and reckless libertine,
Himself the primrose path of dalliance treads
And recks not his own rede.
William Shakespeare (1564–1616) English dramatist.
Hamlet, I:3

9 *Dans ce pays-ci, il est bon de tuer de temps en temps un amiral pour encourager les autres.*
In this country it is good to kill an admiral from time to time, to encourage the others.
Voltaire (François-Marie Arouet; 1694–1778) French writer.
Referring to England: Admiral Byng was executed for failing to defeat the French at Minorca (1757)
Candide, Ch. 23

EXCELLENCE

See also superiority

1 Whatever is worth doing at all is worth doing well.
Earl of Chesterfield (1694–1773) English statesman.
Letter to his son, 10 Mar 1746

2 The danger chiefly lies in acting well,
No crime's so great as daring to excel.
Charles Churchill (1731–64) British poet.
Epistle to William Hogarth

3 If you had been mine when you were seven you would have been the crème de la crème.
Muriel Spark (1918–) British novelist.
The Prime of Miss Jean Brodie, Ch. 2

4 The best is the enemy of the good.
Voltaire (François-Marie Arouet; 1694–1778) French writer.
Dictionnaire philosophique, 'Art dramatique'

EXCESS

See also moderation

1 *L'embarras des richesses.*
A superfluity of good things.
Abbé Lénor Jean d'Allainval (1700–53) French dramatist.
Play title

2 What fun it would be to be poor, as long as one was *excessively* poor! Anything in excess is most exhilarating.
Jean Anouilh (1910–87) French dramatist.
Ring Round the Moon

3 The road of excess leads to the palace of Wisdom.
William Blake (1757–1827) British poet.
The Marriage of Heaven and Hell, 'Proverbs of Hell'

4 I would remind you that extremism in the defence of liberty is no vice. And let me remind you also that moderation in the pursuit of justice is no virtue!
Barry Goldwater (1904–) US politician.
Speech, San Francisco, 17 July 1964

5 No part of the walls is left undecorated. From everywhere the praise of the Lord is drummed into you.
Nikolaus Pevsner (Bernhard Leon; 1902–83) German-born British art historian.
London, except the Cities of London and Westminster

6 In baiting a mouse-trap with cheese, always leave room for the mouse.
Saki (Hector Hugh Munro; 1870–1916) British writer.
The Square Egg

7 'Tis not the drinking that is to be blamed, but the excess.
John Selden (1584–1654) English historian.
Table Talk

8 The lady doth protest too much, methinks.
William Shakespeare (1564–1616) English dramatist.
Hamlet, III:2

9 Well said; that was laid on with a trowel.
William Shakespeare
As You Like It, I:2

10 To gild refined gold, to paint the lily,
To throw a perfume on the violet,
To smooth the ice, or add another hue
Unto the rainbow, or with taper-light
To seek the beauteous eye of heaven to
garnish,
Is wasteful and ridiculous excess.
William Shakespeare
King John, IV:2

11 Heat not a furnace for your foe so hot
That it do singe yourself. We may outrun
By violent swiftness that which we run at,
And lose by over-running.
William Shakespeare
Henry VIII, I:1

12 It out-herods Herod.
William Shakespeare
Hamlet, III:2

13 Extreme *busyness*, whether at school or
college, kirk or market, is a symptom of
deficient vitality.
Robert Louis Stevenson (1850–94) Scottish writer.
Virginibus Puerisque

14 Battering the gates of heaven with storms of
prayer.
Alfred, Lord Tennyson (1809–92) British poet.
St Simeon Stylites

15 Moderation is a fatal thing, Lady Hunstanton.
Nothing succeeds like excess.
Oscar Wilde (1854–1900) Irish-born British dramatist.
A Woman of No Importance, III

EXECUTION

See also last words, martyrdom, punishment

1 It's time for me to enjoy another pinch of
snuff. Tomorrow my hands will be bound, so
as to make it impossible.
Jean Sylvain Bailly (1736–93) French astronomer.
Said on the evening before his execution
Anekdotenschatz (H. Hoffmeister)

2 And almost all things are by the law purged
with blood; and without shedding of blood is
no remission.
Bible: Hebrews
9:22

3 And when they were come to the place,
which is called Calvary, there they crucified
him, and the malefactors, one on the right
hand, and the other on the left.
Bible: Luke
23:33

4 I die a Christian, according to the Profession

of the Church of England, as I found it left
me by my Father.
Charles I (1600–49) King of England.
Speech on the scaffold, 30 Jan 1649

5 Thou wilt show my head to the people: it is
worth showing.
Georges Jacques Danton (1759–94) French political
activist.
Said as he mounted the scaffold, 5 Apr 1794
French Revolution (Carlyle), Bk. VI, Ch. 2

6 It is a far, far, better thing that I do, than I
have ever done; it is a far, far, better rest
that I go to, than I have ever known.
Charles Dickens (1812–70) British novelist.
Said by Sydney Carton
A Tale of Two Cities, Bk. II, Ch. 15

7 To die for faction is a common evil,
But to be hanged for nonsense is the Devil.
John Dryden (1631–1700) British poet and dramatist.
Absalom and Achitophel, II

8 Son of Saint Louis, ascend to heaven.
Abbé Edgeworth de Firmont (1745–1807) Irish-born
confessor to Louis XVI.
Said to Louis XVI as he climbed up to the guillotine
Attrib.

9 Let them bestow on every airth a limb;
Then open all my veins, that I may swim
To thee, my Maker! in that crimson lake;
Then place my parboiled head upon a stake –
Scatter my ashes – strew them in the air; –
Lord! since thou know'st where all these at-
oms are,
I'm hopeful thou'lt recover once my dust,
And confident thou'lt raise me with the just.
James Graham (1612–50) Scottish general.
Lines written on the window of his jail the night before his
execution

10 And have they fixed the where and when?
And shall Trelawny die?
Here's twenty thousand Cornish men
Will know the reason why!
R. S. Hawker (1803–75) British poet.
Referring to the imprisonment (1688) of Trelawny, Bishop of
Bristol, by James II
Song of the Western Men

11 They hang us now in Shrewsbury jail:
The whistles blow forlorn,
And trains all night groan on the rail
To men that die at morn.
A. E. Housman (1859–1936) British scholar and poet.
A Shropshire Lad, 'Reveillé'

12 Depend upon it, Sir, when a man knows he
is to be hanged in a fortnight, it concentrates
his mind wonderfully.
Samuel Johnson (1709–84) British lexicographer.
Life of Johnson (J. Boswell), Vol. III

13 If we are to abolish the death penalty, I
should like to see the first step taken by our
friends the murderers.
Alphonse Karr (1808–90) French writer.
Les Guêpes, Jan 1849

14 'For they're hangin' Danny Deever, you can
hear the Dead March play,
The Regiment's in 'ollow square – they're
hangin' 'im to-day;
They've taken of 'is buttons off an' cut 'is
stripes away,
An' they're hangin' Danny Deever in the
mornin'.'
Rudyard Kipling (1865–1936) Indian-born British writer.
Danny Deever

15 Be of good comfort, Master Ridley, and play
the man; we shall this day light such a
candle, by God's grace, in England as I trust
shall never be put out.
Hugh Latimer (1485–1555) English churchman.
Said to Nicholas Ridley as they were about to be burnt at the
stake for heresy
Famous Last Words (B. Conrad)

16 He nothing common did or mean
Upon that memorable scene,
But with his keener eye
The axe's edge did try.
Andrew Marvell (1621–78) English poet.
Referring to the execution of Charles I
An Horatian Ode upon Cromwell's Return from Ireland

17 Do not hack me as you did my Lord Russell.
Duke of Monmouth (1649–85) An illegitimate son of
Charles II.
Said to the headsman before his execution
History of England (Macaulay), Vol. I, Ch. 5

18 I pray you, Master Lieutenant, see me safe
up, and for coming down let me shift for
myself.
Thomas More (1478–1535) English lawyer and scholar.
On climbing onto the scaffold prior to his execution
Life of Sir Thomas More (William Roper)

19 Pluck up thy spirits, man, and be not afraid
to do thine office; my neck is very short;
take heed therefore thou strike not awry, for
saving of thine honesty.
Thomas More
Said to the headsman
Life of Sir Thomas More (Roper)

20 This hath not offended the king.
Thomas More
Said as he drew his beard aside before putting his head on the
block

21 The sight of it gave me infinite pleasure, as
it proved that I was in a civilized society.
Mungo Park (1771–1806) Scottish explorer.
Remark on finding a gibbet in an unexplored part of Africa
Attrib.

22 I went out to Charing Cross, to see Major-
general Harrison hanged, drawn, and
quartered; which was done there, he looking
as cheerful as any man could do in that
condition.
Samuel Pepys (1633–1703) English diarist.
Diary, 13 Oct 1660

23 The world itself is but a large prison, out of
which some are daily led to execution.
Walter Raleigh (1554–1618) English explorer.
Said after his trial for treason, 1603
Attrib.

24 So the heart be right, it is no matter which
way the head lies.
Walter Raleigh
On laying his head on the executioner's block
Attrib.

25 Tis a sharp remedy, but a sure one for all
ills.
Walter Raleigh
Referring to the executioner's axe just before he was
beheaded
Attrib.

26 If you give me six lines written by the most
honest man, I will find something in them to
hang him.
Cardinal Richelieu (1585–1642) French statesman.
Exact wording uncertain
Attrib.

27 *'O liberté! O liberté! Que de crimes on commet
en ton nom!'*
Oh liberty! Oh liberty! What crimes are com-
mitted in thy name!
Madame Roland (1754–93) French revolutionary.
Said as she mounted the steps of the guillotine
Attrib.

28 Then, with that faint fleeting smile playing
about his lips, he faced the firing squad;
erect and motionless, proud and disdainful,
Walter Mitty, the undefeated, inscrutable to
the last.
James Thurber (1894–1961) US humorist.
My World and Welcome to It, 'The Secret Life of Walter Mitty'

EXISTENCE

1 Dear Sir, Your astonishment's odd:
I am always about in the Quad.
And that's why the tree
Will continue to be,
Since observed by Yours faithfully, God.
Anonymous
The response to KNOX's limerick

2 Let us be moral. Let us contemplate
existence.
Charles Dickens (1812–70) British novelist.
Martin Chuzzlewit, Ch. 10

3 As far as we can discern, the sole purpose of
human existence is to kindle a light in the
darkness of mere being.
Carl Gustav Jung (1875–1961) Swiss psychoanalyst.
Memories, Dreams, Reflections, Ch. 11

4 There once was a man who said 'God
Must think it exceedingly odd
If he find that this tree
Continues to be

When there's no one about in the Quad.'
Ronald Knox (1888–1957) British Roman Catholic priest.
For a reply, *see* ANONYMOUS
Attrib.

5 I know perfectly well that I don't want to do anything; to do something is to create existence – and there's quite enough existence as it is.
Jean-Paul Sartre (1905–80) French writer.
Nausea

EXPECTATION

See also anticipation, disappointment, hope

1 As I know more of mankind I expect less of them, and am ready now to call a man *a good man*, upon easier terms than I was formerly.
Samuel Johnson (1709–84) British lexicographer.
Life of Johnson (J. Boswell), Vol. IV

2 Dear Mary, We all knew you had it in you.
Dorothy Parker (1893–1967) US writer.
Telegram sent to a friend on the successful outcome of her much-publicized pregnancy

3 'Blessed is the man who expects nothing, for he shall never be disappointed' was the ninth beatitude.
Alexander Pope (1688–1744) British poet.
Letter to Fortescue, 23 Sept 1725

4 See yon pale stripling! when a boy,
A mother's pride, a father's joy!
Walter Scott (1771–1832) Scottish novelist.
Rokeby, III

5 Gomer Owen who kissed her once by the pig-sty when she wasn't looking and never kissed her again although she was looking all the time.
Dylan Thomas (1914–53) Welsh poet.
Under Milk Wood

EXPEDIENCY

1 And my parents finally realize that I'm kidnapped and they snap into action immediately: they rent out my room.
Woody Allen (Allen Stewart Konigsberg; 1935–) US film actor.
Woody Allen and His Comedy (E. Lax)

2 I would rather be an opportunist and float than go to the bottom with my principles round my neck.
Stanley Baldwin (1867–1947) British statesman.
Attrib.

3 Nobody is forgotten when it is convenient to remember him.
Benjamin Disraeli (1804–81) British statesman.
Attrib.

4 You can't learn too soon that the most useful thing about a principle is that it can always be sacrificed to expediency.
W. Somerset Maugham (1874–1965) British novelist.
The Circle, III

5 No man is justified in doing evil on the ground of expediency.
Theodore Roosevelt (1858–1919) US Republican president.
The Strenuous Life

6 Well, a widow, I see, is a kind of sinecure.
William Wycherley (1640–1716) English dramatist.
The Plain Dealer, V:3

EXPERIENCE

See also history, past

1 A young physician fattens the churchyard.
Proverb

2 Experience is the best teacher.
Proverb

3 Experience is the mother of wisdom.
Proverb

4 Live and learn.
Proverb

5 Practice makes perfect.
Proverb

6 Experience is a good teacher, but she sends in terrific bills.
Minna Antrim (1861–?) US writer.
Naked Truth and Veiled Allusions

7 One should try everything once, except incest and folk-dancing.
Arnold Bax (1883–1953) British composer.
Farewell to My Youth

8 You will think me lamentably crude: my experience of life has been drawn from life itself.
Max Beerbohm (1872–1956) British writer.
Zuleika Dobson, Ch. 7

9 Experience isn't interesting till it begins to repeat itself – in fact, till it does that, it hardly *is* experience.
Elizabeth Bowen (1899–1973) Irish novelist.
The Death of the Heart, Pt. I, Ch. 1

10 When all is said and done, no literature can outdo the cynicism of real life; you won't intoxicate with one glass someone who has already drunk up a whole barrel.
Anton Chekhov (1860–1904) Russian dramatist.
Letter, 1887

11 If men could learn from history, what lessons it might teach us! But passion and party blind our eyes and the light which experience gives is a lantern on the stern, which shines only on the waves behind us!
Samuel Taylor Coleridge (1772–1834) British poet.
Recollections (Allsop)

12 An experience of women which extends over many nations and three continents.
Arthur Conan Doyle (1856–1930) British writer.
The Sign of Four

13 How many roads must a man walk down Before you call him a man?
Bob Dylan (Robert Allen Zimmerman; 1941–) US popular singer.
Blowin' in the Wind

14 What experience and history teach is this – that people and governments never have learned anything from history, or acted on principles deduced from it.
Hegel (1770–1831) German philosopher.
Philosophy of History, Introduction

15 A moment's insight is sometimes worth a life's experience.
Oliver Wendell Holmes (1809–94) US writer.
The Professor at the Breakfast Table, Ch. 10

16 Experience is never limited, and it is never complete; it is an immense sensibility, a kind of huge spider-web of the finest silken threads suspended in the chamber of consciousness, and catching every air-borne particle in its tissue.
Henry James (1843–1916) US novelist.
Partial Portraits, 'The Art of Fiction'

17 Nothing ever becomes real till it is experienced – even a proverb is no proverb to you till your life has illustrated it.
John Keats (1795–1821) British poet.
Letter to George and Georgiana Keats, 19 Mar 1819

18 He was what I often think is a dangerous thing for a statesman to be – a student of history; and like most of those who study history, he learned from the mistakes of the past how to make new ones.
A. J. P. Taylor (1906–) British historian.
Referring to Napoleon III
The Listener, 6 June 1963

19 Nourishing a youth sublime With the fairy tales of science, and the long result of Time.
Alfred, Lord Tennyson (1809–92) British poet.
Locksley Hall

20 All experience is an arch wherethro' Gleams that untravelled world, whose margin fades
For ever and for ever when I move.
Alfred, Lord Tennyson
Ulysses

21 You don't set a fox to watching the chickens just because he has a lot of experience in the hen house.
Harry S. Truman (1884–1972) US statesman.
Referring to Vice-President Nixon's nomination for President
Speech, 30 Oct 1960

22 I have learned

To look on nature, not as in the hour Of thoughtless youth; but hearing often-times The still, sad music of humanity.
William Wordsworth (1770–1850) British poet.
Lines composed a few miles above Tintern Abbey

EXPERTS

1 By studying the masters - not their pupils.
Niels Henrik Abel (1809–29) Norwegian mathematician.
When asked how he had become a great mathematician so quickly
Men of Mathematics (E. T. Bell)

2 An expert is a man who has made all the mistakes, which can be made, in a very narrow field.
Niels Bohr (1885–1962) Danish physicist.
Attrib.

3 An expert is someone who knows some of the worst mistakes that can be made in his subject, and how to avoid them.
Werner Heisenberg (1901–76) German physicist.
Physics and Beyond

4 An accomplished man to his finger-tips.
Horace (Quintus Horatius Flaccus; 65–8 BC) Roman poet.
Satires, I

5 Specialist – A man who knows more and more about less and less.
William James Mayo (1861–1934) US surgeon.
Also attributed to Nicholas Butler

6 The trouble with specialists is that they tend to think in grooves.
Elaine Morgan (1920–) British writer.
The Descent of Woman, Ch. 1

EXPLANATIONS

1 I am one of those unfortunates to whom death is less hideous than explanations.
D. B. Wyndham Lewis (1891–1969) British journalist and writer.
Welcome to All This

2 There is occasions and causes why and wherefore in all things.
William Shakespeare (1564–1616) English dramatist.
Henry V, V:1

EXPLOITATION

1 Thus the devil played at chess with me, and yielding a pawn, thought to gain a queen of me, taking advantage of my honest endeavours.
Thomas Browne (1605–82) English physician and writer.
Religio Medici, Pt. I

2 Mortals, whose pleasures are their only care, First wish to be imposed on, and then are.
William Cowper (1731–1800) British poet.
The Progress of Error

3 I should be trading on the blood of my men.
Robert E. Lee (1807–70) US general.
Refusing to write his memoirs
Nobody Said It Better (M. Ringo)

EXPLORATION

See also discovery

1 The fair breeze blew, the white foam flew,
The furrow followed free;
We were the first that ever burst
Into that silent sea.
Samuel Taylor Coleridge (1772–1834) British poet.
The Rime of the Ancient Mariner, II

2 Go West, young man, and grow up with the country.
Horace Greeley (1811–72) US politician and journalist.
Also attributed to the US writer John Soule (1815–91), *Terre Haute* (Indiana) *Express*, 1851
Hints toward Reform

3 Nothing easier. One step beyond the pole, you see, and the north wind becomes a south one.
Robert Edwin Peary (1856–1920) US explorer.
Explaining how he knew he had reached the North Pole
Attrib.

EXTRAVAGANCE

See also excess, luxury, money, ostentation, thrift, waste

1 Riches are for spending.
Francis Bacon (1561–1626) English philosopher.
Essays, 'Of Expense'

2 All progress is based upon a universal innate desire on the part of every organism to live beyond its income.
Samuel Butler (1835–1902) British writer.
Notebooks

3 He sometimes forgets that he is Caesar, but I always remember that I am Caesar's daughter.
Julia (39 BC–AD 14) Daughter of Augustus.
Replying to suggestions that she should live in the simple style of her father, which contrasted with her own extravagance
Saturnalia (Macrobius)

4 All decent people live beyond their incomes nowadays, and those who aren't respectable live beyond other people's. A few gifted individuals manage to do both.
Saki (Hector Hugh Munro; 1870–1916) British writer.
The Match-Maker

5 I suppose that I shall have to die beyond my means.
Oscar Wilde (1854–1900) Irish-born British dramatist.
When told that an operation would be expensive. He is also believed to have said 'I am dying beyond my means' on accepting a glass of champagne as he lay on his deathbed
Life of Wilde (Sherard)

EYES

See also appearance

1 It needs no dictionary of quotations to remind me that the eyes are the windows of the soul.
Max Beerbohm (1872–1956) British writer.
Zuleika Dobson, Ch. 4

2 Jeepers Creepers – where'd you get them peepers?
Johnny Mercer (1909–76) US lyricist and composer.
Jeepers Creepers

3 Out vile jelly!
Where is thy lustre now?
William Shakespeare (1564–1616) English dramatist.
Spoken by Cornwall as he puts out Gloucester's remaining eye
King Lear, III:7

F

FACTS

See also truth

1 Now, what I want is Facts . . . Facts alone are wanted in life.
Charles Dickens (1812–70) British novelist.
Hard Times, Bk. I, Ch. 1

2 Facts do not cease to exist because they are ignored.
Aldous Huxley (1894–1964) British novelist.
Proper Studies

3 Facts speak louder than statistics.
Geoffrey Streatfield (1897–1978) British lawyer.
The Observer, 'Sayings of the Week', 19 Mar 1950

FAILURE

See also success

1 A miss is as good as a mile.
Proverb

2 She knows there's no success like failure
And that failure's no success at all.
Bob Dylan (Robert Allen Zimmerman; 1941–) US popular singer.
Love Minus Zero No Limit

3 Here lies Joseph, who failed in everything he undertook.
Joseph II (1741–90) Holy Roman Emperor.
Suggesting his own epitaph when reflecting upon the disappointment of his hopes for reform
Attrib.

4 Like a dull actor now
I have forgot my part and I am out,
Even to a full disgrace.
William Shakespeare (1564–1616) English dramatist.
Coriolanus, V:3

FAIRIES

See also supernatural

1 Every time a child says 'I don't believe in fairies' there is a little fairy somewhere that falls down dead.
J. M. Barrie (1860–1937) British novelist and dramatist.
Peter Pan, I

2 When the first baby laughed for the first time, the laugh broke into a thousand pieces and they all went skipping about, and that was the beginning of fairies.
J. M. Barrie

3 There are fairies at the bottom of our garden.
Rose Fyleman (1877–1957) British writer.
Fairies and Chimneys

FAITH

See also belief, faithfulness, God, religion

1 Faith will move mountains.
Proverb

2 By faith the walls of Jericho fell down, after they were compassed about seven days.
Bible: Hebrews
11:30

3 Now faith is the substance of things hoped for, the evidence of things not seen.
Bible: Hebrews
11:1

4 These all died in faith, not having received the promises, but having seen them afar off, and were persuaded of them, and embraced them, and confessed that they were strangers and pilgrims on the earth.
Bible: Hebrews
11:13

5 For we walk by faith, not by sight.
Bible: II Corinthians
5:7

6 For I am now ready to be offered, and the time of my departure is at hand.
I have fought a good fight, I have finished my course, I have kept the faith:
Henceforth there is laid up for me a crown of righteousness, which the Lord, the righteous judge, shall give me at that day: and not to me only, but unto all them also that love his appearing.
Bible: II Timothy
4:6–8

7 Even so faith, if it hath not works, is dead, being alone.
Bible: James
2:17

8 And Jesus said unto them, I am the bread of life: he that cometh to me shall never hunger; and he that believeth on me shall never thirst.
Bible: John
6:35

9 I feel no need for any other faith than my faith in human beings.
Pearl Buck (1892–1973) US novelist.
I Believe

10 The prayer that reforms the sinner and heals the sick is an absolute faith that all things are possible to God – a spiritual understanding of Him, an unselfed love.
Mary Baker Eddy (1821–1910) US religious leader.
Science and Health, with Key to the Scriptures

11 And I said to the man who stood at the gate of the year:'Give me a light that I may tread safely into the unknown'.And he replied: 'Go out into the darkness and put your hand into the hand of God. That shall be to you better than light and safer than a known way.'
Minnie Louise Haskins (1875–1957) US writer.
Remembered because it was quoted by George VI in his Christmas broadcast, 1939
The Desert, Introduction

12 My dear child, you must believe in God in spite of what the clergy tell you.
Benjamin Jowett (1817–93) British theologian.
Autobiography (Asquith), Ch. 8

13 Booth died blind and still by faith he trod,
Eyes still dazzled by the ways of God.
Vachel Lindsay (1879–1931) US poet.
General William Booth Enters Heaven

14 Faith may be defined briefly as an illogical belief in the occurrence of the improbable.
H. L. Mencken (1880–1956) US journalist.
Prejudices, 'Types of Men'

15 It takes a long while for a naturally trustful person to reconcile himself to the idea that after all God will not help him.
H. L. Mencken
Notebooks, 'Minority Report'

16 Lead, kindly Light, amid the encircling gloom,
Lead thou me on;
The night is dark, and I am far from home,
Lead thou me on.
Cardinal Newman (1801–90) British theologian.
Lead Kindly Light

17 Even such is Time, that takes in trust
Our youth, our joys, our all we have,
And pays us but with age and dust;
Who in the dark and silent grave,
When we have wandered all our ways,
Shuts up the story of our days;
But from this earth, this grave, this dust,
My God shall raise me up, I trust.
Walter Raleigh (1554–1618) English explorer.
Written on the night before his execution
Attrib.

18 'Tis not the dying for a faith that's so hard,

Master Harry — every man of every nation has done that — 'tis the living up to it that is difficult.
William Makepeace Thackeray (1811–63) British novelist.
Henry Esmond, Ch. 6

19 Faith consists in believing when it is beyond the power of reason to believe. It is not enough that a thing be possible for it to be believed.
Voltaire (François-Marie Arouet; 1694–1778) French writer.
Questions sur l'encyclopédie

FAITHFULNESS

See also loyalty

1 It is better to be unfaithful than faithful without wanting to be.
Brigitte Bardot (1934–) French film actress.
The Observer, 'Sayings of the Week', 18 Feb 1968

2 Through perils both of wind and limb,
Through thick and thin she follow'd him.
Samuel Butler (1612–80) English satirist.
Hudibras, Pt. II

3 I have been faithful to thee, Cynara! in my fashion.
Ernest Dowson (1867–1900) British lyric poet.
Non Sum Qualis Eram Bonae Sub Regno Cynarae

4 We only part to meet again.
Change, as ye list, ye winds; my heart shall be
The faithful compass that still points to thee.
John Gay (1685–1732) English poet and dramatist.
Sweet William's Farewell

5 But I'm always true to you, darlin', in my fashion,
Yes, I'm always true to you, darlin', in my way.
Cole Porter (1893–1964) US songwriter.
Kiss Me, Kate, 'Always True to You in My Fashion'

FAME

See also popularity, posterity, reputation

1 A celebrity is a person who works hard all his life to become known, then wears dark glasses to avoid being recognized.
Fred Allen (1894–1956) US comedian.
Treadmill to Oblivion

2 Fame is like a river, that beareth up things light and swollen, and drowns things weighty and solid.
Francis Bacon (1561–1626) English philosopher.
Essays, 'Of Praise'

3 I should like one of these days to be so well known, so popular, so celebrated, so famous, that it would permit me . . . to break wind in society, and society would think it a most natural thing.
Honoré de Balzac (1799–1850) French novelist.
Attrib.

4 The celebrity is a person who is known for his well-knownness.
Daniel J. Boorstin (1914–) US writer.
The Image, 'From Hero to Celebrity: The Human Pseudo-event'

5 A best-seller was a book which somehow sold well simply because it was selling well.
Daniel J. Boorstin
The Image, 'From Shapes to Shadows: Dissolving Forms'

6 I awoke one morning and found myself famous.
Lord Byron (1788–1824) British poet.
Remark made after the publication of *Childe Harold's Pilgrimage* (1812)
Entry in Memoranda

7 Being a star has made it possible for me to get insulted in places where the average Negro could never hope to get insulted.
Sammy Davis Jnr (1925–) Black US singer.
Yes I Can

8 If a man make a better mouse-trap than his neighbour, though he build his house in the woods, the world will make a beaten path to his door.
Ralph Waldo Emerson (1803–82) US poet and essayist.
Attrib.

9 A big man has no time really to do anything but just sit and be big.
F. Scott Fitzgerald (1896–1940) US novelist.
This Side of Paradise, Bk. III, Ch. 2

10 Fame is sometimes like unto a kind of mushroom, which Pliny recounts to be the greatest miracle in nature, because growing and having no root.
Thomas Fuller (1608–61) English historian.
The Holy State and the Profane State

11 Fame is a powerful aphrodisiac.
Graham Greene (1904–) British novelist.
Radio Times, 10 Sept 1964

12 Every man has a lurking wish to appear considerable in his native place.
Samuel Johnson (1709–84) British lexicographer.
Letter to Sir Joshua Reynolds
Life of Johnson (J. Boswell), Vol. II

13 One of the drawbacks of Fame is that one can never escape from it.
Nellie Melba (Helen Porter Mitchell; 1861–1931) Australian soprano.
Melodies and Memories

14 Fame is the spur that the clear spirit doth raise
(That last infirmity of noble mind)
To scorn delights, and live laborious days.
John Milton (1608–74) English poet.
Lycidas

15 'What are you famous *for*?'
'For nothing. I am just famous.'
Iris Murdoch (1919–) Irish-born British novelist.
The Flight from the Enchanter

16 I'm never going to be famous . . . I don't do anything. Not one single thing. I used to bite my nails, but I don't even do that any more.
Dorothy Parker (1893–1967) US writer.
The Little Hours

17 If you have to tell them who you are, you aren't anybody.
Gregory Peck (1916–) US film star.
Remarking upon the failure of anyone in a crowded restaurant to recognize him
Pieces of Eight (S. Harris)

18 The more you are talked about, the more you will wish to be talked about. The condemned murderer who is allowed to see the account of his trial in the Press is indignant if he finds a newspaper which has reported it inadequately. . . . Politicians and literary men are in the same case.
Bertrand Russell (1872–1970) British philosopher.
Human Society in Ethics and Politics

19 Love of fame is the last thing even learned men can bear to be parted from.
Tacitus (c. 55–c. 120 AD) Roman historian.
Histories, IV, 6

20 To famous men all the earth is a sepulchre.
Thucydides (c. 460–c. 400 BC) Greek historian and general.
History of the Peloponnesian War, Bk. II, Ch. 43

21 The only man who wasn't spoilt by being lionized was Daniel.
Herbert Beerbohm Tree (1853–1917) British actor and theatre manager.
Beerbohm Tree (Hesketh Pearson)

22 When I pass my name in such large letters I blush, but at the same time instinctively raise my hat.
Herbert Beerbohm Tree
Beerbohm Tree (Hesketh Pearson)

23 In the future, everyone will be famous for 15 minutes.
Andy Warhol (Andrew Warhola; 1926–87) US pop artist.
Attrib.

24 There is only one thing in the world worse than being talked about, and that is not being talked about.
Oscar Wilde (1854–1900) Irish-born British dramatist.
The Picture of Dorian Gray, Ch. 1

FAMILIARITY

1 Familiarity breeds contempt.
Proverb

2 No man is a hero to his valet.
Anne-Marie Bigot de Cornuel (1605–94) French society hostess.
Lettres de Mlle Aïssé, 13 Aug 1728

3 I've grown accustomed to the trace
Of something in the air,
Accustomed to her face.
Alan Jay Lerner (1918–86) US songwriter.
My Fair Lady, II:6

4 I have been here before.
But when or how I cannot tell:
I know the grass beyond the door,
The sweet keen smell,
The sighing sound, the lights around the shore.
Dante Gabriel Rossetti (1828–82) British painter and poet.
Sudden Light

5 He began to think the tramp a fine, brotherly, generous fellow. He was also growing accustomed to something – shall I call it an olfactory bar – that had hitherto kept them apart.
H. G. Wells (1866–1946) British writer.
Bealby, Pt. VI, Ch. 3

FAMILY

See also children

1 Blood is thicker than water.
Proverb

2 Every family has a skeleton in the cupboard.
Proverb

3 Like father, like son.
Proverb

4 The family that prays together stays together.
Proverb

5 There's a black sheep in every flock.
Proverb

6 Sir Walter, being strangely surprised and put out of his countenance at so great a table, gives his son a damned blow over the face. His son, as rude as he was, would not strike his father, but strikes over the face the gentleman that sat next to him and said 'Box about: 'twill come to my father anon'.
John Aubrey (1626–97) English antiquary.
Brief Lives, 'Sir Walter Raleigh'

7 He that hath wife and children hath given hostages to fortune; for they are impediments to great enterprises, either of virtue or mischief.
Francis Bacon (1561–1626) English philosopher.
See also LUCAN
Essays, 'Of Marriage and Single Life'

8 The joys of parents are secret, and so are their griefs and fears.
Francis Bacon
Essays, 'Of Parents and Children'

9 Fathers, provoke not your children to anger, lest they be discouraged.
Bible: Colossians
3:21

10 Behold, every one that useth proverbs shall use this proverb against thee, saying, As is the mother, so is her daughter.
Bible: Ezekiel
16:44–45

11 I love all my children, but some of them I don't like.
Lillian Carter (1902–) The mother of Jimmy Carter.
In *Woman*, 9 Apr 1977

12 If one is not going to take the necessary precautions to avoid having parents one must undertake to bring them up.
Quentin Crisp (1910–) British model, publicist, and writer.
The Naked Civil Servant

13 Fate chooses your relations, you choose your friends.
Jacques Delille (1738–1813) French abbé and poet.
Malheur et pitié, I

14 It is a melancholy truth that even great men have their poor relations.
Charles Dickens (1812–70) British novelist.
Bleak House, Ch. 28

15 What a marvellous place to drop one's mother-in-law!
Marshal Foch (1851–1929) French soldier.
Remark on being shown the Grand Canyon
Attrib.

16 My father was frightened of his mother. I was frightened of my father, and I'm damned well going to make sure that my children are frightened of me.
George V (1865–1936) King of the United Kingdom (1910–36).
Attrib.

17 And so do his sisters, and his cousins and his aunts!
His sisters and his cousins,
Whom he reckons up by dozens,
And his aunts!
W. S. Gilbert (1836–1911) British dramatist.
HMS Pinafore, I

18 LEONTINE. An only son, sir, might expect more indulgence.
CROAKER. An only father, sir, might expect more obedience.
Oliver Goldsmith (1728–74) Irish-born British writer.
The Good-Natured Man, I

19 A person may be indebted for a nose or an eye, for a graceful carriage or a voluble discourse, to a great-aunt or uncle, whose existence he has scarcely heard of.
William Hazlitt (1778–1830) British essayist.
On Personal Character

20 Good families are generally worse than any others.
Anthony Hope (Sir Anthony Hope Hawkins; 1863–1933) British novelist.
The Prisoner of Zenda, Ch. 1

21 But there, everything has its drawbacks, as the man said when his mother-in-law died, and they came down upon him for the funeral expenses.
Jerome K. Jerome (1859–1927) British humorist.
Three Men in a Boat, Ch. 3

22 A poor relation – is the most irrelevant thing in nature.
Charles Lamb (1775–1834) British essayist.
Last Essays of Elia, 'Poor Relations'

23 They fuck you up, your mum and dad.
They may not mean to, but they do.
They fill you with the faults they had
And add some extra, just for you.
Philip Larkin (1922–85) British poet.
This be the Verse

24 Far from being the basis of the good society, the family, with its narrow privacy and tawdry secrets, is the source of all our discontents.
Edmund Leach (1910–) British social anthropologist.
In the BBC Reith Lectures for 1967. Lecture reprinted in *The Listener*

25 I have a wife, I have sons: all of them hostages given to fate.
Lucan (Marcus Annaeus Lucanus; 39–65 AD) Roman poet.
See also BACON
Works, VII

26 A group of closely related persons living under one roof; it is a convenience, often a necessity, sometimes a pleasure, sometimes the reverse; but who first exalted it as admirable, an almost religious ideal?
Rose Macaulay (1889–1958) British writer.
The World My Wilderness, Ch. 20

27 You're a disgrace to our family name of Wagstaff, if such a thing is possible.
Groucho Marx (Julius Marx; 1895–1977) US comedian.
Horse Feathers

28 The sink is the great symbol of the bloodiness of family life. All life is bad, but family life is worse.
Julian Mitchell (1935–) British writer.
As Far as You Can Go, Pt. I, Ch. 1

29 I cumber you goode Margaret muche, but I woulde be sorye, if it shoulde be any lenger than to morrowe, for it is S. Thomas evin and the vtas of Sainte Peter and therefore to morowe longe I to goe to God, it were a daye very meete and conveniente for me. I neuer liked your maner towarde me better then when you kissed me laste for I loue when doughterly loue and deere charitie hathe no laisor to looke to worldely curtesye. Fare well my deere childe and praye for me, and I

shall for you and all your friendes that we
maie merily meete in heaven.
Thomas More (1478–1535) English lawyer and scholar.
Last letter to Margaret Roper, his daughter, on the eve of his
execution on 6 July 1535

30 Children aren't happy with nothing to ignore,
And that's what parents were created for.
Ogden Nash (1902–71) US poet.
The Parents

31 And Her Mother Came Too.
Ivor Novello (David Ivor Davies; 1893–1951) British
actor, composer, and dramatist.
Title of song

32 Men are generally more careful of the breed
of their horses and dogs than of their children.
William Penn (1644–1718) English preacher.
*Some Fruits of Solitude, in Reflections and Maxims relating to
the conduct of Humane Life*, Pt. I, No 52

33 Parents are sometimes a bit of a
disappointment to their children. They don't
fulfil the promise of their early years.
Anthony Powell (1905–) British novelist.
A Buyer's Market

34 All men are brothers, but, thank God, they
aren't all brothers-in-law.
Anthony Powell
A Dance to the Music of Time: At Lady Molly's, Ch. 4

35 For there is no friend like a sister
In calm or stormy weather;
To cheer one on the tedious way,
To fetch one if one goes astray,
To lift one if one totters down,
To strengthen whilst one stands.
Christina Rossetti (1830–74) British poet.
Goblin Market

36 Two mothers-in-law.
Lord John Russell (1792–1878) British statesman.
His answer when asked what he would consider a proper pun-
ishment for bigamy
Anekdotenschatz (H. Hoffmeister)

37 It is a wise father that knows his own child.
William Shakespeare (1564–1616) English dramatist.
The Merchant of Venice, II:2

38 That dear octopus from whose tentacles we
never quite escape, nor in our innermost
hearts never quite wish to.
Dodie Smith (1896–) British dramatist and novelist.
Dear Octopus

39 I wish either my father or my mother, or
indeed both of them, as they were in duty
both equally bound to it, had minded what
they were about when they begot me.
Laurence Sterne (1713–68) Irish-born British writer.
Tristram Shandy

40 The greatest destroyer of peace is abortion
because if a mother can kill her own child

what is left for me to kill you and you to kill
me? There is nothing between.
Mother Teresa (1910–) Yugoslavian missionary in
Calcutta.
Nobel Peace Prize Lecture

41 If a man's character is to be abused, say
what you will, there's nobody like a relation
to do the business.
William Makepeace Thackeray (1811–63) British
novelist.
Vanity Fair, Ch. 19

42 All happy families resemble one another, each
unhappy family is unhappy in its own way.
Leo Tolstoy (1828–1910) Russian writer.
Anna Karenina, Pt. I, Ch. 1

43 No man is responsible for his father. That is
entirely his mother's affair.
Margaret Turnbull (fl. 1920s–1942) US writer.
Alabaster Lamps

44 Parents are the bones on which children
sharpen their teeth.
Peter Ustinov (1921–) British actor.
Dear Me

45 Don't hold your parents up to contempt.
After all, you are their son, and it is just
possible that you may take after them.
Evelyn Waugh (1903–66) British novelist.
The Tablet, 9 May 1951

46 The thing that impresses me most about
America is the way parents obey their
children.
Duke of Windsor (1894–1972) King of the United
Kingdom; abdicated 1936.
Look Magazine, 5 Mar 1957

47 It is no use telling me that there are bad
aunts and good aunts. At the core they are all
alike. Sooner or later, out pops the cloven
hoof.
P. G. Wodehouse (1881–1975) British humorous
novelist.
The Code of the Woosters

FANATICISM

1 Defined in psychological terms, a fanatic is a
man who consciously over-compensates a
secret doubt.
Aldous Huxley (1894–1964) British novelist.
Vulgarity in Literature, Ch. 4

2 Fanatics have their dreams, wherewith they
weave
A paradise for a sect.
John Keats (1795–1821) British poet.
The Fall of Hyperion, I

3 You are never dedicated to something you
have complete confidence in. No one is
fanatically shouting that the sun is going to
rise tomorrow. They *know* it's going to rise
tomorrow. When people are fanatically
dedicated to political or religious faiths or any

other kind of dogmas or goals, it's always because these dogmas or goals are in doubt.
Robert T. Pirsig (1928–) US writer.
Zen and the Art of Motorcycle Maintenance, Pt. II, Ch. 13

FASCISM

See also Hitler, Nazism

1 I should be pleased, I suppose, that Hitler has carried out a revolution on our lines. But they are Germans. So they will end by ruining our idea.
Benito Mussolini (1883–1945) Italian dictator.
Benito Mussolini (C. Hibbert), Pt. II, Ch. 1

2 Fascism is a religion; the twentieth century will be known in history as the century of Fascism.
Benito Mussolini
On Hitler's seizing power
Sawdust Caesar (George Seldes), Ch. 24

3 Fascism is not an article for export.
Benito Mussolini
Report in the German press, 1932

4 Every communist has a fascist frown, every fascist a communist smile.
Muriel Spark (1918–) British novelist.
The Girls of Slender Means, Ch. 4

5 Fascism means war.
John St Loe Strachey (1901–63) British politician.
Slogan, 1930s

FASHION

See also clothes

1 Fashion is architecture: it is a matter of proportions.
Coco Chanel (1883–1971) French dress designer.
Coco Chanel, Her Life, Her Secrets (Marcel Haedrich)

2 One had as good be out of the world, as out of the fashion.
Colley Cibber (1671–1757) British actor and dramatist.
Love's Last Shift, II

3 I walk down the Strand
With my gloves on my hand,
And I walk down again
With them off.
W. F. Hargreaves (1846–1919) British songwriter.
Burlington Bertie

4 There are few who would not rather be taken in adultery than in provincialism.
Aldous Huxley (1894–1964) British novelist.
Antic Hay, Ch. 10

5 For an idea ever to be fashionable is ominous, since it must afterwards be always old-fashioned.
George Santayana (1863–1952) US philosopher.
Winds of Doctrine, 'Modernism and Christianity'

6 Fashions, after all, are only induced epidemics.
George Bernard Shaw (1856–1950) Irish dramatist and critic.
Doctor's Dilemma, Preface

FEAR

1 It is a miserable state of mind to have few things to desire and many things to fear.
Francis Bacon (1561–1626) English philosopher.
Essays, 'Of Empire'

2 For God hath not given us the spirit of fear; but of power, and of love, and of a sound mind.
Bible: II Timothy
1:7

3 There is no fear in love; but perfect love casteth out fear: because fear hath torment. He that feareth is not made perfect in love.
Bible: I John
4:18

4 Fear has many eyes and can see things underground.
Miguel de Cervantes (1547–1616) Spanish novelist.
Don Quixote, Pt. I, Ch. 20

5 You may take the most gallant sailor, the most intrepid airman, or the most audacious soldier, put them at a table together – what do you get? *The sum of their fears.*
Winston Churchill (1874–1965) British statesman.
Talking about the Chiefs of Staffs system, 16 Nov 1943
The Blast of War (H. Macmillan), Ch. 16

6 Like one, that on a lonesome road
Doth walk in fear and dread,
And having once turned round walks on,
And turns no more his head;
Because he knows, a frightful fiend
Doth close behind him tread.
Samuel Taylor Coleridge (1772–1834) British poet.
The Rime of the Ancient Mariner, VI

7 I'm not frightened of the darkness outside. It's the darkness inside houses I don't like.
Shelagh Delaney (1939–) British dramatist.
A Taste of Honey, I:1

8 I wants to make your flesh creep.
Charles Dickens (1812–70) British novelist.
Pickwick Papers, Ch. 8

9 And I will show you something different from either
Your shadow at morning striding behind you,
Or your shadow at evening rising to meet you
I will show you fear in a handful of dust.
T. S. Eliot (1888–1965) US-born British poet and dramatist.
The Waste Land, 'The Burial of the Dead'

10 Let me assert my firm belief that the only thing we have to fear is fear itself.
Franklin D. Roosevelt (1882–1945) US Democratic president.
First Inaugural Address, 4 Mar 1933

11 I had else been perfect,
Whole as the marble, founded as the rock,
As broad and general as the casing air,
But now I am cabin'd, cribb'd, confin'd, bound in
To saucy doubts and fears.
William Shakespeare (1564–1616) English dramatist.
Macbeth, II:4

12 A lion among ladies is a most dreadful thing; for there is not a more fearful wild-fowl than your lion living.
William Shakespeare
A Midsummer Night's Dream, III:1

13 Fear lent wings to his feet.
Virgil (Publius Vergilius Maro; 70–19 BC) Roman poet.
Aeneid, Bk. VIII

14 He had one peculiar weakness; he had faced death in many forms but he had never faced a dentist. The thought of dentists gave him just the same sick horror as the thought of Socialism.
H. G. Wells (1866–1946) British writer.
Bealby, Pt. VIII, Ch. 1

15 By night an atheist half believes a God.
Edward Young (1683–1765) British poet.
Night Thoughts

FEMINISM

See also equality, sexes, women

Those in favour

1 Old-fashioned ways which no longer apply to changed conditions are a snare in which the feet of women have always become readily entangled.
Jane Addams (1860–1935) US social worker.
In *Newer Ideals of Peace*, 'Utilization of Women in City Government'

2 Men their rights and nothing more; women their rights and nothing less.
Susan B. Anthony (1820–1906) US editor.
The Revolution, Motto

3 . . . there never will be complete equality until women themselves help to make laws and elect lawmakers.
Susan B. Anthony
In *The Arena*, (May 1897) 'The Status of Women, Past, Present and Future'

4 From a timid, shy girl I had become a woman of resolute character, who could not longer be frightened by the struggle with troubles.
Anna Dostoevsky (1846–1918) Russian diarist.
Dostoevsky Portrayed by His Wife

5 The extension of women's rights is the basic principle of all social progress.
Fourier, Charles (1772–1837) French social reformer.
Théorie des Quatre Mouvements

6 Where young boys plan for what they will achieve and attain, young girls plan for whom they will achieve and attain.
Charlotte Perkins Gilman (1860–1935) US writer.
Women and Economics, Ch. 5

7 A woman needs a man like a fish needs a bicycle.
Graffiti

8 Mother is the dead heart of the family, spending father's earnings on consumer goods to enhance the environment in which he eats, sleeps and watches the television.
Germaine Greer (1939–) Australian-born British writer and feminist.
The Female Eunuch

9 Women fail to understand how much men hate them.
Germaine Greer
The Female Eunuch

10 I know you do not make the laws but I also know that you are the wives and mothers, the sisters and daughters of those who do . . .
Angelina Grimké (1805–79) US writer.
The Anti-Slavery Examiner (Sep 1836), 'Appeal to the Christian Women of the South'

11 . . . the emancipation of women is practically the greatest egoistic movement of the nineteenth century, and the most intense affirmation of the right of the self that history has yet seen . . .
Ellen Key (Karolina Sofia Key; 1849–1926) Swedish writer.
The Century of the Child, Ch. 2

12 Can anything be more absurd than keeping women in a state of ignorance, and yet so vehemently to insist on their resisting temptation?
Vicesimus Knox (1752–1821) British essayist.
Liberal Education, Vol. I, 'On the Literary Education of Women'

13 Other books have been written by men physicians . . . One would suppose in reading them that women possess but one class of physical organs, and that these are always diseased. Such teaching is pestiferous, and tends to cause and perpetuate the very evils it professes to remedy.
Mary Ashton Livermore (c. 1820–1905) US writer.
What Shall We Do with Our Daughters?, Ch. 2

14 I'm furious about the Women's Liberationists. They keep getting up on soapboxes and proclaiming that women are brighter than men. That's true, but it should be kept very quiet or it ruins the whole racket.

Anita Loos (1891–1981) US novelist.
The Observer, 'Sayings of the Year', 30 Dec 1973

15 . . . is it to be understood that the principles of the Declaration of Independence bear no relation to half of the human race?

Harriet Martineau (1802–76) British writer.
Society in America, Vol. III, 'Marriage'

16 The most important thing women have to do is to stir up the zeal of women themselves.

John Stuart Mill (1806–73) British philosopher.
Letter to Alexander Bain, 14 July 1869

17 . . . the rumblings of women's liberation are only one pointer to the fact that you already have a discontented work force. And if conditions continue to lag so far behind the industrial norm and the discomfort increases, you will find . . . that you will end up with an inferior product.

Elaine Morgan (1920–) British writer.
The Descent of Woman, Ch. 11

18 No *man*, not even a doctor, ever gives any other definition of what a nurse should be than this – "devoted and obedient." This definition would do just as well for a porter. It might even do for a horse. It would not do for a policeman.

Florence Nightingale (1820–1910) British nurse.
Notes on Nursing

19 The vote, I thought, means nothing to women. We should be armed.

Edna O'Brien (1936–) Irish novelist.
Quoted as epigraph to *Fear of Flying* (Erica Jong), Ch. 16

20 . . . if civilisation is to advance at all in the future, it must be through the help of women, women freed of their political shackles, women with full power to work their will in society. It was rapidly becoming clear to my mind that men regarded women as a servant class in the community, and that women were going to remain in the servant class until they lifted themselves out of it.

Emmeline Pankhurst (1858–1928) British suffragette.
My Own Story

21 Women had always fought for men, and for their children. Now they were ready to fight for their own human rights. Our militant movement was established.

Emmeline Pankhurst
My Own Story

22 We have taken this action, because as women . . . we realize that the condition of our sex is so deplorable that it is our duty even to break the law in order to call attention to the reasons why we do so.

Emmeline Pankhurst
Shoulder to Shoulder (ed. Midge Mackenzie)
Speech in court, 21 Oct 1908

23 The prolonged slavery of women is the darkest page in human history.

Elizabeth Stanton (1815–1902) US suffragette.
History of Woman Suffrage (with Susan B. Anthony and Mathilda Gage), Vol. I

24 Womanhood is the great fact in her life; wifehood and motherhood are but incidental relations.

Elizabeth Stanton
History of Woman Suffrage (with Susan B. Anthony and Mathilda Gage), Vol. I

25 *Declaration of Sentiments:* . . . We hold these truths to be self-evident: that all men and women are created equal . . .

Elizabeth Stanton
History of Woman Suffrage (with Susan B. Anthony and Mathilda Gage), Vol. I

26 People call me a feminist whenever I express sentiments that differentiate me from a doormat or a prostitute.

Rebecca West (1892–) British novelist.
Attrib.

27 Women have always been the guardians of wisdom and humanity which makes them natural, but usually secret, rulers. The time has come for them to rule openly, but together with and not against men.

Charlotte Wolff (1904–) German-born British writer.
Bisexuality: A Study, Ch. 2

28 Women have served all these centuries as looking-glasses possessing the magic and delicious power of reflecting the figure of man at twice its natural size.

Virginia Woolf (1882–1941) British novelist.
A Room of One's Own

29 The *divine right* of husbands, like the divine right of kings, may, it is hoped, in this enlightened age, be contested without danger.

Mary Wollstonecraft 1759–97) British writer.
A Vindication of the Rights of Woman, Ch. 3

30 I do not wish them to have power over men; but over themselves.

Mary Wollstonecraft
A Vindication of the Rights of Woman, Ch. 4
Referring to women

Those against

31 There is a tide in the affairs of women, Which, taken at the flood, leads – God knows where.

Byron, George Gordon, 6th Baron (1788–1824) British poet.
Don Juan, VI

32 Nothing would induce me to vote for giving women the franchise. I am not going to be henpecked into a question of such importance.

Winston Churchill
The Amazing Mr Churchill (Robert Lewis Taylor)

33 The great question . . . which I have not been able to answer, despite my thirty years of research into the feminine soul, is 'What does a woman want'?
Sigmund Freud (1856–1939) Austrian psychoanalyst.
Psychiatry in American Life (Charles Rolo)

34 The First Blast of the Trumpet Against the Monstrous Regiment of Women.
John Knox (c. 1514–72) Scottish religious reformer.
Title of Pamphlet, 1558

35 Women's Liberation is just a lot of foolishness. It's the men who are discriminated against. They can't bear children. And no one's likely to do anything about that.
Golda Meir (1898–1978) Israeli stateswoman.
Attrib.

36 Give women the vote, and in five years there will be a crushing tax on bachelors.
George Bernard Shaw (1856–1950) Irish dramatist.
Man and Superman, Preface

37 The Queen is most anxious to enlist every one who can speak or write to join in checking this mad, wicked folly of 'Woman's Rights', with all its attendant horrors, on which her poor feeble sex is bent, forgetting every sense of womanly feeling and propriety.
Victoria (1819–1901) Queen of England.
Letter to Sir Theodore Martin, 29 May 1870

38 The thought could not be avoided that the best home for a feminist was in another person's lab.
James Dewey Watson (1928–) US geneticist.
The Double Helix, Ch. 2

...and a final word

39 The battle for women's rights has been largely won.
Margaret Thatcher (1925–) British politician.
The Guardian, 1982

40 I do, and I also wash and iron them.
Denis Thatcher (1915–) British businessman, husband of Margaret Thatcher.
Times (Los Angeles), 21 Apr 1981
Replying to the question "Who wears the pants in this house?"

41 WOMEN'S RIGHTS NOW
Followed by
Yes Dear
Exchange of graffiti

FICTION

See also books, literature, novels, writing

1 Science fiction is no more written for scientists than ghost stories are written for ghosts.
Brian Aldiss (1925–) British science-fiction writer.
Penguin Science Fiction, Introduction

2 Sometimes I don't know whether Zelda and I are real or whether we are characters in one of my novels.
F. Scott Fitzgerald (1896–1940) US novelist.
Said of himself and his wife
A Second Flowering (Malcolm Cowley)

3 There are many reasons why novelists write, but they all have one thing in common – a need to create an alternative world.
John Fowles (1926–) British novelist.
The Sunday Times Magazine, 2 Oct 1977

4 Casting my mind's eye over the whole of fiction, the only absolutely original creation I can think of is Don Quixote.
W. Somerset Maugham (1874–1965) British novelist.
10 Novels and Their Authors, Ch. 1

FIRE

1 All things, oh priests, are on fire . . . The eye is on fire; forms are on fire; eye-consciousness is on fire; impressions received by the eye are on fire.
Buddha (Gautama Siddhartha; c. 563–c. 483 BC) Indian religious teacher.
The Fire Sermon

2 Billy, in one of his nice new sashes,
Fell in the fire and was burnt to ashes;
Now, although the room grows chilly,
I haven't the heart to poke poor Billy.
Harry Graham (1874–1936) British writer.
Ruthless Rhymes for Heartless Homes, 'Tender-Heartedness'

3 Whatsoever might be the extent of the private calamity, I hope it will not interfere with the public business of the country.
Richard Brinsley Sheridan (1751–1816) British dramatist.
On learning, whilst in the House of Commons, that his Drury Lane Theatre was on fire
Memoirs of Life of the R. Hon. Richard Brinsley Sheridan (T. Moore)

4 A man may surely be allowed to take a glass of wine by his own fireside.
Richard Brinsley Sheridan
As he sat in a coffeehouse watching his theatre burn down
Memoirs of the Life of the Rt. Hon. Richard Brinsley Sheridan (T. Moore)

5 Arson, after all, is an artificial crime . . . A large number of houses deserve to be burnt.
H. G. Wells (1866–1946) British writer.
The History of Mr Polly, Pt. X, Ch. 1

FIRST IMPRESSIONS

1 First impressions are the most lasting.
Proverb

2 There is a lady sweet and kind,
Was never face so pleased my mind;
I did but see her passing by,
And yet I love her till I die.
Anonymous
Passing By

3   Harris, I am not well; pray get me a glass of brandy.
George IV (1762–1830) King of the United Kingdom.
On seeing Caroline of Brunswick for the first time
Diaries (Earl of Malmesbury)

4   You have sent me a Flanders mare.
Henry VIII (1491–1547) King of England.
Said on meeting his fourth wife, Anne of Cleves, for the first time
Attrib.

5   First feelings are always the most natural.
Louis XIV (1638–1715) French king.
Repeated by Mme de Sévigné

6   Who ever loved, that loved not at first sight?
Christopher Marlowe (1564–93) English dramatist.
Hero and Leander, I

7   Mistrust first impulses; they are nearly always good.
Talleyrand (Charles Maurice de Talleyrand-Périgord; 1754–1838) French politician.
Sometimes attrib. to Count Montrond
Attrib.

FISH

See also fishing, food

1   Fish die belly-upward and rise to the surface; it is their way of falling.
André Gide (1869–1951) French novelist.
Journals

2   Oysters are more beautiful than any religion ... There's nothing in Christianity or Buddhism that quite matches the sympathetic unselfishness of an oyster.
Saki (Hector Hugh Munro; 1870–1916) British writer.
The Match-Maker

FISHING

See also sport

1   Fly fishing may be a very pleasant amusement; but angling or float fishing I can only compare to a stick and a string, with a worm at one end and a fool at the other.
Samuel Johnson (1709–84) British lexicographer.
Attrib. in *Instructions to Young Sportsmen* (Hawker)

2   Angling is somewhat like poetry, men are to be born so.
Izaak Walton
The Compleat Angler, Ch. 1

3   Let the blessing of St Peter's Master be ... upon all that are lovers of virtue; and dare trust in His providence; and be quiet; and go a-Angling.
Izaak Walton
The Compleat Angler, Ch. 21

4   Angling may be said to be so like the mathematics, that it can never be fully learnt.
Izaak Walton
The Compleat Angler, Epistle to the Reader

5   We may say of angling as Dr Boteler said of strawberries, 'Doubtless God could have made a better berry, but doubtless God never did.'
Izaak Walton
The Compleat Angler, Ch. 5

FLATTERY

See also compliments, insincerity, praise, servility

1   Imitation is the sincerest form of flattery.
Proverb

2   It is happy for you that you possess the talent of flattering with delicacy. May I ask whether these pleasing attentions proceed from the impulse of the moment, or are the result of previous study?
Jane Austen (1775–1817) British novelist.
Pride and Prejudice, Ch. 14

3   A rich man's joke is always funny.
Thomas Edward Brown (1830–97) British poet.
The Doctor

4   Every woman is infallibly to be gained by every sort of flattery, and every man by one sort or other.
Earl of Chesterfield (1694–1773) English statesman.
Letter to his son, 16 Mar 1752

5   Madam, before you flatter a man so grossly to his face, you should consider whether or not your flattery is worth his having.
Samuel Johnson (1709–84) British lexicographer.
Diary and Letters (Mme D'Arblay), Vol. I, Ch. 2

6   Be advised that all flatterers live at the expense of those who listen to them.
Jean de La Fontaine (1621–95) French poet.
Fables, I, 'Le Corbeau et le Renard'

7   I will praise any man that will praise me.
William Shakespeare (1564–1616) English dramatist.
Antony and Cleopatra, II:6

8   Flattery is all right so long as you don't inhale.
Adlai Stevenson (1900–65) US statesman.
Attrib.

9   'Tis an old maxim in the schools,
That flattery's the food of fools;
Yet now and then your men of wit
Will condescend to take a bit.
Jonathan Swift (1667–1745) Irish-born Anglican priest and writer.
Cadenus and Vanessa

FLOWERS

See also gardens

1   She wore a wreath of roses,
The night that first we met.
Thomas Haynes Bayly (1797–1839) British writer.
She Wore a Wreath of Roses

2　Just now the lilac is in bloom
All before my little room.
Rupert Brooke (1887–1915) British poet.
The Old Vicarage, Grantchester

3　Tiptoe through the tulips with me.
Al Dubin (20th century) US songwriter.
From the musical, *Gold Diggers of Broadway*
Tiptoe Through the Tulips

4　I sometimes think that never blows so red
The Rose as where some buried Caesar bled;
That every Hyacinth the Garden wears
Dropt in her Lap from some once lovely Head.
Edward Fitzgerald (1809–83) British poet.
The Rubáiyát of Omar Khayyám (1st edn.), XVIII

5　Their smiles,
Wan as primroses gather'd at midnight
By chilly finger'd spring.
John Keats (1795–1821) British poet.
Endymion, IV

6　Good God, I forgot the violets!
Walter Savage Landor (1775–1864) British poet and
writer.
Having thrown his cook out of an open window onto the
flowerbed below
Irreverent Social History (F. Muir)

7　And I will make thee beds of roses
And a thousand fragrant posies.
Christopher Marlowe (1564–93) English dramatist.
The Passionate Shepherd to his Love

8　Gather the flowers, but spare the buds.
Andrew Marvell (1621–78) English poet.
The Picture of Little T.C. in a Prospect of Flowers

9　'Tis the last rose of summer
Left blooming alone;
All her lovely companions
Are faded and gone.
Thomas Moore (1779–1852) Irish poet.
Irish Melodies, ''Tis the Last Rose'

10　Say it with flowers.
Patrick O'Keefe (1872–1934) US advertising agent.
Slogan for Society of American Florists

11　They are for prima donnas or corpses – I
am neither.
Arturo Toscanini (1867–1957) Italian conductor.
Refusing a floral wreath at the end of a performance
The Elephant that Swallowed a Nightingale (C. Galtey)

12　But as we went along there were more and
yet more and there at last under the boughs
of the trees, we saw that there was a long
belt of them along the shore, about the
breadth of a country turnpike road. I never
saw daffodils so beautiful they grew among
the mossy stones about and about them,
some rested their heads upon these stones
as on pillow for weariness and the rest
tossed and reeled and danced and seemed as
if they verily laughed with the wind that blew
upon them over the lake.
Dorothy Wordsworth (1771–1855) British diarist and
sister of William Wordsworth.
The Grasmere Journals, 15 Apr 1802

13　Thou unassuming common-place
Of Nature.
William Wordsworth (1770–1850) British poet.
To the Daisy

14　I wandered lonely as a cloud
That floats on high o'er vales and hills,
When all at once I saw a crowd,
A host, of golden daffodils.
William Wordsworth
I Wandered Lonely as a Cloud

FLYING

See also travel

1　Had I been a man I might have explored the
Poles or climbed Mount Everest, but as it
was my spirit found outlet in the air. . . .
Amy Johnson (1903–41) British flyer.
Myself When Young (ed. Margot Asquith)

2　I feel about airplanes the way I feel about
diets. It seems to me that they are
wonderful things for other people to go on.
Jean Kerr (1923–　) US dramatist.
The Snake Has All the Lines, 'Mirror, Mirror, on the Wall'

3　There are only two emotions in a plane:
boredom and terror.
Orson Welles (1915–85) US film actor.
The Observer, 'Sayings of the Week', 12 May 1985

4　Nor law, nor duty bade me fight,
Nor public men, nor cheering crowds,
A lonely impulse of delight
Drove to this tumult in the clouds;
I balanced all, brought all to mind,
The years to come seemed waste of breath,
A waste of breath the years behind
In balance with this life, this death.
W. B. Yeats (1865–1939) Irish poet.
An Irish Airman Foresees his Death

FOOD

See also etiquette, greed, obesity

1　A meal without flesh is like feeding on grass.
Indian proverb
Proverb

2　An apple-pie without some cheese is like a
kiss without a squeeze.
Proverb

3　Bread is the staff of life.
Proverb

4　Eat to live and not live to eat.
Proverb

5 The nearer the bone, the sweeter the flesh.
Proverb

6 I always eat peas with honey
I've done it all my life,
They do taste kind of funny,
But it keeps them on the knife.
Anonymous
Peas

7 'Oh, my Friends, be warned by me,
That Breakfast, Dinner, Lunch and Tea
Are all the Human Frame requires . . . '
With that the Wretched Child expires.
Hilaire Belloc (1870–1953) French-born British poet.
Cautionary Tales, 'Henry King'

8 The Chief Defect of Henry King
Was chewing little bits of String.
Hilaire Belloc
Cautionary Tales, 'Henry King'

9 I know what I wanted to ask you;
Is trifle sufficient for sweet?
John Betjeman (1906–84) British poet.
How to get on in Society

10 I'm a man
More dined against than dining.
Maurice Bowra (1898–1971) British scholar.
Summoned by Bells (J. Betjeman)

11 Some hae meat, and canna eat,
And some wad eat that want it,
But we hae meat and we can eat,
And sae the Lord be thankit.
Robert Burns (1759–96) Scottish poet.
The Selkirk Grace

12 The Queen of Hearts, she made some tarts,
All on a summer day:
The Knave of Hearts, he stole those tarts,
And took them quite away!
Lewis Carroll (Charles Lutwidge Dodgson; 1832–98)
British writer.
Alice's Adventures in Wonderland, Ch. 11

13 Soup of the evening, beautiful Soup!
Lewis Carroll
Said by the Mock Turtle
Alice's Adventures in Wonderland, Ch. 10

14 Don't eat too many almonds; they add weight
to the breasts
Colette (1873–1954) French novelist.
Gigi

15 Do you *know* what breakfast cereal is made
of? It's made of all those little curly wooden
shavings you find in pencil sharpeners!
Roald Dahl (1916–) British writer.
Charlie and the Chocolate Factory, Ch. 27

16 Bouillabaisse is only good because cooked by
the French, who, if they cared to try, could
produce an excellent and nutritious substitute
out of cigar stumps and empty matchboxes.
Norman Douglas (1868–1952) British novelist.
Siren Land, 'Rain on the Hills'

17 The winter evening settles down
With smell of steaks in passageways.
T. S. Eliot (1888–1965) US-born British poet and
dramatist.
Preludes

18 The way to a man's heart is through his
stomach.
Fanny Fern (1811–72) US writer.
Willis Parton

19 Oh! The roast beef of England.
And old England's roast beef.
Henry Fielding (1707–54) British novelist.
The Grub Street Opera, III:3

20 With my little stick of Blackpool rock,
Along the Promenade I stroll.
It may be sticky but I never complain,
It's nice to have a nibble at it now and again.
George Formby (1905–61) British comedian.
With My Little Stick of Blackpool Rock

21 Take your hare when it is cased . . .
Hannah Glasse (18th century) English writer.
Often misquoted as, 'First catch your hare'
The Art of Cookery Made Plain and Easy, Ch. 1

22 The best number for a dinner party is two –
myself and a dam' good head waiter.
Nubar Gulbenkian (1896–1972) Turkish oil magnate.
Attrib.

23 But one day, one cold winter's day,
He screamed out, 'Take the soup away!'
Heinrich Hoffman (1809–74) German writer.
Struwwelpeter, 'Augustus'

24 This was a good dinner enough, to be sure;
but it was not a dinner to *ask* a man to.
Samuel Johnson (1709–84) British lexicographer.
Life of Johnson (J. Boswell), Vol. I

25 It is as bad as bad can be: it is ill-fed, ill-
killed, ill-kept, and ill-drest.
Samuel Johnson
About the roast mutton at an inn
Life of Johnson (J. Boswell), Vol. IV

26 A cucumber should be well sliced, and
dressed with pepper and vinegar, and then
thrown out, as good for nothing.
Samuel Johnson
Tour to the Hebrides (J. Boswell)

27 I hate a man who swallows it, affecting not
to know what he is eating. I suspect his
taste in higher matters.
Charles Lamb (1775–1834) British essayist.
Referring to food
Essays of Elia, 'Grace before Meat'

28 Any two meals at a boarding-house are
together less than two square meals.
Stephen Leacock (1869–1944) English-born Canadian
economist and humorist.
Literary Lapses, 'Boarding-House Geometry'

29 They dined on mince, and slices of quince,
Which they ate with a runcible spoon;

And hand in hand, on the edge of the sand,
They danced by the light of the moon.
Edward Lear (1812–88) British artist and writer.
The Owl and the Pussy-Cat

30 Food is an important part of a balanced diet.
Fran Lebowitz (1950–) US writer.
Metropolitan Life, 'Food for Thought and Vice Versa'

31 This piece of cod passes all understanding.
Edwin Lutyens (1869–1944) British architect.
Comment made in a restaurant
Attrib.

32 It's a very odd thing –
As odd as can be –
That whatever Miss T eats
Turns into Miss T.
Walter De La Mare (1873–1956) British poet.
Miss T

33 To eat well in England you should have
breakfast three times a day.
W. Somerset Maugham (1874–1965) British novelist.
Attrib.

34 Kissing don't last: cookery do!
George Meredith (1828–1909) British novelist.
The Ordeal of Richard Feverel, Ch. 28

35 One should eat to live, not live to eat.
Molière (Jean Baptiste Poquelin; 1622–73) French
dramatist.
L'Avare, III:2

36 Some breakfast food manufacturer hit upon
the simple notion of emptying out the
leavings of carthorse nosebags, adding a few
other things like unconsumed portions of
chicken layer's mash, and the sweepings of
racing stables, packing the mixture in little
bags and selling them in health food shops.
Frank Muir (1920–) British writer and broadcaster.
Upon My Word!

37 An army marches on its stomach.
Napoleon I (Napoleon Bonaparte; 1769–1821) French
emperor.
Attrib.

38 I think I could eat one of Bellamy's veal pies.
William Pitt the Younger (1759–1806) British
statesman.
Last words
Attrib.

39 The vulgar boil, the learned roast an egg.
Alexander Pope (1688–1744) British poet.
Satires and Epistles of Horace Imitated, Bk II

40 To the old saying that man built the house
but woman made of it a 'home' might be
added the modern supplement that woman
accepted cooking as a chore but man has
made of it a recreation.
Emily Post (1873–1960) US writer.
Etiquette, Ch. 34

41 Dinner at the Huntercombes' possessed 'only

two dramatic features – the wine was a
farce and the food a tragedy'.
Anthony Powell (1905–) British novelist.
A Dance to the Music of Time: The Acceptance World, Ch. 4

42 Great restaurants are, of course, nothing but
mouth-brothels. There is no point in going to
them if one intends to keep one's belt
buckled.
Frederic Raphael (1931–) British author.
The Sunday Times Magazine, 25 Sep 1977

43 The thought of two thousand people
crunching celery at the same time horrified
me.
George Bernard Shaw (1856–1950) Irish dramatist and
critic.
Explaining why he had turned down an invitation to a vegetarian gala dinner
The Greatest Laughs of All Time (G. Lieberman)

44 Yes, cider and tinned salmon are the staple
diet of the agricultural classes.
Evelyn Waugh (1903–66) British novelist.
Scoop, Bk. I, Ch. 1

45 I saw him even now going the way of all
flesh, that is to say towards the kitchen.
John Webster (1580–1625) English dramatist.
Westward Hoe, II:2

46 You breed babies and you eat chips with
everything.
Arnold Wesker (1932–) British dramatist.
Chips with Everything, I:2

47 If I had the choice between smoked salmon
and tinned salmon, I'd have it tinned. With
vinegar.
Harold Wilson (1916–) British politician and prime
minister.
The Observer, 'Sayings of the Week,' 11 Nov 1962

FOOLISHNESS

See also gullibility, ignorance, stupidity, wisdom and foolishness

1 A fool and his money are soon parted.
Proverb

2 A fool at forty is a fool indeed.
Proverb

3 A fool believes everything.
Proverb

4 Better be a fool than a knave.
Proverb

5 Empty vessels make the greatest sound.
Proverb

6 Fools build houses, and wise men buy them.
Proverb

7 Fools live poor to die rich.
Proverb

8 There's no fool like an old fool.
Proverb

9 Give not that which is holy unto the dogs, neither cast ye your pearls before swine, lest they trample them under their feet, and turn again and rend you.
Bible: Matthew
7:6

10 Answer a fool according to his folly, lest he be wise in his own conceit.
Bible: Proverbs
26:5

11 The world is made up for the most part of fools and knaves.
Duke of Buckingham (1628–87) English politician.
To Mr Clifford, on his Humane Reason

12 He's a muddle-headed fool, with frequent lucid intervals.
Miguel de Cervantes (1547–1616) Spanish novelist.
Sancho Panza describing Don Quixote
Don Quixote, Pt. II, Ch. 18

13 The wisest fool in Christendom.
Henri IV (1553–1610) King of France.
Referring to James I of England
Attrib.

14 Mix a little foolishness with your serious plans: it's lovely to be silly at the right moment.
Horace (Quintus Horatius Flaccus; 65–8 BC) Roman poet.
Odes, IV

15 Fools are in a terrible, overwhelming majority, all the wide world over.
Henrik Ibsen (1828–1906) Norwegian dramatist.
An Enemy of the People, IV

16 You cannot fashion a wit out of two half-wits.
Neil Kinnock (1942–) British politician.
The Times, 1983

17 No creature smarts so little as a fool.
Alexander Pope (1688–1744) British poet.
Epistle to Dr. Arbuthnot

18 Lord, what fools these mortals be!
William Shakespeare (1564–1616) English dramatist.
A Midsummer Night's Dream, III:2

19 He was a bold man that first eat an oyster.
Jonathan Swift (1667–1745) Irish-born writer.
Polite conversation, Dialogue 2

FOOTBALL

See also sport

1 I do love cricket – it's so very English.
Sarah Bernhardt (Sarah Henriette Rosine Bernard; 1844–1923) French actress.
On seeing a game of football
Nijinsky (R. Buckle)

2 The goal stands up, the keeper
Stands up to keep the goal.
A. E. Housman (1859–1936) British scholar and poet.
A Shropshire Lad, 'Bredon Hill'

3 I loathed the game . . . it was very difficult for me to show courage at it. Football, it seemed to me, is not really played for the pleasure of kicking a ball about, but is a species of fighting.
George Orwell (Eric Blair; 1903–50) British novelist.
Such, Such Were The Joys

4 The streets were full of footballs.
Samuel Pepys (1633–1703) English diarist.
Diary, 2 Jan 1665

5 A man who had missed the last home match of 't 'United' had to enter social life on tiptoe in Bruddersford.
J. B. Priestley (1894–1984) British novelist and dramatist.
The Good Companions

6 Football isn't a matter of life and death – it's much more important than that.
Bill Shankly (1914–81) British football manager.
Attrib.

7 I will not permit thirty men to travel four hundred miles to agitate a bag of wind.
Andrew Dickson White (1832–1918) US educationalist.
Refusing to allow the Cornell American football team to visit Michigan to play a match
The People's Almanac (D. Wallechinsky)

FORCE

See also oppression, power politics, violence

1 Force is not a remedy.
John Bright (1811–89) British radical politician.
Speech, Birmingham, 16 Nov 1880

2 The use of force alone is but *temporary*. It may subdue for a moment; but it does not remove the necessity of subduing again: and a nation is not governed, which is perpetually to be conquered.
Edmund Burke (1729–97) British politician.
Speech on Conciliation with America (House of Commons, 22 Mar 1775)

FORGIVENESS

1 Forgive and forget.
Proverb

2 Let bygones be bygones.
Proverb

3 Come now, and let us reason together, saith the Lord: though your sins be as scarlet, they shall be as white as snow; though they be red like crimson, they shall be as wool.
Bible: Isaiah
1:18

4 Then said Jesus, Father, forgive them; for they know not what they do. And they parted his raiment, and cast lots.
Bible: Luke
23:34

5 Wherefore I say unto thee, Her sins, which

are many, are forgiven; for she loved much: but to whom little is forgiven, the same loveth little.
Bible: Luke
7:47

6 Then came Peter to him, and said, Lord, how oft shall my brother sin against me, and I forgive him? till seven times?
Jesus saith unto him, I say not unto thee, Until seven times: but, Until seventy times seven.
Bible: Matthew
18:21–22

7 The cut worm forgives the plough.
William Blake (1757–1827) British poet.
The Marriage of Heaven and Hell, 'Proverbs of Hell'

8 The women pardoned all except her face.
Lord Byron (1788–1824) British poet.
Don Juan, V

9 It is the government that should ask me for a pardon.
Eugene Victor Debs (1855–1926) US trade unionist, socialist, and pacifist.
When released from prison (1921) on the orders of President Harding after being jailed for sedition (1918)
The People's Almanac (D. Wallechinsky)

10 Once a woman has forgiven her man, she must not reheat his sins for breakfast.
Marlene Dietrich (Maria Magdalene von Losch; 1904–) German-born film star.
Marlene Dietrich's ABC

11 God may pardon you, but I never can.
Elizabeth I (1533–1603) Queen of England.
To the Countess of Nottingham
History of England under the House of Tudor (Hume), Vol. II, Ch. 7

12 Only lies and evil come from letting people off. . . .
Iris Murdoch (1919–) Irish-born British novelist.
A Severed Head

13 To err is human, to forgive, divine.
Alexander Pope (1688–1744) British poet.
An Essay on Criticism

14 Beware of the man who does not return your blow: he neither forgives you nor allows you to forgive yourself.
George Bernard Shaw (1856–1950) Irish dramatist and critic.
Man and Superman, 'Maxims for Revolutionists'

15 The stupid neither forgive nor forget; the naive forgive and forget; the wise forgive but do not forget.
Thomas Szasz (1920–) US psychiatrist.
The Second Sin

16 I bear no ill-will against those responsible for this. That sort of talk will not bring her back to life. I know there has to be a plan even though we might not understand it. God is good and we shall meet again.
Gordon Wilson Retired businessman.
Speaking of the murder of his daughter, Marie Wilson, in an IRA bombing at the Enniskillen Remembrance Day service, 8 Nov 1987

FRANCE

See also Europe, French Revolution, Paris

1 All Gaul is divided into three parts.
Julius Caesar (100–44 BC) Roman general and statesman.
De Bello Gallico, Vol. I, Ch. 1

2 France was a long despotism tempered by epigrams.
Thomas Carlyle (1795–1881) Scottish historian and essayist.
History of the French Revolution, Pt. I, Bk. I, Ch. 1

3 They are short, blue-vested people who carry their own onions when cycling abroad, and have a yard which is 3.37 inches longer than other people's.
Alan Coren (1938–) British humorist and writer.
The Sanity Inspector, 'All You Need to Know about Europe'

4 There's always something fishy about the French.
Noël Coward (1899–1973) British dramatist.
Conversation Piece, I:6

5 Bouillabaisse is only good because cooked by the French, who, if they cared to try, could produce an excellent and nutritious substitute out of cigar stumps and empty matchboxes.
Norman Douglas (1868–1952) British novelist.
Siren Land, 'Rain on the Hills'

6 The French will only be united under the threat of danger. Nobody can simply bring together a country that has 265 kinds of cheese.
Charles De Gaulle (1890–1970) French general and statesman.
Speech, 1951

7 I hate the French because they are all slaves, and wear wooden shoes.
Oliver Goldsmith (1728–74) Irish-born British writer.
Essays, 'Distresses of a Common Soldier'

8 The best thing I know between France and England is – the sea.
Douglas William Jerrold (1803–57) British dramatist.
Wit and Opinions of Douglas Jerrold, 'The Anglo-French Alliance'

9 A Frenchman must be always talking, whether he knows anything of the matter or not; an Englishman is content to say nothing, when he has nothing to say.
Samuel Johnson (1709–84) British lexicographer.
Life of Johnson (J. Boswell), Vol. IV

10 *Allons, enfants, de la patrie,*
Le jour de gloire est arrivé.
Come, children of our native land,

The day of glory has arrived.

Rouget de Lisle (Claude Joseph Rouget de Lisle; 1760–1836) French military engineer and composer.
La Marseillaise (French national anthem)

11 Yet, who can help loving the land that has taught us
Six hundred and eighty-five ways to dress eggs?

Thomas Moore (1779–1852) Irish poet.
The Fudge Family in Paris

12 There's something Vichy about the French.

Ivor Novello (David Ivor Davies; 1893–1951) British actor, composer, and dramatist.
Ambrosia and Small Beer (Edward Marsh), Ch. 4

13 A mademoiselle from Armenteers,
She hasn't been kissed for forty years,
Hinky, dinky, par-lee-voo.

Edward Rowland (20th century) British songwriter.
Armentières was completely destroyed (1918) in World War I
Mademoiselle from Armentières (song)

14 They are a loyal, a gallant, a generous, an ingenious, and good-temper'd people as is under heaven – if they have a fault, they are too *serious*.

Laurence Sterne (1713–68) Irish-born British writer.
A Sentimental Journey, 'The Character. Versailles'

15 I do not dislike the French from the vulgar antipathy between neighbouring nations, but for their insolent and unfounded airs of superiority.

Horace Walpole (1717–97) British writer.
Letter to Hannah More, 14 Oct 1787

16 France is a country where the money falls apart in your hands and you can't tear the toilet paper.

Billy Wilder (Samuel Wilder; 1906–) Austrian-born US film director.
Attrib.

FRANKNESS

See also honesty, sincerity, truth

1 But of all plagues, good Heaven, thy wrath can send,
Save me, oh, save me, from the candid friend.

George Canning (1770–1827) British statesman.
New Morality

2 I have two very cogent reasons for not printing any list of subscribers; – one, that I have lost all the names, – the other, that I have spent all the money.

Samuel Johnson (1709–84) British lexicographer.
Referring to subscribers to his *Dictionary of the English Language*
Life of Johnson (J. Boswell), Vol. IV

3 The great consolation in life is to say what one thinks.

Voltaire (François-Marie Arouet; 1694–1778) French writer.
Letter, 1765

4 On an occasion of this kind it becomes more than a moral duty to speak one's mind. It becomes a pleasure.

Oscar Wilde (1854–1900) Irish-born British dramatist.
The Importance of Being Earnest, II

FREEDOM

See also human rights, imprisonment

1 I'll have a fling.

Francis Beaumont (1584–1616) English dramatist.
Rule a Wife and have a Wife, III:5

2 My policy is to be able to take a ticket at Victoria Station and go anywhere I damn well please.

Ernest Bevin (1881–1951) British trade-union leader and politician.
The Spectator, 20 Apr 1951

3 Conscience, I say, not thine own, but of the other: for why is my liberty judged of another man's conscience?

Bible: I Corinthians
10:29

4 So free we seem, so fettered fast we are!

Robert Browning (1812–89) British poet.
Andrea del Sarto

5 Liberty, too, must be limited in order to be possessed.

Edmund Burke (1729–97) British politician.
Letter to the Sheriffs of Bristol, 1777

6 Hereditary bondsmen! know ye not
Who would be free themselves must strike the blow?

Lord Byron (1788–1824) British poet.
Childe Harold's Pilgrimage, I

7 England may as well dam up the waters from the Nile with bulrushes as to fetter the step of Freedom, more proud and firm in this youthful land.

Lydia M. Child (1802–80) US abolitionist campaigner.
The Rebels, Ch. 4

8 But what is Freedom? Rightly understood,
A universal licence to be good.

Hartley Coleridge (1796–1849) British poet.
Liberty

9 The condition upon which God hath given liberty to man is eternal vigilance.

John Philpot Curran (1750–1817) Irish judge.
Speech on the Right of Election of Lord Mayor of Dublin, 10 July 1790

10 Yes, 'n' how many years can some people exist
Before they're allowed to be free?
Yes, 'n' how many times can a man turn his head,
Pretending he just doesn't see?

The answer, my friend, is blowin' in the wind.
Bob Dylan (Robert Allen Zimmerman; 1941–) US popular singer.
Blowin' in the Wind

11 My people and I have come to an agreement which satisfies us both. They are to say what they please, and I am to do what I please.
Frederick the Great (1712–86) King of Prussia.
Attrib.

12 This is Liberty-Hall, gentlemen.
Oliver Goldsmith (1728–74) Irish-born British writer.
She Stoops to Conquer, II

13 *Laissez faire, laissez passer.*
Liberty of action, liberty of movement.
Jean Claude Vincent de Gournay (1712–59) French economist.
Speech, Sept 1758

14 Power is so apt to be insolent and Liberty to be saucy, that they are seldom upon good Terms.
George Saville Halifax (1633–95) English statesman.
Political, Moral, and Miscellaneous Thoughts and Reflections

15 The love of liberty is the love of others; the love of power is the love of ourselves.
William Hazlitt (1778–1830) British essayist.
The Times, 1819

16 I know not what course others may take; but as for me, give me liberty or give me death.
Patrick Henry (1736–99) US statesman.
Speech, Virginia Convention, 23 Mar 1775

17 I struck the board, and cried, 'No more;
I will abroad.'
What, shall I ever sigh and pine?
My lines and life are free; free as the road,
Loose as the wind, as large as store.
George Herbert (1593–1633) English poet.
The Collar

18 'Painters and poets alike have always had licence to dare anything.' We know that, and we both claim and allow to others in their turn this indulgence.
Horace (Quintus Horatius Flaccus; 65–8 BC) Roman poet.
Ars Poetica

19 *Nullius addictus iurare in verba magistri,*
Quo me cumque rapit tempestas, deferor hospes.
Not bound to swear allegiance to any master, wherever the wind takes me I travel as a visitor.
Horace
Nullius in verba is the motto of the Royal Society
Epistles, I

20 A man should never put on his best trousers when he goes out to battle for freedom and truth.
Henrik Ibsen (1828–1906) Norwegian dramatist.
An Enemy of the People, V

21 The tree of liberty must be refreshed from time to time with the blood of patriots and tyrants. It is its natural manure.
Thomas Jefferson (1743–1826) US statesman.
Letter to W. S. Smith, 13 Nov 1787

22 I have got no further than this: Every man has a right to utter what he thinks truth, and every other man has a right to knock him down for it. Martyrdom is the test.
Samuel Johnson (1709–84) British lexicographer.
Life of Johnson (J. Boswell), Vol. IV

23 The Liberty of the press is the *Palladium* of all the civil, political and religious rights of an Englishman.
Junius An unidentified writer of letters (1769–72) to the *London Public Advertiser*.
Letters, 'Dedication'

24 It's often safer to be in chains than to be free.
Franz Kafka (1883–1924) Czech novelist.
The Trial, Ch. 8

25 Freedom's just another word for nothing left to lose.
Kris Kristofferson (1936–) US film actor and folk musician.
Me and Bobby McGee

26 It is true that liberty is precious – so precious that it must be rationed.
Lenin (Vladimir Ilich Ulyanov; 1870–1924) Russian revolutionary leader.
Attrib.

27 I intend no modification of my oft-expressed personal wish that all men everywhere could be free.
Abraham Lincoln (1809–65) US statesman.
Letter to Horace Greeley, 22 Aug 1862

28 Those who deny freedom to others, deserve it not for themselves.
Abraham Lincoln
Speech, 19 May 1856

29 Many politicians of our time are in the habit of laying it down as a self-evident proposition, that no people ought to be free till they are fit to use their freedom. The maxim is worthy of the fool in the old story, who resolved not to go into the water till he had learnt to swim. If men are to wait for liberty till they become wise and good in slavery, they may indeed wait for ever.
Lord Macaulay (1800–59) British historian.
Literary Essays Contributed to the 'Edinburgh Review', 'Milton',

30 It would be better that England should be free than that England should be compulsorily sober.
William Connor Magee (1821–91) British clergyman.
Speech on the Intoxicating Liquor Bill, House of Lords, 2 May 1872

31 I cannot and will not give any undertaking at a time when I, and you, the people, are not

free. Your freedom and mine cannot be separated.
Nelson Mandela (1918–) South African lawyer and politician.
Message read by his daughter to a rally in Soweto, 10 Feb 1985

32 Letting a hundred flowers blossom and a hundred schools of thought contend is the policy for promoting the progress of the arts and the sciences.
Mao Tse-Tung (1893–1976) Chinese communist leader.
Quotations from Chairman Mao Tse-Tung, Ch. 32

33 The liberty of the individual must be thus far limited; he must not make himself a nuisance to other people.
John Stuart Mill (1806–73) British philosopher.
On Liberty, Ch. 3

34 None can love freedom heartily, but good men; the rest love not freedom, but licence.
John Milton (1608–74) English poet.
Tenure of Kings and Magistrates

35 Liberty is the right to do everything which the laws allow.
Baron de Montesquieu (1688–1755) French writer.
L'Esprit des lois

36 Before the organization of the Blackshirt movement free speech did not exist in this country.
Oswald Mosley (1896–1980) British politician.
Selections from the *New Statesman, This England*, Pt. I

37 My government will protect all liberties but one – the liberty to do away with other liberties.
Gustavo Diaz Ordaz (1911–) President of Mexico (1964–1970).
Inaugural speech

38 Freedom is the right to tell people what they do not want to hear.
George Orwell (Eric Blair; 1903–50) British novelist.
The Road to Wigan Pier

39 I sometimes think that the price of liberty is not so much eternal vigilance as eternal dirt.
George Orwell
The Road to Wigan Pier, Ch. 4

40 We must plan for freedom, and not only for security, if for no other reason than that only freedom can make security secure.
Karl Popper (1902–) Austrian-born British philosopher.
The Open Society and Its Enemies

41 Now: heaven knows, anything goes.
Cole Porter (1893–1964) US songwriter.
Anything Goes, title song

42 *Laissez faire, laissez passer.*
Let it be, let it pass.
François Quesnay (1694–1774) French economist.
Attrib.

43 In their rules there was only one clause: Do what you will.
François Rabelais (1483–1553) French satirist.
Referring to the fictional Abbey of Thélème
Gargantua, Bk. I, Ch. 57

44 '*O liberté! O liberté! Que de crimes on commet en ton nom!*'
Oh liberty! Oh liberty! What crimes are committed in thy name!
Madame Roland (1754–93) French revolutionary.
Said as she mounted the steps of the guillotine at her execution
Attrib.

45 Man was born free and everywhere he is in chains.
Jean Jacques Rousseau (1712–78) French philosopher.
Du contrat social, Ch. 1

46 No human being, however great, or powerful, was ever so free as a fish.
John Ruskin (1819–1900) British art critic and writer.
The Two Paths, Lecture V

47 Man is condemned to be free.
Jean-Paul Sartre (1905–80) French writer.
Existentialism is a Humanism

48 You took my freedom away a long time ago and you can't give it back because you haven't got it yourself.
Alexander Solzhenitsyn (1918–) Soviet novelist.
The First Circle, Ch. 17

49 My definition of a free society is a society where it is safe to be unpopular.
Adlai Stevenson (1900–65) US statesman.
Speech, Detroit, Oct. 1952

50 It is by the goodness of God that in our country we have those three unspeakably precious things: freedom of speech, freedom of conscience, and the prudence never to practise either of them.
Mark Twain (Samuel Langhorne Clemens; 1835–1910) US writer.
Following the Equator, heading of Ch. 20

51 I disapprove of what you say, but I will defend to the death your right to say it.
Voltaire (François-Marie Arouet; 1694–1778) French writer.
Attrib.

52 Me this unchartered freedom tires;
I feel the weight of chance-desires:
My hopes no more must change their name,
I long for a repose that ever is the same.
William Wordsworth (1770–1850) British poet.
Ode to Duty

53 We must be free or die, who speak the tongue
That Shakspeare spake; the faith and morals hold
Which Milton held.
William Wordsworth
Sonnets, 'It is not to be thought of'

54 Two voices are there; one is of the sea,
One of the mountains; each a mighty voice:
In both from age to age thou didst rejoice,
They were thy chosen music, Liberty!
William Wordsworth
Sonnets, 'Two voices are there'

FRENCH REVOLUTION

See also France, revolution

1 It was the best of times, it was the worst of
times, it was the age of wisdom, it was the
age of foolishness, it was the epoch of belief,
it was the epoch of incredulity, it was the
season of Light, it was the season of
Darkness, it was the spring of hope, it was
the winter of despair, we had everything
before us, we had nothing before us, we
were all going direct to Heaven, we were all
going direct the other way.
Charles Dickens (1812–70) British novelist.
The opening words of the book
A Tale of Two Cities, Bk. I, Ch. 1

2 How much the greatest event it is that ever
happened in the world! and how much the
best!
Charles James Fox (1749–1806) British Whig politician.
Referring to the fall of the Bastille, 14 July 1789
Letter to Fitzpatrick, 30 July 1789

3 Bliss was it in that dawn to be alive,
But to be young was very heaven!
William Wordsworth (1770–1850) British poet.
The Prelude, XI

4 That which sets
. . . The budding rose above the rose full
blown.
William Wordsworth
The Prelude, XI

5 Not in Utopia, – subterranean fields, –
Or some secreted island, Heaven knows
where!
But in the very world, which is the world
Of all of us, – the place where, in the end,
We find our happiness, or not at all!
William Wordsworth
The Prelude, XI

FRIENDS

See also enemies, friendship

1 Books and friends should be few but good.
Proverb

2 Forsake not an old friend; for the new is not
comparable to him: a new friend is as new
wine; when it is old, thou shalt drink it with
pleasure.
Bible: Ecclesiasticus
9:10

3 Cost his enemies a long repentance,
And made him a good friend, but bad
acquaintance.
Lord Byron (1788–1824) British poet.
Don Juan, III

4 Tell me what company thou keepest, and I'll
tell thee what thou art.
Miguel de Cervantes (1547–1616) Spanish novelist.
Don Quixote, Pt. II, Ch. 23

5 Have no friends not equal to yourself.
Confucius (K'ung Fu-tzu; 551–479 BC) Chinese
philosopher.
Analects

6 Fate chooses your relations, you choose your
friends.
Jacques Delille (1738–1813) French abbé and poet.
Malheur et pitié, I

7 A Friend may well be reckoned the
masterpiece of Nature.
Ralph Waldo Emerson (1803–82) US poet and essayist.
Essays, 'Friendship'

8 *Changez vos amis.*
Change your friends.
Charles De Gaulle (1890–1970) French general and
statesman.
Replying to the complaint by Jacques Soustelle that he was be-
ing attacked by his own friends
Attrib.

9 If a man does not make new acquaintance as
he advances through life, he will soon find
himself left alone. A man, Sir, should keep
his friendship in constant repair.
Samuel Johnson (1709–84) British lexicographer.
Life of Johnson (J. Boswell), Vol. I

10 I get by with a little help from my friends.
John Lennon (1940–80) British rock musician.
With a Little Help from My Friends (with Paul McCartney)

11 He's an oul' butty o' mine – oh, he's a
darlin' man, a daarlin' man.
Sean O'Casey (1884–1964) Irish dramatist.
Juno and the Paycock, I

12 It is more shameful to distrust one's friends
than to be deceived by them.
Duc de la Rochefoucauld (1613–80) French writer.
Maximes, 84

13 A friend should bear his friend's infirmities,
But Brutus makes mine greater than they are.
William Shakespeare (1564–1616) English dramatist.
Julius Caesar, IV:3

14 If it is abuse – why one is always sure to
hear of it from one damned good-natured
friend or other!
Richard Brinsley Sheridan (1751–1816) British
dramatist.
The Critic, I

15 Associate yourself with men of good quality if
you esteem your own reputation; for 'tis
better to be alone than in bad company.
George Washington (1732–99) US statesman.
Rules of Civility

FRIENDSHIP

See also friends, love and friendship

1 A friend in need is a friend indeed.
Proverb

2 A good friend is my nearest relation.
Proverb

3 A hedge between keeps friendship green.
Proverb

4 God defend me from my friends; from my enemies I can defend myself.
Proverb

5 Love is blind; friendship closes its eyes.
Proverb

6 The best of friends must part.
Proverb

7 There is no such thing as a free lunch.
Anonymous
Often attributed to Milton Friedman
Attrib.

8 Two are better than one; because they have a good reward for their labour.
For if they fall, the one will lift up his fellow: but woe to him that is alone when he falleth; for he hath not another to help him up.
Bible: Ecclesiastes
4:9–10

9 Saul and Jonathan were lovely and pleasant in their lives, and in their death they were not divided: they were swifter than eagles, they were stronger than lions.
Bible: II Samuel
1:23–24

10 I've noticed your hostility towards him . . . I ought to have guessed you were friends.
Malcolm Bradbury (1932–) British academic and novelist.
The History Man, Ch. 7

11 I don't trust him. We're friends.
Bertolt Brecht (1898–1956) German dramatist.
Mother Courage, III

12 Should auld acquaintance be forgot,
And never brought to min'?
Robert Burns (1759–96) Scottish poet.
Auld Lang Syne

13 We'll tak a cup o' kindness yet,
For auld lang syne.
Robert Burns
Auld Lang Syne

14 Two may talk together under the same roof for many years, yet never really meet; and two others at first speech are old friends.
Mary Catherwood (1847–1901) US writer.
Mackinac and Lake Stories, 'Marianson'

15 A woman can become a man's friend only in the following stages – first an acquaintance, next a mistress, and only then a friend.
Anton Chekhov (1860–1904) Russian dramatist.
Uncle Vanya, II

16 There is nothing in the world I wouldn't do for Hope, and there is nothing he wouldn't do for me . . . We spend our lives doing nothing for each other.
Bing Crosby (Harry Lillis Crosby; 1904–77) US singer.
Referring to Bob Hope
The Observer, 'Sayings of the Week', 7 May 1950

17 It is not so much our friends' help that helps us as the confident knowledge that they will help us.
Epicurus (341–270 BC) Greek philosopher.

18 These are called the pious frauds of friendship.
Henry Fielding (1707–54) British novelist.
Amelia, Bk. III, Ch. 4

19 Always, Sir, set a high value on spontaneous kindness. He whose inclination prompts him to cultivate your friendship of his own accord, will love you more than one whom you have been at pains to attach to you.
Samuel Johnson (1709–84) British lexicographer.
Life of Johnson (J. Boswell), Vol. IV

20 Sir, I look upon every day to be lost, in which I do not make a new acquaintance.
Samuel Johnson
Life of Johnson (J. Boswell), Vol. IV

21 Greater love than this, he said, no man hath that a man lay down his wife for a friend. Go thou and do likewise. Thus, or words to that effect, saith Zarathustra, sometime regius professor of French letters to the University of Oxtail.
James Joyce (1882–1941) Irish novelist.
Ulysses

22 Friendship is unnecessary, like philosophy, like art . . . . It has no survival value; rather it is one of those things that give value to survival.
C. S. Lewis (1898–1963) British academic and writer.
The Four Loves, Friendship

23 Two buttocks of one bum.
T. Sturge Moore (1870–1944) British poet and illustrator.
Referring to Hilaire Belloc and G. K. Chesterton

24 To like and dislike the same things, that is indeed true friendship.
Sallust (Gaius Sallustius Crispus; c. 86–c. 34 BC) Roman historian and politician.
Bellum Catilinae

25 I might give my life for my friend, but he had better not ask me to do up a parcel.
Logan Pearsall Smith (1865–1946) US writer.
Trivia

FUNERALS

See also death

1   Most of the people who will walk after me will be children, so make the beat keep time with short steps.
Hans Christian Andersen (1805–75) Danish writer.
Planning the music for his funeral
Hans Christian Andersen (R. Godden)

2   This is the last time that I will take part as an amateur.
Daniel-François-Esprit Auber (1782–1871) French composer.
Said at a funeral
Das Buch des Lachens (W. Scholz)

3   When we attend the funerals of our friends we grieve for them, but when we go to those of other people it is chiefly our own deaths that we mourn for.
Gerald Brenan (Edward Fitzgerald Brenan; 1894–1987) British writer.
Thoughts in a Dry Season, 'Death'

4   'If you don't go to other men's funerals,' he told Father stiffly, 'they won't go to yours.'
Clarence Shepard Day (1874–1935) US writer.
Life With Father, 'Father plans'

5   I bet you a hundred bucks he ain't in here.
Charles Bancroft Dillingham (1868–1934) US theatrical manager.
Referring to the escapologist Harry Houdini; said at his funeral, while carrying his coffin
Attrib.

6   When I die I want to decompose in a barrel of porter and have it served in all the pubs in Dublin.
J. P. Donleavy (1926–   ) US novelist.
The Ginger Man

7   Why should I go? She won't be there.
Arthur Miller (1915–   ) US dramatist.
When asked if he would attend Marilyn Monroe's funeral
Attrib.

8   It proves what they say, give the public what they want to see and they'll come out for it.
Red Skelton (Richard Bernard Skelton; 1913–   ) US actor and comedian.
Said while attending the funeral in 1958 of Hollywood producer Harry Cohn. It has also been attributed to Samuel Goldwyn while attending Louis B. Mayer's funeral in 1957

9   How Henry would have loved it!
Ellen Terry (1847–1928) British actress.
Referring to Sir Henry Irving's funeral
Yesterdays (Robert Hitchens)

10 Not a drum was heard, not a funeral note, As his corse to the rampart we hurried.
Charles Wolfe (1791–1823) Irish poet.
The Burial of Sir John Moore at Corunna, I

11 We carved not a line, and we raised not a stone –

But we left him alone with his glory.
Charles Wolfe
The Burial of Sir John Moore at Corunna, VIII

FUSSINESS

1   In company with several other old ladies of both sexes.
Charles Dickens (1812–70) British novelist.
Said by Mr Meagles
Little Dorrit, Bk. I, Ch. 17

FUTILITY

See also purpose

1   Why buy a cow when milk is so cheap?
Proverb

2   Why keep a dog and bark yourself?
Proverb

3   You can't get blood out of a stone.
Proverb

4   Mock on, mock on, Voltaire, Rousseau;
Mock on, mock on; 'tis all in vain!
You throw the sand against the wind,
And the wind blows it back again.
William Blake (1757–1827) British poet.
Mock on, mock on, Voltaire, Rousseau

5   It's but little good you'll do a-watering the last year's crop.
George Eliot (Mary Ann Evans; 1819–80) British novelist.
Adam Bede

6   He is very fond of making things which he does not want, and then giving them to people who have no use for them.
Anthony Hope (Sir Anthony Hope Hawkins; 1863–1933) British novelist.
The Dolly Dialogues

7   He's a real Nowhere Man,
Sitting in his Nowhere Land,
Making all his nowhere plans for nobody.
Doesn't have a point of view,
Knows not where he's going to,
Isn't he a bit like you and me?
John Lennon (1940–80) British rock musician.
Nowhere Man (with Paul McCartney)

8   'Tis not necessary to light a candle to the sun.
Algernon Sidney (1622–83) English statesman.
Discourses concerning Government, Ch. 2

9   People talking without speaking,
People listening without hearing,
People writing songs that voices never shared.
Paul Simon (1941–   ) US singer.
Sound of Silence

10 All dressed up, with nowhere to go.
William Allen White (1868–1944) US writer.
Referring to the Progressive Party, after Theodore Roosevelt's withdrawal from the 1916 US Presidential election

FUTURE

See also past, present, promises, prophecy, time

1 Years hence, perhaps, may dawn an age,
More fortunate, alas! than we,
Which without hardness will be sage,
And gay without frivolity.
Matthew Arnold (1822–88) British poet and critic.
The Grande Chartreuse

2 Boast not thyself of tomorrow; for thou
knowest not what a day may bring forth.
Bible: Proverbs
27:1

3 *Future*, n That period of time in which our
affairs prosper, our friends are true and our
happiness is assured.
Ambrose Bierce (1842–?1914) US writer.
The Devil's Dictionary

4 Not a future. At least not in Europe.
America's different, of course, but America's
really only a kind of Russia. You've no idea
how pleasant it is not to have any future. It's
like having a totally efficient contraceptive.
Anthony Burgess (John Burgess Wilson; 1917–)
British novelist.
Honey for the Bears, Pt. II, Ch. 6

5 I never think of the future. It comes soon
enough.
Albert Einstein (1879–1955) German-born US physicist.
Interview, 1930

6 I have seen the future and it works.
Lincoln Steffens (1866–1936) US journalist.
Speaking to Bernard Baruch after visiting the Soviet Union,
1919
Autobiography, Ch. 18

7 The future is made of the same stuff as the
present.
Simone Weil (1909–43) French philosopher.
On Science, Necessity, and the Love of God (ed. Richard Rees),
'Some Thoughts on the Love of God'

G

GARDENS

See also flowers

1 Mary, Mary, quite contrary,
How does your garden grow?
With silver bells and cockle shells,
And pretty maids all in a row.
Anonymous
Tommy Thumb's Pretty Song Book

2 God Almighty first planted a garden. And
indeed it is the purest of human pleasures.
Francis Bacon (1561–1626) English philosopher.
Essays, 'Of Gardens'

3 But there went up a mist from the earth, and
watered the whole face of the ground.
And the Lord God formed man of the dust of
the ground, and breathed into his nostrils the
breath of life; and man became a living soul.
And the Lord God planted a garden eastward
in Eden; and there he put the man whom he
had formed.
And out of the ground made the Lord God to
grow every tree that is pleasant to the sight,
and good for food; the tree of life also in the
midst of the garden, and the tree of knowledge of good and evil.
And a river went out of Eden to water the
garden.
Bible: Genesis
2:6–10

4 A garden is a lovesome thing, God wot!
Thomas Edward Brown (1830–97) British poet.
My Garden

5 To get the best results you must talk to your
vegetables.
Prince Charles (1948–) Eldest son of Elizabeth II.
The Observer, 'Sayings of the Week', 28 Sept 1986

6 God the first garden made, and the first city
Cain.
Abraham Cowley (1618–67) English poet.
The Garden

7 The kiss of sun for pardon,
The song of the birds for mirth –
One is nearer God's Heart in a garden
Than anywhere else on earth.
Dorothy Gurney (1858–1932) British poet.
The Lord God Planted a Garden

8 Oh, Adam was a gardener, and God who
made him sees
That half a proper gardener's work is done up-
on his knees,
So when your work is finished, you can wash
your hands and pray
For the Glory of the Garden, that it may not
pass away!
Rudyard Kipling (1865–1936) Indian-born British writer.
The Glory of the Garden

9 A little thin, flowery border, round, neat, not
gaudy.
Charles Lamb (1775–1834) British essayist.
Letter to Wordsworth, June 1806

10 I have a garden of my own,
But so with roses overgrown,
And lilies, that you would it guess
To be a little wilderness.
Andrew Marvell (1621–78) English poet.
The Nymph Complaining for the Death of her Fawn

GENERALIZATIONS

See also classification

1 To generalize is to be an idiot.
William Blake (1757–1827) British poet.
Life of Blake (Gilchrist)

2 All generalizations are dangerous, even this one.
Alexandre Dumas, fils (1824–95) French writer.
Attrib.

3 Any general statement is like a cheque drawn on a bank. Its value depends on what is there to meet it.
Ezra Pound (1885–1972) US poet.
ABC of Reading, Ch. 2

GENEROSITY

See also charity, gifts, kindness, parasites

1 Every man according as he purposeth in his heart, so let him give; not grudgingly, or of necessity: for God loveth a cheerful giver.
Bible: II Corinthians
9:7

2 Heal the sick, cleanse the lepers, raise the dead, cast out devils: freely ye have received, freely give.
Bible: Matthew
10:8

3 Experience was to be taken as showing that one might get a five-pound note as one got a light for a cigarette; but one had to check the friendly impulse to ask for it in the same way.
Henry James (1843–1916) US novelist.
The Awkward Age

4 In the first place, I have only five guineas in my pocket; and in the second, they are very much at your service.
Lord Peterborough (1658–1735) English military and naval commander.
Persuading an angry mob that he was not the Duke of Marlborough, notorious for his meanness
Dictionary of National Biography

GENIUS

See also talent, talent and genius

1 Genius is an infinite capacity for taking pains.
Proverb

2 Genius (which means transcendent capacity of taking trouble, first of all).
Thomas Carlyle (1795–1881) Scottish historian and essayist.
Frederick the Great, Vol. IV, Ch. 3

3 Great Wits are sure to Madness near alli'd
And thin Partitions do their Bounds divide.
John Dryden (1631–1700) British poet and dramatist.
Absalom and Achitophel, I

4 Genius is one per cent inspiration and ninety-nine per cent perspiration.
Thomas Edison (1847–1931) US inventor.
Attrib.

5 True genius walks along a line, and, perhaps, our greatest pleasure is in seeing it so often near falling, without being ever actually down.
Oliver Goldsmith (1728–74) Irish-born British writer.
The Bee, 'The Characteristics of Greatness'

6 The true genius is a mind of large general powers, accidentally determined to some particular direction.
Samuel Johnson (1709–84) British lexicographer.
Lives of the English Poets, 'Cowley'

7 A genius! For thirty-seven years I've practiced fourteen hours a day, and now they call me a genius!
Pablo Sarasate (1844–1908) Spanish violinist and composer.
On being hailed as a genius by a critic
Attrib.

8 When a true genius appears in the world, you may know him by this sign, that the dunces are all in confederacy against him.
Jonathan Swift (1667–1745) Irish-born Anglican priest and writer.
Thoughts on Various Subjects

GERMANY

See also Europe, Hitler, Nazism, World War II

1 Hamelin Town's in Brunswick,
By famous Hanover city;
The river Weser, deep and wide,
Washes its wall on the southern side;
A pleasanter spot you never spied.
Robert Browning (1812–89) British poet.
The Pied Piper of Hamelin

2 Don't let's be beastly to the Germans.
Noël Coward (1899–1973) British dramatist.
Title of song

3 *Deutschland, Deutschland über alles.*
Germany, Germany before all else.
Heinrich Hoffmann von Fallersleben (1798–1876) German poet.
German national anthem

4 Germany will be either a world power or will not be at all.
Adolf Hitler (1889–1945) German dictator.
Mein Kampf, Ch. 14

5 How appallingly thorough these Germans always managed to be, how emphatic! In sex no less than in war – in scholarship, in science. Diving deeper than anyone else and coming up muddier.
Aldous Huxley (1894–1964) British novelist.

6 All free men, wherever they may live, are citizens of Berlin. And therefore, as a free

man, I take pride in the words *Ich bin ein Berliner*.

John Fitzgerald Kennedy (1917–63) US statesman.
Speech, City Hall, West Berlin, 26 June 1963

7 America . . . is the prize amateur nation of the world. Germany is the prize professional nation.

Woodrow Wilson (1856–1925) US statesman.
Speech, Aug 1917
Mr Wilson's War (John Dos Passos), Pt. III, Ch. 13

GIFTS

See also generosity, materialism

1 Every good gift and every perfect gift is from above, and cometh down from the Father of lights, with whom is no variableness, neither shadow of turning.

Bible: James
1:17

2 Heal the sick, cleanse the lepers, raise the dead, cast out devils: freely ye have received, freely give.

Bible: Matthew
10:8

3 'They gave it me,' Humpty Dumpty continued thoughtfully, . . . 'for an un-birthday present.'

Lewis Carroll (Charles Lutwidge Dodgson; 1832–98)
British writer.
Through the Looking-Glass, Ch. 6

4 The manner of giving is worth more than the gift.

Pierre Corneille (1606–84) French dramatist.
Le Menteur, I:1

5 If one doesn't get birthday presents it can remobilize very painfully the persecutory anxiety which usually follows birth.

Henry Reed (1914–   ) British poet and dramatist.
The Primal Scene, as it were

GLORY

1 Fools! For I also had my hour;
One far fierce hour and sweet;
There was a shout about my ears,
And palms before my feet.

G. K. Chesterton (1874–1936) British writer.
The Donkey

2 May God deny you peace but give you glory!

Miguel de Unamuno y Jugo (1864–1936) Spanish writer.
Closing words
The Tragic Sense of Life

3 *Sic transit gloria mundi.*
Thus the glory of the world passes away.

Thomas à Kempis (Thomas Hemmerken; c. 1380–1471)
German monk.
The Imitation of Christ, I

4 Wi' a hundred pipers an' a', an' a'.

Carolina Nairne (1766–1845) Scottish songwriter.
A romantic glorification of the 1745 Jacobite Rebellion
The Hundred Pipers

5 'Hurrah! hurrah! we bring the Jubilee!
Hurrah! hurrah! the flag that makes you free!'
So we sang the chorus from Atlanta to the sea
As we were marching through Georgia.

Henry Clay Work (1832–84) US songwriter.
Commemorating the march (Nov–Dec 1864) by a Union army under General Sherman through Confederate Georgia
Marching Through Georgia

GOD

See also atheism, creation, faith, prayer, religion

1 God be in my head,
And in my understanding;
God be in my eyes,
And in my looking;
God be in my mouth,
And in my speaking;
God be in my heart,
And in my thinking;
God be at my end,
And at my departing.

Anonymous
Sarum Missal

2 Every man thinks God is on his side. The rich and powerful know that he is.

Jean Anouilh (1910–87) French dramatist.
The Lark

3 It were better to have no opinion of God at all, than such an opinion as is unworthy of him.

Francis Bacon (1561–1626) English philosopher.
Essays, 'Of Superstition'

4 Then Peter opened his mouth, and said, Of a truth I perceive that God is no respecter of persons.

Bible: Acts
10:34

5 For in him we live, and move, and have our being; as certain also of your own poets have said, For we are also his offspring.

Bible: Acts
17:28

6 Seek him that maketh the seven stars and Orion, and turneth the shadow of death into the morning, and maketh the day dark with night: that calleth for the waters of the sea, and poureth them out upon the face of the earth: The Lord is his name.

Bible: Amos
5:8

7 And he changeth the times and the seasons: he removeth kings, and setteth up kings: he giveth wisdom unto the wise, and knowledge to them that know understanding:
He revealeth the deep and secret things: he

knoweth what is in the darkness, and the light dwelleth with him.
Bible: Daniel
2:21–22

8 Be strong and of a good courage, fear not, nor be afraid of them: for the Lord thy God, he it is that doth go with thee; he will not fail thee, nor forsake thee.
Bible: Deuteronomy
31:6

9 Let us hear the conclusion of the whole matter: Fear God, and keep his commandments: for this is the whole duty of man.
Bible: Ecclesiastes
12:13

10 I am the Lord thy God, which have brought thee out of the land of Egypt, out of the house of bondage.
Thou shalt have no other gods before me.
Thou shalt not make unto thee any graven image, or any likeness of any thing that is in heaven above, or that is in the earth beneath, or that is in the water under the earth:
Thou shalt not bow down thyself to them, nor serve them: for Lord thy God am a jealous God, visiting the iniquity of the fathers upon the children unto the third and fourth generation of them that hate me;
And shewing mercy unto thousands of them that love me, and keep my commandments.
Thou shalt not take the name of the Lord thy God in vain; for the Lord will not hold him guiltless that taketh his name in vain.
Remember the sabbath day, to keep it holy.
Six days shalt thou labour, and do all thy work:
But the seventh day is the sabbath of the Lord thy God: in it thou shalt not do any work, thou, nor thy son, nor thy daughter, thy manservant, nor thy maidservant, nor thy cattle, nor thy stranger that is within thy gates:
For in six days the Lord made heaven and earth, the sea, and all that in them is, and rested the seventh day: wherefore the Lord blessed the sabbath day, and hallowed it.
Honour thy father and thy mother: that thy days may be long upon the land which the Lord thy God giveth thee.
Thou shalt not kill.
Thou shalt not commit adultery.
Thou shalt not steal.
Thou shalt not bear false witness against thy neighbour.
Thou shalt not covet thy neighbour's house, thou shalt not covet thy neighbour's wife, nor his manservant, nor his maidservant, nor his ox, nor his ass, nor any thing that is thy neighbour's.
Bible: Exodus
20:2–17

11 And he said, Thou canst not see my face: for there shall no man see me, and live.
Bible: Exodus
33:20

12 For the kingdom of God is not in word, but in power.
Bible: I Corinthians
4:20

13 And he said, Go forth, and stand upon the mount before the Lord. And, behold, the Lord passed by, and a great and strong wind rent the mountains, and brake in pieces the rocks before the Lord; but the Lord was not in the wind: and after the wind an earthquake; but the Lord was not in the earthquake:
And after the earthquake a fire; but the Lord was not in the fire: and after the fire a still small voice.
Bible: I Kings
19:11–12

14 Man has learned to cope with all questions of importance without recourse to God as a working hypothesis.
Dietrich Bonhoeffer (1906–45) German theologian.
Letters and Papers from Prison, 8 June 1944

15 A God who let us prove his existence would be an idol.
Dietrich Bonhoeffer
No Rusty Swords

16 God's gifts put man's best gifts to shame.
Elizabeth Barrett Browning (1806–61) British poet.
Sonnets from the Portuguese, XXVI

17 Thou shalt have one God only; who
Would be at the expense of two?
Arthur Hugh Clough (1819–61) British poet.
The Latest Decalogue, 1

18 God moves in a mysterious way
His wonders to perform;
He plants his footsteps in the sea,
And rides upon the storm.
William Cowper (1731–1800) British poet.
Olney Hymns, 35

19 It is the final proof of God's omnipotence that he need not exist in order to save us.
Peter De Vries (1910–) US novelist.
The Mackerel Plaza, Ch. 2

20 God is subtle but he is not malicious.
Albert Einstein (1879–1955) German-born US physicist. Inscribed over the fireplace in the Mathematical Institute, Princeton. It refers to Einstein's objection to the quantum theory.
Albert Einstein (Carl Seelig), Ch. 8

21 At bottom God is nothing more than an exalted father.
Sigmund Freud (1856–1939) Austrian psychoanalyst.
Totem and Taboo

22 O worship the King, all glorious above!
O gratefully sing his power and his love!

Our Shield and Defender – the Ancient of
Days,
Pavilioned in splendour, and girded with praise.
Robert Grant (1779–1838) British hymn writer.
Hymn

23 Holy, holy, holy, Lord God Almighty!
Early in the morning our song shall rise to
thee.
Reginald Heber (1783–1826) British bishop and hymn
writer.
Holy, Holy, Holy

24 The world is charged with the grandeur of
God.
Gerard Manley Hopkins (1844–99) British Jesuit and
poet.
God's Grandeur

25 Mine eyes have seen the glory of the coming
of the Lord:
He is trampling out the vintage where the
grapes of wrath are stored.
Julia Ward Howe (1819–1910) US writer.
Battle Hymn of the American Republic

26 Operationally, God is beginning to resemble
not a ruler but the last fading smile of a
cosmic Cheshire cat.
Julian Huxley (1887–1975) British biologist.
Religion without Revelation

27 The chess-board is the world; the pieces are
the phenomena of the universe; the rules of
the game are what we call the laws of
Nature. The player on the other side is
hidden from us. We know that his play is
always fair, just, and patient. But also we
know, to our cost, that he never overlooks a
mistake, or makes the smallest allowance for
ignorance.
T. H. Huxley (1825–95) British biologist.
Lay Sermons, 'A Liberal Education'

28 An honest God is the noblest work of man.
Robert G. Ingersoll (1833–99) US lawyer and agnostic.
Gods

29 Man proposes but God disposes.
Thomas à Kempis (Thomas Hemmerken; c. 1380–1471)
German monk.
The Imitation of Christ, I

30 A man with God is always in the majority.
John Knox (c. 1514–72) Scottish religious reformer.
Inscription, Reformation Monument, Geneva, Switzerland

31 What God does, He does well.
Jean de La Fontaine (1621–95) French poet.
Fables, IX, 'Le Gland et la Citrouille'

32 I have no need of that hypothesis.
Marquis de Laplace (1749–1827) French mathematician
and astronomer.
On being asked by Napoleon why he had made no mention of
God in his book about the universe, *Mécanique céleste*.
Men of Mathematics (E. Bell)

33 Though the mills of God grind slowly, yet
they grind exceeding small;

Though with patience He stands waiting, with
exactness grinds He all.
Friedrich von Logau (1604–55) German poet and writer.
Sinngedichte, III

34 God is the immemorial refuge of the
incompetent, the helpless, the miserable.
They find not only sanctuary in His arms, but
also a kind of superiority, soothing to their
macerated egos; He will set them above their
betters.
H. L. Mencken (1880–1956) US journalist.
Notebooks, 'Minority Report'

35 There's a Friend for little children
Above the bright blue sky,
A Friend who never changes,
Whose love will never die.
Albert Midlane (1825–1909) British hymn writer.
Hymn

36 Let us with a gladsome mind
Praise the Lord, for he is kind,
For his mercies ay endure,
Ever faithful, ever sure.
John Milton (1608–74) English poet.
Psalm

37 What in me is dark
Illumine, what is low raise and support;
That, to the height of this great argument,
I may assert Eternal Providence,
And justify the ways of God to men.
John Milton
Paradise Lost, Bk. I

38 God is dead: but considering the state the
species Man is in, there will perhaps be
caves, for ages yet, in which his shadow will
be shown.
Friedrich Wilhelm Nietzsche (1844–1900) German
philosopher.
Die Fröhliche Wissenschaft, Bk. III

39 God is a gentleman. He prefers blondes.
Joe Orton (1933–67) British dramatist.
Loot, II

40 One on God's side is a majority.
Wendell Phillips (1811–84) US reformer.
Speech, Brooklyn, 1 Nov 1859

41 God is really only another artist. He invented
the giraffe, the elephant, and the cat. He has
no real style, He just goes on trying other
things.
Pablo Picasso (1881–1973) Spanish painter.
Life with Picasso Ch. 1 (Françoise Gilot and Carlton Lake)

42 God can stand being told by Professor Ayer
and Marghanita Laski that He doesn't exist.
J. B. Priestley (1894–1984) British novelist.
The Listener, 1 July 1965, 'The BBC's Duty to Society'

43 Write down that they hope they serve God;
and write God first; for God defend but God
should go before such villains!
William Shakespeare (1564–1616) English dramatist.
Much Ado About Nothing, IV:2

44 But already it is time to depart, for me to die, for you to go on living; which of us takes the better course, is concealed from anyone except God.
Socrates (469–399 BC) Athenian philosopher.
Apology (Plato)

45 In the days of my youth I remembered my God!
And He hath not forgotten my age.
Robert Southey (1774–1843) British poet.
The Old Man's Comforts, and how he Gained them

46 Yet her conception of God was certainly not orthodox. She felt towards Him as she might have felt towards a glorified sanitary engineer; and in some of her speculations she seems hardly to distinguish between the Deity and the Drains.
Lytton Strachey (1880–1932) British writer.
Eminent Victorians, 'Florence Nightingale'

47 It is a mistake to assume that God is interested only, or even chiefly, in religion.
William Temple (1881–1944) British archbishop.
Attrib.

48 If God did not exist, it would be necessary to invent Him.
Voltaire (François-Marie Arouet; 1694–1778) French writer.
Épîtres, 'À l'auteur du livre des trois Imposteurs'

49 If God made us in His image, we have certainly returned the compliment.
Voltaire
Le Sottisier

GOLDWYNISMS

Sayings attributed to Samuel Goldwyn (Samuel Goldfish; 1882–1974). Most are apocryphal. *See also* cinema, mixed metaphors

1 Let's have some new clichés.
The Observer, 'Sayings of the Week', 24 Oct 1948

2 Too caustic? To hell with cost; we'll make the picture anyway.

3 We're overpaying him but he's worth it.

4 What we want is a story that starts with an earthquake and works its way up to a climax.

5 I am willing to admit that I may not always be right, but I am never wrong.

6 I don't care if it doesn't make a nickel, I just want every man, woman, and child in America to see it!
Referring to his film *The Best Years of Our Lives*

7 A wide screen just makes a bad film twice as bad.

8 For years I have been known for saying 'Include me out'; but today I am giving it up for ever.
Address, Balliol College, Oxford, 1 Mar 1945

9 In two words: im - possible.
Attrib.

10 Anybody who goes to see a psychiatrist ought to have his head examined.

11 Every director bites the hand that lays the golden egg.

12 I'll give you a definite maybe.

13 A verbal contract isn't worth the paper it's written on.

14 You ought to take the bull between the teeth.

15 We have all passed a lot of water since then.

16 I read part of it all the way through.

17 If Roosevelt were alive he'd turn in his grave.

18 It's more than magnificent – it's mediocre.

19 'Why only twelve?' 'That's the original number.' 'Well, go out and get thousands.'
Referring to the number of disciples whilst filming a scene for *The Last Supper*

20 Yes, I'm going to have a bust made of them.
Replying to an admiring comment about his wife's hands

21 Tell me, how did you love my picture?

GOLF

See also sport

1 It's not in support of cricket but as an earnest protest against golf.
Max Beerbohm (1872–1956) British writer.
Said when giving a shilling towards W. G. Grace's testimonial
Carr's Dictionary of Extraordinary English Cricketers

2 Golf may be played on Sunday, not being a game within the view of the law, but being a form of moral effort.
Stephen Leacock (1869–1944) English-born Canadian economist and humorist.
Other Fancies, 'Why I refuse to play Golf'

3 All I've got against it is that it takes you so far from the club house.
Eric Linklater (1889–1974) Scottish novelist.
Referring to golf
Poet's Pub, Ch. 3

GOOD

See also good and evil, righteousness, virtue

1 Men have never been good, they are not good, they never will be good.
Karl Barth (1886–1968) Swiss Protestant theologian.
Time, 12 Apr 1954

2 He who would do good to another must do it in Minute Particulars.

General Good is the plea of the scoundrel, hypocrite, and flatterer.
William Blake (1757–1827) British poet.
Jerusalem

3   *Summum bonum.*
The greatest good.
Cicero (106–43 BC) Roman orator and statesman.
De Officiis, I

4   Nice guys finish last.
Leo Durocher (1905–   ) US baseball player.
Attrib.

5   What is a weed? A plant whose virtues have not been discovered.
Ralph Waldo Emerson (1803–82) US poet and essayist.
Fortune of the Republic

6   Would to God that we might spend a single day really well!
Thomas à Kempis (Thomas Hemmerken; c. 1380–1471) German monk.
The Imitation of Christ, I

7   Teach us delight in simple things,
And mirth that has no bitter springs;
Forgiveness free of evil done,
And love to all men 'neath the sun!
Rudyard Kipling (1865–1936) Indian-born British writer.
The Children's Song

8   The greatest pleasure I know, is to do a good action by stealth, and to have it found out by accident.
Charles Lamb (1775–1834) British essayist.
The Athenaeum, 'Table Talk by the late Elia', 4 Jan 1834

9   Goodness does not more certainly make men happy than happiness makes them good.
Walter Savage Landor (1775–1864) British poet and writer.
Imaginary Conversations, 'Lord Brooke and Sir Philip Sidney'

10   Dowel, Dobet and Dobest.
William Langland (c. 1330–c. 1400) English poet.
Do well, Do better, and Do Best: three concepts central to the search for Truth in *Piers Plowman,* in which they appear as allegorical characters
The Vision of Piers Plowman

11   Much benevolence of the passive order may be traced to a disinclination to inflict pain upon oneself.
George Meredith (1828–1909) British novelist.
Vittoria, Ch. 42

12   Abashed the devil stood,
And felt how awful goodness is.
John Milton (1608–74) English poet.
Paradise Lost, Bk. IV

13   The good is the beautiful.
Plato (429–347 BC) Greek philosopher.
Lysis

14   Do good by stealth, and blush to find it fame.
Alexander Pope (1688–1744) British poet.
Epilogue to the Satires, Dialogue I

15   How far that little candle throws his beams!

So shines a good deed in a naughty world.
William Shakespeare (1564–1616) English dramatist.
The Merchant of Venice, V:1

16   Nothing can harm a good man, either in life or after death.
Socrates (469–399 BC) Athenian philosopher.
Apology (Plato)

17   – My goodness those diamonds are lovely!
Goodness had nothing whatever to do with it.
Mae West (1892–1980) US actress.
Used in 1959 as the title of the first volume of her autobiography
Diamond Lil, film 1932

18   You shouldn't say it is not good. You should say you do not like it; and then, you know, you're perfectly safe.
James Whistler (1834–1903) US painter.
Whistler Stories (D. Seitz)

GOOD AND EVIL

See also evil, good, virtue and vice

1   There is so much good in the worst of us,
And so much bad in the best of us,
That it hardly becomes any of us
To talk about the rest of us.
Anonymous
Good and Bad

2   Evil comes at leisure like the disease; good comes in a hurry like the doctor.
G. K. Chesterton (1874–1936) British writer.
The Man who was Orthodox

3   The good die early, and the bad die late.
Daniel Defoe (1660–1731) British journalist and writer.
Character of the late Dr. Annesley

4   The web of our life is of a mingled yarn, good and ill together.
William Shakespeare (1564–1616) English dramatist.
All's Well that Ends Well, IV:3

5   The good die first,
And they whose hearts are dry as summer dust
Burn to the socket.
William Wordsworth (1770–1850) British poet.
The Excursion

GOSSIP

See also secrecy

1   A tale never loses in the telling.
Proverb

2   Don't wash your dirty linen in public.
Proverb

3   No names, no pack-drill.
Proverb

4   There's no smoke without fire.
Proverb

5 Throw dirt enough, and some will stick.
Proverb

6 Walls have ears.
Proverb

7 How these curiosities would be quite forgot, did not such idle fellows as I am put them down.
John Aubrey (1626–97) English antiquary.
Brief Lives, 'Venetia Digby'

8 No one gossips about other people's secret virtues.
Bertrand Russell (1872–1970) British philosopher.
On Education

9 Her first economic drive will be to replace X-ray by hearsay.
Gwyn Thomas (1913–81) British writer.
The Keep, II

10 I remember that a wise friend of mine did usually say, 'that which is everybody's business is nobody's business'.
Izaak Walton (1593–1683) English writer.
The Compleat Angler, Ch. 2

GOVERNMENT

See also democracy, Houses of Parliament, monarchy, opposition, politicians, politics

1 I will undoubtedly have to seek what is happily known as gainful employment, which I am glad to say does not describe holding public office.
Dean Acheson (1893–1971) US lawyer and statesman.
Remark made on leaving his post as secretary of state, 1952; he subsequently returned to private legal practice

2 The danger is not that a particular class is unfit to govern. Every class is unfit to govern.
Lord Acton (1834–1902) British historian.
Letter to Mary Gladstone, 1881

3 Whose Finger do you want on the Trigger When the World Situation Is So Delicate?
Anonymous
Headline from the *Daily Mirror* on the day before the General Election, Oct 1951
Publish and Be Damned (Hugh Cudlipp), 1953

4 Where some people are very wealthy and others have nothing, the result will be either extreme democracy or absolute oligarchy, or despotism will come from either of those excesses.
Aristotle (384–322 BC) Greek philosopher.
Politics, Bk. IV

5 One to mislead the public, another to mislead the Cabinet, and the third to mislead itself.
Herbert Henry Asquith (1852–1928) British statesman.
Explaining why the War Office kept three sets of figures
The Price of Glory (Alastair Horne), Ch. 2

6 The object of government in peace and in war is not the glory of rulers or of races, but the happiness of the common man.
Lord Beveridge (1879–1963) British economist.
Social Insurance

7 Too bad all the people who know how to run the country are busy driving cabs and cutting hair.
George Burns (1896–) US comedian.

8 A small acquaintance with history shows that all Governments are selfish and the French Governments more selfish than most.
David Eccles (1904–) British politician.
The Observer, 'Sayings of the Year', 29 Dec 1962

9 He was uniformly of an opinion which, though not a popular one, he was ready to aver, that the right of governing was not property but a trust.
Charles James Fox (1749–1806) British Whig politician.
Referring to William Pitt's plans for parliamentary reform
C.J. Fox (J. L. Hammond)

10 The principles of a free constitution are irrecoverably lost, when the legislative power is nominated by the executive.
Edward Gibbon (1737–94) British historian.
Decline and Fall of the Roman Empire, Ch. 3

11 A government that is big enough to give you all you want is big enough to take it all away.
Barry Goldwater (1904–) US politician.
Bachman's Book of Freedom Quotations (M. Ivens and R. Dunstan)

12 They that are discontented under *monarchy*, call it *tyranny*; and they that are displeased with *aristocracy*, call it *oligarchy*: so also, they which find themselves grieved under a *democracy*, call it *anarchy*, which signifies the want of government; and yet I think no man believes, that want of government, is any new kind of government.
Thomas Hobbes (1588–1679) English philosopher.
Leviathan, Pt. II, Ch. 19

13 I would not give half a guinea to live under one form of government rather than another. It is of no moment to the happiness of an individual.
Samuel Johnson (1709–84) British lexicographer.
Life of Johnson (J. Boswell), Vol. II

14 Any cook should be able to run the country.
Lenin (Vladimir Ilich Ulyanov; 1870–1924) Russian revolutionary leader.
The First Circle (Alexander Solzhenitsyn)

15 What is our task? To make Britain a fit country for heroes to live in.
David Lloyd George (1863–1945) British Liberal statesman.
Speech, 24 Nov 1918

16 The Commons, faithful to their system, remained in a wise and masterly inactivity.
James Mackintosh (1765–1832) Scottish lawyer, philosopher, and historian.
Vindiciae Gallicae

17 Every country has the government it deserves.
Joseph de Maistre (1753–1821) French monarchist.
Lettres et Opuscules Inédits, 15 Aug 1811

18 The worst government is the most moral. One composed of cynics is often very tolerant and human. But when fanatics are on top there is no limit to oppression.
H. L. Mencken (1880–1956) US journalist.
Notebooks, 'Minority Report'

19 One day the don't-knows will get in, and then where will we be?
Spike Milligan (1918–) British comic actor and author.
Attributed remark made about a pre-election poll

20 Do you not know, my son, with how little wisdom the world is governed?
Axel Oxenstierna (1583–1654) Swedish statesman.
Letter to his son, 1648

21 Government, even in its best state, is but a necessary evil; in its worst state, an intolerable one.
Thomas Paine (1737–1809) British writer.
Common Sense, Ch. 1

22 As to religion, I hold it to be the indispensable duty of government to protect all conscientious professors thereof, and I know of no other business which government hath to do therewith.
Thomas Paine
Common Sense, Ch. 4

23 We live under a government of men and morning newspapers.
Wendell Phillips (1811–84) US reformer.
Address: The Press

24 I don't make jokes – I just watch the government and report the facts.
Will Rogers (1879–1935) US actor and humorist.
Saturday Review, 'A Rogers Thesaurus', 25 Aug 1962

25 Hansard is history's ear, already listening.
Herbert Samuel (1870–1963) British Liberal statesman.
The Observer, 'Sayings of the Week', 18 Dec 1949

26 Parliament is the longest running farce in the West End.
Cyril Smith (1928–) British Liberal politician.
The Times, 23 Sept 1977

27 It would be desirable if every government, when it comes to power, should have its old speeches burned.
Philip Snowden (1864–1937) British politician.
Biography (C. E. Bechafer Roberts)

28 Accidentally.
Talleyrand (Charles Maurice de Talleyrand-Périgord; 1754–1838) French politician.
Replying, during the reign of Louis Philippe, to the query 'How do you think this government will end?'
The Wheat and the Chaff (F. Mitterand)

29 Governments needs to have both shepherds and butchers.
Voltaire (François-Marie Arouet; 1694–1778) French writer.
Notebooks

30 Many people consider the things which government does for them to be social progress, but they consider the things government does for others as socialism.
Earl Warren (1891–1971) US lawyer.
Peter's Quotations (Laurence J. Peter)

31 The people's government, made for the people, made by the people, and answerable to the people.
Daniel Webster (1782–1852) US statesman.
Second speech on Foote's resolution, 26 Jan 1830

32 If people behaved in the way nations do they would all be put in straitjackets.
Tennessee Williams (1911–83) US dramatist.
BBC interview

GRAMMAR

See also language, words

1 'Whom are you?' said he, for he had been to night school.
George Ade (1866–1944) US dramatist and humorist.
Bang! Bang!: The Steel Box

2 When I split an infinitive, god damn it, I split it so it stays split.
Raymond Chandler (1888–1959) US novelist.
Letter to his English publisher

3 By being so long in the lowest form I gained an immense advantage over the cleverest boys . . . I got into my bones the essential structure of the normal British sentence – which is a noble thing.
Winston Churchill (1874–1965) British statesman.
My Early Life, Ch. 2

4 This is the sort of English up with which I will not put.
Winston Churchill
The story is that Churchill wrote the comment in the margin of a report in which a Civil Servant had used an awkward construction to avoid ending a sentence with a preposition. An alternative version substitutes 'bloody nonsense' for 'English'
Plain Words (E. Gowers), Ch. 9

5 I will not go down to posterity talking bad grammar.
Benjamin Disraeli (1804–81) British statesman.
Remark made when correcting proofs of his last parliamentary speech, 31 Mar 1881
Disraeli (Blake), Ch. 32

6 Grammar, which can govern even kings.
Molière (Jean Baptiste Poquelin; 1622–73) French dramatist.
Les Femmes savantes, II:6

7 I am the Roman Emperor, and am above grammar.
Sigismund (1368–1437) Holy Roman Emperor.
Responding to criticism of his Latin
Attrib.

8 Why care for grammar as long as we are good?
Artemus Ward (Charles Farrar Browne; 1834–67) US humorous writer.
Pyrotechny

9 Subjunctive to the last, he preferred to ask, 'And that, sir, would be the Hippodrome?'
Alexander Woollcott (1887–1943) US journalist.
While Rome Burns, 'Our Mrs Parker'

GRATITUDE

1 There are minds so impatient of inferiority that their gratitude is a species of revenge, and they return benefits, not because recompense is a pleasure, but because obligation is a pain.
Samuel Johnson (1709–84) British lexicographer.
The Rambler

2 When the messenger who carried the last sheet to Millar returned, Johnson asked him, 'Well, what did he say?' – 'Sir (answered the messenger), he said, thank God I have done with him.' – 'I am glad (replied Johnson, with a smile) that he thanks God for anything.'
Samuel Johnson
After the final page of his *Dictionary* had been delivered
Life of Johnson (J. Boswell)

3 Thank me no thankings, nor proud me no prouds.
William Shakespeare (1564–1616) English dramatist.
Romeo and Juliet, III:5

GREATNESS

1 A truly great man never puts away the simplicity of a child.
Chinese proverb

2 The dullard's envy of brilliant men is always assuaged by the suspicion that they will come to a bad end.
Max Beerbohm (1872–1956) British writer.
Zuleika Dobson

3 Great men are but life-sized. Most of them, indeed, are rather short.
Max Beerbohm
And Even Now

4 Great things are done when men and mountains meet;

This is not done by jostling in the street.
William Blake (1757–1827) British poet.
Gnomic Verses

5 Nothing grows well in the shade of a big tree.
Constantin Brancusi (1876–1957) Romanian sculptor.
Refusing Rodin's invitation to work in his studio
Compton's Encyclopedia

6 No great man lives in vain. The history of the world is but the biography of great men.
Thomas Carlyle (1795–1881) Scottish historian and essayist.
Heroes and Hero-Worship, 'The Hero as Divinity'

7 To be great is to be misunderstood.
Ralph Waldo Emerson (1803–82) US poet and essayist.
Essays, 'Self-Reliance'

8 The world's great men have not commonly been great scholars, nor great scholars great men.
Oliver Wendell Holmes (1809–94) US writer.
The Autocrat of the Breakfast Table, Ch. 6

9 If I am a great man, then a good many of the great men of history are frauds.
Bonar Law (1858–1923) British statesman.
Attrib.

10 You are one of the forces of nature.
Jules Michelet (1798–1874) French historian.
From a letter received by Dumas
Memoirs, Vol. VI, Ch. 138 (Alexandre Dumas)

11 To be alone is the fate of all great minds – a fate deplored at times, but still always chosen as the less grievous of two evils.
Arthur Schopenhauer (1788–1860) German philosopher.
Aphorismen zur Lebensweisheit

12 Some are born great, some achieve greatness, and some have greatness thrust upon 'em.
William Shakespeare (1564–1616) English dramatist.
Twelfth Night, II:5

13 'My name is Ozymandias, king of kings: Look on my works, ye Mighty, and despair!'
Percy Bysshe Shelley (1792–1822) British poet.
Ozymandias

14 Oh, Vanity of vanities!
How wayward the decrees of Fate are;
How very weak the very wise,
How very small the very great are!
William Makepeace Thackeray (1811–63) British novelist.
Vanitas Vanitatum

15 A great city is that which has the greatest men and women.
Walt Whitman (1819–92) US poet.
Song of the Broad-Axe, 5

GREED

See also food, materialism, obesity

1 Give him an inch and he'll take a yard.
Proverb

2 Kill not the goose that lays the golden egg.
Proverb

3 The eye is bigger than the belly.
Proverb

4 Beware that you do not lose the substance
by grasping at the shadow.
Aesop (6th century BC) Reputed Greek writer of fables.
Fables, 'The Dog and the Shadow'

5 But answer came there none –
And this was scarcely odd because
They'd eaten every one.
Lewis Carroll (Charles Lutwidge Dodgson; 1832–98)
British writer.
Through the Looking-Glass, Ch. 4

6 Gluttony is an emotional escape, a sign
something is eating us.
Peter De Vries (1910–   ) US novelist.
Comfort me with Apples, Ch. 7

7 The mountain sheep are sweeter,
But the valley sheep are fatter;
We therefore deemed it meeter
To carry off the latter.
Thomas Love Peacock (1785–1866) British novelist.
The Misfortunes of Elphin, Ch. 11, 'The War-Song of Dinas
Vawr'

8 These citizens are always willing to bet that
what Nicely-Nicely dies of will be over-
feeding and never anything small like
pneumonia, for Nicely-Nicely is known far
and wide as a character who dearly loves to
commit eating.
Damon Runyon (1884–1946) US writer.
Take it Easy, 'Lonely Heart'

9 Wealth is like sea-water; the more we drink,
the thirstier we become; and the same is
true of fame.
Arthur Schopenhauer (1788–1860) German philosopher.
Parerga and Paralipomena

10 He hath eaten me out of house and home.
William Shakespeare (1564–1616) English dramatist.
Henry IV, Part Two, II:1

GREETINGS

1 *Atque in perpetuum, frater, ave atque vale.*
And for ever, brother, hail and farewell!
Catullus (c. 84–c. 54 BC) Roman poet.
Carmina, CI

2 Wery glad to see you indeed, and hope our
acquaintance may be a long 'un, as the
gen'l'm'n said to the fi' pun' note.
Charles Dickens (1812–70) British novelist.
Pickwick Papers, Ch. 25

3 Dr Livingstone, I presume?
Henry Morton Stanley (1841–1904) British explorer.
On finding David Livingstone at Ujiji on Lake Tanganyika, Nov
1871
How I found Livingstone, Ch. 11

4 Lafayette, we are here!
C. E. Stanton (1859–1933) US colonel.
The Marquis de Lafayette (1757–1834) aided the colonists in
the US War of Independence
Address at Lafayette's grave, Paris, 4 July 1917

GUIDANCE

See also leadership

1 Everyman, I will go with thee, and be thy
guide.
In thy most need to go by thy side.
Anonymous
Everyman Pt. 1

2 Wandering in a vast forest at night, I have
only a faint light to guide me. A stranger
appears and says to me: 'My friend, you
should blow out your candle in order to find
your way more clearly.' This stranger is a
theologian.
Denis Diderot (1713–84) French writer.
Addition aux Pensées philosophiques

3 A little onward lend thy guiding hand
To these dark steps, a little further on.
John Milton (1608–74) English poet.
Samson Agonistes

GUILT

See also conscience, regret

1 It is quite gratifying to feel guilty if you
haven't done anything wrong: how noble!
Whereas it is rather hard and certainly
depressing to admit guilt and to repent.
Hannah Arendt (1906–75) German-born US philosopher
and historian.
Eichmann in Jerusalem, Ch. 15

2 Alone, alone, about the dreadful wood
Of conscious evil runs a lost mankind,
Dreading to find its Father.
W. H. Auden (1907–73) British poet.
For the Time Being, 'Chorus'

3 When Pilate saw that he could prevail
nothing, but that rather a tumult was made,
he took water, and washed his hands before
the multitude, saying, I am innocent of the
blood of this just person: see ye to it.
Then answered all the people, and said, His
blood be on us, and on our children.
Bible: Matthew
27:24–25

4 The many men, so beautiful!
And they all dead did lie:
And a thousand thousand slimy things

Lived on; and so did I.
Samuel Taylor Coleridge (1772–1834) British poet.
The Rime of the Ancient Mariner, IV

5   Love bade me welcome; yet my soul drew back,
Guilty of dust and sin.
George Herbert (1593–1633) English poet.
Love

6   You will put on a dress of guilt
and shoes with broken high ideals.
Roger McGough (1937–) British poet.
Comeclose and Sleepnow

7   I am in blood
Stepp'd in so far that, should I wade no more,
Returning were as tedious as go o'er.
William Shakespeare (1564–1616) English dramatist.
Macbeth, III:4

8   Out, damned spot! out, I say!
William Shakespeare
Macbeth, V:1

9   Here's the smell of the blood still. All the perfumes of Arabia will not sweeten this little hand.
William Shakespeare
Macbeth, V:1

GULLIBILITY

See also foolishness, impressionability

1   There's a sucker born every minute.
Phineas Barnum (1810–91) US showman.
Attrib.

2   When lovely woman stoops to folly,
And finds too late that men betray,
What charm can soothe her melancholy,
What art can wash her guilt away?
Oliver Goldsmith (1728–74) Irish-born British writer.
The Vicar of Wakefield, Ch. 9

H

HABIT

See also custom

1   Old habits die hard.
Proverb

2   Habit is a great deadener.
Samuel Beckett (1906–) Irish novelist and dramatist.
Waiting for Godot, III

3   Curious things, habits. People themselves never knew they had them.
Agatha Christie (1891–1976) British detective-story writer.
Witness for the Prosecution

4   Men's natures are alike; it is their habits that carry them far apart.
Confucius (K'ung Fu-tzu; 551–479 BC) Chinese philosopher.
Analects

5   They do those little personal things people sometimes do when they think they are alone in railway carriages; things like smelling their own armpits.
Jonathan Miller (1934–) British doctor and television and stage director.
Beyond the Fringe

HALF MEASURES

1   Two half-truths do not make a truth, and two half-cultures do not make a culture.
Arthur Koestler (1905–83) Hungarian-born British writer.
The Ghost in the Machine, Preface

2   I'm not really a Jew; just Jew-ish, not the whole hog.
Jonathan Miller (1934–) British doctor and television and stage director.
Beyond the Fringe

HAPPINESS

See also contentment, laughter, pleasure

1   One joy scatters a hundred griefs.
Chinese proverb

2   If you haven't been happy very young, you can still be happy later on, but it's much harder. You need more luck.
Simone de Beauvoir (1908–86) French writer.
The Observer, 'Sayings of the Week', 19 May 1975

3   The greatest happiness of the greatest number is the foundation of morals and legislation.
Jeremy Bentham (1748–1832) British philosopher.
The Commonplace Book

4   There was a jolly miller once,
Lived on the river Dee;
He worked and sang from morn till night;
No lark more blithe than he.
Isaac Bickerstaffe (c. 1735–c. 1812) Irish dramatist.
Love in a Village, I

5   When the green woods laugh with
the voice of joy.
William Blake (1757–1827) British poet.
Songs of Innocence, 'Laughing song'

6   In every adversity of fortune, to have been

happy is the most unhappy kind of misfortune.

Boethius (c. 480–524) Roman statesman, philosopher, and scholar.
The Consolation of Philosophy

7 Happiness is a mystery like religion, and should never be rationalized.

G. K. Chesterton (1874–1936) British writer.
Heretics, Ch. 7

8 To marvel at nothing is just about the one and only thing, Numicius, that can make a man happy and keep him that way.

Horace (Quintus Horatius Flaccus; 65–8 BC) Roman poet.
Epistles, I

9 Not the owner of many possessions will you be right to call happy: he more rightly deserves the name of happy who knows how to use the gods' gifts wisely and to put up with rough poverty, and who fears dishonour more than death.

Horace
Odes, IV

10 That action is best, which procures the greatest happiness for the greatest numbers.

Francis Hutcheson (1694–1746) Scottish philosopher.
Inquiry into the Original of our Ideas of Beauty and Virtue, Treatise II, 'Concerning Moral Good and Evil'

11 Happiness is like coke - something you get as a by-product in the process of making something else.

Aldous Huxley (1894–1964) British novelist.
Point Counter Point

12 That all who are happy, are equally happy, is not true. A peasant and a philosopher may be equally *satisfied*, but not equally *happy*. Happiness consists in the multiplicity of agreeable consciousness.

Samuel Johnson (1709–84) British lexicographer.
Life of Johnson (J. Boswell), Vol. II

13 . . . because happiness is not an ideal of reason but of imagination.

Immanuel Kant (1724–1804) German philosopher.
Grundlegung zur Metaphysik der Sitten, II

14 Ask yourself whether you are happy, and you cease to be so.

John Stuart Mill (1806–73) British philosopher.
Autobiography, Ch. 5

15 When a small child . . . I thought that success spelled happiness. I was wrong. Happiness is like a butterfly which appears and delights us for one brief moment, but soon flits away.

Anna Pavlova (1881–1931) Russian ballet dancer.
Pavlova: A Biography (ed. A. H. Franks), 'Pages of My Life'

16 And we suddenly know, what heaven we're in,
When they begin the beguine.

Cole Porter (1893–1964) US songwriter.
Jubilee, 'Begin the Beguine'

17 We are never so happy nor so unhappy as we imagine.

Duc de la Rochefoucauld (1613–80) French writer.
Maximes, 49

18 Happiness is not best achieved by those who seek it directly.

Bertrand Russell (1872–1970) British philosopher.
Mysticism and Logic

19 Every time I talk to a savant I feel quite sure that happiness is no longer a possibility. Yet when I talk with my gardener, I'm convinced of the opposite.

Bertrand Russell
Attrib.

20 One is happy as a result of one's own efforts, once one knows the necessary ingredients of happiness – simple tastes, a certain degree of courage, self denial to a point, love of work, and, above all, a clear conscience. Happiness is no vague dream, of that I now feel certain.

George Sand (Aurore Dupin, Baronne Dudevant; 1804–76) French novelist.
Correspondence, Vol. V

21 Happiness is the only sanction of life; where happiness fails, existence remains a mad and lamentable experiment.

George Santayana (1863–1952) US philosopher.
The Life of Reason

22 A lifetime of happiness: no man alive could bear it: it would be hell on earth.

George Bernard Shaw (1856–1950) Irish dramatist and critic.
Man and Superman, I

23 Mankind are always happy for having been happy, so that if you make them happy now, you make them happy twenty years hence by the memory of it.

Sydney Smith (1771–1845) British clergyman and essayist.
Elementary Sketches of Moral Philosophy

24 There is no duty we so much underrate as the duty of being happy.

Robert Louis Stevenson (1850–94) Scottish writer.
Virginibus Puerisque

25 Happiness is an imaginary condition, formerly often attributed by the living to the dead, now usually attributed by adults to children, and by children to adults.

Thomas Szasz (1920–) US psychiatrist.
The Second Sin

26 If you want to be happy, be.

Leo Tolstoy (1828–1910) Russian writer.
Kosma Prutkov

27 Happiness is no laughing matter.

Richard Whately (1787–1863) British churchman.
Apophthegms

28 Happy Days Are Here Again.
Jack Yellen (1892–) US lyricist.
Used by Roosevelt as a campaign song in 1932
Song title

29 The hell with it. Who never knew the price of happiness will not be happy.
Yevgeny Yevtushenko (1933–) Soviet poet.
Lies

HASTE

See also impetuosity

1 Don't throw the baby out with the bathwater.
Proverb

2 First come, first served.
Proverb

3 Haste makes waste.
Proverb

4 More haste, less speed.
Proverb

5 'Will you walk a little faster?' said a whiting to a snail,
'There's a porpoise close behind us, and he's treading on my tail.'
Lewis Carroll (Charles Lutwidge Dodgson; 1832–98) British writer.
Alice's Adventures in Wonderland, Ch. 10

6 In skating over thin ice, our safety is in our speed.
Ralph Waldo Emerson (1803–82) US poet and essayist.
Essays, 'Prudence'

7 Slow and steady wins the race.
Robert Lloyd (1733–64) British poet.
The Hare and the Tortoise

8 For fools rush in where angels fear to tread.
Alexander Pope (1688–1744) British poet.
An Essay on Criticism

9 Never before have we had so little time in which to do so much.
Franklin D. Roosevelt (1882–1945) US Democratic president.
Radio address, 23 Feb 1942

10 If it were done when 'tis done, then 'twere well
It were done quickly.
William Shakespeare (1564–1616) English dramatist.
Macbeth, I:7

11 Wisely and slow; they stumble that run fast.
William Shakespeare
Romeo and Juliet, II:3

12 Hurry! I never hurry. I have no time to hurry.
Igor Stravinsky (1882–1971) Russian-born US composer.
Responding to his publisher's request that he hurry his completion of a composition
Attrib.

HATE

See also bitterness, love and hate

1 I do not love thee, Doctor Fell,
The reason why I cannot tell;
But this alone I know full well,
I do not love thee, Doctor Fell.
Thomas Brown (1663–1704) English satirist.
Translation of Martial's *Epigrams*

2 Gr-r-r- there go, my heart's abhorrence!
Water your damned flower-pots, do!
Robert Browning (1812–89) British poet.
Soliloquy of the Spanish Cloister

3 I am free of all prejudice. I hate everyone equally.
W. C. Fields (1880–1946) US actor.
Attrib.

4 We can scarcely hate any one that we know.
William Hazlitt (1778–1830) British essayist.
On Criticism

5 If you hate a person, you hate something in him that is part of yourself. What isn't part of ourselves doesn't disturb us.
Hermann Hesse (1877–1962) German novelist and poet.
Demian, Ch. 6

6 With a heavy step Sir Matthew left the room and spent the morning designing mausoleums for his enemies.
Eric Linklater (1889–1974) Scottish novelist.
Juan in America, Prologue

7 Few people can be happy unless they hate some other person, nation or creed.
Bertrand Russell (1872–1970) British philosopher.
Attrib.

8 An intellectual hatred is the worst.
W. B. Yeats (1865–1939) Irish poet.
A Prayer for My Daughter

HEALTH AND HEALTHY LIVING

See also doctors, illness, medicine, remedies

1 An apple a day keeps the doctor away.
Proverb

2 Health is better than wealth.
Proverb

3 It is a fact that not once in all my life have I gone out for a walk. I have been taken out for walks; but that is another matter.
Max Beerbohm (1872–1956) British writer.
Going Out of a Walk

4 I answer 20 000 letters a year and so many couples are having problems because they are not getting the right proteins and vitamins.
Barbara Cartland (1902–) British romantic novelist.
The Observer, 'Sayings of the Week', 31 Aug 1986

5 Exercise is bunk. If you are healthy, you

don't need it: if you are sick you shouldn't take it.
Henry Ford (1863–1947) US industrialist.
Attrib.

6 *Orandum est ut sit mens sana in corpore sano.*
Your prayer must be for a sound mind in a sound body.
Juvenal (Decimus Junius Juvenalis; 60–130 AD) Roman satirist.
Satires, X

7 Some breakfast food manufacturer hit upon the simple notion of emptying out the leavings of carthorse nosebags, adding a few other things like unconsumed portions of chicken layer's mash, and the sweepings of racing stables, packing the mixture in little bags and selling them in health food shops.
Frank Muir (1920–) British writer and broadcaster.
Upon My Word!

HEAVEN

See also afterlife

1 And he dreamed, and behold a ladder set up on the earth, and the top of it reached to heaven: and behold the angels of God ascending and descending on it.
Bible: Genesis
28:12

2 And Jacob awaked out of his sleep, and he said, Surely the Lord is in this place; and I knew it not.
And he was afraid, and said, How dreadful is this place! this is none other but the house of God, and this is the gate of heaven.
Bible: Genesis
28:16–17

3 In my Father's house are many mansions: if it were not so, I would have told you. I go to prepare a place for you.
Bible: John
14:2

4 Then let him receive the new knowledge and wait us,
Pardoned in heaven, the first by the throne!
Robert Browning (1812–89) British poet.
The Lost Leader

5 Probably no invention came more easily to man than Heaven.
Georg Christoph Lichtenberg (1742–99) German physicist and writer.
Aphorisms

6 A heav'n on earth.
John Milton (1608–74) English poet.
Paradise Lost, Bk. IV

7 Glorious things of thee are spoken,
Zion, city of our God.
John Newton (1725–1807) British hymn writer.
Glorious Things

8 For observe, that to hope for Paradise is to live in Paradise, a very different thing from actually getting there.
Vita Sackville-West (Victoria Sackville-West; 1892–1962) British poet and novelist.
Passenger to Tehran, Ch. 1

9 I expect no very violent transition.
Catharine Maria Sedgwick (1789–1867) US writer.
Comparing heaven with her home-town of Stockbridge, Massachussetts
Edie (Jean Stein)

10 If you go to Heaven without being naturally qualified for it you will not enjoy yourself there.
George Bernard Shaw (1856–1950) Irish dramatist and critic.
Man and Superman

11 Heaven, as conventionally conceived, is a place so inane, so dull, so useless, so miserable, that nobody has ever ventured to describe a whole day in heaven, though plenty of people have described a day at the seaside.
George Bernard Shaw
Misalliance, Preface

12 Shall shine the traffic of Jacob's ladder
Pitched between Heaven and Charing Cross.
Francis Thompson (1859–1907) British poet.
The Kingdom of God

13 Grant me paradise in this world; I'm not so sure I'll reach it in the next.
Tintoretto (Jacopo Robusti; 1518–94) Venetian painter.
Arguing that he be allowed to paint the *Paradiso* at the doge's palace in Venice, despite his advanced age
Attrib.

14 There is a happy land,
Far, far away,
Where saints in glory stand,
Bright, bright as day.
Andrew John Young (1885–1971) Scottish poet.
There is a Happy Land

HELL

See also damnation, devil

1 Every wolf's and lion's howl
Raises from Hell a human soul.
William Blake (1757–1827) British poet.
Auguries of Innocence

2 Abandon hope, all ye who enter here.
Dante Alighieri (1265–1321) Italian poet.
The inscription at the entrance to Hell
Divine Comedy, Inferno, III

3 Hell is oneself;
Hell is alone, the other figures in it
Merely projections. There is nothing to escape from
And nothing to escape to. One is always alone.
T. S. Eliot (1888–1965) US-born British poet and dramatist.
The Cocktail Party, I:3

4 Long is the way
And hard, that out of hell leads up to light.
John Milton (1608–74) English poet.
Paradise Lost, Bk. II

5 Which way I fly is Hell; myself am Hell;
And, in the lowest deep, a lower deep
Still threat'ning to devour me opens wide,
To which the Hell I suffer seems a Heaven.
John Milton
Paradise Lost, Bk. IV

6 Hell is other people.
Jean-Paul Sartre (1905–80) French philosopher and
writer.
Huis clos

7 The way down to Hell is easy.
Virgil (Publius Vergilius Maro; 70–19 BC) Roman poet.
Aeneid, Bk. VI

HELP

See also charity, support

1 Every little helps.
Proverb

2 Many hands make light work.
Proverb

3 One good turn deserves another.
Proverb

4 Scratch my back and I'll scratch yours.
Proverb

5 Too many cooks spoil the broth.
Proverb

6 Two heads are better than one.
Proverb

7 People must help one another; it is nature's
law.
Jean de La Fontaine (1621–95) French poet.
Fables, VIII, 'L'Âne et le Chien'

HEROISM

See also courage, endurance, patriotism, war

1 Some talk of Alexander, and some of
Hercules,
Of Hector and Lysander, and such great names
as these;
But of all the world's brave heroes there's
none that can compare
With a tow, row, row, row, row, row for the
British Grenadier.
Anonymous
The British Grenadiers

2 They died to save their country and they
only saved the world.
Hilaire Belloc (1870–1953) French-born British poet.
The English Graves

3 ANDREA. Unhappy the land that has no heroes.

GALILEO. No, unhappy the land that needs
heroes.
Bertolt Brecht (1898–1956) German dramatist.
Galileo, 13

4 In short, he was a perfect cavaliero,
And to his very valet seem'd a hero.
Lord Byron (1788–1824) British poet.
Beppo

5 Every hero becomes a bore at last.
Ralph Waldo Emerson (1803–82) US poet and essayist.
Representative Men, 'Uses of Great Men'

6 Being a hero is about the shortest-lived
profession on earth.
Will Rogers (1879–1935) US actor and humorist.
Saturday Review, 'A Rogers Thesaurus', 25 Aug 1962

HISTORIANS

See also history

1 A good historian is timeless; although he is a
patriot, he will never flatter his country in
any respect.
François Fénelon (1651–1715) French writer and prelate.
Letter to M. Dacier

2 The historian must have . . . some conception
of how men who are not historians behave.
Otherwise he will move in a world of the
dead.
E. M. Forster (1879–1970) British novelist.
Abinger Harvest, 'Captain Edward Gibbon'

3 Great abilities are not requisite for an
Historian . . . Imagination is not required in
any high degree.
Samuel Johnson (1709–84) British lexicographer.
Life of Johnson (J. Boswell), Vol. I

4 History is too serious to be left to historians.
Iain Macleod (1913–70) British politician.
The Observer, 'Sayings of the Week', 16 July 1961

5 And even I can remember
A day when the historians left blanks in their
writings,
I mean for things they didn't know.
Ezra Pound (1885–1972) US poet.
Cantos, XIII

6 A historian is a prophet in reverse.
Friedrich von Schlegel (1772–1829) German diplomat,
writer, and critic.
Das Athenäum

7 Historians are like deaf people who go on
answering questions that no one has asked
them.
Leo Tolstoy (1828–1910) Russian writer.
A Discovery of Australia, 'Being an Historian' (Manning Clark)

HISTORY

See also experience, historians, past

1 History repeats itself.
Proverb

2 Political history is far too criminal and pathological to be a fit subject of study for the young. Children should acquire their heroes and villains from fiction.
W. H. Auden (1907–73) British poet.
A Certain World

3 Man is a history-making creature who can neither repeat his past nor leave it behind.
W. H. Auden
The Dyer's Hand, 'D. H. Lawrence'

4 All things from eternity are of like forms and come round in a circle.
Marcus Aurelius (121–180 AD) Roman emperor.
Meditations, Bk. II, Ch. 14

5 History is the essence of innumerable biographies.
Thomas Carlyle (1795–1881) Scottish historian and essayist.
Critical and Miscellaneous Essays, 'History'

6 No great man lives in vain. The history of the world is but the biography of great men.
Thomas Carlyle
Heroes and Hero-Worship, 'The Hero as Divinity'

7 The history of every country begins in the heart of a man or woman.
Willa Cather (1873–1947) US writer and poet.
O Pioneers!, Pt. II, Ch. 4

8 History is philosophy teaching by examples.
Dionysius of Halicarnassus (40–8 BC) Greek historian.
Ars rhetorica, XI:2

9 History is an endless repetition of the wrong way of living.
Lawrence Durrell (1912–) British novelist.
The Listener, 1978

10 There is properly no history; only biography.
Ralph Waldo Emerson (1803–82) US poet and essayist.
Essays, 'History'

11 History is more or less bunk. It's tradition. We don't want tradition. We want to live in the present and the only history that is worth a tinker's damn is the history we make today.
Henry Ford (1863–1947) US car manufacturer.
Chicago Tribune, 25 May 1916

12 There are moments in history when brooding tragedy and its dark shadows can be lightened by recalling great moments of the past.
Indira Gandhi (1917–84) Indian stateswoman.
Letter to Richard Nixon, 16 Dec 1971

13 History never looks like history when you are living through it. It always looks confusing and messy, and it always feels uncomfortable.
John W. Gardner (1912–) US writer.
No Easy Victories

14 His reign is marked by the rare advantage of furnishing very few materials for history; which is, indeed, little more than the register of the crimes, follies, and misfortunes of mankind.
Edward Gibbon (1737–94) British historian.
Referring to the reign of Antoninus Pius
Decline and Fall of the Roman Empire, Ch. 3

15 What we know of the past is mostly not worth knowing. What is worth knowing is mostly uncertain. Events in the past may roughly be divided into those which probably never happened and those which do not matter.
Dean Inge (1860–1954) British churchman.
Assessments and Anticipations, 'Prognostications'

16 It takes a great deal of history to produce a little literature.
Henry James (1843–1916) US novelist.
Life of Nathaniel Hawthorne, Ch. 1

17 'History', Stephen said, 'is a nightmare from which I am trying to awake'.
James Joyce (1882–1941) Irish novelist.
Ulysses

18 Hegel says somewhere that all great events and personalities in world history reappear in one fashion or another. He forgot to add: the first time as tragedy, the second as farce.
Karl Marx (1818–83) German philosopher and revolutionary.
The Eighteenth Brumaire of Louis Napoleon

19 It is impossible to write ancient history because we do not have enough sources, and impossible to write modern history because we have far too many.
Charles Pierre Péguy (1873–1914) French writer.
Clio

20 There is no history of mankind, there are only many histories of all kinds of aspects of human life. And one of these is the history of political power. This is elevated into the history of the world.
Karl Popper (1902–) Austrian-born British philosopher.
The Open Society and Its Enemies

21 Progress, far from consisting in change, depends on retentiveness. Those who cannot remember the past are condemned to repeat it.
George Santayana (1863–1952) US philosopher.
The Life of Reason

22 I have looked upon the face of Agamemnon.
Heinrich Schliemann (1822–90) German archaeologist.
On discovering a gold death mask at an excavation in Mycenae
The Story of Civilization (W. Durant), Vol. 2

23 History is past politics, and politics present history.
John Robert Seeley (1834–95) British historian.
Quoting the historian E. A. Freeman
The Growth of British Policy

24 The Cavaliers (Wrong but Wromantic) and the Roundheads (Right but Repulsive).
W. C. Sellar (1898–1951) British humorous writer.
1066 And All That

25 1066 And All That.
W. C. Sellar
Book title

26 The Roman Conquest was, however, a *Good Thing*, since the Britons were only natives at the time.
W. C. Sellar
1066 And All That

27 Napoleon's armies used to march on their stomachs, shouting: 'Vive l'intérieur!'
W. C. Sellar
1066 And All That

28 America became top nation and history came to a full stop.
W. C. Sellar
1066 And All That

29 When in the chronicle of wasted time
I see descriptions of the fairest wights.
William Shakespeare (1564–1616) English dramatist.
Sonnet 106

30 History gets thicker as it approaches recent times.
A. J. P. Taylor (1906–) British historian.
English History, 1914–1945, Bibliography

31 All our ancient history, as one of our wits remarked, is no more than accepted fiction.
Voltaire (François-Marie Arouet; 1694–1778) French writer.
Jeannot et Colin

32 Indeed, history is nothing more than a tableau of crimes and misfortunes.
Voltaire
L'Ingénu, Ch. 10

33 Anything but history, for history must be false.
Robert Walpole (1676–1745) British statesman.
Walpoliana

HITLER

See also fascism, Germany, Nazism, World War II

1 The people Hitler never understood, and whose actions continued to exasperate him to the end of his life, were the British.
Alan Bullock (1914–) British academic and historian.
Hitler, A Study in Tyranny, Ch. 8

2 Hitler showed surprising loyalty to Mussolini, but it never extended to trusting him.
Alan Bullock
Hitler, A Study in Tyranny, Ch. 11

3 I have only one purpose, the destruction of Hitler, and my life is much simplified thereby. If Hitler invaded Hell I would make at least a favourable reference to the Devil in the House of Commons.
Winston Churchill (1874–1965) British statesman.
The Grand Alliance

4 The Italians will laugh at me; every time Hitler occupies a country he sends me a message.
Benito Mussolini (1883–1945) Italian dictator.
Hitler (Alan Bullock), Ch. 8

5 A racing tipster who only reached Hitler's level of accuracy would not do well for his clients.
A. J. P. Taylor (1906–) British historian.
The Origins of the Second World War, Ch. 7

HOME

See also homesickness, travel

1 East, west, home's best.
Proverb

2 Home is where the heart is.
Proverb

3 Home is home, though it be never so homely.
John Clarke (fl. 1639) English scholar.
Paroemiologia Anglo-Latina

4 Home is the place where, when you have to go there,
They have to take you in.
Robert Frost (1875–1963) US poet.
The Death of the Hired Man

5 In fact there was but one thing wrong with the Babbitt house; it was not a home.
Sinclair Lewis (1885–1951) US novelist.
Babbitt, Ch. 2

6 A man travels the world over in search of what he needs and returns home to find it.
George Moore (1852–1933) Irish writer and art critic.
The Brook Kerith, Ch. 11

7 Mid pleasures and palaces though we may roam,
Be it ever so humble, there's no place like home;
. . .
Home, home, sweet, sweet home!
There's no place like home! there's no place like home!
John Howard Payne (1791–1852) US actor and dramatist.
Clari, or the Maid of Milan

8 Home-keeping youth have ever homely wits.
William Shakespeare (1564–1616) English dramatist.
The Two Gentlemen of Verona, I:1

9 Seek home for rest,
For home is best.
Thomas Tusser (1524–80) English farmer.
Five Hundred Points of Good Husbandry, 'Instructions to Housewifery'

HOMESICKNESS

See also home, nostalgia

1 They say there's bread and work for all,
And the sun shines always there:
But I'll not forget old Ireland,
Were it fifty times as fair.
Helen Selina Blackwood (1807–67) British poet.
Lament of the Irish Emigrant

2 Weep no more, my lady,
Oh! weep no more today!
We will sing one song for the old Kentucky
Home,
For the old Kentucky Home far away.
Stephen Foster (1826–64) US composer of popular
songs.
My Old Kentucky Home

3 'Way down upon de Swanee Ribber,
Far, far away,
Dere's where my heart is turning ebber:
Dere's where de old folks stay.
All up and down de whole creation
Sadly I roam,
Still longing for de old plantation,
And for de old folks at home.
Stephen Foster
Old Folks at Home

4 Oh give me a home where the buffalo roam,
Where the deer and the antelope play,
Where seldom is heard a discouraging word
And the skies are not cloudy all day.
Brewster Higley (19th century) US songwriter.
Home on the Range

5 The accent of one's birthplace lingers in the
mind and in the heart as it does in one's
speech.
Duc de la Rochefoucauld (1613–80) French writer.
Maximes, 342

6 Breathes there the man, with soul so dead,
Who never to himself hath said,
This is my own, my native land!
Whose heart hath ne'er within him burn'd,
As home his footsteps he hath turn'd
From wandering on a foreign strand!
Walter Scott (1771–1832) Scottish novelist.
The Lay of the Last Minstrel, VI

7 In home-sickness you must keep moving – it
is the only disease that does not require
rest.
H. de Vere Stacpoole (1863–1931) Irish-born novelist.
The Bourgeois

8 Good-bye Piccadilly, Farewell Leicester
Square;
It's a long, long way to Tipperary, but my
heart's right there!
Harry Williams (1874–1924) British songwriter.
Written with Jack Judge (1878–1938)
It's a Long Way to Tipperary

9 I travelled among unknown men
In lands beyond the sea;
Nor, England! did I know till then
What love I bore to thee.
William Wordsworth (1770–1850) British poet.
I Travelled among Unknown Men

HOMOSEXUALITY

See also sex

1 But the men of Sodom were wicked and
sinners before the Lord exceedingly.
Bible: Genesis
13:13

2 I became one of the stately homos of
England.
Quentin Crisp (c. 1910–   ) British model, publicist, and
writer.
The Naked Civil Servant

3 The . . . problem which confronts
homosexuals is that they set out to win the
love of a 'real' man. If they succeed, they
fail. A man who 'goes with' other men is not
what they would call a real man.
Quentin Crisp
The Naked Civil Servant

4 I am the Love that dare not speak its name.
Lord Alfred Douglas (1870–1945) British writer and
poet.
Two Loves

5 The 'homo' is the legitimate child of the
'suffragette'.
Wyndham Lewis (1882–1957) British novelist.
The Art of Being Ruled, Pt. VIII, Ch. 4

6 Well, he looks like a man.
Abraham Lincoln (1809–65) US statesman.
On catching sight of Walt Whitman for the first time
Attrib.

7 This sort of thing may be tolerated by the
French, but we are British – thank God.
Lord Montgomery (1887–1976) British field marshal.
Comment on a bill to relax the laws against homosexuals
Daily Mail, 27 May 1965

8 If Michelangelo had been straight, the Sistine
Chapel would have been wallpapered.
Robin Tyler US comedienne.
Speech to gay-rights rally, Washington, 9 Jan 1988

HONESTY

See also frankness, integrity, sincerity, truth

1 An honest man's word is as good as his
bond.
Proverb

2 Honesty is the best policy.
Proverb

3 It is impossible that a man who is false to his

friends and neighbours should be true to the public.
Bishop Berkeley (1685–1753) Irish churchman and philosopher.
Maxims Concerning Patriotism

4 You see, I always divide people into two groups. Those who live by what they know to be a lie, and those who live by what they believe, falsely, to be the truth.
Christopher Hampton (1946–) British writer and dramatist.
The Philanthropist, Sc. 6

5 Though I be poor, I'm honest.
Thomas Middleton (1580–1627) English dramatist.
The Witch, III:2

6 To make your children *capable of honesty* is the beginning of education.
John Ruskin (1819–1900) British art critic and writer.
Time and Tide, Letter VIII

7 To be honest, as this world goes, is to be one man pick'd out of ten thousand.
William Shakespeare (1564–1616) English dramatist.
Hamlet, II:2

8 I thank God I am as honest as any man living that is an old man and no honester than I.
William Shakespeare
Much Ado About Nothing, III:5

9 Though I am not naturally honest, I am so sometimes by chance.
William Shakespeare
The Winter's Tale, IV:3

10 Father, I cannot tell a lie. I did it with my little hatchet.
George Washington (1732–99) US statesman.
Attrib.

11 Honesty is the best policy; but he who is governed by that maxim is not an honest man.
Richard Whately (1787–1863) British churchman.
Apophthegms

12 It is a terrible thing for a man to find out suddenly that all his life he has been speaking nothing but the truth.
Oscar Wilde (1854–1900) Irish-born British dramatist.
The Importance of Being Earnest, III

13 If you do not tell the truth about yourself you cannot tell it about other people.
Virginia Woolf (1882–1941) British novelist.
The Moment and Other Essays

HONOUR

See also titles

1 And they were offended in him. But Jesus said unto them, A prophet is not without honour, save in his own country, and in his own house.
Bible: Matthew
13:57

2 That chastity of honour, that felt a stain like a wound.
Edmund Burke (1729–97) British politician.
Reflections on the Revolution in France

3 Remember, men, we're fighting for this woman's honour; which is probably more than she ever did.
Groucho Marx (Julius Marx; 1895–1977) US comedian.
Duck Soup

4 Honour pricks me on. Yea, but how if honour prick me off when I come on? How then? Can honour set to a leg? No. Or an arm? No. Or take away the grief of a wound? No. Honour hath no skill in surgery, then? No. What is honour? A word. What is in that word? Honour. What is that honour? Air.
William Shakespeare (1564–1616) English dramatist.
Henry IV, Part One, V:1

5 For Brutus is an honourable man;
So are they all, all honourable men.
William Shakespeare
Julius Caesar, III:2

6 I once had a sparrow alight upon my shoulder for a moment while I was hoeing in a village garden, and I felt that I was more distinguished by that circumstance than I should have been by any epaulet I could have worn.
Henry David Thoreau (1817–62) US writer.
Walden, 'Winter Visitors'

7 Brothers all
In honour, as in one community,
Scholars and gentlemen.
William Wordsworth (1770–1850) British poet.
The Prelude, IX

HOPE

See also ambition, expectation, desire, optimism

1 A drowning man will clutch at a straw.
Proverb

2 Hope for the best.
Proverb

3 It is a long lane that has no turning.
Proverb

4 Still nursing the unconquerable hope,
Still clutching the inviolable shade.
Matthew Arnold (1822–88) British poet and critic.
The Scholar Gipsy

5 Charity is the power of defending that which we know to be indefensible. Hope is the power of being cheerful in circumstances which we know to be desperate.
G. K. Chesterton (1874–1936) British writer.
Heretics, Ch. 12

6 While there is life, there's hope,' he cried;

'Then why such haste?' so groaned and died.
John Gay (1685–1732) English poet and dramatist.
Fables

7   After all, tomorrow is another day.
Margaret Mitchell (1909–49) US novelist.
The closing words of the book
Gone with the Wind

8   Hope springs eternal in the human breast;
Man never is, but always to be blest.
Alexander Pope (1688–1744) British poet.
An Essay on Man, I

9   For hope is but the dream of those that
wake.
Matthew Prior (1664–1721) British poet.
Solomon, II

10 The miserable have no other medicine
But only hope.
William Shakespeare (1564–1616) English dramatist.
Measure for Measure, III:1

HORSES

See also animals, hunting, sport

1   When I appear in public people expect me to
neigh, grind my teeth, paw the ground and
swish my tail – none of which is easy.
Princess Anne (1950–) The Princess Royal, only
daughter of Elizabeth II.
The Observer, 'Sayings of the Week', 22 May 1977

2   I know two things about the horse,
And one of them is rather coarse.
Anonymous
The Horse

3   I sprang to the stirrup, and Joris, and he;
I galloped, Dirck galloped, we galloped all
three.
Robert Browning (1812–89) British poet.
How they brought the Good News from Ghent to Aix

4   As lene was his hors as is a rake.
Geoffrey Chaucer (c. 1342–1400) English poet.
The Canterbury Tales, Prologue

5   The blue ribbon of the turf.
Benjamin Disraeli (1804–81) British statesman.
Describing the Derby
Life of Lord George Bentinck, Ch. 26

6   Gwine to run all night!
Gwine to run all day!
I bet my money on the bob-tail nag.
Somebody bet on the bay.
Stephen Foster (1826–64) US composer of popular
songs.
Camptown Races

7   They say princes learn no art truly, but the
art of horsemanship. The reason is, the
brave beast is no flatterer. He will throw a
prince as soon as his groom.
Ben Jonson (1573–1637) English dramatist.
Timber, or Discoveries made upon Men and Matter

8   It takes a good deal of physical courage to
ride a horse. This, however, I have. I get it
at about forty cents a flask, and take it as
required.
Stephen Leacock (1869–1944) English-born Canadian
economist and humorist.
Literary Lapses, 'Reflections on Riding'

9   To confess that you are totally Ignorant
about the Horse, is social suicide: you will be
despised by everybody, especially the horse.
W. C. Sellar (1898–1951) British humorous writer.
Horse Nonsense

10 A horse! a horse ! my kingdom for a horse.
William Shakespeare (1564–1616) English dramatist.
Richard III, V:4

HOSPITALITY

1   A constant guest is never welcome.
Proverb

2   Fish and guests smell in three days.
Proverb

3   The first day a guest, the second day a
guest, the third day a calamity.
Indian proverb

4   The guest who outstays his fellow-guests
loses his overcoat.
Chinese proverb

5   Let brotherly love continue.
Be not forgetful to entertain strangers: for
thereby some have entertained angels
unawares.
Bible: Hebrews
13:1–2

HOUSES

See also architecture, home, stately homes

1   Houses are built to live in and not to look
on; therefore let use be preferred before
uniformity, except where both may be had.
Francis Bacon (1561–1626) English philosopher.
Essays, 'Of Building'

2   A house is a machine for living in.
Le Corbusier (Charles-Édouard Jeanneret; 1887–1965)
Swiss-born French architect.
Towards an Architecture

3   A hundred and fifty accurate reproductions of
Anne Hathaway's cottage, each complete with
central heating and garage.
Osbert Lancaster (1908–86) British cartoonist.
Pillar to Post, 'Stockbrokers Tudor'

4   They're all made out of ticky-tacky, and they
all look just the same.
Malvina Reynolds (1900–78) US folksinger and
songwriter.
Little Boxes, song describing a housing scheme built in the hills
south of San Francisco
Little Boxes

5 It's 'aving 'ouses built by men, I believe,
   makes all the work and trouble.
   H. G. Wells (1866–1946) British writer.
   Kipps, Bk. III, Ch. 1

HOUSES OF PARLIAMENT

See also aristocracy, government, politics

1 This is a rotten argument, but it should be
   good enough for their lordships on a hot
   summer afternoon.
   Anonymous
   A note on a ministerial brief read out by mistake in the House
   of Lords
   The Way the Wind Blows (Lord Home), 1976

2 The House of Lords is like a glass of
   champagne that has stood for five days.
   Clement Attlee (1883–1967) British statesman and
   Labour prime minister.
   Attrib.

3 A severe though not unfriendly critic of our
   institutions said that 'the cure for admiring
   the House of Lords was to go and look at it.'
   Walter Bagehot (1826–77) British economist and
   journalist.
   The English Constitution, 'The House of Lords'

4 A lot of hard-faced men who look as if they
   had done very well out of the war.
   Stanley Baldwin (1867–1947) British statesman.
   Referring to the first House of Commons elected after World
   War I (1918)
   Economic Consequences of the Peace (J. M. Keynes), Ch. 5

5 The House of Lords is the British Outer
   Mongolia for retired politicians.
   Tony Benn (1925–) British politician.
   Speech, 11 Feb 1962

6 Better than a play.
   Charles II (1630–85) King of England.
   Referring to House of Lords debate on the Divorce Bill
   Attrib.

7 I think . . . that it is the best club in London.
   Charles Dickens (1812–70) British novelist.
   Mr Tremlow describing the House of Commons
   Our Mutual Friend, Bk. II, Ch. 3

8 I am dead: dead, but in the Elysian fields.
   Benjamin Disraeli (1804–81) British statesman.
   Said on his move to the House of Lords
   Attrib.

9 The House of Lords is a model of how to
   care for the elderly.
   Frank Field (1942–) British politician.
   The Observer, 24 May 1981

10 The House of Peers, throughout the war,
   Did nothing in particular,
   And did it very well.
   W. S. Gilbert (1836–1911) British dramatist.
   Iolanthe, II

11 I have neither eye to see, nor tongue to

speak here, but as the House is pleased to
direct me.
William Lenthall (1591–1662) English parliamentarian.
Said on 4 Jan 1642 in the House of Commons when asked by
Charles I if he had seen five MPs whom the King wished to
arrest. It was a succinct restatement of the Speaker's tradi-
tional role
Historical Collections (Rushworth)

12 Mr Balfour's Poodle.
   David Lloyd George (1863–1945) British Liberal
   statesman.
   Referring to the House of Lords and its in-built Conservative
   majority; said in reply to a claim that it was 'the watchdog of
   the nation'
   Remark, House of Commons, 26 June 1907

13 Every man has a House of Lords in his own
   head. Fears, prejudices, misconceptions –
   those are the peers, and they are hereditary.
   David Lloyd George
   Speech, Cambridge, 1927

14 The British, being brought up on team
   games, enter their House of Commons in the
   spirit of those who would rather be doing
   something else. If they cannot be playing golf
   or tennis, they can at least pretend that
   politics is a game with very similar rules.
   Cyril Northcote Parkinson (1919–) British historian
   and writer.
   Parkinson's Law, Ch. 2

15 The House of Lords must be the only
   institution in the world which is kept efficient
   by the persistent absenteeism of most of its
   members.
   Herbert Samuel (1870–1963) British Liberal statesman.
   News Review, 5 Feb 1948

16 A life peer is like a mule – no pride of
   ancestry, no hope of posterity.
   Lord Shackleton (1911–) British politician,
   businessman, and life peer.
   Attrib.

17 The House of Lords is a perfect eventide
   home.
   Mary Stocks (1891–1975) British politician and writer.
   The Observer, 'Sayings of the Week', 4 Oct 1970

18 The House of Lords, an illusion to which I
   have never been able to subscribe –
   responsibility without power, the prerogative
   of the eunuch throughout the ages.
   Tom Stoppard (1937–) Czech-born British dramatist.
   Lord Malquist and Mr Moon, Pt. VI, Ch. 1

19 You must build your House of Parliament
   upon the river: so . . . that the populace
   cannot exact their demands by sitting down
   round you.
   Duke of Wellington (1769–1852) British general and
   statesman.
   Words on Wellington (Sir William Fraser)

HOUSEWORK

See also woman's role

1 Housekeeping ain't no joke.
Louisa May Alcott (1832–88) US novelist.
Little Women, Pt. I

2 Our motto: Life is too short to stuff a mushroom.
Shirley Conran (1932–) Designer and journalist.
Superwoman, Epigraph

3 There was no need to do any housework at all. After the first four years the dirt doesn't get any worse.
Quentin Crisp (c. 1910–) British model, publicist, and writer.
The Naked Civil Servant

4 Cleaning your house while your kids are still growing
Is like shoveling the walk before it stops snowing.
Phyllis Diller (1917–) US writer and comedienne.
Phyllis Diller's Housekeeping Hints

5 I do, and I also wash and iron them.
Denis Thatcher (1915–) British businessman married to Mrs Margaret Thatcher.
Replying to the question 'Who wears the pants in this house?'
Times (Los Angeles), 21 Apr 1981

HUMAN CONDITION

See also human nature, life, mankind

1 A wanderer is man from his birth.
He was born in a ship
On the breast of the river of Time.
Matthew Arnold (1822–88) British poet and critic.
The Future

2 Thou hast created us for Thyself, and our heart is not quiet until it rests in Thee.
St Augustine of Hippo (354–430) Bishop of Hippo.
Confessions, Bk. I, Ch. 1

3 Man that is born of a woman is of few days, and full of trouble.
Bible: Job
14:1

4 We mortals cross the ocean of this world
Each in his average cabin of a life.
Robert Browning (1812–89) British poet.
Bishop Blougram's Apology

5 The human race, to which so many of my readers belong.
G. K. Chesterton (1874–1936) British writer.
The Napoleon of Notting Hill, Vol. I, Ch. 1

6 If God were suddenly condemned to live the life which he has inflicted on men, He would kill Himself.
Alexandre Dumas, fils (1824–95) French writer.
Pensées d'album

7 Every man is wanted, and no man is wanted much.
Ralph Waldo Emerson (1803–82) US poet and essayist.
Essays, 'Nominalist and Realist'

8 Oh wearisome condition of humanity!
Born under one law, to another bound.
Fulke Greville (1554–1628) English poet and politician.
Mustapha, V:6

9 The condition of man . . . is a condition of war of everyone against everyone.
Thomas Hobbes (1588–1679) English philosopher.
Leviathan, Pt. I, Ch. 4

10 No arts; no letters; no society; and which is worst of all, continual fear and danger of violent death; and the life of man, solitary, poor, nasty, brutish, and short.
Thomas Hobbes
Leviathan, Pt. I, Ch. 13

11 Fade far away, dissolve, and quite forget
What thou among the leaves hast never known,
The weariness, the fever, and the fret,
Here, where men sit and hear each other groan.
John Keats (1795–1821) British poet.
Ode to a Nightingale

12 Created half to rise, and half to fall;
Great lord of all things, yet a prey to all;
Sole judge of truth, in endless error hurl'd;
The glory, jest, and riddle of the world!
Alexander Pope (1688–1744) British poet.
An Essay on Man, II

13 Brief and powerless is Man's life; on him and all his race the slow, sure doom falls pitiless and dark.
Bertrand Russell (1872–1970) British philosopher.
Mysticism and Logic, 'A Free Man's Worship'

14 Farewell, a long farewell, to all my greatness!
This is the state of man: to-day he puts forth
The tender leaves of hopes: to-morrow blossoms
And bears his blushing honours thick upon him;
The third day comes a frost, a killing frost,
And when he thinks, good easy man, full surely
His greatness is a-ripening, nips his root,
And then he falls, as I do.
William Shakespeare (1564–1616) English dramatist.
Henry VIII, III:2

15 All the world's a stage,
And all the men and women merely players;
They have their exits and their entrances;
And one man in his time plays many parts,
His acts being seven ages.
William Shakespeare
As You Like It, II:7

16 When we are born, we cry that we are come
To this great stage of fools.
William Shakespeare
King Lear, IV:6

17 We have to believe in free-will. We've got no choice.
Isaac Bashevis Singer (1904–) Polish-born US novelist.
The Times, 21 June 1982

18 But what am I?
An infant crying in the night:
An infant crying for the light:
And with no language but a cry.
Alfred, Lord Tennyson (1809–92) British poet.
In Memoriam A.H.H., LIV

19 For what human ill does not dawn seem to be an alternative?
Thornton Wilder (1897–1975) US novelist and dramatist.
The Bridge of San Luis Rey

HUMAN NATURE

See also mankind

1 Human nature is so well disposed towards those who are in interesting situations, that a young person, who either marries or dies, is sure to be kindly spoken of.
Jane Austen (1775–1817) British novelist.
Emma, Ch. 22

2 A man's nature runs either to herbs, or to weeds; therefore let him seasonably water the one, and destroy the other.
Francis Bacon (1561–1626) English philosopher.
Essays, 'Of Nature in Men'

3 There is in human nature generally more of the fool than of the wise.
Francis Bacon
Essays, 'Of Boldness'

4 Nature is often hidden, sometimes overcome, seldom extinguished.
Francis Bacon
Essays, 'Of Nature in Men'

5 Nature, to be commanded, must be obeyed.
Francis Bacon
Novum Organum

6 I got disappointed in human nature as well and gave it up because I found it too much like my own.
J. P. Donleavy (1926–) US novelist.
Fairy Tales of New York

7 A man so various, that he seem'd to be
Not one, but all Mankind's Epitome.
Stiff in Opinions, always in the wrong;
Was Everything by starts, and Nothing long.
John Dryden (1631–1700) British poet and dramatist.
Absalom and Achitophel, I

8 A person seldom falls sick, but the bystanders are animated with a faint hope that he will die.
Ralph Waldo Emerson (1803–82) US poet and essayist.
Conduct of Life, 'Considerations by the Way'

9 You may drive out nature with a pitchfork, yet she'll be constantly running back.
Horace (Quintus Horatius Flaccus; 65–8 BC) Roman poet.
Epistles, I

10 Most human beings have an almost infinite capacity for taking things for granted.
Aldous Huxley (1894–1964) British novelist.
Themes and Variations

11 We need more understanding of human nature, because the only real danger that exists is man himself . . . We know nothing of man, far too little. His psyche should be studied because we are the origin of all coming evil.
Carl Gustav Jung (1875–1961) Swiss psychoanalyst.
BBC television interview

12 Out of the crooked timber of humanity no straight thing can ever be made.
Immanuel Kant (1724–1804) German philosopher.
Idee zu einer allgemeinen Geschichte in weltbürgerlicher Absicht

13 Scenery is fine – but human nature is finer.
John Keats (1795–1821) British poet.
Letter to Benjamin Bailey, 13 Mar 1818

14 Upon the whole I dislike mankind: whatever people on the other side of the question may advance, they cannot deny that they are always surprised at hearing of a good action and never of a bad one.
John Keats
Letter, 1820

15 No absolute is going to make the lion lie down with the lamb unless the lamb is inside.
D. H. Lawrence (1885–1930) British novelist.
The Later D. H. Lawrence

16 In the misfortune of our best friends we always find something which is not displeasing to us.
Duc de la Rochefoucauld (1613–80) French writer.
Maximes, 99

17 'Tis the way of all flesh.
Thomas Shadwell (1642–92) English dramatist.
The Sullen Lovers, V:2

18 It is part of human nature to hate the man you have hurt.
Tacitus (c. 55–c. 120 AD) Roman historian.
Agricola, 42

19 It is not the ape, nor the tiger in man that I fear, it is the donkey.
William Temple (1881–1944) British churchman.
Attrib.

20 . . . use thought only to justify their injustices, and speech only to conceal their thoughts.
Voltaire (François-Marie Arouet; 1694–1778) French writer.
Referring to men
Dialogue, 'Le Chapon et la poularde'

21 The earth does not argue,

Is not pathetic, has no arrangements,
Does not scream, haste, persuade, threaten,
promise,
Makes no discriminations, has no conceivable
failures,
Closes nothing, refuses nothing, shuts none
out.
Walt Whitman (1819–92) US poet.
To the sayers of words

HUMAN RIGHTS

See also equality, freedom, race

1 All human beings are born free and equal in
dignity and rights.
Anonymous
Universal Declaration of Human Rights (1948), Article 1

2 *Liberté! Égalité! Fraternité!*
Freedom! Equality! Brotherhood!
Anonymous
Motto for French Revolutionaries

3 We hold these truths to be self-evident: that
all men are created equal; that they are
endowed by their Creator with certain
unalienable rights; that among these are life,
liberty, and the pursuit of happiness.
Thomas Jefferson (1743–1826) US statesman.
Declaration of American Independence, 4 July 1776

4 We look forward to a world founded upon
four essential human freedoms. The first is
freedom of speech and expression –
everywhere in the world. The second is
freedom of every person to worship God in
his own way – everywhere in the world.
The third is freedom from want . . .
everywhere in the world. The fourth is
freedom from fear . . . anywhere in the world.
Franklin D. Roosevelt (1882–1945) US Democratic
president.
Speech to Congress, 6 Jan 1941

5 Freedom is an indivisible word. If we want to
enjoy it, and fight for it, we must be
prepared to extend it to everyone, whether
they are rich or poor, whether they agree
with us or not, no matter what their race or
the colour of their skin.
Wendell Lewis Willkie (1892–1944) US lawyer and
businessman.
One World, Ch. 13

HUMILITY

See also service, servility

1 Blessed are the meek: for they shall inherit
the earth.
Bible: Matthew
5:5

2 Humility is only doubt,
And does the sun and moon blot out.
William Blake (1757–1827) British poet.
The Everlasting Gospel

3 I do not consider it an insult but rather a
compliment to be called an agnostic. I do not
pretend to know where many ignorant men
are sure.
Clarence Seward Darrow (1857–1938) US lawyer.
Remark during the trial (1925) of John Scopes for teaching the
theory of evolution in school

4 It is difficult to be humble. Even if you aim
at humility, there is no guarantee that when
you have attained the state you will not be
proud of the feat.
Bonamy Dobrée (1891–) British scholar and writer.
John Wesley

5 Less than the dust beneath thy chariot
wheel,
Less than the weed that grows beside thy
door,
Less than the rust that never stained thy
sword,
Less than the need thou hast in life of me,
Even less am I.
Laurence Hope (Mrs M. H. Nicolson; 1804–1905)
British poet and songwriter.
The Garden of Kama and other Love Lyrics from India, 'Less
than the Dust'

6 The meek do not inherit the earth unless
they are prepared to fight for their
meekness.
H. J. Laski (1893–1950) British political theorist.
Attrib.

7 The humble and meek are thirsting for blood.
Joe Orton (1933–67) British dramatist.
Funeral Games, I

8 Because there's no fourth class.
George Santayana (1863–1952) US philosopher.
On being asked why he always travelled third class
Living Biographies of the Great Philosophers (H. Thomas)

9 I too had thoughts once of being an
intellectual, but I found it too difficult.
Albert Schweitzer (1875–1965) French Protestant
theologian, philosopher, and physician.
Remark made to an African who refused to perform a menial
task on the grounds that he was an intellectual
Attrib.

10 Take physic, pomp;
Expose thyself to feel what wretches feel.
William Shakespeare (1564–1616) English dramatist.
King Lear, III:4

11 We have the highest authority for believing
that the meek shall inherit the Earth; though
I have never found any particular
corroboration of this aphorism in the records
of Somerset House.
F. E. Smith (1872–1930) British lawyer and politician.
Contemporary Personalities, 'Marquess Curzon'

12 When I survey the wondrous Cross,
On which the Prince of Glory died,
My richest gain I count but loss

And pour contempt on all my pride.

Isaac Watts (1674–1748) English theologian and hymn writer.
When I Survey the Wondrous Cross

13 Gentle Jesus, meek and mild,
Look upon a little child;
Pity my simplicity,
Suffer me to come to thee.

Charles Wesley (1707–88) British religious leader.
Hymns and Sacred Poems

HUMOUR

See also laughter, nonsense, puns

On the subject

1 I have a fine sense of the ridiculous, but no sense of humour.

Edward Albee (1928–) US dramatist.
Who's Afraid of Virginia Woolf?, I

2 The marvellous thing about a joke with a double meaning is that it can only mean one thing.

Ronnie Barker (1929–) British comedian.
Sauce, 'Daddie's Sauce'

3 The world would not be in such a snarl, had Marx been Groucho instead of Karl.

Irving Berlin (Israel Baline; 1888–) US composer.
Telegram to Groucho Marx on his seventy-first birthday

4 It's a good deed to forget a poor joke.

Brendan Bracken (1901–58) British newspaper publisher and politician.
The Observer, 'Sayings of the Week', 17 Oct 1943

5 All I need to make a comedy is a park, a policeman and a pretty girl.

Charlie Chaplin (Sir Charles Spencer C.; 1889–1977) British film actor.
My Autobiography

6 A joke's a very serious thing.

Charles Churchill (1731–64) British poet.
The Ghost, Bk. IV

7 Men will confess to treason, murder, arson, false teeth, or a wig. How many of them will own up to a lack of humour?

Frank More Colby (1865–1925) US editor.
Essays, I

8 No mind is thoroughly well organized that is deficient in a sense of humour.

Samuel Taylor Coleridge (1772–1834) British poet.
Table Talk

9 Total absence of humour renders life impossible.

Colette (1873–1954) French novelist.
Chance Acquaintances

10 A different taste in jokes is a great strain on the affections.

George Eliot (Mary Ann Evans; 1819–80) British novelist.
Daniel Deronda

11 Comedy, like sodomy, is an unnatural act.

Marty Feldman (1933–83) British comedian.
The Times, 9 June 1969

12 As for the Freudian, it is a very low, Central European sort of humour.

Robert Graves (1895–1985) British poet and novelist.
Occupation: Writer

13 Funny peculiar, or funny ha-ha?

Ian Hay (John Hay Beith; 1876–1952) British novelist and dramatist.
The Housemaster, III

14 His foe was folly and his weapon wit.

Anthony Hope (Sir Anthony Hope Hawkins; 1863–1933) British novelist.
Written for the inscription on the memorial to W. S. Gilbert, Victoria Embankment, London

15 Every man has, some time in his life, an ambition to be a wag.

Samuel Johnson (1709–84) British lexicographer.
Diary and Letters (Mme D'Arblay), Vol. III, Ch. 46

16 The essence of any blue material is timing. If you sit on it, it becomes vulgar.

Danny La Rue (Daniel Patrick Carroll; 1928–) British entertainer.
Attrib.

17 The coarse joke proclaims that we have here an animal which finds its own animality either objectionable or funny.

C. S. Lewis (1898–1963) British academic and writer.
Miracles

18 Impropriety is the soul of wit.

W. Somerset Maugham (1874–1965) British novelist.
The Moon and Sixpence, Ch. 4

19 It is not for nothing that, in the English language alone, to accuse someone of trying to be funny is highly abusive.

Malcolm Muggeridge (1903–) British writer.
Tread Softly For You Tread on My Jokes

20 Attic wit.

Pliny the Elder (Gaius Plinius Secundus; 23–79 AD) Roman scholar.
Natural History, II

21 True wit is nature to advantage dress'd;
What oft was thought, but ne'er so well express'd.

Alexander Pope (1688–1744) British poet.
An Essay on Criticism

22 Comedy, we may say, is society protecting itself – with a smile.

J. B. Priestley (1894–1984) British novelist.
George Meredith

23 A comedian can only last till he either takes himself serious or his audience takes him serious.

Will Rogers (1879–1935) US actor and humorist.
Newspaper article, 1931

24 Everything is funny, as long as it's happening to somebody else.
Will Rogers
The Illiterate Digest

25 I am not only witty in myself, but the cause that wit is in other men. I do here walk before thee like a sow that hath overwhelm'd all her litter but one.
William Shakespeare (1564–1616) English dramatist.
Henry IV, Part Two, I:2

26 A jest's prosperity lies in the ear
Of him that hears it, never in the tongue
Of him that makes it.
William Shakespeare
Love's Labour's Lost, V:2

27 It's hard to be funny when you have to be clean.
Mae West (1892–1980) US actress.
The Wit and Wisdom of Mae West (ed. J. Weintraub)

Some examples

28 There's a wonderful family called Stein,
There's Gert and there's Epp and there's Ein;
Gert's poems are bunk,
Epp's statues are junk,
And no one can understand Ein.
Anonymous

29 Little Willy from his mirror
Licked the mercury right off,
Thinking in his childish error,
It would cure the whooping cough.
At the funeral his mother
Smartly said to Mrs Brown:
"Twas a chilly day for Willie
When the mercury went down'.
Anonymous
Willie's Epitaph

30 There was an old man from Darjeeling,
Who boarded a bus bound for Ealing,
He saw on the door:
'Please don't spit on the floor',
So he stood up and spat on the ceiling.
Anonymous

31 I do most of my work sitting down; that's where I shine.
Robert Benchley (1889–1945) US humorist.
Attrib.

32 No visit to Dove Cottage, Grasmere, is complete without examining the outhouse where Hazlitt's father, a Unitarian minister of strong liberal views, attempted to put his hand up Dorothy Wordsworth's skirt.
Alan Coren (1938–) British humorist and writer.
All Except the Bastard, 'Bohemia'

33 Dear 338171 (May I call you 338?).
Noël Coward (1899–1973) British dramatist.
Starting a letter to T. E. Lawrence who had retired from public life to become Aircraftsman Brown, 338171
Letters to T. E. Lawrence

34 Miss Bolo rose from the table considerably agitated, and went straight home, in a flood of tears and a Sedan chair.
Charles Dickens (1812–70) British novelist.
Pickwick Papers, Ch. 35

35 It . . . was full of dry rot. An unkind visitor said the only reason Menabilly still stood was that the woodworm obligingly held hands.
Daphne Du Maurier (1907–) British novelist.
Interview – referring to her own house in Cornwall upon which Manderley in *Rebecca* was based

36 Wembley, adj. Suffering from a vague *malaise.* 'I feel a bit w. this morning.'
Paul Jennings (1918–) British humorous writer.
The Jenguin Pennings, 'Ware, Wye, Watford'

37 The desire of the moth for the star.
James Joyce (1882–1941) Irish novelist.
Commenting on the interruption of a music recital when a moth flew into the singer's mouth
James Joyce (R. Ellmann)

38 'When I makes tea I makes tea,' as old mother Grogan said. 'And when I makes water I makes water'.
James Joyce
Ulysses

39 The landlady of a boarding-house is a parallelogram – that is, an oblong angular figure, which cannot be described, but which is equal to anything.
Stephen Leacock (1869–1944) English-born Canadian economist and humorist.
Literary Lapses, 'Boarding-House Geometry'

40 One morning I shot an elephant in my pajamas.
How he got into my pajamas I'll never know.
Groucho Marx (Julius Marx; 1895–1977) US comedian
Animal Crackers

41 I could dance with you till the cows come home. Better still, I'll dance with the cows and *you* come home.
Groucho Marx
Duck Soup

42 Go – and never darken my towels again.
Groucho Marx
Duck Soup

43 I don't have a photograph, but you can have my footprints. They are upstairs in my socks.
Groucho Marx
A Night At the Opera

44 The strains of Verdi will come back to you tonight, and Mrs Claypool's cheque will come back to you in the morning.
Groucho Marx
A Night at the Opera

45 Please accept my resignation. I don't want to

belong to any club that will accept me as a member.
Groucho Marx
Resigning from the Friar's Club in Hollywood
Attrib.

46 Dr Strabismus (Whom God Preserve) of Utrecht is carrying out research work with a view to crossing salmon with mosquitoes. He says it will mean a bite every time for fishermen.
J. B. Morton (1893–1979) British journalist.
By the Way, 'January Tail-piece'

47 Oh, don't worry about Alan . . . Alan will always land on somebody's feet.
Dorothy Parker (1893–1967) US writer.
Said of her husband on the day their divorce became final
You Might As Well Live (J. Keats), Pt. IV, Ch. 1

48 He bit his lip in a manner which immediately awakened my maternal sympathy, and I helped him bite it.
S. J. Perelman (1904–79) US humorous writer.
Crazy Like a Fox, 'The Love Decoy'

49 I have Bright's disease and he has mine.
S. J. Perelman
(Bennet Gerf)

50 A case of the tail dogging the wag.
S. J. Perelman
Having escaped with some difficulty from the persistent attentions of some prostitutes in the street
Another Almanac of Words at Play (W. Espy)

51 The cook was a good cook, as cooks go; and as cooks go she went.
Saki (Hector Hugh Munro; 1870–1916) British writer.
Reginald on Besetting Sins

52 Napoleon's armies used to march on their stomachs, shouting: 'Vive l'intérieur!'
W. C. Sellar (1898–1951) British humorous writer.
1066 And All That

53 You wait here and I'll bring the etchings down.
James Thurber (1894–1961) US humorist.
Cartoon caption

54 Wall is the name – Max Wall. My father was the Great Wall of China. He was a brick.
Max Wall (1908–) British comedian.
Opening line of one of his acts

55 He spoke with a certain what-is-it in his voice, and I could see that, if not actually disgruntled, he was far from being gruntled.
P. G. Wodehouse (1881–1975) British humorous novelist.
The Code of the Woosters

HUNGER

See also desire, food, thirst

1 Hunger is the best sauce.
Proverb

2 Poverty is an anomaly to rich people. It is very difficult to make out why people who want dinner do not ring the bell.
Walter Bagehot (1826–77) British economist and journalist.
Literary Studies, II

3 When he told men to love their neighbour, their bellies were full. Nowadays things are different.
Bertolt Brecht (1898–1956) German dramatist.
Mother Courage, II

4 The best sauce in the world is hunger.
Miguel de Cervantes (1547–1616) Spanish novelist.
Don Quixote, Pt. II, Ch. 5

5 If only it were as easy to banish hunger by rubbing the belly as it is to masturbate.
Diogenes (412–322 BC) Greek philosopher.
Lives and Opinions of Eminent Philosophers (Diogenes Laertius)

6 They that die by famine die by inches.
Matthew Henry (1662–1714) English nonconformist minister.
Exposition of the Old and New Testaments

7 The war against hunger is truly mankind's war of liberation.
John Fitzgerald Kennedy (1917–63) US statesman.
Speech, World Food Congress, 4 June 1963

8 A hungry stomach has no ears.
Jean de La Fontaine (1621–95) French poet.
Fables, IX, 'Le Milan et le Rossignol'

9 I came home . . . hungry as a hunter.
Charles Lamb (1775–1834) British essayist.
Letter to Coleridge, Apr 1800

10 Let them eat cake.
Marie-Antoinette (1755–93) Queen of France.
On being told that the people had no bread to eat; in fact she was repeating a much older saying
Attrib.

HUNTING

See also sport

1 Spirits of well-shot woodcock, partridge, snipe
Flutter and bear him up the Norfolk sky.
John Betjeman (1906–84) British poet.
Death of King George V

2 Detested sport,
That owes its pleasures to another's pain.
William Cowper (1731–1800) British poet.
The Task

3 Wild animals never kill for sport. Man is the only one to whom the torture and death of his fellow-creatures is amusing in itself.
J. A. Froude (1818–94) British historian.
Oceana, Ch. 5

4 D'ye ken John Peel with his coat so gay?
D'ye ken John Peel at the break of the day?

D'ye ken John Peel when he's far far away
With his hounds and his horn in the morning?

'Twas the sound of his horn called me from my
bed,
And the cry of his hounds has me oft-times
led;
For Peel's view-hollo would waken the dead,
Or a fox from his lair in the morning.
John Woodcock Graves (1795–1886) British poet,
huntsman, and songwriter.
John Peel

5   It is very strange, and very melancholy, that
the paucity of human pleasures should
persuade us ever to call hunting one of them.
Samuel Johnson (1709–84) British lexicographer.
Johnsonian Miscellanies (ed. G. B. Hill), Vol. I

6   It isn't mere convention. Everyone can see
that the people who hunt are the right people
and the people who don't are the wrong
ones.
George Bernard Shaw (1856–1950) Irish dramatist and
critic.
Heartbreak House

7   But He was never, well,
What I call
A Sportsman;
For forty days
He went out into the desert
– And never shot anything.
Osbert Sitwell (1892–1969) British writer.
Old Fashioned Sportsmen

8   The English country gentleman galloping after
a fox – the unspeakable in full pursuit of the
uneatable.
Oscar Wilde (1854–1900) Irish-born British dramatist.
A Woman of No Importance, I

HURT

See also cruelty, insensitivity, nastiness, suffering

1   Those have most power to hurt us that we
love.
Francis Beaumont (1584–1616) English dramatist.
The Maid's Tragedy, V:6

2   Mrs Montagu has dropt me. Now, Sir, there
are people whom one should like very well to
drop, but would not wish to be dropped by.
Samuel Johnson (1709–84) British lexicographer.
Life of Johnson (J. Boswell), Vol. IV

3   It takes your enemy and your friend, working
together, to hurt you to the heart; the one
to slander you and the other to get the news
to you.
Mark Twain (Samuel Langhorne Clemens; 1835–1910)
US writer.
Following the Equator

4   We flatter those we scarcely know,
We please the fleeting guest,
And deal full many a thoughtless blow

To those who love us best.
Ella Wheeler Wilcox (1850–1919) US poet.
Life's Scars

HYPOCRISY

See also cant, example, insincerity

1   All are not saints that go to church.
Proverb

2   It is the wisdom of the crocodiles, that shed
tears when they would devour.
Francis Bacon (1561–1626) English philosopher.
Essays, 'Of Wisdom for a Man's Self'

3   Woe unto you, scribes and Pharisees,
hypocrites! for ye are like unto whited
sepulchres, which indeed appear beautiful
outward, but are within full of dead men's
bones, and of all uncleanness.
Bible: Matthew
23:27

4   Prisons are built with stones of Law, brothels
with bricks of Religion.
William Blake (1757–1827) British poet.
The Marriage of Heaven and Hell, 'Proverbs of Hell'

5   God be thanked, the meanest of his
creatures
Boasts two soul-sides, one to face the world
with,
One to show a woman when he loves her!
Robert Browning (1812–89) British poet.
One Word More, XVII

6   Man is the only animal that can remain on
friendly terms with the victims he intends to
eat until he eats them.
Samuel Butler (1835–1902) British writer.
Notebooks

7   The smyler with the knyf under the cloke.
Geoffrey Chaucer (c. 1342–1400) English poet.
The Canterbury Tales, 'The Knight's Tale'

8   We ought to see far enough into a hypocrite
to see even his sincerity.
G. K. Chesterton (1874–1936) British writer.
Heretics, Ch. 5

9   The book written against fame and learning
has the author's name on the title-page.
Ralph Waldo Emerson (1803–82) US poet and essayist.
Journal

10 Man is the only animal that learns by being
hypocritical. He pretends to be polite and
then, eventually, he *becomes* polite.
Jean Kerr (1923–) US dramatist.
Finishing Touches

11 Hypocrisy is the most difficult and nerve-
racking vice that any man can pursue; it
needs an unceasing vigilance and a rare
detachment of spirit. It cannot, like adultery

or gluttony, be practised at spare moments;
it is a whole-time job.
W. Somerset Maugham (1874–1965) British novelist.
Cakes and Ale, Ch. 1

12 For neither man nor angel can discern
Hypocrisy, the only evil that walks
Invisible, except to God alone.
John Milton (1608–74) English poet.
Paradise Lost, Bk. III

13 Hypocrisy is the homage paid by vice to
virtue.
Duc de la Rochefoucauld (1613–80) French writer.
Maximes, 218

14 Well, whiles I am a beggar, I will rail
And say there is no sin but to be rich;
And being rich, my virtue then shall be
To say there is no vice but beggary.
William Shakespeare (1564–1616) English dramatist.
King John, II:1

15 Come not, when I am dead,
To drop thy foolish tears upon my grave,
To trample round my fallen head,

And vex the unhappy dust thou wouldst not
save.
Alfred, Lord Tennyson (1809–92) British poet.
Come Not, When I Am Dead

16 I sit on a man's back, choking him and
making him carry me, and yet assure myself
and others that I am very sorry for him and
wish to ease his lot by all possible means –
except by getting off his back.
Leo Tolstoy (1828–1910) Russian writer.
What Then Must We Do?, Ch. 16

17 I hope you have not been leading a double
life, pretending to be wicked and being really
good all the time. That would be hypocrisy.
Oscar Wilde (1854–1900) Irish-born British dramatist.
The Importance of Being Earnest, II

18 A Christian is a man who feels
Repentance on a Sunday
For what he did on Saturday
And is going to do on Monday.
Thomas Russell Ybarra (born 1880) Venezuelan-born US
writer.
The Christian

IDEALISM

1 If a man hasn't discovered something that he
would die for, he isn't fit to live.
Martin Luther King (1929–68) US Black civil-rights
leader.
Speech, Detroit, 23 June 1963

2 If you can talk with crowds and keep your
virtue,
Or walk with Kings – nor lose the common
touch,
If neither foes nor loving friends can hurt you,
If all men count with you, but none too much;
If you can fill the unforgiving minute
With sixty seconds' worth of distance run,
Yours is the Earth and everything that's in it,
And – which is more – you'll be a Man my
son!
Rudyard Kipling (1865–1936) Indian-born British writer.
If

3 Ideal mankind would abolish death, multiply
itself million upon million, rear up city upon
city, save every parasite alive, until the
accumulation of mere existence is swollen to
a horror.
D. H. Lawrence (1885–1930) British novelist.
St Mawr

4 An idealist is one who, on noticing that a
rose smells better than a cabbage, concludes
that it will also make better soup.
H. L. Mencken (1880–1956) US journalist.
Sententiae

5 Do not despair
For Johnny head-in-air;
He sleeps as sound
As Johnny underground.
John Sleigh Pudney (1909–77) British poet and writer.
For Johnny

6 A radical is a man with both feet firmly
planted in the air.
Franklin D. Roosevelt (1882–1945) US Democratic
president.
Broadcast, 26 Oct 1939

7 If a woman like Eva Peron with no ideals can
get that far, think how far I can go with all
the ideals that I have.
Margaret Thatcher (1925–) British politician and prime
minister.
The Sunday Times, 1980

IDEAS

See also opinions

1 What was once thought can never be
unthought.
Friedrich Dürrenmatt (1921–) Swiss writer.
The Physicists

2 A stand can be made against invasion by an
army; no stand can be made against invasion
by an idea.
Victor Hugo (1802–85) French writer.
Histoire d'un Crime, 'La Chute'

3 Many ideas grow better when transplanted

into another mind than in the one where they sprang up.
Oliver Wendell Holmes Jnr (1841–1935) US jurist.

4 Society goes on and on and on. It is the same with ideas.
Ramsey MacDonald (1866–1937) British statesman and prime minister.
Speech, 1935

5 An idea isn't responsible for the people who believe in it.
Don Marquis (1878–1937) US journalist.
New York Sun

6 A society made up of individuals who were all capable of original thought would probably be unendurable. The pressure of ideas would simply drive it frantic.
H. L. Mencken (1880–1956) US journalist.
Notebooks, 'Minority Report'

IDLENESS

See also bed, laziness, leisure, unemployment

1 The devil finds work for idle hands to do.
Proverb

2 The dreadful burden of having nothing to do.
Nicolas Boileau (1636–1711) French writer.
Épitres, XI

3 Idleness is only the refuge of weak minds.
Earl of Chesterfield (1694–1773) English statesman.
Letter to his son, 20 July 1749

4 What is this life if, full of care,
We have no time to stand and stare?
W. H. Davies (1871–1940) British poet.
Leisure

5 It is impossible to enjoy idling thoroughly unless one has plenty of work to do.
Jerome K. Jerome (1859–1927) British humorist.
Idle Thoughts of an Idle Fellow

6 I like work; it fascinates me. I can sit and look at it for hours. I love to keep it by me; the idea of getting rid of it nearly breaks my heart.
Jerome K. Jerome
Three Men in a Boat, Ch. 15

7 We would all be idle if we could.
Samuel Johnson (1709–84) British lexicographer.
Life of Johnson (J. Boswell), Vol. III

8 Young people ought not to be idle. It is very bad for them.
Margaret Thatcher (1925–) British politician and prime minister.
The Times, 1984

9 I am happiest when I am idle. I could live for months without performing any kind of labour, and at the expiration of that time I should feel fresh and vigorous enough to go

right on in the same way for numerous more months.
Artemus Ward (Charles Farrar Browne; 1834–67) US humorous writer.
Pyrotechny

10 For Satan finds some mischief still
For idle hands to do.
Isaac Watts (1674–1748) English theologian and hymn writer.
Divine Songs for Children, 'Against Idleness and Mischief'

IGNORANCE

See also foolishness, innocence, innocence of childhood, stupidity

1 He that knows little, often repeats it.
Proverb

2 He that knows nothing, doubts nothing.
Proverb

3 What you don't know can't hurt you.
Proverb

4 Happy the hare at morning, for she cannot read
The Hunter's waking thoughts.
W. H. Auden (1907–73) British poet.
The Dog Beneath the Skin (with Christopher Isherwood)

5 She is an excellent creature, but she never can remember which came first, the Greeks or the Romans.
Benjamin Disraeli (1804–81) British statesman.
Referring to his wife
Attrib.

6 To each his suff'rings, all are men,
Condemn'd alike to groan;
The tender for another's pain,
Th' unfeeling for his own.
Yet ah! why should they know their fate?
Since sorrow never comes too late,
And happiness too swiftly flies.
Thought would destroy their paradise.
No more; where ignorance is bliss,
'Tis folly to be wise.
Thomas Gray (1716–71) British poet.
Ode on a Distant Prospect of Eton College

7 Alas, regardless of their doom,
The little victims play!
Thomas Gray
Ode on a Distant Prospect of Eton College

8 I wish you would read a little poetry sometimes. Your ignorance cramps my conversation.
Anthony Hope (Sir Anthony Hope Hawkins; 1863–1933) British novelist.
The Dolly Dialogues

9 Ignorance, madam, pure ignorance.
Samuel Johnson (1709–84) British lexicographer.
His reply on being questioned, by a lady reader of his *Dictionary*, why he had incorrectly defined 'pastern' as the 'knee' of a horse
Life of Johnson (J. Boswell), Vol. I

10 The ignorant man always adores what he cannot understand.
Cesare Lombroso (1853–1909) Italian criminologist.
The Man of Genius, Pt. III, Ch. 3

11 I count religion but a childish toy,
And hold there is no sin but ignorance.
Christopher Marlowe (1564–93) English dramatist.
The Jew of Malta, Prologue

12 From ignorance our comfort flows,
The only wretched are the wise.
Matthew Prior (1664–1721) British poet.
To the Hon. Charles Montague

13 He hath never fed of the dainties that are bred in a book; he hath not eat paper, as it were; he hath not drunk ink; his intellect is not replenished.
William Shakespeare (1564–1616) English dramatist.
Love's Labour's Lost, IV:2

14 He that is robb'd, not wanting what is stol'n,
Let him not know't, and he's not robb'd at all.
William Shakespeare
Othello, III:3

15 What you don't know would make a great book.
Sydney Smith (1771–1845) British clergyman and essayist.
Memoir (Lady Holland)

16 Somebody else's ignorance is bliss.
Jack Vance (1916–) US writer.
Star King

17 Ignorance is like a delicate exotic fruit; touch it, and the bloom is gone.
Oscar Wilde (1854–1900) Irish-born British dramatist.
The Importance of Being Earnest, I

ILLEGITIMACY

1 If you please, ma'am, it was a very little one.
Captain Frederick Marryat (1792–1848) British novelist.
Said by the nurse to excuse the fact that she had had an illegitimate baby
Mr. Midshipman Easy, Ch. 3

2 It serves me right for putting all my eggs in one bastard.
Dorothy Parker (1893–1967) US writer.
Said on going into hospital to get an abortion
You Might as Well Live (J. Keats), Pt. II, Ch. 3

3 There are no illegitimate children – only illegitimate parents.
Léon R. Yankwich US lawyer.
Decision, State District Court, Southern District of California, Jun 1928, quoting columnist O. O. McIntyre

ILLNESS

See also doctors, health, medicine, remedies

1 Across the wires the electric message came:
'He is no better, he is much the same.'
Alfred Austin (1835–1913) British poet.
Generally attrib. to Austin but there is no definite evidence that he wrote it
On the Illness of the Prince of Wales

2 'Ye can call it influenza if ye like,' said Mrs Machin. 'There was no influenza in my young days. We called a cold a cold.'
Arnold Bennett (1867–1931) British novelist.
The Card, Ch. 8

3 My message to the businessmen of this country when they go abroad on business is that there is one thing above all they can take with them to stop them catching Aids, and that is the wife.
Edwina Currie (1946–) British politician.
The Observer, 'Sayings of the Week', 15 Feb 1987

4 Much of the world's work, it has been said, is done by men who do not feel quite well. Marx is a case in point.
John Kenneth Galbraith (1908–) US economist.
The Age of Uncertainty, Ch. 3

5 Hungry Joe collected lists of fatal diseases and arranged them in alphabetical order so that he could put his finger without delay on any one he wanted to worry about.
Joseph Heller (1923–) US novelist.
Catch-22, Ch. 17

6 For that old enemy the gout
Had taken him in toe!
Thomas Hood (1799–1845) British poet.
Lieutenant Luff

7 How few of his friends' houses would a man choose to be at when he is sick.
Samuel Johnson (1709–84) British lexicographer.
Life of Johnson (J. Boswell), Vol. IV

8 Oh what can ail thee, knight at arms
Alone and palely loitering;
The sedge has wither'd from the lake,
And no birds sing.
John Keats (1795–1821) British poet.
La Belle Dame Sans Merci

9 How sickness enlarges the dimensions of a man's self to himself.
Charles Lamb (1775–1834) British essayist.
Last Essays of Elia, 'The Convalescent'

10 I am only half there when I am ill, and so there is only half a man to suffer. To suffer in one's whole self is so great a violation, that it is not to be endured.
D. H. Lawrence (1885–1930) British novelist.
Letter to Catherine Carswell, 16 Apr 1916

11 Too late for fruit, too soon for flowers.
Walter De La Mare (1873–1956) British poet.
On being asked, as he lay seriously ill, whether he would like some fruit or flowers
Attrib.

12 Only do always in health what you have often promised to do when you are sick.
Sigismund (1368–1437) Holy Roman Emperor.
His advice on achieving happiness
Biographiana, Vol. I

13 Illness is the night-side of life, a more onerous citizenship. Everyone who is born holds dual citizenship, in the kingdom of the well and in the kingdom of the sick. Although we all prefer to use only the good passport, sooner or later each of us is obliged, at least for a spell, to identify ourselves as citizens of that other place.
Susan Sontag (1933–) US novelist and essayist.
Illness as Metaphor

14 Most of the time we think we're sick, it's all in the mind.
Thomas Wolfe (1900–38) US novelist.
Look Homeward, Angel, Pt. I, Ch. 1

IMAGINATION

1 The primary imagination I hold to be the living power and prime agent of all human perception, and as a repetition in the finite mind of the eternal act of creation in the infinite I AM.
Samuel Taylor Coleridge (1772–1834) British poet.
Biographia Literaria, Ch. 13

2 The Fancy is indeed no other than a mode of memory emancipated from the order of time and space.
Samuel Taylor Coleridge
Biographia Literaria, Ch. 13

3 Art is ruled uniquely by the imagination.
Benedetto Croce (1866–1952) Italian philosopher.
Esthetic, Ch. 1

4 She has no imagination and that means no compassion.
Michael Foot (1913–) British Labour politician and journalist.
Referring to Margaret Thatcher
Attrib.

5 Were it not for imagination, Sir, a man would be as happy in the arms of a chambermaid as of a Duchess.
Samuel Johnson (1709–84) British lexicographer.
Life of Johnson (J. Boswell), Vol. III

6 I am certain of nothing but the holiness of the heart's affections and the truth of imagination – what the imagination seizes as beauty must be truth – whether it existed before or not.
John Keats (1795–1821) British poet.
Letter to Benjamin Bailey, 22 Nov 1817

7 Picture yourself in a boat on a river with tangerine trees and marmalade skies.

Somebody calls you, you answer quite slowly a girl with kaleidoscope eyes.
John Lennon (1940–80) British rock musician.
Lucy in the Sky with Diamonds (with Paul McCartney)

8 His imagination resembled the wings of an ostrich. It enabled him to run, though not to soar.
Lord Macaulay (1800–59) British historian.
Essays and Biographies, 'John Dryden'. *Edinburgh Review*

IMITATION

See also originality

1 A lotta cats copy the Mona Lisa, but people still line up to see the original.
Louis Armstrong (1900–71) US jazz trumpeter.
When asked whether he objected to people copying his style
Attrib.

2 Imitation is the sincerest form of flattery.
Charles Caleb Colton (?1780–1832) British clergyman and writer.
Lacon, Vol. I

3 When people are free to do as they please, they usually imitate each other.
Eric Hoffer (1902–) US writer.
The Passionate State of Mind

4 A mere copier of nature can never produce anything great.
Joshua Reynolds (1723–92) British portrait painter.
Discourse to Students of the Royal Academy, 14 Dec 1770

5 He who resolves never to ransack any mind but his own, will be soon reduced, from mere barrenness, to the poorest of all imitations; he will be obliged to imitate himself, and to repeat what he has before often repeated.
Joshua Reynolds
Discourse to Students of the Royal Academy, 10 Dec 1774

6 Of all my verse, like not a single line;
But like my title, for it is not mine.
That title from a better man I stole;
Ah, how much better, had I stol'n the whole!
Robert Louis Stevenson (1850–94) Scottish writer.
Underwoods, Foreword

7 You will, Oscar, you will.
James Whistler (1834–1903) US painter.
Replying to Oscar Wilde's exclamation 'I wish I had said that!'
Attrib.

IMMORTALITY

See also eternity, mortality, posterity

1 I don't want to achieve immortality through my work . . . I want to achieve it through not dying.
Woody Allen (Allen Stewart Konigsberg; 1935–) US film actor.
Woody Allen and His Comedy (E. Lax)

2 No young man believes he shall ever die.
William Hazlitt (1778–1830) British essayist.
On the Feeling of Immortality in Youth

3 He had decided to live for ever or die in the attempt.
Joseph Heller (1923–) US novelist.
Catch-22, Ch. 3

4 I detest life-insurance agents; they always argue that I shall some day die, which is not so.
Stephen Leacock (1869–1944) English-born Canadian economist and humorist.
Literary Lapses, 'Insurance. Up to Date'

5 Stuck with placards for 'Deathless', that bitter beer that tastes sweet to its drinkers.
Rainer Maria Rilke (1875–1926) Austrian poet.
Duineser Elegien, X

6 We feel and know that we are eternal.
Benedict Spinoza (Baruch de Spinoza; 1632–77) Dutch philosopher.
Ethics

7 A slumber did my spirit seal;
I had no human fears:
She seemed a thing that could not feel
The touch of earthly years.

No motion has she now, no force;
She neither hears nor sees;
Rolled round in earth's diurnal course,
With rocks, and stones, and trees.
William Wordsworth (1770–1850) British poet.
A Slumber did my Spirit seal

IMPERFECTION

See also mistakes, perfection, weakness

1 Accidents will happen in the best regulated families.
Proverb

2 No man is infallible.
Proverb

3 To err is human.
Proverb

4 Watch and pray, that ye enter not into temptation: the spirit indeed is willing, but the flesh is weak.
Bible: Matthew
26:41

5 He has his talents, his vast and cultivated mind, his vivid imagination, his independence of soul and his high-souled principles of honour. But then – ah, these Buts! Saint Preux never kicked the fireirons, nor made puddings in his tea cup.
Jane Welsh Carlyle (1801–66) The wife of Thomas Carlyle.
Referring to her husband, Thomas Carlyle
Letter to a friend, July 1821

6 When you have faults, do not fear to abandon them.
Confucius (K'ung Fu-tzu; 551–479 BC) Chinese philosopher.
Analects

7 Even imperfection itself may have its ideal or perfect state.
Thomas De Quincey (1785–1859) British writer.
Murder Considered as one of the Fine Arts

8 We must touch his weaknesses with a delicate hand. There are some faults so nearly allied to excellence, that we can scarce weed out the fault without eradicating the virtue.
Oliver Goldsmith (1728–74) Irish-born British writer.
The Good-Natured Man, I

9 I'm aggrieved when sometimes even excellent Homer nods.
Horace (Quintus Horatius Flaccus; 65–8 BC) Roman poet.
Ars Poetica

10 People often say that, by pointing out to a man the faults of his mistress, you succeed only in strengthening his attachment to her, because he does not believe you; yet how much more so if he does!
Marcel Proust (1871–1922) French novelist.
À la recherche du temps perdu: Du côté de chez Swann

11 We only confess our little faults to persuade people that we have no large ones.
Duc de la Rochefoucauld (1613–80) French writer.
Maximes, 327

12 If we had no faults of our own, we would not take so much pleasure in noticing those of others.
Duc de la Rochefoucauld
Maximes, 31

13 Oh. I have got lots of human weaknesses, who hasn't?
Margaret Thatcher (1925–) British politician and prime minister.
The Times, 1983

14 We are none of us infallible – not even the youngest of us.
William Hepworth Thompson (1810–86) British academic.
Referring to G. W. Balfour, who was a junior fellow of Trinity College at the time
Collections and Recollections (G. W. E. Russell), Ch. 18

IMPERTINENCE

See also boldness, frankness, rudeness

1 He has to learn that petulance is not sarcasm, and that insolence is not invective.
Benjamin Disraeli (1804–81) British statesman.
Said of Sir C. Wood
Speech, House of Commons, 16 Dec 1852

2 Must! Is *must* a word to be addressed to princes? Little man, little man! thy father, if

he had been alive, durst not have used that word.
Elizabeth I (1533–1603) Queen of England.
Said to Robert Cecil, on her death bed
A Short History of the English People (J. R. Green), Ch. 7

IMPETUOSITY

See also haste, spontaneity

1 In me the need to talk is a primary impulse, and I can't help saying right off what comes to my tongue.
Miguel de Cervantes (1547–1616) Spanish novelist.
Don Quixote, Pt. I, Ch. 30

2 There are some who speak one moment before they think.
Jean de La Bruyère (1645–96) French satirist.
Les Caractères

3 Celerity is never more admir'd
Than by the negligent.
William Shakespeare (1564–1616) English dramatist.
Antony and Cleopatra, III:7

4 A youth to whom was given
So much of earth – so much of heaven,
And such impetuous blood.
William Wordsworth (1770–1850) British poet.
Ruth

IMPORTANCE

See also triviality

1 Not to be sneezed at.
George Colman, the Younger (1762–1836) British dramatist.
Heir-at-Law, II:1

2 In heaven an angel is nobody in particular.
George Bernard Shaw (1856–1950) Irish dramatist and critic.
Man and Superman, 'Maxims for Revolutionists'

3 Art and religion first; then philosophy; lastly science. That is the order of the great subjects of life, that's their order of importance.
Muriel Spark (1918–) British novelist.
The Prime of Miss Jean Brodie, Ch. 2

IMPOSSIBILITY

See also possibility

1 However, one cannot put a quart in a pint cup.
Charlotte Perkins Gilman (1860–1935) US writer.
The Living of Charlotte Perkins Gilman

IMPRESSIONABILITY

See also gullibility

1 She had
A heart – how shall I say? – too soon made glad,

Too easily impressed.
Robert Browning (1812–89) British poet.
My Last Duchess

2 Like a cushion, he always bore the impress of the last man who sat on him.
David Lloyd George (1863–1945) British Liberal statesman.
Referring to Lord Derby
Attrib. in *The Listener*, 7 Sep 1978. This remark is also credited to Earl Haig

3 Give me a girl at an impressionable age, and she is mine for life.
Muriel Spark (1918–) British novelist.
The Prime of Miss Jean Brodie, Ch. 1

IMPRISONMENT

See also freedom, oppression, slavery

1 A robin redbreast in a cage
Puts all Heaven in a rage.
William Blake (1757–1827) British poet.
Auguries of Innocence

2 O! dreadful is the check – intense the agony
When the ear begins to hear, and the eye begins to see;
When the pulse begins to throb – the brain to think again –
The soul to feel the flesh, and the flesh to feel the chain.
Emily Brontë (1818–48) British novelist.
The Prisoner

3 She's only a bird in a gilded cage.
A. J. Lamb (1870–1928) British songwriter.
Song title

4 Stone walls do not a prison make,
Nor iron bars a cage.
Richard Lovelace (1618–58) English poet.
To Althea, from Prison

5 Forget the outside world. Life has different laws in here. This is Campland, an invisible country. It's not in the geography books, or the psychology books or the history books. This is the famous country where ninety-nine men weep while one laughs.
Alexander Solzhenitsyn (1918–) Soviet novelist.
The Love-Girl and the Innocent, I:3

6 We think caged birds sing, when indeed they cry.
John Webster (1580–1625) English dramatist.
The White Devil, V:4

7 I never saw a man who looked
With such a wistful eye
Upon that little tent of blue
Which prisoners call the sky.
Oscar Wilde (1854–1900) Irish-born British dramatist.
The Ballad of Reading Gaol, I:3

8 The Governor was strong upon
The Regulations Act:

The Doctor said that Death was but
A scientific fact:
And twice a day the Chaplain called,
And left a little tract.
Oscar Wilde
The Ballad of Reading Gaol, III:3

9 Something was dead in each of us,
And what was dead was Hope.
Oscar Wilde
The Ballad of Reading Gaol, III:31

10 I know not whether Laws be right,
Or whether Laws be wrong;
All that we know who lie in gaol
Is that the wall is strong;
And that each day is like a year,
A year whose days are long.
Oscar Wilde
The Ballad of Reading Gaol, V:1

11 If this is the way Queen Victoria treats her
prisoners, she doesn't deserve to have any.
Oscar Wilde
Complaining at having to wait in the rain for transport to take
him to prison
Attrib.

IMPROVEMENT

See also progress

1 He so improved the city that he justly
boasted that he found it brick and left it
marble.
Augustus (63 BC–14 AD) Roman emperor.
Referring to Rome
The Lives of the Caesars (Suetonius), 'Augustus'

2 I've got to admit it's getting better.
It's a little better all the time.
John Lennon (1940–80) British rock musician.
Getting Better (with Paul McCartney)

3 It is a stupidity second to none, to busy
oneself with the correction of the world.
Molière (Jean Baptiste Poquelin; 1622–73) French
dramatist.
Le Misanthrope, I:1

INATTENTION

1 Thank you for the manuscript; I shall lose no
time in reading it.
Benjamin Disraeli (1804–81) British statesman.
His customary reply to those who sent him unsolicited
manuscripts
Irreverent Social History (F. Muir)

2 That should assure us of at least forty-five
minutes of undisturbed privacy.
Dorothy Parker (1893–1967) US writer.
Pressing a button marked NURSE during a stay in hospital
The Algonquin Wits (R. Drennan)

3 Donsmanship . . . 'the art of criticizing without
actually listening'.
Stephen Potter (1900–69) British writer.
Lifemanship, Ch. 6

4 I murdered my grandmother this morning.
Franklin D. Roosevelt (1882–1945) US Democratic
president.
His habitual greeting to any guest at the White House he sus-
pected of paying no attention to what he said
Ear on Washington (D. McClellan)

INCOMPETENCE

1 This island is almost made of coal and
surrounded by fish. Only an organizing genius
could produce a shortage of coal and fish in
Great Britain at the same time.
Aneurin Bevan (1897–1960) British Labour politician.
Speech, Blackpool, 18 May 1945

2 The grotesque chaos of a Labour council – a
Labour council – hiring taxis to scuttle
around a city handing out redundancy notices
to its own workers.
Neil Kinnock (1942–) British politician.
Attacking militant members in Liverpool
Speech, Labour Party Conference, Bournemouth, 1985

3 He really deserves some sort of decoration
. . . a medal inscribed 'For Vaguery in the
Field'.
John Osborne (1929–) British dramatist.
Look Back in Anger, I

4 Work is accomplished by those employees
who have not yet reached their level of
incompetence.
Laurence J. Peter (1919–) Canadian writer.
The Peter Principle

5 Madame, there you sit with that magnificent
instrument between your legs, and all you
can do is *scratch* it!
Arturo Toscanini (1867–1957) Italian conductor.
Rebuking an incompetent woman cellist
Attrib.

6 His ideas of first-aid stopped short at
squirting soda-water.
P. G. Wodehouse (1881–1975) British humorous
novelist.
My Man Jeeves, 'Doing Clarence a Bit of Good'

INCONVENIENCE

1 Death and taxes and childbirth! There's never
any convenient time for any of them!
Margaret Mitchell (1909–49) US novelist.
Gone with the Wind

INDECISION

See also uncertainty

1 I will have nothing to do with a man who can
blow hot and cold with the same breath.
Aesop (6th century BC) Reputed Greek writer of fables.
Fables, 'The Man and the Satyr'

2 I must have a prodigious quantity of mind; it

takes me as much as a week, sometimes, to make it up.
Mark Twain (Samuel Langhorne Clemens; 1835–1910) US writer.
The Innocents Abroad, Ch. 7

INDEPENDENCE

See also self-reliance, society

1 I'm short enough and ugly enough to succeed on my own.
Woody Allen (Allen Stewart Konigsberg; 1935–) US film actor.
Play It Again Sam

2 When in the course of human events, it becomes necessary for one people to dissolve the political bonds which have connected them with another, and to assume among the powers of the earth the separate and equal station to which the laws of nature and of Nature's God entitle them, a decent respect to the opinions of mankind requires that they should declare the causes which impel them to the separation.
Thomas Jefferson (1743–1826) US statesman.
Declaration of Independence, Preamble

3 I think it much better that . . . every man paddle his own canoe.
Captain Frederick Marryat (1792–1848) British novelist.
Settlers in Canada, Ch. 8

INDIFFERENCE

See also insensitivity

1 But what is past my help is past my care.
Francis Beaumont (1584–1616) English dramatist.
With John Fletcher
The Double Marriage, I:1

2 Nothing is so fatal to religion as indifference, which is, at least, half infidelity.
Edmund Burke (1729–97) British politician.
Letter to William Smith, 29 Jan 1795

3 Sir, I view the proposal to hold an international exhibition at San Francisco with an equanimity bordering on indifference.
W. S. Gilbert (1836–1911) British dramatist.
Gilbert, His Life and Strife (Hesketh Pearson)

4 It's no go the picture palace, it's no go the stadium,
It's no go the country cot with a pot of pink geraniums,
It's no go the Government grants, it's no go the elections,
Sit on your arse for fifty years and hang your hat on a pension.
Louis MacNeice (1907–63) Irish-born British poet.
Bagpipe Music

5 At length the morn and cold indifference came.
Nicholas Rowe (1674–1718) English dramatist.
The Fair Penitent, I:1

6 I don't care a twopenny damn what becomes of the ashes of Napoleon Bonaparte.
Duke of Wellington (1769–1852) British general and statesman.
Attrib.

7 I hear it was charged against me that I sought to destroy institutions,
But really I am neither for nor against institutions.
Walt Whitman (1819–92) US poet.
I Hear It was Charged against Me

INDIVIDUALITY

See also difference, opinions, taste

1 Here's tae us wha's like us?
Gey few, and they're a' deid.
Anonymous
Scottish toast

2 Nature made him, and then broke the mould.
Ludovico Ariosto (1474–1533) Italian poet.
Referring to Charlemagne's paladin, Roland
Orlando furioso

3 It is the common wonder of all men, how among so many million of faces, there should be none alike.
Thomas Browne (1605–82) English physician and writer.
Religio Medici, Pt. II

4 We boil at different degrees.
Ralph Waldo Emerson (1803–82) US poet and essayist.
Society and Solitude, 'Eloquence'

INDOCTRINATION

See also education

1 Their teacher had advised them not to read Tolstoy novels, because they were very long and would easily confuse the clear ideas which they had learned from reading critical studies of him.
Alexander Solzhenitsyn (1918–) Soviet novelist.
The First Circle, Ch. 40

2 This universal, obligatory force-feeding with lies is now the most agonizing aspect of existence in our country – worse than all our material miseries, worse than any lack of civil liberties.
Alexander Solzhenitsyn
Letter to Soviet Leaders, 6

3 For us, the tasks of education in socialism were closely integrated with those of fighting. Ideas that enter the mind under fire remain there securely and for ever.
Leon Trotsky (Lev Davidovich Bronstein; 1879–1940) Russian revolutionary.
My Life, Ch. 35

INDULGENCE

1 Love is a boy, by poets styl'd,
Then spare the rod, and spoil the child.
Samuel Butler (1612–80) English satirist.
Hudibras, Pt. II

2 Every luxury was lavished on you – atheism,
breast-feeding, circumcision. I had to make
my own way.
Joe Orton (1933–67) British dramatist.
Loot, I

INDUSTRIAL RELATIONS

See also diplomacy, strikes

1 British management doesn't seem to
understand the importance of the human
factor.
Charles, Prince of Wales (1948–) Eldest son of
Elizabeth II.
Speech, Parliamentary and Scientific Committee lunch, 21 Feb
1979

2 Industrial relations are like sexual relations.
It's better between two consenting parties.
Vic Feather (1908–76) British trade-union leader.
Guardian Weekly, 8 Aug 1976

3 It might be said that it is the ideal of the
employer to have production without
employees and the ideal of the employee is
to have income without work.
E. F. Schumacher (1911–77) German-born economist.
The Observer, 'Sayings of the Week', 4 May 1975

INFERIORITY

See also equality, mediocrity

1 I just met X in the street, I stopped for a
moment to exchange ideas, and now I feel
like a complete idiot.
Heinrich Heine (1797–1856) German poet and writer.
Autant en apportent les mots (Pedrazzini)

2 Wherever an inferiority complex exists, there
is a good reason for it. There is always
something inferior there, although not just
where we persuade ourselves that it is.
Carl Gustav Jung (1875–1961) Swiss psychoanalyst.
Interview, 1943

3 It is an infallible sign of the second-rate in
nature and intellect to make use of
everything and everyone.
Ada Beddington Leverson (1862–1933) British writer.
The Limit

4 There's no such thing as a bad Picasso, but
some are less good than others.
Pablo Picasso (1881–1973) Spanish painter.
Come to Judgment (A. Whitman)

5 No one can make you feel inferior without
your consent.
Eleanor Roosevelt (1884–1962) US writer and lecturer.
This is My Story

6 A king of shreds and patches.
William Shakespeare (1564–1616) English dramatist.
Hamlet, III:4

INFINITY

1 The Desire of Man being Infinite, the
possession is Infinite, and himself Infinite.
William Blake (1757–1827) British poet.
There is no Natural Religion

2 I cannot help it; – in spite of myself, infinity
torments me.
Alfred de Musset (1810–57) French dramatist and poet.
L'Espoir en Dieu

INFLEXIBILITY

See also determination, stubbornness

1 Whenever you accept our views we shall be
in full agreement with you.
Moshe Dayan (1915–81) Israeli general.
Said to Cyrus Vance during Arab-Israeli negotiations
The Observer, 'Sayings of the Week', 14 Aug 1977

2 You cannot shake hands with a clenched fist.
Indira Gandhi (1917–84) Indian stateswoman.
Remark at a press conference, New Delhi, 19 Oct 1971

3 U-turn if you want to. The lady's not for
turning.
Margaret Thatcher (1925–) British politician and prime
minister.
Speech, Conservative Conference, 1980

4 Minds like beds always made up,
(more stony than a shore)
unwilling or unable.
William Carlos Williams (1883–1963) US poet.
Patterson, I, Preface

INFLUENCE

See also inspiration, power

1 Though Rome's gross yoke
Drops off, no more to be endured,
Her teaching is not so obscured
By errors and perversities,
That no truth shines athwart the lies.
Robert Browning (1812–89) British poet.
Christmas Eve, XI

2 How to Win Friends and Influence People.
Dale Carnegie (1888–1955) US lecturer and writer.
Book title

3 The proper time to influence the character of
a child is about a hundred years before he is
born.
Dean Inge (1860–1954) British churchman.
The Observer, 21 June, 1929

4 We have met too late. You are too old for
me to have any effect on you.
James Joyce (1882–1941) Irish novelist.
On meeting W. B. Yeats
James Joyce (R. Ellmann)

5 Practical men, who believe themselves to be quite exempt from any intellectual influences, are usually the slaves of some defunct economist. Madmen in authority, who hear voices in the air, are distilling their frenzy from some academic scribbler of a few years back.
John Maynard Keynes (1883–1946) British economist.
The General Theory of Employment, Interest and Money, Bk. VI, Ch. 24

6 The great man . . . walks across his century and leaves the marks of his feet all over it, ripping out the dates on his goloshes as he passes.
Stephen Leacock (1869–1944) English-born Canadian economist and humorist.
Literary Lapses, 'The Life of John Smith'

7 So you're the little woman who wrote the book that made this great war!
Abraham Lincoln (1809–65) US statesman.
Said on meeting Harriet Beecher Stowe, the author of *Uncle Tom's Cabin* (1852), which stimulated opposition to slavery before the US Civil War
Abraham Lincoln: The War Years (Carl Sandburg), Vol. II, Ch. 39

8 Athens holds sway over all Greece; I dominate Athens; my wife dominates me; our newborn son dominates her.
Themistocles (c. 528–462 BC) Athenian statesman.
Explaining an earlier remark to the effect that his young son ruled all Greece
Attrib.

9 The hand that rocks the cradle
Is the hand that rules the world.
William Ross Wallace (1819–81) US poet and songwriter.
John o'London's Treasure Trove

10 The man who can dominate a London dinner-table can dominate the world.
Oscar Wilde (1854–1900) Irish-born British dramatist.
Attrib. by R. Aldington in his edition of Wilde

INGRATITUDE

1 Never look a gift horse in the mouth.
Proverb

2 And having looked to government for bread, on the very first scarcity they will turn and bite the hand that fed them.
Edmund Burke (1729–97) British politician.
Thoughts and Details on Scarcity

3 Our gratitude to most benefactors is the same as our feeling for dentists who have pulled our teeth. We acknowledge the good they have done and the evil from which they have delivered us, but we remember the pain they occasioned and do not love them very much.
Nicolas Chamfort (1741–94) French writer.
Maximes et pensées

4 Blow, blow, thou winter wind,

Thou art not so unkind
As man's ingratitude.
William Shakespeare (1564–1616) English dramatist.
As You Like It, II:7

5 Ingratitude, thou marble-hearted fiend,
More hideous when thou show'st thee in a child
Than the sea-monster!
William Shakespeare
King Lear I:4

6 I hate ingratitude more in a man
Than lying, vainness, babbling drunkenness,
Or any taint of vice whose strong corruption
Inhabits our frail blood.
William Shakespeare
Twelfth Night, III:4

INJUSTICE

1 Give a dog a bad name and hang him.
Proverb

2 Those who have had no share in the good fortunes of the mighty often have a share in their misfortunes.
Bertolt Brecht (1898–1956) German dramatist.
The Caucasian Chalk Circle

3 When one has been threatened with a great injustice, one accepts a smaller as a favour.
Jane Welsh Carlyle (1801–66) The wife of Thomas Carlyle.
Journal, 21 Nov 1855

4 'No, no!' said the Queen. 'Sentence first – verdict afterwards.'
Lewis Carroll (Charles Lutwidge Dodgson; 1832–98) British writer.
Alice's Adventures in Wonderland, Ch. 12

5 I feel as a horse must feel when the beautiful cup is given to the jockey.
Edgar Degas (1934–17) French artist.
On seeing one of his pictures sold at auction
Attrib.

6 To disarm the strong and arm the weak would be to change the social order which it's my job to preserve. Justice is the means by which established injustices are sanctioned.
Anatole France (Jacques Anatole François Thibault; 1844–1924) French writer.
Crainquebille

7 Undeservedly you will atone for the sins of your fathers.
Horace (Quintus Horatius Flaccus; 65–8 BC) Roman poet.
Odes, III

8 We was robbed!
Joe Jacobs (1896–1940) US boxing manager.
Complaining to the audience when the heavyweight title of Max Schmeling, whom he managed, was passed to Jack Sharkey
Attrib.

9 How could God do this to me after all I have done for him?

Louis XIV (1638–1715) French king.
On receiving news of the French army's defeat at the Battle of Blenheim
Saint-Simon at Versailles (L. Norton)

10 The government burns down whole cities while the people are forbidden to light lamps.

Mao Tse-Tung (1893–1976) Chinese communist leader.
Attrib.

11 That in the captain's but a choleric word Which in the soldier is flat blasphemy.

William Shakespeare (1564–1616) English dramatist.
Measure for Measure, II:2

12 I am a man
More sinn'd against than sinning.

William Shakespeare
King Lear, III:2

13 He was quite sure that he had been wronged. Not to be wronged is to forgo the first privilege of goodness.

H. G. Wells (1866–1946) British writer.
Bealby, Pt. IV, Ch. 1

14 There is something utterly nauseating about a system of society which pays a harlot 25 times as much as it pays its Prime Minister, 250 times as much as it pays its Members of Parliament, and 500 times as much as it pays some of its ministers of religion.

Harold Wilson (1916–) British politician and prime minister.
Referring to the case of Christine Keeler
Speech, House of Commons, June 1963

INNOCENCE

See also conscience, ignorance, innocence of childhood

1 Now I am ashamed of confessing that I have nothing to confess.

Fanny Burney (Frances Burney D'Arblay; 1752–1840) British novelist.
Evelina, Letter 59

2 Now my innocence begins to weigh me down.

Jean Racine (1639–99) French dramatist.
Andromaque, III:1

Innocence of childhood

See also age, children, ignorance, innocence

3 'But the Emperor has nothing on at all!' cried a little child.

Hans Christian Andersen (1805–75) Danish writer.
The Emperor's New Clothes

4 No, it is not only our fate but our business to lose innocence, and once we have lost that, it is futile to attempt a picnic in Eden.

Elizabeth Bowen (1899–1973) Irish novelist.
In *Orion III*, 'Out of a Book'

5 Ralph wept for the end of innocence, the darkness of man's heart, and the fall through the air of the true, wise friend called Piggy.

William Golding (1911–) British novelist.
Lord of the Flies, Ch. 12

6 I remember, I remember,
The fir trees dark and high;
I used to think their slender tops
Were close against the sky:
It was a childish ignorance,
But now 'tis little joy
To know I'm farther off from heav'n
Than when I was a boy.

Thomas Hood (1799–1845) British poet.
I Remember

7 Credulity is the man's weakness, but the child's strength.

Charles Lamb (1775–1834) British essayist.
Essays of Elia, 'Witches and other Night Fears'

8 I'd the upbringing a nun would envy and that's the truth. Until I was fifteen I was more familiar with Africa than my own body.

Joe Orton (1933–67) British dramatist.
Entertaining Mr Sloane, I

9 And the wild boys innocent as strawberries.

Dylan Thomas (1914–53) Welsh poet.
The hunchback in the park

10 There was a time when meadow, grove, and stream,
The earth, and every common sight,
To me did seem
Apparelled in celestial light,
The glory and the freshness of a dream.

William Wordsworth (1770–1850) British poet.
Ode. Intimations of Immortality, I

INNOVATION

See also conservatism, novelty, originality, progress

1 He that will not apply new remedies must expect new evils: for time is the greatest innovator.

Francis Bacon (1561–1626) English philosopher.
Essays, 'Of Innovations'

2 I once knew a chap who had a system of just hanging the baby on the clothes line to dry and he was greatly admired by his fellow citizens for having discovered a wonderful innovation on changing a diaper.

Damon Runyon (1884–1946) US writer.
Short Takes, 'Diaper Dexterity'

INNUENDO

See also meaning

1 There was an old man of Boulogne
Who sang a most topical song.
It wasn't the words
That frightened the birds,

But the horrible double-entendre.
Anonymous

2 I'm one of the ruins that Cromwell knocked about a bit.
Marie Lloyd (1870–1922) British music-hall singer.
Song title

3 Where more is meant than meets the ear.
John Milton (1608–74) English poet.
Il Penseroso

INSENSITIVITY

See also hurt, indifference

1 Miss Buss and Miss Beale
Cupid's darts do not feel.
How different from us,
Miss Beale and Miss Buss.
Anonymous
Written about the headmistresses of North London Collegiate School and Cheltenham Ladies' College, respectively

2 'There's been an accident' they said,
'Your servant's cut in half; he's dead!'
'Indeed!' said Mr Jones, 'and please
Send me the half that's got my keys.'
Harry Graham (1874–1936) British writer.
Ruthless Rhymes for Heartless Homes, 'Mr. Jones'

3 Just as the meanest and most vicious deeds require spirit and talent, so even the greatest deeds require a certain insensitiveness which on other occasions is called stupidity.
Georg Christoph Lichtenberg (1742–99) German physicist and writer.
Aphorisms

4 One would have to have a heart of stone to read the death of Little Nell without laughing.
Oscar Wilde (1854–1900) Irish-born British dramatist.
Lecturing upon Dickens
Lives of the Wits (H. Pearson)

INSIGNIFICANCE

See also triviality

1 There are some people who leave impressions not so lasting as the imprint of an oar upon the water.
Kate Chopin (1851–1904) US writer.
The Awakening, Ch. 34

2 She was one of those indispensables of whom one makes the discovery, when they are gone, that one can get on quite as well without them.
Aldous Huxley (1894–1964) British novelist.
Mortal Coils, 'Nuns at Luncheon'

INSINCERITY

See also cant, hypocrisy

1 Experience teaches you that the man who looks you straight in the eye, particularly if he adds a firm handshake, is hiding something.
Clifton Fadiman (1904–) US writer.
Enter, Conversing

2 He who praises everybody praises nobody.
Samuel Johnson (1709–84) British lexicographer.
Life of Johnson (J. Boswell), Vol. III

3 Went to hear Mrs Turner's daughter . . . play on the harpsichon; but, Lord! it was enough to make any man sick to hear her; yet was I forced to commend her highly.
Samuel Pepys (1633–1703) English diarist.
Diary, 1 May 1663

4 Most friendship is feigning, most loving mere folly.
William Shakespeare (1564–1616) English dramatist.
As You Like It, II:7

INSPIRATION

1 A spur in the head is worth two in the heel.
Proverb

2 Ninety per cent of inspiration is perspiration.
Proverb

3 I dare not alter these things; they come to me from above.
Alfred Austin (1835–1913) British poet.
When accused of writing ungrammatical verse
A Number of People (E. Marsh)

4 That I make poetry and give pleasure (if I give pleasure) are because of you.
Horace (Quintus Horatius Flaccus; 65–8 BC) Roman poet.
Odes, IV

5 Biting my truant pen, beating myself for spite:
'Fool!' said my Muse to me, 'look in thy heart and write.'
Philip Sidney (1554–86) English poet and courtier.
Sonnet, *Astrophel and Stella*

6 I did not write it. God wrote it. I merely did his dictation.
Harriet Beecher Stowe (1811–96) US novelist.
Referring to *Uncle Tom's Cabin*
Attrib.

7 The true God, the mighty God, is the God of ideas.
Alfred de Vigny (1797–1863) French writer.
La Bouteille à la mer

INSULTS

See also actors, criticism, politicians, rudeness

1 Sticks and stones may break my bones, but words will never hurt me.
Proverb

2 Lloyd George could not see a belt without hitting below it.
Margot Asquith (1865–1945) The second wife of Herbert Asquith.
The Autiobiography of Margot Asquith

3 She was a woman of mean understanding, little information, and uncertain temper.
Jane Austen (1775–1817) British novelist.
Pride and Prejudice, Ch. 1

4 I have known many an instance of a man writing a letter and forgetting to sign his name, but this is the only instance I have ever known of a man signing his name and forgetting to write the letter.
Henry Ward Beecher (1813–87) US Congregational minister.
Said on receiving a note containing the single word: 'Fool'
The Best Stories in the World (T. Masson)

5 Of course we all know that Morris was a wonderful all-round man, but the act of walking round him has always tired me.
Max Beerbohm (1872–1956) British writer.
Referring to William Morris
Conversations with Max (S. N. Behrman)

6 Come in, you Anglo-Saxon swine
And drink of my Algerian wine.
'Twill turn your eyeballs black and blue,
And damn well good enough for you.
Brendan Behan (1923–64) Irish playwright.
Painted as an advert on the window of a Paris café (the owner of which could not speak English)
My Life with Brendan (B. Behan)

7 I mock thee not, though I by thee am mockèd;
Thou call'st me madman, but I call thee blockhead.
William Blake (1757–1827) British poet.
To Flaxman

8 If there is anyone here whom I have not insulted, I beg his pardon.
Johannes Brahms (1833–97) German composer.
Said on leaving a gathering of friends
Brahms (P. Latham)

9 Macaulay is well for a while, but one wouldn't *live* under Niagara.
Thomas Carlyle (1795–1881) Scottish historian and essayist.
Notebook (R. M. Milnes)

10 An injury is much sooner forgotten than an insult.
Earl of Chesterfield (1694–1773) English statesman.
Letter to his son, 9 Oct 1746

11 The only time in his life he ever put up a fight was when we asked him for his resignation.
Georges Clemenceau (1841–1929) French statesman.
Referring to Marshal Joffre
Here I Lie (A.M. Thomson)

12 The Cat, the Rat, and Lovell our dog
Rule all England under a hog.
William Collingbourne (d. 1484) English landowner.
The cat was Sir William Catesby; the rat Sir Richard Ratcliffe; the dog Lord Lovell, who had a dog on his crest. The wild boar refers to the emblem of Richard III.
Chronicles (R. Holinshed), III

13 Your dexterity seems a happy compound of the smartness of an attorney's clerk and the intrigue of a Greek of the lower empire.
Benjamin Disraeli (1804–81) British statesman.
Speaking to Lord Palmerston
Attrib.

14 Good-morning, gentlemen both.
Elizabeth I (1533–1603) Queen of England.
When addressing a group of eighteen tailors
Sayings of Queen Elizabeth (Chamberlin)

15 A semi-house-trained polecat.
Michael Foot (1913–) British Labour politician.
Referring to Norman Tebbitt
Speech, House of Commons

16 Like being savaged by a dead sheep.
Denis Healey (1917–) British Labour politician.
Referring to the attack launched by Geoffrey Howe upon his Budget proposals
The Listener, 21 Dec 1978

17 Do you call that thing under your hat a head?
Ludwig Holberg (1684–1754) Danish dramatist.
Reply to the jibe, 'Do you call that thing on your head a hat?'
Anekdotenschatz (H. Hoffmeister)

18 In a disastrous fire in President Reagan's library both books were destroyed. And the real tragedy is that he hadn't finished colouring one.
Jonathan Hunt (1938–) New Zealand politician.
The Observer, 30 Aug 1981

19 Sir, your wife, under pretence of keeping a bawdy-house, is a receiver of stolen goods.
Samuel Johnson (1709–84) British lexicographer.
An example of the customary badinage between travellers on the Thames
Life of Johnson (J. Boswell), Vol. IV

20 Calumnies are answered best with silence.
Ben Jonson (1573–1637) English dramatist.
Volpone, II:2

21 They travel best in gangs, hanging around like clumps of bananas, thick skinned and yellow.
Neil Kinnock (1942–) British politician.
Referring to Tory critics
The Observer, 'Sayings of the Week', 22 Feb 1987

22 She only went to Venice because somebody told her she could walk down the middle of the street.
Neil Kinnock (1942–) British politician.
Referring to Margaret Thatcher who attended a meeting in Venice just before the 1987 election
Speech, Leeds, 9 June 1987

23 I'm sure he had a fork in the other.

Ada Beddington Leverson (1862–1933) British writer.
Reply when told by Oscar Wilde of a devoted *apache* (Parisian gangster) who used to follow him with a knife in one hand
Attrib.

24 When they circumcised Herbert Samuel they threw away the wrong bit.

David Lloyd George (1863–1945) British Liberal statesman.
Attrib. in *The Listener*, 7 Sept 1978

25 The answer is in the plural and they bounce.

Edwin Lutyens (1869–1944) British architect.
Attrib.

26 From the moment I picked up your book until I laid it down, I was convulsed with laughter. Some day I intend reading it.

Groucho Marx (Julius Marx; 1895–1977) US comedian and film actor.
The Last Laugh (S. J. Perelman)

27 I have forgotten more law than you ever knew, but allow me to say, I have not forgotten much.

John Maynard (1602–90) English judge.
Replying to Judge Jeffreys' suggestion that he was so old he had forgotten the law

28 And I don't feel the attraction of the Kennedys at all . . . I don't think they are Christians; they may be Catholics but they are not Christians, in my belief anyway.

Mary McCarthy (1912–) US novelist.
The Observer, 14 Oct 1979

29 Peel's smile: like the silver plate on a coffin.

Daniel O'Connell (1775–1847) Irish politician.
Referring to Sir Robert Peel; quoting J. P. Curran (1750–1817)
Hansard, 26 Feb 1835

30 I remember coming across him at the Grand Canyon and finding him peevish, refusing to admire it or even look at it properly. He was jealous of it.

J. B. Priestley (1894–1984) British novelist.
Referring to George Bernard Shaw
Thoughts In the Wilderness

31 Thou whoreson zed! thou unnecessary letter!

William Shakespeare (1564–1616) English dramatist.
King Lear, II:2

32 He has occasional flashes of silence, that make his conversation perfectly delightful.

Sydney Smith (1771–1845) British clergyman and essayist.
Referring to Lord Macaulay
Memoir (Lady Holland)

33 You silly moo.

Johnny Speight (1920–) British television scriptwriter.
Till Death Do Us Part

34 Okie use' to mean you was from Oklahoma. Now it means you're scum. Don't mean nothing itself, it's the way they say it.

John Steinbeck (1902–68) US novelist.
The Grapes of Wrath, Ch. 18

35 It's too late to apologize.

Arturo Toscanini (1867–1957) Italian conductor.
Retort to the insult 'Nuts to you!' shouted at him by a player he had just ordered from the stage during rehearsal
The Humor of Music (L. Humphrey)

36 A triumph of the embalmer's art.

Gore Vidal (1925–) US novelist.
Referring to Ronald Reagan
The Observer, 26 Apr 1981

37 A typical triumph of modern science to find the only part of Randolph that was not malignant and remove it.

Evelyn Waugh (1903–66) British novelist.
Remarking upon the news that Randolph Churchill had had a noncancerous lung removed
Attrib.

38 Perhaps not, but then you can't call yourself a great work of nature.

James Whistler (1834–1903) US painter.
Responding to a sitter's complaint that his portrait was not a great work of art
Whistler Stories (D. Seitz)

39 I do not mind the Liberals, still less do I mind the Country Party, calling me a bastard. In some circumstances I am only doing my job if they do. But I hope you will not publicly call me a bastard, as some bastards in the Caucus have.

Gough Whitlam (1916–) Australian statesman.
Speech to the Australian Labor Party, 9 June 1974

40 You have Van Gogh's ear for music.

Billy Wilder (Samuel Wilder; 1906–) Austrian-born US film director.
Said to Cliff Osmond
Attrib.

41 I have always said about Tony that he immatures with age.

Harold Wilson (1916–) British politician and prime minister.
Referring to Anthony Wedgwood Benn
The Chariot of Israel

42 If I had had to choose between him and a cockroach as a companion for a walking-tour, the cockroach would have had it by a short head.

P. G. Wodehouse (1881–1975) British humorous novelist.
My Man Jeeves, 'The Spot of Art'

INTEGRITY

See also honesty, morality, principles, righteousness, self, sincerity

1 Be so true to thyself, as thou be not false to others.

Francis Bacon (1561–1626) English philosopher.
Essays, 'Of Wisdom for a Man's Self'

2 Caesar's wife must be above suspicion.

Julius Caesar (100–44 BC) Roman general and statesman.
Said in justification of his divorce from Pompeia, after she was unwittingly involved in a scandal
Lives, 'Julius Caesar' (Plutarch)

3 I cannot and will not cut my conscience to fit this year's fashions, even though I long ago came to the conclusion that I was not a political person and could have no comfortable place in any political group.
Lillian Hellman (1905–84) US dramatist.
Letter to the US House of Representatives Committee on Un-American Activities, *The Nation*, 31 May 1952

4 Integrity without knowledge is weak and useless, and knowledge without integrity is dangerous and dreadful.
Samuel Johnson (1709–84) British lexicographer.
Rasselas, Ch. 41

5 It is necessary to the happiness of man that he be mentally faithful to himself. Infidelity does not consist in believing, or in disbelieving, it consists in professing to believe what one does not believe.
Thomas Paine (1737–1809) British writer.
The Age of Reason, Pt. I

6 Neither a borrower nor a lender be;
For loan oft loses both itself and friend,
And borrowing dulls the edge of husbandry.
This above all: to thine own self be true,
And it must follow, as the night the day,
Thou canst not then be false to any man.
William Shakespeare (1564–1616) English dramatist.
Hamlet, I:3

7 My strength is as the strength of ten,
Because my heart is pure.
Alfred, Lord Tennyson (1809–92) British poet.
Sir Galahad

INTELLECT

See also intelligence, mind, thinking

1 The voice of the intellect is a soft one, but it does not rest till it has gained a hearing.
Sigmund Freud (1856–1939) Austrian psychoanalyst.
The Future of an Illusion

2 Man is an intellectual animal, and therefore an everlasting contradiction to himself. His senses centre in himself, his ideas reach to the ends of the universe; so that he is torn in pieces between the two, without a possibility of its ever being otherwise.
William Hazlitt (1778–1830) British essayist.
Characteristics

3 We are thinking beings, and we cannot exclude the intellect from participating in any of our functions.
William James (1842–1910) US psychologist and philosopher.
Varieties of Religious Experience

4 The highest intellects, like the tops of mountains, are the first to catch and to reflect the dawn.
Lord Macaulay (1800–59) British historian.
Historical Essays Contributed to the 'Edinburgh Review', 'Sir James Mackintosh'

5 The higher the voice the smaller the intellect.
Ernest Newman (1868–1959) British music critic.
Attrib.

6 Intellect is invisible to the man who has none.
Arthur Schopenhauer (1788–1860) German philosopher.
Aphorismen zur Lebensweisheit

INTELLECTUALS

See also academics

1 An intellectual is a man who doesn't know how to park a bike.
Spiro Agnew (1918–) US politician.
Attrib.

2 To the man-in-the-street, who, I'm sorry to say
Is a keen observer of life,
The word Intellectual suggests straight away
A man who's untrue to his wife.
W. H. Auden (1907–73) British poet.
Note on Intellectuals

3 I've been called many things, but never an intellectual.
Tallulah Bankhead (1903–68) US actress.
Tallulah, Ch. 15

4 Intellectuals are people who believe that ideas are of more importance than values. That is to say, their own ideas and other people's values.
Gerald Brenan (Edward Fitzgerald Brenan; 1894–1987) British writer.
Thoughts in a Dry Season, 'Life'

5 An intellectual is someone whose mind watches itself.
Albert Camus (1913–60) French existentialist writer.
Notebooks, 1935–42

6 You will hear more good things on the outside of a stagecoach from London to Oxford than if you were to pass a twelvemonth with the undergraduates, or heads of colleges, of that famous university.
William Hazlitt (1778–1830) British essayist.
The Ignorance of the Learned

7 The trouble with me is, I belong to a vanishing race. I'm one of the intellectuals.
Robert E. Sherwood (1896–1955) US writer and dramatist.
The Petrified Forest

8 Do you think it pleases a man when he looks into a woman's eyes and sees a reflection of the British Museum Reading Room?
Muriel Spark (1918–) British novelist.
The Wit of Women (L. and M. Cowan)

9 What is a highbrow? It is a man who has

found something more interesting than women.

Edgar Wallace (1875–1932) British thriller writer.
Interview

INTELLIGENCE

See also intellect, knowledge, mind, perception, thinking, understanding, wisdom

1 The intelligent are to the intelligentsia what a man is to a gent.

Stanley Baldwin (1867–1947) British statesman.
Attrib.

2 I never heard tell of any clever man that came of entirely stupid people.

Thomas Carlyle (1795–1881) Scottish historian and essayist.
Speech, Edinburgh, 2 Apr 1886

3 A really intelligent man feels what other men only know.

Baron de Montesquieu (1688–1755) French writer.
Essai sur les causes qui peuvent affecter les esprits et les caractères

4 The more intelligence one has the more people one finds original. Commonplace people see no difference between men.

Blaise Pascal (1623–62) French philosopher and mathematician.
Pensées, I

5 The height of cleverness is to be able to conceal it.

Duc de la Rochefoucauld (1613–80) French writer.
Maximes, 245

6 Intelligence is quickness to apprehend as distinct from ability, which is capacity to act wisely on the thing apprehended.

A. N. Whitehead (1861–1947) British philosopher.
Dialogues, 135

7 All the unhappy marriages come from the husbands having brains. What good are brains to a man? They only unsettle him.

P. G. Wodehouse (1881–1975) British humorous novelist.
The Adventures of Sally

INTERFERING

See also curiosity

1 'If everybody minded their own business,' the Duchess said in a hoarse growl, 'the world would go round a deal faster than it does.'

Lewis Carroll (Charles Lutwidge Dodgson; 1832–98) British writer.
Alice's Adventures in Wonderland, Ch. 6

INTERRUPTIONS

1 On awaking he . . . instantly and eagerly wrote down the lines that are here preserved. At this moment he was unfortunately called out by a person on business from Porlock.

Samuel Taylor Coleridge (1772–1834) British poet.
Kubla Khan (preliminary note)

2 As I was saying the other day.

Luis Ponce de Léon (1527–91) Spanish monk.
Said on resuming a lecture interrupted by five years' imprisonment

3 Mr Wordsworth is never interrupted.

Mary Wordsworth (1770–1850) Wife of William Wordsworth.
Rebuking John Keats for interrupting a long monologue by William Wordsworth
Attrib.

INTRIGUE

1 Ay, now the plot thickens very much upon us.

Duke of Buckingham (1628–87) English politician.
The Rehearsal, III:1

2 Everybody was up to something, especially, of course, those who were up to nothing.

Noël Coward (1899–1973) British dramatist.
Future Indefinite

INTRODUCTIONS

1 'You look a little shy; let me introduce you to that leg of mutton,' said the Red Queen. 'Alice – Mutton; Mutton – Alice.'

Lewis Carroll (Charles Lutwidge Dodgson; 1832–98) British writer.
Through the Looking-Glass, Ch. 9

2 Do you suppose I could buy back my introduction to you?

Groucho Marx (Julius Marx; 1895–1977) US comedian.
Monkey Business

INVITATIONS

See also summons

1 'Will you walk into my parlour?' said a spider to a fly:
''Tis the prettiest little parlour that ever you did spy.'

Mary Howitt (1799–1888) British writer.
The Spider and the Fly

2 Come into the garden, Maud,
For the black bat, night, has flown,
Come into the garden, Maud,
I am here at the gate alone.

Alfred, Lord Tennyson (1809–92) British poet.
Maud, I

3 I always did like a man in uniform. And that one fits you grand. Why don't you come up sometime and see me?

Mae West (1892–1980) US actress.
Often misquoted as 'Come up and see me some time'
She Done Him Wrong, film 1933

IRELAND

See also Britain, Irish

1 I met wid Napper Tandy, and he took me by the hand,
And he said, 'How's poor ould Ireland, and how does she stand?'
She's the most disthressful country that iver yet was seen,
For they're hangin' men an' women there for the wearin' o' the Green.
Anonymous
The Wearin' o' the Green

2 Ulster will fight; Ulster will be right.
Randolph Churchill (1849–95) British Conservative politician.
Letter, 7 May 1886

3 By yesterday morning British troops were patrolling the streets of Belfast. I fear that once Catholics and Protestants get used to our presence they will hate us more than they hate each other.
Richard Crossman (1907–74) British politician.
Diaries, 17 Aug 1969

4 Thus you have a starving population, an absentee aristocracy, and an alien Church, and in addition the weakest executive in the world. That is the Irish Question.
Benjamin Disraeli (1804–81) British statesman.
Speech, House of Commons, 16 Feb 1844

5 I never met anyone in Ireland who understood the Irish question, except one Englishman who had only been there a week.
Keith Fraser (1867–1935) British politician.
Speech, House of Commons, May 1919

6 Worth seeing? yes; but not worth going to see.
Samuel Johnson (1709–84) British lexicographer.
Referring to the Giant's Causeway
Life of Johnson (J. Boswell), Vol. III

7 Ireland is the old sow that eats her farrow.
James Joyce (1882–1941) Irish novelist.
A Portrait of the Artist as a Young Man, Ch. 5

8 It is a symbol of Irish art. The cracked looking glass of a servant.
James Joyce
Ulysses

9 The problem with Ireland is that it's a country full of genius, but with absolutely no talent.
Hugh Leonard (1926–) Irish dramatist.
Said during an interview
The Times, Aug 1977

10 The harp that once through Tara's halls
The soul of music shed,
Now hangs as mute on Tara's walls
As if that soul were fled. –
So sleeps the pride of former days,
So glory's thrill is o'er;
And hearts, that once beat high for praise,
Now feel that pulse no more.
Thomas Moore (1779–1852) Irish poet.
Irish Melodies, 'The Harp that Once'

11 It is a city where you can see a sparrow fall to the ground, and God watching it.
Conor Cruise O'Brien (1917–) Irish diplomat and writer.
Referring to Dublin
Attrib.

12 I will drive a coach and six horses through the Act of Settlement.
Stephen Rice (1637–1715) English politician.
State of the Protestants of Ireland (W. King), Ch. 3

13 The English should give Ireland home rule – and reserve the motion picture rights.
Will Rogers (1879–1935) US actor and humorist.
Autobiography (published posthumously)

14 Before Irish Home Rule is conceded by the Imperial Parliament, England as the predominant member of the three kingdoms will have to be convinced of its justice and equity.
Lord Rosebery (1847–1929) British statesman.
Speech, House of Lords, 11 Mar 1894

15 The moment the very name of Ireland is mentioned, the English seem to bid adieu to common feeling, common prudence, and common sense, and to act with the barbarity of tyrants, and the fatuity of idiots.
Sydney Smith (1771–1845) British clergyman and essayist.
The Letters of Peter Plymley

16 I would have liked to go to Ireland, but my grandmother would not let me. Perhaps she thought I wanted to take the little place.
Wilhelm II (1859–1941) King of Prussia and Emperor of Germany.
Queen Victoria was his grandmother
Carson (H. Montgomery Hyde), Ch. 9

IRISH

See also British, Ireland

1 Put an Irishman on the spit, and you can always get another Irishman to baste him.
Proverb

2 Other people have a nationality. The Irish and the Jews have a psychosis.
Brendan Behan (1923–64) Irish playwright.
Richard's Cork Leg, I

3 The English and Americans dislike only *some* Irish – the same Irish that the Irish themselves detest, Irish writers – the ones that *think*.
Brendan Behan
Richard's Cork Leg, I

4 Not in vain is Ireland pouring itself all over the earth . . . The Irish, with their glowing

hearts and reverent credulity, are needed in this cold age of intellect and skepticism.
Lydia M. Child (1802–80) US abolitionist campaigner.
Letters from New York, Vol. I, No. 33, 8 Dec 1842

5 All races have produced notable economists, with the exception of the Irish who doubtless can protest their devotion to higher arts.
John Kenneth Galbraith (1908–) US economist.
The Age of Uncertainty, Ch. 1

6 Irish Americans are about as Irish as Black Americans are African.
Bob Geldof (1952–) Irish rock musician.
The Observer, 'Sayings of the Week', 22 Jun 1986

7 The Irish are a fair people; – they never speak well of one another.
Samuel Johnson (1709–84) British lexicographer.
Life of Johnson (J. Boswell), Vol. II

8 The Irish don't know what they want and are prepared to fight to the death to get it.
Sidney Littlewood (1895–1967) President of The Law Society.
Speech, 13 Apr 1961

IRREVOCABILITY

1 The die is cast.
Julius Caesar (100–44 BC) Roman general and statesman.
Said on crossing the Rubicon (49 BC) at the start of his campaign against Pompey
Attrib.

2 The Gods themselves cannot recall their gifts.
Alfred, Lord Tennyson (1809–92) British poet.
Tithonus

J

JEALOUSY

See also envy

1 For the ear of jealousy heareth all things: and the noise of murmurings is not hid.
Bible: Wisdom
1:10

2 The others were only my wives. But you, my dear, will be my widow.
Sacha Guitry (1885–1957) French actor and dramatist.
Allaying his fifth wife's jealousy of his previous wives
Speaker's and Toastmaster's Handbook (J. Brawle)

3 The secret of my success is that no woman has ever been jealous of me.
Elsa Maxwell (1883–1963) US songwriter, broadcaster, and actress.
The Natives were Friendly (Noël Barber)

4 O, beware, my lord, of jealousy;
It is the green-ey'd monster which doth mock
The meat it feeds on.
William Shakespeare (1564–1616) English dramatist.
Othello, III:3

5 O curse of marriage,
That we can call these delicate creatures ours,
And not their appetites! I had rather be a toad,
And live upon the vapour of a dungeon,
Than keep a corner in the thing I love
For others' uses.
William Shakespeare
Othello, III:3

JEWELLERY

1 Don't ever wear artistic jewellery; it wrecks a woman's reputation.
Colette (1873–1954) French novelist.
Gigi

JEWS

See also Nazism, prejudice, race, religion

1 Other people have a nationality. The Irish and the Jews have a psychosis.
Brendan Behan (1923–64) Irish playwright.
Richard's Cork Leg, I

2 The gentleman will please remember that when his half-civilized ancestors were hunting the wild boar in Silesia, mine were princes of the earth.
Judah Philip Benjamin (1811–84) US politician.
Replying to a senator of Germanic origin who had made an antisemitic remark
Attrib.

3 Now the Lord had said unto Abram, Get thee out of thy country, and from thy kindred, and from thy father's house, unto a land that I will shew thee:
And I will make of thee a great nation, and I will bless thee, and make thy name great; and thou shalt be a blessing:
And I will bless them that bless thee, and curse him that curseth thee: and in thee shall all families of the earth be blessed.
Bible: Genesis
12:1–3

4 How odd
Of God
To choose
The Jews.
William Norman Ewer (1885–1976) British writer.
For a reply see Cecil BROWNE
How Odd

5 But not so odd
As those who choose
A Jewish God,
But spurn the Jews.
Cecil Browne
In reply to EWER (above)

6 It is extremely difficult for a Jew to be converted, for how can he bring himself to believe in the divinity of – another Jew?
Heinrich Heine (1797–1856) German poet and writer.
Attrib.

7 For me this is a vital litmus test: no intellectual society can flourish where a Jew feels even slightly uneasy.
Paul Johnson (1928–) British editor.
The Sunday Times Magazine, 6 Feb 1977

8 The very best that is in the Jewish blood: a faculty for pure disinterestedness, and warm, physically warm love, that seems to make the corpuscles of the blood glow.
D. H. Lawrence (1885–1930) British novelist.
Kangaroo, Ch. 6

9 Pessimism is a luxury that a Jew never can allow himself.
Golda Meir (1898–1978) Russian-born Israeli stateswoman.
The Observer, 'Sayings of the Year', 29 Dec 1974

10 There are not enough prisons and concentration camps in Palestine to hold all the Jews who are ready to defend their lives and property.
Golda Meir
Speech, 2 May 1940

11 And furthermore did you know that behind the discovery of America there was a Jewish financier?
Mordecai Richler (1931–) Canadian novelist.
Cocksure, Ch. 24

12 Doctor, my doctor, what do you say – let's put the id back in yid!
Philip Roth (1933–) US novelist.
Portnoy's Complaint

13 A Jewish man with parents alive is a fifteen-year-old boy, and will remain a fifteen-year-old boy till they die.
Philip Roth
Portnoy's Complaint

14 I believe that the Jews have made a contribution to the human condition out of all proportion to their numbers: I believe them to be an immense people. Not only have they supplied the world with two leaders of the stature of Jesus Christ and Karl Marx, but they have even indulged in the luxury of following neither one nor the other.
Peter Ustinov (1921–) British actor.
Dear Me, Ch. 19

15 The law of dislike for the unlike will always prevail. And whereas the unlike is normally situated at a safe distance, the Jews bring the unlike into the heart of *every milieu*, and must there defend a frontier line as large as the world.
Israel Zangwill (1864–1926) British writer.
Speeches, Articles and Letters, 'The Jewish Race'

JOURNALISM

See also editors, media, newspapers

1 Have you noticed that life, real honest to goodness life, with murders and catastrophes and fabulous inheritances, happens almost exclusively in newspapers?
Jean Anouilh (1910–87) French dramatist.
The Rehearsal

2 What the proprietorship of these papers is aiming at is power, and power without responsibility – the prerogative of the harlot through the ages.
Stanley Baldwin (1867–1947) British statesman.
Attacking the press barons Lords Rothermere and Beaverbrook. It was first used by KIPLING. *See also* DEVONSHIRE (10th Duke)
Speech, election rally, 18 Mar 1931

3 'Christianity, of course but why journalism?'
Arthur Balfour (1848–1930) British statesman.
In reply to Frank Harris's remark, ' . . . all the faults of the age come from Christianity and journalism'
Autobiography (Margot Asquith), Ch. 10

4 Journalists say a thing that they know isn't true, in the hope that if they keep on saying it long enough it will be true.
Arnold Bennett (1867–1931) British novelist.
The Title, II

5 I read the newspaper avidly. It is my one form of continuous fiction.
Aneurin Bevan (1897–1960) British Labour politician.
The Observer, 'Sayings of the Week', 3 Apr 1960

6 When a dog bites a man that is not news, but when a man bites a dog that is news.
John B. Bogart (1845–1920) US journalist.
Sometimes attributed to Charles Dana and Amos Cummings
Attrib.

7 Journalism is the only job that requires no degrees, no diplomas and no specialised knowledge of any kind.
Patrick Campbell (1913–80) British humorous writer and editor.
My Life and Easy Times

8 Journalism largely consists of saying 'Lord Jones is dead' to people who never knew Lord Jones was alive.
G. K. Chesterton (1874–1936) British writer.
Attrib.

9 Literature is the art of writing something that will be read twice; journalism what will be grasped at once.
Cyril Connolly (1903–74) British journalist.
Enemies of Promise, Ch. 3

10 I hesitate to say what the functions of the modern journalist may be; but I imagine that they do not exclude the intelligent anticipation of facts even before they occur.
Lord Curzon (1859–1925) British politician.
Speech, House of Commons, 29 Mar 1898

11 Good God, that's done it. He's lost us the tarts' vote.

Duke of Devonshire (1895–1950) Conservative politician.
Referring to Stanley BALDWIN's attack on newspaper proprietors; recalled by Harold Macmillan
Attrib.

12 I am myself a gentleman of the Press, and I bear no other scutcheon.

Benjamin Disraeli (1804–81) British statesman.
Speech, House of Commons, 18 Feb 1863

13 Blood sport is brought to its ultimate refinement in the gossip columns.

Bernard Ingham (1932–) British journalist.
The Observer, 'Sayings of the Week', 28 Dec 1986

14 Newspapers always excite curiosity. No one ever lays one down without a feeling of disappointment.

Charles Lamb (1775–1834) British essayist.
Last Essays of Elia, 'Detached Thoughts on Books and Reading'

15 On the whole I would not say that our Press is obscene. I would say that it trembles on the brink of obscenity.

Lord Longford (1905–) British politician and social reformer.
The Observer, 'Sayings of the Year', 1963

16 The gallery in which the reporters sit has become a fourth estate of the realm.

Lord Macaulay (1800–59) British historian.
Referring to the press gallery in the House of Commons
Historical Essays Contributed to the 'Edinburgh Review', 'Hallam's 'Constitutional History''

17 Once a newspaper touches a story, the facts are lost forever, even to the protagonists.

Norman Mailer (1923–) US writer.
The Presidential Papers

18 A good newspaper, I suppose, is a nation talking to itself.

Arthur Miller (1915–) US dramatist.
The Observer, 'Sayings of the Week', 26 Nov 1961

19 SIXTY HORSES WEDGED IN A CHIMNEY
The story to fit this sensational headline has not turned up yet.

J. B. Morton (1893–1979) British journalist.
The Best of Beachcomber, 'Mr Justice Cocklecarrot: Home Life'

20 A reporter is a man who has renounced everything in life but the world, the flesh, and the devil.

David Murray (1888–1962) British journalist.
The Observer, 'Sayings of the Week', 5 July 1931

21 We live under a government of men and morning newspapers.

Wendell Phillips (1811–84) US reformer.
Address: The Press

22 Its primary office is the gathering of news. At the peril of its soul it must see that the supply is not tainted. Neither in what it gives, nor in what it does not give, nor in the mode of presentation, must the unclouded face of truth suffer wrong. Comment is free but facts are sacred.

C. P. Scott (1846–1932) British journalist.
Manchester Guardian, 6 May 1926

23 He's someone who flies around from hotel to hotel and thinks the most interesting thing about any story is the fact that he has arrived to cover it.

Tom Stoppard (1937–) Czech-born British dramatist.
Referring to foreign correspondents
Night and Day, I

24 MILNE. No matter how imperfect things are, if you've got a free press everything is correctable, and without it everything is conceivable.
RUTH. I'm with you on the free press. It's the newspapers I can't stand.

Tom Stoppard
Night and Day, I

25 Freedom of the press in Britain is freedom to print such of the proprietor's prejudices as the advertisers don't object to.

Hannen Swaffer (1879–1962) British journalist.
Attrib.

26 Journalism – an ability to meet the challenge of filling the space.

Rebecca West (Cicely Isabel Fairfield; 1892–1983) British novelist and journalist.
The New York Herald Tribune, 22 April 1956

27 There is much to be said in favour of modern journalism. By giving us the opinions of the uneducated, it keeps us in touch with the ignorance of the community.

Oscar Wilde (1854–1900) Irish-born British dramatist.
The Critic as Artist, Pt. 2

28 You cannot hope
to bribe or twist,
thank God! the
British journalist.

But, seeing what
the man will do
unbribed, there's
no occasion to.

Humbert Wolfe (1886–1940) British poet.
The Uncelestial City, Bk. I, 'Over the Fire'

JUDGMENT

1 And this is the writing that was written, MENE, MENE, TEKEL, UPHARSIN.
This is the interpretation of the thing: MENE; God hath numbered thy kingdom, and finished it.
TEKEL; Thou art weighed in the balances, and art found wanting.
PERES; Thy kingdom is divided, and given to the Medes and Persians.

Bible: Daniel
5:25–28

2 Judge not, that ye be not judged.
Bible: Matthew
7:1

3 And why beholdest thou the mote that is in
thy brother's eye, but considerest not the
beam that is in thine own eye?
Bible: Matthew
7:3

4 And I saw a great white throne, and him that
sat on it, from whose face the earth and the
heaven fled away; and there was found no
place for them.
And I saw the dead, small and great, stand
before God; and the books were opened: and
another book was opened, which is the book
of life: and the dead were judged out of
those things which were written in the books,
according to their works.
And the sea gave up the dead which were in it;
and death and hell delivered up the dead
which were in them: and they were judged every man according to their works.
Bible: Revelations
20:11–13

5 No man can justly censure or condemn
another, because indeed no man truly knows
another.
Thomas Browne (1605–82) English physician and writer.
Religio Medici, Pt. II

6 Your representative owes you, not his
industry only, but his judgement; and he
betrays instead of serving you if he sacrifices
it to your opinion.
Edmund Burke (1729–97) British politician.
Speech to the electors of Bristol, 3 Nov 1774

7 You shall judge of a man by his foes as well
as by his friends.
Joseph Conrad (Teodor Josef Konrad Korzeniowski;
1857–1924) Polish-born British novelist.
Lord Jim, Ch. 34

8 Judge not the play before the play be done.
John Davies (1569–1626) English jurist.
Respice Finem

9 Force, if unassisted by judgement, collapses
through its own mass.
Horace (Quintus Horatius Flaccus; 65–8 BC) Roman poet.
Odes, III

10 Let me remind you of the old maxim: people
under suspicion are better moving than at
rest, since at rest they may be sitting in the
balance without knowing it, being weighed
together with their sins.
Franz Kafka (1883–1924) Czech novelist.
The Trial, Ch. 8

11 Consider what you think justice requires, and
decide accordingly. But never give your
reasons; for your judgement will probably be
right, but your reasons will certainly be
wrong.
Lord Mansfield (1705–93) British judge and politician.
Advice given to a new colonial governor
Lives of the Chief Justices (Campbell), Ch. 40

12 Everyone complains of his memory, but no
one complains of his judgement.
Duc de la Rochefoucauld (1613–80) French writer.
Maximes, 89

JUSTICE

See also injustice, judgment, law, lawyers

1 The place of justice is a hallowed place.
Francis Bacon (1561–1626) English philosopher.
Essays, 'Of Judicature'

2 When I came back to Dublin, I was
court-martialled in my absence and sentenced
to death in my absence, so I said they could
shoot me in my absence.
Brendan Behan (1923–64) Irish playwright.
The Hostage, I

3 It is better that ten guilty persons escape
than one innocent suffer.
William Blackstone (1723–80) British jurist.
Commentaries on the Laws of England, Bk. IV, Ch. 27

4 The rain it raineth on the just
And also on the unjust fella:
But chiefly on the just, because
The unjust steals the just's umbrella.
Charles Bowen (1835–94) British judge.
Sands of Time (Walter Sichel)

5 Trial by jury itself, instead of being a security
to persons who are accused, will be a
delusion, a mockery, and a snare.
Thomas Denman (1779–1854) British judge.
Judgment in O'Connell v The Queen, 4 Sept 1844

6 'It is my duty to warn you that it will be
used against you,' cried the Inspector, with
the magnificent fair play of the British
criminal law.
Arthur Conan Doyle (1856–1930) British writer.
The Dancing Men

7 Let justice be done, though the world perish.
Ferdinand I (1503–64) Holy Roman Emperor.
Attrib.

8 Ah, colonel, all's fair in love and war, you
know.
Nathan Bedford Forrest (1821–77) Confederate general.
Remark to a captured enemy officer who had been tricked into
surrendering
A Civil War Treasury (B. Botkin)

9 Let no guilty man escape, if it can be avoided
. . . No personal considerations should stand
in the way of performing a public duty.
Ulysses Simpson Grant (1822–85) US general.
Referring to the Whiskey Ring
Indorsement of a letter, 29 July 1875

10 Justice should not only be done, but should

manifestly and undoubtedly be seen to be done.
Gordon Hewart (1870–1943) British lawyer and politician.
The Chief (R. Jackson)

11 I have come to regard the law courts not as a cathedral but rather as a casino.
Richard Ingrams (1937–) British editor.
The Guardian, 30 July 1977

12 Consider, Sir, how should you like, though conscious of your innocence, to be tried before a jury for a capital crime, once a week.
Samuel Johnson (1709–84) British lexicographer.
Life of Johnson (J. Boswell), Vol. III

13 A lawyer has no business with the justice or injustice of the cause which he undertakes, unless his client asks his opinion, and then he is bound to give it honestly. The justice or injustice of the cause is to be decided by the judge.
Samuel Johnson
Tour to the Hebrides (J. Boswell)

14 Justice is the constant and perpetual wish to render to every one his due.
Justinian I (482–565 AD) Byzantine emperor.
Institutes, I

15 Justice is such a fine thing that we cannot pay too dearly for it.
Alain-René Lesage (1668–1747) French writer.
Crispin rival de son maître, IX

16 I'm arm'd with more than complete steel – The justice of my quarrel.
Christopher Marlowe (1564–93) English dramatist.
Play also attributed to others
Lust's Dominion, IV:3

17 In England, Justice is open to all, like the Ritz hotel.
James Mathew (1830–1908) British judge.
Also attrib. to Lord Darling
Miscellany-at-Law (R. E. Megarry)

18 A judge is not supposed to know anything about the facts of life until they have been presented in evidence and explained to him at least three times.
Hubert Lister Parker (1900–72) Lord Chief Justice of England.
The Observer, 'Sayings of the Week', 12 Mar 1961

19 The hungry judges soon the sentence sign, And wretches hang that jury-men may dine.
Alexander Pope (1688–1744) British poet.
The Rape of the Lock, III

20 The love of justice in most men is simply the fear of suffering injustice.
Duc de la Rochefoucauld (1613–80) French writer.
Maximes, 78

21 A man who is good enough to shed his blood for the country is good enough to be given a square deal afterwards. More than that no man is entitled to, and less than that no man shall have.
Theodore Roosevelt (1858–1919) US Republican president.
Speech at the Lincoln Monument, Springfield, Illinois, 4 June 1903

22 Haste still pays haste, and leisure answers leisure;
Like doth quit like, and Measure still for Measure.
William Shakespeare (1564–1616) English dramatist.
Measure for Measure, V:1

23 This is a British murder inquiry and some degree of justice must be seen to be more or less done.
Tom Stoppard (1937–) Czech-born British dramatist.
Jumpers, II

24 Under a government which imprisons any unjustly, the true place for a just man is also a prison.
Henry David Thoreau (1817–62) US writer.
Civil Disobedience

K

KILLING

See also assassination, death, murder, suicide

1 Euthanasia is a long, smooth-sounding word, and it conceals its danger as long, smooth words do, but the danger is there, nevertheless.
Pearl Buck (1892–1973) US novelist.
The Child Who Never Grew, Ch. 2

2 Thou shalt not kill; but needst not strive Officiously to keep alive.
Arthur Hugh Clough (1819–61) British poet.
The Latest Decalogue, 11

3 To save a man's life against his will is the same as killing him.
Horace (Quintus Horatius Flaccus; 65–8 BC) Roman poet.
Ars Poetica

4 To kill a human being is, after all, the least injury you can do him.
Henry James (1843–1916) US novelist.
My Friend Bingham

5 Killing
Is the ultimate simplification of life.
Hugh MacDiarmid (Christopher Murray Grieve; 1892–1978) Scottish poet.
England's Double Knavery

6 . . . there's no difference between one's killing and making decisions that will send others to kill. It's exactly the same thing, or even worse.

Golda Meir (1898–1978) Russian-born Israeli stateswoman.
L'Europeo (Oriana Fallaci)

7   Kill a man, and you are a murderer. Kill millions of men, and you are a conqueror. Kill everyone, and you are a god.

Jean Rostand (1894–1977) French biologist and writer.
Pensées d'un biologiste

8   Yet each man kills the thing he loves,
By each let this be heard,
Some do it with a bitter look,
Some with a flattering word.
The coward does it with a kiss,
The brave man with a sword!

Oscar Wilde (1854–1900) Irish-born British dramatist.
The Ballad of Reading Gaol, I:7

KINDNESS

See also charity, generosity

1   Recompense injury with justice, and recompense kindness with kindness.

Confucius (K'ung Fu-tzu; 551–479 BC) Chinese philosopher.
Analects

2   I love thee for a heart that's kind –
Not for the knowledge in thy mind.

W. H. Davies (1871–1940) British poet.
Sweet Stay-at-Home

3   Yet do I fear thy nature;
It is too full o' th' milk of human kindness
To catch the nearest way.

William Shakespeare (1564–1616) English dramatist.
Macbeth, I:5

4   This is a way to kill a wife with kindness.

William Shakespeare
The Taming of the Shrew, IV:1

5   So many gods, so many creeds,
So many paths that wind and wind,
While just the art of being kind
Is all the sad world needs.

Ella Wheeler Wilcox (1850–1919) US poet.
The World's Need

6   That best portion of a good man's life,
His little, nameless, unremembered acts
Of kindness and of love.

William Wordsworth (1770–1850) British poet.
Lines composed a few miles above Tintern Abbey

KISSING

1   What of soul was left, I wonder, when the kissing had to stop?

Robert Browning (1812–89) British poet.
A Toccata of Galuppi's

2   Jenny kissed me when we met,
Jumping from the chair she sat in;
Time, you thief, who love to get

Sweets into your list, put that in:
Say I'm weary, say I'm sad,
Say that health and wealth have missed me,
Say I'm growing old, but add,
Jenny kissed me.

Leigh Hunt (1784–1859) British poet.
Writing about Jane Carlyle
Rondeau

3   Being kissed by a man who didn't wax his moustache was –like eating an egg without salt.

Rudyard Kipling (1865–1936) Indian-born British writer.
A similar remark is attributed to the US poet Madison Julius Cawein (1865–1914)
Soldiers Three, 'The Gadsbys, Poor Dear Mamma'

4   A kiss without a moustache, they said then, is like an egg without salt; I will add to it: and it is like Good without Evil.

Jean-Paul Sartre (1905–80) French writer.
Words

KNOWLEDGE

See also learning, self-knowledge, wisdom

1   Knowledge is the mother of all virtue; all vice proceeds from ignorance.

Proverb

2   Learning is a treasure which accompanies its owner everywhere.

Chinese proverb

3   *Nam et ipsa scientia potestas est.*
Knowledge itself is power.

Francis Bacon (1561–1626) English philosopher.
Religious Meditations, 'Of Heresies'

4   I have taken all knowledge to be my province.

Francis Bacon
Letter to Lord Burleigh, 1592

5   For all knowledge and wonder (which is the seed of knowledge) is an impression of pleasure in itself.

Francis Bacon
The Advancement of Learning, Bk. I, Ch. 1

6   For in much wisdom is much grief: and he that increaseth knowledge increaseth sorrow.

Bible: Ecclesiastes
1:18

7   And the Lord God took the man, and put him into the garden of Eden to dress it and to keep it.
And the Lord God commanded the man, saying, Of every tree of the garden thou mayest freely eat:
But of the tree of the knowledge of good and evil, thou shalt not eat of it: for in the day that thou eatest thereof thou shalt surely die.

Bible: Genesis
2:15–17

8   Now as touching things offered unto idols,

we know that we all have knowledge.
Knowledge puffeth up, but charity edifieth.
Bible: I Corinthians
8:1

9 There goes a woman who knows all the
things that can be taught and none of the
things that cannot be taught.
Coco Chanel (1883–1971) French dress designer.
Coco Chanel, Her Life, Her Secrets (Marcel Haedrich)

10 Learning without thought is labour lost;
thought without learning is perilous.
Confucius (K'ung Fu-tzu; 551–479 BC) Chinese
philosopher.
Analects

11 Knowledge dwells
In heads replete with thoughts of other men;
Wisdom in minds attentive to their own.
William Cowper (1731–1800) British poet.
The Task

12 A smattering of everything, and a knowledge
of nothing.
Charles Dickens (1812–70) British novelist.
Sketches by Boz, 'Tales', Ch. 3

13 A man should keep his little brain attic
stocked with all the furniture that he is likely
to use, and the rest he can put away in the
lumber room of his library, where he can get
it if he wants it.
Arthur Conan Doyle (1856–1930) British writer.
Five Orange Pips

14 For lust of knowing what should not be
known,
We take the Golden Road to Samarkand.
James Elroy Flecker (1884–1915) British poet.
Hassan, V:2

15 I am the very model of a modern Major-
General,
I've information vegetable, animal and mineral,
I know the kings of England, and I quote the
fights historical,
From Marathon to Waterloo, in order
categorical.
W. S. Gilbert (1836–1911) British dramatist.
The Pirates of Penzance, I

16 In arguing too, the parson own'd his skill,
For e'en though vanquish'd, he could argue
still;
While words of learned length, and thund'ring
sound
Amazed the gazing rustics rang'd around,
And still they gaz'd, and still the wonder grew,
That one small head could carry all he knew.
Oliver Goldsmith (1728–74) Irish-born British writer.
The Deserted Village

17 The clever men at Oxford
Know all that there is to be knowed.
But they none of them know one half as much
As intelligent Mr Toad.
Kenneth Grahame (1859–1932) Scottish writer.
The Wind in the Willows, Ch. 10

18 It is the province of knowledge to speak and
it is the privilege of wisdom to listen.
Oliver Wendell Holmes (1809–94) US writer.
The Poet at the Breakfast Table, Ch. 10

19 Knowledge is proportionate to being. . . .
You know in virtue of what you are.
Aldous Huxley (1894–1964) British novelist.
Time Must Have a Stop, Ch. 26

20 If a little knowledge is dangerous, where is
the man who has so much as to be out of
danger?
T. H. Huxley (1825–95) British biologist.
On Elementary Instruction in Physiology

21 There was never an age in which useless
knowledge was more important than in our
own.
Cyril Joad (1891–1953) British philosopher and
broadcaster.
The Observer, 'Sayings of the Week', 30 Sept 1951

22 All knowledge is of itself of some value.
There is nothing so minute or inconsiderable,
that I would not rather know it than not.
Samuel Johnson (1709–84) British lexicographer.
Life of Johnson (J. Boswell)

23 Integrity without knowledge is weak and
useless, and knowledge without integrity is
dangerous and dreadful.
Samuel Johnson
Rasselas, Ch. 41

24 In my early years I read very hard. It is a
sad reflection, but a true one, that I knew
almost as much at eighteen as I do now.
Samuel Johnson
Life of Johnson (J. Boswell), Vol. I

25 Knowledge is of two kinds. We know a
subject ourselves, or we know where we can
find information upon it.
Samuel Johnson
Life of Johnson (J. Boswell), Vol. II

26 A study of history shows that civilizations
that abandon the quest for knowledge are
doomed to disintegration.
Bernard Lovell (1913–   ) British astronomer and writer.
The Observer, 'Sayings of the Week', 14 May 1972

27 Knowledge advances by steps, and not by
leaps.
Lord Macaulay (1800–59) British historian.
Essays and Biographies, 'History'. *Edinburgh Review*

28 We have learned the answers, all the
answers:
It is the question that we do not know.
Archibald MacLeish (1892–1982) US poet and dramatist.
The Hamlet of A. Macleish

29 A little learning is a dangerous thing;
Drink deep, or taste not the Pierian spring:
There shallow draughts intoxicate the brain,

And drinking largely sobers us again.

Alexander Pope (1688–1744) British poet.
An Essay on Criticism

30 Our knowledge can only be finite, while our ignorance must necessarily be infinite.

Karl Popper (1902–) Austrian-born British philosopher.
Conjectures and Refutations

31 His had been an intellectual decision founded on his conviction that if a little knowledge was a dangerous thing, a lot was lethal.

Tom Sharpe (1928–) British novelist.
Porterhouse Blue, Ch. 18

32 These things shall be! A loftier race
Than e'er the world hath known shall rise,
With flame of freedom in their souls,

And light of knowledge in their eyes.

John Addington Symonds (1840–93) British art historian.
Hymn

33 Beware you be not swallowed up in books! An ounce of love is worth a pound of knowledge.

John Wesley (1703–91) British religious leader.
Life of Wesley (R. Southey), Ch. 16

34 'I dunno,' Arthur said. 'I forget what I was taught. I only remember what I've learnt.'

Patrick White (1912–) British-born Australian novelist.
The Solid Mandala, Ch. 2

35 I have drunk ale from the Country of the Young
And weep because I know all things now.

W. B. Yeats (1865–1939) Irish poet.
He Thinks of his Past Greatness

L

LANGUAGE

See also class, communication, grammar, Goldwynisms, malapropisms, mixed metaphors, opera, pronunciation, speech, spoonerisms, style, words, writing

1 The Greeks Had a Word for It.

Zoë Akins (1886–1958) US dramatist.
Play title

2 Therefore is the name of it called Babel; because the Lord did there confound the language of all the earth: and from thence did the Lord scatter them abroad upon the face of all the earth.

Bible: Genesis
11:9

3 The cliché is dead poetry. English, being the language of an imaginative race, abounds in clichés, so that English literature is always in danger of being poisoned by its own secretions.

Gerald Brenan (Edward Fitzgerald Brenan; 1894–1987) British writer.
Thoughts in a Dry Season, 'Literature'

4 'Take some more tea,' the March Hare said to Alice, very earnestly.

'I've had nothing yet,' Alice replied in an offended tone, 'so I can't take more.'

'You mean you can't take *less*,' said the Hatter: 'it's very easy to take *more* than nothing.'

Lewis Carroll (Charles Lutwidge Dodgson; 1832–98) British writer.
Alice's Adventures in Wonderland, Ch. 7

5 A silly remark can be made in Latin as well as in Spanish.

Miguel de Cervantes (1547–1616) Spanish novelist.
The Dialogue of the Dogs

6 I speak Spanish to God, Italian to women, French to men, and German to my horse.

Charles V (1500–58) Holy Roman Emperor.
Attrib.

7 The one stream of poetry which is continually flowing is slang.

G. K. Chesterton (1874–1936) British writer.
The Defendant

8 All slang is metaphor, and all metaphor is poetry.

G. K. Chesterton
The Defendant

9 I don't hold with abroad and think that foreigners speak English when our backs are turned.

Quentin Crisp (c. 1910–) British model, publicist, and writer.
The Naked Civil Servant

10 Bring on the empty horses!

Michael Curtiz (1888–1962) Hungarian-born US film director.
Said during the filming of *The Charge of the Light Brigade*. Curtiz, who was not noted for his command of the English language, meant 'riderless horses'. When people laughed at his order he became very angry, shouting, 'You think I know fuck-nothing, when I know fuck-all!' David Niven used the remark as the title of his second volume of autobiography about his experiences in the film industry.
Bring on the Empty Horses (David Niven)

11 Imagine the Lord talking French! Aside from a few odd words in Hebrew, I took it completely for granted that God had never spoken anything but the most dignified English.

Clarence Shepard Day (1874–1935) US writer.
Life With Father, 'Father interferes'

12 What is the prose for God?

Harley Granville-Barker (1877–1946) British actor and dramatist.
Waste, I

13 I have laboured to refine our language to grammatical purity, and to clear it from colloquial barbarisms, licentious idioms, and irregular combinations.

Samuel Johnson (1709–84) British lexicographer.
The Rambler

14 I am always sorry when any language is lost, because languages are the pedigree of nations.

Samuel Johnson
Tour to the Hebrides (J. Boswell)

15 I am not yet so lost in lexicography, as to forget that words are the daughters of earth, and that things are the sons of heaven. Language is only the instrument of science, and words are but the signs of ideas: I wish, however, that the instrument might be less apt to decay, and that signs might be permanent, like the things which they denote.

Samuel Johnson
Dictionary of the English Language

16 The baby doesn't understand English and the Devil knows Latin.

Ronald Knox (1888–1957) British Roman Catholic priest.
Said when asked to conduct a baptism service in English
Ronald Knox (Evelyn Waugh), Pt. I, Ch. 5

17 If the English language had been properly organized . . . then there would be a word which meant both 'he' and 'she', and I could write, 'If John or Mary comes heesh will want to play tennis,' which would save a lot of trouble.

A. A. Milne (1882–1956) British writer.
The Christopher Robin Birthday Book

18 Most of their discourse was about hunting, in a dialect I understand very little.

Samuel Pepys (1633–1703) English diarist.
Diary, 22 Nov 1663

19 I include 'pidgin-English' . . . even though I am referred to in that splendid language as 'Fella belong Mrs Queen'.

Prince Philip (1921–) The consort of Queen Elizabeth II.
Speech, English-Speaking Union Conference, Ottawa, 29 Oct 1958

20 Life is too short to learn German.

Richard Porson (1759–1808) British classicist.
Gryll Grange (T. L. Peacock), Ch. 3

21 Language grows out of life, out of its needs and experiences . . . *Language* and *knowledge* are indissolubly connected; they are interdependent. Good work in language presupposes and depends on a real knowledge of things.

Annie Sullivan (1866–1936) US teacher of the handicapped.
Speech, American Association to Promote the Teaching of Speech to the Deaf, July 1894

22 A foreign swear-word is practically inoffensive

except to the person who has learnt it early in life and knows its social limits.

Paul Theroux (1941–) US-born writer.
Saint Jack, Ch. 12

23 The most attractive sentences are not perhaps the wisest, but the surest and soundest.

Henry David Thoreau (1817–62) US writer.
Journal, 1842

24 I am not like a lady at the court of Versailles, who said: 'What a dreadful pity that the bother at the tower of Babel should have got language all mixed up, but for that, everyone would always have spoken French.

Voltaire (François-Marie Arouet; 1694–1778) French writer.
Letter to Catherine the Great, Empress of Russia, 26 May 1767

25 We should constantly use the most common, little, easy words (so they are pure and proper) which our language affords.

John Wesley (1703–91) British religious leader.
Advice for preaching to 'plain people'
Attrib.

26 We dissect nature along lines laid down by our native language . . . Language is not simply a reporting device for experience but a defining framework for it.

Benjamin Lee Whorf (1897–1941) US linguist.
New Directions in the Study of Language (ed. Hoyer), 'Thinking in Primitive Communities'

LAST WORDS

Not always the actual last words said, but including remarks made when dying. Many are apocryphal, hence the fact that some people have more than one set of attributed 'last words'.
See also death, execution

1 A lot of people, on the verge of death, utter famous last words or stiffen into attitudes, as if the final stiffening in three days' time were not enough; they will have ceased to exist three days' hence, yet they still want to arouse admiration and adopt a pose and tell a lie with their last gasp.

Henry de Montherlant (1896–1972) French novelist.
Explicit Mysterium

some examples

2 I inhabit a weak, frail, decayed tenement; battered by the winds and broken in on by the storms, and, from all I can learn, the landlord does not intend to repair.

John Quincy Adams (1767–1848) Sixth president of the USA.
Said during his last illness
Attrib.

3 See in what peace a Christian can die.

Joseph Addison (1672–1719) British essayist.

4 *Ave Caesar, morituri te salutant.*

Hail Caesar; those who are about to die salute
you.
Anonymous
Greeting to the Roman Emperor by gladiators

5 How were the receipts today in Madison
Square Garden?
Phineas Taylor Barnum (1810–91) US showman.

6 When Jesus therefore had received the
vinegar, he said, It is finished: and he bowed
his head, and gave up the ghost.
Bible: John
19:30

7 And when Jesus had cried with a loud voice,
he said, Father, into thy hands I commend
my spirit: and having said thus, he gave up
the ghost.
Bible: Luke
23:46

8 Jesus, when he had cried again with a loud
voice, yielded up the ghost.
And, behold, the veil of the temple was rent in
twain from the top to the bottom; and the
earth did quake, and the rocks rent;
And the graves were opened; and many bodies
of the saints which slept arose.
Bible: Matthew
27:50–52

9 *Et tu, Brute?*
You too, Brutus?
Julius Caesar (100–44 BC) Roman general and statesman.

10 All right, then, I'll say it: Dante makes me
sick.
Lope Félix de Vega Carpio (1562–1635) Spanish
dramatist and poet.
On being informed he was about to die
Attrib.

11 I realize that patriotism is not enough. I must
have no hatred or bitterness towards anyone.
Edith Cavell (1865–1915) British nurse.
Before her execution by the Germans in 1915

12 Let not poor Nelly starve.
Charles II (1630–85) King of England.
Referring to Nell Gwynne
Said on his death bed

13 Give Dayrolles a chair.
Earl of Chesterfield (1694–1773) English statesman.
Said on his deathbed when visited by his godson, Solomon
Dayrolles
Last words

14 Nurse, it was I who discovered that leeches
have red blood.
Baron Georges Cuvier (1769–1832) French zoologist.
On his deathbed when the nurse came to apply leeches
The Oxford Book of Death (D. Enright)

15 No, it is better not. She will only ask me to
take a message to Albert.
Benjamin Disraeli (1804–81) British statesman.
On his deathbed, declining an offer of a visit from Queen Victoria

16 Shakespeare, I come!
Theodore Dreiser (1871–1945) US novelist.
His intended last words
The Constant Circle (S. Mayfield)

17 All my possessions for a moment of time.
Elizabeth I (1533–1603) Queen of England.

18 I have no pain, dear mother, now;
But oh! I am so dry:
Just moisten poor Jim's lips once more;
And, mother, do not cry!
Edward Farmer (1809–76) British writer.
A typical sentimental verse of the time.
The Collier's Dying Child

19 Now I'll have *eine kleine Pause.*
Kathleen Ferrier (1912–53) British contralto.
Said shortly before her death
Am I Too Loud? (Gerald Moore)

20 It is high time for me to depart, for at my
age I now begin to see things as they really
are.
Bernard de Fontenelle (1657–1757) French philosopher.
Remark on his deathbed
Anekdotenschatz (H. Hoffmeister)

21 I feel nothing, apart from a certain difficulty
in continuing to exist.
Bernard de Fontenelle
Remark on his deathbed
Famous Last Words (B. Conrad)

22 I die happy.
Charles James Fox (1749–1806) British Whig politician.
Life and Times of C. J. Fox (Russell), Vol. III

23 We are all going to Heaven, and Vandyke is
of the company.
Thomas Gainsborough (1727–88) British painter.
Thomas Gainsborough (Boulton), Ch. 9

24 Bugger Bognor.
George V (1865–1936) King of the United Kingdom.
His alleged last words, when his doctor promised him he would
soon be well enough to visit Bognor Regis

25 How is the Empire?
George V
Last words
The Times, 21 Jan 1936

26 We are as near to heaven by sea as by land.
Humphrey Gilbert (c. 1539–83) English navigator.
Remark made shortly before he went down with his ship
Squirrel
A Book of Anecdotes (D. George)

27 *Mehr Licht!*
More light!
Goethe (1749–1832) German poet and dramatist.
Attrib. last words. In fact he asked for the second shutter to
be opened, to allow more light in

28 Well, I've had a happy life.
William Hazlitt (1778–1830) British essayist.

29 You might make that a double.
Neville Heath (1917–46) British murderer.
Comment made when offered a drink before his execution.
Attrib.

30 God will pardon me. It is His trade.

Heinrich Heine (1797–1856) German poet and writer.
Journal (Edmond and Charles Goncourt), 23 Feb 1863

31 Turn up the lights, I don't want to go home in the dark.

O. Henry (William Sidney Porter; 1862–1910) US short-story writer.
Quoting a popular song of the time
O. Henry (C. A. Smith), Ch. 9

32 I am about to take my last voyage, a great leap in the dark.

Thomas Hobbes (1588–1679) English philosopher.

33 If heaven had granted me five more years, I could have become a real painter.

Hokusai (1760–1849) Japanese painter.
Said on his deathbed
Famous Last Words (B. Conrad)

34 On the contrary!

Henrik Ibsen (1828–1906) Norwegian dramatist.
His nurse had just remarked that he was feeling a little better
True Remarkable Occurrences (J. Train)

35 So it has come at last, the distinguished thing.

Henry James (1843–1916) US novelist.
A Backward Glance (Edith Wharton), Ch. 14

36 Don't give up the ship.

James Lawrence (1781–1813) US naval officer.
As he lay dying in his ship, the US frigate *Chesapeake*, during the battle with the British frigate *Shannon*

37 Why are you weeping? Did you imagine that I was immortal?

Louis XIV (1638–1715) French king.
Noticing as he lay on his deathbed that his attendants were crying
Louis XIV (V. Cronin)

38 *Tête d'Armée.*
Chief of the Army.

Napoleon I (Napoleon Bonaparte; 1769–1821) French emperor.
Last words
Attrib.

39 I do not have to forgive my enemies, I have had them all shot.

Ramón Maria Narváez (1800–68) Spanish general and political leader.
Said on his deathbed, when asked by a priest if he forgave his enemies
Famous Last Words (B. Conrad)

40 Kiss me, Hardy.

Lord Nelson (1758–1805) British admiral.
Spoken to Sir Thomas Hardy, captain of the *Victory*, during the Battle of Trafalgar, 1805

41 I am just going outside and may be some time.

Capt. Lawrence Oates (1880–1912) British soldier and explorer.
Before leaving the tent and vanishing into the blizzard on the ill-fated Antarctic expedition (1910–12). Oates was afraid that his lameness would slow down the others.
Journal (R. F. Scott), 17 Mar 1912

42 Die, my dear Doctor, that's the last thing I shall do!

Lord Palmerston (1784–1865) British statesman.

43 I am curious to see what happens in the next world to one who dies unshriven.

Pietro Perugino (1446–1523) Italian painter.
Giving his reasons for refusing to see a priest as he lay dying
Attrib.

44 Oh, my country! How I leave my country!

William Pitt the Younger (1759–1806) British statesman.

45 I think I could eat one of Bellamy's veal pies.

William Pitt the Younger

46 I have not told half of what I saw.

Marco Polo (c. 1254–1324) Venetian traveller.
The Story of Civilization (W. Durant), Vol. I

47 I owe much; I have nothing; the rest I leave to the poor.

François Rabelais (1483–1553) French satirist.

48 Ring down the curtain, the farce is over.

François Rabelais

49 I am going in search of a great perhaps.

François Rabelais

50 I have a long journey to take, and must bid the company farewell.

Walter Raleigh (1554–1618) English explorer.
Sir Walter Raleigh (Edward Thompson), Ch. 26

51 So little done, so much to do.

Cecil Rhodes (1853–1902) South African statesman.

52 You can keep the things of bronze and stone and give me one man to remember me just once a year.

Damon Runyon (1884–1946) US writer.

53 Dear World, I am leaving you because I am bored. I am leaving you with your worries. Good luck.

George Sanders (1906–72) British film actor.
Suicide note

54 Everybody has got to die, but I have always believed an exception would be made in my case. Now what?

William Saroyan (1908–81) US dramatist.
Time, 16 Jan 1984

55 At last I am going to be well!

Paul Scarron (1610–60) French poet.
As he lay dying
Attrib.

56 Nonsense, they couldn't hit an elephant at this distance

John Sedgwick (1813–64) US general.
In response to a suggestion that he should not show himself over the parapet during the Battle of the Wilderness
Attrib.

57 Thank heavens the sun has gone in and I don't have to go out and enjoy it.
Logan Pearsall Smith (1865–1946) US writer.

58 Crito, we owe a cock to Aesculapius; please pay it and don't let it pass.
Socrates (469–399 BC) Athenian philosopher.
Before his execution by drinking hemlock
Phaedo (Plato), 118

59 Beautifully done.
Stanley Spencer (1891–1959) British artist.
Said to the nurse who had injected him, just before he died
Stanley Spencer, a Biography (Maurice Collis), Ch. 19

60 If this is dying, I don't think much of it.
Lytton Strachey (1880–1932) British writer.
Lytton Strachey (Michael Holroyd), Pt. V, Ch. 17

61 Ah, a German and a genius! a prodigy, admit him!
Jonathan Swift (1667–1745) Irish-born Anglican priest and writer.
Learning of the arrival of Handel

62 God bless ... God damn.
James Thurber (1894–1961) US humorist.

63 Even in the valley of the shadow of death, two and two do not make six.
Leo Tolstoy (1828–1910) Russian writer.
Refusing to reconcile himself with the Russian Orthodox Church as he lay dying

64 I have had no real gratification or enjoyment of any sort more than my neighbor on the next block who is worth only half a million.
William Henry Vanderbilt (1821–85) US railway chief.
Famous Last Words (B. Conrad)

65 Dear me, I believe I am becoming a god. An emperor ought at least to die on his feet.
Vespasian (9–79 AD) Roman emperor.
Lives of the Caesars (Suetonius)

66 Either that wall paper goes, or I do.
Oscar Wilde (1854–1900) Irish-born British dramatist.
As he lay dying in a drab Paris bedroom
Time, 16 Jan 1984

67 I expect I shall have to die beyond my means
Oscar Wilde
On accepting a glass of champagne on his deathbed

68 Now God be praised, I will die in peace.
James Wolfe (1727–59) British general.
After being mortally wounded at the Battle of Quebec, 1759
Historical Journal of Campaigns, 1757–60 (J. Knox), Vol. II

LAUGHTER

See also happiness, humour

1 Laugh and grow fat.
Proverb

2 Laugh before breakfast, you'll cry before supper.
Proverb

3 Laughter is the best medicine.
Proverb

4 I make myself laugh at everything, so that I do not weep.
Beaumarchais (1732–99) French dramatist.
Le Barbier de Séville, I:2

5 I said of laughter, It is mad: and of mirth, What doeth it?
Bible: Ecclesiastes
2:2

6 The most wasted of all days is that on which one has not laughed.
Nicolas Chamfort (1741–94) French writer.
Maximes et pensées

7 One must laugh before one is happy, or one may die without ever laughing at all.
Jean de La Bruyère (1645–96) French satirist.
Les Caractères

8 Laughter is pleasant, but the exertion is too much for me.
Thomas Love Peacock (1785–1866) British novelist.
Said by the Hon. Mr Listless
Nightmare Abbey, Ch. 5

9 Laugh, and the world laughs with you;
Weep, and you weep alone,
For the sad old earth must borrow its mirth,
But has trouble enough of its own.
Ella Wheeler Wilcox (1850–1919) US poet.
Solitude

LAW

See also crime, justice, lawyers

1 A judge knows nothing unless it has been explained to him three times.
Proverb

2 Every dog is allowed one bite.
Proverb

3 Every one is innocent until he is proved guilty.
Proverb

4 Possession is nine points of the law.
Proverb

5 The law does not concern itself about trifles.
Proverb

6 One of the Seven was wont to say: 'That laws were like cobwebs; where the small flies were caught, and the great brake through.'
Francis Bacon (1561–1626) English philosopher.
See also SHENSTONE; SOLON; SWIFT
Apothegms

7 The good of the people is the chief law.
Cicero (106–43 BC) Roman orator and statesman.
De Legibus, III

8 The Law of England is a very strange one; it

cannot compel anyone to tell the truth. . . . But what the Law can do is to give you seven years for not telling the truth.
Lord Darling (1849–1936) British judge.
Lord Darling (D. Walker-Smith), Ch. 27

9 'If the law supposes that,' said Mr Bumble . . . , 'the law is a ass – a idiot.'
Charles Dickens (1812–70) British novelist.
Oliver Twist, Ch. 51

10 When I went to the Bar as a very young man,
(Said I to myself – said I),
I'll work on a new and original plan,
(Said I to myself – said I).
W. S. Gilbert (1836–1911) British dramatist.
Iolanthe, I

11 The Law is the true embodiment
Of everything that's excellent.
It has no kind of fault or flaw,
And I, my lords, embody the Law.
W. S. Gilbert
Iolanthe, I

12 There's no better way of exercising the imagination than the study of law. No poet ever interpreted nature as freely as a lawyer interprets truth.
Jean Giraudoux (1882–1944) French dramatist.
Tiger at the Gates, I

13 Laws grind the poor, and rich men rule the law.
Oliver Goldsmith (1728–74) Irish-born British writer.
The Traveller

14 I know no method to secure the repeal of bad or obnoxious laws so effective as their stringent execution.
Ulysses Simpson Grant (1822–85) US president.
Inaugural address, 4 Mar 1869

15 The Common Law of England has been laboriously built about a mythical figure – the figure of 'The Reasonable Man'.
A. P. Herbert (1890–1971) British writer and politician.
Uncommon Law

16 In *this* country, my Lords, . . . the individual subject . . . 'has nothing to do with the laws but to obey them.'
Bishop Samuel Horsley (1733–1806) British bishop.
House of Lords, 13 Nov 1795

17 Oh, Mr. President, do not let so great an achievement suffer from any taint of legality.
Philander Chase Knox (1853–1921) US lawyer and politician.
Responding to Theodore Roosevelt's request for legal justification of his acquisition of the Panama Canal Zone
Violent Neighbours (T. Buckley)

18 In university they don't tell you that the greater part of the law is learning to tolerate fools.
Doris Lessing (1919–) British novelist.
Martha Quest, Pt. III, Ch. 2

19 No brilliance is needed in the law. Nothing but common sense, and relatively clean finger nails.
John Mortimer (1923–) British lawyer and dramatist.
A Voyage Round My Father, I

20 Laws were made to be broken.
Christopher North (John Wilson; 1785–1854) Scottish writer.
Noctes Ambrosianae, 24 May 1830

21 Let us consider the reason of the case. For nothing is law that is not reason.
John Powell (1645–1713) English judge.
Coggs v. Bernard, 2 Lord Raymond, 911

22 Every law is a contract between the king and the people and therefore to be kept.
John Selden (1584–1654) English historian.
Table Talk

23 Ignorance of the law excuses no man; not that all men know the law, but because 'tis an excuse every man will plead, and no man can tell how to confute him.
John Selden
Table Talk

24 Still you keep o' th' windy side of the law.
William Shakespeare (1564–1616) English dramatist.
Twelfth Night, III:4

25 Laws are generally found to be nets of such a texture, as the little creep through, the great break through, and the middle-sized are alone entangled in.
William Shenstone
See also BACON; SOLON; SWIFT
Essays on Men, Manners, and Things, 'On Politics'

26 Laws are like spider's webs: if some poor weak creature come up against them, it is caught; but a bigger one can break through and get away.
Solon (6th century BC) Athenian statesman.
See also BACON; SHENSTONE; SWIFT
Lives of the Eminent Philosophers (Diogenes Laertius), I

27 Laws are like cobwebs, which may catch small flies, but let wasps and hornets break through.
Jonathan Swift (1667–1745) Irish-born Anglican priest and writer.
See also BACON; SHENSTONE; SOLON
A Tritical Essay upon the Faculties of the Mind

LAWYERS

See also law

1 He that is his own lawyer has a fool for a client.
Proverb

2 A lawyer never goes to law himself.
Proverb

3 A lawyer's opinion is worth nothing unless paid for.
Proverb

4 Lawyers are the only persons in whom ignorance of the law is not punished.
Jeremy Bentham (1748–1832) British philosopher.
Attrib.

5 Woe unto you, lawyers! for ye have taken away the key of knowledge: ye entered not in yourselves, and them that were entering in ye hindered.
Bible: Luke
11:52

6 A client is fain to hire a lawyer to keep from the injury of other lawyers – as Christians that travel in Turkey are forced to hire Janissaries, to protect them from the insolencies of other Turks.
Samuel Butler (1835–1902) British writer.
Prose Observations

7 I do not care to speak ill of any man behind his back, but I believe the gentleman is an *attorney.*
Samuel Johnson (1709–84) British lexicographer.
Life of Johnson (J. Boswell), Vol. II

8 It is a very salutary check for a judge to realise that if he does say something silly it is liable to get into the papers.
Mr Justice Templeman (1920–) British judge.
Observer, 20 Aug 1978

LAZINESS

See also bed, idleness

1 I make no secret of the fact that I would rather lie on a sofa than sweep beneath it. But you have to be efficient if you're going to be lazy.
Shirley Conran (1932–) Designer and journalist.
Superwoman, 'The Reason Why'

2 Happy is the man with a wife to tell him what to do and a secretary to do it.
Lord Mancroft (1917–) British businessman and writer.
The Observer, 'Sayings of the Week', 18 Dec 1966

3 For one person who dreams of making fifty thousand pounds, a hundred people dream of being left fifty thousand pounds.
A. A. Milne (1882–1956) British writer.
If I May, 'The Future'

4 It is better to have loafed and lost than never to have loafed at all.
James Thurber (1894–1961) US humorist.
Fables for Our Time, 'The Courtship of Arthur and Al'

5 'Tis the voice of the sluggard, I heard him complain:
'You have waked me too soon, I must slumber again.'
Isaac Watts (1674–1748) English theologian and hymn writer.
The Sluggard

LEADERSHIP

See also guidance

1 The trouble in modern democracy is that men do not approach to leadership until they have lost the desire to lead anyone.
Lord Beveridge (1879–1963) British economist.
The Observer, 'Sayings of the Week', 15 Apr 1934

2 And he shall rule them with a rod of iron; as the vessels of a potter shall they be broken to shivers: even as I received of my Father.
Bible: Revelations
2:27

3 Captains of industry.
Thomas Carlyle (1795–1881) Scottish historian and essayist.
Past and Present, Bk. IV, Ch. 4

4 As the Prime Minister put it to me . . . he saw his role as being that of Moses.
Peter Jay (1937–) British economist and broadcaster.
Referring to a conversation with James Callaghan
Guardian Weekly, 18 Sept 1977

5 Let me pass, I have to follow them, I am their leader.
Alexandre Auguste Ledru-Rollin (1807–74) French lawyer and politician.
Trying to force his way through a mob during the Revolution of 1848, of which he was one of the chief instigators. A similar remark is attributed to Bonar Law.
The Fine Art of Political Wit (L. Harris)

6 A leader who doesn't hesitate before he sends his nation into battle is not fit to be a leader.
Golda Meir (1898–1978) Russian-born Israeli stateswoman.
As Good as Golda (ed. Israel and Mary Shenker)

7 No general in the midst of battle has a great discussion about what he is going to do if defeated.
David Owen (1938–) British politician.
The Observer, 'Sayings of the Week', 6 June 1987

LEARNING

See also education, knowledge

1 What we have to learn to do, we learn by doing.
Aristotle (384–322 BC) Greek philosopher.
Nicomachean Ethics, Bk. II

2 Miss not the discourse of the elders: for they also learned of their fathers, and of them thou shalt learn understanding, and to give answer as need requireth.
Bible: Ecclesiasticus
8:9

3 Read, mark, learn and inwardly digest.
The Book of Common Prayer
Collect, 2nd Sunday in Advent

4 An art can only be learned in the workshop of those who are winning their bread by it.
Samuel Butler (1835–1902) British writer.
Erewhon, Ch. 20

5 LIBOV ANDREEVNA. Are you still a student?
TROFIMOV. I expect I shall be a student to the end of my days.
Anton Chekhov (1860–1904) Russian dramatist.
The Cherry Orchard, I

6 . . . that is what learning is. You suddenly understand something you've understood all your life, but in a new way.
Doris Lessing (1919–) British novelist.
The Four-Gated City

7 He intended, he said, to devote the rest of his life to learning the remaining twenty-two letters of the alphabet.
George Orwell (Eric Blair; 1903–50) British novelist.
Animal Farm, Ch. 9

8 For where is any author in the world
Teaches such beauty as a woman's eye?
Learning is but an adjunct to oneself.
William Shakespeare (1564–1616) English dramatist.
Love's Labour's Lost, IV:3

9 Not with blinded eyesight poring over miserable books.
Alfred, Lord Tennyson (1809–92) British poet.
Locksley Hall

10 One impulse from a vernal wood
May teach you more of man,
Of moral evil and of good,
Than all the sages can.
William Wordsworth (1770–1850) British poet.
The Tables Turned

11 Some for renown, on scraps of learning dote,
And think they grow immortal as they quote.
Edward Young (1683–1765) British poet.
Love of Fame, I

LEISURE

See also idleness, merrymaking, pleasure, rest

1 The wisdom of a learned man cometh by opportunity of leisure: and he that hath little business shall become wise.
How can he get wisdom that holdeth the plough, and that glorieth in the goad, that driveth oxen, and is occupied in their labours, and whose talk is of bullocks?
Bible: Ecclesiasticus
38:24–25

2 Hey! Mr Tambourine Man, play a song for me.
I'm not sleepy and there is no place I'm going to.
Bob Dylan (Robert Allen Zimmerman; 1941–) US popular singer.
Mr Tambourine Man

3 If all the year were playing holidays, To sport would be as tedious as to work.
William Shakespeare (1564–1616) English dramatist.
Henry IV, Part One, I:2

4 Days off.
Spencer Tracy (1900–67) US film star.
Explaining what he looked for in a script
Attrib.

LETTER-WRITING

See also communication

1 . . . a habit the pleasure of which increases with practise, but becomes more urksome with neglect.
Abigail Adams (1744–1818) US feminist.
Letter to her daughter, 8 May 1808

2 When he wrote a letter, he would put that which was most material in the postscript, as if it had been a by-matter.
Francis Bacon (1561–1626) English philosopher.
Essays, 'Of Cunning'

3 His sayings are generally like women's letters; all the pith is in the postscript.
William Hazlitt (1778–1830) British essayist.
Referring to Charles Lamb
Conversations of Northcote

LEXICOGRAPHY

1 To finish is both a relief and a release from an extraordinarily pleasant prison.
Dr. Robert Burchfield (1923–) New Zealand editor.
On completing the supplements to the Oxford English Dictionary
The Observer, 'Sayings of the Week', 11 Sept 1986

2 The responsibility of a dictionary is to record a language, not set its style.
Philip Babcock Gove (1902–72) US dictionary editor.
Letter to *Life Magazine*, 17 Nov 1961

3 But these were the dreams of a poet doomed at last to wake a lexicographer.
Samuel Johnson (1709–84) British lexicographer.
Dictionary of the English Language

4 *Dull.* 8. To make dictionaries is dull work.
Samuel Johnson (1709–84)

5 *Lexicographer.* A writer of dictionaries, a harmless drudge.
Samuel Johnson
Dictionary of the English Language

6 I've been in *Who's Who*, and I know what's what, but this is the first time I ever made the dictionary.
Mae West (1892–1980) US actress.
On having a life-jacket named after her
Attrib.

LIBERALISM

1 To be absolutely honest, what I feel really

bad about is that I don't feel worse. There's the ineffectual liberal's problem in a nutshell.
Michael Frayn (1933–) British journalist and writer.
The Observer, 8 Aug 1965

2   When a liberal is abused, he says: Thank God they didn't beat me. When he is beaten, he thanks God they didn't kill him. When he is killed, he will thank God that his immortal soul has been delivered from its mortal clay.
Lenin (Vladimir Ilich Ulyanov; 1870–1924) Russian revolutionary leader.
Lenin heard this characterization at a meeting, and repeated it with approval
The Government's Falsification of the Duma and the Tasks of the Social-Democrats, 'Proletary', Dec 1906.

3   A pleasant old buffer, nephew to a lord,
Who believed that the bank was mightier than the sword,
And that an umbrella might pacify barbarians abroad:
Just like an old liberal
Between the wars.
William Plomer (1903–73) South African poet and novelist.
Father and Son: 1939

LIFE

See also afterlife, human condition, life and death, mortality, purpose, time, world-weariness

1   Life begins at forty.
Proverb

2   Life is just a bowl of cherries.
Proverb

3   Life is sweet.
Proverb

4   Is it so small a thing
To have enjoy'd the sun,
To have lived light in the spring,
To have loved, to have thought, to have done?
Matthew Arnold (1822–88) British poet and critic.
Empedocles on Etna

5   Before this strange disease of modern life,
With its sick hurry, its divided aims.
Matthew Arnold
The Scholar Gipsy

6   Who saw life steadily, and saw it whole:
The mellow glory of the Attic stage.
Matthew Arnold
Sonnets to a Friend

7   Remember that no man loses any other life than this which he now lives, nor lives any other than this which he now loses.
Marcus Aurelius (121–180 AD) Roman emperor.
Meditations, Bk. II, Ch. 14

8   The universe is transformation; our life is what our thoughts make it.
Marcus Aurelius
Meditations, Bk. IV, Ch. 3

9   The present life of men on earth, O king, as compared with the whole length of time which is unknowable to us, seems to me to be like this: as if, when you are sitting at dinner with your chiefs and ministers in wintertime, . . . one of the sparrows from outside flew very quickly through the hall; as if it came in one door and soon went out through another. In that actual time it is indoors it is not touched by the winter's storm; but yet the tiny period of calm is over in a moment, and having come out of the winter it soon returns to the winter and slips out of your sight. Man's life appears to be more or less like this; and of what may follow it, or what preceded it, we are absolutely ignorant.
St Bede (The Venerable Bede; c. 673–735 AD) English churchman and historian.
Ecclesiastical History of the English People, Bk. II, Ch. 13

10 Life is rather like a tin of sardines – we're all of us looking for the key.
Alan Bennett (1934–) British playwright.
Beyond the Fringe

11 Your whole life is on the other side of the glass. And there is nobody watching.
Alan Bennett
The Old Country, I

12 For everything that lives is holy, life delights in life.
William Blake (1757–1827) British poet.
America

13 At last awake
From life, that insane dream we take
For waking now.
Robert Browning (1812–89) British poet.
Easter-Day, XIV

14 How good is man's life, the mere living! how fit to employ
All the heart and the soul and the senses for ever in joy!
Robert Browning
Saul, IX

15 Life is one long process of getting tired.
Samuel Butler (1835–1902) British writer.
Notebooks

16 Life is the art of drawing sufficient conclusions from insufficient premises.
Samuel Butler
Notebooks

17 Life is a tragedy when seen in close-up, but a comedy in long-shot.
Charlie Chaplin (Sir Charles Spencer C.; 1889–1977) British film actor.
In *The Guardian,* Obituary, 28 Dec 1977

18 Life is a maze in which we take the wrong turning before we have learnt to walk.
Cyril Connolly (1903–74) British journalist.
The Unquiet Grave

19 Life is an incurable disease.
Abraham Cowley (1618–67) English poet.
To Dr Scarborough

20 What a fine comedy this world would be if one did not play a part in it!
Denis Diderot (1713–84) French writer.
Letters to Sophie Volland

21 People do not live nowadays – they get about ten percent out of life.
Isadora Duncan (1878–1927) US dancer.
This Quarter Autumn, 'Memoirs'

22 'Put your shoes at the door, sleep, prepare for life.'
The last twist of the knife.
T. S. Eliot (1888–1965) US-born British poet and dramatist.
Rhapsody on a Windy Night

23 I have measured out my life with coffee spoons.
T. S. Eliot
The Love Song of J. Alfred Prufrock

24 One thing is certain, that Life flies;
One thing is certain, and the Rest is Lies;
The Flower that once has blown for ever dies.
Edward Fitzgerald (1809–83) British poet.
The Rubáiyát of Omar Khayyám (1st edn.), XXVI

25 Life is a jest; and all things show it.
I thought so once; but now I know it.
John Gay (1685–1732) English poet and dramatist.
My Own Epitaph

26 Life's Little Ironies.
Thomas Hardy (1840–1928) British novelist.
Title of book of stories

27 Life is just one damned thing after another.
Elbert Hubbard (1856–1915) US writer.
A Thousand and One Epigrams

28 Life isn't all beer and skittles.
Thomas Hughes (1822–96) British novelist.
Tom Brown's Schooldays, Pt. I, Ch. 2

29 Live all you can; it's a mistake not to. It doesn't so much matter what you do in particular, so long as you have your life. If you haven't had that what *have* you had?
Henry James (1843–1916) US novelist.
The Ambassadors, Bk. V, Ch. 2

30 Life is like a sewer. What you get out of it depends on what you put into it.
Tom Lehrer (1928–) US university teacher and songwriter.
We will all go together when we go

31 Life is what happens to you while you're busy making other plans.
John Lennon (1940–80) British rock musician.
Beautiful Boy

32 Our ingress into the world
Was naked and bare;
Our progress through the world
Is trouble and care.
Henry Wadsworth Longfellow (1807–82) US poet.
Tales of A Wayside Inn, 'The Student's Tale'

33 And thou wilt give thyself relief, if thou doest every act of thy life as if it were the last.
Marcus Aurelius (121–180 AD) Roman emperor.
Meditations, Bk. II, Ch. 5

34 I've looked at life from both sides now
From win and lose and still somehow
It's life's illusions I recall
I really don't know life at all.
Joni Mitchell (1945–) Singer and songwriter.
Both Sides Now

35 There are three ingredients in the good life: learning, earning and yearning.
Christopher Darlington Morley (1890–1957) US writer.
Parnassus on Wheels, Ch. 10

36 Our lives are merely strange dark interludes in the electric display of God the Father.
Eugene O'Neill (1888–1953) US dramatist.
Strange Interlude

37 Most people get a fair amount of fun out of their lives, but on balance life is suffering and only the very young or the very foolish imagine otherwise.
George Orwell (Eric Blair; 1903–50) British novelist.
Shooting an Elephant

38 The vanity of human life is like a river, constantly passing away, and yet constantly coming on.
Alexander Pope (1688–1744) British poet.
Thoughts on Various Subjects

39 Life is not a spectacle or a feast; it is a predicament.
George Santayana (1863–1952) US philosopher.
The Perpetual Pessimist (Sagittarius and George)

40 Life is as tedious as a twice-told tale
Vexing the dull ear of a drowsy man.
William Shakespeare (1564–1616) English dramatist.
King John, III:4

41 Tomorrow, and tomorrow, and tomorrow,
Creeps in this petty pace from day to day
To the last syllable of recorded time,
And all our yesterdays have lighted fools
The way to dusty death. Out, out, brief candle!
Life's but a walking shadow, a poor player,
That struts and frets his hour upon the stage,
And then is heard no more; it is a tale
Told by an idiot, full of sound and fury,
Signifying nothing.
William Shakespeare
Macbeth, V:5

42 And so, from hour to hour, we ripe and ripe,
And then, from hour to hour, we rot and rot;
And thereby hangs a tale.
William Shakespeare
As You Like It, II:7

43 Lift not the painted veil which those who live
Call life.

Percy Bysshe Shelley (1792–1822) British poet.
Lift not the Painted Veil

44 Life is a gamble, at terrible odds – if it was
a bet, you wouldn't take it.

Tom Stoppard (1937–) Czech-born British dramatist.
Rosencrantz and Guildenstern Are Dead, III

45 As our life is very short, so it is very
miserable, and
therefore it is well it is short.

Jeremy Taylor (1613–67) English Anglican theologian.
The Rule and Exercise of Holy Dying, Ch. 1

46 A life that moves to gracious ends
Thro' troops of unrecording friends,
A deedful life, a silent voice.

Alfred, Lord Tennyson (1809–92) British poet.
To – , after reading a Life and Letters

47 Oh, isn't life a terrible thing, thank God?

Dylan Thomas (1914–53) Welsh poet.
Under Milk Wood

48 For life is but a dream whose shapes return,
Some frequently, some seldom, some by night
And some by day.

James Thomson (1834–82) British poet.
The City of Dreadful Night, I

49 The world is a comedy to those who think, a
tragedy to those who feel.

Horace Walpole (1717–97) British writer.
Letter to Sir Horace Mann, 1769

50 I spent the afternoon musing on Life. If you
come to think of it, what a queer thing Life
is! So unlike anything else, don't you know, if
you see what I mean.

P. G. Wodehouse (1881–1975) British humorous
novelist.
My Man Jeeves, 'Rallying Round Old George'

51 When I think of all the books I have read,
and of the wise words I have heard spoken,
and of the anxiety I have given to parents
and grandparents, and of the hopes that I
have had, all life weighed in the scales of my
own life seems to me preparation for
something that never happens.

W. B. Yeats (1865–1939) Irish poet.
Autobiography

52 Never to have lived is best, ancient writers
say;
Never to have drawn the breath of life,
never to have looked into the eye of day
The second best's a gay goodnight and quickly
turn away.

W. B. Yeats
Oedipus at Colonus

LIFE AND DEATH

See also death, life

1 Every moment dies a man,
Every moment one and one sixteenth is born.

Charles Babbage (1792–1871) British mathematician.
A parody of TENNYSON's *Vision of Sin*
Letter to Tennyson

2 I call heaven and earth to record this day
against you, that I have set before you life
and death, blessing and cursing: therefore
choose life, that both thou and thy seed may
live.

Bible: Deuteronomy
30:19

3 This world nis but a thurghfare ful of wo,
And we ben pilgrimes, passinge to and fro;
Deeth is an ende of every worldly sore.

Geoffrey Chaucer (c. 1342–1400) English poet.
The Canterbury Tales, 'The Knight's Tale'

4 Birth, and copulation, and death.
That's all the facts when you come to brass
tacks.

T. S. Eliot (1888–1965) US-born British poet and
dramatist.
Sweeney Agonistes, 'Fragment of an Agon'

5 I came like Water, and like Wind I go.

Edward Fitzgerald (1809–83) British poet.
The Rubáiyát of Omar Khayyám (1st edn.), XXVIII

6 There are only three events in a man's life;
birth, life, and death; he is not conscious of
being born, he dies in pain, and he forgets to
live.

Jean de La Bruyère (1645–96) French satirist.
Les Caractères

7 I strove with none; for none was worth my
strife;
Nature I loved, and, next to Nature, Art;
I warmed both hands before the fire of life;
It sinks, and I am ready to depart.

Walter Savage Landor (1775–1864) British poet and
writer.
I Strove with None

8 Many men would take the death-sentence
without a whimper to escape the life-
sentence which fate carries in her other
hand.

T. E. Lawrence (1888–1935) British soldier and writer.
The Mint, Pt. I, Ch. 4

9 There is no cure for birth and death save to
enjoy the interval.

George Santayana (1863–1952) US philosopher.
Soliloquies in England, 'War Shrines'

10 He hath awakened from the dream of life –
'Tis we, who lost in stormy visions, keep
With phantoms an unprofitable strife,
And in mad trance, strike with our spirit's knife
Invulnerable nothings.

Percy Bysshe Shelley (1792–1822) British poet.
Adonais, XXXIX

11 Every moment dies a man,

Every moment one is born.

Alfred, Lord Tennyson (1809–92) British poet.
For a parody, *see* BABBAGE
The Vision of Sin

12 Because there is no difference.

Thales (c. 624–547 BC) Greek philosopher and astronomer.
His reply when asked why he chose to carry on living after
saying there was no difference between life and death
The Story of Civilization (W. Durant), Vol. 2

LIMBO

1 Wandering between two worlds, one dead,
The other powerless to be born.

Matthew Arnold (1822–88) British poet and critic.
The Grande Chartreuse

LIMERICKS

A small selection

1 There's a wonderful family called Stein,
There's Gert and there's Epp and there's Ein;
Gert's poems are bunk,
Epp's statues are junk,
And no one can understand Ein.

Anonymous

2 There was a faith-healer of Deal,
Who said, 'Although pain isn't real,
If I sit on a pin
And it punctures my skin,
I dislike what I fancy I feel.'

Anonymous

3 There was an old man from Darjeeling,
Who boarded a bus bound for Ealing,
He saw on the door:
'Please don't spit on the floor,'
So he stood up and spat on the ceiling.

Anonymous

4 There was an old man of Boulogne
Who sang a most topical song.
It wasn't the words
That frightened the birds,
But the horrible double-entendre.

Anonymous

5 There was a young lady of Riga,
Who went for a ride on a tiger;
They returned from the ride
With the lady inside,
And a smile on the face of the tiger.

Anonymous

6 There was a young man of Japan
Whose limericks never would scan;
When they said it was so,
He replied, 'Yes, I know,
But I always try to get as many words into the
last line as ever I possibly can.'

Anonymous

7 There once was a man who said 'God
Must think it exceedingly odd

If he find that this tree
Continues to be
When there's no one about in the Quad.'

Ronald Knox (1888–1957) British Roman Catholic priest
and writer.
For a reply, see below
Attrib.

8 Dear Sir, Your astonishment's odd:
I am always about in the Quad.
And that's why the tree
Will continue to be,
Since observed by Yours faithfully, God.

Anonymous
A reply to KNOX

9 There was an Old Man with a beard,
Who said, 'It is just as I feared! –
Two Owls and a Hen,
Four Larks and a Wren,
Have all built their nests in my beard!'

Edward Lear (1812–88) British artist and writer.
Book of Nonsense

LITERACY

See also reading, writing

1 The ratio of literacy to illiteracy is constant,
but nowadays the illiterates can read and
write.

Alberto Moravia (Alberto Pincherle; 1907–) Italian
novelist.
The Observer, 14 Oct 1979

2 To be a well-favoured man is the gift of
fortune; but to write and read comes by
nature.

William Shakespeare (1564–1616) English dramatist.
Much Ado About Nothing, III:3

LITERARY CRITICISM

1 Your works will be read after Shakespeare
and Milton are forgotten – and not till then.

Richard Porson (1759–1808) British classicist.
Giving his opinion of the poems of Robert Southey
Quotable Anecdotes (L. Meissen)

LITERATURE

See also arts, books, criticism, fiction, novels, plays, poetry,
poetry and prose, poets, prose, reading, theatre, writers,
writing

1 Literature is the art of writing something that
will be read twice; journalism what will be
grasped at once.

Cyril Connolly (1903–74) British journalist.
Enemies of Promise, Ch. 3

2 A work that aspires, however humbly, to the
condition of art should carry its justification in
every line.

Joseph Conrad (Teodor Josef Konrad Korzeniowski;
1857–1924) Polish-born British novelist.
The Nigger of the Narcissus, Preface

3 The reading of all good books is like a

conversation with the finest men of past centuries.
René Descartes (1596–1650) French philosopher.
Le Discours de la méthode

4 He knew everything about literature except how to enjoy it.
Joseph Heller (1923–) US novelist.
Catch-22, Ch. 8

5 The proper study of mankind is books.
Aldous Huxley (1894–1964) British novelist.
Chrome Yellow

6 Literature flourishes best when it is half a trade and half an art.
Dean Inge (1860–1954) British churchman.
The Victorian Age

7 It takes a great deal of history to produce a little literature.
Henry James (1843–1916) US novelist.
Life of Nathaniel Hawthorne, Ch. 1

8 Was there ever yet anything written by mere man that was wished longer by its readers, excepting *Don Quixote, Robinson Crusoe,* and the *Pilgrim's Progress*?
Samuel Johnson (1709–84) British lexicographer.
Johnsonian Miscellanies (ed. G. B. Hill), Vol. I

9 *Sturm und Drang.*
Storm and stress.
Friedrich Maximilian von Klinger (1752–1831) German dramatist and novelist.
Used to designate a late 18th-century literary movement in Germany
Play title

10 Our American professors like their literature clear and cold and pure and very dead.
Sinclair Lewis (1885–1951) US novelist.
Speech, on receiving the Nobel Prize, 1930

11 Literature is mostly about having sex and not much about having children; life is the other way round.
David Lodge (1935–) British author.
The British Museum is Falling Down, Ch. 4

12 You understand *Epipsychidion* best when you are in love; *Don Juan* when anger is subsiding into indifference. Why not Strindberg when you have a temperature?
Desmond MacCarthy (1877–1952) British writer and theatre critic.
Theatre, 'Miss Julie and the Pariah'

13 Literature and butterflies are the two sweetest passions known to man.
Vladimir Nabokov (1899–1977) Russian-born US novelist.
Radio Times, Oct 1962

14 Literature is news that STAYS news.
Ezra Pound (1885–1972) US poet.
ABC of Reading, Ch. 2

15 Great Literature is simply language charged with meaning to the utmost possible degree.
Ezra Pound
How to Read

16 Romanticism is the art of presenting people with the literary works which are capable of affording them the greatest possible pleasure, in the present state of their customs and beliefs.
Classicism, on the other hand, presents them with the literature that gave the greatest possible pleasure to their great-grandfathers.
Stendhal (Henri Beyle; 1783–1842) French novelist.
Racine et Shakespeare, Ch. 3

17 Something that everybody wants to have read and nobody wants to read.
Mark Twain (Samuel Langhorne Clemens; 1835–1910) US writer.
Definition of a classic of literature
Speech at Nineteenth Century Club, New York, 20 Nov 1900

18 '*Language,* man!' roared Parsons; 'why, it's LITERATURE!'
H. G. Wells (1866–1946) British writer.
The History of Mr Polly, Pt. I, Ch. 3

19 Literature is the orchestration of platitudes.
Thornton Wilder (1897–1975) US novelist and dramatist.
Time magazine

LOGIC

See also philosophy

1 'Contrariwise,' continued Tweedledee, 'if it was so, it might be; and if it were so, it would be: but as it isn't, it ain't. That's logic.'
Lewis Carroll (Charles Lutwidge Dodgson; 1832–98) British writer.
Through the Looking-Glass, Ch. 4

2 You can only find truth with logic if you have already found truth without it.
G. K. Chesterton (1874–1936) British writer.
The Man who was Orthodox

3 Logical consequences are the scarecrows of fools and the beacons of wise men.
T. H. Huxley (1825–95) British biologist.
Science and Culture, 'On the Hypothesis that Animals are Automata'

4 The world is everything that is the case.
Ludwig Wittgenstein (1889–1951) Austrian philosopher.
Tractatus Logico-Philosophicus, Ch. 1

5 Logic must take care of itself.
Ludwig Wittgenstein
Tractatus Logico-Philosophicus, Ch. 5

LONDON

See also England

1 The streets of London are paved with gold.
Proverb

2 Oranges and lemons,
Say the bells of St Clement's.
You owe me five farthings,
Say the bells of St Martin's.
When will you pay me?
Say the bells of Old Bailey.
When I grow rich,
Say the bells of Shoreditch.
When will that be?
Say the bells of Stepney.
I'm sure I don't know,
Says the great bell at Bow.
Here comes a candle to light you to bed,
Here comes a chopper to chop off your head.
Tommy Thumb's Pretty Song Book

3 Nobody is healthy in London, nobody can be.
Jane Austen (1775–1817) British novelist.
Emma, Ch. 12

4 Let's all go down the Strand.
Harry Castling (19th century) British songwriter.
Song title

5 But what is to be the fate of the great wen of all?
William Cobbett (1763–1835) British journalist and writer.
A wen is a sebaceous cyst
Rural Rides

6 London, that great cesspool into which all the loungers of the Empire are irresistibly drained.
Arthur Conan Doyle (1856–1930) British writer.
A Study in Scarlet

7 Crowds without company, and dissipation without pleasure.
Edward Gibbon (1737–94) British historian.
Autobiography

8 The tourists who come to our island take in the Monarchy along with feeding the pigeons in Trafalgar Square.
William Hamilton (1917–) Scottish MP.
My Queen and I, Ch. 9

9 I think the full tide of human existence is at Charing-Cross.
Samuel Johnson (1709–84) British lexicographer.
Life of Johnson (J. Boswell), Vol. II

10 When a man is tired of London, he is tired of life; for there is in London all that life can afford.
Samuel Johnson
Life of Johnson (J. Boswell), Vol. III

11 London, that great sea, whose ebb and flow
At once is deaf and loud, and on the shore
Vomits its wrecks, and still howls on for more.
Percy Bysshe Shelley (1792–1822) British poet.
Letter to Maria Gisborne, I

12 Hell is a city much like London –
A populous and smoky city.
Percy Bysshe Shelley
Peter Bell the Third

13 Crossing Piccadilly Circus.
Joseph Thomson (1858–95) Scottish explorer.
His reply when asked by J. M. Barrie what was the most hazardous part of his expedition to Africa
J. M. Barrie (D. Dunbar)

14 Earth has not anything to show more fair:
Dull would he be of soul who could pass by
A sight so touching in its majesty:
The City now doth, like a garment, wear
The beauty of the morning; silent, bare,
Ships, towers, domes, theatres, and temples lie
Open unto the fields, and to the sky;
All bright and glittering in the smokeless air.
William Wordsworth (1770–1850) British poet.
Sonnets, 'Composed upon Westminster Bridge'

LONELINESS

See also solitude

1 Oh! why does the wind blow upon me so wild? – It is because I'm nobody's child?
Phila Henrietta Case (fl. 1864) British poet.
Nobody's Child

2 A fav'rite has no friend.
Thomas Gray (1716–71) British poet.
Ode on the Death of a Favourite Cat

3 Pray that your loneliness may spur you into finding something to live for, great enough to die for.
Dag Hammarskjöld (1905–61) Swedish diplomat.
Diaries, 1951

4 Waits at the window, wearing the face that she keeps in a jar by the door
Who is it for? All the lonely people, where do they all come from?
All the lonely people, where do they all belong?
John Lennon (1940–80) British rock musician.
Eleanor Rigby (with Paul McCartney)

5 My heart is a lonely hunter that hunts on a lonely hill.
Fiona Macleod (William Sharp; 1856–1905) Scottish poet and writer.
The Lonely Hunter

6 To be alone is the fate of all great minds – a fate deplored at times, but still always chosen as the less grievous of two evils.
Arthur Schopenhauer (1788–1860) German philosopher.
Aphorismen zur Lebensweisheit

7 Loneliness and the feeling of being unwanted is the most terrible poverty.
Mother Teresa (Agnes Gonxha Bojaxhui; 1910–)
Yugoslavian missionary in Calcutta.
Time, 'Saints Among Us', 29 Dec 1975

8 The hunchback in the park
A solitary mister
Propped between trees and water.
Dylan Thomas (1914–53) Welsh poet.
The Hunchback in the Park

9 She dwelt among the untrodden ways
Beside the springs of Dove,
A maid whom there were none to praise
And very few to love . . .
William Wordsworth (1770–1850) British poet.
She Dwelt Among the Untrodden Ways

10 The wind blows out of the gates of the day,
The wind blows over the lonely of heart,
And the lonely of heart is withered away.
W. B. Yeats (1865–1939) Irish poet.
The Land of Heart's Desire

LONGEVITY

See also age, life, old age

1 Aging seems to be the only available way to
live a long time.
Daniel-François-Esprit Auber (1782–1871) French
composer.
Dictionnaire Encyclopédique (E. Guérard)

2 Get your room full of good air, then shut up
the windows and keep it. It will keep for
years. Anyway, don't keep using your lungs
all the time. Let them rest.
Stephen Leacock (1869–1944) English-born Canadian
economist and humorist.
Literary Lapses, 'How to Live to be 200'

3 If you live long enough, the venerability
factor creeps in; you get accused of things
you never did and praised for virtues you
never had.
I. F. Stone (1907–) US writer and publisher.
Peter's Quotations (Laurence J. Peter)

LOSS

See also defeat, mourning

1 'Tis better to have loved and lost than never
to have lost at all.
Samuel Butler (1835–1902) British writer.
The Way of All Flesh, Ch. 77

2 What's lost upon the roundabouts we pulls up
on the swings!
Patrick Reginald Chalmers (1872–1942) British banker
and novelist.
Green Days and Blue Days: Roundabouts and Swings

3 And much more am I sorrier for my good
knights' loss than for the loss of my fair
queen; for queens I might have enough, but
such a fellowship of good knights shall never
be together in no company.
Thomas Malory (1400–71) English writer.
Morte d'Arthur, Bk. XX, Ch. 9

4 There is a ghost
That eats handkerchiefs;
It keeps you company
On all your travels.
Christian Morgenstern (1871–1914) German poet.
Der Gingganz, 'Gespenst'

5 Where have all the flowers gone?

Young girls picked them every one.
Pete Seeger (1919–) US folksinger and songwriter.
Where Have All the Flowers Gone?

6 I've lost the only playboy of the western
world.
John Millington Synge (1871–1909) Anglo-Irish
dramatist.
The closing words
The Playboy of the Western World, III

7 I've lost one of my children this week.
Joseph Turner (1775–1851) British painter.
His customary remark following the sale of one of his paintings
Sketches of Great Painters (E. Chubb)

8 To lose one parent, Mr Worthing, may be
regarded as a misfortune; to lose both looks
like carelessness.
Oscar Wilde (1854–1900) Irish-born British dramatist.
The Importance of Being Earnest, I

LOVE

See also admiration, love and death, love and friendship, love
and hate, love and marriage, lust, passion, sex

1 All is fair in love and war.
Proverb

2 All the world loves a lover.
Proverb

3 Love laughs at locksmiths.
Proverb

4 Love makes the world go round.
Proverb

5 Love me, love my dog.
Proverb

6 Love will find a way.
Proverb

7 Lucky at cards, unlucky in love.
Proverb

8 No love like the first love.
Proverb

9 Salt water and absence wash away love.
Proverb

10 The way to a man's heart is through his
stomach.
Proverb

11 True love never grows old.
Proverb

12 When poverty comes in at the door, love
flies out of the window.
Proverb

13 In Scarlet town, where I was born,
There was a fair maid dwellin',
Made every youth cry *Well-a-way!*
Her name was Barbara Allen.

All in the merry month of May,

When green buds they were swellin',
Young Jemmy Grove on his death-bed lay,
For love of Barbara Allen.

So slowly, slowly rase she up,
And slowly she came nigh him,
And when she drew the curtain by –
'Young man, I think you're dyin'!'.
Anonymous
Barbara Allen's Cruelty

14 Greensleeves was all my joy,
Greensleeves was my delight,
Greensleeves was my heart of gold,
And who but Lady Greensleeves.
Anonymous
Greensleeves

15 There were twa sisters sat in a bour;
Binnorie, O Binnorie!
There came a knight to be their wooer,
By the bonnie milldams o' Binnorie.
Anonymous
Binnorie

16 Oh, love is real enough, you will find it some
day, but it has one arch-enemy – and that is
life.
Jean Anouilh (1910–87) French dramatist.
Ardèle

17 Love is, above all, the gift of oneself.
Jean Anouilh
Ardèle

18 When it comes, will it come without warning
Just as I'm picking my nose?
Will it knock on my door in the morning,
Or tread in the bus on my toes?
Will it come like a change in the weather?
Will its greeting be courteous or rough?
Will it alter my life altogether?
O tell me the truth about love.
W. H. Auden (1907–73) British poet.
Twelve Songs, XII

19 Nuptial love maketh mankind; friendly love
perfecteth it; but wanton love corrupteth and
embaseth it.
Francis Bacon (1561–1626) English philosopher.
Essays, 'Of Love'

20 Women who love the same man have a kind
of bitter freemasonry.
Max Beerbohm (1872–1956) British writer.
Zuleika Dobson, Ch. 4

21 Love ceases to be a pleasure, when it ceases
to be a secret.
Aphra Behn (1640–89) English novelist and dramatist.
The Lover's Watch, 'Four o'clock'

22 Beloved, let us love one another: for love is
of God; and every one that loveth is born of
God, and knoweth God.

He that loveth not knoweth not God; for God
is love.
Bible: I John
4:7–8

23 If a man say, I love God, and hateth his
brother, he is a liar: for he that loveth not
his brother whom he hath seen, how can he
love God whom he hath not seen?
Bible: I John
4:20

24 There is no fear in love; but perfect love
casteth out fear: because fear hath torment.
He that feareth is not made perfect in love.
Bible: I John
4:18

25 Greater love hath no man than this, that a
man lay down his life for his friends.
Bible: John
15:13

26 Jesus said unto him, Thou shalt love the
Lord thy God with all thy heart, and with all
thy soul, and with all thy mind.
This is the first and great commandment.
And the second is like unto it, Thou shalt love
thy neighbour as thyself.
On these two commandments hang all the law
and the prophets.
Bible: Matthew
22:37–40

27 Love seeketh not itself to please,
Nor for itself hath any care,
But for another gives its ease,
And builds a Heaven in Hell's despair.
William Blake (1757–1827) British poet.
Songs of Experience, 'The Clod and the Pebble'

28 Love seeketh only Self to please,
To bind another to its delight,
Joys in another's loss of ease,
And builds a Hell in Heaven's despite.
William Blake
Songs of Experience, 'The Clod and the Pebble'

29 I love thee with a love I seemed to lose
With my lost saints – I love thee with the
breath,
Smiles, tears, of all my life! – and, if God
choose,
I shall but love thee better after death.
Elizabeth Barrett Browning (1806–61) British poet.
Sonnets from the Portuguese, XLIII

30 Such ever was love's way; to rise, it stoops.
Robert Browning (1812–89) British poet.
A Death in the Desert

31 Green grow the rashes O,
Green grow the rashes O,
The sweetest hours that e'er I spend,
Are spent amang the lasses O!
Robert Burns (1759–96) Scottish poet.
Green Grow the Rashes

32 My love is like a red red rose

That's newly sprung in June:
My love is like the melodie
That's sweetly play'd in tune.
Robert Burns
A Red, Red Rose

33 Gin a body meet a body
Coming through the rye;
Gin a body kiss a body,
Need a body cry?
Robert Burns
Coming through the Rye

34 God is Love – I dare say. But what a
mischievous devil Love is!
Samuel Butler (1835–1902) British writer.
Notebooks

35 Of all the girls that are so smart
There's none like pretty Sally;
She is the darling of my heart
And she lives in our alley.
Henry Carey (c. 1690–1743) English poet and musician.
Sally in our Alley

36 There ain't a lady livin' in the land
As I'd swop for my dear old Dutch!
Albert Chevalier (1861–1923) British music-hall artist.
My Old Dutch

37 Many a man has fallen in love with a girl in a
light so dim he would not have chosen a suit
by it.
Maurice Chevalier (1888–1972) French singer and actor.
Attrib.

38 Love and a cottage! Eh, Fanny! Ah, give me
indifference and a coach and six!
George Colman, the Elder (1732–94) British dramatist.
The Clandestine Marriage, I:2

39 See how love and murder will out.
William Congreve (1670–1729) British Restoration
dramatist.
The Double Dealer, IV:6

40 Lord, what is a lover that it can give? Why
one makes lovers as fast as one pleases, and
they live as long as one pleases, and they die
as soon as one pleases: and then if one
pleases one makes more.
William Congreve
The Way of the World, II:4

41 Say what you will, 'tis better to be left than
never to have been loved.
William Congreve
The Way of the World, II:1

42 Mad about the boy.
Noël Coward (1899–1973) British dramatist.
Title of song

43 Love is a sickness full of woes,
All remedies refusing:
A plant that with most cutting grows,
Most barren with best using.
Why so?
More we enjoy it, more it dies;

If not enjoyed, it sighing cries,
Hey ho.
Samuel Daniel (c. 1562–1619) English poet and dramatist.
Hymen's Triumph, I

44 It has been said that love robs those who
have it of their wit, and gives it to those who
have none.
Denis Diderot (1713–84) French writer.
Paradoxe sur le comédien

45 Come live with me, and be my love,
And we will some new pleasures prove
Of golden sands, and crystal brooks,
With silken lines, and silver hooks.
John Donne (1573–1631) English poet.
The Bait

46 I am two fools, I know,
For loving, and for saying so
In whining Poetry.
John Donne
The Triple Fool

47 O my America! my new-found-land,
My Kingdom, safeliest when with one man
man'd.
John Donne
Elegies, 19, 'Going To Bed'

48 It seems to me that he has never loved, that
he has only imagined that he has loved, that
there has been no real love on his part. I
even think that he is incapable of love; he is
too much occupied with other thoughts and
ideas to become strongly attached to anyone
earthly.
Anna Dostoevsky (1846–1918) Russian diarist and
writer.
Dostoevsky Portrayed by His Wife

49 And I was desolate and sick of an old
passion.
Ernest Dowson (1867–1900) British lyric poet.
Non Sum Qualis Eram Bonae Sub Regno Cynarae

50 You may not be an angel
'Cause angels are so few,
But until the day that one comes along
I'll string along with you.
Al Dubin (20th century) US songwriter.
Twenty Million Sweethearts

51 All mankind love a lover.
Ralph Waldo Emerson (1803–82) US poet and essayist.
Essays, 'Love'

52 Don't you think I was made for you? I feel
like you had me ordered – and I was
delivered to you – to be worn – I want you
to wear me, like a watch-charm or a button
hole bouquet – to the world.
Zelda Fitzgerald (1900–48) US writer.
Letter to F. Scott Fitzgerald, 1919

53 . . . I don't want to live – I want to love
first, and live incidentally . . .
Zelda Fitzgerald
Letter to F. Scott Fitzgerald, 1919

54 *Plaisir d'amour ne dure qu'un moment,*
Chagrin d'amour dure toute la vie.
Love's pleasure lasts but a moment; love's sor-
row lasts all through life.
Jean-Pierre Claris de Florian (1755–94) French writer
of fables.
Celestine

55 I'm leaning on a lamp-post at the corner of
the street,
In case a certain little lady walks by.
George Formby (1905–61) British comedian.
Leaning on a Lamp-post

56 Try thinking of love, or something.
Amor vincit insomnia.
Christopher Fry (1907–   ) British dramatist.
A Sleep of Prisoners

57 If with me you'd fondly stray,
Over the hills and far away.
John Gay (1685–1732) English poet and dramatist.
The Beggar's Opera

58 She who has never loved has never lived.
John Gay
Captives

59 It's a song of a merryman, moping mum,
Whose soul was sad, and whose glance was
glum,
Who sipped no sup, and who craved no crumb,
As he sighed for the love of a ladye.
W. S. Gilbert (1836–1911) British dramatist.
The Yeoman of the Guard, I

60 In love as in sport, the amateur status must
be strictly maintained.
Robert Graves (1895–1985) British poet and novelist.
Occupation: Writer

61 Love, love, love – all the wretched cant of
it, masking egotism, lust, masochism, fantasy
under a mythology of sentimental postures, a
welter of self-induced miseries and joys,
blinding and masking the essential
personalities in the frozen gestures of
courtship, in the kissing and the dating and
the desire, the compliments and the quarrels
which vivify its barrenness.
Germaine Greer (1939–   ) Australian-born British writer
and feminist.
The Female Eunuch

62 If you were the only girl in the world,
And I were the only boy.
George Grossmith the Younger (1874–1935) British
singer, actor, and songwriter.
The Bing Boys, 'If you were the Only Girl' (with Fred Thomp-
son; 1884–1949)

63 Hello, Young Lovers, Wherever You Are.
Oscar Hammerstein (1895–1960) US lyricist.
From the musical *The King and I*
Song title

64 A lover without indiscretion is no lover at all.
Thomas Hardy (1840–1928) British novelist.
The Hand of Ethelberta, Ch. 20

65 'You must sit down,' says Love, 'and taste
My meat,'
So I did sit and eat.
George Herbert (1593–1633) English poet.
Love

66 My love she's but a lassie yet.
James Hogg (1770–1835) Scottish poet and writer.
Title of song

67 Pale hands I loved beside the Shalimar,
Where are you now? Who lies beneath your
spell?
Laurence Hope (Mrs M. H. Nicolson; 1804–1905)
British poet and songwriter.
The Garden of Kama and other Love Lyrics from India, 'Pale
Hands I Loved'

68 Look not in my eyes, for fear
They mirror true the sight I see,
And there you find your face too clear
And love it and be lost like me.
A. E. Housman (1859–1936) British scholar and poet.
A Shropshire Lad, 'March'

69 Love is like the measles; we all have to go
through with it.
Jerome K. Jerome (1859–1927) British humorist.
Idle Thoughts of an Idle Fellow

70 Love's like the measles – all the worse
when it comes late in life.
Douglas William Jerrold (1803–57) British dramatist.
Wit and Opinions of Douglas Jerrold, 'A Philanthropist'

71 Love is the wisdom of the fool and the folly
of the wise.
Samuel Johnson (1709–84) British lexicographer.
Johnsonian Miscellanies (ed. G. B. Hill), Vol. II

72 Drink to me only with thine eyes,
And I will pledge with mine;
Or leave a kiss but in the cup,
And I'll not look for wine.
The thirst that from the soul doth rise
Doth ask a drink divine;
But might I of Jove's nectar sup,
I would not change for thine.

I sent thee late a rosy wreath,
Not so much honouring thee,
As giving it a hope that there
It could not wither'd be.
Ben Jonson (1573–1637) English dramatist.
The Forest, IX, 'To Celia'

73 Come, my Celia, let us prove,
While we can, the sports of love,
Time will not be ours for ever,
He, at length, our good will sever.
Ben Jonson
Volpone, III:6

74 Love in a hut, with water and a crust,
Is – Love, forgive us! – cinders, ashes, dust;
Love in a palace is perhaps at last
More grievous torment than a hermit's fast.
John Keats (1795–1821) British poet.
Lamia, II

75 Soft adorings from their loves receive
Upon the honey'd middle of the night.
John Keats
The Eve of Saint Agnes, VI

76 I love a lassie.
Harry Lauder (Hugh MacLennon; 1870–1950) Scottish
music-hall artist.
Song title

77 You must always be a-waggle with LOVE.
D. H. Lawrence (1885–1930) British novelist.
Bibbles

78 I'm not sure if a mental relation with a
woman doesn't make it impossible to love
her. To know the *mind* of a woman is to end
in hating her. Love means the pre-cognitive
flow . . . it is the honest state before the
apple.
D. H. Lawrence
Letter to Dr Trigant Burrow, 3 Aug 1927

79 If there's anything that you want,
If there's anything I can do,
Just call on me,
And I'll send it along with love from me to you.
John Lennon (1940–80) British rock musician.
From Me to You (with Paul McCartney)

80 She loves you, yeh, yeh, yeh,
And with a love like that you know you should
be glad.
John Lennon
She Loves You (with Paul McCartney)

81 Two souls with but a single thought,
Two hearts that beat as one.
Maria Lovell (1803–77) British actress and dramatist.
Ingomar the Barbarian, II (transl. of Friedrich Halm)

82 Time was away and somewhere else,
There were two glasses and two chairs
And two people with one pulse.
Louis MacNeice (1907–63) Irish-born British poet.
Meeting Point

83 Come live with me, and be my love;
And we will all the pleasures prove
That hills and valleys, dales and fields,
Woods or steepy mountain yields.
Christopher Marlowe (1564–93) English dramatist.
The Passionate Shepherd to his Love

84 Let us roll all our strength and all
Our sweetness up into one ball,
And tear our pleasures with rough strife
Thorough the iron gates of life:
Thus, though we cannot make our sun
Stand still, yet we will make him run.
Andrew Marvell (1621–78) English poet.
To His Coy Mistress

85 Send two dozen roses to Room 424 and put
'Emily, I love you' on the back of the bill.
Groucho Marx (Julius Marx; 1895–1977) US comedian.
A Night in Casablanca

86 Because women can do nothing except love,
they've given it a ridiculous importance.
W. Somerset Maugham (1874–1965) British novelist.
The Moon and Sixpence, Ch. 41

87 My heart shall be thy garden.
Alice Meynell (1847–1922) British poet.
The Garden

88 When a man is in love he endures more than
at other times; he submits to everything.
Friedrich Wilhelm Nietzsche (1844–1900) German
philosopher.
The Antichrist

89 I do not love thee! – no! I do not love thee!
And yet when thou art absent I am sad.
Caroline Elizabeth Sarah Norton (1808–77) British
poet.
I do Not Love Thee

90 K-K-Katy, beautiful Katy,
You're the only g-g-g-girl that I adore,
When the m-m-m-moon shines over the cow-
shed,
I'll be waiting at the k-k-k-kitchen door.
Geoffrey O'Hara (1882–1967) Canadian-born US
songwriter.
K-K-Katy (song)

91 By the time you swear you're his,
Shivering and sighing,
And he vows his passion is
Infinite, undying –
Lady, make a note of this:
One of you is lying.
Dorothy Parker (1893–1967) US writer.
Unfortunate Coincidence

92 Love's perfect blossom only blows
Where noble manners veil defect.
Angels may be familiar; those
Who err each other must respect.
Coventry Patmore (1823–96) British poet.
The Angel in the House, Bk. I, Prelude 2

93 Ye gods! annihilate but space and time.
And make two lovers happy.
Alexander Pope (1688–1744) British poet.
The Art of Sinking in Poetry, 11

94 I've Got You Under My Skin.
Cole Porter (1893–1964) US songwriter.
Born to Dance, song title

95 Night and day, you are the one,
Only you beneath the moon and under the sun.
Cole Porter
The Gay Divorcee, 'Night and Day'

96 Let's Do It; Let's Fall in Love.
Cole Porter
Paris, song title

97 I have sometimes regretted living so close to
Marie . . . because I may be very fond of her,
but I am not quite so fond of her company.
Marcel Proust (1871–1922) French novelist.
À la recherche du temps perdu: Sodome et Gomorrhe

98 There can be no peace of mind in love, since the advantage one has secured is never anything but a fresh starting-point for further desires.
Marcel Proust
À la recherche du temps perdu: À l'ombre des jeunes filles en fleurs

99 I loved you when you were inconstant. What should I have done if you had been faithful?
Jean Racine (1639–99) French dramatist.
Andromaque, IV:5

100 If all the world and love were young,
And truth in every shepherd's tongue,
These pretty pleasures might me move
To live with thee, and be thy love.
Walter Raleigh (1554–1618) English explorer.
Answer to Marlow

101 There are very few people who are not ashamed of having been in love when they no longer love each other.
Duc de la Rochefoucauld (1613–80) French writer.
Maximes, 71

102 It takes a woman twenty years to make a man of her son, and another woman twenty minutes to make a fool of him.
Helen Rowland (1876–1950) US writer.
Reflections of a Bachelor Girl

103 To fear love is to fear life, and those who fear life are already three parts dead.
Bertrand Russell (1872–1970) British philosopher.
Marriage and Morals

104 Of all forms of caution, caution in love is perhaps the most fatal to true happiness.
Bertrand Russell
Marriage and Morals

105 Every little girl knows about love. It is only her capacity to suffer because of it that increases.
Françoise Sagan (1935–) French writer.
Daily Express

106 Liszt said to me today that God alone deserves to be loved. It may be true, but when one has loved a man it is very different to love God.
George Sand (Aurore Dupin, Baronne Dudevant; 1804–76) French novelist.
Intimate Journal

107 True love's the gift which God has given
To man alone beneath the heaven.
Walter Scott (1771–1832) Scottish novelist.
The Lay of the Last Minstrel, V

108 Therefore love moderately: long love doth so;
Too swift arrives as tardy as too slow.
William Shakespeare (1564–1616) English dramatist.
Romeo and Juliet, II:6

109 The triple pillar of the world transform'd

Into a strumpet's fool.
William Shakespeare
Antony and Cleopatra, I:1

110 There's beggary in the love that can be reckon'd.
William Shakespeare
Antony and Cleopatra, I:1

111 If thou rememb'rest not the slightest folly
That ever love did make thee run into,
Thou hast not lov'd.
William Shakespeare
As You Like It, II:4

112 But love is blind, and lovers cannot see
The pretty follies that themselves commit.
William Shakespeare
The Merchant of Venice, II:6

113 For aught that I could ever read,
Could ever hear by tale or history,
The course of true love never did run smooth.
William Shakespeare
A Midsummer Night's Dream, I:1

114 Love looks not with the eyes, but with the mind;
And therefore is wing'd Cupid painted blind.
William Shakespeare
A Midsummer Night's Dream, I:1

115 The lunatic, the lover, and the poet,
Are of imagination all compact.
William Shakespeare
A Midsummer Night's Dream, V:1

116 A woman's face, with Nature's own hand painted,
Hast thou, the Master Mistress of my passion.
William Shakespeare
Sonnet 20

117 Let me not to the marriage of true minds
Admit impediments. Love is not love
Which alters when it alteration finds,
Or bends with the remover to remove.
O, no! it is an ever-fixed mark,
That looks on tempests and is never shaken.
William Shakespeare
Sonnet 116

118 Love alters not with his brief hours and weeks,
But bears it out even to the edge of doom.
If this be error, and upon me prov'd,
I never writ, nor no man ever lov'd.
William Shakespeare
Sonnet 116

119 To be wise and love
Exceeds man's might.
William Shakespeare
Troilus and Cressida, III:2

120 She never told her love,
But let concealment, like a worm i' th' bud,

Feed on her damask cheek. She pin'd in
thought;
And with a green and yellow melancholy
She sat like Patience on a monument,
Smiling at grief.
William Shakespeare
Twelfth Night, II:4

121 Love sought is good, but given unsought is
better.
William Shakespeare
Twelfth Night, III:1

122 Then must you speak
Of one that lov'd not wisely, but too well;
Of one not easily jealous, but, being
wrought,
Perplexed in the extreme; of one whose
hand,
Like the base Indian, threw a pearl away
Richer than all his tribe.
William Shakespeare
Othello, V:2

123 Nowadays we don't think much of a man's
love for an animal; we laugh at people who
are attached to cats. But if we stop loving
animals, aren't we bound to stop loving
humans too?
Alexander Solzhenitsyn (1918–   ) Soviet novelist.
Cancer Ward, Pt. I, Ch. 20

124 A woman despises a man for loving her, unless she returns his love.
Elizabeth Drew Stoddard (1823–1902) US novelist
and poet.
Two Men, Ch. 32

125 I know she likes me,
'Cause she says so.
Eugene Stratton (1861–1918) British music-hall singer.
The Lily of Laguna

126 I hold it true, whate'er befall;
I feel it, when I sorrow most;
'Tis better to have loved and lost
Than never to have loved at all.
Alfred, Lord Tennyson (1809–92) British poet.
In Memoriam A.H.H., XXVII

127 Such a one do I remember, whom to look at
was to love.
Alfred, Lord Tennyson
Locksley Hall

128 The rose was awake all night for your sake,
Knowing your promise to me;
The lilies and roses were all awake,
They sighed for the dawn and thee.
Alfred, Lord Tennyson
Maud, I

129 O tell her, brief is life but love is long.
Alfred, Lord Tennyson
The Princess, IV

130 God gives us love. Something to love
He lends us; but, when love is grown
To ripeness that on which it throve

Falls off, and love is left alone.
Alfred, Lord Tennyson
To J.S.

131 'Tis strange what a man may do, and a woman yet think him an angel.
William Makepeace Thackeray (1811–63) British
novelist.
Henry Esmond, Ch. 7

132 All, everything that I understand, I under-
stand only because I love.
Leo Tolstoy (1828–1910) Russian writer.
War and Peace, Bk. VII, Ch. 16

133 One can't live on love alone; and I am so stu-
pid that I can do nothing but think of him.
Sophie Tolstoy (1844–1919) Russian writer.
A Diary of Tolstoy's Wife, 1860–1891

134 Those who have courage to love should have
courage to suffer.
Anthony Trollope (1815–82) British novelist.
The Bertrams, Ch. 27

135 I doubt whether any girl would be satisfied
with her lover's mind if she knew the whole
of it.
Anthony Trollope
The Small House at Allington, Ch. 4

136 Walking My Baby Back Home.
Roy Turk (20th century) US songwriter.
Title of song

137 Love conquers all things: let us too give in to
Love.
Virgil (Publius Vergilius Maro; 70–19 BC) Roman poet.
Eclogue, Bk. X

138 The boy I love is up in the gallery,
The boy I love is looking now at me.
George Ware (19th century) British songwriter.
The Boy in the Gallery

139 It is like a cigar. If it goes out, you can light
it again but it never tastes quite the same.
Lord Wavell (1883–1950) British field marshall.
Attrib.

140 Beware you be not swallowed up in books!
An ounce of love is worth a pound of
knowledge.
John Wesley (1703–91) British religious leader.
Life of Wesley (R. Southey), Ch. 16

141 I have found it impossible to carry the heavy
burden of responsibility and to discharge my
duties as King as I would wish to do without the help and support of the woman I
love.
Duke of Windsor (1894–1972) King of the United
Kingdom; abdicated 1936.
Radio broadcast, 11 Dec 1936

142 There is a comfort in the strength of love;
'Twill make a thing endurable, which else
Would overset the brain, or break the heart.
William Wordsworth (1770–1850) British poet.
Michael, 448

143 Love fled
And paced upon the mountains overhead
And hid his face amid a crowd of stars.
W. B. Yeats (1865–1939) Irish poet.
When you are Old

144 But Love has pitched his mansion in
The place of excrement.
W. B. Yeats
Crazy Jane Talks with the Bishop

145 A pity beyond all telling
Is hid in the heart of love.
W. B. Yeats
The Pity of Love

LOVE AND DEATH

See also death, love

1 And for bonnie Annie Laurie
I'll lay me doun and dee.
William Douglas (1672–1748) Scottish poet.
Annie Laurie

2 For, Heaven be thanked, we live is such an age,
When no man dies for love, but on the stage.
John Dryden (1631–1700) British poet and dramatist.
Mithridates, Epilogue

3 Love is my religion – I could die for that.
John Keats (1795–1821) British poet.
Letter to Fanny Brawne, 13 Oct 1819

4 How alike are the groans of love to those of the dying.
Malcolm Lowry (1909–57) British novelist.
Under the Volcano, Ch. 12

5 It is very rarely that a man loves
And when he does it is nearly always fatal.
Hugh MacDiarmid (Christopher Murray Grieve; 1892–1978) Scottish poet.
The International Brigade

6 Men have died from time to time, and worms have eaten them, but not for love.
William Shakespeare (1564–1616) English dramatist.
As You Like It, IV:1

7 'Tis said that some have died for love.
William Wordsworth (1770–1850) British poet.
'Tis Said that some have Died

LOVE AND FRIENDSHIP

See also friendship, love

1 Love is blind; friendship closes its eyes.
Proverb

2 Friendship is a disinterested commerce between equals; love, an abject intercourse between tyrants and slaves.
Oliver Goldsmith (1728–74) Irish-born British writer.
The Good-Natured Man, I

3 Friendship is constant in all other things

Save in the office and affairs of love.
William Shakespeare (1564–1616) English dramatist.
Much Ado About Nothing, II:1

LOVE AND HATE

See also hate, love

1 Now hatred is by far the longest pleasure;
Men love in haste, but they detest at leisure.
Lord Byron (1788–1824) British poet.
Don Juan, XIII

2 *Odi et amo.*
I hate and love.
Catullus (c. 84–c. 54 BC) Roman poet.
Carmina, LXXXV

3 Heaven has no rage like love to hatred turned,
Nor hell a fury like a woman scorned.
William Congreve (1670–1729) British Restoration dramatist.
The Mourning Bride, III·

4 Oh, I have loved him too much to feel no hate for him.
Jean Racine (1639–99) French dramatist.
Andromaque, II:1

5 If one judges love by its visible effects, it looks more like hatred than like friendship.
Duc de la Rochefoucauld (1613–80) French writer.
Maximes, 72

LOVE AND MARRIAGE

See also love, marriage

1 Love and marriage, love and marriage,
Go together like a horse and carriage.
Sammy Cahn (Samuel Cohen; 1913–) US songwriter.
Our Town, 'Love and Marriage'

2 ALMA. I rather suspect her of being in love with him.
MARTIN. Her own husband? Monstrous! What a selfish woman!
Jennie Jerome Churchill (1854–1921) US-born British hostess and writer.
His Borrowed Plumes

3 Love is moral even without legal marriage, but marriage is immoral without love.
Ellen Key (Karolina Sofia Key; 1849–1926) Swedish writer.
The Morality of Woman and Other Essays, 'The Morality of Woman'

4 Any one must see at a glance that if men and women marry those whom they do not love, they must love those whom they do not marry.
Harriet Martineau (1802–76) British writer.
Society in America, Vol. III, 'Marriage'

5 Can't you read? The score demands *con*

amore, and what are you doing? You are playing it like married men!

Arturo Toscanini (1867–1957) Italian conductor.
Criticizing the playing of an Austrian orchestra during rehearsal
Attrib.

6 The amount of women in London who flirt with their own husbands is perfectly scandalous. It looks so bad. It is simply washing one's clean linen in public.

Oscar Wilde (1854–1900) Irish-born British dramatist.
The Importance of Being Earnest, I

LOYALTY

See also betrayal, faithfulness, patriotism, support

1 Dog does not eat dog.
Proverb

2 There is honour among thieves.
Proverb

3 You cannot run with the hare and hunt with the hounds.
Proverb

4 Here's a health unto his Majesty . . .
Confusion to his enemies, . . .
And he that will not drink his health,
I wish him neither wit nor wealth,
Nor yet a rope to hang himself.
Anonymous
Here's a Health unto his Majesty

5 And Ruth said, Intreat me not to leave thee, or to return from following after thee: for whither thou goest, I will go; and where thou lodgest, I will lodge: thy people shall be my people, and thy God my God:
Where thou diest, will I die, and there will I be buried: the Lord do so to me, and more also, if ought but death part thee and me.
Bible: Ruth
1:16–17

6 The State, in choosing men to serve it, takes no notice of their opinions. If they be willing faithfully to serve it, that satisfies.
Oliver Cromwell (1599–1658) English soldier and statesman.
Said before the Battle of Marston Moor, 2 July 1644

7 We are all the President's men.
Henry Kissinger (1923–) German-born US politician and diplomat.
Said regarding the invasion of Cambodia, 1970
The Sunday Times Magazine, 4 May 1975

8 A man who will steal *for* me will steal *from* me.
Theodore Roosevelt (1858–1919) US Republican president.
Firing a cowboy who had applied Roosevelt's brand to a steer belonging to a neighbouring ranch
Roosevelt in the Bad Lands (Herman Hagedorn)

9 If this man is not faithful to his God, how can he be faithful to me, a mere man?
Theodoric (c. 445–526) King of the Ostrogoths.
Explaining why he had had a trusted minister, who had said he would adopt his master's religion, beheaded
Dictionnaire Encyclopédique (E. Guérard)

10 When I forget my sovereign, may God forget me!
Lord Thurlow (1731–1806) British lawyer.
Speech, House of Lords, 15 Dec 1778

11 Had I but served God as diligently as I have served the king, he would not have given me over in my gray hairs.
Cardinal Wolsey (1475–1530) English churchman.
Remark to Sir William Kingston
Negotiations of Thomas Wolsey (Cavendish)

LUCK

See also chance, superstition

1 A bad penny always turns up.
Proverb

2 A cat has nine lives.
Proverb

3 Finders keepers, losers weepers.
Proverb

4 It is better to be born lucky than rich.
Proverb

5 The devil looks after his own.
Proverb

6 There, but for the grace of God, goes John Bradford.
John Bradford (c. 1510–55) English Protestant martyr.
Said on seeing some criminals being led to execution
Attrib.

7 This is the temple of Providence where disciples still hourly mark its ways and note the system of its mysteries. Here is the one God whose worshippers prove their faith by their works and in their destruction still trust in Him.
F. H. Bradley (1846–1924) British philosopher.
Referring to Monte Carlo
Aphorisms

8 Fortune, that favours fools.
Ben Jonson (1573–1637) English dramatist.
The Alchemist, Prologue

9 I am a great believer in luck, and I find the harder I work the more I have of it.
Stephen Leacock (1869–1944) English-born Canadian economist and humorist.
Literary Lapses

10 The Eskimo had his own explanation. Said he: 'The devil is asleep or having trouble with his wife, or we should never have come back so easily.'
Robert Edwin Peary (1856–1920) US explorer.
The North Pole

11 We need greater virtues to sustain good fortune than bad.
Duc de la Rochefoucauld (1613–80) French writer.
Maximes, 25

12 'My aunt was suddenly prevented from going a voyage
in a ship what went down – would you call that a case
of Providential interference?'
'Can't tell: didn't know your aunt.'
Frederick Temple (1821–1902) British churchman.
Memoirs of Archbishop Temple (Sandford), Vol. II

LUST

See also animalism, desire, love, sex

1 Licence my roving hands, and let them go,
Before, behind, between, above, below.
John Donne (1573–1631) English poet.
Elegies, 18, 'Love's Progress'

2 What is commonly called love, namely the desire of satisfying a voracious appetite with a certain quantity of delicate white human flesh.
Henry Fielding (1707–54) British novelist.
Tom Jones, Bk. VI, Ch. 1

3 I'll come no more behind your scenes, David; for the silk stockings and white bosoms of your actresses excite my amorous propensities.
Samuel Johnson (1709–84) British lexicographer.
Said to the actor-manager David Garrick
Life of Johnson (J. Boswell), Vol. I

4 Oh, to be seventy again!
Oliver Wendell Holmes Jr. (1841–1935) US jurist.
Said in his eighty-seventh year, while watching a pretty girl
The American Treasury (C. Fadiman)

5 Stand close around, ye Stygian set,
With Dirce in one boat conveyed!
Or Charon, seeing, may forget
That he is old and she a shade.
Walter Savage Landor (1775–1864) British poet and writer.
In Greek mythology, Dirce, a follower of Dionysius, was killed by her great-nephews Amphion and Zethus because of her mistreatment of their mother Antiope; Charon was the ferryman who transported dead souls across the River Styx to the underworld
Dirce

6 Lolita, light of my life, fire of my loins. My sin, my Soul.
Vladimir Nabokov (1899–1977) Russian-born US novelist.
Lolita

7 Th' expense of spirit in a waste of shame
Is lust in action; and till action, lust
Is perjur'd, murd'rous, bloody, full of blame,
Savage, extreme, rude, cruel, not to trust;
Enjoy'd no sooner but despised straight.
William Shakespeare (1564–1616) English dramatist.
Sonnet 129

8 Nonconformity and lust stalking hand in hand through the country, wasting and ravaging.
Evelyn Waugh (1903–66) British novelist.
Decline and Fall, Pt. I, Ch. 5

LUXURY

See also extravagance, wealth

1 It's grand, and ye canna expect to be baith grand and comfortable.
J. M. Barrie (1860–1937) British novelist and dramatist.
The Little Minister, Ch. 10

2 In the affluent society no useful distinction can be made between luxuries and necessaries.
John Kenneth Galbraith (1908–) US economist.
The Affluent Society, Ch. 21

3 Give us the luxuries of life, and we will dispense with its necessities.
John Lothrop Motley (1814–77) US historian and diplomat.
Also quoted by Frank Lloyd Wright
The Autocrat of the Breakfast Table (O. W. Holmes), Ch. 6

4 How many things I can do without!
Socrates (469–399 BC) Athenian philosopher.
Examining the range of goods on sale at a market
Lives of the Eminent Philosophers (Diogenes Laertius), II

5 Beulah, peel me a grape.
Mae West (1892–1980) US actress.
I'm No Angel, film 1933

LYING

See also deception, honesty, truth

1 A liar is worse than a thief.
Proverb

2 The boy cried 'Wolf, wolf!' and the villagers came out to help him.
Aesop (6th century BC) Reputed Greek writer of fables.
Fables, 'The Shepherd's Boy'

3 It contains a misleading impression, not a lie. I was being economical with the truth.
Robert Armstrong (1913–) British civil servant.
Giving evidence on behalf of the British Government in an Australian court case, Nov 1986. Armstrong was, in fact, quoting Edmund Burke (1729–97).

4 Woe unto them that call evil good, and good evil; that put darkness for light, and light for darkness; that put bitter for sweet, and sweet for bitter!
Bible: Isaiah
5:20

5 Nobody speaks the truth when there's something they must have.
Elizabeth Bowen (1899–1973) Irish novelist.
The House in Paris, Ch. 5

6 A lie can be half-way round the world before the truth has got its boots on.
James Callaghan (1912–) British politician and prime minister.
Speech, 1 Nov 1976

7 It cannot in the opinion of His Majesty's Government be classified as slavery in the extreme acceptance of the word without some risk of terminological inexactitude.
Winston Churchill (1874–1965) British statesman.
Speech, House of Commons, 22 Feb 1906

8 The broad mass of a nation . . . will more easily fall victim to a big lie than to a small one.
Adolf Hitler (1889–1945) German dictator.
Mein Kampf, Ch. 10

9 She's too crafty a woman to invent a new lie when an old one will serve.
W. Somerset Maugham (1874–1965) British novelist.
The Constant Wife, II

10 It is hard to believe that a man is telling the truth when you know that you would lie if you were in his place.
H. L. Mencken (1880–1956) US journalist.
Prejudices

11 Unless a man feels he has a good enough memory, he should never venture to lie.
Michel de Montaigne (1533–92) French essayist.
Also quoted in *Le Menteur*, IV:5 by Pierre Corneille (1606–84)
Essais, I

12 He led a double life. Did that make him a liar? He did not feel a liar. He was a man of two truths.
Iris Murdoch (1919–) Irish-born British novelist.
The Sacred and Profane Love Machine

13 He who does not need to lie is proud of not being a liar.
Friedrich Wilhelm Nietzsche (1844–1900) German philosopher.
Nachgelassene Fragmente

14 It has made more liars out of the American people than Golf.
Will Rogers (1879–1935) US actor and humorist.
Referring to income tax
Saturday Review, 'A Rogers Thesaurus', 25 Aug 1962

15 In our country the lie has become not just a moral category but a pillar of the State.
Alexander Solzhenitsyn (1918–) Soviet novelist.
The Observer, 'Sayings of the Year', 29 Dec 1974

16 A lie is an abomination unto the Lord and a very present help in trouble.
Adlai Stevenson (1900–65) US statesman.
Speech, Jan 1951

17 That a lie which is all a lie may be met and fought with outright,
But a lie which is part a truth is a harder matter to fight.
Alfred, Lord Tennyson (1809–92) British poet.
The Grandmother

18 There was things which he stretched, but mainly he told the truth.
Mark Twain (Samuel Langhorne Clemens; 1835–1910) US writer.
The Adventures of Huckleberry Finn, Ch. 1

M

MADNESS

See also psychiatry, psychology

1 We all are born mad. Some remain so.
Samuel Beckett (1906–) Irish novelist and dramatist.
Waiting for Godot, II

2 A knight errant who turns mad for a reason deserves neither merit nor thanks. The thing is to do it without cause.
Miguel de Cervantes (1547–1616) Spanish novelist.
Don Quixote, Pt. I, Ch. 25

3 The madman is not the man who has lost his reason. The madman is the man who has lost everything except his reason.
G. K. Chesterton (1874–1936) British writer.
Orthodoxy, Ch. 1

4 Those whom God wishes to destroy, he first makes mad.
Euripides (c. 480–406 BC) Greek dramatist.
Fragment

5 Show me a sane man and I will cure him for you.
Carl Gustav Jung (1875–1961) Swiss psychoanalyst.
The Observer, 19 July 1975

6 Madness need not be all breakdown. It may also be break-through. It is potential liberation and renewal as well as enslavement and existential death.
R. D. Laing (1927–) British psychiatrist.
The Politics of Experience, Ch. 16

7 The world is becoming like a lunatic asylum run by lunatics.
David Lloyd George (1863–1945) British Liberal statesman.
The Observer, 'Sayings of Our Times', 31 May 1953

8 His father's sister had bats in the belfry and was put away.
Eden Phillpotts (1862–1960) British novelist and dramatist.
Peacock House, 'My First Murder'

9 Though this be madness, yet there is method in't.
William Shakespeare (1564–1616) English dramatist.
Hamlet, II:2

10 Madness in great ones must not unwatch'd go.
William Shakespeare
Hamlet, III:1

11 O, let me not be mad, not mad, sweet heaven!
Keep me in temper; I would not be mad!
William Shakespeare
King Lear, I:5

12 If you talk to God, you are praying; if God talks to you, you have schizophrenia. If the dead talk to you, you are a spiritualist; if God talks to you, you are a schizophrenic.
Thomas Szasz (1920–) US psychiatrist.
The Second Sin

13 Men will always be mad and those who think they can cure them are the maddest of all.
Voltaire (François-Marie Arouet; 1694–1778) French writer.
Letter, 1762

14 I shudder and I sigh to think
That even Cicero
And many-minded Homer were
Mad as the mist and snow.
W. B. Yeats (1865–1939) Irish poet.
Mad as the Mist and Snow

MAJORITY

See also democracy, minority, public

1 It's always best on these occasions to do what the mob do.
'But suppose there are two mobs?' suggested Mr Snodgrass.
'Shout with the largest,' replied Mr Pickwick.
Charles Dickens (1812–70) British novelist.
Pickwick Papers, Ch. 13

2 A majority is always the best repartee.
Benjamin Disraeli (1804–81) British statesman.
Tancred, Bk. II, Ch. 14

3 The majority has the might – more's the pity – but it hasn't right . . . The minority is always right.
Henrik Ibsen (1828–1906) Norwegian dramatist.
An Enemy of the People, IV

4 The worst enemy of truth and freedom in our society is the compact majority. Yes, the damned, compact, liberal majority.
Henrik Ibsen
An Enemy of the People, IV

5 It is time for the great silent majority of Americans to stand up and be counted.
Richard Milhous Nixon (1913–) US president.
Election speech, Oct 1970

MALAPROPISMS

Remarks of a type associated with Mrs Malaprop in Sheridan's play *The Rivals*.

1 Our watch, sir, have indeed comprehended two aspicious persons.
William Shakespeare (1564–1616) English dramatist.
Much Ado About Nothing, III:5

2 Comparisons are odorous.
William Shakespeare
Much Ado About Nothing, III:5

3 A progeny of learning.
Richard Brinsley Sheridan (1751–1816) British dramatist.
The Rivals, I

4 Illiterate him, I say, quite from your memory.
Richard Brinsley Sheridan
The Rivals, II

5 It gives me the hydrostatics to such a degree.
Richard Brinsley Sheridan
The Rivals, III

6 As headstrong as an allegory on the banks of the Nile.
Richard Brinsley Sheridan
The Rivals, III

7 He is the very pine-apple of politeness!
Richard Brinsley Sheridan
The Rivals, III

8 If I reprehend any thing in this world, it is the use of my oracular tongue, and a nice derangement of epitaphs!
Richard Brinsley Sheridan
The Rivals, III

MANKIND

See also evolution, human condition, human nature, men, misanthropy, philanthropy, public, society, women

1 Pray consider what a figure a man would make in the republic of letters.
Joseph Addison (1672–1719) British essayist.
Ancient Medals

2 Either a beast or a god.
Aristotle (384–322 BC) Greek philosopher.
Politics, Bk. I

3 Whatever this is that I am, it is a little flesh and breath, and the ruling part.
Marcus Aurelius (121–180 AD) Roman emperor.
Meditations, Bk. II, Ch. 2

4 Drinking when we are not thirsty and making love all year round, madam; that is all there is to distinguish us from other animals.
Beaumarchais (1732–99) French dramatist.
Le Mariage de Figaro, II:21

5 And God said, Let us make man in our image, after our likeness: and let them have

dominion over the fish of the sea, and over the fowl of the air, and over the cattle, and over all the earth, and over every creeping thing that creepeth upon the earth.
So God created man in his own image, in the image of God created he him; male and female created he them.
And God blessed them, and God said unto them, Be fruitful, and multiply, and replenish the earth, and subdue it: and have dominion over the fish of the sea, and over the fowl of the air, and over every living thing that moveth upon the earth.
Bible: Genesis
1:26–28

6 For Mercy has a human heart,
Pity a human face,
And Love, the human form divine,
And Peace, the human dress.
William Blake (1757–1827) British poet.
Songs of Innocence, 'The Divine Image'

7 Every animal leaves traces of what it was; man alone leaves traces of what he created.
Jacob Bronowski (1908–74) British scientist and writer.
The Ascent of Man, Ch. 1

8 Man is a noble animal, splendid in ashes, and pompous in the grave.
Thomas Browne (1605–82) English physician and writer.
Urn Burial, Ch. 5

9 A single sentence will suffice for modern man: he fornicated and read the papers.
Albert Camus (1913–60) French existentialist writer.
The Fall

10 Carlyle said that men were mostly fools. Christianity, with a surer and more reverend realism, says that they are all fools.
G. K. Chesterton (1874–1936) British writer.
Heretics, Ch. 12

11 Mankind is not a tribe of animals to which we owe compassion. Mankind is a club to which we owe our subscription.
G. K. Chesterton
Daily News, 10 Apr 1906

12 The evolution of the human race will not be accomplished in the ten thousand years of tame animals, but in the million years of wild animals, because man is and will always be a wild animal.
Charles Darwin (1887–1962) British life scientist.
The Next Ten Million Years, Ch. 4

13 On earth there is nothing great but man; in man there is nothing great but mind.
William Hamilton (1788–1856) Scottish philosopher.
Lectures on Metaphysics

14 The majority of men devote the greater part of their lives to making their remaining years unhappy.
Jean de La Bruyère (1645–96) French satirist.
Les Caractères

15 The anthropologist respects history, but he does not accord it a special value. He conceives it as a study complementary to his own: one of them unfurls the range of human societies in time, the other in space.
Claude Lévi-Strauss (1908–) French anthropologist.
The Savage Mind

16 I'll give you my opinion of the human race . . . Their heart's in the right place, but their head is a thoroughly inefficient organ.
W. Somerset Maugham (1874–1965) British novelist.
The Summing Up

17 Clearly, then, the city is not a concrete jungle, it is a human zoo.
Desmond Morris (1928–) British biologist and writer.
The Human Zoo, Introduction

18 There are one hundred and ninety-three living species of monkeys and apes. One hundred and ninety-two of them are covered with hair. The exception is a naked ape self-named *Homo sapiens.*
Desmond Morris
The Naked Ape, Introduction

19 Man, as he is, is not a genuine article. He is an imitation of something, and a very bad imitation.
P. D. Ouspensky (1878–1947) Russian-born occultist.
The Psychology of Man's Possible Evolution, Ch. 2

20 The human face is indeed, like the face of the God of some Oriental theogony, a whole cluster of faces, crowded together but on different surfaces so that one does not see them all at once.
Marcel Proust (1871–1922) French novelist.
À la recherche du temps perdu: À l'ombre des jeunes filles en fleurs

21 I wish I loved the Human Race;
I wish I loved its silly face;
I wish I liked the way it walks;
I wish I liked the way it talks;
And when I'm introduced to one
I wish I thought *What Jolly Fun!*
Walter Raleigh (1861–1922) British scholar.
Laughter from a Cloud, 'Wishes of an Elderly Man'

22 Everything is good when it leaves the Creator's hands; everything degenerates in the hands of man.
Jean Jacques Rousseau (1712–78) French philosopher.
Attrib.

23 I love mankind – it's people I can't stand.
Charles M. Schultz (1922–) US cartoonist.
Go Fly a Kite, Charlie Brown

24 After all, for mankind as a whole there are no exports. We did not start developing by obtaining foreign exchange from Mars or the moon. Mankind is a closed society.
E. F. Schumacher (1911–77) German-born economist.
Small is Beautiful, A Study of Economics as if People Mattered, Ch. 14

25 But man, proud man
Dress'd in a little brief authority,
Most ignorant of what he's most assur'd,
His glassy essence, like an angry ape,
Plays such fantastic tricks before high heaven
As makes the angels weep.
William Shakespeare (1564–1616) English dramatist.
Measure for Measure, II:2

26 What a piece of work is a man! How noble in
reason! how infinite in faculties! in form and
moving, how express and admirable! in
action, how like an angel! in apprehension,
how like a god! the beauty of the world! the
paragon of animals! And yet, to me, what is
this quintessence of dust? Man delights not
me –no, nor woman neither.
William Shakespeare
Hamlet, II:2

27 How beauteous mankind is! O brave new
world
That has such people in't!
William Shakespeare
The Tempest, V:1

28 Physically there is nothing to distinguish
human society from the farm-yard except that
children are more troublesome and costly
than chickens and women are not so
completely enslaved as farm stock.
George Bernard Shaw (1856–1950) Irish dramatist and
critic.
Getting Married, Preface

29 Man, unlike any other thing organic or
inorganic in the universe, grows beyond his
work, walks up the stairs of his concepts,
emerges ahead of his accomplishments.
John Steinbeck (1902–68) US novelist.
The Grapes of Wrath, Ch. 14

30 Glory to Man in the highest! for Man is the
master of things.
Charles Swinburne (1837–1909) British poet.
Hymn of Man

31 I am a man, I count nothing human foreign to
me.
Terence (Publius Terentius Afer; c. 190–159 BC) Roman
poet.
Heauton Timorumenos

32 The highest wisdom has but one science –
the science of the whole – the science
explaining the whole creation and man's place
in it.
Leo Tolstoy (1828–1910) Russian writer.
War and Peace, Bk.V, Ch. 2

33 One thousand years more. That's all *Homo
sapiens* has before him.
H. G. Wells (1866–1946) British writer.
Diary (Harold Nicolson)

34 If anything is sacred the human body is
sacred.
Walt Whitman (1819–92) US poet.
I Sing the Body Electric, 8

35 But there comes a moment in everybody's
life when he must decide whether he'll live
among human beings or not – a fool among
fools or a fool alone.
Thornton Wilder (1897–1975) US novelist and dramatist.
The Matchmaker, IV

36 If this belief from heaven be sent,
If such be Nature's holy plan,
Have I not reason to lament
What man has made of man?
William Wordsworth (1770–1850) British poet.
Lines written in Early Spring

MANNERS

See also courtesy, etiquette

1 Leave off first for manners' sake: and be not
unsatiable, lest thou offend.
Bible: Ecclesiasticus
31:17

2 'Speak when you're spoken to!' the Red
Queen sharply interrupted her.
Lewis Carroll (Charles Lutwidge Dodgson; 1832–98)
British writer.
Through the Looking-Glass, Ch. 9

3 To Americans English manners are far more
frightening than none at all.
Randall Jarrell (1914–65) US author.
Pictures from an Institution, Pt. I, Ch. 5

4 On the Continent people have good food; in
England people have good table manners.
George Mikes (1912–87) Hungarian-born British writer.
How to be an Alien

5 Good breeding consists in concealing how
much we think of ourselves and how little we
think of other persons.
Mark Twain (Samuel Langhorne Clemens; 1835–1910)
US writer.
Notebooks

6 Politeness is organised indifference.
Paul Valéry (1871–1945) French poet and writer.
Tel Quel

7 Manners are especially the need of the plain.
The pretty can get away with anything.
Evelyn Waugh (1903–66) British novelist.
The Observer, 'Sayings of the Year,' 1962

8 Manners maketh man.
William of Wykeham (1324–1404) English churchman.
Motto of Winchester College and New College, Oxford

MARRIAGE

See also adultery, family, love and marriage, unfaithfulness

1 Better be an old man's darling than a young
man's slave.
Proverb

2 Marriages are made in heaven.
Proverb

3 Marry in haste, and repent at leisure.
Proverb

4 Marry in Lent, and you'll live to repent.
Proverb

5 Marry in May, rue for aye.
Proverb

6 The first wife is matrimony, the second company, the third heresy.
Proverb

7 To marry a man out of pity is folly; and, if you think you are going to influence the kind of fellow who has 'never had a chance, poor devil,' you are profoundly mistaken. One can only influence the strong characters in life, not the weak; and it is the height of vanity to suppose that you can make an honest man of anyone.
Margot Asquith (1865–1945) The second wife of Herbert Asquith.
The Autobiography of Margot Asquith, Ch. 6

8 I married beneath me – all women do.
Nancy Astor (1879–1964) American-born British politician.
Dictionary of National Biography

9 It is a truth universally acknowledged, that a single man in possession of a good fortune must be in want of a wife.
Jane Austen (1775–1817) British novelist.
The opening words of the book
Pride and Prejudice, Ch. 1

10 Happiness in marriage is entirely a matter of chance.
Jane Austen
Pride and Prejudice, Ch. 6

11 Mrs Hall of Sherbourne was brought to bed yesterday of a dead child, some weeks before she expected, owing to a fright. I suppose she happened unawares to look at her husband.
Jane Austen
Letter, 27 Oct 1798

12 Wives are young men's mistresses, companions for middle age, and old men's nurses.
Francis Bacon (1561–1626) English philosopher.
Essays, 'Of Marriage and Single Life'

13 He was reputed one of the wise men, that made answer to the question, when a man should marry? A young man not yet, an elder man not at all.
Francis Bacon
Essays, 'Of Marriage and Single Life'

14 I rather think of having a career of my own.
Arthur Balfour (1848–1930) British statesman.
When asked whether he was going to marry Margot Tennant
Autobiography (Margot Asquith), Ch. 9

15 It is easier to be a lover than a husband, for the same reason that it is more difficult to

show a ready wit all day long than to produce an occasional *bon mot*.
Honoré de Balzac (1799–1850) French novelist.
Attrib.

16 The majority of husbands remind me of an orangutang trying to play the violin.
Honoré de Balzac
La Physiologie du mariage

17 My father argued sair – my mother didna speak,
But she looked in my face till my heart was like to break;
They gied him my hand but my heart was in the sea;
And so auld Robin Gray, he was gudeman to me.
Lady Ann Barnard (1750–1825) British poet.
Auld Robin Gray

18 I think weddings is sadder than funerals, because they remind you of your own wedding. You can't be reminded of your own funeral because it hasn't happened. But weddings always make me cry.
Brendan Behan (1923–64) Irish playwright.
Richard's Cork Leg, I

19 Being a husband is a whole-time job. That is why so many husbands fail. They cannot give their entire attention to it.
Arnold Bennett (1867–1931) British novelist.
The Title, I

20 Husbands, love your wives, and be not bitter against them.
Bible: Colossians
3:19

21 Let the husband render unto the wife due benevolence: and likewise also the wife unto the husband.
Bible: I Corinthians
7:3

22 But if they cannot contain, let them marry: for it is better to marry than to burn.
Bible: I Corinthians
7:9

23 But he that is married careth for the things that are of the world, how he may please his wife.
Bible: I Corinthians
7:33

24 Wherefore they are no more twain, but one flesh. What therefore God hath joined together, let not man put asunder.
Bible: Matthew
19:6

25 Even as Sara obeyed Abraham, calling him lord: whose daughters ye are, as long as ye do well, and are not afraid with any amazement.
Likewise, ye husbands, dwell with them according to knowledge, giving honour unto the

wife, as unto the weaker vessel, and as being heirs together of the grace of life; that your prayers be not hindered.
Bible: I Peter
3:6–7

26 *Marriage,* n. The state or condition of a community consisting of a master, a mistress and two slaves, making in all two.
Ambrose Bierce (1842–?1914) US writer and journalist.
The Devil's Dictionary

27 To have and to hold from this day forward, for better for worse, for richer for poorer, in sickness and in health, to love and to cherish, till death us do part.
The Book of Common Prayer
Solemnization of Matrimony

28 'We stay together, but we distrust one another.'
'Ah, yes . . . but isn't that a definition of marriage?'
Malcolm Bradbury (1932–) British academic and novelist.
The History Man, Ch. 3

29 Ah, gentle dames! It gars me greet
To think how mony counsels sweet,
How mony lengthen'd sage advices,
The husband frae the wife despises!
Robert Burns (1759–96) Scottish poet.
Tam o' Shanter

30 Marriage is distinctly and repeatedly excluded from heaven. Is this because it is thought likely to mar the general felicity?
Samuel Butler (1835–1902) British writer.
Notebooks

31 Wedlock – the deep, deep peace of the double bed after the hurly-burly of the chaise-longue.
Mrs Patrick Campbell (Beatrice Stella Tanner; 1865–1940) British actress.
Jennie (Ralph G. Martin), Vol. II

32 She was a worthy womman al hir lyve,
Housbondes at chirche-dore she hadde fyve,
Withouten other companye in youthe.
Geoffrey Chaucer (c. 1342–1400) English poet.
Referring to the wife of Bath
The Canterbury Tales, Prologue

33 An archaeologist is the best husband any woman can have: the older she gets, the more interested he is in her.
Agatha Christie (1891–1976) British detective-story writer.
Attrib.

34 The most happy marriage I can picture or imagine to myself would be the union of a deaf man to a blind woman.
Samuel Taylor Coleridge (1772–1834) British poet.
Recollections (Allsop)

35 SHARPER: Thus grief still treads upon the heels of pleasure:

Marry'd in haste, we may repent at leisure.
SETTER: Some by experience find those words mis-plac'd:
At leisure marry'd, they repent in haste.
William Congreve (1670–1729) British Restoration dramatist.
The Old Bachelor, V:8

36 Courtship to marriage, as a very witty prologue to a very dull Play.
William Congreve
The Old Bachelor, V:10

37 I hope you do not think me prone to any iteration of nuptials.
William Congreve
The Way of the World, IV:12

38 Marriage is a wonderful invention; but then again so is a bicycle repair kit.
Billy Connolly (1942–) British comedian.
The Authorized Version

39 Says John, It is my wedding-day,
And all the world would stare,
If wife should dine at Edmonton,
And I should dine at Ware.
William Cowper (1731–1800) British poet.
John Gilpin

40 To-morrow is our wedding-day,
And we will then repair
Unto the Bell at Edmonton,
All in a chaise and pair.
William Cowper
John Gilpin

41 Daisy, Daisy, give me your answer, do!
I'm half crazy, all for the love of you!
It won't be a stylish marriage,
I can't afford a carriage,
But you'll look sweet upon the seat
Of a bicycle made for two!
Harry Dacre (19th century) British songwriter.
Daisy Bell

42 If a man stays away from his wife for seven years, the law presumes the separation to have killed him; yet according to our daily experience, it might well prolong his life.
Lord Darling (1849–1936) British judge.
Scintillae Juris

43 This man, she reasons, as she looks at her husband, is a poor fish. But he is the nearest I can get to the big one that got away.
Nigel Dennis (1912–) British writer.
Cards of Identity

44 'Old girl,' said Mr Bagnet, 'give him my opinion. You know it.'
Charles Dickens (1812–70) British novelist.
Bleak House, Ch. 27

45 Every woman should marry – and no man.
Benjamin Disraeli (1804–81) British statesman.
Lothair, Ch. 30

46 It destroys one's nerves to be amiable every day to the same human being.
Benjamin Disraeli
The Young Duke

47 Now one of the great reasons why so many husbands and wives make shipwreck of their lives together is because a man is always seeking for happiness, while a woman is on a perpetual still hunt for trouble.
Dorothy Dix (Elizabeth Meriwether Gilmer; 1861–1951) US journalist and writer.
Dorothy Dix, Her Book, Ch. 1

48 The husband was a teetotaller, there was no other woman, and the conduct complained of was that he had drifted into the habit of winding up every meal by taking out his false teeth and hurling them at his wife.
Arthur Conan Doyle (1856–1930) British writer.
A Case of Identity

49 Here lies my wife; here let her lie!
Now she's at rest, and so am I.
John Dryden (1631–1700) British poet and dramatist.
Epitaph Intended for Dryden's Wife

50 I am to be married within these three days; married past redemption.
John Dryden
Marriage à la Mode, I

51 So that ends my first experience with matrimony, which I always thought a highly overrated performance.
Isadora Duncan (1878–1927) US dancer.
The New York Times, 1923

52 Being an old maid is like death by drowning, a really delightful sensation after you cease to struggle.
Edna Ferber (1887–1968) US writer.
Wit's End (R. E. Drennan), 'Completing the Circle'

53 His designs were strictly honourable, as the phrase is; that is, to rob a lady of her fortune by way of marriage.
Henry Fielding (1707–54) British novelist.
Tom Jones, Bk. XI, Ch. 4

54 Composed that monstrous animal a husband and wife.
Henry Fielding
Tom Jones, Bk. XV, Ch. 9

55 When widows exclaim loudly against second marriages, I would always lay a wager, that the man, if not the wedding-day, is absolutely fixed on.
Henry Fielding
Amelia, Bk. VI, Ch. 8

56 One fool at least in every married couple.
Henry Fielding
Amelia, Bk. IX, Ch. 4

57 Most marriages don't add two people together. They subtract one from the other.
Ian Fleming (1908–64) British journalist and author.
Diamonds are Forever

58 Husbands are like fires. They go out when unattended.
Zsa Zsa Gabor (1919–) Hungarian-born US film star.
Newsweek, 28 Mar 1960

59 A man in love is incomplete until he has married. Then he's finished.
Zsa Zsa Gabor
Newsweek, 28 Mar 1960

60 Do you think your mother and I should have liv'd comfortably so long together, if ever we had been married?
John Gay (1685–1732) English poet and dramatist.
The Beggar's Opera

61 No, I shall have mistresses.
George II (1683–1760) King of Great Britain and Ireland. Reply to Queen Caroline's suggestion, as she lay on her deathbed, that he should marry again after her death
Memoirs of George the Second (Hervey), Vol. II

62 I was ever of opinion, that the honest man who married and brought up a large family, did more service than he who continued single and only talked of population.
Oliver Goldsmith (1728–74) Irish-born British writer.
The Vicar of Wakefield, Ch. 1

63 I . . . chose my wife, as she did her wedding gown, not for a fine glossy surface, but such qualities as would wear well.
Oliver Goldsmith
The Vicar of Wakefield, Preface

64 The trouble with my wife is that she is a whore in the kitchen and a cook in bed.
Geoffrey Gorer (1905–) British writer and anthropologist.
Exploring the English Character

65 The concept of two people living together for 25 years without having a cross word suggests a lack of spirit only to be admired in sheep.
A. P. Herbert (1890–1971) British writer and politican.
News Chronicle, 1940

66 The critical period in matrimony is breakfast-time.
A. P. Herbert
Uncommon Law

67 Then be not coy, but use your time;
And while ye may, go marry:
For having lost but once your prime,
You may for ever tarry.
Robert Herrick (1591–1674) English poet.
Hesperides, 'To the Virgins, to Make Much of Time'

68 Marriage has many pains, but celibacy has no pleasures.
Samuel Johnson (1709–84) British lexicographer.
Rasselas, Ch. 26

69 The triumph of hope over experience.

Samuel Johnson
Referring to the hasty remarriage of an acquaintance following
the death of his first wife, with whom he had been most
unhappy
Life of Johnson (J. Boswell), Vol. II

70 Nothing is to me more distasteful than that
entire complacency and satisfaction which
beam in the countenances of a new-married
couple.

Charles Lamb (1775–1834) British essayist.
Essays of Elia, 'A Bachelor's Complaint of Married People'

71 Same old slippers,
Same old rice,
Same old glimpse of
Paradise.

William James Lampton (1859–1917) British writer.
June Weddings

72 There was I, waiting at the church,
Waiting at the church, waiting at the church,
When I found he'd left me in the lurch,
Lor', how it did upset me! . . .
Can't get away to marry you today –
My wife won't let me.

Fred W. Leigh (19th century) British songwriter.
Waiting at the Church

73 I'm getting married in the morning!
Ding dong! the bells are gonna chime.
Pull out the stopper!
Let's have a whopper!
But get me to the church on time!

Alan Jay Lerner (1918–86) US songwriter.
My Fair Lady, II:3

74 I am in truth very thankful for not having
married at all.

Harriet Martineau (1802–76) British writer.
Harriet Martineau's Autobiography, Vol. I

75 . . . the early marriages of silly children . . .
where . . . every woman is married before
she well knows how serious a matter human
life is.

Harriet Martineau
Society in America, Vol. III, 'Marriage'

76 In no country, I believe, are the marriage
laws so iniquitous as in England, and the
conjugal relation, in consequence, so
impaired.

Harriet Martineau
Society in America, Vol. III, 'Marriage'

77 When married people don't get on they can
separate, but if they're not married it's
impossible. It's a tie that only death can
sever.

W. Somerset Maugham (1874–1965) British novelist.
The Circle, III

78 Marriage is like a cage; one sees the birds
outside desperate to get in, and those inside
equally desperate to get out.

Michel de Montaigne (1533–92) French essayist.
Essais, III

79 It has been said that a bride's attitude
towards her betrothed can be summed up in
three words: Aisle. Altar. Hymn.

Frank Muir (1920–) British writer and broadcaster.
Upon My Word! (Frank Muir and Dennis Norden), 'A Jug of
Wine'

80 One doesn't have to get anywhere in a
marriage. It's not a public conveyance.

Iris Murdoch (1919–) Irish-born British novelist.
A Severed Head

81 Writing is like getting married. One should
never commit oneself until one is amazed at
one's luck.

Iris Murdoch
The Black Prince, 'Bradley Pearson's Foreword'

82 It is now known . . . that men enter local
politics solely as a result of being unhappily
married.

Cyril Northcote Parkinson (1919–) British historian
and writer.
Parkinson's Law, Ch. 10

83 Marriage may often be a stormy lake, but
celibacy is almost always a muddy horse-
pond.

Thomas Love Peacock (1785–1866) British novelist.
Melincourt

84 Sir, I have quarrelled with my wife; and a
man who has quarrelled with his wife is
absolved from all duty to his country.

Thomas Love Peacock
Nightmare Abbey, Ch. 11

85 Strange to say what delight we married
people have to see these poor fools decoyed
into our condition.

Samuel Pepys (1633–1703) English diarist.
Diary, 25 Dec 1665

86 A loving wife will do anything for her
husband except stop criticising and trying to
improve him.

J. B. Priestley (1894–1984) British novelist.
Rain on Godshill

87 It doesn't much signify whom one marries,
for one is sure to find next morning that it
was someone else.

Samuel Rogers (1763–1855) British poet.
Table Talk (ed. Alexander Dyce)

88 A married couple are well suited when both
partners usually feel the need for a quarrel at
the same time.

Jean Rostand (1894–1977) French biologist and writer.
Le Mariage

89 Never feel remorse for what you have
thought about your wife; she has thought
much worse things about you.

Jean Rostand
Le Mariage

90 When you see what some girls marry, you

realize how they must hate to work for a living.
Helen Rowland (1876–1950) US writer.
Reflections of a Bachelor Girl

91 The Western custom of one wife and hardly any mistresses.
Saki (Hector Hugh Munro; 1870–1916) British writer.
Reginald in Russia

92 It takes two to make a marriage a success and only one a failure.
Herbert Samuel (1870–1963) British Liberal statesman.
A Book of Quotations

93 Marriage is nothing but a civil contract.
John Selden (1584–1654) English historian.
Table Talk

94 For a light wife doth make a heavy husband.
William Shakespeare (1564–1616) English dramatist.
The Merchant of Venice, V:1

95 Many a good hanging prevents a bad marriage.
William Shakespeare
Twelfth Night, I:5

96 Marriage is popular because it combines the maximum of temptation with the maximum of opportunity.
George Bernard Shaw (1856–1950) Irish dramatist and critic.
Man and Superman

97 It is a woman's business to get married as soon as possible, and a man's to keep unmarried as long as he can.
George Bernard Shaw
Man and Superman, II

98 Have you not heard
When a man marries, dies, or turns Hindoo,
His best friends hear no more of him?
Percy Bysshe Shelley (1792–1822) British poet.
Referring to Thomas Love Peacock, who worked for the East India Company and had recently married
Letter to Maria Gisborne, I

99 Married women are kept women, and they are beginning to find it out.
Logan Pearsall Smith (1865–1946) US writer.
Afterthoughts, 'Other people'

100 My definition of marriage: . . . .it resembles a pair of shears, so joined that they cannot be separated; often moving in opposite directions, yet always punishing anyone who comes between them.
Sydney Smith (1771–1845) British clergyman and essayist.
Memoir (Lady Holland)

101 A little in drink, but at all times yr faithful husband.
Richard Steele (1672–1729) Dublin-born British essayist.
Letter to his wife, 27 Sep 1708

102 Even if we take matrimony at its lowest,

even if we regard it as no more than a sort of friendship recognized by the police.
Robert Louis Stevenson (1850–94) Scottish writer.
Virginibus Puerisque

103 Marriage is a step so grave and decisive that it attracts light-headed, variable men by its very awfulness.
Robert Louis Stevenson
Virginibus Puerisque

104 Marriage is like life in this – that it is a field of battle, and not a bed of roses.
Robert Louis Stevenson
Virginibus Puerisque

105 In marriage, a man becomes slack and selfish and undergoes a fatty degeneration of his moral being.
Robert Louis Stevenson
Virginibus Puerisque

106 Bachelor's fare; bread and cheese, and kisses.
Jonathan Swift (1667–1745) Irish-born Anglican priest and writer.
Polite Conversation, Dialogue 1

107 What they do in heaven we are ignorant of; what they do *not* we are told expressly, that they neither marry, nor are given in marriage.
Jonathan Swift
Thoughts on Various Subjects

108 He that loves not his wife and children, feeds a lioness at home and broods a nest of sorrows.
Jeremy Taylor (1613–67) English Anglican theologian.
Sermons, 'Married Love'

109 Or when the moon was overhead,
Came two young lovers lately wed;
'I am half sick of shadows,' said
The Lady of Shalott.
Alfred, Lord Tennyson (1809–92) British poet.
The Lady of Shalott, Pt. II

110 Remember, it is as easy to marry a rich woman as a poor woman.
William Makepeace Thackeray (1811–63) British novelist.
Pendennis, Ch. 28

111 This I set down as a positive truth. A woman with fair opportunities and without a positive hump, may marry whom she likes.
William Makepeace Thackeray
Vanity Fair, Ch. 4

112 Every night of her married life she has been late for school.
Dylan Thomas (1914–53) Welsh poet.
Under Milk Wood

113 It should be a very happy marriage – they are both so much in love with *him*.
Irene Thomas (1920–) British writer.
Attrib.

114 Divorce? Never. But murder often!
Sybil Thorndike (1882–1976) British actress.
Replying to a query as to whether she had ever considered
divorce during her long marriage to Sir Lewis Casson
Attrib.

115 A man should not insult his wife publicly, at
parties. He should insult her in the privacy
of the home.
James Thurber (1894–1961) US humorist.
Thurber Country

116 Marriage is the only adventure open to the
cowardly.
Voltaire (François-Marie Arouet; 1694–1778) French
writer.
Thoughts of a Philosopher

117 And what would happen to my illusion that I
am a force for order in the home if I wasn't
married to the only man north of the Tiber
who is even untidier than I am?
Katherine Whitehorn (1926–) British journalist.
Sunday Best, 'Husband-Swapping'

118 In married life three is company and two is
none.
Oscar Wilde (1854–1900) Irish-born British dramatist.
The Importance of Being Earnest, I

119 Twenty years of romance makes a woman
look like a ruin; but twenty years of marriage
make her something like a public building.
Oscar Wilde
A Woman of No Importance, I

120 The best part of married life is the fights.
The rest is merely so-so.
Thornton Wilder (1897–1975) US novelist and
dramatist.
The Matchmaker, II

121 Of course, I do have a slight advantage over
the rest of you. It helps in a pinch to be able
to remind your bride that you gave up a
throne for her.
Duke of Windsor (1894–1972) King of the United
Kingdom; abdicated 1936.
Discussing the maintenance of happy marital relations
Attrib.

122 Judges, as a class, display, in the matter of
arranging alimony, that reckless generosity
that is found only in men who are giving
away somebody else's cash.
P. G. Wodehouse (1881–1975) British humorous
novelist.
Louder and Funnier

123 I can honestly say that I always look on Pauline as one of the nicest girls I was ever engaged to.
P. G. Wodehouse
Thank You Jeeves, Ch. 6

MARTYRDOM

See also execution

1 The king has been very good to me. He

promoted me from a simple maid to be a
marchioness. Then he raised me to be a
queen. Now he will raise me to be a martyr.
Anne Boleyn (1507–36) Second wife of Henry VIII.
Notable Women in History (W. Abbot)

2 'Dying for an idea,' again, sounds well
enough, but why not let the idea die instead
of you?
Wyndham Lewis (1882–1957) British novelist.
The Art of Being Ruled, Pt. I, Ch. 1

3 I will burn, but this is a mere incident. We
shall continue our discussion in eternity.
Michael Servetus (1511–53) Spanish physician and
theologian.
Comment to the judges of the Inquisition after being condemned to be burned at the stake as a heretic
Borges: A Reader (E. Monegal)

4 And they blest him in their pain, that they
were not left to Spain,
To the thumbscrew and the stake, for the glo-
ry of the Lord.
Alfred, Lord Tennyson (1809–92) British poet.
The Revenge, III

5 A thing is not necessarily true because a man
dies for it.
Oscar Wilde (1854–1900) Irish-born British dramatist.
Oscariana

MARXISM

See also Communism, socialism

1 Karl Marx wasn't a Marxist all the time. He
got drunk in the Tottenham Court Road.
Michael Foot (1913–) British Labour politician and
journalist.
Behind The Image (Susan Barnes)

2 Marxian Socialism must always remain a
portent to the historians of Opinion – how a
doctrine so illogical and so dull can have
exercised so powerful and enduring an
influence over the minds of men, and,
through them, the events of history.
John Maynard Keynes (1883–1946) British economist.
The End of Laisser-Faire, III

3 The workers have nothing to lose but their
chains. They have a world to gain. Workers
of the world, unite.
Karl Marx (1818–83) German philosopher and
revolutionary.
The Communist Manifesto, 4

4 From each according to his abilities, to each
according to his needs.
Karl Marx
Criticism of the Gotha Programme

5 The dictatorship of the proletariat.
Karl Marx
Attrib.

6 And what a prize we have to fight for: no

less than the chance to banish from our land the dark divisive clouds of Marxist socialism.
Margaret Thatcher (1925–) British politician and prime minister.
Speech, Scottish Conservative Conference, 1983

MASCULINITY

See also men

1 It makes me feel masculine to tell you that I do not answer questions like this without being paid for answering them.
Lillian Hellman (1905–84) US dramatist.
When asked by *Harper's* magazine when she felt most masculine; this question had already been asked of several famous men
Reader's Digest, July 1977

2 You may have my husband, but not my horse. My husband won't need emasculating, and my horse I won't have you meddle with. I'll preserve one last male thing in the museum of this world, if I can.
D. H. Lawrence (1885–1930) British novelist.
St Mawr

MATERIALISM

See also greed, money, wealth

1 Benefits make a man a slave.
Arabic proverb
Proverb

2 Thinking to get at once all the gold that the goose could give, he killed it, and opened it only to find – nothing.
Aesop (6th century BC) Reputed Greek writer of fables.
Fables, 'The Goose with the Golden Eggs'

3 Jesus said unto him, If thou wilt be perfect, go and sell that thou hast, and give to the poor, and thou shalt have treasure in heaven: and come and follow me.
But when the young man heard that saying, he went away sorrowful: for he had great possessions.
Bible: Matthew
19:21–22

4 Maidens, like moths, are ever caught by glare,
And Mammon wins his way where Seraphs might despair.
Lord Byron (1788–1824) British poet.
Childe Harold's Pilgrimage, I

5 For gold in phisik is a cordial,
Therfore he lovede gold in special.
Geoffrey Chaucer (c. 1342–1400) English poet.
Referring to the doctor
The Canterbury Tales, Prologue

6 To be clever enough to get all that money, one must be stupid enough to want it.
G. K. Chesterton (1874–1936) British writer.
The Innocence of Father Brown

7 I never hated a man enough to give him diamonds back.
Zsa Zsa Gabor (1919–) Hungarian-born US film star.
The Observer, 'Sayings of the Week', 28 Aug 1957

8 What female heart can gold despise?
What cat's averse to fish?
Thomas Gray (1716–71) British poet.
Ode on the Death of a Favourite Cat

9 Man must choose whether to be rich in things or in the freedom to use them.
Ivan Illich (1926–) Austrian sociologist.
Deschooling Society, Ch. 4

10 In a consumer society there are inevitably two kinds of slaves: the prisoners of addiction and the prisoners of envy.
Ivan Illich
Tools for Conviviality

11 The almighty dollar, that great object of universal devotion throughout our land, seems to have no genuine devotees in these peculiar villages.
Washington Irving (1783–1859) US writer.
Wolfert's Roost, 'The Creole Village'

12 Good morning to the day: and, next, my gold! –
Open the shrine, that I may see my saint.
Ben Jonson (1573–1637) English dramatist.
Volpone, I:1

13 Kissing your hand may make you feel very very good but a diamond and safire bracelet lasts forever.
Anita Loos (1891–1981) US novelist.
Gentlemen Prefer Blondes, Ch. 4

14 When an American heiress wants to buy a man, she at once crosses the Atlantic. The only really materialistic people I have ever met have been Europeans.
Mary McCarthy (1912–) US novelist.
On the Contrary 1962

15 Years ago a person, he was unhappy, didn't know what to do with himself – he'd go to church, start a revolution – *something.* Today you're unhappy? Can't figure it out? What is the salvation? Go shopping.
Arthur Miller (1915–) US dramatist.
The Price, I

16 Why is it no one ever sent me yet
One perfect limousine, do you suppose?
Ah no, it's always just my luck to get
One perfect rose.
Dorothy Parker (1893–1967) US writer.
One Perfect Rose

17 Diamonds Are A Girl's Best Friend.
Leo Robin (1899–) US songwriter.
Gentlemen Prefer Blondes, song title

18 Bell, book, and candle, shall not drive me back,

When gold and silver becks me to come on.
William Shakespeare (1564–1616) English dramatist.
King John, III:3

19 The want of a thing is perplexing enough, but the possession of it is intolerable.
John Vanbrugh (1664–1726) English architect and dramatist.
The Confederacy, I:2

20 Conspicuous consumption of valuable goods is a means of reputability to the gentleman of leisure.
Thorstein Bunde Veblen (1857–1929) US social scientist.
The Theory of the Leisure Class

21 What do you not drive human hearts into, cursed
craving for gold!
Virgil (Publius Vergilius Maro; 70–19 BC) Roman poet.
Aeneid, Bk. III

22 There's something about a crowd like that that brings a lump to my wallet.
Eli Wallach (1915–   ) US actor.
Remarking upon the long line of people at the box office before one of his performances
Attrib.

23 A gold rush is what happens when a line of chorus girls spot a man with a bank roll.
Mae West (1892–1980) US actress.
Klondike Annie, film 1936

MATHEMATICS

See also numbers

1 What is algebra exactly; is it those three-cornered things?
J. M. Barrie (1860–1937) British novelist and dramatist.
Quality Street, II

2 I never could make out what those damned dots meant.
Lord Randolph Churchill (1849–95) British Conservative politician.
Referring to decimal points
Lord Randolph Churchill (W. S. Churchill)

3 As far as the laws of mathematics refer to reality, they are not certain, and as far as they are certain, they do not refer to reality.
Albert Einstein (1879–1955) German-born US physicist.
The Tao of Physics (F. Capra), Ch. 2

4 There is no 'royal road' to geometry.
Euclid (c. 300 BC) Greek mathematician.
Said to Ptolemy I when asked if there were an easier way to solve theorems
Comment on Euclid (Proclus)

5 About binomial theorems I'm teeming with a lot of news,
With many cheerful facts about the square on the hypoteneuse.
W. S. Gilbert (1836–1911) British dramatist.
The Pirates of Penzance, I

6 MORIARTY. How are you at Mathematics?

HARRY SECOMBE. I speak it like a native.
Spike Milligan (1918–   ) British comic actor and author.
The Goon Show

7 The only way I can distinguish proper from improper fractions is by their actions.
Ogden Nash (1902–71) US poet.
Ask Daddy, He Won't Know

8 One geometry cannot be more true than another; it can only be more convenient. Geometry is not true, it is advantageous.
Robert T. Pirsig (1928–   ) US writer.
Zen and the Art of Motorcycle Maintenance, Pt. III, Ch. 22

9 Let no one ignorant of mathematics enter here.
Plato (429–347 BC) Greek philosopher.
Inscription written over the entrance to the Academy
Biographical Encyclopedia (I. Asimov)

10 The true spirit of delight, the exaltation, the sense of being more than Man, which is the touchstone of the highest excellence is to be found in mathematics as surely as in poetry.
Bertrand Russell (1872–1970) British philosopher.
Mysticism and Logic

11 Mathematics, rightly viewed, possesses not only truth by supreme beauty – a beauty cold and austere like that of sculpture.
Bertrand Russell
Mysticism and Logic

12 Mathematics may be defined as the subject in which we never know what we are talking about, nor whether what we are saying is true.
Bertrand Russell
Mysticism and Logic, Ch. 4

13 Pure mathematics consists entirely of assertions to the effect that, if such and such a proposition is true of *anything*, then such and such another proposition is true of that thing. It is essential not to discuss whether the first proposition is really true, and not to mention what the anything is, of which it is supposed to be true.
Bertrand Russell
Mysticism and Logic, Ch. 5

14 Mathematics possesses not only truth, but supreme beauty –a beauty cold and austere, like that of sculpture.
Bertrand Russell
The Study of Mathematics

15 Numbers constitute the only universal language.
Nathaniel West (1903–40) US novelist and scriptwriter.
Miss Lonelyhearts

MEANING

See also purpose, words

1 'Then you should say what you mean,' the March Hare went on. 'I do,' Alice hastily

replied; 'at least – at least I mean what I say – that's the same thing, you know.'
'Not the same thing a bit!' said the Hatter. 'Why, you might just as well say that "I see what I eat" is the same thing as "I eat what I see!"'
Lewis Carroll (Charles Lutwidge Dodgson; 1832–98) British writer.
Alice's Adventures in Wonderland, Ch. 7

2 Take care of the sense, and the sounds will take care of themselves.
Lewis Carroll
Alice's Adventures in Wonderland, Ch. 9

3 'When *I* use a word,' Humpty Dumpty said in rather a scornful tone, 'it means just what I choose it to mean – neither more nor less.'
Lewis Carroll
Through the Looking-Glass, Ch. 6

4 Where in this small-talking world can I find
A longitude with no platitude?
Christopher Fry (1907–) British dramatist.
The Lady's Not for Burning, III

5 The least of things with a meaning is worth more in life than the greatest of things without it.
Carl Gustav Jung (1875–1961) Swiss psychoanalyst.
Modern Man in Search of a Soul

MEDICINE

See also doctors, health, illness, nurses, remedies

1 Medical men all over the world having merely entered into a tacit agreement to call all sorts of maladies people are liable to, in cold weather, by one name; so that one sort of treatment may serve for all, and their practice thereby be greatly simplified.
Jane Welsh Carlyle (1801–66) The wife of Thomas Carlyle.
Letter to John Welsh, 4 Mar 1837

2 A miracle drug is any drug that will do what the label says it will do.
Eric Hodgins (1899–1971) US writer and editor.
Episode

3 One of the most difficult things to contend with in a hospital is the assumption on the part of the staff that because you have lost your gall bladder you have also lost your mind.
Jean Kerr (1923–) US dramatist.
Please Don't Eat the Daisies

4 The ultimate indignity is to be given a bedpan by a stranger who calls you by your first name.
Maggie Kuhn (1905–) US writer and social activist.
The Observer, 20 Aug 1978

5 Optimistic lies have such immense therapeutic

value that a doctor who cannot tell them convincingly has mistaken his profession.
George Bernard Shaw (1856–1950) Irish dramatist and critic.
Misalliance, Preface

6 I've already had medical attention – a dog licked me when I was on the ground.
Neil Simon (1927–) US playwright.
Only When I Laugh (screenplay)

7 Formerly, when religion was strong and science weak, men mistook magic for medicine, now, when science is strong and religion weak, men mistake medicine for magic.
Thomas Szasz (1920–) US psychiatrist.
The Second Sin

8 Human beings, yes, but not surgeons.
Rudolph Virchow (1821–1902) German pathologist.
Answering a query as to whether human beings could survive appendectomy, which had recently become a widespread practice
Anekdotenschatz (H. Hoffmeister)

9 The art of medicine consists of amusing the patient while Nature cures the disease.
Voltaire (1694–1788) French writer.
Attrib.

MEDIOCRITY

See also inferiority

1 Only mediocrity can be trusted to be always at its best.
Max Beerbohm (1872–1956) British writer.
Conversations with Max (S.N. Behrman)

2 The world is made of people who never quite get into the first team and who just miss the prizes at the flower show.
Jacob Bronowski (1908–74) British scientist and writer.
The Face of Violence, Ch. 6

3 Mediocrity knows nothing higher than itself, but talent instantly recognizes genius.
Arthur Conan Doyle (1856–1930) British writer.
The Valley of Fear

4 Some men are born mediocre, some men achieve mediocrity, and some men have mediocrity thrust upon them. With Major Major it had been all three.
Joseph Heller (1923–) US novelist.
Catch-22, Ch. 9

5 Women want mediocre men, and men are working to be as mediocre as possible.
Margaret Mead (1901–78) US anthropologist.
Quote Magazine, 15 May 1958

6 With first-rate sherry flowing into second-rate whores,
And third-rate conversation without one single pause:
Just like a couple

Between the wars.
William Plomer (1903–73) South African poet and novelist.
Father and Son: 1939

7 It isn't evil that is ruining the earth, but mediocrity. The crime is not that Nero played while Rome burned, but that he played badly.
Ned Rorem (1923–) US composer and writer.
The Final Diary

8 Much of a muchness.
John Vanbrugh (1664–1726) English architect and dramatist.
The Provok'd Husband, I:1

MELANCHOLY

See also despair, sorrow

1 Nothing's so dainty sweet as lovely melancholy.
Francis Beaumont (1584–1616) English dramatist.
The Nice Valour, III:3

2 All my joys to this are folly,
Naught so sweet as Melancholy.
Robert Burton (1577–1640) English scholar and explorer.
Anatomy of Melancholy, Abstract

3 If there is a hell upon earth, it is to be found in a melancholy man's heart.
Robert Burton
Anatomy of Melancholy, Pt. I

4 Twentieth-Century Blues.
Noël Coward (1899–1973) British dramatist.
Title of song

5 I am aware of the damp souls of the housemaids
Sprouting despondently at area gates.
T. S. Eliot (1888–1965) US-born British poet and dramatist.
Morning at the Window

6 I am in that temper that if I were under water I would scarcely kick to come to the top.
John Keats (1795–1821) British poet.
Letter to Benjamin Bailey, 21 May 1818

7 My heart aches, and a drowsy numbness pains
My sense.
John Keats
Ode to a Nightingale

8 Ay, in the very temple of delight
Veil'd Melancholy has her sovran shrine.
Though seen of none save him whose strenuous tongue
Can burst Joy's grape against his palate fine.
John Keats
Ode on Melancholy

9 Where glowing embers through the room
Teach light to counterfeit a gloom,
Far from all resort of mirth,

Save the cricket on the hearth.
John Milton (1608–74) English poet.
Il Penseroso

10 Wrapt in a pleasing fit of melancholy.
John Milton
Comus

11 I was told I am a true cosmopolitan. I am unhappy everywhere.
Stephen Vizinczey (1933–) Hungarian-born British writer.
The Guardian, 7 Mar 1968

MEMORIALS

See also epitaphs, memory, obituaries, reputation

1 When I am dead, and laid in grave,
And all my bones are rotten,
By this may I remembered be
When I should be forgotten.
Anonymous
On a girl's sampler, 1736

2 All your better deeds
Shall be in water writ, but this in marble.
Francis Beaumont (1584–1616) English dramatist.
The Nice Valour, V:3

3 They shall grow not old, as we that are left grow old:
Age shall not weary them, nor the years condemn.
At the going down of the sun and in the morning
We will remember them.
Laurence Binyon (1869–1943) British poet.
Poems For the Fallen

4 John Brown's body lies a-mouldering in the grave,
His soul is marching on!
Charles Sprague Hall (19th century) US songwriter.
The song commemorates the American hero who died in the cause of abolishing slavery
John Brown's Body

5 I have executed a memorial longer lasting than bronze.
Horace (Quintus Horatius Flaccus; 65–8 BC) Roman poet.
Odes, III

6 In a larger sense we cannot dedicate, we cannot consecrate, we cannot hallow this ground. The brave men, living and dead, who struggled here, have consecrated it far above our power to add or detract. The world will little note, nor long remember, what we say here, but it can never forget what they did here. It is for us, the living, rather to be dedicated here to the unfinished work which they who fought here have thus far so nobly advanced. It is rather for us to be here dedicated to the great task remaining before us . . . that we here highly resolve that the dead shall not have died in vain, that this nation, under God, shall have a new birth of

freedom; and that government of the people, by the people, and for the people, shall not perish from the earth.
Abraham Lincoln (1809–65) US statesman.
Report of Lincoln's address at the dedication (19 Nov 1863) of the national cemetery on the site of the Battle of Gettysburg

7 The monument sticks like a fishbone in the city's throat.
Robert Lowell (1917–77) US poet.
For the Union Dead

8 In Flanders fields the poppies blow Between the crosses, row on row, That mark our place.
John McCrae (1872–1918) Canadian poet and doctor.
In Flanders Fields, 'Ypres Salient', 3 May 1915

9 I was told that the Chinese said they would bury me by the Western Lake and build a shrine to my memory. I have some slight regret that this did not happen, as I might have become a god, which would have been very *chic* for an atheist.
Bertrand Russell (1872–1970) British philosopher.
The Autobiography of Bertrand Russell, Vol. II, Ch. 3

10 Men's evil manners live in brass: their virtues We write in water.
William Shakespeare (1564–1616) English dramatist.
Henry VIII, IV:2

11 I met a traveller from an antique land Who said: Two vast and trunkless legs of stone Stand in the desert.
Percy Bysshe Shelley (1792–1822) British poet.
Referring to the legs of a broken statue of the Pharaoh Rameses II (1301–1234 BC; Greek name, Ozymandias)
Ozymandias

12 Move Queen Anne? Most certainly not! Why it might some day be suggested that *my* statue should be moved, which I should much dislike.
Victoria (1819–1901) Queen of the United Kingdom.
Said at the time of her Diamond Jubilee (1897), when it was suggested that the statue of Queen Anne should be moved from outside St. Paul's
Men, Women and Things (Duke of Portland), Ch. 5

MEMORY

See also memorials, nostalgia, past

1 Memories are hunting horns whose sound dies on the wind.
Guillaume Apollinaire (Wilhelm de Kostrowitzky; 1880–1918) Italian-born French poet.
Cors de Chasse

2 I have more memories than if I were a thousand years old.
Charles Baudelaire (1821–67) French poet.
Spleen

3 Time whereof the memory of man runneth not to the contrary.
William Blackstone (1723–80) British jurist.
Commentaries on the Laws of England, Bk. I, Ch. 18

4 Am in Birmingham. Where ought I to be?
G. K. Chesterton (1874–1936) British writer.
Telegram to his wife during a lecture tour
Portrait of Barrie (C. Asquith)

5 When I meet a man whose name I can't remember, I give myself two minutes; then, if it is a hopeless case, I always say, And how is the old complaint?
Benjamin Disraeli (1804–81) British statesman.
Attrib.

6 I have forgot much, Cynara! gone with the wind, Flung roses, roses riotously with the throng.
Ernest Dowson (1867–1900) British lyric poet.
Non Sum Qualis Eram Bonae Sub Regno Cynarae

7 Oh! don't you remember sweet Alice, Ben Bolt, Sweet Alice, whose hair was so brown, Who wept with delight when you gave her a smile, And trembled with fear at your frown?
Thomas Dunn English (1819–1902) US lawyer and writer.
Ben Bolt

8 To endeavour to forget anyone is a certain way of thinking of nothing else.
Jean de La Bruyère (1645–96) French satirist.
Les Caractères

9 I never forget a face, but I'll make an exception in your case.
Groucho Marx (Julius Marx; 1895–1977) US comedian.
The Guardian, 18 June 1965

10 What a strange thing is memory, and hope; one looks backward, the other forward. The one is of today, the other is the Tomorrow. Memory is history recorded in our brain, memory is a painter, it paints pictures of the past and of the day.
Grandma Moses (Anna Mary Robertson Moses; 1860–1961) US primitive painter.
Grandma Moses, My Life's History (ed. Aotto Kallir), Ch. 1

11 The taste was that of the little crumb of madeleine which on Sunday mornings at Combray . . . , when I used to say good-day to her in her bedroom, my aunt Léonie used to give me, dipping it first in her own cup of real or of lime-flower tea.
Marcel Proust (1871–1922) French novelist.
À la recherche du temps perdu: Du côté de chez Swann

12 Thanks For the Memory.
Leo Robin (1899–) US songwriter.
Big Broadcast, song title

13 Remember me when I am gone away,

Gone far away into the silent land.
Christina Rossetti (1830–74) British poet.
Remember

14 Better by far you should forget and smile
Than that you should remember and be sad.
Christina Rossetti
Remember

15 To expect a man to retain everything that he
has ever read is like expecting him to carry
about in his body everything that he has ever
eaten.
Arthur Schopenhauer (1788–1860) German philosopher.
Parerga and Paralipomena

16 Old men forget; yet all shall be forgot,
But he'll remember, with advantages,
What feats he did that day.
William Shakespeare (1564–1616) English dramatist.
Henry V, IV:3

17 Music, when soft voices die,
Rose leaves, when the rose is dead,
Are heaped for the beloved's bed;
And so thy thoughts, when thou art gone,
Love itself shall slumber on.
Percy Bysshe Shelley (1792–1822) British poet.
To –

18 As a perfume doth remain
In the folds where it hath lain,
So the thought of you, remaining
Deeply folded in my brain,
Will not leave me: all things leave me:
You remain.
Arthur Symons (1865–1945) British poet.
Memory

19 I suppose that the high-water mark of my
youth in Columbus, Ohio, was the night the
bed fell on my father.
James Thurber (1894–1961) US humorist.
My Life and Hard Times, Ch. 1

MEN

See also mankind, marriage, masculinity, marriage, sexes,
women

1 One cannot be always laughing at a man
without now and then stumbling on something
witty.
Jane Austen (1775–1817) British novelist.
Pride and Prejudice, Ch. 40

2 A man's a man for a' that.
Robert Burns (1759–96) Scottish poet.
For a' that and a' that

3 A man . . . is *so* in the way in the house!
Elizabeth Gaskell (1810–65) British novelist.
Cranford, Ch. 1

4 Probably the only place where a man can feel
really secure is in a maximum security

prison, except for the imminent threat of
release.
Germaine Greer (1939–) Australian-born British writer
and feminist.
The Female Eunuch

5 How beastly the bourgeois is
especially the male of the species.
D. H. Lawrence (1885–1930) British novelist.
How beastly the bourgeois is

6 One realizes with horror, that the race of
men is almost extinct in Europe. Only Christ-
like heroes and woman-worshipping Don
Juans, and rabid equality-mongrels.
D. H. Lawrence
Sea and Sardinia, Ch. 3

7 Why can't a woman be more like a man?
Men are so honest, so thoroughly square;
Eternally noble, historically fair.
Alan Jay Lerner (1918–86) US songwriter.
My Fair Lady, II:4

8 He was formed for the ruin of our sex.
Tobias Smollett (1721–71) British novelist.
Roderick Random, Ch. 22

9 Sometimes I think if there was a third sex
men wouldn't get so much as a glance from
me.
Amanda Vail (Warren Miller; 1921–66) US writer.
Love Me Little, Ch. 6

10 A man in the house is worth two in the
street.
Mae West (1892–1980) US actress.
Belle of the Nineties, film 1934

MERCY

1 I seem forsaken and alone,
I hear the lion roar;
And every door is shut but one,
And that is Mercy's door.
William Cowper (1731–1800) British poet.
Olney Hymns, 33

2 The quality of mercy is not strain'd;
It droppeth as the gentle rain from heaven
Upon the place beneath. It is twice blest;
It blesseth him that gives and him that takes.
William Shakespeare (1564–1616) English dramatist.
The Merchant of Venice, IV:1

3 And her face so sweet and pleading, yet with
sorrow pale and worn,
Touched his heart with sudden pity – lit his
eye with misty light;
'Go, your lover lives!' said Cromwell; 'Curfew
shall not ring tonight!'
Rose Hartwick Thorpe (1850–1939) US poet and
novelist.
Curfew Shall Not Ring Tonight

MERIT

1 A good dog deserves a good bone.
Proverb

2 I don't deserve this, but I have arthritis, and I don't deserve that either.
Jack Benny (Benjamin Kubelsky; 1894–1974) US actor.
Said when accepting an award
Attrib.

3 But many that are first shall be last; and the last shall be first.
Bible: Matthew
19:30

4 GOLDSMITH: Here's such a stir about a fellow that has written one book, and I have written many.
JOHNSON: Ah, Doctor, there go two-and-forty sixpences you know to one guinea.
Samuel Johnson (1709–84) British lexicographer.
Referring to Beattie's *Essay on Truth*
Johnsonian Miscellanies (ed. G. B. Hill), Vol. I

5 I guess this is the week I earn my salary.
John Fitzgerald Kennedy (1917–63) US statesman.
Comment made during the Cuban missile crisis
Nobody Said It Better (M. Ringo)

6 Use every man after his desert, and who shall scape whipping?
William Shakespeare (1564–1616) English dramatist.
Hamlet, II:2

7 I wasn't lucky. I deserved it.
Margaret Thatcher (1925–) British politician and prime minister.
Said after receiving school prize, aged nine.
Attrib.

8 The Rise of the Meritocracy.
Michael Young (1915–) British political writer.
Book title

MERRIMENT

1 For the good are always the merry,
Save by an evil chance,
And the merry love the fiddle,
And the merry love to dance
W. B. Yeats (1865–1939) Irish poet.
The Fiddler of Dooney

MERRYMAKING

See also parties, pleasure

1 Come lasses and lads, get leave of your dads,
And away to the Maypole hie,
For every he has got him a she,
And the fiddler's standing by.
Anonymous
Come Lasses and Lads

2 There was a sound of revelry by night,
And Belgium's capital had gather'd then
Her Beauty and her Chivalry, and bright

The lamps shone o'er fair women and brave men.
Lord Byron (1788–1824) British poet.
Childe Harold's Pilgrimage, III

3 Dost thou think, because thou art virtuous, there shall be no more cakes and ale?
William Shakespeare (1564–1616) English dramatist.
Twelfth Night, II:3

4 We have heard the chimes at midnight.
William Shakespeare
Henry IV, Part Two, III:2

5 You must wake and call me early, call me early, mother dear;
To-morrow 'ill be the happiest time of all the glad New-year;
Of all the glad New-year, mother, the maddest merriest day;
For I'm to be Queen o' the May, mother, I'm to be Queen o' the May.
Alfred, Lord Tennyson (1809–92) British poet.
The May Queen

6 I love such mirth as does not make friends ashamed to look upon one another next morning.
Izaak Walton (1593–1683) English writer.
The Compleat Angler, Ch. 5

METAPHYSICS

See also philosophy

1 A blind man in a dark room – looking for a black hat– which isn't there.
Lord Bowen (1835–94) British judge.
Characterization of a metaphysician
Attrib.

2 Metaphysics is the finding of bad reasons for what we believe upon instinct; but to find these reasons is no less an instinct.
F. H. Bradley (1846–1924) British philosopher.
Appearance and Reality, Preface

3 We used to think that if we knew one, we knew two, because one and one are two. We are finding that we must learn a great deal more about 'and'.
Arthur Eddington (1882–1944) British astronomer.
The Harvest of a Quiet Eye (A. L. Mackay)

4 In other words, apart from the known and the unknown, what else is there?
Harold Pinter (1930–) British dramatist.
The Homecoming, II

5 Whither is fled the visionary gleam?
Where is it now, the glory and the dream?

Our birth is but a sleep and a forgetting:
The Soul that rises with us, our life's Star,
Hath had elsewhere its setting,
And cometh from afar;
Not in entire forgetfulness,
And not in utter nakedness,

But trailing clouds of glory do we come
From God, who is our home:
Heaven lies about us in our infancy!
Shades of the prison-house begin to close
Upon the growing boy.
William Wordsworth (1770–1850) British poet.
Ode. Intimations of Immortality, IV

6 Hence in a season of calm weather
Though inland far we be,
Our souls have sight of that immortal sea
Which brought us hither . . .
William Wordsworth
Ode. Intimations of Immortality, IX

MIND

See also intellect, intelligence, thinking

1 *Brain*, n. An apparatus with which we think
that we think.
Ambrose Bierce (1842–?1914) US writer and journalist.
The Devil's Dictionary

2 We know the human brain is a device to
keep the ears from grating on one another.
Peter De Vries (1910–) US novelist.
Comfort me with Apples, Ch. 1

3 The pendulum of the mind oscillates between
sense and nonsense, not between right and
wrong.
Carl Gustav Jung (1875–1961) Swiss psychoanalyst.
Memories, Dreams, Reflections, Ch. 5

4 A mind not to be changed by place or time.
The mind is its own place, and in itself
Can make a Heaven of Hell, a Hell of Heaven.
John Milton (1608–74) English poet.
Paradise Lost, Bk. I

5 That's the classical mind at work, runs fine
inside but looks dingy on the surface.
Robert T. Pirsig (1928–) US writer.
Zen and the Art of Motorcycle Maintenance, Pt. III, Ch. 25

6 The dogma of the Ghost in the Machine.
Gilbert Ryle (1900–76) British philosopher.
The Concept of Mind, Ch. 1

7 If it is for mind that we are seaching the
brain, then we are supposing the brain to be
much more than a telephone-exchange. We
are supposing it a telephone-exchange along
with the subscribers as well.
Charles Scott Sherrington (1857–1952) British
physiologist.
Man on his Nature

8 When people will not weed their own minds,
they are apt to be overrun with nettles.
Horace Walpole (1717–97) British writer.
Letter to Lady Ailesbury, 10 July 1779

9 The mind can also be an erogenous zone.
Raquel Welch (Raquel Tejada; 1940–) US film star.
Colombo's Hollywood (J. R. Colombo)

10 Strongest minds

Are often those of whom the noisy world
Hears least.
William Wordsworth (1770–1850) British poet.
The Excursion

MINORITY

See also majority

1 What's a cult? It just means not enough
people to make a minority.
Robert Altman (1922–) US film director.
The Observer, 1981

2 The majority has the might – more's the pity
– but it hasn't right . . . The minority is
always right.
Henrik Ibsen (1828–1906) Norwegian dramatist.
An Enemy of the People, IV

3 Minorities . . . are almost always in the right.
Sydney Smith (1771–1845) British clergyman and
essayist.
The Smith of Smiths (H. Pearson), Ch. 9

MISANTHROPY

See also mankind, philanthropy

1 What though the spicy breezes
Blow soft o'er Ceylon's isle;
Though every prospect pleases,
And only man is vile . . .
Reginald Heber (1783–1826) British bishop and hymn
writer .
From Greenland's Icy Mountains

2 I've always been interested in people, but
I've never liked them.
W. Somerset Maugham (1874–1965) British novelist.
The Observer, 'Sayings of the Week', 28 Aug 1949

3 I love mankind – it's people I can't stand.
Charles M. Schultz (1922–) US cartoonist.
Go Fly a Kite, Charlie Brown

4 Other people are quite dreadful. The only
possible society is oneself.
Oscar Wilde (1854–1900) Irish-born British dramatist.
An Ideal Husband, III

MISFORTUNE

See also accidents, curses, sorrow, suffering

1 It is easy to bear the misfortunes of others.
Proverb

2 It never rains but it pours.
Proverb

3 Prosperity doth best discover vice; but
adversity doth best discover virtue.
Francis Bacon (1561–1626) English philosopher.
Essays, 'Of Adversity'

4 Calamities are of two kinds. Misfortune to
ourselves and good fortune to others.
Ambrose Bierce (1842–?1914) US writer and journalist.
The Devil's Dictionary

5 There remaineth a rest for the people of
God:
And I have had troubles enough, for one.
Robert Browning (1812–89) British poet.
Old Pictures in Florence, XVII

6 Tragedie is to seyn a certeyn storie,
As olde bokes maken us memorie,
Of him that stood in greet prosperitee
And is y-fallen out of heigh degree
Into miserie, and endeth wrecchedly.
Geoffrey Chaucer (c. 1342–1400) English poet.
The Canterbury Tales, 'The Monk's Prologue'

7 For of fortunes sharp adversitee
The worst kinde of infortune is this,
A man to have ben in prosperitee,
And it remembren, what is passed is.
Geoffrey Chaucer
Troilus and Criseyde, 3

8 A chapter of accidents.
Earl of Chesterfield (1694–1773) English statesman.
Letter to his son, 16 Feb 1753

9 'I am a lone lorn creetur,' were Mrs
Gummidge's words . . . 'and everythink goes
contrairy with me.'
Charles Dickens (1812–70) British novelist.
David Copperfield, Ch. 3

10 Life is mostly froth and bubble;
Two things stand like stone,
Kindness in another's trouble,
Courage in your own.
Adam Lindsay Gordon (1833–70) Australian poet.
Ye Wearie Wayfarer, Fytte 8

11 Depend upon it that if a man talks of his
misfortunes there is something in them that
is not disagreeable to him; for where there is
nothing but pure misery there never is any
recourse to the mention of it.
Samuel Johnson (1709–84) British lexicographer.
Life of Johnson (J. Boswell), Vol. IV

12 There exist some evils so terrible and some
misfortunes so horrible that we dare not
think of them, whilst their very aspect makes
us shudder; but if they happen to fall on us,
we find ourselves stronger than we imagined,
we grapple with our ill luck, and behave
better than we expected we should.
Jean de La Bruyère (1645–96) French satirist.
Les Caractères

13 I never knew any man in my life who could
not bear another's misfortunes perfectly like
a Christian.
Alexander Pope (1688–1744) British poet.
Thoughts on Various Subjects

14 We are all strong enough to bear the
misfortunes of others.
Duc de la Rochefoucauld (1613–80) French writer.
Maximes, 19

15 In the misfortune of our best friends, we
always find something which is not
displeasing to us.
Duc de la Rochefoucauld
Maximes, 99

16 Misery acquaints a man with strange
bedfellows.
William Shakespeare (1564–1616) English dramatist.
The Tempest, II:2

17 When sorrows come, they come not single
spies,
But in battalions!
William Shakespeare
Hamlet, IV:5

18 This is the excellent foppery of the world,
that, when we are sick in fortune, often the
surfeits of our own behaviour, we make
guilty of our disasters the sun, the moon,
and stars.
William Shakespeare
King Lear, I:2

MISOGYNY

See also women

1 I'd be equally as willing
For a dentist to be drilling
Than to ever let a woman in my life.
Alan Jay Lerner (1918–86) US songwriter.
My Fair Lady, I:2

2 How can I possibly dislike a sex to which
Your Majesty belongs?
Cecil Rhodes (1853–1902) South African statesman.
Replying to Queen Victoria's suggestion that he disliked
women
Rhodes (Lockhart)

3 Would you have me speak after my custom,
as being a professed tyrant to their sex?
William Shakespeare (1564–1616) English dramatist.
Much Ado About Nothing, I:1

MISTAKES

See also imperfection

1 Two wrongs do not make a right.
Proverb

2 It is worse than immoral, it's a mistake.
Dean Acheson (1893–1971) US lawyer and statesman.
Describing the Vietnam war. *See also* BOULAY DE LA MEURTHE.
Quoted by Alistair Cooke in his radio programme *Letter from
America*

3 The weak have one weapon: the errors of
those who think they are strong.
Georges Bidault (1899–1983) French statesman.
The Observer, 1962

4 It is worse than a crime, it is a blunder.
Antoine Boulay de la Meurthe (1761–1840) French
politician.
See also ACHESON. Referring to the summary execution of the
Duc d'Enghien by Napoleon, 1804
Attrib.

5 I beseech you, in the bowels of Christ, think it possible you may be mistaken.
Oliver Cromwell (1599–1658) English soldier and statesman.
Letter to the General Assembly of the Church of Scotland, 3 Aug 1650

6 Better send them a Papal Bull.
Lord Curzon (1859–1925) British politician.
Written in the margin of a Foreign Office document. The phrase 'the monks of Mount Athos were violating their vows' had been misprinted as ' . . . violating their cows'.
Life of Lord Curzon (Ronaldshay), Vol. III, Ch. 15

7 Yes, once – many, many years ago. I thought I had made a wrong decision. Of course, it turned out that I had been right all along. But I was wrong to have *thought* that I was wrong.
John Foster Dulles (1888–1959) US politician.
On being asked whether he had ever been wrong
Facing the Music (H. Temianka)

8 Pardon me, madam, but *I* am my brother.
Karl Gustav Jacob Jacobi (1804–51) German mathematician.
On being mistaken by a lady for his brother
Men of Mathematics (M. H. Jacobi)

9 The man who makes no mistakes does not usually make anything.
Edward John Phelps (1822–1900) US lawyer and diplomat.
Speech, Mansion House, London, 24 Jan 1899

10 A man should never be ashamed to own he has been in the wrong, which is but saying, in other words, that he is wiser to-day than he was yesterday.
Alexander Pope (1688–1744) British poet.
Thoughts on Various Subjects

11 To err is human, to forgive, divine.
Alexander Pope
An Essay on Criticism

12 The follies which a man regrets the most in his life, are those which he didn't commit when he had the opportunity.
Helen Rowland (1876–1950) US writer.
Guide To Men

13 What time is the next swan?
Leo Slezak (1873–1946) Czechoslovakian-born tenor.
When the mechanical swan left the stage without him during a performance of *Lohengrin*
What Time Is the Next Swan? (Walter Slezak)

14 We often discover what *will* do, by finding out what will not do; and probably he who never made a mistake never made a discovery.
Samuel Smiles (1812–1904) British writer.
Self-Help, Ch. 11

15 Well, if I called the wrong number, why did you answer the phone?
James Thurber (1894–1961) US humorist.
Cartoon caption

16 If we had more time for discussion we should probably have made a great many more mistakes.
Leon Trotsky (Lev Davidovich Bronstein; 1879–1940) Russian revolutionary.
My Life

17 The physician can bury his mistakes, but the architect can only advise his client to plant vines.
Frank Lloyd Wright (1869–1959) US architect.
New York Times Magazine, 4 Oct 1953

MISTRUST

See also suspicion, trust

1 After shaking hands with a Greek, count your fingers.
Proverb

2 While I see many hoof-marks going in, I see none coming out.
Aesop (6th century BC) Reputed Greek writer of fables.
Fables, 'The Lion, the Fox, and the Beasts'

3 The lion and the calf shall lie down together but the calf won't get much sleep.
Woody Allen (Allen Stewart Konigsberg; 1935–   ) US film actor.
Without Feathers 'The Scrolls'

4 The louder he talked of his honour, the faster we counted our spoons.
Ralph Waldo Emerson (1803–82) US poet and essayist.
Conduct of Life, 'Worship'

5 Let me remind you what the wary fox said once upon a time to the sick lion: 'Because those footprints scare me, all directed your way, none coming back.'
Horace (Quintus Horatius Flaccus; 65–8 BC) Roman poet.
Epistles, I

6 But if he does really think that there is no distinction between virtue and vice, why, Sir, when he leaves our houses let us count our spoons.
Samuel Johnson (1709–84) British lexicographer.
Life of Johnson (J. Boswell), Vol. I

7 *Quis custodiet ipsos custodes?*
Who is to guard the guards themselves?
Juvenal (Decimus Junius Juvenalis; 60–130 AD). Roman satirist.
Satires, VI

8 Ye diners-out from whom we guard our spoons.
Lord Macaulay (1800–59) British historian.
Letter to Hannah Macaulay, 29 June 1831

9 Let me have men about me that are fat;
Sleek-headed men, and such as sleep o' nights.
Yon Cassius has a lean and hungry look;
He thinks too much. Such men are dangerous.
William Shakespeare (1564–1616) English dramatist.
Julius Caesar, I:2

10 An ally has to be watched just like an enemy.
Leon Trotsky (Lev Davidovich Bronstein; 1879–1940) Russian revolutionary.
Expansion and Coexistence (A. Ulam)

11 *Equo ne credite, Teucri.*
Quidquid id est timeo Danaos et dona ferentis.
Do not trust the horse, Trojans. Whatever it is, I fear the Greeks even when they bring gifts.
Virgil (Publius Vergilius Maro; 70–19 BC) Roman poet.
Aeneid, Bk. II

MIXED METAPHORS

See also Goldwynisms

1 If you open that Pandora's Box you never know what Trojan 'orses will jump out.
Ernest Bevin (1881–1951) British trade-union leader and politician.
Referring to the Council of Europe
Ernest Bevin and the Foreign Office (Sir Roderick Barclay)

2 Every director bites the hand that lays the golden egg.
Samuel Goldwyn (Samuel Goldfish; 1882–1974) Polish-born US film producer.
Attrib.

3 You ought to take the bull between the teeth.
Samuel Goldwyn
Attrib.

4 Mr Speaker, I smell a rat; I see him forming in the air and darkening the sky; but I'll nip him in the bud.
Boyle Roche (1743–1807) British politician.
Attrib.

MODERATION

See also excess

1 Moderation in all things.
Proverb

2 You can have too much of a good thing.
Proverb

3 By God, Mr Chairman, at this moment I stand astonished at my own moderation!
Clive of India (1725–74) British soldier and governor of Bengal.
Reply during Parliamentary Inquiry, 1773

4 Not too much zeal.
Talleyrand (Charles Maurice de Talleyrand-Périgord; 1754–1838) French politician.
Attrib.

5 Moderation is a fatal thing, Lady Hunstanton. Nothing succeeds like excess.
Oscar Wilde (1854–1900) Irish-born British dramatist.
A Woman of No Importance, III

MODESTY

1 Nurse, take away the candle and spare my blushes.
Henry James (1843–1916) US novelist.
On being informed, whilst confined to his bed, that he had been awarded the Order of Merit
The American Treasury (C. Fadiman)

2 It was involuntary. They sank my boat.
John Fitzgerald Kennedy (1917–63) US statesman.
Responding to praise of his courage whilst serving in the US navy against the Japanese in World War II
Nobody Said It Better (M. Ringo)

3 In some remote regions of Islam it is said, a woman caught unveiled by a stranger will raise her skirt to cover her face.
Raymond Mortimer (1895–) British literary critic and writer.
Colette

4 If you want people to think well of you, do not speak well of yourself.
Blaise Pascal (1623–62) French philosopher and mathematician.
Pensées, I

5 Be modest! It is the kind of pride least likely to offend.
Jules Renard (1894–1910) French writer.
Journal

6 . . . the nuns who never take a bath without wearing a bathrobe all the time. When asked why, since no man can see them, they reply 'Oh, but you forget the good God.'
Bertrand Russell (1872–1970) British philosopher.
The Basic Writings, Pt. II, Ch. 7

7 I have often wished I had time to cultivate modesty . . . But I am too busy thinking about myself.
Edith Sitwell (1887–1964) British poet and writer.
The Observer, 'Sayings of the Week', 30 Apr 1950

MONARCHY

See also royalty

1 The best reason why Monarchy is a strong government is that it is an intelligible government. The mass of mankind understand it, and they hardly anywhere in the world understand any other.
Walter Bagehot (1826–77) British economist and journalist.
The English Constitution, 'The Monarchy'

2 The Sovereign has, under a constitutional monarchy such as ours, three rights – the right to be consulted, the right to encourage, the right to warn.
Walter Bagehot
The English Constitution, 'The Monarchy'

3 God grant him peace and happiness but never understanding of what he has lost.
Stanley Baldwin (1867–1947) British politician and prime minister.
Referring to Edward VIII's abdication

4 That the king can do no wrong, is a necessary and fundamental principle of the English constitution.
William Blackstone (1723–80) British jurist.
Commentaries on the Laws of England, Bk. III, Ch. 17

5 The king never dies.
William Blackstone
Commentaries on the Laws of England, Bk. I, Ch. 7

6 I would rather hew wood than be a king under the conditions of the King of England.
Charles X (1757–1836) King of France.
Encyclopaedia Britannica

7 There is no middle course between the throne and the scaffold.
Charles X
Said to Talleyrand, who is said to have replied 'You are forgetting the postchaise'.
Attrib.

8 Magna Charta is such a fellow, that he will have no sovereign.
Edward Coke (1552–1634) English lawyer and politician.
Speaking on the Lords Amendment to the Petition of Right, 17 May 1628
Hist. Coll. (Rushworth), I

9 The influence of the Crown has increased, is increasing, and ought to be diminished.
John Dunning (1731–83) British lawyer and politician.
Motion passed by the House of Commons, 1780

10 There will soon be only five kings left – the Kings of England, Diamonds, Hearts, Spades and Clubs.
Farouk I (1920–65) The last king of Egypt.
Remark made to Lord Boyd-Orr

11 Kings govern by means of popular assemblies only when they cannot do without them.
Charles James Fox (1749–1806) British Whig politician.
Attrib.

12 I will govern according to the common weal, but not according to the common will.
James I (1566–1625) King of England.
History of the English People (J. R. Green)

13 A constitutional king must learn to stoop.
Leopold II (1835–1909) King of the Belgians.
Instructing Prince Albert, the heir apparent, to pick up some papers that had fallen onto the floor
The Mistress (Betty Kelen)

14 L'État c'est moi.
I am the State.
Louis XIV (1638–1715) French king.
Attrib.

15 There is something behind the throne greater than the King himself.
William Pitt the Elder (1708–78) British statesman.
Speech, House of Lords, 2 Mar 1770

16 The right divine of kings to govern wrong.
Alexander Pope (1688–1744) British poet.
The Dunciad, IV

17 A king is a thing men have made for their own sakes, for quietness' sake. Just as if in a family one man is appointed to buy the meat.
John Selden (1584–1654) English historian.
Table Talk

18 Every subject's duty is the King's; but every subject's soul is his own.
William Shakespeare (1564–1616) English dramatist.
Henry V, IV:1

19 There's such divinity doth hedge a king That treason can but peep to what it would.
William Shakespeare
Hamlet, IV:5

20 Not all the water in the rough rude sea Can wash the balm from an anointed king; The breath of worldly men cannot depose The deputy elected by the Lord.
William Shakespeare
Richard II, III:2

21 Uneasy lies the head that wears a crown.
William Shakespeare
Henry IV, Part Two, III:1

22 The king reigns, and the people govern themselves.
Louis Adolphe Thiers (1797–1877) French statesman and historian.
In an unsigned article attributed to Thiers
Le National, 20 Jan 1830

23 As guardian of His Majesty's conscience.
Lord Thurlow (1731–1806) British lawyer.
Speech, House of Lords, 1779

24 The monarchy is a labour-intensive industry.
Harold Wilson (1916–) British politician and prime minister.
The Observer, 13 Feb 1977

25 The king reigns, but does not govern.
Jan Zamoyski (1541–1605) Grand chancellor of Poland.
Speech, Polish Parliament, 1605

MONEY

See also bribery, economics, extravagance, greed, materialism, thrift, wealth

1 Easy come, easy go.
Proverb

2 Out of debt, out of danger.
Proverb

3 Take care of the pence, and the pounds will take care of themselves.
Proverb

4 I can't afford to waste my time making money.

Jean Louis Rodolphe Agassiz (1807–73) Swiss naturalist.
When asked to give a lecture for a fee
Attrib.

5 Business, you know, may bring money, but friendship hardly ever does.

Jane Austen (1775–1817) British novelist.
Emma, Ch. 34

6 Money is like muck, not good except it be spread.

Francis Bacon (1561–1626) English philosopher.
See also MURCHISON
Essays, 'Of Seditions and Troubles'

7 Money, it turned out, was exactly like sex, you thought of nothing else if you didn't have it and thought of other things if you did.

James Baldwin (1924–87) US writer.
Nobody Knows My Name

8 I'm tired of Love: I'm still more tired of Rhyme.
But Money gives me pleasure all the Time.

Hilaire Belloc (1870–1953) French-born British poet.
Fatigue

9 A feast is made for laughter, and wine maketh merry: but money answereth all things.

Bible: Ecclesiastes
10:19

10 For the love of money is the root of all evil: which while some coveted after, they have erred from the faith, and pierced themselves through with many sorrows.

Bible: I Timothy
6:10

11 Straighteners, managers and cashiers of the Musical Banks.

Samuel Butler (1835–1902) British writer.
Erewhon, Ch. 9

12 It has been said that the love of money is the root of all evil. The want of money is so quite as truly.

Samuel Butler
Erewhon, Ch. 20

13 What makes all doctrines plain and clear?
About two hundred pounds a year.

Samuel Butler
Hudibras, Pt. III

14 It is a kind of spiritual snobbery that makes people think that they can be happy without money.

Albert Camus (1913–60) French existentialist writer.
Notebooks, 1935–1942

15 Where large sums of money are concerned, it is advisable to trust nobody.

Agatha Christie (1891–1976) British detective-story writer.
Endless Night, Bk. II, Ch. 15

16 How pleasant it is to have money.

Arthur Hugh Clough (1819–61) British poet.
Dipsychus, Bk. I

17 But then one is always excited by descriptions of money changing hands. It's much more fundamental than sex.

Nigel Dennis (1912–) British writer.
Cards of Identity

18 Buy an annuity cheap, and make your life interesting to yourself and everybody else that watches the speculation.

Charles Dickens (1812–70) British novelist.
Martin Chuzzlewit, Ch. 18

19 Ah, take the Cash in hand and waive the Rest;
Oh, the brave Music of a *distant* Drum!

Edward Fitzgerald (1809–83) British poet.
The Rubáiyát of Omar Khayyám (1st edn.), XII

20 It is only the poor who pay cash, and that not from virtue, but because they are refused credit.

Anatole France (Jacques Anatole François Thibault; 1844–1924) French writer.
A Cynic's Breviary (J. R. Solly)

21 Money differs from an automobile, a mistress or cancer in being equally important to those who have it and those who do not.

John Kenneth Galbraith (1908–) US economist.
Attrib.

22 If possible honestly, if not, somehow, make money.

Horace (Quintus Horatius Flaccus; 65–8 BC) Roman poet.
Epistles, I

23 We all know how the size of sums of money appears to vary in a remarkable way according as they are being paid in or paid out.

Julian Huxley (1887–1975) British biologist.
Essays of a Biologist, 5

24 Money is like manure. If you spread it around it does a lot of good. But if you pile it up in one place it stinks like hell.

Clint Murchison Jnr (1895–1969) US industrialist.
Following BACON
Time Magazine, 16 June 1961

25 There are few ways in which a man can be more innocently employed than in getting money.

Samuel Johnson (1709–84) British lexicographer.
Life of Johnson (J. Boswell), Vol. II

26 You don't seem to realize that a poor person who is unhappy is in a better position than a rich person who is unhappy. Because the poor person has hope. He thinks money would help.

Jean Kerr (1923–) US dramatist.
Poor Richard

27 Clearly money has something to do with life

– In fact, they've a lot in common, if you enquire:
You can't put off being young until you retire.
Philip Larkin (1922–85) British poet.
Money

28 For I don't care too much for money,
For money can't buy me love.
John Lennon (1940–80) British rock musician.
Can't Buy Me Love (with Paul McCartney)

29 What's a thousand dollars? Mere chicken feed. A poultry matter.
Groucho Marx (Julius Marx; 1895–1977) US comedian.
The Cocoanuts

30 Do they allow tipping on the boat?
  – Yes, sir.
Have you got two fives?
  – Oh, yes, sir.
Then you won't need the ten cents I was going to give you.
Groucho Marx
A Night at the Opera

31 Money is like a sixth sense without which you cannot make a complete use of the other five.
W. Somerset Maugham (1874–1965) British novelist.
Of Human Bondage, Ch. 51

32 Money can't buy friends, but you can get a better class of enemy.
Spike Milligan (1918–) British comic actor and author.
Puckoon, Ch. 6

33 Some people's money is merited
And other people's is inherited.
Ogden Nash (1902–71) US poet.
The Terrible People

34 Check enclosed.
Dorothy Parker (1893–1967) US writer.
Giving her version of the two most beautiful words in the English language
Attrib.

35 Money is good for bribing yourself through the inconveniences of life.
Gottfried Reinhardt (1911–) Austrian film producer.
Picture, 'Looks Like We're Still in Business' (Lillian Ross)

36 My boy . . . always try to rub up against money, for if you rub up against money long enough, some of it may rub off on you.
Damon Runyon (1884–1946) US writer.
Furthermore, 'A Very Honourable Guy'

37 He that wants money, means, and content, is without three good friends.
William Shakespeare (1564–1616) English dramatist.
As You Like It, III:2

38 I can get no remedy against this consumption of the purse; borrowing only lingers and lingers it out, but the disease is incurable.
William Shakespeare
Henry IV, Part Two, I:2

39 Put money in thy purse.
William Shakespeare
Othello, I:3

40 Lack of money is the root of all evil.
George Bernard Shaw (1856–1950) Irish dramatist and critic.
Man and Superman, 'Maxims for Revolutionists.'

41 The trouble, Mr Goldwyn is that you are only interested in art and I am only interested in money.
George Bernard Shaw
Turning down Goldwyn's offer to buy the screen rights of his plays
The Movie Moguls (Philip French), Ch. 4

42 Nothing links man to man like the frequent passage from hand to hand of cash.
Walter Richard Sickert (1860–1942) British impressionist painter.
A Certain World (W. H. Auden)

43 Pieces of eight!
Robert Louis Stevenson (1850–94) Scottish writer.
Treasure Island, Ch. 10

44 I think I could be a good woman if I had five thousand a year.
William Makepeace Thackeray (1811–63) British novelist.
Vanity Fair, Ch. 36

45 No one would have remembered the Good Samaritan if he'd only had good intentions. He had money as well.
Margaret Thatcher (1925–) British politician and prime minister.
Television interview, 1980

46 The easiest way for your children to learn about money is for you not to have any.
Katherine Whitehorn (1926–) British journalist.
How to Survive Children

47 You can be young without money but you can't be old without it.
Tennessee Williams (1911–83) US dramatist.
Cat on a Hot Tin Roof, I

48 All these financiers, all the little gnomes of Zürich and the other financial centres, about whom we keep on hearing.
Harold Wilson (1916–) British politician and prime minister.
Speech, House of Commons, 12 Nov 1956

MONTHS

See also autumn, spring, summer, winter

1 March comes in like a lion and goes out like a lamb.
Proverb

2 Ne'er cast a clout till May be out.
Proverb

3 The cuckoo comes in April, and stays the

month of May; sings a song at midsummer, and then goes away.
Proverb

4 Thirty days hath September,
April, June, and November;
All the rest have thirty-one,
Excepting February alone,
And that has twenty-eight days clear
And twenty-nine in each leap year.
Anonymous
See also GRAFTON
Stevins Manuscript, c. 1555

5 There are twelve months in all the year,
As I hear many men say,
But the merriest month in all the year
Is the merry month of May.
Anonymous
Robin Hood and the Widow's Three Sons

6 And after April, when May follows,
And the whitethroat builds, and all the swallows!
Robert Browning (1812–89) British poet.
Home Thoughts from Abroad

7 Whan that Aprille with his shoures sote
The droghte of Marche hath perced to the rote.
Geoffrey Chaucer (c. 1342–1400) English poet.
The Canterbury Tales, Prologue

8 April is the cruellest month, breeding
Lilacs out of the dead land, mixing
Memory and desire, stirring
Dull roots with spring rain.
T. S. Eliot (1888–1965) US-born British poet and dramatist.
The Waste Land, 'The Burial of the Dead'

9 Thirty days hath November,
April, June and September,
February hath twenty-eight alone,
And all the rest have thirty-one.
Richard Grafton (d. c. 1572) English chronicler and printer.
Abridgement of the Chronicles of England, Introduction

10 No warmth, no cheerfulness, no healthful ease,
No comfortable feel in any member –
No shade, no shine, no butterflies, no bees,
No fruits, no flowers, no leaves, no birds, –
November!
Thomas Hood (1799–1845) British poet.
No!

11 February, fill the dyke
With what thou dost like.
Thomas Tusser (1524–80) English farmer.
Five Hundred Points of Good Husbandry, 'February's Husbandry'

12 Sweet April showers
Do spring May flowers.
Thomas Tusser
Five Hundred Points of Good Husbandry, 'April's Husbandry'

MOON

See also astronomy, space, universe

1 I saw the new moon late yestreen
Wi' the auld moon in her arm;
And if we gang to sea master;
I fear we'll come to harm.
Anonymous
The 'new moon in the old moon's arms' is generally regarded as a sign of bad weather
Sir Patrick Spens

2 The moving Moon went up the sky,
And no where did abide:
Softly she was going up,
And a star or two beside.
Samuel Taylor Coleridge (1772–1834) British poet.
The Rime of the Ancient Mariner, IV

3 who knows if the moon's
a balloon, coming out of a keen city
in the sky – filled with pretty people?
e. e. cummings (1894–1962) US poet.
Used for the title and epigraph of David Niven's first volume of autobiography, *The Moon's a Balloon*, about his experiences in the film industry

4 So sicken waning moons too near the sun,
And blunt their crescents on the edge of day.
John Dryden (1631–1700) British poet and dramatist.
Annus Mirabilis

5 For years politicians have promised the moon, I'm the first one to be able to deliver it.
Richard Milhous Nixon (1913–) US president.
Radio message to astronaughts on the moon, 20 Jul 1969

6 Oh! shine on, shine on, harvest moon
Up in the sky.
I ain't had no lovin'
Since April, January, June or July.
Jack Norworth (1879–1959) US vaudeville comedian and songwriter.
Shine On, Harvest Moon (song)

MORALITY

See also integrity, principles, righteousness

1 In his own way each man must struggle, lest the moral law become a far-off abstraction utterly separated from his active life.
Jane Addams (1860–1935) US social worker.
Twenty Years at Hull House

2 No morality can be founded on authority, even if the authority were divine.
A. J. Ayer (1910–) British philosopher.
Essay on Humanism

3 Morality's not practical. Morality's a gesture. A complicated gesture learnt from books.
Robert Bolt (1924–) British playwright.
A Man for All Seasons

4 The propriety of some persons seems to

consist in having improper thoughts about their neighbours.

F. H. Bradley (1846–1924) British philosopher.
Aphorisms

5 What is moral is what you feel good after, and what is immoral is what you feel bad after.

Ernest Hemingway (1899–1961) US novelist.
Death in the Afternoon

6 The quality of moral behaviour varies in inverse ratio to the number of human beings involved.

Aldous Huxley (1894–1964) British novelist.
Grey Eminence, Ch. 10

7 Finally, there is an imperative which commands a certain conduct immediately . . . This imperative is Categorical . . . This imperative may be called that of Morality.

Immanuel Kant (1724–1804) German philosopher.
Grundlegung zur Metaphysik der Sitten, II

8 Morality which is based on ideas, or on an ideal, is an unmitigated evil.

D. H. Lawrence (1885–1930) British novelist.
Fantasia of the Unconscious, Ch. 7

9 We know no spectacle so ridiculous as the British public in one of its periodical fits of morality.

Lord Macaulay (1800–59) British historian.
Literary Essays Contributed to the 'Edinburgh Review', 'Moore's 'Life of Lord Byron''

10 It is a public scandal that gives offence, and it is no sin to sin in secret.

Molière (Jean Baptiste Poquelin; 1622–73) French dramatist.
Tartuffe, IV:5

11 Morality in Europe today is herd-morality.

Friedrich Wilhelm Nietzsche (1844–1900) German philosopher.
Jenseits von Gut und Böse

12 We have, in fact, two kinds of morality side by side; one which we preach but do not practise, and another which we practise but seldom preach.

Bertrand Russell (1872–1970) British philosopher.
Sceptical Essays

13 All universal moral principles are idle fancies.

Marquis de Sade (1740–1814) French novelist.
The 120 Days of Sodom

14 Without doubt the greatest injury . . . was done by basing morals on myth, for sooner or later myth is recognized for what it is, and disappears. Then morality loses the foundation on which it has been built.

Herbert Samuel (1870–1963) British Liberal statesman.
Romanes Lecture, 1947

15 Morality consists in suspecting other people of not being legally married.

George Bernard Shaw (1856–1950) Irish dramatist and critic.
The Doctor's Dilemma

16 He never does a proper thing without giving an improper reason for it.

George Bernard Shaw
Major Barbara, III

17 The so-called new morality is too often the old immorality condoned.

Lord Shawcross (1902–) British Labour politician and lawyer.
The Observer, 17 Nov 1963

18 'Twas Peter's drift
To be a kind of moral eunuch.

Percy Bysshe Shelley (1792–1822) British poet.
Peter Bell the Third

19 Moral indignation is in most cases 2 percent moral, 48 percent indignation and 50 percent envy.

Vittorio De Sica (1901–74) Italian film director.
The Observer, 1961

20 If your morals make you dreary, depend upon it, they are wrong.

Robert Louis Stevenson (1850–94) Scottish writer.
Across the Plains

21 Victorian values . . . were the values when our country became great.

Margaret Thatcher (1925–) British politician and prime minister.
Television interview, 1982

22 Morals are an acquirement – like music, like a foreign language, like piety, poker, paralysis – no man is born with them.

Mark Twain (Samuel Langhorne Clemens; 1835–1910) US writer.
Seventieth Birthday

MORTALITY

See also death, equality in death, human condition, immortality, life, life and death, time, transience

1 All men are mortal.
Proverb

2 Mortality, behold and fear!
What a change of flesh is here!

Francis Beaumont (1584–1616) English dramatist.
On the Tombs in Westminster Abbey

3 That lyf so short, the craft so long to lerne,
Th' assay so hard, so sharp the conquerynge.

Geoffrey Chaucer (c. 1342–1400) English poet.
See also HIPPOCRATES
The Parliament of Fowls

4 What argufies pride and ambition?
Soon or late death will take us in tow:
Each bullet has got its commission,

And when our time's come we must go.

Charles Dibdin (1745–1814) British actor and dramatist.
Each Bullet has its Commission

5 All humane things are subject to decay,
And, when Fate summons, Monarchs must obey.

John Dryden (1631–1700) British poet and dramatist.
Mac Flecknoe

6 The Wine of Life keeps oozing drop by drop,
The Leaves of Life keep falling one by one.

Edward Fitzgerald (1809–83) British poet.
The Rubáiyát of Omar Khayyám (4th edn.), VIII

7 Is life a boon?
If so, it must befall
That Death, whene'er he call,
Must call too soon.

W. S. Gilbert (1836–1911) British dramatist.
The lines are written on Arthur Sullivan's memorial in the Embankment gardens
The Yeoman of the Guard, I

8 I was not unaware that I had begotten a mortal.

Goethe (1749–1832) German poet and dramatist.
On learning of his son's death
The Story of Civilization (W. Durant), Vol. X

9 Man wants but little here below,
Nor wants that little long.

Oliver Goldsmith (1728–74) Irish-born British writer.
Edwin and Angelina, or the Hermit

10 The boast of heraldry, the pomp of pow'r,
And all that beauty, all that wealth e'er gave,
Awaits alike th' inevitable hour,
The paths of glory lead but to the grave.

Thomas Gray (1716–71) British poet.
Elegy Written in a Country Churchyard

11 I expect to pass through this world but once;
any good thing therefore that I can do, or
any kindness that I can show to any fellow-
creature, let me do it now; let me not defer
or neglect it, for I shall not pass this way again.

Stephen Grellet (1773–1855) French-born US missionary.
Attrib.
Treasure Trove (John o'London)

12 The life so short, the craft so long to learn.

Hippocrates (c. 460–c. 377 BC) Greek physician.
Describing medicine. It is often quoted in Latin as *Ars longa, vita brevis*, and interpreted as 'Art lasts, life is short'. *See also* CHAUCER.
Aphorisms, I

13 Life's short span forbids us to enter on far-
reaching hopes.

Horace (Quintus Horatius Flaccus; 65–8 BC) Roman poet.
Odes, I

14 Art is long, and Time is fleeting,
And our hearts, though stout and brave,
Still, like muffled drums, are beating

Funeral marches to the grave.

Henry Wadsworth Longfellow (1807–82) US poet.
See also HIPPOCRATES
A Psalm of Life

15 *Inque brevi spatio mutantur saecla animantum
Et quasi cursores vitai lampada tradunt.*
The generations of living things pass in a short
time, and like runners hand on the torch of life.

Lucretius (Titus Lucretius Carus; c. 99–55 BC) Roman philosopher.
On the Nature of the Universe, II

16 Fear no more the heat o' th' sun
Nor the furious winter's rages;
Thou thy worldly task hast done,
Home art gone, and ta'en thy wages.
Golden lads and girls all must,
As chimney-sweepers, come to dust.

William Shakespeare (1564–1616) English dramatist.
Cymbeline, IV:2

17 Our revels now are ended. These our actors,
As I foretold you, were all spirits, and
Are melted into air, into thin air;
And, like the baseless fabric of this vision,
The cloud-capp'd towers, the gorgeous palaces,
The solemn temples, the great globe itself,
Yea, all which it inherit, shall dissolve,
And, like this insubstantial pageant faded,
Leave not a rack behind. We are such stuff
As dreams are made on; and our little life
Is rounded with a sleep.

William Shakespeare
The Tempest, IV:1

18 Old and young, we are all on our last cruise.

Robert Louis Stevenson (1850–94) Scottish writer.
Virginibus Puerisque

19 The woods decay, the woods decay and fall,
The vapours weep their burthen to the ground,
Man comes and tills the field and lies beneath,
And after many a summer dies the swan.

Alfred, Lord Tennyson (1809–92) British poet.
Tithonus

20 A power is passing from the earth
To breathless Nature's dark abyss;
But when the great and good depart,
What is it more than this –

That Man who is from God sent forth,
Doth yet again to God return? –
Such ebb and flow must ever be,
Then wherefore should we mourn?

William Wordsworth (1770–1850) British poet.
Referring to Charles James Fox, the hero of the liberal Whigs, who died in 1806
Lines on the Expected Dissolution of Mr. Fox

21 The clouds that gather round the setting sun
Do take a sober colouring from an eye
That hath kept watch o'er man's mortality.

William Wordsworth
Ode. Intimations of Immortality, XI

22 I am moved to pity, when I think of the brevity of human life, seeing that of all this host of men not one will still be alive in a hundred years' time.
Xerxes (d. 465 BC) King of Persia.
On surveying his army

23 That is no country for old men. The young
In one another's arms, birds in the trees
– Those dying generations – at their song,
The salmon-falls, the mackerel-crowded seas,
Fish, flesh, or fowl, commend all summer long
Whatever is begotten, born, and dies.
W. B. Yeats (1865–1939) Irish poet.
Sailing to Byzantium, I

24 Man wants but little, nor that little long.
Edward Young (1683–1765) British poet.
Night Thoughts

MOTIVE

See also purpose

1 Never ascribe to an opponent motives meaner than your own.
J. M. Barrie (1860–1937) British novelist and dramatist.
Speech, St Andrews, 3 May 1922

2 The last temptation is the greatest treason:
To do the right deed for the wrong reason.
T. S. Eliot (1888–1965) US-born British poet and dramatist.
Murder in the Cathedral, I

3 Because it is there.
George Mallory (1886–1924) British mountaineer.
Answer to the question 'Why do you want to climb Mt. Everest?'
George Mallory (D. Robertson)

4 Nobody ever did anything very foolish except from some strong principle.
Lord Melbourne (1779–1848) British statesman.
The Young Melbourne (Lord David Cecil)

5 The heart has its reasons which reason does not know.
Blaise Pascal (1623–62) French philosopher and mathematician.
Pensées, IV

6 Men are rewarded and punished not for what they do, but rather for how their acts are defined. This is why men are more interested in better justifying themselves than in better behaving themselves.
Thomas Szasz (1920–) US psychiatrist.
The Second Sin

MOUNTAINS

1 Mountains interposed
Make enemies of nations, who had else,
Like kindred drops, been mingled into one.
William Cowper (1731–1800) British poet.
The Task

2 Separate from the pleasure of your company,

I don't much care if I never see another mountain in my life.
Charles Lamb (1775–1834) British essayist.
Letter to William Wordsworth, 30 Jan 1801

3 Mountains are the beginning and the end of all natural scenery.
John Ruskin (1819–1900) British art critic and writer.
Modern Painters, Vol. IV

4 They say that if the Swiss had designed these mountains they'd be rather flatter.
Paul Theroux (1941–) US-born writer.
Referring to the Alps
The Great Railway Bazaar, Ch. 28

MOURNING

See also death, loss, regret, sorrow

1 We met . . . Dr Hall in such very deep mourning that either his mother, his wife, or himself must be dead.
Jane Austen (1775–1817) British novelist.
Letter to Cassandra Austen, 17 May 1799

2 I am distressed for thee, my brother Jonathan: very pleasant hast thou been unto me: thy love to me was wonderful, passing the love of women.
How are the mighty fallen, and the weapons of war perished!
Bible: II Samuel
1:26–27

3 With proud thanksgiving, a mother for her children,
England mourns for her dead across the sea.
Laurence Binyon (1869–1943) British poet.
In response to the slaughter of World War I
Poems For the Fallen

4 MEDVEDENKO. Why do you wear black all the time?
MASHA. I'm in mourning for my life, I'm unhappy.
Anton Chekhov (1860–1904) Russian dramatist.
The Seagull, I

5 There's a one-eyed yellow idol to the north of Khatmandu,
There's a little marble cross below the town;
There's a broken-hearted woman tends the grave of Mad Carew
And the Yellow God forever gazes down.
J. Milton Hayes (1884–1940) British writer.
The Green Eye of the Yellow God

6 What we call mourning for our dead is perhaps not so much grief at not being able to call them back as it is grief at not being able to want to do so.
Thomas Mann (1875–1955) German novelist.
The Magic Mountain

7 In a cavern, in a canyon,
Excavating for a mine
Dwelt a miner, Forty-niner,
And his daughter, Clementine.

Oh, my darling, Oh, my darling, Oh, my darling Clementine!
Thou art lost and gone for ever, dreadful sorry, Clementine.

Percy Montrose (19th century) US songwriter.
Clementine

8 She is far from the land where her young hero sleeps,
And lovers are round her, sighing:
But coldly she turns from their gaze, and weeps,
For her heart in his grave is lying.

Thomas Moore (1779–1852) Irish poet.
Irish Melodies, 'She is Far'

9 And my poor fool is hang'd! No, no, no life!
Why should a dog, a horse, a rat have life,
And thou no breath at all? Thou'lt come no more,
Never, never, never, never.

William Shakespeare (1564–1616) English dramatist.
King Lear, V:3

10 Alas, poor Yorick! I knew him, Horatio: a fellow of infinite jest, of most excellent fancy.

William Shakespeare
Hamlet, V:1

11 O, wither'd is the garland of the war,
The soldier's pole is fall'n! Young boys and girls
Are level now with men. The odds is gone,
And there is nothing left remarkable
Beneath the visiting moon.

William Shakespeare
Antony and Cleopatra, IV:13

12 But I have that within which passes show –
these but the trappings and the suits of woe.

William Shakespeare
Hamlet, I:2

13 If thou didst ever hold me in thy heart,
Absent thee from felicity awhile,
And in this harsh world draw thy breath in pain,
To tell my story.

William Shakespeare
Hamlet, V:2

14 I weep for Adonais – he is dead!
O, weep for Adonais! though our tears
Thaw not the frost which binds so dear a head!

Percy Bysshe Shelley (1792–1822) British poet.
Prompted by the death of Keats
Adonais, I

15 A lady asked me why, on most occasions, I wore black. 'Are you in mourning?'
'Yes.'
'For whom are you in mourning?'
'For the world.'

Edith Sitwell (1887–1964) British poet and writer.
Taken Care Of, Ch. 1

16 Home they brought her warrior dead.
She nor swoon'd, nor utter'd cry:

All her maidens, watching said,
'She must weep or she will die.'

Alfred, Lord Tennyson (1809–92) British poet.
The Princess, VI

MURDER

See also assassination, crime, killing

1 Lizzie Borden took an axe
And gave her mother forty whacks;
When she saw what she had done
She gave her father forty-one!

Anonymous
On 4 Aug 1892 in Fall River, Massachusetts, Lizzie Borden was acquitted of the murder of her stepmother and her father

2 And the Lord said unto Cain, Where is Abel thy brother? And he said, I know not: Am I my brother's keeper?
And he said, What hast thou done? the voice of thy brother's blood crieth unto me from the ground.

Bible: Genesis
4:9–10

3 I've been accused of every death except the casualty list of the World War.

Al Capone (1899–1947) Italian-born US gangster.
The Bootleggers (Kenneth Allsop), Ch. 11

4 Mordre wol out, that see we day by day.

Geoffrey Chaucer (c. 1342–1400) English poet.
The Canterbury Tales, 'The Nun's Priest's Tale'

5 See how love and murder will out.

William Congreve (1670–1729) British Restoration dramatist.
The Double Dealer, IV:6

6 Murder considered as one of the Fine Arts.

Thomas De Quincey (1785–1859) British writer.
Essay title

7 I made a remark a long time ago. I said I was very pleased that television was now showing murder stories, because it's bringing murder back into its rightful setting – in the home.

Alfred Hitchcock (1889–1980) British film director.
The Observer, 'Sayings of the Week', 17 Aug 1969

8 It takes two to make a murder. There are born victims, born to have their throats cut.

Aldous Huxley (1894–1963) British novelist.
Point Counter Point

9 Murder, like talent, seems occasionally to run in families.

G. H. Lewes (1817–78) British philosopher and writer.
The Physiology of Common Life, Ch. 12

10 Put out the light, and then put out the light.
If I quench thee, thou flaming minister,
I can again thy former light restore,
Should I repent me; but once put out thy light,
Thou cunning'st pattern of excelling nature,
I know not where is that Promethean heat

That can thy light relume.
William Shakespeare (1564–1616) English dramatist.
Othello, V:2

11 Murder most foul, as in the best it is;
But this most foul, strange, and unnatural.
William Shakespeare
Hamlet, I:5

12 I met Murder on the way –
He had a mask like Castlereagh.
Percy Bysshe Shelley (1792–1822) British poet.
Viscount Castlereagh (1769–1822) was British foreign secretary (1812–22); he was highly unpopular and became identified with such controversial events as the Peterloo massacre of 1819.
The Mask of Anarchy, 5

13 Other sins only speak; murder shrieks out.
John Webster (1580–1625) English dramatist.
The Duchess of Malfi, IV:2

MUSEUMS

1 The Arab who builds himself a hut out of the marble fragments of a temple in Palmyra is more philosophical than all the curators of the museums in London, Munich or Paris.
Anatole France (Jacques Anatole François Thibault; 1844–1924) French writer.
The Crime of Sylvestre Bonnard

2 If there was a little room somewhere in the British Museum that contained only about twenty exhibits and good lighting, easy chairs, and a notice imploring you to smoke, I believe I should become a museum man.
J. B. Priestley (1894–1984) British novelist.
Self-Selected Essays, 'In the British Museum'

3 There is in the British Museum an enormous mind. Consider that Plato is there cheek by jowl with Aristotle; and Shakespeare with Marlowe. This great mind is hoarded beyond the power of any single mind to possess it.
Virginia Woolf (1882–1941) British novelist.
Jacob's Room, Ch. 9

MUSIC

See also criticism, musicians, opera, singing

1 Music helps not the toothache.
Proverb

2 Nothing is capable of being well set to music that is not nonsense.
Joseph Addison (1672–1719) British essayist.
The Spectator, 18

3 The music teacher came twice each week to bridge the awful gap between Dorothy and Chopin.
George Ade (1866–1944) US dramatist and humorist.
Attrib.

4 Brass bands are all very well in their place – outdoors and several miles away.
Thomas Beecham (1879–1961) British conductor.
Attrib.

5 The English may not like music – but they absolutely love the noise it makes.
Thomas Beecham
The Wit of Music (L. Ayre)

6 The sound of the harpsichord resembles that of a bird-cage played with toasting-forks.
Thomas Beecham
Attrib.

7 A musicologist is a man who can read music but can't hear it.
Thomas Beecham
Beecham Remembered (H. Procter-Gregg)

8 When I composed that, I was conscious of being inspired by God Almighty. Do you think I can consider your puny little fiddle when He speaks to me?
Ludwig van Beethoven (1770–1827) German composer.
Said when a violinist complained that a passage was unplayable
Music All Around Me (A. Hopkins)

9 *Fiddle, n.* An instrument to tickle human ears by function of a horse's tail on the entrails of a cat.
Ambrose Bierce (1842–?1914) US writer and journalist.
The Devil's Dictionary

10 Down South where I come from you don't go around hitting too many white keys.
Eubie Blake (1883–1983) US pianist and ragtime composer.
When asked why his compositions contained so many sharps and flats
Attrib.

11 Piping down the valleys wild,
Piping songs of pleasant glee,
On a cloud I saw a child.
William Blake (1757–1827) British poet.
Songs of Innocence, Introduction

12 'Pipe a song about a Lamb!'
So I piped with merry cheer.
William Blake
Songs of Innocence, Introduction

13 No one really understood music unless he was a scientist, her father had declared, and not just a scientist, either, oh, no, only the real ones, the theoreticians, whose language was mathematics.
Pearl Buck (1892–1973) US novelist.
The Goddess Abides, Pt. I

14 Music has charms to soothe a savage breast.
William Congreve (1670–1729) British Restoration dramatist.
The Mourning Bride, I

15 Strange how potent cheap music is.
Noël Coward (1899–1973) British dramatist.
Private Lives

16 Music is the arithmetic of sounds as optics is the geometry of light.
Claude Debussy (1862–1918) French composer.
Attrib.

17 Music was invented to confirm human loneliness.
Lawrence Durrell (1912–) British novelist.
Clea

18 Beethoven's Fifth Symphony is the most sublime noise that has ever penetrated into the ear of man.
E. M. Forster (1879–1970) British novelist.
Howards End, Ch. 5

19 The hills are alive with the sound of music
With the songs they have sung
For a thousand years.
Oscar Hammerstein (1895–1960) US lyricist.
The Sound of Music, title song

20 I do not see any reason why the devil should have all the good tunes.
Rowland Hill (1744–1833) British clergyman.
Attrib.

21 Never compose anything unless the not composing of it becomes a positive nuisance to you.
Gustav Holst (1874–1934) British composer.
Letter to W. G. Whittaker

22 Since Mozart's day composers have learned the art of making music throatily and palpitatingly sexual.
Aldous Huxley (1894–1964) British novelist.
Along the Road, 'Popular music'

23 The only sensual pleasure without vice.
Samuel Johnson (1709–84) British lexicographer.
Referring to music
Johnsonian Miscellanies (ed. G. B. Hill), Vol. II

24 Heard melodies are sweet, but those unheard
Are sweeter; therefore, ye soft pipes, play on.
John Keats (1795–1821) British poet.
Ode on a Grecian Urn

25 There's sure no passion in the human soul,
But finds its food in music.
George Lillo (1693–1739) English dramatist.
Fatal Curiosity, I:2

26 Music, Maestro, Please.
Herb Magidson (20th century) US songwriter.
Song title

27 Music is not written in red, white and blue. It is written in the heart's blood of the composer.
Nellie Melba (Helen Porter Mitchell; 1861–1931) Australian soprano.
Melodies and Memories

28 Music creates order out of chaos; for rhythm imposes unanimity upon the divergent, melody imposes continuity upon the disjointed, and harmony imposes compatibility upon the incongruous.
Yehudi Menuhin (1916–) US-born British violinist.
The Sunday Times, 10 Oct 1976

29 The melting voice through mazes running;
Untwisting all the chains that tie
The hidden soul of harmony.
John Milton (1608–74) English poet.
L'Allegro

30 The song that we hear with our ears is only the song that is sung in our hearts.
Ouida (Marie Louise de la Ramée; 1839–1908) British novelist.
Wisdom, Wit and Pathos, 'Ariadne'

31 What a terrible revenge by the culture of the Negroes on that of the whites.
Ignacy Paderewski (1860–1941) Polish pianist, composer, and statesman.
Referring to jazz
Attrib.

32 Music is your own experience, your thoughts, your wisdom. If you don't live it, it won't come out of your horn.
Charlie Parker (1920–55) US black jazz musician.
Hear Me Talkin' to Ya (Nat Shapiro and Nat Hentoff)

33 Music and women I cannot but give way to, whatever my business is.
Samuel Pepys (1633–1703) English diarist.
Diary, 9 Mar 1666

34 The basic difference between classical music and jazz is that in the former the music is always greater than its performance – whereas the way jazz is performed is always more important than what is being played.
André Previn (1929–) German-born conductor.
An Encyclopedia of Quotations about Music (Nat Shapiro)

35 Seated one day at the organ,
I was weary and ill at ease,
And my fingers wandered idly
Over the noisy keys.
. . .
But I struck one chord of music,
Like the sound of a great Amen.
Adelaide Anne Procter (1825–64) British poet.
Better known in the setting by Sir Arthur Sullivan
Legends and Lyrics, 'A Lost Chord'

36 I have already heard it. I had better not go: I will start to get accustomed to it and finally like it.
Nikolai Rimsky-Korsakov (1844–1908) Russian composer.
Referring to music by Debussy
Conversations with Stravinsky (Robert Craft and Igor Stravinsky)

37 Give me a laundry-list and I'll set it to music.
Gioacchino Rossini (1792–1868) Italian operatic composer.
Attrib.

38 To be played with both hands in the pocket.
Erik Satie (1866–1925) French composer.
Direction on one of his piano pieces
The Unimportance of Being Oscar (O. Levant)

39 The sonatas of Mozart are unique; they are too easy for children, and too difficult for artists.
Artur Schnabel (1882–1951) Austrian concert pianist.
An Encyclopedia of Quotations about Music (Nat Shapiro)

40 I am never merry when I hear sweet music.
William Shakespeare (1564–1616) English dramatist.
The Merchant of Venice, V:1

41 The man that hath no music in himself,
Nor is not mov'd with concord of sweet sounds,
Is fit for treasons, stratagems, and spoils.
William Shakespeare
The Merchant of Venice, V:1

42 If music be the food of love, play on,
Give me excess of it, that, surfeiting,
The appetite may sicken and so die.
William Shakespeare
Twelfth Night, I:1

43 I wish the Government would put a tax on pianos for the incompetent.
Edith Sitwell (1887–1964) British poet and writer.
Letters, 1916–1964

44 Jazz will endure just as long as people hear it through their feet instead of their brains.
John Philip Sousa (1854–1932) US composer, conductor, and writer.
Attrib.

45 I don't write modern music. I only write good music.
Igor Stravinsky (1882–1971) Russian-born US composer.
To journalists on his first visit to America, 1925

46 My music is best understood by children and animals.
Igor Stravinsky
The Observer, 'Sayings of the Week', 8 Oct 1961

47 Music that gentlier on the spirit lies,
Than tir'd eyelids upon tir'd eyes.
Alfred, Lord Tennyson (1809–92) British poet.
The Lotos-Eaters, 'Choric Song'

48 Oh I'm a martyr to music.
Dylan Thomas (1914–53) Welsh poet.
Under Milk Wood

49 The cello is not one of my favourite instruments. It has such a lugubrious sound, like someone reading a will.
Irene Thomas (1920–) British writer.
Attrib.

50 God tells me how he wants this music played – and you get in his way.
Arturo Toscanini (1867–1957) Italian conductor.
Etude (Howard Tubman)

51 When I play on my fiddle in Dooney,

Folk dance like a wave of the sea.
W. B. Yeats (1865–1939) Irish poet.
The Fiddler of Dooney

MUSICIANS

See also composers, critics, singers

1 Musicians don't retire; they stop when there's no more music in them.
Louis Armstrong (1900–71) US jazz trumpeter.
The Observer, 'Sayings of the Week', 21 Apr 1968

2 Of all musicians, flautists are most obviously the ones who know something we don't know.
Paul Jennings (1918–) British humorous writer.
The Jenguin Pennings, 'Flautists Flaunt Afflatus'

3 The conductor has the advantage of not seeing the audience.
André Kostalenetz (1903–80) Russian-born conductor.
Attrib.

4 You see, our fingers are circumcised, which gives it a very good dexterity, you know, particularly in the pinky.
Itzhak Perlman (1945–) Israeli violinist.
Responding to an observation that many great violinists are Jewish
Close Encounters (M. Wallace)

5 My dear hands. Farewell, my poor hands.
Sergei Rachmaninov (1873–1943) Russian composer.
On being informed that he was dying from cancer
The Great Pianists (H. Schonberg)

6 Sometimes I think, not so much am I a pianist, but a vampire. All my life I have lived off the blood of Chopin.
Arthur Rubinstein (1887–1982) Polish-born US pianist.
Attrib.

7 When a piece gets difficult make faces.
Artur Schnabel (1882–1951) Austrian concert pianist.
Advice given to the pianist Vladimir Horowitz
The Unimportance of Being Oscar (O. Levant)

8 The notes I handle no better than many pianists. But the pauses between the notes – ah, that is where the art resides.
Artur Schnabel
Chicago Daily News, 11 June 1958

9 He was the only pianist I have ever seen who did not grimace. That is a great deal.
Igor Stravinsky (1882–1971) Russian-born US composer.
Referring to Rachmaninov
Conversations with Igor Stravinsky (Igor Stravinsky and Robert Craft)

MYTHS

1 Science must begin with myths, and with the criticism of myths.
Karl Popper (1902–) Austrian-born British philosopher.
British Philosophy in the Mid-Century (ed. C. A. Mace)

2 A myth is, of course, not a fairy story. It is the presentation of facts belonging to one category in the idioms appropriate to another.

To explode a myth is accordingly not to deny the facts but to re-allocate them.

Gilbert Ryle (1900–76) British philosopher.
The Concept of Mind, Introduction

N

NAKEDNESS

1 Nakedness is uncomely as well in mind, as body.
Francis Bacon (1561–1626) English philosopher.
Essays, 'Of Simulation and Dissimulation'

2 Lives there the man that can figure a naked Duke of Windlestraw addressing a naked House of Lords?
Thomas Carlyle (1795–1881) Scottish historian and essayist.
Sartor Resartus, Bk. I, Ch. 9

3 a pretty girl who naked is is worth a million statues.
e. e. cummings (1894–1962) US poet.
Collected Poems, 133

4 No woman so naked as one you can see to be naked underneath her clothes.
Michael Frayn (1933–) British journalist and writer.
Constructions

5 How idiotic civilization is! Why be given a body if you have to keep it shut up in a case like a rare, rare fiddle?
Katherine Mansfield (1888–1923) New-Zealand-born British writer.
Bliss and Other Stories, 'Bliss'

6 JOURNALIST. Didn't you have anything on?
M. M. I had the radio on.
Marilyn Monroe (Norma-Jean Baker; 1926–62) US film star.
Attrib.

NAMES

1 Known by the *sobriquet* of 'The artful Dodger.'
Charles Dickens (1812–70) British novelist.
Oliver Twist, Ch. 8

2 I'm called Little Buttercup – dear Little Buttercup,
Though I could never tell why.
W. S. Gilbert (1836–1911) British dramatist.
HMS Pinafore, I

3 A nickname is the heaviest stone that the devil can throw at a man.
William Hazlitt (1778–1830) British essayist.
Nicknames

4 No, Groucho is not my real name. I'm breaking it in for a friend.
Groucho Marx (Julius Marx; 1895–1977) US comedian.
Attrib.

5 O Romeo, Romeo! wherefore art thou Romeo?
William Shakespeare (1564–1616) English dramatist.
Romeo and Juliet, II:2

6 What's in a name? That which we call a rose By any other name would smell as sweet.
William Shakespeare
Romeo and Juliet, II:2

7 'It's giving girls names like that', said Buggins, 'that nine times out of ten makes 'em go wrong. It unsettles 'em. If ever I was to have a girl, if ever I was to have a dozen girls, I'd call 'em all Jane.'
H. G. Wells (1866–1946) British writer.
Referring to the name Euphemia
Kipps, Bk. I, Ch. 4

NASTINESS

See also cruelty, hurt

1 But are they all horrid, are you sure they are all horrid?
Jane Austen (1775–1817) British novelist.
Northanger Abbey, Ch. 6

2 I do not want people to be very agreeable, as it saves me the trouble of liking them a great deal.
Jane Austen
Letter, 24 Dec 1798

3 There is an unseemly exposure of the mind, as well as of the body.
William Hazlitt (1778–1830) British essayist.
On Disagreeable People

4 Because I am a bastard.
Ernest Hemingway (1899–1961) US novelist.
When asked why he had deserted his wife for another woman
Americans in Paris (B. Morton)

5 He was one of those born neither to obey nor to command, but to be evil to the commander and the obeyer alike. Perhaps there was nothing in life that he had much wanted to do, except to shoot rabbits and hit his father on the jaw, and both these things he had done.
John Masefield (1878–1967) British poet.
The Bird of Dawning

6 One of the worst things about life is not how nasty the nasty people are. You know that already. It is how nasty the nice people can be.
Anthony Powell (1905–) British novelist.
A Dance to the Music of Time: The Kindly Ones, Ch. 4

7 I can't see that she could have found anything nastier to say if she'd thought it out with both hands for a fortnight.
Dorothy L. Sayers (1893–1957) British writer.
Busman's Holiday, 'Prothalamion'

8 'I grant you that he's not two-faced,' I said. 'But what's the use of that when the one face he has got is so peculiarly unpleasant?'
C. P. Snow (1905–80) British novelist.
The Affair, Ch. 4

9 Malice is like a game of poker or tennis; you don't play it with anyone who is manifestly inferior to you.
Hilde Spiel (1911–) Austrian writer.
The Darkened Room

NATIONALITY

See also Americans, British

1 He was born an Englishman and remained one for years.
Brendan Behan (1923–64) Irish playwright.
The Hostage, I

2 PAT. He was an Anglo-Irishman.
MEG. In the blessed name of God, what's that?
PAT. A Protestant with a horse.
Brendan Behan
The Hostage, I

3 England is a paradise for women, and hell for horses: Italy a paradise for horses, hell for women.
Robert Burton (1577–1640) English scholar and explorer.
Anatomy of Melancholy, Pt. III

4 The Almighty in His infinite wisdom did not see fit to create Frenchmen in the image of Englishmen.
Winston Churchill (1874–1965) British statesman.
Speech, House of Commons, 10 Dec 1942

5 For he might have been a Roosian,
A French, or Turk, or Proosian,
Or perhaps Ital-ian!
But in spite of all temptations
To belong to other nations,
He remains an Englishman!
W. S. Gilbert (1836–1911) British dramatist.
HMS Pinafore, II

6 The Saxon is not like us Normans. His manners are not so polite.
But he never means anything serious till he talks about justice and right,
When he stands like an ox in the furrow with his sullen set eyes on your own,
And grumbles, 'This isn't fair dealing,' my son, leave the Saxon alone.
Rudyard Kipling (1865–1936) Indian-born British writer.
Norman and Saxon

7 Great artists have no country.
Alfred de Musset (1810–57) French dramatist and poet.
Lorenzaccio, I:5

8 I am not an Athenian or a Greek, but a citizen of the world.
Socrates (469–399 BC) Athenian philosopher.
Of Banishment (Plutarch)

9 Men of England! You wish to kill me because I am a Frenchman. Am I not punished enough in not being born an Englishman?
Voltaire (François-Marie Arouet; 1694–1778) French writer.
Addressing an angry London mob who desired to hang him because he was a Frenchman
Attrib.

10 We are all American at puberty; we die French.
Evelyn Waugh (1903–66) British novelist.
Diaries, 'Irregular Notes', 18 July 1961

NATIONS

See also places

1 The day of small nations has long passed away. The day of Empires has come.
Joseph Chamberlain (1836–1914) British politician.
Speech, Birmingham, 12 May 1904

2 The nations which have put mankind and posterity most in their debt have been small states – Israel, Athens, Florence, Elizabethan England.
Dean Inge (1860–1954) British churchman.
Wit and Wisdom of Dean Inge (ed. Marchant)

3 This agglomeration which was called and which still calls itself the Holy Roman Empire was neither holy, nor Roman, nor an empire.
Voltaire (François-Marie Arouet; 1694–1778) French writer.
Essai sur les moeurs et l'esprit des nations, LXX

NATURE

See also animals, birds, countryside, ecology, fish, flowers, human nature, insects, science

1 All things are artificial, for nature is the art of God.
Thomas Browne (1605–82) English physician and writer.
Religio Medici, Pt. I

2 Ye banks and braes o' bonnie Doon,
How can ye bloom sae fresh and fair?
How can ye chant, ye little birds,
And I sae weary fu' o' care?
Robert Burns (1759–96) Scottish poet.
Ye Banks and Braes

3 There is a pleasure in the pathless woods,
There is a rapture on the lonely shore,
There is society, where none intrudes,
By the deep Sea, and music in its roar:
I love not Man the less, but Nature more.
Lord Byron (1788–1824) British poet.
Childe Harold's Pilgrimage, IV

4 Nature admits no lie.
Thomas Carlyle (1795–1881) Scottish historian and essayist.
Latter-Day Pamphlets, 5

5 Is ditchwater dull? Naturalists with microscopes have told me that it teems with quiet fun.
G. K. Chesterton (1874–1936) British writer.
The Spice of Life

6 Nature is but a name for an effect
Whose cause is God.
William Cowper (1731–1800) British poet.
The Task

7 All my life through, the new sights of Nature made me rejoice like a child.
Marie Curie (1867–1934) Polish chemist.
Pierre Curie

8 By viewing Nature, Nature's handmaid, art,
Makes mighty things from small beginnings grow.
John Dryden (1631–1700) British poet and dramatist.
Annus Mirabilis

9 All Nature wears one universal grin.
Henry Fielding (1707–54) British novelist.
Tom Thumb the Great, I:1

10 Natural science does not simply describe and explain nature, it is part of the interplay between nature and ourselves.
Werner Heisenberg (1901–76) German physicist.
Physics and Philosophy

11 In nature there are neither rewards nor punishments – there are consequences.
Robert G. Ingersoll (1833–99) US lawyer and agnostic.
Lectures & Essays, 'Some Reasons Why'

12 Nature is very consonant and conformable with herself.
Isaac Newton (1642–1727) British scientist.
Opticks, Bk. III

13 It is far from easy to determine whether she has proved a kind parent to man or a merciless step-mother.
Pliny the Elder (Gaius Plinius Secundus; 23–79 AD) Roman scholar.
Natural History, VII

14 Nature abhors a vacuum.
François Rabelais (1483–1553) French satirist.
Attrib.

15 Are God and Nature then at strife
That Nature lends such evil dreams?
So careful of the type she seems,
So careless of the single life.
Alfred, Lord Tennyson (1809–92) British poet.
In Memoriam A.H.H.

16 Nature is usually wrong.
James Whistler (1834–1903) US painter.
The Gentle Art of Making Enemies

17 After you have exhausted what there is in business, politics, conviviality, and so on – have found that none of these finally satisfy, or permanently wear – what remains?
Nature remains.
Walt Whitman (1819–92) US poet.
Specimen Days, 'New Themes Entered Upon'

18 Nature never did betray
The heart that loved her.
William Wordsworth (1770–1850) British poet.
Lines composed a few miles above Tintern Abbey

19 Earth fills her lap with pleasures of her own:
Yearnings she hath in her own natural kind.
William Wordsworth
Ode. Intimations of Immortality, VI

20 Come forth into the light of things,
Let Nature be your Teacher.
William Wordsworth
The Tables Turned

21 Another race hath been, and other palms are won.
Thanks to the human heart by which we live,
Thanks to its tenderness, its joys and fears,
To me the meanest flower that blows can give
Thoughts that do often lie too deep for tears.
William Wordsworth
Ode. Intimations of Immortality, IX

22 O chestnut tree, great rooted blossomer,
Are you the leaf, the blossom or the bole?
O body swayed to music; O brightening glance,
How can we know the dancer from the dance?
W. B. Yeats (1865–1939) Irish poet.
Among School Children

NAVY

See also boats, officers, sea, war

1 Ye Mariners of England
That guard our native seas,
Whose flag has braved, a thousand years,
The battle and the breeze –
Your glorious standard launch again
To match another foe!
And sweep through the deep,
While the stormy winds do blow, –
While the battle rages loud and long,
And the stormy winds do blow.
Thomas Campbell (1777–1844) British poet.
Ye Mariners of England

2 Don't talk to me about naval tradition. It's nothing but rum, sodomy, and the lash.
Winston Churchill (1874–1965) British statesman.
Former Naval Person (Sir Peter Gretton), Ch. 1

3 There were gentlemen and there were seamen in the navy of Charles the Second. But the seamen were not gentlemen; and the gentlemen were not seamen.
Lord Macaulay (1800–59) British historian.
History of England, Vol. I, Ch. 3

4 The Fleet's lit up. It is like fairyland; the ships are covered with fairy lights.
Thomas Woodroofe (1899–1978) British radio broadcaster.
Said during commentary at the Coronation Review of the Royal Navy, May 1937

NAZISM

See also fascism, Germany, Hitler, Jews, World War II

1 I herewith commission you to carry out all preparations with regard to . . . a *total solution* of the Jewish question, in those territories of Europe which are under German influence.
Hermann Goering (1893–1946) German leader.
The Rise and Fall of the Third Reich (William Shirer)

2 *Kraft durch Freude.*
Strength through joy.
Robert Ley (1890–1945) German Nazi.
German Labour Front slogan

3 The former allies had blundered in the past by offering Germany too little, and offering even that too late, until finally Nazi Germany had become a menace to all mankind.
Allan Nevins (1890–1971) US historian.
Current History, May 1935

4 In Germany, the Nazis came for the Communists and I didn't speak up because I was not a Communist. Then they came for the Jews and I didn't speak up because I was not a Jew. Then they came for the trade unionists and I didn't speak up because I was not a trade unionist. Then they came for the Catholics and I was a Protestant so I didn't speak up. Then they came for me . . . By that time there was no one to speak up for anyone.
Martin Niemöller (1892–1984) German pastor.
Concise Dictionary of Religious Quotations (W. Neil)

NECESSITY

1 Beggars can't be choosers.
Proverb

2 Necessity is the mother of invention.
Proverb

3 Needs must when the devil drives.
Proverb

4 Necessity is the plea for every infringement of human freedom. It is the argument of tyrants; it is the creed of slaves.
William Pitt the Younger (1759–1806) British statesman.
Speech, House of Commons, 18 Nov 1783

5 O, reason not the need! Our basest beggars Are in the poorest thing superfluous.
Allow not nature more than nature needs,

Man's life is cheap as beast's.
William Shakespeare (1564–1616) English dramatist.
King Lear, II:4

6 Teach thy necessity to reason thus:
There is no virtue like necessity.
William Shakespeare
Richard II, I:3

7 Necessity knows no law.
Publilius Syrus (1st century BC) Roman dramatist.
Attrib.

8 I find no hint throughout the universe
Of good or ill, of blessing or of curse;
I find alone Necessity Supreme.
James Thomson (1834–82) British poet.
The City of Dreadful Night, XIV

NEGLECT

1 A little neglect may breed mischief, . . . for want of a nail, the shoe was lost; for want of a shoe the horse was lost; and for want of a horse the rider was lost.
Benjamin Franklin (1706–90) US scientist and statesman.
Poor Richard's Almanack

2 The general idea, of course, in any first-class laundry is to see that no shirt or collar ever comes back twice.
Stephen Leacock (1869–1944) English-born Canadian economist and humorist.
Winnowed Wisdom, Ch. 6

3 The dust and silence of the upper shelf.
Lord Macaulay (1800–59) British historian.
Literary Essays Contributed to the 'Edinburgh Review', 'Milton'

4 What time he can spare from the adornment of his person he devotes to the neglect of his duties.
William Hepworth Thompson (1810–86) British academic.
Referring to the Cambridge Professor of Greek, Sir Richard Jebb
With Dearest Love to All (M. R. Bobbit), Ch. 7

NEIGHBOURS

See also boundaries

1 Love your neighbour, yet pull not down your hedge.
Proverb

2 Thou shalt love thy neighbour as thy self.
Bible: Matthew
22:39

3 My apple trees will never get across
And eat the cones under his pines, I tell him.
He only says, 'Good fences make good neighbours.'
Robert Frost (1875–1963) US poet.
North of Boston, 'Mending Wall'

4 For it is your business, when the wall next door catches fire.
Horace (Quintus Horatius Flaccus; 65–8 BC) Roman poet.
Epistles, I

NEPOTISM

1 I am against government by crony.
Harold L. Ickes (1874–1952) US Republican politician.
Comment on his resignation as Secretary of the Interior (1946) after a dispute with President Truman

2 I can't see that it's wrong to give him a little legal experience before he goes out to practice law.
John Fitzgerald Kennedy (1917–63) US statesman.
On being criticized for making his brother Robert attorney general
Nobody Said It Better (M. Ringo)

NEUROSIS

See also psychiatry, psychology

1 Neurosis has an absolute genius for malingering. There is no illness which it cannot counterfeit perfectly . . . If it is capable of deceiving the doctor, how should it fail to deceive the patient?
Marcel Proust (1871–1922) French novelist.
À la recherche du temps perdu: Le Côté de Guermantes

2 Everything great in the world is done by neurotics; they alone founded our religions and created our masterpieces.
Marcel Proust
The Perpetual Pessimist (Sagittarius and George)

3 Neurosis is the way of avoiding non-being by avoiding being.
Paul Tillich (1886–1965) German-born US theologian.
The Courage to Be

NEWSPAPERS

See also journalism

1 *The Times* has made many ministries.
Walter Bagehot (1826–77) British economist and journalist.
The English Constitution, 'The Cabinet'

2 Deleted by French censor.
James Gordon Bennett (1841–1918) US newspaper owner and editor.
Used to fill empty spaces in his papers during World War I when news was lacking
Americans in Paris (B. Morton)

3 Price of Herald three cents daily. Five cents Sunday. Bennett.
James Gordon Bennett
Telegram to William Randolph Hearst, when he heard that Hearst was trying to buy his paper
The Life and Death of the Press Barons (P. Brandon)

4 Reading someone else's newspaper is like sleeping with someone else's wife. Nothing seems to be precisely in the right place, and when you find what you are looking for, it is not clear then how to respond to it.
Malcolm Bradbury (1932–) British academic and novelist.
Stepping Westward, Bk. I, Ch. 1

5 *The Times* is speechless and takes three columns to express its speechlessness.
Winston Churchill (1874–1965) British statesman.
Referring to Irish Home Rule
Speech, Dundee, 14 May 1908

6 I believe it has been said that one copy of *The Times* contains more useful information than the whole of the historical works of Thucydides.
Richard Cobden (1804–65) British politician.
Speech, Manchester, 27 Dec 1850

7 Nothing is news until it has appeared in *The Times*.
Ralph Deakin (1888–1952) Foreign News Editor of *The Times*.
Attrib.

8 All the news that's fit to print.
Adolph Simon Ochs (1858–1935) US newspaper publisher.
The motto of the *New York Times*

9 Well, there are only two posh papers on a Sunday – the one you're reading and this one.
John Osborne (1929–) British dramatist.
Look Back in Anger, I

10 Written by office boys for office boys.
Marquess of Salisbury (1830–1903) British statesman.
Reaction to the launch of the *Daily Mail*, 1896
Northcliffe, an Intimate Biography (Hamilton Fyfe), Ch. 4

11 The *Pall Mall Gazette* is written by gentlemen for gentlemen.
William Makepeace Thackeray (1811–63) British novelist.
Pendennis, Ch. 32

12 'The Beast stands for strong mutually antagonistic governments everywhere', he said. 'Self-sufficiency at home, self-assertion abroad.'
Evelyn Waugh (1903–66) British novelist.
Scoop, Bk. I, Ch. 1

13 News is what a chap who doesn't care much about anything wants to read. And it's only news until he's read it. After that it's dead.
Evelyn Waugh
Scoop, Bk. I, Ch. 5

14 They were not so much published as carried screaming into the street.
H. G. Wells (1866–1946) British writer.
War In the Air

NOBILITY

See also aristocracy, honour

1 There is surely a piece of divinity in us,

something that was before the elements, and owes no homage unto the sun.

Thomas Browne (1605–82) English physician and writer.
Religio Medici, Pt. II

2 *Noblesse oblige.*
Nobility has its own obligations.

Duc de Lévis (1764–1830) French writer and soldier.
Maximes et Réflexions

3 The high sentiments always win in the end, the leaders who offer blood, toil, tears and sweat always get more out of their followers than those who offer safety and a good time. When it comes to the pinch, human beings are heroic.

George Orwell (Eric Blair; 1903–50) British novelist.
The Art of Donald McGill

4 This was the noblest Roman of them all.
All the conspirators save only he
Did that they did in envy of great Caesar.

William Shakespeare (1564–1616) English dramatist.
Julius Caesar, V:5

5 His life was gentle, and the elements
So mixed in him that Nature might stand up
And say to all the world, 'This was a man!'

William Shakespeare
Julius Caesar, V:5

6 There is
One great society alone on earth:
The noble living and the noble dead.

William Wordsworth (1770–1850) British poet.
The Prelude, XI

7 Thy soul was like a star, and dwelt apart.

William Wordsworth
Sonnets, 'Milton! thou shouldst'

NONCOMMITMENT

1 We know what happens to people who stay in the middle of the road. They get run over.

Aneurin Bevan (1897–1960) British Labour politician.
The Observer, 'Sayings of the Week', 9 Dec 1953

2 Let them eat the lie and swallow it with their bread. Whether the two were lovers or no, they'll have accounted to God for it by now. I have my own fish to fry.

Miguel de Cervantes (1547–1616) Spanish novelist.
Don Quixote, Pt. I, Ch. 25

3 The Right Hon. gentleman has sat so long on the fence that the iron has entered his soul.

David Lloyd George (1863–1945) British Liberal statesman.
Referring to Sir John Simon
Attrib.

NONSENSE

See also humour

1 If all the world were paper,
And all the sea were ink,
And all the trees were bread and cheese,

What should we do for drink?

Anonymous
If All the World were Paper

2 If ever there was a case of clearer evidence than this of persons acting in concert together, this case is that case.

William Arabin (1773–1841) British judge.
Arabinesque at Law (Sir R. Megarry)

3 The fleas that tease in the high Pyrenees.

Hilaire Belloc (1870–1953) French-born British poet.
Tarantella

4 What happens to the hole when the cheese is gone?

Bertolt Brecht (1898–1956) German dramatist.
Mother Courage, VI

5 Twinkle, twinkle, little bat!
How I wonder what you're at!
Up above the world you fly!
Like a teatray in the sky.

Lewis Carroll (Charles Lutwidge Dodgson; 1832–98) British writer.
Alice's Adventures in Wonderland, Ch. 7

6 For the Snark *was* a Boojum, you see.

Lewis Carroll
The Hunting of the Snark

7 'Twas brillig, and the slithy toves
Did gyre and gimble in the wabe;
All mimsy were the borogoves,
And the mome raths outgrabe.

Lewis Carroll
Through the Looking-Glass, Ch. 1

8 Now, *here*, you see, it takes all the running *you* can do, to keep in the same place. If you want to get somewhere else, you must run at least twice as fast as that!

Lewis Carroll
Through the Looking-Glass, Ch. 2

9 'The time has come,' the Walrus said,
'To talk of many things:
Of shoes – and ships – and sealing-wax –
Of cabbages – and kings –
And why the sea is boiling hot –
And whether pigs have wings.'

Lewis Carroll
Through the Looking-Glass, Ch. 4

10 Colourless green ideas sleep furiously.

Noam Chomsky (1928–) US academic linguist.
Used by Chomsky to demonstrate that an utterance can be grammatical without having meaning
Syntactic Structures

11 Go, and catch a falling star,
Get with child a mandrake root,
Tell me, where all past years are,
Or who cleft the Devil's foot.

John Donne (1573–1631) English poet.
Go and Catch a Falling Star

12 So she went into the garden to cut a cabbage-leaf; to make an apple-pie; and at the same time a great she-bear, coming up

the street, pops its head into the shop.
'What! no soap?' So he died, and she very
imprudently married the barber; and there
were present the Picninnies, and the
Joblillies, and the Garyalies, and the grand
Panjandrum himself, with the little round
button at top, and they all fell to playing the
game of catch as catch can, till the gun
powder ran out at the heels of their boots.
Samuel Foote (1720–77) British actor and dramatist.
Nonsense composed to test the actor Charles Macklin's claim
that he could memorize anything

13 If the man who turnips cries,
Cry not when his father dies,
'Tis a proof that he had rather
Have a turnip than his father.
Samuel Johnson (1709–84) British lexicographer.
Johnsonian Miscellanies (ed. G. B. Hill), Vol. I

14 Three quarks for Muster Mark!
James Joyce (1882–1941) Irish novelist.
The word quark has since been adopted by physicists for hypo-
thetical elementary particles
Finnegans Wake

15 Lord Ronald said nothing; he flung himself
from the room, flung himself upon his horse
and rode madly off in all directions.
Stephen Leacock (1869–1944) English-born Canadian
economist and humorist.
Nonsense Novels, 'Gertrude the Governess'

16 On the Coast of Coromandel
Where the early pumpkins blow,
In the middle of the woods
Lived the Yonghy-Bonghy-Bò.
Edward Lear (1812–88) British artist and writer.
The Courtship of the Yonghy-Bonghy-Bò

17 The Dong! – the Dong!
The wandering Dong through the forest goes!
The Dong! – the Dong!
The Dong with a luminous Nose!
Edward Lear
The Dong with a Luminous Nose

18 Far and few, far and few,
Are the lands where the Jumblies live;
Their heads are green, and their hands are
blue,
And they went to sea in a sieve.
Edward Lear
The Jumblies

19 He has many friends, laymen and clerical.
Old Foss is the name of his cat:
His body is perfectly spherical,
He weareth a runcible hat.
Edward Lear
Nonsense Songs, preface

20 The Owl and the Pussy-Cat went to sea
In a beautiful pea-green boat,
They took some honey, and plenty of money,
Wrapped up in a five-pound note.
Edward Lear
The Owl and the Pussy-Cat

21 Serve up in a clean dish, and throw the
whole out of the window as fast as possible.
Edward Lear
To make an Amblongus Pie

22 As I was going up the stair
I met a man who wasn't there.
He wasn't there again to-day.
I wish, I wish he'd stay away.
Hughes Mearns (1875–1965) US writer.
The Psychoed

23 I'm walking backwards till Christmas.
Spike Milligan (1918–) British comic actor and author.
The Goon Show

NORMALITY

1 She always says she dislikes the abnormal, it
is so obvious. She says the normal is so
much more simply complicated and
interesting.
Gertrude Stein (1874–1946) US writer.
The Autobiography of Alice B. Toklas

2 My suit is pale yellow. My nationality is
French, and my normality has been often
subject to question.
Tennessee Williams (1911–83) US dramatist.
Camino Real, Block 4

NOSTALGIA

See also homesickness, memory, past, regret

1 Were we closer to the ground as children, or
is the grass emptier now?
Alan Bennett (1934–) British playwright.
Forty Years On

2 Play it, Sam. Play 'As Time Goes By'.
Humphrey Bogart (1899–1957) US film star.
Often misquoted as 'Play it again, Sam'
Casablanca

3 Stands the Church clock at ten to three?
And is there honey still for tea?
Rupert Brooke (1887–1915) British poet.
The Old Vicarage, Grantchester

4 John Anderson my jo, John,
When we were first acquent,
Your locks were like the raven,
Your bonnie brow was brent.
Robert Burns (1759–96) Scottish poet.
John Anderson My Jo

5 The 'good old times' – all times when old
are good –
Are gone.
Lord Byron (1788–1824) British poet.
The Age of Bronze, I

6 Nothing recalls the past so potently as a
smell.
Winston Churchill (1874–1965) British statesman.
My Early Life

7 What peaceful hours I once enjoyed!

How sweet their memory still!
But they have left an aching void
The world can never fill.
William Cowper (1731–1800) British poet.
Olney Hymns, 1

8 I'm sitting on the stile, Mary,
Where we sat, side by side.
Countess of Dufferin (1807–67) British poet.
Lament of the Irish Emigrant

9 I remember, I remember,
The house where I was born,
The little window where the sun
Came peeping in at morn;
He never came a wink too soon,
Nor brought too long a day,
But now, I often wish the night
Had borne my breath away!
Thomas Hood (1799–1845) British poet.
I Remember

10 Into my heart an air that kills
From yon far country blows:
What are those blue remembered hills,
What spires, what farms are those?
A. E. Housman (1859–1936) British scholar and poet.
A Shropshire Lad, 'The Welsh Marches'

11 With rue my heart is laden
For golden friends I had,
For many a rose-lipt maiden
And many a lightfoot lad.
A. E. Housman
A Shropshire Lad, 'The Welsh Marches'

12 I have had playmates, I have had companions
In my days of childhood, in my joyful school-
days –
All, all are gone, the old familiar faces.
Charles Lamb (1775–1834) British essayist.
The Old Familiar Faces

13 For love that time was not as love is
nowadays.
Thomas Malory (1400–71) English writer.
Morte d'Arthur, Bk. XX, Ch. 3

14 Oft in the stilly night,
Ere Slumber's chain has bound me,
Fond Memory brings the light
Of other days around me;
The smiles, the tears,
Of boyhood's years,
The words of love then spoken;
The eyes that shone,
Now dimmed and gone,
The cheerful hearts now broken!
Thomas Moore (1779–1852) Irish poet.
National Airs, 'Oft in the Stilly Night'

15 Fings Ain't Wot They Used T'Be.
Frank Norman (1931–) British dramatist and
broadcaster.
Title of musical

16 Before the war, and especially before the
Boer War, it was summer all the year round.
George Orwell (Eric Blair; 1903–50) British novelist.
Coming Up for Air, Pt. II, Ch. 1

17 They spend their time mostly looking forward
to the past.
John Osborne (1929–) British dramatist.
Look Back in Anger, II:1

18 Come to me in the silence of the night;
Come in the speaking silence of a dream;
Come with soft rounded cheeks and eyes as
bright
As sunlight on a stream;
Come back in tears,
O memory, hope, love of finished years.
Christina Rossetti (1830–74) British poet.
Echo

19 For now I see the true old times are dead,
When every morning brought a noble chance,
And every chance brought out a noble knight.
Alfred, Lord Tennyson (1809–92) British poet.
Idylls of the King, 'The Passing of Arthur'

20 Dear as remembered kisses after death,
And sweet as those by hopeless fancy feign'd
On lips that are for others: deep as love,
Deep as first love, and wild with all regret;
O Death in Life, the days that are no more.
Alfred, Lord Tennyson
The Princess, IV

21 And the stately ships go on
To their haven under the hill;
But O for the touch of a vanish'd hand,
And the sound of a voice that is still!
Alfred, Lord Tennyson
Break, Break, Break

22 *Mais où sont les neiges d'antan?*
But where are the snows of yesteryear?
François Villon (1431–85) French poet.
Ballade des dames du temps jadis

23 Where are the boys of the Old Brigade?
Frederic Edward Weatherly (1848–1929) British lawyer
and songwriter.
The Old Brigade

24 Sweet childish days, that were as long
As twenty days are now.
William Wordsworth (1770–1850) British poet.
To a Butterfly, I've Watched you now

NOTHING

1 Nothing can be created out of nothing.
Lucretius (Titus Lucretius Carus; c. 99–55 BC) Roman
philosopher.
On the Nature of the Universe, I

2 Nothing will come of nothing. Speak again.
William Shakespeare (1564–1616) English dramatist.
King Lear, I:1

NOVELS

See also books, criticism, fiction, literature, writers, writing

1   My scrofulous French novel
    On grey paper with blunt type!
    Robert Browning (1812–89) British poet.
    Soliloquy of the Spanish Cloister

2   A good novel tells us the truth about its
    hero; but a bad novel tells us the truth about
    its author.
    G. K. Chesterton (1874–1936) British writer.
    Heretics, Ch. 15

3   When I want to read a novel I write one.
    Benjamin Disraeli (1804–81) British statesman.
    Attrib.

4   Yes – oh dear, yes – the novel tells a
    story.
    E. M. Forster (1879–1970) British novelist.
    Aspects of the Novel, Ch. 2

5   The romance of *Tom Jones*, that exquisite
    picture of human manners, will outlive the
    palace of the Escurial and the imperial eagle
    of the house of Austria.
    Edward Gibbon (1737–94) British historian.
    Autobiography

6   Historians tell the story of the past, novelists
    the story of the present.
    Edmond de Goncourt (1822–96) French novelist.
    Journal

7   The only obligation to which in advance we
    may hold a novel, without incurring the
    accusation of being arbitrary, is that it be
    interesting.
    Henry James (1843–1916) US novelist.
    Partial Portraits, 'The Art of Fiction'

8   Far too many relied on the classic formula of
    a beginning, a muddle, and an end.
    Philip Larkin (1922–85) British poet.
    Referring to modern novels
    New Fiction, 15 (January 1978)

9   I am a man, and alive . . . For this reason I
    am a novelist. And being a novelist, I
    consider myself superior to the saint, the
    scientist, the philosopher, and the poet, who
    are all great masters of different bits of man
    alive, but never get the whole hog.
    D. H. Lawrence (1885–1930) British novelist.
    Phoenix, 'Why the Novel Matters'

10 I would sooner read a time-table or a
    catalogue than nothing at all. They are much
    more entertaining than half the novels that
    are written.
    W. Somerset Maugham (1874–1965) British novelist.
    The Summing Up

11 An interviewer asked me what book I
    thought best represented the modern

American woman. All I could think of to
answer was: *Madame Bovary*.
Mary McCarthy (1912–) US novelist.
On the Contrary

12 People think that because a novel's invented,
    it isn't true. Exactly the reverse is the case.
    Biography and memoirs can never be wholly
    true, since they cannot include every
    conceivable circumstance of what happened.
    The novel can do that.
    Anthony Powell (1905–) British novelist.
    A Dance to the Music of Time: Hearing Secret Harmonies, Ch.
    3

13 The detective novel is the art-for-art's-sake
    of yawning Philistinism.
    V. S. Pritchett (1900–) British short-story writer.
    Books in General, 'The Roots of Detection'

14 It is the sexless novel that should be
    distinguished: the sex novel is now normal.
    George Bernard Shaw (1856–1950) Irish dramatist and
    critic.
    Table-Talk of G.B.S.

15 A novel is a mirror walking along a main
    road.
    Stendhal (Henri Beyle; 1783–1842) French novelist.
    Le Rouge et le noir, Ch. 49

16 A novel is a static thing that one moves
    through; a play is a dynamic thing that moves
    past one.
    Kenneth Tynan (1927–80) British theatre critic.
    Curtains

17 The novel being dead, there is no point to
    writing made-up stories. Look at the French
    who will not and the Americans who cannot.
    Gore Vidal (1925–) US novelist.
    Myra Breckinridge, Ch. 2

NOVELTY

See also conservatism, innovation, progress

1   All the rivers run into the sea; yet the sea is
    not full; unto the place from whence the
    rivers come, thither they return again.
    All things are full of labour; man cannot utter
    it: the eye is not satisfied with seeing, nor
    the ear filled with hearing.
    The thing that hath been, it is that which shall
    be; and that which is done is that which shall
    be done: and there is no new thing under
    the sun.
    Bible: Ecclesiastes
    1:7–9

2   Most of the change we think we see in life
    Is due to truths being in and out of favour.
    Robert Frost (1875–1963) US poet.
    The Black Cottage

3   There are three things which the public will

always clamour for, sooner or later: namely, Novelty, novelty, novelty.
Thomas Hood (1799–1845) British poet.
Announcement of *Comic Annual*, 1836

4 It is the customary fate of new truths to begin as heresies and to end as superstitions.
T. H. Huxley (1825–95) British biologist.
The Coming of Age of the Origin of Species

5 New opinions are always suspected, and usually opposed, without any other reason but because they are not already common.
John Locke (1632–1704) English philosopher.
An Essay Concerning Human Understanding, dedicatory epistle

6 Rummidge . . . had lately suffered the mortifying fate of most English universities of its type (civic redbrick): having competed strenuously for fifty years with two universities chiefly valued for being old, it was, at the moment of drawing level, rudely overtaken in popularity and prestige by a batch of universities chiefly valued for being new.
David Lodge (1935–) British author.
Changing Places, Ch. 1

7 There are no new truths, but only truths that have not been recognized by those who have perceived them without noticing.
Mary McCarthy (1912–) US novelist.
On the Contrary

8 There is always something new out of Africa.
Pliny the Elder (Gaius Plinius Secundus; 23–79 AD) Roman scholar.
Natural History, VIII

9 All great truths begin as blasphemies.
George Bernard Shaw (1856–1950) Irish dramatist and critic.
Annajanska

10 If we do not find anything pleasant, at least we shall find something new.
Voltaire (François-Marie Arouet; 1694–1778) French writer.
Candide, Ch. 17

NUCLEAR WEAPONS

See also weapons

1 Now we are all sons of bitches.
Kenneth Bainbridge (1904–) US physicist.
After the first atomic test
The Decision to Drop the Bomb

2 If you carry this resolution and follow out all its implications and do not run away from it you will send a Foreign Minister, whoever he may be, naked into the conference chamber.
Aneurin Bevan (1897–1960) British Labour politician.
Opposing a motion advocating unilateral nuclear disarmament
Speech, Labour Party Conference, 3 Oct 1957

3 The way to win an atomic war is to make certain it never starts.
Omar Nelson Bradley (1893–1981) US general.
The Observer, 'Sayings of the Week', 20 Apr 1952

4 If only I had known, I should have become a watchmaker.
Albert Einstein (1879–1955) German-born US physicist.
Reflecting on his role in the development of the atom bomb
New Statesman, 16 Apr 1965

5 Surely the right course is to test the Russians, not the bombs.
Hugh Gaitskell (1906–63) British Labour politician.
Observer, 'Sayings of the Week', 23 June 1957

6 We thus denounce the false and dangerous programme of the arms race, of the secret rivalry between peoples for military superiority.
John Paul II (Karol Wojtyla; 1920–) Polish pope (1978–).
The Observer, 'Sayings of the Week', 19 Dec 1976

7 Preparing for suicide is not a very intelligent means of defence.
Bruce Kent (1929–) British campaigner for nuclear disarmament.
The Observer, 'Sayings of the Week', 10 Aug 1986

8 Hitherto man had to live with the idea of death as an individual; from now onward mankind will have to live with the idea of its death as a species.
Arthur Koestler (1905–83) Hungarian-born British writer.
Referring to the development of the atomic bomb
Peter's Quotations (Laurence J. Peter)

9 The statesmen of the world who boast and threaten that they have Doomsday weapons are far more dangerous, and far more estranged from 'reality', than many of the people on whom the label 'psychotic' is affixed.
R. D. Laing (1927–) British psychiatrist.
The Divided Self, Preface

10 At first it was a giant column that soon took the shape of a supramundane mushroom.
William L. Laurence (1888–1977) US journalist.
Referring to the explosion of the first atomic bomb, over Hiroshima, 6 Aug 1945
The New York Times, 26 Sept 1945

11 The atom bomb is a paper tiger which the United States reactionaries use to scare people.
Mao Tse-Tung (1893–1976) Chinese communist leader.
Interview, Aug 1946

12 We knew the world would not be the same.
J. Robert Oppenheimer (1904–67) US physicist.
After the first atomic test
The Decision to Drop the Bomb

13 It was on this issue, the nuclear defence of Britain, on which I left the Labour Party, and on this issue I am prepared to stake my entire political career.

David Owen (1938–) British politician.
The Observer, 'Sayings of the Week', 9 Nov 1986

14 You may reasonably expect a man to walk a tightrope safely for ten minutes; it would be unreasonable to do so without accident for two hundred years.

Bertrand Russell (1872–1970) British philosopher.
On the subject of nuclear war between the USA and the Soviets
The Tightrope Men (D. Bagley)

15 There is no evil in the atom; only in men's souls.

Adlai Stevenson (1900–65) US statesman.
Speech, Hartford, Connecticut, 18 Sept 1952

16 For Hon. Members opposite the deterrent is a phallic symbol. It convinces them that they are men.

George Wigg (1900–76) British politician.
The Observer, 'Sayings of the Week', 8 Mar 1964

NUMBERS

See also mathematics, statistics

1 Round numbers are always false.

Samuel Johnson (1709–84) British lexicographer.
Life of Johnson (J. Boswell), Vol. III

2 No, I don't know his telephone number. But it was up in the high numbers.

John Maynard Keynes (1883–1946) British economist.
Attrib.

3 No, it is a very interesting number, it is the smallest number expressible as a sum of two cubes in two different ways.

Srinivasa Ramanujan (1887–1920) Indian mathematician.
The mathematician G. H. Hardy had referred to the number 1729 as 'dull'.
Collected Papers of Srinivasa Ramanujan

4 Oh, quite easy! The Septuagint minus the Apostles.

Arthur Woollgar Verrall (1851–1912) British classicist.
Reply to a person who thought the number 58 difficult to remember

NURSERY RHYMES

A selection is given here. The form used is that most commonly used today – not the one in the original publication.

1 A frog he would a-wooing go,
Heigh ho! says Rowley,
A frog he would a-wooing go,
Whether his mother would let him or no.
With a rowley, powley, gammon and spinach,
Heigh ho! says Anthony Rowley.

Melismata (Thomas Ravenscroft)

2 All the birds of the air
Fell a-sighing and a-sobbing,
When they heard the bell toll

For poor Cock Robin.

Tommy Thumb's Pretty Song Book

3 As I was going to St Ives,
I met a man with seven wives.
Each wife had seven sacks
Each sack had seven cats,
Each cat had seven kits,
How many were going to St Ives?

Mother Goose's Quarto

4 Baa, baa, black sheep,
Have you any wool?
Yes, sir, yes, sir,
Three bags full;
One for the master,
And one for the dame,
And one for the little boy
Who lives down the lane.

Tommy Thumb's Pretty Song Book

5 Bobby Shafto's gone to sea,
Silver buckles on his knee;
He'll come back and marry me,
Bonny Bobby Shafto! ·

Songs for the Nursery

6 Boys and girls come out to play,
The moon doth shine as bright as day.

Useful Transactions in Philosophy (William King)

7 Come, let's to bed
Says Sleepy-head;
Tarry a while, says Slow;
Put on the pan;
Says Greedy Nan,
Let's sup before we go.

Gammer Gurton's Garland (R. Christopher)

8 Curly locks, Curly locks,
Wilt thou be mine?
Thou shalt not wash dishes
Nor yet feed the swine,
But sit on a cushion
And sew a fine seam,
And feed upon strawberries,
Sugar and cream

Infant Institutes

9 Ding dong, bell,
Pussy's in the well.
Who put her in?
Little Johnny Green.
Who pulled her out?
Little Tommy Stout.

Mother Goose's Melody

10 Doctor Foster went to Gloucester
In a shower of rain:
He stepped in a puddle,
Right up to his middle,
And never went there again.

The Nursery Rhymes of England (J. O. Halliwell)

11 Eena, meena, mina, mo,
Catch a nigger by his toe;
If he hollers, let him go,

Eena, meena, mina, mo.
Games and Songs of American Children (Newell)

12 Georgie Porgie, pudding and pie,
Kissed the girls and made them cry;
When the boys came out to play,
Georgie Porgie ran away.
The Nursery Rhymes of England (J. O. Halliwell)

13 Goosey, goosey gander,
Whither shall I wander?
Upstairs and downstairs
And in my lady's chamber.
Gammer Gurton' Garland

14 Hey diddle diddle,
The cat and the fiddle,
The cow jumped over the moon;
The little dog laughed
To see such sport,
And the dish ran away with the spoon.
Mother Goose's Melody

15 Hickory, dickory, dock,
The mouse ran up the clock.
The clock struck one,
The mouse ran down,
Hickory, dickory, dock.
Tommy Thumb's Pretty Song Book

16 Hot cross buns!
Hot cross buns!
One a penny, two a penny,
Hot cross buns!
Christmas Box

17 How many miles to Babylon?
Three score miles and ten.
Can I get there by candle-light?
Yes, and back again.
If your heels are nimble and light,
You may get there by candle-light.
Songs for the Nursery

18 Humpty Dumpty sat on a wall,
Humpty Dumpty had a great fall.
All the king's horses,
And all the king's men,
Couldn't put Humpty together again.
Gammer Gurton's Garland

19 Hush-a-bye, baby, on the tree top,
When the wind blows the cradle will rock;
When the bough breaks the cradle will fall,
Down will come baby, cradle, and all.
Mother Goose's Melody

20 I had a little nut tree,
Nothing would it bear
But a silver nutmeg
And a golden pear;
The King of Spain's daughter
Came to visit me,
And all for the sake
Of my little nut tree.
Newest Christmas Box

21 I had a little pony,

His name was Dapple Grey;
I lent him to a lady
To ride a mile away.
She whipped him, she lashed him,
She rode him through the mire;
I would not lend my pony now,
For all the lady's hire.
Poetical Alphabet

22 I love sixpence, jolly little sixpence,
I love sixpence better than my life;
I spent a penny of it, I lent a penny of it,
And I took fourpence home to my wife.
Gammer Gurton's Garland

23 I'm the king of the castle,
Get down you dirty rascal.
Brand's Popular Antiquities

24 Jack and Jill went up the hill
To fetch a pail of water;
Jack fell down and broke his crown,
And Jill came tumbling after.
Mother Goose's Melody

25 Jack Sprat could eat no fat,
His wife could eat no lean,
And so between them both you see,
They licked the platter clean.
Paroemiologia Anglo-Latina (John Clark)

26 Ladybird, ladybird,
Fly away home,
Your house is on fire
And your children all gone.
Tommy Thumb's Pretty Song Book

27 Little Bo-peep has lost her sheep,
And can't tell where to find them;
Leave them alone, and they'll come home,
Bringing their tails behind them.
Gammer Gurton's Garland

28 Little Boy Blue,
Come blow your horn,
The sheep's in the meadow,
The cow's in the corn.
Famous Tommy Thumb's Little Story Book

29 Little Jack Horner
Sat in the corner,
Eating a Christmas pie;
He put in his thumb,
And pulled out a plum,
And said, What a good boy am I!
Namby Pamby (Henry Carey)

30 Little Miss Muffet
Sat on a tuffet,
Eating her curds and whey;
There came a big spider,
Who sat down beside her
And frightened Miss Muffet away.
Songs for the Nursery

31 Little Tommy Tucker,
Sings for his supper:
What shall we give him?

White bread and butter
How shall he cut it
Without a knife?
How will be be married
Without a wife?
Tommy Thumb's Pretty Song Book

32 London Bridge is broken down,
My fair lady.
Namby Pamby (Henry Carey)

33 Monday's child is fair of face,
Tuesday's child is full of grace,
Wednesday's child is full of woe,
Thursday's child has far to go,
Friday's child is loving and giving,
Saturday's child works hard for his living,
And the child that is born on the Sabbath day
Is bonny and blithe, and good and gay.
Traditions of Devonshire (A. E. Bray)

34 My mother said that I never should
Play with the gypsies in the wood;
If I did, she would say,
Naughty girl to disobey.
Come Hither (Walter de la Mare)

35 Old Mother Hubbard
Went to the cupboard,
To fetch her poor dog a bone;
But when she got there
The cupboard was bare
And so the poor dog had none.
The Comic Adventures of Old Mother Hubbard and Her Dog

36 One, two,
Buckle my shoe;
Three, four,
Knock at the door.
Songs for the Nursery

37 Pat-a-cake, pat-a-cake, baker's man,
Bake me a cake as fast as you can;
Pat it and prick it, and mark it with B,
Put it in the oven for baby and me.
The Campaigners (Tom D'Urfey)

38 Peter Piper picked a peck of pickled pepper;
A peck of pickled pepper Peter Piper picked;
If Peter Piper picked a peck of pickled pepper,
Where's the peck of pickled pepper Peter Piper picked?
Peter Piper's Practical Principles of Plain and Perfect Pronunciation

39 Polly put the kettle on,
Sukey take it off again,
Sukey take it off again,
Sukey take it off again,
They've all gone away.
Traditional

40 Pussy cat, pussy cat, where have you been?
I've been to London to look at the queen.
Pussy cat, pussy cat, what did you there?
I frightened a little mouse under her chair.
Songs for the Nursery

41 Ride a cock-horse to Banbury Cross,
To see a fine lady upon a white horse;
Rings on her fingers and bells on her toes,
And she shall have music wherever she goes.
Gammer Gurton's Garland

42 Ring-a-ring o'roses,
A pocket full of posies,
A-tishoo! A-tishoo!
We all fall down.
Mother Goose (Kate Greenway)

43 Round and round the garden
Like a teddy bear;
One step, two step,
Tickle you under there!
Traditional

44 Rub-a-dub-dub,
Three men in a tub,
And who do you think they be?
The butcher, the baker,
The candlestick-maker,
And they all sailed out to sea.
Christmas Box

45 See-saw, Margery Daw,
Jacky shall have a new master;
Jacky shall have put a penny a day,
Because he can't work any faster.
Mother Goose's Melody

46 Simple Simon met a pieman,
Going to the fair;
Says Simple Simon to the pieman,
Let me taste your ware.
Says the pieman to Simple Simon,
Show me first your penny;
Says Simple Simon to the pieman,
Indeed I have not any.
Simple Simon (Chapbook Advertisement)

47 The king was in his counting-house,
Counting out his money;
The queen was in the parlour,
Eating bread and honey.
The maid was in the garden,
Hanging out the clothes,
When down came a blackbird,
And pecked off her nose.
Tommy Thumb's Pretty Song Book

48 Solomon Grundy,
Born on a Monday,
Christened on Tuesday,
Married on Wednesday,
Took ill on Thursday,
Worse on Friday,
Died on Saturday,
Buried on Sunday.
This is the end
Of Solomon Grundy.
The Nursery Rhymes of England (J. O. Halliwell)

49 The first day of Christmas,
My true love sent to me

A partridge in a pear tree.
Mirth without Mischief

50 The lion and the unicorn
Were fighting for the crown;
The lion beat the unicorn
All round about the town.
Useful Transactions in Philosophy (William King)

51 The Queen of Hearts
She made some tarts,
All on a summer's day;
The Knave of Hearts
He stole the tarts,
And took them clean away.
The European Magazine

52 There was a crooked man, and he walked a crooked mile,
He found a crooked sixpence against a crooked stile;
He bought a crooked cat, which caught a crooked mouse,
And they all lived together in a little crooked house.
The Nursery Rhymes of England (J. O. Halliwell)

53 There was an old woman
Lived under a hill,
And if she's not gone
She lives there still.
Academy of Complements

54 There was an old woman who lived in a shoe,
She had so many children she didn't know what to do;
She gave them some broth without any bread;
She whipped them all soundly and put them to bed.
Gammer Gurton's Garland

55 The twelfth day of Christmas,
My true love sent to me
Twelve lords a-leaping,
Eleven ladies dancing,
Ten pipers piping,
Nine drummers drumming,
Eight maids a-milking,
Seven swans a-swimming,
Six geese a-laying,
Five gold rings,
Four colly birds,
Three French hens,
Two turtle doves, and
A partridge in a pear tree.
Mirth without Mischief

56 Thirty days hath September,
April, June, and November;
All the rest have thirty-one,
Excepting February alone
And that has twenty-eight days clear
And twenty-nine in each leap year.
Abridgement of the Chronicles of England (Richard Grafton)

57 This is the farmer sowing his corn,

That kept the cock that crowed in the morn,
That waked the priest all shaven and shorn,
That married the man all tattered and torn,
That kissed the maiden all forlorn,
That milked the cow with the crumpled horn,
That tossed the dog,
That worried the cat,
That killed the rat,
That ate the corn,
That lay in the house that Jack built.
Nurse Truelove's New-Year-Gift

58 This little piggy went to market,
This little piggy stayed at home,
This little piggy had roast beef,
This little piggy had none,
And this little piggy cried, Wee-wee-wee-wee-wee,
I can't find my way home.
The Famous Tommy Thumb's Little Story Book

59 Three blind mice, see how they run!
They all run after the farmer's wife,
Who cut off their tails with a carving knife,
Did you ever see such a thing in your life,
As three blind mice?
Deuteromelia (Thomas Ravenscroft)

60 Tinker,
Tailor,
Soldier,
Sailor,
Rich man,
Poor man,
Beggarman,
Thief.
Popular Rhymes and Nursery Tales (J. O. Halliwell)

61 Tom, he was a piper's son,
He learnt to play when he was young,
And all the tune that he could play
Was 'Over the hills and far away'.
Tom, The Piper's Son

62 Tom, Tom, the piper's son,
Stole a pig and away he run;
The pig was eat
And Tom was beat,
And Tom went howling down the street.
Tom, The Piper's Son

63 Two little dicky birds,
Sitting on a wall;
One named Peter,
The other named Paul,
Fly away, Peter!
Fly away, Paul!
Come back, Peter!
Come back, Paul!
Mother Goose's Melody

64 Wee Willie Winkie runs through the town
upstairs and downstairs and in his nightgown,
Rapping at the window, crying through the lock,

Are the children all in bed? It's past eight
o'clock.
In *Whistle-Binkie* (W. Miller)

65 What are little boys made of?
Frogs and snails
And puppy-dogs' tails,
That's what little boys are made of.
What are little girls made of?
Sugar and spice
And all that's nice,
That's what little girls are made of.
Nursery Rhymes (J. O. Halliwell)

66 What is your fortune, my pretty maid?
My face is my fortune, sir, she said.
Then I can't marry you, my pretty maid.
Nobody asked you, sir, she said.
Archaeologia Cornu-Britannica (William Pryce)

67 Where are you going to, my pretty maid?
I'm going a-milking, sir, she said.
Archaeologia Cornu-Britannica (William Pryce)

68 Who killed Cock Robin?
I, said the Sparrow,

With my bow and arrow,
I killed Cock Robin.
Who saw him die?
I, said the Fly,
With my little eye,
I saw him die.
Tommy Thumb's Pretty Song Book

69 Yankee Doodle came to town,
Riding on a pony;
He stuck a feather in his cap
And called it macaroni.
Gammer Gurton's Garland

NURSES

1 No *man*, not even a doctor, ever gives any
other definition of what a nurse should be
than this – 'devoted and obedient.' This
definition would do just as well for a porter.
It might even do for a horse. It would not do
for a policeman.
Florence Nightingale (1820–1910) British nurse.
Notes on Nursing

O

OBEDIENCE

1 Children, obey your parents in the Lord: for
this is right.
Bible: Ephesians
6:1

2 'She still seems to me in her own way a
person born to command,' said Luce . . .
'I wonder if anyone is born to obey,' said
Isabel.
'That may be why people command rather bad-
ly, that
they have no suitable material to work on.'
Ivy Compton-Burnett (1892–1969) British novelist.
Parents and Children, Ch. 3

3 It is much safer to obey than to rule.
Thomas à Kempis (Thomas Hemmerken; c. 1380–1471)
German monk.
The Imitation of Christ, I

4 'Forward the Light Brigade!'
Was there a man dismay'd?
Not tho' the soldier knew
Some one had blunder'd:
Their's not to make reply,
Their's not to reason why,
Their's but to do and die:
Into the valley of Death
Rode the six hundred.
Alfred, Lord Tennyson (1809–92) British poet.
The Charge of the Light Brigade

OBESITY

See also food, greed

1 Outside every fat man there is an even fatter
man trying to close in.
Kingsley Amis (1922–) British novelist.
See also CONNOLLY, ORWELL
One Fat Englishman, Ch. 3

2 Who's your fat friend?
'Beau' Brummel (George Bryan Brummell; 1778–1840)
British dandy.
Referring to George, Prince of Wales
Reminiscences (Gronow)

3 Just the other day in the Underground I
enjoyed the pleasure of offering my seat to
three ladies.
G. K. Chesterton (1874–1936) British writer.
Suggesting that fatness had its consolations
Das Buch des Lachens (W. Scholz)

4 I want to reassure you I am not this size,
really – dear me no, I'm being amplified by
the mike.
G. K. Chesterton
At a lecture in Pittsburgh
The Outline of Sanity: A Life of G. K. Chesterton (S. D. Dale)

5 Imprisoned in every fat man a thin one is
wildly signalling to be let out.
Cyril Connolly (1903–74) British journalist.
See also AMIS, ORWELL.
The Unquiet Grave

6 O fat white woman whom nobody loves,
Why do you walk through the fields in gloves . . .
Missing so much and so much?
F. M. Cornford (1886–1960) British poet.
To a Fat Lady Seen from a Train

7 I see no objection to stoutness, in
moderation.
W. S. Gilbert (1836–1911) British dramatist.
Iolanthe, I

8 I'm fat, but I'm thin inside. Has it ever
struck you that there's a thin man inside
every fat man, just as they say there's a
statue inside every block of stone?
George Orwell (Eric Blair; 1903–50)
See also AMIS, CONNOLLY British novelist.
Coming Up For Air, Pt. I, Ch. 3

9 My advice if you insist on slimming: Eat as
much as you like – just don't swallow it.
Harry Secombe (1921–) Welsh singer, actor, and
comedian.
Daily Herald, 5 Oct 1962

10 Falstaff sweats to death
And lards the lean earth as he walks along.
William Shakespeare (1564–1616) English dramatist.
Henry IV, Part One, II:2

11 I have more flesh than another man, and
therefore more frailty.
William Shakespeare
Henry IV, Part One, III:3

12 She fitted into my biggest armchair as if it
had been built round her by someone who
knew they were wearing armchairs tight
about the hips that season.
P. G. Wodehouse (1881–1975) British humorous
novelist.
My Man Jeeves, 'Jeeves and the Unbidden Guest'

13 The Right Hon. was a tubby little chap who
looked as if he had been poured into his
clothes and had forgotten to say 'When!'
P. G. Wodehouse
Very Good Jeeves!, 'Jeeves and the Impending Doom'

OBITUARIES

See also death, epitaphs, memorials

1 With the newspaper strike on I wouldn't
consider it.
Bette Davis (Ruth Elizabeth Davis; 1908–) US film
star.
When told that a rumour was spreading that she had died
Book of Lists (I. Wallace)

2 I've just read that I am dead. Don't forget to
delete me from your list of subscribers.
Rudyard Kipling (1865–1936) Indian-born British writer.
Writing to a magazine that had mistakenly published an an-
nouncement of his death
Anekdotenschatz (H. Hoffmeister)

3 In these days a man is nobody unless his
biography is kept so far posted up that it
may be ready for the national breakfast-table
on the morning after his demise.
Anthony Trollope (1815–82) British novelist.
Doctor Thorne, Ch. 25

4 Reports of my death are greatly exaggerated.
Mark Twain (Samuel Langhorne Clemens; 1835–1910)
US writer.
On learning that his obituary had been published
Cable to the Associated Press

OBJECTIVITY

See also perspective, subjectivity

1 *Sir Roger* told them, with the air of a man
who would not give his judgment rashly, that
'much might be said on both sides'.
Joseph Addison (1672–1719) British essayist.
Sir Roger de Coverley was a fictional archetype of the old-fashioned and eccentric country squire
The Spectator, 122

2 Thus I live in the world rather as a Spectator
of mankind, than as one of the species, by
which means I have made myself a
speculative statesman, soldier, merchant, and
artisan, without ever meddling with any
practical part of life.
Joseph Addison
The Spectator, 1

3 Only reason can convince us of those three
fundamental truths without a recognition of
which there can be no effective liberty: that
what we believe is not necessarily true; that
what we like is not necessarily good; and
that all questions are open.
Clive Bell (1881–1964) British art critic.
Civilization, Ch. 5

4 I am a camera with its shutter open, quite
passive, recording, not thinking.
Christopher Isherwood (1904–86) British novelist.
Goodbye to Berlin

5 The man who sees both sides of a question
is a man who sees absolutely nothing at all.
Oscar Wilde (1854–1900) Irish-born British dramatist.
The Critic as Artist, Pt. 2

OBLIGATION

See also duty

1 The debt which cancels all others.
Charles Caleb Colton (?1780–1832) British clergyman
and writer.
Lacon, Vol. II

2 It is the nature of men to be bound by the
benefits they confer as much as by those
they receive.
Machiavelli (1469–1527) Italian statesman.
The Prince

OBLIVION

1 Many brave men lived before Agamemnon's
time; but they are all, unmourned and

unknown, covered by the long night, because they lack their sacred poet.
Horace (Quintus Horatius Flaccus; 65–8 BC) Roman poet.
Odes, IV

2 No, no, go not to Lethe, neither twist Wolf's-bane, tight-rooted, for its poisonous wine.
John Keats (1795–1821) British poet.
Ode on Melancholy

3 Annihilating all that's made
To a green thought in a green shade.
Andrew Marvell (1621–78) English poet.
The Garden

OBSESSIONS

1 I have three phobias which, could I mute them, would make my life as slick as a sonnet, but as dull as ditch water: I hate to go to bed, I hate to get up, and I hate to be alone.
Tallulah Bankhead (1903–68) US actress.
Tallulah, Ch. 1

2 *Papyromania* – compulsive accumulation of papers . . .
Papyrophobia – abnormal desire for 'a clean desk'.
Laurence J. Peter (1919–) Canadian writer.
The Peter Principle, Glossary

OBSTRUCTION

1 I'll put a spoke among your wheels.
Francis Beaumont (1584–1616) English dramatist.
The Mad Lover, III:6

2 If any of you know cause, or just impediment.
The Book of Common Prayer
Solemnization of Matrimony

3 There was only one catch and that was Catch-22, which specified that a concern for one's own safety in the face of dangers that were real and immediate was the process of a rational mind.
Joseph Heller (1923–) US novelist.
Catch-22, Ch. 5

OCCUPATIONS

See also doctors, lawyers, nurses, police

1 A priest sees people at their best, a lawyer at their worst, but a doctor sees them as they really are.
Proverb

2 Every man to his trade.
Proverb

3 Jack of all trades, master of none.
Proverb

4 Old soldiers never die, they simply fade away.
Proverb

5 Once a parson always a parson.
Proverb

6 Sailors have a port in every storm.
Proverb

7 The ugliest of trades have their moments of pleasure. Now, if I were a grave-digger, or even a hangman, there are some people I could work for with a great deal of enjoyment.
Douglas William Jerrold (1803–57) British dramatist.
Wit and Opinions of Douglas Jerrold, 'Ugly Trades'

8 He did not know that a keeper is only a poacher turned outside in, and a poacher a keeper turned inside out.
Charles Kingsley (1819–75) British writer.
The Water Babies, Ch. 1

9 Under the spreading chestnut tree
The village smithy stands;
The smith, a mighty man is he,
With large and sinewy hands;
And the muscles of his brawny arms
Are strong as iron bands.
Henry Wadsworth Longfellow (1807–82) US poet.
The Village Blacksmith

10 I have nothing against undertakers personally. It's just that I wouldn't want one to bury my sister.
Jessica Mitford (1917–) British writer.
Attrib. in *Saturday Review*, 1 Feb 1964

11 If I didn't start painting, I would have raised chickens.
Grandma Moses (Anna Mary Robertson Moses; 1860–1961) US primitive painter.
Grandma Moses, My Life's History (ed. Aotto Kallir), Ch. 3

12 A doctor who doesn't say too many foolish things is a patient half-cured, just as a critic is a poet who has stopped writing verse and a policeman a burglar who has retired from practice.
Marcel Proust (1871–1922) French novelist.
À la recherche du temps perdu: Le Côté de Guermantes

13 Everybody hates house-agents because they have everybody at a disadvantage. All other callings have a certain amount of give and take; the house-agent simply takes.
H. G. Wells (1866–1946) British writer.
Kipps, Bk. III, Ch. 1

14 The best careers advice to give to the young is 'Find out what you like doing best and get someone to pay you for doing it.'
Katherine Whitehorn (1926–) British journalist.
The Observer, 1975

OFFICERS

See also army, navy, soldiers, war

1 Any officer who shall behave in a scandalous manner, unbecoming the character of an officer and a gentleman shall . . . be cashiered.

Anonymous
The words 'conduct unbecoming the character of an officer' are a direct quotation from the Naval Discipline Act (10 Aug 1860), Article 24
Articles of War (1872), *Disgraceful Conduct*, 79

2 If Kitchener was not a great man, he was, at least, a great poster.

Margot Asquith (1865–1945) The second wife of Herbert Asquith.
Kitchener: Portrait of an Imperialist (Sir Philip Magnus), Ch. 14

3 In defeat unbeatable; in victory unbearable.

Winston Churchill (1874–1965) British statesman.
Referring to Viscount Montgomery
Ambrosia and Small Beer (E. Marsh), Ch. 5

4 Jellicoe was the only man on either side who could lose the war in an afternoon.

Winston Churchill
The Observer, 'Sayings of the Week', 13 Feb 1927

5 War is too important to be left to the generals.

Georges Clemenceau (1841–1929) French statesman.
A similar remark is attributed to Talleyrand
Attrib.

6 When I was a lad I served a term
As office boy to an Attorney's firm.
I cleaned the windows and I swept the floor,
And I polished up the handle of the big front door.
I polished up that handle so carefullee
That now I am the Ruler of the Queen's Navee!

W. S. Gilbert (1836–1911) British dramatist.
HMS Pinafore, 1

7 Stick close to your desks and never go to sea,
And you all may be Rulers of the Queen's Navee!

W. S. Gilbert
HMS Pinafore, 1

8 LUDENDORFF: The English soldiers fight like lions.
HOFFMANN: True. But don't we know that they are lions led by donkeys.

Max Hoffmann (1869–1927) German general.
Referring to the performance of the British army in World War I
The Donkeys (A. Clark)

9 I can't spare this man; he fights.

Abraham Lincoln (1809–65) US statesman.
Resisting demands for the dismissal of Ulysses Grant
Attrib.

10 The Nelson touch.

Lord Nelson (1758–1805) British admiral.
Diary, 9 Oct 1805

11 Nelson, born in a fortunate hour for himself and for his country, was always in his element and always on his element.

George Macaulay Trevelyan (1876–1962) British historian.
History of England, Bk. V, Ch. 5

12 I didn't fire him because he was a dumb son of a bitch, although he was, but that's not against the law for generals. If it was, half to three-quarters of them would be in gaol.

Harry S. Truman (1884–1972) US statesman.
Referring to General MacArthur
Plain Speaking (Merle Miller)

13 I don't know what effect these men will have on the enemy, but, by God, they frighten me.

Duke of Wellington (1769–1852) British general and statesman.
Referring to his generals
Attrib.

14 It is not the business of generals to shoot one another.

Duke of Wellington
Refusing an artillery officer permission to fire upon Napoleon himself during the Battle of Waterloo, 1815
Attrib.

15 Not upon a man from the colonel to the private in a regiment –both inclusive. We may pick up a marshal or two perhaps; but not worth a damn.

Duke of Wellington
Said during the Waterloo campaign, when asked whether he anticipated any desertions from Napoleon's army
Creevey Papers, Ch. X

16 I used to say of him that his presence on the field made the difference of forty thousand men.

Duke of Wellington
Referring to Napoleon
Notes of Conversations with the Duke of Wellington (Stanhope), 2 Nov 1831

OLD AGE

See also age, longevity

1 Grey hairs are death's blossoms.
Proverb

2 You can't teach an old dog new tricks.
Proverb

3 I will never be an old man. To me, old age is always fifteen years older than I am.

Bernard Baruch (1870–1965) US financier and presidential adviser.
The Observer 'Sayings of the Week', 21 Aug 1955

4 Better is a poor and a wise child than an old and foolish king, who will no more be admonished.

Bible: Ecclesiastes
4:13

5 With the ancient is wisdom; and in length of days understanding.
Bible: Job
12:12

6 To be old is to be part of a huge and ordinary multitude ... the reason why old age was venerated in the past was because it was extraordinary.
Ronald Blythe (1922–) British author.
The View in Winter

7 Old age takes away from us what we have inherited and gives us what we have earned.
Gerald Brenan (Edward Fitzgerald Brenan; 1894–1987) British writer.
Thoughts in a Dry Season, 'Life'

8 As a white candle
In a holy place,
So is the beauty
Of an aged face.
Joseph Campbell (1879–1944) Irish poet.
The Old Woman

9 'You are old, Father William,' the young man said,
'And your hair has become very white;
And yet you incessantly stand on your head –
Do you think at your age, it is right?'
Lewis Carroll (Charles Lutwidge Dodgson; 1832–98) British writer.
See also Robert SOUTHEY
Alice's Adventures in Wonderland, Ch. 5

10 Old age is the out-patients' department of purgatory.
Lord Cecil (1869–1956) British politician.
The Cecils of Hatfield House (David Cecil)

11 I prefer old age to the alternative.
Maurice Chevalier (1888–1972) French singer and actor.
Attrib.

12 Old-age, a second child, by Nature curs'd
With more and greater evils than the first,
Weak, sickly, full of pains; in ev'ry breath
Railing at life, and yet afraid of death.
Charles Churchill (1731–64) British poet.
Gotham, I

13 Oh to be seventy again.
Georges Clemenceau (1841–1929) French statesman.
Remark on his eightieth birthday, noticing a pretty girl in the Champs Elysées
Ego 3 (James Agate)

·14 So, perhaps, I may escape otherwise than by death the last humiliation of an aged scholar, when his juniors conspire to print a volume of essays and offer it to him as a sign that they now consider him senile.
Robin George Collingwood (1889–1943) British philosopher and archaeologist.
Autobiography

15 When a man fell into his anecdotage it was a sign for him to retire from the world.
Benjamin Disraeli (1804–81) British statesman.
Lothair, Ch. 28

16 I grow old . . . I grow old . . .
I shall wear the bottoms of my trousers rolled.
T. S. Eliot (1888–1965) US-born British poet and dramatist.
The Love Song of J. Alfred Prufrock

17 Shall I part my hair behind? Do I dare to eat a peach?
I shall wear white flannel trousers, and walk upon the beach.
I have heard the mermaids singing, each to each.
T. S. Eliot
The Love Song of J. Alfred Prufrock

18 Old age brings along with its uglinesses the comfort that you will soon be out of it, – which ought to be a substantial relief to such discontented pendulums as we are.
Ralph Waldo Emerson (1803–82) US poet and essayist.
Journal

19 He cannot bear old men's jokes. That is not new. But now he begins to think of them himself.
Max Frisch (1911–) Swiss dramatist and novelist.
Sketchbook 1966–71

20 Time goes by: reputation increases, ability declines.
Dag Hammarskjöld (1905–61) Swedish diplomat.
Diaries, 1964

21 And now in age I bud again,
After so many deaths I live and write;
I once more smell the dew and rain,
And relish versing; O, my only Light,
It cannot be
That I am he
On whom Thy tempests fell all night.
George Herbert (1593–1633) English poet.
The Flower

22 It is so comic to hear oneself called old, even at ninety I suppose!
Alice James (1848–92) US diarist.
Letter to William James, 14 June 1889
The Diary of Alice James (ed. Leon Edel)

23 There is a wicked inclination in most people to suppose an old man decayed in his intellects. If a young or middle-aged man, when leaving a company, does not recollect where he laid his hat, it is nothing; but if the same inattention is discovered in an old man, people will shrug up their shoulders, and say, 'His memory is going.'
Samuel Johnson (1709–84) British lexicographer.
Life of Johnson (J. Boswell), Vol. IV

24 Perhaps being old is having lighted rooms
Inside your head, and people in them, acting.
People you know, yet can't quite name.
Philip Larkin (1922–85) British poet.
The Old Fools

25 A 'Grand Old Man'. That means on our

continent any one with snow white hair who has kept out of jail till eighty.

Stephen Leacock (1869–1944) English-born Canadian economist and humorist.
The Score and Ten

26 Old age is woman's hell.

Ninon de Lenclos (1620–1705) French courtesan.
Attrib.

27 From the earliest times the old have rubbed it into the young that they are wiser than they, and before the young had discovered what nonsense this was they were old too, and it profited them to carry on the imposture.

W. Somerset Maugham (1874–1965) British novelist.
Cakes and Ale, Ch. 9

28 Being seventy is not a sin.

Golda Meir (1898–1978) Russian-born Israeli stateswoman.
Reader's Digest (July 1971), 'The Indestructible Golda Meir'

29 I prefer to forget both pairs of glasses and pass my declining years saluting strange women and grandfather clocks.

Ogden Nash (1902–71) US poet.
Peekaboo, I Almost See You

30 Age only matters when one is ageing. Now that I have arrived at a great age, I might just as well be twenty.

Pablo Picasso (1881–1973) Spanish painter.
The Observer, Shouts and Murmurs, 'Picasso in Private' (John Richardson)

31 See how the world its veterans rewards!
A youth of frolics, an old age of cards.

Alexander Pope (1688–1744) British poet.
Moral Essays, II

32 Growing old is like being increasingly penalized for a crime you haven't committed.

Anthony Powell (1905–) British novelist.
A Dance to the Music of Time: Temporary Kings, Ch. 1

33 Darling, I am growing old,
Silver threads among the gold.

Eben Rexford (1848–1916) British songwriter.
Silver Threads Among the Gold

34 Age seldom arrives smoothly or quickly. It's more often a succession of jerks.

Jean Rhys (1894–1979) Dominican-born British novelist.
The Observer, 'Sayings of the Week', 25 May 1975

35 As I grow older and older,
And totter towards the tomb,
I find that I care less and less
Who goes to bed with whom.

Dorothy L. Sayers (1893–1957) British writer.
That's Why I Never Read Modern Novels

36 Last scene of all,
That ends this strange eventful history,
Is second childishness and mere oblivion;

Sans teeth, sans eyes, sans taste, sans every thing.

William Shakespeare (1564–1616) English dramatist.
As You Like It, II:7

37 I have liv'd long enough.
My way of life
Is fall'n into the sear, the yellow leaf;
And that which should accompany old age,
As honour, love, obedience, troops of friends,
I must not look to have.

William Shakespeare
Macbeth, V:3

38 That time of year thou mayst in me behold
When yellow leaves, or none, or few, do hang
Upon those boughs which shake against the cold,
Bare ruin'd choirs, where late the sweet birds sang.

William Shakespeare
Sonnet 73

39 Old men are dangerous; it doesn't matter to them what is going to happen to the world.

George Bernard Shaw (1856–1950) Irish dramatist and critic.
Heartbreak House

40 You are old, Father William, the young man cried,
The few locks which are left you are grey;
You are hale, Father William, a hearty old man,
Now tell me the reason, I pray.

Robert Southey (1774–1843) British poet.
See also Lewis CARROLL
The Old Man's Comforts, and how he Gained them

41 Being over seventy is like being engaged in a war. All our friends are going or gone and we survive amongst the dead and the dying as on a battlefield.

Muriel Spark (1918–) British novelist.
Memento Mori, Ch. 4

42 The greatest problem about old age is the fear that it may go on too long.

A. J. P. Taylor (1906–) British historian.
Observer 'Sayings of the Week', 1 Nov 1981

43 Sleeping as quiet as death, side by wrinkled side, toothless, salt and brown, like two old kippers in a box.

Dylan Thomas (1914–53) Welsh poet.
Under Milk Wood

44 Old age is the most unexpected of all the things that happen to a man.

Leon Trotsky (Lev Davidovich Bronstein; 1879–1940) Russian revolutionary.
Diary in Exile, 8 May 1935

45 The gods bestowed on Max the gift of perpetual old age.

Oscar Wilde (1854–1900) Irish-born British dramatist.
Referring to Max Beerbohm
Attrib.

46 It is a terrible thing for an old woman to outlive her dogs.
Tennessee Williams (1911–83) US dramatist.
Camino Real

47 He was either a man of about a hundred and fifty who was rather young for his years or a man of about a hundred and ten who had been aged by trouble.
P. G. Wodehouse (1881–1975) British humorous novelist.
Wodehouse at Work to the End (Richard Usborne), Ch. 6

48 The wiser mind
Mourns less for what age takes away
Than what it leaves behind.
William Wordsworth (1770–1850) British poet.
The Fountain

49 Provoke
The years to bring the inevitable yoke.
William Wordsworth
Ode. Intimations of Immortality, VIII

50 When you are old and gray and full of sleep,
And nodding by the fire, take down this book,
And slowly read, and dream of the soft look
Your eyes had once, and of their shadows deep
. . .
W. B. Yeats (1865–1939) Irish poet.
When you are Old

ONE-UPMANSHIP

See also snobbery, superiority

1 Keeping up with the Joneses was a full-time job with my mother and father. It was not until many years later when I lived alone that I realized how much cheaper it was to drag the Joneses down to my level.
Quentin Crisp (c. 1910–) British model, publicist, and writer.
The Naked Civil Servant

2 There is no doubt that basic weekendmanship should contain some reference to Important Person Play.
Stephen Potter (1900–69) British writer.
Lifemanship, Ch. 2

3 *How to be one up* – how to make the other man feel that something has gone wrong, however slightly.
Stephen Potter
Lifemanship, Introduction

OPERA

See also music, singing

1 I do not mind what language an opera is sung in so long as it is a language I don't understand.
Edward Appleton (1892–1965) British physicist.
The Observer, 'Sayings of the Week,' 28 Aug 1955

2 No good opera plot can be sensible, for people do not sing when they are feeling sensible.
W. H. Auden (1907–73) British poet.
Time, 29 Dec 1961

3 People are wrong when they say the opera isn't what it used to be. It is what it used to be. That's what's wrong with it.
Noël Coward (1899–1973) British dramatist.
Design for Living

4 Opera in English, is, in the main, just about as sensible as baseball in Italian.
H. L. Mencken (1880–1956) US journalist.
The Frank Muir Book (Frank Muir)

5 I sometimes wonder which would be nicer – an opera without an interval, or an interval without an opera.
Ernest Newman (1868–1959) British music critic.
Berlioz, Romantic and Classic, (ed. Peter Heyworth)

6 His vocal cords were kissed by God.
Harold Schoenberg (1915–) US music critic.
Referring to Luciano Pavarotti
The Times, 30 June 1981

7 Like German opera, too long and too loud.
Evelyn Waugh (1903–66) British novelist.
Giving his opinions of warfare after the Battle of Crete, 1941
Attrib.

8 An unalterable and unquestioned law of the musical world required that the German text of French operas sung by Swedish artists should be translated into Italian for the clearer understanding of English speaking audiences.
Edith Wharton (1862–1937) US novelist.
The Age of Innocence, Bk. I, Ch. 1

OPINIONS

See also ideas

1 They that approve a private opinion, call it opinion; but they that mislike it, heresy: and yet heresy signifies no more than private opinion.
Thomas Hobbes (1588–1679) English philosopher.
Leviathan, Pt. I, Ch. 11

2 The superiority of one man's opinion over another's is never so great as when the opinion is about a woman.
Henry James (1843–1916) US novelist.
The Tragic Muse, Ch. 9

3 'Tis with our judgments as our watches, none Go just alike, yet each believes his own.
Alexander Pope (1688–1744) British poet.
An Essay on Criticism

4 It is folly of too many to mistake the echo of a London coffee-house for the voice of the kingdom.
Jonathan Swift (1667–1745) Irish-born Anglican priest and writer.
The Conduct of the Allies

5 So many men, so many opinions.
Terence (Publius Terentius Afer; c. 190–159 BC) Roman poet.
Phormio

6 I agree with no man's opinion. I have some of my own.
Ivan Turgenev (1818–83) Russian novelist.
Fathers and Sons, Ch. 13

OPPORTUNITY

See also present

1 All's grist that comes to the mill.
Proverb

2 Every dog has his day.
Proverb

3 Hoist your sail when the wind is fair.
Proverb

4 Make hay while the sun shines.
Proverb

5 Nothing ventured, nothing gained.
Proverb

6 Opportunity seldom knocks twice.
Proverb

7 Strike while the iron is hot.
Proverb

8 Whenever you fall, pick up something.
Oswald Theodore Avery (1877–1955) Canadian bacteriologist.
Attrib.

9 A wise man will make more opportunities than he finds.
Francis Bacon (1561–1626) English philosopher.
Essays, 'Of Ceremonies and Respects'

10 Cast thy bread upon the waters: for thou shalt find it after many days.
Bible: Ecclesiastes
11:1

11 Let him now speak, or else hereafter for ever hold his peace.
The Book of Common Prayer
Solemnization of Matrimony

12 One can present people with opportunities. One cannot make them equal to them.
Rosamond Lehmann (1901–) British novelist.
The Ballad and the Source

13 Equality of opportunity means equal opportunity to be unequal.
Iain Macleod (1913–70) British politician.
Way Of Life (John Boyd Carpenter)

14 There is a tide in the affairs of men
Which, taken at the flood, leads on to fortune;
Omitted, all the voyage of their life
Is bound in shallows and in miseries.
On such a full sea are we now afloat,
And we must take the current when it serves,
Or lose our ventures.
William Shakespeare (1564–1616) English dramatist.
Julius Caesar, IV:3

15 Why, then the world's mine oyster,
Which I with sword will open.
William Shakespeare
The Merry Wives of Windsor, II:2

16 I missed the chance of a lifetime, too. Fifty lovelies in the rude and I'd left my Bunsen burner home.
Dylan Thomas (1914–53) Welsh poet.
Portrait of the Artist as a Young Dog, 'One Warm Saturday'

OPPOSITES

See also conflict, difference, doublethink

1 It takes all sorts to make a world.
Proverb

2 The poet and the dreamer are distinct,
Diverse, sheer opposite, antipodes.
The one pours out a balm upon the world,
The other vexes it.
John Keats (1795–1821) British poet.
The Fall of Hyperion, I

3 Oh, East is East, and West is West, and never the twain shall meet.
Rudyard Kipling (1865–1936) Indian-born British writer.
The Ballad of East and West

4 The sublime and the ridiculous are often so nearly related that it is difficult to class them separately. One step above the sublime makes the ridiculous; and one step above the ridiculous makes the sublime again.
Thomas Paine (1737–1809) British writer.
The Age of Reason, Pt. 2

OPPOSITION

See also government, politics

1 It has been said that England invented the phrase, 'Her Majesty's Opposition'.
Walter Bagehot (1826–77) British economist and journalist.
See HOBHOUSE
The English Constitution, 'The Monarchy'

2 The duty of an opposition is to oppose.
Lord Randolph Churchill (1849–95) British Conservative politician.
Lord Randolph Churchill (W. S. Churchill)

3 When I invented the phrase 'His Majesty's Opposition' he paid me a compliment on the fortunate hit.
John Cam Hobhouse (1786–1869) British politician.
Speaking about Canning
Recollections of a Long Life, II, Ch. 12

4 One-fifth of the people are against everything all the time.
Robert Kennedy (1925–68) US politician.
The Observer, 'Sayings of the Week', 10 May 1964

5 . . . I have spent many years of my life in opposition and I rather like the role.
Eleanor Roosevelt (1884–1962) US writer and lecturer.
Letter to Bernard Baruch, 18 Nov 1952

OPPRESSION

See also imprisonment, indoctrination, power politics, slavery, tyranny

1 When Israel was in Egypt land,
Let my people go,
Oppressed so hard they could not stand,
Let my people go.
Go down, Moses,
Way-down in Egypt land,
Tell old Pharaoh
To let my people go.
Anonymous
Negro spiritual

2 Christ in this country would quite likely have been arrested under the Suppression of Communism Act.
Joost de Blank (1908–68) Dutch-born British churchman.
Referring to South Africa
The Observer, 'Sayings of the Week', 27 Oct 1963

3 The enemies of Freedom do not argue; they shout and they shoot.
Dean Inge (1860–1954) British churchman.
The End of an Age, Ch. 4

4 If you want a picture of the future, imagine a boot stamping on a human face – for ever.
George Orwell (Eric Blair; 1903–50) British novelist.
Nineteen Eighty-Four

5 In the first days of the revolt you must kill: to shoot down a European is to kill two birds with one stone, to destroy an oppressor and the man he oppresses at the same time: there remain a dead man, and a free man.
Jean-Paul Sartre (1905–80) French writer.
The Wretched of the Earth (F. Fanon), Preface

OPTIMISM

See also hope

1 After a storm comes a calm.
Proverb

2 Every cloud has a silver lining.
Proverb

3 It's an ill wind that blows nobody any good.
Proverb

4 It will all come right in the wash.
Proverb

5 Look on the bright side.
Proverb

6 No news is good news.
Proverb

7 Nothing so bad but it might have been worse.
Proverb

8 The darkest hour is just before the dawn.
Proverb

9 Tomorrow is another day.
Proverb

10 When one door shuts, another opens.
Proverb

11 While there's life there's hope.
Proverb

12 Are we downhearted? No!
Anonymous
A favourite expression of the British soldiers during World War I
Attrib.

13 What's the use of worrying?
It never was worth while,
So, pack up your troubles in your old kit-bag,
And smile, smile, smile.
George Asaf (George H. Powell; 1880–1951) US songwriter.
Pack up Your Troubles in Your Old Kit-bag

14 Let other pens dwell on guilt and misery.
Jane Austen (1775–1817) British novelist.
Mansfield Park, Ch. 48

15 *Future*, n. That period of time in which our affairs prosper, our friends are true and our happiness is assured.
Ambrose Bierce (1842–?1914) US writer and journalist.
The Devil's Dictionary

16 My sun sets to rise again.
Robert Browning (1812–89) British poet.
At the 'Mermaid'

17 No, at noonday in the bustle of man's worktime
Greet the unseen with a cheer!
Robert Browning
Epilogue to Asolando

18 Don't you know each cloud contains Pennies from Heaven?
Johnny Burke (1908–64) US songwriter.
Pennies from Heaven

19 The optimist proclaims we live in the best of all possible worlds; and the pessimist fears this is true.
James Cabell (1879–1958) US novelist and journalist.
The Silver Stallion

20 The place where optimism most flourishes is the lunatic asylum.
Havelock Ellis (1859–1939) British sexologist.
The Dance of Life

21 Two men look out through the same bars:
One sees the mud, and one the stars.
Frederick Langbridge (1849–1923) British religious writer.
A Cluster of Quiet Thoughts

22 The worst is not
So long as we can say 'This is the worst'.
William Shakespeare (1564–1616) English dramatist.
King Lear, IV:1

23 Now is the winter of our discontent
Made glorious summer by this sun of York.
William Shakespeare
Richard III, I:1

24 Life may change, but it may fly not;
Hope may vanish, but can die not;
Truth be veiled, but still it burneth;
Love repulsed, – but it returneth!
Percy Bysshe Shelley (1792–1822) British poet.
Hellas, I

25 The latest definition of an optimist is one
who fills up his crossword puzzle in ink.
Clement King Shorter (1857–1926) British journalist and
critic.
The Observer, 'Sayings of the Week', 22 Feb 1925

26 I am an optimist, unrepentant and militant.
After all, in order not to be a fool an optimist
must know how sad a place the world can
be. It is only the pessimist who finds this out
anew every day.
Peter Ustinov (1921–) British actor.
Dear Me, Ch. 9

27 All is for the best in the best of possible
worlds.
Voltaire (François-Marie Arouet; 1694–1778) French
writer.
Candide, Ch. 30

28 We are all in the gutter, but some of us are
looking at the stars.
Oscar Wilde (1854–1900) Irish-born British dramatist.
Lady Windermere's Fan, III

29 Nor greetings where no kindness is, nor all
The dreary intercourse of daily life,
Shall e'er prevail against us, or disturb
Our cheerful faith, that all which we behold
Is full of blessings.
William Wordsworth (1770–1850) British poet.
Lines composed a few miles above Tintern Abbey

ORDER

1 'Where shall I begin, please your Majesty?'
he asked.
'Begin at the beginning' the King said, gravely,
'and go on till you come to the end: then
stop.'
Lewis Carroll (Charles Lutwidge Dodgson; 1832–98)
British writer.
Alice's Adventures in Wonderland, Ch. 11

2 Order is heaven's first law.
Alexander Pope (1688–1744) British poet.
An Essay on Man, IV

3 O, when degree is shak'd,
Which is the ladder of all high designs,

The enterprise is sick!
William Shakespeare (1564–1616) English dramatist.
Troilus and Cressida, I:3

4 How sour sweet music is
When time is broke and no proportion kept!
So is it in the music of men's lives.
William Shakespeare
Richard II, V:5

5 A place for everything, and everything in its
place.
Samuel Smiles (1812–1904) British writer.
Thrift, Ch. 5

ORIGINALITY

See also imitation, innovation

1 Anything that is worth doing has been done
frequently. Things hitherto undone should be
given, I suspect, a wide berth.
Max Beerbohm (1872–1956) British writer.
Mainly on the Air

2 An original writer is not one who imitates
nobody, but one whom nobody can imitate.
Vicomte de Chateaubriand (1768–1848) French
diplomat and writer.
Génie du Christianisme

3 A thought is often original, though you have
uttered it a hundred times.
Oliver Wendell Holmes (1809–94) US writer.
The Autocrat of the Breakfast Table, Ch. 1

4 All good things which exist are the fruits of
originality.
John Stuart Mill (1806–73) British philosopher.
On Liberty, Ch. 3

5 Nothing has yet been said that's not been
said before.
Terence (Publius Terentius Afer; c. 190–159 BC) Roman
poet.
Eunuchus, Prologue

6 Another unsettling element in modern art is
that common symptom of immaturity, the
dread of doing what has been done before.
Edith Wharton (1862–1937) US novelist.
The Writing of Fiction, Ch. 1

ORTHODOXY

See also conformity

1 The difference between Orthodoxy or My-
doxy and Heterodoxy or Thy-doxy.
Thomas Carlyle (1795–1881) Scottish historian and
essayist.
A similar remark is attributed to the British churchman William
Warburton (1698–1779)
History of the French Revolution, Pt. II, Bk. IV, Ch. 2

2 The word 'orthodoxy' not only no longer
means being right; it practically means being
wrong.
G. K. Chesterton (1874–1936) British writer.
Heretics, Ch. 1

3 Worldly wisdom teaches that it is better for the reputation to fail conventionally than to succeed unconventionally.
John Maynard Keynes (1883–1946) British economist.
The General Theory of Employment, Interest and Money, Bk. IV, Ch. 12

OSTENTATION

See also affectation

1 That's it, baby, if you've got it, flaunt it.
Mel Brooks (Melvyn Kaminsky; 1926–) US film director.
The Producers

2 The possession of a book becomes a substitute for reading it.
Anthony Burgess (John Burgess Wilson; 1917–) British novelist.
New York Times Book Review

3 Wealth has never been a sufficient source of honour in itself. It must be advertised, and the normal medium is obtrusively expensive goods.
John Kenneth Galbraith (1908–) US economist.
The Affluent Society, Ch. 7

4 When I meet those remarkable people whose company is coveted, I often wish they would show off a little more.
Desmond MacCarthy (1877–1952) British writer and theatre critic.
Theatre, 'Good Talk'

5 She's like the old line about justice – not only must be done but must be seen to be done.
John Osborne (1929–) British dramatist.
Time Present, I

6 With the great part of rich people, the chief employment of riches consists in the parade of riches.
Adam Smith (1723–90) Scottish economist.
The Wealth of Nations

OXFORD

See also education, England

1 Home of lost causes, and forsaken beliefs, and unpopular names, and impossible loyalties!
Matthew Arnold (1822–88) British poet and critic.
Essays in Criticism, First Series, Preface

2 That sweet City with her dreaming spires She needs not June for beauty's heightening.
Matthew Arnold
Thyrsis

3 Oxford is on the whole more attractive than Cambridge to the ordinary visitor; and the traveller is therefore recommended to visit Cambridge first, or to omit it altogether if he cannot visit both.
Karl Baedeker (1801–59) German publisher.
Baedeker's Great Britain, 'From London to Oxford'

4 The King to Oxford sent a troop of horse, For Tories own no argument but force: With equal skill to Cambridge books he sent, For Whigs admit no force but argument.
William Browne (1692–1774) English physician.
A reply to TRAPP
Literary Anecdotes (Nichols), Vol. III

5 Very nice sort of place, Oxford, I should think, for people that like that sort of place.
George Bernard Shaw (1856–1950) Irish dramatist and critic.
Man and Superman, II

6 The King, observing with judicious eyes The state of both his universities, To Oxford sent a troop of horse, and why? That learned body wanted loyalty; To Cambridge books, as very well discerning How much that loyal body wanted learning.
Joseph Trapp (1679–1747) English churchman and academic.
Written after George I donated the Bishop of Ely's library to Cambridge; for reply see BROWNE
Literary Anecdotes (Nichols), Vol. III

7 Oxford is, and always has been, full of cliques, full of factions, and full of a particular non-social snobbiness.
Mary Warnock (1924–) British philosopher and educationalist.
The Observer, 2 Nov 1980

P

PAINTING

See also art, artists

1 Buy old masters. They fetch a better price than old mistresses.
Lord Beaverbrook (1879–1964) Canadian-born British newspaper proprietor.
Attrib.

2 *Painting, n.* The art of protecting flat surfaces from the weather and exposing them to the critic.
Ambrose Bierce (1842–?1914) US writer and journalist.
The Devil's Dictionary

3 Good painters imitate nature, bad ones spew it up.
Miguel de Cervantes (1547–1616) Spanish novelist.
El Licenciado Vidriera

4 It's either easy or impossible.
Salvador Dali (1904–) Spanish painter.
Reply when asked if he found it hard to paint a picture
Attrib.

5 Never mind about my soul, just make sure you get my tie right.
James Joyce (1882–1941) Irish novelist.
Responding to the painter Patrick Tuohy's assertion that he wished to capture Joyce's soul in his portrait of him
James Joyce (R. Ellmann)

6 If people only knew as much about painting as I do, they would never buy my pictures.
Edwin Landseer (1802–73) British painter and sculptor.
Said to W. P. Frith
Landseer the Victorian Paragon (Campbell Lennie), Ch. 12

7 I mix them with my brains, sir.
John Opie (1761–1807) British painter.
When asked what he mixed his colours with
Self-Help (Samuel Smiles), Ch. 4

8 A picture has been said to be something between a thing and a thought.
Samuel Palmer (1805–81) British landscape painter.
Life of Blake (Arthur Symons)

9 If I like it, I say it's mine. If I don't I say it's a fake.
Pablo Picasso (1881–1973) Spanish painter.
When asked how he knew which paintings were his
The Sunday Times, 10 Oct 1965

10 I paint objects as I think them, not as I see them.
Pablo Picasso
Attrib.

11 Painting is a blind man's profession. He paints not what he sees, but what he feels, what he tells himself about what he has seen.
Pablo Picasso
Journals (Jean Cocteau), 'Childhood'

12 It's better like that, if you want to kill a picture all you have to do is to hang it beautifully on a nail and soon you will see nothing of it but the frame. When it's out of place you see it better.
Pablo Picasso
Explaining why a Renoir in his apartment was hung crooked
Picasso: His Life and Work (Ronald Penrose)

13 It is bad enough to be condemned to drag around this image in which nature has imprisoned me. Why should I consent to the perpetuation of the image of this image?
Plotinus (205–270 AD) Egyptian-born Greek philosopher.
Refusing to have his portrait painted
Attrib.

14 I just keep painting till I feel like pinching. Then I know it's right.
Pierre Auguste Renoir (1841–1919) French impressionist painter.
Explaining how he achieved such lifelike flesh tones in his nudes
Attrib.

15 Every time I paint a portrait I lose a friend.
John Singer Sargent (1856–1925) US portrait painter.
Attrib.

16 Portraits of famous bards and preachers, all fur and wool from the squint to the kneecaps.
Dylan Thomas (1914–53) Welsh poet.
Under Milk Wood

17 My business is to paint not what I know, but what I see.
Joseph Turner (1775–1851) British painter.
Responding to a criticism of the fact that he had painted no portholes on the ships in a view of Plymouth
Proust: The Early Years (G. Painter)

PARASITES

1 Many a man who thinks to found a home discovers that he has merely opened a tavern for his friends.
Norman Douglas (1868–1952) British novelist.
South Wind, Ch. 24

2 A free-loader is a confirmed guest. He is the man who is always willing to come to dinner.
Damon Runyon (1884–1946) US writer.
Short Takes, 'Free-Loading Ethics'

3 So, naturalist observe, a flea
Hath smaller fleas that on him prey,
And these have smaller fleas to bite 'em.
And so proceed *ad infinitum*.
Jonathan Swift (1667–1745) Irish-born Anglican priest and writer.
On Poetry

4 But was there ever dog that praised his fleas?
   W. B. Yeats (1865–1939) Irish poet.
   To a Poet, who would have me Praise certain Bad Poets, Imitators of His and Mine

PARIS

See also France

1 If you are lucky enough to have lived in Paris as a young man, then wherever you go for the rest of your life, it stays with you, for Paris is a moveable feast.
   Ernest Hemingway (1899–1961) US novelist.
   A Moveable Feast, Epigraph

2 Paris is worth a mass.
   Henri IV (1553–1610) King of France.
   Said on entering Paris (March 1594), having secured its submission to his authority by becoming a Roman Catholic
   Attrib.

3 Is Paris burning?
   Adolf Hitler (1889–1945) German dictator.
   Referring to the liberation of Paris, 1944

4 As an artist, a man has no home in Europe save in Paris.
   Friedrich Wilhelm Nietzsche (1844–1900) German philosopher.
   Ecce Homo

5 I love Paris in the springtime.
   Cole Porter (1893–1964) US songwriter.
   Can-Can, 'I Love Paris'

PAROCHIALISM

See also self-interest, selfishness

1 This fellow did not see further than his own nose.
   Jean de La Fontaine (1621–95) French poet.
   Fables, III, 'Le Renard et le Bouc'

2 A broken head in Cold Bath Fields produces a greater sensation among us than three pitched battles in India.
   Lord Macaulay (1800–59) British historian.
   Speech, 10 July 1833

3 'That is well said,' replied Candide, 'but we must cultivate our garden.'
   Voltaire (François-Marie Arouet; 1694–1778) French writer.
   Candide, Ch. 30

PARTIES

See also society

1 The sooner every party breaks up the better.
   Jane Austen (1775–1817) British novelist.
   Emma, Ch. 25

2 And bring hither the fatted calf, and kill it; and let us eat, and be merry:

For this my son was dead, and is alive again; he was lost, and is found. And they began to be merry.
   Bible: Luke
   15:23–24

3 I entertained on a cruising trip that was so much fun that I had to sink my yacht to make my guests go home.
   F. Scott Fitzgerald (1896–1940) US novelist.
   The Crack-Up, 'Notebooks, K'

4 I was one of the few guests who had actually been invited. People were not invited – they went there.
   F. Scott Fitzgerald
   The Great Gatsby, Ch. 3

5 HE. Have you heard it's in the stars
   Next July we collide with Mars?
   SHE. Well, did you evah! What a swell party this is.
   Cole Porter (1893–1964) US songwriter.
   High Society 'Well, Did You Evah!'

6 Certainly, there is nothing else here to enjoy.
   George Bernard Shaw (1856–1950) Irish dramatist and critic.
   Said at a party when his hostess asked him whether he was enjoying himself
   Pass the Port (Oxfam)

7 'So like one's first parties' said Miss Runcible 'being sick with other people singing.'
   Evelyn Waugh (1903–66) British novelist.
   Vile Bodies

8 She had heard someone say something about an Independent Labour Party, and was furious that she had not been asked.
   Evelyn Waugh
   Vile Bodies

9 The Life and Soul, the man who will never go home while there is one man, woman or glass of anything not yet drunk.
   Katherine Whitehorn (1926–   ) British journalist.
   Sunday Best, 'Husband-Swapping'

PARTING

See also departure, greetings, separation

1 Adieu, adieu, kind friends, adieu, adieu, adieu,
   I can no longer stay with you, stay with you.
   I'll hang my harp on a weeping willow-tree.
   And may the world go well with thee.
   Anonymous
   There is a Tavern in the Town

2 There is a tavern in the town,
   And there my dear love sits him down,
   And drinks his wine 'mid laughter free,
   And never, never thinks of me.

   Fare thee well, for I must leave thee,
   Do not let this parting grieve thee,

And remember that the best of friends must part.
Anonymous
There is a Tavern in the Town

3 Farewell and adieu to you,
Fair Spanish Ladies
Farewell and adieu to you, Ladies of Spain.
Anonymous
Spanish Ladies

4 Forty years on, when afar and asunder
Parted are those who are singing to-day.
E. E. Bowen (1836–1901) British writer.
Forty Years On (the Harrow school song)

5 Parting is all we know of heaven,
And all we need of hell.
Emily Dickinson (1830–86) US poet.
My Life Closed Twice Before its Close

6 Since there's no help, come let us kiss and part –
Nay, I have done, you get no more of me;
And I am glad, yea glad with all my heart
That thus so cleanly I myself can free.
Michael Drayton (1563–1631) English poet.
Sonnets, 61

7 But tha mun dress thysen, an' go back to thy stately homes of England, how beautiful they stand. Time's up! Time's up for Sir John, an' for little Lady Jane! Put thy shimmy on, Lady Chatterley!
D. H. Lawrence (1885–1930) British novelist.
Lady Chatterley's Lover, Ch. 15

8 It was not like your great and gracious ways!
Do you, that have nought other to lament,
Never, my Love, repent
Of how, that July afternoon,
You went,
With sudden, unintelligible phrase, – And frightened eye,
Upon your journey of so many days,
Without a single kiss or a good-bye?
Coventry Patmore (1823–96) British poet.
The Unknown Eros, Bk. I, 'Departure'

9 It is seldom indeed that one parts on good terms, because if one were on good terms one would not part.
Marcel Proust (1871–1922) French novelist.
À la recherche du temps perdu: La Prisonnière

10 Good night, good night! Parting is such sweet sorrow
That I shall say good night till it be morrow.
William Shakespeare (1564–1616) English dramatist.
Romeo and Juliet, II:2

11 Farewell! thou art too dear for my possessing,
And like enough thou know'st thy estimate:
The charter of thy worth gives thee releasing;
My bonds in thee are all determinate.
William Shakespeare
Sonnet 87

12 Good-by-ee! – good-bye-ee!
Wipe the tear, baby dear, from your eye-ee.
Tho' it's hard to part, I know,
I'll be tickled to death to go.
Don't cry-ee! – don't sigh-ee!
There's a silver lining in the sky-ee! –
Bonsoir, old thing! cheerio! chin-chin!
Nahpoo! Toodle-oo! Good-bye-ee!
R. P. Weston (20th century) British songwriter.
Good-bye-ee! (with Bert Lee)

PASSION

See also emotion, love

1 The man who is master of his passions is Reason's slave.
Cyril Connolly (1903–74) British journalist.
Turnstile One (ed. V. S. Pritchett)

2 A man who has not passed through the inferno of his passions has never overcome them.
Carl Gustav Jung (1875–1961) Swiss psychoanalyst.
Memories, Dreams, Reflections, Ch. 9

3 For ever warm and still to be enjoy'd,
For ever panting and for ever young;
All breathing human passion far above,
That leaves a heart high-sorrowful and cloy'd,
A burning forehead, and a parching tongue.
John Keats (1795–1821) British poet.
Ode on a Grecian Urn

4 It is with our passions as it is with fire and water, they are good servants, but bad masters.
Roger L'Estrange (1616–1704) English journalist and writer.
Aesop's Fables, 38

5 And hence one master-passion in the breast,
Like Aaron's serpent,
swallows up the rest.
Alexander Pope (1688–1744) British poet.
An Essay on Man, II

6 The ruling passion, be it what it will
The ruling passion conquers reason still.
Alexander Pope
Moral Essays, III

7 Passion, you see, can be destroyed by a doctor. It cannot be created.
Peter Shaffer (1926–) British dramatist.
Equus, II:35

8 So I triumphed ere my passion, sweeping thro' me, left me dry,
Left me with the palsied heart, and left me with the jaundiced eye.
Alfred, Lord Tennyson (1809–92) British poet.
Locksley Hall

9 Strange fits of passion have I known:
And I will dare to tell,
But in the lover's ear alone,

What once to me befell.
William Wordsworth (1770–1850) British poet.
Strange Fits of Passion

PAST

See also experience, future, history, memory, nostalgia, present, regret, time

1 Even God cannot change the past.
Agathon (c. 446–401 BC) Athenian poet and playwright.
Nicomachean Ethics (Aristotle), VI

2 There is always something rather absurd about the past.
Max Beerbohm (1872–1956) British writer.
1880

3 A king lived long ago,
In the morning of the world,
When earth was nigher heaven than now.
Robert Browning (1812–89) British poet.
Pippa Passes, Pt. I

4 Study the past, if you would divine the future.
Confucius (K'ung Fu-tzu; 551–479 BC) Chinese philosopher.
Analects

5 The past is a foreign country: they do things differently there.
L. P. Hartley (1895–1972) British novelist.
The Go-Between

6 Look back, and smile at perils past.
Walter Scott (1771–1832) Scottish novelist.
The Bridal of Triermain, Introduction

7 The past is the only dead thing that smells sweet.
Edward Thomas (1878–1917) British poet.
Early One Morning

8 Keep off your thoughts from things that are past and done;
For thinking of the past wakes regret and pain.
Arthur Waley (1889–1966) British poet and translator.
Translation from the Chinese of Po-Chü-I
Resignation

9 The past, at least, is secure.
Daniel Webster (1782–1852) US statesman.
Speech, US Senate, 26 Jan 1830

PATIENCE

See also endurance, persistence

1 A watched pot never boils.
Proverb

2 Everything comes to him who waits.
Proverb

3 First things first.
Proverb

4 Patience is a virtue.
Proverb

5 Rome was not built in a day.
Proverb

6 We must learn to walk before we can run.
Proverb

7 Wait and see.
Herbert Henry Asquith (1852–1928) British statesman.
In various speeches, 1910

8 *Patience*, n. A minor form of despair, disguised as a virtue.
Ambrose Bierce (1842–?1914) US writer and journalist.
The Devil's Dictionary

9 The bud may have a bitter taste,
But sweet will be the flower.
William Cowper (1731–1800) British poet.
Olney Hymns, 35

10 Beware the Fury of a Patient Man.
John Dryden (1631–1700) British poet and dramatist.
Absalom and Achitophel, I

11 Patience and passage of time do more than strength and fury.
Jean de La Fontaine (1621–95) French poet.
Fables, II, 'Le Lion et le Rat'

12 Though patience be a tired mare, yet she will plod.
William Shakespeare (1564–1616) English dramatist.
Henry V, II:1

13 It is very strange . . . that the years teach us patience; that the shorter our time, the greater our capacity for waiting.
Elizabeth Taylor (1912–75) British writer.
A Wreath of Roses, Ch. 10

PATRIOTISM

See also homesickness, loyalty, war

1 What pity is it
That we can die but once to serve our country!
Joseph Addison (1672–1719) British essayist.
Cato, IV:4

2 Speak for England.
Leopold Amery (1873–1955) British statesman.
Shouted to Arthur Greenwood, Labour Party spokesman, before he began to speak in a House of Commons debate immediately preceding the declaration of war, 2 Sept 1939

3 That this house will in no circumstances fight for its King and country.
Anonymous
Motion passed at the Oxford Union, 9 Feb 1933

4 'My country, right or wrong' is a thing that no patriot would think of saying, except in a desperate case. It is like saying 'My mother, drunk or sober.'
G. K. Chesterton (1874–1936) British writer.
The Defendant

5 Be England what she will,

With all her faults, she is my country still.
Charles Churchill (1731–64) British poet.
The Farewell

6 England, with all thy faults, I love thee still,
My country.
William Cowper (1731–1800) British poet.
The Task

7 Our country! In her intercourse with foreign
nations, may she always be in the right; but
our country, right or wrong.
Stephen Decatur (1779–1820) US naval officer.
Speech, Norfolk, Virginia, Apr 1816

8 I have never understood why one's affections
must be confined, as once with women, to a
single country.
John Kenneth Galbraith (1908–) US economist.
A Life in our Times

9 Anyone who wants to carry on the war
against the outsiders, come with me. I can't
offer you either honours or wages; I offer
you hunger, thirst, forced marches, battles
and death. Anyone who loves his country,
follow me.
Giuseppe Garibaldi (1807–82) Italian general and political
leader.
Garibaldi (Guerzoni)

10 That kind of patriotism which consists in
hating all other nations.
Elizabeth Gaskell (1810–65) British novelist.
Sylvia's Lovers, Ch. 1

11 I only regret that I have but one life to lose
for my country.
Nathan Hale (1755–76) US revolutionary hero.
Speech before his execution, 22 Sept 1776

12 Unlike so many who find success, she
remained a 'dinkum hard-swearing Aussie' to
the end.
Arnold Haskell (1903–80) English writer on ballet.
Referring to Dame Nellie Melba
Waltzing Matilda

13 *Dulce et decorum est pro patria mori.*
It is a sweet and seemly thing to die for one's
country.
Horace (Quintus Horatius Flaccus; 65–8 BC) Roman poet.
Odes, III

14 We don't want to fight, but, by jingo if we
do,
We've got the ships, we've got the men, we've
got the money too.
We've fought the Bear before, and while
Britons shall be true,
The Russians shall not have Constantinople.
George William Hunt (c. 1829–1904) British writer.
We Don't Want to Fight

15 Patriotism is the last refuge of a scoundrel.
Samuel Johnson (1709–84) British lexicographer.
Life of Johnson (J. Boswell), Vol. II

16 And so, my fellow Americans: ask not what

your country can do for you – ask what you
can do for your country. My fellow citizens
of the world: ask not what America will do
for you, but what together we can do for the
freedom of man.
John Fitzgerald Kennedy (1917–63) US statesman.
Inaugural address, 20 Jan 1961

17 Those who prate about Blimpish patriotism in
the mode of Margaret Thatcher are also the
ones who will take millions off the caring
services of this country.
Neil Kinnock (1942–) British politician.
Speech, Labour Party Conference, Brighton, 1983

18 I would die for my country . . . but I would
not let my country die for me.
Neil Kinnock
Speech on nuclear disarmament, 1987

19 'Take my drum to England, hang et by the
shore,
Strike et when your powder's runnin' low;
If the Dons sight Devon, I'll quit the port o'
Heaven,
An' drum them up the Channel as we drummed
them long ago.'
Henry John Newbolt (1862–1938) British poet.
Drake's Drum

20 But cared greatly to serve God and the King,
And keep the Nelson touch.
Henry John Newbolt
Minora Sidera

21 The old Lie: *Dulce et decorum est
Pro patria mori.*
Wilfred Owen (1893–1918) British poet.
Dulce et decorum est

22 If I were an American, as I am an
Englishman, while a foreign troop was landed
in my country, I never would lay down my
arms, – never – never – never!
William Pitt the Elder (1708–78) British statesman.
Speech, House of Lords, 18 Nov 1777

23 There is no room in this country for
hyphenated Americanism.
Theodore Roosevelt (1858–1919) US Republican
president.
Speech, New York, 12 Oct 1915

24 There can be no fifty-fifty Americanism in
this country. There is room here for only
one hundred per cent Americanism.
Theodore Roosevelt
Speech, Saratoga, 19 July 1918

25 Patriots always talk of dying for their country
and never of killing for their country.
Bertrand Russell (1872–1970) British philosopher.
The Autobiography of Bertrand Russell

26 Not that I lov'd Caesar less, but that I lov'd
Rome more.
William Shakespeare (1564–1616) English dramatist.
Julius Caesar, III:2

27 True patriotism is of no party.
Tobias Smollett (1721–71) British novelist.
The Adventures of Sir Launcelote Greaves

28 Patriotism to the Soviet State is a revolutionary duty, whereas patriotism to a bourgeois State is treachery.
Leon Trotsky (Lev Davidovich Bronstein; 1879–1940) Russian revolutionary.
Disputed Barricade (Fitzroy Maclean)

29 I was born an American; I will live an American; I shall die an American.
Daniel Webster (1782–1852) US statesman.
Speech, US Senate, 17 July 1850

30 'Shoot, if you must, this old gray head,
But spare your country's flag,' she said.

A shade of sadness, a blush of shame,
Over the face of the leader came.
John Greenleaf Whittier (1807–92) US poet.
Barbara Frietchie

31 There is one certain means by which I can be sure never to see my country's ruin; I will die in the last ditch.
William III (1650–1702) King of Great Britain.
History of England (Hume)

PATRONAGE

See also promotion

1 *Patron.* Commonly a wretch who supports with insolence, and is paid with flattery.
Samuel Johnson (1709–84) British lexicographer.
Dictionary of the English Language

2 Is not a Patron, my Lord, one who looks with unconcern on a man struggling for life in the water, and, when he has reached ground, encumbers him with help? The notice which you have been pleased to take of my labours, had it been early, had been kind; but it has been delayed till I am indifferent, and cannot enjoy it; till I am solitary, and cannot impart it; till I am known, and do not want it.
Samuel Johnson
Letter to Lord Chesterfield, 7 Feb 1755
Life of Johnson (J. Boswell), Vol. I

PEACE

See also war and peace

1 The wolf also shall dwell with the lamb, and the leopard shall lie down with the kid; and the calf and the young lion and the fatling together: and a little child shall lead them. And the cow and the bear shall feed; their young ones shall lie down together: and the lion shall eat straw like the ox.
And the sucking child shall play on the hole of the asp, and the weaned child shall put his hand on the cockatrice' den.
They shall not hurt nor destroy in all my holy mountain: for the earth shall be full of the knowledge of the Lord, as the waters cover the sea.
Bible: Isaiah
11:6–9

2 There is no peace, saith the Lord, unto the wicked.
Bible: Isaiah
48:22

3 Peace I leave with you, my peace I give unto you: not as the world giveth, give I unto you. Let not your heart be troubled, neither let it be afraid.
Bible: John
14:27

4 *Peace,* n. In international affairs, a period of cheating between two periods of fighting.
Ambrose Bierce (1842–?1914) US writer and journalist.
The Devil's Dictionary

5 Give peace in our time, O Lord.
The Book of Common Prayer
Morning Prayer, Versicles

6 Don't tell me peace has broken out.
Bertolt Brecht (1898–1956) German dramatist.
Mother Courage, VIII

7 I believe it is peace for our time . . . peace with honour.
Neville Chamberlain (1869–1940) British statesman.
Broadcast after Munich Agreement, 1 Oct 1938

8 Anythin' for a quiet life, as the man said wen he took the sitivation at the lighthouse.
Charles Dickens (1812–70) British novelist.
Pickwick Papers, Ch. 43

9 Lord Salisbury and myself have brought you back peace – but a peace I hope with honour.
Benjamin Disraeli (1804–81) British statesman.
Speech, House of Commons, 16 July 1878

10 Let us have peace.
Ulysses Simpson Grant (1822–85) US general.
On accepting nomination
Letter, 29 May 1868

11 Arms alone are not enough to keep the peace – it must be kept by men.
John Fitzgerald Kennedy (1917–63) US president.
The Observer, 'Sayings of the Decade', 1962

12 And who will bring white peace
That he may sleep upon his hill again?
Vachel Lindsay (1879–1931) US poet.
Abraham Lincoln Walks at Midnight

13 The issues are the same. We wanted peace on earth, love, and understanding between everyone around the world. We have learned that change comes slowly.
Paul McCartney (1943–) British rock musician.
The Observer, 'Sayings of the Week', 7 June 1987

14 Roll up that map: it will not be wanted these ten years.
William Pitt the Younger (1759–1806) British statesman.
On learning that Napoleon had won the Battle of Austerlitz
Attrib.

15 Nation shall speak peace unto nation.
Montague John Rendall (1862–1950) British schoolmaster.
Motto of BBC, 1927

16 Here, where the world is quiet;
Here, where all trouble seems
Dead winds' and spent waves' riot
In doubtful dreams of dreams.
Algernon Charles Swinburne (1837–1909) British poet.
The Garden of Proserpine

17 We are the true peace movement.
Margaret Thatcher (1925–) British politician and prime minister.
The Times, 1983

18 And I shall have some peace there, for peace comes dropping slow,
Dropping from the veils of the morning to where the cricket sings.
W. B. Yeats (1865–1939) Irish poet.
The Lake Isle of Innisfree

PERCEPTION

1 If the doors of perception were cleansed everything would appear to man as it is, infinite.
William Blake (1757–1827) British poet.
The Marriage of Heaven and Hell, 'A Memorable Fancy'

2 Man's Desires are limited by his Perceptions; none can desire what he has not perceived.
William Blake
There is no Natural Religion

3 'What,' it will be questioned, 'when the sun rises, do you not see a round disc of fire somewhat like a guinea?' 'O no, no, I see an innumerable company of the heavenly host crying, 'Holy, Holy, Holy is the Lord God Almighty!''
William Blake
Descriptive Catalogue, 'The Vision of Judgment'

4 I saw it, but I did not realize it.
Elizabeth Peabody (1804–94) US educationalist.
Giving a Transcendentalist explanation for her accidentally walking into a tree
The Peabody Sisters of Salem (L. Tharp)

PERFECTION

See also imperfection

1 The pursuit of perfection, then, is the pursuit of sweetness and light. . . . He who works for sweetness and light united, works to make reason and the will of God prevail.
Matthew Arnold (1822–88) British poet and critic.
Culture and Anarchy, Ch. 1

2 The year's at the spring,
And day's at the morn;
Morning's at seven;
The hill-side's dew-pearled;
The lark's on the wing;
The snail's on the thorn;
God's in His heaven –
All's right with the world.
Robert Browning (1812–89) British poet.
Pippa Passes, Pt. I

3 What's come to perfection perishes.
Things learned on earth, we shall practise in heaven.
Works done least rapidly, Art most cherishes.
Robert Browning
Old Pictures in Florence, XVII

4 You would attain to the divine perfection,
And yet not turn your back upon the world.
Henry Wadsworth Longfellow (1807–82) US poet.
Michael Angelo

5 Perfection has one grave defect; it is apt to be dull.
W. Somerset Maugham (1874–1965) British novelist.
The Summing Up

6 Whoever thinks a faultless piece to see,
Thinks what ne'er was, nor is, nor e'er shall be.
Alexander Pope (1688–1744) British poet.
An Essay on Criticism

7 Everything's Coming Up Roses.
Stephen Sondheim (1930–) US composer and lyricist.
Song title

8 Finality is death. Perfection is finality.
Nothing is perfect. There are lumps in it.
James Stephens (1882–1950) Irish novelist.
The Crock of Gold

PERSISTENCE

See also determination, endurance, patience

1 If the mountain will not come to Mahomet, Mahomet must go to the mountain.
Proverb

2 Never say die.
Proverb

3 Slow but sure wins the race.
Proverb

4 And ye shall be hated of all men for my name's sake: but he that endureth to the end shall be saved.
Bible: Matthew
10:22

5 If at first you don't succeed,
Try, try again.
William Edward Hickson (1803–70) British educationalist.
Try and Try Again

6 A man may write at any time, if he will set himself doggedly to it.
Samuel Johnson (1709–84) British lexicographer.
Life of Johnson (J. Boswell), Vol. I

7 The drop of rain maketh a hole in the stone, not by violence, but by oft falling.
Hugh Latimer (1485–1555) English churchman.
See also LUCRETIUS; OVID
Sermon preached before Edward VI

8 Keep right on to the end of the road.
Harry Lauder (Hugh MacLennon; 1870–1950) Scottish music-hall artist.
Song title

9 You persisted for a certain number of years like a stammer. You were a *stammer*, if you like, of Space-Time.
Wyndham Lewis (1882–1957) British novelist.
The Human Age, 'The Childermass'

10 Constant dripping hollows out a stone.
Lucretius (Titus Lucretius Carus; c. 99–55 BC) Roman philosopher.
On the Nature of the Universe, I. *See also* LATIMER; OVID

11 Dripping water hollows out a stone, a ring is worn away by use.
Ovid (Publius Ovidius Naso; 43 BC–17 AD) Roman poet.
See also LATIMER; LUCRETIUS
Epistulae Ex Ponto, Bk. IV

12 I am a kind of burr; I shall stick.
William Shakespeare (1564–1616) English dramatist.
Measure for Measure, IV:3

PERSPECTIVE

See also objectivity

1 'Tis distance lends enchantment to the view, And robes the mountain in its azure hue.
Thomas Campbell (1777–1844) British poet.
Pleasures of Hope, I

2 One sees great things from the valley; only small things from the peak.
G. K. Chesterton (1874–1936) British writer.
The Hammer of God

3 Fleas know not whether they are upon the body of a giant or upon one of ordinary size.
Walter Savage Landor (1775–1864) British poet and writer.
Imaginary Conversations, 'Southey and Porson'

4 Everything must be taken seriously, nothing tragically.
Louis Adolphe Thiers (1797–1877) French statesman and historian.
Speech, French National Assembly, 24 May 1873

PERSUASION

1 They will conquer, but they will not convince.
Miguel de Unamuno y Jugo (1864–1936) Spanish writer.
Referring to the Franco rebels
Attrib.

2 There is a holy, mistaken zeal in politics, as well as religion. By persuading others we convince ourselves.
Junius An unidentified writer of letters (1769–72) to the *London Public Advertiser*.
Letter, 19 Dec 1769

3 For a priest to turn a man when he lies a-dying, is just like one that has a long time solicited a woman, and cannot obtain his end; at length makes her drunk, and so lies with her.
John Selden (1584–1654) English historian.
Table Talk

4 The President spends most of his time kissing people on the cheek in order to get them to do what they ought to do without getting kissed.
Harry S. Truman (1884–1972) US statesman.
The Observer, 'Sayings of the Week', 6 Feb 1949

PERVERSITY

See also petulance, stubbornness

1 If it's heaven for climate, it's hell for company.
J. M. Barrie (1860–1937) British novelist and dramatist.
The Little Minister, Ch. 3

2 Never the time and the place
And the loved one all together!
Robert Browning (1812–89) British poet.
Never the Time and the Place

3 For 'tis a truth well known to most,
That whatsoever thing is lost –
We seek it, ere it come to light,
In every cranny but the right.
William Cowper (1731–1800) British poet.
The Retired Cat

4 Let's find out what everyone is doing,
And then stop everyone from doing it.
A. P. Herbert (1890–1971) British writer and politician.
Let's Stop Somebody

5 I had never had a piece of toast
Particularly long and wide,
But fell upon the sanded floor,
And always on the buttered side.
James Payn (1830–98) British writer and editor.
Chambers's Journal, 2 Feb 1884

6 Adam was but human – this explains it all.
He did not want the apple for the apple's

sake, he wanted it only because it was forbidden.

Mark Twain (Samuel Langhorne Clemens; 1835–1910) US writer.
Pudd'nhead Wilson's Calendar, Ch. 2

PESSIMISM

1 Pessimism, when you get used to it, is just as agreeable as optimism.
Arnold Bennett (1867–1931) British novelist.
Things that have Interested Me, 'The Slump in Pessimism'

2 Scratch a pessimist, and you find often a defender of privilege.
Lord Beveridge (1879–1963) British economist.
The Observer, 'Sayings of the Week', 17 Dec 1943

3 The optimist proclaims we live in the best of all possible worlds; and the pessimist fears this is true.
James Cabell (1879–1958) US novelist and journalist.
The Silver Stallion

4 He who despairs over an event is a coward, but he who holds hopes for the human condition is a fool.
Albert Camus (1913–60) French existentialist writer.
The Rebel

5 A Hard Rain's A-Gonna Fall.
Bob Dylan (Robert Allen Zimmerman; 1941–) US popular singer.
Song title

6 Sleep is good, death is better; but of course, the best thing would be never to have been born at all.
Heinrich Heine (1797–1856) German poet and writer.
Morphine

7 Nothing to do but work,
Nothing to eat but food,
Nothing to wear but clothes,
To keep one from going nude.
Benjamin Franklin King (1857–94) American humorist.
The Pessimist

8 If we see light at the end of the tunnel it is the light of an oncoming train.
Robert Lowell (1917–77) US poet.
Day by Day

9 How many pessimists end up by desiring the things they fear, in order to prove that they are right.
Robert Mallet (1915–) French writer.
Apostilles

10 A pessimist is a man who looks both ways before crossing a one-way street.
Laurence J. Peter (1919–) Canadian writer.
Peter's Quotations

11 It is not, nor it cannot come to good.
William Shakespeare (1564–1616) English dramatist.
Hamlet, I:2

PETULANCE

See also perversity, stubbornness

1 She refused to begin the 'Beguine'
Tho' they besought her to
And with language profane and obscene
She curs'd the man who taught her to
She curs'd Cole Porter too!
Noël Coward (1899–1973) British dramatist.
Sigh No More, 'Nina'

2 He has to learn that petulance is not sarcasm, and that insolence is not invective.
Benjamin Disraeli (1804–81) British statesman.
Said of Sir C. Wood
Speech, House of Commons, 16 Dec 1852

3 I am the emperor, and I want dumplings.
Ferdinand I (1793–1875) Emperor of Austria.
The Fall of the House of Habsburg (E. Crankshaw)

4 I hate a fellow whom pride, or cowardice, or laziness drives into a corner, and who does nothing when he is there but sit and *growl*; let him come out as I do, and *bark*.
Samuel Johnson (1709–84) British lexicographer.
Life of Johnson (J. Boswell), Vol. IV

PHILISTINISM

See also arts, books, culture

1 For this class we have a designation which now has become pretty well known, and which we may as well still keep for them, the designation of Philistines.
Matthew Arnold (1822–88) British poet and critic.
Referring to the middle class
Culture and Anarchy, Ch. 3

2 The great apostle of the Philistines, Lord Macaulay.
Matthew Arnold
Joubert

3 The finest collection of frames I ever saw.
Humphry Davy (1778–1829) British chemist.
When asked what he thought of the Paris art galleries
Attrib.

4 When I hear anyone talk of Culture, I reach for my revolver.
Hermann Goering (1893–1946) German leader.
Attrib. to Goering but probably said by Hanns Johst

5 I've never been in there . . . but there are only three things to see, and I've seen colour reproductions of all of them.
Harold W. Ross (1892–1951) US journalist.
Referring to the Louvre
A Farewell to Arms (Ernest Hemingway)

6 All my wife has ever taken from the Mediterranean – from that whole vast intuitive culture – are four bottles of Chianti

to make into lamps, and two china condiment donkeys labelled Sally and Peppy.

Peter Shaffer (1926–) British dramatist.
Equus, I:18

7 Particularly against books the Home Secretary is. If we can't stamp out literature in the country, we can at least stop it being brought in from outside.

Evelyn Waugh (1903–66) British novelist.
Vile Bodies, Ch. 2

8 Listen! There never was an artistic period. There never was an Art-loving nation.

James Whistler (1834–1903) US painter.
Attrib.

PHILOSOPHERS

See also philosophy

1 There is nothing so absurd but some philosopher has said it.

Cicero (106–43 BC) Roman orator and statesman.
De Divinatione, II

2 To a philosopher no circumstance, however trifling, is too minute.

Oliver Goldsmith (1728–74) Irish-born British writer.
The Citizen of the World

3 Philosophers never balance between profit and honesty, because their decisions are general, and neither their passions nor imaginations are interested in the objects.

David Hume (1711–76) Scottish philosopher.
A Treatise of Human Nature

4 I doubt if the philosopher lives, or ever has lived, who could know himself to be heartily despised by a street boy without some irritation.

T. H. Huxley (1825–95) British biologist.
Evolution and Ethics

5 In the philosopher there is nothing whatever impersonal; and, above all, his morality bears decided and decisive testimony to *who he is* – that is to say, to the order of rank in which the innermost drives of his nature stand in relation to one another.

Friedrich Wilhelm Nietzsche (1844–1900) German philosopher.
Jenseits von Gut und Böse

6 Not to care for philosophy is to be a true philosopher.

Blaise Pascal (1623–62) French philosopher and mathematician.
Pensées, I

7 Three passions, simple but overwhelmingly strong, have governed my life: the longing for love, the search for knowledge, and unbearable pity for the suffering of mankind.

Bertrand Russell (1872–1970) British philosopher.
The Autobiography of Bertrand Russell, Prologue

8 Philosophers are as jealous as women. Each wants a monopoly of praise.

George Santayana (1863–1952) US philosopher.
Dialogues In Limbo

9 There are now-a-days professors of philosophy but not philosophers.

Henry David Thoreau (1817–62) US writer.
Walden, 'Economy'

PHILOSOPHY

See also logic, metaphysics, philosophers

1 The principles of logic and metaphysics are true simply because we never allow them to be anything else.

A. J. Ayer (1910–) British philosopher.
Language, Truth and Logic

2 The formula 'Two and two make five' is not without its attractions.

Fedor Mikhailovich Dostoevsky (1821–81) Russian novelist.
Notes from the Underground

3 If we take in our hand any volume; of divinity or school metaphysics, for instance; let us ask, *Does it contain any abstract reasoning concerning quantity or number?* No. *Does it contain any experimental reasoning, concerning matter of fact and existence?* No. Commit it then to the flames: for it can contain nothing but sophistry and illusion.

David Hume (1711–76) Scottish philosopher.
An Enquiry Concerning Human Understanding

4 We are perpetually moralists, but we are geometricians only by chance. Our intercourse with intellectual nature is necessary; our speculations upon matter are voluntary, and at leisure.

Samuel Johnson (1709–84) British lexicographer.
Lives of the English Poets, 'Milton'

5 I refute it *thus*.

Samuel Johnson
Replying to Boswell's contention that they were unable to refute Bishop Berkeley's theory of matter, by kicking a large stone with his foot
Life of Johnson (J. Boswell), Vol. I

6 There are innumerable questions to which the inquisitive mind can in this state receive no answer: Why do you and I exist? Why was this world created? Since it was to be created, why was it not created sooner?

Samuel Johnson
Life of Johnson (J. Boswell), Vol. III

7 Do not all charms fly
At the mere touch of cold philosophy?

John Keats (1795–1821) British poet.
Lamia, II

8 Axioms in philosophy are not axioms until they are proved upon our pulses; we read fine things but never feel them to the full

until we have gone the same steps as the author.
John Keats
Letter to J. H. Reynolds, 3 May 1818

9 There will be no end to the troubles of states, or indeed, my dear Glaucon, of humanity itself, till philosophers become kings in this world, or till those we now call kings and rulers really and truly become philosophers.
Plato (429–347 BC) Greek philosopher.
Republic, Bk. 5

10 We thought philosophy ought to be patient and unravel people's mental blocks. Trouble with doing that is, once you've unravelled them, their heads fall off.
Frederic Raphael (1931–) British author.
The Glittering Prizes: A Double Life, III:2

11 Matter . . . a convenient formula for describing what happens where it isn't.
Bertrand Russell (1872–1970) British philosopher.
An Outline of Philosophy

12 Philosophy is the replacement of category-habits by category-disciplines.
Gilbert Ryle (1900–76) British philosopher.
The Concept of Mind, Introduction

13 It is a great advantage for a system of philosophy to be substantially true.
George Santayana (1863–1952) US philosopher.
The Unknowable

14 Philosophy is the product of wonder.
A. N. Whitehead (1861–1947) British philosopher.
Nature and Life, Ch. 1

15 The history of Western philosophy is, after all, no more than a series of footnotes to Plato's philosophy.
A. N. Whitehead
Attrib.

16 My advice to you is not to inquire why or whither, but just enjoy your ice-cream while it's on your plate, – that's my philosophy.
Thornton Wilder (1897–1975) US novelist and dramatist.
The Skin of Our Teeth, I

17 Philosophy, as we use the word, is a fight against the fascination which forms of expression exert upon us.
Ludwig Wittgenstein (1889–1951) Austrian philosopher.
The Blue Book

18 Philosophy is not a theory but an activity.
Ludwig Wittgenstein
Tractatus Logico-Philosophicus, Ch. 4

PHOTOGRAPHY

1 Photography can never grow up if it imitates some other medium. It has to walk alone; it has to be itself.
Berenice Abbott (1898–) US photographer.
Infinity, 'It Has to Walk Alone'

2 The camera cannot lie. But it can be an accessory to untruth.
Harold Evans (1928–) British journalist.
Pictures on a Page

3 As far as I knew, he had never taken a photograph before, and the summit of Everest was hardly the place to show him how.
Edmund Hillary (1919–) New Zealand mountaineer.
Referring to Tenzing Norgay, his companion on the conquest of Mt Everest (1953)
High Adventure

4 The modern pantheist not only sees the god in everything, he takes photographs of it.
D. H. Lawrence (1885–1930) British novelist.
St Mawr

5 I have for instance among my purchases . . . several original Mona Lisas and all painted (according to the Signature) by the great artist Kodak.
Spike Milligan (1918–) British comic actor and author.
A Dustbin of Milligan, 'Letters to Harry Secombe'

6 A photograph is not only an image (as a painting is an image), an interpretation of the real; it is also a trace, something directly stencilled off the real, like a footprint or a death mask.
Susan Sontag (1933–) US novelist and essayist.
On Photography

PLACES

See also Britain, Europe

1 Nothing and no one can destroy the Chinese people. They are relentless survivors. They are the oldest civilized people on earth. Their civilization passes through phases but its basic characteristics remain the same. They yield, they bend to the wind, but they never break.
Pearl Buck (1892–1973) US novelist.
China, Past and Present, Ch. 1

2 India is a geographical term. It is no more a united nation than the Equator.
Winston Churchill (1874–1965) British statesman.
Speech, Royal Albert Hall, 18 Mar 1931

3 There are few virtues which the Poles do not possess and there are few errors they have ever avoided.
Winston Churchill
Speech, House of Commons, 1945

4 Latins are tenderly enthusiastic. In Brazil they throw flowers at you. In Argentina they throw themselves.
Marlene Dietrich (Maria Magdalene von Losch; 1904–) German-born film star.
Newsweek, 24 Aug 1959

5 I find it hard to say, because when I was there it seemed to be shut.
Clement Freud (1924–) British Liberal politician and broadcaster.
On being asked for his opinion of New Zealand. Similar remarks have been attributed to others
BBC radio, 12 Apr 1978

6 From Greenland's icy mountains,
From India's coral strand,
Where Afric's sunny fountains
Roll down their golden sand.
Reginald Heber (1783–1826) British bishop and hymn writer.
From Greenland's Icy Mountains

7 Dublin, though a place much worse than London, is not so bad as Iceland.
Samuel Johnson (1709–84) British lexicographer.
Letter to Mrs Christopher Smart
Life of Johnson (J. Boswell), Vol. IV

8 Asia is not going to be civilized after the methods of the West. There is too much Asia and she is too old.
Rudyard Kipling (1865–1936) Indian-born British writer.
Life's Handicap, 'The Man Who Was'

9 On the road to Mandalay
Where the flyin'-fishes play.
Rudyard Kipling
The Road to Mandalay

10 And all lying mysteriously within the Australian underdark, that peculiar, lost weary aloofness of Australia. There was the vast town of Sydney. And it didn't seem to be real, it seemed to be sprinkled on the surface of a darkness into which it never penetrated.
D. H. Lawrence (1885–1930) British novelist.
Kangaroo, Ch. 1

11 So you're going to Australia! Well, I made twenty thousand pounds on my tour there, but of course *that* will never be done again. Still, it's a wonderful country, and you'll have a good time. What are you going to sing? All I can say is – sing 'em muck! It's all they can understand!
Nellie Melba (Helen Porter Mitchell; 1861–1931) Australian soprano.
Speaking to Clara Butt
Clara Butt: Her Life Story (W. H. Ponder)

12 I shook hands with a friendly Arab . . . I still have my right hand to prove it.
Spike Milligan (1918–) British comic actor and author.
A Dustbin of Milligan, 'Letters to Harry Secombe'

13 Jerusalem the golden,
With milk and honey blest,
Beneath thy contemplation
Sink heart and voice opprest.
John Mason Neale (1818–66) British churchman.
Jerusalem the Golden

14 Once a jolly swagman camped by a billy-bong,

Under the shade of a coolibah tree,
And he sang as he sat and waited for his billy-boil,
'You'll come a-waltzing, Matilda, with me.'
Andrew Barton Paterson (1864–1941) Australian journalist and poet.
Waltzing Matilda

15 Even the Hooligan was probably invented in China centuries before we thought of him.
Saki (Hector Hugh Munro; 1870–1916) British writer.
Reginald on House-Parties

16 Great God! this is an awful place.
Captain Robert Falcon Scott (1868–1912) British explorer.
Referring to the South Pole
Journal, 17 Jan 1912

17 The South African Police would leave no stone unturned to see that nothing disturbed the even terror of their lives.
Tom Sharpe (1928–) British novelist.
Indecent Exposure, Ch. 1

18 Cusins is a very nice fellow, certainly: nobody would ever guess that he was born in Australia.
George Bernard Shaw (1856–1950) Irish dramatist and critic.
Major Barbara, I

19 The Japanese have perfected good manners and made them indistinguishable from rudeness.
Paul Theroux (1941–) US-born writer.
The Great Railway Bazaar, Ch. 2

20 I'm Charley's aunt from Brazil, where the nuts come from.
Brandon Thomas (1856–1914) British actor and dramatist.
Charley's Aunt, I

PLAYS

See also acting, actors, criticism, literature, Shakespeare, theatre, writers, writing

1 Now a whole is that which has a beginning, a middle, and an end.
Aristotle (384–322 BC) Greek philosopher.
Referring specifically to the dramatic form of tragedy
Poetics, Ch. 7

2 One of Edward's Mistresses was Jane Shore, who has had a play written about her, but it is a tragedy and therefore not worth reading.
Jane Austen (1775–1817) British novelist.
The History of England

3 In the theatre the audience want to be surprised – but by things that they expect.
Tristan Bernard (1866–1947) French dramatist.
Contes, Repliques et Bon Mots

4 Prologues precede the piece – in mournful verse;

As undertakers – walk before the hearse.
David Garrick (1717–79) British actor and manager.
Apprentice, Prologue

5 He always hurries to the main event and
whisks his audience into the middle of things
as though they knew already.
Horace (Quintus Horatius Flaccus; 65–8 BC) Roman poet.
Ars Poetica

6 I think you would have been very glad if I
had written it.
Alexis Piron (1689–1773) French poet and dramatist.
Discussing Voltaire's *Sémiramis* with him after its poor recep-
tion on the first night
Cyclopaedia of Anecdotes (K. Arvine)

7 Depending upon shock tactics is easy,
whereas writing a good play is difficult. Pubic
hair is no substitute for wit.
J. B. Priestley (1894–1984) British novelist.
Outcries and Asides

8 My soul; sit thou a patient looker-on;
Judge not the play before the play is done:
Her plot hath many changes, every day
Speaks a new scene; the last act crowns the
play.
Francis Quarles (1592–1644) English poet.
Epigram, Respice Finem

9 Rehearsing a play is making the word flesh.
Publishing a play is reversing the process.
Peter Shaffer (1926–) British dramatist.
Equus, Note

10 If it be true that good wine needs no bush,
'tis true that a good play needs no epilogue.
William Shakespeare (1564–1616) English dramatist.
As You Like It, Epilogue

11 The play's the thing
Wherein I'll catch the conscience of the King.
William Shakespeare
Hamlet, II:2

12 A good many inconveniences attend play-
going in any large city, but the greatest of
them is usually the play itself.
Kenneth Tynan (1927–80) British theatre critic.
New York Herald Tribune

13 A novel is a static thing that one moves
through; a play is a dynamic thing that moves
past one.
Kenneth Tynan
Curtains

14 The play was a great success, but the
audience was a disaster.
Oscar Wilde (1854–1900) Irish-born British dramatist.
Referring to a play that had recently failed
Attrib.

PLEASURE

See also debauchery, happiness, leisure, merrymaking

1 No pleasure without pain.
Proverb

2 And if the following day, he chance to find
A new repast, or an untasted spring,
Blesses his stars, and thinks it luxury.
Joseph Addison (1672–1719) British essayist.
Cato, I:4

3 One half of the world cannot understand the
pleasures of the other.
Jane Austen (1775–1817) British novelist.
Emma, Ch. 9

4 Then I commended mirth, because a man
hath no better thing under the sun, than to
eat, and to drink, and to be merry: for that
shall abide with him of his labour the days of
his life, which God giveth him under the sun.
Bible: Ecclesiastes
8:15

5 He who bends to himself a Joy
Doth the wingèd life destroy;
But he who kisses the Joy as it flies
Lives in Eternity's sunrise.
William Blake (1757–1827) British poet.
Gnomic Verses

6 Pleasure after all is a safer guide than either
right or duty.
Samuel Butler (1835–1902) British writer.
The Way of All Flesh, Ch. 19

7 Though sages may pour out their wisdom's
treasure,
There is no sterner moralist than Pleasure.
Lord Byron (1788–1824) British poet.
Don Juan, III

8 In Xanadu did Kubla Khan
A stately pleasure-dome decree:
Where Alph, the sacred river, ran
Through caverns measureless to man
Down to a sunless sea.
Samuel Taylor Coleridge (1772–1834) British poet.
Kubla Khan

9 It was a miracle of rare device,
A sunny pleasure-dome with caves of ice!
Samuel Taylor Coleridge
Kubla Khan

10 Nothing can permanently please, which does
not contain in itself the reason why it is so,
and not otherwise.
Samuel Taylor Coleridge
Biographia Literaria, Ch. 14

11 For present joys are more to flesh and blood
Than a dull prospect of a distant good.
John Dryden (1631–1700) British poet and dramatist.
The Hind and the Panther, III

12 The art of pleasing consists in being pleased.
William Hazlitt (1778–1830) British essayist.
On Manner

13 People must not do things for fun. We are

not here for fun. There is no reference to fun in any Act of Parliament.

A. P. Herbert (1890–1971) British writer and politician.
Uncommon Law

14 Pleasure is very seldom found where it is sought; our brightest blazes of gladness are commonly kindled by unexpected sparks.

Samuel Johnson (1709–84) British lexicographer.
The Idler

15 No man is a hypocrite in his pleasures.

Samuel Johnson
Life of Johnson (J. Boswell), Vol. IV

16 If I had no duties, and no reference to futurity, I would spend my life in driving briskly in a post-chaise with a pretty woman.

Samuel Johnson
Life of Johnson (J. Boswell), Vol. III

17 Give me books, fruit, French wine and fine weather and a little music out of doors, played by somebody I do not know.

John Keats (1795–1821) British poet.
Letter to Fanny Keats, 29 Aug 1819

18 Life would be tolerable, were it not for its amusements.

George Cornewall Lewis (1806–63) British statesman and writer.
The Perpetual Pessimist (Sagittarius and George)

19 A little of what you fancy does you good.

Marie Lloyd (1870–1922) British music-hall singer.
Song title

20 Who loves not wine, woman and song, Remains a fool his whole life long.

Martin Luther (1483–1546) German Protestant.
Attrib.

21 My candle burns at both ends;
It will not last the night;
But ah, my foes, and oh my friends –
It gives a lovely light!

Edna St Vincent Millay (1892–1950) US poet.
A Few Figs from Thistles, 'First Fig'

22 To sport with Amaryllis in the shade, Or with the tangles of Neaera's hair.

John Milton (1608–74) English poet.
Lycidas

23 Hence, vain deluding Joys,
The brood of Folly without father bred!

John Milton
Il Penseroso

24 Great lords have their pleasures, but the people have fun.

Baron de Montesquieu (1688–1755) French writer.
Pensées diverses

25 I wish thee as much pleasure in the reading, as I had in the writing.

Francis Quarles (1592–1644) English poet.
Emblems, 'To the Reader'

26 Pleasures are all alike simply considered in

themselves . . . He that takes pleasure to hear sermons enjoys himself as much as he that hears plays.

John Selden (1584–1654) English historian.
Table Talk

27 Pleasure is nothing else but the intermission of pain.

John Selden
Table Talk

28 A Good Time Was Had by All.

Stevie Smith (Florence Margaret Smith; 1902–71) British poet.
Book title

29 Everyone is dragged on by their favourite pleasure.

Virgil (Publius Vergilius Maro; 70–19 BC) Roman poet.
Eclogue, Bk. II

30 All the things I really like to do are either immoral, illegal, or fattening.

Alexander Woollcott (1887–1943) US journalist.
Attrib.

31 Pleasures newly found are sweet When they lie about our feet.

William Wordsworth (1770–1850) British poet.
To the Small Celandine

POETRY

See also criticism, inspiration, literature, poetry and prose, poets

1 For this reason poetry is something more philosophical and more worthy of serious attention than history.

Aristotle (384–322 BC) Greek philosopher.
Poetics, Ch. 9

2 A criticism of life under the conditions fixed for such a criticism by the laws of poetic truth and poetic beauty.

Matthew Arnold (1822–88) British poet and critic.
Essays in Criticism, Second Series, 'The Study of Poetry'

3 I think it will be found that the grand style arises in poetry, when a noble nature, poetically gifted, treats with simplicity or with severity a serious subject.

Matthew Arnold
Closing words
On Translating Homer

4 The difference between genuine poetry and the poetry of Dryden, Pope, and all their school, is briefly this: their poetry is conceived and composed in their wits, genuine poetry is conceived and composed in the soul.

Matthew Arnold
Thomas Gray

5 Now Ireland has her madness and her weather still,

For poetry makes nothing happen.
W. H. Auden (1907–73) British poet.
In Memory of W. B. Yeats, II

6 Poetry is as much a part of the universe as mathematics and physics. It is not a cleverer device or recreation, unless the Eternal is clever.
Edmund Blunden (1896–1974) British poet.
Speech on his election as Professor of Poetry at Oxford University, 1966

7 Nothing so difficult as a beginning
In poesy, unless perhaps the end.
Lord Byron (1788–1824) British poet.
Don Juan, IV

8 I have nothing to say, I am saying it, and that is poetry.
John Cage (1912–) US composer.
In *The Sunday Times* (quoted by Cyril Connolly), 10 Sept 1972

9 For the godly poet must be chaste himself, but there is no need for his verses to be so.
Catullus (c. 84–c. 54 BC) Roman poet.
Carmina, XVI

10 That willing suspension of disbelief for the moment, which constitutes poetic faith.
Samuel Taylor Coleridge (1772–1834) British poet.
Biographia Literaria, Ch. 14

11 Poetry's unnat'ral; no man ever talked poetry 'cept a beadle on boxin' day.
Charles Dickens (1812–70) British novelist.
Pickwick Papers, Ch. 33

12 I am afeered that werges on the poetical, Sammy.
Charles Dickens
Said by Sam Weller
Pickwick Papers, Ch. 33

13 Poetry is not a turning loose of emotion, but an escape from emotion; it is not the expression of personality, but an escape from personality.
T. S. Eliot (1888–1965) US-born British poet and dramatist.
Tradition and the Individual Talent

14 All one's inventions are true, you can be sure of that. Poetry is as exact a science as geometry.
Gustave Flaubert (1821–80) French novelist.
Letter to Louise Colet, 14 Aug 1853

15 We all write poems; it is simply that poets are the ones who write in words.
John Fowles (1926–) British novelist.
The French Lieutenant's Woman, Ch. 19

16 Writing free verse is like playing tennis with the net down.
Robert Frost (1875–1963) US poet.
Speech, Milton Academy, 17 May 1935

17 Rightly thought of there is poetry in peaches . . . even when they are canned.
Harley Granville-Barker (1877–1946) British actor and dramatist.
The Madras House, I

18 If Galileo had said in verse that the world moved, the Inquisition might have let him alone.
Thomas Hardy (1840–1928) British novelist.
The Later Years of Thomas Hardy (F. E. Hardy)

19 Even when poetry has a meaning, as it usually has, it may be inadvisable to draw it out . . . Perfect understanding will sometimes almost extinguish pleasure.
A. E. Housman (1859–1936) British scholar and poet.
The Name and Nature of Poetry

20 'Why Sir, it is much easier to say what it is not. We all *know* what light is; but it is not easy to *tell* what it is.'
Samuel Johnson (1709–84) British lexicographer.
When asked, 'What is poetry'
Life of Johnson (J. Boswell), Vol. III

21 A drainless shower
Of light is poesy; 'tis the supreme of power;
'Tis might half slumb'ring on its own right arm.
John Keats (1795–1821) British poet.
Sleep and Poetry

22 A long poem is a test of invention which I take to be the Polar star of poetry, as fancy is the sails, and imagination the rudder.
John Keats
Letter to Benjamin Bailey, 8 Oct 1817

23 We hate poetry that has a palpable design upon us – and if we do not agree, seems to put its hand in its breeches pocket. Poetry should be great and unobtrusive, a thing which enters into one's soul, and does not startle or amaze it with itself, but with its subject.
John Keats
Letter to J. H. Reynolds, 3 Feb 1818

24 If poetry comes not as naturally as leaves to a tree it had better not come at all.
John Keats
Letter to John Taylor, 27 Feb 1818

25 When power narrows the areas of man's concern, poetry reminds him of the richness and diversity of his existence.
John Fitzgerald Kennedy (1917–63) US statesman.
Address at Dedication of the Robert Frost Library, 26 Oct 1963

26 Perhaps no person can be a poet, or can even enjoy poetry, without a certain unsoundness of mind.
Lord Macaulay (1800–59) British historian.
Literary Essays Contributed to the 'Edinburgh Review', 'Milton'

27 Poem me no poems.
Rose Macaulay (1889–1958) British writer.
Poetry Review, Autumn 1963

28 Poetry is a comforting piece of fiction set to more or less lascivious music.

H. L. Mencken (1880–1956) US journalist.
Prejudices, 'The Poet and his Art'

29 Blest pair of Sirens, pledges of Heaven's joy, Sphere-born harmonious sisters, Voice and Verse.

John Milton (1608–74) English poet.
At a Solemn Music

30 Rhyme being no necessary adjunct or true ornament of poem or good verse, in longer works especially, but the invention of a barbarous age, to set off wretched matter and lame metre.

John Milton
Paradise Lost, The Verse. Preface to 1668 ed.

31 The troublesome and modern bondage of Rhyming.

John Milton
Paradise Lost, The Verse. Preface to 1668 ed.

32 . . . poetry, 'The Cinderella of the Arts.'

Harriet Monroe (1860–1936) US poet and editor.
Famous American Women (Hope Stoddard), 'Harriet Monroe'

33 Above all I am not concerned with Poetry. My subject is War, and the pity of War. The Poetry is in the pity.

Wilfred Owen (1893–1918) British poet.
Poems, Preface

34 Curst be the verse, how well so'er it flow, That tends to make one worthy man my foe.

Alexander Pope (1688–1744) British poet.
Epistle to Dr. Arbuthnot

35 For three years, out of key with his time, He strove to resuscitate the dead art Of poetry to maintain 'the sublime' In the old sense. Wrong from the start.

Ezra Pound (1885–1972) US poet.
Pour l'élection de son sépulcre

36 It is a perfectly possible means of overcoming chaos.

I. A. Richards (1893–1979) British critic.
Science and Poetry

37 A sonnet is a moment's monument, – Memorial from the Soul's eternity To one dead deathless hour.

Dante Gabriel Rossetti (1828–82) British painter and poet.
The House of Life, Introduction

38 What is poetry? The suggestion, by the imagination, of noble grounds for the noble emotions.

John Ruskin (1819–1900) British art critic and writer.
Modern Painters, Vol. III

39 The truest poetry is the most feigning.

William Shakespeare (1564–1616) English dramatist.
As You Like It, III:3

40 The poet's eye, in a fine frenzy rolling, Doth glance from heaven to earth, from earth to heaven; And as imagination bodies forth The forms of things unknown, the poet's pen Turns them to shapes, and gives to airy nothing A local habitation and a name.

William Shakespeare
A Midsummer Night's Dream, V:1

41 Not marble, nor the gilded monuments Of princes, shall outlive this powerful rhyme.

William Shakespeare
Sonnet 55

42 The lunatic, the lover, and the poet, Are of imagination all compact.

William Shakespeare
A Midsummer Night's Dream, V:1

43 Poetry is the record of the best and happiest moments of the happiest and best minds.

Percy Bysshe Shelley (1792–1822) British poet.
A Defence of Poetry

44 One of the purposes of poetry is to show the dimensions of man that are, as Sir Arthur Eddington said 'midway in scale between the atom and the star.'

Edith Sitwell (1887–1964) British poet and writer.
Rhyme and Reason

45 My poems are hymns of praise to the glory of life.

Edith Sitwell
Collected Poems, 'Some Notes on My Poetry'

46 A man does not write poems about what he knows, but about what he does not know.

Robin Skelton (1925–) British academic.
Teach Yourself Poetry

47 These poems, with all their crudities, doubts, and confusions, are written for the love of Man and in praise of God, and I'd be a damn' fool if they weren't.

Dylan Thomas (1914–53) Welsh poet.
Collected Poems, Note

48 Having verse set to music is like looking at a painting through a stained glass window.

Paul Valéry (1871–1945) French poet and writer.
Attrib.

49 Hence no force however great can stretch a cord however fine into an horizontal line which is accurately straight: there will always be a bending downwards.

William Whewell (1794–1866) British philosopher and mathematician.
An example of unintentional versification
Elementary Treatise on Mechanics (1819 edition), Ch. 4

50 No one will ever get at my verses who insists upon viewing them as a literary performance.

Walt Whitman (1819–92) US poet.
A Backward Glance O'er Travel'd Roads

51 I would rather have written those lines than take Quebec.

James Wolfe (1727–59) British general.
Referring to Gray's Elegy, on the eve of the Battle of Quebec, 1759
Attrib.

52 Poetry is the spontaneous overflow of powerful feelings: it takes its origin from emotion recollected in tranquillity.

William Wordsworth (1770–1850) British poet.
Lyrics Ballads, Preface

53 Out of the quarrel with others we make rhetoric; out of the quarrel with ourselves we make poetry.

W. B. Yeats (1865–1939) Irish poet.
Essay

POETRY AND PROSE

See also poetry, prose

1 Poetry is not the proper antithesis to prose, but to science. Poetry is opposed to science, and prose to metre.

Samuel Taylor Coleridge (1772–1834) British poet.
Lectures and Notes of 1818, I

2 I wish our clever young poets would remember my homely definitions of prose and poetry; that is, prose = words in their best order; – poetry = the best words in the best order.

Samuel Taylor Coleridge
Table Talk

3 Prose on certain occasions can bear a great deal of poetry: on the other hand, poetry sinks and swoons under a moderate weight of prose.

Walter Savage Landor (1775–1864) British poet and writer.
Imaginary Conversations, 'Archdeacon Hare and Walter Landor'

4 For to write good prose is an affair of good manners. It is, unlike verse, a civil art.... Poetry is baroque.

W. Somerset Maugham (1874–1965) British novelist.
The Summing Up

5 Poetry is to prose as dancing is to walking.

John Wain (1925–) British novelist and poet.
Talk, BBC radio, 13 Jan 1976

6 The poet gives us his essence, but prose takes the mould of the body and mind entire.

Virginia Woolf (1882–1941) British novelist.
The Captain's Death Bed, 'Reading'

7 There neither is, nor can be, any *essential* difference between the language of prose and metrical composition.

William Wordsworth (1770–1850) British poet.
Lyrical Ballads, Preface

8 O'CONNOR. How are you?

w.b.y. Not very well, I can only write prose today.

W. B. Yeats (1865–1939) Irish poet.
Attrib.

POETS

See also Byron, criticism, poetry, Shakespeare, writers

1 It always seems to me that the right sphere for Shelley's genius was the sphere of music, not of poetry.

Matthew Arnold (1822–88) British poet and critic.
Maurice de Guérin, Footnote

2 He spoke, and loos'd our heart in tears.
He laid us as we lay at birth
On the cool flowery lap of earth.

Matthew Arnold
Referring to Wordsworth
Memorial Verses

3 Time may restore us in his course
Goethe's sage mind and Byron's force:
But where will Europe's latter hour
Again find Wordsworth's healing power?

Matthew Arnold
Memorial Verses

4 Earth, receive an honoured guest:
William Yeats is laid to rest.
Let the Irish vessel lie
Emptied of its poetry.

W. H. Auden (1907–73) British poet.
In Memory of W. B. Yeats, III

5 Poets and painters are outside the class system, or rather they constitute a special class of their own, like the circus people and the gipsies.

Gerald Brenan (Edward Fitzgerald Brenan; 1894–1987) British writer.
Thoughts in a Dry Season, 'Writing'

6 The Fleshly School of Poetry.

Robert Williams Buchanan (1841–1901) British poet and writer.
Referring to Swinburne, William Morris, D. G. Rossetti, etc.
Title of article in the *Contemporary Review*, Oct 1871

7 A poet without love were a physical and metaphysical impossibility.

Thomas Carlyle (1795–1881) Scottish historian and essayist.
Critical and Miscellaneous Essays, 'Burns'

8 He could not think up to the height of his own towering style.

G. K. Chesterton (1874–1936) British writer.
Speaking of Tennyson
The Victorian Age in Literature, Ch. 3

9 A true poet does not bother to be poetical. Nor does a nursery gardener scent his roses.

Jean Cocteau (1889–1963) French poet and artist.
Professional Secrets

10 With Donne, whose muse on dromedary trots,

Wreathe iron pokers into true-love knots.
Samuel Taylor Coleridge (1772–1834) British poet.
On Donne's Poetry

11 The misfortune is, that he has begun to write verses without very well understanding what metre is.
Samuel Taylor Coleridge
Referring to Tennyson
Table Talk

12 Immature poets imitate; mature poets steal.
T. S. Eliot (1888–1965) US-born British poet and dramatist.
Philip Massinger

13 *Hugo – hélas!*
André Gide (1869–1951) French novelist.
Replying to an inquiry as to whom he considered the finest poet of the 19th century.
André Gide–Paul Valéry Correspondence 1890–1942

14 To be a poet is a condition rather than a profession.
Robert Graves (1895–1985) British poet and novelist.
Horizon

15 Shelley and Keats were the last English poets who were at all up to date in their chemical knowledge.
J. B. S. Haldane (1892–1964) British geneticist.
Daedalus or Science and the Future

16 He talked on for ever; and you wished him to talk on for ever.
William Hazlitt (1778–1830) British essayist.
Referring to Coleridge
Lectures on the English Poets, Lecture VIII, 'On the Living Poets'

17 Not gods, nor men, nor even booksellers have put up with poets' being second-rate.
Horace (Quintus Horatius Flaccus; 65–8 BC) Roman poet.
Ars Poetica

18 Sir, there is no settling the point of precedency between a louse and a flea.
Samuel Johnson (1709–84) British lexicographer.
When Maurice Morgann asked him who he considered to be the better poet – Smart or Derrick
Life of Johnson (J. Boswell), Vol. IV

19 He was dull in a new way, and that made many people think him *great*.
Samuel Johnson
Referring to the poet Thomas Gray
Life of Johnson (J. Boswell), Vol. II

20 Milton, Madam, was a genius that could cut a Colossus from a rock; but could not carve heads upon cherry-stones.
Samuel Johnson
When Miss Hannah More had wondered why Milton could write the epic *Paradise Lost* but only very poor sonnets
Life of Johnson (J. Boswell), Vol. IV

21 Walt Whitman who laid end to end words never seen in each other's company before outside of a dictionary.
David Lodge (1935–) British author.
Changing Places, Ch. 5

22 For ne'er
Was flattery lost on poet's ear:
A simple race! they waste their toil
For the vain tribute of a smile.
Walter Scott (1771–1832) Scottish novelist.
The Lay of the Last Minstrel, IV

23 There have been many most excellent poets that have never versified, and now swarm many versifiers that need never answer to the name of poets.
Philip Sidney (1554–86) English poet and courtier.
The Defence of Poesy

24 People sometimes divide others into those you laugh at and those you laugh with. The young Auden was someone you could laugh-at-with.
Stephen Spender (1909–) British poet.
Address, W. H. Auden's memorial service, Oxford, 27 Oct 1973

25 I hate the whole race . . . There is no believing a word they say – your professional poets, I mean – there never existed a more worthless set than Byron and his friends for example.
Duke of Wellington (1769–1852) British general and statesman.
Lady Salisbury's diary, 26 Oct 1833

26 That William Blake
Who beat upon the wall
Till Truth obeyed his call.
W. B. Yeats (1865–1939) Irish poet.
An Acre of Grass

POLICE

1 When constabulary duty's to be done –
A policeman's lot is not a happy one.
W. S. Gilbert (1836–1911) British dramatist.
The Pirates of Penzance, II

2 Policemen are numbered in case they get lost.
Spike Milligan (1918–) British comic actor and author.
The Last Goon Show of All

3 A thing of duty is a boy for ever.
Flann O'Brien (Brian O'Nolan; 1911–66) Irish novelist and journalist.
About policemen always seeming to be young-looking
The Listener, 24 Feb 1977

4 Reading isn't an occupation we encourage among police officers. We try to keep the paper work down to a minimum.
Joe Orton (1933–67) British dramatist.
Loot, II

5 My father didn't create you to arrest me.
Lord Peel (1829–1912) British politician.
Protesting against his arrest by the police, recently established by his father
Attrib.

6 One always has the air of someone who is lying when one speaks to a policeman.
Charles-Louis Philippe (1874–1909) French novelist.
Les Chroniques du canard sauvage

POLITICIANS

See also Churchill, compliments, government, Hitler, Houses of Parliament, insults, politics

1 It is fitting that we should have buried the Unknown Prime Minister by the side of the Unknown Soldier.
Herbert Henry Asquith (1852–1928) British statesman.
Said at Bonar Law's funeral, 5 Nov 1923
Attrib.

2 No man has come so near our definition of a constitutional statesman – the powers of a first-rate man and the creed of a second-rate man.
Walter Bagehot (1826–77) British economist and journalist.
Historical Essays, 'The Character of Sir Robert Peel'

3 He believes, with all his heart and soul and strength, that there *is* such a thing as truth; he has the soul of a martyr with the intellect of an advocate.
Walter Bagehot
Referring to Gladstone
Historical Essays, 'Mr Gladstone'

4 If I rescued a child from drowning, the Press would no doubt headline the story 'Benn grabs child'.
Tony Benn (1925–) British politician.
The Observer, 'Sayings of the Week', 2 Mar 1975

5 A dessicated calculating machine.
Aneurin Bevan (1897–1960) British Labour politician.
Referring to Hugh Gaitskell
Hugh Gaitskell (W. T. Rodgers)

6 There is no reason to attack the monkey when the organ-grinder is present.
Aneurin Bevan
The 'monkey' was Selwyn Lloyd; the 'organ-grinder' was Harold Macmillan
Speech, House of Commons

7 She is trying to wear the trousers of Winston Churchill.
Leonid Brezhnev (1906–82) Soviet statesman.
Referring to Margaret Thatcher
Speech, 1979

8 He was not merely a chip of the old block, but the old block itself.
Edmund Burke (1729–97) British politician.
Referring to William Pitt the Younger's first speech in the House of Commons, 26 Feb 1781
Attrib.

9 Mr Macmillan is the best prime minister we have.
R. A. Butler (1902–82) British Conservative politician.
Often quoted in the form above. In fact, Butler simply answered 'Yes' to the question 'Would you say that this is the best prime minister we have?'
Interview, London Airport, Dec 1955

10 Politics and the fate of mankind are shaped by men without ideals and without greatness. Men who have greatness within them don't go in for politics.
Albert Camus (1913–60) French existentialist writer.
Notebooks, 1935–42

11 Pitt is to Addington
As London is to Paddington.
George Canning (1770–1827) British statesman.
The Oracle

12 The seagreen Incorruptible.
Thomas Carlyle (1795–1881) Scottish historian and essayist.
Referring to Robespierre
History of the French Revolution, Pt. II, Bk. IV, Ch. 4

13 She is clearly the best man among them.
Barbara Castle (1910–) British politician.
Referring to Margaret Thatcher
The Castle Diaries

14 An old man in a hurry.
Lord Randolph Churchill (1849–95) British Conservative politician.
Referring to Gladstone
Speech, June 1886

15 I remember, when I was a child, being taken to the celebrated Barnum's circus, which contained an exhibition of freaks and monstrosities, but the exhibit . . . which I most desired to see was the one described as 'The Boneless Wonder'. My parents judged that that spectacle would be too revolting and demoralising for my youthful eyes, and I have waited 50 years to see the boneless wonder sitting on the Treasury Bench.
Winston Churchill (1874–1965) British statesman.
Referring to Ramsey MacDonald
Speech, House of Commons, 28 Jan 1931

16 I have never seen a human being who more perfectly represented the modern conception of a robot.
Winston Churchill
Referring to the Soviet statesman Molotov
The Second World War

17 In Franklin Roosevelt there died the greatest American friend we have ever known and the greatest champion of freedom who has ever brought help and comfort from the New World to the Old.
Winston Churchill
The Second World War

18 a politician is an arse upon which everyone has sat except a man
e. e. cummings (1894–1962) US poet.
A Politician

19 In private conversation he tries on speeches like a man trying on ties in his bedroom to see how he would look in them.
Lionel Curtis (1872–1955) British writer.
Referring to Winston Churchill
Letter to Nancy Astor, 1912

20 Not even a public figure. A man of no experience. And of the utmost insignificance.
Lord Curzon (1859–1925) British politician.
Referring to Stanley Baldwin on his appointment as Prime Minister
Curzon: The Last Phase (Harold Nicolson)

21 When I was a boy I was told that anybody could become President of the United States. I am beginning to believe it.
Clarence Darrow (1857–1938) US lawyer.
Attrib.

22 If a traveller were informed that such a man was leader of the House of Commons, he may well begin to comprehend how the Egyptians worshipped an insect.
Benjamin Disraeli (1804–81) British statesman.
Referring to Lord John Russell
Attrib.

23 There are two problems in my life. The political ones are insoluble and the economic ones are incomprehensible.
Alec Douglas-Home (1903–) British statesman.
Speech, Jan 1964

24 He is used to dealing with estate workers. I cannot see how anyone can say he is out of touch.
Lady Caroline Douglas-Home (1937–) Daughter of Alec Douglas-Home.
Referring to her father's suitability for his new role as prime minister
Daily Herald, 21 Oct 1963 (Jon Akass)

25 For Politicians neither love nor hate.
John Dryden (1631–1700) British poet and dramatist.
Absalom and Achitophel, I

26 Since a politician never believes what he says, he is surprised when others believe him.
Charles De Gaulle (1890–1970) French general and statesman.
Attrib.

27 In order to become the master, the politician poses as the servant.
Charles De Gaulle
Attrib.

28 I have come to the conclusion that politics are too serious a matter to be left to the politicians.
Charles De Gaulle
Attrib.

29 I always voted at my party's call,
And I never thought of thinking for myself at all.
W. S. Gilbert (1836–1911) British dramatist.
HMS Pinafore, I

30 The prospect of a lot
Of dull MPs in close proximity,
All thinking for themselves is what
No man can face with equanimity.
W. S. Gilbert
Iolanthe, I

31 'Do you pray for the senators, Dr Hale?' 'No, I look at the senators and I pray for the country.'
Edward Everett Hale (1822–1909) US author and clergyman.
New England Indian Summer (Van Wyck Brooks)

32 For the past few months she has been charging about like some bargain-basement Boadicea.
Denis Healey (1917–) British Labour politician.
Referring to Margaret Thatcher
Observer, 'Sayings of the Week', 7 Nov 1982

33 I am the Gromyko of the Labour party.
Denis Healey
Alluding to Andrei Gromyko (1909–), Soviet statesman who was foreign minister from 1957 to 1985
Attrib.

34 There is one statesman of the present day, of whom I always say that he would have escaped making the blunders that he has made if he had only ridden more in omnibuses.
Arthur Helps (1813–75) British historian.
Friends in Council

35 He would rather follow public opinion than lead it.
Harry Hopkins (1890–1946) US politician.
Referring to Roosevelt
Attrib.

36 If a man were to go by chance at the same time with Burke under a shed, to shun a shower, he would say – 'this is an extraordinary man.'
Samuel Johnson (1709–84) British lexicographer.
Referring to Edmund Burke
Life of Johnson (J. Boswell), Vol. IV

37 Do you realize the responsibility I carry? I'm the only person standing between Nixon and the White House.
John Fitzgerald Kennedy (1917–63) US statesman.
Said to Arthur Schlesinger, 13 Oct 1960; Richard Nixon was the Republican candidate in the 1960 US Presidential election
A Thousand Days (Arthur M. Schlesinger, Jnr)

38 This goat-footed bard, this half-human visitor to our age from the hag-ridden magic and enchanted woods of Celtic antiquity.
John Maynard Keynes (1883–1946) British economist.
Referring to Lloyd George
Essays and Sketches in Biography

39 Politicians are the same everywhere. They promise to build bridges even where there are no rivers.
Nikita Khrushchev (1894–1971) Soviet statesman.
Attrib., Oct 1960

40 We will bury you.
Nikita Khrushchev
Said at a reception at the Kremlin, 26 Nov 1956

41 Political renegades always start their career

of treachery as 'the best men of all parties' and end up in the Tory knackery.

Neil Kinnock (1942–) British politician.
Speech, Welsh Labour Party Conference, 1985

42 We have heard of people being thrown to the wolves, but never before have we heard of a man being thrown to the wolves with a bargain on the part of the wolves that they would not eat him.

Bonar Law (1858–1923) British statesman.
Referring to the fact that the then war minister, Col Seely, had offered his resignation
Speech, House of Commons, Mar 1914

43 Look at that man's eyes. You will hear more of him later.

Bonar Law
Referring to Mussolini
Attrib.

44 A politician is a person with whose politics you don't agree; if you agree with him he is a statesman.

David Lloyd George (1863–1945) British Liberal statesman.
Attrib.

45 Poor Bonar can't bear being called a liar. Now I don't mind.

David Lloyd George
Referring to Bonar Law, prime minister 1922–23
Stanley Baldwin (G. M. Young)

46 He saw foreign policy through the wrong end of a municipal drainpipe.

David Lloyd George
Referring to Neville Chamberlain
The Fine Art of Political Wit (Harris), Ch. 6

47 When you're abroad you're a statesman: when you're at home you're just a politician.

Harold Macmillan (1894–1986) British statesman.
Speech, 1958

48 So restless Cromwell could not cease
In the inglorious arts of peace.

Andrew Marvell (1621–78) English poet.
An Horatian Ode upon Cromwell's Return from Ireland

49 It is very unfair to expect a politician to live in private up to the statements he makes in public.

W. Somerset Maugham (1874–1965) British novelist.
The Circle

50 Sit down, man. You're a bloody tragedy.

James Maxton (1885–1946) Scottish Labour leader.
Said to Ramsay MacDonald when he made his last speech in Parliament
Attrib.

51 The rogue elephant among British prime ministers.

Dr Kenneth Morgan (1934–) British historian.
Referring to Lloyd George
Life of David Lloyd George

52 I am not and never have been, a man of the

right. My position was on the left and is now in the centre of politics.

Oswald Mosley (1896–1980) British politician.
The Times, 26 Apr 1968

53 Argue as you please, you are nowhere, that grand old man, the Prime Minister, insists on the other thing.

Lord Northcote (1818–87) British statesman.
Referring to Gladstone; the phrase, and its acronym GOM, became his nickname – temporarily reversed to MOG ('Murderer of Gordon') in 1885, after the death of General Gordon at Khartoum
Speech, Liverpool, 12 Apr 1882

54 How could they tell?

Dorothy Parker (1893–1967) US writer.
Reaction to news of the death of Calvin Coolidge, US President 1923–29; also attributed to H. L. Mencken
You Might As Well Live (J. Keats)

55 A statesman is a politician who places himself at the service of the nation. A politician is a statesman who places the nation at his service.

Georges Pompidou (1911–74) French statesman.
The Observer, 'Sayings of the Year', 30 Dec 1973

56 All political lives, unless they are cut off in mid-stream at a happy juncture, end in failure.

Enoch Powell (1912–) British politician.
Sunday Times, 6 Nov 1977

57 Above any other position of eminence, that of Prime Minister is filled by fluke.

Enoch Powell
The Observer, 'Sayings of the Week', 8 Mar 1987

58 A number of anxious dwarfs trying to grill a whale.

J. B. Priestley (1894–1984) British novelist.
Outcries and Asides

59 Coolidge is a better example of evolution than either Bryan or Darrow, for he knows when not to talk, which is the biggest asset the monkey possesses over the human.

Will Rogers (1879–1935) US actor and humorist.
Saturday Review, 'A Rogers Thesaurus', 25 Aug 1962

60 Stalin hates the guts of all your top people. He thinks he likes me better, and I hope he will continue to do so.

Franklin D. Roosevelt (1882–1945) US Democratic president.
The Hinge of Fate (Winston S. Churchill), Ch. 11

61 Get thee glass eyes,
And, like a scurvy politician, seem
To see the things thou dost not.

William Shakespeare (1564–1616) English dramatist.
King Lear, IV:6

62 He knows nothing; and he thinks he knows everything. That points clearly to a political career.

George Bernard Shaw (1856–1950) Irish dramatist and critic.
Major Barbara, III

63 The Right Honourable gentleman is indebted to his memory for his jests, and to his imagination for his facts.

Richard Brinsley Sheridan (1751–1816) British dramatist.
Replying to a speech in the House of Commons
Attrib.

64 I will not accept if nominated, and will not serve if elected.

General William Sherman (1820–91) US politician and president.
Replying to a request that he accept the Republican presidential nomination
Attrib.

65 He was the Messiah of the new age, and his crucifixion was yet to come.

George Edward Slocombe (1894–1963) British journalist.
Referring to Woodrow Wilson and his visit to the Versailles conference
Mirror to Geneva

66 All politicians have vanity. Some wear it more gently than others.

David Steel (1938–) British politician.
The Observer, 'Sayings of the Week', 14 July 1985

67 Nixon is the kind of politician who would cut down a redwood tree, then mount the stump for a conservation speech.

Adlai Stevenson (1900–65) US statesman.
Attrib.

68 A politician is a statesman who approaches every question with an open mouth.

Adlai Stevenson
Also attrib. to Arthur Goldberg
The Fine Art of Political Wit (L. Harris)

69 Whoever could make two ears of corn or two blades of grass to grow upon a spot of ground where only one grew before would deserve better of mankind and do more essential service to his country than the whole race of politicians put together.

Jonathan Swift (1667–1745) Irish-born Anglican priest and writer.
Gulliver's Travels, 'Voyage to Brobdingnag', Ch. 7

70 I hope Mrs Thatcher will go until the turn of the century looking like Queen Victoria.

Norman Tebbitt (1931–) British Conservative politician.
The Observer, 'Sayings of the Week', 17 May 1987

71 In politics, if you want anything said, ask a man; if you want anything done, ask a woman.

Margaret Thatcher (1925–) British politician and prime minister.
The Changing Anatomy of Britain (Anthony Sampson)

72 If a woman like Eva Peron with no ideals can get that far, think how far I can go with all the ideals that I have.

Margaret Thatcher
The Sunday Times, 1980

73 A politician is a man who understands

government, and it takes a politician to run a government. A statesman is a politician who's been dead ten or fifteen years.

Harry S. Truman (1884–1972) US statesman.
New York World Telegram and Sun, 12 Apr 1958

74 Introducing Super-Mac.

Vicky (Victor Weisz; 1913–66) German-born British cartoonist.
Cartoon caption depicting Harold Macmillan as Superman
Evening Standard, 6 Nov 1958

75 The danger to the country, to Europe, to her vast Empire, which is involved in having all these great interests entrusted to the shaking hand of an old, wild, and incomprehensible man of 82½, is very great!

Victoria (1819–1901) Queen of the United Kingdom.
Reaction to Gladstone's fourth and last appointment as prime minister, 1892
Letter to Lord Lansdowne, 12 Aug 1892

76 He speaks to Me as if I was a public meeting.

Victoria
Referring to Gladstone
Collections and Recollections (G. W. E. Russell), Ch. 14

77 Politicians can forgive almost anything in the way of abuse; they can forgive subversion, revolution, being contradicted, exposed as liars, even ridiculed, but they can never forgive being ignored.

Auberon Waugh (1939–) British novelist and critic.
The Observer, 11 Oct 1981

78 It is a pity, as my husband says, that more politicians are not bastards by birth instead of vocation.

Katherine Whitehorn (1926–) British journalist.
The Observer, 1964

POLITICS

See also Communism, democracy, diplomacy, government, Houses of Parliament, monarchy, opposition, politicians, power politics, socialism

1 He warns the heads of parties against believing their own lies.

John Arbuthnot (1667–1735) Scottish writer and physician.
The Art of Political Lying

2 Man is by nature a political animal.

Aristotle (384–322 BC) Greek philosopher.
Politics, Bk. I

3 The accursed power which stands on Privilege
(And goes with Women, and Champagne, and Bridge)
Broke – and Democracy resumed her reign:
(Which goes with Bridge, and Women and Champagne).

Hilaire Belloc (1870–1953) French-born British poet.
Epigrams, 'On a Great Election'

4 Every Briton is at heart a Tory – especially every British Liberal.
Arnold Bennett (1867–1931) British novelist.
Journal

5 Politics is a blood sport.
Aneurin Bevan (1897–1960) British Labour politician.
My Life with Nye (Jennie Lee)

6 No attempt at ethical or social seduction can eradicate from my heart a deep burning hatred for the Tory Party . . . So far as I am concerned they are lower than vermin.
Aneurin Bevan
Speech, Manchester, 4 July 1949

7 Politics is not an exact science.
Bismarck (1815–98) German statesman.
Speech, Prussian Chamber, 18 Dec 1863

8 Politics is not a science . . . but an art.
Bismarck
Speech, Reichstag, 15 Mar 1884

9 Politics are usually the executive expression of human immaturity.
Vera Brittain (1893–1970) British writer and feminist.
The Rebel Passion

10 Party loyalty lowers the greatest of men to the petty level of the masses.
Jean de La Bruyère (1645–96) French satirist.
Les Caractères

11 Politics is the art of the possible.
R. A. Butler (1902–82) British Conservative politician.
Often attrib. to Butler but used earlier by others, including Bismarck
The Art of the Possible, Epigraph

12 The healthy stomach is nothing if not conservative. Few radicals have good digestions.
Samuel Butler (1835–1902) British writer.
Notebooks

13 I am not made for politics because I am incapable of wishing for, or accepting the death of my adversary.
Albert Camus (1913–60) French existentialist writer.
The Rebel

14 What a genius the Labour Party has for cutting itself in half and letting the two parts writhe in public.
Cassandra (William Neil Cannon; 1910–67) Irish journalist.
The Daily Mirror

15 Labour is not fit to govern.
Winston Churchill (1874–1965) British statesman.
Election speech, 1920

16 The disastrous element in the Labour party is its intellectuals.
George Norman Clark (1890–1979) British historian.
A Man of the Thirties (A. L. Rowse)

17 We now are, as we always have been, decidedly and conscientiously attached to what is called the Tory, and which might with more propriety be called the Conservative, party.
John Wilson Croker (1780–1857) British Tory politician.
The first use of the term 'Conservative Party'
In *Quarterly Review*, Jan 1830

18 A Conservative government is an organized hypocrisy.
Benjamin Disraeli (1804–81) British statesman.
Speech, 17 Mar 1845

19 The right honourable gentleman caught the Whigs bathing, and walked away with their clothes.
Benjamin Disraeli
Referring to Sir Robert Peel
Speech, House of Commons, 28 Feb 1845

20 During the last few weeks I have felt that the Suez Canal was flowing through my drawing room.
Clarissa Eden (1920–85) Wife of Anthony Eden.
Said during the Suez crisis of 1956
Attrib.

21 All terrorists, at the invitation of the Government, end up with drinks at the Dorchester.
Hugh Gaitskell (1906–63) British Labour politician.
Letter to *The Guardian*, 23 Aug 1977 (Dora Gaitskell)

22 There are some of us . . . who will fight, fight, fight, and fight again to save the party we love.
Hugh Gaitskell
After his policy for a nuclear deterrent had been defeated.
Speech, Labour Party conference, Scarborough, 3 Oct 1960

23 There are times in politics when you must be on the right side and lose.
John Kenneth Galbraith (1908–) US economist.
The Observer, 'Sayings of the Week', 11 Feb 1968

24 Few things are as immutable as the addiction of political groups to the ideas by which they have once won office.
John Kenneth Galbraith
The Affluent Society, Ch. 13

25 There is just one rule for politicians all over the world. Don't say in Power what you say in Opposition: if you do you only have to carry out what the other fellows have found impossible.
John Galsworthy (1867–1933) British novelist.
Maid in Waiting

26 I myself have become a Gaullist only little by little.
Charles De Gaulle (1890–1970) French general and statesman.
The Observer, 'Sayings of the Year', 29 Dec 1963

27 I often think it's comical
How Nature always does contrive
That every boy and every gal
That's born into the world alive
Is either a little Liberal

Or else a little Conservative!
W. S. Gilbert (1836–1911) British dramatist.
Iolanthe, II

28 If the British public falls for this, I say it will
be stark, staring bonkers.
Lord Hailsham (1907–   ) British Conservative politician.
Referring to Labour policy in the 1964 general-election
campaign
Press conference, Conservative Central Office, 12 Oct 1964

29 A great party is not to be brought down
because of a scandal by a woman of easy
virtue and a proved liar.
Lord Hailsham
Referring to the Profumo affair, in BBC interview, 13 June
1963
The Pendulum Years, Ch. 3 (Bernard Levin)

30 Their Europeanism is nothing but imperialism
with an inferiority complex.
Denis Healey (1917–   ) British Labour politician.
Referring to the policies of the Conservative party
The Observer, 'Sayings of the Week', 7 Oct 1962

31 The essential thing is the formation of the
political will of the nation: that is the starting
point for political action.
Adolf Hitler (1889–1945) German dictator.
Speech, Düsseldorf, 27 Jan 1932

32 If you're in politics and you can't tell when
you walk into a room who's for you and
who's against you, then you're in the wrong
line of work.
Lyndon B. Johnson (1908–73) US statesman.
The Lyndon Johnson Story (B. Mooney)

33 Sir, I perceive you are a vile Whig.
Samuel Johnson (1709–84) British lexicographer.
Speaking to Sir Adam Fergusson
Life of Johnson (J. Boswell), Vol. II

34 Why, Sir, most schemes of political
improvement are very laughable things.
Samuel Johnson
Life of Johnson (J. Boswell), Vol. II

35 Politics are now nothing more than a means
of rising in the world.
Samuel Johnson
Life of Johnson (J. Boswell), Vol. II

36 The idea that there is a model Labour voter,
a blue-collar council house tenant who
belongs to a union and has 2.4 children, a
five-year-old car and a holiday in Blackpool, is
patronizing and politically immature.
Neil Kinnock (1942–   ) British politician.
Speech, 1986

37 Proportional Representation, I think, is
fundamentally counter-democratic.
Neil Kinnock
Marxism Today, 1983

38 States, like men, have their growth, their
manhood, their decrepitude, their decay.
Walter Savage Landor (1775–1864) British poet and
writer.
Imaginary Conversations, 'Pollio and Calvus'

39 If it were necessary to give the briefest
possible definition of imperialism we should
have to say that imperialism is the monopoly
stage of capitalism.
Lenin (Vladimir Ilich Ulyanov; 1870–1924) Russian
revolutionary leader.
Imperialism, the Highest Stage of Capitalism, Ch. 7

40 In every age the vilest specimens of human
nature are to be found among demagogues.
Lord Macaulay (1800–59) British historian.
History of England, Vol. I, Ch. 5

41 I thought the best thing to do was to settle
up these little local difficulties, and then turn
to the wider vision of the Commonwealth.
Harold Macmillan (1894–1986) British politician and
prime minister.
Referring to resignation of ministers
Attrib., London Airport, 7 Jan 1958

42 There are three groups that no prime
minister should provoke: the Treasury, the
Vatican, and the National Union of
Mineworkers.
Harold Macmillan
First used by Stanley Baldwin
Attrib.

43 Selling the family silver.
Harold Macmillan
Referring to privatization of profitable nationalized industries
Speech, House of Lords, 1986

44 In politics, as in grammar, one should be able
to tell the substantives from the adjectives.
Hitler was a substantive; Mussolini only an
adjective. Hitler was a nuisance. Mussolini
was bloody. Together a bloody nuisance.
Salvador de Madariaga y Rogo (1886–1978) Spanish
diplomat and writer.
Attrib.

45 Every intellectual attitude is latently political.
Thomas Mann (1875–1955) German novelist.
The Observer, 11 Aug 1974

46 All reactionaries are paper tigers.
Mao Tse-Tung (1893–1976) Chinese communist leader.
Quotations from Chairman Mao Tse-Tung, Ch. 6

47 McCarthyism is Americanism with its sleeves
rolled.
Joseph R. McCarthy (1908–57) US senator.
Speech, 1952

48 The expression 'positive neutrality' is a
contradiction in terms. There can be no more
positive neutrality than there can be a
vegetarian tiger.
V. K. Krishna Menon (1897–   ) Indian barrister and
writer.
The New York Times, 18 Oct 1960

49 We cannot change our policy now. After all, we are not political whores.

Benito Mussolini (1883–1945) Italian dictator.
Hitler (Alan Bullock), Ch. 8

50 I still love you, but in politics there is no heart, only head.

Napoleon I (Napoleon Bonaparte; 1769–1821) French emperor.
Referring to his divorce, for reasons of state, from the Empress Josephine (1809)
Bonaparte (C. Barnett)

51 In our time, political speech and writing are largely the defence of the indefensible.

George Orwell (Eric Blair; 1903–50) British novelist.
Politics and the English Language

52 I used to say that politics was the second lowest profession and I have come to know that it bears a great similarity to the first.

Ronald Reagan (1911–   ) US politician and president.
The Observer, 13 May 1979

53 Please assure me that you are all Republicans!

Ronald Reagan
Addressing the surgeons on being wheeled into the operating theatre for an emergency operation after an assassination attempt
Presidential Anecdotes (P. Boller)

54 Remember this, Griffin. The revolution eats its own. Capitalism re-creates itself.

Mordecai Richler (1931–   ) Canadian novelist.
Cocksure, Ch. 22

55 The more you read about politics, you got to admit that each party is worse than the other.

Will Rogers (1879–1935) US actor and humorist.
Saturday Review, 'A Rogers Thesaurus', 25 Aug 1962

56 England elects a Labour Government. When a man goes in for politics over here, he has no time to labour, and any man that labours has no time to fool with politics. Over there politics is an obligation; over here it's a business.

Will Rogers
Autobiography, Ch. 14

57 You have to clean your plate.

Lord Rosebery (1847–1929) British statesman.
Said to the Liberal Party
Speech, Chesterfield, 16 Dec 1901

58 The collection of prejudices which is called political philosophy is useful provided that it is not called philosophy.

Bertrand Russell (1872–1970) British philosopher.
The Observer, 'Sayings of the Year', 1962

59 History is past politics, and politics present history.

John Robert Seeley (1834–95) British historian.
Quoting the historian E. A. Freeman
The Growth of British Policy

60 If Her Majesty stood for Parliament – if the

Tory Party had any sense and made Her its leader instead of that grammar school twit Heath – us Tories, mate, would win every election we went in for.

Johnny Speight (1920–   ) British television scriptwriter.
Till Death Do Us Part

61 The Republican form of Government is the highest form of government; but because of this it requires the highest type of human nature– a type nowhere at present existing.

Herbert Spencer (1820–1903) British philosopher.
Essays, 'The Americans'

62 The tasks of the party are . . . to be cautious and not allow our country to be drawn into conflicts by warmongers who are accustomed to have others pull the chestnuts out of the fire for them.

Joseph Stalin (J. Dzhugashvili; 1879–1953) Soviet statesman.
Speech, 8th Congress of the Communist Party, 6 Jan 1941

63 Disdain is the wrong word, but perhaps affection is too strong a word

David Steel (1938–   ) British politician.
Referring to his attitude to the Liberal party
The Observer, 'Sayings of the Week', 22 Sept 1985

64 Go back to your constituencies and prepare for government!

David Steel
Speech to party conference, 1985

65 I sense that the British electorate is now itching to break out once and for all from the discredited straight-jacket of the past.

David Steel
The Times, 2 June 1987

66 An independent is a guy who wants to take the politics out of politics.

Adlai Stevenson (1900–65) US statesman.
The Art Of Politics.

67 Politics is perhaps the only profession for which no preparation is thought necessary.

Robert Louis Stevenson (1850–94) Scottish writer.
Familiar Studies of Men and Books, 'Yoshida-Torajiro'

68 Socialists treat their servants with respect and then wonder why they vote Conservative.

Tom Stoppard (1937–   ) Czech-born British dramatist.
Lord Malquist and Mr Moon, Pt. V, Ch. 1

69 Revolts, republics, revolutions, most No graver than a schoolboy's barring out.

Alfred, Lord Tennyson (1809–92) British poet.
The Princess, Conclusion

70 Any woman who understands the problems of running a home will be nearer to understanding the problems of running a country.

Margaret Thatcher (1925–   ) British politician and prime minister.
The Observer, 8 May 1979

71 I can trust my husband not to fall asleep on a

public platform and he usually claps in the right places.
Margaret Thatcher
Observer, 20 Aug 1978

72 Britain is no longer in the politics of the pendulum, but of the ratchet.
Margaret Thatcher
Speech, Institute of Public Relations, 1977

73 Politics is the art of preventing people from taking part in affairs which properly concern them.
Paul Valéry (1871–1945) French poet and writer.
Tel quel

74 Any American who is prepared to run for President should automatically, by definition, be disqualified from ever doing so.
Gore Vidal (1925–) US novelist.
Attrib.

75 Politics come from man. Mercy, compassion and justice come from God.
Terry Waite (1939–) British churchman.
The Observer, 'Sayings of the Week', 13 Jan 1985

76 A writer of crook stories ought never to stop seeking new material.
Edgar Wallace (1875–1932) British thriller writer.
Said when a candidate for Parliament
The Long Weekend (Alan Hodge)

77 He stood twice for Parliament, but so diffidently that his candidature passed almost unnoticed.
Evelyn Waugh (1903–66) British novelist.
Decline and Fall, Pt. III, Ch. 1

78 Pappenhacker says that every time you are polite to a proletarian you are helping to bolster up the capitalist system.
Evelyn Waugh
Scoop, Bk. I, Ch. 5

79 The Labour Party is going about the country stirring up apathy.
William Whitelaw (1918–) British politician.
Attrib.

80 The Labour party is like a stage-coach. If you rattle along at great speed everybody inside is too exhilarated or too seasick to cause any trouble. But if you stop everybody gets out and argues about where to go next.
Harold Wilson (1916–) British politician and prime minister.
Harold Wilson, The Authentic Portrait (Leslie Smith)

81 Hence the practised performances of latter-day politicians in the game of musical daggers: never be left holding the dagger when the music stops.
Harold Wilson
The Governance of Britain, Ch. 2

82 A week is a long time in politics.
Harold Wilson
First said in 1965 or 1966, and repeated on several occasions
Attrib.

POLLUTION

See ecology, environment

POP MUSIC

1 Rock'n'roll is part of a pest to undermine the morals of the youth of our nation. It . . . brings people of both races together.
Anonymous
Statement by the North Alabama Citizens' Council in the 1950s.

2 Listen kid, take my advice, never hate a song that has sold half a million copies.
Irving Berlin (Israel Baline; 1888–) Russian-born US composer.
Giving advice to Cole Porter
Attrib.

3 Do they merit vitriol, even a drop of it? Yes, because they corrupt the young, persuading them that the mature world, which produced Beethoven and Schweitzer, sets an even higher value on the transient anodynes of youth than does youth itself . . . They are the Hollow Men. The are electronic lice.
Anthony Burgess (1917–) British novelist.
Punch, 20 Sept 1967
Referring to disc jockeys

4 Canned music is like audible wallpaper.
Alistair Cooke (1908–) British broadcaster.
Attrib.

5 Strange how potent cheap music is.
Noël Coward (1899–1973) British dramatist.
Private Lives

6 I think popular music in this country is one of the few things in the twentieth century that have made giant strides in reverse.
Bing Crosby (Harry Lillis Crosby; 1904–77) US singer.
Interview in *This Week*

7 Yeah, some of them are about ten minutes long, others five or six.
Bob Dylan (Robert Allen Zimmerman; 1941–) US songwriter.
On being asked in an interview, to say something about his songs
Attrib.

8 We're more popular than Jesus Christ now. I don't know which will go first, Rock and Roll or Christianity.
John Lennon (1940–80) British rock musician.
The Beatles Illustrated Lyrics

9 What a terrible revenge by the culture of the Negroes on that of the Whites.
Ignacy Paderewski (1860–1941) Polish pianist.
Referring to jazz
Attrib.

10 Every popular song has at least one line or sentence that is perfectly clear – the line that fits the music.
Ezra Pound (1885–1972) US poet and critic.
Attrib.

11 Jazz will endure just as long as people hear it through their feet instead of their brains.
John Philip Sousa (1854–1932) US composer, conductor, and writer.
Attrib.

POPULARITY

See also fame

1 Do not let that trouble Your Excellency; perhaps the greetings are intended for me.
Ludwig van Beethoven (1770–1827) German composer.
Said when walking with Goethe, when Goethe complained about greetings from passers-by
Thayer's Life of Beethoven (E. Forbes)

2 Everybody hates me because I'm so universally liked.
Peter De Vries (1910–) US novelist.
The Vale of Laughter, Pt. I

3 Popularity is a crime from the moment it is sought; it is only a virtue where men have it whether they will or no.
Lord Halifax (1633–95) English statesman.
Political, Moral and Miscellaneous Thoughts and Reflections

4 Popularity? It's glory's small change.
Victor Hugo (1802–85) French writer.
Ruy Blas, III

5 The worse I do, the more popular I get.
John Fitzgerald Kennedy (1917–63) US statesman.
Referring to his popularity following the failure of the US invasion of Cuba
The People's Almanac (D. Wallechinsky)

6 We're more popular than Jesus Christ now. I don't know which will go first. Rock and roll or Christianity.
John Lennon (1940–80) British rock musician.
The Beatles Illustrated Lyrics

7 He's liked, but he's not well liked.
Arthur Miller (1915–) US dramatist.
Death of a Salesman, I

8 He hasn't an enemy in the world, and none of his friends like him.
Oscar Wilde (1854–1900) Irish-born British dramatist.
Said of G. B. Shaw
Sixteen Self Sketches (Shaw), Ch. 17

PORNOGRAPHY

See also censorship, prudery, sex

1 I don't think pornography is very harmful, but it is terribly, terribly boring.
Noël Coward (1899–1973) British dramatist.
The Observer, 'Sayings of the Week', 24 Sept 1972

2 Pornography is the attempt to insult sex, to do dirt on it.
D. H. Lawrence (1885–1930) British novelist.
Phoenix, 'Pornography and Obscenity'

3 Its avowed purpose is to excite sexual desire, which, I should have thought, is unnecessary in the case of the young, inconvenient in the case of the middle aged, and unseemly in the old.
Malcolm Muggeridge (1903–) British writer.
Tread Softly For You Tread On My Jokes, 1966

4 *Lady Chatterley's Lover* is a book that all Christians might read with profit.
John Robinson (1919–83) Bishop of Woolwich.
Said in the court case against Penguin Books
Attrib.

5 Don't be daft. You don't get any pornography on there, not on the telly. Get filth, that's all. The only place you get pornography is in yer Sunday papers.
Johnny Speight (1920–) British television scriptwriter.
Till Death Do Us Part

POSSIBILITY

See also impossibility

1 The grand Perhaps!
Robert Browning (1812–89) British poet.
Bishop Blougram's Apology

2 Your If is the only peace-maker; much virtue in If.
William Shakespeare (1564–1616) English dramatist.
As You Like It, V:4

POSTERITY

See also death, fame, future, immortality, reputation

1 Think of your forefathers! Think of your posterity!
John Quincy Adams (1767–1848) Sixth president of the USA.
Speech, Plymouth, Massachusetts, 22 Dec 1802

2 We are always doing something for posterity, but I would fain see posterity do something for us.
Joseph Addison (1672–1719) British essayist.
The Spectator, 583

3 Let us honour if we can
The vertical man
Though we value none
But the horizontal one.
W. H. Auden (1907–73) British poet.
Epigraph for Poems

4 When a man is in doubt about this or that in his writing, it will often guide him if he asks himself how it will tell a hundred years hence.

Samuel Butler (1835–1902) British writer.
Notebooks

5 I think I shall be among the English Poets after my death.

John Keats (1795–1821) British poet.
Letter to George and Georgiana Keats, 14 Oct 1818

6 A writer's ambition should be to trade a hundred contemporary readers for ten readers in ten years' time and for one reader in a hundred years' time.

Arthur Koestler (1905–83) Hungarian-born British writer.
New York Times Book Review, 1 Apr 1951

7 Damn the age. I'll write for antiquity.

Charles Lamb (1775–1834) British essayist.
Referring to his lack of payment for the *Essays of Elia*
English Wits (L. Russell)

8 Now I'm dead in the grave with my lips moving
And every schoolboy repeating my words by heart.

Osip Mandelstam (1891–1938) Russian poet.
Poems, No. 306

9 My time has not yet come either; some are born posthumously.

Friedrich Wilhelm Nietzsche (1844–1900) German philosopher.
Ecce Homo

POVERTY

See also hunger, poverty and wealth

1 From clogs to clogs is only three generations.
Proverb

2 Poverty is not a crime.
Proverb

3 To some extent, if you've seen one city slum you've seen them all.

Spiro Agnew (1918–) US politician.
Election speech, Detroit, 18 Oct 1968

4 To be poor and independent is very nearly an impossibility.

William Cobbett (1763–1835) British journalist and writer.
Advice to Young Men

5 He found it inconvenient to be poor.

William Cowper (1731–1800) British poet.
Charity

6 Poverty and oysters always seem to go together.

Charles Dickens (1812–70) British novelist.
Pickwick Papers, Ch. 22

7 There's no scandal like rags, nor any crime so shameful as poverty.

George Farquhar (1678–1707) Irish dramatist.
The Beaux' Stratagem, I:1

8 The very poor are unthinkable and only to be approached by the statistician and the poet.

E. M. Forster (1879–1970) British novelist.
Howards End

9 It is only the poor who are forbidden to beg.

Anatole France (Jacques Anatole François Thibault; 1844–1924) French writer.
Crainquebille

10 No sir, tho' I was born and bred in England, I can dare to be poor, which is the only thing now-a-days men are asham'd of.

John Gay (1685–1732) English poet and dramatist.
Polly

11 Is it possible that my people live in such awful conditions? . . . I tell you, Mr Wheatley, that if I had to live in conditions like that I would be a revolutionary myself.

George V (1865–1936) King of the United Kingdom.
On being told Mr Wheatley's life story
The Tragedy of Ramsay MacDonald (L. MacNeill Weir), Ch. 16

12 Let not Ambition mock their useful toil,
Their homely joys, and destiny obscure;
Nor Grandeur hear with a disdainful smile,
The short and simple annals of the poor.

Thomas Gray (1716–71) British poet.
Elegy Written in a Country Churchyard

13 I want there to be no peasant in my kingdom so poor that he is unable to have a chicken in his pot every Sunday.

Henri IV (1553–1610) King of France.
Hist. de Henry le Grand (Hardouin de Péréfixe)

14 Seven cities warr'd for Homer, being dead,
Who, living, had no roof to shroud his head.

Thomas Heywood (c. 1574–1641) English dramatist.
The Hierarchy of the Blessed Angels

15 Oh! God! that bread should be so dear,
And flesh and blood so cheap!

Thomas Hood (1799–1845) British poet.
The Song of the Shirt

16 Hard to train to accept being poor.

Horace (Quintus Horatius Flaccus; 65–8 BC) Roman poet.
Odes, I

17 It is easy enough to say that poverty is no crime. No; if it were men wouldn't be ashamed of it. It is a blunder, though, and is punished as such. A poor man is despised the whole world over.

Jerome K. Jerome (1859–1927) British humorist.
Idle Thoughts of an Idle Fellow

18 Resolve not to be poor: whatever you have, spend less. Poverty is a great enemy to human happiness; it certainly destroys liberty, and it makes some virtues impracticable and others extremely difficult.

Samuel Johnson (1709–84) British lexicographer.
Life of Johnson (J. Boswell), Vol. IV

19 The misfortunes of poverty carry with them

nothing harder to bear than that it exposes men to ridicule.
Juvenal (Decimus Junius Juvenalis; 60–130 AD) Roman satirist.
Satires, III

20 It's not easy for people to rise out of obscurity when they have to face straitened circumstances at home.
Juvenal
Satires, III

21 We're really all of us bottomly broke. I haven't had time to work in weeks.
Jack Kerouac (1922–69) US novelist.
On the Road, Pt. I

22 Few, save the poor, feel for the poor.
Letitia Landon (1802–38) British poet and novelist.
The Poor

23 Look at me: I worked my way up from nothing to a state of extreme poverty.
Groucho Marx (Julius Marx; 1895–1977) US comedian.
Monkey Business

24 The forgotten man at the bottom of the economic pyramid.
Franklin D. Roosevelt (1882–1945) US Democratic president.
Speech on radio, 7 Apr 1932

25 The poor don't know that their function in life is to exercise our generosity.
Jean-Paul Sartre (1905–80) French writer.
Words

26 The heart of the matter, as I see it, is the stark fact that world poverty is primarily a problem of two million villages, and thus a problem of two thousand million villagers.
E. F. Schumacher (1911–77) German-born economist.
Small is Beautiful, A Study of Economics as if People Mattered, Ch. 13

27 CUSINS. Do you call poverty a crime?
UNDERSHAFT. The worst of all crimes. All the other crimes are virtues beside it.
George Bernard Shaw (1856–1950) Irish dramatist and critic.
Major Barbara, IV

28 . . . the poor are our brothers and sisters. . . . people in the world who need love, who need care, who have to be wanted.
Mother Teresa (Agnes Gonxha Bojaxhui; 1910–   ) Yugoslavian missionary in Calcutta.
Time, 'Saints Among Us', 29 Dec 1975

29 There were times my pants were so thin I could sit on a dime and tell if it was heads or tails.
Spencer Tracy (1900–67) US film star.
Spencer Tracy (L. Swindell)

30 As for the virtuous poor, one can pity them, of course, but one cannot possibly admire them.
Oscar Wilde (1854–1900) Irish-born British dramatist.
The Soul of Man under Socialism

31 But I, being poor, have only my dreams; I have spread my dreams under your feet; Tread softly because you tread on my dreams.
W. B. Yeats (1865–1939) Irish poet.
He Wishes for the Cloths of Heaven

POVERTY AND WEALTH

See also money, poverty, wealth

1 She was poor but she was honest Victim of a rich man's game. First he loved her, then he left her, And she lost her maiden name.

See her on the bridge at midnight, Saying 'Farewell, blighted love.' Then a scream, a splash and goodness, What is she a-doin' of?

It's the same the whole world over, It's the poor wot gets the blame, It's the rich wot gets the gravy. Ain't it all a bleedin' shame?
Anonymous
She was Poor but she was Honest

2 There was a certain rich man, which was clothed in purple and fine linen, and fared sumptuously every day: And there was a certain beggar named Lazarus, which was laid at his gate, full of sores, And desiring to be fed with the crumbs which fell from the rich man's table: moreover the dogs came and licked his sores. And it came to pass, that the beggar died, and was carried by the angels into Abraham's bosom: the rich man also died, and was buried; And in hell he lift up his eyes, being in torments, and seeth Abraham afar off, and Lazarus in his bosom.
Bible: Luke
16:19–23

3 There are only two families in the world, my old grandmother used to say, The *Haves* and the *Have-Nots*.
Miguel de Cervantes (1547–1616) Spanish novelist.
Don Quixote, Pt. II, Ch. 20

4 'Two nations; between whom there is no intercourse and no sympathy; who are as ignorant of each other's habits, thoughts, and feelings, as if they were dwellers in different zones, or inhabitants of different planets; who are formed by a different breeding, are fed by a different food, are ordered by different manners, and are not governed by the same laws.'
'You speak of –' said Egremont, hesitatingly 'THE RICH AND THE POOR.'
Benjamin Disraeli (1804–81) British statesman.
Sybil, Bk. II, Ch. 5

5 Errors look so very ugly in persons of small means – one feels they are taking quite a liberty in going astray; whereas people of

fortune may naturally indulge in a few delinquencies.
George Eliot (Mary Ann Evans; 1819–80) British novelist.
Janet's Repentance, Ch. 25

6 Whereas it has long been known and declared that the poor have no right to the property of the rich, I wish it also to be known and declared that the rich have no right to the property of the poor.
John Ruskin (1819–1900) British art critic and writer.
Unto this Last, Essay III

7 When the rich wage war it is the poor who die.
Jean-Paul Sartre (1905–80) French writer.
The Devil and the Good Lord

8 As long as men are men, a poor society cannot be too poor to find a right order of life, nor a rich society too rich to have need to seek it.
R. H. Tawney (1880–1962) British economist and historian.
The Acquisitive Society

POWER

See also influence, leadership, responsibility

1 Divide and rule.
Proverb

2 He who pays the piper calls the tune.
Proverb

3 Power tends to corrupt, and absolute power corrupts absolutely. Great men are almost always bad men . . . There is no worse heresy than that the office sanctifies the holder of it.
Lord Acton (1834–1902) British historian.
Often misquoted as 'Power corrupts . . . '
Letter to Bishop Mandell Creighton, 5 Apr 1887

4 Nothing destroyeth authority so much as the unequal and untimely interchange of power pressed too far, and relaxed too much.
Francis Bacon (1561–1626) English philosopher.
Essays, 'Of Empire'

5 He did not care in which direction the car was travelling, so long as he remained in the driver's seat.
Lord Beaverbrook (1879–1964) Canadian-born British newspaper proprietor.
Referring to Lloyd George
New Statesman, 14 June 1963

6 The strongest poison ever known
Came from Caesar's laurel crown.
William Blake (1757–1827) British poet.
Auguries of Innocence

7 The greater the power, the more dangerous the abuse.
Edmund Burke (1729–97) British politician.
Speech, House of Commons, 7 Feb 1771

8 There is one thing about being President – nobody can tell you when to sit down.
Dwight D. Eisenhower (1890–1969) US general and statesman.
The Observer, 'Sayings of the Week', 9 Aug 1953

9 Men of power have not time to read; yet men who do not read are unfit for power.
Michael Foot (1913–) British Labour politician and journalist.
Debts Of Honour

10 Power is so apt to be insolent and Liberty to be saucy, that they are seldom upon good Terms.
Lord Halifax (1633–95) English statesman.
Political, Moral, and Miscellaneous Thoughts and Reflections

11 Power is the ultimate aphrodisiac.
Henry Kissinger (1923–) German-born US politician and diplomat.
The Guardian, 28 Nov 1976

12 To reign is worth ambition, though in Hell:
Better to reign in Hell than serve in Heaven.
John Milton (1608–74) English poet.
Paradise Lost, Bk. I

13 Who controls the past controls the future. Who controls the present controls the past.
George Orwell (Eric Blair; 1903–50) British novelist.
Nineteen Eighty-Four

14 Unlimited power is apt to corrupt the minds of those who possess it.
William Pitt the Elder (1708–78) British statesman.
See also Lord ACTON
Speech, House of Lords, 9 Jan 1770

15 The megalomaniac differs from the narcissist by the fact that he wishes to be powerful rather than charming, and seeks to be feared rather than loved. To this type belong many lunatics and most of the great men of history.
Bertrand Russell (1872–1970) British philosopher.
The Conquest of Happiness

16 We are the masters at the moment – and not only for the moment, but for a very long time to come.
Lord Shawcross (1902–) British Labour politician and lawyer.
Sometimes quoted as, 'We are the masters now!'
House of Commons, 2 Apr 1946

17 The official world, the corridors of power, the dilemmas of conscience and egotism – she disliked them all.
C. P. Snow (1905–80) British novelist.
Homecomings, Ch. 22

18 You only have power over people so long as you don't take *everything* away from them. But when you've robbed a man of everything he's no longer in your power – he's free again.
Alexander Solzhenitsyn (1918–) Soviet novelist.
The First Circle, Ch. 17

19 Power corrupts, but lack of power corrupts absolutely.
Adlai Stevenson (1900–65) US statesman.
The Observer, Jan 1963

20 He aspired to power instead of influence, and as a result forfeited both.
A. J. P. Taylor (1906–) British historian.
Referring to Lord Northcliffe
English History, 1914–1945, Ch. 1

21 One Ring to rule them all, One Ring to find them,
One Ring to bring them all and in the darkness bind them.
J. R. R. Tolkien (1892–1973) British writer.
The Lord of the Rings, Pt. I: *The Fellowship of the Ring*, Ch. 2

22 The balance of power.
Robert Walpole (1676–1745) British statesman.
Speech, House of Commons

23 The good old rule
Sufficeth them, the simple plan,
That they should take, who have the power,
And they should keep who can.
William Wordsworth (1770–1850) British poet.
Rob Roy's Grave

24 The wrong sort of people are always in power because they would not be in power if they were not the wrong sort of people.
Jon Wynne-Tyson (1924–) British humorous writer.
Times Literary Supplement

POWER POLITICS

See also force, oppression, violence, weapons

1 Whatever happens, we have got
The Maxim Gun, and they have not.
Hilaire Belloc (1870–1953) French-born British poet.
Referring to African natives
The Modern Traveller

2 The great questions of our day cannot be solved by speeches and majority votes . . . but by iron and blood.
Bismarck (1815–98) German statesman.
Usually misquoted as 'blood and iron' – a form Bismarck himself used in 1886
Speech, Prussian Chamber, 30 Sept 1862

3 Guns will make us powerful; butter will only make us fat.
Hermann Goering (1893–1946) German leader.
Radio broadcast, 1936

4 A man may build himself a throne of bayonets, but he cannot sit on it.
Dean Inge (1860–1954) British churchman.
Wit and Wisdom of Dean Inge (ed. Marchant)

5 Every Communist must grasp the truth, 'Political power grows out of the barrel of a gun.'
Mao Tse-Tung (1893–1976) Chinese communist leader.
Selected Works, Vol II, 'Problems of War and Strategy', 6 Nov 1938

6 There is a homely adage which runs 'Speak softly and carry a big stick, you will go far'.
Theodore Roosevelt (1858–1919) US Republican president.
Speech, Minnesota State Fair, 2 Sept 1901

7 God is always on the side of the big battalions.
Vicomte de Turenne (1611–75) French marshal.
Attrib.

8 God is on the side not of the heavy battalions, but of the best shots.
Voltaire (François-Marie Arouet; 1694–1778) French writer.
Notebooks

PRACTICALITY

1 I have no dress except the one I wear every day. If you are going to be kind enough to give me one, please let it be practical and dark so that I can put it on afterwards to go to the laboratory.
Marie Curie (1867–1934) Polish chemist.
Referring to a wedding dress
Letter to a friend

2 What would you do with it? It is full of leprosy.
Father Damien (Joseph de Veuster; 1840–89) Belgian Roman Catholic missionary.
When asked on his deathbed whether he would leave another priest his mantle, like Elijah
Memoirs of an Aesthete (H. Acton)

3 The Arab who builds himself a hut out of the marble fragments of a temple in Palmyra is more philosophical than all the curators of the museums in London, Munich or Paris.
Anatole France (Jacques Anatole François Thibault; 1844–1924) French writer.
The Crime of Sylvestre Bonnard

4 Talk to him of Jacob's ladder, and he would ask the number of the steps.
Douglas William Jerrold (1803–57) British dramatist.
Wit and Opinions of Douglas Jerrold, 'A Matter-of-fact Man'

5 Don't carry away that arm till I have taken off my ring.
Lord Raglan (1788–1855) British field marshal.
Request immediately after his arm had been amputated following the battle of Waterloo
Dictionary of National Biography

6 Very well, then I shall not take off my boots.
Duke of Wellington (1769–1852) British general and statesman.
Responding to the news, as he was going to bed, that the ship in which he was travelling seemed about to sink
Attrib.

PRAISE

See also admiration, boasts, compliments, flattery

1 Self-praise is no recommendation.
Proverb

2 Just as it is always said of slander that something always sticks when people boldly slander, so it might be said of self-praise (if it is not entirely shameful and ridiculous) that if we praise ourselves fearlessly, something will always stick.

Francis Bacon (1561–1626) English philosopher.
The Advancement of Learning

3 Let us now praise famous men, and our fathers that begat us.

Bible: Ecclesiasticus
44:1

4 The advantage of doing one's praising for oneself is that one can lay it on so thick and exactly in the right places.

Samuel Butler (1835–1902) British writer.
The Way of All Flesh, Ch. 34

5 Fondly we think we honour merit then,
When we but praise ourselves in other men.

Alexander Pope (1688–1744) British poet.
An Essay on Criticism

6 To refuse praise reveals a desire to be praised twice over.

Duc de la Rochefoucauld (1613–80) French writer.
Maximes, 149

PRAYER

See also Christianity, faith, God, religion

1 Hail Mary, full of grace, the Lord is with thee: Blessed art thou among women, and blessed is the fruit of thy womb, Jesus.

Anonymous
Ave Maria, 11th century

2 From ghoulies and ghosties and long-leggety beasties
And things that go bump in the night,
Good Lord, deliver us!

Anonymous
Cornish

3 O Lord! thou knowest how busy I must be this day: if I forget thee, do not thou forget me.

Lord Astley (1579–1652) English Royalist general.
Prayer before taking part in the Battle of Edgehill
Memoires (Sir Philip Warwick)

4 But when ye pray, use not vain repetitions, as the heathen do: for they think that they shall be heard for their much speaking.
Be not ye therefore like unto them: for your Father knoweth what things ye have need of, before ye ask him.
After this manner therefore pray ye: Our Father which art in heaven, Hallowed be thy name.
Thy kingdom come. Thy will be done in earth, as it is in heaven.
Give us this day our daily bread.
And forgive us our debts, as we forgive our debtors.

And lead us not into temptation, but deliver us from evil: For thine is the kingdom, and the power, and the glory, for ever. Amen.

Bible: Matthew
6:7–13

5 To Mercy, Pity, Peace, and Love
All pray in their distress.

William Blake (1757–1827) British poet.
Songs of Innocence, 'The Divine Image'

6 When two or three are gathered together in thy Name thou wilt grant their requests.

The Book of Common Prayer
Morning Prayer, Prayer of St Chrysostom

7 A leap over the hedge is better than good men's prayers.

Miguel de Cervantes (1547–1616) Spanish novelist.
Don Quixote, Pt. I, Ch. 21

8 He prayeth well, who loveth well
Both man and bird and beast.

Samuel Taylor Coleridge (1772–1834) British poet.
The Rime of the Ancient Mariner, VII

9 He prayeth best, who loveth best
All things both great and small;
For the dear God who loveth us,
He made and loveth all.

Samuel Taylor Coleridge
The Rime of the Ancient Mariner, VII

10 Prayer makes the Christian's armour bright;
And Satan trembles when he sees
The weakest saint upon his knees.

William Cowper (1731–1800) British poet.
Olney Hymns, 29

11 The idea that He would take his attention away from the universe in order to give me a bicycle with three speeds is just so unlikely I can't go along with it.

Quentin Crisp (?1910–) British model, publicist, and writer.
The Sunday Times, 18 Dec 1977

12 Forgive, O Lord, my little jokes on Thee
And I'll forgive Thy great big one on me.

Robert Frost (1875–1963) US poet.
In the clearing, 'Cluster of Faith'

13 Religion's in the heart, not in the knees.

Douglas William Jerrold (1803–57) British dramatist.
The Devil's Ducat, I.2

14 The Beadsman, after thousand aves told,
For aye unsought-for slept among his ashes cold.

John Keats (1795–1821) British poet.
The Eve of Saint Agnes, I

15 I am just going to pray for you at St Paul's, but with no very lively hope of success.

Sydney Smith (1771–1845) British clergyman and essayist.
On meeting an acquaintance
The Smith of Smiths (H. Pearson), Ch. 13

16 If thou shouldst never see my face again,

Pray for my soul. More things are wrought by prayer
Than this world dreams of.
Alfred, Lord Tennyson (1809–92) British poet.
Idylls of the King, 'The Passing of Arthur'

17 Whatever a man prays for, he prays for a miracle. Every prayer reduces itself to this: 'Great God grant that twice two be not four.'
Ivan Turgenev (1818–83) Russian novelist.
Prayer

PRECOCITY

See also children, youth

1 One of those men who reach such an acute limited excellence at twenty-one that everything afterward savours of anti-climax.
F. Scott Fitzgerald (1896–1940) US novelist.
The Great Gatsby, Ch. 1

2 Thank you, madam, the agony is abated.
Lord Macaulay (1800–59) British historian.
Replying, aged four, to a lady who asked if he had hurt himself
Life and Letters of Macaulay (Trevelyan), Ch. 1

PREJUDICE

See also equality, feminism, Jews, objectivity, race, racism, religion, subjectivity

1 I am a Catholic. As far as possible I go to Mass every day. As far as possible I kneel down and tell these beads every day. If you reject me on account of my religion, I shall thank God that he has spared me the indignity of being your representative.
Hilaire Belloc (1870–1953) French-born British poet.
Said in his first election campaign
Speech, Salford, 1906

2 Mother is far too clever to understand anything she does not like.
Arnold Bennett (1867–1931) British novelist.
The Title

3 Common sense is the collection of prejudices acquired by age eighteen.
Albert Einstein (1879–1955) German-born US physicist.
Scientific American, Feb 1976

4 Vegetarians have wicked, shifty eyes, and laugh in a cold and calculating manner. They pinch little children, steal stamps, drink water, favour beards . . . wheeze, squeak, drawl and maunder.
J. B. Morton (1893–1979) British journalist.
By the Way, '4 June'

5 . . . I *too well* know its truth, from experience, that whenever any poor Gipsies are encamped anywhere and crimes and robberies &c. occur, it is invariably laid to their account, which is shocking; and if they are always looked upon as vagabonds, how *can* they become good people?
Victoria (1819–1901) Queen of the United Kingdom.
Journal, 29 Dec 1836

6 I do not intend to prejudge the past.
William Whitelaw (1918–) British politician.
Said on arriving in Ulster as Minister for Northern Ireland
The Times, 3 Dec 1973

7 No Jewish blood runs among my blood,
but I am as bitterly and hardly hated
by every anti-semite
as if I were a Jew. By this
I am a Russian.
Yevgeny Yevtushenko (1933–) Soviet poet.
Babi Yar

PRESENT

See also future, opportunity, past, time

1 No time like the present.
Proverb

2 The past was nothing to her; offered no lesson which she was willing to heed. The future was a mystery which she never attempted to penetrate. The present alone was significant . . .
Kate Chopin (1851–1904) US writer.
The Awakening, Ch. 15

3 I have learned to live each day as it comes, and not to borrow trouble by dreading tomorrow. It is the dark menace of the future that makes cowards of us.
Dorothy Dix (Elizabeth Meriwether Gilmer; 1861–1951) US journalist and writer.
Dorothy Dix, Her Book, Introduction

4 Happy the Man, and happy he alone,
He who can call today his own:
He who, secure within, can say,
Tomorrow do thy worst, for I have liv'd today.
John Dryden (1631–1700) British poet and dramatist.
Translation of Horace, III

5 Ah, my Belovéd, fill the Cup that clears
TO-DAY of past Regrets and Future Fears:
To-morrow! – Why, To-morrow I may be
Myself with Yesterday's Sev'n thousand Years.
Edward Fitzgerald (1809–83) British poet.
The Rubáiyát of Omar Khayyám (1st edn.), XX

6 Gather ye rosebuds while ye may,
Old time is still a-flying:
And this same flower that smiles today
Tomorrow will be dying.
Robert Herrick (1591–1674) English poet.
Hesperides, 'To the Virgins, to Make Much of Time'

7 *Carpe diem.*
Seize the day.
Horace (Quintus Horatius Flaccus; 65–8 BC) Roman poet.
Odes, I

8 Drop the question what tomorrow may bring, and count as profit every day that Fate allows you.
Horace
Odes, I

9 While we're talking, time will have meanly

run on: pick today's fruits, not relying on the future in the slightest.
Horace
Odes, I

10 Believe each day that has dawned is your last. Some hour to which you have not been looking forward will prove lovely. As for me, if you want a good laugh, you will come and find me fat and sleek, in excellent condition, one of Epicurus' herd of pigs.
Horace
Epistles, I

11 We live in stirring times – tea-stirring times.
Christopher Isherwood (1904–86) British novelist.
Mr Norris Changes Trains

12 Redeem thy mis-spent time that's past;
Live this day, as if 'twere thy last.
Thomas Ken (1637–1711) English bishop.
A Morning Hymn

13 What is love? 'Tis not hereafter;
Present mirth hath present laughter;
What's to come is still unsure.
In delay there lies no plenty,
Then come kiss me, sweet and twenty;
Youth's a stuff will not endure.
William Shakespeare (1564–1616) English dramatist.
Twelfth Night, II:3

PRIDE

See also arrogance, conceit, egotism, self-respect

1 Pride goeth before destruction, and an haughty spirit before a fall.
Bible: Proverbs
16:18

2 He that is down needs fear no fall;
He that is low, no pride.
John Bunyan (1628–88) English writer.
The Pilgrim's Progress, 'Shepherd Boy's Song'

3 When the Lord sent me forth into the world, He forbade me to put off my hat to any high or low.
George Fox (1624–91) English religious leader.
Journal

4 And if you include me among the lyric poets, I'll hold my head so high it'll strike the stars.
Horace (Quintus Horatius Flaccus; 65–8 BC) Roman poet.
Odes, I

5 We are not ashamed of what we have done, because, when you have a great cause to fight for, the moment of greatest humiliation is the moment when the spirit is proudest.
Christabel Pankhurst (1880–1958) British suffragette.
Speech, Albert Hall, London, 19 Mar 1908

6 Yes; I am proud, I must be proud to see
Men not afraid of God, afraid of me.
Alexander Pope (1688–1744) British poet.
Epilogue to the Satires, Dialogue II

7 Of all the causes which conspire to blind
Man's erring judgment, and misguide the mind,
What the weak head with strongest bias rules,
Is Pride, the never-failing vice of fools.
Alexander Pope
An Essay on Criticism

8 There is false modesty, but there is no false pride.
Jules Renard (1894–1910) French writer.
Journal

9 The French want no-one to be their *superior*. The English want *inferiors*. The Frenchman constantly raises his eyes above him with anxiety. The Englishman lowers his beneath him with satisfaction. On either side it is pride, but understood in a different way.
Alexis de Tocqueville (1805–59) French writer, historian, and politician.
Voyage en Angleterre et en Irlande de 1835, 18 May

10 We cannot bring ourselves to believe it possible that a foreigner should in any respect be wiser than ourselves. If any such point out to us our follies, we at once claim those follies as the special evidences of our wisdom.
Anthony Trollope (1815–82) British novelist.
Orley Farm, Ch. 18

PRINCIPLES

See also integrity, morality

1 It is easier to fight for one's principles than to live up to them.
Alfred Adler (1870–1937) Austrian psychiatrist.
Alfred Adler (P. Bottome)

2 If one sticks too rigidly to one's principles one would hardly see anybody.
Agatha Christie (1891–1976) British detective-story writer.
Towards Zero, I

3 Whenever two good people argue over principles, they are both right.
Marie Ebner von Eschenbach (1830–1916) Austrian writer.
Aphorism

4 Well, sir, you never can tell. That's a principle in life with me, sir, if you'll excuse my having such a thing, sir.
George Bernard Shaw (1856–1950) Irish dramatist and critic.
You Never Can Tell, II

PRIVACY

1 The house of every one is to him as his castle and fortress.
Edward Coke (1552–1634) English lawyer and politician.
Semayne's Case

2 I never said, 'I want to be alone.' I only said,

'I want to be *left* alone.' There is all the difference.

Greta Garbo (1905–) Swedish-born US film star.
Garbo (John Bainbridge)

3 The poorest man may in his cottage bid defiance to all the forces of the Crown. It may be frail – its roof may shake – the wind may blow through it – the storm may enter – the rain may enter – but the King of England cannot enter! – all his force dares not cross the threshold of the ruined tenement!

William Pitt the Elder (1708–78) British statesman.
Statesmen in the Time of George III (Lord Brougham), Vol. I

4 This is a free country, madam. We have a right to share your privacy in a public place.

Peter Ustinov (1921–) British actor.
Romanoff and Juliet, I

PROCRASTINATION

1 Never put off till tomorrow what you can do today.

Proverb

2 Put off the evil hour as long as you can.

Proverb

3 The road to hell is paved with good intentions.

Proverb

4 Give me chastity and continence, but not yet.

St Augustine of Hippo (354–430) Bishop of Hippo.
Confessions, Bk. VIII, Ch. 7

5 Procrastination is the thief of time.

Edward Young (1683–1765) British poet.
Night Thoughts

PROGRESS

See also change, conservatism, improvement, innovation, novelty, technology

1 The people who live in the past must yield to the people who live in the future. Otherwise the world would begin to turn the other way round.

Arnold Bennett (1867–1931) British novelist.
Milestones

2 All progress is based upon a universal innate desire on the part of every organism to live beyond its income.

Samuel Butler (1835–1902) British writer.
Notebooks

3 As enunciated today, 'progress' is simply a comparative of which we have not settled the superlative.

G. K. Chesterton (1874–1936) British writer.
Heretics, Ch. 2

4 New roads: new ruts.

G. K. Chesterton
Attrib.

5 What we call progress is the exchange of one nuisance for another nuisance.

Havelock Ellis (1859–1939) British sexologist.
Attrib.

6 All that is human must retrograde if it does not advance.

Edward Gibbon (1737–94) British historian.
Decline and Fall of the Roman Empire, Ch. 71

7 You cannot fight against the future. Time is on our side.

William Ewart Gladstone (1809–98) British statesman.
Advocating parliamentary reform
Speech, 1866

8 One step forward, two steps back . . . It happens in the lives of individuals, and it happens in the history of nations and in the development of parties.

Lenin (Vladimir Ilich Ulyanov; 1870–1924) Russian revolutionary leader.
One Step Forward, Two Steps Back

9 If I have seen further it is by standing on the shoulders of giants.

Isaac Newton (1642–1727) British scientist.
Letter to Robert Hooke, 5 Feb 1675

10 You can't say civilization don't advance, however, for in every war they kill you a new way.

Will Rogers (1879–1935) US actor and humorist.
Autobiography, Ch. 12

11 Organic life, we are told, has developed gradually from the protozoon to the philosopher, and this development, we are assured, is indubitably an advance. Unfortunately it is the philosopher, not the protozoon, who gives us this assurance.

Bertrand Russell (1872–1970) British philosopher.
Mysticism and Logic, Ch. 6

12 Man's 'progress' is but a gradual discovery that his questions have no meaning.

Antoine de Saint-Exupéry (1900–44) French novelist and aviator.
The Wisdom of the Sands

PROMISCUITY

See also sex

1 I see – she's the original good time that was had by all.

Bette Davis (Ruth Elizabeth Davis; 1908–) US film star.
Referring to a starlet of the time
The Filmgoer's Book of Quotes (Leslie Halliwell)

2 Lady Capricorn, he understood, was still keeping open bed.

Aldous Huxley (1894–1964) British novelist.
Antic Hay, Ch. 21

3 The woman's a whore, and there's an end on't.
Samuel Johnson (1709–84) British lexicographer.
Referring to Lady Diana Beauclerk
Life of Johnson (J. Boswell), Vol. II

4 You were born with your legs apart. They'll send you to the grave in a Y-shaped coffin.
Joe Orton (1933–67) British dramatist.
What the Butler Saw, I

5 You know, she speaks eighteen languages. And she can't say 'No' in any of them.
Dorothy Parker (1893–1967) US writer.
Speaking of an acquaintance
Attrib.

6 I'm glad you like my Catherine. I like her too. She ruled thirty million people and had three thousand lovers. I do the best I can in two hours.
Mae West (1892–1980) US actress.
After her performance in *Catherine the Great*
Speech from the stage

PROMISES

1 Better is it that thou shouldest not vow, than that thou shouldest vow and not pay.
Bible: Ecclesiastes
5:5

2 I do set my bow in the cloud, and it shall be for a token of a covenant between me and the earth.
Bible: Genesis
9:13

3 The rule is, jam tomorrow and jam yesterday – but never jam today.
Lewis Carroll (Charles Lutwidge Dodgson; 1832–98) British writer.
Through the Looking-Glass, Ch. 5

4 If you feed people just with revolutionary slogans they will listen today, they will listen tomorrow, they will listen the day after tomorrow, but on the fourth day they will say 'To hell with you!'
Nikita Khrushchev (1894–1971) Soviet statesman.
Attrib.

5 A promise made is a debt unpaid.
Robert William Service (1874–1958) Canadian poet.
The Cremation of Sam McGee

6 Jam today, and men aren't at their most exciting: Jam tomorrow, and one often sees them at their noblest.
C. P. Snow (1905–80) British novelist.
The Two Cultures and the Scientific Revolution, 4

7 Promises and pie-crust are made to be broken.
Jonathan Swift (1667–1745) Irish-born Anglican priest and writer.
Polite Conversation, Dialogue 1

PROMOTION

See also patronage

1 Tired of knocking at Preferment's door.
Matthew Arnold (1822–88) British poet and critic.
The Scholar Gipsy

2 He had said he had known many kicked down stairs, but he never knew any kicked up stairs before.
Lord Halifax (1633–95) English statesman.
Original Memoirs (Burnet)

PROMPTNESS

1 Liberality lies less in giving liberally than in the timeliness of the gift.
Jean de La Bruyère (1645–96) French satirist.
Les Caractères

2 Punctuality is the politeness of kings.
Louis XVIII (1755–1824) French king.
Attrib.

3 Better never than late.
George Bernard Shaw (1856–1950) Irish dramatist and critic.
Responding to an offer by a producer to present one of Shaw's plays, having earlier rejected it
The Unimportance of Being Oscar (Oscar Levant)

4 He gives twice who gives promptly.
Publilius Syrus (1st century BC) Roman dramatist.
Attrib.

5 Punctuality is the virtue of the bored.
Evelyn Waugh (1903–66) British novelist.
Diaries, 'Irregular Notes', 26 Mar 1962

PRONUNCIATION

See also class, language, speech, spelling

1 Everybody has a right to pronounce foreign names as he chooses.
Winston Churchill (1874–1965) British statesman.
The Observer, 'Sayings of the Week', 5 Aug 1951

2 Oh my God! Remember you're in Egypt. The *skay* is only seen in Kensington.
Herbert Beerbohm Tree (1853–1917) British actor and theatre manager.
To a leading lady
Beerbohm Tree (Hesketh Pearson)

3 They spell it Vinci and pronounce it Vinchy; foreigners always spell better than they pronounce.
Mark Twain (Samuel Langhorne Clemens; 1835–1910) US writer.
The Innocents Abroad, Ch. 19

PROOF

1 One swallow does not make a summer.
Proverb

2 What is now proved was once only imagined.
William Blake (1757–1827) British poet.
The Marriage of Heaven and Hell, 'Proverbs of Hell'

3 If a man could pass through Paradise in a dream, and have a flower presented to him as a pledge that his soul had really been there, and if he found that flower in his hand when he awoke – Aye, and what then?
Samuel Taylor Coleridge (1772–1834) British poet.
Anima Poetae

4 Of course, before we *know* he is a saint, there will have to be miracles.
Graham Greene (1904–) British novelist.
The Power and the Glory, Pt. IV

5 If only I could get down to Sidcup! I've been waiting for the weather to break. He's got my papers, this man I left them with, it's got it all down there, I could prove everything.
Harold Pinter (1930–) British dramatist.
The Caretaker, I

6 Some circumstantial evidence is very strong, as when you find a trout in the milk.
Henry David Thoreau (1817–62) US writer.
Journal, 1850

PROPAGANDA

1 Propaganda is that branch of the art of lying which consists in nearly deceiving your friends without quite deceiving your enemies.
F. M. Cornford (1886–1960) British poet.
New Statesman, 15 Sept 1978

2 The greater the lie, the greater the chance that it will be believed.
Adolf Hitler (1889–1945) German dictator.
Mein Kampf

3 I wonder if we could contrive . . . some magnificent myth that would in itself carry conviction to our whole community.
Plato (429–347 BC) Greek philosopher.
Republic, Bk. 5

PROPHECY

See also beginning, future

1 'I saw the new moon late yestreen
Wi' the auld moon in her arm;
And if we gang to sea master,
I fear we'll come to harm.'
Anonymous
Sir Patrick Spens

2 And there arose not a prophet since in Israel like unto Moses, whom the Lord knew face to face.
Bible: Deuteronomy
34:10

3 I am signing my death warrant.
Michael Collins (1890–1922) Irish nationalist.
Said on signing the agreement with Great Britain, 1921, that

established the Irish Free State. He was assassinated in an ambush some months later.
Peace by Ordeal (Longford), Pt. 6, Ch. 1

4 I will sit down now, but the time will come when you will hear me.
Benjamin Disraeli (1804–81) British statesman.
Maiden Speech, House of Commons, 7 Dec 1837

5 The lamps are going out over all Europe; we shall not see them lit again in our lifetime.
Lord Grey (1862–1933) British statesman.
Remark made on 3 Aug 1914, the eve of World War I

6 You ain't heard nothin' yet, folks.
Al Jolson (Asa Yoelson; 1886–1950) US actor and singer.
In the film *The Jazz Singer*, July 1927
The Jazz Singer

7 *Après nous le déluge.*
After us the deluge.
Madame de Pompadour (1721–64) The mistress of Louis XV of France.
After the Battle of Rossbach, 1757

8 As I look ahead, I am filled with foreboding. Like the Roman, I seem to see 'the River Tiber foaming with much blood'.
Enoch Powell (1912–) British politician.
Talking about immigration
Speech in Birmingham, 20 Apr 1968

9 Beware the ides of March.
William Shakespeare (1564–1616) English dramatist.
Julius Caesar, I:2

10 Mr Turnbull had predicted evil consequences . . . and was now doing the best in his power to bring about the verification of his own prophecies.
Anthony Trollope (1815–82) British novelist.
Phineas Finn, Ch. 25

11 I see wars, horrible wars, and the Tiber foaming with much blood.
Virgil (Publius Vergilius Maro; 70–19 BC) Roman poet.
Part of the Sibyl's prophecy to Aeneas, foretelling his difficulties in winning a home in Italy.
Aeneid, Bk. VI

PROSE

See also books, criticism, fiction, literature, novels, poetry and prose, writing

1 Yet no one hears his own remarks as prose.
W. H. Auden (1907–73) British poet.
At a Party

2 Men will forgive a man anything except bad prose.
Winston Churchill (1874–1965) British statesman.
Election speech, Manchester, 1906

3 Good heavens! I have been talking prose for over forty years without realizing it.
Molière (Jean Baptiste Poquelin; 1622–73) French dramatist.
Le Bourgeois Gentilhomme, II:4

PROTESTANTISM

See also Catholicism, Christianity, religion

1 The chief contribution of Protestantism to human thought is its massive proof that God is a bore.
H. L. Mencken (1880–1956) US journalist.
Notebooks, 'Minority Report'

2 'You're a Christian?' 'Church of England,' said Mr Polly. 'Mm,' said the employer, a little checked. 'For good all round business work, I should have preferred a Baptist.'
H. G. Wells (1866–1946) British writer.
The History of Mr Polly, Pt. III, Ch. 1

3 Take heed of thinking. *The farther you go from the church of Rome, the nearer you are to God.*
Henry Wotton (1568–1639) English poet and diplomat.
Reliquiae Wottonianae (Izaak Walton)

PROVOCATION

1 My wife hath something in her gizzard, that only waits an opportunity of being provoked to bring up.
Samuel Pepys (1633–1703) English diarist.
Diary, 17 June 1668

2 Ask you what provocation I have had?
The strong antipathy of good to bad.
Alexander Pope (1688–1744) British poet.
Epilogue to the Satires, Dialogue II

PRUDENCE

See also caution, wisdom

1 A bird in the hand is worth two in the bush.
Proverb

2 Forewarned is forearmed.
Proverb

3 For want of a nail the shoe was lost; for want of a shoe the horse was lost; for want of a horse the rider was lost.
Proverb

4 Prevention is better than cure.
Proverb

5 It is always good
When a man has two irons in the fire.
Francis Beaumont (1584–1616) English dramatist.
The Faithful Friends, I:2

6 Put your trust in God, my boys, and keep your powder dry.
Valentine Blacker (1778–1823) British soldier.
Oliver Cromwell's Advice

7 I'd much rather have that fellow inside my tent pissing out, than outside my tent pissing in.
Lyndon B. Johnson (1908–73) US statesman.
When asked why he retained J. Edgar Hoover at the FBI
Guardian Weekly, 18 Dec 1971

8 One should oblige everyone to the extent of one's ability. One often needs someone smaller than oneself.
Jean de La Fontaine (1621–95) French poet.
Fables, II, 'Le Lion et le Rat'

9 Any girl who was a lady would not even think of having such a good time that she did not remember to hang on to her jewelry.
Anita Loos (1891–1981) US novelist.
Gentlemen Prefer Blondes, Ch. 4

10 Be nice to people on your way up because you'll meet 'em on your way down.
Wilson Mizner (1876–1933) US writer and wit.
Also attributed to Jimmy Durante
A Dictionary of Catch Phrases (Eric Partridge)

PRUDERY

See also censorship, pornography, puritanism

1 Would you allow your wife or your servant to read this book?
Mervyn Griffith-Jones (1909–78) British lawyer.
As counsel for the prosecution in the *Lady Chatterley's Lover* trial

2 Age will bring all things, and everyone knows, Madame, that twenty is no age to be a prude.
Molière (Jean Baptiste Poquelin; 1622–73) French dramatist.
Le Misanthrope, III:4

3 An orgy looks particularly alluring seen through the mists of righteous indignation.
Malcolm Muggeridge (1903–) British writer.
The Most of Malcolm Muggeridge, 'Dolce Vita in a Cold Climate'

4 Obscenity is what happens to shock some elderly and ignorant magistrate.
Bertrand Russell (1872–1970) British philosopher.
Look magazine

PSYCHIATRY

See also madness, neurosis, psychology

1 To us he is no more a person
Now but a climate of opinion.
W. H. Auden (1907–73) British poet.
In Memory of Sigmund Freud

2 The trouble with Freud is that he never played the Glasgow Empire Saturday night.
Ken Dodd (1931–) British comedian.
TV interview, 1965

3 The psychic development of the individual is

a short repetition of the course of development of the race.

Sigmund Freud (1856–1939) Austrian psychoanalyst.
Leonardo da Vinci

4 Anybody who goes to see a psychiatrist ought to have his head examined.

Samuel Goldwyn (Samuel Goldfish; 1882–1974) Polish-born US film producer.
Attrib.

5 Schizophrenic behaviour is a special strategy that a person invents in order to live in an unlivable situation.

R. D. Laing (1927–) British psychiatrist.
The Politics of Experience

6 Schizophrenia cannot be understood without understanding despair.

R. D. Laing
The Divided Self, Ch. 2

7 The mystic sees the ineffable, and the psychopathologist the unspeakable.

W. Somerset Maugham (1874–1965) British novelist.
The Moon and Sixpence, Ch. 1

8 If the nineteenth century was the age of the editorial chair, ours is the century of the psychiatrist's couch.

Marshall McLuhan (1911–81) Canadian sociologist.
Understanding Media, Introduction

9 A psychiatrist is a man who goes to the Folies-Bergère and looks at the audience.

Mervyn Stockwood (1913–) British churchman.
The Observer, 'Sayings of the Week', 15 Oct 1961

10 Psychiatrists classify a person as neurotic if he suffers from his problems in living, and a psychotic if he makes others suffer.

Thomas Szasz (1920–) US psychiatrist.
The Second Sin

11 He was meddling too much in my private life.

Tennessee Williams (1911–83) US dramatist.
Explaining why he had given up visiting his psychoanalyst
Attrib.

12 He is always called a nerve specialist because it sounds better, but everyone knows he's a sort of janitor in a looney bin.

P. G. Wodehouse (1881–1975) British humorous novelist.
The Inimitable Jeeves

PSYCHOLOGY

See also mind, psychiatry

1 What progress we are making. In the Middle Ages they would have burned me. Now they are content with burning my books.

Sigmund Freud (1856–1939) Austrian psychoanalyst.
Referring to the public burning of his books in Berlin.
Letter to Ernest Jones, 1933

2 I don't think the profession of historian fits a man for psychological analysis. In our work we have to deal only with simple feelings to

which we give generic names such as Ambition and Interest.

Jean-Paul Sartre (1905–80) French writer.
Nausea

PUBLIC

See also class, majority

1 *Vox populi, vox dei.*
The voice of the people is the voice of God.

Alcuin (c. 735–804) English theologian.
Letter to Charlemagne

2 But that vast portion, lastly, of the working-class which, raw and half-developed, has long lain half-hidden amidst its poverty and squalor, and is now issuing from its hiding-place to assert an Englishman's heaven-born privilege of doing as he likes, and is beginning to perplex us by marching where it likes, meeting where it likes, bawling what it likes, breaking what it likes – to this vast residuum we may with great propriety give the name of Populace.

Matthew Arnold (1822–88) British poet and critic.
Culture and Anarchy, Ch. 3

3 Our researchers into Public Opinion are content
That he held the proper opinions for the time of year;
When there was peace, he was for peace; when there was war, he went.

W. H. Auden (1907–73) British poet.
The Unknown Citizen

4 You cannot make a man by standing a sheep on its hind legs. But by standing a flock of sheep in that position you can make a crowd of men.

Max Beerbohm (1872–1956) British writer.
Zuleika Dobson, Ch. 9

5 The great Unwashed.

Henry Peter Brougham (1778–1868) Scottish lawyer and politician.
Attrib.

6 The people are the masters.

Edmund Burke (1729–97) British politician.
Speech on the Economical Reform (House of Commons, 11 Feb 1780)

7 The public buys its opinions as it buys its meat, or takes in its milk, on the principle that it is cheaper to do this than to keep a cow. So it is, but the milk is more likely to be watered.

Samuel Butler (1835–1902) British writer.
Notebooks

8 The Public is an old woman. Let her maunder and mumble.

Thomas Carlyle (1795–1881) Scottish historian and essayist.
Journal, 1835

9 The people would be just as noisy if they were going to see me hanged.
Oliver Cromwell (1599–1658) English soldier and statesman.
Referring to a cheering crowd

10 If by the people you understand the multitude, the *hoi polloi*, 'tis no matter what they think; they are sometimes in the right, sometimes in the wrong; their judgement is a mere lottery.
John Dryden (1631–1700) British poet and dramatist.
Essay of Dramatic Poesy

11 Nor is the Peoples Judgment always true:
The Most may err as grosly as the Few.
John Dryden
Absalom and Achitophel, I

12 Ill fares the land, to hast'ning ills a prey,
Where wealth accumulates, and men decay;
Princes and lords may flourish, or may fade;
A breath can make them, as a breath has made;
But a bold peasantry, their country's pride,
When once destroy'd, can never be supplied.
Oliver Goldsmith (1728–74) Irish-born British writer.
The Deserted Village

13 There is not a more mean, stupid, dastardly, pitiful, selfish, spiteful, envious, ungrateful animal than the public. It is the greatest of cowards, for it is afraid of itself.
William Hazlitt (1778–1830) British essayist.
On Living to Oneself

14 Only constant repetition will finally succeed in imprinting an idea on the memory of the crowd.
Adolf Hitler (1889–1945) German dictator.
Mein Kampf, Ch. 6

15 The people long eagerly for just two things – bread and circuses.
Juvenal (Decimus Junius Juvenalis; 60–130 AD) Roman satirist.
Satires, X

16 They are only ten.
Lord Northcliffe (1865–1922) Irish-born British newspaper proprietor.
Rumoured to have been a notice to remind his staff of his opinion of the mental age of the general public.
Attrib.

17 The multitude is always in the wrong.
Earl of Roscommon (1633–85) Irish-born English poet.
Essay on Translated Verse

18 Once the people begin to reason, all is lost.
Voltaire (François-Marie Arouet; 1694–1778) French writer.
Letter to Damilaville, 1 Apr 1766

19 The century on which we are entering – the century which will come out of this war – can be and must be the century of the common man.
Henry Wallace (1888–1965) US economist and politician.
Speech, 'The Price of Free World Victory', 8 May 1942

20 Our supreme governors, the mob.
Horace Walpole (1717–97) British writer.
Letter to Sir Horace Mann, 7 Sept 1743

21 I have no concern for the common man except that he should not be so common.
Angus Wilson (1913–) British novelist.
No Laughing Matter

PUBLIC HOUSES

See also alcohol, drunkenness

1 A tavern chair is the throne of human felicity.
Samuel Johnson (1709–84) British lexicographer.
Johnsonian Miscellanies (ed. G. B. Hill), Vol. II

2 There is nothing which has yet been contrived by man, by which so much happiness is produced as by a good tavern or inn.
Samuel Johnson
Life of Johnson (J. Boswell), Vol. II

3 Souls of poets dead and gone,
What Elysium have ye known,
Happy field or mossy cavern,
Choicer than the Mermaid Tavern?
Have ye tippled drink more fine
Than mine host's Canary wine?
John Keats (1795–1821) British poet.
Lines on the Mermaid Tavern

4 The hands of the clock have stayed still at half past eleven for fifty years. It is always opening time in the Sailors Arms.
Dylan Thomas (1914–53) Welsh poet.
Under Milk Wood

5 Come, Come, Come and have a drink with me
Down at the old 'Bull and Bush'.
Harry Tilzer (Albert von Tilzer; 1878–1956) British songwriter.
The Old Bull and Bush

PUBLISHING

See also books, editors

1 Publication is the male equivalent of childbirth.
Richard Acland (1906–) British politician and writer.
The Observer, 'Sayings of the Week', 19 May 1974

2 I'll publish, right or wrong:
Fools are my theme, let satire be my song.
Lord Byron (1788–1824) British poet.
English Bards and Scotch Reviewers

3 Now Barabbas was a publisher.
Thomas Campbell (1777–1844) British poet.
Attrib.

4 Gentlemen, you must not mistake me. I admit that he is the sworn foe of our nation, and, if you will, of the whole human race. But, gentlemen, we must be just to our

enemy. We must not forget that he once shot a bookseller.

Thomas Campbell
Excusing himself in proposing a toast to Napoleon at a literary dinner
The Life and Letters of Lord Macaulay (G. O. Trevelyan)

5 As repressed sadists are supposed to become policemen or butchers so those with irrational fear of life become publishers.

Cyril Connolly (1903–74) British journalist.
Enemies of Promise, Ch. 3

6 Let it be kept till the ninth year, the manuscript put away at home: you may destroy whatever you haven't published; once out, what you've said can't be stopped.

Horace (Quintus Horatius Flaccus; 65–8 BC) Roman poet.
Ars Poetica

7 My own motto is publish and be sued.

Richard Ingrams (1937–) British editor.
Referring to his editorship of *Private Eye*
BBC radio broadcast, 4 May 1977

8 The booksellers are generous liberal-minded men.

Samuel Johnson (1709–84) British lexicographer.
Life of Johnson (J. Boswell), Vol. I

9 Publish and be damned!

Duke of Wellington (1769–1852) British general and statesman.
On being offered the chance to avoid mention in the memoirs of Harriette Wilson by giving her money
Attrib.

PUNISHMENT

See also education, execution, imprisonment, retribution

1 Wherefore putting away lying, speak every man truth with his neighbour: for we are members one of another.
Be ye angry, and sin not: let not the sun go down upon your wrath:
Neither give place to the devil.
Let him that stole steal no more: but rather let him labour, working with his hands the thing which is good, that he may have to give to him that needeth.

Bible: Ephesians
4:25–28

2 When thou tillest the ground, it shall not henceforth yield unto thee her strength; a fugitive and a vagabond shalt thou be in the earth.
And Cain said unto the Lord, My punishment is greater than I can bear.

Bible: Genesis
4:12–13

3 Then the Lord rained upon Sodom and upon Gomorrah brimstone and fire from the Lord out of heaven.

Bible: Genesis
19:24

4 And surely your blood of your lives will I require; at the hand of every beast will I require it, and at the hand of man; at the hand of every man's brother will I require the life of man.
Whoso sheddeth man's blood, by man shall his blood be shed: for in the image of God made he man.

Bible: Genesis
9:5–6

5 There is no peace, saith the Lord, unto the wicked.

Bible: Isaiah
48:22

6 Love is a boy, by poets styl'd,
Then spare the rod, and spoil the child.

Samuel Butler (1612–80) English satirist.
Hudibras, Pt. II

7 Quoth he, 'The man hath penance done,
And penance more will do.'

Samuel Taylor Coleridge (1772–1834) British poet.
The Rime of the Ancient Mariner, V

8 As some day it may happen that a victim must be found
I've got a little list – I've got a little list
Of society offenders who might well be underground,
And who never would be missed – who never would be missed!

W. S. Gilbert (1836–1911) British dramatist.
The Mikado, I

9 My object all sublime
I shall achieve in time –
To let the punishment fit the crime –
The punishment fit the crime.

W. S. Gilbert
The Mikado, II

10 The billiard sharp whom any one catches,
His doom's extremely hard –
He's made to dwell –
In a dungeon cell
On a spot that's always barred.
And there he plays extravagant matches
In fitless finger-stalls
On a cloth untrue
With a twisted cue
And elliptical billiard balls.

W. S. Gilbert
The Mikado, II

11 The door flew open, in he ran,
The great, long, red-legged scissor-man.

Heinrich Hoffman (1809–74) German writer.
Struwwelpeter, 'The Little Suck-a-Thumb'

12 Corporal punishment is as humiliating for him who gives it as for him who receives it; it is ineffective besides. Neither shame nor

physical pain have any other effect than a hardening one . . .

Ellen Key (Karolina Sofia Key; 1849–1926) Swedish writer.
The Century of the Child, Ch. 8

13 The refined punishments of the spiritual mode are usually much more indecent and dangerous than a good smack.

D. H. Lawrence (1885–1930) British novelist.
Fantasia of the Unconscious, Ch. 4

14 He must have known me had he seen me as he was wont to see me, for he was in the habit of flogging me constantly. Perhaps he did not recognize me by my face.

Anthony Trollope (1815–82) British novelist.
Autobiography, Ch. 1

15 I'm all for bringing back the birch, but only between consenting adults.

Gore Vidal (1925–) US novelist.
Said when asked by David Frost in a TV interview for his views about corporal punishment

---

PUNS

See also humour

1 When I am dead, I hope it may be said: 'His sins were scarlet, but his books were read.'

Hilaire Belloc (1870–1953) French-born British poet.
Epigrams, 'On His Books'

2 VISITOR. Ah, Bottomley, sewing?
BOTTOMLEY. No, reaping.

Horatio William Bottomley (1860–1933) British newspaper editor.
When found sewing mail bags
Horatio Bottomley (Julian Symons)

3 A man who could make so vile a pun would not scruple to pick a pocket.

John Dennis (1657–1734) British critic and dramatist.
The Gentleman's Magazine, 1781

4 Any stigma will do to beat a dogma.

Philip Guedalla (1889–1944) British writer.
Attrib.

5 His death, which happen'd in his berth,
At forty-odd befell:
They went and told the sexton, and
The sexton toll'd the bell.

Thomas Hood (1799–1845) British poet.
Faithless Sally Brown

6 For that old enemy the gout
Had taken him in toe!

Thomas Hood
Lieutenant Luff

7 The love that loves a scarlet coat
Should be more uniform.

Thomas Hood
Faithless Nelly Gray

8 Ben Battle was a soldier bold,
And used to war's alarms:

But a cannon-ball took off his legs,
So he laid down his arms!

Thomas Hood
Faithless Nelly Gray

9 For here I leave my second leg,
And the Forty-second Foot!

Thomas Hood
Faithless Nelly Gray

10 It is a pistol let off at the ear; not a feather to tickle the intellect.

Charles Lamb (1775–1834) British essayist.
Referring to the nature of a pun
Last Essays of Elia, 'Popular Fallacies'

11 Thou canst not serve both cod and salmon.

Ada Beddington Leverson (1862–1933) British writer.
Reply when offered a choice of fish at dinner
The Times, 7 Nov 1970

12 You know it's hard to hear what a bearded man is saying. He can't speak above a whisker.

Herman J. Mankiewicz (1897–1953) US journalist and screenwriter.
Wit's End (R. E. Drennan)

13 What's a thousand dollars? Mere chicken feed. A poultry matter.

Groucho Marx (Julius Marx; 1895–1977) US comedian.
The Cocoanuts

14 It has been said that a bride's attitude towards her betrothed can be summed up in three words: Aisle. Altar. Hymn.

Frank Muir (1920–) British writer and broadcaster.
Upon My Word! (Frank Muir and Dennis Norden), 'A Jug of Wine'

15 A thing of duty is a boy for ever.

Flann O'Brien (Brian O'Nolan; 1911–66) Irish novelist and journalist.
About policemen always seeming to be young-looking
The Listener, 24 Feb 1977

16 You can lead a whore to culture but you can't make her think.

Dorothy Parker (1893–1967) US writer.
Speech to American Horticultural Society

17 You can't teach an old dogma new tricks.

Dorothy Parker
Wit's End (R. E. Drennan)

18 I tried to resist his overtures, but he plied me with symphonies, quartettes, chamber music and cantatas.

S. J. Perelman (1904–79) US humorous writer.
Crazy Like a Fox, 'The Love Decoy'

19 Mother always told me my day was coming, but I never realized that I'd end up being the shortest knight of the year.

Gordon Richards (1904–86) British champion jockey.
Referring to his diminutive size, on learning of his knighthood
Attrib.

20 Private Means is dead,
God rest his soul,

Officers and fellow-rankers said.

Stevie Smith (Florence Margaret Smith; 1902–71) British poet.
Private Means is Dead

21 That's right. 'Taint yours, and 'taint mine.

Mark Twain (Samuel Langhorne Clemens; 1835–1910) US writer.
Agreeing with a friend's comment that the money of a particular rich industrialist was 'tainted'.
Attrib.

22 To me Adler will always be Jung.

Max Wall (1908–   ) British comedian.
Telegram to Larry Adler on his 60th birthday

PURITANISM

See also prudery

1 A puritan's a person who pours righteous indignation into the wrong things.

G. K. Chesterton (1874–1936) British writer.
Attrib.

2 To the Puritan all things are impure, as somebody says.

D. H. Lawrence (1885–1930) British novelist.
Etruscan Places, 'Cerveteri'

3 The Puritan hated bear-baiting, not because it gave pain to the bear, but because it gave pleasure to the spectators.

Lord Macaulay (1800–59) British historian.
History of England, Vol. I, Ch. 2

4 Puritanism – The haunting fear that someone, somewhere, may be happy.

H. L. Mencken (1880–1956) US journalist.
A Book of Burlesques

PURITY

1 Caesar's wife must be above suspicion.

Proverb

2 I'm as pure as the driven slush.

Tallulah Bankhead (1903–68) US actress.
The Observer, 'Sayings of the Week', 24 Feb 1957

3 A simple maiden in her flower
Is worth a hundred coats-of-arms.

Alfred, Lord Tennyson (1809–92) British poet.
Lady Clara Vere de Vere, II

4 It is one of the superstitions of the human mind to have imagined that virginity could be a virtue.

Voltaire (François-Marie Arouet; 1694–1778) French writer.
Notebooks

5 Age cannot wither her, nor custom stale her infinite virginity.

Daniel Webster (1782–1852) US statesman.
Paraphrasing a line from Shakespeare's *Antony and Cleopatra*

on hearing of Andrew Jackson's steadfast maintenance that his friend Peggy Eaton did not deserve her scandalous reputation
Presidential Anecdotes (P. Boller)

6 I used to be Snow White . . . but I drifted.

Mae West (1892–1980) US actress.
The Wit and Wisdom of Mae West (ed. J. Weintraub)

PURPOSE

See also futility, motive

1 Everything's got a moral, if only you can find it.

Lewis Carroll (Charles Lutwidge Dodgson; 1832–98) British writer.
Alice's Adventures in Wonderland, Ch. 9

2 What is the use of a new-born child?

Benjamin Franklin (1706–90) US scientist and statesman.
Response when asked the same question of a new invention
Life and Times of Benjamin Franklin (J. Parton), Pt. IV

3 A useless life is an early death.

Goethe (1749–1832) German poet and dramatist.
Iphegenie, I:2

4 Fortunately, in her kindness and patience, Nature has never put the fatal question as to the meaning of their lives into the mouths of most people. And where no one asks, no one needs to answer.

Carl Gustav Jung (1875–1961) Swiss psychoanalyst.
The Development of Personality

5 I go among the fields and catch a glimpse of a stoat or a fieldmouse peeping out of the withered grass – the creature hath a purpose and its eyes are bright with it. I go amongst the buildings of a city and I see a man hurrying along –to what? the Creature has a purpose and his eyes are bright with it.

John Keats (1795–1821) British poet.
Letter, 1819

6 Riddle of destiny, who can show
What thy short visit meant, or know
What thy errand here below?

Charles Lamb (1775–1834) British essayist.
On an Infant Dying as soon as Born

7 Yes there is a meaning; at least for me, there is one thing that matters – to set a chime of words tinkling in the minds of a few fastidious people.

Logan Pearsall Smith (1865–1946) US writer.
Attrib.

8 It should not merely be useful and ornamental; it should preach a high moral lesson.

Lytton Strachey (1880–1932) British writer.
Referring to Prince Albert's plans for the Great Exhibition
Queen Victoria, Ch. 4

Q

QUOTATIONS

1 It is a good thing for an uneducated man to read books of quotations.
Winston Churchill (1874–1965) British statesman.
My Early Life, Ch. 9

2 We prefer to believe that the absence of inverted commas guarantees the originality of a thought, whereas it may be merely that the utterer has forgotten its source.
Clifton Fadiman (1904–) US writer.
Any Number Can Play

3 When a thing has been said and said well, have no scruple. Take it and copy it.
Anatole France (1844–1924)
In *The Routledge Dictionary of Quotations* (Robert Andrews)

4 Classical quotation is the *parole* of literary men all over the world.
Samuel Johnson (1709–84) British lexicographer.
Life of Johnson (J. Boswell), Vol. IV

5 Every quotation contributes something to the stability or enlargement of the language.
Samuel Johnson
Dictionary of the English Language

6 To be amused at what you read – that is the great spring of happy quotation
C. E. Montague (1867–1928) British editor and writer.
A Writer's Notes on his Trade

7 If with the literate I am
Impelled to try an epigram
I never seek to take the credit

We all assume that Oscar said it.
Dorothy Parker (1893–1967) US writer.
Oscar Wilde

8 I might repeat to myself . . . a list of quotations from minds profound – if I can remember any of the damn things.
Dorothy Parker
The Little Hours

9 A book that furnishes no quotations is, *me judice*, no book – it is a plaything.
Thomas Love Peacock (1785–1866) British novelist.
Crotchet Castle, Ch. 9

10 To say that anything was a quotation was an excellent method, in Eleanor's eyes, for withdrawing it from discussion.
Saki (Hector Hugh Munro; 1870–1916) British writer.
The Jesting of Arlington Stringham

11 The devil can cite Scripture for his purpose.
William Shakespeare (1564–1616) English dramatist.
The Merchant of Venice, I:3

12 It's better to be quotable than to be honest.
Tom Stoppard (1937–) Czech-born British dramatist.
The Guardian

13 In the dying world I come from quotation is a national vice. It used to be the classics, now it's lyric verse.
Evelyn Waugh (1903–66) British novelist.
The Loved One

14 The nicest thing about quotes is that they give us a nodding acquaintance with the originator which is often socially impressive.
Kenneth Williams (1926–88) British comic actor.
Acid Drops

R

RABBITS

See also animals

1 The rabbit has a charming face;
Its private life is a disgrace.
Anonymous
The Rabbit

2 I shall tell you a tale of four little rabbits whose names were Flopsy, Mopsy, Cottontail and Peter.
Beatrix Potter (1866–1943) British children's writer.
The Tale of Peter Rabbit

RACE

See also equality, freedom, human rights, Jews, oppression, prejudice, racism, slavery

1 There was a young woman called Starkie,
Who had an affair with a darky.
The result of her sins
Was quadruplets, not twins –

One black, and one white, and two khaki.
Anonymous

2 It is a great shock at the age of five or six to find that in a world of Gary Coopers you are the Indian.
James Baldwin (1924–87) US writer.
Speech, Cambridge Union, 17 Feb 1965

3 The future is . . . black.
James Baldwin
The Observer, 'Sayings of the Week', 25 Aug 1963

4 My mother bore me in the southern wild.
And I am black, but O! my soul is white;
White as an angel is the English child,
But I am black, as if bereav'd of light.
William Blake (1757–1827) British poet.
Songs of Innocence, 'The Little Black Boy'

5 I suffer from an incurable disease – colour blindness.
Joost de Blank (1908–68) Dutch-born British churchman.
Attrib.

6 I'm a coloured, one-eyed Jew.
Sammy Davis Jnr (1925–) Black US singer.
When asked what his handicap was during a game of golf
Attrib.

7 The so-called white races are really pinko-gray.
E. M. Forster (1879–1970) British novelist.
A Passage to India, Ch. 7

8 When the white man came we had the land and they had the Bibles; now they have the land and we have the Bibles.
Dan George (1899–1982) Canadian Indian chief.
Attrib.

9 I want to be the white man's brother, not his brother-in-law.
Martin Luther King (1929–68) US Black civil-rights leader.
New York Journal-American, 10 Sept 1962

10 Take up the White Man's burden –
And reap his old reward:
The blame of those ye better,
The hate of those ye guard.
Rudyard Kipling (1865–1936) Indian-born British writer.
The White Man's Burden

11 So 'ere's to you, Fuzzy-Wuzzy, at your 'ome in the Soudan;
You're a pore benighted 'eathen but a first-class fightin' man;
An' 'ere's to you, Fuzzy-Wuzzy, with your 'ayrick 'ead of 'air –
You big black boundin' beggar – for you broke a British square!
Rudyard Kipling
Fuzzy-Wuzzy

12 When old settlers say 'One has to understand the country', what they mean is, 'You have to get used to our ideas about the native.' They are saying, in effect, 'Learn our ideas, or otherwise get out; we don't want you.'
Doris Lessing (1919–) British novelist.
Referring specifically to South Africa
The Grass is Singing, Ch. 1

13 When a white man in Africa by accident looks into the eyes of a native and sees the human being (which it is his chief preoccupation to avoid), his sense of guilt, which he denies, fumes up in resentment and he brings down the whip.
Doris Lessing
The Grass is Singing, Ch. 8

14 It's just like when you've got some coffee that's too black, which means it's too strong. What do you do? You integrate it with cream, you make it weak . . . It used to wake you up, now it puts you to sleep.
Malcolm X (1925–65) US Black leader.
Referring to Black Power and the Civil Rights movement
Malcolm X Speaks, Ch. 14

15 He's really awfully fond of coloured people.

Well, he says himself, he wouldn't have white servants.
Dorothy Parker (1893–1967) US writer.
Arrangements in Black and White

16 As I look ahead, I am filled with foreboding. Like the Roman, I seem to see 'the River Tiber foaming with much blood'.
Enoch Powell (1912–) British politician.
Talking about immigration
Speech in Birmingham, 20 Apr 1968

17 He liked to patronise coloured people and treated them as equals because he was quite sure they were not.
Bertrand Russell (1872–1970) British philosopher.
The Autobiography of Bertrand Russell

18 I don't believe in black majority rule ever in Rhodesia . . . not in a thousand years.
Ian Smith (1919–) Rhodesian (Zimbabwe) politician.
Speech, Mar 1976

19 There are two kinds of blood, the blood that flows in the veins and the blood that flows out of them.
Julian Tuwim (1894–1954) Polish writer and poet.
We, the Polish Jews

RACISM

See also equality, freedom, human rights, Jews, oppression, prejudice, racism, slavery

1 All those who are not racially pure are mere chaff.
Adolf Hitler (1889–1945) German dictator.
Mein Kampf, Ch. 2

2 A coloured man can tell, in five seconds dead, whether a white man likes him or not. If the white man *says* he does, he is instantly – and usually quite rightly – mistrusted.
Colin MacInnes (1914–76) British novelist.
England, Half English, 'A Short Guide for Jumbles'

3 One of the things that makes a Negro unpleasant to white folk is the fact that he suffers from their injustice. He is thus a standing rebuke to them.
H. L. Mencken (1880–1956) US journalist.
Notebooks, 'Minority Report'

4 We don't want apartheid liberalized. We want it dismantled. You can't improve something that is intrinsically evil.
Bishop Desmond Tutu (1931–) South African clergyman.
The Observer, 'Sayings of the Week', 10 Mar 1985

5 It seems that the British Government sees black people as expendable.
Bishop Desmond Tutu
Speech, June 1986

READING

See also books, criticism, fiction, literacy, literature, novels, writing

1 Reading maketh a full man; conference a ready man; and writing an exact man.
Francis Bacon (1561–1626) English philosopher.
Essays, 'Of Studies'

2 He has only half learned the art of reading who has not added to it the even more refined accomplishments of skipping and skimming.
Arthur Balfour (1848–1930) British statesman; Conservative prime minister (1902–05).
Mr. Balfour (E. T. Raymond)

3 I read, much of the night, and go south in the winter.
T. S. Eliot (1888–1965) US-born British poet and dramatist.
The Waste Land, 'The Burial of the Dead'

4 A lonesome man on a rainy day who does not know how to read.
Benjamin Franklin (1706–90) US scientist and statesman.
On being asked what condition of man he considered the most pitiable
Wit, Wisdom, and Foibles of the Great (C. Shriner)

5 As writers become more numerous, it is natural for readers to become more indolent.
Oliver Goldsmith (1728–74) Irish-born British writer.
The Bee, 'Upon Unfortunate Merit'

6 Reading is sometimes an ingenious device for avoiding thought.
Arthur Helps (1813–75) British historian.
Friends in Council

7 ELPHINSTON. What, have you not read it through? . . .
JOHNSON. No, Sir, do *you* read books *through*?
Samuel Johnson (1709–84) British lexicographer.
Life of Johnson (J. Boswell), Vol. II

8 A man ought to read just as inclination leads him; for what he reads as a task will do him little good.
Samuel Johnson
Life of Johnson (J. Boswell), Vol. I

9 I love to lose myself in other men's minds. When I am not walking, I am reading; I cannot sit and think. Books think for me.
Charles Lamb (1775–1834) British essayist.
Last Essays of Elia, 'Detached Thoughts on Books and Reading'

10 I'm re-reading it with a slow deliberate carelessness.
T. E. Lawrence (1888–1935) British soldier and writer.
Letter to Edward Marsh, 18 Apr 1929

11 To read too many books is harmful.
Mao Tse-Tung (1893–1976) Chinese communist leader.
The New Yorker, 7 Mar 1977

12 I have only read one book in my life and that is *White Fang*. It's so frightfully good I've never bothered to read another.
Nancy Mitford (1904–73) British writer.
The Pursuit Of Love

13 There are two motives for reading a book: one, that you enjoy it, the other that you can boast about it.
Bertrand Russell (1872–1970) British philosopher.
The Conquest of Happiness

14 People say that life is the thing, but I prefer reading.
Logan Pearsall Smith (1865–1946) US writer.
Afterthoughts, 'Myself'

15 Reading is to the mind what exercise is to the body.
Richard Steele (1672–1729) Dublin-born British essayist.
The Tatler, 147

16 Education . . . has produced a vast population able to read but unable to distinguish what is worth reading.
George Macaulay Trevelyan (1876–1962) British historian.
English Social History, Ch. 18

17 I have led a life of business so long that I have lost my taste for reading, and now – what shall I do?
Horace Walpole (1717–97) British writer.
Thraliana (K. Balderston)

18 Lady Peabury was in the morning room reading a novel; early training gave a guilty spice to this recreation, for she had been brought up to believe that to read a novel before luncheon was one of the gravest sins it was possible for a gentlewoman to commit.
Evelyn Waugh (1903–66) British novelist.
Work Suspended, 'An Englishman's Home'

19 As in the sexual experience, there are never more than two persons present in the act of reading – the writer who is the impregnator, and the reader who is the respondent.
Elwyn Brooks White (1899–1985) US journalist and humorist.
The Second Tree from the Corner

REALISM

1 Mr Lely, I desire you would use all your skill to paint my picture truly like me, and not flatter me at all; but remark all these roughnesses, pimples, warts, and everything as you see me, otherwise I will never pay a farthing for it.
Oliver Cromwell (1599–1658) English soldier and statesman.
The origin of the expression 'warts and all'
Anecdotes of Painting (Horace Walpole), Ch. 12

2 We must rediscover the distinction between hope and expectation.
Ivan Illich (1926–) Austrian sociologist.
Deschooling Society, Ch. 7

3 Better by far
For Johnny-the-bright-star,
To keep your head

And see his children fed.
John Sleigh Pudney (1909–77) British poet and writer.
For Johnny

REALITY

1 For I see now that I am asleep that I dream when I am awake.
Pedro Calderón de la Barca (1600–81) Spanish dramatist.
La Vida es Sueño, II

2 Human kind
Cannot bear very much reality.
T. S. Eliot (1888–1965) US-born British poet and dramatist.
Four Quartets, 'Burnt Norton'

3 Dear friend, theory is all grey,
And the golden tree of life is green.
Goethe (1749–1832) German poet and dramatist.
Faust, Pt. I

4 I fancy, for myself, that they are rather out of touch with reality; by reality I mean shops like Selfridges, and motor buses, and the *Daily Express*.
T. E. Lawrence (1888–1935) British soldier and writer.
Referring to expatriate authors living in Paris, such as James Joyce
Letter to W. Hurley, 1 Apr 1929

5 If this were play'd upon a stage now, I could condemn it as an improbable fiction.
William Shakespeare (1564–1616) English dramatist.
Twelfth Night, III:4

REASON

See also motive

1 Some who had received a liberal education at the Colleges of Unreason, and taken the highest degrees in hypothetics, which are their principal study.
Samuel Butler (1835–1902) British writer.
Erewhon, Ch. 9

2 Reason is itself a matter of faith. It is an act of faith to assert that our thoughts have any relation to reality at all.
G. K. Chesterton (1874–1936) British writer.
Orthodoxy, Ch. 3

3 My dear friend, clear your *mind* of cant . . . You may *talk* in this manner; it is a mode of talking in Society: but don't *think* foolishly.
Samuel Johnson (1709–84) British lexicographer.
Life of Johnson (J. Boswell), Vol. IV

4 A man who does not lose his reason over certain things has none to lose.
Gotthold Ephraim Lessing (1729–81) German dramatist.
Emilia Galotti, IV:7

REBELLION

See also revolution

1 The defiance of established authority, religious and secular, social and political, as a world-wide phenomenon may well one day be accounted the outstanding event of the last decade.
Hannah Arendt (1906–75) German-born US philosopher and historian.
Crises of the Republic, 'Civil Disobedience'

2 What is a rebel? A man who says no.
Albert Camus (1913–60) French existentialist writer.
The Rebel

3 No one can go on being a rebel too long without turning into an autocrat.
Lawrence Durrell (1912–) British novelist.
Balthazar, II

4 When the People contend for their Liberty, they seldom get anything by their Victory but new masters.
Lord Halifax (1633–95) English statesman.
Political, Moral, and Miscellaneous Thoughts and Reflections

5 A little rebellion now and then is a good thing.
Thomas Jefferson (1743–1826) US statesman.
Letter to James Madison, 30 Jan 1787

6 A riot is at bottom the language of the unheard.
Martin Luther King (1929–68) US Black civil-rights leader.
Chaos or Community, Ch. 4

7 Angry Young Man.
Leslie Paul (1905–) British writer.
Book title

REGRET

See also apologies, memory, mourning, nostalgia, past, sorrow

1 It is no use crying over spilt milk.
Proverb

2 It's too late to shut the stable door after the horse has bolted.
Proverb

3 What's done cannot be undone.
Proverb

4 One doesn't recognize in one's life the really important moments – not until it's too late.
Agatha Christie (1891–1976) British detective-story writer.
Endless Night, Bk. II, Ch. 14

5 This hand hath offended.
Thomas Cranmer (1489–1556) English churchman.
Memorials of Cranmer (Strype)

6 Were it not better to forget
Than but remember and regret?
Letitia Landon (1802–38) British poet and novelist.
Despondency

7 We might have been – These are but common words,

And yet they make the sum of life's bewailing.
Letitia Landon
Three Extracts from the Diary of a Week

8 And so, I missed my chance with one of the lords
Of life.
And I have something to expiate;
A pettiness.
D. H. Lawrence (1885–1930) British novelist.
Snake

9 Maybe it would have been better if neither of us had been born.
Napoleon I (Napoleon Bonaparte; 1769–1821) French emperor.
Said while looking at the tomb of the philosopher Jean-Jacques Rousseau, whose theories had influenced the French Revolution
The Story of Civilization (W. Durant), Vol. II

10 Good-bye, I've barely said a word to you, it is always like that at parties, we never see the people, we never say the things we should like to say, but it is the same everywhere in this life. Let us hope that when we are dead things will be better arranged.
Marcel Proust (1871–1922) French novelist.
À la recherche du temps perdu: Sodome et Gomorrhe

11 The follies which a man regrets most in his life are those which he didn't commit when he had the opportunity.
Helen Rowland (1876–1950) US writer.
Reflections of a Bachelor Girl

12 But with the morning cool repentance came.
Walter Scott (1771–1832) Scottish novelist.
Rob Roy, Ch. 12

13 Things sweet to taste prove in digestion sour.
William Shakespeare (1564–1616) English dramatist.
Richard II, I:3

14 What's gone and what's past help
Should be past grief.
William Shakespeare
The Winter's Tale, III:2

15 O, pardon me, thou bleeding piece of earth,
That I am meek and gentle with these butchers!
Thou art the ruins of the noblest man
That ever lived in the tide of times.
William Shakespeare
Julius Caesar, III:1

16 To mourn a mischief that is past and gone
Is the next way to draw new mischief on.
William Shakespeare
Othello, I:3

17 When to the sessions of sweet silent thought
I summon up remembrance of things past,
I sigh the lack of many a thing I sought,

And with old woes new wail my dear time's waste.
William Shakespeare
Sonnet 30

18 Had I but serv'd my God with half the zeal
I serv'd my King, he would not in mine age
Have left me naked to mine enemies.
William Shakespeare
Henry VIII, III:2

19 The bitterest tears shed over graves are for words left unsaid and deeds left undone.
Harriet Beecher Stowe (1811–96) US novelist.
Little Foxes, Ch. 3

20 I never wonder to see men wicked, but I often wonder to see them not ashamed.
Jonathan Swift (1667–1745) Irish-born Anglican priest and writer.
Thoughts on Various Subjects

21 Though nothing can bring back the hour
Of splendour in the grass, of glory in the flower;
We will grieve not, rather find
Strength in what remains behind . . .
William Wordsworth (1770–1850) British poet.
Ode. Intimations of Immortality, IX

22 Men are we, and must grieve when even the shade
Of that which once was great is passed away.
William Wordsworth
Sonnets, 'Once did she hold'

RELIABILITY

1 He's the Man Who Delivers the Goods.
Walt Mason (1862–1939) Canadian poet and humorist.
The Man Who Delivers the Goods

RELIGION

See also atheism, belief, Bible, Catholicism, Christianity, Christmas, Church, damnation, devil, doomsday, faith, God, heaven, hell, Jews, martyrdom, prayer, Protestantism, Sunday

1 Nearer, my God, to thee,
Nearer to thee!
Sarah F. Adams (1805–48) British poet and hymn writer.
Nearer My God to Thee

2 There is no salvation outside the church.
St Augustine of Hippo (354–430) Bishop of Hippo.
De Bapt., IV

3 The Jews and Arabs should sit down and settle their differences like good Christians.
Warren Austin (1877–1962) US politician and diplomat.
Attrib.

4 If the concept of God has any validity or use, it can only be to make us larger, freer, and more loving. If God cannot do this, then it is time we got rid of Him.
James Baldwin (1924–1987) US writer.
The Fire next Time

5 Every day people are straying away from the church and going back to God. Really.
Lenny Bruce (1925–66) US comedian.
The Essential Lenny Bruce (ed. J. Cohen), 'Religions Inc.'

6 This Ariyan Eightfold Path, that is to say: Right view, right aim, right speech, right action, right living, right effort, right mindfulness, right contemplation.
Buddha (Gautama Siddhartha; c. 563 – c. 483 BC) Indian religious teacher.
Some Sayings of the Buddha (F. L. Woodward)

7 Man is by his constitution a religious animal.
Edmund Burke (1729–97) British politician.
Reflections on the Revolution in France

8 One religion is as true as another.
Robert Burton (1577–1640) English scholar and explorer.
Anatomy of Melancholy, Pt. III

9 To be at all is to be religious more or less.
Samuel Butler (1835–1902) British writer.
Notebooks

10 Not a religion for gentlemen.
Charles II (1630–85) King of England.
Referring to Presbyterianism
History of My Own Time (Burnet), Vol. I, Bk. II, Ch. 2

11 Religion is by no means a proper subject of conversation in a mixed company.
Earl of Chesterfield (1694–1773) English statesman.
Letter to his godson

12 When your ladyship's faith has removed them, I will go thither with all my heart.
Earl of Chesterfield
Said to his sister, Lady Gertrude Hotham, when she suggested he go to a Methodist seminary in Wales to recuperate, recommending the views
Attrib.

13 Talk about the pews and steeples
And the cash that goes therewith!
But the souls of Christian peoples . . .
Chuck it, Smith!
G. K. Chesterton (1874–1936) British writer.
Antichrist, or the Reunion of Christendom

14 Men will wrangle for religion; write for it; fight for it; anything but – live for it.
Charles Caleb Colton (?1780–1832) British clergyman and writer.
Lacon, Vol. I

15 Pray remember, Mr Dean, no dogma, no Dean.
Benjamin Disraeli (1804–81) British statesman.
Attrib.

16 'Sensible men are all of the same religion.'
'And pray what is that?' inquired the prince.
'Sensible men never tell.'
Benjamin Disraeli
Endymion, Bk. I, Ch. 81

17 In pious times, e'r Priest-craft did begin, Before Polygamy was made a Sin.
John Dryden (1631–1700) British poet and dramatist.
Absalom and Achitophel, I

18 Christian Science explains all cause and effect as mental, not physical.
Mary Baker Eddy (1821–1910) US religious leader.
Science and Health, with Key to the Scriptures

19 Sickness, sin and death, being inharmonious, do not originate in God, nor belong to His government.
Mary Baker Eddy
Science and Health, with Key to the Scriptures

20 Science without religion is lame, religion without science is blind.
Albert Einstein (1879–1955) German-born US physicist.
Out of My Later Years

21 The religions we call false were once true.
Ralph Waldo Emerson (1803–82) US poet and essayist.
Essays, 'Character'

22 Religion is an illusion and it derives its strength from the fact that it falls in with our instinctual desires.
Sigmund Freud (1856–1939) Austrian psychoanalyst.
New Introductory Lectures on Psychoanalysis, 'A Philosophy of Life'

23 Religion
Has made an honest woman of the supernatural,
And we won't have it kicking over the traces again.
Christopher Fry (1907–) British dramatist.
The Lady's Not for Burning, II

24 There exists no politician in India daring enough to attempt to explain to the masses that cows can be eaten.
Indira Gandhi (1917–84) Indian stateswoman.
New York Review of Books, 'Indira's Coup' (Oriana Fallaci)

25 The various modes of worship, which prevailed in the Roman world, were all considered by the people as equally true; by the philosopher, as equally false; and by the magistrate, as equally useful. And thus toleration produced not only mutual indulgence, but even religious concord.
Edward Gibbon (1737–94) British historian.
Decline and Fall of the Roman Empire, Ch. 2

26 As I take my shoes from the shoemaker, and my coat from the tailor, so I take my religion from the priest.
Oliver Goldsmith (1728–74) Irish-born British writer.
Life of Johnson (J. Boswell)

27 Those who marry God . . . can become domesticated too – it's just as humdrum a marriage as all the others.
Graham Greene (1904–) British novelist.
A Burnt-Out Case, Ch. 1

28 Pray, good people, be civil. I am the Protestant whore.
Nell Gwyn (1650–87) English actress.
On being surrounded in her coach by an angry mob in Oxford at the time of the Popish Plot
Nell Gwyn (Bevan), Ch. 13

29 But as I rav'd and grew more fierce and wild
At every word,
Methought I heard one calling, 'Child';
And I replied, 'My Lord.'
George Herbert (1593–1633) English poet.
The Collar

30 The sedate, sober, silent, serious, sad-coloured sect.
Thomas Hood (1799–1845) British poet.
Referring to the Quakers
The Doves and the Crows

31 To become a popular religion, it is only necessary for a superstition to enslave a philosophy.
Dean Inge (1860–1954) British churchman.
Outspoken Essays

32 Many people believe that they are attracted by God, or by Nature, when they are only repelled by man.
Dean Inge
More Lay Thoughts of a Dean

33 Among all my patients in the second half of life ... there has not been one whose problem in the last resort was not that of finding a religious outlook on life.
Carl Gustav Jung (1875–1961) Swiss psychoanalyst.
Modern Man in Search of a Soul

34 But I suppose even God was born too late to trust the old religion –
all those setting out
that never left the ground,
beginning in wisdom, dying in doubt.
Robert Lowell (1917–77) US poet.
Tenth Muse

35 Here stand I. I can do no other. God help me. Amen.
Martin Luther (1483–1546) German Protestant.
Speech at the Diet of Worms, 18 Apr 1521

36 Abide with me; fast falls the eventide;
The darkness deepens; Lord, with me abide;
When other helpers fail, and comforts flee,
Help of the helpless, O, abide with me.
Henry Francis Lyte (1793–1847) British hymn writer.
Abide with Me

37 Religion ... is the opium of the people.
Karl Marx (1818–83) German philosopher and revolutionary.
Criticism of the Hegelian Philosophy of Right, Introduction

38 Things have come to a pretty pass when religion is allowed to invade the sphere of private life.
Lord Melbourne (1779–1848) British statesman.
Attrib.

39 There are many who stay away from church these days because you hardly ever mention God any more.
Arthur Miller (1915–) US dramatist.
The Crucible, I

40 New Presbyter is but old Priest writ large.
John Milton (1608–74) English poet.
Sonnet: 'On the New Forcers of Conscience under the Long Parliament'

41 Man is quite insane. He wouldn't know how to create a maggot and he creates Gods by the dozen.
Michel de Montaigne (1533–92) French essayist.
Essais, II

42 There is a very good saying that if triangles invented a god, they would make him three-sided.
Baron de Montesquieu (1688–1755) French writer.
Lettres persanes

43 There's no reason to bring religion into it. I think we ought to have as great a regard for religion as we can, so as to keep it out of as many things as possible.
Sean O'Casey (1884–1964) Irish dramatist.
The Plough and the Stars, I

44 Organized religion is making Christianity political rather than making politics Christian.
Laurens Van der Post (1906–) South African novelist.
The Observer, 'Sayings of the Week', 9 Nov 1986

45 Unlike Christianity, which preached a peace that it never achieved, Islam unashamedly came with a sword.
Steven Runciman (1903–) British academic and diplomat.
A History of the Crusades, 'The First Crusade'

46 I have been into many of the ancient cathedrals – grand, wonderful, mysterious. But I always leave them with a feeling of indignation because of the generations of human beings who have struggled in poverty to build these altars to the unknown god.
Elizabeth Stanton (1815–1902) US suffragette.
Diary

47 Whenever a man talks loudly against religion, – always suspect that it is not his reason, but his passions which have got the better of his creed.
Laurence Sterne (1713–68) Irish-born British writer.
Tristram Shandy

48 I believe in the Church, One Holy, Catholic and Apostolic, and I regret that it nowhere exists.
William Temple (1881–1944) British churchman.
Attrib.

49 Alas, O Lord, to what a state dost Thou bring those who love Thee!
St Teresa of Ávila (1515–82) Spanish mystic.
The Interior Castle, VI

50 It is spring, moonless night in the small town, starless and bible-black.
Dylan Thomas (1914–53) Welsh poet.
Under Milk Wood

51 I fled Him, down the nights and down the days;
I fled Him, down the arches of the years;
I fled Him, down the labyrinthine ways
Of my own mind; and in the mist of tears
I hid from Him, and under running laughter.
Francis Thompson (1859–1907) British poet.
The Hound of Heaven

52 Rock of ages, cleft for me,
Let me hide myself in Thee.
Augustus Montague Toplady (1740–78) British hymn writer.
Rock of Ages

53 Beware when you take on the Church of God. Others have tried and have bitten the dust.
Bishop Desmond Tutu (1931–) South African clergyman.
Speech, Apr 1987

54 In general the churches, visited by me too often on weekdays . . . bore for me the same relation to God that billboards did to Coca-Cola: they promoted thirst without quenching it.
John Updike (1932–) US novelist.
A Month of Sundays, Ch. 2

55 Jesus loves me – this I know,
For the Bible tells me so.
Susan Warner (1819–85) US novelist.
The Love of Jesus

56 Lord, I ascribe it to Thy grace,
And not to chance, as others do,
That I was born of Christian race,
And not a Heathen, or a Jew.
Isaac Watts (1674–1748) English theologian and hymn writer.
Divine Songs for Children, 'Praise for the Gospel'

57 Our God, our help in ages past,
Our hope for years to come,
Our shelter from the stormy blast,
And our eternal home.
Isaac Watts
Our God, Our Help in Ages Past

58 I have noticed again and again since I have been in the Church that lay interest in ecclesiastical matters is often a prelude to insanity.
Evelyn Waugh (1903–66) British novelist.
Decline and Fall, Pt. I, Ch. 8

59 There is a species of person called a 'Modern Churchman' who draws the full salary of a beneficed clergyman and need not commit himself to any religious belief.
Evelyn Waugh
Decline and Fall, Pt. II, Ch. 4

60 Religion is love; in no case is it logic.
Beatrice Webb (1858–1943) British economist and writer.
My Apprenticeship, Ch. 2

61 I look upon all the world as my parish.
John Wesley (1703–91) British religious leader.
Journal, 11 June 1739

62 Why do born-again people so often make you wish they'd never been born the first time?
Katherine Whitehorn (1926–) British journalist.
The Observer, 20 May 1979

63 So many gods, so many creeds,
So many paths that wind and wind,
While just the art of being kind
Is all the sad world needs.
Ella Wheeler Wilcox (1850–1919) US poet.
The World's Need

64 The itch of disputing will prove the scab of churches.
Henry Wotton (1568–1639) English poet and diplomat.
A Panegyric to King Charles

65 The Ethiopians say that their gods are snub-nosed and black, the Thracians that theirs have light blue eyes and red hair.
Xenophanes (c. 560–c. 478 BC) Greek poet and philosopher.
Fragment 15

66 No Jew was ever fool enough to turn Christian unless he was a clever man.
Israel Zangwill (1864–1926) British writer.
Children of the Ghetto, Ch. 1

REMEDIES

See also doctors, illness, medicine

1 Cure the disease and kill the patient.
Francis Bacon (1561–1626) English philosopher.
Essays, 'Of Friendship'

2 The remedy is worse than the disease.
Francis Bacon
Essays, 'Of Seditions and Troubles'

3 Then Peter said, Silver and gold have I none; but such as I have give I thee: In the name of Jesus Christ of Nazareth rise up and walk.
Bible: Acts
3:6

4 And besought him that they might only touch the hem of his garment: and as many as touched were made perfectly whole.
Bible: Matthew
14:36

5 My father invented a cure for which there was no disease and unfortunately my mother caught it and died of it.
Victor Borge (1909–) Danish-born US composer, actor, and musical comedian.
In Concert

6 Well, now, there's a remedy for everything except death.
Miguel de Cervantes (1547–1616) Spanish novelist.
Don Quixote, Pt. II, Ch. 10

7 When a lot of remedies are suggested for a disease, that means it can't be cured.
Anton Chekhov (1860–1904) Russian dramatist.
The Cherry Orchard, II

8 Every day, in every way, I am getting better and better.
Émile Coué (1857–1920) French doctor.
Formula for a cure by autosuggestion

9 Extreme remedies are most appropriate for extreme diseases.
Hippocrates (c. 460–c. 377 BC) Greek physician.
Aphorisms, I

10 As soon as he ceased to be mad he became merely stupid. There are maladies we must not seek to cure because they alone protect us from others that are more serious.
Marcel Proust (1871–1922) French novelist.
À la recherche du temps perdu: Le Côté de Guermantes

11 They all thought she was dead; but my father he kept ladling gin down her throat till she came to so sudden that she bit the bowl off the spoon.
George Bernard Shaw (1856–1950) Irish dramatist and critic.
Pygmalion, III

12 Our body is a machine for living. It is organized for that, it is its nature. Let life go on in it unhindered and let it defend itself, it will do more than if you paralyse it by encumbering it with remedies.
Leo Tolstoy (1828–1910) Russian writer.
War and Peace, Bk. X, Ch. 29

13 Sparrowhawks, Ma'am.
Duke of Wellington (1769–1852) British general and statesman.
Advice when asked by Queen Victoria how to remove sparrows from the Crystal Palace
Attrib.

14 There is only one cure for grey hair. It was invented by a Frenchman. It is called the guillotine.
P. G. Wodehouse (1881–1975) British humorous novelist.
The Old Reliable

RENUNCIATION

See also dismissal

1 Renounce the devil and all his works.
The Book of Common Prayer
Publick Baptism of Infants

2 I would rather be a brilliant memory than a curiosity.
Emma Eames (1865–1952) US opera singer.
Referring to her retirement at the age of 47
The Elephant that Swallowed a Nightingale (C. Galtey)

3 You won't have Nixon to kick around any more, gentlemen. This is my last Press Conference.
Richard Milhous Nixon (1913–) US president.
Press conference, after losing the election for the governorship of California, 2 Nov 1962

4 I'll break my staff,
Bury it certain fathoms in the earth,
And deeper than did ever plummet sound
I'll drown my book.
William Shakespeare (1564–1616) English dramatist.
The Tempest, V:1

5 It is very simple. The artists retired. The British remained.
James Whistler (1834–1903) US painter.
Explaining his resignation as president of the Royal Society of British Artists
Whistler Stories (D. Seitz)

REPARTEE

1 This is very true: for my words are my own, and my actions are my ministers'.
Charles II (1630–85) King of Great Britain and Ireland.
Replying to Lord Rochester's suggested epitaph
King Charles II (A. Bryant)

2 Stand a little less between me and the sun.
Diogenes (412–322 BC) Greek philosopher.
When Alexander the Great asked if there was anything he wanted
Life of Alexander (Plutarch)

3 Oh! he is mad, is he? Then I wish he would bite some other of my generals.
George II (1683–1760) King of Great Britain and Ireland.
Replying to advisors who told him that General James Wolfe was mad
Attrib.

4 JUDGE WILLIS. What do you suppose I am on the Bench for, Mr Smith?
SMITH. It is not for me to attempt to fathom the inscrutable workings of Providence.
F. E. Smith (1872–1930) British lawyer.
Frederick Elwin, Earl of Birkenhead (Lord Birkenhead), Vol. I, Ch. 9

5 LORD SANDWICH. You will die either on the gallows, or of the pox.
WILKES. That must depend on whether I embrace your lordship's principles or your mistress.
John Wilkes (1725–97) British politician.
Sometimes attrib. to Samuel Foote
Portrait of a Patriot (Charles Chenevix-Trench), Ch. 3

REPRESENTATION

1 Taxation without representation is tyranny.
James Otis (1725–83) US political activist.
As 'No taxation without representation' this became the principal slogan of the American Revolution
Attrib.

2 No annihilation without representation.
Arnold Toynbee (1889–1975) British historian.
Urging the need for a greater British influence in the UN 1947

REPUBLIC

See also democracy, State

1 Our object in the construction of the state is the greatest happiness of the whole, and not that of any one class.
Plato (429–347 BC) Greek philosopher.
Republic, Bk. 4

2 As there was no form of government common to the peoples thus segregated, nor tie of language, history, habit, or belief, they were called a Republic.
Evelyn Waugh (1903–66) British novelist.
Scoop, Bk. II, Ch. 1

REPUTATION

See also fame, posterity

1 For my name and memory, I leave it to men's charitable speeches, and to foreign nations, and the next ages.
Francis Bacon (1561–1626) English philosopher.
Will, 19 Dec 1625

2 I hold it as certain, that no man was ever written out of reputation but by himself.
Richard Bentley (1662–1742) English academic.
The Works of Alexander Pope (W. Warburton), Vol. IV

3 Die when I may, I want it said of me by those who know me best, that I have always plucked a thistle and planted a flower where I thought a flower would grow.
Abraham Lincoln (1809–65) US statesman.
Presidential Anecdotes (P. Boller)

4 Until you've lost your reputation, you never realize what a burden it was or what freedom really is.
Margaret Mitchell (1909–49) US novelist.
Gone with the Wind

5 Reputation, reputation, reputation! O, I have lost my reputation! I have lost the immortal part of myself, and what remains is bestial.
William Shakespeare (1564–1616) English dramatist.
Othello, II:3

6 Good name in man and woman, dear my lord,
Is the immediate jewel of their souls:
Who steals my purse steals trash; 'tis something, nothing;
'Twas mine, 'tis his, and has been slave to thousands;
But he that filches from me my good name
Robs me of that which not enriches him
And makes me poor indeed.
William Shakespeare
Othello, III:3

7 The purest treasure mortal times afford
Is spotless reputation; that away,

Men are but gilded loam or painted clay.
William Shakespeare
Richard II, I:1

8 I'm called away by particular business. But I leave my character behind me.
Richard Brinsley Sheridan (1751–1816) British dramatist.
The School for Scandal, II

9 Everything.
Mae West (1892–1980) US actress.
When asked what she wanted to be remembered for
Attrib.

RESEARCH

1 Research! A mere excuse for idleness; it has never achieved, and will never achieve any results of the slightest value.
Benjamin Jowett (1817–93) British theologian.
Unforgotten Years (Logan Pearsall Smith)

2 Always verify your references.
Martin Joseph Routh (1755–1854) British scholar.
Attrib.

3 We haven't the money, so we've got to think.
Ernest Rutherford (1871–1937) British physicist.
Attrib.

4 The outcome of any serious research can only be to make two questions grow where only one grew before.
Thorstein Bunde Veblen (1857–1929) US social scientist.
The Place of Science in Modern Civilization

RESPECT

See also courtesy, self-respect

1 Let them hate, so long as they fear.
Lucius Accius (170–c. 85 BC) Roman tragic playwright.
Atreus, 'Seneca'

2 One does not arrest Voltaire.
Charles De Gaulle (1890–1970) French general and statesman.
Explaining why he had not arrested Jean-Paul Sartre for urging French soldiers in Algeria to desert
Attrib.

3 I hate victims who respect their executioners.
Jean-Paul Sartre (1905–80) French writer.
Altona

4 We owe respect to the living; to the dead we owe only truth.
Voltaire (François-Marie Arouet; 1694–1778) French writer.
Oeuvres, 'Première lettre sur Oedipe'

5 The old-fashioned respect for the young is fast dying out.
Oscar Wilde (1854–1900) Irish-born British dramatist.
The Importance of Being Earnest, I

RESPECTABILITY

1 Since when was genius found respectable?
Elizabeth Barrett Browning (1806–61) British poet.
Aurora Leigh, Bk. VI

2 Let them cant about decorum
Who have characters to lose.
Robert Burns (1759–96) Scottish poet.
The Jolly Beggars

3 Respectable means rich, and decent means poor. I should die if I heard my family called decent.
Thomas Love Peacock (1785–1866) British novelist.
Crotchet Castle, Ch. 3

4 So live that you wouldn't be ashamed to sell the family parrot to the town gossip.
Will Rogers (1879–1935) US actor and humorist.
Attrib.

RESPONSIBILITY

See also accusation

1 A bad workman always blames his tools.
Proverb

2 What the proprietorship of these papers is aiming at is power, and power without responsibility – the prerogative of the harlot through the ages.
Stanley Baldwin (1867–1947) British statesman.
Attacking the press barons Lords Rothermere and Beaverbrook. It was first used by KIPLING. *See also* DUKE OF DEVONSHIRE; STOPPARD
Speech, election rally, 18 Mar 1931

3 Each man the architect of his own fate.
Appius Caecus (4th–3rd century BC) Roman statesman.
De Civitate (Sallust), Bk. I

4 Everyone threw the blame on me. I have noticed that they nearly always do. I suppose it is because they think I shall be able to bear it best.
Winston Churchill (1874–1965) British statesman.
My Early Life, Ch. 17

5 Perhaps it is better to be irresponsible and right than to be responsible and wrong.
Winston Churchill
Party Political Broadcast, London, 26 Aug 1950

6 Good God, that's done it. He's lost us the tarts' vote.
Duke of Devonshire (1895–1950) Conservative politician.
Referring to Stanley BALDWIN's attack on newspaper proprietors; recalled by Harold Macmillan
Attrib.

7 It matters not how strait the gate,
How charged with punishments the scroll,
I am the master of my fate:
I am the captain of my soul.
William Ernest Henley (1849–1903) British writer.
Echoes, IV, 'Invictus. In Mem. R.T.H.B.'

8 Power without responsibility – the prerogative of the harlot throughout the ages.
Rudyard Kipling (1865–1936) Indian-born British writer.
Better known for its subsequent use by BALDWIN
Attrib.

9 Accuse not Nature, she hath done her part;
Do thou but thine.
John Milton (1608–74) English poet.
Paradise Lost, Bk. VIII

10 *We can believe what we choose.* We are answerable for what we choose to believe.
Cardinal Newman (1801–90) British theologian.
Letter to Mrs Froude, 27 June 1848

11 You become responsible, forever, for what you have tamed. You are responsible for your rose.
Antoine de Saint-Exupéry (1900–44) French novelist and aviator.
The Little Prince, Ch. 21

12 The salvation of mankind lies only in making everything the concern of all.
Alexander Solzhenitsyn (1918–) Soviet novelist.
Nobel Lecture, 1970

13 The House of Lords, an illusion to which I have never been able to subscribe – responsibility without power, the prerogative of the eunuch throughout the ages.
Tom Stoppard (1937–) Czech-born British dramatist.
See also BALDWIN
Lord Malquist and Mr Moon, Pt. VI, Ch. 1

14 For man is man and master of his fate.
Alfred, Lord Tennyson (1809–92) British poet.
Idylls of the King, 'The Marriage of Geraint'

15 The buck stops here.
Harry S. Truman (1884–1972) US statesman.
Sign kept on his desk during his term as president
Presidential Anecdotes (P. Boller)

16 In dreams begins responsibility.
W. B. Yeats (1865–1939) Irish poet.
Old Play, Epigraph, Responsibilities

REST

See also bed, idleness, leisure, sleep

1 Will there be beds for me and all who seek?
Yea, beds for all who come.
Christina Rossetti (1830–74) British poet.
Up-Hill

2 Unarm, Eros; the long day's task is done,
And we must sleep.
William Shakespeare (1564–1616) English dramatist.
Antony and Cleopatra, IV:12

3 It is well to lie fallow for a while.
Martin Farquhar Tupper (1810–89) British writer.
Proverbial Philosophy, 'Of Recreation'

RESULTS

1 Desperate cuts must have desperate cures.
Proverb

2 The little bit (two inches wide) of ivory on which I work with so fine a brush as produces little effect after much labour.
Jane Austen (1775–1817) British novelist.
Letter, 16 Dec 1816

3 Ye shall know them by their fruits. Do men gather grapes of thorns, or figs of thistles? Even so every good tree bringeth forth good fruit; but a corrupt tree bringeth forth evil fruit.
A good tree cannot bring forth evil fruit, neither can a corrupt tree bring forth good fruit.
Every tree that bringeth not forth good fruit is hewn down, and cast into the fire.
Wherefore by their fruits ye shall know them.
Bible: Matthew
7:16–20

4 Our love of what is beautiful does not lead to extravagance; our love of the things of the mind does not make us soft.
Pericles (c. 495–429 BC) Greek statesman.
Part of the funeral oration, 430 BC, for the dead of the first year of the Peloponnesian War
Attrib. in *Histories* Bk. II, Ch. 40 (Thucydides)

5 What dire offence from am'rous causes springs,
What mighty contests rise from trivial things.
Alexander Pope (1688–1744) British poet.
The Rape of the Lock, I

RETRIBUTION

See also punishment, revenge

1 Give a thief enough rope and he'll hang himself.
Proverb

2 *Nemo me impune lacessit.*
No one provokes me with impunity.
Anonymous
Motto of the Crown of Scotland

3 And if any mischief follow, then thou shalt give life for life,
Eye for eye, tooth for tooth, hand for hand, foot for foot,
Burning for burning, wound for wound, stripe for stripe.
Bible: Exodus
21:23–25

4 Be not deceived: God is not mocked: for whatsoever a man soweth, that shall he also reap.
For he that soweth to his flesh shall of the flesh reap corruption; but he that soweth to the Spirit shall of the Spirit reap life everlasting.

And let us not be weary in well doing: for in due season we shall reap, if we faint not.
Bible: Galatians
6:7–9

5 For they have sown the wind, and they shall reap the whirlwind: it hath no stalk: the bud shall yield no meal: if so be it yield, the strangers shall swallow it up.
Bible: Hosea
8:7

6 For I say unto you, That except your righteousness shall exceed the righteousness of the scribes and Pharisees, ye shall in no case enter into the kingdom of heaven.
Bible: Matthew
5:20

7 And if thy right eye offend thee, pluck it out, and cast it from thee: for it is profitable for thee that one of thy members should perish, and not that thy whole body should be cast into hell.
Bible: Matthew
5:29

8 For thou shalt heap coals of fire upon his head, and the Lord shall reward thee.
Bible: Proverbs
25:22

9 But men never violate the laws of God without suffering the consequences, sooner or later.
Lydia M. Child (1802–80) US abolitionist campaigner.
The Freedmen's Book, 'Toussaint L'Ouverture'

10 The Germans, if this Government is returned, are going to pay every penny; they are going to be squeezed, as a lemon is squeezed – until the pips squeak. My only doubt is not whether we can squeeze hard enough, but whether there is enough juice.
Eric Campbell Geddes (1875–1937) British politician.
Speech, Cambridge, 10 Dec 1918

RETURN

1 Poor wandering one!
Though thou hast surely strayed,
Take heart of grace,
Thy steps retrace,
Poor wandering one!
W. S. Gilbert (1836–1911) British dramatist.
The Pirates of Penzance, I

2 Ten o'clock . . . and back he'll come. I can just see him.
With vine leaves in his hair. Flushed and confident.
Henrik Ibsen (1828–1906) Norwegian dramatist.
Hedda Gabler, II

3 Better lo'ed ye canna be,

Will ye no come back again?

Carolina Nairne (1766–1845) Scottish songwriter.
Referring to Bonnie Prince Charlie
Bonnie Charlie's now awa!

REVENGE

See also retribution

1 Don't cut off your nose to spite your face.
Proverb

2 Revenge is a dish that tastes better cold.
Proverb

3 Revenge is sweet.
Proverb

4 Revenge is a kind of wild justice; which the more man's nature runs to, the more ought law to weed it out.
Francis Bacon (1561–1626) English philosopher.
Essays, 'Of Revenge'

5 A man that studieth revenge keeps his own wounds green.
Francis Bacon
Essays, 'Of Revenge'

6 Perish the Universe, provided I have my revenge.
Cyrano de Bergerac (1619–55) French writer.
La Mort d'Agrippine, IV

7 And the Lord said unto him, Therefore whosoever slayeth Cain, vengeance shall be taken on him sevenfold. And the Lord set a mark upon Cain, lest any finding him should kill him.
And Cain went out from the presence of the Lord, and dwelt in the land of Nod, on the east of Eden.
Bible: Genesis
4:15–16

8 I make war on the living, not on the dead.
Charles V (1500–58) Holy Roman Emperor.
After the death of Martin Luther, when it was suggested that he hang the corpse on a gallows
Attrib.

9 Rome shall perish – write that word
In the blood that she has spilt.
William Cowper (1731–1800) British poet.
Boadicea

10 Wisdom has taught us to be calm and meek,
To take one blow, and turn the other cheek;
It is not written what a man shall do
If the rude caitiff smite the other too!
Oliver Wendell Holmes (1809–94) US writer.
Non-Resistance

11 No one delights more in vengeance than a woman.
Juvenal (Decimus Junius Juvenalis; 60–130 AD) Roman satirist.
Satires, XIII

12 We had no use for the policy of the Gospels: if someone slaps you, just turn the other cheek. We had shown that anyone who slapped us on our cheek would get his head kicked off.
Nikita Khrushchev (1894–1971) Soviet statesman.
Khrushchev Remembers, Vol. II

13 Revenge, at first though sweet,
Bitter ere long back on itself recoils.
John Milton (1608–74) English poet.
Paradise Lost, Bk. IX

14 Those who offend us are generally punished for the offence they give; but we so frequently miss the satisfaction of knowing that we are avenged!
Anthony Trollope (1815–82) British novelist.
The Small House at Allington, Ch. 50

REVOLUTION

See also French Revolution, rebellion, Russian Revolution

1 Inferiors revolt in order that they may be equal and equals that they may be superior. Such is the state of mind which creates revolutions.
Aristotle (384–322 BC) Greek philosopher.
Politics, Bk. V

2 All modern revolutions have ended in a reinforcement of the power of the State.
Albert Camus (1913–60) French existentialist writer.
The Rebel

3 The uprising of the masses implies a fabulous increase of vital possibilities; quite the contrary of what we hear so often about the decadence of Europe.
José Ortega y Gasset (1883–1955) Spanish philosopher.
The Revolt of the Masses, Ch. 2

4 Revolution is not the uprising against pre-existing order, but the setting-up of a new order contradictory to the traditional one.
José Ortega y Gasset
The Revolt of the Masses, Ch. 6

5 We are dancing on a volcano.
Comte de Salvandy (1795–1856) French nobleman.
A remark made before the July Revolution in 1830

6 Insurrection is an art, and like all arts it has its laws.
Leon Trotsky (Lev Davidovich Bronstein; 1879–1940) Russian revolutionary.
History of the Russian Revolution, Pt. III, Ch. 6

7 Revolutions are always verbose.
Leon Trotsky
History of the Russian Revolution, Pt. II, Ch. 12

8 The fundamental premise of a revolution is that the existing social structure has become incapable of solving the urgent problems of development of the nation.
Leon Trotsky
History of the Russian Revolution, Pt. III, Ch. 6

9 Revolution by its very nature is sometimes compelled to take in more territory than it is capable of holding. Retreats are possible – when there is territory to retreat from.
Leon Trotsky
Diary in Exile, 15 Feb 1935

10 The word 'revolution' is a word for which you kill, for which you die, for which you send the labouring masses to their death, but which does not possess any content.
Simone Weil (1909–43) French philosopher.
Oppression and Liberty, 'Reflections Concerning the Causes of Liberty and Social Oppression'

11 We invented the Revolution
but we don't know how to run it.
Peter Weiss (1916–82) German novelist and dramatist.
Marat Sade, 15

12 Where the populace rise at once against the never-ending audacity of elected persons.
Walt Whitman (1819–92) US poet.
Song of the Broad Axe, 5

RIDICULE

See also contempt, satire

1 For what do we live, but to make sport for our neighbours, and laugh at them in our turn?
Jane Austen (1775–1817) British novelist.
Pride and Prejudice, Ch. 57

2 Few women care to be laughed at and men not at all, except for large sums of money.
Alan Ayckbourn (1939–) British dramatist.
The Norman Conquests, Preface

3 Ridicule often checks what is absurd, and fully as often smothers that which is noble.
Walter Scott (1771–1832) Scottish novelist.
Quentin Durward

RIGHT

1 This the grave of Mike O'Day
Who died maintaining his right of way.
His right was clear, his will was strong.
But he's just as dead as if he'd been wrong.
Anonymous
Epitaph

2 A child becomes an adult when he realizes that he has a right not only to be right but also to be wrong.
Thomas Szasz (1920–) US psychiatrist.
The Second Sin

3 While I'd rather be right than president, at any time I'm ready to be both.
Norman M. Thomas (1884–1968) US politician.
Referring to his lack of success in presidential campaigns. The expression 'I'd rather be right than president' is also attributed to the US politician Henry Clay (1777–1852).
Come to Judgment (A. Whitman)

4 Right is more precious than peace.
Woodrow Wilson (1856–1925) US statesman.
Radio Times, 10 Sept 1964

RIGHTEOUSNESS

See also good, integrity, morality, virtue

1 The eternal *not ourselves* that makes for righteousness.
Matthew Arnold (1822–88) British poet and critic.
Literature and Dogma, Ch. 8

2 Righteous people terrify me . . . Virtue is its own punishment.
Aneurin Bevan (1897–1960) British Labour politician.
Aneurin Bevan 1897–1945 (Michael Foot)

3 Ye must leave righteous ways behind, not to speak of unrighteous ways.
Buddha (Gautama Siddhartha; c. 563–c. 483 BC) Indian religious teacher.
Some Sayings of the Buddha (F. L. Woodward)

4 The man of life upright,
Whose guiltless heart is free
From all dishonest deeds
Or thought of vanity.
Thomas Campion (1567–1620) English poet.
The Man of Life Upright

5 Good thoughts his only friends,
His wealth a well-spent age,
The earth his sober inn
And quiet pilgrimage.
Thomas Campion
The Man of Life Upright

6 Perhaps it is better to be irresponsible and right than to be responsible and wrong.
Winston Churchill (1874–1965) British statesman.
Party Political Broadcast, London, 26 Aug 1950

7 Looks the whole world in the face,
For he owes not any man.
Henry Wadsworth Longfellow (1807–82) US poet.
The Village Blacksmith

8 Live among men as if God beheld you; speak to God as if men were listening.
Seneca (c. 4 BC–65 AD) Roman author.
Epistles

RIVERS

1 Ol' man river, dat ol' man river,
He must know sumpin', but don't say nothin',
He just keeps rollin', he keeps on rollin' along.
Oscar Hammerstein (1895–1960) US lyricist.
From the musical *Show Boat*
Ol' Man River

2 What is there to make so much of in the Thames? I am quite tired of it. Flow, flow, flow, always the same.
Duke of Queensberry (1724–1810) British peer.
Century of Anecdote (J. Timbs)

3 *Die Wacht am Rhein.*

The Watch on the Rhine.
Max Schneckenburger (1819–49) German poet.
Song title

4 Sweet Thames! run softly, till I end my
Song.
Edmund Spenser (1552–99) English poet.
Prothalamion, 18

5 I come from haunts of coot and hern,
I make a sudden sally
And sparkle out among the fern,
To bicker down a valley.
Alfred, Lord Tennyson (1809–92) British poet.
The Brook

ROYALTY

See also monarchy

1 The King over the Water.
Anonymous
Jacobite toast

2 'How different, how very different from the
home life of our own dear Queen!'
Anonymous
Remark about the character of Cleopatra as performed by Sarah Bernhardt

3 Here lies Fred,
Who was alive and is dead:
Had it been his father,
I had much rather;
Had it been his brother,
Still better than another;
Had it been his sister,
No one would have missed her;
Had it been the whole generation,
Still better for the nation:
But since 'tis only Fred,
Who was alive and is dead, –
There's no more to be said.
Anonymous
Referring to Frederick, Prince of Wales, eldest son of George II and father of George III
Memoirs of George II (Horace Walpole)

4 The house is well, but it is you, Your
Majesty, who have made me too great for
my house.
Francis Bacon (1561–1626) English philosopher.
Reply when Elizabeth I remarked on the smallness of his house
After-dinner Stories and Anecdotes (L. Meissen)

5 Speed, bonny boat, like a bird on the wing;
'Onward', the sailors cry;
Carry the lad that's born to be king
Over the sea to Skye.
H. E. Boulton (1859–1935) Scottish songwriter.
Referring to Bonnie Prince Charlie
Skye Boat Song

6 Such grace had kings when the world begun!
Robert Browning (1812–89) British poet.
Pippa Passes, Pt. I

7 Kings are naturally lovers of low company.
Edmund Burke (1729–97) British politician.
Speech on the Economical Reform (House of Commons, 11 Feb 1780)

8 A better farmer ne'er brushed dew from
lawn,
A worse king never left a realm undone!
Lord Byron (1788–1824) British poet.
Referring to George III
The Vision of Judgment, VIII

9 Conquering kings their titles take.
John Chandler (1806–76) British clergyman and writer.
Poem title

10 Brother, I am too old to go again to my
travels.
Charles II (1630–85) King of England.
Referring to his exile, 1651–60
History of Great Britain (Hume), Vol. II, Ch. 7

11 The monarchy is the oldest profession in the
world.
Charles, Prince of Wales (1948–) Eldest son of Elizabeth II.
Attrib.

12 Her Majesty is not a subject.
Benjamin Disraeli (1804–81) British statesman.
Responding to Gladstone's taunt that Disraeli could make a joke out of any subject, including Queen Victoria
Attrib.

13 I know I have the body of a weak and feeble
woman, but I have the heart and stomach of
a King, and of a King of England too.
Elizabeth I (1533–1603) Queen of England.
Speech at Tilbury on the approach of the Spanish Armada

14 Though God hath raised me high, yet this I
count the glory of my crown: that I have
reigned with your loves.
Elizabeth I
The Golden Speech, 1601

15 I will make you shorter by a head.
Elizabeth I
Sayings of Queen Elizabeth (Chamberlin)

16 I should like to be a horse.
Elizabeth II (1926–) Queen of the United Kingdom.
When asked about her ambitions when a child.
Attrib.

17 I think that everyone will conceed that –
today of all days –I should begin by saying,
'My husband and I'.
Elizabeth II
On her silver-wedding
Speech, Guildhall, 1972

18 We're not a family; we're a firm.
George VI (1895–1952) King of the United Kingdom.
Our Future King (Peter Lane)

19 I'm prepared to take advice on leisure from
Prince Philip. He's a world expert on leisure.
He's been practising for most of his adult life.
Neil Kinnock (1942–) British politician.
Western Mail, 1981

20 I don't mind your being killed, but I object to your being taken prisoner.

Lord Kitchener (1850–1916) British field marshal.
Said to the Prince of Wales (later Edward VIII) when he asked to go to the Front
Journal (Viscount Esher), 18 Dec 1914

21 Ah, if I were not king, I should lose my temper.

Louis XIV (1638–1715) French king.
Attrib.

22 For God's sake, ma'am, let's have no more of that. If you get the English people into the way of making kings, you'll get them into the way of *un*making them.

Lord Melbourne (1779–1848) British statesman.
Advising Queen Victoria against granting Prince Albert the title of King Consort
Lord M. (Lord David Cecil)

23 He will go from resort to resort getting more tanned and more tired.

Westbrook Pegler (1894–1969) US journalist.
On the abdication of Edward VIII
Six Men (Alistair Cooke), Pt. II

24 I'm self-employed.

Prince Philip (1921–) The consort of Queen Elizabeth II.
Answering a query as to what nature of work he did
Attrib.

25 Kings and such like are just as funny as politicians.

Theodore Roosevelt (1858–1919) US Republican president.
Mr Wilson's War (John Dos Passos), Ch. 1

26 The sun does not set in my dominions.

Friedrich von Schiller (1759–1805) German dramatist.
Said by Philip II
Don Carlos, I:6

27 Kings are earth's gods; in vice their law's their will.

William Shakespeare (1564–1616) English dramatist.
Pericles, I:1

28 For God's sake let us sit upon the ground
And tell sad stories of the death of kings:
How some have been depos'd, some slain in war,
Some haunted by the ghosts they have depos'd,
Some poison'd by their wives, some sleeping kill'd,
All murder'd – for within the hollow crown
That rounds the mortal temples of a king
Keeps Death his court.

William Shakespeare
Richard II, III:2

29 Ay, every inch a king.

William Shakespeare
King Lear, IV:6

30 I would not be a queen

For all the world.

William Shakespeare
Henry VIII, II:3

31 Albert was merely a young foreigner, who suffered from having no vices, and whose only claim to distinction was that he had happened to marry the Queen of England.

Lytton Strachey (1880–1932) British writer.
Queen Victoria, Ch. 5

32 Authority forgets a dying king.

Alfred, Lord Tennyson (1809–92) British poet.
Idylls of the King, 'The Passing of Arthur'

33 We are not amused!

Victoria (1819–1901) Queen of the United Kingdom.
Attrib.

34 I sat between the King and Queen. We left supper soon. My health was drunk. I then danced one more quadrille with Lord Paget. . . . I was *very* much amused.

Victoria
Journal, 16 June 1833

35 It has none, your Highness. Its history dates from today.

James Whistler (1834–1903) US painter.
Replying to a query from the Prince of Wales about the history of the Society of British Artists, which he was visiting for the first time
Whistler Stories (D. Seitz)

36 Now what do I do with *this*?

Duke of Windsor (1894–1972) King of the United Kingdom; abdicated 1936.
On being handed the bill after a lengthy stay in a luxury hotel
Attrib.

RUDENESS

See also impertinence, insults

1 The right people are rude. They can afford to be.

W. Somerset Maugham (1874–1965) British novelist.
Our Betters, II

2 JUDGE WILLIS. You are extremely offensive, young man.

F. E. SMITH. As a matter of fact, we both are, and the only difference between us is that I am trying to be, and you can't help it.

F. E. Smith (1872–1930) British lawyer and politician.
Frederick Elwin, Earl of Birkenhead (Lord Birkenhead), Vol. I, Ch. 9

RULES

1 The exception proves the rule.

Proverb

2 Rules and models destroy genius and art.

William Hazlitt (1778–1830) British essayist.
On Taste

3 The golden rule is that there are no golden rules.
George Bernard Shaw (1856–1950) Irish dramatist and critic.
Man and Superman, 'Maxims for Revolutionists'

RUSSIA

See also Cold War, oppression, Russian Revolution

1 I cannot forecast to you the action of Russia. It is a riddle wrapped in a mystery inside an enigma.
Winston Churchill (1874–1965) British statesman.
Broadcast talk, 1 Oct 1939

2 Russia will certainly inherit the future. What we already call the greatness of Russia is only her pre-natal struggling.
D. H. Lawrence (1885–1930) British novelist.
Phoenix, Preface, 'All Things are Possible' by Leo Shostov

3 Neither can you expect a revolution, because there is no new baby in the womb of our society. Russia is a collapse, not a revolution.
D. H. Lawrence
Phoenix, 'The Good Man'

4 Scratch the Russian and you will find the Tartar.
Joseph de Maistre (1753–1821) French monarchist.
Attributed also to Napoleon and Prince de Ligne

5 Absolutism tempered by assassination.
Ernst Friedrich Herbert Münster (1766–1839) Hanoverian statesman.
Referring to the Russian Constitution
Letter

6 It was the supreme expression of the mediocrity of the apparatus that Stalin himself rose to his position.
Leon Trotsky (Lev Davidovich Bronstein; 1879–1940) Russian revolutionary.
My Life, Ch. 40

7 From being a patriotic myth, the Russian people have become an awful reality.
Leon Trotsky
History of the Russian Revolution, Pt. III, Ch. 7

RUSSIAN REVOLUTION

See also revolution, Russia

1 The 23rd of February was International

Woman's Day . . . It had not occurred to anyone that it might become the first day of the revolution.
Leon Trotsky (Lev Davidovich Bronstein; 1879–1940) Russian revolutionary.
History of the Russian Revolution, Pt. I, Ch. 7

2 The revolution does not choose its paths: it made its first steps towards victory under the belly of a Cossack's horse.
Leon Trotsky
History of the Russian Revolution, Pt. I, Ch. 7

RUTHLESSNESS

1 Would that the Roman people had but one neck!
Caligula ((Gaius Caesar; 12–41 AD)) Roman Emperor.
Life of Caligula (Suetonius), Ch. 30

2 What millions died – that Caesar might be great!
Thomas Campbell (1777–1844) British poet.
Pleasures of Hope, II

3 Exterminate all brutes.
Joseph Conrad (Teodor Josef Konrad Korzeniowski; 1857–1924) Polish-born British novelist.
Heart of Darkness

4 I do not have to forgive my enemies, I have had them all shot.
Ramón Maria Narváez (1800–68) Spanish general and political leader.
Said on his deathbed, when asked by a priest if he forgave his enemies
Famous Last Words (B. Conrad)

5 3RD FISHERMAN. Master, I marvel how the fishes live in the sea.
1ST FISHERMAN. Why, as men do a-land – the great ones eat up the little ones.
William Shakespeare (1564–1616) English dramatist.
Pericles, II:1

6 The world continues to offer glittering prizes to those who have stout hearts and sharp swords.
F. E. Smith (1872–1930) British lawyer and politician.
Speech, Glasgow University, 7 Nov 1923

7 It is not enough to succeed. Others must fail.
Gore Vidal (1925–) US novelist.
Antipanegyric for Tom Driberg (G. Irvine)

S

SARCASM

1 Sarcasm I now see to be, in general, the language of the devil.
Thomas Carlyle (1795–1881) Scottish historian and essayist.
Sartor Resartus, Bk. II, Ch. 4

2 If you don't want to use the army, I should

like to borrow it for a while. Yours respectfully, A. Lincoln.
Abraham Lincoln (1809–65) US statesman.
Letter to General George B. McClellan, whose lack of activity during the US Civil War irritated Lincoln

SATIRE

See also ridicule, sarcasm

1 It's hard not to write satire.
Juvenal (Decimus Junius Juvenalis; 60–130 AD) Roman satirist.
Satires, I

2 Satire should, like a polished razor keen,
Wound with a touch that's scarcely felt or seen.
Lady Mary Wortley Montagu (1689–1762) English writer.
To the Imitator of the First Satire of Horace, Bk. II

3 Satire is a sort of glass, wherein beholders do generally discover everybody's face but their own.
Jonathan Swift (1667–1745) Irish-born Anglican priest and writer.
The Battle of the Books, 'Preface'

SATISFACTION

See also contentment

1 Youth will be served, every dog has his day, and mine has been a fine one.
George Henry Borrow (1803–81) British writer.
Lavengro, Ch. 92

2 I wasna fou, but just had plenty.
Robert Burns (1759–96) Scottish poet.
Death and Doctor Hornbrook

3 The reward of a thing well done is to have done it.
Ralph Waldo Emerson (1803–82) US poet and essayist.
Essays, 'New England Reformers'

SAYINGS

See also quotations

1 A platitude is simply a truth repeated till people get tired of hearing it.
Stanley Baldwin (1867–1947) British statesman.
Attrib.

2 The hunter for aphorisms on human nature has to fish in muddy water, and he is even condemned to find much of his own mind.
F. H. Bradley (1846–1924) British philosopher.
Aphorisms

3 The great writers of aphorisms read as if they had all known each other well.
Elias Canetti (1905–) Bulgarian-born novelist.
The Human Province

4 A proverb is much matter decorated into few words.
Thomas Fuller (1608–61) English historian.
The History of the Worthies of England, Ch. 2

5 A new maxim is often a brilliant error.
Chrétien Guillaume de Lamoignonde Malesherbes (1721–94) French statesman.
Pensées et maximes

6 A proverb is one man's wit and all men's wisdom.
Lord John Russell (1792–1878) British statesman.
Attrib.

7 A truism is on that account none the less true.
Herbert Samuel (1870–1963) British Liberal statesman.
A Book of Quotations

SCEPTICISM

See also doubt, proof

1 We don't believe in rheumatism and true love until after the first attack.
Marie Ebner von Eschenbach (1830–1916) Austrian writer.
Aphorism

2 I am too much of a sceptic to deny the possibility of anything.
T. H. Huxley (1825–95) British biologist.
Letter to Herbert Spencer, 22 Mar 1886

3 Truth, Sir, is a cow, which will yield such people no more milk, and so they are gone to milk the bull.
Samuel Johnson (1709–84) British lexicographer.
Life of Johnson (J. Boswell), Vol. I
Referring to sceptics

4 It is undesirable to believe a proposition when there is no ground whatever for supposing it true.
Bertrand Russell (1872–1970) British philosopher.
Sceptical Essays

5 She believed in nothing; only her scepticism kept her from being an atheist.
Jean-Paul Sartre (1905–80) French writer.
Words

6 The temerity to believe in nothing.
Ivan Turgenev (1818–83) Russian novelist.
Fathers and Sons, Ch. 14

SCIENCE

See also discovery, mathematics, Nature, progress, research, scientists, technology

1 That is the essence of science: ask an impertinent question, and you are on the way to the pertinent answer.
Jacob Bronowski (1908–74) British scientist and writer.
The Ascent of Man, Ch. 4

2 Physics becomes in those years the greatest collective work of science – no, more than that, the great collective work of art of the twentieth century.
Jacob Bronowski
The Ascent of Man, Ch. 10
Referring to the period around the turn of the century marked by the elucidation of atomic structure and the development of the quantum theory

3 There was a young lady named Bright, Whose speed was far faster than light;

She set out one day
In a relative way,
And returned home the previous night.
Arthur Henry Reginald Buller (1874–1944) British botanist.
Limerick

4 It is, of course, a bit of a drawback that science was invented after I left school.
Lord Carrington (1919–) British statesman.
The Observer, 23 Jan 1983

5 When a distinguished but elderly scientist states that something is possible, he is almost certainly right. When he states that something is impossible, he is very probably wrong.
Arthur C. Clarke (1917–) British science-fiction writer.
Profiles of the Future

6 After all, science is essentially international, and it is only through lack of the historical sense that national qualities have been attributed to it.
Marie Curie (1867–1934) Polish chemist.
Memorandum, 'Intellectual Co-operation'

7 And new Philosophy calls all in doubt,
The Element of fire is quite put out;
The Sun is lost, and th' earth, and no man's wit
Can well direct him where to look for it.
John Donne (1573–1631) English poet.
An Anatomy of the World, 205

8 Electrical force is defined as something which causes motion of electrical charge; an electrical charge is something which exerts electric force.
Arthur Eddington (1882–1944) British astronomer.
The Nature of the Physical World

9 Man is slightly nearer to the atom than the stars. From his central position he can survey the grandest works of Nature with the astronomer, or the minutest works with the physicist.
Arthur Eddington
Stars and Atoms

10 When you are courting a nice girl an hour seems like a second. When you sit on a red-hot cinder a second seems like an hour. That's relativity.
Albert Einstein (1879–1955) German-born US physicist.
News Chronicle, 14 Mar 1949

11 The whole of science is nothing more than a refinement of everyday thinking.
Albert Einstein
Out of My Later Years

12 Science without religion is lame, religion without science is blind.
Albert Einstein
Out of My Later Years

13 God does not play dice.
Albert Einstein
Albert Einstein, Creator and Rebel (B. Hoffman), Ch. 10
Einstein's objection to the quantum theory, in which physical events can only be known in terms of probabilities. It is sometimes quoted as 'God does not play dice with the Universe'

14 A vacuum can only exist, I imagine, by the things which enclose it.
Zelda Fitzgerald (1900–48) US writer.
Journal, 1932

15 Shelley and Keats were the last English poets who were at all up to date in their chemical knowledge.
J. B. S. Haldane (1892–1964) British geneticist.
Daedalus or Science and the Future

16 MASTER: They split the atom by firing particles at it, at 5,500 miles a second.
BOY: Good heavens. And they only split it?
Will Hay (1888–1949) British comedian.
The Fourth Form at St Michael's

17 Science has 'explained' nothing; the more we know the more fantastic the world becomes and the profounder the surrounding darkness.
Aldous Huxley (1894–1964) British novelist.
Views Of Holland

18 Science is nothing but trained and organized common sense, differing from the latter only as a veteran may differ from a raw recruit: and its methods differ from those of common sense only as far as the guardsman's cut and thrust differ from the manner in which a savage wields his club.
T. H. Huxley (1825–95) British biologist.
Collected Essays, 'The Method of Zadig'

19 The great tragedy of Science – the slaying of a beautiful hypothesis by an ugly fact.
T. H. Huxley
Collected Essays, 'Biogenesis and Abiogenesis'

20 Life exists in the universe only because the carbon atom possesses certain exceptional properties.
James Jeans (1877–1946) British scientist.
The Mysterious Universe, Ch. 1

21 Science should leave off making pronouncements: the river of knowledge has too often turned back on itself.
James Jeans
The Mysterious Universe, Ch. 5

22 In everything that relates to science, I am a whole Encyclopaedia behind the rest of the world.
Charles Lamb (1775–1834) British essayist.
Essays of Elia, 'The Old and the New Schoolmaster'

23 Water is H_2O, hydrogen two parts, oxygen one,
but there is also a third thing, that makes it water

and nobody knows what that is.
D. H. Lawrence (1885–1930) British novelist.
Pansies, 'The Third Thing'

24 Scientific discovery is a private event, and the delight that accompanies it, or the despair of finding it illusory does not travel.
Peter Medawar (1915–87) British immunologist.
Hypothesis and Imagination

25 *Laboratorium est oratorium.* The place where we do our scientific work is a place of prayer.
Joseph Needham (1900–) British biochemist.
The Harvest of a Quiet Eye (A. L. Mackay)

26 Do you really believe that the sciences would ever have originated and grown if the way had not been prepared by magicians, alchemists, astrologers and witches whose promises and pretensions first had to create a thirst, a hunger, a taste for *hidden* and *forbidden* powers? Indeed, infinitely more had to be *promised* than could ever be fulfilled in order that anything at all might be fulfilled in the realms of knowledge.
Friedrich Wilhelm Nietzsche (1844–1900) German philosopher.
The Gay Science

27 There are no such things as applied sciences, only applications of science.
Louis Pasteur (1822–95) French scientist.
Address, 11 Sept 1872

28 Traditional scientific method has always been at the very *best*, 20-20 hindsight. It's good for seeing where you've been.
Robert T. Pirsig (1928–) US writer.
Zen and the Art of Motorcycle Maintenance, Pt. III, Ch. 24

29 Science must begin with myths, and with the criticism of myths.
Karl Popper (1902–) Austrian-born British philosopher.
British Philosophy in the Mid-Century (ed. C. A. Mace)

30 Should we force science down the throats of those that have no taste for it? Is it our duty to drag them kicking and screaming into the twenty-first century? I am afraid that it is.
George Porter (1920–) British chemist.
Speech, Sept 1986

31 If all the arts aspire to the condition of music, all the sciences aspire to the condition of mathematics.
George Santayana (1863–1952) US philosopher.
The Observer, 'Sayings of the Week', 4 Mar 1928

32 Her own mother lived the latter years of her life in the horrible suspicion that electricity was dripping invisibly all over the house.
James Thurber (1894–1961) US humorist.
My Life and Hard Times, Ch. 2

33 Modern Physics is an instrument of Jewry for

the destruction of Nordic science . . . True physics is the creation of the German spirit.
Rudolphe Tomaschek (20th century) German scientist.
The Rise and Fall of the Third Reich (W. L. Shirer), Ch. 8

34 The term Science should not be given to anything but the aggregate of the recipes that are always successful. All the rest is literature.
Paul Valéry (1871–1945) French poet and writer.
Moralités

35 Classical physics has been superseded by quantum theory: quantum theory is verified by experiments. Experiments must be described in terms of classical physics.
C. F. von Weizsäcker (1912–) German physicist and philosopher.
Attrib.

36 A science which hesitates to forget its founders is lost.
A. N. Whitehead (1861–1947) British philosopher.
Attrib.

37 The airplane stays up because it doesn't have the time to fall.
Orville Wright (1871–1948) US aviator.
Attrib.
Explaining the principles of powered flight

SCIENTISTS

See also science

1 When I find myself in the company of scientists, I feel like a shabby curate who has strayed by mistake into a drawing-room full of dukes.
W. H. Auden (1907–73) British poet.
The Dyer's Hand

2 The true men of action in our time, those who transform the world, are not the politicians and statesmen, but the scientists. Unfortunately, poetry cannot celebrate them, because their deeds are concerned with things, not persons and are, therefore, speechless.
W. H. Auden
The Dyer's Hand

3 Sir Humphry Davy
Abominated gravy.
He lived in the odium
Of having discovered Sodium.
Edmund Clerihew Bentley (1875–1956) British writer.
Biography for Beginners

4 I believe the souls of five hundred Sir Isaac Newtons would go to the making up of a Shakespeare or a Milton.
Samuel Taylor Coleridge (1772–1834) British poet.
Letter to Thomas Poole, 23 Mar 1801

5 If you want to find out anything from the theoretical physicists about the methods they use, I advise you to stick closely to one principle: Don't listen to their words fix your attention on their deeds.

Albert Einstein (1879–1955) German-born US physicist.
The World As I See It

6 Einstein – the greatest Jew since Jesus. I have no doubt that Einstein's name will still be remembered and revered when Lloyd George, Foch and William Hohenzollern share with Charlie Chaplin that ineluctable oblivion which awaits the uncreative mind.

J. B. S. Haldane (1892–1964) British geneticist.
Daedalus or Science and the Future

7 The physicists have known sin; and this is a knowledge which they cannot lose.

J. Robert Oppenheimer (1904–67) US physicist.
Lecture, Massachusetts Institute of Technology, 25 Nov 1947

8 Nature, and Nature's laws lay hid in night: God said, *Let Newton be!* and all was light.

Alexander Pope (1688–1744) British poet.
Epitaphs, 'Intended for Sir Isaac Newton'
For a reply, *see* John Collings SQUIRE

9 It did not last: the Devil howling 'Ho! Let Einstein be!' restored the status quo.

John Collings Squire (1884–1958) British journalist.
Epigrams, 'The Dilemma'
Answer to POPE's Epitaph for Newton

10 He snatched the lightning shaft from heaven, and the sceptre from tyrants.

Anne-Robert-Jacques Turgot (1727–81) French economist.
Vie de Turgot (A. N. de Condorcet)
An inscription for a bust of Benjamin Franklin, alluding both to Franklin's invention of the lightning conductor and to his role in the American Revolution

11 Already for thirty-five years he had not stopped talking and almost nothing of fundamental value had emerged.

James Dewey Watson (1928–) US geneticist.
The Double Helix, Ch. 8
Referring to Francis Crick

12 He doubted the existence of the Deity but accepted Carnot's cycle, and he had read Shakespeare and found him weak in chemistry.

H. G. Wells (1866–1946) British writer.
Short Stories, 'The Lord of the Dynamos'

SCOTLAND

See also Britain, Scots

1 O ye'll tak' the high road, and I'll tak' the low road,
And I'll be in Scotland afore ye,
But me and my true love will never meet again,
On the bonnie, bonnie banks o' Loch Lomon'.

Anonymous
The Bonnie Banks o' Loch Lomon'

2 My heart's in the Highlands, my heart is not here;

My heart's in the Highlands a-chasing the deer
Chasing the wild deer, and following the roe,
My heart's in the Highlands, wherever I go.

Robert Burns (1759–96) Scottish poet.
My Heart's in the Highlands

3 *Oats.* A grain, which in England is generally given to horses, but in Scotland supports the people.

Samuel Johnson (1709–84) British lexicographer.
Dictionary of the English Language

4 Norway, too, has noble wild prospects; and Lapland is remarkable for prodigious noble wild prospects. But, Sir, let me tell you, the noblest prospect which a Scotchman ever sees, is the high road that leads him to England!

Samuel Johnson
Life of Johnson (J. Boswell), Vol. I

5 Seeing Scotland, Madam, is only seeing a worse England.

Samuel Johnson
Life of Johnson (J. Boswell), Vol. III

6 Roamin' in the gloamin',
By the bonny banks of Clyde.

Harry Lauder (Hugh MacLennon; 1870–1950) Scottish music-hall artist.
Song

7 O Caledonia! stern and wild,
Meet nurse for a poetic child!
Land of brown heath and shaggy wood,
Land of the mountain and the flood,
Land of my sires! what mortal hand
Can e'er untie the filial band
That knits me to thy rugged strand!

Walter Scott (1771–1832) Scottish novelist.
The Lay of the Last Minstrel, VI

8 That knuckle-end of England – that land of Calvin, oat-cakes, and sulphur.

Sydney Smith (1771–1845) British clergyman and essayist.
Memoir (Lady Holland)

SCOTS

See also British, Scotland

1 You've forgotten the grandest moral attribute of a Scotsman, Maggie, that he'll do nothing which might damage his career.

J. M. Barrie (1860–1937) British novelist and dramatist.
What Every Woman Knows, II

2 There are few more impressive sights in the world than a Scotsman on the make.

J. M. Barrie
What Every Woman Knows, II

3 A Scotchman must be a very sturdy moralist who does not love Scotland better than truth.

Samuel Johnson (1709–84) British lexicographer.
Journey to the Western Islands of Scotland, 'Col'

4 BOSWELL. I do indeed come from Scotland, but I cannot help it . . .
JOHNSON. That, Sir, I find, is what a very great many of your countrymen cannot help.
Samuel Johnson
Life of Johnson (J. Boswell), Vol. I

5 Much may be made of a Scotchman, if he be *caught* young.
Samuel Johnson
Life of Johnson (J. Boswell), Vol. II
Referring to Lord Mansfield

6 Their learning is like bread in a besieged town: every man gets a little, but no man gets a full meal.
Samuel Johnson
Life of Johnson (J. Boswell), Vol. II
Referring to education in Scotland

7 I have been trying all my life to like Scotchmen, and am obliged to desist from the experiment in despair.
Charles Lamb (1775–1834) British essayist.
Essays of Elia, 'Imperfect Sympathies'

8 In all my travels I never met with any one Scotchman but what was a man of sense. I believe everybody of that country that has any, leaves it as fast as they can.
Francis Lockier (1667–1740) English writer.
Anecdotes (Joseph Spence)

9 Join a Highland regiment, me boy. The kilt is an unrivalled garment for fornication and diarrhoea.
John Masters (1914–) British writer.
Bugles and a Tiger

10 It's ill taking the breeks aff a wild Highlandman.
Walter Scott (1771–1832) Scottish novelist.
The Fair Maid of Perth, Ch. 5

11 It is never difficult to distinguish between a Scotsman with a grievance and a ray of sunshine.
P. G. Wodehouse (1881–1975) British humorous novelist.
Wodehouse at Work to the End (Richard Usborne), Ch. 8

SCULPTURE

See also art, artists

1 If people dug up the remains of this civilization a thousand years hence, and found Epstein's statues and that man Ellis, they would think we were just savages.
Doris Lessing (1919–) British novelist.
Martha Quest, Pt. I, Ch. 1

2 See what will happen to you if you don't stop biting your fingernails.
Will Rogers (1879–1935) US actor and humorist.
Message written on a postcard of the Venus de Milo that he sent to his young niece

SEA

See also boats, Navy, seaside

1 The sea is calm to-night,
The tide is full, the moon lies fair
Upon the Straits.
Matthew Arnold (1822–88) British poet and critic.
Dover Beach

2 For all at last return to the sea – to Oceanus, the ocean river, like the ever-flowing stream of time, the beginning and the end.
Rachel Carson (1907–64) US biologist.
The Sea Around Us
The closing words of the book

3 The voice of the sea speaks to the soul. The touch of the sea is sensuous, enfolding the body in its soft, close embrace.
Kate Chopin (1851–1904) US writer.
The Awakening, Ch. 6

4 The ice was here, the ice was there,
The ice was all around:
It cracked and growled, and roared and howled,
Like noises in a swound!
Samuel Taylor Coleridge (1772–1834) British poet.
The Rime of the Ancient Mariner, I

5 We are as near to heaven by sea as by land.
Humphrey Gilbert (c. 1539–83) English navigator.
A Book of Anecdotes (D. George)
Remark made shortly before he went down with his ship *Squirrel*

6 When men come to like a sea-life, they are not fit to live on land.
Samuel Johnson (1709–84) British lexicographer.
Life of Johnson (J. Boswell), Vol. II

7 The snotgreen sea. The scrotumtightening sea.
James Joyce (1882–1941) Irish novelist.
Ulysses

8 It keeps eternal whisperings around Desolate shores, and with its mighty swell Gluts twice ten thousand Caverns.
John Keats (1795–1821) British poet.
On the Sea

9 'Wouldst thou' – so the helmsman answered –
'Learn the secret of the sea?
Only those who brave its dangers
Comprehend its mystery!'
Henry Wadsworth Longfellow (1807–82) US poet.
The Secret of the Sea

10 I must down to the seas again, to the lonely sea and the sky,
And all I ask is a tall ship and a star to steer her by,
And the wheel's kick and the wind's song and the white sail's shaking,

And a grey mist on the sea's face and a grey dawn breaking.

John Masefield (1878–1967) British poet.
Sea Fever
Often quoted using 'sea' rather than 'seas', and 'I must go down' rather than 'I must down'

11 Rocked in the cradle of the deep.

Emma Millard (1787–1870) British songwriter.
Song

12 A life on the ocean wave,
A home on the rolling deep.

Epes Sargent (1813–80) US writer and dramatist.
A Life on the Ocean Wave

13 O hear us when we cry to Thee
For those in peril on the sea.

William Whiting (1825–78) British hymn writer.
Eternal Father Strong to Save

14 The sea! the sea!

Xenophon (430–354 BC) Greek historian.
Anabasis, IV:7

SEASIDE

See also sea

1 The Walrus and the Carpenter
Were walking close at hand;
They wept like anything to see
Such quantities of sand:
'If this were only cleared away,'
They said, 'it *would* be grand!'

Lewis Carroll (Charles Lutwidge Dodgson; 1832–98) British writer.
Through the Looking-Glass, Ch. 4

2 It is the drawback of all sea-side places that half the landscape is unavailable for purposes of human locomotion, being covered by useless water.

Norman Douglas (1868–1952) British novelist.
Alone, 'Mentone'

3 I do Like to be Beside the Seaside.

John A. Glover-Kind (19th century) US songwriter.
Song title

SEASONS

See also autumn, months, spring, summer, winter

1 Four seasons fill the measure of the year;
There are four seasons in the mind of men.

John Keats (1795–1821) British poet.
Four Seasons

2 No one thinks of winter when the grass is green!

Rudyard Kipling (1865–1936) Indian-born British writer.
A St Helena Lullaby

3 If Winter comes, can Spring be far behind?

Percy Bysshe Shelley (1792–1822) British poet.
Ode to the West Wind

SECRECY

See also gossip

1 Only the nose knows
Where the nose goes
When the door close.

Muhammad Ali (Cassius Clay; 1942–   ) US boxer.
Remark, reported by Al Silverman
When asked whether a boxer should have sex before a big fight

2 I have seldom spoken with greater regret, for my lips are not yet unsealed. Were these troubles over I would make a case, and I guarantee that not a man would go into the Lobby against us.

Stanley Baldwin (1867–1947) British statesman.
Speech, House of Commons, 10 Dec 1935
Referring to the Abyssinian crisis; usually misquoted as 'My lips are sealed'

3 Curse not the king, no not in thy thought; and curse not the rich in thy bedchamber: for a bird of the air shall carry the voice, and that which hath wings shall tell the matter.

Bible: Ecclesiastes
10:20

4 If thou hast heard a word, let it die with thee; and be bold, it will not burst thee.

Bible: Ecclesiasticus
19:10

5 Stolen waters are sweet, and bread eaten in secret is pleasant.

Bible: Proverbs
9:17

6 Mum's the word.

George Colman the Younger (1762–1836) British dramatist.
The Battle of Hexham, II:1

7 O fie miss, you must not kiss and tell.

William Congreve (1670–1729) British Restoration dramatist.
Love for Love, II:10

8 I know that's a secret, for it's whispered every where.

William Congreve
Love for Love, III:3

9 Three may keep a secret, if two of them are dead.

Benjamin Franklin (1706–90) US scientist and statesman.
Poor Richard's Almanack

10 It is a secret in the Oxford sense: you may tell it to only one person at a time.

Oliver Franks (1905–   ) British philosopher and administrator.
Sunday Telegraph, 30 Jan 1977

SELF

See also self-confidence, etc.

1 Every man is his own worst enemy.
Proverb

2 God helps them that help themselves.
Proverb

3 He helps little that helps not himself.
Proverb

4 He travels fastest who travels alone.
Proverb

5 Lord, deliver me from myself.
Thomas Browne (1605–82) English physician and writer.
Religio Medici, Pt. II

6 I have always disliked myself at any given moment; the total of such moments is my life.
Cyril Connolly (1903–74) British journalist.
Enemies of Promise, Ch. 18

7 But I do nothing upon myself, and yet I am mine own Executioner.
John Donne (1573–1631) English poet.
Devotions, 12

8 We never remark any passion or principle in others, of which, in some degree or other, we may not find a parallel in ourselves.
David Hume (1711–76) Scottish philosopher.
A Treatise of Human Nature

9 Whenever I look inside myself I am afraid.
Cyril Joad (1891–1953) British writer and broadcaster.
The Observer, 'Sayings of the Week', 8 Nov 1942

10 All censure of a man's self is oblique praise. It is in order to shew how much he can spare.
Samuel Johnson (1709–84) British lexicographer.
Life of Johnson (J. Boswell), Vol. III

11 One should examine oneself for a very long time before thinking of condemning others.
Molière (Jean Baptiste Poquelin; 1622–73) French dramatist.
Le Misanthrope, III:4

12 Self-love seems so often unrequited.
Anthony Powell (1905–) British novelist.
The Acceptance World

13 Do not love your neighbour as yourself. If you are on good terms with yourself it is an impertinence; if on bad, an injury.
George Bernard Shaw (1856–1950) Irish dramatist and critic.
Man and Superman, 'Maxims for Revolutionists'

14 The unexamined life is not worth living.
Socrates (469–399 BC) Athenian philosopher.
Apology (Plato)

15 I am always with myself, and it is I who am my tormentor.
Leo Tolstoy (1828–1910) Russian writer.
Memoirs of a Madman

16 Meanwhile you will write an essay on 'self-indulgence'. There will be a prize of half a crown for the longest essay, irrespective of any possible merit.
Evelyn Waugh (1903–66) British novelist.
Decline and Fall, Pt. I, Ch. 5

17 I can't quite explain it, but I don't believe one can ever be unhappy for long provided one does just exactly what one wants to and when one wants to.
Evelyn Waugh
Decline and Fall, Pt. I, Ch. 5

18 I celebrate myself, and sing myself,
And what I assume you shall assume.
Walt Whitman (1819–92) US poet.
Song of Myself, 1

19 Behold, I do not give lectures or a little charity,
When I give I give myself.
Walt Whitman
Song of Myself, 40

20 I have said that the soul is not more than the body,
And I have said that the body is not more than the soul,
And nothing, but God, is greater to one than one's self is.
Walt Whitman
Song of Myself, 48

21 Do I contradict myself?
Very well then I contradict myself,
(I am large, I contain multitudes).
Walt Whitman
Song of Myself, 51

SELF-CONFIDENCE

See also shyness

1 Those who believe that they are exclusively in the right are generally those who achieve something.
Aldous Huxley (1894–1964) British novelist.
Proper Studies

2 I can honestly say that I was never affected by the question of the success of an undertaking. If I felt it was the right thing to do, I was for it regardless of the possible outcome.
Golda Meir (1898–1978) Russian-born Israeli stateswoman.
Golda Meir: Woman with a Cause (Marie Syrkin)

3 I wish I was as cocksure of anything as Tom Macaulay is of everything.
Lord Melbourne (1779–1848) British statesman.
Preface to Lord Melbourne's Papers (Earl Cowper)

4 'Tis an ill cook that cannot lick his own fingers.
William Shakespeare (1564–1616) English dramatist.
Romeo and Juliet, IV:2

5 'Are you not,' a Rugby master had asked him in discussing one of his essays, 'a little out of

your depth here?' 'Perhaps, Sir,' was the confident reply, 'but I can swim.'
William Temple (1881–1944) British churchman.
William Temple (F. A. Iremonger)

6 I am certain that we will win the election with a good majority. Not that I am ever over-confident.
Margaret Thatcher (1925–) British politician and prime minister.
Evening Standard, 1987

7 If I ever felt inclined to be timid as I was going into a room full of people, I would say to myself, 'You're the cleverest member of one of the cleverest families in the cleverest class of the cleverest nation in the world, why should you be frightened?'
Beatrice Webb (1858–1943) British economist and writer.
Portraits from Memory (Bertrand Russell), 'Sidney and Beatrice Webb'

SELF-CONTROL

1 He that is slow to anger is better than the mighty; and he that ruleth his spirit than he that taketh a city.
Bible: Proverbs
16:32

2 No one who cannot limit himself has ever been able to write.
Nicolas Boileau (1636–1711) French writer.
L'Art poétique, I

3 The highest possible stage in moral culture is when we recognize that we ought to control our thoughts.
Charles Darwin (1809–82) British life scientist.
Descent of Man, Ch. 4

4 When things are steep, remember to stay level-headed.
Horace (Quintus Horatius Flaccus; 65–8 BC) Roman poet.
Odes, II

5 If you can keep your head when all about you Are losing theirs and blaming it on you.
Rudyard Kipling (1865–1936) Indian-born British writer.
If

6 He that would govern others, first should be The master of himself.
Philip Massinger (1583–1640) English dramatist.
The Bondman, I

7 Never lose your temper with the Press or the public is a major rule of political life.
Christabel Pankhurst (1880–1958) British suffragette.
Unshackled

SELF-DENIAL

See also abstinence, selflessness

1 Self-denial is not a virtue; it is only the effect of prudence on rascality.
George Bernard Shaw (1856–1950) Irish dramatist and critic.
Man and Superman, 'Maxims for Revolutionists'

2 Thy need is yet greater than mine.
Philip Sidney (1554–86) English poet and courtier.
Attrib.
Giving his own water bottle to a humble wounded soldier after he had himself been wounded

SELF-INTEREST

See also parochialism, selfishness

1 Every man for himself, and the devil take the hindmost.
Proverb

2 The land self-interest groans from shore to shore,
For fear that plenty should attain the poor.
Lord Byron (1788–1824) British poet.
The Age of Bronze, XIV

3 Anyone informed that the universe is expanding and contracting in pulsations of eighty billion years has a right to ask, 'What's in it for me?'
Peter De Vries (1910–) US novelist.
The Glory of the Hummingbird, Ch. 1

4 The least pain in our little finger gives us more concern and uneasiness than the destruction of millions of our fellow-beings.
William Hazlitt (1778–1830) British essayist.
American Literature, 'Dr Channing'

5 Self-interest speaks all sorts of tongues, and plays all sorts of roles, even that of disinterestedness.
Duc de la Rochefoucauld (1613–80) French writer.
Maximes, 39

SELFISHNESS

See also self-interest

1 I have been a selfish being all my life, in practice, though not in principle.
Jane Austen (1775–1817) British novelist.
Pride and Prejudice, Ch. 58

2 And this the burthen of his song,
For ever us'd to be,
I care for nobody, not I,
If no one cares for me.
Isaac Bickerstaffe (c. 1735–c. 1812) Irish dramatist.
Love in a Village, I

3 It's 'Damn you, Jack – I'm all right!' with you chaps.
David Bone (1874–1959) British sea captain and writer.
The Brassbounder, Ch. 3

4 The proud, the cold untroubled heart of stone,

That never mused on sorrow but its own.
Thomas Campbell (1777–1844) British poet.
Pleasures of Hope, I

SELF-KNOWLEDGE

1 Resolve to be thyself: and know, that he
Who finds himself, loses his misery.
Matthew Arnold (1822–88) British poet and critic.
Self-Dependence

2 We confess our bad qualities to others out of
fear of appearing naive or ridiculous by not
being aware of them.
Gerald Brenan (Edward Fitzgerald Brenan; 1894–1987)
British writer.
Thoughts in a Dry Season

3 'I know myself,' he cried, 'but that is all.'
F. Scott Fitzgerald (1896–1940) US novelist.
This Side of Paradise, Bk. II, Ch. 5

4 I do not know myself, and God forbid that I
should.
Goethe (1749–1832) German poet and dramatist.
Conversations with Eckermann, 10 Apr 1829

5 Know then thyself, presume not God to
scan,
The proper study of Mankind is Man.
Alexander Pope (1688–1744) British poet.
An Essay on Man, II

6 That true self-love and social are the same;
That virtue only makes our bliss below;
And all our knowledge is, ourselves to know.
Alexander Pope
An Essay on Man, IV

SELFLESSNESS

See also charity, self-denial

1 The way to get things done is not to mind
who gets the credit of doing them.
Benjamin Jowett (1817–93) British theologian.
Attrib.

2 To give and not to count the cost;
To fight and not to heed the wounds;
To toil and not to seek for rest;
To labour and not ask for any reward
Save that of knowing that we do Thy will.
St Ignatius Loyola (1491–1556) Spanish priest.
Prayer for Generosity

3 There is nothing in Christianity or Buddhism
that quite matches the sympathetic
unselfishness of an oyster.
Saki (Hector Hugh Munro; 1870–1916) British writer.
Chronicles of Clovis

SELF-MADE MEN

1 I know he is, and he adores his maker.
Benjamin Disraeli (1804–81) British statesman.
The Fine Art of Political Wit (L. Harris)
Replying to a remark made in defence of John Bright that he
was a self-made man

2 He was a self-made man who owed his lack
of success to nobody.
Joseph Heller (1923–) US novelist.
Catch-22, Ch. 3

3 A self-made man is one who believes in luck
and sends his son to Oxford.
Christina Stead (1902–83) Australian novelist.
House of All Nations, 'Credo'

SELF-PRESERVATION

See also survival

1 Look after number one.
Proverb

2 He that fights and runs away
May live to fight another day.
Anonymous
Musarum Deliciae

3 This animal is very bad; when attacked it
defends itself.
Anonymous
La Ménagerie (P. K. Théodore), 1828

4 In good King Charles's golden days,
When loyalty no harm meant,
A zealous High Churchman was I,
And so I got preferment.

And this is law, that I'll maintain,
Unto my dying day, Sir,
That whatsoever King shall reign,
I'll be the Vicar of Bray, Sir.
Anonymous
The Vicar of Bray

5 There was only one catch and that was
Catch-22, which specified that a concern for
one's own safety in the face of dangers that
were real and immediate was the process of
a rational mind.
Joseph Heller (1923–) US novelist.
Catch-22, Ch. 5

6 If a madman were to come into this room
with a stick in his hand, no doubt we should
pity the state of his mind; but our primary
consideration would be to take care of
ourselves. We should knock him down first,
and pity him afterwards.
Samuel Johnson (1709–84) British lexicographer.
Life of Johnson (J. Boswell), Vol. III

7 We intend to remain alive. Our neighbors

want to see us dead. This is not a question that leaves much room for compromise.
Golda Meir (1898–1978) Russian-born Israeli stateswoman.
Reader's Digest (July 1971), 'The Indestructible Golda Meir'

8 The better part of valour is discretion; in the which better part I have saved my life.
William Shakespeare (1564–1616) English dramatist.
Henry IV, Part One, V:4

9 *J'ai vécu.*
I survived.
Abbé de Sieyès (1748–1836) French churchman.
Dictionnaire Encyclopédique (E. Guérard)
Replying to an enquiry concerning what he had done during the Terror

10 Greater love hath no man than this, that he lay down his friends for his life.
Jeremy Thorpe (1929–) British politician.
The Pendulum Years (Bernard Levin), Ch. 12
After Macmillan's 1962 Cabinet reshuffle

11 Scheherazade is the classical example of a woman saving her head by using it.
Esme Wynne-Tyson (1898–) British writer.
Attrib.

SELF-RELIANCE

See also independence

1 If you want a thing well done, do it yourself.
Proverb

2 The gods help them that help themselves.
Aesop (6th century BC) Reputed Greek writer of fables.
Fables, 'Hercules and the Waggoner'

3 They do most by Books, who could do much without them, and he that chiefly owes himself unto himself, is the substantial Man.
Thomas Browne (1605–82) English physician and writer.
Christian Morals, Pt. II

4 Let the boy win his spurs.
Edward III (1312–77) King of England.
Attrib.
Replying to a suggestion that he should send reinforcements to his son, the Black Prince, during the Battle of Crécy, 1346

5 The first rule in opera is the first rule in life: see to everything yourself.
Nellie Melba (Helen Porter Mitchell; 1861–1931) Australian soprano.
Melodies and Memories

6 The greatest thing in the world is to know how to be self-sufficient.
Michel de Montaigne (1533–92) French essayist.
Essais, I

7 Our remedies oft in ourselves do lie, Which we ascribe to heaven.
William Shakespeare (1564–1616) English dramatist.
All's Well that Ends Well, I:1

SELF-RESPECT

See also pride, respect

1 It is better to die on your feet than to live on your knees.
Dolores Ibarruri (1895–) Spanish politician.
Speech, Paris, 1936

2 As for conceit, what man will do any good who is not conceited? Nobody holds a good opinion of a man who has a low opinion of himself.
Anthony Trollope (1815–82) British novelist.
Orley Farm, Ch. 22

3 And, above all things, never think that you're not good enough yourself. A man should never think that. My belief is that in life people will take you very much at your own reckoning.
Anthony Trollope
The Small House at Allington, Ch. 32

4 When people do not respect us we are sharply offended; yet deep down in his heart no man much respects himself.
Mark Twain (Samuel Langhorne Clemens; 1835–1910) US writer.
Notebooks

SENSATION

1 O for a life of sensations rather than of thoughts!
John Keats (1795–1821) British poet.
Letter to Benjamin Bailey, 22 Nov 1817

2 'The story is like the wind', the Bushman prisoner said. 'It comes from a far off place, and we feel it.'
Laurens Van der Post (1906–) South African novelist.
A Story Like the Wind

SENTIMENTALITY

See also emotion

1 They had been corrupted by money, and he had been corrupted by sentiment. Sentiment was the more dangerous, because you couldn't name its price. A man open to bribes was to be relied upon below a certain figure, but sentiment might uncoil in the heart at a name, a photograph, even a smell remembered.
Graham Greene (1904–) British novelist.
The Heart of the Matter

2 Sentimentality is a superstructure covering brutality.
Carl Gustav Jung (1875–1961) Swiss psychoanalyst.
Reflections

3 One may not regard the world as a sort of metaphysical brothel for emotions.
Arthur Koestler (1905–83) Hungarian-born British writer.
Darkness at Noon, 'The Second Hearing'

4 Sentimentality is only sentiment that rubs you up the wrong way.
W. Somerset Maugham (1874–1965) British novelist.
A Writer's Notebook

5 She likes stories that make her cry – I think we all do, it's so nice to feel sad when you've nothing particular to be sad about.
Annie Sullivan (1866–1936) US teacher of the handicapped.
Letter, 12 Dec 1887
Referring to Helen Keller

SEPARATION

See also absence, parting

1 My Bonnie lies over the ocean,
My Bonnie lies over the sea,
My Bonnie lies over the ocean,
Oh, bring back my Bonnie to me.
Anonymous
My Bonnie

2 If I should meet thee
After long years,
How should I greet thee? –
With silence and tears.
Lord Byron (1788–1824) British poet.
When we two parted

3 Absence from whom we love is worse than death.
William Cowper (1731–1800) British poet.
'Hope, like the Short-lived Ray'

4 As it will be the right of all, so it will be the duty of some, definitely to prepare for a separation, amicably if they can, violently if they must.
Josiah Quincy (1772–1864) US statesman.
Abridgement of Debates of Congress, Vol. IV, 14 Jan 1811

5 Every parting gives a foretaste of death; every coming together again a foretaste of the resurrection.
Arthur Schopenhauer (1788–1860) German philosopher.
Gedanken über vielerlei Gegenstände, XXVI

6 I do desire we may be better strangers.
William Shakespeare (1564–1616) English dramatist.
As You Like It, III:2

SERIOUSNESS

1 Angels can fly because they take themselves lightly.
G. K. Chesterton (1874–1936) British writer.
Orthodoxy, Ch. 7

2 Though this may be play to you, 'tis death to us.
Roger L'Estrange (1616–1704) English journalist and writer.
Aesop's Fables, 398

3 You must not think me necessarily foolish because I am facetious, nor will I consider you necessarily wise because you are grave.
Sydney Smith (1771–1845) British clergyman and essayist.
Letter to Bishop Blomfield

4 He rose by gravity; I sank by levity.
Sydney Smith
Attrib.
Comparing his career with that of his brother, Robert Percy Smith

SERMONS

See also brevity, speeches, verbosity

1 They are written as if sin were to be taken out of man like Eve out of Adam – by putting him to sleep.
Sydney Smith (1771–1845) British clergyman and essayist.
Anecdotes of the Clergy (J. Larwood)
Referring to boring sermons

2 I never quite forgave Mahaffy for getting himself suspended from preaching in the College Chapel. Ever since his sermons were discontinued, I suffer from insomnia in church.
George Tyrrell (1861–1909) Irish Catholic theologian.
As I Was Going Down Sackville Street (Oliver St John Gogarty), Ch. 25

3 Yes, about ten minutes.
Duke of Wellington (1769–1852) British general and statesman.
Attrib.
Responding to a vicar's query as to whether there was anything he would like his forthcoming sermon to be about

SERVICE

See also help

1 His lord said unto him, Well done, thou good and faithful servant: thou hast been faithful over a few things, I will make thee ruler over many things: enter thou into the joy of thy lord.
Bible: Matthew
25:21

2 Oh that I were an orange-tree,
That busy plant!
Then I should ever laden be,
And never want
Some fruit for Him that dressed me.
George Herbert (1593–1633) English poet.
Employment

3 God doth not need
Either man's work or his own gifts. Who best
Bear his mild yoke, they serve him best: his state
Is kingly; thousands at his bidding speed,
And post o'er land and ocean without rest;
They also serve who only stand and wait.
John Milton (1608–74) English poet.
Sonnet: 'On his Blindness'

4 Small service is true service, while it lasts.
William Wordsworth (1770–1850) British poet.
To a Child, Written in her Album

SERVILITY

See also flattery, humility

1 Fine words and an insinuating appearance are seldom associated with true virtue.
Confucius (K'ung Fu-tzu; 551–479 BC) Chinese philosopher.
Analects

2 I am well aware that I am the 'umblest person going . . . .My mother is likewise a very 'umble person. We live in a numble abode.
Charles Dickens (1812–70) British novelist.
David Copperfield, Ch. 16
Said by Uriah Heep

3 Uriah, with his long hands slowly twining over one another, made a ghastly writhe from the waist upwards.
Charles Dickens
David Copperfield, Ch. 17

4 A pious man is one who would be an atheist if the king were.
Jean de La Bruyère (1645–96) French satirist.
Les Caractères

5 Wit that can creep, and pride that licks the dust.
Alexander Pope (1688–1744) British poet.
Epistle to Dr. Arbuthnot

6 You know that nobody is strongminded around a President . . . it is always: 'yes sir', 'no sir' (the 'no sir' comes when he asks whether you're dissatisfied).
George Edward Reedy (1917–) US government official.
The White House (ed. R. Gordon Hoxie)

7 Whenever he met a great man he grovelled before him, and my-lorded him as only a free-born Briton can do.
William Makepeace Thackeray (1811–63) British novelist.
Vanity Fair, Ch. 13

SEX

See also abstinence, adultery, animalism, contraception, debauchery, illegitimacy, lust, pornography, promiscuity, prudery, purity, sexes

1 Is sex dirty? Only if it's done right.
Woody Allen (Allen Stewart Konigsberg; 1935–) US film actor.
All You've Ever Wanted to Know About Sex

2 It was the most fun I ever had without laughing.
Woody Allen
Annie Hall

3 Don't knock it, it's sex with someone you love.
Woody Allen
Annie Hall
Referring to masturbation

4 She sighed, she cried, she damned near died: she said 'What shall I do?'
So I took her into bed and covered up her head
Just to save her from the foggy, foggy dew.
Anonymous
Weaver's Song

5 Money, it turned out, was exactly like sex, you thought of nothing else if you didn't have it and thought of other things if you did.
James Baldwin (1924–87) US writer.
Nobody Knows My Name

6 If God had meant us to have group sex, I guess he'd have given us all more organs.
Malcolm Bradbury (1932–) British academic and novelist.
Who Do You Think You Are?, 'A Very Hospitable Person'

7 It doesn't matter what you do in the bedroom as long as you don't do it in the street and frighten the horses.
Mrs Patrick Campbell (Beatrice Stella Tanner; 1865–1940) British actress.
The Duchess of Jermyn Street (Daphne Fielding), Ch. 2

8 The Summer hath his joys,
And Winter his delights.
Though Love and all his pleasures are but toys,
They shorten tedious nights.
Thomas Campion (1567–1620) English poet.
Now Winter Nights Enlarge

9 I'll wager you that in 10 years it will be fashionable again to be a virgin.
Barbara Cartland (1902–) British romantic novelist.
The Observer, 'Sayings of the Week', 20 June 1976

10 I answer 20 000 letters a year and so many couples are having problems because they are not getting the right proteins and vitamins.
Barbara Cartland
The Observer, 'Sayings of the Week', 31 Aug 1986

11 I said 10 years ago that in 10 years time it would be smart to be a virgin. Now everyone is back to virgins again.
Barbara Cartland
The Observer, 'Sayings of the Week', 12 July 1987

12 She gave me a smile I could feel in my hip pocket.
Raymond Chandler (1888–1959) US novelist.
Farewell, My Lovely, Ch. 18

13 When she raises her eyelids it's as if she were taking off all her clothes.
Colette (1873–1954) French novelist.
Claudine and Annie

14 No more about sex, it's too boring.
Lawrence Durrell (1912–) British novelist.
Tunc

15 He in a few minutes ravished this fair
creature, or at least would have ravished
her, if she had not, by a timely compliance,
prevented him.
Henry Fielding (1707–54) British novelist.
Jonathan Wild, Bk. III, Ch. 7

16 Older women are best because they always
think they may be doing it for the last time.
Ian Fleming (1908–64) British journalist and author.
Life of Ian Fleming (John Pearson)

17 Personally I know nothing about sex because
I've always been married.
Zsa Zsa Gabor (1919–) Hungarian-born US film star.
The Observer, 'Sayings of the Week', 16 Aug 1987

18 Prostitution gives her an opportunity to meet
people. It provides fresh air and wholesome
exercise, and it keeps her out of trouble.
Joseph Heller (1923–) US novelist.
Catch-22, Ch. 33

19 But did thee feel the earth move?
Ernest Hemingway (1899–1961) US novelist.
For Whom the Bell Tolls, Ch. 13

20 My life with girls has ended, though till lately
I was up to it and soldiered on not
ingloriously; now on this wall will hang my
weapons and my lyre, discharged from the
war.
Horace (Quintus Horatius Flaccus; 65–8 BC) Roman poet.
Odes, III

21 People will insist . . . on treating the *mons
Veneris* as though it were Mount Everest.
Aldous Huxley (1894–1964) British novelist.
Eyeless in Gaza, Ch. 30

22 A million million spermatozoa,
All of them alive:
Out of their cataclysm but one poor Noah
Dare hope to survive.
Aldous Huxley
Fifth Philosopher's Song

23 'Bed,' as the Italian proverb succinctly puts
it, 'is the poor man's opera.'
Aldous Huxley
Heaven and Hell

24 When Eve ate this particular apple, she
became aware of her own womanhood,
mentally. And mentally she began to
experiment with it. She has been
experimenting ever since. So has man. To
the rage and horror of both of them.
D. H. Lawrence (1885–1930) British novelist.
Fantasia of the Unconscious, Ch. 7

25 No sex without responsibility.
Lord Longford (1905–) British politician and social
reformer.
The Observer, 'Sayings of the Week', 3 May 1954

26 The Duke returned from the wars today and
did pleasure me in his top-boots.
Sarah, Duchess of Marlborough (1660–1744) Wife of
John Churchill, 1st Duke of Marlborough.
Attributed to her in various forms; a more ambitious version
goes '. . . pleasure me three times in his top-boots'

27 FRIAR BARNARDINE. Thou hast committed –
BARABAS. Fornication: but that was in another
country;
And beside the wench is dead.
Christopher Marlowe (1564–93) English dramatist.
The Jew of Malta, IV:1

28 Whoever named it necking was a poor judge
of anatomy.
Groucho Marx (Julius Marx; 1895–1977) US comedian.
Attrib.

29 Sex is one of the nine reasons for
reincarnation . . . The other eight are
unimportant.
Henry Miller (1891–1980) US novelist.
Big Sur and the Oranges of Hieronymus Bosch

30 There was a little girl
Who had a little curl
Right in the middle of her forehead,
When she was good she was very very good
And when she was bad she was very very
popular.
Max Miller (Harold Sargent; 1895–1963) British music-hall
comedian.
The Max Miller Blue Book

31 The daughter-in-law of Pythagoras said that a
woman who goes to bed with a man ought to
lay aside her modesty with her skirt, and put
it on again with her petticoat.
Michel de Montaigne (1533–92) French essayist.
Essais, I

32 Why do they put the Gideon Bibles only in
the bedrooms where it's usually too late?
Christopher Darlington Morley (1890–1957) US writer.
Quotations for Speakers and Writers

33 The orgasm has replaced the Cross as the
focus of longing and the image of fulfilment.
Malcolm Muggeridge (1903–) British writer.
The Most of Malcolm Muggeridge, 'Down with Sex'

34 It's all any reasonable child can expect if the
dad is present at the conception.
Joe Orton (1933–67) British dramatist.
Entertaining Mr Sloane, III

35 If all the young ladies who attended the Yale
promenade dance were laid end to end, no
one would be the least surprised.
Dorothy Parker (1893–1967) US writer.
While Rome Burns (Alexander Woollcott)

36 I know it does make people happy but to me
it is just like having a cup of tea.
Cynthia Payne (1934–) London housewife
After her acquittal on a charge of controlling prostitutes in a
famous 'sex-for-luncheon-vouchers' case, 8 Nov 1987

37 Love is not the dying moan of a distant violin – it's the triumphant twang of a bedspring.
S. J. Perelman (1904–79) US humorous writer.
Quotations for Speakers and Writers (A. Andrews)

38 On a sofa upholstered in panther skin
Mona did researches in original sin.
William Plomer (1903–73) South African poet and novelist.
Mews Flat Mona

39 A PUSHING LADY. What are your views on love?
MME LEROI. Love? I make it constantly but I never talk about it.
Marcel Proust (1871–1922) French novelist.
À la recherche du temps perdu: Le Côté de Guermantes

40 The Christian view of sex is that it is, indeed, a form of holy communion.
John Robinson (1919–83) Bishop of Woolwich.
Giving evidence in the prosecution of Penguin Books for publishing *Lady Chatterly's Lover*

41 Sex is something I really don't understand too hot. You never know *where* the hell you are. I keep making up these sex rules for myself, and then I break them right away.
J. D. Salinger (1919–) US novelist.
The Catcher in the Rye, Ch. 9

42 Is it not strange that desire should so many years outlive performance?
William Shakespeare (1564–1616) English dramatist.
Henry IV, Part Two, II:4

43 Lechery, lechery! Still wars and lechery! Nothing else holds fashion.
William Shakespeare
Troilus and Cressida, V:2

44 Someone asked Sophocles, 'How do you feel now about sex? Are you still able to have a woman?' He replied, 'Hush, man; most gladly indeed am I rid of it all, as though I had escaped from a mad and savage master.'
Sophocles (c. 496–406 BC) Greek dramatist.
Republic (Plato), Bk. I

45 Masturbation: the primary sexual activity of mankind. In the nineteenth century it was a disease; in the twentieth, it's a cure.
Thomas Szasz (1920–) US psychiatrist.
The Second Sin

46 Traditionally, sex has been a very private, secretive activity. Herein perhaps lies its powerful force for uniting people in a strong bond. As we make sex less secretive, we may rob it of its power to hold men and women together.
Thomas Szasz
The Second Sin

47 Chasing the naughty couples down the grassgreen gooseberried double bed of the wood.
Dylan Thomas (1914–53) Welsh poet.
Under Milk Wood

48 Old Nat Burge sat . . . He was . . . watching the moon come up lazily out of the old cemetery in which nine of his daughters were lying, and only two of them were dead.
James Thurber (1894–1961) US humorist.
Let Your Mind Alone, 'Bateman Comes Home'

49 Surely you don't mean by unartificial insemination!
James Thurber
Attrib.
On being accosted at a party by a drunk woman who claimed she would like to have a baby by him

50 Familiarity breeds contempt – and children.
Mark Twain (Samuel Langhorne Clemens; 1835–1910) US writer.
Notebooks

51 All this fuss about sleeping together. For physical pleasure I'd sooner go to my dentist any day.
Evelyn Waugh (1903–66) British novelist.
Vile Bodies, Ch. 6

52 When women go wrong, men go right after them.
Mae West (1892–1980) US actress.
The Wit and Wisdom of Mae West (ed. J. Weintraub)

53 It's not the men in my life that count; it's the life in my men.
Mae West
Attrib.

54 When I'm good I'm very good, but when I'm bad I'm better.
Mae West
Attrib.

55 I shall not say why and how I became, at the age of fifteen, the mistress of the Earl of Craven.
Harriette Wilson (1789–1846) British writer and courtesan.
Memoirs, Opening

56 A mistress should be like a little country retreat near the town, not to dwell in constantly, but only for a night and away.
William Wycherley (1640–1716) English dramatist.
The Country Wife, I:1

SEXES

See also feminism, marriage, men, sex, woman's role, women

1 As men
Do walk a mile, women should talk an hour,
After supper. 'Tis their exercise.
Francis Beaumont (1584–1616) English dramatist.
Philaster, II:4

2 And the man said, The woman whom thou gavest to be with me, she gave me of the tree, and I did eat.
And the Lord God said unto the woman, What is this that thou hast done? And the woman said, The serpent beguiled me, and I did eat.

And the Lord God said unto the serpent, Because thou hast done this, thou art cursed above all cattle, and above every beast of the field; upon thy belly shalt thou go, and dust shalt thou eat all the days of thy life:

And I will put enmity between thee and the woman, and between thy seed and her seed; it shall bruise thy head, and thou shalt bruise his heel.

Unto the woman he said, I will greatly multiply thy sorrow and thy conception; in sorrow thou shalt bring forth children; and thy desire shall be to thy husband, and he shall rule over thee.

And unto Adam he said, Because thou hast hearkened unto the voice of thy wife, and has eaten of the tree, of which I commanded thee, saying, Thou shalt not eat of it: cursed is the ground for thy sake; in sorrow shalt thou eat of it all the days of thy life.

Bible: Genesis
3:12–17

3 Mr. Darwin . . . has failed to hold definitely before his mind the principle that the difference of sex, whatever it may consist in, must itself be subject to natural selection and to evolution.
Antoinette Brown Blackwell (1825–1921) US feminist writer.
The Sexes Throughout Nature

4 Man's love is of man's life a thing apart,
'Tis woman's whole existence.
Lord Byron (1788–1824) British poet.
Don Juan, I

5 There is more difference within the sexes than between them.
Ivy Compton-Burnett (1892–1969) British novelist.
Mother and Son

6 In the sex-war thoughtlessness is the weapon of the male, vindictiveness of the female.
Cyril Connolly (1903–74) British journalist.
The Unquiet Grave

7 The average man is more interested in a woman who is interested in him than he is in a woman – any woman – with beautiful legs.
Marlene Dietrich (Maria Magdalene von Losch; 1904–) German-born film star.
News item, 13 Dec 1954

8 The reason that husbands and wives do not understand each other is because they belong to different sexes.
Dorothy Dix (Elizabeth Meriwether Gilmer; 1861–1951) US journalist and writer.
News item

9 Where young boys plan for what they will achieve and attain, young girls plan for whom they will achieve and attain.
Charlotte Perkins Gilman (1860–1935) US writer.
Women and Economics, Ch. 5

10 Man has his will, – but woman has her way.
Oliver Wendell Holmes (1809–94) US writer.
The Autocrat of the Breakfast Table, Prologue

11 Boys will be boys – '
'And even that . . . wouldn't matter if we could only prevent girls from being girls.'
Anthony Hope (Anthony Hope Hawkins; 1863–1933) British novelist.
The Dolly Dialogues

12 For men must work, and women must weep,
And there's little to earn, and many to keep,
Though the harbour bar be moaning.
Charles Kingsley (1819–75) British writer.
The Three Fishers

13 The silliest woman can manage a clever man; but it needs a very clever woman to manage a fool.
Rudyard Kipling (1865–1936) Indian-born British writer.
Plain Tales from the Hills, 'Three and – an Extra'

14 Perhaps at fourteen every boy should be in love with some ideal woman to put on a pedestal and worship. As he grows up, of course, he will put her on a pedestal the better to view her legs.
Barry Norman (1933–) British cinema critic and broadcaster.
The Listener

15 The seldom female in a world of males!
Ruth Pitter (1897–) British poet.
The Kitten's Eclogue, IV

16 I often want to cry. That is the only advantage women have over men – at least they can cry.
Jean Rhys (1894–1979) Dominican-born British novelist.
Good Morning, Midnight, Pt. II

17 Woman's virtue is man's greatest invention.
Cornelia Otis Skinner (1901–79) US stage actress.
Attrib.

18 Man is a creature who lives not upon bread alone, but principally by catchwords; and the little rift between the sexes is astonishingly widened by simply teaching one set of catchwords to the girls and another to the boys.
Robert Louis Stevenson (1850–94) Scottish writer.
Virginibus Puerisque

19 Man is the hunter; woman is his game:
The sleek and shining creatures of the chase,
We hunt them for the beauty of their skins.
Alfred, Lord Tennyson (1809–92) British poet.
The Princess, V

20 Man for the field and woman for the hearth:
Man for the sword and for the needle she:
Man with the head and woman with the heart:
Man to command and woman to obey;
All else confusion.
Alfred, Lord Tennyson
The Princess, V

21 There are some meannesses which are too mean even for man – woman, lovely woman alone, can venture to commit them.
William Makepeace Thackeray (1811–63) British novelist.
A Shabby-Genteel Story, Ch. 3

22 The War between Men and Women.
James Thurber (1894–1961) US humorist.
Title of a series of cartoons

23 When a man confronts catastrophe on the road, he looks in his purse – but a woman looks in her mirror.
Margaret Turnbull (fl. 1920s–1942) US writer.
The Left Lady

24 Instead of this absurd division into sexes they ought to class people as static and dynamic.
Evelyn Waugh (1903–66) British novelist.
Decline and Fall, Pt. III, Ch. 7

25 All women become like their mothers. That is their tragedy. No man does. That's his.
Oscar Wilde (1854–1900) Irish-born British dramatist.
The Importance of Being Earnest, I

26 Women represent the triumph of matter over mind, just as men represent the triumph of mind over morals.
Oscar Wilde
The Picture of Dorian Gray, Ch. 4

27 Why are women . . . so much more interesting to men than men are to women?
Virginia Woolf (1882–1941) British novelist.
A Room of One's Own

SHAKESPEARE

See also critcism, poets, writers

1 Others abide our question, Thou art free,
We ask and ask: Thou smilest and art still,
Out-topping knowledge.
Matthew Arnold (1822–88) British poet and critic.
Shakespeare

2 Our myriad-minded Shakespeare.
Samuel Taylor Coleridge (1772–1834) British poet.
Biographia Literaria, Ch. 15

3 I have tried lately to read Shakespeare, and found it so intolerably dull that it nauseated me.
Charles Darwin (1809–82) British life scientist.
Autobiography

4 He was the man who of all modern, and perhaps ancient poets had the largest and most comprehensive soul.
John Dryden (1631–1700) British poet and dramatist.
Essay of Dramatic Poesy

5 He was naturally learned; he needed not the spectacles of books to read nature; he looked inwards, and found her there.
John Dryden
Essay of Dramatic Poesy

6 We can say of Shakespeare, that never has a man turned so little knowledge to such great account.
T. S. Eliot (1888–1965) US-born British poet and dramatist.
The Classics and the Man of Letters (lecture)

7 The remarkable thing about Shakespeare is that he is really very good – in spite of all the people who say he is very good.
Robert Graves (1895–1985) British poet and novelist.
The Observer, 'Sayings of the Week', 6 Dec 1964

8 Shakespeare never had six lines together without a fault. Perhaps you may find seven, but this does not refute my general assertion.
Samuel Johnson (1709–84) British lexicographer.
Life of Johnson (J. Boswell), Vol. II

9 He was not of an age, but for all time!
Ben Jonson (1573–1637) English dramatist.
To the Memory of William Shakespeare

10 Sweet Swan of Avon!
Ben Jonson
To the Memory of William Shakespeare

11 When I read Shakespeare I am struck with wonder
That such trivial people should muse and thunder
In such lovely language.
D. H. Lawrence (1885–1930) British novelist.
When I Read Shakespeare

12 Or sweetest Shakespeare, Fancy's child,
Warble his native wood-notes wild.
John Milton (1608–74) English poet.
L'Allegro

13 Shakespeare – the nearest thing in incarnation to the eye of God.
Laurence Olivier (1907–) British actor.
Kenneth Harris Talking To, 'Sir Laurence Olivier'

14 A man can be forgiven a lot if he can quote Shakespeare in an economic crisis.
Prince Philip (1921–) The consort of Queen Elizabeth II.
Attrib.

15 With the single exception of Homer, there is no eminent writer, not even Sir Walter Scott, whom I can despise so entirely as I despise Shakespeare when I measure my mind against his . . . It would positively be a relief to me to dig him up and throw stones at him.
George Bernard Shaw (1856–1950) Irish dramatist and critic.
Dramatic Opinions and Essays, Vol. 2

16 Wonderful women! Have you ever thought how much we all, and women especially, owe to Shakespeare for his vindication of women in these fearless, high-spirited, resolute and intelligent heroines?

Ellen Terry (1847–1928) British actress.
Four Lectures on Shakespeare, 'The Triumphant Women'

17 One of the greatest geniuses that ever existed, Shakespeare, undoubtedly wanted taste.

Horace Walpole (1717–97) British writer.
Letter to Wren, 9 Aug 1764

SHYNESS

See also self-confidence

1 I'm really a timid person – I was beaten up by Quakers.

Woody Allen (Allen Stewart Konigsberg; 1935–) US film actor.
Sleeper

2 A timid question will always receive a confident answer.

Lord Darling (1849–1936) British judge.
Scintillae Juris

3 Why so shy, my pretty Thomasina?
Thomasin, O Thomasin,
Once you were so promisin'.

Christopher Fry (1907–) British dramatist.
The Dark Is Light Enough, II

4 Had we but world enough, and time,
This coyness, lady, were no crime.

Andrew Marvell (1621–78) English poet.
To His Coy Mistress

SIGNATURES

1 Never sign a walentine with your own name.

Charles Dickens (1812–70) British novelist.
Pickwick Papers, Ch. 33
Said by Sam Weller

2 There, I guess King George will be able to read that.

John Hancock (1737–93) US revolutionary.
The American Treasury (C. Fadiman)
Referring to his signature, written in a bold hand, on the US Declaration of Independence

3 The hand that signed the treaty bred a fever,
And famine grew, and locusts came;
Great is the hand that holds dominion over
Man by a scribbled name.

Dylan Thomas (1914–53) Welsh poet.
The hand that signed the paper

SILENCE

See also speech

1 A still tongue makes a wise head.
Proverb

2 Speech is silver, silence is golden.
Proverb

3 No voice; but oh! the silence sank

Like music on my heart.

Samuel Taylor Coleridge (1772–1834) British poet.
The Rime of the Ancient Mariner, VI

4 When you have nothing to say, say nothing.

Charles Caleb Colton (?1780–1832) British clergyman and writer.
Lacon, Vol. I

5 For God's sake hold your tongue and let me love.

John Donne (1573–1631) English poet.
The Canonization

6 Silence is become his mother tongue.

Oliver Goldsmith (1728–74) Irish-born British writer.
The Good-Natured Man, II

7 That man's silence is wonderful to listen to.

Thomas Hardy (1840–1928) British novelist.
Under the Greenwood Tree, Ch. 14

8 Silence is as full of potential wisdom and wit as the unhewn marble of great sculpture.

Aldous Huxley (1894–1964) British novelist.
Point Counter Point

9 Thou still unravish'd bride of quietness,
Thou foster-child of silence and slow time.

John Keats (1795–1821) British poet.
Ode on a Grecian Urn

10 Silence is the best tactic for him who distrusts himself.

Duc de la Rochefoucauld (1613–80) French writer.
Maximes, 79

11 You get the impression that their normal condition is silence and that speech is a slight fever which attacks them now and then.

Jean-Paul Sartre (1905–80) French writer.
Nausea

12 Silence is the perfectest herald of joy: I were but little happy if I could say how much.

William Shakespeare (1564–1616) English dramatist.
Much Ado About Nothing, II:1

13 Silence is the most perfect expression of scorn.

George Bernard Shaw (1856–1950) Irish dramatist and critic.
Back to Methuselah

14 The cruellest lies are often told in silence.

Robert Louis Stevenson (1850–94) Scottish writer.
Virginibus Puerisque

15 Whereof one cannot speak, thereon one must remain silent.

Ludwig Wittgenstein (1889–1951) Austrian philosopher.
Tractatus Logico-Philosophicus, Ch. 7

SIMILARITY

See also analogy, difference

1 Birds of a feather flock together.
Proverbs

2 Great minds think alike.
Proverb

3 Like breeds like.
Proverb

4 Never mind, dear, we're all made the same, though some more than others.
Noël Coward (1899–1973) British dramatist.
The Café de la Paix

5 I never knows the children. It's just six of one and half-a-dozen of the other.
Captain Frederick Marryat (1792–1848) British novelist.
The Pirate, Ch. 4

SIMPLICITY

1 'Excellent!' I cried. 'Elementary,' said he.
Arthur Conan Doyle (1856–1930) British writer.
The Crooked Man
Watson talking to Sherlock Holmes; Holmes's reply is often misquoted as 'Elementary my dear Watson'

2 The ability to simplify means to eliminate the unnecessary so that the necessary may speak.
Hans Hofmann (1880–1966) German-born US painter.
Search for the Real

3 O holy simplicity!
John Huss (Jan Hus; c. 1369–1415) Bohemian religious reformer.
Apophthegmata (Zincgreff-Weidner), Pt. III
On noticing a peasant adding a faggot to the pile at his execution

4 The trivial round, the common task,
Would furnish all we ought to ask;
Room to deny ourselves; a road
To bring us, daily, nearer God.
John Keble (1792–1866) British poet and clergyman.
The Christian Year, 'Morning'

5 A child of five would understand this. Send somebody to fetch a child of five.
Groucho Marx (Julius Marx; 1895–1977) US comedian.
Duck Soup

6 Entities should not be multiplied unnecessarily.
No more things should be presumed to exist than are absolutely necessary.
William of Okham (c. 1280–1349) English philosopher.
'Okham's Razor'. Despite its attribution to William of Okham, it was in fact a repetition of an ancient philosophical maxim

7 Anybody can shock a baby, or a television audience. But it's too easy, and the effect is disproportionate to the effort.
Richard G. Stern (1928–) US writer.
Golk, Ch. 4

8 Our life is frittered away by detail . . .
Simplify, simplify.
Henry David Thoreau (1817–62) US writer.
Walden, 'Where I lived, and What I Lived For'

SIN

See also evil, vice

1 Old sins cast long shadows.
Proverb

2 All sin tends to be addictive, and the terminal point of addiction is what is called damnation.
W. H. Auden (1907–73) British poet.
A Certain World

3 Wherefore putting away lying, speak every man truth with his neighbour: for we are members one of another.
Be ye angry, and sin not: let not the sun go down upon your wrath:
Neither give place to the devil.
Let him that stole steal no more: but rather let him labour, working with his hands the thing which is good, that he may have to give to him that needeth.
Bible: Ephesians
4:25–28

4 So when they continued asking him, he lifted up himself, and said unto them, He that is without sin among you, let him first cast a stone at her.
Bible: John
8:7

5 If we say that we have no sin, we deceive ourselves, and the truth is not in us.
If we confess our sins, he is faithful and just to forgive us our sins, and to cleanse us from all unrighteousness.
Bible: I John
1:8–9

6 Wherefore I say unto thee, Her sins, which are many, are forgiven; for she loved much: but to whom little is forgiven, the same loveth little.
Bible: Luke
7:47

7 But if ye will not do so, behold, ye have sinned against the Lord: and be sure your sin will find you out.
Bible: Numbers
32:23

8 We have erred, and strayed from thy ways like lost sheep.
The Book of Common Prayer
Morning Prayer, General Confession

9 We have left undone those things which we ought to have done; and we have done those things we ought not to have done.
The Book of Common Prayer
Morning Prayer, General Confession

10 A private sin is not so prejudicial in the world as a public indecency.
Miguel de Cervantes (1547–1616) Spanish novelist.
Don Quixote, Pt. II, Ch. 22

11 He said he was against it.

Calvin Coolidge (1872–1933) US president.
Attrib.
Reply when asked what a clergyman had said regarding sin in his sermon

12 It is my belief, Watson, founded upon my experience, that the lowest and vilest alleys of London do not present a more dreadful record of sin than does the smiling and beautiful countryside.

Arthur Conan Doyle (1856–1930) British writer.
Copper Beeches

13 Did wisely from Expensive Sins refrain,
And never broke the Sabbath, but for Gain.

John Dryden (1631–1700) British poet and dramatist.
Absalom and Achitophel, I

14 Sin brought death, and death will disappear with the disappearance of sin.

Mary Baker Eddy (1821–1910) US religious leader.
Science and Health, with Key to the Scriptures

15 There's nothing so artificial as sinning nowadays. I suppose it once was real.

D. H. Lawrence (1885–1930) British novelist.
St Mawr

16 Of Man's first disobedience, and the fruit
Of that forbidden tree, whose mortal taste
Brought death into the World, and all our woe
. . .

John Milton (1608–74) English poet.
Paradise Lost, Bk. I

17 She holds that it were better for sun and moon to drop from heaven, for the earth to fail, and for all the many millions who are upon it to die of starvation in extremest agony, as far as temporal affliction goes, than that one soul, I will not say, should be lost, but should commit one single venial sin, should tell one wilful untruth, . . . or steal one poor farthing without excuse.

Cardinal Newman (1801–90) British theologian.
Lectures on Anglican Difficulties, VIII
Referring to the Roman Catholic Church

18 At such an hour the sinners are still in bed resting up from their sinning of the night before, so they will be in good shape for more sinning a little later on.

Damon Runyon (1884–1946) US writer.
Runyon à la carte, 'The Idyll of Miss Sarah Brown'

19 Were't not for gold and women, there would be no damnation.

Cyril Tourneur (1575–1626) English dramatist.
The Revenger's Tragedy, II:1

SINCERITY

See also frankness, honesty, integrity

1 Best be yourself, imperial, plain and true!

Robert Browning (1812–89) British poet.
Bishop Blougram's Apology

2 What comes from the heart, goes to the heart.

Samuel Taylor Coleridge (1772–1834) British poet.
Table Talk

3 Some of the worst men in the world are sincere and the more sincere they are the worse they are.

Lord Hailsham (1907–) British Conservative politician.
The Observer, 'Sayings of the Week', 7 Jan 1968

4 I'm afraid of losing my obscurity. Genuineness only thrives in the dark. Like celery.

Aldous Huxley (1894–1964) British novelist.
Those Barren Leaves, Pt. I, Ch. 1

5 What's a man's first duty? The answer's brief: To be himself.

Henrik Ibsen (1828–1906) Norwegian dramatist.
Peer Gynt, IV:1

6 A little sincerity is a dangerous thing, and a great deal of it is absolutely fatal.

Oscar Wilde (1854–1900) Irish-born British dramatist.
The Critic as Artist, Pt. 2

SINGERS

See also musicians, singing

1 Swans sing before they die – 'twere no bad thing,
Did certain persons die before they sing.

Samuel Taylor Coleridge (1772–1834) British poet.
Epigram on a Volunteer Singer

2 A wandering minstrel I –
A thing of shreds and patches,
Of ballads, songs and snatches,
And dreamy lullaby!

W. S. Gilbert (1836–1911) British dramatist.
The Mikado, I

3 The Last of the Red-Hot Mamas.

Sophie Tucker (Sophia Abuza; 1884–1966) Russian-born US singer.
Dictionary of Biographical Quotation (J. Wintle and R. Kenin)
Description of herself

SINGING

See also music, opera, singers

1 You know whatta you do when you shit?
Singing, it's the same thing, only up!

Enrico Caruso (1873–1921) Italian tenor.
Whose Little Boy Are You? (H. Brown)

2 I have a song to sing O!
Sing me your song, O!

W. S. Gilbert (1836–1911) British dramatist.
The Yeoman of the Guard, I

3 Just a little more reverence, please, and not so much astonishment.

Malcolm Sargent (1895–1967) British conductor.
2500 Anecdotes (E. Fuller)
Rehearsing the female chorus in 'For Unto Us a Child is Born' from Handel's *Messiah*

SLAVERY

See also oppression

1 The future is the only kind of property that the masters willingly concede to slaves.
Albert Camus (1913–60) French existentialist writer.
The Rebel

2 There they are cutting each other's throats, because one half of them prefer hiring their servants for life, and the other by the hour.
Thomas Carlyle (1795–1881) Scottish historian and essayist.
Attrib.
Referring to the American Civil War

3 Slaves cannot breathe in England; if their lungs
Receive our air, that moment they are free;
They touch our country, and their shackles fall.
William Cowper (1731–1800) British poet.
The Task
A situation resulting from a judicial decision in 1772

4 The compact which exists between the North and the South is a covenant with death and an agreement with hell.
William Lloyd Garrison (1805–79) US abolitionist.
Resolution, Massachusetts Anti-Slavery Society, 27 Jan 1843

SLEEP

See also bed, dreams

1 One hour's sleep before midnight, is worth two after.
Proverb

2 Now I lay me down to sleep,
I pray the Lord my soul to keep.
If I should die before I wake,
I pray the Lord my soul to take.
Anonymous
New England Primer, 1781

3 Lay your sleeping head, my love,
Human on my faithless arm.
W. H. Auden (1907–73) British poet.
Lullaby

4 Rock-a-bye baby on the tree top,
When the wind blows the cradle will rock,
When the bough bends the cradle will fall,
Down comes the baby, cradle and all.
Charles Dupee Blake (1846–1903) British writer of nursery rhymes.
Attrib.

5 Laugh and the world laughs with you; snore and you sleep alone.
Anthony Burgess (1917–) British novelist and critic.
Inside Mr. Enderby

6 Oh sleep! it is a gentle thing,
Beloved from pole to pole!
Samuel Taylor Coleridge (1772–1834) British poet.
The Rime of the Ancient Mariner, V

7 Golden slumbers kiss your eyes,

Smiles awake you when you rise.
Thomas Dekker (c. 1572–1632) English dramatist.
Patient Grissil, IV:2

8 Try thinking of love, or something.
Amor vincit insomnia.
Christopher Fry (1907–) British dramatist.
A Sleep of Prisoners

9 He's a wicked man that comes after children when they won't go to bed and throws handfuls of sand in their eyes.
Ernst Hoffmann (1776–1822) German composer.
The Sandman

10 O soft embalmer of the still midnight.
John Keats (1795–1821) British poet.
To Sleep

11 Turn the key deftly in the oiled wards,
And seal the hushed casket of my soul.
John Keats
To Sleep

12 How do people go to sleep? I'm afraid I've lost the knack. I might try busting myself smartly over the temple with the nightlight. I might repeat to myself, slowly and soothingly, a list of quotations beautiful from minds profound; if I can remember any of the damn things.
Dorothy Parker (1893–1967) US writer.
The Little Hours

13 Sleep that knits up the ravell'd sleave of care,
The death of each day's life, sore labour's bath,
Balm of hurt minds, great nature's second course,
Chief nourisher in life's feast.
William Shakespeare (1564–1616) English dramatist.
Macbeth, II:2

14 Sleep, Death's twin-brother, knows not Death,
Nor can I dream of thee as dead.
Alfred, Lord Tennyson (1809–92) British poet.
In Memoriam A.H.H., LXVIII

15 There ain't no way to find out why a snorer can't hear himself snore.
Mark Twain (Samuel Langhorne Clemens; 1835–1910) US writer.
Tom Sawyer Abroad, Ch. 10

16 It was the time when first sleep begins for weary
mortals and by the gift of the gods creeps over them
most welcomely.
Virgil (Publius Vergilius Maro; 70–19 BC) Roman poet.
Aeneid, Bk. II

17 I haven't been to sleep for over a year. That's why I go to bed early. One needs more rest if one doesn't sleep.
Evelyn Waugh (1903–66) British novelist.
Decline and Fall, Pt. II, Ch. 3

18 I believe the greatest asset a head of state can have is the ability to get a good night's sleep.
Harold Wilson (1916–) British politician and prime minister.
The World Tonight, BBC Radio, 16 Apr 1975

19 Dear God! the very houses seem asleep;
And all that mighty heart is lying still!
William Wordsworth (1770–1850) British poet.
Sonnets, 'Composed upon Westminster Bridge'

SMALLNESS

See also triviality

1 The best things come in small parcels.
Proverb

2 The Microbe is so very small
You cannot make him out at all.
Hilaire Belloc (1870–1953) French-born British poet.
More Beasts for Worse Children, 'The Microbe'

3 One cubic foot less of space and it would have constituted adultery.
Robert Benchley (1889–1945) US humorist.
Attrib.
Describing an office shared with Dorothy Parker

4 Small is beautiful.
E. F. Schumacher (1911–77) German-born economist.
Title of book

SMOKING

See also abstinence

1 Certainly not – if you don't object if I'm sick.
Thomas Beecham (1879–1961) British conductor.
When asked whether he minded if someone smoked in a non-smoking compartment
Attrib.

2 Jones – (who, I'm glad to say,
Asked leave of Mrs J. –)
Daily absorbs a clay
After his labours.
C. S. Calverley (1831–84) British poet.
Ode to Tobacco

3 I must point out that my rule of life prescribed as an absolutely sacred rite smoking cigars and also the drinking of alcohol before, after, and if need be during all meals and in the intervals between them.
Winston Churchill (1874–1965) British statesman.
The Second World War
Said during a lunch with the Arab leader Ibn Saud, when he heard that the king's religion forbade smoking and alcohol

4 It is quite a three-pipe problem.
Arthur Conan Doyle (1856–1930) British writer.
The Red-Headed League

5 What a blessing this smoking is! perhaps the greatest that we owe to the discovery of America.
Arthur Helps (1813–75) British historian.
Friends in Council

6 A custom loathsome to the eye, hateful to the nose, harmful to the brain, dangerous to the lungs, and in the black, stinking fume thereof, nearest resembling the horrible Stygian smoke of the pit that is bottomless.
James I (1566–1625) King of England.
A Counterblast to Tobacco

7 Neither do thou lust after that tawney weed tobacco.
Ben Jonson (1573–1637) English dramatist.
Bartholomew Fair, II:6

8 Ods me, I marvel what pleasure or felicity they have in taking their roguish tobacco. It is good for nothing but to choke a man, and fill him full of smoke and embers.
Ben Jonson
Every Man in His Humour, III:5

9 This very night I am going to leave off tobacco! Surely there must be some other world in which this unconquerable purpose shall be realized. The soul hath not her generous aspirings implanted in her in vain.
Charles Lamb (1775–1834) British essayist.
Letter to Thomas Manning, 26 Dec 1815

10 Dr Parr . . . asked him, how he had acquired his power of smoking at such a rate? Lamb replied, 'I toiled after it, sir, as some men toil after virtue.'
Charles Lamb
Memoirs of Charles Lamb (Talfourd)

11 He who lives without tobacco is not worthy to live.
Molière (Jean Baptiste Poquelin; 1622–73) French dramatist.
Don Juan, I:1

12 This vice brings in one hundred million francs in taxes every year. I will certainly forbid it at once – as soon as you can name a virtue that brings in as much revenue.
Napoleon III (1808–73) French emperor.
Anekdotenschatz (H. Hoffmeister)
Reply when asked to ban smoking

13 My doctor has always told me to smoke. He even explains himself: 'Smoke, my friend. Otherwise someone else will smoke in your place.'
Erik Satie (1866–1925) French composer.
Mémoires d'un amnésique

14 I've done it a hundred times!
Mark Twain (Samuel Langhorne Clemens; 1835–1910) US writer.
Attrib.
Referring to giving up smoking

15 A cigarette is the perfect type of a perfect pleasure. It is exquisite, and it leaves one unsatisfied. What more can one want?
Oscar Wilde (1854–1900) Irish-born British dramatist.
The Picture of Dorian Gray, Ch. 6

SNOBBERY

See also aristocracy, class, one-upmanship

1 In our way we were both snobs, and no snob welcomes another who has risen with him.
Cecil Beaton (1904–80) British photographer.
Referring to Evelyn Waugh
Attrib.

2 And this is good old Boston,
The home of the bean and the cod,
Where the Lowells talk only to Cabots,
And the Cabots talk only to God.
John Collins Bossidy (1860–1928) US writer.
Toast at Holy Cross Alumni dinner, 1910

3 Of course they have, or I wouldn't be sitting here talking to someone like you.
Barbara Cartland (1902–) British romantic novelist.
Class (J. Cooper)
When asked in a radio interview whether she thought that British class barriers had broken down

4 I've danced with a man, who's danced with a girl, who's danced with the Prince of Wales.
Herbert Farjeon (1887–1945) British writer.
Picnic

5 His hatred of snobs was a derivative of his snobbishness, but made the simpletons (in other words, everyone) believe that he was immune from snobbishness.
Marcel Proust (1871–1922) French novelist.
À la recherche du temps perdu: Le Côté de Guermantes

6 I mustn't go on singling out names. One must not be a name-dropper, as Her Majesty remarked to me yesterday.
Norman St John Stevas (1929–) British politician.
Speech, Museum of the Year luncheon, 20 June 1979

7 He who meanly admires mean things is a Snob.
William Makepeace Thackeray (1811–63) British novelist.
The Book of Snobs, Ch. 2

8 It is impossible, in our condition of society, not to be sometimes a Snob.
William Makepeace Thackeray
The Book of Snobs, Ch. 3

9 She was – but I assure you that she was a very bad cook.
Louis Adolphe Thiers (1797–1877) French statesman and historian.
Attrib.
Defending his social status after someone had remarked that his mother had been a cook

10 My dear – the people we should have been seen dead with.
Rebecca West (Cicely Isabel Fairfield; 1892–1983) British novelist and journalist.
Times Literary Supplement, 1 Oct 1982
Cable sent to Noël Coward after learning they had both been on a Nazi death list

11 CECILY: When I see a spade I call it a spade.
GWENDOLEN: I am glad to say I have never seen a spade. It is obvious that our social spheres have been widely different.
Oscar Wilde (1854–1900) Irish-born British dramatist.
The Importance of Being Earnest, II

12 Never speak disrespectfully of Society, Algernon. Only people who can't get into it do that.
Oscar Wilde
The Importance of Being Earnest, III

SOCIALISM

See also Communism, Marxism

1 The language of priorities is the religion of Socialism.
Aneurin Bevan (1897–1960) British Labour politician.
Aneurin Bevan (Vincent Brome), Ch. 1

2 The people's flag is deepest red;
It shrouded oft our martyred dead,
And ere their limbs grew stiff and cold,
Their heart's blood dyed its every fold.
Then raise the scarlet standard high!
Within its shade we'll live or die.
Tho' cowards flinch and traitors sneer,
We'll keep the red flag flying here.
James Connell (1852–1929) British socialist.
The Red Flag, in *Songs that made History* (H. E. Piggot), Ch. 6
Traditionally sung at the close of annual conferences of the British Labour Party

3 Socialism can only arrive by bicycle.
José Antonio Viera Gallo (1943–) Chilean politician.
Energy and Equity (Ivan Illich)

4 Only socialism would put up with it for so long. Capitalism would have gone bankrupt years ago.
Mikhail Gorbachov (1931–) Soviet statesman.
Talking of sub-standard workmanship in the Soviet Union
TV documentary, 23 March 1987

5 Well, what are you socialists going to do about me?
George V (1865–1936) King of the United Kingdom.
To Ramsay MacDonald at his first meeting as prime minister
Attrib.

6 We are all Socialists now.
William Harcourt (1827–1904) British statesman.
Attrib.

7 Compassion is not a sloppy, sentimental feeling for people who are underprivileged or sick . . . it is an absolutely practical belief that, regardless of a person's background, ability or ability to pay, he should be provided with the best that society has to offer.
Neil Kinnock (1942–) British politician.
Maiden speech, House of Commons, 1970

8 It is inconceivable that we could transform this society without a major extension of public ownership.
Neil Kinnock
Marxism Today, 1983

9 Under socialism *all* will govern in turn and will soon become accustomed to no one governing.
Lenin (Vladimir Ilich Ulyanov; 1870–1924) Russian revolutionary leader.
The State and Revolution, Ch. 6

10 As with the Christian religion, the worst advertisement for Socialism is its adherents.
George Orwell (Eric Blair; 1903–50) British novelist.
The Road to Wigan Pier, Ch. 11

11 To the ordinary working man, the sort you would meet in any pub on Saturday night, Socialism does not mean much more than better wages and shorter hours and nobody bossing you about.
George Orwell
The Road to Wigan Pier, Ch. 11

12 The higher-water mark, so to speak, of Socialist literature is W. H. Auden, a sort of gutless Kipling.
George Orwell
The Road to Wigan Pier, Ch. 11

13 State socialism is totally alien to the British character.
Margaret Thatcher (1925–) British politician and prime minister.
The Times, 1983

14 We are redefining and we are restating our socialism in terms of the scientific revolution . . . the Britain that is going to be forged in the white heat of this revolution will be no place for restrictive practices or out-dated methods on either side of industry.
Harold Wilson (1916–) British politician and prime minister.
Speech, Labour Party Conference, 1 Oct 1963

SOCIETY

See also mankind

1 I am a sociable worker.
Brendan Behan (1923–64) Irish playwright.
The Hostage, II

2 Man was formed for society.
William Blackstone (1723–80) British jurist.
Commentaries on the Laws of England, Introduction

3 No man is an Island, entire of itself; every man is a piece of the Continent, a part of the main.
John Donne (1573–1631) English poet.
Devotions, 17

4 People who need people are the luckiest people in the world.
Bob Merrill (Robert Merrill; 1890–1977) US lyricist and composer.
People Who Need People

5 Our civilization . . . has not yet fully recovered from the shock of its birth – the transition from the tribal or 'closed society', with its submission to magical forces, to the 'open society' which sets free the critical powers of man.
Karl Popper (1902–) Austrian-born British philosopher.
The Open Society and Its Enemies

6 Man is not a solitary animal, and so long as social life survives, self-realization cannot be the supreme principle of ethics.
Bertrand Russell (1872–1970) British philosopher.
History of Western Philosophy, 'Romanticism'

7 Society is no comfort
To one not sociable.
William Shakespeare (1564–1616) English dramatist.
Cymbeline, IV:2

8 Man is a social animal.
Benedict Spinoza (Baruch de Spinoza; 1632–77) Dutch philosopher.
Ethics

9 What men call social virtues, good fellowship, is commonly but the virtue of pigs in a litter, which lie close together to keep each other warm. It brings men together in crowds and mobs in bar-rooms and elsewhere, but it does not deserve the name of virtue.
Henry David Thoreau (1817–62) US writer.
Journal, 1852

SOLDIERS

See also army, officers, war

1 It's Tommy this, an' Tommy that, an' 'Chuck him out, the brute!'
But it's 'Saviour of 'is country' when the guns begin to shoot.
Rudyard Kipling (1865–1936) Indian-born British writer.
Tommy

2 Oh, it's Tommy this, an' Tommy that, an' 'Tommy, go away';
But it's 'Thank you, Mister Atkins,' when the band begins to play.
Rudyard Kipling
Tommy

3 They're changing guard at Buckingham Palace
Christopher Robin went down with Alice.
Alice is marrying one of the guard.
'A soldier's life is terrible hard,'
Says Alice.
A. A. Milne (1882–1956) British writer.
When We Were Very Young, 'Buckingham Palace'

4 Soldiers are citizens of death's grey land,
Drawing no dividend from time's tomorrows.
Siegfried Sassoon (1886–1967) British poet.
Dreamers

5 You are a very poor soldier: a chocolate cream soldier!
George Bernard Shaw (1856–1950) Irish dramatist and critic.
Arms and the Man, I

6 I never expect a soldier to think.
George Bernard Shaw
The Devil's Disciple, III

7 They're overpaid, overfed, oversexed and over here.
Tommy Trinder (1909–) British entertainer.
Attrib.
Referring to the G.I.s

8 He (the recruiting officer) asked me 'Why tanks?' I replied that I preferred to go into battle sitting down.
Peter Ustinov (1921–) British actor.
Dear Me

9 It all depends upon that article there.
Duke of Wellington (1769–1852) British general and statesman.
The Age of Elegance (A. Bryant)
Indicating a passing infantryman when asked if he would be able to defeat Napoleon

SOLITUDE

See also loneliness

1 Whosoever is delighted in solitude is either a wild beast or a god.
Francis Bacon (1561–1626) English philosopher.
Essays, 'Of Friendship'

2 Alone, alone, all, all alone,
Alone on a wide wide sea!
And never a saint took pity on
My soul in agony.
Samuel Taylor Coleridge (1772–1834) British poet.
The Rime of the Ancient Mariner, IV

3 Oh for a lodge in some vast wilderness,
Some boundless contiguity of shade,
Where rumour of oppression and deceit,
Of unsuccessful or successful war,
Might never reach me more!
William Cowper (1731–1800) British poet.
The Task

4 Society, friendship, and love,
Divinely bestowed upon man,
Oh, had I the wings of a dove,
How soon would I taste you again!
William Cowper
Verses supposed to be written by Alexander Selkirk

5 I am monarch of all I survey,
My right there is none to dispute;
From the centre all round to the sea
I am lord of the fowl and the brute.
Oh, solitude! where are the charms
That sages have seen in thy face?
Better dwell in the midst of alarms,
Than reign in this horrible place.
William Cowper
Verses supposed to be written by Alexander Selkirk

6 I want to be alone.
Greta Garbo (1905–) Swedish-born US film star.
Words spoken by Garbo in the film *Grand Hotel*, and associated with her for the rest of her career.

7 Far from the madding crowd's ignoble strife,
Their sober wishes never learn'd to stray;
Along the cool sequester'd vale of life
They kept the noiseless tenor of their way.
Thomas Gray (1716–71) British poet.
Elegy Written in a Country Churchyard

8 One of the pleasantest things in the world is going on a journey; but I like to go by myself.
William Hazlitt (1778–1830) British essayist.
On Going a Journey

9 It is a fine thing to be out on the hills alone. A man can hardly be a beast or a fool alone on a great mountain.
Francis Kilvert (1840–79) British diarist and clergyman.
Diary, 29 May 1871

10 In solitude
What happiness? who can enjoy alone,
Or, all enjoying, what contentment find?
John Milton (1608–74) English poet.
Paradise Lost, Bk. VIII

11 I want to be a movement
But there's no one on my side.
Adrian Mitchell (1932–) British writer and dramatist.
Loose Leaf Poem

12 A man must keep a little back shop where he can be himself without reserve. In solitude alone can he know true freedom.
Michel de Montaigne (1533–92) French essayist.
Essais, I

13 I never found the companion that was so companionable as solitude.
Henry David Thoreau (1817–62) US writer.
Walden, 'Solitude'

14 Alas, Lord, I am powerful but alone. Let me sleep the sleep of the earth.
Alfred de Vigny (1797–1863) French writer.
Moise

15 For oft, when on my couch I lie
In vacant or in pensive mood,
They flash upon that inward eye
Which is the bliss of solitude.
William Wordsworth (1770–1850) British poet.
I Wandered Lonely as a Cloud

16 Behold her, single in the field,
Yon solitary Highland lass!
William Wordsworth
The Solitary Reaper

17 I will arise and go now, and go to Innisfree,
And a small cabin build there, of clay and wattles made;
Nine bean rows will I have there, a hive for the honey bee,
And live alone in the bee-loud glade.
W. B. Yeats (1865–1939) Irish poet.
The Lake Isle of Innisfree

SORROW

See also despair, melancholy, mourning, regret

1 Every tear from every eye
Becomes a babe in Eternity.
William Blake (1757–1827) British poet.
Auguries of Innocence

2 Do you hear the children weeping, O my brothers,
Ere the sorrow comes with years?
Elizabeth Barrett Browning (1806–61) British poet.
The Cry of the Children

3 Follow thy fair sun, unhappy shadow.
Thomas Campion (1567–1620) English poet.
Follow Thy Fair Sun

4 One often calms one's grief by recounting it.
Pierre Corneille (1606–84) French dramatist.
Polyeucte, I:3

5 Tears were to me what glass beads are to African traders.
Quentin Crisp (?1910–) Model, publicist, and writer.
The Naked Civil Servant

6 There is no greater sorrow than to recall a time of happiness when in misery.
Dante (1265–1321) Italian poet.
Divine Comedy, Inferno, V

7 *Adieu tristesse*
Bonjour tristesse
Tu es inscrite dans les lignes du plafond.
Farewell sadness
Good day sadness
You are written in the lines of the ceiling.
Paul Éluard (Eugène Grindel; 1895–1952) French surrealist poet.
La Vie immédiate

8 A moment of time may make us unhappy for ever.
John Gay (1685–1732) English poet and dramatist.
The Beggar's Opera

9 Sadness is almost never anything but a form of fatigue.
André Gide (1869–1951) French novelist.
Journals, 1922

10 They say my verse is sad: no wonder;
Its narrow measure spans
Tears of eternity, and sorrow,
Not mine, but man's.
A. E. Housman (1859–1936) British scholar and poet.
Last Poems, 'Fancy's Knell'

11 Then Sir Launcelot saw her visage, but he wept not greatly, but sighed!
Thomas Malory (1400–71) English writer.
Morte d'Arthur, Bk. XXI, Ch. 11

12 Tears such as angels weep, burst forth.
John Milton (1608–74) English poet.
Paradise Lost, Bk. I

13 Art thou weary, art thou languid,
Art thou sore distressed?
John Mason Neale (1818–66) British churchman.
Art thou Weary?

14 Sorrow is tranquillity remembered in emotion.
Dorothy Parker (1893–1967) US writer.
Sentiment

15 Line after line my gushing eyes o'erflow,
Led through a sad variety of woe.
Alexander Pope (1688–1744) British poet.
Eloisa to Abelard

16 Not louder shrieks to pitying heav'n are cast,
When husbands, or when lap-dogs breathe their last.
Alexander Pope
The Rape of the Lock, III

17 As soon as one is unhappy one becomes moral.
Marcel Proust (1871–1922) French novelist.
À la recherche du temps perdu: À l'ombre des jeunes filles en fleurs

18 Happiness is beneficial for the body, but it is grief that develops the powers of the mind.
Marcel Proust
À la recherche du temps perdu: Le Temps retrouvé

19 It is such a secret place, the land of tears.
Antoine de Saint-Exupéry (1900–44) French novelist and aviator.
The Little Prince, Ch. 7

20 He's simply got the instinct for being unhappy highly developed.
Saki (Hector Hugh Munro; 1870–1916) British writer.
The Match-Maker

21 If you have tears, prepare to shed them now.
William Shakespeare (1564–1616) English dramatist.
Julius Caesar, III:2

22 Down, thou climbing sorrow,
Thy element's below.
William Shakespeare
King Lear, II:4

23 The secret of being miserable is to have leisure to bother about whether you are happy or not.
George Bernard Shaw (1856–1950) Irish dramatist and critic.
Misalliance, Preface

24 'Tis held that sorrow makes us wise.
Alfred, Lord Tennyson (1809–92) British poet.
In Memoriam A.H.H., CXIII

25 My regret
Becomes an April violet,
And buds and blossoms like the rest.
Alfred, Lord Tennyson
In Memoriam A.H.H., CXV

26 Tears, idle tears, I know not what they mean,

Tears from the depth of some divine despair.
Alfred, Lord Tennyson
The Princess, IV

27 A grief too much to be told, O queen, you
bid me renew.
Virgil (Publius Vergilius Maro; 70–19 BC) Roman poet.
Aeneid, Bk. II
The opening words of Aeneas' account to Dido of the fall of
Troy

SOUL

1 The eyes are the window of the soul.
Proverb

2 We cannot kindle when we will
The fire which in the heart resides,
The spirit bloweth and is still,
In mystery our soul abides.
Matthew Arnold (1822–88) British poet and critic.
Morality

3 And see all sights from pole to pole,
And glance, and nod, and bustle by;
And never once possess our soul
Before we die.
Matthew Arnold
A Southern Night

4 Man has no Body distinct from his Soul; for
that called Body is a portion of Soul
discerned by the five Senses, the chief inlets
of Soul in this age.
William Blake (1757–1827) British poet.
The Marriage of Heaven and Hell, 'The Voice of the Devil'

5 Leave the flesh to the fate it was fit for! the
spirit be thine!
Robert Browning (1812–89) British poet.
Saul, XIII

6 In the real dark night of the soul it is always
three o'clock in the morning.
F. Scott Fitzgerald (1896–1940) US novelist.
The Crack-Up
See ST JOHN OF THE CROSS

7 That night, that year
Of now done darkness I wretch lay wrestling
with (my God!) my God.
Gerard Manley Hopkins (1844–99) British Jesuit and
poet.
Carrion Comfort

8 The dark night of the soul.
St John of the Cross (Juan de Yepes y Alvarez; 1542–
91) Spanish churchman and poet.
English translation of *Noche obscura del alma*, the title of a
poem; *see also* F. SCOTT FITZGERALD

9 Nor let the beetle, nor the death-moth be
Your mournful Psyche.
John Keats (1795–1821) British poet.
Ode on Melancholy

10 And looks commercing with the skies,
Thy rapt soul sitting in thine eyes.
John Milton (1608–74) English poet.
Il Penseroso

11 I am positive I have a soul; nor can all the
books with which materialists have pestered
the world ever convince me of the contrary.
Laurence Sterne (1713–68) Irish-born British writer.
A Sentimental Journey, 'Maria, Moulines'

12 Fair seed-time had my soul, and I grew up
Fostered alike by beauty and by fear.
William Wordsworth (1770–1850) British poet.
The Prelude, I

SPACE

See also astronomy, discovery, exploration, moon, science,
stars, sun, technology, universe

1 That's one small step for man, one giant leap
for mankind.
Neil Armstrong (1930–) US astronaut.
Remark, 21 July 1969
Said on stepping onto the moon. Often quoted as, 'small step
for a man . . . ' (which is probably what he intended)

2 Outer space is no place for a person of
breeding.
Violet Bonham Carter (1887–1969) British politician.
The New Yorker

3 I am a passenger on the spaceship, Earth.
Richard Buckminster Fuller (1895–1983) US architect
and inventor.
Operating Manual for Spaceship Earth

4 Space isn't remote at all. It's only an hour's
drive away if your car could go straight
upwards.
Fred Hoyle (1915–) British astronomer.
The Observer, 9 Sept 1979

5 This is the greatest week in the history of
the world since the creation.
Richard Milhous Nixon (1913–) US president.
Attrib., 24 July 1969
Said when men first landed on the moon

6 The astronauts! . . . Rotarians in outer space.
Gore Vidal (1925–) US novelist.
Two Sisters

SPARSENESS

1 As for the grass, it grew as scant as hair
In leprosy.
Robert Browning (1812–89) British poet.
Childe Roland to the Dark Tower Came, XIII

SPECULATION

1 While to deny the existence of an unseen
kingdom is bad, to pretend that we know
more about it than its bare existence is no
better.
Samuel Butler (1835–1902) British writer.
Erewhon, Ch. 15

2 If the world were good for nothing else, it is
a fine subject for speculation.
William Hazlitt (1778–1830) British essayist.
Characteristics

SPEECH

See also silence, speeches, verbosity, words

1 Save your breath to cool your porridge.
Proverb

2 Speak when you are spoken to.
Proverb

3 Let your speech be alway with grace, seasoned with salt, that ye may know how ye ought to answer every man.
Bible: Colossians
4:6

4 Let thy speech be short, comprehending much in few words; be as one that knoweth and yet holdeth his tongue.
Bible: Ecclesiasticus
32:8

5 Even so the tongue is a little member, and boasteth great things. Behold, how great a matter a little fire kindleth!
Bible: James
3:5

6 But the tongue can no man tame; it is an unruly evil, full of deadly poison.
Bible: James
3:8

7 To know how to say what others only know how to think is what makes men poets or sages; and to dare to say what others only dare to think makes men martyrs or reformers – or both.
Elizabeth Charles (1828–96) British writer.
Chronicle of the Schönberg-Cotta Family

8 No, Sir, because I have time to think before I speak, and don't ask impertinent questions.
Erasmus Darwin (1731–1802) British physician, biologist, and poet.
Reminiscences of My Father's Everyday Life (Sir Francis Darwin)
Reply when asked whether he found his stammer inconvenient

9 The true use of speech is not so much to express our wants as to conceal them.
Oliver Goldsmith (1728–74) Irish-born British writer.
Essays, 'The Use of Language'

10 Most men make little use of their speech than to give evidence against their own understanding.
Lord Halifax (1633–95) English statesman.
Political, Moral, and Miscellaneous Thoughts and Reflections

11 Talking and eloquence are not the same: to speak, and to speak well, are two things.
Ben Jonson (1573–1637) English dramatist.
Timber, or Discoveries made upon Men and Matter

12 The most precious things in speech are pauses.
Ralph Richardson (1902–83) British actor.
Attrib.

13 But words once spoke can never be recall'd.
Earl of Roscommon (1633–85) Irish-born English poet.
Art of Poetry

14 Words may be false and full of art,
Sighs are the natural language of the heart.
Thomas Shadwell (1642–92) English dramatist.
Psyche, III

15 Speech was given to man to disguise his thoughts.
Talleyrand (Charles Maurice de Talleyrand-Périgord; 1754–1838) French politician.
Attrib.

SPEECHES

See also brevity, sermons, verbosity

1 I take the view, and always have done, that if you cannot say what you have to say in twenty minutes, you should go away and write a book about it.
Lord Brabazon of Tara (1910–74) British businessman and Conservative politician.
Attrib.

2 He is one of those orators of whom it was well said, 'Before they get up they do not know what they are going to say; when they are speaking, they do not know what they are saying; and when they sit down, they do not know what they have said'.
Winston Churchill (1874–1965) British statesman.
Speech, House of Commons, 20 Dec 1912
Referring to Lord Charles Beresford

3 I dreamt that I was making a speech in the House. I woke up, and by Jove I was!
Duke of Devonshire (1833–1908) Conservative politician.
Thought and Adventures (W. S. Churchill)

4 For I have neither wit, nor words, nor worth,
Action, nor utterance, nor the power of speech,
To stir men's blood; I only speak right on.
William Shakespeare (1564–1616) English dramatist.
Julius Caesar, III:2

5 Don't quote Latin; say what you have to say, and then sit down.
Duke of Wellington (1769–1852) British general and statesman.
Attrib.
Advice to a new Member of Parliament

SPELLING

See also language, pronunciation, words, writing

1 Put it down a we, my lord, put it down a we!
Charles Dickens (1812–70) British novelist.
Pickwick Papers, Ch. 34

2 They spell it Vinci and pronounce it Vinchy;

foreigners always spell better than they
pronounce.

Mark Twain (Samuel Langhorne Clemens; 1835–1910)
US writer.
The Innocents Abroad, Ch. 19

SPONTANEITY

See also impetuosity

1 Spontaneity is only a term for man's
ignorance of the gods.

Samuel Butler (1835–1902) British writer.
Erewhon, Ch. 25

2 *L'acte gratuite.*
The unmotivated action.

André Gide (1869–1951) French novelist.
Les Caves du Vatican

3 Away with all ideals. Let each individual act
spontaneously from the for ever incalculable
prompting of the creative wellhead within
him. There is no universal law.

D. H. Lawrence (1885–1930) British novelist.
Phoenix, Preface to 'All Things are Possible' by Leo Shostov

4 Nothing prevents us from being natural so
much as the desire to appear so.

Duc de la Rochefoucauld (1613–80) French writer.
Maximes, 431

SPOONERISMS

Sayings associated with the Oxford clergyman and academic
William Archibald Spooner (1844–1930).

1 You will find as you grow older that the
weight of rages will press harder and harder
on the employer.

Spooner (Sir W. Hayter), Ch. 6

2 I remember your name perfectly, but I just
can't think of your face.

3 Kinquering Congs their titles take.

A scrambled announcement of the hymn in New College Chapel (probably apocryphal)

4 Let us drink to the queer old Dean.

5 Sir, you have tasted two whole worms; you
have hissed all my mystery lectures and have
been caught fighting a liar in the quad; you
will leave Oxford by the town drain.

SPORT AND GAMES

See also cricket, fishing, football, golf, horses, hunting

1 Float like a butterfly
Sting like a bee.

Muhammad Ali (Cassius Clay; 1942–) US boxer.
Remark
Describing his boxing style

2 Follow up! Follow up! Follow up! Follow up!
Follow up!

Till the field ring again and again,
With the tramp of the twenty-two men,
Follow up!

E. E. Bowen (1836–1901) British writer.
Forty Years On (the Harrow school song)

3 Life's too short for chess.

Henry James Byron (1834–84) British dramatist and
actor.
Our Boys, I

4 There is plenty of time to win this game, and
to thrash the Spaniards too.

Francis Drake (1540–96) British navigator and admiral.
Attrib.
Referring to the sighting of the Armada during a game of
bowls, 20 July 1588

5 Exercise is bunk. If you are healthy, you
don't need it: if you are sick, you shouldn't
take it.

Henry Ford (1863–1947) US car manufacturer.
Attrib.

6 Bullfighting is the only art in which the artist
is in danger of death and in which the degree
of brilliance in the performance is left to the
fighter's honour.

Ernest Hemingway (1899–1961) US novelist.
Death in the Afternoon, Ch. 9

7 When in doubt, win the trick.

Edmond Hoyle (1672–1769) English writer on card
games.
Hoyle's Games, 'Whist, Twenty-four Short Rules for Learners'

8 The only athletic sport I ever mastered was
backgammon.

Douglas William Jerrold (1803–57) British dramatist.
Douglas Jerrold (W. Jerrold), Vol. I, Ch. 1

9 It is unbecoming for a cardinal to ski badly.

John Paul II (Karol Wojtyla; 1920–) Polish pope
(1978–).
John Paul II
Replying to the suggestion that it was inappropriate for him, a
cardinal, to ski

10 I am sorry I have not learned to play at
cards. It is very useful in life: it generates
kindness and consolidates society.

Samuel Johnson (1709–84) British lexicographer.
Tour to the Hebrides (J. Boswell)

11 At what time does the dissipation of energy
begin?

Lord Kelvin (1824–1907) British physicist.
Memories of a Scientific Life (A. Fleming)
On realizing that his wife was planning an afternoon excursion

12 Man is a gaming animal. He must always be
trying to get the better in something or
other.

Charles Lamb (1775–1834) British essayist.
Essays of Elia, 'Mrs Battle's Opinions on Whist'

13 O, he flies through the air with the greatest
of ease,
This daring young man on the flying trapeze.

George Leybourne (?–1884) British songwriter.
The Man on the Flying Trapeze

14 I don't like this game.

Spike Milligan (1918–) British comic actor and author.
The Goon Show

15 Serious sport has nothing to do with fair play. It is bound up with hatred, jealousy, boastfulness, disregard of all rules and sadistic pleasure in witnessing violence; in other words it is war minus the shooting.

George Orwell (Eric Blair; 1903–50) British novelist.
The Sporting Spirit

16 Gamesmanship or The Art of Winning Games Without Actually Cheating.

Stephen Potter (1900–69) British writer.
Book title

17 For when the One Great Scorer comes
To write against your name,
He marks – not that you won or lost –
But how you played the game.

Grantland Rice (1880–1954) US sportswriter.
Alumnus Football

18 It was remarked to me by the late Mr Charles Roupell . . . that to play billiards well was a sign of an ill-spent youth.

Herbert Spencer (1820–1903) British philosopher.
Life and Letters of Spencer (Duncan), Ch. 20

19 I wanted a play that would paint the full face of sensuality, rebellion and revivalism. In South Wales these three phenomena have played second fiddle only to the Rugby Union which is a distillation of all three.

Gwyn Thomas (1913–1981) British writer.
Jackie the Jumper (Introduction), 'Plays and Players' 19 Jan 1963

20 There's no secret. You just press the accelerator to the floor and steer left.

Bill Vukovich (1918–55) US motor-racing driver.
Attrib.
Explaining his success in the Indianapolis 500

SPRING

See also months, seasons

1 My beloved spake, and said unto me, Rise up, my love, my fair one, and come away. For, lo, the winter is past, the rain is over and gone;
The flowers appear on the earth; the time of the singing of birds is come, and the voice of the turtle is heard in our land.

Bible: Song of Solomon
2:10–12

2 Now Spring, sweet laxative of Georgian strains,
Quickens the ink in literary veins,
The Stately Homes of England ope their doors
To piping Nancy-boys and Crashing Bores.

Roy Campbell (1901–57) South African poet.
The Georgiad

3 Where are the songs of Spring? Ay, where are they?

John Keats (1795–1821) British poet.
To Autumn

4 Spring has returned. The earth is like a child that knows poems.

Rainer Maria Rilke (1875–1926) Austrian poet.
Die Sonette an Orpheus, I, 21

5 The country habit has me by the heart,
For he's bewitched for ever who has seen,
Not with his eyes but with his vision, Spring
Flow down the woods and stipple leaves with sun.

Vita Sackville-West (Victoria Sackville-West; 1892–1962) British poet and novelist.
The Land, 'Winter'

6 When the hounds of spring are on winter's traces,
The mother of months in meadow or plain
Fills the shadows and windy places
With lisp of leaves and ripple of rain . . .

Algernon Charles Swinburne (1837–1909) British poet.
Atlanta in Calydon

7 In the Spring a young man's fancy lightly turns to thoughts of love.

Alfred, Lord Tennyson (1809–92) British poet.
Locksley Hall

8 Spring is come home with her world-wandering feet.
And all the things are made young with young desires.

Francis Thompson (1859–1907) British poet.
The Night of Forebeing, 'Ode to Easter'

9 Like an army defeated
The snow hath retreated.

William Wordsworth (1770–1850) British poet.
Written in March

STARING

1 It is better to be looked over than overlooked.

Mae West (1892–1980) US actress.
The Wit and Wisdom of Mae West (ed. J. Weintraub)

2 Don't go on looking at me like that, because you'll wear your eyes out.

Émile Zola (1840–1902) French novelist.
La Bête Humaine, Ch. 5

STARS

See also astronomy, moon, space, sun, universe

1 And God made two great lights: the greater light to rule the day, and the lesser light to rule the night: he made the stars also.

Bible: Genesis
1:16

2 Look at the stars! look, look up at the skies!
O look at all the fire-folk sitting in the air!

The bright boroughs, the circle-citadels there!
Gerard Manley Hopkins (1844–99) British Jesuit and poet.
The Starlight Night

3 Bright star, would I were steadfast as thou art.
John Keats (1795–1821) British poet.
Bright Star

4 Twinkle, twinkle, little star,
How I wonder what you are!
Up above the world so high,
Like a diamond in the sky!
Jane Taylor (1783–1824) British writer.
Rhymes for the Nursery (with Ann Taylor), 'The Star'

5 For still I looked on that same star,
That fitful, fiery Lucifer,
Watching with mind as quiet as moss
Its light nailed to a burning cross.
Andrew John Young (1885–1971) Scottish poet.
The Evening Star

6 Stars lay like yellow pollen
That from a flower has fallen;
And single stars I saw
Crossing themselves in awe;
Some stars in sudden fear
Fell like a falling tear.
Andrew John Young
The Stars

STATE

See also democracy, government, republic

1 The only way to erect such a common power, as may be able to defend them from the invasion of foreigners, and the injuries of one another . . . is, to confer all their power and strength upon one man, or upon one assembly of men, that may reduce all their wills, by plurality of voices, unto one will . . . This is the generation of that great Leviathan, or rather (to speak more reverently) of that *Mortal God*, to which we owe under the *Immortal God*, our peace and defence.
Thomas Hobbes (1588–1679) English philosopher.
Leviathan, Pt. II, Ch. 17

2 So long as the state exists there is no freedom. When there is freedom there will be no state.
Lenin (Vladimir Ilich Ulyanov; 1870–1924) Russian revolutionary leader.
The State and Revolution, Ch. 5

3 In a free society the state does not administer the affairs of men. It administers justice among men who conduct their own affairs.
Walter Lippman (1889–1974) US editor and writer.
An Enquiry into the Principles of a Good Society

4 The worth of a State in the long run is the worth of the individuals composing it.
John Stuart Mill (1806–73) British philosopher.
On Liberty, Ch. 5

5 The state is an instrument in the hands of the ruling class for suppressing the resistance of its class enemies.
Joseph Stalin (J. Dzhugashvili; 1879–1953) Soviet statesman.
Stalin's Kampf (ed. M. R. Werner)

STATELY HOMES

See also architecture, aristocracy, houses

1 Now Spring, sweet laxative of Georgian strains,
Quickens the ink in literary veins,
The Stately Homes of England ope their doors
To piping Nancy-boys and Crashing Bores.
Roy Campbell (1901–57) South African poet.
The Georgiad

2 The Stately Homes of England
How beautiful they stand,
To prove the upper classes
Have still the upper hand.
Noël Coward (1899–1973) British dramatist.
Operette, 'The Stately Homes of England'

3 And though the Van Dycks have to go
And we pawn the Bechstein grand,
We'll stand by the Stately Homes of England.
Noël Coward
Operette, The Stately Homes of England

4 The stately homes of England,
How beautiful they stand!
Amidst their tall ancestral trees,
O'er all the pleasant land.
Felicia Dorothea Hemans (1793–1835) British poet.
The Homes of England

5 Those comfortably padded lunatic asylums which are known, euphemistically, as the stately homes of England.
Virginia Woolf (1882–1941) British novelist.
The Common Reader, 'Lady Dorothy Nevill'

STATISTICS

1 A witty statesman said, you might prove anything by figures.
Thomas Carlyle (1795–1881) Scottish historian and essayist.
Critical and Miscellaneous Essays, 'Chartism'

2 There are three kinds of lies: lies, damned lies and statistics.
Benjamin Disraeli (1804–81) British statesman.
Autobiography (Mark Twain)

3 We are just statistics, born to consume resources.
Horace (Quintus Horatius Flaccus; 65–8 BC) Roman poet.
Epistles, I

4 He uses statistics as a drunken man uses

lamp-posts – for support rather than illumination.
Andrew Lang (1844 – 1912) Scottish writer and poet.
Treasury of Humorous Quotations

5 You cannot feed the hungry on statistics.
David Lloyd George (1863 – 1945) British Liberal statesman.
Speech, 1904
Advocating Tariff Reform

6 Statistics will prove anything, even the truth.
Noël Moynihan (1916 –) British doctor and writer.
Attrib.

7 To understand God's thoughts we must study statistics, for these are the measure of his purpose.
Florence Nightingale (1820 – 1910) British nurse.
Life . . . of Francis Galton (K. Pearson), Vol. II, Ch. 13

8 I am one of the unpraised, unrewarded millions without whom Statistics would be a bankrupt science. It is we who are born, who marry, who die, in constant ratios.
Logan Pearsall Smith (1865 – 1946) US writer.
Trivia

9 A single death is a tragedy; a million is a statistic.
Joseph Stalin (J. Dzhugashvili; 1879 – 1953) Soviet statesman.
Attrib.

10 There are two kinds of statistics, the kind you look up and the kind you make up.
Rex Todhunter Stout (1886 – 1975) US writer.
Death of a Doxy, Ch. 9

11 Facts speak louder than statistics.
Geoffrey Streatfield (1897 – 1978) British lawyer.
The Observer, 'Sayings of the Week', 19 Mar 1950

STRIKES

See also industrial relations

1 Not a penny off the pay; not a minute on the day.
A. J. Cook (1885 – 1931) British trade-union leader.
Slogan used in the miners' strike, 1925

2 There is no right to strike against the public safety by anybody, anywhere, any time.
Calvin Coolidge (1872 – 1933) US President.
Remark, 14 Sept 1919
Referring to the Boston police strike

3 Another fact of life that will not have escaped you is that, in this country, the twenty-four-hour strike is like the twenty-four-hour flu. You have to reckon on it lasting at least five days.
Frank Muir (1920 –) British writer and broadcaster.
You Can't Have Your Kayak and Heat It (Frank Muir and Dennis Norden), 'Great Expectations'

4 Have you noticed, the last four strikes we've had, it's pissed down? It wouldn't be a bad idea to check the weather reports before they pull us out next time.
Johnny Speight (1920 –) British television scriptwriter.
Till Death Do Us Part

STUBBORNNESS

See also determination, inflexibility, petulance

1 You can lead a horse to the water, but you can't make him drink.
Proverb

2 Obstinate people can be divided into the opinionated, the ignorant, and the boorish.
Aristotle (384 – 322 BC) Greek philosopher.
Nicomachean Ethics, Bk. VII

3 'Tis known by the name of perseverance in a good cause, – and of obstinacy in a bad one.
Laurence Sterne (1713 – 68) Irish-born British writer.
Tristram Shandy

STUPIDITY

See also foolishness, ignorance

1 His mind is open; yes, it is so open that nothing is retained; ideas simply pass through him.
F. H. Bradley (1846 – 1924) British philosopher.
Attrib.

2 The trouble with Senator Long is that he is suffering from halitosis of the intellect. That's presuming Emperor Long has an intellect.
Harold L. Ickes (1874 – 1952) US Republican politician.
The Politics of Upheaval (A. M. Schlesinger Jnr), Pt. II, Ch. 14

3 Jerry Ford is so dumb that he can't fart and chew gum at the same time.
Lyndon B. Johnson (1908 – 73) US statesman.
A Ford, Not a Lincoln (R. Reeves), Ch. 1
Sometimes quoted as ' . . . can't walk and chew gum'

4 That fellow seems to me to possess but one idea, and that is a wrong one.
Samuel Johnson (1709 – 84) British lexicographer.
Life of Johnson (J. Boswell), Vol. II

5 I've been married six months. She looks like a million dollars, but she only knows a hundred and twenty words and she's only got two ideas in her head. The other one's hats.
Eric Linklater (1889 – 1974) Scottish novelist.
Juan in America, Pt. II, Ch. 5

6 You've got the brain of a four-year-old boy, and I bet he was glad to get rid of it.
Groucho Marx (Julius Marx; 1895 – 1977) US comedian.
Horse Feathers

7 Music-hall songs provide the dull with wit, just as proverbs provide them with wisdom.
W. Somerset Maugham (1874 – 1965) British novelist.
A Writer's Notebook

8 Stupidity does not consist in being without ideas. Such stupidity would be the sweet,

blissful stupidity of animals, molluscs and the gods. Human Stupidity consists in having lots of ideas, but stupid ones.
Henry de Montherlant (1896–1972) French novelist.
Notebooks

9 She has a Rolls body and a Balham mind.
J. B. Morton (1893–1979) British journalist.
The Best of Beachcomber, 'A Foul Innuendo'

10 I've examined your son's head, Mr Glum, and there's nothing there.
Frank Muir (1920–) British writer and broadcaster.
Take It from Here (Frank Muir and Dennis Norden), 1957

11 You beat your pate, and fancy wit will come;
Knock as you please, there's nobody at home.
Alexander Pope (1688–1744) British poet.
Epigram

12 Against stupidity the gods themselves struggle in vain.
Friedrich von Schiller (1759–1805) German dramatist.
Die Jungfrau von Orleans, III:6

13 There is no sin except stupidity.
Oscar Wilde (1854–1900) Irish-born British dramatist.
The Critic as Artist, Pt. 2

STYLE

1 Style is the man himself.
Comte de Buffon (1707–88) French naturalist.
Discours sur le style

2 Style, like sheer silk, too often hides eczema.
Albert Camus (1913–60) French existentialist writer.
The Fall

3 An author arrives at a good style when his language performs what is required of it without shyness.
Cyril Connolly (1903–74) British journalist.
Enemies of Promise, Ch. 3

4 He has never been known to use a word that might send the reader to the dictionary.
William Faulkner (1897–1962) US novelist.
Attrib.
Referring to Ernest HEMINGWAY

5 Poor Faulkner. Does he really think big emotions come from big words? He thinks I don't know the ten-dollar words. I know them all right. But there are older and simpler and better words, and those are the ones I use.
Ernest Hemingway (1899–1961) US novelist.
Attrib.
In response to a jibe by William FAULKNER

6 All styles are good except the tiresome sort.
Voltaire (François-Marie Arouet; 1694–1778) French writer.
L'Enfant prodigue, Preface

7 In matters of grave importance, style, not sincerity, is the vital thing.
Oscar Wilde (1854–1900) Irish-born British dramatist.
The Importance of Being Earnest, III

SUBJECTIVITY

See also objectivity, prejudice

1 She was one of the people who say, 'I don't know anything about music really, but I know what I like'.
Max Beerbohm (1872–1956) British writer.
Zuleika Dobson, Ch. 16

2 An apology for the Devil – it must be remembered that we have only heard one side of the case. God has written all the books.
Samuel Butler (1835–1902) British writer.
Notebooks

3 It is a general mistake to think the men we like are good for everything, and those we do not, good for nothing.
Lord Halifax (1633–95) English statesman.
Political, Moral and Miscellaneous Thoughts and Reflections

4 He who knows only his own side of the case knows little of that.
John Stuart Mill (1806–73) British philosopher.
On Liberty, Ch. 2

5 All the world is queer save thee and me, and even thou art a little queer.
Robert Owen (1771–1858) British social reformer.
Attrib., 1828
Referring to William Allen, his partner in business

6 To observations which ourselves we make
We grow more partial for th' observer's sake.
Alexander Pope (1688–1744) British poet.
Moral Essays, I

7 Partisanship is our great curse. We too readily assume that everything has two sides and that it is our duty to be on one or the other.
James Harvey Robinson (1863–1936) US historian and educator.
The Mind in the Making

SUBURBIA

1 I come from suburbia, Dan, personally, I don't ever want to go back. It's the one place in the world that's further away than anywhere else.
Frederic Raphael (1931–) British author.
The Glittering Prizes: A Sex Life, I:3

2 She was more than ever proud of the position of the bungalow, so almost in the country.
Angus Wilson (1913–) British novelist.
A Bit Off the Map, 'A Flat Country Christmas'

SUCCESS

See also achievement, victory

1 Nothing succeeds like success.
Proverb

2 'Tis not in mortals to command success,
But we'll do more, Sempronius; we'll deserve it.
Joseph Addison (1672–1719) British essayist.
Cato, I:2

3 The penalty of success is to be bored by people who used to snub you.
Nancy Astor (1879–1964) American-born British politician.
Sunday Express, 12 Jan 1956

4 One's religion is whatever he is most interested in, and yours is Success.
J. M. Barrie (1860–1937) British novelist and dramatist.
The Twelve-Pound Look

5 The only infallible criterion of wisdom to vulgar minds – success.
Edmund Burke (1729–97) British politician.
Letter to a Member of the National Assembly

6 Success is counted sweetest
By those who ne'er succeed.
Emily Dickinson (1830–86) US poet.
Success is Counted Sweetest

7 The moral flabbiness born of the bitch-goddess Success.
William James (1842–1910) US psychologist and philosopher.
Letter to H. G. Wells, 11 Sept 1906

8 Victory has a thousand fathers but defeat is an orphan.
John Fitzgerald Kennedy (1917–63) US statesman.
Attrib.

9 The shortest and best way to make your fortune is to let people see clearly that it is in their interests to promote yours.
Jean de La Bruyère (1645–96) French satirist.
Les Caractères

10 Sweet Smell of Success.
Ernest Lehman (1920–) US screenwriter.
Novel and film title

11 As is the case in all branches of art, success depends in a very large measure upon individual initiative and exertion, and cannot be achieved except by dint of hard work.
Anna Pavlova (1881–1931) Russian ballet dancer.
Pavlova: A Biography (ed. A. H. Franks), 'Pages of My Life'

12 To succeed in the world, we do everything we can to appear successful.
Duc de la Rochefoucauld (1613–80) French writer.
Maximes, 50

13 The only place where success comes before work is a dictionary.
Vidal Sassoon (1928–) British hair stylist.
Quoting one of his teachers in a BBC radio broadcast

14 There are no gains without pains.
Adlai Stevenson (1900–65) US statesman.
Speech, Chicago, 26 July 1952

SUFFERING

1 He that lives long suffers much.
Proverb

2 There was a faith-healer of Deal,
Who said, 'Although pain isn't real,
If I sit on a pin
And it punctures my skin,
I dislike what I fancy I feel.'
Anonymous

3 One does not love a place the less for having suffered in it unless it has all been suffering, nothing but suffering.
Jane Austen (1775–1817) British novelist.
Persuasion, Ch. 20

4 Once drinking deep of that divinest anguish,
How could I seek the empty world again?
Emily Brontë (1818–48) British novelist.
Remembrance

5 I am convinced that we have a degree of delight, and that no small one, in the real misfortunes and pains of others.
Edmund Burke (1729–97) British politician.
On the Sublime and Beautiful, Pt. I

6 If suffer we must, let's suffer on the heights.
Victor Hugo (1802–85) French writer.
Contemplations, 'Les Malheureux'

7 The music, yearning like a God in pain.
John Keats (1795–1821) British poet.
The Eve of Saint Agnes, VII

8 Rather suffer than die is man's motto.
Jean de La Fontaine (1621–95) French poet.
Fables, I, 'La Mort et le Bûcheron'

9 A man who fears suffering is already suffering from what he fears.
Michel de Montaigne (1533–92) French essayist.
Essais, III

10 Every reformation must have its victims. You can't expect the fatted calf to share the enthusiasm of the angels over the prodigal's return.
Saki (Hector Hugh Munro; 1870–1916) British writer.
Reginald on the Academy

11 Thou art a soul in bliss; but I am bound
Upon a wheel of fire, that mine own tears
Do scald like molten lead.
William Shakespeare (1564–1616) English dramatist.
King Lear, IV:7

SUICIDE

See also death

1 The strangest whim has seized me . . . After all
I think I will not hang myself today.
G. K. Chesterton (1874–1936) British writer.
A Ballade of Suicide

2 Not only is suicide a sin, it is the sin. It is the ultimate and absolute evil, the refusal to take the oath of loyalty to life. The man who kills a man, kills a man. The man who kills himself kills all men; as far as he is concerned he wipes out the world.
G. K. Chesterton
Orthodoxy

3 There are many who dare not kill themselves for fear of what the neighbours might say.
Cyril Connolly (1903–74) British journalist.
The Unquiet Grave

4 The thought of suicide is a great source of comfort: with it a calm passage is to be made across many a bad night.
Friedrich Wilhelm Nietzsche (1844–1900) German philosopher.
Jenseits von Gut und Böse

5 Razors pain you
Rivers are damp;
Acids stain you;
And drugs cause cramp.
Guns aren't lawful;
Nooses give;
Gas smells awful;
You might as well live.
Dorothy Parker (1893–1967) US writer.
Enough Rope, 'Resumé'

6 When you're between any sort of devil and the deep blue sea, the deep blue sea sometimes looks very inviting.
Terence Rattigan (1911–77) British dramatist.
The Deep Blue Sea

7 Next week, or next month, or next year I'll kill myself. But I might as well last out my month's rent, which has been paid up, and my credit for breakfast in the morning.
Jean Rhys (1894–1979) Dominican-born British novelist.
Good Morning, Midnight, Pt. II

8 It is against the law to commit suicide in this man's town . . . although what the law can do to a guy who commits suicide I am never able to figure out.
Damon Runyon (1884–1946) US writer.
Guys and Dolls

9 Dost thou not see my baby at my breast
That sucks the nurse asleep?
William Shakespeare (1564–1616) English dramatist.
Antony and Cleopatra, V:2
Holding the asp to her breast

10 To be, or not to be – that is the question;
Whether 'tis nobler in the mind to suffer
The slings and arrows of outrageous fortune,
Or to take arms against a sea of troubles,
And by opposing end them? To die, to sleep –
No more; and by a sleep to say we end
The heart-ache and the thousand natural shocks
That flesh is heir to, 'tis a consummation
Devoutly to be wish'd. To die, to sleep;

To sleep, perchance to dream. Ay, there's the rub;
For in that sleep of death what dreams may come,
When we have shuffled off this mortal coil,
Must give us pause.
William Shakespeare
Hamlet, III:1

11 A still small voice spake unto me,
'Thou art so full of misery,
Were it not better not to be?'
Alfred, Lord Tennyson (1809–92) British poet.
The Two Voices

12 Never murder a man who is committing suicide.
Woodrow Wilson (1856–1925) US statesman.
Mr Wilson's War (John Dos Passos), Pt. II, Ch. 10

SUITABILITY

1 In seed time learn, in harvest teach, in winter enjoy.
William Blake (1757–1827) British poet.
The Marriage of Heaven and Hell, 'Proverbs of Hell'

2 A cow is a very good animal in the field; but we turn her out of a garden.
Samuel Johnson (1709–84) British lexicographer.
The Personal History of Samuel Johnson (C. Hibbert)
Responding to Boswell's objections to the expulsion of six Methodists from Oxford University

3 Today I dressed to meet my father's eyes; yesterday it was for my husband's.
Julia (39 BC–AD 14) Daughter of Augustus.
Saturnalia (Macrobius)
On being complimented by her father, the emperor Augustus, on her choice of a more modest dress than the one she had worn the previous day

4 At Christmas I no more desire a rose
Than wish a snow in May's newfangled shows.
William Shakespeare (1564–1616) English dramatist.
Love's Labour's Lost, I:1

SUMMER

See also months, seasons

1 Sumer is icumen in,
Lhude sing cuccu!
Groweth sed, and bloweth med,
And springth the wude nu.
Anonymous
Cuckoo Song

2 All the live murmur of a summer's day.
Matthew Arnold (1822–88) British poet and critic.
The Scholar Gipsy

3 It is time for the destruction of error.
The chairs are being brought in from the garden,
The summer talk stopped on that savage coast
Before the storms.
W. H. Auden (1907–73) British poet.
It is time

4 Summer has set in with its usual severity.
Samuel Taylor Coleridge (1772–1834) British poet.
Quoted in Lamb's letter to V. Novello, 9 May 1826

5 Summer afternoon – summer afternoon; to me those have always been the two most beautiful words in the English language.
Henry James (1843–1916) US novelist.
A Backward Glance (Edith Wharton), Ch. 10

6 In a somer season, when soft was the sonne.
William Langland (c. 1330–c. 1400) English poet.
The Vision of Piers Plowman, Prologue

7 The moans of doves in immemorial elms,
And murmuring of innumerable bees.
Alfred, Lord Tennyson (1809–92) British poet.
The Princess, VII

SUMMONS

See also invitations

1 Go, for they call you, Shepherd, from the hill.
Matthew Arnold (1822–88) British poet and critic.
The Scholar Gipsy

2 Whistle and she'll come to you.
Francis Beaumont (1584–1616) English dramatist.
Wit Without Money, IV:4

3 Mr Watson, come here; I want you.
Alexander Graham Bell (1847–1922) Scottish scientist.
Attrib.
The first telephone conversation, 10 Mar 1876, in Boston

4 Dauntless the slug-horn to my lips I set,
And blew. *Childe Roland to the Dark Tower came.*
Robert Browning (1812–89) British poet.
Childe Roland to the Dark Tower Came, XXXIV

SUN

See also weather

1 The Sun came up upon the left,
Out of the sea came he!
And he shone bright, and on the right
Went down into the sea.
Samuel Taylor Coleridge (1772–1834) British poet.
The Rime of the Ancient Mariner, I

2 Busy old fool, unruly Sun,
Why dost thou thus,
Through windows and through curtains call on us?
John Donne (1573–1631) English poet.
The Sun Rising

3 I have a horror of sunsets, they're so romantic, so operatic.
Marcel Proust (1871–1922) French novelist.
À la recherche du temps perdu: Sodome et Gomorrhe

SUNDAY

1 And on the seventh day God ended his work

which he had made; and he rested on the seventh day from all his work which he had made.
Bible: Genesis
2:2

2 And he said unto them, The sabbath was made for man, and not man for the sabbath: Therefore the Son of man is Lord also of the sabbath.
Bible: Mark
2:27–28

3 Of all the days that's in the week
I dearly love but one day –
And that's the day that comes betwixt
A Saturday and Monday.
Henry Carey (c. 1690–1743) English poet and musician.
Sally in our Alley

4 The better day, the worse deed.
Matthew Henry (1662–1714) English nonconformist minister.
Exposition of the Old and New Testaments

5 The feeling of Sunday is the same everywhere, heavy, melancholy, standing still. Like when they say, 'As it was in the beginning, is now, and ever shall be, world without end.'
Jean Rhys (1894–1979) Dominican-born British novelist.
Voyage in the Dark, Ch. 4

SUPERIORITY

See also equality, excellence, one-upmanship, snobbery

1 My name is George Nathaniel Curzon,
I am a most superior person.
My face is pink, my hair is sleek,
I dine at Blenheim once a week.
Anonymous
The Masque of Balliol

2 The superior man is satisfied and composed; the mean man is always full of distress.
Confucius (K'ung Fu-tzu; 551–479 BC) Chinese philosopher.
Analects

3 The superior man is distressed by his want of ability.
Confucius
Analects

4 When you meet someone better than yourself, turn your thoughts to becoming his equal. When you meet someone not as good as you are, look within and examine your own self.
Confucius
Analects

5 And lo! Ben Adhem's name led all the rest.
Leigh Hunt (1784–1859) British poet.
Abou Ben Adhem and the Angel

6 Though I've belted you an' flayed you,
By the livin' Gawd that made you,

You're a better man than I am, Gunga Din!
Rudyard Kipling (1865–1936) Indian-born British writer.
Gunga Din

7 Sir, you have the advantage of me.
– Not yet I haven't, but wait till I get you outside.
Groucho Marx (Julius Marx; 1895–1977) US comedian.
Monkey Business

8 Above the vulgar flight of common souls.
Arthur Murphy (1727–1805) Irish dramatist, writer, and actor.
Zenobia, V

9 I teach you the Superman. Man is something that is to be surpassed.
Friedrich Wilhelm Nietzsche (1844–1900) German philosopher.
Thus Spake Zarathustra

10 It is brought home to you . . . that it is only because miners sweat their guts out that superior persons can remain superior.
George Orwell (Eric Blair; 1903–50) British novelist.
The Road to Wigan Pier, Ch. 2

11 'I believe I take precedence,' he said coldly; 'you are merely the club Bore: I am the club Liar.'
Saki (Hector Hugh Munro; 1870–1916) British writer.
A Defensive Diamond

12 In the Country of the Blind the One-eyed Man is King.
H. G. Wells (1866–1946) British writer.
The Country of the Blind

SUPERNATURAL

See also fairies

1 From ghoulies and ghosties and long-leggety beasties
And things that go bump in the night,
Good Lord, deliver us!
Anonymous
Cornish prayer

2 Open Sesame!
The Arabian Nights (c. 1500) A collection of tales from the East.
The History of Ali Baba

3 Thou shalt not suffer a witch to live.
Bible: Exodus
22:18

4 For my part, I have ever believed, and do now know, that there are witches.
Thomas Browne (1605–82) English physician and writer.
Religio Medici, Pt. I

5 This time it vanished quite slowly, beginning with the end of the tail, and ending with the grin, which remained some time after the rest of it had gone.
Lewis Carroll (Charles Lutwidge Dodgson; 1832–98) British writer.
Alice's Adventures in Wonderland, Ch. 6
Describing the Cheshire Cat

6 A savage place! as holy and enchanted
As e'er beneath a waning moon was haunted
By woman wailing for her demon-lover!
Samuel Taylor Coleridge (1772–1834) British poet.
Kubla Khan

7 Religion
Has made an honest woman of the supernatural,
And we won't have it kicking over the traces again.
Christopher Fry (1907–) British dramatist.
The Lady's Not for Burning, II

8 All argument is against it; but all belief is for it.
Samuel Johnson (1709–84) British lexicographer.
Life of Johnson (J. Boswell), Vol. III
Of the ghost of a dead person

9 'La belle Dame sans Merci
Hath thee in thrall!'
John Keats (1795–1821) British poet.
La Belle Dame Sans Merci

10 That old black magic has me in its spell.
Johnny Mercer (1909–76) US lyricist and composer.
That Old Black Magic

11 Once upon a midnight dreary, while I pondered, weak and weary,
Over many a quaint and curious volume of forgotten lore,
While I nodded, nearly napping, suddenly there came a tapping,
As of some one gently rapping, rapping at my chamber door.
Edgar Allan Poe (1809–49) US poet and writer.
The Raven

12 There are more things in heaven and earth, Horatio,
Than are dreamt of in your philosophy.
William Shakespeare (1564–1616) English dramatist.
Hamlet, I:5

13 This supernatural soliciting
Cannot be ill; cannot be good.
William Shakespeare
Macbeth, I:3

SUPERSTITION

See also luck

1 A dimple in the chin, a devil within.
Proverb

2 Meet on the stairs and you won't meet in heaven.
Proverb

3 One for sorrow, two for mirth; three for a wedding, four for a birth; five for silver, six for gold; seven for a secret, not to be told; eight for heaven, nine for hell; and ten for the devil's own sel.
Proverb
Referring to magpies or crows; there are numerous variants

4 See a pin and pick it up, all the day you'll have good luck; see a pin and let it lie, you'll want a pin before you die.
Proverb

5 Third time lucky.
Proverb

6 Of course I don't believe in it. But I understand that it brings you luck whether you believe in it or not.
Niels Bohr (1885–1962) Danish physicist.
Attrib.
When asked why he had a horseshoe on his wall

7 Superstition is the religion of feeble minds.
Edmund Burke (1729–97) British politician.
Reflections on the Revolution in France

8 Superstition is the poetry of life.
Goethe (1749–1832) German poet and dramatist.
Sprüche in Prosa, III

9 And some of the bigger bears try to pretend
That they came round the corner to look for a friend;
And they'll try to pretend that nobody cares
Whether you walk on the lines or the squares.
A. A. Milne (1882–1956) British writer.
When We Were Very Young, 'Lines and Squares'

10 They say there is divinity in odd numbers, either in nativity, chance, or death.
William Shakespeare (1564–1616) English dramatist.
The Merry Wives of Windsor, V:1

11 Superstition sets the whole world in flames; philosophy quenches them.
Voltaire (François-Marie Arouet; 1694–1778) French writer.
Dictionnaire philosophique, 'Superstition'

SUPPORT

See also loyalty

1 He found him in a desert land, and in the waste howling wilderness; he led him about, he instructed him, he kept him as the apple of his eye.
Bible: Deuteronomy
32:10

2 The finest plans have always been spoiled by the littleness of those that should carry them out. Even emperors can't do it all by themselves.
Bertolt Brecht (1898–1956) German dramatist.
Mother Courage, VI

3 Either back us or sack us.
James Callaghan (1912–) British politician and prime minister.
Speech, Labour Party Conference, Brighton, 5 Oct 1977

4 What I want is men who will support me when I am in the wrong.
Lord Melbourne (1779–1848) British statesman.
Lord M. (Lord David Cecil)
Replying to someone who said he would support Melbourne as long as he was in the right

5 While I cannot be regarded as a pillar, I must be regarded as a buttress of the church, because I support it from the outside.
Lord Melbourne
Attrib.

6 Ladies and gentleman, it takes more than one to make a ballet.
Ninette de Valois (Edris Stannus; 1898–) British ballet dancer and choreographer.
New Yorker

SURVIVAL

See also evolution, self-preservation

1 I haven't asked you to make me young again. All I want is to go on getting older.
Konrad Adenauer (1876–1967) German statesman.
Attrib.
Replying to his doctor

2 The perpetual struggle for room and food.
Thomas Robert Malthus (1766–1834) British clergyman and economist.
Essays on the Principle of Population

3 The thing-in-itself, the will-to-live, exists whole and undivided in every being, even in the tiniest; it is present as completely as in all that ever were, are, and will be, taken together.
Arthur Schopenhauer (1788–1860) German philosopher.
Parerga and Paralipomena

4 This is the Law of the Yukon, that only the strong shall thrive;
That surely the weak shall perish, and only the Fit survive.
Robert William Service (1874–1958) Canadian poet.
The Law of the Yukon

SUSPENSE

1 This suspense is terrible. I hope it will last.
Oscar Wilde (1854–1900) Irish-born British dramatist.
The Importance of Being Earnest, III

SUSPICION

See also mistrust

1 Suspicions amongst thoughts are like bats amongst birds, they ever fly by twilight.
Francis Bacon (1561–1626) English philosopher.
Essays, 'Of Suspicion'

SWITZERLAND

See also Europe

1 Since both its national products, snow and chocolate, melt, the cuckoo clock was invented solely in order to give tourists something solid to remember it by.
Alan Coren (1938–) British humorist and writer.
The Sanity Inspector, 'And Though They Do Their Best'

2 The Swiss who are not a people so much as a neat clean quite solvent business.
William Faulkner (1897–1962) US novelist.
Intruder in the Dust, Ch. 7

3 I look upon Switzerland as an inferior sort of Scotland.
Sydney Smith (1771–1845) British clergyman and essayist.
Letter to Lord Holland, 1815

4 They say that if the Swiss had designed these mountains they'd be rather flatter.
Paul Theroux (1941–) US-born writer.
The Great Railway Bazaar, Ch. 28
Referring to the Alps

5 In Italy for thirty years under the Borgias they had warfare, terror, murder, bloodshed – they produced Michelangelo, Leonardo da Vinci and the Renaissance. In Switzerland they had brotherly love, five hundred years of democracy and peace, and what did they produce . . . ? The cuckoo clock.
Orson Welles (1915–85) US film actor.
The Third Man

SYMPATHY

See also comfort

1 Sympathy – for all these people, for being foreigners – lay over the gathering like a woolly blanket; and no one was enjoying it at all.
Malcolm Bradbury (1932–) British academic and novelist.
Eating People is Wrong, Ch. 2

2 To be sympathetic without discrimination is so very debilitating.
Ronald Firbank (1886–1926) British novelist.
Vainglory

3 She was a machine-gun riddling her hostess with sympathy.
Aldous Huxley (1894–1964) British novelist.
Mortal Coils, 'The Gioconda Smile'

4 I can sympathize with people's pains, but not with their pleasures. There is something curiously boring about somebody else's happiness.
Aldous Huxley
Limbo, 'Cynthia'

5 To show pity is felt as a sign of contempt because one has clearly ceased to be an object of *fear* as soon as one is pitied.
Friedrich Wilhelm Nietzsche (1844–1900) German philosopher.
The Wanderer and His Shadow

6 I can sympathize with everything, except suffering.
Oscar Wilde (1854–1900) Irish-born British dramatist.
The Picture of Dorian Gray, Ch. 3

T

TACT

See also diplomacy

1 Leave well alone.
Proverb

2 Let sleeping dogs lie.
Proverb

3 One shouldn't talk of halters in the hanged man's house.
Miguel de Cervantes (1547–1616) Spanish novelist.
Don Quixote, Pt. I, Ch. 25

4 Tact consists in knowing how far we may go too far.
Jean Cocteau (1889–1963) French poet and artist.
In *Treasury of Humorous Quotations*

5 My advice was delicately poised between the cliché and the indiscretion.
Robert Runcie (1921–) British churchman (Archbishop of Canterbury).
Comment to the press concerning his advice to the Prince of Wales and Lady Diana Spencer on their approaching wedding, 13 July 1981

TALENT

See also genius, talent and genius

1 Whom the gods wish to destroy they first call promising.
Cyril Connolly (1903–74) British journalist.
Enemies of Promise, Ch. 3

2 Talent develops in quiet places, character in the full current of human life.
Goethe (1749–1832) German poet and dramatist.
Torquato Tasso, I

3 There is no substitute for talent. Industry and all the virtues are of no avail.
Aldous Huxley (1894–1964) British novelist.
Point Counter Point

4 I think it's the most extraordinary collection of talent, of human knowledge, that has ever been gathered together at the White House – with the possible exception of when Thomas Jefferson dined alone.
John Fitzgerald Kennedy (1917–63) US statesman.
Said at a dinner for Nobel Prizewinners, 29 Apr 1962

5 It's not enough to be Hungarian, you must have talent too.
Alexander Korda (Sandor Kellner; 1893–1956) Hungarian-born British film director.
Alexander Korda (K. Kulik)

6 Let our children grow tall, and some taller than others if they have it in them to do so.
Margaret Thatcher (1925–) British politician and prime minister.
Speech, US tour, 1975

TALENT AND GENIUS

See also genius, talent

1 It takes people a long time to learn the difference between talent and genius, especially ambitious young men and women.
Louisa May Alcott (1832–88) US novelist.
Little Women, Pt. II

2 Mediocrity knows nothing higher than itself, but talent instantly recognizes genius.
Arthur Conan Doyle (1856–1930) British writer.
The Valley of Fear

3 Genius does what it must, and Talent does what it can.
Owen Meredith (Robert Bulmer-Lytton, 1st Earl of Lytton; 1831–91) British statesman and poet.
Last Words of a Sensitive Second-rate Poet

TASTE

See also difference, individuality

1 Good taste is better than bad taste, but bad taste is better than no taste.
Arnold Bennett (1867–1931) British novelist.
The Observer, 'Sayings of the Week', 24 Aug 1930

2 Taste is the feminine of genius.
Edward Fitzgerald (1809–83) British poet.
Letter to J. R. Lowell, Oct 1877

3 Our tastes greatly alter. The lad does not care for the child's rattle, and the old man does not care for the young man's whore.
Samuel Johnson (1709–84) British lexicographer.
Life of Johnson (J. Boswell), Vol. II

4 What is food to one man is bitter poison to others.
Lucretius (Titus Lucretius Carus; c. 99–55 BC) Roman philosopher.
On the Nature of the Universe, IV

5 The kind of people who always go on about whether a thing is in good taste invariably have very bad taste.
Joe Orton (1933–67) British dramatist.
Attrib.

6 The play, I remember, pleas'd not the million; 'twas caviare to the general.
William Shakespeare (1564–1616) English dramatist.
Hamlet, II:2

7 You had no taste when you married me.
Richard Brinsley Sheridan (1751–1816) British dramatist.
The School for Scandal, I

TAXATION

1 They can't collect legal taxes from illegal money.
Al Capone (1899–1947) Italian-born US gangster.
Objecting to the US Bureau of Internal Revenue claiming large sums in unpaid back tax
Capone (J. Kobler)

2 The hardest thing in the world to understand is income tax.
Albert Einstein (1879–1955) German-born US physicist.
Attrib.

3 In this world nothing is certain but death and taxes.
Benjamin Franklin (1706–90) US scientist and statesman.
Letter to Jean-Baptiste Leroy, 13 Nov 1789

4 *Excise.* A hateful tax levied upon commodities.
Samuel Johnson (1709–84) British lexicographer.
Dictionary of the English Language

5 Sir, I now pay you this exorbitant charge, but I must ask you to explain to her Majesty that she must not in future look upon me as a source of income.
Charles Kemble (1775–1854) British actor.
On being obliged to hand over his income tax to the tax collector
Humour in the Theatre (J. Aye)

6 The avoidance of taxes is the only pursuit that still carries any reward.
John Maynard Keynes (1883–1946) British economist.
Attrib.

7 The Chancellor of the Exchequer is a man whose duties make him more or less of a taxing machine. He is intrusted with a certain amount of misery which it is his duty to distribute as fairly as he can.
Robert Lowe (1811–92) British lawyer and politician.
Speech, House of Commons, 11 Apr 1870

8 The taxpayer is someone who works for the federal government but doesn't have to take a civil service examination.
Ronald Reagan (1911–) US politician and president.
Attrib.

9 There is no art which one government

sooner learns of another than that of draining money from the pockets of the people.

Adam Smith (1723–90) Scottish economist.
The Wealth of Nations

10 For God's sake, madam, don't say that in England for if you do, they will surely tax it.

Jonathan Swift (1667–1745) Irish-born Anglican priest and writer.
Responding to Lady Carteret's admiration for the quality of the air in Ireland
Lives of the Wits (H. Pearson)

TECHNOLOGY

See also progress, science

1 Give me a firm place to stand, and I will move the earth.

Archimedes (c. 287–212 BC) Greek mathematician.
On the Lever

2 Man is a tool-using animal.

Thomas Carlyle (1795–1881) Scottish historian and essayist.
Sartor Resartus, Bk. I, Ch. 5

3 Any sufficiently advanced technology is indistinguishable from magic.

Arthur C. Clarke (1917–) British science-fiction writer.
The Lost Worlds of 2001

4 Man is a tool-making animal.

Benjamin Franklin (1706–90) US scientist and statesman.
Life of Johnson (J. Boswell), 7 Apr 1778

5 One machine can do the work of fifty ordinary men. No machine can do the work of one extraordinary man.

Elbert Hubbard (1856–1915) US writer.
Roycroft Dictionary and Book of Epigrams

6 The new electronic interdependence recreates the world in the image of a global village.

Marshall McLuhan (1911–81) Canadian sociologist.
The Gutenberg Galaxy

7 For tribal man space was the uncontrollable mystery. For technological man it is time that occupies the same role.

Marshall McLuhan
The Mechanical Bride, 'Magic that Changes Mood'

8 The machine threatens all achievement.

Rainer Maria Rilke (1875–1926) Austrian poet.
Die Sonette an Orpheus, II, 10

9 Pylons, those pillars
Bare like nude giant girls that have no secret.

Stephen Spender (1909–) British poet.
The Pylons

10 No man . . . who has wrestled with a self-adjusting card table can ever quite be the man he once was.

James Thurber (1894–1961) US humorist.
Let Your Mind Alone, 'Sex ex Machina'

11 I see no reason to suppose that these machines will ever force themselves into general use.

Duke of Wellington (1769–1852) British general and statesman.
Referring to steam locomotives
Geoffrey Madan's Notebooks (J. Gere)

TEETH

1 For years I have let dentists ride roughshod over my teeth: I have been sawed, hacked, chopped, whittled, bewitched, bewildered, tattooed, and signed on again; but this is cuspid's last stand.

S. J. Perelman (1904–79) US humorous writer.
Crazy Like a Fox, 'Nothing but the Tooth'

2 I'll dispose of my teeth as I see fit, and after they've gone, I'll get along. I started off living on gruel, and by God, I can always go back to it again.

S. J. Perelman
Crazy Like a Fox, 'Nothing but the Tooth'

3 Certain people are born with natural false teeth.

Robert Robinson (1927–) British writer and broadcaster.
BBC radio programme, *Stop the Week*, 1977

4 To lose a lover or even a husband or two during the course of one's life can be vexing. But to lose one's teeth is a catastrophe.

Hugh Wheeler (1912–) British-born US writer.
A Little Night Music

TELEVISION

See also media

1 Television is more interesting than people. If it were not, we should have people standing in the corners of our rooms.

Alan Coren (1938–) British humorist and writer.
In *The Times*

2 If any reader of this book is in the grip of some habit of which he is deeply ashamed, I advise him not to give way to it in secret but to do it on television. No-one will pass him with averted gaze on the other side of the street. People will cross the road at the risk of losing their own lives in order to say 'We saw you on the telly'.

Quentin Crisp (?1910–) Model, publicist, and writer.
How to Become a Virgin

3 Television is an invention that permits you to be entertained in your living room by people you wouldn't have in your home.

David Frost (1939–) British television personality.
Attrib., CBS television, 1971 home

4 Television brought the brutality of war into the comfort of the living room. Vietnam was lost in the living rooms of America – not on the battlefields of Vietnam.

Marshall McLuhan (1911–81) Canadian sociologist.
Montreal *Gazette*, 16 May 1975

5 Television? No good will come of this device. The word is half Greek and half Latin.

C. P. Scott (1846–1932) British journalist.
Attrib.

TEMPTATION

1 Forbidden fruit is sweet.

Proverb

2 If you can't be good, be careful.

Proverb

3 I am not over-fond of resisting temptation.

William Beckford (1759–1844) British writer.
Vathek

4 Blessed is the man that endureth temptation: for when he is tried, he shall receive the crown of life, which the Lord hath promised to them that love him.

Bible: James
1:12

5 All the deceits of the world, the flesh, and the devil.

The Book of Common Prayer
Morning Prayer, Prayer of St Chrysostom

6 Not all that tempts your wand'ring eyes
And heedless hearts, is lawful prize;
Nor all, that glisters, gold.

Thomas Gray (1716–71) British poet.
Ode on the Death of a Favourite Cat

7 'You oughtn't to yield to temptation.'
'Well, somebody must, or the thing becomes absurd.'

Anthony Hope (Sir Anthony Hope Hawkins; 1863–1933) British novelist.
The Dolly Dialogues

8 . . . with peaches and women, it's only the side next the sun that's tempting.

Ouida (Marie Louise de la Ramée; 1839–1908) British novelist.
Strathmore

9 I never resist temptation because I have found that things that are bad for me never tempt me.

George Bernard Shaw (1856–1950) Irish dramatist and critic.
The Apple Cart

10 I can resist everything except temptation.

Oscar Wilde (1854–1900) Irish-born British dramatist.
Lady Windermere's Fan, I

11 The only way to get rid of a temptation is to yield to it.

Oscar Wilde
Repeating a similar sentiment expressed by Clementina Stirling Graham (1782–1877)
The Picture of Dorian Gray, Ch. 2

THEATRE

See also acting, actors, audiences, criticism, literature, plays, Shakespeare

1 The reason why Absurdist plays take place in No Man's Land with only two characters is primarily financial.

Arthur Adamov (1908–70) Russian-born French dramatist.
Said at the Edinburgh International Drama Conference, 13 Sept 1963

2 It's one of the tragic ironies of the theatre that only one man in it can count on steady work – the night watchman.

Tallulah Bankhead (1903–68) US actress.
Tallulah, Ch. 1

3 Tragedy is if I cut my finger. Comedy is if I walk into an open sewer and die.

Mel Brooks (Melvyn Kaminsky; 1926–) US film director.
New Yorker, 30 Oct 1978

4 All tragedies are finish'd by a death,
All comedies are ended by a marriage.

Lord Byron (1788–1824) British poet.
Don Juan, III

5 You know, I go to the theatre to be entertained . . . I don't want to see plays about rape, sodomy and drug addiction . . . I can get all that at home.

Peter Cook (1937–) British writer and entertainer.
The Observer, caption to cartoon, 8 July 1962

6 Don't put your daughter on the stage, Mrs Worthington.

Noël Coward (1899–1973) British dramatist.
Title of song

7 Farce is the essential theatre. Farce refined becomes high comedy: farce brutalized becomes tragedy.

Gordon Craig (1872–1966) British actor.
The Story of my Days, Index

8 We participate in a tragedy; at a comedy we only look.

Aldous Huxley (1894–1964) British novelist.
The Devils of Loudon, Ch. 11

9 I never deliberately set out to shock, but when people don't walk out of my plays I think there is something wrong.

John Osborne (1929–) British dramatist.
The Observer, 'Sayings of the Week', 19 Jan 1975

10 I depict men as they ought to be, but Euripides portrays them as they are.

Sophocles (c. 496–406 BC) Greek dramatist.
Poetics (Aristotle)

11 The bad end unhappily, the good unluckily. That is what tragedy means.

Tom Stoppard (1937–) Czech-born British dramatist.
Rosencrantz and Guildenstern Are Dead, II

12 I would just like to mention Robert Houdin

who in the eighteenth century invented the vanishing bird-cage trick and the theater matinée – may he rot and perish. Good afternoon.

Orson Welles (1915–85) US film actor.
Addressing the audience at the end of a matinée performance
Great Theatrical Disasters (G. Brandreth)

THEFT

See also crime

1 The fault is great in man or woman
Who steals a goose from off a common;
But what can plead that man's excuse
Who steals a common from a goose?
Anonymous
The Tickler Magazine, 1 Feb 1821

2 They will steal the very teeth out of your mouth as you walk through the streets. I know it from experience.
William Arabin (1773–1841) British judge.
Referring to the people of Uxbridge
Arabinesque at Law (Sir R. Megarry)

3 Prisoner, God has given you good abilities, instead of which you go about the country stealing ducks.
William Arabin
Arabinesque at Law (Sir R. Megarry)

4 I am laughing to think what risks you take to try to find money in a desk by night where the legal owner can never find any by day.
Honoré de Balzac (1799–1850) French novelist.
Said on waking to find a burglar in the room
Attrib.

5 Stolen sweets are best.
Colley Cibber (1671–1757) British actor and dramatist.
The Rival Fools, I

6 Travel light and you can sing in the robber's face.
Juvenal (Decimus Junius Juvenalis; 60–130 AD) Roman satirist.
Satires, X

7 Stolen sweets are always sweeter,
Stolen kisses much completer,
Stolen looks are nice in chapels,
Stolen, stolen, be your apples.
Hunt Leigh (1784–1859) British poet.
Song of Fairies Robbing an Orchard

THEORY

See also ideas

1 A thing may look specious in theory, and yet be ruinous in practice; a thing may look evil in theory, and yet be in practice excellent.
Edmund Burke (1729–97) British politician.
Impeachment of Warren Hastings, 19 Feb 1788

2 A theory can be proved by experiment; but no path leads from experiment to the birth of a theory.
Albert Einstein (1879–1955) German-born US physicist.
The Sunday Times, 18 July 1976

3 For hundreds of pages the closely-reasoned arguments unroll, axioms and theorems interlock. And what remains with us in the end? A general sense that the world can be expressed in closely-reasoned arguments, in interlocking axioms and theorems.
Michael Frayn (1933–) British journalist and writer.
Constructions

4 Dear friend, theory is all grey,
And the golden tree of life is green.
Goethe (1749–1832) German poet and dramatist.
Faust, Pt. I

5 You know very well that unless you're a scientist, it's much more important for a theory to be shapely, than for it to be true.
Christopher Hampton (1946–) British writer and dramatist.
The Philanthropist, Sc. 1

6 It is a good morning exercise for a research scientist to discard a pet hypothesis every day before breakfast. It keeps him young.
Konrad Lorenz (1903–) Austrian zoologist.
On Aggression, Ch. 2

7 When the torrent sweeps a man against a boulder, you must expect him to scream, and you need not be surprised if the scream is sometimes a theory.
Robert Louis Stevenson (1850–94) Scottish writer.
Virginibus Puerisque

THINKING

See also intellect, intelligence, mind, philosophy

1 I have always found that the man whose second thoughts are good is worth watching.
J. M. Barrie (1860–1937) British novelist and dramatist.
What Every Woman Knows, III

2 *Cogito, ergo sum.*
I think, therefore I am.
René Descartes (1596–1650) French philosopher.
Le Discours de la méthode

3 The most fluent talkers or most plausible reasoners are not always the justest thinkers.
William Hazlitt (1778–1830) British essayist.
On Prejudice

4 Most of one's life . . . is one prolonged effort to prevent oneself thinking.
Aldous Huxley (1894–1964) British novelist.
Mortal Coils, 'Green Tunnels'

5 You can't think rationally on an empty stomach, and a whole lot of people can't do it on a full one either.
Lord Reith (1889–1971) British administrator.
Attrib.

6 People don't seem to realize that it takes time and effort and preparation to think. Statesmen are far too busy making speeches to think.
Bertrand Russell (1872–1970) British philosopher.
Kenneth Harris Talking To: 'Bertrand Russell' (Kenneth Harris)

7 Many people would sooner die than think. In fact they do.
Bertrand Russell
Thinking About Thinking (A. Flew)

8 My thought is *me*: that is why I can't stop. I exist by what I think . . . and I can't prevent myself from thinking.
Jean-Paul Sartre (1905–80) French writer.
Nausea

9 There is nothing either good or bad, but thinking makes it so.
William Shakespeare (1564–1616) English dramatist.
Hamlet, II:2

10 Thinking is to me the greatest fatigue in the world.
John Vanbrugh (1664–1726) English architect and dramatist.
The Relapse, II:1

11 Great thoughts come from the heart.
Marquis de Vauvenargues (1715–47) French soldier and writer.
Réflexions et maximes

12 In order to draw a limit to thinking, we should have to be able to think both sides of this limit.
Ludwig Wittgenstein (1889–1951) Austrian philosopher.
Tractatus Logico-Philosophicus, Preface

THIRST

See also alcohol, desire, drinks, hunger

1 There are two reasons for drinking; one is, when you are thirsty, to cure it; the other, when you are not thirsty, to prevent it . . . Prevention is better than cure.
Thomas Love Peacock (1785–1866) British novelist.
Melincourt

2 I drink for the thirst to come.
François Rabelais (1483–1553) French satirist.
Gargantua, Bk. I, Ch. 5

3 As pants the hart for cooling streams When heated in the chase.
Nahum Tate (1652–1715) Irish-born English poet.
New Version of the Psalms, 'As Pants the Hart'

THREATS

1 Violet Elizabeth dried her tears. She saw that they were useless and she did not believe in wasting her effects. 'All right,' she said

calmly, 'I'll thcream then. I'll thcream, an' thcream, an' thcream till I'm thick.'
Richmal Crompton (Richmal Crompton Lamburn; 1890–1969) British writer.
Violet Elizabeth Bott, a minor character in the *William* books, had both a lisp and an exceptional ability to get her own way
Just William

2 If you start throwing hedgehogs under me, I shall throw two porcupines under you.
Nikita Khrushchev (1894–1971) Soviet statesman.
The Observer, 'Sayings of the Week', 10 Nov 1963

3 After I die, I shall return to earth as a gatekeeper of a bordello and I won't let any of you – not a one of you – enter!
Arturo Toscanini (1867–1957) Italian conductor.
Rebuking an incompetent orchestra
The Maestro: The Life of Arturo Toscanini (Howard Taubman)

THRIFT

See also extravagance, money

1 A penny saved is a penny earned.
Proverb

2 Keep something for a rainy day.
Proverb

3 Penny wise, pound foolish.
Proverb

4 I knew once a very covetous, sordid fellow, who used to say, 'Take care of the pence, for the pounds will take care of themselves.'
Earl of Chesterfield (1694–1773) English statesman.
Possibly referring to William Lowndes
Letter to his son, 6 Nov 1747

5 . . . we owe something to extravagance, for thrift and adventure seldom go hand in hand. . . .
Jennie Jerome Churchill (1854–1921) US-born British hostess and writer.
Pearson's, 'Extravagance'

6 Everybody is always in favour of general economy and particular expenditure.
Anthony Eden (1897–1977) British statesman.
The Observer, 'Sayings of the Week', 17 June 1956

7 Economy is going without something you do want in case you should, some day, want something you probably won't want.
Anthony Hope (Sir Anthony Hope Hawkins; 1863–1933) British novelist.
The Dolly Dialogues

8 What! Can't a fellow even enjoy a biscuit any more?
Duke of Portland (1857–1943) British peer.
On being informed that as one of several measures to reduce his own expenses he would have to dispense with one of his two Italian pastry cooks
Their Noble Lordships (S. Winchester)

9 A hole is the accident of a day, while a darn is premeditated poverty.
Edward Shuter (1728–76) British actor.
Explaining why he did not mend the holes in his stocking
Dictionary of National Biography

10 Beware of all enterprises that require new clothes.
Henry David Thoreau (1817–62) US writer.
Walden, 'Economy'

TIME

See also eternity, future, life, past, present, transience

1 An hour in the morning is worth two in the evening.
Proverb

2 There are only twenty-four hours in the day.
Proverb

3 There is a time and place for everything.
Proverb

4 Time and tide wait for no man.
Proverb

5 Time is a great healer.
Proverb

6 Time will tell.
Proverb

7 To choose time is to save time.
Francis Bacon (1561–1626) English philosopher.
Essays, 'Of Dispatch'

8 VLADIMIR. That passed the time.
ESTRAGON. It would have passed in any case.
VLADIMIR. Yes, but not so rapidly.
Samuel Beckett (1906–) Irish novelist and dramatist.
Waiting for Godot, I

9 I believe the twenty-four hour day has come to stay.
Max Beerbohm (1872–1956) British writer.
A Christmas Garland, 'Perkins and Mankind'

10 Time is a great teacher, but unfortunately it kills all its pupils.
Hector Berlioz (1803–69) French composer.
Almanach des lettres françaises

11 To every thing there is a season, and a time to every purpose under the heaven:
A time to be born, and a time to die; a time to plant, and a time to pluck up that which is planted;
A time to kill, and a time to heal; a time to break down, and a time to build up;
A time to weep, and a time to laugh; a time to mourn, and a time to dance;
A time to cast away stones, and a time to gather stones together; a time to embrace, and a time to refrain from embracing;
A time to get, and a time to lose; a time to keep, and a time to cast away;
A time to rend, and a time to sew; a time to keep silence, and a time to speak;
A time to love, and a time to hate; a time of war, and a time of peace.
Bible: Ecclesiastes
3:1–8

12 Men talk of killing time, while time quietly kills them.
Dion Boucicault (Dionysius Lardner Boursiquot; 1820–90) Irish-born US actor and dramatist.
London Assurance, II:1

13 I recommend you to take care of the minutes: for hours will take care of themselves.
Earl of Chesterfield (1694–1773) English statesman.
Letter to his son, 6 Nov 1747

14 Time present and time past
Are both perhaps present in time future
And time future contained in time past.
T. S. Eliot (1888–1965) US-born British poet and dramatist.
Four Quartets

15 Come, fill the Cup, and in the Fire of Spring
The Winter Garment of Repentance fling:
The Bird of Time has but a little way
To fly – and Lo! the Bird is on the Wing.
Edward Fitzgerald (1809–83) British poet.
The Rubáiyát of Omar Khayyám

16 Ah, fill the Cup: – what boots it to repeat
How Time is slipping underneath our Feet:
Unborn TOMORROW, and dead YESTERDAY,
Why fret about them if TODAY be sweet!
Edward Fitzgerald
The Rubáiyát of Omar Khayyám

17 Dost thou love life? Then do not squander time, for that's the stuff life is made of.
Benjamin Franklin (1706–90) US scientist and statesman.
Poor Richard's Almanack

18 You must remember this;
A kiss is just a kiss,
A sigh is just a sigh –
The fundamental things apply
As time goes by.
Herman Hupfeld (20th century) US songwriter.
From the film *Casablanca*
As Time Goes By

19 O aching time! O moments big as years!
John Keats (1795–1821) British poet.
Hyperion, I

20 We must use time as a tool, not as a couch.
John Fitzgerald Kennedy (1917–63) US statesman.
The Observer, 'Sayings of the Week', 10 Dec 1961

21 They shut the road through the woods
Seventy years ago.
Weather and rain have undone it again,
And now you would never know
There was once a road through the woods.
Rudyard Kipling (1865–1936) Indian-born British writer.
The Way Through the Woods

22 The Future is something which everyone reaches at the rate of sixty minutes an hour, whatever he does, whoever he is.
C. S. Lewis (1898–1963) British academic and writer.
The Screwtape Letters

23 I stood on the bridge at midnight,
As the clocks were striking the hour.
Henry Wadsworth Longfellow (1807–82) US poet.
The Bridge

24 The man is killing time – there's nothing else.
Robert Lowell (1917–77) US poet.
The Drinker

25 Time wounds all heels.
Groucho Marx (Julius Marx; 1895–1977) US comedian.
Attrib.

26 They do that to pass the time, nothing more. But Time is too large, it refuses to let itself be filled up.
Jean-Paul Sartre (1905–80) French writer.
Nausea

27 Ah! the clock is always slow;
It is later than you think.
Robert William Service (1874–1958) Canadian poet.
It is Later than You Think

28 Come what come may,
Time and the hour runs through the roughest day.
William Shakespeare (1564–1616) English dramatist.
Macbeth, I:3

29 Th' inaudible and noiseless foot of Time.
William Shakespeare
All's Well that Ends Well, V:3

30 Like as the waves make towards the pebbled shore,
So do our minutes hasten to their end.
William Shakespeare
Sonnet 60

31 Time hath, my lord, a wallet at his back,
Wherein he puts alms for oblivion,
A great-siz'd monster of ingratitudes.
William Shakespeare
Troilus and Cressida, III:3

32 In reality, *killing time*
Is only the name for another of the multifarious ways
By which Time kills us.
Osbert Sitwell (1892–1969) British writer.
Milordo Inglese

33 Time driveth onward fast,
And in a little while our lips are dumb.
Let us alone. What is it that will last?
All things are taken from us, and become
Portions and parcels of the dreadful Past.
Alfred, Lord Tennyson (1809–92) British poet.
The Lotos-Eaters, 'Choric Song'

34 Time is but the stream I go a-fishing in.
Henry David Thoreau (1817–62) US writer.
Walden, 'Where I Lived, and What I Lived For'

35 As if you could kill time without injuring eternity.
Henry David Thoreau
Walden, 'Economy'

36 But meanwhile it is flying, irretrievable time is flying.
Virgil (Publius Vergilius Maro; 70–19 BC) Roman poet.
Georgics, Bk. III

37 Time drops in decay,
Like a candle burnt out.
W. B. Yeats (1865–1939) Irish poet.
The Moods

38 The bell strikes one. We take no note of time
But from its loss.
Edward Young (1683–1765) British poet.
Night Thoughts

39 Time flies, death urges, knells call, heaven invites,
Hell threatens.
Edward Young
Night Thoughts

TITLES

See also aristocracy, courtesy, honour, nobility

1 As far as the 14th Earl is concerned, I suppose Mr Wilson, when you come to think of it, is the 14th Mr Wilson.
Alec Douglas-Home (1903–) British statesman.
On renouncing his peerage (as 14th Earl of Home) to become prime minister
TV interview, 21 Oct 1963

2 Madam I may not call you; mistress I am ashamed to call you; and so I know not what to call you; but howsoever, I thank you.
Elizabeth I (1533–1603) Queen of England.
Writing to the wife of the Archbishop of Canterbury, expressing her disapproval of married clergy
Brief View of the State of the Church (Harington)

3 Tyndall, I must remain plain Michael Faraday to the last; and let me now tell you, that if I accepted the honour which the Royal Society desires to confer upon me, I would not answer for the integrity of my intellect for a single year.
Michael Faraday (1791–1867) British scientist.
Said when Faraday was offered the Presidency of the Royal Society
Faraday as a Discoverer (J. Tyndall), 'Illustrations of Character'

4 Pooh-Bah (Lord High Everything Else)
W. S. Gilbert (1836–1911) British dramatist.
The Mikado, Dramatis Personae

5 I like the Garter; there is no damned merit in it.
Lord Melbourne (1779–1848) British statesman.
Lord Melbourne (H. Dunckley), 'On the Order of the Garter'

6 When I want a peerage, I shall buy one like an honest man.
Lord Northcliffe (1865–1922) Irish-born British newspaper proprietor.
Attrib.

7 Call me madame.
Francis Perkins (1882–1965) US social worker and politician.
Deciding the term of address she would prefer when made the first woman to hold a cabinet office in the USA
Familiar Quotations (J. Bartlett)

8 Mother always told me my day was coming, but I never realized that I'd end up being the shortest knight of the year.
Gordon Richards (1904–86) British champion jockey.
Referring to his diminutive size, on learning of his knighthood
Attrib.

9 Members rise from CMG (known sometimes in Whitehall as 'Call me God') to the KCMG ('Kindly Call me God') to . . . The GCMG ('God Calls me God').
Anthony Sampson (1926–) British writer and journalist.
Anatomy of Britain, Ch. 18

10 Titles distinguish the mediocre, embarrass the superior, and are disgraced by the inferior.
George Bernard Shaw (1856–1950) Irish dramatist and critic.
Man and Superman, 'Maxims for Revolutionists'

11 I've been offered titles, but I think they get one into disreputable company.
George Bernard Shaw
Gossip (A. Barrow)

12 After half a century of democratic advance, the whole process has ground to a halt with a 14th Earl.
Harold Wilson (1916–) British politician and prime minister.
Speech, Manchester, 19 Oct 1963

TOLERANCE

1 There is, however, a limit at which forbearance ceases to be a virtue.
Edmund Burke (1729–97) British politician.
Observations on a Publication, 'The Present State of the Nation'

2 It is flattering some men to endure them.
Lord Halifax (1633–95) English statesman.
Political, Moral and Miscellaneous Thoughts and Reflections

3 If you cannot mould yourself as you would wish, how can you expect other people to be entirely to your liking?
Thomas à Kempis (Thomas Hemmerken; c. 1380–1471) German monk.
The Imitation of Christ, I

4 We must respect the other fellow's religion, but only in the sense and to the extent that we respect his theory that his wife is beautiful and his children smart.
H. L. Mencken (1880–1956) US journalist.
Notebooks, 'Minority Report'

5 Steven's mind was so tolerant that he could have attended a lynching every day without becoming critical.
Thorne Smith (1892–1934) US humorist.
The Jovial Ghosts, Ch. 11

6 So long as a man rides his hobby-horse peaceably and quietly along the king's highway, and neither compels you or me to get up behind him, – pray, Sir, what have either you or I to do with it?
Laurence Sterne (1713–68) Irish-born British writer.
Tristram Shandy

7 It is because we put up with bad things that hotel-keepers continue to give them to us.
Anthony Trollope (1815–82) British novelist.
Orley Farm, Ch. 18

TRANSIENCE

See also life, mortality, time

1 Everything is only for a day, both that which remembers and that which is remembered.
Marcus Aurelius (121–180 AD) Roman emperor.
Meditations, Bk. IV, Ch. 35

2 Time is like a river made up of the events which happen, and its current is strong; no sooner does anything appear than it is swept away, and another comes in its place, and will be swept away too.
Marcus Aurelius
Meditations, Bk. IV, Ch. 43

3 Faith, Sir, we are here to-day, and gone to-morrow.
Aphra Behn (1640–89) English novelist and dramatist.
The Lucky Chance, IV

4 Vanity of vanities, saith the Preacher, vanity of vanities; all is vanity.
What profit hath a man of all his labour which he taketh under the sun?
One generation passeth away, and another generation cometh: but the earth abideth for ever.
Bible: Ecclesiastes
1:2–4

5 And I gave my heart to seek and search out by wisdom concerning all things that are done under heaven: this sore travail hath God given to the sons of man to be exercised therewith.
I have seen all the works that are done under the sun; and, behold, all is vanity and vexation of spirit.
Bible: Ecclesiastes
1:13–14

6 Whatsoever thy hand findeth to do, do it with

thy might; for there is no work, nor device, nor knowledge, nor wisdom, in the grave, whither thou goest.
Bible: Ecclesiastes
9:10

7 And behold joy and gladness, slaying oxen, and killing sheep, eating flesh, and drinking wine: let us eat and drink; for tomorrow we shall die.
Bible: Isaiah
A similar sentiment is expressed in Corinthians 15:32–33
22:13

8 Heaven and earth shall pass away, but my words shall not pass away.
Bible: Matthew
24:35

9 Suddenly, as rare things will, it vanished.
Robert Browning (1812–89) British poet.
One Word More, IV

10 Now the peak of summer's past, the sky is overcast
And the love we swore would last for an age seems deceit.
C. Day Lewis (1904–72) British poet.
Hornpipe

11 They are not long, the days of wine and roses.
Ernest Dowson (1867–1900) British lyric poet.
Vitae Summa Brevis Spem Nos Vetat Incohare Longam

12 A little rule, a little sway,
A sunbeam in a winter's day,
Is all the proud and mighty have
Between the cradle and the grave.
John Dyer (1700–58) British poet.
Grongar Hill

13 The Worldly Hope men set their Hearts upon
Turns Ashes – or it prospers; and anon,
Like Snow upon the Desert's dusty face,
Lighting a little Hour or two – is gone.
Edward Fitzgerald (1809–83) British poet.
The Rubáiyát of Omar Khayyám, XIV

14 Fair daffodils, we weep to see
You haste away so soon:
As yet the early-rising sun
Has not attain'd his noon.
Stay, stay,
Until the hasting day
Has run
But to the even-song;
And, having pray'd together, we
Will go with you along.

We have short time to stay, as you,
We have as short a Spring;
As quick a growth to meet decay,
As you or any thing.
Robert Herrick (1591–1674) English poet.
Hesperides, 'To Daffodils'

15 Not to hope for things to last for ever, is

what the year teaches and even the hour which snatches a nice day away.
Horace (Quintus Horatius Flaccus; 65–8 BC) Roman poet.
Odes, IV

16 Ships that pass in the night, and speak each other in passing;
Only a signal shown and a distant voice in the darkness;
So on the ocean of life we pass and speak one another,
Only a look and a voice; then darkness again and a silence.
Henry Wadsworth Longfellow (1807–82) US poet.
Tales of a Wayside Inn, 'The Theologian's Tale. Elizabeth'

17 But she was of the world where the fairest things have the worst fate. Like a rose, she has lived as long as roses live, the space of one morning.
François de Malherbe (1555–1628) French poet.
Consolation à M. du Périer

18 Our little systems have their day;
They have their day and cease to be.
Alfred, Lord Tennyson (1809–92) British poet.
In Memoriam A.H.H., Prologue

TRANSLATION

1 The original is unfaithful to the translation.
Jorge Luis Borges (1899–1986) Argentinian writer.
Referring to Henley's translation of Beckford's Vathek
Sobre el 'Vathek' de William Beckford

2 Translations (like wives) are seldom faithful if they are in the least attractive.
Roy Campbell (1901–57) South African poet.
Poetry Review

3 Poetry is what gets lost in translation.
Robert Frost (1875–1963) US poet.
Attrib.

4 An idea does not pass from one language to another without change.
Miguel de Unamuno y Jugo (1864–1936) Spanish writer.
The Tragic Sense of Life

5 Humour is the first of the gifts to perish in a foreign tongue.
Virginia Woolf (1882–1941) British novelist.
The Common Reader

TRAVEL

See also boats, flying

1 Travel broadens the mind.
Proverb

2 Travel, in the younger sort, is a part of education; in the elder, a part of experience.
Francis Bacon (1561–1626) English philosopher.
Essays, 'Of Travel'

3 I have recently been all round the world and have formed a very poor opinion of it.
Thomas Beecham (1879–1961) British conductor.
Speech at the Savoy
The News Review, 22 Aug 1946

4 Rumbling under blackened girders, Midland, bound for Cricklewood,
Puffed its sulphur to the sunset where the Land of Laundries stood.
Rumble under, thunder over, train and tram alternate go.
John Betjeman (1906–84) British poet.
Parliament Hill Fields

5 Before the Roman came to Rye or out to Severn strode,
The rolling English drunkard made the rolling English road.
G. K. Chesterton (1874–1936) British writer.
The Rolling English Road

6 The only way to be sure of catching a train is to miss the one before it.
G. K. Chesterton
Vacances à tous prix, 'Le Supplice de l'heure' (P. Daninos)

7 Travelling is almost like talking with men of other centuries.
René Descartes (1596–1650) French philosopher.
Le Discours de la méthode

8 How does it feel
To be without a home
Like a complete unknown
Like a rolling stone?
Bob Dylan (Robert Allen Zimmerman; 1941–) US popular singer.
Like a Rolling Stone

9 I read, much of the night, and go south in the winter.
T. S. Eliot (1888–1965) US-born British poet and dramatist.
The Waste Land, 'The Burial of the Dead'

10 The woods are lovely, dark, and deep,
But I have promises to keep,
And miles to go before I sleep,
And miles to go before I sleep.
Robert Frost (1875–1963) US poet.
Stopping by Woods on a Snowy Evening

11 He gave the impression that very many cities had rubbed him smooth.
Graham Greene (1904–) British novelist.
A Gun for Sale, Ch. 4

12 One of the pleasantest things in the world is going on a journey; but I like to go by myself.
William Hazlitt (1778–1830) British essayist.
On Going a Journey

13 They change their clime, not their frame of mind, who rush across the sea. We work hard at doing nothing: we look for happiness in boats and carriage rides. What you are

looking for is here, is at Ulubrae, if only peace of mind doesn't desert you.
Horace (Quintus Horatius Flaccus; 65–8 BC) Roman poet.
Epistles, I

14 A man who has not been in Italy, is always conscious of an inferiority, from his not having seen what it is expected a man should see. The grand object of travelling is to see the shores of the Mediterranean.
Samuel Johnson (1709–84) British lexicographer.
Life of Johnson (J. Boswell), Vol. III

15 Much have I travell'd in the realms of gold, And many goodly states and kingdoms seen.
John Keats (1795–1821) British poet.
On first looking into Chapman's Homer

16 Like Brighton pier, all right as far as it goes, but inadequate for getting to France.
Neil Kinnock (1942–) British politician.
Speech, House of Commons, 1981

17 Oh, mister porter, what shall I do?
I wanted to go to Birmingham, but they've carried me on to Crewe.
Marie Lloyd (1870–1922) British music-hall singer.
Oh, Mister Porter

18 The great and recurrent question about abroad is, is it worth getting there?
Rose Macaulay (1889–1958) British writer.
Attrib.

19 Whenever I prepare for a journey I prepare as though for death. Should I never return, all is in order. This is what life has taught me.
Katherine Mansfield (1888–1923) New-Zealand-born British writer.
The Journal of Katherine Mansfield, 1922

20 The car has become the carapace, the protective and aggressive shell, of urban and suburban man.
Marshall McLuhan (1911–81) Canadian sociologist.
Understanding Media, Ch. 22

21 It is the overtakers who keep the undertakers busy.
William Ewart Pitts (1900–) British chief constable.
The Observer, 'Sayings of the Week', 22 Dec 1963

22 Travel is the most private of pleasures. There is no greater bore than the travel bore. We do not in the least want to hear what he has seen in Hong-Kong.
Vita Sackville-West (Victoria Sackville-West; 1892–1962) British poet and novelist.
Passenger to Tehran, Ch. 1

23 A man should know something of his own country, too, before he goes abroad.
Laurence Sterne (1713–68) Irish-born British writer.
Tristram Shandy

24 Wealth I ask not; hope nor love,
Nor a friend to know me;
All I seek, the heaven above

And the road below me.
Robert Louis Stevenson (1850–94) Scottish writer.
Songs of Travel, 'The Vagabond'

25 For my part, I travel not to go anywhere,
but to go. I travel for travel's sake. The
great affair is to move.
Robert Louis Stevenson
Travels with a Donkey, 'Cheylard and Luc'

26 Yes – around Concord.
Henry David Thoreau (1817–62) US writer.
On being asked whether he had travelled much
Attrib.

27 Commuter – one who spends his life
In riding to and from his wife;
A man who shaves and takes a train,
And then rides back to shave again.
Elwyn Brooks White (1899–1985) US journalist and
humorist.
The Commuter

28 The Victorians had not been anxious to go
away for the weekend. The Edwardians, on
the contrary, were nomadic.
T. H. White (1906–64) British novelist.
Farewell Victoria, Ch. 4

TREASON

See also betrayal

1 Please to remember the Fifth of November,
Gunpowder Treason and Plot.
We know no reason why gunpowder treason
Should ever be forgot.
Anonymous
Traditional

2 During his Office, Treason was no Crime.
The Sons of Belial had a Glorious Time.
John Dryden (1631–1700) British poet and dramatist.
Absalom and Achitophel, I

3 Treason doth never prosper: what's the
reason?
For if it prosper, none dare call it treason.
John Harington (1561–1612) English writer.
Epigrams, 'Of Treason'

4 Caesar had his Brutus – Charles the First,
his Cromwell – and George the Third –
('Treason,' cried the Speaker) . . . *may profit
by their example*. If *this* be treason, make the
most of it.
Patrick Henry (1736–99) US statesman.
Speech, Virginia Convention, May 1765

TREES

See also countryside, Nature

1 And the Lord God took the man, and put him
into the garden of Eden to dress it and to
keep it.
And the Lord God commanded the man, saying, Of every tree of the garden thou mayest
freely eat:

But of the tree of the knowledge of good and
evil, thou shalt not eat of it: for in the day
that thou eatest thereof thou shalt surely die.
Bible: Genesis
2:15–17

2 O leave this barren spot to me!
Spare, woodman, spare the beechen tree.
Thomas Campbell (1777–1844) British poet.
The Beech-Tree's Petition

3 The poplars are felled, farewell to the shade,
And the whispering sound of the cool
colonnade!
William Cowper (1731–1800) British poet.
The Poplar Field

4 On Wenlock Edge the wood's in trouble;
His forest fleece the Wrekin heaves;
The gale, it plies the saplings double,
And thick on Severn snow the leaves.
A. E. Housman (1859–1936) British scholar and poet.
A Shropshire Lad, 'The Welsh Marches'

5 Loveliest of trees, the cherry now
Is hung with bloom along the bough,
And stands about the woodland ride
Wearing white for Eastertide.
A. E. Housman
A Shropshire Lad, '1887'

6 As when, upon a trancèd summer-night,
Those green-rob'd senators of mighty woods,
Tall oaks, branch-charmèd by the earnest
stars,
Dream, and so dream all night without a stir.
John Keats (1795–1821) British poet.
Hyperion, I

7 I think that I shall never see
A poem lovely as a tree.
Alfred Joyce Kilmer (1886–1918) US poet.
Trees

8 Poems are made by fools like me,
But only God can make a tree.
Alfred Joyce Kilmer
Trees

9 Yet once more, O ye laurels, and once more,
Ye myrtles brown, with ivy never sere,
I come to pluck your berries harsh and crude,
And with forced fingers rude
Shatter your leaves before the mellowing year.
John Milton (1608–74) English poet.
Lycidas

10 Woodman, spare that tree!
Touch not a single bough!
In youth it sheltered me,
And I'll protect it now.
George Pope Morris (1802–64) US journalist.
Woodman, Spare That Tree

11 I think that I shall never see
A billboard lovely as a tree.
Perhaps unless the billboards fall,

I'll never see a tree at all.
Ogden Nash (1902–71) US poet.
Song of the Open Road

12 The difference between a gun and a tree is a difference of tempo. The tree explodes every spring.
Ezra Pound (1885–1972) US poet.
Criterion, July 1937

TRIVIALITY

See also insignificance

1 Nothing matters very much, and very few things matter at all.
Arthur Balfour (1848–1930) British statesman.
Attrib.

2 A Storm in a Teacup.
W. B. Bernard (1807–75) British dramatist.
Play title

3 As she frequently remarked when she made any such mistake, it would be all the same a hundred years hence.
Charles Dickens (1812–70) British novelist.
Said by Mrs Squeers
Martin Chuzzlewit, Ch. 9

4 Little things affect little minds.
Benjamin Disraeli (1804–81) British statesman.
Sybil, Bk. III, Ch. 2

5 You know my method. It is founded upon the observance of trifles.
Arthur Conan Doyle (1856–1930) British writer.
The Boscombe Valley Mystery

6 It has long been an axiom of mine that the little things are infinitely the most important.
Arthur Conan Doyle
A Case of Identity

7 Depend upon it, there is nothing so unnatural as the commonplace.
Arthur Conan Doyle
A Case of Identity

8 'Is there any point to which you would wish to draw my attention?'
'To the curious incident of the dog in the night-time.'
'The dog did nothing in the night-time.'
'That was the curious incident,' remarked Sherlock Holmes.
Arthur Conan Doyle
The Silver Blaze

9 To great evils we submit; we resent little provocations.
William Hazlitt (1778–1830) British essayist.
On Great and Little Things

10 Little minds are interested in the extraordinary; great minds in the commonplace.
Elbert Hubbard (1856–1915) US writer.
Roycroft Dictionary and Book of Epigrams

11 What should I do? I think the best thing is to order a new stamp to be made with my face on it.
Charles Francis Joseph (1887–1922) Emperor of Austria.
On hearing of his accession to emperor
Anekdotenschatz (H. Hoffmeister)

12 To suckle fools and chronicle small beer.
William Shakespeare (1564–1616) English dramatist.
Othello, II:1

13 It's deadly commonplace, but, after all, the commonplaces are the great poetic truths.
Robert Louis Stevenson (1850–94) Scottish writer.
Weir of Hermiston, Ch. 6

14 Ah God! the petty fools of rhyme
That shriek and sweat in pigmy wars.
Alfred, Lord Tennyson (1809–92) British poet.
Literary Squabbles

TRUST

See also faith, mistrust

1 Trust ye not in a friend, put ye not confidence in a guide: keep the doors of thy mouth from her that lieth in thy bosom.
Bible: Micah
7:5

2 Never trust the man who hath reason to suspect that you know he hath injured you.
Henry Fielding (1707–54) British novelist.
Jonathan Wild, Bk III, Ch. 4

3 We are inclined to believe those whom we do not know because they have never deceived us.
Samuel Johnson (1709–84) British lexicographer.
The Idler

4 Never trust a husband too far, nor a bachelor too near.
Helen Rowland (1876–1950) US writer.
The Rubaiyat of a Bachelor

5 Would you buy a second-hand car from this man?
Mort Sahl (1926–) US political comedian.
Referring to President Nixon
Attrib.

TRUTH

See also facts, frankness, honesty, lying, sincerity

1 Better a lie that heals than a truth that wounds.
Proverb

2 Many a true word is spoken in jest.
Proverb

3 Tell the truth and shame the devil.
Proverb

4 Truth fears no trial.
Proverb

5 Truth is stranger than fiction.
Proverb

6 Truth will out.
Proverb

7 The truth that makes men free is for the most part the truth which men prefer not to hear.
Herbert Sebastian Agar (1897–1980) US writer.
A Time for Greatness

8 Plato is dear to me, but dearer still is truth.
Aristotle (384–322 BC) Greek philosopher.
Attrib.

9 Truth sits upon the lips of dying men.
Matthew Arnold (1822–88) British poet and critic.
Sohrab and Rustum

10 What is truth? said jesting Pilate, and would not stay for an answer.
Francis Bacon (1561–1626) English philosopher.
Essays, 'Of Truth'

11 And ye shall know the truth, and the truth shall make you free.
Bible: John
8:32

12 Pilate saith unto him, What is truth? And when he had said this, he went out again unto the Jews, and saith unto them, I find in him no fault at all.
Bible: John
18:38

13 A truth that's told with bad intent
Beats all the lies you can invent.
William Blake (1757–1827) British poet.
Auguries of Innocence

14 To treat your facts with imagination is one thing, to imagine your facts is another.
John Burroughs (1837–1921) US naturalist.
The Heart of Burroughs Journals

15 Some men love truth so much that they seem to be in continual fear lest she should catch a cold on overexposure.
Samuel Butler (1835–1902) British writer.
Notebooks

16 Agree to a short armistice with truth.
Lord Byron (1788–1824) British poet.
Don Juan, III

17 'Tis strange – but true; for truth is always strange;
Stranger than fiction: if it could be told,
How much would novels gain by the exchange!
Lord Byron
Don Juan, XIV

18 You can only find truth with logic if you have already found truth without it.
G. K. Chesterton (1874–1936) British writer.
The Man who was Orthodox

19 Much truth is spoken, that more may be concealed.
Lord Darling (1849–1936) British judge.
Scintillae Juris

20 Perjury is often bold and open. It is truth that is shamefaced – as, indeed, in many cases is no more than decent.
Lord Darling
Scintillae Juris

21 It is an old maxim of mine that when you have excluded the impossible, whatever remains, however improbable, must be the truth.
Arthur Conan Doyle (1856–1930) British writer.
The Beryl Coronet

22 Errors, like Straws, upon the surface flow;
He who would search for Pearls must dive below.
John Dryden (1631–1700) British poet and dramatist.
All for Love, Prologue

23 A man is to be cheated into passion, but to be reasoned into truth.
John Dryden
Religio Laici, Preface

24 Ethical axioms are found and tested not very differently from the axioms of science. Truth is what stands the test of experience.
Albert Einstein (1879–1955) German-born US physicist.
Out of My Later Years

25 Truth, like a torch, the more it's shook it shines.
William Hamilton (1788–1856) Scottish philosopher.
Discussions on Philosophy, title page

26 True and False are attributes of speech, not of things. And where speech is not, there is neither Truth nor Falsehood.
Thomas Hobbes (1588–1679) English philosopher.
Leviathan, Pt. I, Ch. 4

27 It's easy to make a man confess the lies he tells to himself; it's far harder to make him confess the truth.
Geoffrey Household (1900–) British writer.
Rogue Male

28 I am certain of nothing but the holiness of the heart's affections and the truth of imagination – what the imagination seizes as beauty must be truth – whether it existed before or not.
John Keats (1795–1821) British poet.
Letter to Benjamin Bailey, 22 Nov 1817

29 I never can feel certain of any truth but from a clear perception of its beauty.
John Keats
Letter to George and Georgiana Keats, 16 Dec 1818–4 Jan 1819

30 'Beauty is truth, truth beauty,' – that is all

Ye know on earth, and all ye need to know.
John Keats
Ode on a Grecian Urn

31 It is one thing to show a man that he is in an error, and another to put him in possession of truth.
John Locke (1632–1704) English philosopher.
An Essay Concerning Human Understanding, Bk. IV, Ch. 7

32 Let her and Falsehood grapple; who ever knew Truth put to the worse, in a free and open encounter?
John Milton (1608–74) English poet.
Areopagitica

33 There can be no whitewash at the White House.
Richard Milhous Nixon (1913–) US president.
Referring to the Watergate scandal
The Observer, 'Sayings of the Week', 30 Dec 1973

34 Let us begin by committing ourselves to the truth, to see it like it is and to tell it like it is, to find the truth, to speak the truth and live with the truth. That's what we'll do.
Richard Milhous Nixon
Nomination acceptance speech, Miami, 8 Aug 1968

35 Truth has no special time of its own. Its hour is now – always.
Albert Schweitzer (1875–1965) French Protestant theologian, philosopher, physician, and musician.
Out of My Life and Thought

36 Truth telling is not compatible with the defence of the realm.
George Bernard Shaw (1856–1950) Irish dramatist and critic.
Heartbreak House

37 My way of joking is to tell the truth. It's the funniest joke in the world.
George Bernard Shaw
John Bull's Other Island, II

38 When truth is discovered by someone else, it loses something of its attractiveness.
Alexander Solzhenitsyn (1918–) Soviet novelist.
Candle in the Wind, 3

39 It takes two to speak the truth – one to speak, and another to hear.
Henry David Thoreau (1817–62) US writer.
A Week on the Concord and Merrimack Rivers

40 The only truths which are universal are those gross enough to be thought so.
Paul Valéry (1871–1945) French poet and writer.
Mauvaises Pensées et autres

41 But not even Marx is more precious to us than the truth.
Simone Weil (1909–43) French philosopher.
Oppression and Liberty, 'Revolution Proletarienne'

42 There are no whole truths; all truths are half-truths. It is trying to treat them as whole truths that plays the devil.
A. N. Whitehead (1861–1947) British philosopher.
Dialogues, 16

43 I believe that in the end the truth will conquer.
John Wycliffe (1329–84) English religious reformer.
Said to John of Gaunt, Duke of Lancaster, 1381
Short History of the English People (J. R. Green)

44 Truth is on the march; nothing can stop it now.
Émile Zola (1840–1902) French novelist.
Referring to the Dreyfus scandal
Attrib.

TYRANNY

See also authoritarianism, oppression

1 Nature has left this tincture in the blood,
That all men would be tyrants if they could.
Daniel Defoe (1660–1731) British journalist and writer.
The Kentish Petition, Addenda

2 'Twixt kings and tyrants there's this difference known;
Kings seek their subjects' good: tyrants their own.
Robert Herrick (1591–1674) English poet.
Hesperides, 'Kings and Tyrants'

3 A country governed by a despot is an inverted cone.
Samuel Johnson (1709–84) British lexicographer.
Life of Johnson (J. Boswell), Vol. III

4 It is better that a man should tyrannize over his bank balance than over his fellow citizens.
John Maynard Keynes (1883–1946) British economist.
The General Theory of Employment, Interest and Money, Bk. VI, Ch. 24

5 Where laws end, tyranny begins.
William Pitt the Elder (1708–78) British statesman.
Speech, House of Lords, referring to the Wilkes case, 9 Jan 1770

U

UNCERTAINTY

See also doubt, indecision

1 If ifs and ans were pots and pans, there'd be no trade for tinkers.
Proverb

2 I have known uncertainty: a state unknown to the Greeks.
Jorge Luis Borges (1899–1986) Argentinian writer.
Ficciones, 'The Babylonian Lottery'

3 Of course not. After all, I may be wrong.

Bertrand Russell (1872–1970) British philosopher.
On being asked whether he would be prepared to die for his beliefs
Attrib.

UNDERSTANDING

See also intelligence, wisdom

1   And come hither, and I shall light a candle of understanding in thine heart, which shall not be put out, till the things be performed which thou shalt begin to write.
Bible: II Esdras
14:25

2   It is good to know what a man is, and also what the world takes him for. But you do not understand him until you have learnt how he understands himself.
F. H. Bradley (1846–1924) British philosopher.
Aphorisms

3   The people may be made to follow a course of action, but they may not be made to understand it.
Confucius (K'ung Fu-tzu; 551–479 BC) Chinese philosopher.
Analects

4   Only one man ever understood me. . . . And he didn't understand me.
Hegel (1770–1831) German philosopher.
Said on his deathbed
Famous Last Words (B. Conrad)

5   Even when poetry has a meaning, as it usually has, it may be inadvisable to draw it out . . . Perfect understanding will sometimes almost extinguish pleasure.
A. E. Housman (1859–1936) British scholar and poet.
The Name and Nature of Poetry

6   Thought must be divided against itself before it can come to any knowledge of itself.
Aldous Huxley (1894–1964) British novelist.
Do What You Will

7   She did her work with the thoroughness of a mind that reveres details and never quite understands them.
Sinclair Lewis (1885–1951) US novelist.
Babbitt, Ch. 18

8   I used to tell my husband that, if he could make me understand something, it would be clear to all the other people in the country.
Eleanor Roosevelt (1884–1962) US writer and lecturer.
Newspaper column, 'My Day', 12 Feb 1947

9   I have striven not to laugh at human actions, not to weep at them, nor to hate them, but to understand them.
Benedict Spinoza (Baruch de Spinoza; 1632–77) Dutch philosopher.
Tractatus Theologico-Politicus, Ch. 1

10   All, everything that I understand, I understand only because I love.
Leo Tolstoy (1828–1910) Russian writer.
War and Peace, Bk. VII, Ch. 16

UNEMPLOYMENT

See also idleness, work

1   My father did not wait around . . . he got on his bike and went out looking for work.
Norman Tebbitt (1931–) British Conservative politician.
Speech, Conservative Party conference, 1981

2   It's a recession when your neighbour loses his job; it's a depression when you lose your own.
Harry S. Truman (1884–1972) US statesman.
The Observer, 'Sayings of the Week', 6 Apr 1958

3   Something must be done.
Duke of Windsor (1894–1972) King of the United Kingdom; abdicated 1936.
Said while visiting areas of high unemployment in South Wales during the 1930s
Attrib.

UNFAITHFULNESS

See also adultery

1   Swore to be true to each other, true as the stars above;
He was her man, but he done her wrong.
Anonymous
Frankie and Johnny

2   But I kissed her little sister,
And forgot my Clementine.
Percy Montrose (19th century) US songwriter.
Clementine

3   O, swear not by the moon, th' inconstant moon,
That monthly changes in her circled orb,
Lest that thy love prove likewise variable.
William Shakespeare (1564–1616) English dramatist.
Romeo and Juliet, II:2

4   His honour rooted in dishonour stood,
And faith unfaithful kept him falsely true.
Alfred, Lord Tennyson (1809–92) British poet.
Idylls of the King, 'Lancelot and Elaine'

5   No man worth having is true to his wife, or can be true to his wife, or ever was, or ever will be so.
John Vanbrugh (1664–1726) English architect and dramatist.
The Relapse, III:2

UNITY

1   A chain is no stronger than its weakest link.
Proverb

2 Union is strength.
Proverb

3 United we stand, divided we fall.
Proverb

4 That typically English characteristic for which there is no English name – *esprit de corps*.
Frank Ezra Adcock (1886–1968) British classicist.
Presidential address

5 And if one prevail against him, two shall withstand him; and a threefold cord is not quickly broken.
Bible: Ecclesiastes
4:12

6 And the whole earth was of one language, and of one speech.
Bible: Genesis
11:1

7 When bad men combine, the good must associate; else they will fall one by one, an unpitied sacrifice in a contemptible struggle.
Edmund Burke (1729–97) British politician.
Thoughts on the Cause of the Present Discontents

8 All for one, and one for all.
Alexandre Dumas, père (1802–70) French novelist and dramatist.
The Three Musketeers

9 We must indeed all hang together, or most assuredly, we shall all hang separately.
Benjamin Franklin (1706–90) US scientist and statesman.
Remark on signing the Declaration of Independence, 4 July 1776

10 Everyone has observed how much more dogs are animated when they hunt in a pack, than when they pursue their game apart. We might, perhaps, be at a loss to explain this phenomenon, if we had not experience of a similar in ourselves.
David Hume (1711–76) Scottish philosopher.
A Treatise of Human Nature

11 Now, is it to lower the price of corn, or isn't it? It is not much matter which we say, but mind, we must all say *the same*.
Lord Melbourne (1779–1848) British statesman.
Said at a cabinet meeting
The English Constitution (Bagehot), Ch. 1

UNIVERSE

See also astronomy, moon, space, stars, sun, world

1 Had I been present at the Creation, I would have given some useful hints for the better ordering of the universe.
Alfonso the Wise (c. 1221–84) King of Castile and León.
Referring to the complicated Ptolemaic model of the universe. Often quoted as, 'Had I been consulted I would have recommended something simpler'.
Attrib.

2 The visible universe was an illusion or, more precisely, a sophism. Mirrors and fatherhood are abominable because they multiply it and extend it.
Jorge Luis Borges (1899–1986) Argentinian writer.
Ficciones, 'Tlön, Uqbar, Orbis Tertius'

3 I don't pretend to understand the Universe – it's a great deal bigger than I am . . . People ought to be modester.
Thomas Carlyle (1795–1881) Scottish historian and essayist.
Attrib.

4 MARGARET FULLER. I accept the universe.
CARLYLE. Gad! she'd better!
Thomas Carlyle
Attrib.

5 The cosmos is about the smallest hole that a man can hide his head in.
G. K. Chesterton (1874–1936) British writer.
Orthodoxy, Ch. 1

6 I am very interested in the Universe – I am specializing in the universe and all that surrounds it.
Peter Cook (1937–) British writer and entertainer.
Beyond the Fringe

7 My own suspicion is that the universe is not only queerer than we suppose, but queerer than we *can* suppose.
J. B. S. Haldane (1892–1964) British geneticist.
Possible Worlds, 'On Being the Right Size'

8 The universe is not hostile, nor yet is it friendly. It is simply indifferent.
John Haynes Holmes (1879–1964) US clergyman.
A Sensible Man's View of Religion

9 The universe begins to look more like a great thought than like a great machine.
James Jeans (1877–1946) British scientist.
The Mysterious Universe

10 The universe ought to be presumed too vast to have any character.
C. S. Peirce (1839–1914) US physicist.
Collected Papers, VI

V

VENICE

See also Europe

1 Streets full of water. Please advise.
Robert Benchley (1889–1945) US humorist.
Telegram sent to his editor on arriving in Venice
Attrib.

2 Venice is like eating an entire box of chocolate liqueurs at one go.
Truman Capote (1924–84) US novelist.
The Observer, 'Sayings of the Week', 26 Nov 1961

3 Venice, the eldest Child of Liberty.
She was a maiden City, bright and free.
William Wordsworth (1770–1850) British poet.
Venice, a republic since the Middle Ages, was conquered by Napoleon in 1797 and absorbed into his Kingdom of Italy in 1805
Sonnets, 'Once did she hold'

4 Once did she hold the gorgeous east in fee;
And was the safeguard of the west.
William Wordsworth
Sonnets, 'Once did she hold'

5 When she took unto herself a mate,
She must espouse the everlasting sea.
William Wordsworth
Sonnets, 'Once did she hold'

VERBOSITY

See also brevity, sermons, speech, speeches, writing

1 There was a young man of Japan
Whose limericks never would scan;
When they said it was so,
He replied, 'Yes, I know,
But I always try to get as many words into the last line as ever I possibly can.'
Anonymous

2 A sophistical rhetorician inebriated with the exuberance of his own verbosity.
Benjamin Disraeli (1804–81) British statesman.
Referring to Gladstone
Speech, 27 July 1878

3 But far more numerous was the Herd of such,
Who think too little, and who talk too much.
John Dryden (1631–1700) British poet and dramatist.
Absalom and Achitophel, I

4 Nothing is more despicable than a professional talker who uses his words as a quack uses his remedies.
Françços Fénelon (1651–1715) French writer and prelate.
Letter to M. Dacier

5 I have made this letter longer than usual, only because I have not had the time to make it shorter.
Blaise Pascal (1623–62) French philosopher and mathematician.
Lettres provinciales, XVI

6 Words are like leaves; and where they most abound,
Much fruit of sense beneath is rarely found.
Alexander Pope (1688–1744) British poet.
An Essay on Criticism

VICE

See also crime, evil, sin, virtue and vice

1 When vice prevails, and impious men bear sway,
The post of honour is a private station.
Joseph Addison (1672–1719) British essayist.
Cato, IV:1

2 We make ourselves a ladder out of our vices if we trample the vices themselves underfoot.
St Augustine of Hippo (354–430) Bishop of Hippo.
Sermons, Bk. III, 'De Ascensione'

3 Often the fear of one evil leads us into a worse.
Nicolas Boileau (1636–1711) French writer.
L'Art poétique, I

4 The wickedness of the world is so great you have to run your legs off to avoid having them stolen from under you.
Bertolt Brecht (1898–1956) German dramatist.
The Threepenny Opera, I:3

5 Vice itself lost half its evil, by losing all its grossness.
Edmund Burke (1729–97) British politician.
Reflections on the Revolution in France

6 Vice is its own reward.
Quentin Crisp (c. 1910–) Model, publicist, and writer.
The Naked Civil Servant

7 In my time, the follies of the town crept slowly among us, but now they travel faster than a stagecoach.
Oliver Goldsmith (1728–74) Irish-born British writer.
She Stoops to Conquer, I

8 Wrongdoing can only be avoided if those who are not wronged feel the same indignation at it as those who are.
Solon (6th century BC) Athenian statesman.
Greek Wit (F. Paley)

9 Whenever I'm caught between two evils, I take the one I've never tried.
Mae West (1892–1980) US actress.
Attrib.

10 Never support two weaknesses at the same time. It's your combination sinners – your lecherous liars and your miserly drunkards – who dishonour the vices and bring them into bad repute.
Thornton Wilder (1897–1975) US novelist and dramatist.
The Matchmaker, III

VICTORY

See also war

1 *Veni, vidi, vici.*
I came, I saw, I conquered.
Julius Caesar (100–44 BC) Roman general and statesman.
The Twelve Caesars (Suetonius)

2 Victory at all costs, victory in spite of all

terror, victory however long and hard the road may be; for without victory there is no survival.

Winston Churchill (1874–1965) British statesman.
Speech, House of Commons, 13 May 1940

3 We triumph without glory when we conquer without danger.

Pierre Corneille (1606–84) French dramatist.
Le Cid, II:2

4 The most important thing in the Olympic Games is not winning but taking part . . . The essential thing in life is not conquering but fighting well.

Pierre de Coubertin (1863–1937) French educator and sportsman.
Speech, Banquet to Officials of Olympic Games, London, 24 July 1908

5 A game which a sharper once played with a dupe, entitled 'Heads I win, tails you lose.'

John Wilson Croker (1780–1857) British Tory politician.
Croker Papers

6 The happy state of getting the victor's palm without the dust of racing.

Horace (Quintus Horatius Flaccus; 65–8 BC) Roman poet.
Epistles, I

7 They talk about who won and who lost. Human reason won. Mankind won.

Nikita Khrushchev (1894–1971) Soviet statesman.
Referring to the Cuban missiles crisis
The Observer, 'Sayings of the Week', 11 Nov 1962

8 Winning isn't everything, but wanting to win is.

Vince Lombardi (1913–70) US football coach.

9 How vainly men themselves amaze
To win the palm, the oak, or bays.

Andrew Marvell (1621–78) English poet.
The Garden

10 Who overcomes
By force, hath overcome but half his foe.

John Milton (1608–74) English poet.
Paradise Lost, Bk. I

11 See, the conquering hero comes!
Sound the trumpets, beat the drums!

Thomas Morell (1703–84) British classicist.
The libretto for Handel's oratorio
Joshua, Pt. III

12 We have met the enemy, and they are ours.

Oliver Hazard Perry (1785–1819) US naval officer.
Message sent reporting his victory in a naval battle on Lake Erie
Familiar Quotations (J. Bartlett)

13 Such another victory and we are ruined.

Pyrrhus (319–272 BC) King of Epirus.
Commenting upon the costliness of his victory at the Battle of Asculum, 279 BC
Life of Pyrrhus (Plutarch)

14 For when the One Great Scorer comes

To write against your name,
He marks – not that you won or lost –
But how you played the game.

Grantland Rice (1880–1954) US sportswriter.
Alumnus Football

15 I came; I saw; God conquered.

John III Sobieski (1624–96) King of Poland.
Announcing his victory over the Turks at Vienna to the pope (paraphrasing Caesar's 'veni, vidi, vici')
Attrib.

16 'And everybody praised the Duke,
Who this great fight did win.'
'But what good came of it at last?'
Quoth little Peterkin.
'Why that I cannot tell,' said he,
'But 'twas a famous victory.'

Robert Southey (1774–1843) British poet.
The Battle of Blenheim

17 The next greatest misfortune to losing a battle is to gain such a victory as this.

Duke of Wellington (1769–1852) British general and statesman.
Recollections (S. Rogers)

18 I always say that, next to a battle lost, the greatest misery is a battle gained.

Duke of Wellington
Diary (Frances, Lady Shelley)

19 By the splendour of God I have taken possession of my realm; the earth of England is in my two hands.

William the Conqueror (1027–87) King of England.
Said after falling over when coming ashore at Pevensey with his army of invasion
Attrib.

VIOLENCE

See also cruelty, force

1 A bit of shooting takes your mind off your troubles – it makes you forget the cost of living.

Brendan Behan (1923–64) Irish playwright.
The Hostage

2 So soon as the man overtook me, he was but a word and a blow.

John Bunyan (1628–88) English writer.
The Pilgrim's Progress, Pt. I

3 Two lovely black eyes,
Oh, what a surprise!
Only for telling a man he was wrong.
Two lovely black eyes!

Charles Coborn (1852–1945) US songwriter.
Two Lovely Black Eyes

4 It's possible to disagree with someone about the ethics of non-violence without wanting to kick his face in.

Christopher Hampton (1946–) British writer and dramatist.
Treats, Sc. 4

5 We are effectively destroying ourselves by violence masquerading as love.

R. D. Laing (1927–) British psychiatrist.
The Politics of Experience, Ch. 13

6 If you strike a child, take care that you strike it in anger, even at the risk of maiming it for life. A blow in cold blood neither can nor should be forgiven.

George Bernard Shaw (1856–1950) Irish dramatist and critic.
Man and Superman, 'Maxims for Revolutionists'

VIRTUE

See also good, morality, purity, righteousness, virtue and vice

1 Virtue is like a rich stone, best plain set.

Francis Bacon (1561–1626) English philosopher.
Essays, 'Of Beauty'

2 As in nature things move violently to their place and calmly in their place, so virtue in ambition is violent, in authority settled and calm.

Francis Bacon
Essays, 'Of Great Place'

3 A good name is better than precious ointment; and the day of death than the day of one's birth.
It is better to go to the house of mourning, than to go to the house of feasting: for that is the end of all men; and the living will lay it to his heart.

Bible: Ecclesiastes
7:1–2

4 Finally, brethren, whatsoever things are true, whatsoever things are honest, whatsoever things are just, whatsoever things are pure, whatsoever things are lovely, whatsoever things are of good report; if there be any virtue; and if there be any praise, think on these things.

Bible: Philippians
4:8

5 Virtue consisted in avoiding scandal and venereal disease.

Robert Cecil (1913–) British writer.
Life in Edwardian England

6 My virtue's still far too small, I don't trot it out and about yet.

Colette (1873–1954) French novelist.
Claudine at School

7 To be able to practise five things everywhere under heaven constitutes perfect virtue . . . gravity, generosity of soul, sincerity, earnestness, and kindness.

Confucius (K'ung Fu-tzu; 551–479 BC) Chinese philosopher.
Analects

8 Good, but not religious-good.

Thomas Hardy (1840–1928) British novelist.
Under the Greenwood Tree, Ch. 2

9 The greatest offence against virtue is to speak ill of it.

William Hazlitt (1778–1830) British essayist.
On Cant and Hypocrisy

10 Only a sweet and virtuous soul,
Like season'd timber, never gives;
But though the whole world turn to coal,
Then chiefly lives.

George Herbert (1593–1633) English poet.
Virtue

11 Be good, sweet maid, and let who can be clever;
Do lovely things, not dream them, all day long;
And so make Life, and Death, and that For Ever,
One grand sweet song.

Charles Kingsley (1819–75) British writer.
A Farewell. To C. E. G.

12 To be discontented with the divine discontent, and to be ashamed with the noble shame, is the very germ and first upgrowth of all virtue.

Charles Kingsley
Health and Education

13 Most men admire
Virtue, who follow not her lore.

John Milton (1608–74) English poet.
Paradise Regained, Bk. I

14 When men grow virtuous in their old age, they only make a sacrifice to God of the devil's leavings.

Alexander Pope (1688–1744) British poet.
Thoughts on Various Subjects

VIRTUE AND VICE

See also good and evil, vice, virtue

1 ·Our virtues and vices couple with one another, and get children that resemble both their parents.

Lord Halifax (1633–95) English statesman.
Political, Moral and Miscellaneous Thoughts and Reflections

2 Most usually our virtues are only vices in disguise.

Duc de la Rochefoucauld (1613–80) French writer.
Maximes, added to the 4th edition

3 Vice and virtues are products like sulphuric acid and sugar.

Hippolyte Adolphe Taine (1828–93) French writer and philosopher.
Histoire de la littérature anglaise, Introduction

VULGARITY

See also humour

1 You gotta have a swine to show you where the truffles are.

Edward Albee (1928–) US dramatist.
Who's Afraid of Virginia Woolf?, I

2 The aristocratic pleasure of displeasing is not the only delight that bad taste can yield. One can love a certain kind of vulgarity for its own sake.
Aldous Huxley (1894–1964) British novelist.
Vulgarity in Literature, Ch. 4

3 That fellow would vulgarize the day of judgment.
Douglas William Jerrold (1803–57) British dramatist.
Wit and Opinions of Douglas Jerrold, 'A Comic Author'

4 With our James vulgarity begins at home, and should be allowed to stay there.
Oscar Wilde (1854–1900) Irish-born British dramatist.
Referring to the artist James Whistler
Letter to the *World*

5 I can't stand a naked light bulb, any more than I can a rude remark or a vulgar action.
Tennessee Williams (1911–83) US dramatist.
A Streetcar Named Desire, II:3

W

WALES

See also Britain, Welsh

1 The thing I value about Wales and Welsh background is that it has always been a genuinely more classless society than many people present England as being.
Geoffrey Howe (1926–) British politician.
The Observer, 'Sayings of the Week', 9 Nov 1986

2 The land of my fathers. My fathers can have it.
Dylan Thomas (1914–53) Welsh poet.
Referring to Wales
Dylan Thomas (John Ackerman)

3 Too many of the artists of Wales spend too much time about the position of the artist of Wales. There is only one position for an artist anywhere: and that is, upright.
Dylan Thomas
New Statesman, 18 Dec 1964

4 Make me content
With some sweetness
From Wales
Whose nightingales
Have no wings.
Edward Thomas (1878–1917) British poet.
Words

5 We can trace almost all the disasters of English history to the influence of Wales.
Evelyn Waugh (1903–66) British novelist.
Decline and Fall, Pt. I, Ch. 8

WAR

See also army, Cold War, defeat, navy, nuclear weapons, officers, patriotism, soldiers, victory, war and peace, weapons, World War II

1 Give them the cold steel, boys!
Lewis Addison Arminstead (1817–63) US general.
Exhortation given to his troops during the US Civil War
Attrib.

2 And we are here as on a darkling plain
Swept with confused alarms of struggle and flight,
Where ignorant armies clash by night.
Matthew Arnold (1822–88) British poet and critic.
Dover Beach

3 To save your world you asked this man to die:
Would this man, could he see you now, ask why?
W. H. Auden (1907–73) British poet.
Epitaph for an Unknown Soldier

4 Well, if you knows of a better 'ole, go to it.
Bruce Bairnsfather (1888–1959) British cartoonist.
Fragments from France

5 The only defence is in offence, which means that you have to kill more women and children more quickly than the enemy if you want to save yourselves.
Stanley Baldwin (1867–1947) British statesman.
Speech, Nov 1932

6 I have never understood this liking for war. It panders to instincts already catered for within the scope of any respectable domestic establishment.
Alan Bennett (1934–) British playwright.
Forty Years On, I

7 And ye shall hear of wars and rumours of wars: see that ye be not troubled: for all these things must come to pass, but the end is not yet.
For nation shall rise against nation, and kingdom against kingdom: and there shall be famines, and pestilences, and earthquakes, in divers places.
All these are the beginning of sorrows.
Bible: Matthew
24:6–8

8 Then said Jesus unto him, Put up again thy sword into his place: for all they that take the sword shall perish with the sword.
Bible: Matthew
26:52

9 If there is ever another war in Europe, it will come out of some damned silly thing in the Balkans.
Bismarck (1815–98) German statesman.
Remark to Ballen, shortly before Bismarck's death

10 *C'est magnifique, mais ce n'est pas la guerre.*

It is magnificent, but it is not war.
Pierre Bosquet (1810–61) French marshal.
Referring to the Charge of the Light Brigade at the Battle of
Balaclava, 25 Oct 1854
Attrib.

11 The wrong war, at the wrong place, at the
wrong time, and with the wrong enemy.
Omar Nelson Bradley (1893–1981) US general.
Said in evidence to a Senate inquiry, May 1951, over a proposal by MacArthur that the Korean war should be extended
into China

12 What they could do with round here is a
good war.
Bertolt Brecht (1898–1956) German dramatist.
Mother Courage, I

13 A war of which we could say it left nothing
to be desired will probably never exist.
Bertolt Brecht
Mother Courage, VI

14 War is like love, it always finds a way.
Bertolt Brecht
Mother Courage, VI

15 The Angel of Death has been abroad
throughout the land: you may almost hear the
beating of his wings.
John Bright (1811–89) British radical politician.
Referring to the Crimean War
Speech, House of Commons, 23 Feb 1855

16 If I should die, think only this of me:
That there's some corner of a foreign field
That is forever England.
Rupert Brooke (1887–1915) British poet.
The Soldier

17 War knows no power. Safe shall be my
going,
Secretly armed against all death's endeavour;
Safe though all safety's lost; safe where men
fall;
And if these poor limbs die, safest of all.
Rupert Brooke
Safety

18 Scots, wha hae wi' Wallace bled,
Scots, wham Bruce has aften led,
Welcome to your gory bed,
Or to victorie.
Robert Burns (1759–96) Scottish poet.
Scots, Wha Hae

19 When civil fury first grew high,
And men fell out they knew not why.
Samuel Butler (1612–80) English satirist.
Hudibras, Pt. I

20 War, war is still the cry, 'War even to the
knife!'
Lord Byron (1788–1824) British poet.
Childe Harold's Pilgrimage, I

21 Tweedledum and Tweedledee
Agreed to have a battle;

For Tweedledum said Tweedledee
Had spoiled his nice new rattle.
Lewis Carroll (Charles Lutwidge Dodgson; 1832–98)
British writer.
Through the Looking-Glass, Ch. 4

22 Carthage must be destroyed.
Cato the Elder (Marcius Porcius C; 234–149 BC) Roman
statesman.
Life of Cato (Plutarch)

23 In war, whichever side may call itself the
victor, there are no winners, but all are
losers.
Neville Chamberlain (1869–1940) British statesman.
Speech, Kettering, 3 July 1938

24 Wars, conflict, it's all business. One murder
makes a villain. Millions a hero. Numbers
sanctify.
Charlie Chaplin (Sir Charles Spencer C.; 1889–1977)
British film actor.
Monsieur Verdoux

25 The redress of the grievances of the
vanquished should precede the disarmament
of the victors.
Winston Churchill (1874–1965) British statesman.
The Gathering Storm, Ch. 3

26 I said that the world must be made safe for
at least fifty years. If it was only for fifteen
to twenty years then we should have
betrayed our soldiers.
Winston Churchill
Closing the Ring, Ch. 20

27 No one can guarantee success in war, but
only deserve it.
Winston Churchill
Their Finest Hour

28 War is the continuation of politics by other
means.
Karl von Clausewitz (1780–1831) Prussian general.
The usual misquotation of 'War is nothing but a continuation of
politics with the admixture of other means'
Vom Kriege

29 Now, gentlemen, let us do something today
which the world may talk of hereafter.
Lord Collingwood (1750–1810) British admiral.
Said before Trafalgar, 21 Oct 1805
Correspondence and Memoir of Lord Collingwood (G. L. Newn-
ham; ed. Collingwood)

30 Come on, you sons of bitches! Do you want
to live for ever?
Dan Daly (20th century) Sergeant in the US Marines.
Remark during Allied resistance at Belleau Wood, June 1918.
See also FREDERICK THE GREAT
Attrib.

31 If we lose this war, I'll start another in my
wife's name.
Moshe Dayan (1915–81) Israeli general.
Attrib.

32 There is plenty of time to win this game, and to thrash the Spaniards too.

Francis Drake (1540–96) British navigator.
Referring to the sighting of the Armada during a game of bowls, 20 July 1588
Attrib.

33 I have singed the Spanish king's beard.

Francis Drake
Referring to the raid on Cadiz harbour, 1587
Attrib.

34 We are not at war with Egypt. We are in an armed conflict.

Anthony Eden (1897–1977) British statesman.
Speech, House of Commons, 4 Nov 1956

35 My centre is giving way, my right is in retreat; situation excellent. I shall attack.

Marshal Foch (1851–1929) French soldier.
Message sent during the second battle of the Marne, 1918
Biography of Foch (Aston), Ch. 13

36 Praise the Lord and pass the ammunition!

Howell Maurice Forgy (1908–) US naval lieutenant.
Remark made during the Japanese attack on Pearl Harbor, 7 Dec 1941
Attrib. in *The Los Angeles Times*

37 I got there fustest with the mostest.

Nathan Bedford Forrest (1821–77) Confederate general.
Popular misquotation of his explanation of his success in capturing Murfreesboro; his actual words were, 'I just took the short cut and got there first with the most men'
A Civil War Treasury (B. Botkin)

38 Rascals, would you live for ever?

Frederick the Great (1712–86) King of Prussia.
Addressed to reluctant soldiers at the Battle of Kolin, 18 June 1757. *See also* DALY

39 Madam, I am the civilization they are fighting to defend.

Heathcote William Garrod (1878–1960) British classical scholar.
Replying to criticism that he was not fighting to defend civilization, during World War I
Oxford Now and Then (D. Balsdon)

40 I have many times asked myself whether there can be more potent advocates of peace upon earth through the years to come than this massed multitude of silent witnesses to the desolation of war.

George V (1865–1936) King of the United Kingdom.
Referring to the massed World War I graves in Flanders, 1922
Silent Cities (ed. Gavin Stamp)

41 You've got to forget about this civilian. Whenever you drop bombs, you're going to hit civilians.

Barry Goldwater (1904–) US politician.
Speech, New York, 23 Jan 1967

42 No terms except unconditional and immediate surrender can be accepted. I propose to move immediately upon your works.

Ulysses Simpson Grant (1822–85) US general.
Message to opposing commander, Simon Bolivar Buckner, during siege of Fort Donelson, 16 Feb 1862

43 Every position must be held to the last man: there must be no retirement. With our backs to the wall, and believing in the justice of our cause, each one of us must fight on to the end.

Earl Haig (1861–1928) British general.
Order to the British Army, 12 Apr 1918

44 Gentlemen of the French Guard, fire first!

Lord Charles Hay (d. 1760) British soldier.
Said at the Battle of Fontenoy, 1745
Attrib.

45 I'd like to see the government get out of war altogether and leave the whole feud to private industry.

Joseph Heller (1923–) US novelist.
Catch 22

46 In starting and waging a war it is not right that matters, but victory.

Adolf Hitler (1889–1945) German dictator.
The Rise and Fall of the Third Reich (W. L. Shirer), Ch. 16

47 War? War is an organized bore.

Oliver Wendell Holmes Jnr (1841–1935) US jurist.
Yankee from Olympus (C. Bowen)

48 Older men declare war. But it is youth that must fight and die.

Herbert Clark Hoover (1874–1964) US statesman.
Speech, Republican National Convention, Chicago, 27 June 1944

49 East and west on fields forgotten
Bleach the bones of comrades slain,
Lovely lads and dead and rotten;
None that go return again.

A. E. Housman (1859–1936) British scholar and poet.
A Shropshire Lad, 'The Welsh Marches'

50 Elevate them guns a little lower.

Andrew Jackson (1767–1845) US statesman.
Order given whilst watching the effect of the US artillery upon the British lines at the Battle of New Orleans
Attrib.

51 I had always to remember that I could have lost the war in an afternoon.

Lord Jellicoe (1859–1935) British admiral.
Referring to the Battle of Jutland

52 The first casualty when war comes is truth.

Hiram Warren Johnson (1866–1945) US politician.
Speech, U.S. Senate, 1917

53 Formerly, a nation that broke the peace did not trouble to try and prove to the world that it was done solely from higher motives . . . *Now war has a bad conscience.* Now every nation assures us that it is bleeding for a human cause, the fate of which hangs in the balance of its victory. . . . No nation dares to admit the guilt of blood before the world.

Ellen Key (Karolina Sofia Key; 1849–1926) Swedish writer.
War, Peace, and the Future, Preface

54 Everything, everything in war is barbaric . . . But the worst barbarity of war is that it forces men collectively to commit acts against which individually they would revolt with their whole being.

Ellen Key
War, Peace, and the Future, Ch. 6

55 Our scientific power has outrun our spiritual power. We have guided missiles and misguided men.

Martin Luther King (1929–68) US Black civil-rights leader.
Strength to Love

56 The conventional army loses if it does not win. The guerrilla wins if he does not lose.

Henry Kissinger (1923–) German-born US politician and diplomat.
Foreign Affairs, XIII (Jan 1969), 'The Vietnam Negotiations'

57 The most persistent sound which reverberates through men's history is the beating of war drums.

Arthur Koestler (1905–83) Hungarian-born British writer.
Janus: A Summing Up, Prologue

58 If, therefore, war should ever come between these two countries, which Heaven forbid! it will not, I think, be due to irresistible natural laws, it will be due to the want of human wisdom.

Bonar Law (1858–1923) British statesman.
Referring to the UK and Germany
Speech, House of Commons, 27 Nov 1911

59 We have all lost the war. All Europe.

D. H. Lawrence (1885–1930) British novelist.
The Ladybird, 'The Ladybird'

60 It is well that war is so terrible; else we would grow too fond of it.

Robert E. Lee (1807–70) US general.
Speaking to another general during the battle of Fredericksburg
The American Treasury (C. Fadiman)

61 This war, like the next war, is a war to end war.

David Lloyd George (1863–1945) British Liberal statesman.
Referring to the popular opinion that World War I would be the last major war

62 'War is the continuation of politics'. In this sense war is politics and war itself is a political action.

Mao Tse-Tung (1893–1976) Chinese communist leader.
See also CLAUSEWITZ
Quotations from Chairman Mao Tse-Tung, Ch. 5

63 We are advocates of the abolition of war, we do not want war; but war can only be abolished through war, and in order to get rid of the gun it is necessary to take up the gun.

Mao Tse-Tung
Quotations from Chairman Mao Tse-Tung, Ch. 5

64 Television brought the brutality of war into the comfort of the living room. Vietnam was lost in the living rooms of America – not on the battlefields of Vietnam.

Marshall McLuhan (1911–81) Canadian sociologist.
Montreal *Gazette*, 16 May 1975

65 War will never cease until babies begin to come into the world with larger cerebrums and smaller adrenal glands.

H. L. Mencken (1880–1956) US journalist.
Notebooks, 'Minority Report'

66 War is the national industry of Prussia.

Comte de Mirabeau (1749–91) French statesman.
Attrib.

67 Fighting is like champagne. It goes to the heads of cowards as quickly as of heroes. Any fool can be brave on a battle field when it's be brave or else be killed.

Margaret Mitchell (1909–49) US novelist.
Gone with the Wind

68 War hath no fury like a non-combatant.

C. E. Montague (1867–1928) British editor and writer.
Disenchantment, Ch. 15

69 An empire founded by war has to maintain itself by war.

Baron de Montesquieu (1688–1755) French writer.
Considérations sur les causes de la grandeur et de la décadence des romains, Ch. 8

70 The U.S. has broken the second rule of war. That is, don't go fighting with your land army on the mainland of Asia. Rule One is don't march on Moscow. I developed these two rules myself.

Lord Montgomery (1887–1976) British field marshal.
Referring to the Vietnam war
Montgomery of Alamein (Chalfont)

71 The Minstrel Boy to the war has gone,
In the ranks of death you'll find him;
His father's sword he has girded on,
And his wild harp slung behind him.

Thomas Moore (1779–1852) Irish poet.
Irish Melodies, 'The Minstrel Boy'

72 It's the most beautiful battlefield I've ever seen.

Napoleon I (Napoleon Bonaparte; 1769–1821) French emperor.
Referring to carnage on the field of Borodino, near Moscow, after the battle (7 Sept 1812)
Attrib.

73 There rises the sun of Austerlitz.

Napoleon I
Said at the Battle of Borodino (7 Sept 1812), near Moscow; the Battle of Austerlitz (2 Dec 1805) was Napoleon's great victory over the Russians and Austrians

74 I don't care for war, there's far too much luck in it for my liking.

Napoleon III (1808–73) French emperor.
Said after the narrow but bloody French victory at Solferino (24 June 1859)
The Fall of the House of Habsburg (E. Crankshaw)

75 The sand of the desert is sodden red, –
Red with the wreck of a square that broke; –

The gatling's jammed and the colonel dead,
And the regiment blind with the dust and
smoke.
The river of death has brimmed its banks
And England's far and honour a name.
But the voice of a schoolboy rallies the ranks:
'Play up! play up! and play the game!'
Henry John Newbolt (1862–1938) British poet.
Vitaï Lampada

76 Drake he's in his hammock till the great
Armadas come.
(Capten, art tha sleepin' there below?)
Slung atween the round shot, listenin' for the
drum,
An dreamin' arl the time o' Plymouth Hoe.
Henry John Newbolt
Drake's Drum

77 War is war. The only good human being is a
dead one.
George Orwell (Eric Blair; 1903–50) British novelist.
Animal Farm, Ch. 4

78 Probably the Battle of Waterloo *was* won on
the playing-fields of Eton, but the opening
battles of all subsequent wars have been lost
there.
George Orwell
The Lion and the Unicorn, 'England, Your England'

79 The quickest way of ending a war is to lose
it.
George Orwell
Second Thoughts on James Burnham

80 The pallor of girls' brows shall be their pall;
Their flowers the tenderness of patient minds,
And each slow dusk a drawing-down of blinds.
Wilfred Owen (1893–1918) British poet.
Anthem for Doomed Youth

81 Red lips are not so red
As the stained stones kissed by the English
dead.
Wilfred Owen
Greater Love

82 I could not give my name to aid the slaughter
in this war, fought on both sides for grossly
material ends, which did not justify the
sacrifice of a single mother's son. Clearly I
must continue to oppose it, and expose it, to
all whom I could reach with voice or pen.
Sylvia Pankhurst (1882–1960) British suffragette.
The Home Front, Ch. 25

83 Stand your ground. Don't fire unless fired
upon, but if they mean to have a war, let it
begin here!
John Parker (1729–75) US general.
Command given at the start of the Battle of Lexington
Familiar Quotations (J. Bartlett)

84 War should belong to the tragic past, to

history: it should find no place on humanity's
agenda for the future.
John Paul II (Karol Wojtyla; 1920–) Polish pope
(1978–).
Speech, 1982

85 Don't cheer, boys; the poor devils are dying.
John Woodward Philip (1840–1900) US naval officer.
Restraining his victorious crew during the naval battle off Santiago in the Spanish-American War.
Attrib.

86 Don't fire until you see the whites of their
eyes.
William Prescott (1726–95) US revolutionary soldier.
Command given at the Battle of Bunker Hill

87 War is, after all, the universal perversion.
We are all tainted: if we cannot experience
our perversion at first hand we spend our
time reading war stories, the pornography of
war; or seeing war films, the blue films of
war; or titillating our senses with the
imagination of great deeds, the masturbation
of war.
John Rae (1931–) British schoolmaster and writer.
The Custard Boys, Ch. 6

88 In a civil war, a general must know – and
I'm afraid it's a thing rather of instinct than of
practice – he must know exactly when to
move over to the other side.
Henry Reed (1914–) British poet and dramatist.
Not a Drum was Heard: The War Memoirs of General Gland

89 And the various holds and rolls and throws
and breakfalls
Somehow or other I always seemed to put
In the wrong place. And as for war, my wars
Were global from the start.
Henry Reed
A Map of Verona, 'Lessons of the War', III

90 All Quiet on the Western Front.
Erich Maria Remarque (1898–1970) German novelist.
Title of novel

91 All wars are planned by old men
In council rooms apart.
Grantland Rice (1880–1954) US sportswriter.
Two Sides of War

92 (Fire – without hatred).
Antonio Rivera (d. 1936) Spanish Nationalist hero.
Giving the order to open fire at the siege of the Alcázar
The Siege of the Alcázar (C. Eby)

93 More than an end to war, we want an end to
the beginnings of all wars.
Franklin D. Roosevelt (1882–1945) US Democratic
president.
Speech broadcast on the day after his death (13 Apr 1945)

94 They dashed on towards that *thin red line
tipped with steel.*
William Howard Russell (1820–1907) British journalist.
Description of the Russian charge against the British at the
Battle of Balaclava, 1854
The British Expedition to the Crimea

95 War is not an adventure. It is a disease. It is like typhus.

Antoine de Saint-Exupéry (1900–44) French novelist and aviator.
Flight to Arras

96 Sometime they'll give a war and nobody will come.

Carl Sandburg (1878–1967) US author and poet.
The People, Yes

97 Man, it seemed, had been created to jab the life out of Germans.

Siegfried Sassoon (1886–1967) British poet.
Memoirs of an Infantry Officer, Pt. I, Ch. 1

98 Safe with his wound, a citizen of life,
He hobbled blithely through the garden gate,
And thought: 'Thank God they had to amputate!'

Siegfried Sassoon
The One-Legged Man

99 If I were fierce and bald and short of breath,
I'd live with scarlet Majors at the Base,
And speed glum heroes up the line to death.

Siegfried Sassoon
Base Details

100 And when the war is done and youth stone dead
I'd toddle safely home and die – in bed.

Siegfried Sassoon
Base Details

101 'Good morning; good morning!' the general said
When we met him last week on our way to the line.
Now the soldiers he smiled at are most of 'em dead,
And we're cursing his staff for incompetent swine.

Siegfried Sassoon
The General

102 I am making this statement as a wilful defiance of military authority because I believe that the War is being deliberately prolonged by those who have the power to end it.

Siegfried Sassoon
Memoirs of an Infantry Officer, Pt. X, Ch. 3

103 All wars are popular for the first thirty days.

Arthur Schlesinger Jnr (1917–) US historian, educator, and author.
Attrib.

104 When you march into France, let the last man on the right brush the Channel with his sleeve.

Alfred Graf von Schlieffen (1833–1913) German general.
Referring to the Schlieffen plan
August 1914 (Barbara Tuchman), Ch. 2

105 When we, the Workers, all demand: 'What are we fighting for? . . .

Then, then we'll end that stupid crime, that devil's madness – War.

Robert William Service (1874–1958) Canadian poet.
Michael

106 Cry 'Havoc!' and let slip the dogs of war.

William Shakespeare (1564–1616) English dramatist.
Julius Caesar, III:1

107 Farewell the neighing steed and the shrill trump,
The spirit-stirring drum, th'ear piercing fife,
The royal banner, and all quality,
Pride, pomp, and circumstance, of glorious war!

William Shakespeare
Othello, III:3

108 The British soldier can stand up to anything except the British War Office.

George Bernard Shaw (1856–1950) Irish dramatist and critic.
The Devil's Disciple, II

109 I am tired and sick of war. Its glory is all moonshine . . . War is hell.

General William Sherman (1820–91) US general.
Attrib. in address, Michigan Military Academy, 19 June 1879

110 Who live under the shadow of a war,
What can I do that matters?

Stephen Spender (1909–) British poet.
Who live under the Shadow

111 To win in Vietnam, we will have to exterminate a nation.

Dr Benjamin Spock (1903–) US paediatrician and psychiatrist.
Dr Spock on Vietnam, Ch. 7

112 Yonder are the Hessians. They were bought for seven pounds and tenpence a man. Are you worth more? Prove it. Tonight the American flag floats from yonder hill or Molly Stark sleeps a widow!

John Stark (1728–1822) US general.
Urging on his troops at the Battle of Bennington in 1777
The American Treasury (C. Fadiman)

113 That's what you are. That's what you all are. All of you young people who served in the war. You are a lost generation.

Gertrude Stein (1874–1946) US writer.
A Moveable Feast (E. Hemingway)

114 War is capitalism with the gloves off.

Tom Stoppard (1937–) Czech-born British dramatist.
Travesties

115 Most sorts of diversion in men, children, and other animals, are an imitation of fighting.

Jonathan Swift (1667–1745) Irish-born Anglican priest and writer.
Thoughts on Various Subjects

116 The guerrilla fights the war of the flea, and his military enemy suffers the dog's disadvantages: too much to defend; too small,

117 They make a wilderness and call it peace.
Tacitus (c. 55–c. 120 AD) Roman historian.
Agricola, 30

118 Now all roads lead to France
And heavy is the tread
Of the living; but the dead
Returning lightly dance.
Edward Thomas (1878–1917) British poet.
Roads

119 Dead battles, like dead generals, hold the military mind in their dead grip.
Barbara W. Tuchman (1912–) US editor and writer.
August 1914, Ch. 2

120 They now *ring* the bells, but they will soon *wring* their hands.
Robert Walpole (1676–1745) British statesman.
Said when war was declared in 1739 with Spain, against Walpole's wishes
Memoirs of Sir Robert Walpole (W. Coxe)

121 I heard the bullets whistle, and believe me, there is something charming in the sound.
George Washington (1732–99) US statesman.
Referring to a recent skirmish in the French and Indian War
Presidential Anecdotes (P. Boller)

122 When the war broke out she took down the signed photograph of the Kaiser and, with some solemnity, hung it in the menservants' lavatory; it was her one combative action.
Evelyn Waugh (1903–66) British novelist.
Vile Bodies, Ch. 3

123 Like German opera, too long and too loud.
Evelyn Waugh
Giving his opinions of warfare after the Battle of Crete, 1941
Attrib.

124 It has been a damned serious business – Blücher and I have lost 30,000 men. It has been a damned nice thing – the nearest run thing you ever saw in your life . . . By God! I don't think it would have done if I had not been there.
Duke of Wellington (1769–1852) British general and statesman.
Referring to the Battle of Waterloo
Creevey Papers, Ch. X

125 Yes, and they went down very well too.
Duke of Wellington
Replying to the observation that the French cavalry had come up very well during the Battle of Waterloo
The Age of Elegance (A. Bryant)

126 A battle of giants.
Duke of Wellington
Referring to the Battle of Waterloo; said to Samuel Rogers
Attrib.

Ubiquitous, and agile an enemy to come to grips with.
Robert Taber (20th century) US writer.
The War of the Flea, Ch. 2

127 Up, Guards, and at 'em.
Duke of Wellington
Order given at the battle of Waterloo, 18 June 1815
Attrib.

128 The military don't start wars. The politicians start wars.
William Westmorland (1914–) US army officer.
Attrib.

129 As long as war is regarded as wicked, it will always have its fascination. When it is looked upon as vulgar, it will cease to be popular.
Oscar Wilde (1854–1900) Irish-born British dramatist.
The Critic as Artist, Pt. 2

130 You will be home before the leaves have fallen from the trees.
Wilhelm II (1859–1941) King of Prussia and Emperor of Germany.
Said to troops leaving for the Front, Aug 1914
August 1914 (Barbara Tuchman), Ch. 9

131 It is my Royal and Imperial Command that you . . . exterminate first the treacherous English, and . . . walk over General French's contemptible little Army.
Wilhelm II
Referring to the British Expeditionary Force; veterans of this force became known as 'Old Contemptibles'
The Times, 1 Oct 1914

132 There is such a thing as a man being too proud to fight.
Woodrow Wilson (1856–1925) US statesman.
Address to foreign-born citizens, 10 May 1915

133 The war we have just been through, though it was shot through with terror, is not to be compared with the war we would have to face next time.
Woodrow Wilson
Mr Wilson's War (John Dos Passos), Pt. V, Ch. 22

134 Once lead this people into war and they'll forget there ever was such a thing as tolerance.
Woodrow Wilson
Mr Wilson's War (John Dos Passos), Pt. III, Ch. 2

WAR AND PEACE

See also peace, war

1 Since wars begin in the minds of men, it is in the minds of men that the defences of peace must be constructed.
Anonymous
Constitution of UNESCO

2 And he shall judge among the nations, and shall rebuke many people: and they shall beat their swords into plowshares, and their spears into pruning-hooks: nation shall not lift up sword against nation, neither shall they learn war any more.
Bible: Isaiah
2:4

3 In war, resolution; in defeat, defiance; in victory, magnanimity; in peace, goodwill.
Winston Churchill (1874–1965) British statesman.
Epigram used by Sir Edward Marsh after World War II; used as 'a moral of the work' in Churchill's book
The Second World War

4 Those who can win a war well can rarely make a good peace and those who could make a good peace would never have won the war.
Winston Churchill
My Early Life, Ch. 26

5 My pacifism is not based on any intellectual theory but on a deep antipathy to every form of cruelty and hatred.
Albert Einstein (1879–1955) German-born US physicist.
Said on the outbreak of World War I
Attrib.

6 There never was a good war or a bad peace.
Benjamin Franklin (1706–90) US scientist and statesman.
Letter to Josiah Quincy, 11 Sept 1783

7 My argument is that War makes rattling good history; but Peace is poor reading.
Thomas Hardy (1840–1928) British novelist.
The Dynasts, II:5

8 He that makes a good war makes a good peace.
George Herbert (1593–1633) English poet.
Outlandish Proverbs, 420

9 The statistics of suicide show that, for non-combatants at least, life is more interesting in war than in peace.
Dean Inge (1860–1954) British churchman.
The End of an Age

10 Peace hath her victories
No less renowned than war.
John Milton (1608–74) English poet.
Sonnet: 'To the Lord General Cromwell, May 1652'

11 Peace is not only better than war, but infinitely more arduous.
George Bernard Shaw (1856–1950) Irish dramatist and critic.
Heartbreak House (Preface)

12 Let him who desires peace, prepare for war.
Vegetius (Flavius Vegetius Renatus; 4th century AD) Roman writer.
Epitoma Rei Militaris, 3, 'Prologue'

13 When you're at war you think about a better life; when you're at peace you think about a more comfortable one.
Thornton Wilder (1897–1975) US novelist and dramatist.
The Skin of Our Teeth, III

WASTE

See also extravagance

1 Waste not, want not.
Proverb

2 Full many a gem of purest ray serene,
The dark unfathom'd caves of ocean bear:
Full many a flower is born to blush unseen,
And waste its sweetness on the desert air.
Thomas Gray (1716–71) British poet.
Elegy Written in a Country Churchyard

3 The world is too much with us; late and soon,
Getting and spending, we lay waste our powers:
Little we see in Nature that is ours.
William Wordsworth (1770–1850) British poet.
Sonnets, 'The world is too much with us'

WATER

See also drinks

1 Well, the principle seems the same. The water still keeps falling over.
Winston Churchill (1874–1965) British statesman.
When asked whether the Niagara Falls looked the same as when he first saw them
Closing the Ring, Ch. 5

2 Water, water, every where,
And all the boards did shrink;
Water, water, every where,
Nor any drop to drink.
Samuel Taylor Coleridge (1772–1834) British poet.
The Rime of the Ancient Mariner, II

3 Fish fuck in it.
W. C. Fields (1880–1946) US actor.
His reason for not drinking water
Attrib.

4 For any ceremonial purposes the otherwise excellent liquid, water, is unsuitable in colour and other respects.
A. P. Herbert (1890–1971) British writer and politician.
Uncommon Law

5 If you believe Cratinus from days of old, Maecenas, (as you must know) no verse can give pleasure for long, nor last, that is written by drinkers of water.
Horace (Quintus Horatius Flaccus; 65–8 BC) Roman poet.
Epistles, I

6 The biggest waste of water in the country by far. You spend half a pint and flush two gallons.
Prince Philip (1921–) The consort of Queen Elizabeth II.
Speech, 1965

7 Human beings were invented by water as a device for transporting itself from one place to another.
Tom Robbins (1936–) US novelist.
Another Roadside Attraction

8 He who drinks a tumbler of London water has literally in his stomach more animated

beings than there are men, women and children on the face of the globe.
Sydney Smith (1771–1845) British clergyman and essayist.
Letter

WEAKNESS

See also imperfection, yielding

1 The weakest goes to the wall.
Proverb

2 Oh, your precious 'lame ducks'!
John Galsworthy (1867–1933) British novelist.
The Man of Property, Pt. II, Ch. 12

3 A sheep in sheep's clothing.
Edmund Gosse (1849–1928) British writer and critic.
Referring to T. Sturge Moore. Sometimes attributed to Winston Churchill, referring to Clement Attlee.
Under the Bridge (Ferris Greenslet), Ch. 12

4 Frailty, thy name is woman!
William Shakespeare (1564–1616) English dramatist.
Hamlet, I:2

WEALTH

See also capitalism, extravagance, materialism, money, ostentation, poverty and wealth

1 The best things in life are free.
Proverb

2 You can't take it with you when you go.
Proverb

3 Rich men's houses are seldom beautiful, rarely comfortable, and never original. It is a constant source of surprise to people of moderate means to observe how little a big fortune contributes to Beauty.
Margot Asquith (1865–1945) The second wife of Herbert Asquith.
The Autobiography of Margot Asquith, Ch. 17

4 A man who has a million dollars is as well off as if he were rich.
John Jacob Astor (1763–1848) US millionaire.
Attrib.

5 For the Lord thy God bringeth thee into a good land, a land of brooks of water, of fountains and depths that spring out of valleys and hills;
A land of wheat, and barley, and vines, and fig trees, and pomegranates; a land of oil olive, and honey;
A land wherein thou shalt eat bread without scarceness, thou shalt not lack any thing in it; a land whose stones are iron, and out of whose hills thou mayest dig brass.
When thou hast eaten and art full, then thou shalt bless the Lord thy God for the good land which he hath given thee.
Bible: Deuteronomy
8:7–10

6 For what shall it profit a man, if he shall gain the whole world, and lose his own soul? Or what shall a man give in exchange for his soul?
Bible: Mark
8:36–37

7 Lay not up for yourselves treasures upon earth, where moth and rust doth corrupt, and where thieves break through and steal:
But lay up for yourselves treasures in heaven, where neither moth nor rust doth corrupt, and where thieves do not break through nor steal:
For where your treasure is, there will your heart be also.
Bible: Matthew
6:19–21

8 Then said Jesus unto his disciples, Verily I say unto you, That a rich man shall hardly enter into the kingdom of heaven.
And again I say unto you, It is easier for a camel to go through the eye of a needle, than for a rich man to enter into the kingdom of God.
Bible: Matthew
19:23–24

9 The rich are the scum of the earth in every country.
G. K. Chesterton (1874–1936) British writer.
The Flying Inn

10 Poor Little Rich Girl.
Noël Coward (1899–1973) British dramatist.
Title of song

11 Riches have wings, and grandeur is a dream.
William Cowper (1731–1800) British poet.
The Task

12 FITZGERALD. The rich are different from us.
HEMINGWAY. Yes, they have more money.
F. Scott Fitzgerald (1896–1940) US novelist.
The Crack-Up, 'Notebooks, E'

13 Wealth is not without its advantages, and the case to the contrary, although it has often been made, has never proved widely persuasive.
John Kenneth Galbraith (1908–) US economist.
The Affluent Society, Ch. 1

14 The meek shall inherit the earth but not the mineral rights.
J. Paul Getty (1892–1976) US oil magnate.
Attrib.

15 If you can actually count your money you are not really a rich man.
J. Paul Getty
Gossip (A. Barrow)

16 As I walk along the Bois Bou-long,
With an independent air,
You can hear the girls declare,
'He must be a millionaire',
You can hear them sigh and wish to die,

You can see them wink the other eye
At the man who broke the Bank at Monte
Carlo.

Fred Gilbert (1850–1903) British songwriter.
The Bois de Boulogne was a fashionable recreational area on
the outskirts of Paris
The Man who Broke the Bank at Monte Carlo (song)

17 Sir, the insolence of wealth will creep out.

Samuel Johnson (1709–84) British lexicographer.
Life of Johnson (J. Boswell), Vol. III

18 Most of our people have never had it so
good.

Harold Macmillan (1894–1986) British politician and
prime minister.
Speech, Bedford Football Ground, 20 July 1957

19 And, as their wealth increaseth, so inclose
Infinite riches in a little room.

Christopher Marlowe (1564–93) English dramatist.
The Jew of Malta, I:1

20 He must have killed a lot of men to have
made so much money.

Molière (Jean Baptiste Poquelin; 1622–73) French
dramatist.
Le Malade imaginaire, I:5

21 I am rich beyond the dreams of avarice.

Edward Moore (1712–57) British dramatist.
The Gamester, II

22 God shows his contempt for wealth by the
kind of person he selects to receive it.

Austin O'Malley (1858–1932) US writer.

23 Who Wants to Be a Millionaire? I don't.

Cole Porter (1893–1964) US songwriter.
Who Wants to be a Millionaire?, title song

24 I am a millionaire. That is my religion.

George Bernard Shaw (1856–1950) Irish dramatist and
critic.
Major Barbara

25 With the great part of rich people, the chief
employment of riches consists in the parade
of riches.

Adam Smith (1723–90) Scottish economist.
The Wealth of Nations

26 It is the wretchedness of being rich that you
have to live with rich people.

Logan Pearsall Smith (1865–1946) US writer.
Afterthoughts, 'In the World'

27 If Heaven had looked upon riches to be a
valuable thing, it would not have given them
to such a scoundrel.

Jonathan Swift (1667–1745) Irish-born Anglican priest and
writer.
Letter to Miss Vanhomrigh, 12–13 Aug 1720

28 I have had no real gratification or enjoyment
of any sort more than my neighbor on the
next block who is worth only half a million.

William Henry Vanderbilt (1821–85) US railway chief.
Famous Last Words (B. Conrad)

29 One can never be too thin or too rich.

Duchess of Windsor (Wallis Warfield Simpson; 1896–
1986) The wife of the Duke of Windsor (formerly Edward
VIII).
Attrib.

30 Just what God would have done if he had the
money.

Alexander Woollcott (1887–1943) US journalist.
On being shown round Moss Hart's elegant country house and
grounds
Attrib.

WEAPONS

See also nuclear weapons, power politics, war

1 If you carry this resolution and follow out all
its implications and do not run away from it,
you will send a Foreign Secretary, whoever
he may be, naked into the conference
chamber.

Aneurin Bevan (1897–1960) British Labour politician.
Referring to unilateral disarmament
Speech, Labour Party Conference, 2 Oct 1957

2 It was very successful, but it fell on the
wrong planet.

Wernher von Braun (1912–77) German rocket engineer.
Referring to the first V2 rocket to hit London during World
War II
Attrib.

3 We may find in the long run that tinned food
is a deadlier weapon than the machine-gun.

George Orwell (Eric Blair; 1903–50) British novelist.
The Road to Wigan Pier, Ch. 6

4 Today we have naming of parts. Yesterday,
We had daily cleaning. And tomorrow morning
We shall have what to do after firing. But
today,
Today we have naming of parts.

Henry Reed (1914–) British poet and dramatist.
Naming of Parts

5 They call it easing the Spring: it is perfectly
easy
If you have any strength in your thumb: like
the bolt,
And the breech, and the cocking-piece, and the
point of balance,
Which in our case we have not got.

Henry Reed
Naming of Parts

6 Though loaded firearms were strictly
forbidden at St Trinian's to all but Sixth-
Formers . . . one or two of them carried
automatics acquired in the holidays, generally
the gift of some indulgent relative.

Ronald Searle (1920–) British cartoonist.
The Terror of St Trinian's, Ch. 3

7 But bombs *are* unbelievable until they actually
fall.

Patrick White (1912–) British-born Australian novelist.
Riders in the Chariot, I:4

WEATHER

See also sun

1 Mackerel sky and mares' tails make lofty
ships carry low sails.
Proverb

2 Rain before seven: fine before eleven.
Proverb

3 Rain, rain, go away, come again another day.
Proverb

4 Red sky at night, shepherd's delight; red sky
in the morning, shepherd's warning.
Proverb

5 St. Swithin's Day, if thou dost rain, for forty
days it will remain; St. Swithin's Day, if thou
be fair, for forty days 'twill rain no more.
Proverb

6 The north wind does blow, and we shall have
snow.
Proverb

7 What dreadful hot weather we have! It keeps
me in a continual state of inelegance.
Jane Austen (1775–1817) British novelist.
Letter, 18 Sept 1796

8 I like the weather, when it is not rainy,
That is, I like two months of every year.
Lord Byron (1788–1824) British poet.
Beppo

9 This is a London particular . . . A fog, miss.
Charles Dickens (1812–70) British novelist.
Bleak House, Ch. 3

10 It ain't a fit night out for man or beast.
W. C. Fields (1880–1946) US actor.
The Fatal Glass of Beer

11 I'm singing in the rain, just singing in the
rain;
What a wonderful feeling, I'm happy again.
Arthur Freed (1894–1973) US film producer and
songwriter.
From the musical, *Hollywood Revue of 1929*
Singing in the Rain

12 This is the weather the cuckoo likes,
And so do I;
When showers betumble the chestnut spikes,
And nestlings fly:
And the little brown nightingale bills his best,
And they sit outside at 'The Travellers' Rest'.
Thomas Hardy (1840–1928) British novelist.
Weathers

13 This is the weather the shepherd shuns,
And so do I.
Thomas Hardy
Weathers

14 When two Englishmen meet, their first talk is
of the weather.
Samuel Johnson (1709–84) British lexicographer.
The Idler

15 A snake came to my water-trough
On a hot, hot day, and I in pyjamas for the
heat,
To drink there.
D. H. Lawrence (1885–1930) British novelist.
Snake

16 The British, he thought, must be gluttons for
satire: even the weather forecast seemed to
be some kind of spoof, predicting every
possible combination of weather for the next
twenty-four hours without actually committing
itself to anything specific.
David Lodge (1935–) British author.
Changing Places, Ch. 2

17 Who has seen the wind?
Neither you nor I:
But when the trees bow down their heads,
The wind is passing by.
Christina Rossetti (1830–74) British poet.
Who Has Seen the Wind?

18 Blow, winds, and crack your cheeks; rage,
blow.
You cataracts and hurricanoes, spout
Till you have drench'd our steeples, drown'd
the cocks.
William Shakespeare (1564–1616) English dramatist.
King Lear, III:2

19 Rumble thy bellyful. Spit, fire; spout rain.
Nor rain, wind, thunder, fire, are my
daughters
I tax not you, you elements, with unkindness.
William Shakespeare
King Lear, III:2

20 Poor naked wretches, wheresoe'er you are,
That bide the pelting of this pitiless storm,
How shall your houseless heads and unfed
sides,
Your loop'd and window'd raggedness, defend
you
From seasons such as these?
William Shakespeare
King Lear, III:4

21 So foul and fair a day I have not seen.
William Shakespeare
Macbeth, I:3

22 I am the daughter of Earth and Water,
And the nursling of the Sky;
I pass through the pores of the ocean and
shores;
I change, but I cannot die,
For after the rain when with never a stain
The pavilion of Heaven is bare,
And the winds and sunbeams with their convex
gleams
Build up the blue dome of air,
I silently laugh at my own cenotaph,

And out of the caverns of rain,
Like a child from the womb, like a ghost from the tomb,
I arise and unbuild it again.
Percy Bysshe Shelley (1792–1822) British poet.
The Cloud

23 I wield the flail of the lashing hail,
And whiten the green plains under,
And then again I dissolve it in rain,
And laugh as I pass in thunder.
Percy Bysshe Shelley
The Cloud

24 O Wild West Wind, thou breath of Autumn's being,
Thou, from whose unseen presence the leaves dead
Are driven, like ghosts from an enchanter fleeing,
Yellow, and black, and pale, and hectic red,
Pestilence-stricken multitudes.
Percy Bysshe Shelley
Ode to the West Wind

25 Heat, madam! It was so dreadful that I found there was nothing for it but to take off my flesh and sit in my bones.
Sydney Smith (1771–1845) British clergyman and essayist.
Discussing the hot weather with a lady acquaintance
Lives of the Wits (H. Pearson)

26 Willows whiten, aspens quiver,
Little breezes dusk and shiver.
Alfred, Lord Tennyson (1809–92) British poet.
The Lady of Shalott, Pt. I

WELSH

See also British, Wales

1 Eddy was a tremendously tolerant person, but he wouldn't put up with the Welsh. He always said, surely there's enough English to go round.
John Mortimer (1923–) British lawyer and dramatist.
Two Stars for Comfort, I:2

2 There are still parts of Wales where the only concession to gaiety is a striped shroud.
Gwyn Thomas (1913–81) British writer.
Punch, 18 June 1958

3 . . . an impotent people,
Sick with inbreeding,
Worrying the carcase of an old song.
R. S. Thomas (1913–) Welsh poet.
Welsh Landscape

4 'The Welsh,' said the Doctor, 'are the only nation in the world that has produced no graphic or plastic art, no architecture, no drama. They just sing,' he said with disgust, sing and blow down wind instruments of plated silver.'
Evelyn Waugh (1903–66) British novelist.
Decline and Fall, Pt. I, Ch. 8

WHISTLING

See also fear

1 The schoolboy, with his satchel in his hand,
Whistling aloud to bear his courage up.
Robert Blair (1699–1746) Scottish poet.
The Grave

2 I Whistle a Happy Tune.
Oscar Hammerstein (1895–1960) US lyricist.
From the musical *The King and I*
Song title

WINTER

See also months, seasons

1 Many human beings say that they enjoy the winter, but what they really enjoy is feeling proof against it.
Richard Adams (1920–) British novelist.
Watership Down, Ch. 50

2 St Agnes' Eve – Ah, bitter chill it was!
The owl, for all his feathers, was a-cold;
The hare limp'd trembling through the frozen grass,
And silent was the flock in woolly fold.
John Keats (1795–1821) British poet.
The Eve of Saint Agnes, I

3 Russia has two generals in whom she can confide – Generals Janvier and Février.
Nicholas I (1796–1855) Tsar of Russia.
Referring to the Russian winter. Nicholas himself succumbed to a February cold in 1855 – the subject of the famous *Punch* Cartoon, 'General Février turned traitor', 10 Mar 1855
Attrib.

4 Winter is icummen in,
Lhude sing Goddamm,
Raineth drop and staineth slop
And how the wind doth ramm!
Sing: Goddamm.
Ezra Pound (1885–1972) US poet.
Ancient Music

5 In the bleak mid-winter
Frosty wind made moan,
Earth stood hard as iron,
Water like a stone;
Snow had fallen, snow on snow,
Snow on snow,
In the bleak mid-winter,
Long ago.
Christina Rossetti (1830–74) British poet.
Mid-Winter

6 When icicles hang by the wall,
And Dick the shepherd blows his nail,
And Tom bears logs into the hall,
And milk comes frozen home in pail,
When blood is nipp'd, and ways be foul,
Then nightly sings the staring owl:
'Tu-who;
Tu-whit, Tu-who' – A merry note,

While greasy Joan doth keel the pot.
William Shakespeare (1564–1616) English dramatist.
Love's Labour's Lost, V:2

7 It is a winter's tale
That the snow blind twilight ferries over the lakes
And floating fields from the farm in the cup of the vales.
Dylan Thomas (1914–53) Welsh poet.
A Winter's Tale

8 The comic almanacs give us dreadful pictures of January and February; but, in truth, the months which should be made to look gloomy in England are March and April. Let no man boast himself that he has got through the perils of winter till at least the seventh of May.
Anthony Trollope (1815–82) British novelist.
Doctor Thorne, Ch. 47

WISDOM

See also intelligence, knowledge, prudence, wisdom and foolishness

1 It is easy to be wise after the event.
Proverb

2 For in much wisdom is much grief: and he that increaseth knowledge increaseth sorrow.
Bible: Ecclesiastes
1:18

3 The words of wise men are heard in quiet more than the cry of him that ruleth among fools.
Bible: Ecclesiastes
9:17

4 The wisdom of a learned man cometh by opportunity of leisure: and he that hath little business shall become wise.
How can he get wisdom that holdeth the plough, and that glorieth in the goad, that driveth oxen, and is occupied in their labours, and whose talk is of bullocks?
Bible: Ecclesiasticus
38:24–25

5 With the ancient is wisdom; and in length of days understanding.
Bible: Job
12:12

6 No mention shall be made of coral, or of pearls: for the price of wisdom is above rubies.
Bible: Job
28:18

7 A wise man will hear, and will increase learning; and a man of understanding shall attain unto wise counsels:
To understand a proverb, and the interpretation; the words of the wise, and their dark sayings.

The fear of the Lord is the beginning of knowledge: but fools despise wisdom and instruction.
Bible: Proverbs
1:5–7

8 Wisdom is the principal thing; therefore get wisdom: and with all thy getting get understanding.
Bible: Proverbs
4:7

9 Wisdom reacheth from one end to another mightily: and sweetly doth she order all things.
Bible: Wisdom
8:1

10 Does the Eagle know what is in the pit
Or wilt thou go ask the Mole?
Can Wisdom be put in a silver rod,
Or love in a golden bowl?
William Blake (1757–1827) British poet.
The Book of Thel, 'Thel's Motto'

11 I care not whether a man is Good or Evil; all that I care
Is whether he is a Wise Man or a Fool. Go! put off Holiness,
And put on Intellect.
William Blake
Jerusalem

12 Be wiser than other people if you can, but do not tell them so.
Earl of Chesterfield (1694–1773) English statesman.
Letter to his son, 19 Nov 1745

13 A sadder and a wiser man,
He rose the morrow morn.
Samuel Taylor Coleridge (1772–1834) British poet.
The Rime of the Ancient Mariner, VII

14 Knowledge dwells
In heads replete with thoughts of other men;
Wisdom in minds attentive to their own.
William Cowper (1731–1800) British poet.
The Task

15 Some are weather-wise, some are otherwise.
Benjamin Franklin (1706–90) US scientist and statesman.
Poor Richard's Almanack

16 Knowledge can be communicated but not wisdom.
Hermann Hesse (1877–1962) German novelist and poet.
Siddhartha

17 It is the province of knowledge to speak and it is the privilege of wisdom to listen.
Oliver Wendell Holmes (1809–94) US writer.
The Poet at the Breakfast Table, Ch. 10

18 Vain wisdom all, and false philosophy.
John Milton (1608–74) English poet.
Paradise Lost, Bk. II

19 The young man who has not wept is a

savage, and the old man who will not laugh is a fool.
George Santayana (1863–1952) US philosopher.
Dialogues in Limbo, Ch. 3

20 Some folk are wise, and some are otherwise.
Tobias Smollett (1721–71) British novelist.
Roderick Random, Ch. 6

21 An ounce of a man's own wit is worth a ton of other people's.
Laurence Sterne (1713–68) Irish-born British writer.
Tristram Shandy

22 Oh, Vanity of vanities!
How wayward the decrees of Fate are;
How very weak the very wise,
How very small the very great are!
William Makepeace Thackeray (1811–63) British novelist.
Vanitas Vanitatum

23 It is never wise to try to appear to be more clever than you are. It is sometimes wise to appear slightly less so.
William Whitelaw (1918–   ) British politician.
The Observer, 'Sayings of the Year', 1975

WISDOM AND FOOLISHNESS

1 Then I saw that wisdom excelleth folly, as far as light excelleth darkness.
The wise man's eyes are in his head; but the fool walketh in darkness: and I myself perceived also that one event happeneth to them all.
Bible: Ecclesiastes
2:13–14

2 But God hath chosen the foolish things of the world to confound the wise; and God hath chosen the weak things of the world to confound the things which are mighty.
Bible: I Corinthians
1:27

3 For ye suffer fools gladly, seeing ye yourselves are wise.
Bible: II Corinthians
11:19

4 A fool sees not the same tree that a wise man sees.
William Blake (1757–1827) British poet.
The Marriage of Heaven and Hell, 'Proverbs of Hell'

5 Many have been the wise speeches of fools, though not so many as the foolish speeches of wise men.
Thomas Fuller (1608–61) English historian.
The Holy State and the Profane State

6 Give me the young man who has brains enough to make a fool of himself!
Robert Louis Stevenson (1850–94) Scottish writer.
Virginibus Puerisque

WOMAN'S ROLE

See also feminism, housework, marriage, women, sexes

1 Mother is the dead heart of the family, spending father's earnings on consumer goods to enhance the environment in which he eats, sleeps and watches the television.
Germaine Greer (1939–   ) Australian-born British writer and feminist.
The Female Eunuch

2 These are rare attainments for a damsel, but pray tell me, can she spin?
James I (1566–1625) King of England.
On being introduced to a young girl proficient in Latin, Greek, and Hebrew
Attrib.

3 A man is in general better pleased when he has a good dinner upon his table, than when his wife talks Greek.
Samuel Johnson (1709–84) British lexicographer.
Johnsonian Miscellanies (ed. G. B. Hill), Vol. II

WOMEN

See also feminism

1 A man of straw is worth a woman of gold.
Proverb

2 A woman's place is in the home.
Proverb

3 A woman's work is never done.
Proverb

4 The hand that rocks the cradle rules the world.
Proverb

5 Old-fashioned ways which no longer apply to changed conditions are a snare in which the feet of women have always become readily entangled.
Jane Addams (1860–1935) US social worker.
In *Newer Ideals of Peace*, 'Utilization of Women in City Government'

6 The woman that deliberates is lost.
Joseph Addison (1672–1719) British essayist.
Cato, IV:1

7 A woman seldom asks advice until she has bought her wedding clothes.
Joseph Addison
The Spectator, 475

8 . . . girls are so queer you never know what they mean. They say No when they mean Yes, and drive a man out of his wits for the fun of it . . .
Louisa May Alcott (1832–88) US novelist.
Little Women, Pt. II

9 Next to being married, a girl likes to be crossed in love a little now and then.
Jane Austen (1775–1817) British novelist.
Pride and Prejudice, Ch. 24

10 A woman, especially if she have the misfortune of knowing anything, should conceal it as well as she can.
Jane Austen
Northanger Abbey, Ch. 14

11 A lady's imagination is very rapid; it jumps from admiration to love, from love to matrimony in a moment.
Jane Austen
Pride and Prejudice, Ch. 6

12 Women – one half the human race at least – care fifty times more for a marriage than a ministry.
Walter Bagehot (1826–77) British economist and journalist.
The English Constitution, 'The Monarchy'

13 One is not born a woman, one becomes one.
Simone de Beauvoir (1908–86) French writer.
Le Deuxième Sexe (trans. The Second Sex)

14 You will find that the woman who is really kind to dogs is always one who has failed to inspire sympathy in men.
Max Beerbohm (1872–1956) British writer.
Zuleika Dobson, Ch. 6

15 And the Lord God caused a deep sleep to fall upon Adam, and he slept: and he took one of his ribs, and closed up the flesh instead thereof;
And the rib, which the Lord God had taken from man, made he a woman, and brought her unto the man.
And Adam said, This is now bone of my bones, and flesh of my flesh: she shall be called Woman, because she was taken out of Man.
Therefore shall a man leave his father and his mother, and shall cleave unto his wife: and they shall be one flesh.
And they were both naked, the man and his wife, and were not ashamed.
Bible: Genesis
2:21–25

16 For the lips of a strange woman drop as an honeycomb, and her mouth is smoother than oil:
But her end is bitter as wormwood, sharp as a two-edged sword.
Bible: Proverbs
5:3–4

17 Who can find a virtuous woman? for her price is far above rubies
The heart of her husband doth safely trust in her, so that he shall have no need of spoil.
She will do him good and not evil all the days of her life.
Bible: Proverbs
31:10–12

18 Why need the other women know so much?
Robert Browning (1812–89) British poet.
Any Wife to any Husband

19 The souls of women are so small,
That some believe they've none at all.
Samuel Butler (1612–80) English satirist.
Miscellaneous Thoughts

20 Brigands demand your money or your life; women require both.
Samuel Butler
Attrib.

21 I thought it would appear
That there had been a lady in the case.
Lord Byron (1788–1824) British poet.
Don Juan, V

22 Women are much more like each other than men: they have, in truth, but two passions, vanity and love; these are their universal characteristics.
Earl of Chesterfield (1694–1773) English statesman.
Letter to his son, 19 Dec 1749

23 There is no fury like an ex-wife searching for a new lover.
Cyril Connolly (1903–74) British journalist.
The Unquiet Grave

24 Certain women should be struck regularly, like gongs.
Noël Coward (1899–1973) British dramatist.
Private Lives

25 Women never have young minds. They are born three thousand years old.
Shelagh Delaney (1939–) British dramatist.
A Taste of Honey, I:1

26 'She's the sort of woman now,' said Mould, ... 'one would almost feel disposed to bury for nothing: and to do it neatly, too!'
Charles Dickens (1812–70) British novelist.
Martin Chuzzlewit, Ch. 25

27 It is only the women whose eyes have been washed clear with tears who get the broad vision that makes them little sisters to all the world.
Dorothy Dix (Elizabeth Meriwether Gilmer; 1861–1951) US journalist and writer.
Dorothy Dix, Her Book, Introduction

28 She takes just like a woman, yes, she does
She makes love just like a woman, yes, she does
And she aches just like a woman
But she breaks just like a little girl.
Bob Dylan (Robert Allen Zimmerman; 1941–) US popular singer.
Just Like a Woman

29 I should like to know what is the proper function of women, if it is not to make reasons for husbands to stay at home, and still stronger reasons for bachelors to go out.
George Eliot (Mary Ann Evans; 1819–80) British novelist.
The Mill on the Floss, Ch. 6

30 In the room the women come and go

Talking of Michelangelo.
T. S. Eliot (1888–1965) US-born British poet and dramatist.
The Love Song of J. Alfred Prufrock

31 When a woman behaves like a man, why doesn't she behave like a nice man?
Edith Evans (1888–1976) British actress.
The Observer, 'Sayings of the Week', 30 Sept 1956

32 The great question . . . which I have not been able to answer, despite my thirty years of research into the feminine soul, is 'What does a woman want'?
Sigmund Freud (1856–1939) Austrian psychoanalyst.
Psychiatry in American Life (Charles Rolo)

33 How, like a moth, the simple maid Still plays about the flame!
John Gay (1685–1732) English poet and dramatist.
The Beggar's Opera

34 Fighting is essentially a masculine idea; a woman's weapon is her tongue.
Hermione Gingold (1897–1987) British actress.
Attrib.

35 I know you do not make the laws but I also know that you are the wives and mothers, the sisters and daughters of those who do . . .
Angelina Grimké (1805–79) US writer and reformer.
The Anti-Slavery Examiner (Sep 1836), 'Appeal to the Christian Women of the South'

36 If men knew how women pass their time when they are alone, they'd never marry.
O. Henry (William Sidney Porter; 1862–1910) US short-story writer.
The Four Million Memoirs of a Yellow Dog

37 O! men with sisters dear,
O! men with mothers and wives!
It is not linen you're wearing out,
But human creatures' lives!
Thomas Hood (1799–1845) British poet.
The Song of the Shirt

38 A woman's preaching is like a dog's walking on his hinder legs. It is not done well; but you are surprised to find it done at all.
Samuel Johnson (1709–84) British lexicographer.
Life of Johnson (J. Boswell), Vol. I

39 No one delights more in vengeance than a woman.
Juvenal (Decimus Junius Juvenalis; 60–130 AD) Roman satirist.
Satires, XIII

40 When the Himalayan peasant meets the he-bear in his pride,
He shouts to scare the monster, who will often turn aside.
But the she-bear thus accosted rends the peasant tooth and nail

For the female of the species is more deadly than the male.
Rudyard Kipling (1865–1936) Indian-born British writer.
The Female of the Species

41 And a woman is only a woman, but a good cigar is a smoke.
Rudyard Kipling
The Betrothed

42 The First Blast of the Trumpet Against the Monstrous Regiment of Women.
John Knox (c. 1514–72) Scottish religious reformer.
Title of Pamphlet, 1558

43 Women run to extremes; they are either better or worse than men.
Jean de La Bruyère (1645–96) French satirist.
Les Caractères

44 So this gentleman said a girl with brains ought to do something else with them besides think.
Anita Loos (1891–1981) US novelist.
Gentlemen Prefer Blondes, Ch. 1

45 Women do not find it difficult nowadays to behave like men; but they often find it extremely difficult to behave like gentlemen.
Compton Mackenzie (1883–1972) British writer.
On Moral Courage

46 The Professor of Gynaecology began his course of lectures as follows: Gentlemen, woman is an animal that micturates once a day, defecates once a week, menstruates once a month, parturates once a year and copulates whenever she has the opportunity.
W. Somerset Maugham (1874–1965) British novelist.
A Writer's Notebook

47 A woman will always sacrifice herself if you give her the opportunity. It is her favourite form of self-indulgence.
W. Somerset Maugham
The Circle, III

48 Because women can do nothing except love, they've given it a ridiculous importance.
W. Somerset Maugham
The Moon and Sixpence, Ch. 41

49 I expect that Woman will be the last thing civilized by Man.
George Meredith (1828–1909) British novelist.
The Ordeal of Richard Feverel, Ch. 1

50 One tongue is sufficient for a woman.
John Milton (1608–74) English poet.
On being asked whether he would allow his daughters to learn foreign languages
Attrib.

51 Women would rather be right than reasonable.
Ogden Nash (1902–71) US poet.
Frailty, Thy Name Is a Misnomer

52 God created woman. And boredom did indeed cease from that moment – but many other

things ceased as well! Woman was God's *second* mistake.
Friedrich Wilhelm Nietzsche (1844–1900) German philosopher.
The Antichrist

53 Whether a pretty woman grants or withholds her favours, she always likes to be asked for them.
Ovid (Publius Ovidius Naso; 43 BC–17 AD) Roman poet.
Ars Amatoria

54 Most good women are hidden treasures who are only safe because nobody looks for them.
Dorothy Parker (1893–1967) US writer.
Obituary, *The New York Times*, 8 June 1967

55 My wife, who, poor wretch, is troubled with her lonely life.
Samuel Pepys (1633–1703) English diarist.
Diary, 19 Dec 1662

56 There are two kinds of women – goddesses and doormats.
Pablo Picasso (1881–1973) Spanish painter.
Attrib.

57 Most women have no characters at all.
Alexander Pope (1688–1744) British poet.
Moral Essays, II

58 Men, some to business, some to pleasure take;
But every woman is at heart a rake.
Alexander Pope
Moral Essays, II

59 Woman's at best a contradiction still.
Alexander Pope
Moral Essays, II

60 Bah! I have sung women in three cities,
But it is all the same;
And I will sing of the sun.
Ezra Pound (1885–1972) US poet.
Cino

61 The fundamental fault of the female character is that it has no sense of justice.
Arthur Schopenhauer (1788–1860) German philosopher.
Gedanken über vielerlei Gegenstände, XXVII

62 Do you not know I am a woman? When I think, I must speak.
William Shakespeare (1564–1616) English dramatist.
As You Like It, III:2

63 Frailty, thy name is woman!
William Shakespeare
Hamlet, I:2

64 I have no other but a woman's reason:
I think him so, because I think him so.
William Shakespeare
The Two Gentlemen of Verona, I:2

65 This Englishwoman is so refined

She has no bosom and no behind.
Stevie Smith (Florence Margaret Smith; 1902–71) British poet.
This Englishwoman

66 Womanhood is the great fact in her life; wifehood and motherhood are but incidental relations.
Elizabeth Stanton (1815–1902) US suffragette.
History of Woman Suffrage (with Susan B. Anthony and Mathilda Gage), Vol. I

67 The really original woman is the one who first imitates a man.
Italo Svevo (Ettore Schmitz; 1861–1928) Italian writer.
A Life, Ch. 8

68 God made the woman for the man,
And for the good and increase of the world.
Alfred, Lord Tennyson (1809–92) British poet.
Edwin Morris

69 How sweet are looks that ladies bend
On whom their favours fall!
Alfred, Lord Tennyson
Sir Galahad

70 It is a great glory in a woman to show no more weakness than is natural to her sex, and not be talked of, either for good or evil by men.
Thucydides (c. 460–c. 400 BC) Greek historian and general.
History of the Peloponnesian War, Bk. II, Ch. 45

71 I was seized by the stern hand of Compulsion, that dark, unseasonable Urge that impels women to clean house in the middle of the night.
James Thurber (1894–1961) US humorist.
Alarms and Diversions, 'There's a Time for Flags'

72 I am a source of satisfaction to him, a nurse, a piece of furniture, a *woman* – nothing more.
Sophie Tolstoy (1844–1919) Russian writer.
A Diary of Tolstoy's Wife, 1860–1891

73 With many women I doubt whether there be any more effectual way of touching their hearts than ill-using them and then confessing it. If you wish to get the sweetest fragrance from the herb at your feet, tread on it and bruise it.
Anthony Trollope (1815–82) British novelist.
Miss Mackenzie, Ch. 10

74 Scarce, sir. Mighty scarce.
Mark Twain (Samuel Langhorne Clemens; 1835–1910) US writer.
Responding to the question 'In a world without women what would men become?'
Attrib.

75 As if a woman of education bought things because she wanted 'em.
John Vanbrugh (1664–1726) English architect and dramatist.
The Confederacy, II:1

76 Once a woman has given you her heart you can never get rid of the rest of her.
John Vanbrugh
The Relapse, II:1

77 Woman is always fickle and changing.
Virgil (Publius Vergilius Maro; 70–19 BC) Roman poet.
Aeneid, Bk. IV

78 I have often observed in women of her type a tendency to regard all athletics as inferior forms of fox-hunting.
Evelyn Waugh (1903–66) British novelist.
Decline and Fall, Pt. I, Ch. 10

79 'I will not stand for being called a woman in my own house,' she said.
Evelyn Waugh
Scoop, Bk. I, Ch. 5

80 There is nothing in the whole world so unbecoming to a woman as a Nonconformist conscience.
Oscar Wilde (1854–1900) Irish-born British dramatist.
Lady Windermere's Fan, III

81 I would venture to guess that Anon, who wrote so many poems without signing them, was often a woman.
Virginia Woolf (1882–1941) British novelist.
A Room of One's Own

82 Women have served all these centuries as looking-glasses possessing the magic and delicious power of reflecting the figure of man at twice its natural size.
Virginia Woolf
A Room of One's Own

WONDER

See also admiration, curiosity

1 For all knowledge and wonder (which is the seed of knowledge) is an impression of pleasure in itself.
Francis Bacon (1561–1626) English philosopher.
The Advancement of Learning, Bk. I, Ch. 1

2 To see a World in a grain of sand,
And a Heaven in a wild flower,
Hold Infinity in the palm of your hand,
And Eternity in an hour.
William Blake (1757–1827) British poet.
Auguries of Innocence

3 Two things fill the mind with ever new and increasing wonder and awe, the more often and the more seriously reflection concentrates upon them: the starry heaven above me and the moral law within me.
Immanuel Kant (1724–1804) German philosopher.
Critique of Practical Reason, Conclusion

4 Philosophy is the product of wonder.
A. N. Whitehead (1861–1947) British philosopher.
Nature and Life, Ch. 1

WORDS

See also language, speech, verbosity

1 In the beginning was the Word, and the Word was with God, and the Word was God.
1:1

2 Actions speak louder than words.
Proverb

3 He said true things, but called them by wrong names.
Robert Browning (1812–89) British poet.
Bishop Blougram's Apology

4 Oaths are but words, and words but wind.
Samuel Butler (1612–80) English satirist.
Hudibras, Pt. II

5 Be not the slave of Words.
Thomas Carlyle (1795–1881) Scottish historian and essayist.
Sartor Resartus, Bk I, Ch. 8

6 We must have a better word than 'prefabricated'. Why not 'ready-made'?
Winston Churchill (1874–1965) British statesman.
Closing the Ring, Appendix C

7 Words as is well known, are great foes of reality.
Joseph Conrad (Teodor Josef Konrad Korzeniowski; 1857–1924) Polish-born British novelist.
Under Western Eyes

8 You can stroke people with words.
F. Scott Fitzgerald (1896–1940) US novelist.
The Crack-up

9 It was in the barbarous, gothic times when words had a meaning; in those days, writers expressed thoughts.
Anatole France (Jacques Anatole François Thibault; 1844–1924) French writer.
The Literary Life, 'M. Charles Morice'

10 Many terms which have now dropped out of favour, will be revived, and those that are at present respectable will drop out, if usage so choose, with whom resides the decision and the judgement and the code of speech.
Horace (Quintus Horatius Flaccus; 65–8 BC) Roman poet.
Ars Poetica

11 Thanks to words, we have been able to rise above the brutes; and thanks to words, we have often sunk to the level of the demons.
Aldous Huxley (1894–1964) British novelist.
Adonis and the Alphabet

12 *Net.* Anything reticulated or decussated at equal distances, with interstices between the intersections.
Samuel Johnson (1709–84) British lexicographer.
Dictionary of the English Language

13 Words are, of course, the most powerful drug used by mankind.
Rudyard Kipling (1865–1936) Indian-born British writer.
Speech, 14 Feb 1923

14 Words are men's daughters, but God's sons are things.
Samuel Madden (1686–1765) Irish writer.
Boulter's Monument

15 Until we learn the use of living words we shall continue to be waxworks inhabited by gramophones.
Walter De La Mare (1873–1956) British poet.
The Observer, 'Sayings of the Week', 12 May 1929

16 I am a Bear of Very Little Brain, and long words Bother me.
A. A. Milne (1882–1956) British writer.
Winnie-the-Pooh, Ch. 4

17 It is an important general rule always to refer to your friend's country establishment as a 'cottage'.
Stephen Potter (1900–69) British writer.
Lifemanship, Ch. 2

18 There is a Southern proverb, – fine words butter no parsnips.
Walter Scott (1771–1832) Scottish novelist.
The Legend of Montrose, Ch. 3

19 For words, like Nature, half reveal
And half conceal the Soul within.
Alfred, Lord Tennyson (1809–92) British poet.
In Memoriam A.H.H., V

20 No, my dear, it is *I* who am surprised; you are merely astonished.
Noah Webster (1758–1843) US lexicographer.
Responding to his wife's comment that she had been surprised to find him embracing their maid
Attrib.

WORK

See also effort, unemployment

1 All work and no play makes Jack a dull boy.
Proverb

2 No bees, no honey; no work, no money.
Proverb

3 Whatsoever thy hand findeth to do, do it with thy might; for there is no work, nor device, nor knowledge, nor wisdom, in the grave, whither thou goest.
Bible: Ecclesiastes
9:10

4 For even when we were with you, this we commanded you, that if any would not work, neither should he eat.
Bible: II Thessalonians
3:10

5 There is dignity in work only when it is work freely accepted.
Albert Camus (1913–60) French existentialist writer.
Notebooks, 1935–42

6 Work is the grand cure of all the maladies and miseries that ever beset mankind.
Thomas Carlyle (1795–1881) Scottish historian and essayist.
Speech, Edinburgh, 2 Apr 1886

7 Work is much more fun than fun.
Noël Coward (1899–1973) British dramatist.
The Observer, 'Sayings of the Week', 21 June 1963

8 By working faithfully eight hours a day you may eventually get to be a boss and work twelve hours a day.
Robert Frost (1875–1963) US poet.
Attrib.

9 When work is a pleasure, life is a joy! When work is a duty, life is slavery.
Maxim Gorky (Aleksei Maksimovich Peshkov; 1868–1936) Russian writer.
The Lower Depths

10 That one must do some work seriously and must be independent and not merely amuse oneself in life – this our mother has told us always, but never that science was the only career worth following.
Iréne Joliot-Curie (1897–1956) French scientist.
Recalling the advice of her mother, Marie Curie
A Long Way from Missouri (Mary Margaret McBride), Ch. 10

11 Horny-handed sons of toil.
Denis Kearney (1847–1907) US Labor leader.
Speech, San Francisco, c. 1878

12 It's been a hard day's night.
John Lennon (1940–80) British rock musician.
A Hard Day's Night (with Paul McCartney)

13 Life is too short to do anything for oneself that one can pay others to do for one.
W. Somerset Maugham (1874–1965) British novelist.
The Summing Up

14 The rise in the total of those employed is governed by Parkinson's Law and would be much the same whether the volume of work were to increase, diminish or even disappear.
Cyril Northcote Parkinson (1919–) British historian and writer.
Parkinson's Law, Ch. 1

15 Work expands so as to fill the time available for its completion.
Cyril Northcote Parkinson
Parkinson's Law, Ch. 1

16 Work is necessary for man. Man invented the alarm clock.
Pablo Picasso (1881–1973) Spanish painter.
Attrib.

17 They say hard work never hurt anybody, but I figure why take the chance.
Ronald Reagan (1911–) US Republican president.
Attrib.

18 If you have great talents, industry will improve them: if you have but moderate abilities, industry will supply their deficiency.
Joshua Reynolds (1723–92) British portrait painter.
Discourse to Students of the Royal Academy, 11 Dec 1769

19 I wish to preach, not the doctrine of ignoble ease, but the doctrine of the strenuous life.
Theodore Roosevelt (1858–1919) US Republican president.
Speech, Chicago, 10 Apr 1899

20 One of the symptoms of approaching nervous breakdown is the belief that one's work is terribly important. If I were a medical man, I should prescribe a holiday to any patient who considered his work important.
Bertrand Russell (1872–1970) British philosopher.
The Autobiography of Bertrand Russell, Vol. II, Ch. 5

21 The only place where success comes before work is a dictionary.
Vidal Sassoon (1928–) British hair stylist.
Quoting one of his teachers in a BBC radio broadcast

22 Pennies do not come from heaven. They have to be earned here on earth.
Margaret Thatcher (1925–) British politician and prime minister.
Sunday Telegraph, 1982

23 Work banishes those three great evils, boredom, vice, and poverty.
Voltaire (François-Marie Arouet; 1694–1778) French writer.
Candide, Ch. 30

24 How doth the little busy bee
Improve each shining hour,
And gather honey all the day
From every opening flower!
Isaac Watts (1674–1748) English theologian and hymn writer.
Divine Songs for Children, 'Against Idleness and Mischief'

25 Work is the curse of the drinking classes.
Oscar Wilde (1854–1900) Irish-born British dramatist.
Attrib.

26 I haven't got time to be tired.
Wilhelm I (1797–1888) King of Prussia and Emperor of Germany.
Said during his last illness

WORLD

See also confusion

1 For the world, I count it not an inn, but an hospital, and a place, not to live, but to die in.
Thomas Browne (1605–82) English physician and writer.
Religio Medici, Pt. II

2 As I walked through the wilderness of this world.
John Bunyan (1628–88) English writer.
The Pilgrim's Progress, Pt. I

WORLD WAR II

See also Churchill, Germany, Hitler, Nazism, war

1 How horrible, fantastic, incredible, it is that we should be digging trenches and trying on gas-masks here because of a quarrel in a far-away country between people of whom we know nothing.
Neville Chamberlain (1869–1940) British statesman.
Referring to Germany's annexation of the Sudetenland
Radio broadcast, 27 Sept 1938

2 Hitler has missed the bus.
Neville Chamberlain
Speech, House of Commons, 4 Apr 1940

3 We have sustained a defeat without a war.
Winston Churchill (1874–1965)
Speech, House of Commons, 5 Oct 1938

4 We shall not flag or fail. We shall fight in France, we shall fight on the seas and oceans, we shall fight with growing confidence and growing strength in the air, we shall defend our island, whatever the cost may be, we shall fight on the beaches, we shall fight on the landing grounds, we shall fight in the fields and in the streets, we shall fight in the hills; we shall never surrender.
Winston Churchill
Speech, House of Commons, 4 June 1940

5 This was their finest hour.
Winston Churchill
Referring to the Dunkirk evacuation
Speech, House of Commons, 18 June 1940

6 The battle of Britain is about to begin.
Winston Churchill
Speech, House of Commons, 1 July 1940

7 Never in the field of human conflict was so much owed by so many to so few.
Winston Churchill
Referring to the Battle of Britain pilots
Speech, House of Commons, 20 Aug 1940

8 We are waiting for the long-promised invasion. So are the fishes.
Winston Churchill
Radio broadcast to the French people, 21 Oct 1940

9 Give us the tools, and we will finish the job.
Winston Churchill
Referring to Lend-lease, which was being legislated in the USA
Radio broadcast, 9 Feb 1941

10 You do your worst, and we will do our best.
Winston Churchill
Addressed to Hitler
Speech, 14 July 1941

11 Do not let us speak of darker days; let us

rather speak of sterner days. These are not dark days: these are great days – the greatest days our country has ever lived.
Winston Churchill
Address, Harrow School, 29 Oct 1941

12 When I warned them that Britain would fight on alone whatever they did, their Generals told their Prime Minister and his divided Cabinet: 'In three weeks England will have her neck wrung like a chicken.'
Some chicken! Some neck!
Winston Churchill
Referring to the French Government; see WEYGAND
Speech, Canadian Parliament, 30 Dec 1941

13 This is not the end. It is not even the beginning of the end. But it is, perhaps, the end of the beginning.
Winston Churchill
Referring to the Battle of Egypt
Speech, Mansion House, 10 Nov 1942

14 Wars are not won by evacuations.
Winston Churchill
Referring to Dunkirk
Their Finest Hour

15 Before Alamein we never had a victory. After Alamein we never had a defeat.
Winston Churchill
The Hinge of Fate, Ch. 33

16 Peace with Germany and Japan on our terms will not bring much rest. . . . As I observed last time, when the war of the giants is over the wars of the pygmies will begin.
Winston Churchill
Triumph and Tragedy, Ch. 25

17 Now we can look the East End in the face.
Elizabeth the Queen Mother (1900–) The wife of King George VI.
Surveying the damage caused to Buckingham Palace by a bomb during the Blitz in World War II
Attrib.

18 This was the Angel of History! We felt its wings flutter through the room. Was that not the fortune we awaited so anxiously?
Joseph Goebbels (1897–1945) German politician.
Referring to Roosevelt's death
Diary

19 They entered the war to prevent us from going into the East, not to have the East come to the Atlantic.
Hermann Goering (1893–1946) German leader.
Referring to the war aims of the British in World War II
Nuremberg Diary (G. M. Gilbert)

20 The little ships, the unforgotten Homeric catalogue of *Mary Jane* and *Peggy IV*, of *Folkestone Belle, Boy Billy*, and *Ethel Maud*, of *Lady Haig* and *Skylark* . . . the little ships of England brought the Army home.
Philip Guedalla (1889–1944) British writer.
Referring to the evacuation of Dunkirk
Mr. Churchill

21 When Barbarossa commences, the world will hold its breath and make no comment.
Adolf Hitler (1889–1945) German dictator.
Referring to the planned invasion of the USSR, Operation Barbarossa, which began on 22 June 1941
Attrib.

22 If we are going in without the help of Russia we are walking into a trap.
David Lloyd George (1863–1945) British Liberal statesman.
Speech, House of Commons, 3 Apr 1939

23 Dear Ike, Today I spat in the Seine.
General George Patton (1885–1945) US general.
Message sent to Eisenhower reporting his crossing of the Seine in World War II
The American Treasury (C. Fadiman)

24 To make a union with Great Britain would be fusion with a corpse.
Marshal Pétain (1856–1951) French marshal.
On hearing Churchill's suggestion for an Anglo-French union, 1940
Their Finest Hour (Winston S. Churchill), Ch. 10

25 Our great-grandchildren, when they learn how we began this war by snatching glory out of defeat . . . may also learn how the little holiday steamers made an excursion to hell and came back glorious.
J. B. Priestley (1894–1984) British novelist.
Referring to the British Expeditionary Force's evacuation from Dunkirk
Broadcast, 5 June 1940

26 The best immediate defence of the United States is the success of Great Britain defending itself.
Franklin D. Roosevelt (1882–1945) US Democratic president.
At press conference, 17 Dec 1940.
Their Finest Hour (Winston S. Churchill), Ch. 28

27 Defeat of Germany means the defeat of Japan, probably without firing a shot or losing a life.
Franklin D. Roosevelt
The Hinge of Fate (Winston S. Churchill), Ch. 25

28 We have finished the job, what shall we do with the tools?
Haile Selassie (1892–1975) Emperor of Ethiopia.
Telegram sent to Winston Churchill, mimicking his 'Give us the tools, and we will finish the job'
Ambrosia and Small Beer, Ch. 4 (Edward Marsh)

29 If we see that Germany is winning the war we ought to help Russia, and if Russia is winning we ought to help Germany, and in that way let them kill as many as possible.
Harry S. Truman (1884–1972) US statesman.
New York Times, 24 July 1941, when Russia was invaded by Germany

30 In three weeks England will have her neck wrung like a chicken.
Maxime Weygand (1867–1965) French general.
Said at the fall of France; see CHURCHILL
Their Finest Hour (Winston S. Churchill)

31 I fear we have only awakened a sleeping giant, and his reaction will be terrible.
Isoroku Yamamoto (1884–1943) Japanese admiral.
Said after the Japanese attack on Pearl Harbor, 1941

WORLD-WEARINESS

1 Bankrupt of Life, yet Prodigal of Ease.
John Dryden (1631–1700) British poet and dramatist.
Absalom and Achitophel, I

2 Spare all I have, and take my life.
George Farquhar (1678–1707) Irish dramatist.
The Beaux' Strategem, V:2

3 I am sick of this way of life. The weariness and sadness of old age make it intolerable. I have walked with death in hand, and death's own hand is warmer than my own. I don't wish to live any longer.
W. Somerset Maugham (1874–1965) British novelist.
Said on his ninetieth birthday
Familiar Medical Quotations (M. B. Strauss)

4 Stop the World, I Want to Get Off.
Anthony Newley (1931–) British actor, composer, singer, and comedian.
With Leslie Bricusse
Title of musical

5 How weary, stale, flat, and unprofitable, Seem to me all the uses of this world!
William Shakespeare (1564–1616) English dramatist.
Hamlet, I:2

6 I have supp'd full with horrors.
William Shakespeare
Macbeth, V:5

7 I gin to be aweary of the sun, And wish th' estate o' th' world were now undone.
William Shakespeare
Macbeth, V:5

WORRY

See also misfortune

1 A trouble shared is a trouble halved.
Proverb

2 Don't meet troubles half-way.
Proverb

3 It will be all the same in a hundred years.
Proverb

4 Take things as they come.
Proverb

5 Begone, dull care! I prithee begone from me! Begone, dull care, you and I shall never agree.
Anonymous
Begone Dull Care

6 Behold the fowls of the air: for they sow not, neither do they reap, nor gather into barns; yet your heavenly Father feedeth them. Are ye not much better than they?

Which of you by taking thought can add one cubit unto his stature?
And why take ye thought for raiment? Consider the lilies of the field, how they grow; they toil not, neither do they spin:
And yet I say unto you, That even Solomon in all his glory was not arrayed like one of these.
Wherefore, if God so clothe the grass of the field, which today is, and tomorrow is cast into the oven, shall he not much more clothe you, O ye of little faith?
Therefore take no thought, saying, What shall we eat? or, What shall we drink? or, Wherewithal shall we be clothed?
Bible: Matthew
6:26–31

7 But seek ye first the kingdom of God, and his righteousness; and all these things shall be added unto you.
Take therefore no thought for the morrow: for the morrow shall take thought for the things of itself. Sufficient unto the day is the evil thereof.
Bible: Matthew
6:33–34

8 Just when we are safest, there's a sunset-touch,
A fancy from a flower-bell, some one's death,
A chorus-ending from Euripides, –
And that's enough for fifty hopes and fears
As old and new at once as Nature's self,
To rap and knock and enter in our soul.
Robert Browning (1812–89) British poet.
Bishop Blougram's Apology

9 Before the cherry orchard was sold everybody was worried and upset, but as soon as it was all settled finally and once for all, everybody calmed down, and felt quite cheerful.
Anton Chekhov (1860–1904) Russian dramatist.
The Cherry Orchard, IV

10 When I look back on all these worries I remember the story of the old man who said on his deathbed that he had had a lot of trouble in his life, most of which had never happened.
Winston Churchill (1874–1965) British statesman.
Their Finest Hour

11 Care
Sat on his faded cheek.
John Milton (1608–74) English poet.
Paradise Lost, Bk. I

12 Worrying is the most natural and spontaneous of all human functions. It is time to acknowledge this, perhaps even to learn to do it better.
Lewis Thomas (1913–) US pathologist.
More Notes of a Biology Watcher, 'The Medusa and the Snail'

WRITERS

See also criticism, Dickens, poets, Shakespeare, writing

1 A reader seldom peruses a book with pleasure until he knows whether the writer of it be a black man or a fair man, of a mild or choleric disposition, married or a bachelor.
Joseph Addison (1672–1719) British essayist.
The Spectator, 1

2 Writers, like teeth, are divided into incisors and grinders.
Walter Bagehot (1826–77) British economist and journalist.
Estimates of some Englishmen and Scotchmen, 'The First Edinburgh Reviewers'

3 I have been told by hospital authorities that more copies of my works are left behind by departing patients than those of any other author.
Robert Benchley (1889–1945) US humorist.
Chips off the Old Benchley, 'Why Does Nobody Collect Me?'

4 Miller is not really a writer but a non-stop talker to whom someone has given a typewriter.
Gerald Brenan (Edward Fitzgerald Brenan; 1894–1987) British writer.
Referring to Henry Miller
Thoughts in a Dry Season, 'Literature'

5 The idea that it is necessary to go to a university in order to become a successful writer, or even a man or woman of letters (which is by no means the same thing), is one of those phantasies that surround authorship.
Vera Brittain (1893–1970) British writer and feminist.
On Being an Author, Ch. 2

6 And, Robert Browning, you writer of plays,
Here's a subject made to your hand!
Robert Browning (1812–89) British poet.
A Light Woman, XIV

7 Literary men are . . . a perpetual priesthood.
Thomas Carlyle (1795–1881) Scottish historian and essayist.
Critical and Miscellaneous Essays, 'The State of German Literature'

8 Mr Shaw is (I suspect) the only man on earth who has never written any poetry.
G. K. Chesterton (1874–1936) British writer.
Referring to George Bernard Shaw
Orthodoxy, Ch. 3

9 The faults of great authors are generally excellences carried to an excess.
Samuel Taylor Coleridge (1772–1834) British poet.
Miscellanies, 149

10 I believe the souls of five hundred Sir Isaac Newtons would go to the making up of a Shakespeare or a Milton.
Samuel Taylor Coleridge
Letter to Thomas Poole, 23 Mar 1801

11 The only way for writers to meet is to share a quick pee over a common lamp-post.
Cyril Connolly (1903–74) British journalist.
The Unquiet Grave

12 A great writer creates a world of his own and his readers are proud to live in it. A lesser writer may entice them in for a moment, but soon he will watch them filing out.
Cyril Connolly
Enemies of Promise, Ch. 1

13 Talent alone cannot make a writer. There must be a man behind the book.
Ralph Waldo Emerson (1803–82) US poet and essayist.
Goethe

14 Creative writers are always greater than the causes that they represent.
E. M. Forster (1879–1970) British novelist.
Gide and George

15 There is no arguing with Johnson; for when his pistol misses fire, he knocks you down with the butt end of it.
Oliver Goldsmith (1728–74) Irish-born British writer.
Life of Johnson (J. Boswell)

16 The work of Henry James has always seemed divisible by a simple dynastic arrangement into three reigns: James I, James II, and the Old Pretender.
Philip Guedalla (1889–1944) British writer.
Collected Essays, 'Men of Letters: Mr. Henry James'

17 His worst is better than any other person's best.
William Hazlitt (1778–1830) British essayist.
English Literature, Ch. XIV, 'Sir Walter Scott'

18 He writes as fast as they can read, and he does not write himself down.
William Hazlitt
English Literature, Ch. XIV, 'Sir Walter Scott'

19 Dr Johnson's sayings would not appear so extraordinary, were it not for his *bow-wow way*.
Henry Herbert (1734–94) British general.
Life of Johnson (J. Boswell)

20 He was unperfect, unfinished, inartistic; he was worse than provincial – he was parochial.
Henry James (1843–1916) US novelist.
Referring to Thoreau
Life of Nathaniel Hawthorne, Ch. 4

21 The reciprocal civility of authors is one of the most risible scenes in the farce of life.
Samuel Johnson (1709–84) British lexicographer.
Life of Sir Thomas Browne

22 He is the richest author that ever grazed the common of literature.
Samuel Johnson
Referring to Dr John Campbell
Life of Johnson (J. Boswell), Vol. I

23 Authors are easy to get on with – if you're fond of children.
Michael Joseph (1897–1958) British publisher.
The Observer, 1949

24 One man is as good as another until he has written a book.
Benjamin Jowett (1817–93) British theologian.
Letters of B. Jowett (Abbott and Campbell)

25 A good man fallen among Fabians.
Lenin (Vladimir Ilich Ulyanov; 1870–1924) Russian revolutionary leader.
Referring to Bernard Shaw
Attrib.

26 The last gentleman in Europe.
Ada Beddington Leverson (1862–1933) British writer.
Said of Oscar Wilde
Letters to the Sphinx (Wilde), 'Reminiscences', 2

27 Our principal writers have nearly all been fortunate in escaping regular education.
Hugh MacDiarmid (Christopher Murray Grieve; 1892–1978) Scottish poet.
The Observer, 'Sayings of the Week', 29 Mar 1953

28 The trouble with our younger authors is that they are all in the sixties.
W. Somerset Maugham (1874–1965) British novelist.
The Observer, 'Sayings of the Week', 14 Oct 1951

29 A novelist is, like all mortals, more fully at home on the surface of the present than in the ooze of the past.
Vladimir Nabokov (1899–1977) Russian-born US novelist.
Strong Opinions, Ch. 20

30 English literature's performing flea.
Sean O'Casey (1884–1964) Irish dramatist.
Referring to P. G. Wodehouse
Attrib.

31 He is pretty certain to come back into favour. One of the surest signs of his genius is that women dislike his books.
George Orwell (Eric Blair; 1903–50) British novelist.
Referring to Conrad
New English Weekly, 23 Jul 1936

32 The poor son-of-a-bitch!
Dorothy Parker (1893–1967) US writer.
Quoting from *The Great Gatsby* on paying her last respects to F. Scott Fitzgerald
Thalberg: Life and Legend (B. Thomas)

33 A list of authors who have made themselves most beloved and therefore, most comfortable financially, shows that it is our national joy to mistake for the first-rate, the fecund rate.
Dorothy Parker
Wit's End (R. E. Drennan)

34 Now that the old lion is dead, every ass thinks he may kick at him.
Samuel Parr (1747–1825) British writer and scholar.
Referring to Dr Johnson
Life of Johnson (J. Boswell)

35 A novelist who writes nothing for 10 years finds his reputation rising. Because I keep on producing books they say there must be something wrong with this fellow.
J. B. Priestley (1894–1984) British novelist.
The Observer, 'Sayings of the Week', 21 Sept 1969

36 Everybody writes a book too many.
Mordecai Richler (1931–   ) Canadian novelist.
The Observer, 'Sayings of the Week', 9 Jan 1985

37 Among the many problems which beset the novelist, not the least weighty is the choice of the moment at which to begin his novel.
Vita Sackville-West (Victoria Sackville-West; 1892–1962) British poet and novelist.
The Edwardians, Ch. 1

38 Waldo is one of those people who would be enormously improved by death.
Saki (Hector Hugh Munro; 1870–1916) British writer.
Referring to Ralph Waldo Emerson
The Feast of Nemesis

39 Sherard Blaw, the dramatist who had discovered himself, and who had given so ungrudgingly of his discovery to the world.
Saki
The Unbearable Bassington, Ch. 13

40 The Big Bow-Wow strain I can do myself like any now going; but the exquisite touch, which renders ordinary commonplace things and characters interesting, from the truth of the description and the sentiment, is denied to me.
Walter Scott (1771–1832) Scottish novelist.
In praise of Jane Austen
Journal, 14 Mar 1826

41 I enjoyed talking to her, but thought *nothing* of her writing. I considered her 'a beautiful little knitter'.
Edith Sitwell (1887–1964) British poet and writer.
Referring to Virginia Woolf
Letter to G. Singleton

42 That great Cham of literature, Samuel Johnson.
Tobias Smollett (1721–71) British novelist.
Letter to John Wilkes, 16 Mar 1759

43 No regime has ever loved great writers, only minor ones.
Alexander Solzhenitsyn (1918–   ) Soviet novelist.
The First Circle, Ch. 57

44 William Congreve is the only sophisticated playwright England has produced; and like Shaw, Sheridan, and Wilde, his nearest rivals, he was brought up in Ireland.
Kenneth Tynan (1927–80) British theatre critic.
Curtains, 'The Way of the World'

45 I wouldn't give up writing about God at this stage, if I was you. It would be like P. G.

Wodehouse dropping Jeeves half-way through the Wooster series.

Evelyn Waugh (1903–66) British novelist.
Said to Graham Greene, who proposed to write a political novel
Evelyn Waugh (Christopher Sykes)

46 In my situation as Chancellor of the University of Oxford, I have been much exposed to authors.

Duke of Wellington (1769–1852) British general and statesman.
Collections and Recollections (G. W. E. Russell)

47 I think it's good for a writer to think he's dying; he works harder.

Tennessee Williams (1911–83) US dramatist.
The Observer, 'Sayings of the Week', 31 Oct 1976

48 Of all the great Victorian writers, he was probably the most antagonistic to the Victorian age itself.

Edmund Wilson (1895–1972) US critic and writer.
Referring to Dickens
The Wound and the Bow, 'The Two Scrooges'

49 Literature is strewn with the wreckage of men who have minded beyond reason the opinions of others.

Virginia Woolf (1882–1941) British novelist.
A Room of One's Own

50 It's not a writer's business to hold opinions.

W. B. Yeats (1865–1939) Irish poet.
Speaking to playwright, Denis Johnston
The Guardian, 5 May 1977

WRITING

See also books, criticism, fiction, inspiration, letter-writing, literacy, literature, novels, plays, poetry, poetry and prose, prose, reading, style, writers

1 Every book must be chewed to get out its juice.

Chinese proverb
Proverb

2 The style is the man.

Proverb

3 Beneath the rule of men entirely great,
The pen is mightier than the sword.

Edward Bulwer-Lytton (1803–73) British novelist and politician.
Richelieu, II:2

4 From this it is clear how much more cruel the pen is than the sword.

Robert Burton (1577–1640) English scholar and explorer.
Anatomy of Melancholy, Pt. I

5 NINA. Your play's hard to act, there are no living people in it.

TREPLEV. Living people! We should show life neither as it is nor as it ought to be, but as we see it in our dreams.

Anton Chekhov (1860–1904) Russian dramatist.
The Seagull, I

6 Better to write for yourself and have no public, than write for the public and have no self.

Cyril Connolly (1903–74) British journalist.
Turnstile One (ed. V. S. Pritchett)

7 All good writing is *swimming under water* and holding your breath.

F. Scott Fitzgerald (1896–1940) US novelist.
Letter to Frances Scott Fitzgerald

8 No tears in the writer, no tears in the reader.

Robert Frost (1875–1963) US poet.
Collected Poems, Preface

9 Another damned, thick, square book! Always scribble, scribble, scribble! Eh! Mr Gibbon?

William, Duke of Gloucester (1743–1805) The brother of George III.
Addressing Edward Gibbon, author of *The History of the Decline and Fall of the Roman Empire*
Literary Memorials (Best)

10 You must write for children in the same way as you do for adults, only better.

Maxim Gorky (Aleksei Maksimovich Peshkov; 1868–1936) Russian writer.
Attrib.

11 You will have written exceptionally well if, by skilful arrangement of your words, you have made an ordinary one seem original.

Horace (Quintus Horatius Flaccus; 65–8 BC) Roman poet.
Ars Poetica

12 A bad book is as much a labour to write as a good one; it comes as sincerely from the author's soul.

Aldous Huxley (1894–1964) British novelist.
Point Counter Point

13 A man will turn over half a library to make one book.

Samuel Johnson (1709–84) British lexicographer.
Life of Johnson (J. Boswell), Vol. II

14 What is written without effort is in general read without pleasure.

Samuel Johnson
Johnsonian Miscellanies (ed. G. B. Hill), Vol. II

15 Read over your compositions, and where ever you meet with a passage which you think is particularly fine, strike it out.

Samuel Johnson
Recalling the advice of a college tutor
Life of Johnson (J. Boswell), Vol. II

16 No man but a blockhead ever wrote, except for money.

Samuel Johnson
Life of Johnson (J. Boswell), Vol. III

17 Many suffer from the incurable disease of writing, and it becomes chronic in their sick minds.

Juvenal (Decimus Junius Juvenalis; 60–130 AD) Roman satirist.
Satires, VII

18 Clear writers, like clear fountains, do not seem so deep as they are; the turbid look the most profound.
Walter Savage Landor (1775–1864) British poet and writer.
Imaginary Conversations, 'Southey and Porson'

19 I like to write when I feel spiteful: it's like having a good sneeze.
D. H. Lawrence (1885–1930) British novelist.
Letter to Lady Cynthia Asquith, Nov 1913

20 When once the itch of literature comes over a man, nothing can cure it but the scratching of a pen.
Samuel Lover (1797–1868) Irish novelist.
Handy Andy, Ch. 36

21 I shall not be satisfied unless I produce something that shall for a few days supersede the last fashionable novel on the tables of young ladies.
Lord Macaulay (1800–59) British historian.
Letter to Macvey Napier, 5 Nov 1841

22 There is an impression abroad that everyone has it in him to write one book; but if by this is implied a good book the impression is false.
W. Somerset Maugham (1874–1965) British novelist.
The Summing Up

23 I suffer from the disease of writing books and being ashamed of them when they are finished.
Baron de Montesquieu (1688–1755) French writer.
Pensées diverses

24 Writing is like getting married. One should never commit oneself until one is amazed at one's luck.
Iris Murdoch (1919–) Irish-born British novelist.
The Black Prince, 'Bradley Pearson's Foreword'

25 Poor Knight! he really had two periods, the first – a dull man writing broken English, the second – a broken man writing dull English.
Vladimir Nabokov (1899–1977) Russian-born US novelist.
The Real Life of Sebastian Knight, Ch. 1

26 True ease in writing comes from art, not chance,
As those move easiest who have learn'd to dance.
'Tis not enough no harshness gives offence,
The sound must seem an echo to the sense.
Alexander Pope (1688–1744) British poet.
An Essay on Criticism

27 Make 'em laugh; make 'em cry; make 'em wait.
Charles Reade (1911–77) British novelist and dramatist.
Advice to an aspiring writer
Attrib.

28 The profession of letters is, after all, the only one in which one can make no money without being ridiculous.
Jules Renard (1894–1910) French writer.
Journal

29 My scribbling pays me zero francs per line – not including the white spaces.
Marquis de Rochefort (1830–1913) French journalist.
Referring to his salary as a writer
Autant en apportent les mots (Pedrazzini)

30 No, this right hand shall work it all off.
Walter Scott (1771–1832) Scottish novelist.
Refusing offers of help following his bankruptcy in 1826
Century of Anecdote (J. Timbs)

31 Writing, when properly managed, (as you may be sure I think mine is) is but a different name for conversation.
Laurence Sterne (1713–68) Irish-born British writer.
Tristram Shandy

32 Whatever sentence will bear to be read twice, we may be sure was thought twice.
Henry David Thoreau (1817–62) US writer.
Journal, 1842

33 Not that the story need be long, but it will take a long while to make it short.
Henry David Thoreau
Letter, 16 Nov 1867

34 Three hours a day will produce as much as a man ought to write.
Anthony Trollope (1815–82) British novelist.
Autobiography, Ch. 15

35 I put the words down and push them a bit.
Evelyn Waugh (1903–66) British novelist.
Obituary, *New York Times*, 11 Apr 1966

36 All my novels are an accumulation of detail. I'm a bit of a bower-bird.
Patrick White (1912–) British-born Australian novelist.
Southerly, 139

37 Every great and original writer, in proportion as he is great and original, must himself create the taste by which he is to be relished.
William Wordsworth (1770–1850) British poet.
Lyrical Ballads, Preface

YIELDING

See also determination, weakness

1 The concessions of the weak are the concessions of fear.
Edmund Burke (1729–97) British politician.
Speech on Conciliation with America (House of Commons, 22 Mar 1775)

2 He that complies against his will,
Is of his own opinion still.
Samuel Butler (1612–80) English satirist.
Hudibras, Pt. III

YOUTH

See also age, children

1 Better is a poor and a wise child than an old and foolish king, who will no more be admonished.
Bible: Ecclesiastes
4:13

2 It is good for a man that he bear the yoke in his youth.
Bible: Lamentations
3:27

3 Youth is something very new: twenty years ago no one mentioned it.
Coco Chanel (1883–1971) French dress designer.
Coco Chanel, Her Life, Her Secrets (Marcel Haedrich)

4 I remember my youth and the feeling that will never come back any more – the feeling that I could last for ever, outlast the sea, the earth, and all men; the deceitful feeling that lures us on to perils, to love, to vain effort – to death . . .
Joseph Conrad (Teodor Josef Konrad Korzeniowski; 1857–1924) Polish-born British novelist.
Youth

5 The young always have the same problem – how to rebel and conform at the same time. They have now solved this by defying their parents and copying one another.
Quentin Crisp (?1910–   ) Model, publicist, and writer.
The Naked Civil Servant

6 Almost everything that is great has been done by youth.
Benjamin Disraeli (1804–81) British statesman.
Coningsby, Bk. III, Ch. 1

7 I never dared be radical when young, for fear it would make me conservative when old.
Robert Frost (1875–1963) US poet.
Precaution

8 *Les enfants terribles.*
The embarrassing young.
Paul Gavarni (1801–66) French illustrator.
Title of a series of prints

9 Youth will come here and beat on my door, and force its way in.
Henrik Ibsen (1828–1906) Norwegian dramatist.
The Master Builder, I

10 Young men make great mistakes in life; for one thing, they idealize love too much.
Benjamin Jowett (1817–93) British theologian.
Letters of B. Jowett (Abbott and Campbell)

11 When all the world is young, lad,
And all the trees are green;
And every goose a swan, lad,
And every lass a queen;
Then hey for boot and horse, lad,
And round the world away:
Young blood must have its course, lad,
And every dog his day.
Charles Kingsley (1819–75) British writer.
Songs from The Water Babies, 'Young and Old'

12 Youth is a malady of which one becomes cured a little every day.
Benito Mussolini (1883–1945) Italian dictator.
Said on his 50th birthday

13 The atrocious crime of being a young man . . . I shall neither attempt to palliate nor deny.
William Pitt the Elder (1708–78) British statesman.
Speech, House of Commons, 27 Jan 1741

14 My salad days,
When I was green in judgment, cold in blood,
To say as I said then!
William Shakespeare (1564–1616) English dramatist and critic.
Antony and Cleopatra, I:5

15 I would there were no age between ten and three and twenty, or that youth would sleep out the rest; for there is nothing in the between but getting wenches with child, wronging the ancientry, stealing, fighting.
William Shakespeare
The Winter's Tale, III:3

16 Far too good to waste on children.
George Bernard Shaw (1856–1950) Irish dramatist and critic.
10,000 Jokes, Toasts, and Stories (L. Copeland)

17 Live as long as you may, the first twenty years are the longest half of your life.
Robert Southey (1774–1843) British poet.
The Doctor, Ch. 130

18 Young people ought not to be idle. It is very bad for them.
Margaret Thatcher (1925–   ) British politician and prime minister.
The Times, 1984

KEYWORD INDEX

amiable It destroys one's nerves to be a. every day
MARRIAGE, 46

amis *Changez vos a.* FRIENDS, 8

ammunition Praise the Lord and pass the a. WAR, 36

amo *Odi et a.* LOVE AND HATE, 2

amor *A. vincit insomnia* LOVE, 56; SLEEP, 8

amorous the silk stockings and white bosoms . . . excite my a.
propensities LUST, 3

amplified I'm being a. by the mike OBESITY, 4

amputate Thank God they had to a.! WAR, 98

am'rous dire offence from a. causes springs RESULTS, 5

amused how to be a. rather than shocked AGE, 14

I was *very* much a. ROYALTY, 34

one has to be very old before one learns how to be a. AGE, 14

We are not a. ROYALTY, 33

amusing Any a. deaths DEATH, 32

analogy Though a. is often misleading ANALOGY, 1

analysis historian fits a man for psychological a. PSYCHOLOGY, 2

anarchy a well-bred sort of emotional a. CLASSIFICATION, 2

grieved under a *democracy*, call it a. GOVERNMENT, 12

ancestor I am my own a. ANCESTRY, 1

ancestors a. on either side of the Battle of Hastings
ANCESTRY, 4

when his half-civilized a. were hunting the wild boar JEWS, 2

ancestry I can trace my a. back to a . . . globule ANCESTRY, 2

ancient with the a. is wisdom OLD AGE, 5; WISDOM, 5

anecdotage man fell into his a. OLD AGE, 15

angel An a. writing in a book of gold DREAMS, 11

A. of Death has been abroad WAR, 15

A. of the Lord came down CHRISTMAS, 17

in action, how like an a. MANKIND, 26

in comparison with which . . . I am a A. EVIL, 8

In heaven an a. is nobody in particular IMPORTANCE, 2

Is man an ape or an a. EVOLUTION, 7

This was the A. of History WORLD WAR II, 18

woman yet think him an a. LOVE, 131

You may not be an a. LOVE, 50

angels A. can fly SERIOUSNESS, 1

fools rush in where a. fear to tread HASTE, 4

I . . . am on the side of the a. EVOLUTION, 7

Its visits, Like those of a. DEATH, 30

Not Angles, but a. ENGLISH, 14

One more devils'-triumph and sorrow for a. DAMNATION, 1

People are not fallen a. CRITICISM, 25

Tears such as a. weep SORROW, 12

the tongues of men and of a. CHARITY, 5

anger A. is one of the sinews of the soul ANGER, 4

a. makes us all stupid ANGER, 6

A. supplies the arms ANGER, 7

Grief and disappointment give rise to a. EMOTION, 3

he that is slow to a. is better than the mighty SELF-CONTROL, 1

Juno's never-forgetting a. ENDURANCE, 23

Angles Not A., but angels ENGLISH, 14

angling A. is somewhat like poetry FISHING, 8

A. may be said to be . . . like the mathematics FISHING, 4

lovers of virtue; . . . and go a-A. FISHING, 3

We may say of a. as Dr Boteler FISHING, 5

Anglo-Catholic Becoming an A. must . . . be a sad business
CATHOLICISM, 11

Anglo-Saxon Come in, you A. swine INSULTS, 6

those are A. attitudes ENGLISH, 10

angry A. Young Man REBELLION, 7

The man who gets a. . . . in the right way . . . is commended
ANGER, 1

anguish drinking deep of that divinest a. SUFFERING, 4

angular an oblong a. figure HUMOUR, 39

animal information vegetable, a. and mineral KNOWLEDGE, 15

Man is a gaming a. SPORT AND GAMES, 12

man is and will always be a wild a. MANKIND, 24

Man is an intellectual a. INTELLECT, 2

Man is a noble a. MANKIND, 8

man is . . . a religious a. RELIGION, 8

Man is a social a. SOCIETY, 8

Man is by nature a political a. POLITICS, 2

Man is the only a. . . . on friendly terms with the victims
HYPOCRISY, 6

This a. is very bad SELF-PRESERVATION, 3

true to your a. instincts ANIMALISM, 3

Whenever you observe an a. closely ANIMALS, 4

animality its own a. either objectionable or funny HUMOUR, 17

animals A. are such agreeable friends ANIMALS, 10

a. . . . know nothing . . . of what people say about them
ANIMALS, 19

All a. are equal EQUALITY, 15

all a. were created . . . for the use of man ANIMALS, 17

all there is to distinguish us from other a. MANKIND, 4

But if we stop loving a. LOVE, 123

I could . . . live with a. ANIMALS, 22

My music . . . understood by children and a. MUSIC, 46

paragon of a. MANKIND, 26

some a. are more equal than others EQUALITY, 15

There are two things for which a. are . . . envied ANIMALS, 19

Wild a. never kill for sport HUNTING, 3

Anna great A.! whom three realms obey DRINKS, 7

annals short and simple a. of the poor POVERTY, 12

Anne Move Queen A.? Most certainly not MEMORIALS, 12

Annie for bonnie A. Laurie LOVE AND DEATH, 1

annihilating A. all that's made OBLIVION, 3

annihilation No a. REPRESENTATION, 2

anno A. domini . . . the most fatal complaint DEATH, 58

annual A. income twenty pounds ECONOMICS, 5

annuity Buy an a. cheap MONEY, 18

anomaly Poverty is an a. to rich people HUNGER, 2

anon I would . . . guess that A. . . . was often a woman
WOMEN, 81

another A. year! – a. deadly blow DEFEAT, 9

He who would do good to a. GOOD, 2

I would have given you a.! CHIVALRY, 5

Life is just one damned thing after a. LIFE, 27

No man can . . . condemn a. JUDGMENT, 5

answer a. a fool according to his folly FOOLISHNESS, 10

A timid question will . . . receive a confident a. SHYNESS, 2

But a. came there none GREED, 5

give a. as need requireth LEARNING, 2

I do not a. questions like this without being paid
MASCULINITY, 1

more than the wisest man can a. EXAMINATIONS, 1

The a. . . . is blowin' in the wind FREEDOM, 10

the inquisitive mind can . . . receive no a. PHILOSOPHY, 6

where no one asks, no one needs to a. PURPOSE, 4

would not stay for an a. TRUTH, 10

antagonistic the most a. to the Victorian age WRITERS, 48

antan *les neiges d'a.* NOSTALGIA, 22

anthology a. is like all the plums and orange peel BOOKS, 28

antic dance an a. hay DANCING, 6

anticipation the intelligent a. of facts JOURNALISM, 10

anti-clerical it makes me understand a. things CLERGY, 1

anti-climax everything afterward savours of a. PRECOCITY, 1

antidote the a. to desire DESIRE, 5

antipathy dislike the French from . . . vulgar a. FRANCE, 4

strong a. of good to bad PROVOCATION, 2

antiquity Damn the age. I'll write for a. POSTERITY, 7

anti-Semite An American is either a Jew, or an a.
AMERICANS, 9

hated by every a. as if I were a Jew PREJUDICE, 7

anxious a. to do the wrong thing correctly ETIQUETTE, 5

anybody who you are, you aren't a. FAME, 17

anyone a. here whom I have not insulted INSULTS, 8

anywhere go a. I damn well please FREEDOM, 2

apartheid We don't want a. liberalized RACISM, 4

apathy going about the country stirring up a. POLITICS, 79

sheer a. and boredom DISCOVERY, 4

ape having an a. for his grandfather EVOLUTION, 9

Is man an a. or an angel EVOLUTION, 7

It is not the a., nor the tiger HUMAN NATURE, 19

the a. from which he is descended EVOLUTION, 10

The exception is a naked a. MANKIND, 18

ape-like The a. virtues without which EDUCATION, 13

aphorisms The great writers of a. SAYINGS, 3

The hunter for a. . . . has to fish in muddy water SAYINGS, 2

aphrodisiac Fame is a powerful a. FAME, 11

Power is the ultimate a. POWER, 11

apologize a good rule in life never to a. APOLOGIES, 5

It's too late to a. INSULTS, 35

apology Never make a defence or a. ACCUSATION, 1

apostates that peculiar malignity . . . characteristic of a.
BETRAYAL, 1

apostle great a. of the Philistines PHILISTINISM, 2

apostles The Septuagint minus the A. NUMBERS, 4

apparatus *Brain*, n. An a. with which we think MIND, 1

apparel a. oft proclaims the man CLOTHES, 16

appeal The whole of art is an a. to a reality ARTS, 6

appear Things are . . . what they a. to be APPEARANCES, 18

only one position for an a. anywhere — WALES, 3
Remember I'm an a. — ARTISTS, 3
the gentleman from both the a. and the aristocrat — CLASS, 34
What is an a.? — ARTISTS, 9
artistic a. temperament . . . afflicts amateurs — ARTS, 2
There never was an a. period — PHILISTINISM, 8
artists A. are not engineers of the soul — ART, 10
Great a. have no country — NATIONALITY, 7
The a. retired. The British remained — RENUNCIATION, 5
art-loving an A. nation — PHILISTINISM, 8
arts If all the a. aspire to the condition of music — SCIENCE, 31
Murder . . . one of the Fine A. — MURDER, 6
secret of the a. is to correct nature — ARTS, 8
ashamed I am a. of confessing — INNOCENCE, 1
not a. of having been in love — LOVE, 101
some habit of which he is deeply a. — TELEVISION, 2
to see them not a. — REGRET, 20
We are not a. of what we have done — PRIDE, 5
ashes a. of Napoleon — INDIFFERENCE, 6
Asia There is too much A. — PLACES, 8
ask A. no questions — CURIOSITY, 1
To labour and not a. for any reward — SELFLESSNESS, 2
asks where no one a., no one needs to answer — PURPOSE, 4
asleep The devil is a. — LUCK, 10
aspect Meet in her a. — BEAUTY, 13
aspens Willows whiten, a. quiver — WEATHER, 26
aspicious two a. persons — MALAPROPISMS, 1
aspirations The young have a. — AGE, 47
aspires art constantly a. towards . . . music — ART, 19
a. . . . to the condition of art — LITERATURE, 2
aspirings The soul hath not her generous a. — SMOKING, 9
ass every a. thinks he may kick at him — WRITERS, 34
the law is a a. — LAW, 9
assassination Absolutism tempered by a. — RUSSIA, 5
A. has never changed — ASSASSINATION, 1
A. . . . the extreme form of censorship — ASSASSINATION, 5
assemblance Care I for the . . . a. of a man — APPEARANCES, 19
assemblies Kings govern by . . . a. only when — MONARCHY, 11
assertions Pure mathematics consists entirely of a. — MATHEMATICS, 13
asset the greatest a. a head of state can have — SLEEP, 18
assigned purpose of God and the doom a. — DESTINY, 9
associate good must a. — UNITY, 7
I . . . like to a. with . . . priests — CLERGY, 1
assure a. him that he'd live tomorrow — DESTINY, 16
astonished a. at my own moderation — MODERATION, 3
you are merely a. — WORDS, 20
astonishment a little more reverence . . . and not so much a. — SINGING, 3
Dear Sir, Your a.'s odd — EXISTENCE, 1
astound Austria will a. the world — DIPLOMACY, 18
astronauts The a.! . . . Rotarians in outer space — SPACE, 6
astronomy A. teaches the correct use — ASTRONOMY, 3
asunder afar and a. — PARTING, 4
let not man put a. — MARRIAGE, 24
asylum world is . . . like a lunatic a. — MADNESS, 7
asylums lunatic a. . . . the stately homes — STATELY HOMES, 1
atheism a., breast-feeding, circumcision — INDULGENCE, 2
miracle to convince a. — ATHEISM, 2
atheist an a. half believes a God — FEAR, 15
An a. . . . has no invisible means of support — ATHEISM, 5
an a. if the king were — SERVILITY, 4
An a. is one point — ATHEISM, 1
He was an embittered a. — ATHEISM, 8
I am an a. . . . thank God — ATHEISM, 4
scepticism kept her from being an a. — SCEPTICISM, 5
very *chic* for an a. — MEMORIALS, 1
Athens A. arose — EUROPE, 17
A. holds sway over all Greece — INFLUENCE, 8
athletic The only a. sport I ever mastered — SPORT AND GAMES, 8
athletics a. as inferior forms of fox-hunting — WOMEN, 78
Atlantic The Admiral of the A. salutes — ARROGANCE, 10
to have the East come to the A. — WORLD WAR II, 19
atom carbon a. possesses certain exceptional properties — SCIENCE, 20
nearer to the a. than the stars — SCIENCE, 9
The a. bomb is a paper tiger — NUCLEAR WEAPONS, 11
There is no evil in the a. — NUCLEAR WEAPONS, 15
They split the a. by firing particles — SCIENCE, 16
atomic The way to win an a. war — NUCLEAR WEAPONS, 3
atoms fortuitous concurrence of a. — CHANCE, 4

atone a. for the sins of your fathers — INJUSTICE, 7
atrophy Music begins to a. — ARTS, 7
attached a. even to Widnes — ENGLAND, 37
attack A. is the best form — CONFLICT, 1
love until after the first a. — SCEPTICISM, 1
situation excellent. I shall a. — WAR, 35
attainments rare a. . . . but . . . can she spin — WOMAN'S ROLE, 2
attention a. to the inside . . . contempt for the outside — BOOKS, 13
take his a. away from the universe — PRAYER, 11
attic A. wit — HUMOUR, 20
brain a. stocked with all the furniture that he is likely to use — KNOWLEDGE, 13
glory of the A. stage — LIFE, 6
attitudes Anglo-Saxon a. — ENGLISH, 10
attorney the gentleman is an *a.* — LAWYERS, 7
attraction Every arrow . . . feels the a. of earth — AMBITION, 13
The chief a. of military service — ARMY, 3
attractive if they are in the least a. — TRANSLATION, 2
The most a. sentences are not perhaps the wisest — LANGUAGE, 23
audacity a. of elected persons — REVOLUTION, 12
Auden A. was someone you could laugh-at-with — POETS, 24
W. H. A., a sort of gutless Kipling — SOCIALISM, 12
audience I know two kinds of a. — AUDIENCES, 5
the a. want to be surprised . . . by things that they expect — PLAYS, 3
the a. was a disaster — PLAYS, 14
auld a. acquaintance be forgot — FRIENDSHIP, 12
for a. lang syne — FRIENDSHIP, 13
aunt Charley's a. from Brazil — PLACES, 20
aunts bad a. and good a. — FAMILY, 47
Aussie a dinkum hard-swearing A. — PATRIOTISM, 12
Austen Jane A. — WRITERS, 40
Austerlitz There rises the sun of A. — WAR, 73
Australia guess . . . he was born in A. — PLACES, 18
So you're going to A. — PLACES, 10
Australian I'm going to write the Great A. Novel — AMBITION, 19
Austria A. is Switzerland . . . with history added — EUROPE, 12
A. will astound the world with . . . her ingratitude — DIPLOMACY, 18
author An a. who speaks about his own books — EGOTISM, 5
bad novel tells us . . . about its a. — NOVELS, 2
He is the richest a. that ever grazed — WRITERS, 22
authority a. be a stubborn bear — BRIBERY, 4
A. forgets a dying king — ROYALTY, 32
man Dress'd in a little brief a. — MANKIND, 25
No morality can be founded on a. — MORALITY, 2
Nothing destroyeth a. so much — POWER, 4
The defiance of established a. — REBELLION, 1
the highest a. for believing that the meek shall inherit the Earth — HUMILITY, 11
authors A. are easy to get on with — WRITERS, 23
much exposed to a. — WRITERS, 46
The faults of great a. — WRITERS, 9
their a. could not endure being wrong — CRIME, 1
The reciprocal civility of a. — WRITERS, 21
The trouble with our younger a. is — WRITERS, 28
automobile Money differs from an a. — MONEY, 21
avarice rich beyond the dreams of a. — WEALTH, 21
ave *a. atque vale* — GREETINGS, 1
avenged the satisfaction of knowing that we are a. — REVENGE, 14
average Take the life-lie away from the a. man — DELUSION, 4
aves Beadsman, after thousand a. told — PRAYER, 14
Avilion To the island-valley of A. — AFTERLIFE, 9
avoidance The a. of taxes . . . still carries . . . reward — TAXATION, 6
avoiding Reading . . . ingenious device for a. thought — READING, 6
Avon Sweet Swan of A. — SHAKESPEARE, 10
a-waggle You must always be a. — LOVE, 77
awake A.! for Morning in the Bowl of Night — DAY, 5
At last a. — LIFE, 13
I dream when I am a. — REALITY, 1
The lilies and roses were all a. — LOVE, 128
We're very wide a., The moon and I — APPEARANCES, 15
away Over the hills and far a. — LOVE, 57
Take the soup a. — FOOD, 23
the big one that got a. — MARRIAGE, 43
aweary I gin to be a. of the sun — WORLD-WEARINESS, 7

beefsteak Dr Johnson's morality was as English . . . as a b.
ENGLAND, 19

beer chronicle small b.
TRIVIALITY, 12
Did you ever taste b.?
ALCOHOL, 23
Life isn't all b. and skittles
LIFE, 28
that bitter b. that tastes sweet
IMMORTALITY, 5
Beerbohm Max B.
OLD AGE, 45
bees No b., no honey
WORK, 2
No shade, no shine, no butterflies, no b.
MONTHS, 10
Beethoven B.'s Fifth Symphony is the most sublime noise
MUSIC, 18
before I have been here b.
FAMILIARITY, 4
beg only the poor . . . are forbidden to b.
POVERTY, 9
beggar'd b. all description
ADMIRATION, 13
beggars B. can't be choosers
NECESSITY, 1
beggary b. in the love that can be reckon'd
LOVE, 110
no vice but b.
HYPOCRISY, 14
begin Are you sitting comfortably? Then I'll b.
BEGINNING, 12
B. at the beginning
ORDER, 1
beginning a b., a muddle, and an end
NOVELS, 4
As it was in the b.
ETERNITY, 2
a whole is that which has a b., a middle, and an end
PLAYS, 1
Begin at the b.
ORDER, 1
b. of fairies
FAIRIES, 2
end of the b.
WORLD WAR II, 13
every man at the b. doth set forth good wine
ALCOHOL, 14
I like a film to have a b., a middle and an end
CINEMA, 3
in the b. God
CREATION, 2
in the b. was the word
WORDS, 1
Nothing so difficult as a b.
POETRY, 7
the b. of the end
DEFEAT, 8
beginnings end to the b. of all wars
WAR, 93
mighty things from small b.
NATURE, 8
begins my family b. with me
ANCESTRY, 3
begot what they were about when they b. me
FAMILY, 39
begotten Whatever is b., born, and dies
MORTALITY, 23
beguine She refused to begin the 'B.'
PETULANCE, 1
When they begin the b.
HAPPINESS, 16
begun There is an old saying 'well b. is half done'
BEGINNING, 10
behaving men are more interested in . . . justifying themselves
than in . . . b.
MOTIVE, 6
behaviour The quality of moral b. varies
MORALITY, 6
behind In the dusk, with a light b. her
AGE, 27
led his regiment from b.
COWARDICE, 3
part my hair b.
OLD AGE, 17
behold all which we b. Is full of blessings
OPTIMISM, 29
B. her, single in the field
SOLITUDE, 16
b. it was a dream
DREAMS, 3
beholder Beauty is . . . in the eye of the b.
BEAUTY, 21
beige It's b.! My color!
ARCHITECTURE, 12
being in him we live, and move, and have our b.
GOD, 5
Knowledge is proportionate to b.
KNOWLEDGE, 19
To kill a human b.
KILLING, 4
Belfast British troops were patrolling the streets of B.
IRELAND, 8
belfry bats in the b.
MADNESS, 8
belief Action will furnish b.
BELIEF, 5
believe a verb meaning 'to b. falsely'
BELIEF, 8
b. in the life to come
AFTERLIFE, 1
B. it or not
BELIEF, 6
B. nothing of what you hear
BELIEF, 1
don't b. in . . . true love until after the first attack
SCEPTICISM, 1
I b. because it is impossible
BELIEF, 7
I b. I am becoming a god
LAST WORDS, 65
I b. in the Church
RELIGION, 48
I don't b. in fairies
FAIRIES, 1
inclined to b. those whom we do not know
TRUST, 3
Infidelity . . . consists in professing to b.
INTEGRITY, 5
it brings you luck whether you b. . . . or not
SUPERSTITION, 6
They didn't b. me!
BEAUTY, 29
undesirable to b. a proposition
SCEPTICISM, 4
We can b. what we choose
RESPONSIBILITY, 10
what we b. is not necessarily true
OBJECTIVITY, 3
you must b. in God
FAITH, 12
believes He b., . . . that there is such a thing as truth
POLITICIANS, 3
politician never b. what he says
POLITICIANS, 26
bell B., book, and candle
MATERIALISM, 4
for whom the b. tolls
DEATH, 43
I'll b. the cat
COURAGE, 8

The b. strikes one
TIME, 38
The sexton toll'd the b.
PUNS, 5
Unto the B. at Edmonton
MARRIAGE, 40
Bellamy I could eat one of B.'s veal pies
FOOD, 38; LAST WORDS, 45
belle La b. Dame sans Merci
SUPERNATURAL, 9
bellies their b. were full
HUNGER, 3
bells Ring out, wild b., and let him die
ENDING, 7
Rings on her fingers and b. on her toes
NURSERY RHYMES, 41
The b. of hell go ting-a-ling-a-ling
DEATH, 15
'Twould ring the b. of Heaven
ANIMALS, 12
With silver b. and cockle shells
GARDENS, 1
belly Every man with a b. full of the classics
CLASSICS, 7
to banish hunger by rubbing the b.
HUNGER, 6
upon thy b. shalt thou go
SEXES, 2
victory under the b. of a Cossack's horse
RUSSIAN REVOLUTION, 2
bellyful Rumble thy b.
WEATHER, 19
below Capten, art tha sleepin' there b.?
WAR, 76
Down and away b.
DEPARTURE, 1
What thy errand here b.
PURPOSE, 6
Ben Adhem And lo! B.'s name led all the rest
SUPERIORITY, 5
Ben Battle B. was a soldier bold
bench What do you suppose I am on the B. for
REPARTEE, 4
benefactors Our gratitude to most b. is the same as . . . for
dentists
INGRATITUDE, 3
benefits B. make a man slave
MATERIALISM, 1
It is the nature of men to be bound by the b. they confer
OBLIGATION, 2
benevolence husband render unto the wife due b.
MARRIAGE, 21
bereav'd I am black, as if b. of light
RACE, 4
Berkeley A Nightingale Sang in B. Square
BIRDS, 7
Berliner Ich bin ein B.
GERMANY, 6
berries I come to pluck your b.
TREES, 3
berth His death, which happen'd in his b.
PUNS, 5
Things hitherto undone should be given . . . a wide b.
ORIGINALITY, 1
Bertie I'm Burlington B.
BED, 3
best all that's b. of dark and bright
BEAUTY, 13
as in the b. it is
MURDER, 1
beauty being the b. of all we know
BEAUTY, 9
b. of life is but intoxication
DRUNKENNESS, 10
b. that is known and thought in the world
CRITICISM, 4
b. words in the b. order
POETRY AND PROSE, 2
Culture, the acquainting ourselves with the b.
CULTURE, 1
For home is b.
HOME, 9
His worst is better than any other person's b.
WRITERS, 17
It was the b. of times
FRENCH REVOLUTION, 1
look at the b. book . . . price of a turbot
BOOKS, 34
Men of few words are the b.
BREVITY, 8
Stolen sweets are b.
THEFT, 5
The b. is the enemy of the good
EXCELLENCE, 4
The b. of friends
FRIENDSHIP, 6
the b. of possible worlds
OPTIMISM, 27
The b. things in life
WEALTH, 1
the shortest works are always the b.
BREVITY, 4
we live in the b. of all possible worlds
OPTIMISM, 19; PESSIMISM, 3
we will do our b.
WORLD WAR II, 10
bestial what remains is b.
REPUTATION, 5
bestow Let them on every airth a limb
EXECUTION, 9
best-seller A b. . . . because it was selling well
FAME, 5
A b. is the gilded tomb of a mediocre talent
BOOKS, 37
bet I b. my money on the bob-tail nag
HORSES, 4
Bethlehem O come ye to B.
CHRISTMAS, 15
O little town of B.
CHRISTMAS, 11
betimes to be up b.
BED, 8
betray Nature never did b.
NATURE, 18
betraying if I had to choose between b. my country and b. my
friend
BETRAYAL, 2
betrothed a bride's attitude towards her b.
MARRIAGE, 79; PUNS, 14
better a far, far, b. thing
EXECUTION, 6
always . . . trying to get the b.
SPORT AND GAMES, 12
b. is he . . . who hath not seen the evil work . . . under the sun
EVIL, 3
b. strangers
SEPARATION, 6
B. than a play
HOUSES OF PARLIAMENT, 6
b. to have loved and lost
LOVE, 126
b. to have no opinion of God
GOD, 3
b. to marry than to burn
MARRIAGE, 22

blocks philosophy ought to . . . unravel people's mental b.
PHILOSOPHY, 10
blonde A b. to make a bishop kick a hole APPEARANCE, 8
springing from b. to b. like the chamois of the Alps
AMERICANS, 14
blondes Gentlemen always seem to remember b.
APPEARANCE, 22
blood b. and iron POWER POLITICS, 2
B. is thicker FAMILY, 1
B. sport is brought to its ultimate refinement JOURNALISM, 13
b., toil, tears and sweat EFFORT, 3
critics . . . desire our b., not our pain CRITICS, 11
He is all b., dirt and sucked sugar stick CRITICISM, 55
his b. be on us GUILT, 3
humble and meek are thirsting for b. HUMILITY, 7
I am in b. Stepp'd in so far GUILT, 7
leeches have red b. LAST WORDS, 14
rather have b. on my hands COMMITMENT, 4
Seas of B. CHRISTIANITY, 39
shed his b. for the country JUSTICE, 21
The b. of the martyrs is the seed of the Church
CHRISTIANITY, 44
the b. that she has spilt REVENGE, 9
the old savage England, whose last b. flows still ENGLAND, 22
There are two kinds of b. RACE, 2
the River Tiber foaming with much b. PROPHECY, 8; RACE, 16
thy brother's b. crieth unto me MURDER, 2
trading on the b. of my men EXPLOITATION; 3
without shedding of b. is no remission EXECUTION, 2
You can't get b. FUTILITY, 3
your b. of your lives will I require CRIME, 1; PUNISHMENT, 4
bloodiness The sink is the great symbol of the b. of family life
FAMILY, 28
bloody All the faces . . . seem to be b. Poms ENGLISH, 11
My head is b., but unbowed ENDURANCE, 6
bloom It's a sort of b. on a woman CHARM, 1
lilac is in b. FLOWERS, 2
blossom Love's perfect b. LOVE, 92
blow A b. in cold blood VIOLENCE, 6
Another year! – another deadly b. DEFEAT, 9
B., blow, thou winter wind INGRATITUDE, 4
Beware of the man who does not return your b.
FORGIVENESS, 14
B. . . . till you burst CONTEMPT, 2
but a word and a b. VIOLENCE, 2
B., winds, and crack your cheeks WEATHER, 18
themselves must strike the b. FREEDOM, 6
this b. Might be the be-all and the end-all here ENDING, 5
bludgeoning the b. of the people DEMOCRACY, 2
blue Little Boy B., Come blow your horn NURSERY RHYMES, 28
that little tent of b. IMPRISONMENT, 7
The b. ribbon of the turf HORSES, 5
The essence of any b. material HUMOUR, 16
What are those b. remembered hills NOSTALGIA, 10
blues Twentieth-Century B. MELANCHOLY, 4
blue-vested short, b. people FRANCE, 3
blunder poverty . . . is a b. POVERTY, 17
worse than a crime, it is a b. MISTAKES, 4
Youth is a b. AGE, 17
blunders escaped making the b. that he has made
POLITICIANS, 34
blush a b. to the cheek of a young person EMBARRASSMENT, 1
b. to find it fame GOOD, 14
flower is born to b. unseen WASTE, 2
blushes Man is the only animal that b. EMBARRASSMENT, 2
take away the candle and spare my b. MODESTY, 1
Boadicea some bargain-basement B. POLITICIANS, 32
boar when his half-civilized ancestors were hunting the wild b.
JEWS, 2
boarding-house Any two meals at a b. FOOD, 28
boat a beautiful pea-green b. NONSENSE, 20
Do they allow tipping on the b. MONEY, 30
It was involuntary. They sank my b. MODESTY, 2
On a slow b. to China BOATS, 10
boating Jolly b. weather BOATS, 4
boats messing about in b. BOATS, 7
we look for happiness in b. and carriage rides TRAVEL, 3
Bobby B. Shafto's gone to sea NURSERY RHYMES, 5
bob-tail I bet my money on the b. nag HORSES, 6
bodies many b. of the saints which slept arose LAST WORDS, 8
our dead b. must tell the tale ENDURANCE, 16

well-developed b., fairly developed minds, and undeveloped
hearts EDUCATION, 18
body a sound mind in a sound b. HEALTH AND HEALTHY LIVING, 6
b. of a weak and feeble woman ROYALTY, 13
company, . . . have neither a soul to lose nor a b. to kick
BUSINESS, 17
Happiness is beneficial for the b. SORROW, 18
Man has no B. distinct from his Soul SOUL, 4
mind that makes the b. rich APPEARANCES, 21
more familiar with Africa than my own b. INNOCENCE, 8
Our b. is a machine for living REMEDIES, 12
the human b. is sacred MANKIND, 34
the soul is not more than the b. SELF, 20
Why be given a b. if you . . . keep it shut up NAKEDNESS, 5
Bognor Bugger B. LAST WORDS, 24
boil b. at different degrees INDIVIDUALITY, 4
boiler The United States is like a gigantic b. AMERICA, 16
boldness B., and again b. and always b. BOLDNESS, 1
bombs b. *are* unbelievable until they . . . fall WEAPONS, 7
Come, friendly b., and fall on Slough ENGLAND, 3
drop b. . . . hit civilians WAR, 41
Ears like b. APPEARANCE, 7
test the Russians, not the b. NUCLEAR WEAPONS, 5
bon to produce an occasional *b. mot* MARRIAGE, 15
Bonaparte The three-o'-clock in the morning courage, which B.
thought was the rarest COURAGE, 21
Bonar Poor B. can't bear being called a liar POLITICIANS, 45
bone The nearer the b. FOOD, 5
boneless the b. wonder POLITICIANS, 15
bones Bleach the b. of comrades slain WAR, 49
Heat, madam! . . . to take off my flesh and sit in my b.
WEATHER, 25
Of his b. are coral made DEATH, 100
The healthy b. of a single Pomeranian grenadier DIPLOMACY, 4
bonhomie Overcame his natural b. ECONOMICS, 2
Bonjour B. *tristesse* SORROW, 7
bonkers If the British public falls for this . . . it will be . . . b.
POLITICS, 28
bonnie *By the b. milldams o' Binnorie* LOVE, 15
My B. lies over the ocean SEPARATION, 1
bonny the child that is born on the Sabbath day Is b. NURSERY
RHYMES, 33
bonum *Summum b.* GOOD, 3
Boojum Snark *was* a B. NONSENSE, 6
book A b. may be amusing BOOKS, 18
A b.'s a b., although there's nothing in't BOOKS, 9
A b. that furnishes no quotations is, . . . a plaything
QUOTATIONS, 9
a b. that is a b. flowers once BOOKS, 21
a b. to kill time CRITICISM, 30
A good b. is the best of friends BOOKS, 41
A good b. is the precious life-blood BOOKS, 25
An angel writing in a b. of gold: – DREAMS, 11
Another damned, thick, square b. WRITING, 9
any b. should be banned CENSORSHIP, 3
Bell, b., and candle MATERIALISM, 18
dainties that are bred in a b. IGNORANCE, 1
do not throw this b. about BOOKS, 6
Every b. must be chewed WRITING, 1
Everybody writes a b. too many WRITERS, 36
go away and write a b. about it SPEECHES, 1
Go, litel b. BOOKS, 12
half a library to make one b. WRITING, 13
he who destroys a good b., kills reason BOOKS, 24
If a b. is worth reading BOOKS, 32
I have only read one b. READING, 12
I'll drown my b. RENUNCIATION, 4
moral or an immoral b. BOOKS, 43
never got around to reading the b. CRITICISM, 31
Never judge a cover by its b. BOOKS, 22
that everyone has it in him to write one b. WRITING, 22
The number one b. . . . was written by a committee BIBLE, 6
The possession of a b. OSTENTATION, 2
There are two motives for reading a b. READING, 13
There is not any b. Or face DEATH, 118
There must be a man behind the b. WRITERS, 13
unprintable b. that is readable BOOKS, 2
What is the use of a b. BOOKS, 11
What you don't know would make a great b. IGNORANCE, 15
When a b. is boring, they yawn openly BOOKS, 36
without mentioning a single b. BOOKS, 29
Would you allow your wife . . . to read this b. PRUDERY, 1

I hope it will not interfere with the public b. of the country FIRE, 3
it is . . . our b. to lose innocence INNOCENCE, 4
That's the true b. precept BUSINESS, 4
The b. of America is b. AMERICA, 10
The Swiss . . . are not a people so much as a . . . b. SWITZERLAND, 2
To b. that we love we rise betime ENTHUSIASM, 7
Your b. is to put me out of b. ADVICE, 6
businessmen My message to the b. of this country ILLNESS, 3
Buss Miss B. and Miss Beale Cupid's darts do not feel INSENSITIVITY, 1
bust It's a funny thing about that b. AGE, 54
bustle the b. of man's worktime OPTIMISM, 17
busy How doth the little b. bee WORK, 24
It is a stupidity . . . to b. oneself with the correction of the world IMPROVEMENT, 3
The English are b. ENGLISH, 26
thou knowest how b. I must be this day PRAYER, 3
busyness Extreme b. EXCESS, 13
butcher The b., the baker, The candlestick-maker NURSERY RHYMES, 44
butchers Governments needs to have both shepherds and b. GOVERNMENT, 29
butter b. will only make us fat POWER POLITICS, 3
b. wouldn't melt in her mouth ACTORS, 7
fine words b. no parsnips WORDS, 18
Buttercup I'm called Little B. NAMES, 2
buttered a piece of toast . . . fell . . . always . . . on the b. side PERVERSITY, 5
butterflies Literature and b. are the two sweetest passions LITERATURE, 13
No shade, no shine, no b., no bees MONTHS, 10
butterfly a man dreaming I was a b. DREAMS, 4
Float like a b. SPORT AND GAMES, 1
Happiness is like a b. HAPPINESS, 15
buttocks Two b. of one bum FRIENDSHIP, 23
buttress a b. of the church SUPPORT, 5
buy American heiress wants to b. a man MATERIALISM, 14
I could b. back my introduction INTRODUCTIONS, 2
would never b. my pictures PAINTING, 6
bygones Let b. be b. FORGIVENESS, 2
Byron a more worthless set than B. POETS, 25
the words: B. is dead BYRON, 2
When B.'s eyes were shut in death BYRON, 1

C

cabbages c. and kings NONSENSE, 9
The c. are coming now ENGLAND, 3
cabin'd c., cribb'd, confin'd, bound in FEAR, 11
cabs busy driving c. and cutting hair GOVERNMENT, 7
Caesar Ave C., morituri te salutant LAST WORDS, 5
C.! dost thou lie so low DEATH, 98
C. had his Brutus – Charles the First, his Cromwell TREASON, 4
C.'s laurel crown POWER, 6
C.'s wife PURITY, 1
C.'s wife must be above suspicion INTEGRITY, 4
I always remember that I am C.'s daughter EXTRAVAGANCE, 3
I come to bury C. EVIL, 15
Not that I lov'd C. less PATRIOTISM, 26
Regions C. never knew ENGLAND, 12
Rose . . . where some buried C. bled FLOWERS, 4
that C. might be great RUTHLESSNESS, 2
cage Marriage is like a c. MARRIAGE, 78
Nor iron bars a c. IMPRISONMENT, 4
robin redbreast in a c. IMPRISONMENT, 1
She's only a bird in a gilded c. IMPRISONMENT, 3
caged We think c. birds sing, when indeed they cry IMPRISONMENT, 6
Cain the Lord set a mark upon C. REVENGE, 7
caitiff If the rude c. smite the other too REVENGE, 10
cake Bake me a c. as fast as you can NURSERY RHYMES, 37
Let them eat c. HUNGER, 6
cakes no more c. and ale MERRYMAKING, 3
Calais 'C.' lying in my heart DEFEAT, 5
calamities C. are of two kinds MISFORTUNE, 4
the c. of life CLASS, 8
calamity Whatsoever . . . the private c., I hope it will not interfere with the public business of the country FIRE, 3
calculating A dessicated c. machine POLITICIANS, 5

Caledonia C.! stern and wild SCOTLAND, 7
calf but the c. won't get much sleep MISTRUST, 3
the fatted c. PARTIES, 2
call one clear c. for me DUTY, 5
called c. a cold a cold ILLNESS, 2
calm sea is c. to-night SEA, 1
Wisdom has taught us to be c. and meek REVENGE, 10
calumnies C. are answered best INSULTS, 20
Calvary the place, which is called C. EXECUTION, 3
Calvin land of C., oat-cakes, and sulphur SCOTLAND, 8
Cambridge Oxford is on the whole more attractive than C. CAMBRIDGE, 1; OXFORD, 3
Spring and summer did happen in C. CAMBRIDGE, 3
The young C. group CLASSIFICATION, 2
To C. books CAMBRIDGE, 5; OXFORD 6
With equal skill to C. books he sent CAMBRIDGE, 2; OXFORD 4
came I c.; I saw; God conquered VICTORY, 15
I c., I saw, I conquered VICTORY, 1
I c. like Water LIFE AND DEATH, 5
camel easier for a c. to go through the eye of a needle WEALTH, 8
Camelot many-tower'd C. ARTHURIAN LEGEND, 2
To look down to C. CURSES, 4
camera I am a c. OBJECTIVITY, 4
The c. cannot lie. But PHOTOGRAPHY, 2
Campland This is C., an invisible country IMPRISONMENT, 5
campus three major administrative problems on a c. EDUCATION, 28
can Talent does what it c. TALENT AND GENIUS, 3
cancel to c. half a Line DESTINY, 7
cancels debt which c. all others OBLIGATION, 1
candid save me, from the c. friend FRANKNESS, 1
candidates C. should not attempt more than six BIBLE, 2
candle a c. of understanding UNDERSTANDING, 1
Bell, book, and c. MATERIALISM, 18
blow out your c. . . . to find your way GUIDANCE, 2
It is burning a farthing c. at Dover CRITICISM, 17
light a c. to the sun FUTILITY, 8
Like a c. burnt out TIME, 37
little c. throws his beams GOOD, 15
My c. burns at both ends PLEASURE, 21
Out, out, brief c. LIFE, 41
take away the c. and spare my blushes MODESTY, 1
we shall this day light such a c. EXECUTION, 15
candle-light Can I get there by c. NURSERY RHYMES, 17
candles She would rather light c. than curse the darkness COMPLIMENTS, 6
candlestick The butcher, the baker, The c.-maker NURSERY RHYMES, 44
canem Cave c. DOGS, 1
canker killing as the c. to the rose CORRUPTION, 4
cannibal Better sleep with a sober c. than a drunken Christian DRUNKENNESS, 16
cannon-ball c. took off his legs PUNS, 8
canoe every man paddle his own c. INDEPENDENCE, 3
Canossa We will not go to C. DETERMINATION, 8
cant clear your mind of c. . . . REASON, 3
love – all the wretched c. of it LOVE, 61
can't 'C.' will be the epitaph of the British Empire BRITISH EMPIRE, 3
where the Greeks had modesty, we have c. CANT, 1
capability Negative C. DOUBT, 6
capable c. of being well set to music MUSIC, 2
capital Boys are c. fellows in their own way CHILDREN, 30
capitalism C. re-creates POLITICS, 54
c. . . . : the process whereby American girls turn into American women CAPITALISM, 3
I am going to fight c. CAPITALISM, 11
imperialism is the monopoly stage of c. POLITICS, 39
Lenin was the first to discover that c. 'inevitably' caused war CAPITALISM, 14
militarism . . . is one of the chief bulwarks of c. CAPITALISM, 5
unacceptable face of c. CAPITALISM, 4
We cannot remove the evils of c. CAPITALISM, 6
capitalist C. production begets . . . its own negation CAPITALISM, 9
Not every problem someone has with his girlfriend is . . . due to . . . c. . . . production CAPITALISM, 8
capitulate I will be conquered; I will not c. DETERMINATION, 8
Capricorn Lady C., . . . was . . . keeping open bed PROMISCUITY, 2
captain C. of the Pinafore CONCEIT, 9

I am the c. of my soul	RESPONSIBILITY, 7
captains C. of industry	LEADERSHIP, 3
capten C., art tha sleepin' there below?	WAR, 76
captive Beauty stands . . . Led c.	BEAUTY, 27
car The c. has become the carapace	TRAVEL, 20
carapace The car has become the c.	TRAVEL, 20
carbon c. atom possesses certain exceptional properties	
	SCIENCE, 20
carbuncle Like a c. on the face of an old and valued friend	
	ARCHITECTURE, 4
card wrestled with a self-adjusting c. table	TECHNOLOGY, 10
cardinal unbecoming for a c. to ski badly	SPORT AND GAMES, 9
cards an old age of c.	OLD AGE, 31
I have not learned to play at c.	SPORT AND GAMES, 10
care age is full of c.	AGE, 52
Begone, dull c.	WORRY, 5
C. Sat on his faded cheek	WORRY, 11
I c. for nobody	SELFISHNESS, 2
I don't c. for war	WAR, 74
Our progress . . . Is trouble and c.	LIFE, 32
pleasures are their only c.	EXPLOITATION, 2
Sleep that knits up the ravell'd sleave of c.	SLEEP, 13
so vain . . . c. for the opinion of those we don't c. for	
	CONCEIT, 8
take c. of the minutes	TIME, 13
Take c. of the pence	THRIFT, 4
what is past my help is past my c.	INDIFFERENCE, 1
career a lover with any other c. in view	COMMITMENT, 6
having a c. of my own	MARRIAGE, 14
Miss Madeleine Philips . . . was a c.	COMMITMENT, 6
nothing which might damage his c.	SCOTS, 1
science was the only c. worth following	WORK, 10
careers The best c. advice to give to the young	
	OCCUPATIONS, 14
careful be very c. o' vidders	CAUTION, 11
careless first fine c. rapture	BIRDS, 1
carelessness To lose one parent, . . . a misfortune; to lose	
both looks like c.	LOSS, 8
with a slow deliberate c.	READING, 10
cares the earth where c. abound?	BIRDS, 11
careth he that is married c. . . . how he may please his wife	
	MARRIAGE, 23
cargo With a c. of ivory	BOATS, 12
With a c. of Tyne coal	BOATS, 13
caring take millions off the c. services	PATRIOTISM, 17
carpe C. diem	PRESENT, 7
carpenter Walrus and the C.	SEASIDE, 1
carpet a Turkey c. bears to a picture	CRITICISM, 29
only men in rags . . . Mistake themselves for c. bags	
	ETIQUETTE, 3
carriage Go together like a horse and c.	LOVE AND MARRIAGE, 1
very small second-class c.	BOATS, 6
we look for happiness in boats and c. rides	TRAVEL, 13
carriages when they think they are alone in railway c.	
	HABIT, 5
Carthage C. must be destroyed	WAR, 22
case If ever there was a c. of clearer evidence	NONSENSE, 2
in our c. we have not got	WEAPONS, 5
the c. is still before the courts	ARGUMENTS, 6
the reason of the c.	LAW, 21
there had been a lady in the c.	WOMEN, 21
The world is everything that is the c.	LOGIC, 4
casements Charm'd magic c.	BIRDS, 5
cash Nothing links man to man like . . . c.	MONEY, 42
One cannot assess in terms of c. . . . a church tower	
	ENVIRONMENT, 1
only the poor who pay c.	MONEY, 20
take the C. in hand	MONEY, 19
cashiers c. of the Musical Banks	MONEY, 11
casino I have come to regard . . . courts . . . as a c.	
	JUSTICE, 11
cask A c. of wine	ALCOHOL, 1
casket seal the hushed c. of my soul	SLEEP, 11
Cassius C. has a lean and hungry look	MISTRUST, 9
cassock C., band, and hymn-book too	CLERGY, 14
cassowary If I were a c.	CLERGY, 14
cast c. thy bread upon the waters	OPPORTUNITY, 10
he that is without sin . . . let him first c. a stone	SIN, 4
pale c. of thought	CONSCIENCE, 5
The die is c.	IRREVOCABILITY, 1
caste measure the social c. of a person	CLASS, 2
casteth perfect love c. out fear	FEAR, 3; LOVE, 24
casting It is no good c. out devils	DEVIL, 9
castle A c. called Doubting C.	DESPAIR, 3
The house of every one is to him as his c.	PRIVACY, 1
Castlereagh Murder . . . had a mask like C.	MURDER, 12
castles C. in the air	DREAMS, 8
Pale Death kicks his way . . . into . . . the c. of kings	
	EQUALITY, 23
the c. I have, are built with air	DREAMS, 9
casualty except the c. list of the World War	MURDER, 3
The first c. when war comes	WAR, 52
cat A c. has nine lives	LUCK, 2
A c. may look	EQUALITY, 1
a C. of such deceitfulness	CATS, 2
c. is a diagram and pattern of subtle air	CATS, 5
God . . . a cosmic Cheshire c.	GOD, 26
Had Tiberius been a c.	CATS, 1
He bought a crooked c.	NURSERY RHYMES, 52
he is a very fine c.	CATS, 4
Hey diddle diddle, The c. and the fiddle	NURSERY RHYMES, 14
I'll bell the c.	COURAGE, 4
More ways of killing a c.	CHOICE, 3
That tossed the dog, That worried the c.	NURSERY RHYMES, 57
The C., the Rat, and Lovell our dog	INSULTS, 12
What c.'s averse to fish	MATERIALISM, 8
When I play with my c.	CATS, 6
When the c.'s away	ABSENCE, 3
cataclysm Out of their c. but one poor Noah Dare hope to	
survive	SEX, 22
catastrophe to lose one's teeth is a c.	TEETH, 4
When a man confronts c. . . . a woman looks in her mirror	
	SEXES, 23
catch Go, and c. a falling star	NONSENSE, 11
only one c. and that was Catch-22	OBSTRUCTION, 3;
	SELF-PRESERVATION, 5
Catch-22 only one catch and that was C.	OBSTRUCTION, 3;
	SELF-PRESERVATION, 5
catchwords Man is a creature who lives . . . by c.	SEXES, 18
categorical This imperative is C.	MORALITY, 7
cathedrals the ancient c. – grand, wonderful, mysterious	
	RELIGION, 46
Catherine I'm glad you like my C.	PROMISCUITY, 6
Catholic I am a C. . . . . I go to Mass every day	PREJUDICE, 1
I have a C. soul, but a Lutheran stomach	CATHOLICISM, 4
I'm still a C.	CATHOLICISM, 12
quite lawful for a C. woman to avoid pregnancy by . . .	
mathematics	CONTRACEPTION, 3
who, like you, your Holiness, is a Roman C.	CATHOLICISM, 3
Catholics C. and Communists have committed great crimes	
	COMMITMENT, 4
they may be C. but they are not Christians	INSULTS, 7
We know these new English C.	CATHOLICISM, 7
cats All c. are grey	EQUALITY, 2
A lotta c. copy the Mona Lisa	IMITATION, 1
what c. most appreciate . . . is . . . entertainment value	CATS, 3
cattle Actors should be treated like c.	ACTORS, 5
O Mary, go and call the c. home	AGRICULTURE, 4
cause for what high c. This darling of the Gods	DESTINY, 13
the name of perseverance in a good c.	STUBBORNNESS, 3
causes Home of lost c.	OXFORD, 1
they should declare the c. which impel them to . . . separation	
	INDEPENDENCE, 2
cavaliero a perfect c.	HEROISM, 4
Cavaliers C. (Wrong but Wromantic)	HISTORY, 24
cave C. canem	DOGS, 1
I should be like a lion in a c. of savage Daniels	ENEMIES, 5
caverns Gluts twice ten thousand C.	SEA, 8
Through c. measureless to man	PLEASURE, 8
caves be c. . . . in which his shadow will be shown	GOD, 38
sunny pleasure-dome with c. of ice	PLEASURE, 9
caviare c. to the general	TASTE, 6
cease have their day and c. to be	TRANSIENCE, 18
I will not c. from mental fight	ENGLAND, 4
restless Cromwell could not c.	POLITICIANS, 48
ceases forbearance c. to be a virtue	TOLERANCE, 1
celebrate I c. myself	SELF, 18
poetry cannot c. them	SCIENTISTS, 2
celebrity A c. . . . works hard . . . to become known	FAME, 4
The c. . . . known for his well-knownness	FAME, 4
celerity C. is never more admir'd	IMPETUOSITY, 3
celery Genuineness . . . Like c.	SINCERITY, 4
two thousand people crunching c. at the same time	FOOD, 43
Celia Come, my C., let us prove	LOVE, 73

celibacy c. is . . . a muddy horse-pond — MARRIAGE, 83
cello The c. is not one of my favourite instruments — MUSIC, 49
cemetery old c. in which nine of his daughters were lying — SEX, 48
censor Deleted by French c. — NEWSPAPERS, 2
censorship Assassination . . . the extreme form of c. — ASSASSINATION, 5
C. . . . depraving and corrupting — CENSORSHIP, 2
censure All c. of a man's self — SELF, 10
centre I love being at the c. of things — COMMITMENT, 5
century The c. on which we are entering . . . must be the c. of the common man — PUBLIC, 19
The great man . . . walks across his c. — INFLUENCE, 6
the twentieth c. will be . . . the c. of Fascism — FASCISM, 2
cereal Do you *know* what breakfast c. is made of — FOOD, 15
cerebrums larger c. and smaller adrenal glands — WAR, 65
certain I am c. that we will win the election with a good majority — SELF-CONFIDENCE, 6
Nothing is c. but death — DEATH, 9
nothing is c. but death and taxes — TAXATION, 3
One thing is c. — LIFE, 24
certainties begin with c. — CERTAINTY, 1; DOUBT, 1
His doubts are better than . . . c. — DOUBT, 5
cesspool London, that great c. — LONDON, 6
Ceylon spicy breezes Blow soft o'er C.'s isle — MISANTHROPY, 1
chaff An editor . . . separates the wheat from the c. — EDITORS, 3
chain A c. is no stronger — UNITY, 1
the flesh to feel the c. — IMPRISONMENT, 2
chains c. that tie The hidden soul of harmony — MUSIC, 29
It's often safer to be in c. — FREEDOM, 24
Man . . . everywhere he is in c. — FREEDOM, 45
nothing to lose but their c. — MARXISM, 3
chair Give Dayrolles a c. — LAST WORDS, 13
the nineteenth century was the age of the editorial c. — PSYCHIATRY, 8
chairs The c. are being brought in from the garden — SUMMER, 3
chaise All in a c. and pair — MARRIAGE, 40
chaise-longue Wedlock – the . . . deep peace of the double bed after the . . . c. — MARRIAGE, 31
chalices In old time we had treen c. and golden priests — CLERGY, 7
Cham That great C. of literature, Samuel Johnson — WRITERS, 42
chamber rapping at my c. door — SUPERNATURAL, 11
Upstairs and downstairs And in my lady's c. — NURSERY RHYMES, 13
chambermaid a man would be as happy in the arms of a c. — IMAGINATION, 5
chamois springing from blonde to blonde like the c. of the Alps — AMERICANS, 14
champagne Fighting is like c. — WAR, 67
like a glass of c. that has stood — HOUSES OF PARLIAMENT, 2
water flowed like c. — ABSTINENCE, 3
chance every c. brought out a noble knight — NOSTALGIA, 19
time and c. happeneth to them all — CHANCE, 2
Chancellor C. of the Exchequer — TAXATION, 7
change C. is not made without inconvenience — CHANGE, 10
I c., but I cannot die — WEATHER, 22
If you leave a thing alone you leave it to a torrent of c. — CONSERVATISM, 1
Most of the c. we think we see — NOVELTY, 2
Most women set out to try to c. a man — CHANGE, 5
Plus ça c. — CONSTANCY, 3
Popularity? . . . glory's small c. — POPULARITY, 4
The more things c. — CONSTANCY, 3
There is a certain relief in c. — CHANGE, 11
The wind of c. — CHANGE, 14
changed All c., c. utterly — BEAUTY, 40
changeth The old order c. — CHANGE, 18
changez C. vos amis — FRIENDS, 9
changing c. scenes of life — CHANGE, 17
Woman is always fickle and c. — WOMEN, 77
Channel dream you are crossing the C. — BOATS, 6
let the last man . . . brush the C. with his sleeve — WAR, 104
chaos a perfectly possible means of overcoming c. — POETRY, 36
The grotesque c. of a Labour council – a *Labour* council — INCOMPETENCE, 2
chapel Devil always builds a c. there — DEVIL, 7
chapels c. had been churches — ACTION, 11
chaplain twice a day the C. called — IMPRISONMENT, 8
Chaplin C. is no business man — ACTORS, 4
chaps Biography is about C. — BIOGRAPHY, 1
chapter c. of accidents — MISFORTUNE, 8

c. of accidents is the longest . . . in the book — ACCIDENTS, 7
character I had become a woman of . . . c. — CHARACTER, 5
I leave my c. behind — REPUTATION, 8
What is c. but the determination of incident? — CHARACTER, 12
characteristic typically English c. — ENGLISH, 3; UNITY, 4
characters c. in one of my novels — FICTION, 5
Most women have no c. — WOMEN, 57
charge Electrical force . . . causes motion of electrical c. — SCIENCE, 8
charged it was c. against me — INDIFFERENCE, 7
Charing Cross between Heaven and C. — HEAVEN, 12
I went out to C., to see Major-general Harrison hanged — EXECUTION, 22
the full tide of human existence is at C. — LONDON, 9
chariot Swing low sweet c. — DEATH, 16
the dust beneath thy c. wheel — HUMILITY, 5
Time's winged c. — AGE, 35
charity C. begins at home — CHARITY, 1; CHARITY, 9
C. is the power of defending that which we know to be indefensible — CHARITY, 11; HOPE, 5
c. never faileth — CHARITY, 5
c. suffereth long, and is kind — CHARITY, 5
In c. there is no excess — CHARITY, 3
knowledge puffeth up, but c. edifieth — CHARITY, 6; KNOWLEDGE, 8
lectures or a little c. — SELF, 19
now abideth faith, hope, c. — CHARITY, 5
the greatest of these is c. — CHARITY, 5
The living need c. — CHARITY, 5
The man who leaves money to c. in his will — BEQUESTS, 3
without c. are nothing worth — CHARITY, 8
Charles Caesar had his Brutus – C. the First, his Cromwell — TREASON, 4
There were gentlemen and . . . seamen in the navy of C. the Second — NAVY, 3
Charley I'm C.'s aunt from Brazil — PLACES, 20
Charlie C. is my darling — ADMIRATION, 9
charm Conversation has a kind of c. — CONVERSATION, 7
Oozing c. from every pore, He oiled his way — CHARM, 3
the c. . . . of a nomadic existence — CAMPING, 1
charming c. people have something to conceal — CHARM, 2
I heard the bullets whistle, ... c. in the sound — WAR, 121
It is c. to totter into vogue — AGE, 62
People are either c. or tedious — CHARM, 4
charms Whose c. all other maids surpass — ADMIRATION, 7
Charon C., seeing, may forget — LUST, 5
Chartreuse religious system that produced green C. — ALCOHOL, 49
chaste godly poet must be c. himself — POETRY, 9
chastity Give me c. and continence — PROCRASTINATION, 4
Chatterley Put thy shimmy on, Lady C. — PARTING, 7
cheap flesh and blood so c. — POVERTY, 15
cheating *Peace*, n. . . . a period of c. — PEACE, 4
check C. enclosed — MONEY, 34
dreadful is the c. — IMPRISONMENT, 4
cheek Care Sat on his faded c. — WORRY, 11
the c. that doth not fade — APPEARANCE, 17
turn the other c. — REVENGE, 10
whosoever shall smite thee on thy right c. — ENEMIES, 2
cheeks Blow, winds, and crack your c. — WEATHER, 18
cheer cups, That c. but not inebriate — DRINKS, 4
Don't c., boys; the poor devils are dying — WAR, 85
cheerful God loveth a c. giver — GENEROSITY, 1
cheerfulness No warmth, no c., no healthful ease — MONTHS, 10
cheese 265 kinds of c. — FRANCE, 6
bread and c., and kisses — MARRIAGE, 106
c. – toasted, mostly — DREAMS, 12
when the c. is gone — NONSENSE, 4
chemical c. barrage has been hurled against the fabric of life — ECOLOGY, 2
Shelley and Keats were . . . up to date in . . . c. knowledge — POETS, 15; SCIENCE, 15
chemistry he had read Shakespeare and found him weak in c. — SCIENTISTS, 12
cheque Any general statement is like a c. — GENERALIZATIONS, 3
Mrs Claypool's c. will come back to you — HUMOUR, 44
chequer-board a C. of Nights and Days — DESTINY, 6
cherish to love and to c. — MARRIAGE, 27
cherry Before the c. orchard was sold — WORRY, 9
C. ripe, ripe, ripe — BUSINESS, 9
Loveliest of trees, the c. — TREES, 5
Till 'C. ripe' themselves do cry — ADMIRATION, 4
chess Life's too short for c. — SPORT AND GAMES, 3

several young women . . . would render the C. life intensely
difficult CHRISTIANITY, 31
The C. religion cannot be believed by any reasonable person
without one CHRISTIANITY, 29
Christianity C. accepted as given a metaphysical system
CHRISTIANITY, 30
C., . . . but why journalism CHRISTIANITY, 2; JOURNALISM, 3
C. has done a great deal for love CHRISTIANITY, 24
C. has made of death a terror CHRISTIANITY, 36
C. is part of the Common Law of England CHRISTIANITY, 26
C. is the most materialistic of all great religions
CHRISTIANITY, 42
C. . . . says that they are all fools MANKIND, 10
C. the one great curse CHRISTIANITY, 35
C. . . . the one immortal blemish of mankind CHRISTIANITY, 35
decay of C. ALCOHOL, 49
His C. was muscular CHRISTIANITY, 23
local cult called C. CHRISTIANITY, 28
loving C. better than Truth CHRISTIANITY, 22
nothing in C. or Buddhism that quite matches FISH, 2
Rock and roll or C. POPULARITY, 6
Christians C. awake, salute the happy morn CHRISTMAS, 12
Onward, C., onward go ENDURANCE, 24
settle their differences like good C. RELIGION, 3
these C. love one another CHRISTIANITY, 45
they may be Catholics but they are not C. INSULTS, 28
Christ-like C. heroes and woman-worshipping Don Juans
MEN, 6
Christmas At C. I no more desire a rose SUITABILITY, 4
C. should fall out in the Middle of Winter CHRISTMAS, 1
Eating a C. pie NURSERY RHYMES, 29
For C. comes but once a year CHRISTMAS, 18
I'm walking backwards till C. NONSENSE, 23
perceive C. through its wrapping CHRISTMAS, 19
The first day of C., My true love sent to me NURSERY
RHYMES, 49
'Twas the night before C. CHRISTMAS, 13
Christopher C. Robin went down with Alice SOLDIERS, 3
chronicle c. small beer TRIVIALITY, 12
the c. of wasted time HISTORY, 29
church an alien C. IRELAND, 4
Beware when you take on the C. of God RELIGION, 53
But get me to the c. on time MARRIAGE, 73
he'd go to c., start a revolution – *something* MATERIALISM, 15
I believe in the C. RELIGION, 48
straying away from the c. RELIGION, 5
The blood of the martyrs is the seed of the C.
CHRISTIANITY, 44
The C. exists CHURCH, 5
The C.'s one foundation CHRISTIANITY, 40
The farther you go from the c. of Rome PROTESTANTISM, 3
There are many who stay away from c. RELIGION, 39
There is no salvation outside the c. RELIGION, 2
There was I, waiting at the c. MARRIAGE, 72
where MCC ends and the C. of England begins CHURCH, 4
churches chapels had been c. ACTION, 11
c. have kill'd their Christ CLERGY, 13
the c. . . . bore for me the same relation to God that billboards
did to Coca-Cola RELIGION, 54
The itch of disputing will prove the scab of c. RELIGION, 64
churchman a species of person called a 'Modern C.'
RELIGION, 59
churchyard A piece of c. fits everybody DEATH, 2
Cicero C. And . . . Homer were *Mad as the mist and snow*
MADNESS, 14
cider c. and tinned salmon FOOD, 44
cigar a good c. is a smoke WOMEN, 41
It is like a c. . . . it never tastes quite the same LOVE, 139
cigarette A c. is . . . a perfect pleasure SMOKING, 15
Cinderella poetry, 'The C. of the Arts.' POETRY, 32
cinema c. is truth twenty-four times a second CINEMA, 4
circle All things from eternity . . . come round in a c.
HISTORY, 4
circumcised our fingers are c. MUSICIANS, 4
When they c. Herbert Samuel INSULTS, 24
circumcision Every luxury . . . – atheism, breast-feeding, c.
INDULGENCE, 2
circumlocution C. Office BUREAUCRACY, 4
circumstance Pride, pomp, and c. WAR, 107
To a philosopher no c., . . . is too minute PHILOSOPHERS, 2
circumstances to face straitened c. at home POVERTY, 20
circumstantial Some c. evidence is very strong PROOF, 6

circuses bread and c. PUBLIC, 15
cities I have sung women in three c. WOMEN, 60
many c. had rubbed him smooth TRAVEL, 11
The government burns down whole c. INJUSTICE, 10
citizen a c. of the world COURTESY, 2; NATIONALITY, 8
citizens All free men, . . . are c. of Berlin GERMANY, 6
city first c. Cain GARDENS, 6
great c. . . . has the greatest men and women GREATNESS, 15
hiring taxis to scuttle around a c. INCOMPETENCE, 2
I go amongst the buildings of a c. PURPOSE, 5
It is a c. where you can see a sparrow fall IRELAND, 11
the c. is not a concrete jungle, it is a human zoo MANKIND, 17
the c. of perspiring dreams CAMBRIDGE, 4
civil In a c. war, a general must know WAR, 88
civilian forget about this c. WAR, 41
civilians drop bombs . . . hit c. WAR, 41
civilisation Disinterested intellectual curiosity . . . life blood of
. . . c. CURIOSITY, 8
civility C. costs nothing COURTESY, 1
The reciprocal c. of authors WRITERS, 21
civilization As c. advances, poetry . . . declines CIVILIZATION, 8
C. is a method of living CIVILIZATION, 1
C. is . . . equal respect for all men CIVILIZATION, 1
How idiotic c. is NAKEDNESS, 5
It is so stupid of modern c. DEVIL, 8
little in c. to appeal to a Yeti CIVILIZATION, 7
Madam, I am the c. they are fighting to defend WAR, 39
Our c. is founded on the shambles DEATH, 60
The degree of a nation's c. CIVILIZATION, 9
the Renaissance was . . . the green end of one of c.'s hardest
winters CIVILIZATION, 5
without the usual interval of c. AMERICA, 8
You can't say c. don't advance PROGRESS, 10
civilized it proved that I was in a c. society EXECUTION, 21
Woman will be the last thing c. by Man WOMEN, 49
clap Don't c. too hard ENTHUSIASM, 5
clapped c. the glass to his sightless eye BLINDNESS, 6
claret C. is the liquor for boys ALCOHOL, 30
drink a dozen of C. on my Tomb ALCOHOL, 33
look for the second cheapest c. . . . and say, 'Number 22 . . .'
ALCOHOL, 46
said of c. ALCOHOL, 11
class an . . . young Englishman of our upper c. ARISTOCRACY, 1
a special machine for the suppression of one c. by another
CAPITALISM, 7
Because there's no fourth c. HUMILITY, 8
Discussion in c., which means EDUCATION, 38
Every c. is unfit to govern GOVERNMENT, 2
for one c. to appreciate the wrongs of another CLASS, 31
For this c. we have . . . the designation of Philistines
PHILISTINISM, 1
Like many of the upper c. He liked the sound of broken glass
ARISTOCRACY, 2
Poets and painters . . . constitute a special c. ARTISTS, 2;
POETS, 5
The constitution . . . first and second c. citizens CLASS, 39
The history of all . . . society is the history of c. struggles
CLASS, 22
The one c. you do *not* belong to CLASS, 23
the proletariat will . . . wage a c. struggle for Socialism
CLASS, 18
The state is an instrument . . . of the ruling c. STATE, 5
Without c. differences, . . . living theatre ENGLAND, 8
classes back the masses against the c. CLASS, 14
Hats divide generally into three c. CLOTHES, 19
I'm not interested in c. CLASS, 20
responsible and the irresponsible c. CLASS, 17
classical C. quotation is the *parole* of literary men
QUOTATIONS, 4
That's the c. mind at work MIND, 5
The basic difference between c. music and jazz MUSIC, 34
classicism C., . . . presents . . . the literature that gave . . .
pleasure to their great-grandfathers LITERATURE, 16
classics Every man with a belly full of the c. CLASSICS, 7
The c. are only primitive literature CLASSICS, 6
clay absorbs a c. After his labours SMOKING, 2
clean Bath . . . once a day to be passably c. CLEANNESS, 1
c. your plate POLITICS, 57
hard to be funny when you have to be c. HUMOUR, 27
clear His right was c., his will was strong RIGHT, 1
if he could make *me* understand . . . it would be c. to all
UNDERSTANDING, 8

clearing-house the C. of the World ECONOMICS, 4
cleft Rock of ages, c. for me RELIGION, 52
Clementine In a cavern, in a canyon, Excavating for a mine
Dwelt a miner, Forty-niner, And his daughter, C.
MOURNING, 7
clenched You cannot shake hands with a c. fist
INFLEXIBILITY, 2
Cleopatra Had C.'s nose been shorter APPEARANCE, 4
clergy c. are men CLERGY, 5
I never saw . . . the c. were beloved in any nation CLERGY, 11
clergyman c. whose mendicity is only equalled by their
mendacity CLERGY, 12
good enough to be a c. CLERGY, 8
clerk the smartness of an attorney's c. INSULTS, 13
clever Be good, sweet maid, and let who can be c. VIRTUE, 11
c. man . . . came of . . . stupid people INTELLIGENCE, 2
It's c., but is it art ART, 11
never wise to try to appear . . . more c. WISDOM, 23
no use trying to be c. ACADEMICS, 3
To be c. enough to get . . . money, one must be stupid
MATERIALISM, 6
cleverest You're the c. member of . . . the c. nation in the
world SELF-CONFIDENCE, 7
cleverness height of c. is . . . to conceal it INTELLIGENCE, 5
cliché The c. is dead poetry LANGUAGE, 3
cliffs the chalk c. of Dover BOUNDARIES, 1
climate common where the c.'s sultry ADULTERY, 1
If it's heaven for c. PERVERSITY, 1
climb Fain would I c., yet fear I to fall AMBITION, 14
clime change their c., not their frame of mind, who rush across
the sea TRAVEL, 13
Clive What I like about C. DEATH, 24
clock c. in the steeple strikes one ALCOHOL, 65
grandfather's c. CLOCKS, 2
Stands the Church c. at ten to three NOSTALGIA, 6
The mouse ran up the c. NURSERY RHYMES, 15
clocks hands of c. in railway stations CHILDREN, 19
pass my declining years saluting . . . grandfather c. OLD AGE, 29
the c. were striking the hour TIME, 23
clogs From c. to c. POVERTY, 1
cloke knyf under the c. HYPOCRISY, 7
Clootie Satan, Nick, or C. DEVIL, 6
close a breathless hush in the C. tonight CRICKET, 5
I have sometimes regretted living so c. to Marie LOVE, 97
closed Mankind is a c. society MANKIND, 24
the transition from the . . . 'c. society', . . . to the 'open society'
SOCIETY, 1
close-up Life is a tragedy . . . in c. LIFE, 17
closing c. time in the gardens of the West CAPITALISM, 1
clothes After that you just take the girl's c. off ALCOHOL, 18
as if she were taking off all her c. SEX, 13
bought her wedding c. WOMEN, 7
enterprises that require new c. THRIFT, 10
Fine c. are good CLOTHES, 9
hanging the baby on the c. line to dry INNOVATION, 2
Have you ever taken anything out of the c. basket
CLEANNESS, 3
if it be our c. alone which fit us for society CLOTHES, 4
Nothing to wear but c. PESSIMISM, 7
No woman so naked as . . . underneath her c. NAKEDNESS, 4
walked away with their c. POLITICS, 19
wrapped him in swaddling c. CHRISTMAS, 7
cloud Every c. has a silver lining OPTIMISM, 2
fiend hid in a c. BIRTH, 3
I wandered lonely as a c. FLOWERS, 14
clouds But trailing c. of glory METAPHYSICS, 5
c. that gather round the setting sun MORTALITY, 21
clout Ne'er cast a c. MONTHS, 2
clown I remain . . . a c. CLOWNS, 1
clowns Send in the C. CLOWNS, 2
club I don't want to belong to any c. HUMOUR, 45
Mankind is a c. MANKIND, 11
takes you so far from the c. house GOLF, 3
the best c. in London HOUSES OF PARLIAMENT, 1
the most exclusive c. there is ENGLISH, 29
cluster The human face is . . . a whole c. of faces MANKIND, 20
Clyde the bonny banks of C. SCOTLAND, 6
CMG Members rise from C. TITLES, 9
coach c. and six horses through the Act of Settlement
IRELAND, 12
indifference and a c. and six LOVE, 38
coal though the whole world turn to c. VIRTUE, 10

coals heap c. of fire upon his head RETRIBUTION, 8
coaster Dirty British c. BOATS, 13
cobwebs Laws are like c. LAW, 27
laws were like c. LAW, 6
Coca-Cola the churches . . . bore for me the same relation to
God that billboards did to C. RELIGION, 54
cocaine C. isn't habit-forming ADDICTION, 1
cock He was like a c. ARROGANCE, 2
That kept the c. that crowed in the morn NURSERY RHYMES, 57
waiting for the c. to crow BETRAYAL, 4
we owe a c. to Aesculapius LAST WORDS, 58
cockles Crying, C. and mussels! alive, alive, O! BUSINESS, 1
cockroach to choose between him and a c. as a companion
INSULTS, 42
cocksure as c. of anything SELF-CONFIDENCE, 3
cod piece of c. passes all understanding FOOD, 31
serve both c. and salmon PUNS, 11
the c.'s wallop is always fresh made COMMUNISM, 5
The home of the bean and the c. SNOBBERY, 2
codfish Unlike the male c. . . . the British aristocracy is
ARISTOCRACY, 15
coffee c. that's too black . . . You integrate it with cream
RACE, 4
C. which makes the politician wise DRINKS, 3
measured out my life with c. spoons LIFE, 23
coffee-house It is folly . . . to mistake the echo of a . . . c. for
the . . . kingdom OPINIONS, 4
coffin the silver plate on a c. INSULTS, 29
cogito C., ergo sum THINKING, 7
coil shuffled off this mortal c. SUICIDE, 10
coke Happiness is like c. HAPPINESS, 11
cold a period of c. peace COLD WAR, 1
blow hot and c. with the same breath INDECISION, 1
C. Pastoral ETERNITY, 1
I beg c. comfort COMFORT, 3
she should catch a c. on overexposure TRUTH, 15
The Irish, . . . are needed in this c. age IRISH, 4
we are . . . in the midst of a c. war COLD WAR, 1
We called a c. a c. ILLNESS, 2
coldly c. she turns from their gaze, and weeps MOURNING, 8
Coliseum While stands the C., Rome shall stand EUROPE, 5
collapse Russia is a c., not a revolution RUSSIA, 7
collapses Force . . . c. through its own mass JUDGMENT, 9
collar no shirt or c. ever comes back twice NEGLECT, 2
collections those mutilators of c. BORROWING, 2
collective the greatest c. work of science SCIENCE, 2
college I am Master of this c.: What I don't know isn't
knowledge ACADEMICS, 1
Like so many ageing c. people ACADEMICS, 2
Colleges of Unreason a liberal education at the C. REASON, 1
colonel The gatling's jammed and the c. dead WAR, 75
colonnade whispering sound of the cool c. TREES, 3
colour an incurable disease – c. blindness RACE, 8
Any c., so long as it's black CHOICE, 1
water, is unsuitable in c. WATER, 4
coloured I'm a c., one-eyed Jew DISABILITY, 2; RACE, 6
colourless C. green ideas NONSENSE, 10
colours All c. will agree in the dark DIFFERENCE, 2
combine When bad men c. UNITY, 7
combustion the Immaculate Conception was spontaneous c.
CATHOLICISM, 3
come C. what come may TIME, 28
Mr Watson, c. here; I want you SUMMONS, 1
O c. all ye faithful CHRISTMAS, 15
Thou'lt c. no more MOURNING, 9
Whistle and she'll c. to you SUMMONS, 2
Why don't you c. up sometime and see me INVITATIONS, 1
Will ye no c. back again RETURN, 3
comedian A c. can only last HUMOUR, 1
comedies c. are ended by a marriage THEATRE, 4
comedy All I need to make a c. HUMOUR, 5
at a c. we only look THEATRE, 4
C. is if I walk into an open sewer and die THEATRE, 3
C., like sodomy, is an unnatural act HUMOUR, 11
C., we may say, is society HUMOUR, 2
Farce refined becomes high c. THEATRE, 7
Life is . . . a c. in long-shot LIFE, 17
What a fine c. this world would be LIFE, 20
world is a c. to those who think LIFE, 49
comes Everything c. to him who waits PATIENCE, 2
comfort carrion c., Despair, not feast on thee DESPAIR, 4
From ignorance our c. flows IGNORANCE, 12

I beg cold c.   COMFORT, 3
thought of suicide is a great . . . c.   SUICIDE, 4
Two loves I have, of c. and despair   CONFLICT, 7
until his friends came to c. him   ENDURANCE, 8
comfortable to be baith grand and c.   LUXURY, 1
comfortably Are you sitting c.? Then I'll begin   BEGINNING, 12
comic It is so c. to hear oneself called old   OLD AGE, 22
coming C. through the rye   LOVE, 33
he . . . c. after me is preferred before me   CHRISTIANITY, 11
command mortals to c. success   SUCCESS, 2
one of those born neither to obey nor to c.   NASTINESS, 5
people c. rather badly   OBEDIENCE, 2
commandments fear God, and keep his c.   GOD, 9
Where there aren't no Ten C.   DESIRE, 8
commas absence of inverted c. guarantees . . . originality
                                                               QUOTATIONS, 2
commend forced to c. her highly   INSINCERITY, 3
into thy hands I c. my spirit   LAST WORDS, 7
commended The man who gets angry . . . in the right way . . .
is c.   ANGER, 1
commendeth obliquely c. himself   CRITICISM, 6
comment C. is free but facts are sacred   JOURNALISM, 22
commentators rather give me c. plain   CLARITY, 1
commerce Friendship is a disinterested c. between equals
                                                               LOVE AND FRIENDSHIP, 2
honour sinks where c. long prevails   BUSINESS, 8
commercing looks c. with the skies   SOUL, 10
commission A Royal C. is a broody hen   BUREAUCRACY, 5
Each bullet has got its c.   MORTALITY, 4
commit woman alone, can . . . c. them   SEXES, 21
committee A c. is a cul-de-sac   BUREAUCRACY, 3
The number one book . . . was written by a c.   BIBLE, 6
commodity C., Firmness, and Delight   ARCHITECTURE, 1
common C. Law of England   LAW, 15
C. sense is the collection of prejudices   PREJUDICE, 3
good thing, to make it too c.   ENGLAND, 35
He nothing c. did or mean   EXECUTION, 16
I have no concern for the c. man   PUBLIC, 21
lose the c. touch   IDEALISM, 2
seldom attribute c. sense   AGREEMENT, 4
the happiness of the c. man   GOVERNMENT, 6
The trivial round, the c. task   SIMPLICITY, 4
'Tis education forms the c. mind   EDUCATION, 42
trained and organized c. sense   SCIENCE, 18
common-looking The Lord prefers c. people   APPEARANCE, 20
commonplace nothing so unnatural as the c.   TRIVIALITY, 7
renders . . . c. things and characters interesting   WRITERS, 40
unassuming c. Of Nature   FLOWERS, 13
commonplaces c. are the great poetic truths   TRIVIALITY, 13
Commons The C., faithful to their system   GOVERNMENT, 16
Commonwealth a C. of Nations   BRITISH EMPIRE, 5
turn to the wider vision of the C.   POLITICS, 41
communism arrested under the Suppression of C. Act
                                                               OPPRESSION, 4
C. continued to haunt Europe as a spectre   COMMUNISM, 10
C. is like prohibition   COMMUNISM, 6
C. is Soviet power plus the electrification   COMMUNISM, 4
C. with a human face   COMMUNISM, 2
For us in Russia c. is a dead dog   COMMUNISM, 7
communist Every c. has a fascist frown   COMMUNISM, 8;
                                                               FASCISM, 4
your grandson will . . . be a C.   COMMUNISM, 3
communists Catholics and C. have committed great crimes
                                                               COMMITMENT, 4
In Germany, the Nazis came for the C.   NAZISM, 4
community journalism. . . . keeps us in touch with the ignorance
of the c.   JOURNALISM, 27
Marriage, n. . . . a c. . . . making in all two   MARRIAGE, 26
the c. of Europe   EUROPE, 15
commute the agricultural labourers round here c. from London
                                                               COUNTRYSIDE, 7
commuter C. . . . riding to and from his wife   TRAVEL, 2
compact the damned, c., liberal majority   MAJORITY, 4
companion to choose between him and a cockroach as a c.
                                                               INSULTS, 42
companionable so c. as solitude   SOLITUDE, 13
companions Boys . . . are unwholesome c. for grown people
                                                               CHILDREN, 30
c. for middle age   MARRIAGE, 12
company better to be alone than in bad c.   FRIENDS, 15
c., . . . have neither a soul to lose nor a body to kick
                                                               BUSINESS, 17

Crowds without c.   LONDON, 7
I've been offered titles, . . . get one into disreputable c.
                                                               TITLES, 11
pleasure of your c.   MOUNTAINS, 2
Take the tone of the c.   CONFORMITY, 3
Tell me what c. thou keepest   FRIENDS, 4
You never expected justice from a c.   BUSINESS, 17
comparative progress is simply a c.   PROGRESS, 3
compare any she belied with false c.   ANALOGY, 4
c. thee to a summer's day   COMPLIMENTS, 4
compared The war we have just been through, . . . is not to be
c.   WAR, 133
comparisons c. are odious   ANALOGY, 2
C. are odorous   MALAPROPISMS, 2
compass my heart shall be The faithful c.   FAITHFULNESS, 4
compassion But a certain Samaritan . . . had c. on him
                                                               CHARITY, 7
C. is not a sloppy, sentimental feeling   SOCIALISM, 7
complacency c. and satisfaction . . . in . . . a new-married couple
                                                               MARRIAGE, 70
complain one hardly knows to whom to c.   COMPLAINTS, 2
complaint Anno domini . . . the most fatal c.   DEATH, 58
how is the old c.   MEMORY, 5
I want to register a c.   COMPLAINTS, 5
complete now I feel like a c. idiot   INFERIORITY, 1
complex Wherever an inferiority c. exists, there is . . . reason
                                                               INFERIORITY, 1
compliance by a timely c.   SEX, 15
compliment returned the c.   GOD, 49
compose Never c. . . . unless . . . not composing . . . becomes a
positive nuisance   MUSIC, 21
composed When I c. that, I was . . . inspired by God   MUSIC, 8
composer A good c. . . . steals   COMPOSERS, 6
demands of a c. is that he be dead   COMPOSERS, 3
composition difference between . . . prose and metrical c.
                                                               POETRY AND PROSE, 7
comprehended c. two aspicious persons   MALAPROPISMS, 1
compromise All government . . . is founded on c. and barter
                                                               COMPROMISE, 3
C. used to mean that half a loaf   COMPROMISE, 4
not a question that leaves much room for c.
                                                               SELF-PRESERVATION, 7
compulsion seized by the stern hand of C.   WOMEN, 71
compulsory c. and irreproachable idleness   ARMY, 3
comrade stepping where his c. stood   COURAGE, 15
comrades Bleach the bones of c. slain   WAR, 49
conceal Addresses . . . c. our whereabouts   ADDRESSES, 1
height of cleverness is . . . to c. it   INTELLIGENCE, 5
speech only to . . . their thoughts   HUMAN NATURE, 20
concealed Much truth is spoken, . . . more . . . c.   TRUTH, 19
concealing Good breeding consists in c. how . . . we think of
ourselves   MANNERS, 5
concealment c., like a worm i' th' bud   LOVE, 120
conceit C. is the finest armour   CONCEIT, 12
conceited I would grow intolerably c.   CONCEIT, 19
what man will do any good who is not c.   SELF-RESPECT, 2
concept If the c. of God has   RELIGION, 4
conception if the dad is present at the c.   SEX, 34
the Immaculate C. was spontaneous combustion   CATHOLICISM, 9
concepts walks up the stairs of his c.   MANKIND, 29
concessions C. of the weak are the c. of fear   YIELDING, 1
conclusions Life is the art of drawing . . . c.   LIFE, 16
concord toleration produced . . . religious c.   RELIGION, 25
Yes – around C.   TRAVEL, 26
concurrence Accidental and fortuitous c. of atoms   CHANCE, 4
condemn No man can justly censure or c. another
                                                               JUDGMENT, 5
condemned If God were suddenly c. to live the life   HUMAN
                                                               CONDITION, 6
Man is c. to be free   FREEDOM, 47
condemning One should examine oneself . . . before . . . c.
others   SELF, 11
condition fools decoyed into our c.   MARRIAGE, 85
hopes for the human c.   PESSIMISM, 4
The c. of man . . . is a c. of war   HUMAN CONDITION, 9
the Jews have made a contribution to the human c.   JEWS, 14
To be a poet is a c.   POETS, 4
wearisome c. of humanity   HUMAN CONDITION, 8
conditioned Americans have been c. to respect newness
                                                               AMERICANS, 11
conditions my people live in such awful c.   POVERTY, 11

conduct C. . . . to the prejudice of good order and military discipline ARMY, 2
conductor The c. . . . advantage of not seeing the audience MUSICIANS, 3
conference naked into the c. chamber WEAPONS, 1
confess It's easy to make a man c. . . . lies TRUTH, 27
Men will c. HUMOUR, 7
only c. our little faults IMPERFECTION, 11
We c. our bad qualities . . . out of fear SELF-KNOWLEDGE, 2
confessing I am ashamed of c. INNOCENCE, 1
women . . . ill-using them and then c. it WOMEN, 73
confidence never dedicated to something you have complete c. in FANATICISM, 3
Three addresses always inspire c. ADDRESSES, 2
confident There are two things which I am c. I can do very well CRITICISM, 16
confin'd cabin'd, cribb'd, c., bound in FEAR, 11
conflict We are in an armed c. WAR, 34
conform how to rebel and c. at the same time YOUTH, 5
conformable Nature is very consonant and c. NATURE, 12
confound the weak things of the world to c. the . . . mighty WISDOM AND FOOLISHNESS, 2
Congreve C. is the only sophisticated playwright WRITERS, 44
congs Kinquering C. their titles take SPOONERISMS, 3
connect Only c.! COMMUNICATION, 1
conquer in the end the truth will c. TRUTH, 43
They will c., but . . . not convince PERSUASION, 1
We'll fight and we'll c. COURAGE, 11
when we c. without danger VICTORY, 3
conquered I came; I saw; God c. VICTORY, 15
I came, I saw, I c. VICTORY, 1
I will be c.; I will not capitulate DETERMINATION, 8
the English seem . . . to have c. and peopled half the world BRITISH EMPIRE, 6
conquering C. kings ROYALTY, 9
not c. but fighting well VICTORY, 4
See, the c. hero comes VICTORY, 11
conquest The Roman C. was, however, a *Good Thing* HISTORY, 26
conscience a Nonconformist c. WOMEN, 80
As guardian of His Majesty's c. MONARCHY, 23
c. does make cowards of us all CONSCIENCE, 5
C. is a coward CONSCIENCE, 3
C. is the inner voice CONSCIENCE, 4
C. is the internal perception of the rejection of a particular wish CONSCIENCE, 2
dilemmas of c. and egotism POWER, 17
freedom of speech, freedom of c., and the prudence never to practise . . . them FREEDOM, 50
I cannot . . . cut my c. to fit this year's fashions INTEGRITY, 3
I'll catch the c. of the King PLAYS, 11
Now war has a bad c. WAR, 53
why is my liberty judged of another man's c.? CONSCIENCE, 1; FREEDOM, 3
consent deep c. of all great men ARTISTS, 7
No one can make you feel inferior without your c. INFERIORITY, 5
consequence physicians . . . mistake subsequence for c. DOCTORS, 5
consequences Logical c. are the scarecrows of fools LOGIC, 3
men never violate the laws of God without suffering the c. RETRIBUTION, 9
conservatism c. . . . adherence to the old and tried CONSERVATISM, 5
c. is based upon the idea CONSERVATISM, 1
Conservative C. government is an organized hypocrisy POLITICS, 18
Or else a little C. POLITICS, 27
to what is called the Tory, and which might . . . be called the C., party POLITICS, 17
conservative The radical invents the views . . . the c. adopts them CONSERVATISM, 7
which makes a man more c. CONSERVATISM, 4
consider When I c. how my light is spent BLINDNESS, 5
considerable to appear in his native place FAME, 12
consistency C. is contrary to nature CONSTANCY, 2
consonant Nature is very c. and conformable NATURE, 12
conspiracy not a Party, it is a c. COMMUNISM, 1
People of the same trade . . . conversation ends in a c. BUSINESS, 16
conspirators All the c. NOBILITY, 4
constabulary When c. duty's to be done POLICE, 1

constant A c. guest HOSPITALITY, 1
Friendship is c. in all other things LOVE AND FRIENDSHIP, 3
constitution The c. . . . first and second class citizens CLASS, 39
The principles of a free c. GOVERNMENT, 10
constitutional A c. king must learn to stoop MONARCHY, 13
c. right DEMOCRACY, 8
definition of a c. statesman POLITICIANS, 2
construction Our object in the c. of the state REPUBLIC, 1
consultations dictator . . . always take some c. AUTHORITARIANISM, 6
consulted the right to be c., . . . to encourage, . . . to warn MONARCHY, 2
consume more history than they can c. EUROPE, 14
statistics, born to c. resources STATISTICS, 3
consumer In a c. society there are . . . two kinds of slaves MATERIALISM, 10
consumes Man . . . c. without producing CAPITALISM, 10
consummation a c. Devoutly to be wish'd SUICIDE, 10
consumption Conspicuous c. . . . is a means of reputability MATERIALISM, 20
this c. of the purse MONEY, 38
contemplate the only passers-by who can c. it . . . are those . . . with a white stick and a dog ARCHITECTURE, 6
contemplates Beauty in things exists in the mind which c. them BEAUTY, 20
contemplation right mindfulness, right c. RELIGION, 6
contemporary I am no one's c. – ever DENIAL, 2
to trade a hundred c. readers for POSTERITY, 6
contempt attention to the inside . . . c. for the outside BOOKS, 13
she was only an Object of C. CONTEMPT, 1
To show pity is felt as a sign of c. SYMPATHY, 5
contemptible c. little Army WAR, 131
content desire is got without c. CONTENTMENT, 6
contented How is it . . . that no one lives c. with his lot DISCONTENT, 4
If you are foolish enough to be c., don't show it COMPLAINTS, 3
With what I most enjoy c. least DISCONTENT, 8
contentment Where wealth and freedom reign, c. fails BUSINESS, 8
contests mighty c. rise from trivial things RESULTS, 5
continence Give me chastity and c. PROCRASTINATION, 4
that melancholy sexual perversion known as c. ABSTINENCE, 5
Continent On the C. people have good food MANNERS, 4
Continental C. people have sex life ENGLISH, 24
continual c. state of inelegance WEATHER, 7
continuation All diplomacy is a c. of war DIPLOMACY, 14
War is the c. of politics WAR, 28
contraception a terrific story about oral c. CONTRACEPTION, 1
contraceptive It's like having a totally efficient c. FUTURE, 4
contraceptives C. should be used CONTRACEPTION, 4
Skullion had little use for c. CONTRACEPTION, 5
contract Every law is a c. LAW, 22
Marriage is . . . but a civil c. MARRIAGE, 93
contradict Do I c. myself SELF, 21
contradiction brook no c. DOCTORS, 3
Man is . . . an everlasting c. to himself INTELLECT, 2
Woman's at best a c. WOMEN, 59
contradictory Doublethink . . . holding two c. beliefs DOUBLETHINK, 2
contrary everythink goes c. with me MISFORTUNE, 1
contraries Without C. is no progression CONFLICT, 4
contrariwise 'C.,' continued Tweedledee LOGIC, 1
contrary Mary, Mary, quite c. GARDENS, 1
On the c. LAST WORDS, 34
control we ought to c. our thoughts SELF-CONTROL, 3
controversies savage c. . . . no good evidence either way ARGUMENTS, 13
controversy that c. is either superfluous or hopeless ARGUMENTS, 11
convenient Nobody is forgotten when it is c. to remember him EXPEDIENCY, 3
convent To enter the . . . Ballet is to enter a c. DANCING, 4
conventional The c. army loses if it does not win WAR, 56
conventionally to fail c. ORTHODOXY, 3
conversation a c. with the finest men LITERATURE, 3
And third-rate c. MEDIOCRITY, 6
a proper subject of c. RELIGION, 11
C. . . . elicits secrets from us CONVERSATION, 7
c. must be an exchange of thought CONVERSATION, 6
make his c. perfectly delightful INSULTS, 32

Questioning is not the mode of c.   CONVERSATION, 4
There is no such thing as c.   CONVERSATION, 9
Writing . . . is but a different name for c.   WRITING, 31
Your ignorance cramps my c.   IGNORANCE, 8
conversationalist   the c. who adds 'in other words'
                                                      CONVERSATION, 5
converted   difficult for a Jew to be c.   JEWS, 6
convince   They will conquer, but . . . not c.   PERSUASION, 1
cook   a good c., as cooks go   HUMOUR, 51
Any c. should be able to   GOVERNMENT, 14
C. is a little unnerved   ETIQUETTE, 1
ill c. that cannot lick his own fingers   SELF-CONFIDENCE, 4
she was a very bad c.   SNOBBERY, 9
cookery   c. do   FOOD, 34
cooking   woman accepted c. . . . but man . . . made of it a
recreation   FOOD, 40
cooks   Too many c.   HELP, 5
Coolidge   C. is a better example of evolution   POLITICIANS, 59
copier   c. of nature can never produce anything great
                                                      IMITATION, 4
copies   more c. of my works are left behind   WRITERS, 3
copulation   Birth, and c., and death   LIFE AND DEATH, 4
copy   A lotta cats c. the Mona Lisa   IMITATION, 1
copying   by defying their parents and c. one another   YOUTH, 5
coral   C. is far more red   ANALOGY, 8
Of his bones are c. made   DEATH, 100
cord   a threefold c. is not quickly broken   UNITY, 5
cordial   gold in phisik is a c.   MATERIALISM, 5
cordiale   La c. entente   DIPLOMACY, 15
corn   amid the alien c.   BIRDS, 5
make two ears of c. . . . grow . . . where only one grew before
                                                      POLITICIANS, 69
That ate the c.   NURSERY RHYMES, 57
the meadows rich with c.   AMERICA, 35
corner   a c. in the thing I love   JEALOUSY, 5
some c. of a foreign field   WAR, 16
corners   people standing in the c. of our rooms TELEVISION, 1
Cornish   twenty thousand C. men   EXECUTION, 10
Coromandel   On the Coast of C.   NONSENSE, 16
coronets   Kind hearts are more than c.   ARISTOCRACY, 12
corps   English characteristic . . . *esprit de c.*   ENGLISH, 3
corpse   He'd make a lovely c.   DEATH, 50
he makes a very handsome c.   DEATH, 53
corpses   They are for prima donnas or c.   FLOWERS, 11
corpuscles   make the c. of the blood glow   JEWS, 8
correct   Astronomy teaches the c. use   ASTRONOMY, 9
correction   It is a stupidity . . . to busy oneself with the c. of
the world   IMPROVEMENT, 5
correctly   anxious to do the wrong thing c.   ETIQUETTE, 5
corridors   c. of power   POWER, 17
corroboration   c. . . . in the records of Somerset House
                                                      HUMILITY, 11
corrupt   Among a people generally c.   CORRUPTION, 1
power is apt to c.   POWER, 14
Power tends to c.   POWER, 3
corrupted   They had been c. by money   SENTIMENTALITY, 1
corruptible   born again, not of c. seed   DEATH, 27
corruption   C., the most infallible symptom of constitutional
liberty   CORRUPTION, 2
corrupts   lack of power c. absolutely   POWER, 19
corse   As his c. to the rampart   FUNERALS, 10
cosmetics   In the factory we make c.   COSMETICS, 3
cosmopolitan   I was told I am a true c.   MELANCHOLY, 11
cosmos   c. is about the smallest hole   UNIVERSE, 5
cost   To give and not to count the c.   SELFLESSNESS, 2
cottage   Love and a c.   LOVE, 38
poorest man may in his c. bid defiance to . . . the Crown
                                                      PRIVACY, 3
to refer to your friend's country establishment as a 'c.'
                                                      WORDS, 17
cottages   Pale Death kicks his way equally into the c. of the
poor   EQUALITY, 23
couch   the century of the psychiatrist's c.   PSYCHIATRY, 8
time as a tool not as a c.   TIME, 20
when on my c. I lie   SOLITUDE, 15
cough   Jeeves coughed one soft, low, gentle c.   ANALOGY, 7
coughing   The art of acting consists in keeping people from c.
                                                      ACTING, 6
council   The grotesque chaos of a Labour c.   INCOMPETENCE, 2
counsel   C. of her country's gods   BRITAIN, 6
sometimes c. take – and sometimes Tea   DRINKS, 7
count   Don't c. your chickens   ANTICIPATION, 4

If you can . . . c. your money you are not . . . rich man
                                                      WEALTH, 15
To give and not to c. the cost   SELFLESSNESS, 2
countenance   the Lord lift up his c. upon thee   BLESSING, 4
counter-democratic   Proportional Representation, . . . is
fundamentally c.   POLITICS, 37
counterpoint   Too much c.; what is worse, Protestant c.
                                                      CRITICISM, 1
counties   see the coloured c.   COUNTRYSIDE, 6
countries   preferreth all c. before his own   DISCONTENT, 7
country   absolved from all duty to his c.   MARRIAGE, 84
a c. diversion   COUNTRYSIDE, 8
A c. governed by a despot   TYRANNY, 3
a c. of young men   AMERICA, 13
affections must be confined . . . to a single c.   PATRIOTISM, 8
A man should know something of his own c.   TRAVEL, 23
an honest man sent to lie abroad for . . . his c.   DIPLOMACY, 21
Anybody can be good in the c.   COUNTRYSIDE, 10
Anyone who loves his c., follow me   PATRIOTISM, 9
c. from whose bourn no traveller returns   AFTERLIFE, 8
Counsel of her c.'s gods   BRITAIN, 6
God made the c.   COUNTRYSIDE, 2
go down into the c.   DECEPTION, 7
Great artists have no c.   NATIONALITY, 7
How I leave my c.   LAST WORDS, 44
I have but one life to lose for my c.   PATRIOTISM, 11
I love thee still, My c.   PATRIOTISM, 6
I would die for my c.   PATRIOTISM, 18
loathe the c.   COUNTRYSIDE, 1
'My c., right or wrong'   PATRIOTISM, 4
nothing good . . . in the c.   COUNTRYSIDE, 4
Our c. is the world   AMERICA, 14
our c., right or wrong   PATRIOTISM, 7
proud of the position of the bungalow, . . . in the c.   SUBURBIA, 2
she is my c. still   PATRIOTISM, 5
That is no c. for old men   MORTALITY, 23
The history of every c. begins in the heart   HISTORY, 7
The idiot who praises . . . every c. but his own   DISCONTENT, 2
The past is a foreign c.   PAST, 5
The undiscover'd c.   AFTERLIFE, 8
This c. . . . belongs to the people who inhabit it   DEMOCRACY, 8
to leave his c. as good as he had found it   DUTY, 1
understanding the problems of running a c.   POLITICS, 70
we can die but once to serve our c.   PATRIOTISM, 1
what was good for our c.   BUSINESS, 22
When I am in the c. I wish to vegetate   COUNTRYSIDE, 5
countryside   a more dreadful record of sin than . . . c.   SIN, 12
county   The sound of the English c. families   ARISTOCRACY, 14
couple   A married c. are well suited   MARRIAGE, 88
couples   so many c. . . . not getting the right proteins   SEX, 10
courage   be strong and of a good c.   GOD, 3
C. is the price . . . for granting peace   COURAGE, 10
c. to love . . . courage to suffer   LOVE, 134
good deal of physical c. to ride a horse   ALCOHOL, 39; HORSES, 8
tale . . . of . . . c. of my companions   ENDURANCE, 16
The Red Badge of C.   COURAGE, 6
three o'clock in the morning c.   COURAGE, 21
Whistling aloud to bear his c. up   WHISTLING, 1
course   c. of true love never did run smooth   LOVE, 113
courteous   If a man be . . . c. to strangers   COURTESY, 3
courtesy   C. is not dead   COURTESY, 4
courting   When you are c. a nice girl   SCIENCE, 10
courts   I have come to regard . . . c. . . . as a casino   JUSTICE, 11
the case is still before the c.   ARGUMENTS, 6
courtship   C. to marriage   MARRIAGE, 36
covenant   a c. between me and the earth   PROMISES, 2
a c. with death   SLAVERY, 4
cover   Never judge a c. by its book   BOOKS, 22
covet   thou shalt not c.   GOD, 10
cow   A c. is a very good animal in the field   SUITABILITY, 2
That milked the c. with the crumpled horn   NURSERY RHYMES, 57
The c. is of the bovine ilk   ANIMALS, 16
The c. jumped over the moon   NURSERY RHYMES, 14
till the c. comes home   ETERNITY, 1
Truth, Sir, is a c.   SCEPTICISM, 3
Why buy a c.   FUTILITY, 1
coward   better to be the widow of a hero than the wife of a c.
                                                      COURAGE, 13
Conscience is a c.   CONSCIENCE, 3
No c. soul is mine   COURAGE, 2
None but a c. . . . has never known fear   COWARDICE, 2
The c. does it with a kiss   KILLING, 8

Cowardice guilty of Noël C. — COWARDICE, 1
cowardly Marriage is the only adventure open to the c. — MARRIAGE, 116
cowards C. die many times — COWARDICE, 9
the future . . . makes c. of us — PRESENT, 3
Thus conscience does make c. of us all — CONSCIENCE, 5
cowboy easier to get an actor to be a c. — ACTING, 4
cows daring . . . to explain . . . that c. can be eaten — RELIGION, 24
The c. in the corn — NURSERY RHYMES, 28
coxcomb to hear a c. ask two hundred guineas — CRITICISM, 43
coyness This c., lady, were no crime — SHYNESS, 4
cracked The c. looking glass of a servant — IRELAND, 8
cradle Between the c. and the grave — TRANSIENCE, 12
Rocked in the c. of the deep — SEA, 11
The hand that rocks the c. — INFLUENCE, 9
cradles bit the babies in the c. — ANIMALS, 3
craft the c. so long to lerne — MORTALITY, 3
The life so short, the c. so long to learn — MORTALITY, 12
craftsmanship Skill without imagination is c. — ART, 25
crafty too c. a woman to invent a new lie — LYING, 9
cranny We seek . . . In every c. but the right — PERVERSITY, 3
crap Books are a load of c. — BOOKS, 20
Craven why and how I became . . . mistress of the Earl of C. — SEX, 55
cream coffee that's too black . . . You integrate it with c. — RACE, 14
create My father didn't c. you to arrest me — POLICE, 5
created God c. . . . the earth — CREATION, 2
man alone leaves traces of what he c. — MANKIND, 7
Man, . . . had been c. to jab the life out of Germans — WAR, 97
Thou hast c. us for Thyself — HUMAN CONDITION, 1
we cannot be c. for this sort of suffering — AFTERLIFE, 5
creates he c. Gods by the dozen — RELIGION, 41
creation greatest week . . . since the c. — SPACE, 5
Had I been present at the C. — UNIVERSE, 1
The art of c. is older — CREATION, 14
creator All right, my lord c., Don Miguel — DEATH, 5
Man . . . hasn't been a c., only a destroyer — ECOLOGY, 3
creature No c. smarts . . . as a fool — FOOLISHNESS, 17
the c. hath a purpose and its eyes are bright with it — PURPOSE, 5
Who kills a man kills a reasonable c. — BOOKS, 24
creatures call these delicate c. ours — JEALOUSY, 4
From fairest c. we desire increase — BEAUTY, 35
credentials no c. . . . not even . . . a certificate of birth — ARISTOCRACY, 8
credit The way to get things done is not to mind who gets the c. — SELFLESSNESS, 1
creditors my oldest c. would hardly know me — APPEARANCE, 14
not everyone who wishes makes c. — BORROWING, 7
credits c. would still read 'Rubinstein, God, and Piatigorsky' — EGOTISM, 6
credulity C. is . . . the child's strength — INNOCENCE, 7
creed got the better of his c. — RELIGION, 47
the c. of a second-rate man — POLITICIANS, 2
wrought . . . the c. of creeds — CHRISTIANITY, 43
creeds So many gods, so many c. — KINDNESS, 5; RELIGION, 63
Vain are the thousand c. — BELIEF, 3
creep I wants to make your flesh c. — FEAR, 8
Wit that can c. — SERVILITY, 5
Creepers Jeepers C. — EYES, 2
creetur lone lorn c. — MISFORTUNE, 9
crème you would have been the c. de la c. — EXCELLENCE, 3
Crete The people of C. . . . make more history — EUROPE, 14
cricket c. as organised loafing — CRICKET, 6
I do love c. – it's so very English — CRICKET, 2; FOOTBALL, 1
It's not in support of c. — CRICKET, 1; GOLF, 1
the c. on the hearth — MELANCHOLY, 9
where the c. sings — PEACE, 18
Cricklewood Midland, bound for C. — TRAVEL, 9
cried I c. all the way to the bank — CRITICISM, 27
crieth thy brother's blood c. unto me — MURDER, 2
crime all c. is due to the repressed desire for aesthetic expression — CRIME, 6
Arson, after all, is an artificial c. — FIRE, 5
C., like virtue, has its degrees — CRIME, 5
Do you call poverty a c. — POVERTY, 27
If poverty is the mother of c., stupidity is its father — CRIME, 4
man's greatest c. — BIRTH, 4
no . . . c. so shameful as poverty — POVERTY, 7
The atrocious c. of being a young man — YOUTH, 13

the Napoleon of c. — CRIME, 3
The punishment fit the c. — PUNISHMENT, 9
This coyness, lady, were no C. — SHYNESS, 4
Treason was no C. — TREASON, 2
worse than a c., it is a blunder — MISTAKES, 4
crimes Catholics and Communists have committed great c. — COMMITMENT, 4
history is . . . a tableau of c. and misfortunes — HISTORY, 32
how many c. committed — CRIME, 2
Oh liberty! . . . What c. are committed in thy name — EXECUTION, 27; FREEDOM, 44
crippled I don't advise any one to take it up . . . unless they . . . are c. — ARTISTS, 5
crisp Deep and c. and even — CHRISTMAS, 14
critic A c. is a man who — CRITICS, 17
A good c. . . . narrates the adventures of his mind — CRITICS, 4
A good drama c. is — CRITICS, 18
c. spits on what is done — CRITICS, 7
Nor in the c. let the man be lost — CRITICS, 12
the function of the c. — CRITICS, 1
critical c. judgement is so exquisite — CRITICS, 5
nothing if not c. — CRITICISM, 44
criticism A great deal of contemporary c. — CRITICISM, 7
As far as c. is concerned — CRITICISM, 50
c. is a letter to the public — CRITICISM, 39
my own definition of c. — CRITICISM, 1
People ask you for c. — CRITICISM, 32
The Stealthy School of C. — CRITICISM, 41
criticize don't c. What you can't understand — CHANGE, 6
criticizing The pleasure of c. — CRITICISM, 24
critics Asking a working writer . . . about c. — CRITICS, 6
c. all are ready made — CRITICS, 2
c. . . . desire our blood, not our pain — CRITICS, 11
music c. . . . . small and rodent-like with padlocked ears — CRITICS, 15
crocodile An appeaser is one who feeds a c. — DIPLOMACY, 6
crocodiles wisdom of the c. — HYPOCRISY, 2
Cromwell Caesar had his Brutus – Charles the First, his C. — TREASON, 4
restless C. could not cease — POLITICIANS, 48
ruins that C. knocked about a bit — INNUENDO, 1
crony government by c. — NEPOTISM, 1
crook A writer of c. stories — POLITICS, 76
I am not a c. — DENIAL, 3
the symbol of a bishop is a c. — CLERGY, 4
crooked the c. timber of humanity — HUMAN NATURE, 1
There was a c. man, and he walked a c. mile — NURSERY RHYMES, 52
crop watering the last year's c. — FUTILITY, 5
crops Man . . . Laid the c. low — AGRICULTURE, 5
cross Don't c. the bridge — ANTICIPATION, 2
Hot c. buns! . . . One a penny, two a penny — NURSERY RHYMES, 16
no c., no crown — ENDURANCE, 12
The orgasm has replaced the C. — SEX, 33
When I survey the wondrous C. — HUMILITY, 12
cross-bow With my c. I shot — BIRDS, 2
crossed a girl likes to be c. in love a little now and then — WOMEN, 9
crossword an optimist . . . fills up his c. puzzle in ink — OPTIMISM, 25
crow sun had risen to hear him c. — ARROGANCE, 4
waiting for the cock to c. — BETRAYAL, 2
crowd a c. like that . . . brings a lump to my wallet — MATERIALISM, 22
And hid his face amid a c. of stars — LOVE, 143
Far from the madding c. — SOLITUDE, 7
crowds C. without company — LONDON, 7
If you can talk with c. and keep your virtue — IDEALISM, 2
It brings men together in c. and mobs in bar-rooms — SOCIETY, 9
crown no cross, no c. — ENDURANCE, 12
poorest man may . . . bid defiance to . . . the C. — PRIVACY, 3
the c. of life — TEMPTATION, 2
The influence of the C. has increased — MONARCHY, 9
Uneasy lies the head that wears a c. — MONARCHY, 21
within the hollow c. — ROYALTY, 28
crucible America is God's C. — AMERICA, 40
crucified Where the dear Lord was c. — CHRISTIANITY, 1
you might try getting c. — CHRISTIANITY, 41
crucify Do you want to c. the boy? — CHRISTIANITY, 25
cruel A c. story runs on wheels — CRUELTY, 4
C., but composed and bland — CATS, 1

cruellest April is the c. month — MONTHS, 8
cruelty Fear is the parent of c. — CRUELTY, 3
cruise we are all on our last c. — MORTALITY, 18
crumbs c. which fell from the rich man's table — POVERTY AND WEALTH, 2
cry I often want to c. — SEXES, 16
make 'em c. — WRITING, 27
mother, do not c. — LAST WORDS, 18
She likes stories that make her c. — SENTIMENTALITY, 5
the c. of him that ruleth among fools — WISDOM, 3
the only advantage women have over men – . . . they can c. — SEXES, 16
We think caged birds sing, when indeed they c. — IMPRISONMENT, 6
when we c. to Thee — SEA, 13
crying An infant c. in the night — HUMAN CONDITION, 18
It is no use c. — REGRET, 1
cubic One c. foot less — SMALLNESS, 3
cuckoo the c. clock was invented . . . to give tourists something solid — SWITZERLAND, 1
The c. comes in April — MONTHS, 3
This is the weather the c. likes — WEATHER, 12
cucumber A c. should be well sliced — FOOD, 26
cucumbers they are but c. after all — CRITICISM, 23
cul-de-sac A committee is a c. — BUREAUCRACY, 3
cult local c. called Christianity — CHRISTIANITY, 28
What's a c. — MINORITY, 1
cultivate c. our garden — PAROCHIALISM, 3
cultivated I do not want to die . . . until I have . . . c. the seed — ACHIEVEMENT, 4
culture C. is an instrument wielded by professors — CULTURE, 3
C. is the passion for sweetness and light — CULTURE, 2
C., the acquainting ourselves with the best — CULTURE, 1
ladies who pursue C. in bands — CULTURE, 4
two half-cultures do not make a c. — HALF MEASURES, 1
When I hear anyone talk of C. — PHILISTINISM, 4
You can lead a whore to c. — PUNS, 16
cup Ah, fill the C. — TIME, 16
Come, fill the C., and in the Fire of Spring — TIME, 15
tak a c. o' kindness yet — FRIENDSHIP, 13
the c. of the vales — WINTER, 7
cupboard But when she got there The c. was bare — NURSERY RHYMES, 35
Cupid wing'd C. painted blind — LOVE, 114
cups c., That cheer but not inebriate — DRINKS, 4
curators more philosophical than . . . c. of the museums — MUSEUMS, 1; PRACTICALITY, 1
cur'd C. . . . of my disease — DOCTORS, 7
curds Eating her c. and whey — NURSERY RHYMES, 30
cure a c. for which there was no disease — REMEDIES, 5
C. the disease — REMEDIES, 1
no c. for birth and death — LIFE AND DEATH, 9
Show me a sane man and I will c. him for you — MADNESS, 5
the c. for admiring the House of Lords — HOUSES OF PARLIAMENT, 3
There are maladies we must not seek to c. — REMEDIES, 10
Work is the grand c. — WORK, 6
cured the only disease you don't look forward to being c. of — DEATH, 75
What can't be c. — ENDURANCE, 3
curfew 'C. shall not ring tonight!' — MERCY, 3
The C. tolls the knell of parting day — DAY, 6
curiosities How these c. would be quite forgot — GOSSIP, 7
curiosity C. killed the cat — CURIOSITY, 2
C. will conquer fear — CURIOSITY, 7
Disinterested intellectual c. . . . life blood of . . . civilisation — CURIOSITY, 8
I would rather be a brilliant memory than a c. — RENUNCIATION, 2
curious Be not c. in unnecessary matters — CURIOSITY, 3
I am c. to see what happens . . . to one who dies unshriven — LAST WORDS, 43
'That was the c. incident,' remarked . . . Holmes — TRIVIALITY, 8
curiouser C. and c. — CONFUSION, 3
curl There was a little girl Who had a little c. — SEX, 30
curly C. locks, C. locks, Wilt thou be mine — NURSERY RHYMES, 8
currency I will not be a party to debasing the c. — ECONOMICS, 7
curse A c. is on her if she stay — CURSES, 4
Christianity the one great c. — CHRISTIANITY, 35
c. not the king, no not in thy thought — SECRECY, 3
She would rather light candles than c. the darkness — COMPLIMENTS, 6
The c. is come upon me — CURSES, 3

Work is the c. of the drinking classes — WORK, 25
cursed thou art c. above all cattle — SEXES, 2
curses C. . . . always come home to roost — CURSES, 2
curst C. be the verse — POETRY, 34
curtain An iron c. — COLD WAR, 2
I saw it at a disadvantage – the c. was up — CRITICISM, 52
Ring down the c. — LAST WORDS, 48
cushion Like a c., he always bore — IMPRESSIONABILITY, 2
custodiet Quis c. ipsos custodes — MISTRUST, 7
custom A c. loathsome to the eye, hateful to the nose — SMOKING, 6
Age . . . nor c. stale her infinite virginity — PURITY, 5
C. calls me to't — CUSTOM, 4
c. More honour'd in the breach than the observance — CUSTOM, 3
c. stale Her infinite variety — ADMIRATION, 14
C., then, is the great guide of human life — CUSTOM, 2
customer The c. is always right — BUSINESS, 13
customers When you are skinning your c. — BUSINESS, 10
cut c. to the heart — ANGER, 2
Don't c. off your nose — REVENGE, 1
the human pack is shuffled and c. — EDUCATION, 31
cuts he that c. off twenty years of life — DEATH, 97
cutting busy driving cabs and c. hair — GOVERNMENT, 7
cymbal a tinkling c. — CHARITY, 5
Cynara faithful to thee, C. — FAITHFULNESS, 3
cynicism C. is an unpleasant way of saying the truth — CYNICISM, 2
C. is humour in ill-health — CYNICISM, 3
no literature can outdo the c. of real life — EXPERIENCE, 10

D

dad if the d. is present at the conception — SEX, 34
They fuck you up, your mum and d. — FAMILY, 23
daddy D. wouldn't buy me a bow-wow — DOGS, 14
daffodils Fair d., we weep to see — TRANSIENCE, 14
host, of golden d. — FLOWERS, 14
I never saw d. so beautiful — FLOWERS, 12
dagger never be left holding the d. — POLITICS, 81
dainties d. that are bred in a book — IGNORANCE, 13
dainty Nothing's so d. sweet — MELANCHOLY, 1
Daisy D., give me your answer, do — MARRIAGE, 41
Dalhousie Alas! Lord and Lady D. are dead — DEATH, 81
dalliance primrose path of d. — EXAMPLE, 8
damage nothing which might d. his career — SCOTS, 1
dame La belle D. sans Merci — SUPERNATURAL, 9
one for the d. — NURSERY RHYMES, 4
dammed Holland . . . lies so low they're only saved by being d. — EUROPE, 8
damn D. the age. I'll write for antiquity — POSTERITY, 7
D. with faint praise — CRITICISM, 38
I don't care a twopenny d. — INDIFFERENCE, 6
not worth a d. — OFFICERS, 15
damnation there would be no d. — SIN, 19
the terminal point of addiction is . . . d. — SIN, 2
damnations Twenty-nine distinct d. — BIBLE, 3
damn'd thou must be d. perpetually — DAMNATION, 3
damned a d. serious business — WAR, 124
d. good-natured friend — FRIENDS, 14
d. if you do – And . . . d. if you don't — DAMNATION, 2
Life is just one d. thing after another — LIFE, 27
Publish and be d. — PUBLISHING, 9
The public be d.. I am working for my stockholders — CAPITALISM, 15
Danaos timeo D. et dona ferentis — MISTRUST, 11
dance d. an antic hay — DANCING, 6
D., d., d. little lady — DANCING, 3
I could d. with you till the cows come home — HUMOUR, 41
I have discovered the d. — DANCING, 4
On with the d. — DANCING, 1
will you join the d.? — DANCING, 2
danced I've d. with a man — SNOBBERY, 4
dancers a perfectly ghastly season . . . for you Spanish d. — CHARITY, 4
dancing And d. dogs and bears — ANIMALS, 12
d. on a volcano — REVOLUTION, 5
the morals of a whore, and the manners of a d. master — CRITICISM, 20
danger A nation is not in d. . . . because it owes itself money — ECONOMICS, 10
d. . . . lies in acting well — EXCELLENCE, 2
I realized there was a measure of d. — DANGER, 5

Oft in d., oft in woe	ENDURANCE, 24
the only real d. that exists is man himself	HUMAN NATURE, 11
when we conquer without d.	VICTORY, 3
dangerous A little learning is a d. thing	KNOWLEDGE, 29
He thinks too much. Such men are d.	MISTRUST, 9
If a little knowledge is d., where is the man . . . out of danger	KNOWLEDGE, 20
if a little knowledge was a d. thing	KNOWLEDGE, 31
more d. the abuse	POWER, 7
dangerously live d.!	DANGER, 6
dangers D. by being despised	DANGER, 4
Daniels I should be like a lion in a cave of savage D.	ENEMIES, 9
Danny Deever they're hangin' D. in the mornin'.	EXECUTION, 14
Dante D. makes me sick	LAST WORDS, 10
dappled Glory be to God for d. things	BEAUTY, 19
dare d. to eat a peach	OLD AGE, 17
Darien Silent, upon a peak in D.	DISCOVERY, 5
daring d. to excel	EXCELLENCE, 2
Darjeeling There was an old man from D.	HUMOUR, 30
dark A blind man in a d. room	METAPHYSICS, 1
children fear . . . the d.	DEATH, 21
colours will agree in the d.	DIFFERENCE, 7
d. sayings	WISDOM, 7
Genuineness only thrives in the d.	SINCERITY, 4
great leap in the d.	LAST WORDS, 32
never to refuse a drink after d.	ALCOHOL, 41
O d., d., d., amid the blaze of noon	BLINDNESS, 4
slow, sure doom falls pitiless and d.	HUMAN CONDITION, 13
The d. night of the soul	SOUL, 8
Turn up the lights, I don't want to go home in the d.	LAST WORDS, 31
we are for the d.	ENDING, 4
What in me is d. Illumine	GOD, 37
darken never d. my towels again	DISMISSAL, 5
darkest The d. hour	OPTIMISM, 8
darkling as on a d. plain	WAR, 2
D. I listen	DEATH, 66
darkly through a glass, d.	CHARITY, 5
darkness Before us pass'd the door of D.	DEATH, 47
d. was upon the face of the deep	CREATION, 2
men loved d. . . . because their deeds were evil	EVIL, 5
She would rather light candles than curse the d.	COMPLIMENTS, 6
The d. falls at Thy behest	DAY, 4
the d. inside houses	FEAR, 7
darlin' he's a d. man	FRIENDS, 11
darling Charlie is my d.	ADMIRATION, 9
d. of the Gods was born	DESTINY, 13
Thrice welcome, d. of the spring	BIRDS, 14
darn A hole is the accident . . . a d. is . . . poverty	THRIFT, 9
dates Its history d. from today	ROYALTY, 35
daughter as is the mother, so is her d.	FAMILY, 10
d. of Earth and Water	WEATHER, 22
Don't put your d. on the stage	THEATRE, 6
Dwelt a miner, Forty-niner, And his d., Clementine	MOURNING, 7
I always remember that I am Caesar's d.	EXTRAVAGANCE, 3
skipper had taken his little d.	BOATS, 11
daughters old cemetery in which nine of his d. were lying	SEX, 48
Words are men's d.	WORDS, 14
dauntless faithful in love, . . . d. in war	CHIVALRY, 10
David's Once in royal D. city	CHRISTMAS, 2
Davy Sir Humphry D. Abominated gravy	SCIENTISTS, 3
dawn a grey d. breaking	SEA, 10
Bliss was it in that d. to be alive	FRENCH REVOLUTION, 3
the dappled d. doth rise	BIRDS, 8
They sighed for the d. and thee	LOVE, 128
dawned each day that has d. is your last	PRESENT, 10
day As I was saying the other d.	INTERRUPTIONS, 2
compare thee to a summer's d.	COMPLIMENTS, 4
count as profit every d. that Fate allows you	PRESENT, 8
each d. is like a year	IMPRISONMENT, 10
each d. that has dawned is your last	PRESENT, 10
every dog has his d.	SATISFACTION, 1
from this d. forward	MARRIAGE, 27
God called the light D.	CREATION, 2
Good morning to the d.: and, next, my gold	MATERIALISM, 12
If every d. in the life of a school	EDUCATION, 30
I look upon every d. to be lost	FRIENDSHIP, 20
in the d. of judgement	DEATH, 31

It takes place every d.	DOOMSDAY, 4
It was such a lovely d.	BED, 6
live murmur of a summer's d.	SUMMER, 2
Live this d., as . . . thy last	PRESENT, 12
long d.'s task is done	REST, 2
Night and d.	LOVE, 95
Now the d. is over	DAY, 1
Our little systems have their d.	TRANSIENCE, 18
Seize the d.	PRESENT, 7
So foul and fair a d.	WEATHER, 21
spend a single d. really well	GOOD, 6
Stay, stay, Until the hasting d. Has run	TRANSIENCE, 14
Sweet d., so cool, so calm	DAY, 8
That fellow would vulgarize the d. of judgment	VULGARITY, 3
The bright d. is done	ENDING, 6
The d. begins to droop	DAY, 2
the twenty-four hour d.	TIME, 9
thou knowest not what a d. may bring forth	FUTURE, 2
Without all hope of d.	BLINDNESS, 4
daylight a rule never to drink by d.	ALCOHOL, 41
Dayrolles Give D. a chair	LAST WORDS, 9
days D. and moments quickly flying	DEATH, 35
D. off	LEISURE, 4
d. of wine and roses	TRANSIENCE, 4
Do not let us speak of darker d.	WORLD WAR II, 11
Shuts up the story of our d.	FAITH, 17
Sweet childish d.	NOSTALGIA, 24
Thirty d. hath November	MONTHS, 9
dead Add: 'provided he is really d.'	ADMIRATION, 6
A master is d.	COMPOSERS, 2
And what was d. was Hope	IMPRISONMENT, 9
A statesman is a politician who's been d.	POLITICIANS, 73
But he's just as d. as if he'd been wrong	RIGHT, 1
Come not, when I am d.	HYPOCRISY, 15
D.! and . . . never called me mother	DEATH, 123
d., but in the Elysian fields	HOUSES OF PARLIAMENT, 8
D. men tell no tales	DEATH, 4
Either he's d. or my watch has stopped	DEATH, 78
England mourns for her d. across the sea	MOURNING, 3
Fifteen men on the d. man's chest	ALCOHOL, 57
for those who like it better d.	CRITICISM, 30
God is d.	GOD, 38
great deal to be said for being d.	DEATH, 24
Here lies Fred, Who was alive and is d.	ROYALTY, 3
He was a great patriot . . . provided . . . that he really is d.	ADMIRATION, 17
if I am d. he would like to see me	DEATH, 51
If the d. talk to you, you are a spiritualist	MADNESS, 12
I have been drinking it for sixty-five years and I am not d. yet	DRINKS, 9
I've just read that I am d.	OBITUARIES, 2
more to say when I am d.	DEATH, 91
most of 'em d.	WAR, 101
Mother is the d. heart of the family	WOMAN'S ROLE, 1
move in a world of the d.	HISTORIANS, 2
My husband is d.	DEATH, 79
Nobody heard him, the d. man	DROWNING, 3
Now he is d.!	DEATH, 18
Now I'm d. in the grave with my lips moving	POSTERITY, 8
O pity the d. that are d.	DEATH, 71
she was d.; but my father he kept ladling gin	REMEDIES, 11
The d. . . . look on and help	DEATH, 72
the d. shall be raised incorruptible	DEATH, 26
The noble living and the noble d.	NOBILITY, 6
The novel being d.	NOVELS, 17
The only completely consistent people are the d.	CONSTANCY, 4
The only good Indians I ever saw were d.	ENEMIES, 7
The past is the only d. thing	PAST, 7
the people we should have been seen d. with	SNOBBERY, 3
To one d. deathless hour	POETRY, 37
to resuscitate the d. art Of poetry	POETRY, 35
to the d. we owe only truth	RESPECT, 4
we are all d.	DEATH, 69
we survive amongst the d. and the dying as on a battlefield	OLD AGE, 41
When I am d., and laid in grave	MEMORIALS, 1
When I am d., my dearest	DEATH, 92
who quoted d. languages	CRITICS, 16
deadener Habit is a great d.	HABIT, 2
deadly Soap and education . . . are more d.	EDUCATION, 53
the female of the species is more d. than the male	WOMEN, 40
deaf Historians are like d. people	HISTORIANS, 7

union of a d. man to a blind woman — MARRIAGE, 34
deal a new d. for the American people — AMERICA, 28
Shed his blood . . . given a square d. — JUSTICE, 21
dean no dogma, no D. — RELIGION, 15
the queer old D. — SPOONERISMS, 4
dear D. 338171 — HUMOUR, 33
that bread should be so d. — POVERTY, 15
dearer d. still is truth — TRUTH, 8
death a covenant with d. — SLAVERY, 4
added another terror to d. — BIOGRAPHY, 4
After the first d., there is no other — DEATH, 116
After your d. you will be — AFTERLIFE, 7
Angel of D. has been abroad — WAR, 15
Any man's d. diminishes me — DEATH, 43
a Reaper whose name is D. — DEATH, 74
a remedy for everything except d. — REMEDIES, 6
artist is in danger of d. — SPORT AND GAMES, 6
A single d. is a tragedy — STATISTICS, 9
a tie that only d. can sever — MARRIAGE, 77
A useless life is an early d. — PURPOSE, 3
Because I could not stop for D. — DEATH, 40
Birth, and copulation, and d. — LIFE AND DEATH, 4
Christianity has made of d. a terror — CHRISTIANITY, 36
d. after life does greatly please — DEATH, 111
D. and taxes and childbirth — INCONVENIENCE, 1
D. be not proud — DEATH, 42
D. cometh soon or late — COURAGE, 14
D. defies the doctor — DEATH, 5
D. destroys a man — DEATH, 49
D. is my neighbour now — DEATH, 45
D. is still working like a mole — DEATH, 57
D. is the great leveller — DEATH, 6
D. is the veil — DEATH, 106
d. itself must be . . . a mockery — DEATH, 107
dread of something after d. — AFTERLIFE, 8
d.'s own hand is warmer than my own — WORLD-WEARINESS, 3
d. . . . the least of all evils — DEATH, 19
D. took him by the heart — DEATH, 85
D. was but A scientific fact — IMPRISONMENT, 8
D. . . . we haven't succeeded in . . . vulgarizing — DEATH, 59
D. will disprove you — DEATH, 119
easy d. only to the just — DEATH, 14
enormously improved by d. — WRITERS, 38
Football isn't a matter of life and d. — FOOTBALL, 6
give me liberty or give me d. — FREEDOM, 16
Go and try to disprove it — DEATH, 119
Growth is a greater mystery than d. — AGE, 34
half in love with easeful D. — DEATH, 66
His d., which happen'd in his berth — PUNS, 5
I am able to follow my own d. step by step — DEATH, 63
I am signing my d. warrant — PROPHECY, 3
Ideal mankind would abolish d. — IDEALISM, 3
I do really think that d. will be marvellous — DEATH, 109
in their d. they were not divided — FRIENDSHIP, 9
Into the jaws of D. — COURAGE, 19
Into the valley of D. — OBEDIENCE, 4
I prepare for a journey . . . as though for d. — TRAVEL, 19
I shall but love thee better after d. — LOVE, 29
it is not d., but dying, which is terrible — DEATH, 46
it may be so the moment after d. — AFTERLIFE, 4
I've been accused of every d. — MURDER, 3
I wanted to be bored to d. — BOREDOM, 2
man fears . . . only the stroke of d. — DEATH, 20
Many men would take the d.-sentence — LIFE AND DEATH, 8
Men fear d. — DEATH, 21
no cure for birth and d. — LIFE AND DEATH, 9
no drinking after d. — ALCOHOL, 25
nothing is certain but d. and taxes — TAXATION, 3
O d., where is thy sting? — DEATH, 26; DEATH, 87
O D., where is thy sting-a-ling-a-ling — DEATH, 15
one of those unfortunates to whom d. is — EXPLANATIONS, 1
one that had been studied in his d. — DEATH, 102
Pale D. kicks his way equally — EQUALITY, 23
Railing at life, and yet afraid of d. — OLD AGE, 12
Reports of my d. are greatly exaggerated — OBITUARIES, 4
sad stories of the d. of kings — ROYALTY, 28
sentenced to d. in my absence — JUSTICE, 2
Sickness, sin and d. . . . do not originate in God — RELIGION, 19
Sin brought d. — DEATH, 44; SIN, 1
Sleeping as quiet as d. — OLD AGE, 43
Sleep is good, d. is better — PESSIMISM, 6
Sleep . . . knows not D. — SLEEP, 14

Soldiers are citizens of d.'s grey land — SOLDIERS, 4
Swarm over, D. — ENGLAND, 3
the idea of d. as an individual — NUCLEAR WEAPONS, 8
the last enemy . . . is d. — AUTHORITARIANISM, 2
there's always d. — DEATH, 84
this is d., and the sole d. — DEATH, 33
this may be play to you, 'tis d. to us — SERIOUSNESS, 2
Thou wast not born for d. — BIRDS, 5
till d. us do part — MARRIAGE, 27
Time flies, d. urges — TIME, 39
to abolish the d. penalty — EXECUTION, 13
to read the d. of Little Nell without laughing — DICKENS, 3
— INSENSITIVITY, 4
tragedies are finished by a d. — THEATRE, 4
turneth the shadow of d. into the morning — GOD, 6
valiant never taste of d. but once — COWARDICE, 9
way to dusty d. — LIFE, 41
we all contain failure and d. within us — AGE, 34
we owe God a d. — DEATH, 105
what a man still plans . . . shows the . . . injustice in his d. — DEATH, 34
When Byron's eyes were shut in d. — BYRON, 1
who fears dishonour more than d. — HAPPINESS, 9
worse than d. — SEPARATION, 3
deaths Any amusing d. — DEATH, 32
it is chiefly our own d. that we mourn for — FUNERALS, 3
debasing I will not be a party to d. the currency — ECONOMICS, 7
debate I love argument, I love d. — ARGUMENTS, 14
debauchee D., n. One who has . . . pursued pleasure — DEBAUCHERY, 3
debt A promise made is a d. unpaid — PROMISES, 5
d. which cancels all others — OBLIGATION, 1
Out of d. — MONEY, 2
The nations which have put mankind . . . most in their d. — NATIONS, 2
debtor Not everyone is a d. — BORROWING, 7
debts He that dies pays all d. — DEATH, 101
decade fun to be in the same d. — AGE, 49
decadence The difference between our d. and the Russians' — DECLINE, 12
decades D. have a delusive edge — CLASSIFICATION, 3
decay as short a Spring; As quick a growth to meet d. — TRANSIENCE, 14
Macmillan seemed . . . to embody the national d. — DECLINE, 5
Time drops in d. — TIME, 37
woods d. and fall — MORTALITY, 19
deceit love we swore . . . seems d. — TRANSIENCE, 10
philosophy and vain d. — CHRISTIANITY, 4
temper discretion with d. — EDUCATION, 57
Where rumour of oppression and d. — SOLITUDE, 1
deceitfulness a Cat of such d. — CATS, 2
deceive if we say that we have no sin, we d. — SIN, 5
To d. oneself — DECEPTION, 1
deceived take heed . . . that your heart be not d. — CHRISTIANITY, 6
deceiving Propaganda . . . consists in nearly d. your friends — PROPAGANDA, 1
decent d. means poor — RESPECTABILITY, 3
riff-raff apply to what is respectable, . . . aristocracy to what is d. — CLASS, 16
the only d. thing . . . is to die at once — BEQUESTS, 1
decision he is going to make 'a realistic d.', . . . resolved to do something bad — DECISION, 3
if usage so choose, with whom resides the d. — WORDS, 10
decisive Marriage is a step so grave and d. — MARRIAGE, 103
declaim Nay, Madam, when you are declaiming, d. — COMPLAINTS, 4
declare they should d. the causes which impel them to . . . separation — INDEPENDENCE, 2
declining pass my d. years saluting strange women and grandfather clocks — OLD AGE, 29
decompose d. in a barrel of porter . . . in Dublin — FUNERALS, 6
decomposing d. in the eternity of print — CRITICISM, 53
decorated proverb . . . much matter d. — SAYINGS, 4
decorum *Dulce et d. est* — PATRIOTISM, 13
Let them cant about d. — RESPECTABILITY, 2
decrepit you are not yet d. enough — AGE, 20
decussated Anything reticulated or d. at equal distances — WORDS, 12
dedicated never d. to something you have complete confidence in — FANATICISM, 3

Dee Across the sands of D.   AGRICULTURE, 4
deed a good d. to forget a poor joke   HUMOUR, 4
good d. in a naughty world   GOOD, 15
right d. for the wrong reason   MOTIVE, 2
The better day, the worse d.   SUNDAY, 4
deeds better d. shall be in water writ   MEMORIALS, 2
Don't listen to their words fix your attention on their d.
   SCIENTISTS, 5
The bitterest tears . . . are for words . . . unsaid and d. . . .
undone   REGRET, 19
deep beauty is only sin d.   BEAUTY, 33
D. and crisp and even   CHRISTMAS, 14
Rocked in the cradle of the d.   SEA, 11
what a very singularly d. young man   ARROGANCE, 4
deeper d. than did ever plummet sound   RENUNCIATION, 2
whelm'd in d. gulphs   DEATH, 38
deeth D. is an ende of every worldly sore   LIFE AND DEATH, 3
defeat a d. without a war   WORLD WAR II, 3
d. is an orphan   SUCCESS, 8
D. of Germany means   WORLD WAR II, 27
every victory turns into a d.   DISILLUSION, 2
In d. unbeatable   OFFICERS, 3
defeated Like an army d. The snow hath retreated   SPRING, 9
man can be destroyed . . . not d.   DEFEAT, 3
defect Chief D. of Henry King   FOOD, 8
defence Never make a d. or apology   ACCUSATION, 2
Preparing for suicide . . . means of d.   NUCLEAR WEAPONS, 7
The best immediate d. of the United States   WORLD WAR II, 26
the d. of England   BOUNDARIES, 1
The only d. is in offence   WAR, 5
Truth telling is not compatible with the d. of the realm
   TRUTH, 36
defend I disapprove of what you say, but I will d. . . . your
right to say it   FREEDOM, 51
defiance in defeat, d.   WAR AND PEACE, 3
poorest man may in his cottage bid d. to . . . the Crown
   PRIVACY, 3
The d. of established authority   REBELLION, 1
defied Age will not be d.   AGE, 5
defining Language is . . . a d. framework   LANGUAGE, 26
definition This d. . . . would not do for a policeman   NURSES, 1
defying by d. their parents and copying one another   YOUTH, 5
degenerates everything d. in the hands of man   MANKIND, 22
degeneration fatty d. of his moral being   MARRIAGE, 105
degradation a . . . sense of intellectual d. after an interview
with a doctor   DOCTORS, 4
degree d. of delight   SUFFERING, 5
when d. is shak'd   ORDER, 3
degrees Crime, like virtue, has its d.   CRIME, 5
We boil at different d.   INDIVIDUALITY, 4
dei Vox populi, vox d.   PUBLIC, 1
deid Gey few, and they're a' d.   INDIVIDUALITY, 1
deities the d. so kindly   DESTINY, 16
deity to distinguish between the D. and the Drains   GOD, 46
deleted D. by French censor   NEWSPAPERS, 2
deliberate with a slow d. carelessness   READING, 10
deliberates woman that d. is lost   WOMEN, 6
deliberation D. is the work of many men   ACTION, 9
delicacy the talent of flattering with d.   FLATTERY, 2
delight a degree of d.   SUFFERING, 5
Commodity, Firmness, and D.   ARCHITECTURE, 13
Energy is Eternal D.   EFFORT, 2
go to't with d.   ENTHUSIASM, 7
Studies serve for d.   EDUCATION, 5
Teach us d. in simple things   GOOD, 7
The leaping light for your d. discovers   DISCOVERY, 2
very temple of d.   MELANCHOLY, 8
wept with d. when you gave her a smile   MEMORY, 7
delighted Whosoever is d. in solitude   SOLITUDE, 4
You have d. us long enough   DISMISSAL, 2
delightful make his conversation perfectly d.   INSULTS, 32
What a d. thing this perspective is!   ART, 27
delights Man d. not me   MANKIND, 26
deliver d. me from myself   SELF, 5
delivers the Man Who D. the Goods   RELIABILITY, 1
deluge After us the d.   PROPHECY, 7
Après nous le d.   PROPHECY, 7
delusions Many people have d. of grandeur   DELUSION, 5
delusive Decades have a d. edge   CLASSIFICATION, 3
delved When Adam d.   CLASS, 4
demagogues the vilest specimens of human nature are . . .
found among d.   POLITICS, 40

demands the populace cannot exact their d.   HOUSES OF
PARLIAMENT, 19
democracy arsenal of d.   DEMOCRACY, 13
D. . . . government by the uneducated   ARISTOCRACY, 5;
DEMOCRACY, 3
D. is only an experiment in government   DEMOCRACY, 5
D. means government by discussion   DEMOCRACY, 1
D. passes into despotism   DEMOCRACY, 11
D. resumed her reign   POLITICS, 3
extreme d. or absolute oligarchy, or despotism will come
   GOVERNMENT, 4
In Switzerland they had . . . five hundred years of d. and peace
   SWITZERLAND, 5
Man's capacity for evil makes d. necessary   DEMOCRACY, 10
not the voting that's d.   DEMOCRACY, 5
they which find themselves grieved under a d., call it anarchy
   GOVERNMENT, 12
world . . . made safe for d.   DEMOCRACY, 18
democratic thoroughly d. and patronise everybody
   DEMOCRACY, 14
demon woman wailing for her d.-lover   SUPERNATURAL, 6
demons we have often sunk to the level of the d.   WORDS, 11
denial the highest praise of God consists in the d. of Him
   ATHEISM, 9
denies spirit that always d.   DENIAL, 1
Denmark rotten in the state of D.   CORRUPTION, 6
denounce We thus d. . . . the arms race   NUCLEAR WEAPONS, 6
dentist fuss about sleeping together . . . sooner go to my d.
   SEX, 51
dentists gratitude to most benefactors is the same as . . . for d.
   INGRATITUDE, 3
I have let d. ride roughshod over my teeth   TEETH, 1
The thought of d. gave him just the same sick horror   FEAR, 14
deny let him d. himself   CHRISTIANITY, 19
Those who d. freedom   FREEDOM, 28
depart D., . . . and let us have done with you   DISMISSAL, 1
lettest thou thy servant d. in peace   DEATH, 28
when the great and good d.   MORTALITY, 20
departure the time of my d. is at hand   FAITH, 9
depends It all d. upon that article there   SOLDIERS, 9
depraved No one . . . suddenly became d.   DEBAUCHERY, 6
depression Recession . . . a neighbour loses . . . d. . . . you lose
   ECONOMICS, 11
depth out of your d.   SELF-CONFIDENCE, 5
derangement a nice d. of epitaphs   MALAPROPISMS, 8
derision Ambition, Distraction, Uglification, and D.
   EDUCATION, 9
descend Never d. to the ways of those above you
   EQUALITY, 14
descended D. from the apes . . . hope it is not true
   EVOLUTION, 1
description beggar'd all d.   ADMIRATION, 13
descriptions d. of the fairest wights   HISTORY, 29
desert The sand of the d. is sodden red   WAR, 75
Use every man after his d.   MERIT, 6
deserts D. of vast eternity   AGE, 35
deserve I have arthritis, and I don't d. that either   MERIT, 2
deserved I wasn't lucky. I d. it   MERIT, 7
deserves At 50, everyone has the face he d.   AGE, 40
the government it d.   GOVERNMENT, 17
designing I am d. St Paul's   ARCHITECTURE, 1
desire antidote to d.   DESIRE, 5
a universal innate d.   EXTRAVAGANCE, 2; PROGRESS, 2
d. is got without content   CONTENTMENT, 6
D. is the very essence of man   DESIRE, 15
d. should so many years outlive performance   SEX, 3
d. to be praised twice over   PRAISE, 6
It provokes the d.   ALCOHOL, 51
nothing like d. for preventing the thing one says   DESIRE, 1
The D. of Man being Infinite   INFINITY, 1
Those who restrain D.   DESIRE, 1
to have few things to d.   FEAR, 1
to lose your heart's d.   DESIRE, 14
desired war which . . . left nothing to be d.   WAR, 13
desires He who d. but acts not   ACTION, 7
made young with young d.   SPRING, 8
Man's D. are limited by his Perceptions   DESIRE, 3;
PERCEPTION, 2
Strong enough to answer back to d.   CHARACTER, 10
than nurse unacted d.   DESIRE, 2
desiring pessimists end up by d. the things they fear
   PESSIMISM, 9

disreputable I've been offered titles . . . get one into d.
company   TITLES, 11
disrespectfully Never speak d. of Society SNOBBERY, 12
dissipated still keep looking so d.   DEBAUCHERY, 2
dissipation At what time does the d. of energy begin SPORT
                                           AND GAMES, 11
d. without pleasure   LONDON, 7
other things than d. . . . thicken the features APPEARANCE, 38
dissolve Fade far away, d.   HUMAN CONDITION, 11
distance The d. doesn't matter   BEGINNING, 7
disthressful She's the most d. country that iver yet was seen
                                           IRELAND, 1
distinguish all there is to d. us from other animals MANKIND, 4
distinguished a sparrow alight on my shoulder . . . I was more
d. by that   HONOUR, 6
So it has come at last, the d. thing   LAST WORDS, 35
When a d. but elderly scientist states   SCIENCE, 4
distraction Ambition, D., Uglification, and Derision.
                                           EDUCATION, 9
distress All pray in their d.   PRAYER, 5
the mean man is always full of d.   SUPERIORITY, 2
distrust shameful to d. one's friends   FRIENDS, 12
stay together, but we d. one another   MARRIAGE, 28
distrusts him who d. himself   SILENCE, 10
disturb What isn't part of ourselves doesn't d. us HATE, 5
ditchwater Is d. dull   NATURE, 5
diversion Most sorts of d. . . . are an imitation of fighting
                                           WAR, 115
'tis a country d.   COUNTRYSIDE, 1
diversity make the world safe for d.   DIFFERENCE, 8
divide D. and rule   POWER, 1
divided in their death they were not d.   FRIENDSHIP, 9
Obstinate people can be d. into   STUBBORNNESS, 2
Thought must be d. against itself   UNDERSTANDING, 6
divine attain to the d. perfection   PERFECTION, 4
The Hand that made us is d.   CREATION, 1
The right d. of kings to govern wrong   MONARCHY, 16
To be discontented with the d. discontent   VIRTUE, 12
To err is human, to forgive, d.   FORGIVENESS, 13; MISTAKES, 11
divines Many a long dispute among d.   ARGUMENTS, 4
divinity a d. that shapes our ends   DESTINY, 17
a piece of d. in us   NOBILITY, 1
d. in odd numbers   SUPERSTITION, 10
There's such d. doth hedge a king   MONARCHY, 19
divisions How many d. has he got?   CATHOLICISM, 10
divorce D.? Never. But murder often   MARRIAGE, 114
do D. as you would be done by   EXAMPLE, 3
D. other men   BUSINESS, 4
d. what the mob d.   MAJORITY, 1
either d., or die   ACTION, 6
for they know not what they d.   FORGIVENESS, 4
I am to d. what I please   FREEDOM, 11
Let us d. or die   ACTION, 8
Nature . . . hath done her part; D. thou but thine
                                           RESPONSIBILITY, 9
Now what d. I d. with this   ROYALTY, 36
Preachers say, D. as I say, not as I d.   EXAMPLE, 7
so much to d., So little done   ACTION, 12
they would d. you   BUSINESS, 4
to d. something is to create existence   EXISTENCE, 5
Dobest Dowel, Dobet and D.   GOOD, 10
Dobet Dowel, D. and Dobest   GOOD, 10
doctor A d. . . . is a patient half-cured OCCUPATIONS, 12
a . . . sense of intellectual degradation after an interview with a
d.   DOCTORS, 4
D. Foster went to Gloucester   NURSERY RHYMES, 10
Evil comes . . . like the disease; good . . . like the d. GOOD AND
                                           EVIL, 2
I do not love thee, D. Fell   HATE, 1
Knocked down a d.? With an ambulance?   ACCIDENTS, 6
Passion . . . can be destroyed by a d.   PASSION, 7
The d. found . . . Her last disorder mortal DOCTORS, 3
doctors Who shall decide when d. disagree? DOCTORS, 6
doctrine a d. so illogical and so dull   MARXISM, 2
doctrines What makes all d. plain   MONEY, 13
documents sign d. which they do not read   BORROWING, 4
Dodger artful D.   NAMES, 1
does It's dogged as d. it   ACTION, 13
dog A door is what a d. is . . . on the wrong side of DOGS, 10
A good d.   MERIT, 1
America is a large, friendly d.   AMERICA, 33
And every d. his day   YOUTH, 11

A woman's preaching is like a d.'s walking on his hinder legs
                                           WOMEN, 38
Beware of the d.   DOGS, 1
D. does not eat d.   LOYALTY, 1
d. that praised his fleas   PARASITES, 4
end up eating our d.   ECOLOGY, 6
Every d. has his day   OPPORTUNITY, 2; SATISFACTION, 1
Every d. is allowed   LAW, 2
Give a d. a bad name   INJUSTICE, 1
I am His Highness' d. at Kew   DOGS, 11
If a d. jumps . . . but if a cat   CATS, 7
I ope my lips let no d. bark   EGOTISM, 8
That tossed the d., That worried the cat   NURSERY RHYMES, 57
The d. it was that died   DOGS, 8
The d. . . . Went mad and bit the man   DOGS, 7
The great pleasure of a d.   DOGS, 4
The little d. laughed To see such sport   NURSERY RHYMES, 14
the only passers-by who can contemplate it . . . are those . . .
with a white stick and a d.   ARCHITECTURE, 6
The world regards such a person as . . . an unmuzzled d.
                                           CLASSIFICATION, 1
whose d. are you   DOGS, 11
Why keep a d.   FUTILITY, 2
dogged It's d. as does it   ACTION, 13
dogging A case of the tail d. the wag   HUMOUR, 50
no d., no Dean   PUNS, 4
You can't teach an old d.   CONSERVATISM, 6; PUNS, 17
dogmas these d. or goals are in doubt   FANATICISM, 3
dogs And dancing d. and bears   ANIMALS, 12
Anybody who hates children and d.   CHILDREN, 21; DOGS, 6
d. delight to bark and bite   ANIMALS, 20
D., like horses, are quadrupeds   ANIMALS, 15
how much more d. are animated when they hunt in a pack
                                           UNITY, 10
I loathe people who keep d.   DOGS, 13
let slip the d. of war   WAR, 106
like asking a lamp-post . . . about d.   CRITICS, 6
more careful of the breed of their horses and d. than of their
children   FAMILY, 32
Rats . . . fought the d.   ANIMALS, 5
Stop . . . those d. . . . peeing on my cheapest rug DOGS, 9
The woman who is really kind to d.   DOGS, 2; WOMEN, 14
doing Anything that is worth d.   ORIGINALITY, 1
D. is better than saying   ACTION, 2
Find out what you like d. best and get someone to pay you for
d. it.   OCCUPATIONS, 14
let us not be weary in well d.   RETRIBUTION, 4
we learn by d.   LEARNING, 1
Whatever is worth d.   EXCELLENCE, 1
doings All our d. without charity   CHARITY, 8
dollar The almighty d., that great object of universal devotion
                                           MATERIALISM, 11
dollars What's a thousand d.   MONEY, 29; PUNS, 13
dominate d. the world   INFLUENCE, 10
dominions The sun does not set in my d.   ROYALTY, 26
dona timeo Danaos et d. ferentis   MISTRUST, 11
done bright day is d.   ENDING, 6
Do as you would be d. by   EXAMPLE, 3
d. those things we ought not   SIN, 9
If it were d. when 'tis d.   HASTE, 10
Justice should . . . be seen to be d.   JUSTICE, 10
Let justice be d.   JUSTICE, 7
long day's task is d.   REST, 2
One never notices what has been d.   ACHIEVEMENT, 3
so little d.   ACTION, 12
the dread of doing what has been d. before ORIGINALITY, 6
The way to get things d. is not to mind who gets the credit
                                           SELFLESSNESS, 1
thy worldly task hast d.   MORTALITY, 16
What's d. cannot be undone   REGRET, 3
What you do not want d. to yourself   EXAMPLE, 4
Dong The D. with a luminous Nose   NONSENSE, 17
Don Juan D. when anger is subsiding into indifference
                                           LITERATURE, 12
Don Juans Christ-like heroes and woman-worshipping D.
                                           MEN, 6
donkeys lions led by d.   OFFICERS, 8
Don Miguel All right, my lord creator, D. DEATH, 65
Don Quixote the only absolutely original creation . . . is D.
                                           FICTION, 4
dons If the D. sight Devon   PATRIOTISM, 19

E

more things in heaven and e. SUPERNATURAL, 12
passenger on the spaceship, E. SPACE, 3
so much of e. . . . of heaven IMPETUOSITY, 4
the cool flowery lap of e. POETS, 2
The e. does not argue HUMAN NATURE, 21
the e. of England is in my two hands VICTORY, 19
the e. where cares abound? BIRDS, 11
The meek do not inherit the e. HUMILITY, 6
This e. of majesty ENGLAND, 34
When e. was nigher heaven PAST, 3
ease done with so much e. CHARACTER, 6
Joys in another's loss of e. LOVE, 28
No warmth, no cheerfulness, no healthful e. MONTHS, 10
Prodigal of E. WORLD-WEARINESS, 1
True e. in writing comes from art WRITING, 26
easeful half in love with e. Death DEATH, 66
easier E. said than done ACTION, 3
it is much e. to say what it is not POETRY, 20
east E. is E., and West is West OPPOSITES, 3
E., west HOME, 1
hold the gorgeous e. in fee VENICE, 4
Now we can look the E. End in the face WORLD WAR II, 17
the e. wind made flesh AMERICANS, 2
to have the E. come to the Atlantic WORLD WAR II, 19
to prevent us from going into the E. WORLD WAR II, 19
wise men from the e. CHRISTMAS, 9
easy E. come MONEY, 1
It is e. to bear MISFORTUNE, 1
It is e. to be wise WISDOM, 1
It's either e. or impossible PAINTING, 4
eat Don't e. too many almonds FOOD, 14
E. as much as you like OBESITY, 9
E. to live FOOD, 4
e. to live, not live to e. FOOD, 35
great ones e. up the little ones RUTHLESSNESS, 5
I commended mirth . . . to e. . . . to drink, and to be merry
PLEASURE, 1
I could e. one of Bellamy's veal pies FOOD, 38; LAST WORDS, 45
if any would not work, neither should he e. WORK, 4
Let them e. the lie NONCOMMITMENT, 2
let us e. and drink; for tomorrow we . . . die TRANSIENCE, 1
So I did sit and e. LOVE, 65
Some hae meat, and canna e. FOOD, 14
To e. well in England FOOD, 33
eaten daring . . . to explain . . . that cows can be e.
RELIGION, 24
e. me out of house and home GREED, 10
eating Appetite comes with e. DESIRE, 12
E. people is wrong CANNIBALISM, 1
sign something is e. us GREED, 6
eats e., sleeps and watches the television WOMAN'S ROLE, 1
Man is the only animal that can remain on friendly terms with
the victims . . . he e. HYPOCRISY, 6
ecclesiastic E. tyranny's the worst CHURCH, 3
ecclesiastical lay interest in e. matters . . . often a prelude to
insanity RELIGION, 58
echo The sound must seem an e. to the sense WRITING, 26
economic bottom of the e. pyramid POVERTY, 1
economist Give me a one-handed e. ECONOMICS, 13
Jesus was . . . a first-rate political e. CHRISTIANITY, 38
Practical men, . . . are usually the slaves of some defunct e.
INFLUENCE, 5
economists All races have . . . e., with the exception of the
Irish IRISH, 5
If all e. were laid end to end ECONOMICS, 12
economy E. is going without something you do want THRIFT, 7
Everybody is always in favour of general e. THRIFT, 3
eczema style . . . often hides e. STYLE, 2
Eden a garden eastward in E. GARDENS, 3
futile to attempt a picnic in E. INNOCENCE, 4
Sir Anthony E. BORES, 4
the garden of E. KNOWLEDGE, 7; TREES, 1
This other E., demi-paradise ENGLAND, 8
edge his keener eye The axe's e. did try EXECUTION, 16
We stand today on the e. of a new frontier BEGINNING, 11
editor An e. . . . separates the wheat from the chaff EDITORS, 3
editorial the nineteenth century was the age of the e. chair
PSYCHIATRY, 8
Edmonton If wife should dine at E. MARRIAGE, 39
Unto the Bell at E. MARRIAGE, 40
Edna Aunt E. is universal AUDIENCES, 4
educate e. a woman you e. a family EDUCATION, 32

e. with the head instead of with the hand EDUCATION, 29
got to e. him first EDUCATION, 44
'tis the schoolboys that e. my son EDUCATION, 15
education a liberal e. at the Colleges of Unreason REASON, 1
E. . . . has produced a vast population able to read READING, 16
e. is a leading out of what is . . . in the pupil's soul
EDUCATION, 52
E. is . . . the soul of a society EDUCATION, 11
E. is what survives EDUCATION, 51
E. made us what we are EDUCATION, 21
fortunate in escaping regular e. WRITERS, 27
His English e. . . . preserved his intellect . . . at the stage of
boyhood EDUCATION, 10
if e. is . . . a mere transmission of knowledge EDUCATION, 36
make your children *capable of honesty* is the beginning of e.
HONESTY, 6
one of the ultimate advantages of an e. EDUCATION, 50
part of English middle-class e. is devoted to the training of
servants EDUCATION, 62
Soap and e. are not as sudden as a massacre, but they are
more deadly EDUCATION, 53
'Tis e. forms the common mind EDUCATION, 42
Travel . . . is a part of e. TRAVEL, 2
with e. and whisky the price it is CHARACTER, 4
woman of e. WOMEN, 75
educations last resort of feeble minds with classical e.
EDUCATION, 23
Edwardian plants left over from the E. Wilderness CHANGE, 16
Edwardians The E., . . . , were nomadic TRAVEL, 28
eena E., meena, mina, mo NURSERY RHYMES, 11
effect little e. after much labour RESULTS, 2
efficient be e. if you're going to be lazy LAZINESS, 1
effort What is written without e. WRITING, 14
efforts One is happy as a result of one's own e. HAPPINESS, 2
egalitarianism The majestic e. of the law EQUALITY, 8
égalité *Liberté! É.! Fraternité!* HUMAN RIGHTS, 2
egg a broody hen sitting on a china e. BUREAUCRACY, 5
hand that lays the golden e. MIXED METAPHORS, 2
the learned roast an e. FOOD, 39
throw an e. into an electric fan AMBITION, 9
eggs Don't put all your e. in one basket CAUTION, 4
I've met a lot of hardboiled e. CHARACTER, 25
putting all my e. in one bastard ILLEGITIMACY, 2
to cook himself a couple of e. EGOTISM, 2
ways to dress e. FRANCE, 11
eggyellow his nicotine e. weeping walrus Victorian moustache
APPEARANCE, 35
egotism dilemmas of conscience and e. POWER, 17
egotist E. . . . A person . . . more interested in himself
EGOTISM, 3
Egypt Remember you're in E. PRONUNCIATION, 2
We are not at war with E. WAR, 34
Egyptians the E. worshipped an insect POLITICIANS, 22
eight E. maids a-milking NURSERY RHYMES, 55
Pieces of e. MONEY, 43
eighteen From birth to age e., a girl needs good parents
AGE, 60
I knew almost as much at e. as I do now KNOWLEDGE, 24
she speaks e. languages. And she can't say 'No' in any of them
PROMISCUITY, 5
Ein There's Gert and there's Epp and there's E. HUMOUR, 28
Einstein E. – the greatest Jew since Jesus SCIENTISTS, 1
Let E. be! SCIENTISTS, 9
elations the impalpable e. and apprehensions of growth
AGE, 34
elderly When a distinguished but e. scientist states SCIENCE, 5
elders miss not the discourse of the e. LEARNING, 2
elected audacity of e. persons REVOLUTION, 12
election I am certain that we will win the e. with a good
majority SELF-CONFIDENCE, 6
electric the e. display of God the Father LIFE, 36
electrical E. force . . . causes motion of e. charge SCIENCE, 8
electricity e. was dripping invisibly SCIENCE, 32
electrification Communism is Soviet power plus the e.
COMMUNISM, 4
elegant English women are e. ENGLISH, 25
element One God, one law, one e. DESTINY, 20
elementary 'E.,' said he SIMPLICITY, 1
elements I tax not you, you e., with unkindness WEATHER, 19
something that was before the e. NOBILITY, 1
elephant I shot an e. in my pajamas HUMOUR, 4

Nonsense, they couldn't hit an e. at this distance LAST WORDS, 56
elevate E. them guns a little lower WAR, 50
eleven E. ladies dancing NURSERY RHYMES, 55
eloquence Talking and e. are not the same SPEECH, 11
else Lord High Everything E. TITLES, 4
Suppose it had been someone e. who found you like this ADULTERY, 5
elusive One's prime is e. AGE, 55
Elysian dead, but in the E. fields HOUSES OF PARLIAMENT, 1
emancipated e. from . . . time and space IMAGINATION, 2
embalmer A triumph of the e.'s art INSULTS, 36
soft e. of the still midnight SLEEP, 10
embarras l'e. des richesses EXCESS, 1
embarrassment God could cause us considerable e. DISCOVERY, 4
embittered He was an e. atheist ATHEISM, 8
embody I, my lords, e. the Law LAW, 11
embrace I e. the purpose of God DESTINY, 21
none, I think, do there e. DEATH, 77
whether I e. your lordship's principles or your mistress REPARTEE, 5
emotion Poetry is not a turning loose of e. POETRY, 13
Sorrow is tranquillity remembered in e. SORROW, 14
the degree of my aesthetic e. CRITICS, 1
emotional a well-bred sort of e. anarchy CLASSIFICATION, 2
emotions a sort of metaphysical brothel for e. SENTIMENTALITY, 3
big e. come from big words STYLE, 5
noble grounds for the noble e. POETRY, 38
She ran . . . e. from A to B CRITICISM, 35
emperor An e. ought at least to die on his feet LAST WORDS, 65
I am the e., and I want dumplings PETULANCE, 3
the E. has nothing on INNOCENCE, 2
emperors e. can't do it all by themselves SUPPORT, 2
empire An e. founded by war WAR, 69
Great Britain has lost an E. BRITAIN, 1
How is the E.? BRITISH EMPIRE, 2; LAST WORDS, 25
the Holy Roman Empire was neither holy, nor Roman, nor an e. NATIONS, 3
to the French the e. of the land EUROPE, 13
empires The day of e. has come NATIONS, 1
employed innocently e. than in getting money MONEY, 25
The rise in the . . . e. is governed by Parkinson's Law WORK, 14
employees Work . . . by those e. who have not yet reached . . . incompetence INCOMPETENCE, 4
employer ideal of the e. . . . production without employees INDUSTRIAL RELATIONS, 3
employment I will undoubtedly have to seek . . . gainful e. GOVERNMENT, 1
empty Bring on the e. horses LANGUAGE, 10
E. vessels FOOLISHNESS, 5
You can't think rationally on an e. stomach THINKING, 5
enchantment distance lends e. to the view PERSPECTIVE, 1
enclose A vacuum can only exist . . . by the things which e. it SCIENCE, 14
enclosed Check e. MONEY, 34
encourage the right to be consulted, . . . to e., . . . to warn MONARCHY, 2
to e. the others EXAMPLE, 9
encourager pour e. les autres EXAMPLE, 9
encyclopaedia a whole E. behind the rest of the world SCIENCE, 22
end a beginning, a muddle, and an e. NOVELS, 8
an e. to the beginnings of all wars WAR, 93
a whole is that which has a beginning, a middle, and an e. PLAYS, 1
beginning of the e. DEFEAT, 8
God be at my e., And at my departing GOD, 1
I like a film to have a beginning, a middle and an e. CINEMA, 3
I move softly towards the e. DEATH, 63
Keep right on to the e. of the road PERSISTENCE, 8
of making many books there is no e. BOOKS, 7
our minutes hasten to their e. TIME, 30
the e. is not yet WAR, 7
The e. is to build well ARCHITECTURE, 13
the e. of the beginning WORLD WAR II, 13
Walt Whitman who laid e. to e. POETS, 21
we're forbidden to know – what e. the gods have in store DESTINY, 12
world without e. ETERNITY, 2

Yes, to the very e. ENDURANCE, 15
endeavour To e. to forget anyone MEMORY, 8
ended My life with girls has e. SEX, 20
The day Thou gavest, Lord, is e. DAY, 4
ending The quickest way of e. a war WAR, 79
endless History is an e. repetition HISTORY, 9
ends divinity that shapes our e. DESTINY, 17
my family begins . . . yours e. with you ANCESTRY, 3
endurance patient e. is godlike ENDURANCE, 9
endure For his mercies ay e. GOD, 36
It is flattering some men to e. them TOLERANCE, 2
Youth's a stuff will not e. PRESENT, 13
endured Job e. everything – until his friends came ENDURANCE, 8
endures When a man is in love he e. more LOVE, 88
endureth blessed is the man that e. temptation TEMPTATION, 4
enemies Better a thousand e. ENEMIES, 1
designing mausoleums for his e. HATE, 6
do not have to forgive my e. LAST WORDS, 39; RUTHLESSNESS, 4
Even a paranoid can have e. ENEMIES, 4
love your e. ENEMIES, 3
Mountains interposed Make e. of nations MOUNTAINS, 1
The e. of Freedom OPPRESSION, 3
we have been mortal e. ever since ENEMIES, 5
enemy Every man is his own worst e. SELF, 1
hasn't an e. in the world POPULARITY, 8
It takes your e. and your friend . . . , to hurt you HURT, 3
no more sombre e. of good art BABIES, 1
Poverty is a great e. to human happiness POVERTY, 18
We have met the e., and they are ours VICTORY, 12
we must be just to our e. PUBLISHING, 4
energies quarrel . . . e. displayed in it are fine ARGUMENTS, 10
energy At what time does the dissipation of e. begin SPORT AND GAMES, 11
E. is Eternal Delight EFFORT, 2
enfants Allons, e., de la patrie FRANCE, 10
Les e. terribles YOUTH, 8
engaged one of the nicest girls I was ever e. to MARRIAGE, 123
engine indefatigable and unsavoury e. of pollution DOGS, 12
England A grain, which in E. is generally given to horses SCOTLAND, 3
Be E. what she will PATRIOTISM, 5
but the King of E. cannot enter PRIVACY, 3
Christianity is part of the Common Law of E. CHRISTIANITY, 26
Common Law of E. LAW, 15
E. elects a Labour Government POLITICS, 56
E. expects every man will do his duty DUTY, 3
E. is a nation of shopkeepers ENGLISH, 28
E. is a paradise for women NATIONALITY, 3
E. is the mother of parliaments ENGLAND, 5
E. is the paradise of individuality ENGLAND, 33
E. is the paradise of women ENGLAND, 16
E. mourns for her dead across the sea MOURNING, 3
E.'s green and pleasant land ENGLAND, 4
E.'s pleasant pastures ENGLAND, 4
E. . . . the envy of less happy lands ENGLAND, 13
E. . . . the workshop of the world ENGLAND, 15
E.! . . . What love I bore to thee HOMESICKNESS, 9
E. will have her neck wrung like a chicken WORLD WAR II, 30
E., with all thy faults PATRIOTISM, 6
For E.'s the one land ENGLAND, 6
For God's sake, madam, don't say that in E. for . . . they will surely tax it TAXATION, 10
go back to thy stately homes of E. PARTING, 7
hardly be a town in the South of E. ENGLAND, 30
he bores for E. BORES, 4
in E. people have good table manners MANNERS, 4
In E., pop art and fine art ART, 14
In E. there is only silence or scandal ENGLAND, 26
It was twenty-one years ago that E. and I ENGLAND, 28
Living in E., . . . must be like being married to a stupid . . . wife ENGLAND, 17
no man in E. will take away my life ARROGANCE, 2
occurred nowhere but in E. ENGLAND, 10
Oh, to be in E. ENGLAND, 7
Old E. is lost BRITAIN, 9
rather hew wood than be . . . King of E. MONARCHY, 6
should they know of E. who only E. know ENGLAND, 21
Speak for E. PATRIOTISM, 2
Stately Homes of E. ARISTOCRACY, 6; STATELY HOMES, 2; STATELY HOMES, 4

Look not in my e., for fear They mirror true the sight I see LOVE, 68
Love looks not with the e. LOVE, 114
Mine e. have seen the glory of the coming of the Lord GOD, 25
pearls that were his e. DEATH, 100
the creature hath a purpose and its e. are bright with it PURPOSE, 5
The e. are the window SOUL, 1
the e. are the windows of the soul EYES, 1
The e. that shone, Now dimmed and gone NOSTALGIA, 14
the whites of their e. WAR, 86
Thy rapt soul sitting in thine e. SOUL, 10
Two lovely black e. VIOLENCE, 3
you'll wear your e. out STARING, 2
Your e. shine like the pants COMPLIMENTS, 3
eyesight with blinded e. LEARNING, 9

F

Fabian Britain . . . F. Society writ large BRITAIN, 7
Fabians A good man fallen among F. WRITERS, 25
fabric chemical barrage has been hurled against the f. of life ECOLOGY, 2
the baseless f. of this vision MORTALITY, 17
face Accustomed to her f. FAMILIARITY, 3
a garden in her f. ADMIRATION, 4
A good f. is a letter of recommendation BEAUTY, 1
And hid his f. amid a crowd of stars LOVE, 143
At 50, everyone has the f. he deserves AGE, 40
Communism with a human f. COMMUNISM, 2
everybody's f. but their own SATIRE, 9
every man is responsible for his f. APPEARANCE, 6
False f. must hide DECEPTION, 5
from whose f. the earth and the heaven fled JUDGMENT, 4
I have looked upon the f. of Agamemnon HISTORY, 22
I never forget a f., but I'll make an exception MEMORY, 9
Look in my f.; my name is Might-have-been DISAPPOINTMENT, 6
Looks the whole world in the f. RIGHTEOUSNESS, 7
My f. is my fortune, sir, she said NURSERY RHYMES, 66
painting a f. and not washing APPEARANCE, 15
the f. that launch'd a thousand ships BEAUTY, 24
The human f. is . . . a whole cluster of faces MANKIND, 20
There is not any book Or f. DEATH, 118
to order a new stamp . . . with my f. on it TRIVIALITY, 11
faces All, all are gone, the old familiar f. NOSTALGIA, 12
among so many million of f. INDIVIDUALITY, 3
make f. MUSICIANS, 7
facetious You must not think me . . . foolish because I am f. SERIOUSNESS, 3
fact the slaying of a beautiful hypothesis by an ugly f. SCIENCE, 19
faction To die for f. EXECUTION, 7
factory In the f. we make cosmetics COSMETICS, 3
facts Comment is free but f. are sacred JOURNALISM, 22
F. alone are wanted in life FACTS, 1
F. do not cease to exist FACTS, 2
F. speak louder than statistics FACTS, 3; STATISTICS, 11
Once a newspaper touches a story, the f. are lost JOURNALISM, 17
fade the cheek that doth not f. APPEARANCE, 17
fail If they succeed, they f. HOMOSEXUALITY, 3
Others must f. RUTHLESSNESS, 7
to f. conventionally ORTHODOXY, 3
failed Here lies Joseph, who f. in everything he undertook FAILURE, 3
faileth charity never f. CHARITY, 5
fails If thy heart f. thee AMBITION, 7
failure All political lives . . . end in f. POLITICIANS, 56
no success like f. FAILURE, 2
we all contain f. and death within us AGE, 34
faint Damn with f. praise CRITICISM, 38
fair All is f. LOVE, 1
all's f. in love and war JUSTICE, 8
F. stood the wind for France BOATS, 5
Grief has turned her f. APPEARANCE, 39
Monday's child is f. of face NURSERY RHYMES, 33
Serious sport has nothing to do with f. play SPORT AND GAMES, 15
So foul and f. a day WEATHER, 21
the Brave deserves the F. COURAGE, 9
There was a f. maid dwellin' LOVE, 13
faire Laissez f. FREEDOM, 42

fairer thou art f. than the evening air BEAUTY, 25
fairest the f. things have the worst fate TRANSIENCE, 17
fairies I don't believe in f. FAIRIES, 1
the beginning of f. FAIRIES, 2
There are f. at the bottom of our garden FAIRIES, 3
fairy A myth is, of course, not a f. story MYTHS, 7
the f. tales of science EXPERIENCE, 19
fairyland The Fleet's lit up. It is like f. NAVY, 4
faith a life of doubt diversified by f. DOUBT, 1
an absolute f. that all things are possible to God FAITH, 10
And f. shines equal COURAGE, 2
by f. the walls of Jericho fell down FAITH, 2
F. . . . an illogical belief in . . . the improbable FAITH, 14
F. consists in believing when it is beyond the power of reason to believe FAITH, 19
f., if it hath not works, is dead FAITH, 7
f. is the substance of things hoped for FAITH, 3
f. unfaithful kept him falsely true UNFAITHFULNESS, 1
F. will move mountains FAITH, 1
no need for any other f. than . . . f. in human beings FAITH, 9
now abideth f., hope, charity CHARITY, 3
O thou of little f., wherefore didst thou doubt? DOUBT, 2
Reason is itself a matter of f. REASON, 2
the f. and morals Which Milton held FREEDOM, 53
'Tis not the dying for a f. FAITH, 18
we walk by f., not by sight FAITH, 5
When your ladyship's f. has removed them RELIGION, 40
whoever is moved by f. to assent CHRISTIANITY, 29
faithful f. in love, . . . dauntless in war CHIVALRY, 10
f. to thee, Cynara FAITHFULNESS, 3
happiness of man that he be mentally f. INTEGRITY, 5
If this man is not f. to his God LOYALTY, 9
if you had been f. LOVE, 99
my heart shall be The f. compass FAITHFULNESS, 4
O come all ye f. CHRISTMAS, 15
thou good and f. servant SERVICE, 1
Translations (like wives) are seldom f. TRANSLATION, 2
fake If I like it, . . . it's mine. If I don't . . . it's a f. PAINTING, 9
fall and an haughty spirit before a f. PRIDE, 1
Fain would I climb, yet fear I to f. AMBITION, 14
The airplane stays up because it doesn't have the time to f. SCIENCE, 37
Whenever you f., pick up something OPPORTUNITY, 8
fallen A good man f. among Fabians WRITERS, 25
y-f. out of heigh degree. Into miserie MISFORTUNE, 4
falleth woe to him that is alone when he f. FRIENDSHIP, 8
falling Fish die belly-upward and rise . . . their way of f. FISH, 1
fallow lie f. for a while REST, 3
false beware of f. prophets DECEPTION, 2
F. face must hide what the false heart DECEPTION, 5
f. to his friends . . . true to the public HONESTY, 3
natural f. teeth TEETH, 3
The religions we call f. were once true RELIGION, 21
Thou canst not then be f. BORROWING, 8; INTEGRITY, 6
thou shalt not bear f. witness GOD, 10
True and F. are attributes of speech, not of things TRUTH, 26
Vain wisdom all, and f. philosophy WISDOM, 18
falsehood Let her and F. grapple TRUTH, 32
falsely a verb meaning 'to believe f.' BELIEF, 8
Falstaff F. sweats to death OBESITY, 10
fame blush to find it f. GOOD, 14
F. is a powerful aphrodisiac FAME, 4
F. is like a river FAME, 2
F. is sometimes like unto a . . . mushroom FAME, 10
F. is the spur FAME, 14
Here rests . . . A youth to fortune and to f. unknown DEATH, 55
Love of f. is the last thing . . . to be parted from FAME, 19
One of the drawbacks of F. FAME, 13
The book written against f. . . . has the author's name on the title-page HYPOCRISY, 9
familiar old f. faces NOSTALGIA, 12
familiarity F. breeds contempt FAMILIARITY, 1
F. breeds contempt – and children SEX, 50
families All happy f. resemble one another FAMILY, 42
Good f. are generally worse than any others FAMILY, 20
Murder, like talent, seems . . . to run in f. MURDER, 9
the best-regulated f. ACCIDENTS, 2
There are only two f. in the world POVERTY AND WEALTH, 3
family A f. with the wrong members in control ENGLAND, 29
a tense and peculiar f., the Oedipuses CLASSICS, 1
educate a woman you educate a f. EDUCATION, 32

Mother is the dead heart of the f.   WOMAN'S ROLE, 1
my f. begins with me   ANCESTRY, 3
the f. . . . source of all our discontents   FAMILY, 24
The f. that prays together   FAMILY, 4
The sink is the great symbol of the bloodiness of f. life
    FAMILY, 28
famine They that die by f. die by inches   HUNGER, 6
you look as if there were f. in the land   APPEARANCE, 32
famous everyone will be f. for 15 minutes   FAME, 23
I awoke . . . found myself f.   FAME, 6
I'm never going to be f.   FAME, 16
let us now praise f. men   PRAISE, 3
so f., that it would permit me . . . to break wind in society
    FAME, 3
What are you f. *for*?   FAME, 15
fan 'F. vaulting' . . . belongs to the 'Last-supper-carved-on-a-
peach-stone'   ARCHITECTURE, 5
throw an egg into an electric f.   AMBITION, 9
fanatic f. . . . over-compensates a . . . doubt   FANATICISM, 1
fanatics F. have their dreams   FANATICISM, 2
when f. are on top there is no limit to oppression
    GOVERNMENT, 18
fancies All universal moral principles are idle f.   MORALITY, 13
fancy a young man's f. . . . turns to . . . love   SPRING, 7
Ever let the f. roam   DISCONTENT, 5
F. is . . . a mode of memory   IMAGINATION, 2
f. wit will come   STUPIDITY, 11
hopeless f. feign'd   NOSTALGIA, 20
little of what you f. does you good   PLEASURE, 19
sweetest Shakespeare, F.'s child   SHAKESPEARE, 12
fantastic the light f. toe   DANCING, 1
far a f., f., better thing   EXECUTION, 6
how f. we may go too f.   TACT, 4
The night is dark, and I am f. from home   FAITH, 16
Thursday's child has f. to go   NURSERY RHYMES, 33
Faraday remain plain Michael F. to the last   TITLES, 3
farce F. is the essential theatre   THEATRE, 7
Parliament is the longest running f.   GOVERNMENT, 26
the f. is over   LAST WORDS, 48
the wine was a f. and the food a tragedy   FOOD, 41
farewell F., a long f., to all my greatness   HUMAN
    CONDITION, 14
F., my poor hands   MUSICIANS, 5
F.! thou art too dear for my possession   PARTING, 11
hail and f.   GREETINGS, 1
long journey . . . must bid the company f.   LAST WORDS, 50
farmer This is the f. sowing his corn   NURSERY RHYMES, 57
farm-yard nothing to distinguish human society from the f.
    MANKIND, 28
the f. world of sex   ANIMALISM, 5
far-reaching Life's short span forbids us to enter on f. hopes
    MORTALITY, 13
fart he can't f. and chew gum at the same time   STUPIDITY, 3
farthing It is burning a f. candle at Dover   CRITICISM, 17
steal one poor f. without excuse   SIN, 17
fascinates I like work; it f. me   IDLENESS, 6
fascination Philosophy, . . . is a fight against . . . f.
    PHILOSOPHY, 17
war . . . will always have its f.   WAR, 129
fascism F. is a religion   FASCISM, 2
F. is not an article for export   FASCISM, 3
F. means war   FASCISM, 5
the twentieth century will be . . . the century of F.   FASCISM, 2
fascist Every communist has a f. frown   COMMUNISM, 8;
    FASCISM, 4
fashion after the f. of their country   ENGLAND, 36
as . . . be . . . out of the f.   FASHION, 2
Every man after his f.   DIFFERENCE, 1
faithful to thee, Cynara! in my f.   FAITHFULNESS, 3
F. is architecture   FASHION, 1
Nothing else holds f.   SEX, 43
the unreasoning laws of markets and f.   ART, 1
true to you, darlin', in my f.   FAITHFULNESS, 5
fashionable an idea . . . to be f. is ominous   FASHION, 5
fashions F., . . . only induced epidemics   FASHION, 6
I cannot . . . cut my conscience to fit this year's f.   INTEGRITY, 3
fast none so f. as stroke   BOATS, 2
they stumble that run f.   HASTE, 11
US has to move very f.   AMERICA, 19
faster the world would go round a deal f.   INTERFERING, 1
Will you walk a little f.   HASTE, 5

fastidious to set a chime of words tinkling in . . . a few f.
people   PURPOSE, 7
fat butter will only make us f.   POWER POLITICS, 3
Enclosing every thin man, there's a f. man   APPEARANCE, 37
in every f. man a thin one   OBESITY, 5
Let me have men about me that are f.   MISTRUST, 9
O f. white woman   OBESITY, 6
Outside every f. man . . . an even fatter man   OBESITY, 1
there's a thin man inside every f. man   OBESITY, 8
Who's your f. friend   OBESITY, 2
you will come and find me f. and sleek   PRESENT, 10
fatal Anno domini . . . the most f. complaint   DEATH, 58
Nature has never put the f. question as to the meaning of their
lives   PURPOSE, 4
when he does it is nearly always f.   LOVE AND DEATH, 4
fate count as profit every day that F. allows you   PRESENT, 8
Each man the architect of his own f.   RESPONSIBILITY, 3
hostages given to f.   FAMILY, 25
How wayward the decrees of F.   GREATNESS, 14; WISDOM, 22
it is not only our f. but our business to lose innocence
    INNOCENCE, 4
jeers at F.   ENVY, 2
Leave the flesh to the f. it was fit for   SOUL, 5
master of his f.   RESPONSIBILITY, 14
mortifying f. of most English universities   NOVELTY, 6
the fairest things have the worst f.   TRANSIENCE, 17
the life-sentence which f. carries   LIFE AND DEATH, 8
the master of my f.   RESPONSIBILITY, 7
the severity of f.   DESTINY, 10
We may become the makers of our f.   DESTINY, 15
when F. summons   MORTALITY, 5
father a wise f. that knows his own child   FAMILY, 37
Box about: 'twill come to my f. anon   FAMILY, 6
brood of Folly without f.   PLEASURE, 23
Dreading to find its F.   GUILT, 2
except to shoot rabbits and hit his f. on the jaw   NASTINESS, 5
F., . . . come home with me now   ALCOHOL, 65
Full fathom five thy f. lies   DEATH, 100
God is . . . an exalted f.   GOD, 21
he had rather Have a turnip than his f.   NONSENSE, 13
If poverty is the mother of crime, stupidity is its f.   CRIME, 4
in my F.'s house are many mansions   HEAVEN, 5
left me by my F.   EXECUTION, 4
Like f., like son   FAMILY, 3
My f. didn't create you to arrest me   POLICE, 5
No man is responsible for his f.   FAMILY, 43
our F.   PRAYER, 4
The Child is F. of the Man   AGE, 66
the electric display of God the F.   LIFE, 36
the F. of lights   GIFTS, 1
the night the bed fell on my f.   MEMORY, 19
Today I dressed to meet my f.'s eyes   SUITABILITY, 3
You are old, F. William   OLD AGE, 40
fatherhood Mirrors and f. are abominable   UNIVERSE, 2
fathers atone for the sins of your f.   INJUSTICE, 7
Come mothers and f. Throughout the land   CHANGE, 6
f., provoke not your children   FAMILY, 9
land of my f.   WALES, 2
Victory has a thousand f.   SUCCESS, 8
fathom f. the inscrutable workings of Providence   REPARTEE, 4
Full f. five thy father lies   DEATH, 100
fatted the f. calf   PARTIES, 1
fattening the things I really like . . . are either
immoral, illegal, or f.   PLEASURE, 30
fatter But the valley sheep are f.   GREED, 7
fatty f. degeneration of his moral being   MARRIAGE, 105
fatuity the English seem . . . to act with . . . the f. of idiots
    IRELAND, 15
fault only one f.. It was . . . lousy   CRITICISM, 47
Shakespeare never had six lines together without a f.
    SHAKESPEARE, 8
The fundamental f. of the female character   WOMEN, 61
the f. were on only one side   ARGUMENTS, 12
faultless Whoever thinks a f. piece to see   PERFECTION, 6
faults by pointing out to a man the f. of his mistress
    IMPERFECTION, 10
Don't tell your friends their social f.   ADVICE, 10
England, with all thy f.   PATRIOTISM, 6
f., do not fear to abandon them   IMPERFECTION, 6
If we had no f. of our own   IMPERFECTION, 12
only confess our little f.   IMPERFECTION, 11
When you have f.   IMPERFECTION, 6

FIGURE · 465

favour accepts a smaller as a f.	INJUSTICE, 3
Many terms . . . out of f., will be revived	WORDS, 10
truths being in and out of f.	NOVELTY, 2
favoured they're a f. race	ACTORS, 3
Whether a pretty woman grants or withholds her f.	WOMEN, 53
fav'rite A f. has no friend	LONELINESS, 2
fear concessions of f.	YIELDING, 1
Curiosity will conquer f.	CURIOSITY, 7
do I f. thy nature	KINDNESS, 3
f. God, and keep his commandments	GOD, 9
F. has many eyes	FEAR, 4
f. in a handful of dust	FEAR, 9
F. is the parent of cruelty	CRUELTY, 3
F. lent wings to his feet	FEAR, 13
F. no more the heat o' th' sun	MORTALITY, 16
F. of death	DEATH, 7
fools rush in where angels f. to tread	HASTE, 8
Fostered alike by beauty and by f.	SOUL, 12
freedom from f.	HUMAN RIGHTS, 4
have . . . many things to f.	FEAR, 1
Men f. death	DEATH, 21
None but a coward . . . has never known f.	COWARDICE, 2
one has . . . ceased to be an object of *f.* as soon as one is pitied	SYMPATHY, 5
only thing we have to f. is f. itself	FEAR, 10
perfect love casteth out f.	FEAR, 3; LOVE, 24
Perhaps your f. in passing judgement	COURAGE, 1
pessimists end up by desiring the things they f.	PESSIMISM, 9
the f. of one evil	VICE, 3
fearful facing f. odds	COURAGE, 14
thy f. symmetry	ANIMALS, 4
fears A man who f. suffering	SUFFERING, 9
enough for fifty hopes and f.	WORRY, 8
man f. . . . only the stroke of death	DEATH, 20
The sum of their f.	FEAR, 5
feast Life is not a . . . f.	LIFE, 39
Paris is a moveable f.	PARIS, 1
feather a f. to tickle the intellect	PUNS, 1
feathers Fine f.	APPEARANCE, 1
not only fine f.	CLOTHES, 1
February dreadful pictures of January and F.	WINTER, 8
Excepting F. alone And that has twenty-eight days clear	NURSERY RHYMES, 56
F., fill the dyke	MONTHS, 11
fecund to mistake for the first-rate, the f. rate	WRITERS, 33
fed bite the hand that f. them	INGRATITUDE, 2
fee hold the gorgeous east in f.	VENICE, 4
feed he shall f. his flock	CHRISTIANITY, 10
Why rob one to f. the other?	DEATH, 64
You cannot f. the hungry on statistics	STATISTICS, 5
feeding Spoon f. . . . teaches us nothing but the shape of the spoon	EDUCATION, 19
feel Englishman . . . is afraid to f.	EDUCATION, 17
I draw what I f. in my body	ART, 9
what I f. really bad about	LIBERALISM, 1
feeling A man is as old as he's f.	AGE, 16
Compassion is not a sloppy, sentimental f.	SOCIALISM, 7
feelings First f. are always the most natural	FIRST IMPRESSIONS, 5
feels A really intelligent man f. what other men . . . know	INTELLIGENCE, 3
feet Alan will always land on somebody's f.	HUMOUR, 4
An emperor ought at least to die on his f.	LAST WORDS, 65
better to die on your f. than to live on your knees	SELF-RESPECT, 1
both f. firmly planted in the air	IDEALISM, 6
Fear lent wings to his f.	FEAR, 13
those f. in ancient time	ENGLAND, 4
feigning truest poetry is the most f.	POETRY, 39
felicity likely to mar the general f.	MARRIAGE, 30
Fell Doctor F.	HATE, 1
fell by faith the walls of Jericho f. down	FAITH, 2
crumbs which f. from the rich man's table	POVERTY AND WEALTH, 2
men f. out	WAR, 19
felled The poplars are f.	TREES, 3
fellow f. of infinite jest	MOURNING, 10
fellows Boys are capital f. in their own way	CHILDREN, 30
fellowship such a f. of good knights shall never be together	LOSS, 3
female male and f. created he them	CREATION, 6; MANKIND, 5

the f. character . . . has no sense of justice	WOMEN, 61
the f. of the species is more deadly than the male	WOMEN, 40
The fundamental fault of the f. character	WOMEN, 61
The seldom f.	SEXES, 15
What f. heart can gold despise	MATERIALISM, 8
feminine Taste is the f. of genius	TASTE, 2
fence The . . . gentleman has sat so long on the f.	NONCOMMITMENT, 3
fences Good f. make good neighbours	NEIGHBOURS, 3
ferries the snow blind twilight f.	WINTER, 7
fettered so f. fast we are	FREEDOM, 4
fever hand that signed the treaty bred a f.	SIGNATURES, 3
Février Generals Janvier and F.	WINTER, 3
few err as grosly as the F.	PUBLIC, 11
How f. of his friends' houses	ILLNESS, 7
owed by so many to so f.	WORLD WAR II, 7
fickle Woman is always f. and changing	WOMEN, 77
fiction ancient history, . . . is no more than accepted f.	HISTORY, 31
an improbable f.	REALITY, 5
Children should acquire . . . heroes and villains from f.	HISTORY, 2
one form of continuous f.	JOURNALISM, 5
Poetry is a comforting piece of f.	POETRY, 28
Science f. is no more written for scientists	FICTION, 1
Stranger than f.	TRUTH, 17
fiddle consider your puny little f. when He speaks to me	MUSIC, 8
Hey diddle diddle, The cat and the f.	NURSERY RHYMES, 14
keep it shut up . . . like a rare, rare f.	NAKEDNESS, 5
When I play on my f. in Dooney	MUSIC, 51
field A cow is a very good animal in the f.	SUITABILITY, 2
Behold her, single in the f.	SOLITUDE, 16
Man for the f. and woman for the hearth	SEXES, 20
shepherds abiding in the f.	CHRISTMAS, 8
some corner of a foreign f.	WAR, 16
What though the f. be lost?	DETERMINATION, 11
fields 'a babbl'd of green f.	DEATH, 104
East and west on f. forgotten	WAR, 49
Now there are f. where Troy once was	DECLINE, 8
We plough the f., and scatter	AGRICULTURE, 1
fiend a f. hid in a cloud	BIRTH, 3
a frightful f. Doth close behind him tread	FEAR, 6
fierce f. and bald and short of breath	WAR, 99
fiery Nightingale, . . . A creature of a f. heart	BIRDS, 12
fifteen F. men on the dead man's chest	ALCOHOL, 57
fifth Beethoven's F. Symphony is the most sublime noise	MUSIC, 18
One f. of the people are against everything	OPPOSITION, 4
fifty For one person who dreams of making f. thousand pounds	LAZINESS, 3
Sit on your arse for f. years	INDIFFERENCE, 4
You'll see, when you're f.	AGE, 49
fifty-fifty There can be no f. Americanism	PATRIOTISM, 20
fight a great cause to f. for	PRIDE, 5
easier to f. for one's principles	PRINCIPLES, 1
f., f., f., and f. again	POLITICS, 22
F. fire	CONFLICT, 2
F. the good f. with all thy might	CHRISTIANITY, 33
I dare not f.	COWARDICE, 4
I have not yet begun to f.	DETERMINATION, 9
I purpose to f. it out on this line	DETERMINATION, 7
I will not cease from mental f.	ENGLAND, 4
Nor law, nor duty bade me f.	FLYING, 4
The only time . . . ever put up a f.	INSULTS, 11
To f. and not to heed the wounds	SELFLESSNESS, 2
too proud to f.	WAR, 132
Ulster will f.	IRELAND, 2
We don't want to f., but, by jingo if we do	PATRIOTISM, 14
We'll f. and we'll conquer	COURAGE, 11
we shall f. on the beaches	WORLD WAR II, 4
when the f. begins within	CONFLICT, 5
With our backs to the wall . . . each . . . must f. on to the end	WAR, 43
You cannot f. against the future	PROGRESS, 7
fighting F. is like champagne	WAR, 67
Most sorts of diversion . . . are an imitation of f.	WAR, 115
not conquering but f. well	VICTORY, 4
What are we f. for	WAR, 105
fights He that f. and runs away	SELF-PRESERVATION, 2
I can't spare this man; he f.	OFFICERS, 9
figure an oblong angular f.	HUMOUR, 39

figures   prove anything by f.   STATISTICS, 1
film   A wide screen . . . makes a bad f. twice as bad   CINEMA, 6
I like a f. to have a beginning, a middle and an end   CINEMA, 3
films   Why . . . pay money to see bad f.   CINEMA, 5
finality   F. is death. Perfection is finality   PERFECTION, 8
find   terrible thing for a man to f. out   HONESTY, 12
your sin will f. you out   SIN, 7
finders   F. keepers   LUCK, 3
fine   f. feathers that make f. birds   CLOTHES, 1
In England, pop art and f. art   ART, 14
The big print giveth and the f. print taketh away   BUSINESS, 15
finer   every baby . . . is a f. one   BABIES, 2
finest   their f. hour   WORLD WAR II, 5
finger   Moving F. writes   DESTINY, 7
The least pain in our little f.   SELF-INTEREST, 4
fingernails   See what will happen . . . if you don't stop biting
your f.   SCULPTURE, 2
fingers   F. were made before forks   BEGINNING, 1
ill cook that cannot lick his own f.   SELF-CONFIDENCE, 4
our f. are circumcised   MUSICIANS, 4
finger-tips   An accomplished man to his f.   EXPERTS, 4
fings   F. Ain't Wot They Used T'Be   NOSTALGIA, 15
finished   it is f.   LAST WORDS, 6
finite   Our knowledge can only be f.   KNOWLEDGE, 30
fir   The f. trees dark and high   INNOCENCE, 6
fire   All things, oh priests, are on f.   FIRE, 1
Billy . . . Fell in the f.   FIRE, 2
bound Upon a wheel of f.   SUFFERING, 11
French Guard, f. first   WAR, 44
F. – without hatred   WAR, 92
heap coals of f. upon his head   RETRIBUTION, 8
how great a matter a little f. kindleth   SPEECH, 5
Ideas that enter the mind under f.   INDOCTRINATION, 4
It is with our passions as it is with f. and water   PASSION, 4
it is your business, when the wall next door catches f.
                                                       NEIGHBOURS, 4
I warmed both hands before the f. of life   LIFE AND DEATH, 7
The f. which in the heart resides   SOUL, 2
two irons in the f.   PRUDENCE, 5
what wind is to f.   ABSENCE, 6
firearms   Though loaded f. were strictly forbidden at St
Trinian's   WEAPONS, 6
fire-folk   the f. sitting in the air   STARS, 2
fireirons   Saint Preux never kicked the f.   IMPERFECTION, 5
fires   Husbands are like f.   MARRIAGE, 58
fireside   A man may surely be allowed to take a glass of wine
by his own f.   FIRE, 4
firing   he faced the f. squad; erect and motionless
                                                       EXECUTION, 28
firm   not a family; we're a f.   ROYALTY, 18
firmness   Commodity, F., and Delight   ARCHITECTURE, 13
first   Because of my title, I was the f.   COURAGE, 7
F. come   HASTE, 2
F. impressions   FIRST IMPRESSIONS, 1
F. things f.   PATIENCE, 3
If at f. you don't succeed   PERSISTENCE, 5
many that are f. shall be last   MERIT, 3
The constitution . . . f. and second class citizens   CLASS, 39
The f. day a guest   HOSPITALITY, 3
there is no last or f.   EQUALITY, 6
which came f., the Greeks or the Romans   IGNORANCE, 5
Who ever loved, that loved not at f. sight   FIRST IMPRESSIONS, 6
first-aid   His ideas of f.   INCOMPETENCE, 5
first-rate   the powers of a f. man and the creed of a second-
rate man   POLITICIANS, 2
to mistake for the f., the fecund rate   WRITERS, 33
fish   F. and guests   HOSPITALITY, 2
F. die belly-upward and rise . . . their way of falling   FISH, 1
F. fuck in it   WATER, 3
I have my own f. to fry   NONCOMMITMENT, 2
No human being, . . . was ever so free as a f.   FREEDOM, 46
Phone for the f. knives Norman   ETIQUETTE, 1
This man . . . is a poor f.   MARRIAGE, 43
What cat's averse to f.   MATERIALISM, 8
fishbone   The monument sticks like a f.   MEMORIALS, 2
fishermen   a bite every time for f.   HUMOUR, 46
fishes   f. live in the sea   RUTHLESSNESS, 5
So are the f.   WORLD WAR II, 8
fishing   Time is but the stream I go a-f. in   TIME, 34
fishmonger   She was a f., but sure 'twas no wonder
                                                       BUSINESS, 1
fishy   something f. about the French   FRANCE, 4

fist   You cannot shake hands with a clenched f.   INFLEXIBILITY, 2
fit   a pleasing f. of melancholy   MELANCHOLY, 10
It is not f. that you should sit here   DISMISSAL, 3
let the punishment f. the crime   PUNISHMENT, 9
news that's f. to print   NEWSPAPERS, 8
only the F. survive   SURVIVAL, 4
fits   periodical f. of morality   MORALITY, 9
Strange f. of passion   PASSION, 9
fittest   Survival of the F.   EVOLUTION, 6
five   child of f. would understand this   SIMPLICITY, 5
F. gold rings   NURSERY RHYMES, 55
If you don't find a God by f. o'clock this afternoon   ATHEISM, 7
practise f. things   VIRTUE, 7
The formula 'Two and two make f.'   PHILOSOPHY, 2
five-pound   get a f. note as . . . a light for a cigarette
                                                       GENEROSITY, 3
five-year-old   real menace in dealing with a f.   CHILDREN, 28
flabbiness   The moral f. born of . . . Success   SUCCESS, 7
flag   But spare your country's f.   PATRIOTISM, 30
keep the red f. flying here   SOCIALISM, 2
Tonight the American f. floats from yonder hill   WAR, 112
flame   like a moth, the simple maid Still plays about the f.
                                                       WOMEN, 33
flames   Commit it then to the f.   PHILOSOPHY, 3
Superstition sets the whole world in f.   SUPERSTITION, 11
Flanders   In F. fields   MEMORIALS, 8
You have sent me a F. mare   FIRST IMPRESSIONS, 4
flashing   His f. eyes, his floating hair!   CAUTION, 9
flat   Very f., Norfolk   ENGLAND, 11
Vile snub-nose, f.-nosed ass   APPEARANCE, 30
flatter   not f. me   REALISM, 1
We f. those we scarcely know   HURT, 4
flatterer   the brave beast is no f.   HORSES, 7
flatterers   f. live at the expense of those who listen
                                                       FLATTERY, 6
Self-love . . . greatest of all f.   CONCEIT, 14
flattering   It is f. some men to endure them   TOLERANCE, 2
the talent of f. with delicacy   FLATTERY, 2
flattery   consider whether . . . your f. is worth his having
                                                       FLATTERY, 5
F. is all right   FLATTERY, 8
f.'s the food of fools   FLATTERY, 9
Imitation is the sincerest form of f.   IMITATION, 2
ne'er Was f. lost   POETS, 22
woman . . . to be gained by . . . f.   FLATTERY, 4
flaunt   if you've got it, f. it   OSTENTATION, 1
flautists   f. . . . know something we don't know   MUSICIANS, 2
flea   English literature's performing f.   WRITERS, 30
man's whole frame is obvious to a f.   CLARITY, 3
The guerrilla fights the war of the f.   WAR, 116
the point of precedency between a louse and a f.   POETS, 18
fleas   dog that praised his f.   PARASITES, 4
F. . . . upon the body of a giant   PERSPECTIVE, 3
the f. in my bed were as good   COMPLIMENTS, 1
The f. that tease in the high Pyrenees   NONSENSE, 4
these have smaller f. to bite 'em   PARASITES, 3
fled   I f. Him, down the nights   RELIGION, 51
fleece   On Wenlock Edge the wood's in trouble; His forest f.
the Wrekin heaves   TREES, 4
fleet   The F.'s lit up. It is like fairyland   NAVY, 4
flesh   all f. is as grass   DEATH, 27
f. and blood so cheap   POVERTY, 15
f. to feel the chain   IMPRISONMENT, 2
Heat, madam! . . . to take off my f. and sit in my bones
                                                       WEATHER, 25
I, born of f. and ghost   DEATH, 115
I have more f. than another man   OBESITY, 11
Ishmaelites . . . will not publicly eat human f. uncooked in Lent
                                                       CANNIBALISM, 2
I wants to make your f. creep   FEAR, 8
Leave the f. to the fate it was fit for   SOUL, 5
Rehearsing a play is making the word f.   PLAYS, 9
the f. is weak   IMPERFECTION, 4
the f. lusteth against the Spirit   COMPROMISE, 2
the way of all f.   DEATH, 37; HUMAN NATURE, 17
the way of all f. . . . towards the kitchen   FOOD, 45
the world, the f., and the devil   JOURNALISM, 20; TEMPTATION, 5
fleshly   The F. School of Poetry   POETS, 5
flies   As f. to wanton boys   DESTINY, 18
certain, that Life f.   LIFE, 24
Time f., death urges   TIME, 39
flight   Above the vulgar f. of common souls   SUPERIORITY, 8

Work is much more f. than f. WORK, 7
you feel as if a human being sitting inside were making f. of
you ANIMALS, 8
function f. of the critic CRITICS, 1
funeral F. marches to the grave MORTALITY, 14
funerals If you don't go to other men's f. FUNERALS, 4
weddings is sadder than f. MARRIAGE, 18
funny Everything is f. HUMOUR, 24
F. peculiar, or f. ha-ha HUMOUR, 19
F. without being vulgar CRITICISM, 13
hard to be f. when you have to be clean HUMOUR, 27
its own animality either objectionable or f. HUMOUR, 17
Kings . . . are just as f. ROYALTY, 25
to accuse someone of trying to be f. is highly abusive
HUMOUR, 19
furiously sleep f. NONSENSE, 10
furnace a burning fiery f. DOOMSDAY, 1
Heat not a f. for your foe EXCESS, 11
furniture brain attic stocked with all the f. that he is likely to
use KNOWLEDGE, 13
fury full of sound and f. LIFE, 41
hell a f. like a woman scorned LOVE AND HATE, 3
no f. like an ex-wife searching for a new lover WOMEN, 23
strength and f. PATIENCE, 11
the F. of a Patient Man PATIENCE, 11
fustest I got there f. with the mostest WAR, 37
future F., n. That period of time in which OPTIMISM, 15
how pleasant . . . not to have any f. FUTURE, 4
If you want a picture of the f. OPPRESSION, 4
if you would divine the f. PAST, 4
I have seen the f. FUTURE, 6
I mean a F. Life AFTERLIFE, 2
I never think of the f. FUTURE, 5
people who live in the f. PROGRESS, 1
pick today's fruits, not relying on the f. in the slightest
PRESENT, 9
The f. is . . . black RACE, 3
The f. is made of the same stuff FUTURE, 7
The f. is the only kind of property SLAVERY, 1
the f. . . . makes cowards of us PRESENT, 3
The past was nothing . . . The f. was a mystery PRESENT, 1
Who controls the past controls the f. POWER, 13
You cannot fight against the f. PROGRESS, 7
Fuzzy-Wuzzy to you, F., at your 'ome in the Soudan RACE, 11

G

gaiety the only concession to g. WELSH, 2
gain never broke the Sabbath, but for G. SIN, 13
richest g. I count but loss HUMILITY, 12
gained learning hath g. most BOOKS, 17
gainful I will undoubtedly have to seek . . . g. employment
GOVERNMENT, 1
gains no g. without pains ENDURANCE, 19; SUCCESS, 14
Galatians a great text in G. BIBLE, 3
Galileo If G. had said in verse that the world moved
POETRY, 18
gallant a loyal, a g., a generous, an ingenious, and good-
temper'd people FRANCE, 14
gallantry What men call g. ADULTERY, 1
gallery The boy I love is up in the g. LOVE, 138
galloped I g., Dirck g. HORSES, 3
gallows You will die either on the g., or of the pox
REPARTEE, 5
gamble Life is a g. LIFE, 44
game how you played the g. SPORT AND GAMES, 17; VICTORY, 14
I don't like this g. SPORT AND GAMES, 14
It's more than a g.. It's an institution CRICKET, 4
Play up! play up! and play the g.! WAR, 75
win this g. and thrash the Spaniards SPORT AND GAMES, 4;
WAR, 32
woman is his g. SEXES, 19
games The most important thing in the Olympic G. VICTORY, 4
gamesmanship G. or The Art of Winning Games SPORT AND
GAMES, 16
gaming Man is a g. animal SPORT AND GAMES, 12
gangsters The great nations have always acted like g.
DIPLOMACY, 13
Garbo one sees in G. sober COMPLIMENTS, 7
garden a g. in her face ADMIRATION, 4
A g. is a lovesome thing GARDENS, 4
Come into the g., Maud INVITATIONS, 2

cultivate our g. PAROCHIALISM, 3
Don't go into Mr McGregor's g. CAUTION, 12
God Almighty first planted a g. GARDENS, 2
God the first g. made GARDENS, 6
I have a g. of my own GARDENS, 10
My heart shall be thy g. LOVE, 87
nearer God's Heart in a g. GARDENS, 7
The chairs are being brought in from the g. SUMMER, 3
the g. of Eden KNOWLEDGE, 7; TREES, 1
There are fairies at the bottom of our g. FAIRIES, 3
gardener Every time I talk to . . . my g., I'm convinced of the
opposite HAPPINESS, 19
Nor does a . . . g. scent his roses POETS, 9
Oh, Adam was a g. GARDENS, 8
gardens closing time in the g. of the West CAPITALISM, 1
garland wither'd is the g. of the war MOURNING, 11
garlands gather g. there COUNTRYSIDE, 8
Garter I like the G. TITLES, 5
gas If silicon had been a g. I should have been a major-general
EXAMINATIONS, 3
gas-masks digging trenches and trying on g. WORLD WAR II, 1
gate I am here at the g. alone INVITATIONS, 2
I said to the man who stood at the g. of the year FAITH, 11
matters not how strait the g. RESPONSIBILITY, 7
the g. of heaven HEAVEN, 2
gatekeeper After I die, I shall return to earth as a g. of a
bordello THREATS, 3
gates Battering the g. of heaven EXCESS, 14
the g. of the day LONELINESS, 10
the iron g. of life LOVE, 84
gather G. the flowers FLOWERS, 8
G. ye rosebuds while ye may PRESENT, 6
gathered two or three are g. together CHURCH, 2; PRAYER, 6
gatling The g.'s jammed and the colonel dead WAR, 75
gaudy round, neat, not g. GARDENS, 9
Gaul G. is divided into three FRANCE, 4
Gaullist I . . . have become a G. . . . little by little POLITICS, 26
gave God . . . g. his only begotten Son CHRISTIANITY, 13
gay g. without frivolity FUTURE, 1
Gaza Eyeless in G. BLINDNESS, 3
gazelle never nurs'd a dear g. ANIMALS, 14
general caviare to the g. TASTE, 6
In a civil war, a g. must know WAR, 88
generalizations All g. are dangerous GENERALIZATIONS, 2
generalize To g. is to be an idiot GENERALIZATIONS, 1
General Motors was good for G. BUSINESS, 22
generals at the age of four with paper hats and wooden swords
we're all G. AUTHORITARIANISM, 8
Dead battles, like dead g. WAR, 119
It is not the business of g. to shoot one another OFFICERS, 14
that's not against the law for g. OFFICERS, 12
to be left to the g. OFFICERS, 5
wish he would *bite* . . . my g. REPARTEE, 3
generation Each g. imagines itself . . . more intelligent AGE, 41
You are a lost g. WAR, 113
generations g. . . . have struggled in poverty to build these
altars RELIGION, 46
g. . . . pass in a short time MORTALITY, 15
No hungry g. tread thee down BIRDS, 5
generosity The poor . . . their function . . . is to exercise our g.
POVERTY, 25
generous a loyal, a gallant, a g., an ingenious, and good-
temper'd people FRANCE, 14
genius a country full of g., but with absolutely no talent
IRELAND, 9
a German and a g.! COMPOSERS, 7; LAST WORDS, 61
A g.! For thirty-seven years I've practiced . . . and now they
call me a g. GENIUS, 7
G. . . . capacity of taking trouble GENIUS, 2
G. does what it must TALENT AND GENIUS, 3
G. is an infinite capacity GENIUS, 1
G. is one per cent inspiration GENIUS, 1
Milton, Madam, was a g. POETS, 20
Nothing, except my g. CONCEIT, 23
Only an organizing g. INCOMPETENCE, 1
Rules and models destroy g. and art RULES, 2
Since when was g. . . . respectable RESPECTABILITY, 1
talent instantly recognizes g. MEDIOCRITY, 3; TALENT AND
GENIUS, 1
Taste is the feminine of g. TASTE, 2
the difference between talent and g. TALENT AND GENIUS, 1
true g. is a mind of large general powers GENIUS, 6

gloamin' Roamin' in the g.	SCOTLAND, 6
global my wars Were g.	WAR, 89
the world in the image of a g. village	TECHNOLOGY, 6
globe the great g. itself	MORTALITY, 17
globule I can trace my ancestry back to a . . . g.	ANCESTRY, 2
gloire Le jour de g. est arrivé	FRANCE, 10
gloria Sic transit g. mundi	GLORY, 3
glorious G. things of thee are spoken	HEAVEN, 7
Happy and g.	BRITAIN, 5
glory But trailing clouds of g.	METAPHYSICS, 5
G. be to God for dappled things	BEAUTY, 19
g., jest, and riddle of the world	HUMAN CONDITION, 12
It is a great g. in a woman	WOMEN, 70
Land of Hope and G.	BRITAIN, 3
Mine eyes have seen the g. of the coming of the Lord	GOD, 25
paths of g. lead but to the grave	MORTALITY, 10
Popularity? . . . g.'s small change	POPULARITY, 4
the g. of Europe is extinguished for ever	EUROPE, 2
the Son of man coming . . . with power and great g.	
	DOOMSDAY, 2
To the greater g. of God	CATHOLICISM, 2
we left him alone with his g.	FUNERALS, 11
Where is it now, the g. and the dream	METAPHYSICS, 5
Gloucester Doctor Foster went to G.	NURSERY RHYMES, 10
glow make the corpuscles of the blood g.	JEWS, 8
Glum I've examined your son's head, Mr G.	STUPIDITY, 10
glum speed g. heroes . . . to death	WAR, 99
gluttony G. is an emotional escape	GREED, 6
gnomes the little g. of Zürich	MONEY, 48
go a good cook, as cooks g.	HUMOUR, 51
In the name of God, g.!	DISMISSAL, 1
I shall be the last to g. out	COURAGE, 7
Let us g. then, you and I	DEPARTURE, 5
not to g. anywhere, but to g.	TRAVEL, 25
stopped short – never to g. again	CLOCKS, 3
whither thou goest, I will g.	LOYALTY, 5
goal The g. stands up	FOOTBALL, 2
goat-footed This g. bard	POLITICIANS, 38
God Act of G. . . . something which no reasonable man could	
have expected	DISASTER, 3
A G. who let us prove his existence	GOD, 15
a kind of Providence will . . . end . . . the acts of G.	DISASTER, 2
A man with G.	GOD, 30
America is G.'s Crucible	AMERICA, 40
an absolute faith that all things are possible to G.	FAITH, 10
an atheist half believes a G.	FEAR, 15
An honest G.	GOD, 28
Are G. and Nature then at strife	NATURE, 15
better to have no opinion of G.	GOD, 3
but for the grace of G. goes	LUCK, 6
charged with the grandeur of G.	GOD, 24
concept of G. has any validity	RELIGION, 4
effect Whose cause is G.	NATURE, 6
Either a beast or a g.	MANKIND, 2
either a wild beast or a g.	SOLITUDE, 1
Even G. cannot change the past	PAST, 1
even G. was born too late	RELIGION, 34
Every man thinks G. is on his side	GOD, 2
final proof of G.'s omnipotence	GOD, 1
for which . . . the good G. prepare me!	BLINDNESS, 7
G. alone deserves to be loved	LOVE, 106
G. as a working hypothesis	GOD, 14
G. bless . . . G. damn	LAST WORDS, 62
G. bless us every one!	BLESSING, 6
G. can stand being told	GOD, 42
G. could cause us considerable embarrassment	DISCOVERY, 4
G. defend me from my friends	FRIENDSHIP, 4
G. disposes	GOD, 29
G. does not play dice	SCIENCE, 13
G. erects a house of prayer	DEVIL, 7
G. . . . first planted a garden	GARDENS, 2
G. has written all the books	SUBJECTIVITY, 2
G. helps them	SELF, 2
G. is a gentleman	GOD, 39
G. is always on the side of the big battalions	POWER POLITICS, 7
G. is beginning to resemble . . . the last fading smile of a cosmic	
Cheshire cat	GOD, 26
G. is dead	GOD, 38
G. is nothing more than an exalted father	GOD, 21
G. is on the side not of the heavy battalions, but of the best	
shots	POWER POLITICS, 8
G. is really only another artist	GOD, 41

G. is subtle but he is not malicious	GOD, 20
G. is the immemorial refuge of the incompetent	GOD, 34
G. made everything out of nothing	CREATION, 13
G. made the country	COUNTRYSIDE, 2
going back to G.	RELIGION, 5
Great G. grant that twice two be not four.	PRAYER, 17
G. said, Let Newton be	SCIENTISTS, 8
G. save our gracious King	BRITAIN, 5
G.'s gifts put man's best gifts	GOD, 16
G. should go before such villains	GOD, 43
G.'s in His heaven	PERFECTION, 2
G. the first garden made	GARDENS, 6
G. will cease to dream you!	DEATH, 65
G. will grant an end to these too	ENDURANCE, 2
G. will pardon me. It is His trade	LAST WORDS, 30
Had I but serv'd my G. with half the zeal I serv'd my King	
	REGRET, 18
Had I . . . served G. as diligently as I have served the king	
	LOYALTY, 11
have one G. only	GOD, 17
her conception of G. was certainly not orthodox	GOD, 46
Holy, holy, holy, Lord G. Almighty	GOD, 23
How could G. do this to me	INJUSTICE, 9
I am glad . . . he thanks G. for anything.	GRATITUDE, 2
I believe I am becoming a g.	LAST WORDS, 65
I did not write it. G. wrote it.	INSPIRATION, 6
If G. did not exist	GOD, 48
If G. made us in His image	GOD, 49
If G. were suddenly condemned to live the life	HUMAN
	CONDITION, 6
If this man is not faithful to his G.	LOYALTY, 9
if triangles invented a g., they would make him three-sided	
	RELIGION, 42
If you don't find a G. by five o'clock this afternoon	ATHEISM, 7
If you talk to G., you are praying	MADNESS, 12
It takes a long while for a . . . trustful person to reconcile	
himself to . . . G.	FAITH, 15
I wouldn't give up writing about G.	WRITERS, 45
I wretch lay wrestling with . . . my G.	SOUL, 7
justify the ways of G. to men	GOD, 37
Just what G. would have done if he had the money	WEALTH, 30
Kill everyone, and you are a g.	KILLING, 7
Know then thyself, presume not G. to scan	SELF-KNOWLEDGE, 5
Live among men as if G. beheld you	RIGHTEOUSNESS, 8
Many people believe that they are attracted by G.	RELIGION, 30
May G. deny you peace	GLORY, 2
nature is the art of G.	NATURE, 1
Nearer, my G., to thee	RELIGION, 1
none deny there is a G.	ATHEISM, 3
One G., one law, one element	DESTINY, 20
One on G.'s side is a majority	GOD, 40
only G. can make a tree	TREES, 8
Our G., our help in ages past	RELIGION, 5
poems . . . for the love of Man and in praise of G.	POETRY, 47
proof that G. is a bore	PROTESTANTISM, 1
prose for G.	LANGUAGE, 12
put your hand into the hand of G.	FAITH, 11
Sickness, sin and death . . . do not originate in G.	RELIGION, 19
Since G. has given us the papacy . . . enjoy it	CATHOLICISM, 8
speak to G. as if men were listening	RIGHTEOUSNESS, 8
that G. is interested only . . . in religion	GOD, 47
that great Leviathan, or rather . . . that Mortal G.	STATE, 1
The Act of G. designation	ACCIDENTS, 1
the dear G. who loveth us	PRAYER, 9
the electric display of G. the Father	LIFE, 36
the highest praise of G. consists in the denial of Him	
	ATHEISM, 9
the nearer you are to G.	PROTESTANTISM, 3
the one G. whose worshippers . . . still trust in Him	LUCK, 7
There, but for the Grace of G., goes G.	ARROGANCE, 5
There once was a man who said G.	EXISTENCE, 4
The true G., . . . G. of ideas	INSPIRATION, 7
Those who marry G. . . . can become domesticated too	
	RELIGION, 27
To understand G.'s thoughts	STATISTICS, 7
we come From G., who is our home	METAPHYSICS, 5
we owe G. a death	DEATH, 105
What G. does, He does well	GOD, 31
When I composed that, I was . . . inspired by G.	MUSIC, 8
when one has loved a man it is very different to love G.	
	LOVE, 106
whom G. wishes to destroy	MADNESS, 4

yearning like a G. in pain SUFFERING, 7
you hardly ever mention G. any more RELIGION, 39
you must believe in G. FAITH, 12
goddamm Lhude sing G. WINTER, 4
godlike patient endurance is g. ENDURANCE, 9
gods Against stupidity the g. . . . struggle in vain STUPIDITY, 12
by force of the g. ENDURANCE, 23
deserves the name of happy who knows how to use the g.'
gifts wisely HAPPINESS, 9
for what high cause This darling of the G. DESTINY, 13
G. help them SELF-RELIANCE, 2
Kings are earth's g. ROYALTY, 27
leave the rest to the G. DUTY, 2
Live with the g. CONTENTMENT, 1
man's ignorance of the g. SPONTANEITY, 1
no other g. before me GOD, 10
So many g., so many creeds KINDNESS, 5; RELIGION, 63
The Ethiopians say that their g. are . . . black RELIGION, 65
The G. themselves cannot recall their gifts IRREVOCABILITY, 2
we're forbidden to know – what end the g. have in store
DESTINY, 12
Whom the g. love DEATH, 82
Whom the g. wish to destroy TALENT, 1
goe to morowe longe I to g. to God FAMILY, 29
going I am just g. outside LAST WORDS, 41
Men must endure Their g. hence ENDURANCE, 17
Stand not upon the order of your g. DISMISSAL, 8
gold A g. rush is what happens when MATERIALISM, 23
all the g. that the goose could give MATERIALISM, 2
An angel writing in a book of g. – DREAMS, 11
cursed craving for g. MATERIALISM, 21
For g. in phisik is a cordial MATERIALISM, 5
gild refined g. EXCESS, 10
Good morning to the day: and next my g. MATERIALISM, 12
Nor all that glisters g. TEMPTATION, 6
silver and g. have I none REMEDIES, 3
Silver threads among the g. OLD AGE, 33
The ring so worn . . . is yet of g. APPEARANCE, 10
To a shower of g. BRIBERY, 2
travell'd in the realms of g. TRAVEL, 15
Were't not for g. and women SIN, 19
What female heart can g. despise MATERIALISM, 8
When every . . . thing you hold Is made of silver, or of g.
ECONOMICS, 6
golden G. slumbers kiss your eyes SLEEP, 7
In good King Charles's g. days SELF-PRESERVATION, 4
In old time we had treen chalices and g. priests CLERGY, 7
Jerusalem the g. PLACES, 13
perhaps, the g. rule ABSTINENCE, 8
The g. apples of the sun DESIRE, 16
the G. Road to Samarkand KNOWLEDGE, 14
there are no g. rules RULES, 3
Goldwyn Mr G. . . . you are only interested in art ART, 24;
MONEY, 41
golf an earnest protest against g. CRICKET, 1; GOLF, 1
G. . . . a form of moral effort GOLF, 2
Gomorrah Sodom and . . . G. PUNISHMENT, 3
gone g. with the wind MEMORY, 4
gongs women should be struck . . . like g. WOMEN, 24
good a gigantic reservoir of g. will AMERICA, 36
A g. man fallen among Fabians WRITERS, 25
A g. novel tells us the truth NOVELS, 2
A G. Time Was Had by All PLEASURE, 28
All g. writing WRITING, 7
Anybody can be g. in the country COUNTRYSIDE, 10
Be g., sweet maid, and let who can be clever VIRTUE, 11
being really g. all the time HYPOCRISY, 17
dedicate this nation to the policy of the g. neighbor CHARITY, 15
Do g. by stealth GOOD, 14
doing g. . . . professions which are full CHARITY, 21
doing g. to base fellows CHARITY, 10
dull prospect of a distant g. PLEASURE, 11
every man at the beginning doth set forth g. wine ALCOHOL, 14
Every man loves what he is g. at ENTHUSIASM, 6
Evil, be thou my G. EVIL, 11
Evil comes . . . like the disease; g. . . . like the doctor GOOD
AND EVIL, 2
Far too g. to waste on children YOUTH, 16
G., but not religious-good VIRTUE, 8
General G. is the plea of the scoundrel GOOD, 2
G. isn't the word! CRITICISM, 14
God saw that it was g. CREATION, 3

Good, but not religious-g. VIRTUE, 8
greatest g. GOOD, 3
g. shepherd giveth his life for the sheep CHRISTIANITY, 15
G. things, when short, are twice as good BREVITY, 1
g. tidings of great joy CHRISTMAS, 8
happiness makes them g. GOOD, 9
He who would do g. to another GOOD, 2
how *can* they become g. people PREJUDICE, 5
How g. is man's life, the mere living LIFE, 14
If . . . 'feeling g.' could decide, drunkenness would be
DRUNKENNESS, 13
If to do were as easy as to know what were g. ACTION, 11
If you can't be g. TEMPTATION, 2
I have fought a g. fight FAITH, 6
it cannot come to g. PESSIMISM, 11
It is g. to know what a man is UNDERSTANDING, 2
It is seldom . . . one parts on g. terms PARTING, 9
little of what you fancy does you g. PLEASURE, 19
Men have never been g. GOOD, 1
never was a g. war WAR AND PEACE, 6
no hint throughout the universe Of g. or ill NECESSITY, 8
Nothing can harm a g. man GOOD, 16
Nothing either g. or bad THINKING, 9
nothing g. to be had in the country COUNTRYSIDE, 4
One man is as g. as another WRITERS, 24
Only g. girls keep diaries DIARIES, 2
our people have never had it so g. WEALTH, 18
Roman Conquest . . . a G. Thing HISTORY, 26
strong antipathy of g. to bad PROVOCATION, 2
suppose the people g. CORRUPTION, 5
the g. are always the merry MERRIMENT, 1
The g. die early GOOD AND EVIL, 3
The g. die first GOOD AND EVIL, 5
The g. die young DEATH, 10
The g. is oft interred with their bones EVIL, 15
The g. is the beautiful GOOD, 13
the g. must associate UNITY, 7
The g. of the people LAW, 7
The 'g. old times' NOSTALGIA, 5
The king has been very g. to me MARTYRDOM, 1
the name of perseverance in a g. cause STUBBORNNESS, 3
The only g. Indians I ever saw were dead ENEMIES, 7
There is so much g. in the worst of us GOOD AND EVIL, 1
the thing which is g. PUNISHMENT, 1; SIN, 3
those who go about doing g. CHARITY, 12
thou g. and faithful servant SERVICE, 1
three ingredients in the g. life LIFE, 35
to write g. prose is an affair of g. manners POETRY AND
PROSE, 4
what g. came of it at last VICTORY, 16
What's the g. of a home ABSENCE, 7
Whenever two g. people argue over principles PRINCIPLES, 3
When I'm g. I'm very g. SEX, 54
when the great and g. depart MORTALITY, 20
Why care for grammar as long as we are g. GRAMMAR, 8
You shouldn't say it is not g. GOOD, 18
good-bye Without a single kiss or a g. PARTING, 8
good-by-ee G.! – g. PARTING, 12
goodness Abashed the devil stood, And felt how awful g. is
GOOD, 12
G. does not . . . make men happy GOOD, 9
My g. those diamonds are lovely GOOD, 17
Not to be wronged is to forgo . . . g. INJUSTICE, 13
goods isn't a bad bit of g., the Queen! COMPLIMENTS, 1
the Man Who Delivers the G. RELIABILITY, 1
good-temper'd a loyal, a gallant, a generous, an ingenious, and
g. people FRANCE, 14
goodwill in peace, g. WAR AND PEACE, 3
goose all the gold that the g. could give MATERIALISM, 2
goosey G., g. gander NURSERY RHYMES, 13
gored you tossed and g. several persons CONVERSATION, 3
gorgeous hold the g. east in fee VENICE, 4
Gospels We had no use for the policy of the G. REVENGE, 12
gossips No one g. about . . . secret virtues GOSSIP, 8
got Which in our case we have not g. WEAPONS, 5
gout A taste for drink, combined with g. ALCOHOL, 27
that old enemy the g. Had taken him in toe ILLNESS, 6; PUNS, 6
govern Every class is unfit to g. GOVERNMENT, 2
Grammar, which can g. even kings GRAMMAR, 6
He that would g. others SELF-CONTROL, 6
I will g. according to the common weal MONARCHY, 12
king reigns, but does not g. MONARCHY, 25

Kings g. by . . . assemblies only when · MONARCHY, 11
Labour is not fit to g. · POLITICS, 15
No man is good enough to g. another man · DEMOCRACY, 6
Under socialism *all* will g. · SOCIALISM, 9
governed with how little wisdom the world is g.
· GOVERNMENT, 20
governing become accustomed to no one g. · SOCIALISM, 9
the right of g. was not property but a trust · GOVERNMENT, 9
government A g. . . . big enough to give you all you want
· GOVERNMENT, 11
a g. organization could do it that quickly · BUREAUCRACY, 2
All g. . . . is founded on compromise and barter · COMPROMISE, 3
As to religion, . . . duty of g. to protect all . . . professors
thereof · GOVERNMENT, 22
Democracy is only an experiment in g. · DEMOCRACY, 5
every g. . . . should have its old speeches burned
· GOVERNMENT, 27
g. by crony · NEPOTISM, 1
G., . . . is but a necessary evil · GOVERNMENT, 21
g. of the people, by the people, and for the people
· DEMOCRACY, 9; MEMORIALS, 6
I would not give half a guinea to live under one form of g.
· GOVERNMENT, 13
Monarchy is a strong g. · MONARCHY, 1
no man believes, that want of g., is any new kind of g.
· GOVERNMENT, 12
people's g. · GOVERNMENT, 31
prepare for g. · POLITICS, 64
The g. burns down whole cities · INJUSTICE, 10
the g. it deserves · GOVERNMENT, 17
the President is dead, but the G. lives · ASSASSINATION, 2
there was no form of g. common to the peoples · REPUBLIC, 2
the things which g. does . . . social progress · GOVERNMENT, 30
The worst g. is the most moral · GOVERNMENT, 18
We live under a g. of men and . . . newspapers
· GOVERNMENT, 23; JOURNALISM, 21
governments all G. are selfish · GOVERNMENT, 8
G. needs to have both shepherds and butchers
· GOVERNMENT, 29
The Beast stands for strong mutually antagonistic g.
· NEWSPAPERS, 12
governors Our supreme g., the mob · PUBLIC, 20
Gower moral G. · BOOKS, 12
grace but for the g. of God, goes · LUCK, 6
g. a summer queen · COUNTRYSIDE, 8
God in his mercy lend her g. · BEAUTY, 38
He had at least the g. · BRIBERY, 1
Lord, I ascribe it to Thy g. · RELIGION, 56
Such g. had kings · ROYALTY, 6
Tuesday's child is full of g. · NURSERY RHYMES, 33
graces the G. do not seem . . . natives of Great Britain
· BRITISH, 4
gracious A life that moves to g. ends · LIFE, 46
gradually Boys do not grow up g. · CHILDREN, 19
Grail What were they going to do with the G. · ARTHURIAN
LEGEND, 1
grain A g., which in England is generally given to horses
· SCOTLAND, 3
He reaps the bearded g. at a breath · DEATH, 74
grammar down to posterity talking bad g. · GRAMMAR, 5
G., which can govern even kings · GRAMMAR, 6
I am . . . above g. · GRAMMAR, 7
Why care for g. as long as we are good · GRAMMAR, 8
grammatical I have laboured to refine our language to g. purity
· LANGUAGE, 13
gramophones waxworks inhabited by g. · WORDS, 15
grand A 'G. Old Man' · OLD AGE, 25
that g. old man · POLITICIANS, 53
The g. Perhaps · POSSIBILITY, 1
the g. style arises in poetry · POETRY, 3
to be baith g. and comfortable · LUXURY, 1
Grand Canyon coming across him at the G. · INSULTS, 30
grandeur g. is a dream · WEALTH, 11
g. of God · GOD, 24
Many people have delusions of g. · DELUSION, 5
grandfather g.'s clock · CLOCKS, 2
I don't know who my g. was · ANCESTRY, 5
no reason to be ashamed of having an ape for his g.
· EVOLUTION, 9
pass my declining years saluting strange women and g. clocks
· OLD AGE, 29
grandmother I murdered my g. this morning · INATTENTION, 4

grandson I am much more concerned to know what his g. will
be · ANCESTRY, 5
your g. will . . . be a Communist · COMMUNISM, 3
Grant 'Old Cary G. fine' · AGE, 28
granted human beings have an . . . infinite capacity for taking
things for g. · HUMAN NATURE, 10
grape Beulah, peel me a g. · LUXURY, 5
grapes I am sure the g. are sour · ENVY, 4
trampling out the vintage where the g. of wrath · GOD, 25
grasp man's reach should exceed his g. · AMBITION, 3
grass all flesh is as g. · DEATH, 27
There's a snake hidden in the g. · DANGER, 7
grassgreen down the g. gooseberried double bed · SEX, 47
gratification I have had no real g. . . . more than my neighbor
· LAST WORDS, 64; WEALTH, 28
gratifying It is quite g. to feel guilty · GUILT, 1
gratuite *L'acte g.* · SPONTANEITY, 2
grave a-mouldering in the g. · MEMORIALS, 4
And digs my g. at each remove · DEATH, 57
And on his g., with shining eyes · DEATH, 18
Between the cradle and the g. · TRANSIENCE, 12
Dig the g. and let me lie · DEATH, 112
Funeral marches to the g. · MORTALITY, 14
her heart in his g. is lying · MOURNING, 8
I may dread The g. as little · DEATH, 68
I shall soon be laid in the quiet g. · DEATH, 67
Marriage is a step so g. and decisive · MARRIAGE, 103
no work, nor device, nor knowledge . . . in the g.
· TRANSIENCE, 6; WORK, 3
O g., where is thy victory? · DEATH, 26; DEATH, 87
paths of glory lead but to the g. · MORTALITY, 10
The g.'s a fine and private place · DEATH, 77
the g. yawns for him · BORES, 7
To that dark inn, the g. · DEATH, 93
grave-digger if I were a g., or . . . a hangman · OCCUPATIONS, 7
graven any g. image · GOD, 10
graves The bitterest tears shed over g. · REGRET, 19
The dust of great persons' g. · EQUALITY, 21
gravity He rose by g.; I sank by levity · SERIOUSNESS, 4
gravy Sir Humphry Davy Abominated g. · SCIENTISTS, 3
Gray Robin G., he was gudeman to me · MARRIAGE, 17
gray When you are old and g. · OLD AGE, 50
grazed He is the richest author that ever g. · WRITERS, 22
great All my shows are g. · CONCEIT, 11
All things both g. and small · PRAYER, 9
deep consent of all g. men · ARTISTS, 7
Everything g. in the world is done by neurotics · NEUROSIS, 2
everything that is g. . . . done by youth · YOUTH, 6
fate of the g. wen · LONDON, 5
G. men are but life-sized · GREATNESS, 3
g. men have not commonly been g. scholars · GREATNESS, 4
G. oaks · BEGINNING, 3
History is full of ignominious getaways by the g. · COWARDICE, 5
how g. a matter a little fire kindleth · SPEECH, 5
How very small the very g. · GREATNESS, 14; WISDOM, 22
If I am a g. man · GREATNESS, 9
many of the g. men of history are frauds · GREATNESS, 9
No g. man lives in vain · GREATNESS, 6; HISTORY, 6
On earth there is nothing g. but man · MANKIND, 13
Some are born g. · GREATNESS, 12
the g. break through · LAW, 25
The g. man . . . walks across his century · INFLUENCE, 6
the g. ones eat up the little ones · RUTHLESSNESS, 5
the shade Of that which once was g. · REGRET, 22
To be g. is to be misunderstood · GREATNESS, 7
when the g. and good depart · MORTALITY, 20
you, . . . who have made me too g. for my house · ROYALTY, 4
great-aunt A person may be indebted for a nose or an eye, . . .
to a g. · FAMILY, 19
Great Britain G. could say that she supported both sides
· DIPLOMACY, 17
G. has lost an Empire · BRITAIN, 1
To make a union with G. · WORLD WAR II, 24
greater g. love hath no man · LOVE, 25
The g. the power · POWER, 7
Thy need is yet g. than mine · SELF-DENIAL, 2
greatest great city . . . has the g. men and women
· GREATNESS, 15
I'm the g.! · CONCEIT, 1
the g. deeds require a certain insensitiveness · INSENSITIVITY, 3
The g. happiness of the g. number · HAPPINESS, 3
the g. of these is charity · CHARITY, 5

great-grandfathers Classicism, . . . the literature that gave . . .
pleasure to their g. LITERATURE, 16
greatness long farewell to all my g. HUMAN CONDITION, 14
Men who have g. . . . don't go in for politics POLITICIANS, 6
some have g. thrust upon 'em GREATNESS, 12
Greece Athens holds sway over all G. INFLUENCE, 8
G. might still be free EUROPE, 4
The isles of G. EUROPE, 3
Greek I . . . impress upon you the study of G. literature
CLASSICS, 3
it was G. to me CONFUSION, 8
neither Jew nor G. CHRISTIANITY, 7
Nobody can say a word against G. CLASSICS, 8
small Latin and less G. CLASSICS, 5
the intrigue of a G. of the lower empire INSULTS, 13
The word is half Latin TELEVISION, 5
We were taught . . . Latin and G. CLASSICS, 9
Greeks G. Had a Word LANGUAGE, 1
I fear the G. even when they bring gifts MISTRUST, 11
The Romans and G. found everything human
ANTHROPOMORPHISM, 1
To the G. the Muse gave native wit CLASSICS, 4
uncertainty: a state unknown to the G. UNCERTAINTY, 2
where the G. had modesty, we have cant CANT, 1
which came first, the G. or the Romans IGNORANCE, 6
green a g. thought in a g. shade OBLIVION, 3
for the wearin' o' the G. IRELAND, 1
G. grow the rashes O LOVE, 31
I was g. in judgment YOUTH, 14
religious system that produced g. Chartreuse ALCOHOL, 49
There is a g. hill far away CHRISTIANITY, 1
tree of life is g. REALITY, 3; THEORY, 4
When the g. woods laugh HAPPINESS, 5
green-ey'd jealousy . . . g. monster JEALOUSY, 4
Greenland From G.'s icy mountains PLACES, 6
green-rob'd g. senators of mighty woods TREES, 6
Greensleeves G. was all my joy LOVE, 14
greenwood Under the g. tree COUNTRYSIDE, 9
greetings g. where no kindness is OPTIMISM, 29
perhaps the g. are intended for me POPULARITY, 1
grenadier The healthy bones of a single Pomeranian g.
DIPLOMACY, 4
With a tow, . . . row for the British G. HEROISM, 1
grew Three years she g. DEATH, 124
grey G. hairs are death's blossoms OLD AGE, 1
theory is all g. REALITY, 3; THEORY, 4
There is only one cure for g. hair. . . . the guillotine
REMEDIES, 14
well-belovèd's hair has threads of g. AGE, 67
grief A g. too much to be told SORROW, 27
calms one's g. by recounting it SORROW, 4
G. and disappointment give rise to anger EMOTION, 4
G. has turned her fair APPEARANCE, 39
heart which g. hath cankered ALCOHOL, 17
in much wisdom is much g. KNOWLEDGE, 6; WISDOM, 2
Should be past g. REGRET, 14
grievances redress of the g. of the vanquished WAR, 25
grieve G. not that I die young DEATH, 56
Men are we, and must g. REGRET, 22
grill be careful not to look like a mixed g. APPEARANCE, 9
grimace the only pianist . . . who did not g. MUSICIANS, 9
grin All Nature wears one universal g. NATURE, 9
ending with the g., which remained some time
SUPERNATURAL, 5
grind mills of God g. slowly GOD, 33
grinders Writers, like teeth, are divided into incisors and g.
WRITERS, 2
grist All's g. that comes to the mill OPPORTUNITY, 1
groan men sit and hear each other g. HUMAN CONDITION, 11
groans How alike are the g. of love to those of the dying
LOVE AND DEATH, 4
Gromyko the G. of the Labour party POLITICIANS, 33
grooves specialists . . . tend to think in g. EXPERTS, 6
Groucho had Marx been G. instead of Karl HUMOUR, 3
No, G. is not my real name NAMES, 4
group A g. of closely related persons FAMILY, 26
grovelled Whenever he met a great man he g. SERVILITY, 7
groves And seek for truth in the g. of Academe EDUCATION, 22
grow Green the rashes O LOVE, 31
make two questions g. where only one RESEARCH, 4
some of us never g. out AUTHORITARIANISM, 8
They shall g. not old MEMORIALS, 3

two ears of corn . . . g. . . . where only one grew before
POLITICIANS, 69
grow'd 'I 'spect I g..' CREATION, 12
growing G. old is like being increasingly penalized OLD AGE, 32
growl I hate a fellow . . . who does nothing . . . but sit and g.
PETULANCE, 4
grown Boys . . . are unwholesome companions for g. people
CHILDREN, 30
one of the few English novels for g. up people CRITICISM, 54
grows Nothing g. well in the shade GREATNESS, 5
growth as short a Spring; As quick a g. to meet decay
TRANSIENCE, 14
G. is a greater mystery than death AGE, 34
the impalpable elations and apprehensions of g. AGE, 34
grub it is poor g., poor pay, and easy work AMERICA, 23;
ENGLAND, 24
grumbling the muttering grew to a g. ANIMALS, 6
gruntled far from feeling g. DISCONTENT, 9; HUMOUR, 55
guarantee No one can g. success in war WAR, 27
guard That g. our native seas NAVY, 1
guardian As g. of His Majesty's conscience MONARCHY, 23
guards Up, G., and at 'em WAR, 127
Who is to guard the g. themselves MISTRUST, 7
gudeman Robin Gray, he was g. to me MARRIAGE, 17
guerre ce n'est pas la g. WAR, 10
guerrilla The g. fights the war of the flea WAR, 116
The g. wins if he does not lose WAR, 56
guest A free-loader is a confirmed g. PARASITES, 2
Earth, receive an honoured g. POETS, 4
The g. who outstays HOSPITALITY, 4
guests the g. must be chosen as carefully as the wine
ALCOHOL, 50
guide Custom, then, is the great g. of human life CUSTOM, 2
Everyman, I will go with thee, and be thy g. GUIDANCE, 1
I have only a faint light to g. me GUIDANCE, 2
guiding little onward lend thy g. hand GUIDANCE, 3
guillotine There is only one cure for grey hair. . . . the g.
REMEDIES, 14
guilt Let other pens dwell on g. and misery OPTIMISM, 14
Life without industry is g. ART, 22
put on a dress of g. GUILT, 6
guiltless Whose g. heart is free RIGHTEOUSNESS, 4
guilty g. of Noël Cowardice COWARDICE, 1
It is quite gratifying to feel g. GUILT, 1
Let no g. man escape JUSTICE, 9
ten g. persons escape than one innocent suffer JUSTICE, 3
tremble like a g. thing surprised DOUBT, 8
guinea a round disc of fire somewhat like a g. PERCEPTION, 3
I would not give half a g. to live under one form of government
GOVERNMENT, 13
there go two-and-forty sixpences . . . to one g. MERIT, 4
guineas I have only five g. in my pocket GENEROSITY, 4
gulphs whelm'd in deeper g. than he DEATH, 38
gun it is necessary to take up the g. WAR, 63
The difference between a g. and a tree TREES, 12
we have got The Maxim G. POWER POLITICS, 1
gunfire Thanks to the movies, g. has always sounded unreal
CINEMA, 9
Gunga Din You're a better man than I am, G. SUPERIORITY, 6
gunpowder G., Printing, and the Protestant Religion
CIVILIZATION, 3
guns Elevate them g. a little lower WAR, 50
G. will make us powerful POWER POLITICS, 3
Saviour of 'is country when the g. SOLDIERS, 1
gutless W. H. Auden, a sort of g. Kipling SOCIALISM, 12
gutter We are all in the g. OPTIMISM, 28
gypsies My mother said that I never should Play with the g. in
the wood NURSERY RHYMES, 34

H

H Drop thy 'H's' CLASS, 5
habit a h. the pleasure of which increases with practise
LETTER-WRITING, 1
H. is a great deadener HABIT, 2
honour peereth in the meanest h. APPEARANCES, 21
some h. of which he is deeply ashamed TELEVISION, 2
habitation to airy nothing A local h. POETRY, 40
habits Curious things, h. HABIT, 3
h. that carry them far apart HABIT, 4
Old h. die hard HABIT, 1
hack Do not h. me EXECUTION, 17

our h. is not quiet until it rests in Thee — HUMAN CONDITION, 2
She had A h. . . . too soon made glad — IMPRESSIONABILITY, 1
So the h. be right — EXECUTION, 24
strings . . . in the human h. — EMOTION, 2
take heed . . . that your h. be not deceived — CHRISTIANITY, 6
Take thy beak from out my h. — EVIL, 12
that mighty h. is lying still — SLEEP, 19
The fire which in the h. resides — SOUL, 2
The h. has its reasons — MOTIVE, 5
The history of every country begins in the h. — HISTORY, 7
The h. that loved her — NATURE, 18
The intellect is always fooled by the h. — EMOTION, 4
Their h.'s in the right place — MANKIND, 16
There is a road from the eye to the h. — EMOTION, 1
the waters of the h. Push in their tides — EMOTION, 5
The way to a man's h. is through his stomach — FOOD, 18
to lose your h.'s desire — DESIRE, 14
What comes from the h. — SINCERITY, 2
With rue my h. is laden — NOSTALGIA, 11
with the palsied h. — PASSION, 8
hearth Man for the field and woman for the h. — SEXES, 20
the cricket on the h. — MELANCHOLY, 9
hearts Kind h. are more than coronets — ARISTOCRACY, 12
One equal temper of heroic h. — DETERMINATION, 14
The Queen of H. She made some tarts — FOOD, 12; NURSERY RHYMES, 51

the song that is sung in our h. — MUSIC, 30
The Worldly Hope men set their H. upon — TRANSIENCE, 13
those who have stout h. and sharp swords — RUTHLESSNESS, 6
Two h. that beat as one — LOVE, 81
well-developed bodies, fairly developed minds, and undeveloped h. — EDUCATION, 18
heat Britain . . . is going to be forged in the white h. of this revolution — SOCIALISM, 14
can't stand the h., get out of the kitchen — ENDURANCE, 20
H., madam! . . . to take off my flesh and sit in my bones — WEATHER, 25

heathen I was born of Christian race, And not a H., or a Jew — RELIGION, 56

heaven a H. in Hell's despair — LOVE, 27
all H. in a rage — IMPRISONMENT, 1
All place shall be hell that is not h. — DOOMSDAY, 5
ascend to h. — EXECUTION, 8
between H. and Charing Cross — HEAVEN, 12
from whose face the earth and the h. fled — JUDGMENT, 4
God created the h. — CREATION, 2
h. and earth shall pass away — TRANSIENCE, 8
H. has granted me no offspring — CONCEIT, 22
H. in a wild flower — WONDER, 2
H. . . . , is a place so inane, so dull — HEAVEN, 11
Home is h. — DEBAUCHERY, 8
H. was in him, before he was in h. — COMPLIMENTS, 8
H. without being naturally qualified — HEAVEN, 10
If it's h. for climate — PERVERSITY, 1
If Max gets to H. — BUSINESS, 21
If this belief from h. be sent — MANKIND, 36
In h. an angel is nobody in particular — IMPORTANCE, 2
it were better for sun and moon to drop from h. — SIN, 17
make a H. of Hell, a Hell of H. — MIND, 4
man is as H. made him — CHARACTER, 2
Marriage is . . . excluded from h. — MARRIAGE, 30
more things in h. and earth — SUPERNATURAL, 12
no invention came more easily to man than H. — HEAVEN, 5
Now: h. knows — FREEDOM, 41
Order is h.'s first law — ORDER, 2
Parting is all we know of h. — PARTING, 5
Pennies do not come from h. — WORK, 22
Pennies from H. — OPTIMISM, 18
so much of earth . . . of h. — IMPETUOSITY, 4
steep and thorny way to h. — EXAMPLE, 8
the Hell I suffer seems a H. — HELL, 5
The mind . . . Can make a H. of Hell — MIND, 4
there was war in h. — DEVIL, 4
the starry h. above me — WONDER, 3
to be young was very h. — FRENCH REVOLUTION, 3
'Twould ring the bells of H. — ANIMALS, 12
We are all going to H. — LAST WORDS, 23
We are as near to h. by sea as by land — LAST WORDS, 26; SEA, 5
what's a h. for — AMBITION, 3
What they do in h. — MARRIAGE, 107
When earth was nigher h. — PAST, 3

heavenward A homely face . . . aided many women h. — APPEARANCE, 3
heavier O you who have borne even h. things — ENDURANCE, 21
heaviest nickname is the h. stone that the devil can throw — NAMES, 3
heav'n h. on earth — HEAVEN, 6
'tis little joy To know I'm farther off from h. Than when . . . a boy — INNOCENCE, 6
hedge A leap over the h. — PRAYER, 7
hedgehogs If you start throwing h. under me — THREATS, 2
heed To fight and not to h. the wounds — SELFLESSNESS, 2
heels Time wounds all h. — TIME, 25
heesh If John or Mary comes h. will want to play — LANGUAGE, 17

heights If suffer we must, let's suffer on the h. — SUFFERING, 6
heiress American h. wants to buy a man — MATERIALISM, 14
hell a H. in Heaven's despite — LOVE, 28
A lifetime of happiness . . . h. on earth — HAPPINESS, 22
All place shall be h. that is not heaven — DOOMSDAY, 5
all we need of h. — PARTING, 5
Better to reign in H. — POWER, 12
h. a fury like a woman scorned — LOVE AND HATE, 3
H. is a city much like London — LONDON, 12
H. is other people — HELL, 6
h. upon earth . . . in a melancholy man's heart — MELANCHOLY, 3
Italy . . . h. for women — NATIONALITY, 3
make a Heaven of H., a H. of Heaven — MIND, 4
Old age is woman's h. — OLD AGE, 26
on the fourth day they will say 'To h. with you!' — PROMISES, 4
out of h. leads up to light — HELL, 4
Raises from H. a human soul — HELL, 1
The h. I am — ACTORS, 1
the H. I suffer seems a Heaven — HELL, 5
the h. of horses — ENGLAND, 16
the little holiday steamers made an excursion to h. — WORLD WAR II, 25

The mind . . . Can make a Heaven of H. — MIND, 4
The road to h. is paved — PROCRASTINATION, 3
though h. should bar the way! — DETERMINATION, 12
Ugly h., gape not — DAMNATION, 4
War is h. — WAR, 109
way down to H. is easy — HELL, 7
Which way I fly is H.; myself am H. — HELL, 5
help gods h. them that h. themselves — SELF-RELIANCE, 2
going in without the h. of Russia — WORLD WAR II, 22
I am trying to be, and you can't h. it — RUDENESS, 2
not so much our friends' h. that helps us — FRIENDSHIP, 17
People must h. one another — HELP, 7
Since there's no h. — PARTING, 6
The dead . . . look on and h. — DEATH, 72
the h. of too many physicians — DOCTORS, 1
what is past my h. is past my care — INDIFFERENCE, 1
with a little h. from my friends — FRIENDS, 10
helpless Help of the h. — RELIGION, 36
helps He h. little — SELF, 1
not so much our friends' help that h. us — FRIENDSHIP, 17
hem only touch the h. of his garment — REMEDIES, 4
hen a broody h. sitting on a china egg — BUREAUCRACY, 5
Two Owls and a H. — APPEARANCE, 19
Henry He is without strict doubt a Hoorah H. — ARISTOCRACY, 11
How H. would have loved it — FUNERALS, 9
Herald Price of H. three cents daily — NEWSPAPERS, 3
herb sweetest fragrance from the h. . . . tread on it and bruise it — WOMEN, 73
herbs nature runs either to h., or to weeds — HUMAN NATURE, 2
Hercules Some talk of Alexander, and some of H. — HEROISM, 1
herd the H. of such, Who think too little — VERBOSITY, 5
herd-morality Morality . . . is h. — MORALITY, 11
here bet you a hundred bucks he ain't in h. — ESCAPE, 1; FUNERALS, 5

h. today and gone tomorrow — TRANSIENCE, 3
What you are looking for is h., is at Ulubrae — TRAVEL, 13
heresies new truths . . . begin as h. — NOVELTY, 4
heresy h. signifies no more than private opinion — OPINIONS, 1
heritage I summon age To grant youth's h. — AGE, 13
hero Being a h. — HEROISM, 6
better to be the widow of a h. than the wife of a coward — COURAGE, 13
Every h. becomes a bore — HEROISM, 5
No man is a h. to his valet — FAMILIARITY, 2
The h. is strangely akin — DEATH, 90
to his very valet seem'd a h. — HEROISM, 4

Many a man who thinks to found a h.   PARASITES, 1
no h. . . . save in Paris   PARIS, 4
permits you to be entertained . . . by people you wouldn't have
  in your h.   TELEVISION, 3
Pleasure never is at h.   DISCONTENT, 5
She's leaving h.   DEPARTURE, 7
The Life and Soul, the man who will never go h.   PARTIES, 9
there's no place like h.   HOME, 7
till the cow comes h.   ETERNITY, 1
we come From God, who is our h.   METAPHYSICS, 5
What's the good of a h.   ABSENCE, 7
home-keeping h. youth   HOME, 8
homely A h. face . . . aided many women heavenward
     APPEARANCE, 3
be never so h.   HOME, 3
h. wits   HOME, 8
Homer Cicero And . . . H. were *Mad as the mist and snow*
     MADNESS, 14
even excellent H. nods   IMPERFECTION, 9
Mr Gladstone read H. for fun   CLASSICS, 2
Seven cities warr'd for H., being dead   POVERTY, 14
The author of that poem is either H.   ARGUMENTS, 7
homes go back to thy stately h. of England   PARTING, 7
the Stately H. of England   DECLINE, 1; STATELY HOMES, 3
home-sickness In h. you must keep moving   HOMESICKNESS, 7
homo The 'h.' is the legitimate child   HOMOSEXUALITY, 5
homos one of the stately h. of England   HOMOSEXUALITY, 2
homosexuals h. . . . set out to win the love of a 'real' man
     HOMOSEXUALITY, 1
honest An h. broker   DIPLOMACY, 3
An h. God   GOD, 28
an h. man sent to lie abroad for . . . his country   DIPLOMACY, 21
An h. man's word   HONESTY, 1
give me six lines . . . by the most h. man   EXECUTION, 26
I am as h. as any man living   HONESTY, 8
It's better to be quotable than . . . h.   QUOTATIONS, 12
not an h. man   HONESTY, 11
She was poor but she was h.   POVERTY AND WEALTH, 1
then they get *h.*   DOCTORS, 8
Though I am not naturally h.   HONESTY, 9
Though I be poor, I'm h.   HONESTY, 5
honestly If possible h., if not, somehow, make money
     MONEY, 22
honesty H. is the best policy   HONESTY, 2; HONESTY, 11
make your children *capable of h.* is the beginning of education
     HONESTY, 6
Philosophers never balance between profit and h.
     PHILOSOPHERS, 3
honey a land of oil olive, and h.   WEALTH, 5
gather h. all the day   WORK, 24
h. still for tea   NOSTALGIA, 3
They took some h., and plenty of money   NONSENSE, 20
honey'd the h. middle of the night   LOVE, 75
honey-dew on h. hath fed   CAUTION, 9
honi *H. soit qui mal y pense*   EVIL, 1
honour All is lost save h.   DEFEAT, 1
a prophet is not without h.   HONOUR, 1
Brothers all In h.   HONOUR, 7
His h. rooted in dishonour   UNFAITHFULNESS, 4
H. pricks me on   HONOUR, 4
h. sinks where commerce long prevails   BUSINESS, 8
h. thy father and thy mother   GOD, 10
if I accepted the h. . . . I would not answer for the integrity of
  my intellect   TITLES, 3
Let us h. if we can   POSTERITY, 4
only h. and life have been spared   DEFEAT, 2
peace I hope with h.   PEACE, 9
So h. peereth in the meanest habit   APPEARANCES, 21
That chastity of h.   HONOUR, 2
then they get *h.*   DOCTORS, 8
There is h. among thieves   LOYALTY, 2
To h. we call you   COURAGE, 11
Wealth has never been a sufficient source of h.   OSTENTATION, 3
we're fighting for this woman's h.   HONOUR, 3
honourable His designs were strictly h.   MARRIAGE, 53
hoof I see many h.-marks going in   MISTRUST, 2
hooligan Even the H. was probably invented in China
     PLACES, 15
hoorah He is without strict doubt a H. Henry   ARISTOCRACY, 11
hoo-ray H. and up she rises   DRUNKENNESS, 4
hope Abandon h., all ye who enter here   HELL, 1
a faint h. that he will die   HUMAN NATURE, 8

And what was dead was H.   IMPRISONMENT, 9
H. for the best   HOPE, 2
h. is . . . the dream of those that wake   HOPE, 9
H. is the power of being cheerful   CHARITY, 11; HOPE, 5
H. may vanish, but can die not   OPTIMISM, 24
H. springs eternal in the human breast   HOPE, 8
Land of H. and Glory   BRITAIN, 3
no other medicine but only h.   HOPE, 1
Not to h. for things to last for ever, is what the year teaches
     TRANSIENCE, 15
now abideth faith, h., charity   CHARITY, 5
Our h. for years to come   RELIGION, 57
the distinction between h. and expectation   REALISM, 2
The triumph of h. over experience   MARRIAGE, 69
The Worldly H. men set their Hearts upon   TRANSIENCE, 13
unconquerable h.   HOPE, 4
What a strange thing is memory, and h.   MEMORY, 10
While there is life, there's h.   HOPE, 6
Without all h. of day   BLINDNESS, 4
hopeless that controversy is either superfluous or h.
     ARGUMENTS, 11
hopes enough for fifty h. and fears   WORRY, 8
Life's short span forbids us to enter on far-reaching h.
     MORTALITY, 13
My h. no more must change their name   FREEDOM, 52
Horatius brave H.   COURAGE, 14
horde Society is now one polish'd h.   BORES, 4
horizontal we value none But the h. one   POSTERITY, 3
Horner Little Jack H. Sat in the corner   NURSERY RHYMES, 29
Hornie Auld H., Satan, Nick   DEVIL, 6
horns Memories are hunting h.   MEMORY, 1
When you take the bull by the h.   CHANCE, 5
horny-handed H. sons of toil   WORK, 11
Horowitz Vladimir H.   MUSICIANS, 7
horrible A strange, h. business, . . . good enough for
  Shakespeare's day   CRITICISM, 48
horrid are they all h.   NASTINESS, 1
horror I have a h. of sunsets   SUN, 3
mere existence is swollen to a h.   IDEALISM, 3
The thought of dentists gave him just the same sick h.
     FEAR, 14
horrors I have supp'd full with h.   WORLD-WEARINESS, 6
horse A fly, Sir, may sting a stately h.   CRITICS, 9
a pale h.   DEATH, 29
A Protestant with a h.   NATIONALITY, 4
Do not trust the h., Trojans   MISTRUST, 11
good deal of physical courage to ride a h.   ALCOHOL, 39;
  HORSES, 8
Go together like a h. and carriage   LOVE AND MARRIAGE, 1
I feel as a h. must feel   INJUSTICE, 5
I know two things about the h.   HORSES, 1
like to be a h.   ROYALTY, 16
my kingdom for a h.   HORSES, 10
nobody has any business to go around looking like a h.
     APPEARANCE, 27
Ride a cock-h. to Banbury Cross   NURSERY RHYMES, 41
To confess that you are totally Ignorant about the H.
     HORSES, 9
victory under the belly of a Cossack's h.   RUSSIAN
     REVOLUTION, 2
You can be in the H. Guards   CLASS, 26
You can lead a h. to the water   STUBBORNNESS, 1
You may have my husband, but not my h.   MASCULINITY, 2
horsemanship They say princes learn no art truly, but . . . h.
     HORSES, 7
horse-pond celibacy is . . . a muddy h.   MARRIAGE, 83
horses A grain, which in England is generally given to h.
     SCOTLAND, 2
Bring on the empty h.   LANGUAGE, 10
Dogs, like h., are quadrupeds   ANIMALS, 15
England . . . hell for h.   NATIONALITY, 4
England . . . hell of h.   ENGLAND, 16
frighten the h.   SEX, 7
Men are . . . more careful of the breed of their h.   FAMILY, 32
sixty h. wedged in a chimney   JOURNALISM, 19
swap h. in mid-stream   CHANGE, 12
hospital h. is the assumption on the part of the staff
     MEDICINE, 3
the world, I count it not an inn, but an h.   WORLD, 1
host an innumerable company of the heavenly h.   PERCEPTION, 3
of all this h. of men not one will still be alive in a hundred
  years' time   MORTALITY, 22

hurrah h.! we bring the Jubilee	GLORY, 5
hurricanoes You cataracts and h.	WEATHER, 18
hurries h. to the main event	PLAYS, 5
hurry An old man in a h.	POLITICIANS, 14
H.! I never h. I have no time to h.	HASTE, 12
So who's in a h.?	ALCOHOL, 10
hurrying I see a man h. along – to what	PURPOSE, 5
hurt it h. too much to laugh	DISAPPOINTMENT, 8
It takes your enemy and your friend . . . , to h. you	HURT, 3
Those have most power to h.	HURT, 1
wish to h.	CRUELTY, 1
hurting Art . . . can go on mattering once it has stopped h.	ART, 5
husband An archaeologist is the best h.	MARRIAGE, 33
at all times yr faithful h.	MARRIAGE, 101
Being a h. is a whole-time job	MARRIAGE, 19
easier to be a lover than a h.	MARRIAGE, 15
happened unawares to look at her h.	MARRIAGE, 11
h. render unto the wife due benevolence	MARRIAGE, 21
in love with . . . Her own h.	LOVE AND MARRIAGE, 2
light wife doth make a heavy h.	MARRIAGE, 94
My h. and I	ROYALTY, 17
My h. is dead	DEATH, 79
Never trust a h. too far	TRUST, 4
that monstrous animal a h. and wife	MARRIAGE, 54
The h. frae the wife despises	MARRIAGE, 29
trust my h. not to fall asleep	POLITICS, 71
You may have my h., but not my horse	MASCULINITY, 2
husbandry borrowing dulls the edge of h.	BORROWING, 8; INTEGRITY, 6
husbands flirt with their own h.	LOVE AND MARRIAGE, 6
h. and wives . . . belong to different sexes	SEXES, 8
h. and wives make shipwreck of their lives	MARRIAGE, 47
H. are like fires	MARRIAGE, 58
h., love your wives	MARRIAGE, 20
h. remind me of an orangutang	MARRIAGE, 16
h. to stay at home	WOMEN, 29
hush a breathless h. in the Close tonight	CRICKET, 5
hut Love in a h.	LOVE, 74
The Arab who builds . . . a h. out of . . . a temple	MUSEUMS, 1; PRACTICALITY, 3
hyacinth Children with H.'s temperament . . . merely know more	CHARACTER, 17
every H. the Garden wears	FLOWERS, 4
hydrostatics It gives me the h.	MALAPROPISMS, 5
hymn Aisle. Altar. H.	MARRIAGE, 79; PUNS, 14
hymn-book Cassock, band, and h. too	CLERGY, 14
hymns My poems are h. of praise	POETRY, 45
hyper-thyroid Shelley had a h. face	APPEARANCE, 34
hyphenated h. Americanism	PATRIOTISM, 23
hypocrisy an organized h.	POLITICS, 18
H. . . . is a whole-time job	HYPOCRISY, 11
H. is the homage paid by vice to virtue	HYPOCRISY, 3
H. is the most . . . nerve-racking vice	HYPOCRISY, 11
neither man nor angel can discern H.	HYPOCRISY, 12
That would be h.	HYPOCRISY, 17
hypocrite No man is a h. in his pleasures	PLEASURE, 15
see . . . into a h.	HYPOCRISY, 8
hypocritical Man . . . learns by being h.	HYPOCRISY, 10
hypothesis I have no need of that h.	GOD, 32
the slaying of a beautiful h. by an ugly fact	SCIENCE, 19
to discard a pet h. every day	THEORY, 6

I I also had my hour	GLORY, 1
in the infinite I AM	IMAGINATION, 1
I would have done it differently	ARROGANCE, 9
ice skating over thin i.	HASTE, 6
The i. was all around	SEA, 4
ice-cream just enjoy your i. while it's on your plate	PHILOSOPHY, 16
iced three parts i. over	AGE, 4
icicles When i. hang by the wall	WINTER, 6
id put the i. back in yid	JEWS, 12
idea An i. does not pass from one language	TRANSLATION, 4
An i. isn't responsible for the people	IDEAS, 5
constant repetition . . . in imprinting an i.	PUBLIC, 14
Dying for an i.	MARTYRDOM, 2
I think it would be a good i.	CIVILIZATION, 6
no stand can be made against invasion by an i.	IDEAS, 2
That fellow seems to me to possess but one i.	STUPIDITY, 4

the i. of death as an individual	NUCLEAR WEAPONS, 8
they will end by ruining our i.	FASCISM, 1
ideal at fourteen every boy should be in love with some i.	SEXES, 14
woman . . . on a pedestal	SEXES, 14
the i. American	AMERICANS, 3
idealist An i. . . . , on noticing that a rose smells better than a cabbage	IDEALISM, 4
people call me an i.	AMERICA, 37
ideals Away with all i.	SPONTANEITY, 3
think how far I can go with all the i. that I have	IDEALISM, 7; POLITICIANS, 72
ideas down which i. are lured and . . . strangled	BUREAUCRACY, 3
Human Stupidity consists in having lots of i.	STUPIDITY, 8
i. are of more importance than values	INTELLECTUALS, 4
i. simply pass through him	STUPIDITY, 1
I stopped . . . to exchange i.	INFERIORITY, 1
I. that enter the mind under fire	INDOCTRINATION, 3
Learn our i., or otherwise get out	RACE, 12
Many i. grow better when transplanted into another mind	IDEAS, 3
Morality which is based on i.	MORALITY, 8
she's only got two i. in her head	STUPIDITY, 5
the addiction of political groups to the i.	POLITICS, 24
The true God, . . . God of i.	INSPIRATION, 5
ides Beware the i. of March	PROPHECY, 9
idiot now I feel like a complete i.	INFERIORITY, 1
tale told by an i.	LIFE, 41
The i. who praises . . . every country but his own	DISCONTENT, 2
To generalize is to be an i.	GENERALIZATIONS, 1
idiots the English seem . . . to act with . . . the fatuity of i.	IRELAND, 15
idle As i. as a painted ship	BOATS, 3
I am happiest when I am i.	IDLENESS, 9
Satan finds . . . mischief . . . For i. hands	IDLENESS, 10
We would all be i.	IDLENESS, 3
Young people ought not to be i.	IDLENESS, 8; YOUTH, 18
idleness compulsory and irreproachable i.	ARMY, 3
i. and indifference	CHANGE, 3
I. . . . the refuge of weak minds	IDLENESS, 3
Research! A mere excuse for i.	RESEARCH, 1
idling It is impossible to enjoy i.	IDLENESS, 5
idol one-eyed yellow i. to the north of Khatmandu	MOURNING, 5
idolatry There is no i. in the Mass	CATHOLICISM, 6
if I. you can keep your head	SELF-CONTROL, 6
much virtue in I.	POSSIBILITY, 2
ifs If i. and ands	UNCERTAINTY, 1
ignominious History is full of i. getaways by the great	COWARDICE, 5
ignorance From i. our comfort flows	IGNORANCE, 12
I. is like a delicate exotic fruit	IGNORANCE, 17
I. is Strength	DOUBLETHINK, 1
I., madam, pure i.	IGNORANCE, 9
I. of the law excuses	LAW, 23
journalism. . . . keeps us in touch with the i. of the community	JOURNALISM, 27
Lawyers are the only persons in whom i. . . . is not punished	LAWYERS, 4
man's i. of the gods	SPONTANEITY, 1
no sin but i.	IGNORANCE, 11
Somebody else's i. is bliss	IGNORANCE, 16
where i. is bliss, 'Tis folly to be wise	IGNORANCE, 6
Your i. cramps my conversation	IGNORANCE, 8
ignorant Let no one i. of mathematics enter here	MATHEMATICS, 9
The i. man always adores	IGNORANCE, 10
the opinionated, the i., and the boorish	STUBBORNNESS, 2
To confess that you are totally I. about the Horse	HORSES, 1
what may follow it, or what preceded it, we are absolutely i.	LIFE, 9
ill Cannot be i.; cannot be good	SUPERNATURAL, 13
human i. does not dawn seem . . . an alternative	HUMAN CONDITION, 19
I am only half there when I am i.	ILLNESS, 10
If . . . someone is speaking i. of you	CRITICISM, 11
no hint throughout the universe Of good or i.	NECESSITY, 8
very fine country to be acutely i.	BRITAIN, 10
woman colour'd i.	CONFLICT, 7
illegal collect legal taxes from i. money	TAXATION, 1

the things I really like . . . are either immoral, i., or fattening
PLEASURE, 30
illegitimate There are no i. children ILLEGITIMACY, 3
ill-health Cynicism is humour in i. CYNICISM, 3
illiteracy The ratio of literacy to i. LITERACY, 1
illiterate I. him . . . from your memory MALAPROPISMS, 4
illness I. is the night-side of life ILLNESS, 13
illogical Faith . . . an i. belief in . . . the improbable FAITH, 14
ills sharp remedy . . . for all i. EXECUTION, 25
ill-spent sign of an i. youth SPORT AND GAMES, 18
illumine What in me is dark I. GOD, 37
illusion Commit it then to the flames: for it can contain nothing
but sophistry and i. PHILOSOPHY, 3
Religion is an i. RELIGION, 22
The House of Lords, an i. HOUSES OF PARLIAMENT, 18;
RESPONSIBILITY, 13
visible universe was an i. UNIVERSE, 2
illusions It's life's i. I recall LIFE, 34
ill-will I bear no i. against those responsible for this
FORGIVENESS, 16
image any graven i. GOD, 10
A photograph is not only an i. PHOTOGRAPHY, 6
fall down and worship the golden i. DOOMSDAY, 1
If God made us in His i. GOD, 49
make man in our own i. CREATION, 6; MANKIND, 5
Why should I consent to the perpetuation of the i. of this i.
PAINTING, 13
imaginary Happiness is an i. condition HAPPINESS, 25
imagination A lady's i. is very rapid WOMEN, 11
Art is ruled . . . by the i. IMAGINATION, 3
I.! . . . I put it first years ago ACTING, 8
indebted to his . . . i. for his facts POLITICIANS, 63
I. without skill gives us modern art ART, 25
no i. and . . . no compassion IMAGINATION, 4
not an ideal of reason but of i. HAPPINESS, 13
of i. all compact LOVE, 115; POETRY, 42
The primary i. IMAGINATION, 1
treat your facts with i. is one thing TRUTH, 14
truth of i. IMAGINATION, 6; TRUTH, 28
imagine never so happy . . . as we i. HAPPINESS, 17
imagined What is now proved was . . . i. PROOF, 2
imagining How reconcile this world . . . with . . . my i.?
BLINDNESS, 2
imitate An original writer is . . . one whom nobody can i.
ORIGINALITY, 2
never failed to i. CHILDREN, 6
obliged to i. himself, and to repeat IMITATION, 5
people . . . usually i. each other IMITATION, 3
imitates Photography can never grow up if it i.
PHOTOGRAPHY, 1
imitation I. is the sincerest form of flattery FLATTERY, 1;
IMITATION, 2
Man . . . is an i. MANKIND, 19
Immaculate the I. Conception was spontaneous combustion
CATHOLICISM, 9
Immanuel call his name I. CHRISTIANITY, 9
immature the i. man . . . wants to die nobly for a cause
AGE, 56
immaturity common symptom of i. ORIGINALITY, 6
the executive expression of human i. POLITICS, 9
immoral moral or an i. book BOOKS, 43
the things I really like . . . are either i., illegal, or fattening
PLEASURE, 30
worse than i. MISTAKES, 2
immorality the most rigid code of i. ENGLISH, 6
immortal I have lost the i. part REPUTATION, 9
make me i. with a kiss BEAUTY, 24
Our souls have sight of that i. sea METAPHYSICS, 4
Why are you weeping? Did you imagine that I was i. LAST
WORDS, 37
immortality I . . . want to achieve i. . . . through not dying
IMMORTALITY, 1
just ourselves And I. DEATH, 40
immutable Few things are as i. POLITICS, 24
impediment cause, or just i. OBSTRUCTION, 2
imperative This i. is Categorical MORALITY, 7
imperfection i. itself may have its . . . perfect state
IMPERFECTION, 7
imperial be yourself, i., plain and true SINCERITY, 1
imperialism i. is the monopoly stage of capitalism POLITICS, 39
Their Europeanism is . . . i. with an inferiority complex
POLITICS, 30

impersonal In the philosopher there is nothing whatever i.
PHILOSOPHERS, 5
impertinent ask an i. question SCIENCE, 1
impetuous such i. blood IMPETUOSITY, 4
importance Official dignity . . . in inverse ratio to . . . i.
DIPLOMACY, 12
important One doesn't recognize . . . the really i. moments . . .
until it's too late REGRET, 4
that basic weekendmanship should contain some reference to I.
Person Play ONE-UPMANSHIP, 2
the little things are infinitely the most i. TRIVIALITY, 6
imposed wish to be i. on, and then are EXPLOITATION, 2
impossibility a physical and metaphysical i. POETS, 7
impossible complete sorrow is as i. EMOTION, 6
I believe because it is i. BELIEF, 7
It's either easy or i. PAINTING, 4
something is i., he is . . . wrong SCIENCE, 5
when you have excluded the i. TRUTH, 21
impotent an i. people, Sick with inbreeding WELSH, 3
impregnator the writer . . . is the i. READING, 19
impression knowledge and wonder . . . is an i. of pleasure
KNOWLEDGE, 5; WONDER, 1
impressionable Give me a girl at an i. age
IMPRESSIONABILITY, 3
impressions i. . . . lasting as . . . an oar upon the water
INSIGNIFICANCE, 1
improbable an i. fiction REALITY, 5
Faith . . . an illogical belief in . . . the i. FAITH, 14
whatever remains, however i., must be the truth TRUTH, 21
improper I only hope it is not i. ETIQUETTE, 2
impropriety I. is the soul of wit HUMOUR, 18
improved enormously i. by death WRITERS, 38
improvement most schemes of political i. are very laughable
POLITICS, 34
impulse the i. of the moment FLATTERY, 2
the need to talk is a primary i. IMPETUOSITY, 1
impulses Mistrust first i. FIRST IMPRESSIONS, 7
impure To the Puritan all things are i. PURITANISM, 2
in you had it i. you EXPECTATION, 2
inactivity wise and masterly i. GOVERNMENT, 16
inadequate Like Brighton pier, . . . i. for getting to France
TRAVEL, 16
inartistic He was unperfect, unfinished, i. WRITERS, 20
inbreeding an impotent people, Sick with i. WELSH, 3
incest except i. and folk-dancing EXPERIENCE, 7
inch every i. a king ROYALTY, 29
Give him an i. GREED, 1
inches They that die by famine die by i. HUNGER, 6
incident What is i. but the illustration of character?
CHARACTER, 12
incisors Writers, like teeth, are divided into i. and grinders
WRITERS, 2
inclination A man ought to read just as i. leads him
READING, 8
incoherent I'm not i. CONFUSION, 7
income Annual i. twenty pounds ECONOMICS, 5
hardest thing . . . to understand is i. tax TAXATION, 7
her Majesty . . . must not . . . look upon me as a source of i.
TAXATION, 5
live beyond its i. EXTRAVAGANCE, 2; PROGRESS, 2
incomes people live beyond their i. EXTRAVAGANCE, 4
incompetence Work . . . by those employees who have not yet
reached . . . i. INCOMPETENCE, 1
incompetent a tax on pianos for the i. MUSIC, 43
God is the immemorial refuge of the i. GOD, 34
i. swine WAR, 101
incomplete A man in love is i. until . . . married MARRIAGE, 59
incomprehensible an old, wild, and i. man POLITICIANS, 75
inconvenience Change is not made without i. CHANGE, 10
inconveniences A good many i. attend play-going PLAYS, 12
inconvenient i. to be poor POVERTY, 5
incorruptible seagreen I. POLITICIANS, 12
the dead shall be raised i. DEATH, 26
increase from fairest creatures we desire i. BEAUTY, 35
increased influence of the Crown has i. MONARCHY, 9
incurable the i. disease of writing WRITING, 17
Ind Outshone the wealth of Ormus and of I. DEVIL, 19
indecency prejudicial . . . as a public i. SIN, 10
The older one grows the more one likes i. AGE, 65
indecent It requires one to assume such i. postures
CRICKET, 7
much more i. . . . than a good smack PUNISHMENT, 13

sent down for i. behaviour — EDUCATION, 55
indefatigable i. and unsavoury engine of pollution — DOGS, 12
indefensible political speech and writing are largely the defence of the i. — POLITICS, 51
independent an I. Labour Party — PARTIES, 8
An i. . . . wants to take the politics out of politics — POLITICS, 66
To be poor and i. — POVERTY, 4
India From I.'s coral strand — PLACES, 6
I. is a geographical term — PLACES, 2
What have we to say to I.? — COMMUNICATION, 4
Indian base I., threw a pearl away — LOVE, 122
in a world of Gary Coopers you are the I. — RACE, 2
lay out ten to see a dead I. — CHARITY, 16
Indians The only good I. I ever saw were dead — ENEMIES, 7
indictment an i. against an whole people — ACCUSATION, 1
indifference and cold i. came — INDIFFERENCE, 5
equanimity bordering on i. — INDIFFERENCE, 3
i. and a coach and six — LOVE, 38
idleness and i. — CHANGE, 3
Nothing is so fatal to religion as i. — INDIFFERENCE, 2
indignation 2 percent moral, 48 percent i. and 50 percent envy — MORALITY, 19
puritan pours righteous i. — PURITANISM, 1
the mists of righteous i. — PRUDERY, 3
Wrongdoing can only be avoided if those who are not wronged feel the same i. — VICE, 8
indignity ultimate i. is to be given a bedpan — MEDICINE, 4
indiscretion lover without i. — LOVE, 64
indispensables She was one of those i. — INSIGNIFICANCE, 2
indistinguishable in America the successful writer or picture-painter is i. from any other decent business man — AMERICA, 22
individual gesture by the i. himself — BUSINESS, 7
It is of no moment to the happiness of an i. — GOVERNMENT, 13
the idea of death as an i. — NUCLEAR WEAPONS, 8
The liberty of the i. must be thus far limited — FREEDOM, 33
The psychic development of the i. — PSYCHIATRY, 3
individualism American system of rugged i. — AMERICA, 18
Art is the most intense mode of i. — ART, 32
individuality England is the paradise of i. — ENGLAND, 33
indulgence An only son, sir, might expect more i. — FAMILY, 18
industrial I. relations are like sexual relations — INDUSTRIAL RELATIONS, 2
industry Captains of i. — LEADERSHIP, 3
i. will supply their deficiency — WORK, 18
Life without i. is guilt — ART, 22
national i. of Prussia — WAR, 66
inebriated i. with . . . his own verbosity — VERBOSITY, 2
inelegance a continual state of i. — WEATHER, 7
inexactitude terminological i. — LYING, 7
infallible an i. sign of the second-rate — INFERIORITY, 4
No man is i. — IMPERFECTION, 2
The only i. criterion of wisdom — SUCCESS, 5
We are none of us i. — IMPERFECTION, 4
infancy Heaven lies about us in our i. — METAPHYSICS, 5
infant a mixed i. — CHILDREN, 8
An i. crying in the night — HUMAN CONDITION, 18
Sooner murder an i. in its cradle — DESIRE, 2
infanticide as indefensible as i. — CENSORSHIP, 3
inferior No one can make you feel i. without your consent — INFERIORITY, 5
Switzerland . . . an i. sort of Scotland — SWITZERLAND, 3
inferiority minds so impatient of i. — GRATITUDE, 1
Their Europeanism is . . . imperialism with an i. complex — POLITICS, 30
Wherever an i. complex exists, there is . . . reason for it — INFERIORITY, 2
inferiors I. revolt in order that they may be equal — REVOLUTION, 1
The English want i. — PRIDE, 9
inferno A man who has not passed through the i. of his passions — PASSION, 2
infidelity I. . . . consists in professing to believe — INTEGRITY, 5
infinite The Desire of Man being I. — INFINITY, 1
The sight . . . gave me i. pleasure — EXECUTION, 21
infinitive When I split an i. — GRAMMAR, 2
infinity I cannot help it; . . . i. torments me — INFINITY, 2
I. in the palm of your hand — WONDER, 2
infirmities friend should bear his friend's i. — FRIENDS, 13
infirmity last i. of noble mind — FAME, 14
inflation I. in the Sixties was a nuisance — ECONOMICS, 8
influence How to . . . I. People — INFLUENCE, 2
i. of the Crown has increased — MONARCHY, 9
influenza call it i. if ye like — ILLNESS, 2

inform not to i. the reader — BUREAUCRACY, 1
infortune The worst kinde of i. is this — MISFORTUNE, 7
infringement Necessity is the plea for every i. of human freedom — NECESSITY, 4
infusion The i. of a China plant — DRINKS, 1
ingenious a loyal, a gallant, a generous, an i., and good-temper'd people — FRANCE, 14
inglorious the i. arts of peace — POLITICIANS, 48
ingratitude Austria will astound the world with . . . her i. — DIPLOMACY, 18
I hate i. more in a man — INGRATITUDE, 6
I., thou marble-hearted fiend — INGRATITUDE, 5
man's i. — INGRATITUDE, 4
ingress Our i. . . . Was naked and bare — LIFE, 32
inherit Russia will certainly i. the future — RUSSIA, 7
inhumanity Man's i. to man — CRUELTY, 2
initiative success depends . . . upon individual i. and exertion — EFFORT, 5; SUCCESS, 11
injured Never trust the man who . . . hath i. you — TRUST, 2
injury An i. is much sooner forgotten — INSULTS, 10
Recompense i. with justice — KINDNESS, 1
injustice A lawyer has no business with . . . justice or i. — JUSTICE, 13
fear of suffering i. — JUSTICE, 20
threatened with a great i. — INJUSTICE, 3
what a man still plans . . . shows the . . . i. in his death — DEATH, 34
injustices thought only to justify their i. — HUMAN NATURE, 20
ink an optimist . . . fills up his crossword puzzle in i. — OPTIMISM, 25
inn no room for them in the i. — CHRISTMAS, 7
To that dark i., the grave — DEATH, 93
inner Conscience is the i. voice — CONSCIENCE, 4
Innisfree I will arise and . . . go to I. — SOLITUDE, 17
innocence it is not only our fate but our business to lose i. — INNOCENCE, 4
my i. begins to weigh me down — INNOCENCE, 2
Ralph wept for the end of i. — INNOCENCE, 5
innocent Every one is i. — LAW, 3
ten guilty persons escape than one i. suffer — JUSTICE, 3
innocently i. employed in getting money — MONEY, 7
innovator time is the greatest i. — INNOVATION, 1
inquiry The world is but a school of i. — CURIOSITY, 5
inquisitive There are innumerable questions to which the i. mind can . . . receive no answer — PHILOSOPHY, 6
insane Man is quite i. — RELIGION, 41
insanity lay interest in ecclesiastical matters . . . often a prelude to i. — RELIGION, 58
inscrutable Dumb, i. and grand — CATS, 1
fathom the i. workings of Providence — REPARTEE, 4
insect the Egyptians worshipped an i. — POLITICIANS, 22
insemination Surely you don't mean by unartificial i. — SEX, 49
insensitiveness the greatest deeds require a certain i. — INSENSITIVITY, 3
inside attention to the i. . . . contempt for the outside — BOOKS, 13
insight moment's i. . . . worth a life's experience — EXPERIENCE, 15
insignificance A man of . . . the utmost i. — POLITICIANS, 20
insignificant as i. men as any in England — ARISTOCRACY, 13
insolence a wretch who supports with i. — PATRONAGE, 1
i. is not invective — IMPERTINENCE, 1; PETULANCE, 2
the i. of wealth — WEALTH, 17
insolent their i. and unfounded airs of superiority — FRANCE, 15
insomnia Amor vincit i. — LOVE, 56; SLEEP, 8
inspiration Genius is one per cent i. — GENIUS, 4
Ninety per cent of i. — INSPIRATION, 2
instinct the i. for being unhappy — SORROW, 20
institution Any i. which does not suppose the people good — CORRUPTION, 5
more than a game. It's an i. — CRICKET, 4
institutions working of great i. — BUREAUCRACY, 7
instrument An i. to tickle human ears — MUSIC, 9
there you sit with that magnificent i. between your legs — INCOMPETENCE, 5
The state is an i. . . . of the ruling class — STATE, 5
insufferable It is Oxford that has made me i. — EDUCATION, 6
insult adding i. to injuries — AGGRAVATION, 1
A man should not i. his wife publicly — MARRIAGE, 115
sooner forgotten than an i. — INSULTS, 10
insulted anyone here whom I have not i. — INSULTS, 8
insured you cannot be i. for the accidents . . . most likely to happen — ACCIDENTS, 1

insurrection I. is an art   REVOLUTION, 6
integrate I i. the current export drive   BUSINESS, 3
integrity if I accepted the honour . . . I would not answer for
  the i. of my intellect   TITLES, 3
  I. without knowledge is weak   INTEGRITY, 4; KNOWLEDGE, 23
intellect a feather to tickle the i.   PUNS, 10
  a road . . . that does not go through the i.   EMOTION, 1
  halitosis of the i.   STUPIDITY, 2
  his i. is not replenished   IGNORANCE, 13
  i. is . . . fooled by the heart   EMOTION, 4
  I. is invisible   INTELLECT, 6
  put on I.   WISDOM, 11
  the soul of a martyr with the i. of an advocate   POLITICIANS, 3
  The voice of the i. is a soft one   INTELLECT, 1
  we cannot exclude the i. from . . . any of our functions
     INTELLECT, 3
intellects highest i., like the tops of mountains   INTELLECT, 4
  There is a wicked inclination . . . to suppose an old man decayed
  in his i.   OLD AGE, 23
intellectual an i. . . . mind watches itself   INTELLECTUALS, 5
  artist who's an i.   ARTISTS, 4
  Every i. attitude is latently political   POLITICS, 45
  i., but I found it too difficult   HUMILITY, 9
  i. . . . doesn't know how to park a bike   INTELLECTUALS, 1
  I've been called many things, but never an i.   INTELLECTUALS, 3
  Man is an i. animal   INTELLECT, 2
  The word I. suggests   INTELLECTUALS, 2
  thirdly, i. ability   EDUCATION, 2
intellectuals vanishing race. . . . the i.   INTELLECTUALS, 7
intelligence I. is quickness to apprehend   INTELLIGENCE, 6
  i. is the great polluter   ENVIRONMENT, 4
  The more i. . . . the more . . . one finds original
     INTELLIGENCE, 4
intelligent A really i. man feels what other men . . . know
     INTELLIGENCE, 3
  Each generation imagines itself . . . more i. than the one . . .
  before   AGE, 41
  stupid are cocksure . . . i. full of doubt   DOUBT, 7
  The i. are to the intelligentsia   INTELLIGENCE, 1
intelligentsia intelligent are to the i.   INTELLIGENCE, 1
intelligible to aim at being i.   COMMUNICATION, 2
intended i. to give you some advice   ADVICE, 7
intensity excellence of every art is its i.   ARTS, 5
intent A truth that's told with bad i.   TRUTH, 13
  prick the sides of my i.   AMBITION, 16
intercourse dreary i. of daily life   OPTIMISM, 29
interest How can I take an i. in my work   ENTHUSIASM, 1
  It is not my i. to pay the principal, nor my principle to pay the
  i.   BORROWING, 10
interested always been i. in people   MISANTHROPY, 2
  The average man is . . . i. in a woman who is i. in him
     SEXES, 7
interests all these great i. entrusted to the shaking hand
     POLITICIANS, 75
intérieur Vive l'i.   HISTORY, 27; HUMOUR, 52
intermission Pleasure is . . . i. of pain   PLEASURE, 27
international I. Woman's Day   RUSSIAN REVOLUTION, 1
  science is essentially i.   SCIENCE, 6
interrupted Mr Wordsworth is never i.   INTERRUPTIONS, 3
interval an opera without an i., or an i. without an opera
     OPERA, 5
intolerably I would grow i. conceited   CONCEIT, 19
intoxicate you won't i. with one glass someone who has . . .
  drunk . . . a . . . barrel   EXPERIENCE, 10
intoxicated A man who exposes himself when he is i.
     DRUNKENNESS, 15
  No, thank you, I was born i.   DRUNKENNESS, 18
intoxication best of life is . . . i.   DRUNKENNESS, 10
intrigue the i. of a Greek of the lower empire   INSULTS, 13
introduce let me i. you to that leg of mutton   INTRODUCTIONS, 1
introduction I could buy back my i.   INTRODUCTIONS, 2
intrudes society, where none i.   NATURE, 3
invade when religion is allowed to i. . . . private life
     RELIGION, 38
invalid an invaluable permanent i. called Bunbury   DECEPTION, 7
invasion no stand can be made against i. by an idea   IDEAS, 2
  the long-promised i.   WORLD WAR II, 8
invective insolence is not i.   IMPERTINENCE, 1; PETULANCE, 2
invent it would be necessary to i. Him   GOD, 48
inventing Prolonged . . . reviewing of books involves constantly
  i. reactions   CRITICISM, 34
invention A long poem is a test of i.   POETRY, 22
  Woman's virtue is man's greatest i.   SEXES, 17

inventions All one's i. are true   POETRY, 14
investment There is no finer i.   CHILDREN, 18
  To bear many children is considered . . . an i.   CHILDREN, 22
inviolable the i. shade   HOPE, 4
invisible the only evil that walks I.   HYPOCRISY, 12
invisibly electricity was dripping i.   SCIENCE, 32
invited People were not i. – they went there   PARTIES, 4
involuntary It was i.. They sank my boat   MODESTY, 2
inward They flash upon that i. eye   SOLITUDE, 15
inwards he looked i., and found her   SHAKESPEARE, 5
Ireland a picture of a relief map of I.   APPEARANCE, 4
  English should give I. home rule   IRELAND, 13
  How's poor ould I., and how does she stand?   IRELAND, 1
  I. is the old sow   IRELAND, 7
  I'll not forget old I.   HOMESICKNESS, 1
  I never met anyone in I. who understood the Irish question
     IRELAND, 5
  I would have liked to go to I.   IRELAND, 16
  Now I. has her madness   POETRY, 3
  The moment . . . I. is mentioned   IRELAND, 15
  The problem with I.   IRELAND, 9
Irish All races have . . . economists, with the exception of the I.
     IRISH, 5
  as I. as Black Americans   IRISH, 6
  I. . . . devotion to higher arts   IRISH, 5
  That is the I. Question   IRELAND, 4
  The English and Americans dislike only *some* I.   IRISH, 3
  The I. and the Jews have a psychosis   IRISH, 2; JEWS, 1
  The I. are a fair people   IRISH, 7
  The I., . . . are needed in this cold age   IRISH, 4
  The I. don't know what they want   IRISH, 8
Irishman Put an I. on the spit   IRISH, 1
iron An i. curtain   COLD WAR, 2
  blood and i.   POWER POLITICS, 2
  I do, and I also wash and i. them   HOUSEWORK, 5
  muscles . . . Are strong as i. bands   OCCUPATIONS, 9
  rule them with a rod of i.   LEADERSHIP, 2
  the i. enter into his soul!   BITTERNESS, 3
  the i. has entered his soul   NONCOMMITMENT, 3
  will wink and hold out mine i.   COWARDICE, 8
ironies Life's Little I.   LIFE, 26
irons two i. in the fire   PRUDENCE, 5
irrelevant the most i. thing in nature   FAMILY, 22
irreproachable compulsory and i. idleness   ARMY, 3
irresponsible better to be i. and right   RESPONSIBILITY, 5;
     RIGHTEOUSNESS, 6
Ishmaelites I. . . . will not publicly eat human flesh uncooked in
  Lent   CANNIBALISM, 2
Islam In some remote regions of I.   MODESTY, 5
  I. unashamedly came with a sword   RELIGION, 45
island No man is an I.   SOCIETY, 3
islands less known by the British than these selfsame British I.
     BRITISH, 2
isle Kelly from the I. of Man   ABSENCE, 8
  this sceptred i.   ENGLAND, 34
isles The i. of Greece   EUROPE, 3
Israel When I. was in Egypt land   OPPRESSION, 1
Italian as sensible as baseball in I.   OPERA, 4
  I speak . . . I. to women, French to men   LANGUAGE, 6
Italians The I. will laugh at me   HITLER, 4
Italy A man who has not been in I.   TRAVEL, 14
  I. a paradise for horses   NATIONALITY, 3
itch The i. of disputing will prove the scab of churches
     RELIGION, 64
  the i. of literature   WRITING, 20
iteration i. of nuptials   MARRIAGE, 37
itself Love seeketh not i. to please   LOVE, 27
ivy The holly and the i.   CHRISTMAS, 5

J

jab Man, . . . had been created to j. the life out of Germans
     WAR, 97
J'accuse *J.*   ACCUSATION, 3
Jack Damn you, J. – I'm all right   SELFISHNESS, 3
  J. and Jill went up the hill   NURSERY RHYMES, 24
  J. of all trades   OCCUPATIONS, 3
  J. Sprat could eat no fat   NURSERY RHYMES, 25
  Little J. Horner Sat in the corner   NURSERY RHYMES, 29
  the house that J. built   NURSERY RHYMES, 57
jackals J. piss at their foot   BOOKS, 16
Jackson J. standing like a stone wall   DETERMINATION, 4
Jacob Talk to him of J.'s ladder   PRACTICALITY, 4

the traffic of J.'s ladder — HEAVEN, 12
jail being in a ship is being in a j. — BOATS, 9
jam J. today, and men aren't at their most exciting — PROMISES, 6
The rule is, j. tomorrow and j. yesterday — PROMISES, 3
James The work of Henry J. has always seemed divisible — WRITERS, 16
Jane if ever I was to have a dozen girls, I'd call 'em all J. — NAMES, 7
Time's up for Sir John, an' for little Lady J. — PARTING, 7
January dreadful pictures of J. and February — WINTER, 3
Janvier Generals J. and Février — WINTER, 3
Japan There was a young man of J. — VERBOSITY, 1
Japanese The J. have perfected good manners — PLACES, 19
jaundiced with the j. eye — PASSION, 8
jaw-jaw To j. is better than to war-war — DIPLOMACY, 5
jazz J. . . . people hear it through their feet — MUSIC, 44
The basic difference between classical music and j. — MUSIC, 34
the J. Age . . . became less and less an affair of youth — AGE, 24
jealous a j. God — GOD, 10
Art is a j. mistress — ART, 7
jealousy of j.; It is the green-ey'd monster — JEALOUSY, 3
the ear of j. heareth all things — JEALOUSY, 1
Jeepers J. Creepers — EYES, 2
jeering laughing and j. at everything . . . strange — ENGLISH, 30
jeers j. at Fate — ENVY, 2
Jeeves J. coughed one soft, low, gentle cough — ANALOGY, 5
like P. G. Wodehouse dropping J. — WRITERS, 45
Jefferson when Thomas J. dined alone — TALENT, 4
jelly Out vile j. — EYES, 3
Jemmy Young J. Grove on his death-bed lay — LOVE, 13
Jenny J. kissed me when we met — KISSING, 2
Jericho by faith the walls of J. fell down — FAITH, 2
Jerusalem J. — ENGLAND, 4
J. the golden — PLACES, 13
Till we have built J. — ENGLAND, 4
jest a fellow of infinite j. — MOURNING, 8
A j.'s prosperity lies in the ear — HUMOUR, 26
glory, j., and riddle of the world — HUMAN CONDITION, 12
Life is a j. — LIFE, 25
jesting j. Pilate — TRUTH, 10
Jesus All hail, the power of J.' name — CHRISTIANITY, 37
Gentle J. — HUMILITY, 13
If J. Christ were to come to-day — BELIEF, 4
J. loves me – this I know — RELIGION, 55
J. was . . . a first-rate political economist — CHRISTIANITY, 38
when J. was born in Bethlehem of Judaea — CHRISTMAS, 9
jeunesse Si j. savait — AGE, 22
Jew An American is either a J., or an anti-Semite — AMERICANS, 9
difficult for a J. to be converted — JEWS, 6
Einstein – the greatest J. since Jesus — SCIENTISTS, 6
hated by every anti-semite as if I were a J. — PREJUDICE, 7
Hath not a J. eyes — EQUALITY, 18
I'm a coloured, one-eyed J. — DISABILITY, 2; RACE, 6
I'm not really a J.; just J.-ish — HALF MEASURES, 2
I was born of Christian race, And not a Heathen, or a J. — RELIGION, 56
neither J. nor Greek — CHRISTIANITY, 7
no intellectual society can flourish where a J. feels . . . uneasy — JEWS, 7
No J. was ever fool enough to turn Christian — RELIGION, 66
Pessimism is a luxury that a J. never can allow himself — JEWS, 9
jewellery Don't ever wear artistic j. — JEWELLERY, 1
j. . . . wrecks a woman's reputation — JEWELLERY, 1
jewelry she did not remember . . . her j. — PRUDENCE, 9
jewels a capital bosom to hang j. upon — APPEARANCE, 13
Jewish A J. man with parents alive — JEWS, 13
a total solution of the J. question — NAZISM, 1
best that is in the J. blood — JEWS, 8
I'm not really a Jew; just' J. — HALF MEASURES, 2
Jewry Modern Physics is an instrument of J. — SCIENCE, 1
Jews But spurn the J. — JEWS, 5
King of the J. — CHRISTMAS, 9
not enough prisons . . . in Palestine to hold all the J. — JEWS, 10
The Irish and the J. have a psychosis — IRISH, 2; JEWS, 1
The J. and Arabs should . . . settle their differences — RELIGION, 3
the J. bring the unlike into the heart of every milieu — JEWS, 15
the J. have made a contribution to the human condition out of all proportion — JEWS, 14
The J. have produced . . . Christ, Spinoza, and myself — CONCEIT, 16
To choose The J. — JEWS, 4

Jill Jack and J. went up the hill To fetch a pail of water — NURSERY RHYMES, 24
jingo We don't want to fight, but, by j. if we do — PATRIOTISM, 14
jo John Anderson my j. — NOSTALGIA, 4
Joan greasy J. doth keel the pot — WINTER, 6
Job J. endured everything – until his friends came — ENDURANCE, 8
job Being a husband is a whole-time j. — MARRIAGE, 19
If two men on the same j. agree — AGREEMENT, 8
We have finished the j. — WORLD WAR II, 28
we will finish the j. — WORLD WAR II, 9
jockey the . . . cup is given to the j. — INJUSTICE, 5
Joe Hungry J. collected lists of fatal diseases — ILLNESS, 5
John D'ye ken J. Peel — HUNTING, 4
J. Anderson my jo — NOSTALGIA, 4
J. Brown's body — MEMORIALS, 4
Matthew, Mark, Luke and J. — BLESSING, 1
Time's up for Sir J., an' for little Lady Jane — PARTING, 7
Johnny J. head-in-air — IDEALISM, 5
J.-the-bright-star — REALISM, 5
J. underground — IDEALISM, 5
Little J. Head-in-Air — CHILDREN, 24
Johnson Dr J.'s morality was as English . . . as a beefsteak — ENGLAND, 19
Dr J.'s sayings — WRITERS, 19
That great Cham of literature, Samuel J. — WRITERS, 42
There is no arguing with J. — WRITERS, 15
join He's gone to j. the majority — DEATH, 17
will you j. the dance — DANCING, 2
joined what . . . God hath j. together, let not man put asunder — MARRIAGE, 24
joke a j. with a double meaning — HUMOUR, 2
A rich man's j. is always funny — FLATTERY, 3
good deed to forget a poor j. — HUMOUR, 4
Housekeeping ain't no j. — HOUSEWORK, 1
The coarse j. proclaims — HUMOUR, 17
jokes A different taste in j. is a . . . strain on the affections — HUMOUR, 10
A j. a very serious thing — HUMOUR, 6
Forgive . . . my little j. on Thee — PRAYER, 12
He cannot bear old men's j. — OLD AGE, 19
I don't make j. — GOVERNMENT, 24
joking My way of j. is to tell the truth — TRUTH, 37
jolly There was a j. miller — HAPPINESS, 4
Joneses drag the J. down to my level — ONE-UPMANSHIP, 1
Joseph Here lies J., who failed in everything he undertook — FAILURE, 3
journalism Christianity, . . . but why j. — CHRISTIANITY, 2; JOURNALISM, 3
J. is the only job that requires no degrees — JOURNALISM, 7
j. . . . . keeps us in touch with the ignorance of the community — JOURNALISM, 27
J. largely consists of saying 'Lord Jones is dead' — JOURNALISM, 8
J. . . . the challenge of filling . . . space — JOURNALISM, 26
j. what will be grasped at once — JOURNALISM, 9; LITERATURE, 1
journalist the functions of the modern j. — JOURNALISM, 10
You cannot hope to bribe or twist . . . the British j. — JOURNALISM, 28
journalists J. say a thing that they know isn't true — JOURNALISM, 4
journey I prepare for a j. . . . as though for death — TRAVEL, 19
long j. . . . . must bid the company farewell — LAST WORDS, 50
One of the pleasantest things in the world is going on a j. — SOLITUDE, 8; TRAVEL, 12
Our j. had advanced — DEATH, 41
Jowett First come I; my name is J. — ACADEMICS, 2
joy a father's j. — EXPECTATION, 6
A thing of beauty is a j. for ever — BEAUTY, 22
let j. be unconfined — DANCING, 1
One j. scatters a hundred griefs — HAPPINESS, 9
Silence is the perfectest herald of j. — SILENCE, 12
Strength through j. — NAZISM, 2
'tis little j. To know I'm farther off from heav'n — INNOCENCE, 6
we could never learn to be brave . . . if there were only j. — ENDURANCE, 7
you'll give happiness and j. to many other people — COMPOSERS, 1
joys For present j. — PLEASURE, 11
Hence, vain deluding J. — PLEASURE, 23
j. of parents are secret — FAMILY, 8
jubilee hurrah! we bring the J. — GLORY, 1
judge A j. is not supposed to know — JUSTICE, 18
A j. knows nothing — LAW, 1

j. not, that ye be not judged | JUDGMENT, 2
J. not the play | JUDGMENT, 8
j. of a man by his foes | JUDGMENT, 7
Never j. from appearances | APPEARANCES, 3
salutary check for a j. | LAWYERS, 8
shallow people . . . do not j. by appearances | APPEARANCES, 22
judged they were j. every man according to their works | JUDGMENT, 4
why is my liberty j. of another man's conscience? | CONSCIENCE, 1; FREEDOM, 3
judgement day of j. | DEATH, 31
Don't wait for the Last J. | DOOMSDAY, 4
Force, if unassisted by j., collapses | JUDGMENT, 9
let my will replace reasoned j. | AUTHORITARIANISM, 4
no one complains of his j. | JUDGMENT, 12
Perhaps your fear in passing j. | COURAGE, 3
your j. will probably be right | JUDGMENT, 11
Your representative owes you . . . his j. | JUDGMENT, 6
judgment That fellow would vulgarize the day of j. | VULGARITY, 3
'Tis the Last J.'s fire | DOOMSDAY, 3
judgments 'Tis with our j. as our watches | OPINIONS, 3
jug Little brown j., don't I love thee! | DRUNKENNESS, 5
Julia Whenas in silks my J. goes | CLOTHES, 8
Jumblies far and few, Are the lands where the J. live | NONSENSE, 18
jump We'd j. the life to come | ENDING, 5
Juno fierce J.'s never-forgetting anger | ENDURANCE, 23
jury how should you like . . . to be tried before a j. | JUSTICE, 12
Trial by j. itself . . . will be a delusion | JUSTICE, 5
jury-men wretches hang that j. may dine | JUSTICE, 19
just it raineth on the j. | JUSTICE, 4
rain on the j. and on the unjust | ENEMIES, 3
justice A lawyer has no business with . . . j. or injustice | JUSTICE, 13
In a free society the state . . . administers j. among men | STATE, 3
J. is open to all | JUSTICE, 17
J. is such a fine thing | JUSTICE, 15
J. is the means by which established injustices are sanctioned | INJUSTICE, 6
J. is the . . . perpetual wish | JUSTICE, 14
j. must be seen to be more or less done | JUSTICE, 23
J. should not only be done | JUSTICE, 10
Let j. be done | JUSTICE, 7
moderation in the pursuit of j. is no virtue | EXCESS, 4
Recompense injury with j. | KINDNESS, 1
Revenge is a kind of wild j. | REVENGE, 4
She's like the old line about j. | OSTENTATION, 5
the female character . . . has no sense of j. | • WOMEN, 61
The j. of my quarrel | JUSTICE, 16
The love of j. in most men | JUSTICE, 20
The place of j. is a hallowed place | JUSTICE, 1
You never expected j. from a company | BUSINESS, 17
justification carry its j. in every line | LITERATURE, 2
justified No man is j. in doing evil | EXPEDIENCY, 5
justify thought only to j. their injustices | HUMAN NATURE, 20
justifying men are more interested in . . . j. themselves | MOTIVE, 6

K

Kaiser she took down the signed photograph of the K. | WAR, 122
kaleidoscope a girl with k. eyes | IMAGINATION, 7
Karl had Marx been Groucho instead of K. | HUMOUR, 3
Keats K.'s vulgarity with a Public School accent | CRITICISM, 26
Mister John K. five feet high | ADMIRATION, 5
Shelley and K. were . . . up to date in . . . chemical knowledge | POETS, 15; SCIENCE, 15
keen out of a k. city in the sky | MOON, 1
Satire should, like a polished razor k. | SATIRE, 2
keep if they k. on saying it . . . it will be true | JOURNALISM, 4
K. up appearances | APPEARANCES, 11
they should k. who can | POWER, 23
keeper am I my brother's k. | MURDER, 2
a poacher a k. turned inside out | OCCUPATIONS, 8
k. stands up | FOOTBALL, 2
Kelly Has anybody here seen K. | ABSENCE, 8
ken When a new planet swims into his k. | DISCOVERY, 5
Kennedy the kind of nation . . . President K. died for | AMBITION, 10
Kennedys I don't feel the attraction of the K. at all | INSULTS, 28

Kent K., sir – everybody knows K. | ENGLAND, 14
Kentucky For the old K. Home far away | HOMESICKNESS, 3
kept Married women are k. women | MARRIAGE, 99
kettle Polly put the k. on | NURSERY RHYMES, 39
Kew I am His Highness' dog at K. | DOGS, 11
key lawyers . . . have taken away the k. of knowledge | LAWYERS, 5
turn the k. deftly | SLEEP, 11
keys don't go around hitting too many white k. | MUSIC, 10
the k. of the kingdom of heaven | CHURCH, 1
khaki One black, and one white, and two k. | RACE, 1
Khatmandu one-eyed yellow idol to the north of K. | MOURNING, 5
kick every ass thinks he may k. at him | WRITERS, 34
if I were under water I would scarcely k. | MELANCHOLY, 6
k. you out, but . . . never let you down | EDUCATION, 58
kicked anyone who slapped us . . . would get his head k. off | REVENGE, 12
he had known many k. down stairs | PROMOTION, 2
Saint Preux never k. the fireirons | IMPERFECTION, 6
kid Here's looking at you, k. | ADMIRATION, 2
kiddies k. have crumpled the serviettes | ETIQUETTE, 1
kidnapped my parents finally realize that I'm k. | EXPEDIENCY, 1
kids Cleaning your house while your k. are still growing | HOUSEWORK, 4
kill a man can't step up and k. a woman | CHIVALRY, 2
churchmen fain would k. their church | CLERGY, 13
good to k. an admiral | EXAMPLE, 9
He would k. Himself | HUMAN CONDITION, 4
K. a man, and you are a murderer | KILLING, 7
k. a wife with kindness | KINDNESS, 4
K. everyone, and you are a god | KILLING, 7
K. not the goose | GREED, 2
k. the patient | REMEDIES, 1
k. us for their sport | DESTINY, 18
Next week . . . I'll k. myself | SUICIDE, 7
only k. you once | COMFORT, 1
The bullet that is to k. me | ARROGANCE, 6
The word 'revolution' is a word for which you k. | REVOLUTION, 10
they k. you a new way | PROGRESS, 10
thou shalt not k. | GOD, 10
To k. a human being | KILLING, 4
When you have to k. a man | DIPLOMACY, 7
killed He must have k. a lot of men | WEALTH, 20
I don't mind your being k. | ROYALTY, 20
killing K. Is the ultimate | KILLING, 5
k. time Is only . . . another of the multifarious ways By which Time kills us | TIME, 32
More ways of k. a cat | CHOICE, 4
no difference between . . . k. and making decisions that . . . kill | KILLING, 6
The man is k. time | TIME, 7
To save a man's life against his will is . . . k. him | KILLING, 3
kills Time is a great teacher, but . . . k. all its pupils | TIME, 10
time quietly k. them | TIME, 12
Who k. a man k. a reasonable creature | BOOKS, 24
Yet each man k. the thing he loves | KILLING, 8
kilt The k. is an unrivalled garment for fornication | SCOTS, 9
kind a k. parent . . . or a merciless step-mother | NATURE, 13
being k. all the sad world needs | KINDNESS, 5; RELIGION, 63
charity suffereth long, and is k. | CHARITY, 1
He was a vicious man, but very k. | CHARACTER, 13
I love thee for a heart that's k. | KINDNESS, 2
try to be k. | ACADEMICS, 3
kindle the sole purpose of human existence is to k. a light | EXISTENCE, 3
kindly a young person, who . . . marries or dies, is sure to be k. spoken of | HUMAN NATURE, 1
the deities so k. | DESTINY, 16
kindness a cup o' k. yet | FRIENDSHIP, 13
full o' th' milk of human k. | KINDNESS, 3
greetings where no k. is | OPTIMISM, 29
kill a wife with k. | KINDNESS, 4
recompense k. with k. | KINDNESS, 1
set a high value on spontaneous k. | FRIENDSHIP, 19
the k. of strangers | CHARITY, 22
unremembered acts Of k. and of love | KINDNESS, 6
kindred Like k. drops, then mingled | MOUNTAINS, 1
king A constitutional k. must learn to stoop | MONARCHY, 13
A k. is a thing | MONARCHY, 17
a k. may make a nobleman | CHIVALRY, 3
A k. of shreds and patches | INFERIORITY, 6

lasses Come l. and lads, get leave of your dads
MERRYMAKING, 1
lassie I love a l.
LOVE, 76
last as if it were the l.
LIFE, 33
Die, . . . the l. thing I shall do
LAST WORDS, 42
Don't wait for the L. Judgement
DOOMSDAY, 4
each day that has dawned is your l.
PRESENT, 10
'Fan vaulting' . . . belongs to the 'L.-supper-carved-on-a-peach-stone'
ARCHITECTURE, 5
for the l. time in my life, Your Humble Servant
ARGUMENTS, 16
hoping that it will eat him l.
DIPLOMACY, 6
I hope it will l.
SUSPENSE, 1
I shall be the l. to go out
COURAGE, 7
l. act crowns the play
PLAYS, 8
l. day but one
EDUCATION, 30
l. words . . . name of – Michael Angelo
ARTISTS, 6
Nice guys finish l.
GOOD, 4
the feeling that I could l. for ever
YOUTH, 4
the l. shall be first
MERIT, 3
The l. straw
ENDURANCE, 2
the l. time that I will take part as an amateur
FUNERALS, 2
there is no l. or first
EQUALITY, 6
'Tis the L. Judgment's fire
DOOMSDAY, 3
we are all on our l. cruise
MORTALITY, 18
What is it that will l.
TIME, 33
late Better never than l.
PROMPTNESS, 3
Never too l. to learn
AGE, 1
One doesn't recognize . . . the really important moments . . . until it's too l.
REGRET, 4
So l. into the night
DEBAUCHERY, 4
We have met too l.. You are too old
INFLUENCE, 4
later It is l. than you think
TIME, 27
Latin A gentleman need not know L.
EDUCATION, 33
A silly remark can be made in L.
LANGUAGE, 5
Don't quote L.
SPEECHES, 5
small L., and less Greek
CLASSICS, 5
the Devil knows L.
LANGUAGE, 16
The word is half Greek and half L.
TELEVISION, 5
We were taught . . . L. and Greek
CLASSICS, 9
Latins L. are tenderly enthusiastic
PLACES, 4
latrine used as a l. by some small animal
DRUNKENNESS, 2
laudanum Whipping and abuse are like l.
CRUELTY, 5
laugh I make myself l. at everything
LAUGHTER, 4
L. and grow fat
LAUGHTER, 1
L., and the world laughs with you
LAUGHTER, 9
L. before breakfast
LAUGHTER, 2
l. before one is happy
LAUGHTER, 7
Make 'em l.
WRITING, 27
not to l. at human actions
UNDERSTANDING, 9
old man who will not l.
AGE, 48; WISDOM, 19
The Italians will l. at me
HITLER, 4
laughable most schemes of political improvement are very l.
POLITICS, 34
laugh-at-with Auden was someone you could l.
POETS, 24
laughed Few women care to be l. at
RIDICULE, 2
on which one has not l.
LAUGHTER, 6
When the first baby l.
FAIRIES, 2
laughing Happiness is no l. matter
HAPPINESS, 27
l. and jeering at everything . . . strange
ENGLISH, 30
One cannot be always l. at a man
MEN, 1
one may die without ever l.
LAUGHTER, 7
the most fun I ever had without l.
SEX, 2
to read the death of Little Nell without l.
DICKENS, 3; INSENSITIVITY, 4
laughter I said of l., it is mad
LAUGHTER, 5
I was convulsed with l.
INSULTS, 26
L. is pleasant
LAUGHTER, 8
L. is the best medicine
LAUGHTER, 3
present l.
PRESENT, 13
Launcelot Sir L. saw her visage, but he wept not greatly
SORROW, 11
laundries Land of L.
TRAVEL, 4
laundry Give me a l.-list
MUSIC, 37
The general idea, . . . in any first-class l.
NEGLECT, 2
laurel Caesar's l. crown
POWER, 6
laurel-bough burned is Apollo's l.
DEATH, 76
laurels once more, O ye l.
TREES, 9
The l. all are cut
ENDING, 4
Laurie for bonnie Annie L.
LOVE AND DEATH, 1
law Born under one l.
HUMAN CONDITION, 8
Common L. of England
LAW, 15
each man must struggle, lest the moral l. become . . . separated
MORALITY, 1

Every l. is a contract
LAW, 22
Ignorance of the l.
LAW, 23
I have forgotten more l. than you ever knew
INSULTS, 27
No brilliance is needed in the l.
LAW, 19
Nor l., nor duty bade me fight
FLYING, 4
nothing is l. that is not reason
LAW, 21
Order is heaven's first l.
ORDER, 2
Or lesser breeds without the L.
BOASTS, 4
Prisons are built with stones of L.
HYPOCRISY, 4
rich men rule the l.
LAW, 13
The army ages men sooner than the l.
ARMY, 6
the greater part of the l. is learning to tolerate fools
LAW, 18
The l. does not concern itself
LAW, 5
the l. is a ass –
LAW, 9
The L. is the true embodiment
LAW, 11
The l. of dislike for the unlike
JEWS, 15
The L. of England is a very strange one
LAW, 8
the L. of the Yukon
SURVIVAL, 4
the magnificent fair play of the British criminal l.
JUSTICE, 6
The majestic egalitarianism of the l.
EQUALITY, 8
the moral l.
WONDER, 3
There is no universal l.
SPONTANEITY, 3
There's one l. for the rich
CLASS, 1
The rise in the . . . employed is governed by Parkinson's L.
WORK, 14
th' windy side of the l.
LAW, 24
laws I know not whether L. be right
IMPRISONMENT, 10
L. are generally found to be nets
LAW, 25
L. are like cobwebs
LAW, 27
L. are like spider's webs
LAW, 26
L. grind the poor
LAW, 13
l. were like cobwebs
LAW, 6
L. were made to be broken
LAW, 20
Nature's l. lay hid in night
SCIENTISTS, 8
rules of the game are what we call the l. of Nature
GOD, 27
the individual subject . . . 'has nothing to do with the l. but to obey them.'
LAW, 16
the l. of poetic truth and poetic beauty
POETRY, 2
the repeal of bad or obnoxious l.
LAW, 14
Where l. end, tyranny begins
TYRANNY, 5
who are . . . not governed by the same l.
POVERTY AND WEALTH, 4
you do not make the l. but . . . are the wives . . . of those who do
WOMEN, 35
lawyer A client is fain to hire a l. to keep from . . . other lawyers
LAWYERS, 6
A l. has no business with . . . justice or injustice
JUSTICE, 13
A l. never goes
LAWYERS, 2
A l.'s opinion
LAWYERS, 3
He that is his own l.
LAWYERS, 1
No poet ever interpreted nature . . . as a l. interprets truth
LAW, 12
lawyers L. are the only persons in whom ignorance . . . is not punished
LAWYERS, 4
woe unto you, l.
LAWYERS, 5
laxative sweet l. of Georgian strains
SPRING, 2; STATELY HOMES, 1
lay I never would l. down my arms
PATRIOTISM, 22
L. your sleeping head
SLEEP, 3
Lazarus L. . . . laid at his gate, full of sores
POVERTY AND WEALTH, 2
lazy be efficient if you're going to be l.
LAZINESS, 1
There are no ugly women, only l. ones
BEAUTY, 30
lead L., kindly Light
FAITH, 16
leader A l. who doesn't hesitate . . . is not fit to be a l.
LEADERSHIP, 6
I have to follow them, I am their l.
LEADERSHIP, 5
leadership men do not approach to l.
LEADERSHIP, 1
leap a great l. in the dark
LAST WORDS, 32
A l. over the hedge
PRAYER, 7
And twenty-nine in each l. year
NURSERY RHYMES, 56
one giant l. for mankind
SPACE, 1
leapt Into the dangerous world I l.
BIRTH, 3
learn The life so short, the craft so long to l.
MORTALITY, 12
we could never l. to be brave . . . if there were only joy
ENDURANCE, 7
What we have to l. to do
LEARNING, 1
learned A l. man is an idler
EDUCATION, 47
He was naturally l.
SHAKESPEARE, 5
I am . . . of the opinion with the l.
AGREEMENT, 2
people . . . never have l. anything from history
EXPERIENCE, 14
the l. roast an egg
FOOD, 39
learning A little l. is a dangerous thing
KNOWLEDGE, 29

M

half of the nation is m. ENGLISH, 33
he ceased to be m. he became merely stupid REMEDIES, 10
he first makes m. MADNESS, 4
I said of laughter, it is m. LAUGHTER, 5
let me not be m. MADNESS, 11
M. about the boy LOVE, 42
M. as the mist and snow MADNESS, 14
M., bad, and dangerous to know BYRON, 3
Men will always be m. MADNESS, 13
Never go to bed m. ANGER, 3
The dog, . . . Went m. and bit the man DOGS, 7
We all are born m. MADNESS, 3
who turns m. for a reason MADNESS, 2
madam M. I may not call you TITLES, 6
madame All I could think of . . . was: *M. Bovary* NOVELS, 11
Call me m. TITLES, 7
maddest those who think they can cure them are the m.
MADNESS, 13
made Annihilating all that's m. OBLIVION, 3
Don't you think I was m. for you LOVE, 52
Do you know who m. you? CREATION, 12
Little Lamb, who m. thee? CREATION, 8
we're all m. the same SIMILARITY, 4
Madeira We're from M. EUROPE, 16
madeleine The taste was that of the little crumb of m.
MEMORY, 11
mademoiselle A m. from Armenteers FRANCE, 13
Madison How were the receipts today in M. Square Garden
LAST WORDS, 5
madman If a m. were to come into this room
SELF-PRESERVATION, 6
The m. . . . has lost everything except his reason MADNESS, 3
Thou call'st me m. INSULTS, 1
madness devil's m. – War WAR, 105
Great Wits . . . to M. near alli'd GENIUS, 3
M. in great ones MADNESS, 10
M. need not be all breakdown MADNESS, 6
Now Ireland has her m. POETRY, 5
maestro Music, M., Please MUSIC, 26
maggot how to create a m. RELIGION, 41
magic men mistook m. for medicine MEDICINE, 7
That old black m. SUPERNATURAL, 10
magicians if the way had not been prepared by m.
SCIENCE, 26
magistrate Obscenity . . . happens to shock some elderly . . . m.
PRUDERY, 4
suppose . . . the m. corruptible CORRUPTION, 5
Magna Charta M. is such a fellow MONARCHY, 8
magnanimity in victory, m. WAR AND PEACE, 3
magnificent some m. myth PROPAGANDA, 3
there you sit with that m. instrument between your legs
INCOMPETENCE, 5
magnifique *c'est m., mais* WAR, 10
Mahomet If the hill will not come to M. ADAPTABILITY, 2
maid Being an old m. is like death by drowning MARRIAGE, 52
like a moth, the simple m. WOMEN, 33
The m. was in the garden NURSERY RHYMES, 47
Where are you going to, my pretty m. NURSERY RHYMES, 67
maiden A simple m. in her flower PURITY, 3
I've a neater, sweeter m. DISCONTENT, 6
many a rose-lipt m. NOSTALGIA, 11
That kissed the m. all forlorn NURSERY RHYMES, 57
maids And pretty m. all in a row GARDENS, 1
Three little m. from school CHILDREN, 23
majesty A sight so touching in its m. LONDON, 14
Her M. is not a subject ROYALTY, 12
her M. . . . must not . . . look upon me as a source of income
TAXATION, 5
Her M.'s Opposition OPPOSITION, 1
How can I . . . dislike a sex to which Your M. belongs
MISOGYNY, 2
If Her M. stood for Parliament POLITICS, 60
Ride on! ride on in m.! CHRISTIANITY, 32
This earth of m. ENGLAND, 34
When I invented the phrase 'His M.'s Opposition'
OPPOSITION, 3
major-general very model of a modern M. KNOWLEDGE, 15
majority A m. is always the best repartee MAJORITY, 2
Fools are in a terrible . . . m. FOOLISHNESS, 15
He's gone to join the m. DEATH, 17
I am certain that we will win the election with a good m.
SELF-CONFIDENCE, 6

No candidate . . . elected ex-president by such a large m.!
DEFEAT, 7
One on God's side is a m. GOD, 40
the damned, compact, liberal m. MAJORITY, 4
the great silent m. MAJORITY, 5
The m. has the might MAJORITY, 3; MINORITY, 2
majors scarlet M. WAR, 99
make a Scotsman on the m. SCOTS, 2
Love? I m. it constantly SEX, 39
The white man knows how to m. everything CHARITY, 18
maker he adores his m. CONCEIT, 7; SELF-MADE MEN, 1
making He is very fond of m. things FUTILITY, 6
If you get the English people into the way of m. kings
ROYALTY, 22
maladies all the m. and miseries WORK, 6
Medical men . . . call all sorts of m. . . . by one name
MEDICINE, 1
There are m. we must not seek to cure REMEDIES, 10
malaise Wembley, adj. Suffering from a vague *m.* HUMOUR, 36
male especially the m. of the species MEN, 5
In the sex-war thoughtlessness is the weapon of the m.
SEXES, 6
m. and female created he them CREATION, 6; MANKIND, 5
more deadly than the m. WOMEN, 40
preserve one last m. thing MASCULINITY, 2
malice M. is like a game of poker NASTINESS, 9
malicious God is subtle but he is not m. GOD, 20
malign rather m. oneself EGOTISM, 7
malignant the only part of Randolph that was not m.
INSULTS, 37
malignity that peculiar m. . . . characteristic of apostates
BETRAYAL, 5
malingering Neurosis has an absolute genius for m.
NEUROSIS, 1
malt M. does more than Milton ALCOHOL, 29
mamas The Last of the Red-Hot M. SINGERS, 3
mammon M. wins his way where Seraphs might despair
MATERIALISM, 4
man A 'Grand Old M.' OLD AGE, 25
all animals were created . . . for the use of m. ANIMALS, 17
a m. can die but once DEATH, 105
a m. has no reason to be ashamed of having an ape for his
grandfather EVOLUTION, 9
A m. in the house is worth two MEN, 10
A m. is always seeking for happiness MARRIAGE, 47
A m. is only as old as the woman AGE, 36
A m. . . . is *so* in the way MEN, 3
A m. must serve his time to every trade CRITICS, 2
A m. of straw WOMEN, 1
A m.'s a m. for a' that MEN, 2
A m. should never put on his best trousers FREEDOM, 20
A m. should . . . own he has been in the wrong MISTAKES, 10
A m. with God GOD, 30
an old m. in a dry month AGE, 21
apparel oft proclaims the m. CLOTHES, 16
'A was a m., take him for all in all ADMIRATION, 15
big m. has no time FAME, 9
Brutus is an honourable m. HONOUR, 5
condition of m. is a condition of war HUMAN CONDITION, 9
England expects every m. will do his duty DUTY, 3
Every m. is as Heaven made him CHARACTER, 4
Every m. is wanted HUMAN CONDITION, 7
Every m. meets his Waterloo DEFEAT, 6
figure of 'The Reasonable M.' LAW, 15
follies which a m. regrets the most MISTAKES, 12
for m. or beast WEATHER, 10
Glory to M. in the highest MANKIND, 30
God made the woman for the m. WOMEN, 68
Go West, young m. EXPLORATION, 2
hate ingratitude more in a m. INGRATITUDE, 6
He is a m. of brick CHARACTER, 23
he owes not any m. RIGHTEOUSNESS, 7
He was her m., but he done her wrong UNFAITHFULNESS, 1
I care not whether a m. is Good WISDOM, 11
If a m. be gracious and courteous COURTESY, 2
If a m. stays away from his wife MARRIAGE, 42
I love not M. the less NATURE, 3
I said to the m. who stood at the gate of the year FAITH, 11
I see a m. hurrying along – to what PURPOSE, 5
I sing of arms and the m. ENDURANCE, 23
It is good to know what a m. is UNDERSTANDING, 2
It takes . . . twenty years to make a m. LOVE, 102
Kelly from the Isle of M. ABSENCE, 8

that the m. willingly concede to slaves — SLAVERY, 1
We are the m. at the moment — POWER, 16
masturbation m. of war — WAR, 87
M.: the primary sexual activity — SEX, 45
match man who had missed the last home m. — FOOTBALL, 5
material that which was most m. in the postscript — LETTER-WRITING, 2
materialistic Christianity is the most m. of all great religions — CHRISTIANITY, 42
only really m. people . . . Europeans — MATERIALISM, 14
materialists all the books with which m. have pestered the world — SOUL, 11
mates moves, and m., and slays — DESTINY, 6
mathematics Angling may be said to be . . . like the m. — FISHING, 4
As far as the laws of m. refer to reality — MATHEMATICS, 3
How are you at M. — MATHEMATICS, 6
Let no one ignorant of m. enter here — MATHEMATICS, 9
M. may be defined as the subject — MATHEMATICS, 12
M. possesses not only truth, but supreme beauty — MATHEMATICS, 14
M. . . . possesses . . . supreme beauty — MATHEMATICS, 11
Pure m. consists entirely of assertions — MATHEMATICS, 13
quite lawful for a Catholic woman to avoid pregnancy by . . . m. — CONTRACEPTION, 3
spirit of delight . . . in m. — MATHEMATICS, 10
Matilda You'll come a-waltzing, M. — PLACES, 14
matinée Robert Houdin who . . . invented the . . . theater m. — THEATRE, 12
mating Only in the m. season — ANIMALISM, 6
matrimony critical period in m. is breakfast-time — MARRIAGE, 66
it jumps from . . . love to m. — WOMEN, 11
m., which I always thought a highly overrated performance — MARRIAGE, 51
matter It is not much m. which we say — UNITY, 11
M. . . . a convenient formula — PHILOSOPHY, 11
proverb is much m. decorated — SAYINGS, 4
We die – does it m. when? — DEATH, 114
Women represent . . . m. over mind — SEXES, 26
mattering Art . . . can go on m. once it has stopped hurting — ART, 5
matters Nothing m. very much — TRIVIALITY, 1
Matthew M., Mark, Luke and John — BLESSING, 7
maturing Do you think my mind is m. late — AGE, 39
maturity m. is only a short break in adolescence — AGE, 23
Maud Come into the garden, M. — INVITATIONS, 2
maunder m. and mumble — PUBLIC, 8
mausoleums designing m. for his enemies — HATE, 6
Max If M. gets to Heaven — BUSINESS, 21
maxim A new m. is often a brilliant error — SAYINGS, 5
we have got The M. Gun — POWER POLITICS, 1
May And after April, when M. follows — MONTHS, 6
as fresh as is the month of M. — CHARACTER, 3
darling buds of M. — COMPLIMENTS, 4
Do spring M. flowers — MONTHS, 12
got through the perils of winter till at least the seventh of M. — WINTER, 8
I'm to be Queen o' the M. — MERRYMAKING, 5
the merry month of M. — MONTHS, 5
wish a snow in M. — SUITABILITY, 6
maze Life is a m. — LIFE, 18
mazes The melting voice through m. running — MUSIC, 29
MCC where M. ends and the Church of England begins — CHURCH, 4
McCarthyism M. is Americanism — POLITICS, 47
McGregor Don't go into Mr M.'s garden — CAUTION, 4
me Besides Shakespeare and m., who do you think there is? — CONCEIT, 15
between m. and the sun — REPARTEE, 2
My thought is m. — THINKING, 8
we never talk about anything except m. — CONCEIT, 21
meal A m. without flesh — FOOD, 1
meals Any two m. at a boarding-house — FOOD, 28
mean Down these m. streets — COURAGE, 5
He nothing common did or m. — EXECUTION, 16
He who meanly admires m. things is a Snob — SNOBBERY, 7
it means just what I choose it to m. — MEANING, 3
She was a woman of m. understanding — INSULTS, 3
'you should say what you m.,' the March Hare went on — MEANING, 1
meaner A patronizing disposition . . . has its m. side — CHARACTER, 7
motives m. than your own — MOTIVE, 1

meanest the m. . . . deeds require spirit and talent — INSENSITIVITY, 3
the m. of his creatures Boasts two soul-sides — HYPOCRISY, 5
meaning Even when poetry has a m. — POETRY, 19; UNDERSTANDING, 5
Literature is simply language charged with m. — LITERATURE, 15
Nature has never put the fatal question as to the m. of their lives — PURPOSE, 4
The least of things with a m. is worth more . . . than the greatest — MEANING, 5
meannesses some m. . . . too mean even for man — SEXES, 21
means Errors look so very ugly in persons of small m. — POVERTY AND WEALTH, 5
I shall have to die beyond my m. — EXTRAVAGANCE, 5
Let us all be happy, and live within our m. — BORROWING, 12
m. just what I choose it to mean — MEANING, 3
Private M. is dead — PUNS, 20
We are living beyond our m. — ECOLOGY, 5
measles Love is like the m. — LOVE, 69
Love's like the m. — LOVE, 70
measure M. still for M. — JUSTICE, 22
Shrunk to this little m. — DEATH, 98
measureless caverns m. to man — PLEASURE, 8
meat man loves the m. in his youth — AGE, 51
one man is appointed to buy the m. — MONARCHY, 17
One man's m. — DIFFERENCE, 3
Some hae m., and canna eat — FOOD, 11
The public buys its opinions as it buys its m. — PUBLIC, 7
meddling He was m. too much in my private life — PSYCHIATRY, 11
medical m. attention – a dog licked me — MEDICINE, 6
medicine men mistook magic for m. — MEDICINE, 7
miserable have no other m. — HOPE, 10
medieval disillusionments in the lives of the m. saints — DECLINE, 9
mediocre A best-seller is the gilded tomb of a m. talent — BOOKS, 37
Some men are born m. — MEDIOCRITY, 4
Titles distinguish the m. — TITLES, 10
Women want m. men — MEDIOCRITY, 5
mediocrity It isn't evil . . . but m. — MEDIOCRITY, 7
m. . . . always at its best — MEDIOCRITY, 1
M. knows nothing higher — MEDIOCRITY, 3; TALENT AND GENIUS, 2
supreme expression of the m. — RUSSIA, 6
Mediterranean All my wife has ever taken from the M. — PHILISTINISM, 6
medium The m. is the message — COMMUNICATION, 3
meek Blessed are the m. — HUMILITY, 1
humble and m. are thirsting for blood — HUMILITY, 7
m. and lowly in heart — CHRISTIANITY, 18
m. and mild — HUMILITY, 13
the highest authority for believing that the m. shall inherit the Earth — HUMILITY, 11
The m. do not inherit the earth — HUMILITY, 6
The m. . . . not the mineral rights — WEALTH, 14
Wisdom has taught us to be calm and m. — REVENGE, 10
meet M. on the stairs — SUPERSTITION, 2
never the twain shall m. — OPPOSITES, 3
The only way for writers to m. — WRITERS, 11
Two may talk . . . yet never really m. — FRIENDSHIP, 14
We only part to m. again — FAITHFULNESS, 4
meeting as if I was a public m. — POLITICIANS, 76
My life's been a m., Dad — BUREAUCRACY, 3
this m. is drunk — DRUNKENNESS, 11
megalomaniac m. . . . seeks to be feared — POWER, 15
melancholy a pleasing fit of m. — MELANCHOLY, 10
hell upon earth . . . in a m. man's heart — MELANCHOLY, 3
M. has her sovran shrine — MELANCHOLY, 8
Most musical, most m. — BIRDS, 9
so sweet as M. — MELANCHOLY, 2
Melba Dame Nellie M. — PATRIOTISM, 12
mellows A tart temper never m. with age — CHARACTER, 11
melodies Heard m. are sweet — MUSIC, 24
melody m. imposes continuity upon the disjointed — MUSIC, 28
melting the races of Europe are m. — AMERICA, 40
melting-pot America is . . . the great M. — AMERICA, 40
member the tongue is a little m. — SPEECH, 5
même plus c'est la m. chose — CONSTANCY, 3
memorandum A m. is written — BUREAUCRACY, 1
memorial executed a m. longer lasting than bronze — MEMORIALS, 5
memories M. are hunting horns — MEMORY, 1
memory Everyone complains of his m. — JUDGMENT, 12

mislead   One to m. the public, another to m. the Cabinet
                                                          GOVERNMENT, 5
misleading   Though analogy is often m.   ANALOGY, 1
miss   A m. is as good   FAILURE, 1
to m. the one before it   TRAVEL, 6
missed   who never would be m.   PUNISHMENT, 8
missiles   We have guided m. and misguided men   WAR, 55
missionary   I would eat a m.   CLERGY, 14
mist   Cicero And . . . Homer were *Mad as the m. and snow*
                                                          MADNESS, 14
The rolling m. came down   DROWNING, 1
mistake   he who never made a m. never made a discovery
                                                          MISTAKES, 14
Live all you can; it's a m. not to   LIFE, 29
Woman was God's *second* m.   WOMEN, 52
mistaken   think it possible you may be m.   MISTAKES, 5
mistakes   An expert . . . knows some of the worst m. that can
be made   EXPERTS, 3
The man who makes no m.   MISTAKES, 9
Young men make great m. in life   YOUTH, 10
mistress   a m., and only then a friend   FRIENDSHIP, 15
A m. should be like a . . . retreat   SEX, 56
Art is a jealous m.   ART, 7
by pointing out to a man his faults of him. m.   IMPERFECTION, 10
Master M. of my passion   LOVE, 116
m. I am ashamed to call you   TITLES, 2
whether I embrace your lordship's principles or your m.
                                                          REPARTEE, 5
why and how I became . . . m. of the Earl of Craven   SEX, 55
mistresses   a better price than old m.   PAINTING, 1
No, I shall have m.   MARRIAGE, 61
one wife and hardly any m.   MARRIAGE, 91
Wives are young men's m.   MARRIAGE, 12
mistrust   M. first impulses   FIRST IMPRESSIONS, 7
mistrusted   If the white man *says* he does, he is instantly . . .
m.   RACISM, 2
mists   Season of m.   AUTUMN, 1
misunderstood   To be great is to be m.   GREATNESS, 7
Mitty   Walter M., the undefeated   EXECUTION, 28
mix   I m. them with my brains   PAINTING, 7
mixed   a m. infant   CHILDREN, 8
not to look like a m. grill   APPEARANCE, 9
mob   do what the m. do   MAJORITY, 1
Our supreme governors, the m.   PUBLIC, 20
mobs   It brings men together in crowds and m. in bar-rooms
                                                          SOCIETY, 9
mock   Let not Ambition m.   POVERTY, 12
M. on, m. on, Voltaire, Rousseau   FUTILITY, 4
mockery   death itself must be . . . a m.   DEATH, 107
mode   Fancy is . . . a m. of memory   IMAGINATION, 2
model   The idea that there is a m. Labour voter, . . . is
patronizing   POLITICS, 36
very m. of a modern Major-General   KNOWLEDGE, 15
models   Rules and m. destroy genius and art   RULES, 2
moderation   astonished at my own m.   MODERATION, 3
M. in all things   MODERATION, 1
m. in the pursuit of justice is no virtue   EXCESS, 4
modern   Imagination without skill gives us m. art   ART, 25
It is so stupid of m. civilization   DEVIL, 8
The m. pantheist not only   PHOTOGRAPHY, 4
modest   and is m. about it   ENGLISH, 1
Be m.! It is the kind of pride least likely to offend MODESTY, 5
modester   People ought to be m.   UNIVERSE, 3
modesty   a woman . . . ought to lay aside . . . m. with her skirt
                                                          SEX, 31
Enough for m.   CLOTHES, 2
I have often wished I had time to cultivate m.   MODESTY, 7
lay aside . . . m. . . . and put it on again with her petticoat
                                                          SEX, 31
There is false m., but there is no false pride   PRIDE, 8
where the Greeks had m., we have cant   CANT, 1
Mohammed   If the mountain will not come to M.
                                                          ADAPTABILITY, 2
moi   *L'État c'est m.*   MONARCHY, 14
mole   Death is still working like a m.   DEATH, 57
Molly   Tonight the American flag floats from yonder hill or M.
Stark sleeps a widow   WAR, 112
moment   a m. of time   LAST WORDS, 17
A m. of time may make us unhappy for ever   SORROW, 8
Every m. one is born   LIFE AND DEATH, 11
Mona   A lotta cats copy the M. Lisa   IMITATION, 1
I have . . . . . . several original M. Lisas   PHOTOGRAPHY, 5
monarch   m. of all I survey   SOLITUDE, 5

monarchy   M. is a strong government   MONARCHY, 1
The m. is a labour-intensive industry   MONARCHY, 24
The m. . . . . oldest profession in the world   ROYALTY, 11
The Sovereign has, under a constitutional m. . . . . three rights
                                                          MONARCHY, 2
They that are discontented under *m.*, call it *tyranny*
                                                          GOVERNMENT, 12
tourists . . . take in the M. . . . with . . . the pigeons   LONDON, 8
Monday   is going to do on M.   HYPOCRISY, 18
M.'s child   CHARACTER, 1; NURSERY RHYMES, 33
Solomon Grundy, Born on a M.   NURSERY RHYMES, 48
money   a bank that would lend m. to such a poor risk
                                                          BORROWING, 2
a licence to print your own m.   BUSINESS, 19
always try to rub up against m.   MONEY, 36
art . . . of draining m.   TAXATION, 9
Brigands demand your m. or your life   WOMEN, 20
Business . . . may bring m., . . . friendship hardly ever does
                                                          MONEY, 5
collect legal taxes from illegal m.   TAXATION, 1
descriptions of m. changing hands   MONEY, 17
easiest way for your children to learn about m.   MONEY, 46
except for large sums of m.   RIDICULE, 2
France is a country where the m. falls apart   FRANCE, 16
Good Samaritan . . . had m. as well   MONEY, 45
He that wants m., means, and content   MONEY, 37
If possible honestly, if not, somehow, make m.   MONEY, 22
If you can . . . count your m. you are not . . . rich man
                                                          WEALTH, 15
innocently employed than in getting m.   MONEY, 25
Just what God would have done if he had the m.   WEALTH, 30
killed a lot of men to have made so much m.   WEALTH, 20
Lack of m.   MONEY, 40
love of m. is the root of all evil   MONEY, 10
m. answereth all things   MONEY, 9
M. can't buy friends   MONEY, 28
m. can't buy me love   MONEY, 28
M. gives me pleasure   MONEY, 8
m. has something to do with life   MONEY, 27
M. is good for bribing yourself   MONEY, 35
M. is like a sixth sense   MONEY, 31
M. is like manure   MONEY, 24
M. is like muck   MONEY, 6
M., it turned out, was exactly like sex   MONEY, 7; SEX, 5
M. . . . . source of anxiety   MONEY, 21
pleasant it is to have m.   MONEY, 16
Put m. in thy purse   MONEY, 39
Some people's m. is merited   MONEY, 33
spiritual snobbery . . . happy without m.   MONEY, 14
the love of m. is the root of all evil   MONEY, 12
The man who leaves m. to charity in his will   BEQUESTS, 3
the poor person . . . thinks m. would help   MONEY, 26
The profession . . . in which one can make no m. without being
ridiculous   WRITING, 28
They had been corrupted by m.   SENTIMENTALITY, 1
they have more m.   WEALTH, 12
time is m.   BUSINESS, 6
To be clever enough to get . . . . m., one must be stupid
                                                          MATERIALISM, 6
to waste my time making m.   MONEY, 4
We all know how the size of sums of m. appears to vary
                                                          MONEY, 23
We haven't the m., so we've got to think   RESEARCH, 3
We've got the ships, we've got the men, we've got the m. too
                                                          PATRIOTISM, 14
what risks you take . . . to find m. in a desk   THEFT, 4
Where large sums of m. are concerned, . . . trust nobody
                                                          MONEY, 15
with m. . . . . they have not got   BORROWING, 4
You can be young without m.   MONEY, 47
monkey   no reason to attack the m. when the organ-grinder is
present   POLITICIANS, 6
the biggest asset the m. possesses   POLITICIANS, 59
monopoly   imperialism is the m. stage of capitalism   POLITICS, 39
Monroe   Marilyn M.'s   FUNERALS, 7
mons   treating the *m. Veneris* as . . . Mount Everest   SEX, 21
monster   jealousy . . . green-ey'd m.   JEALOUSY, 4
Montagu   Mrs M. has dropt me   HURT, 2
Monte Carlo   M.   LUCK, 7
the man who broke the Bank at M.   WEALTH, 16
month   April is the cruellest m.   MONTHS, 8
months   two m. of every year   WEATHER, 8
monument   like Patience on a m.   LOVE, 120

sonnet is a moment's m. — POETRY, 37
The m. sticks like a fishbone — MEMORIALS, 7
monuments Not marble, nor the gilded m. — POETRY, 41
moo You silly m. — INSULTS, 33
moon For years politicians have promised the m. — MOON, 5
If they had said the sun and the m. was gone — BYRON, 2
I saw the new m. late yestreen — MOON, 1; PROPHECY, 1
I see the m., And the m. sees me — BLESSING, 2
moving M. went up the sky — MOON, 2
nothing left remarkable beneath the . . . m. — MOURNING, 11
shine on, shine on, harvest m. — MOON, 6
The m. doth shine as bright as day — NURSERY RHYMES, 6
They danced by the light of the m. — FOOD, 29
th' inconstant m. — UNFAITHFULNESS, 3
We're very wide awake, The m. and I — APPEARANCES, 15
moonlight Look for me by m. — DETERMINATION, 12
moons So sicken waning m. too near the sun — MOON, 4
the m. a balloon — MOON, 3
moral All universal m. principles are idle fancies — MORALITY, 13
each man must struggle, lest the m. law become . . . separated — MORALITY, 1
Everything's got a m. — PURPOSE, 1
it should preach a high m. lesson — PURPOSE, 8
Let us be m. — EXISTENCE, 2
Love is m. even without . . . marriage — LOVE AND MARRIAGE, 3
m. attribute of a Scotsman — SCOTS, 1
M. indignation is in most cases 2 percent m. — MORALITY, 19
m. is what you feel good after — MORALITY, 5
m. or an immoral book — BOOKS, 43
more than a m. duty to speak one's mind — FRANKNESS, 4
one is unhappy one becomes m. — SORROW, 17
The highest possible stage in m. culture — SELF-CONTROL, 2
the m. law — WONDER, 3
The worst government is the most m. — GOVERNMENT, 18
moralist A Scotchman must be a very sturdy m. — SCOTS, 3
no sterner m. than Pleasure — PLEASURE, 7
morality Dr Johnson's m. was as English . . . as a beefsteak — ENGLAND, 19
live for others . . . middle class m. — CLASS, 30
M. consists in suspecting — MORALITY, 15
M. . . . . is herd-morality — MORALITY, 11
M.'s a gesture. . . . learnt from books — MORALITY, 3
M.'s not practical — MORALITY, 3
M. which is based on ideas — MORALITY, 17
new m. . . . . the old immorality condoned — MORALITY, 2
No m. can be founded on authority — MORALITY, 9
periodical fits of m. — MORALITY, 7
This imperative may be called that of M. — MORALITY, 12
two kinds of m. — MORALITY, 14
morals basing m. on myth — MORALITY, 20
If your m. make you dreary — MORALITY, 22
M. are an acquirement — SEXES, 26
men represent . . . mind over m. — FREEDOM, 53
the faith and m. hold Which Milton held — CRITICISM, 20
the m. of a whore, and the manners of a dancing master — MURDER, 4
mordre M. wol out — EXPECTATION, 4
more As I know m. of mankind — BOLDNESS, 2
Oliver Twist has asked for m. — EXPERTS, 5
Specialist – A man who knows m. and m. about less and less — LANGUAGE, 4
take *m*. than nothing — CUSTOM, 1
mores O tempora! O m. — ENDURANCE, 15
morn From m. to night, my friend — DECLINE, 4
From m. To noon he fell — WISDOM, 13
He rose the morrow m. — DAY, 10
the opening eye-lids of the m. — BED, 5
mornin' nice to get up in the m. — UNFAITHFULNESS, 1
morning Early one m., just as the sun was rising — FAME, 6
I awoke one m. — MARRIAGE, 73
I'm getting married in the m. — DAY, 5
M. in the Bowl of Night — DAY, 7
Oh, what a beautiful m.! — TRANSIENCE, 17
she has lived . . . the space of one m. — GOD, 6
that . . . turneth the shadow of death into the m. — BEGINNING, 9
'Tis always m. somewhere — WORRY, 7
morrow take . . . no thought for the m. — MORTALITY, 1
mortal All men are m. — MORTALITY, 8
I was not unaware that I had begotten a m. — ARROGANCE, 11
men think all men m. — STATE, 1
that *M. God* — DOCTORS, 3
The doctor found, . . . Her last disorder m.

we have been m. enemies ever since — ENEMIES, 5
mortality kept watch o'er man's m. — MORTALITY, 21
M., behold and fear — MORTALITY, 2
mortals A novelist is, like all m. — WRITERS, 29
We m. cross the ocean — HUMAN CONDITION, 4
what fools these m. be — FOOLISHNESS, 18
Moscow don't march on M. — WAR, 70
Moses he saw his role as being that of M. — LEADERSHIP, 4
there arose not a prophet . . . like unto M. — PROPHECY, 2
most The M. may err as grosly — PUBLIC, 11
mostest I got there fustest with the m. — WAR, 37
mote the m. that is in thy brother's eye — CRITICISM, 5; JUDGMENT, 3
moth like a m., the simple maid — WOMEN, 33
The desire of the m. for the star — HUMOUR, 37
mother And Her M. Came Too — FAMILY, 31
as is the m., so is her daughter — FAMILY, 10
Dead! and . . . never called me m. — DEATH, 123
I am old enough to be – in fact am – your m. — AGE, 37
If poverty is the m. of crime, stupidity is its father — CRIME, 4
I was born . . . at an extremely tender age because my m. needed a fourth at meals — BIRTH, 6
I wished to be near my m. — BIRTH, 8
May you be the m. of a bishop! — BLESSING, 3
M. is far too clever to understand — PREJUDICE, 2
M. is the dead heart of the family — WOMAN'S ROLE, 1
M. of the Free — BRITAIN, 5
My m., drunk or sober. — PATRIOTISM, 4
the m. of parliaments — ENGLAND, 5
this war, . . . which did not justify the sacrifice of a single m.'s son — WAR, 82
motherhood wifehood and m. are but incidental relations — WOMEN, 66
mother-in-law as the man said when his m. died — FAMILY, 21
What a marvellous place to drop one's m. — FAMILY, 15
mothers Come m. and fathers Throughout the land — CHANGE, 6
O! men with m. and wives — WOMEN, 37
women become like their m. — SEXES, 25
mothers-in-law Two m. — FAMILY, 36
motives m. meaner than your own — MOTIVE, 1
motors was good for General M. — BUSINESS, 22
mould If you cannot m. yourself — TOLERANCE, 3
Nature made him, and then broke the m. — INDIVIDUALITY, 2
mountain A m. in labour shouted so loud — DISAPPOINTMENT, 4
hardly be a beast or a fool alone on a great m. — SOLITUDE, 9
If the m. will not come to Mohammed — ADAPTABILITY, 2
Land of the m. and the flood — SCOTLAND, 7
never see another m. — MOUNTAINS, 2
mountains all faith, so that I could remove m. — CHARITY, 5
England's m. green — ENGLAND, 4
highest intellects, like the tops of m. — INTELLECT, 9
if the Swiss had designed these m. — MOUNTAINS, 4; SWITZERLAND, 4
M. interposed Make enemies of nations — MOUNTAINS, 1
m. look on Marathon — EUROPE, 4
M. . . . . the beginning and the end of all natural scenery — MOUNTAINS, 3
M. will heave in childbirth — DISAPPOINTMENT, 3
Two voices . . . one is of the sea, One of the m. — FREEDOM, 54
when men and m. meet — GREATNESS, 2
mourn countless thousands m. — CRUELTY, 2
it is chiefly our own deaths that we m. for — FUNERALS, 3
To m. a mischief that is past — REGRET, 16
mourning I'm in m. for my life — MOURNING, 4
in m. . . . for the world — MOURNING, 15
tedium is the very basis of m. — BOREDOM, 4
We met . . . Dr Hall in such very deep m. — MOURNING, 1
What we call m. for our dead — MOURNING, 6
with my m. . . . and new periwig — APPEARANCE, 29
mouse a silly little m. will be born — DISAPPOINTMENT, 3
He bought a crooked cat, which caught a crooked m. — NURSERY RHYMES, 52
leave room for the m. — EXCESS, 6
she brought forth a m. — DISAPPOINTMENT, 4
The m. ran up the clock — NURSERY RHYMES, 15
mouse-trap If a man make a better m. — FAME, 8
moustache A kiss without a m. — KISSING, 4
a man outside with a big black m. — APPEARANCE, 24
Being kissed by a man who didn't wax his m. — KISSING, 3
his nicotine eggyellow weeping walrus Victorian m. — APPEARANCE, 35
mouth A politician is a statesman . . . with an open m. — POLITICIANS, 68

butter wouldn't melt in her m.   ACTORS, 7
God be in my m., And in my speaking   GOD, 1
Keep your m. shut and your eyes open   CAUTION, 6
mouth-brothels Great restaurants are . . . nothing but m.   FOOD, 42
move But did thee feel the earth m.   SEX, 19
in him we live, and m., and have our being   GOD, 5
I will m. the earth   TECHNOLOGY, 1
The great affair is to m.   TRAVEL, 25
movement I want to be a m.   SOLITUDE, 11
We are the true peace m.   PEACE, 1
moves m., and mates, and slays   DESTINY, 6
Yet it m.   ASTRONOMY, 2
movie This is a m., not a lifeboat   EQUALITY, 19
movies Thanks to the m., gunfire has always sounded unreal   CINEMA, 9
moving In home-sickness you must keep m.   HOMESICKNESS, 7
m. Moon went up the sky   MOON, 2
people under suspicion are better m.   JUDGMENT, 10
The M. Finger writes   DESTINY, 7
Mozart The sonatas of M. are unique   MUSIC, 39
when M. was my age   AGE, 32
MPs The prospect of a lot Of dull M.   POLITICIANS, 30
much m. . . . said on both sides   OBJECTIVITY, 1
So little done, so m. to do   LAST WORDS, 51
so m. owed by so many to so few   WORLD WAR II, 7
muchness Much of a m.   MEDIOCRITY, 8
muck Money is like m.   MONEY, 4
sing 'em m.   PLACES, 11
mud One sees the m., and one the stars   OPTIMISM, 21
muddle a beginning, a m., and an end   NOVELS, 8
muddle-headed He's a m. fool   FOOLISHNESS, 12
muddy The hunter for aphorisms . . . has to fish in m. water   SAYINGS, 1
Muffet Little Miss M. Sat on a tuffet   NURSERY RHYMES, 30
multiplied Entities should not be m.   SIMPLICITY, 6
multiply be fruitful and m.   CREATION, 6; MANKIND, 5
multitude long dresses, . . . cover a m. of shins   CLOTHES, 18
The m. is always in the wrong   PUBLIC, 17
this massed m. of silent witnesses to . . . war   WAR, 40
multitudes I contain m.   SELF, 21
mum M.'s the word   SECRECY, 6
They fuck you up, your m. and dad   FAMILY, 23
mumble maunder and m.   PUBLIC, 8
mundi Sic transit gloria m.   GLORY, 3
murder Divorce? Never. But m. often   MARRIAGE, 114
love and m. will out   LOVE, 39; MURDER, 5
m. back into its rightful setting – in the home   MURDER, 7
M. considered as one of the Fine Arts   MURDER, 6
M. . . . had a mask like Castlereagh   MURDER, 12
M., like talent, seems . . . to run in families   MURDER, 9
M. most foul   MURDER, 11
m. shrieks out   MURDER, 13
Never m. a man who is committing suicide   SUICIDE, 12
So it was m.   DEATH, 79
Sooner m. an infant in its cradle   DESIRE, 2
murdered I m. my grandmother this morning   INATTENTION, 4
murderer Kill a man, and you are a m.   KILLING, 1
murmur live m. of a summer's day   SUMMER, 2
muscular His Christianity was m.   CHRISTIANITY, 23
Muse To the Greeks the M. gave native wit   CLASSICS, 4
mused Lancelot m. a little space   BEAUTY, 38
museum the m. of this world   MASCULINITY, 2
museums The Arab . . . is more philosophical than . . . curators of the m.   MUSEUMS, 1; PRACTICALITY, 3
mushroom a supramundane m.   NUCLEAR WEAPONS, 10
Fame is sometimes like unto a . . . m.   FAME, 10
to stuff a m.   HOUSEWORK, 2
music a martyr to m.   MUSIC, 48
Architecture . . . is frozen m.   ARCHITECTURE, 10
art constantly aspires towards . . . m.   ART, 19
capable of being well set to m.   MUSIC, 2
chord of m.   MUSIC, 35
food in m.   MUSIC, 25
God tells me how he wants this m. played   MUSIC, 50
Having verse set to m.   POETRY, 48
how potent cheap m. is   MUSIC, 15
How sour sweet m. is   ORDER, 4
I don't write modern m.   MUSIC, 45
If all the arts aspire to the condition of m.   SCIENCE, 31
If m. be the food of love   MUSIC, 42
I'll set it to m.   MUSIC, 37
In m., the punctuation is absolutely strict   ACTING, 7
making m. throatily and palpitatingly sexual   MUSIC, 22
M. and women I cannot but give way to   MUSIC, 33
man that hath no m. in himself   MUSIC, 41
M. begins to atrophy   ARTS, 7
M. . . . confirm human loneliness   MUSIC, 17
M. creates order out of chaos   MUSIC, 28
m. critics. . . . small and rodent-like with padlocked ears   CRITICS, 15
M. has charms to soothe   MUSIC, 14
M. helps not   MUSIC, 1
M. is not written in red, white and blue   MUSIC, 27
M. is the arithmetic of sounds   MUSIC, 16
M. is your own experience   MUSIC, 32
M., Maestro, Please   MUSIC, 26
M. that gentlier on the spirit lies   MUSIC, 47
M., when soft voices die   MEMORY, 17
never merry when I hear sweet m.   MUSIC, 40
no more m. in them   MUSICIANS, 1
Poetry . . . set to more or less lascivious m.   POETRY, 28
silence sank like m.   SILENCE, 3
The English may not like m.   MUSIC, 5
The hills are alive with the sound of m.   MUSIC, 19
The m. teacher came twice each week   MUSIC, 3
thy chosen m., Liberty   FREEDOM, 54
Van Gogh's ear for m.   INSULTS, 40
musical cashiers of the M. Banks   MONEY, 11
Most m., most melancholy   BIRDS, 9
music-hall M. songs provide the dull with wit   STUPIDITY, 7
musicologist A m. . . . can read music but can't hear it   MUSIC, 7
Mussolini Hitler was a nuisance. M. was bloody   POLITICS, 44
must Genius does what it m.   TALENT AND GENIUS, 3
Is m. a word to be addressed to princes   IMPERTINENCE, 2
muttering the m. grew to a grumbling   ANIMALS, 6
mutton Alice – M.; M. – Alice   INTRODUCTIONS, 1
I could no longer stand their eternal cold m.   ENGLAND, 32
myriad-minded m. Shakespeare   SHAKESPEARE, 2
myself deliver me from m.   SELF, 5
I am always with m.   SELF, 15
I have always disliked m.   SELF, 6
I know m.   SELF-KNOWLEDGE, 3
I like to go by m.   SOLITUDE, 8; TRAVEL, 12
I've over-educated m.   DEBAUCHERY, 5
not only witty in m.   HUMOUR, 25
The Jews have produced . . . Christ, Spinoza, and m.   CONCEIT, 16
mysteries disciples . . . mark its ways and note . . . its m.   LUCK, 7
mysterious God moves in a m. way   GOD, 18
the ancient cathedrals – grand, wonderful, m.   RELIGION, 46
mystery a riddle wrapped in a m. inside an enigma   RUSSIA, 1
Growth is a greater m. than death   AGE, 34
Happiness is a m. like religion   HAPPINESS, 7
In m. our soul abides   SOUL, 2
mystic The m. sees the ineffable   PSYCHIATRY, 7
myth A m. is, of course, not a fairy story   MYTHS, 2
basing morals on m.   MORALITY, 14
some magnificent m.   PROPAGANDA, 1
myths Science must begin with m.   MYTHS, 1; SCIENCE, 29

N

nails I used to bite my n.   FAME, 16
naive the n. forgive   FORGIVENESS, 15
naked a n. Duke of Windlestraw addressing a n. House of Lords   NAKEDNESS, 2
a pretty girl who n. is   NAKEDNESS, 3
I can't stand a n. light bulb   VULGARITY, 5
n. into the conference chamber   NUCLEAR WEAPONS, 2; WEAPONS, 1
No woman so n. as . . . underneath her clothes   NAKEDNESS, 4
Our ingress . . . Was n. and bare   LIFE, 32
Poor n. wretches   WEATHER, 20
The exception is a n. ape   MANKIND, 18
they were both n.   WOMEN, 15
nakedness N. is uncomely   NAKEDNESS, 1
name a good n. is better than precious ointment   VIRTUE, 3
And lo! Ben Adhem's n. led all the rest   SUPERIORITY, 5
Good n. in man and woman   REPUTATION, 6
his n. shall be called, Wonderful, Counsellor   CHRISTMAS, 6
How I loathe that other with my n.   DENIAL, 2
I remember your n. perfectly   SPOONERISMS, 2
local habitation and a n.   POETRY, 40

No, Groucho is not my real n. NAMES, 4
Oh liberty! . . . What crimes are committed in thy n.
EXECUTION, 27; FREEDOM, 44
People you know, yet can't quite n. OLD AGE, 24
rose by any other n. NAMES, 6
signing his n. and forgetting to write the letter INSULTS, 4
the n. of which was Beautiful ARCHITECTURE, 2
thou shalt not take the n. of . . . God in vain GOD, 10
two or three . . . gathered together in my n. CHURCH, 2
What's in a n. NAMES, 6
When I pass my n. in such large letters FAME, 22
name-dropper One must not be a n. SNOBBERY, 6
names No n., no pack-drill GOSSIP, 3
naming Today we have n. of parts WEAPONS, 4
Napoleon ashes of N. INDIFFERENCE, 6
N. OFFICERS, 16
the N. of crime CRIME, 3
narcissist megalomaniac differs from the n. POWER, 15
nastier she could have found anything n. to say NASTINESS, 7
nasty how n. the nice people can be NASTINESS, 6
Something n. in the woodshed EVIL, 9
nation America became top n. HISTORY, 28
An army is a n. within a n. ARMY, 4
A n. is not in danger ECONOMICS, 10
a n. of amateurs BRITISH, 8
dedicate this n. to the policy of the good neighbor CHARITY, 15
England is a n. of shopkeepers ENGLISH, 28
he is the sworn foe of our n. PUBLISHING, 4
I will make of thee a great n. JEWS, 3
n. . . . fall victim to a big lie LYING, 8
n. had the lion's heart CHURCHILL, 5
No n. is fit to sit in judgement DIPLOMACY, 10
No n. was ever ruined by trade BUSINESS, 5
n. shall not lift up sword against n. WAR AND PEACE, 2
n. shall rise against n. WAR, 7
N. shall speak peace PEACE, 15
the English are . . . the least a n. of pure philosophers
ENGLISH, 5
the kind of n. . . . President Kennedy died for AMBITION, 10
the kind of n. that President Roosevelt hoped for AMBITION, 10
nationality My n. is French NORMALITY, 2
Other people have a n. IRISH, 2; JEWS, 1
nations Commonwealth of N. BRITISH EMPIRE, 5
extends over many n. and three continents EXPERIENCE, 12
If people behaved in the way n. do GOVERNMENT, 32
languages are the pedigree of n. LANGUAGE, 14
The day of small n. has long passed away NATIONS, 1
The great n. have always acted like gangsters DIPLOMACY, 13
The n. which have put mankind and posterity most in their debt
NATIONS, 2
Two n. POVERTY AND WEALTH, 4
native My n. Land – Good Night DEPARTURE, 4
my own, my n. land HOMESICKNESS, 6
to appear considerable in his n. place FAME, 12
white man . . . looks into the eyes of a n. RACE, 13
natives Britons were only n. HISTORY, 26
natural First feelings are always the most n. FIRST
IMPRESSIONS, 5
It is n. to die DEATH, 22
n. false teeth TEETH, 3
Nothing prevents us from being n. SPONTANEITY, 4
N. Selection EVOLUTION, 5
'twas N. to please CHARACTER, 6
naturally Though I am not n. honest HONESTY, 9
nature Accuse not N., she hath done her part
RESPONSIBILITY, 9
All N. wears one universal grin NATURE, 9
Allow not n. more than n. needs NECESSITY, 5
a noble n., . . . treats . . . a serious subject POETRY, 3
but N. more NATURE, 3
Consistency is contrary to n. CONSTANCY, 2
drive out n. with a pitchfork HUMAN NATURE, 9
fortress built by N. ENGLAND, 34
Friend . . . masterpiece of N. FRIENDS, 7
God and N. then at strife NATURE, 15
Human n. is so well disposed HUMAN NATURE, 1
I got disappointed in human n. HUMAN NATURE, 6
I have learned To look on n. EXPERIENCE, 22
In n. there are neither rewards nor punishments NATURE, 11
It is a wonderful case of n. imitating art ACTORS, 10
Let N. be your Teacher NATURE, 20
Little we see in N. that is ours WASTE, 3
N. abhors a vacuum NATURE, 14

N. admits no lie NATURE, 4
new sights of N. made me rejoice NATURE, 7
N. has left this tincture TYRANNY, 8
N. has never put the fatal question as to the meaning of their
lives PURPOSE, 4
N. is but a name for an effect NATURE, 6
N. is creeping up ARROGANCE, 8
N. is often hidden HUMAN NATURE, 4
n. is the art of God NATURE, 1
N. is usually wrong NATURE, 16
N. is very consonant and conformable NATURE, 12
N. made him, and then broke the mould INDIVIDUALITY, 6
N., . . . must be obeyed HUMAN NATURE, 5
N. never did betray NATURE, 18
not formed by n. to bear ENDURANCE, 4
N. remains NATURE, 17
N.'s ancient power was lost DECLINE, 11
N.'s handmaid, art NATURE, 8
n.'s law HELP, 7
N.'s laws lay hid in night SCIENTISTS, 8
o'erstep not the modesty of n. ACTION, 10
one of N.'s Gentlemen CHIVALRY, 7
one of the forces of n. GREATNESS, 10
rules of the game are what we call the laws of N. GOD, 27
science . . . is . . . the interplay between n. and ourselves
NATURE, 10
secret of the arts is to correct n. ARTS, 8
the most irrelevant thing in n. FAMILY, 22
the spectacles of books to read n. SHAKESPEARE, 5
to see the absurd n. of Englishmen ENGLISH, 30
True wit is n. to advantage dress'd HUMOUR, 21
unassuming common-place Of N. FLOWERS, 13
We need more understanding of human n. HUMAN NATURE, 11
you can't call yourself a great work of n. INSULTS, 38
natures Men's n. are alike HABIT, 4
naught N. so sweet as Melancholy MELANCHOLY, 2
nauseate I n. walking COUNTRYSIDE, 1
Navee Ruler of the Queen's N. OFFICERS, 6
navy There were gentlemen and . . . seamen in the n. of
Charles the Second NAVY, 3
Nazi N. Germany had become a menace to all mankind
NAZISM, 3
Nazis In Germany, the N. came for the Communists NAZISM, 4
near I wished to be n. my mother BIRTH, 8
nearer N., my God, to thee RELIGION, 1
the n. you are to God PROTESTANTISM, 3
nearest the n. run thing you ever saw WAR, 124
nearsighted don't raise your hands because I am also n.
DISABILITY, 1
neat round, n., not gaudy GARDENS, 9
necessary Government, . . . is but a n. evil GOVERNMENT, 21
necessities disregard for the n. of existence CIVILIZATION, 9
we will dispense with its n. LUXURY, 3
necessity I find alone N. Supreme NECESSITY, 8
N. is the mother NECESSITY, 2
N. is the plea for every infringement of human freedom
NECESSITY, 4
N. knows no law NECESSITY, 7
no virtue like n. NECESSITY, 6
neck A short n. denotes a good mind APPEARANCE, 33
England will have her n. wrung like a chicken WORLD WAR II, 30
equipping us with a n. BOLDNESS, 3
go to the bottom with my principles round my n.
EXPEDIENCY, 2
my n. is very short EXECUTION, 19
Some n. WORLD WAR II, 12
the Roman people had but one n. RUTHLESSNESS, 1
necking Whoever named it n. SEX, 28
neckties men wore their beards, like they wear their n.
APPEARANCE, 18
Ned no more work for poor old N. DEATH, 50
need An artist . . . produces things that people don't n.
ARTISTS, 11
reason not the n. NECESSITY, 5
Thy n. is yet greater than mine SELF-DENIAL, 2
needle easier for a camel to go through the eye of a n.
WEALTH, 8
needs N. must NECESSITY, 3
to each according to his n. MARXISM, 4
negation Capitalist production begets . . . its own n.
CAPITALISM, 9
negative Europe is the unfinished n. AMERICA, 26
N. Capability DOUBT, 6

neglect A little n. may breed mischief NEGLECT, 1
he devotes to the n. of his duties NEGLECT, 4
negligent Celerity . . . admired . . . by the n. IMPETUOSITY, 3
Negro One of the things that makes a N. unpleasant to white
folk RACISM, 3
Negroes revenge by the culture of the N. MUSIC, 31
neiges les n. d'antan NOSTALGIA, 22
neighbor I have had no real gratification . . . more than my n.
LAST WORDS, 64; WEALTH, 28
neighbour better mouse-trap than his n. FAME, 8
death . . . had been his next-door n. DEATH, 94
Death is my n. now DEATH, 45
Do not love your n. as yourself SELF, 13
It's a recession when your n. UNEMPLOYMENT, 2
love thy n. as thyself LOVE, 26
told men to love their n. HUNGER, 3
neighbours fear of what the n. might say SUICIDE, 3
improper thoughts about . . . n. MORALITY, 4
make sport for our n. RIDICULE, 1
neither better if n. of us had been born REGRET, 9
Nell to read the death of Little N. without laughing DICKENS, 3;
INSENSITIVITY, 4
Nelly let not poor N. starve LAST WORDS, 12
Nelson keep the N. touch PATRIOTISM, 20
N., born in a fortunate hour OFFICERS, 11
The N. touch OFFICERS, 10
nerve called a n. specialist because it sounds better
PSYCHIATRY, 12
nerves It destroys one's n. to be amiable every day
MARRIAGE, 46
nervous One of the symptoms of approaching n. breakdown
WORK, 20
nest broods a n. of sorrows MARRIAGE, 108
nets Laws are generally found to be n. LAW, 25
nettle stroke a n., And it stings you for your pains DECISION, 1
nettles apt to be overrun with n. MIND, 8
neurosis N. has an absolute genius for malingering NEUROSIS, 1
N. is the way of avoiding non-being NEUROSIS, 3
neurotic Psychiatrists classify a person as n. PSYCHIATRY, 10
neurotics Everything great in the world is done by n.
NEUROSIS, 2
neutrality 'positive n.' is a contradiction in terms POLITICS, 48
never Better n. than late PROMPTNESS, 3
I n. would lay down my arms PATRIOTISM, 22
Love? I make it constantly but I n. talk about it SEX, 39
N., n., n., n. MOURNING, 9
our people have n. had it so good WEALTH, 18
Than n. to have loved at all LOVE, 126
nevermore Quoth the Raven, 'N.' EVIL, 12
Nevershit like you was Lady N. AFFECTATION, 1
new He that will not apply n. remedies INNOVATION, 1
He was dull in a n. way POETS, 19
He was the Messiah of the n. age POLITICIANS, 65
n. book is published, read an old one BOOKS, 30
n. deal for the American people AMERICA, 28
N. roads: n. ruts PROGRESS, 4
Revolution is . . . the setting-up of a n. order REVOLUTION, 4
something n. out of Africa NOVELTY, 8
There are no n. truths NOVELTY, 7
there is no n. thing under the sun NOVELTY, 1
we shall find something n. NOVELTY, 10
We stand today on the edge of a n. frontier BEGINNING, 11
You suddenly understand something . . . in a n. way
LEARNING, 6
Youth is something very n. YOUTH, 3
new-found-land my n. LOVE, 47
newness Americans have been conditioned to respect n.
AMERICANS, 11
news Bad n. travels fast DISASTER, 1
Literature is n. LITERATURE, 14
No n. is good n. OPTIMISM, 6
Nothing is n. until it has appeared in The Times NEWSPAPERS, 7
n. that's fit to print NEWSPAPERS, 8
only n. until he's read it. After that it's dead NEWSPAPERS, 13
when a man bites a dog that is n. JOURNALISM, 6
newspaper good n., . . . is a nation talking to itself
JOURNALISM, 18
I read the n. avidly JOURNALISM, 5
Once a n. touches a story, the facts are lost JOURNALISM, 17
Reading someone else's n. NEWSPAPERS, 4
With the n. strike on OBITUARIES, 1
newspapers I'm with you on the free press. It's the n.
JOURNALISM, 24

life, . . . happens almost exclusively in n. JOURNALISM, 1
N. always excite curiosity JOURNALISM, 14
We live under a government of men and . . . n.
GOVERNMENT, 23; JOURNALISM, 21
Newton God said, Let N. be SCIENTISTS, 8
Newtons the souls of five hundred . . . N. SCIENTISTS, 4;
WRITERS, 10
New York N. is a small place AMERICA, 39
N. . . . that unnatural city . . . where every one is an exile
AMERICA, 15
Niagara one wouldn't live under N. INSULTS, 9
nice Be n. to people on your way up PRUDENCE, 10
how nasty the n. people can be NASTINESS, 6
N. guys finish last GOOD, 4
Sugar and spice And all that's n. NURSERY RHYMES, 65
Nicely-Nicely what N. dies of will be over-feeding GREED, 8
nicest English people . . . are surely the n. people in the world
ENGLISH, 21
Nicholas St N. soon would be there CHRISTMAS, 13
Nick Satan, N., or Clootie DEVIL, 6
nickname n. is the heaviest stone NAMES, 3
nicotine his n. eggyellow weeping walrus Victorian moustache
APPEARANCE, 35
nigger Catch a n. by his toe NURSERY RHYMES, 11
niggers He's gone whar de good n. go DEATH, 50
night An infant crying in the n. HUMAN CONDITION, 18
calm passage . . . across many a bad n. SUICIDE, 4
Come to me in the silence of the n. NOSTALGIA, 18
Do not go gentle into that good n. DEATH, 117
From morn to n., my friend ENDURANCE, 15
Gwine to run all n. HORSES, 6
ignorant armies clash by n. WAR, 2
It ain't a fit n. out WEATHER, 10
money in a desk by n. THEFT, 4
moonless n. in the small town RELIGION, 50
Morning in the Bowl of N. DAY, 5
N. and day LOVE, 95
Nature's laws lay hid in n. SCIENTISTS, 8
Oft in the stilly n., Ere Slumber's chain NOSTALGIA, 14
only one man . . . can count on steady work – the n. watchman
THEATRE, 2
perils . . . of this n. DANGER, 3
real dark n. of the soul SOUL, 6
returned home the previous n. SCIENCE, 3
Ships that pass in the n. TRANSIENCE, 16
So late into the n. DEBAUCHERY, 4
sound of revelry by n. MERRYMAKING, 5
the black bat, n., has flown INVITATIONS, 2
the darkness he called N. CREATION, 2
The dark n. of the soul SOUL, 8
the honey'd middle of the n. LOVE, 75
The n. is dark, and I am far from home FAITH, 16
wish the n. Had borne my breath away NOSTALGIA, 9
nightingale A N. Sang in Berkeley Square BIRDS, 7
N., . . . A creature of a fiery heart BIRDS, 12
The n. does sit so late BIRDS, 9
nightingales From Wales Whose n. WALES, 4
nightmare 'History', Stephen said, 'is a n.' HISTORY, 17
nights a Chequer-board of N. and Days DESTINY, 6
The weariest n. . . . must . . . end ENDURANCE, 11
They shorten tedious n. SEX, 8
nihilist a part-time n. COMMITMENT, 3
Nile England may as well dam . . . the N. with bulrushes
FREEDOM, 7
nine N. drummers drumming NURSERY RHYMES, 55
ninepence I have but n. in ready money CONVERSATION, 2
ninety stood n. years on the floor CLOCKS, 2
Nineveh Quinquireme of N. BOATS, 12
nip I'll n. him in the bud MIXED METAPHORS, 4
Nixon N. . . . would cut down a redwood tree POLITICIANS, 67
standing between N. and the White House POLITICIANS, 37
You won't have N. to kick around RENUNCIATION, 3
no become accustomed to n. one governing SOCIALISM, 9
girls . . . say N. when they mean Yes WOMEN, 8
It's n. go the picture palace INDIFFERENCE, 4
rebel . . . man who says n. REBELLION, 2
she speaks eighteen languages. And she can't say 'N.' in any of
them PROMISCUITY, 5
why Absurdist plays take place in N. Man's Land THEATRE, 1
Noah Out of their cataclysm but one poor N. SEX, 22
nobility N. has its own obligations NOBILITY, 2
The n. . . . snored through the Sermon ARISTOCRACY, 3
noble a n. nature, . . . treats . . . a serious subject POETRY, 3

Englishman never enjoys himself except for a n. purpose

ENGLISH, 19

n. grounds for the n. emotions POETRY, 38
Ridicule . . . smothers that which is n. RIDICULE, 3
The n. living and the n. dead NOBILITY, 6
nobleman a king may make a n. CHIVALRY, 3
nobleness perfect plainness of speech . . . perfect n. BIBLE, 1
noblest n. man That ever lived in the tide of times REGRET, 15
n. Roman of them all NOBILITY, 4
nobly the immature man . . . wants to die n. for a cause

AGE, 56

nobody a man is n. unless his biography OBITUARIES, 3
I care for n., . . . If no one cares for me SELFISHNESS, 2
N. asked you, sir, she said NURSERY RHYMES, 66
whom n. loves OBESITY, 6
Nod the land of N. REVENGE, 7
nod A n. is as good as a wink BLINDNESS, 1
nods even excellent Homer n. IMPERFECTION, 9
noise A loud n. at one end BABIES, 4
dreadful n. of waters in my ears DROWNING, 2
the less they have . . . the more n. they make

CHARACTER, 16

they . . . love the n. it makes MUSIC, 5
Those people . . . are making such a n. AUDIENCES, 3
noises Like n. in a swound SEA, 4
noisy Strongest minds . . . the n. world Hears least MIND, 10
The people would be just as n. PUBLIC, 9
nomadic the charm . . . of a n. existence CAMPING, 1
nominated I will not accept if n. POLITICIANS, 64
No-more I am also called N. DISAPPOINTMENT, 6
non-being Neurosis is the way of avoiding n. NEUROSIS, 3
non-combatant War hath no fury like a n. WAR, 68
nonconformist a N. conscience WOMEN, 80
man must be a n. CONFORMITY, 4
Why do you have to be a n.? CONFORMITY, 5
nonconformity N. and lust stalking hand in hand LUST, 8
none N. but the Brave COURAGE, 9
nonsense you intend to talk n. AMERICANS, 6
non-U U and N. CLASS, 27
non-violence to disagree . . . about . . . n. without wanting to
kick VIOLENCE, 4
noon From morn To n. he fell DECLINE, 4
from n. to dewy eve DECLINE, 4
O dark, dark, dark, amid the blaze of n. BLINDNESS, 4
Norfolk bear him up the N. sky HUNTING, 1
Very flat, N. ENGLAND, 11
Norgay Tenzing N. PHOTOGRAPHY, 3
Norma Jean Goodbye N. ACTORS, 9
normal the n. is so . . . interesting NORMALITY, 1
Normans The Saxon is not like us N. NATIONALITY, 6
north The n. wind does blow WEATHER, 6
nose A custom loathsome to the eye, hateful to the n.

SMOKING, 6

A person may be indebted for a n. . . . to a great-aunt

FAMILY, 19

Dong with a luminous N. NONSENSE, 17
Had Cleopatra's n. been shorter APPEARANCE, 28
led by the n. with gold BRIBERY, 4
My n. is huge! APPEARANCE, 30
Only the n. knows SECRECY, 1
This fellow did not see further than his . . . n. PAROCHIALISM, 1
will it come without warning Just as I'm picking my n. LOVE, 18
nostrils God . . . breathed into his n. GARDENS, 1
not Believe it or n. BELIEF, 6
HOW N. TO DO IT BUREAUCRACY, 4
note The world will little n., nor long remember MEMORIALS, 8
notes the pauses between the n. MUSICIANS, 8
nothin' You ain't heard n. yet PROPHECY, 6
nothing Blessed is the man who expects n. EXPECTATION, 1
Certainly, there is n. else here to enjoy PARTIES, 6
Children aren't happy with n. to ignore FAMILY, 30
doing n. for each other FRIENDSHIP, 16
from n. to a state of extreme poverty POVERTY, 23
God made everything out of n. CREATION, 13
have n. whatever to do with it DEATH, 80
N. can be created out of n. NOTHING, 1
n. can bring back the hour REGRET, 21
n. either good or bad THINKING, 9
N., except my genius CONCEIT, 23
N. happens BOREDOM, 1
n. if not critical CRITICISM, 44
n. is certain but death and taxes TAXATION, 3
n., . . . is greater . . . than one's self SELF, 20

n. is had for n. EFFORT, 4
n. is law that is not reason LAW, 21
N. long HUMAN NATURE, 7
N. matters very much TRIVIALITY, 1
N. to do but work PESSIMISM, 7
n. to do with the case APPEARANCE, 16
N. will come of n. NOTHING, 2
opened it only to find – n. MATERIALISM, 2
Signifying n. LIFE, 41
sooner read a time-table . . . than n. NOVELS, 10
take *more* than n. LANGUAGE, 4
The House of Peers . . . Did n. in particular HOUSES OF
PARLIAMENT, 10
the sort of woman . . . one would almost feel disposed to bury
for n. WOMEN, 26
The temerity to believe in n. SCEPTICISM, 6
those who were up to n. INTRIGUE, 2
To marvel at n. is just about the one and only thing

HAPPINESS, 8

When you have n. to say, say n. SILENCE, 4
Where some people are very wealthy and others have n.

GOVERNMENT, 4

nothingness the n. shows through CREATION, 13
notice The State, in choosing men . . . takes no n. of their
opinions LOYALTY, 6
notices One never n. what has been done ACHIEVEMENT, 2
nought N.'s had, all's spent CONTENTMENT, 6
nourisher Chief n. in life's feast SLEEP, 1
novel Among the many problems . . . the choice of the moment
. . . to begin his n. WRITERS, 37
A n. is a mirror NOVELS, 15
A n. is a static thing NOVELS, 16; PLAYS, 13
because a n.'s invented, it isn't true NOVELS, 12
good n. tells us the truth NOVELS, 2
I'm going to write the Great Australian N. AMBITION, 19
not a n. to be tossed aside lightly CRITICISM, 36
scrofulous French n. NOVELS, 1
The detective n. is NOVELS, 13
the last fashionable n. on the tables of young ladies WRITING, 21
The n. being dead NOVELS, 17
the n. tells a story NOVELS, 4
The only obligation to which . . . we may hold a n. NOVELS, 7
the sex n. is now normal NOVELS, 14
to read a n. before luncheon was one of the gravest sins

READING, 18

When I want to read a n. NOVELS, 8
novelist A n. is, like all mortals WRITERS, 29
n. who writes nothing for 10 years WRITERS, 35
novelists n. the story of the present NOVELS, 6
There are many reasons why n. write FICTION, 3
novels characters in one of my n. FICTION, 2
one of the few English n. for grown up people CRITICISM, 54
novelty N., n., n. NOVELTY, 3
November MONTHS, 10
Please to remember the Fifth of N. TREASON, 1
Thirty days hath N. MONTHS, 9
now We are all Socialists n. SOCIALISM, 6
nowhere All dressed up, with n. to go FUTILITY, 10
He's a real N. Man FUTILITY, 7
noxious the most n. is a tourist BRITISH, 7
nude To keep one from going n. PESSIMISM, 7
nudity you don't need the n. CINEMA, 11
nuisance exchange of one n. for another n. PROGRESS, 5
Inflation in the Sixties was a n. ECONOMICS, 8
Never compose . . . unless . . . not composing . . . becomes a
positive n. MUSIC, 21
nuisances a change of n. is as good as a vacation CHANGE, 13
number a very interesting n. NUMBERS, 3
Does it contain any abstract reasoning concerning quantity or n.?

PHILOSOPHY, 3

Look after n. one SELF-PRESERVATION, 1
numbers divinity in odd n. SUPERSTITION, 1
N. . . . only universal language MATHEMATICS, 15
Round n. NUMBERS, 1
the greatest happiness for the greatest n. HAPPINESS, 10
up in the high n. NUMBERS, 2
numble We live in a n. abode SERVILITY, 8
numbness drowsy n. pains My sense MELANCHOLY, 9
nun the upbringing a n. would envy INNOCENCE, 8
nuns the n. who never take a bath MODESTY, 6
nuptials prone to any iteration of n. MARRIAGE, 37
nurse definition of . . . a n. . . . 'devoted and obedient.'

NURSES, 1

N. unupblown | BREVITY, 9
nurseries n. of all vice | EDUCATION, 16
nurses old men's n. | MARRIAGE, 12
nut I had a little n. tree | NURSERY RHYMES, 20
nut-brown the spicy n. ale | ALCOHOL, 43
nutmeg But a silver n. | NURSERY RHYMES, 20

O

oak Heart of o. are our ships | COURAGE, 11
To win the palm, the o., or bays | VICTORY, 9
oar impressions . . . lasting as . . . an o. upon the water | INSIGNIFICANCE, 1
oat This bread I break was once the o. | AGRICULTURE, 5
oat-cakes land of Calvin, o., and sulphur | SCOTLAND, 8
oaths O. are but words | WORDS, 4
obedience The reluctant o. of distant provinces | DIPLOMACY, 16
obedient definition of . . . a nurse . . . 'devoted and o.' | NURSES, 1
obey born to o. | OBEDIENCE, 2
children, o. your parents | OBEDIENCE, 1
one of those born neither to o. nor to command | NASTINESS, 5
safer to o. than to rule | OBEDIENCE, 3
obeyed Nature, . . . must be o. | HUMAN NATURE, 5
object o. will be, if possible to form Christian men | EDUCATION, 3
objectionable its own animality either o. or funny | HUMOUR, 17
obligation The only o. to which . . . we may hold a novel | NOVELS, 7
To the University of Oxford I acknowledge no o. | EDUCATION, 20
oblige One should o. everyone to . . . one's ability | PRUDENCE, 4
oblivion alms for o. | TIME, 31
that ineluctable o. which awaits the uncreative mind | SCIENTISTS, 6
oblong an o. angular figure | HUMOUR, 39
obscene would not say that our Press is o. | JOURNALISM, 15
obscenity O. . . . happens to shock some elderly . . . magistrate | PRUDERY, 4
obscure I strive to be brief, and I become o. | BREVITY, 2
observance More honour'd in the breach than the o. | CUSTOM, 3
the o. of trifles | TRIVIALITY, 5
observations To o. which ourselves we make | SUBJECTIVITY, 6
observe Whenever you o. an animal closely | ANIMALS, 8
obstinacy the name of . . . o. in a bad one | STUBBORNNESS, 3
obstinate O. people can be divided into | STUBBORNNESS, 4
occupation for ever apologizing for his o. | BUSINESS, 11
occur Accidents will o. | ACCIDENTS, 2
ocean A life on the o. wave | SEA, 12
on the o. of life we pass | TRANSIENCE, 16
We mortals cross the o. | HUMAN CONDITION, 4
whilst the great o. of truth lay all undiscovered before me | DISCOVERY, 6
o'clock Three o. is always too late or too early | DAY, 13
octopus dear o. from whose tentacles we never quite escape | FAMILY, 38
odd How o. Of God | JEWS, 4
This world is very o. we see | CONFUSION, 4
odds The o. is gone | MOURNING, 11
odi O. et amo | LOVE AND HATE, 2
odious comparisons are o. | ANALOGY, 2
little o. vermin | ENGLISH, 34
One is not superior . . . because one sees the world in an o. light | CYNICISM, 1
odium He lived in the o. | SCIENTISTS, 3
odorous Comparisons are o. | MALAPROPISMS, 2
Oedipuses a tense and peculiar family, the O. | CLASSICS, 1
o'er Returning were as tedious as go o. | GUILT, 7
o'er-leaps Vaulting ambition, which o. itself | AMBITION, 5
off Days o. | LEISURE, 4
offence dire o. from am'rous causes springs | RESULTS, 5
greatest o. against virtue | VIRTUE, 7
It is a public scandal that gives o. | MORALITY, 10
The only defence is in o. | WAR, 5
offend the kind of pride least likely to o. | MODESTY, 5
Those who o. us are generally punished | REVENGE, 14
offended This hath not o. the king | REGRET, 5
When people do not respect us we are sharply o. | EXECUTION, 20 / SELF-RESPECT, 4
offensive extremely o., young man | RUDENESS, 2
office not describe holding public o. | GOVERNMENT, 1

o. sanctifies the holder | POWER, 3
Written by o. boys for o. boys | NEWSPAPERS, 10
officer unbecoming the character of an o. | OFFICERS, 1
official O. dignity . . . in inverse ratio to . . . importance | DIPLOMACY, 12
offspring Heaven has granted me no o. | CONCEIT, 22
often Do you come here o. | ANIMALISM, 6
oiled Oozing charm . . . He o. his way | CHARM, 3
ointment a good name is better than precious o. | VIRTUE, 3
Okie O. use' to mean you was from Oklahoma | INSULTS, 34
Oklahoma Okie use' to mean you was from O. | INSULTS, 34
old All evil comes from the o. | AGE, 3
an o., wild, and incomprehensible man | POLITICIANS, 75
a sight to make an o. man young | BEAUTY, 37
Before we grow o. and die | AGE, 70
being o. is having lighted rooms | OLD AGE, 24
Better be an o. man's darling | MARRIAGE, 1
first sign of o. age | AGE, 29
for de o. folks at home | HOMESICKNESS, 3
gift of perpetual o. age | OLD AGE, 45
Growing o. is like being increasingly penalized | OLD AGE, 32
He cannot bear o. men's jokes | OLD AGE, 19
I am o. enough to be – in fact am – your mother | AGE, 37
I grow o. . . . I grow o. | OLD AGE, 16
I love everything that's o. | CONSERVATISM, 2
inclination . . . to suppose an o. man decayed in his intellects | OLD AGE, 23
I prefer o. age to the alternative | OLD AGE, 11
It is so comic to hear oneself called o. | OLD AGE, 22
I was born o. | AGE, 58
I will never be an o. man | OLD AGE, 3
man . . . as o. as the woman he feels | AGE, 36
new book is published, read an o. one | BOOKS, 30
no more work for poor o. Ned | DEATH, 50
o. age a regret | AGE, 17
O. age brings . . . the comfort that you will soon be out of it | OLD AGE, 18
O. age is . . . crossed off names in an address book | AGE, 11
o. age is . . . older than I am | OLD AGE, 3
O. age is the out-patients' department | OLD AGE, 10
o. age . . . the fear that it may go on too long | OLD AGE, 42
O. men are dangerous | OLD AGE, 39
O. men forget | MEMORY, 16
one has to be very o. before one learns how to be amused | AGE, 14
O. sins | SIN, 1
redress the balance of the O. | AMERICA, 5
Say I'm growing o., but add, Jenny kissed me | KISSING, 2
Tell me the o., o. story | CHRISTIANITY, 27
terrible thing for an o. woman to outlive her dogs | OLD AGE, 46
that grand o. man | POLITICIANS, 53
That is no country for o. men | MORTALITY, 23
that o. serpent | DEVIL, 4
the o. have reminiscences | AGE, 47
the o. have rubbed it into the young that they are wiser | OLD AGE, 27
the o. is better | AGE, 10; ALCOHOL, 15
The o. man has his death | DEATH, 11
There are no o. men any more | AGE, 61
There is too much Asia and she is too o. | PLACES, 8
They shall grow not o. | MEMORIALS, 3
they think he is growing o. | AGE, 31
To be o. is to be part of a . . . multitude | OLD AGE, 6
too o. to go again to my travels | ROYALTY, 10
When you are o. and gray | OLD AGE, 50
Where are the boys of the O. Brigade | NOSTALGIA, 23
You are o., Father William | OLD AGE, 9
older make way for an o. man | DISMISSAL, 6
O. men declare war | WAR, 48
The o. one grows the more one likes indecency | AGE, 65
to go on getting o. | SURVIVAL, 2
old-fashioned o. respect for the young | RESPECT, 5
O. ways which no longer apply | WOMEN, 5
olfactory an o. bar | FAMILIARITY, 5
oligarchy extreme democracy or absolute o. . . . will come | GOVERNMENT, 4
they that are displeased with *aristocracy*, call it o. | GOVERNMENT, 12
olive a land of oil o., and honey | WEALTH, 5
Oliver O. Twist has asked for more | BOLDNESS, 2
Olympic The most important thing in the O. Games | VICTORY, 4
ominous an idea . . . to be fashionable is o. | FASHION, 5
omnibuses if he had only ridden more in o. | POLITICIANS, 34

omnipotence final proof of God's o. GOD, 19
on O. with the dance DANCING, 1
they get o., then they get *honour* DOCTORS, 8
once For Christmas comes but o. a year CHRISTMAS, 18
O. more unto the breach, dear friends COURAGE, 16
One dies only o. DEATH, 83
you have dined in every house in London – o. BORES, 9
you shall drink twice while I drink o. DRUNKENNESS, 20
one All for o., and o. for all UNITY, 8
How to be o. up ONE-UPMANSHIP, 3
if we knew o., we knew two METAPHYSICS, 3
The number o. book . . . was written by a committee BIBLE, 6
one-eyed o. yellow idol to the north of Khatmandu MOURNING, 5
the O. Man is King SUPERIORITY, 12
one-handed Give me a o. economist ECONOMICS, 13
oneself It is a stupidity . . . to busy o. with the correction of the world IMPROVEMENT, 3
One should examine o. . . . before . . . condemning others SELF, 11
only possible society is o. MISANTHROPY, 4
onions carry their own o. when cycling abroad FRANCE, 3
onward little o. lend thy guiding hand GUIDANCE, 3
O., Christian soldiers CHRISTIANITY, 3
O., Christians, onward go ENDURANCE, 24
open I declare this thing o. – whatever it is ARCHITECTURE, 7
O. Sesame SUPERNATURAL, 2
the transition from the . . . 'closed society', . . . to the 'o. society' SOCIETY, 5
opening It is always o. time in the Sailors Arms PUBLIC HOUSES, 4
opera an o. without an interval, or an interval without an o. OPERA, 5
Bed . . . is the poor man's o. SEX, 23
Like German o., too long and too loud OPERA, 7; WAR, 123
No good o. plot can be sensible OPERA, 2
O. in English OPERA, 4
o. isn't what it used to be OPERA, 3
The first rule in o. is the first rule in life SELF-RELIANCE, 8
what language an o. is sung in OPERA, 1
operas the German text of French o. OPERA, 8
opinion A man . . . must have a very good o. of himself CONCEIT, 2
better to have no o. of God GOD, 3
give him my o. MARRIAGE, 44
he is . . . Now but a climate of o. PSYCHIATRY, 1
heresy signifies no more than private o. OPINIONS, 1
He would rather follow public o. POLITICIANS, 35
I agree with no man's o. OPINIONS, 6
I am . . . of the o. with the learned AGREEMENT, 2
Nobody holds a good o. of a man who has a low o. of himself SELF-RESPECT, 2
nothing to admire except his o. CRITICS, 5
of his own o. still YIELDING, 5
so vain . . . care for the o. of those we don't care for CONCEIT, 8
the English think of an o. as something . . . to hide ENGLISH, 17
The superiority of one man's o. over another's OPINIONS, 2
They that approve . . . call it o. OPINIONS, 1
opinionated the o., the ignorant, and the boorish STUBBORNNESS, 2
opinions a decent respect to the o. of mankind INDEPENDENCE, 2
New o. are always suspected NOVELTY, 5
not a writer's business to hold o. WRITERS, 50
So many men, so many o. OPINIONS, 5
the proper o. for the time of year PUBLIC, 3
The public buys its o. as it buys its meat PUBLIC, 7
The State, in choosing men . . . takes no notice of their o. LOYALTY, 6
The wish to spread those o. that we hold ENGLISH, 7
opium Religion . . . is the o. of the people RELIGION, 37
opium-dose an o. for keeping beasts of burden BIBLE, 4
opponent Never ascribe to an o. motives meaner than your own MOTIVE, 1
opportunist rather be an o. and float EXPEDIENCY, 2
opportunities A wise man will make more o. OPPORTUNITY, 9
One can present people with o. OPPORTUNITY, 12
opportunity Equality of o. OPPORTUNITY, 13
follies . . . he didn't commit when he had the o. REGRET, 11
O. seldom knocks twice OPPORTUNITY, 6
oppose duty . . . to o. OPPOSITION, 2
opposition Her Majesty's O. OPPOSITION, 1

I have spent many years . . . in o. OPPOSITION, 5
The duty of an o. OPPOSITION, 2
When I invented the phrase 'His Majesty's O.' OPPOSITION, 3
oppression when fanatics are on top there is no limit to o. GOVERNMENT, 18
Where rumour of o. and deceit SOLITUDE, 3
optimism Pessimism, . . . is just as agreeable as o. PESSIMISM, 1
The place where o. most flourishes OPTIMISM, 20
optimist an o. . . . fills up his crossword puzzle in ink OPTIMISM, 25
I am an o., unrepentant and militant OPTIMISM, 26
The o. proclaims OPTIMISM, 19; PESSIMISM, 1
optimistic O. lies MEDICINE, 5
Oracle I am Sir O. EGOTISM, 8
oracular the use of my o. tongue MALAPROPISMS, 8
oral a terrific story about o. contraception CONTRACEPTION, 1
orange Oh that I were an o.-tree SERVICE, 2
oranges O. and lemons, Say the bells of St Clement's LONDON, 2
orangutang an o. trying to play the violin MARRIAGE, 38
oratorium *Laboratorium est o.* SCIENCE, 25
orchard Before the cherry o. was sold WORRY, 9
orchestration Literature is the o. of platitudes LITERATURE, 19
order O. is heaven's first law ORDER, 2
The old o. changeth CHANGE, 18
upon the o. of your going DISMISSAL, 8
wisdom . . . sweetly doth . . . o. all things WISDOM, 9
words in the best o. POETRY AND PROSE, 2
ordered a side dish he hadn't o. CONTEMPT, 3
ordering the better o. of the universe UNIVERSE, 1
ordinary One machine can do the work of fifty o. men TECHNOLOGY, 5
organ my second favourite o. ANIMALISM, 1
Seated . . . at the o. MUSIC, 35
organ-grinder no reason to attack the monkey when the o. is present POLITICIANS, 6
organic O. life . . . has developed . . . from the protozoon to the philosopher PROGRESS, 11
organization a government o. could do it that quickly BUREAUCRACY, 2
organized War is an o. bore WAR, 47
organs he'd have given us all more o. SEX, 6
orgasm The o. has replaced the Cross SEX, 33
orgies o. are vile DEBAUCHERY, 3
orgy An o. looks particularly alluring PRUDERY, 3
you need an o., once in a while DEBAUCHERY, 8
Orientals If . . . O. . . . drank a liquor which . . . made them vomit ALCOHOL, 37
origin the indelible stamp of his lowly o. EVOLUTION, 3
original An o. writer is . . . one whom nobody can imitate ORIGINALITY, 2
Mona did researches in o. sin SEX, 38
o. is unfaithful to the translation TRANSLATION, 1
The more intelligence . . . the more . . . one finds o. INTELLIGENCE, 4
the only absolutely o. creation . . . is Don Quixote FICTION, 4
thought is often o. ORIGINALITY, 3
originality absence of inverted commas guarantees . . . o. QUOTATIONS, 2
All good things . . . are the fruits of o. ORIGINALITY, 4
without o. or moral courage CHARACTER, 14
originator quotes . . . give us a nodding acquaintance with the o. QUOTATIONS, 14
Ormus Outshone the wealth of O. and of Ind DEVIL, 10
ornamental not merely . . . useful and o. PURPOSE, 8
orphan defeat is an o. SUCCESS, 8
orthodoxy 'o.' . . . no longer means being right ORTHODOXY, 2
O. or My-doxy ORTHODOXY, 1
Oscar We all assume that O. said it QUOTATIONS, 7
ostrich the wings of an o. IMAGINATION, 8
other O. people are quite dreadful MISANTHROPY, 4
you expect o. people to be . . . to your liking TOLERANCE, 3
others By persuading o. we convince ourselves PERSUASION, 2
delight in . . . misfortunes . . . of o. SUFFERING, 5
some more than o. SIMILARITY, 4
tell the o. by their hunted expression CHARITY, 14
to encourage the o. EXAMPLE, 9
otherwise Some folk . . . are o. WISDOM, 20
Otis Miss O. regrets APOLOGIES, 1
ounce An o. of a man's own wit WISDOM, 21
ours We have met the enemy, and they are o. VICTORY, 12
ourselves all our knowledge is, o. to know SELF-KNOWLEDGE, 6

By persuading others we convince o. — PERSUASION, 2
In every friend we lose a part of o. — DEATH, 89
remedies of in o. do lie — SELF-RELIANCE, 7
we but praise o. in other men — PRAISE, 5
What isn't part of o. doesn't disturb us — HATE, 5
out Mordre wol o. — MURDER, 4
O., damned spot — GUILT, 8
once o., what you've said can't be stopped — PUBLISHING, 6
outlive o. this powerful rhyme — POETRY, 41
outlook religious o. on life — RELIGION, 33
outrun We may o. — EXCESS, 11
outside I am just going o. — LAST WORDS, 41
I support it from the o. — SUPPORT, 5
outward I may not hope from o. forms — APPEARANCES, 12
over Now the day is o. — DAY, 1
overcomes Who o. By force — VICTORY, 10
over-confident Not that I am ever o. — SELF-CONFIDENCE, 6
over-educated I've o. myself in all the things — DEBAUCHERY, 5
overexposure she should catch a cold on o. — TRUTH, 15
overfed They're overpaid, o., oversexed and over here — SOLDIERS, 7
over-feeding what Nicely-Nicely dies of will be o. — GREED, 8
overlooked better to be looked over than o. — STARING, 1
overpaid They're o., overfed, oversexed and over here — SOLDIERS, 7
overrated matrimony, which I always thought a highly o. performance — MARRIAGE, 51
overrun apt to be o. with nettles — MIND, 8
over-running and lose by o. — EXCESS, 11
oversexed They're overpaid, overfed, o. and over here — SOLDIERS, 7
overtakers It is the o. who — TRAVEL, 21
overthrown Another mighty empire o. — DEFEAT, 9
overtures I tried to resist his o. — PUNS, 18
owe I don't o. a penny to a single soul — BORROWING, 13
owed so much o. by so many to so few — WORLD WAR II, 7
owes A nation is not in danger . . . because it o. itself money — ECONOMICS, 10
he o. not any man — RIGHTEOUSNESS, 7
owl The O. and the Pussy-Cat went to sea — NONSENSE, 20
owls Two O. and a Hen — APPEARANCE, 19
own mine o. Executioner — SELF, 7
ownership its source of power: o. — CAPITALISM, 6
transform this society without . . . extension of public o. — SOCIALISM, 8
ox When he stands like an o. in the furrow — NATIONALITY, 6
Oxford a secret in the O. sense — SECRECY, 10
It is O. that has made me insufferable — EDUCATION, 6
nice sort of place, O. — OXFORD, 5
O. . . . full of a particular non-social snobbiness — OXFORD, 7
O. is on the whole more attractive than Cambridge — CAMBRIDGE, 1; OXFORD, 3
The clever men at O. Know all that there is to be known — KNOWLEDGE, 17
The King to O. sent a troop of horse — CAMBRIDGE, 2; OXFORD, 4
To O. sent a troop of horse — CAMBRIDGE, 5; OXFORD, 6
To the University of O. I acknowledge no obligation — EDUCATION, 20
You will hear more good things on . . . a stagecoach from London to O. — INTELLECTUALS, 6
you will leave O. by the town drain — SPOONERISMS, 5
oyster bold man that first eat an o. — COURAGE, 17; FOOLISHNESS, 19
sympathetic unselfishness of an o. — FISH, 2
the sort of eye that can open an o. at sixty paces — APPEARANCE, 40
world's mine o. — OPPORTUNITY, 15
oysters Poverty and o. — POVERTY, 6

P

pace this petty p. from day to day — LIFE, 41
Pacific The Admiral of the Atlantic salutes the Admiral of the P. — ARROGANCE, 10
pacifism My p. is not based on . . . intellectual theory — WAR AND PEACE, 5
pack how much more dogs are animated when they hunt in a p. — UNITY, 10
the human p. is shuffled and cut — EDUCATION, 31
paddle every man p. his own canoe — INDEPENDENCE, 3
padlocked music critics. . . . small and rodent-like with p. ears — CRITICS, 15
pagan A P. suckled in a creed outworn — DISCONTENT, 10

pageant insubstantial p. faded — MORTALITY, 17
paid I do not answer questions like this without being p. — MASCULINITY, 1
pain a gentleman . . . never inflicts p. — CHIVALRY, 8
Although p. isn't real — SUFFERING, 2
critics . . . desire our blood, not our p. — CRITICS, 11
disinclination to inflict p. upon oneself — GOOD, 11
I feel no p., dear mother, now — ALCOHOL, 9
I have no p., dear mother, now — LAST WORDS, 18
momentary intoxication with p. — CRUELTY, 1
Neither shame nor physical p. have any . . . effect — PUNISHMENT, 12
owes its pleasures to another's p. — HUNTING, 2
Pleasure is . . . intermission of p. — PLEASURE, 27
The least p. in our little finger — SELF-INTEREST, 4
The p. passes, but the beauty remains — ENDURANCE, 14
they blest him in their p. — MARTYRDOM, 4
what p. it was to drown — DROWNING, 2
yearning like a God in p. — SUFFERING, 7
pains no gains without p. — ENDURANCE, 19
paint A professional is someone whose wife works to enable him to p. — ARTISTS, 8
flinging a pot of p. in the public's face — CRITICISM, 43
I p. objects as I think them — PAINTING, 10
My business is to p. . . . what I see — PAINTING, 17
to p. the lily — EXCESS, 10
painted As idle as a p. ship — BOATS, 1
I am p. as the greatest little dictator — AUTHORITARIANISM, 6
Most women are not so young as they are p. — COSMETICS, 1
p. . . . by the great artist Kodak — PHOTOGRAPHY, 5
painter I am married to Beatrice Salkeld, a p. — CHILDREN, 7
I could have become a real p. — LAST WORDS, 33
memory is a p. — MEMORY, 10
who is not a great sculptor or p. can be an architect — ARCHITECTURE, 8
painters Good p. imitate nature — PAINTING, 3
P. and poets . . . licence to dare anything — FREEDOM, 18
Poets and p. are outside the class system — ARTISTS, 2; POETS, 5
painting a great difference between p. a face — APPEARANCE, 15
If I didn't start p., I would have raised chickens — OCCUPATIONS, 11
If people only knew . . . about p. — PAINTING, 6
I just keep p. till I feel like pinching. Then I know it's right — PAINTING, 14
P. is a blind man's profession — PAINTING, 11
P., . . . protecting flat surfaces from the weather — PAINTING, 2
pajamas I shot an elephant in my p. — HUMOUR, 40
palace Love in a p. — LOVE, 74
palaces Mid pleasures and p. though we may roam — HOME, 7
pale a p. horse — DEATH, 29
Palestine not enough prisons . . . in P. to hold all the Jews — JEWS, 10
pall The pallor of girls' brows shall be their p. — WAR, 80
Palladium Liberty of the press is the P. of . . . rights — FREEDOM, 23
pallor The p. of girls' brows shall be their pall — WAR, 80
palm happy state of getting the victor's p. without the dust of racing — VICTORY, 6
To win the p., the oak, or bays — VICTORY, 9
palms p. before my feet — GLORY, 1
palsied with the p. heart — PASSION, 8
pan Put on the p.; Says Greedy Nan — NURSERY RHYMES, 7
Pandora open that P.'s Box . . . Trojan 'orses will jump out — MIXED METAPHORS, 1
Panjandrum the grand P. — NONSENSE, 12
pantheist The modern p. not only — PHOTOGRAPHY, 4
pants There were times my p. were so thin — POVERTY, 29
Your eyes shine like the p. — COMPLIMENTS, 3
papacy Since God has given us the p. . . . enjoy it — CATHOLICISM, 8
The P. is not other than the Ghost of the deceased Roman Empire — CATHOLICISM, 5
paper reactionaries are p. tigers — POLITICS, 46
The atom bomb is a p. tiger — NUCLEAR WEAPONS, 11
This p. will no doubt be found interesting — CRITICISM, 10
Where were you fellows when the p. was blank — EDITORS, 1
papers fornicated and read the p. — MANKIND, 9
only two posh p. on a Sunday — NEWSPAPERS, 9
papyromania P. – compulsive accumulation — OBSESSIONS, 2
papyrophobia P. – abnormal desire — OBSESSIONS, 2
parables great p., . . . , but false art — CRITICISM, 25
parade the chief employment of riches consists in the p. of riches — OSTENTATION, 6; WEALTH, 25

paradise A p. for a sect | FANATICISM, 2
drunk the milk of P. | CAUTION, 9
England is a p. for women | NATIONALITY, 3
England is the p. of individuality | ENGLAND, 33
England is the p. of women | ENGLAND, 16
Grant me p. in this world | HEAVEN, 13
If a man could pass through P. | PROOF, 3
Same old glimpse of P. | MARRIAGE, 71
to hope for P. is to live in P. | HEAVEN, 8
Wilderness is P. enow | CONTENTMENT, 3
paragon the p. of animals | MANKIND, 26
parallel We never remark any passion . . . in others, of which,
. . . we may not find a p. | SELF, 8
parallelogram The landlady . . . is a p. | HUMOUR, 39
paralyse p. it by encumbering it with remedies | REMEDIES, 12
paranoid Even a p. can have enemies | ENEMIES, 4
parcels Portions and p. of the dreadful Past | TIME, 33
pardon God may p. you, but I never can | FORGIVENESS, 11
God will p. me. It is His trade | LAST WORDS, 30
the government that should ask me for a p. | FORGIVENESS, 9
pardoned The women p. all | FORGIVENESS, 8
parent a kind p. . . . or a merciless step-mother | NATURE, 13
To lose one p., . . . a misfortune; to lose both looks like
carelessness | LOSS, 8
parents A Jewish man with p. alive | JEWS, 13
by defying their p. and copying one another | YOUTH, 5
children, obey your p. | OBEDIENCE, 1
Don't hold your p. up to contempt | FAMILY, 45
From birth to age eighteen, a girl needs good p. | AGE, 60
joys of p. are secret | FAMILY, 8
necessary precautions to avoid having p. | FAMILY, 12
P. . . . a disappointment to their children | FAMILY, 33
P. . . . bones on which children sharpen their teeth | FAMILY, 44
P. learn a lot from their children | CHILDREN, 34
the way p. obey their children | FAMILY, 46
what p. were created for | FAMILY, 30
Paris delivered of a city bigger than P. | DISAPPOINTMENT, 4
Good Americans, when they die, go to P. | AMERICANS, 1
I love P. | PARIS, 5
Is P. burning | PARIS, 3
no home . . . save in P. | PARIS, 4
P. is worth a mass | PARIS, 2
when good Americans die they go to P. | AMERICANS, 13
parish all the world as my p. | RELIGION, 61
park The hunchback in the p. | LONELINESS, 8
Parkinson The rise in the . . . employed is governed by P.'s
Law | WORK, 14
par-lee-voo Hinky, dinky, p. | FRANCE, 11
Parliament build your House of P. upon the river | HOUSES OF
PARLIAMENT, 19
He stood twice for P. | POLITICS, 77
If Her Majesty stood for P. | POLITICS, 60
no reference to fun in any Act of P. | PLEASURE, 13
P. is the longest running farce | GOVERNMENT, 26
parliaments England . . . mother of p. | ENGLAND, 5
parlour Will you walk into my p.? | INVITATIONS, 1
parochial worse than provincial – he was p. | WRITERS, 20
parody devil's walking p. | ANIMALS, 9
parole Classical quotation is the p. of literary men
QUOTATIONS, 4
parrot to sell the family p. | RESPECTABILITY, 4
parsnips fine words butter no p. | WORDS, 18
parson If P. lost his senses | ANIMALS, 12
In arguing too, the p. own'd his skill | KNOWLEDGE, 16
Once a p. | OCCUPATIONS, 5
part I have forgot my p. | FAILURE, 4
In every friend we lose a p. of ourselves | DEATH, 89
it is a little flesh and breath, and the ruling p. | MANKIND, 3
let us kiss and p. | PARTING, 6
till death us do p. | MARRIAGE, 27
We only p. to meet again | FAITHFULNESS, 4
particular a London p. . . . A fog | WEATHER, 9
did nothing in p. | HOUSES OF PARLIAMENT, 10
particulars Minute P. | GOOD, 2
parties it is always like that at p. | REGRET, 10
one of those p. which got out of hand | CHRISTIANITY, 21
parting Every p. gives a foretaste of death | SEPARATION, 5
P. is all we know of heaven | PARTING, 5
P. is such sweet sorrow | PARTING, 10
partisanship P. is our great curse | SUBJECTIVITY, 7
partly Man p. is | AMBITION, 4
partridge A p. in a pear tree | NURSERY RHYMES, 49
well-shot woodcock, p., snipe | HUNTING, 1

parts It is seldom . . . one p. on good terms | PARTING, 9
one man in his time plays many p. | HUMAN CONDITION, 15
Today we have naming of p. | WEAPONS, 4
part-time p. nihilist | COMMITMENT, 3
party A great p. is not to be brought down | POLITICS, 29
best number for a dinner p. is two | FOOD, 22
Heard there was a p. | ACCIDENTS, 4
I always voted at my p.'s call | POLITICIANS, 29
The p. is the rallying-point for the . . . working class
COMMUNISM, 9
The sooner every p. breaks up the better | PARTIES, 1
Well, did you evah! What a swell p. | PARTIES, 5
pass ideas simply p. through him | STUPIDITY, 5
I shall not p. this way again | MORTALITY, 11
p. for forty-three | AGE, 27
Praise the Lord and p. the ammunition | WAR, 36
They shall not p. | DETERMINATION, 13
To p. away ere life hath lost its brightness | DEATH, 56
passage calm p. . . . across many a bad night | SUICIDE, 4
patience and p. of time | PATIENCE, 11
passageways smell of steaks in p. | FOOD, 17
passed That p. the time | TIME, 8
passengers fools and p. drink at sea | BOATS, 15
passeront Ils ne p. pas | DETERMINATION, 13
passes Men seldom make p. | APPEARANCE, 26
passeth the peace of God, which p. all understanding
BLESSING, 5
passion All breathing human p. far above | PASSION, 3
cheated into p., but . . . reasoned into truth | TRUTH, 23
Culture is the p. for sweetness and light | CULTURE, 2
desolate and sick of an old p. | LOVE, 49
Master Mistress of my p. | LOVE, 116
one master-p. . . . swallows up the rest | PASSION, 5
p. and party blind our eyes | EXPERIENCE, 11
P. . . . can be destroyed by a doctor | PASSION, 7
p. in the human soul | MUSIC, 25
So I triumphed ere my p. | PASSION, 8
Strange fits of p. | PASSION, 9
The p. and the life, whose fountains are within
APPEARANCES, 12
The ruling p. conquers reason still | PASSION, 6
We never remark any p. . . . in others, of which, . . . we may
not find a parallel | SELF, 8
passions A man who has not passed through the inferno of his
p. | PASSION, 2
It is with our p. as it is with fire and water | PASSION, 4
Literature and butterflies are the two sweetest p.
LITERATURE, 13
not his reason, but his p. | RELIGION, 47
The man who is master of his p. | PASSION, 1
Three p., simple but overwhelmingly strong, have governed my
life | PHILOSOPHERS, 7
past Even God cannot change the p. | PAST, 1
Historians tell the story of the p. | NOVELS, 6
I do not . . . prejudge the p. | PREJUDICE, 6
Keep off your thoughts from things that are p. | PAST, 8
looking forward to the p. | NOSTALGIA, 17
Nothing recalls the p. so potently as a smell | NOSTALGIA, 6
people who live in the p. | PROGRESS, 1
Portions and parcels of the dreadful P. | TIME, 33
remembrance of things p. | REGRET, 17
something . . . absurd about the p. | PAST, 2
Study the p. | PAST, 4
The only thing I regret about my p. life | AGE, 7
The p., at least, is secure | PAST, 9
The p. is a foreign country | PAST, 5
The p. is the only dead thing | PAST, 7
The p. was a sleep | BEGINNING, 4
The p. was nothing . . . The future was a mystery | PRESENT, 2
Those who cannot remember the p. | HISTORY, 21
to know nothing but the p. | CONSERVATISM, 2
what is p. my help is p. my care | INDIFFERENCE, 1
what's p. help Should be p. grief | REGRET, 14
What we know of the p. is | HISTORY, 15
Who controls the p. controls the future | POWER, 13
Pastoral Cold P. | ETERNITY, 3
pastures fresh woods, and p. new | CHANGE, 15
pat P.-a-cake, p.-a-cake, baker's man | NURSERY RHYMES, 37
P. it and prick it, and mark it with B | NURSERY RHYMES, 37
patches king of shreds and p. | INFERIORITY, 6
thing of shreds and p. | SINGERS, 2
pate You beat your p. | STUPIDITY, 11
patent The people – could you p. the sun? | DISCOVERY, 7

P., . . . is a fight against . . . fascination | PHILOSOPHY, 17
P. is not a theory | PHILOSOPHY, 18
P. is the product of wonder | PHILOSOPHY, 17; WONDER, 4
P. is the replacement | PHILOSOPHY, 12
p. ought to . . . unravel people's mental blocks | PHILOSOPHY, 10
Vain wisdom all, and false p. | WISDOM, 18
Western p. is, . . . a series of footnotes to Plato's p. | PHILOSOPHY, 15

phobias I have three p. which . . . would make my life as slick
  as a sonnet | OBSESSIONS, 1
phonus is nothing but a p. bolonus | APPEARANCES, 17
photograph A p. is not only an image | PHOTOGRAPHY, 6
  she took down the signed p. of the Kaiser | WAR, 122
photography P. can never grow up if it imitates | PHOTOGRAPHY, 1
P. is truth | CINEMA, 4
physic Take p., pomp | HUMILITY, 10
physical a p. and metaphysical impossibility | POETS, 7
physician I died . . . of my p. | DOCTORS, 7
  if the p. had the same disease upon him that I have | EXAMPLE, 7
p., heal thyself | DOCTORS, 2
The p. can bury his mistakes | MISTAKES, 17
the p. cutteth off a long disease | DEATH, 25
physicians P. are like kings | DOCTORS, 9
the help of too many p. | DOCTORS, 1
physicists The p. have known sin | SCIENTISTS, 7
to find out anything from the theoretical p. | SCIENTISTS, 5
physics Classical p. . . . superseded by quantum theory | SCIENCE, 35
Modern P. is an instrument of Jewry | SCIENCE, 33
pianist do not shoot the p. | EFFORT, 7
not so much . . . a p., but a vampire | MUSICIANS, 6
the only p. . . . who did not grimace | MUSICIANS, 9
Piatigorsky Gregor P. | EGOTISM, 6
Picardy Roses are flowering in P. | COMPLIMENTS, 9
Picasso Nothing divides them like P. | ART, 16
There's no such thing as a bad P. | INFERIORITY, 4
Piccadilly Crossing P. Circus | LONDON, 13
Good-bye P., Farewell Leicester Square | HOMESICKNESS, 8
pick Whenever you fall, p. up something | OPPORTUNITY, 3
pickle weaned on a p. | APPEARANCE, 21
picnic futile to attempt a p. in Eden | INNOCENCE, 4
picture If you want a p. of the future | OPPRESSION, 4
It's no go the p. palace | INDIFFERENCE, 4
pictures book . . . without p. | BOOKS, 11
would never buy my p. | PAINTING, 6
pidgin-English I include 'p.' | LANGUAGE, 19
pie Amblongus P. | NONSENSE, 21
piece p. of cod passes all understanding | FOOD, 31
p. of divinity in us | NOBILITY, 1
Prologues precede the p. | PLAYS, 4
What a p. of work is a man | MANKIND, 26
When a p. gets difficult | MUSICIANS, 7
pieces P. of eight | MONEY, 43
pie-crust Promises and p. are made to be broken | PROMISES, 1
pieman Simple Simon met a p. | NURSERY RHYMES, 46
pier Like Brighton p. | TRAVEL, 16
Pierian Drink deep, or taste not the P. spring | KNOWLEDGE, 7
pies I could eat one of Bellamy's veal p. | FOOD, 38; LAST WORDS, 45
pigeons tourists . . . take in the Monarchy . . . with . . . the p. | LONDON, 8
piggy This little p. went to market | NURSERY RHYMES, 58
pigmy That shriek and sweat in p. wars | TRIVIALITY, 14
pigs And whether p. have wings | NONSENSE, 9
one of Epicurus' herd of p. | PRESENT, 10
What men call social virtues, . . . is . . . but the virtue of p. in a
  litter | SOCIETY, 9
pig-sty kissed her once by the p. | EXPECTATION, 5
Pilate jesting P. | TRUTH, 10
P. . . . washed his hands | GUILT, 3
rather have blood on my hands . . . P. | COMMITMENT, 4
pilgrim P. of the sky | BIRDS, 11
pilgrims strangers and p. on the earth | FAITH, 4
Pill Protestant women may take the P. | CONTRACEPTION, 1
pillar the lie has become . . . a p. of the State | LYING, 15
triple p. of the world | LOVE, 109
pilot Dropping the p. | DISMISSAL, 3
Pimpernel That damned elusive P.? | ABSENCE, 9
pin If I sit on a p. And it punctures my skin | SUFFERING, 2
See a p. and pick it up | SUPERSTITION, 4
you are like a p., but without . . . head or . . . point | BORES, 3

Pinafore Captain of the P. | CONCEIT, 9
pinch time for me to enjoy another p. of snuff | EXECUTION, 1
pinching I just keep painting till I feel like p.. Then I know it's
  right | PAINTING, 14
pine-apple p. of politeness | MALAPROPISMS, 7
pinko-gray white races are . . . p. | RACE, 7
pint one cannot put a quart in a p. cup | IMPOSSIBILITY, 1
You spend half a p. and flush two gallons | WATER, 6
pious A p. man . . . would be an atheist if the king were | SERVILITY, 4
p. bird with the scarlet breast | BIRDS, 13
p. frauds of friendship | FRIENDSHIP, 18
pipe Blow your p. there | CONTEMPT, 2
piped their fountains p. an answer | ANTHROPOMORPHISM, 1
Piper Peter P. picked a peck of pickled pepper | NURSERY RHYMES, 38
pipers Wi' a hundred p. an' a', an' a' | GLORY, 4
piping Helpless, naked, p. loud | BIRTH, 3
P. down the valleys wild | MUSIC, 11
pips squeezed – until the p. squeak | RETRIBUTION, 10
piss I can p. the old boy | BOASTS, 5
pissed the last four strikes we've had, it's p. down | STRIKES, 4
pissing inside my tent p. out | PRUDENCE, 7
pistol a p. let off at the ear | PUNS, 10
pit And wretched, blind, p. ponies | ANIMALS, 12
pitchfork drive out nature with a p. . . . she'll be constantly
  running back | HUMAN NATURE, 9
pith all the p. is in the postscript | LETTER-WRITING, 3
pitied one has . . . ceased to be an object of *fear* as soon as
  one is p. | SYMPATHY, 5
pitiless slow, sure doom falls p. and dark | HUMAN CONDITION, 13
Pitt P. is to Addington | POLITICIANS, 11
pity A p. beyond all telling | LOVE, 145
I thought it was a p. to get up | BED, 6
knock him down first, and p. him afterwards | SELF-PRESERVATION, 6
My subject is War, and the p. of War | POETRY, 33
P. a human face | MANKIND, 6
p. for the suffering of mankind | PHILOSOPHERS, 4
The Poetry is in the p. | POETRY, 33
To marry a man out of p. is folly | MARRIAGE, 2
To show p. is felt as a sign of contempt | SYMPATHY, 5
place everything in its p. | ORDER, 5
firm p. to stand | TECHNOLOGY, 1
give p. to better men | DISMISSAL, 3
Home is the p. where | HOME, 4
I go to prepare a p. for you | HEAVEN, 3
Never the time and the p. | PERVERSITY, 2
running . . . to keep in the same p. | NONSENSE, 8
there's no p. like home | HOME, 7
the summit of Everest was hardly the p. | PHOTOGRAPHY, 3
this is an awful p. | PLACES, 16
Upon the p. beneath | MERCY, 2
plague A p. o' both your houses! | CURSES, 1
plagues of all p. with which mankind are curst | CHURCH, 3
plain be yourself, imperial, p. and true | SINCERITY, 1
making things p. to uninstructed people was . . . best means of
  clearing . . . one's own mind | EDUCATION, 24
Manners are . . . the need of the p. | MANNERS, 7
plainness perfect p. of speech . . . perfect nobleness | BIBLE, 1
plaisir P. d'amour | LOVE, 54
plane only two emotions in a p.: boredom and terror | FLYING, 3
planet I have lived some thirty years on this p. | ADVICE, 13
it fell on the wrong p. | WEAPONS, 2
When a new p. swims into his ken | DISCOVERY, 5
plans Life . . . happens . . . while you're busy making other p. | LIFE, 31
The finest p. have always been spoiled | SUPPORT, 3
what a man still p. . . . shows the . . . injustice in his death | DEATH, 34
plant Is thy love a p. Of such weak fibre | ABSENCE, 10
The infusion of a China p. | DRINKS, 1
plants bottinney means a knowledge of p. | EDUCATION, 14
p. left over from the Edwardian Wilderness | CHANGE, 16
plashy p. fen passes the questing vole | ANIMALS, 21
plate clean your p. | POLITICS, 57
the silver p. on a coffin | INSULTS, 29
platitude A longitude with no p. | MEANING, 4
A p. is simply a truth repeated | SAYINGS, 1
platitudes Literature is the orchestration of p. | LITERATURE, 19
Plato P. is dear to me | TRUTH, 8
Western philosophy is, . . . a series of footnotes to P.'s
  philosophy | PHILOSOPHY, 15

play a good p. needs no epilogue | PLAYS, 10
a p. is a dynamic thing | NOVELS, 16; PLAYS, 13
behold the Englishman . . . p. tip-and-run | ENGLISH, 13
Better than a p. | HOUSES OF PARLIAMENT, 6
If you p. with fire | DANGER, 2
Judge not the p. | JUDGMENT, 8; PLAYS, 8
p., I remember, pleas'd not the million | TASTE, 6
p.'s the thing | PLAYS, 11
'P. up! p. up! and p. the game!' | WAR, 75
Rehearsing a p. is making the word flesh | PLAYS, 9
The little victims p. | IGNORANCE, 7
this may be p. to you, 'tis death to us | SERIOUSNESS, 2
unless the p. is stopped, the child cannot . . . go on | AUDIENCES, 2
writing a good p. is difficult | PLAYS, 7
playboy p. of the western world | LOSS, 6
player poor p., That struts and frets his hour | LIFE, 41
players men and women merely p. | HUMAN CONDITION, 15
to conceal the fact that the p. cannot act | ACTING, 1
play-going A good many inconveniences attend p. | PLAYS, 12
plays p. about rape, sodomy and drug addiction | THEATRE, 5
Robert Browning, you writer of p. | WRITERS, 6
plaything A book that furnishes no quotations is, . . . a p. | QUOTATIONS, 9
A child's a p. for an hour | CHILDREN, 31
pleasant If we do not find anything p. | NOVELTY, 10
lovely and p. in their lives | FRIENDSHIP, 9
p. it is to have money | MONEY, 16
please go anywhere I damn well p. | FREEDOM, 2
he that is married careth . . . how he may p. his wife | MARRIAGE, 23
I . . . do what I p. | FREEDOM, 11
Music, Maestro, P. | MUSIC, 26
Natural to p. | CHARACTER, 6
Nothing can permanently p. | PLEASURE, 10
They . . . say what they p. | FREEDOM, 11
pleases every prospect p. | MISANTHROPY, 1
one makes lovers as fast as one p. | LOVE, 40
pleasing The art of p. consists in | PLEASURE, 12
the surest method . . . of p. | EXAMPLE, 3
pleasure A fool bolts p., then complains of . . . indigestion | DEBAUCHERY, 1
a p. in the pathless woods | NATURE, 3
as much p. in the reading | PLEASURE, 25
Debauchee, . . . One who has . . . pursued p. | DEBAUCHERY, 3
did p. me in his top-boots | SEX, 26
dissipation without p. | LONDON, 7
Everyone is dragged on by their favourite p. | PLEASURE, 29
gave p. to the spectators | PURITANISM, 3
greatest p. . . . to do a good action | GOOD, 8
hatred is by far the longest p. | LOVE AND HATE, 1
He that takes p. to hear sermons | PLEASURE, 26
I make poetry and give p. . . . because of you | INSPIRATION, 4
knowledge and wonder . . . is an impression of p. | KNOWLEDGE, 5; WONDER, 1
Love ceases to be a p. | LOVE, 21
Money gives me p. | MONEY, 8
No p. without pain | PLEASURE, 1
no sterner moralist than P. | PLEASURE, 7
P. after all is a safer guide | PLEASURE, 6
P. is . . . intermission of pain | PLEASURE, 27
P. is . . . seldom found where it is sought | PLEASURE, 14
P. never is at home | DISCONTENT, 1
p. of your company | MOUNTAINS, 2
Romanticism is . . . presenting people with the literary works . . . affording . . . the greatest . . . p. | LITERATURE, 16
The only sensual p. without vice | MUSIC, 23
The p. of criticizing | CRITICISM, 24
the p. of offering my seat to three ladies | OBESITY, 3
The sight . . . gave me infinite p. | EXECUTION, 21
The ugliest of trades have their moments of p. | OCCUPATIONS, 7
understanding will . . . extinguish p. | POETRY, 19; UNDERSTANDING, 5
what p. . . . they have in taking their roguish tobacco | SMOKING, 8
Youth is full of p. | AGE, 52
pleasure-dome A stately p. decree | PLEASURE, 8
sunny p. with caves of ice | PLEASURE, 9
pleasures Earth fills her lap with p. | NATURE, 19
interfering with the p. of others | ABSTINENCE, 7
Love and all his p. | SEX, 8
Mid p. and palaces though we may roam | HOME, 7
No man is a hypocrite in his p. | PLEASURE, 15

One half . . . cannot understand the p. | PLEASURE, 3
One of the p. of middle age is to *find out* that one WAS right | AGE, 43
P. are all alike | PLEASURE, 26
p. are their only care | EXPLOITATION, 2
P. newly found are sweet | PLEASURE, 31
purest of human p. | GARDENS, 2
The English take their p. | ENGLAND, 36
the paucity of human p. | HUNTING, 5
plenty but just had p. | SATISFACTION, 2
that p. should attain the poor | SELF-INTEREST, 2
plods plowman homeward p. his weary way | DAY, 6
plot hath many changes | PLAYS, 8
the p. thickens | INTRIGUE, 1
plough To get it ready for the p. | ENGLAND, 3
We p. the fields, and scatter | AGRICULTURE, 1
ploughing Is my team p. | AGRICULTURE, 3
plowman The p. homeward plods his weary way | DAY, 6
plowshares beat their swords into p. | WAR AND PEACE, 2
pluck if thy right eye offend thee, p. it out | RETRIBUTION, 7
p. till time and times are done | DESIRE, 16
plural in the p. and they bounce | INSULTS, 25
plus P. *ça change* | CONSTANCY, 3
Plymouth dreamin' . . . o' P. Hoe | WAR, 76
poacher a p. a keeper turned inside out | OCCUPATIONS, 8
pocket carried a . . . brick in his p. | BUSINESS, 18
smile I could feel in my hip p. | SEX, 12
To be played with both hands in the p. | MUSIC, 38
pockets the p. of the people | TAXATION, 9
Podduyev life had prepared P. for living | DEATH, 110
poem A long p. is a test of invention | POETRY, 22
A p. lovely as a tree | TREES, 7
I do not think this p. will reach its destination | CRITICISM, 49
P. me no poems | POETRY, 27
poems A man does not write p. | POETRY, 46
My p. are hymns of praise | POETRY, 45
p. . . . for the love of Man and in praise of God | POETRY, 47
that Anon, who wrote so many p. | WOMEN, 81
The bad p. . . . created during abstinence | ABSTINENCE, 6
We all write p. | POETRY, 15
poet a modern p.'s fate? | CRITICS, 7
A true p. does not bother to be poetical | POETS, 9
godly p. must be chaste himself | POETRY, 9
lunatic, the lover, and the p. | LOVE, 115; POETRY, 42
Many brave men . . . unmourned and unknown, . . . because they lack their sacred p. | OBLIVION, 1
no person can be a p. . . . without . . . unsoundness of mind | POETRY, 76
No p., no artist of any sort, has his complete meaning alone | ARTS, 3
p.'s eye, in a fine frenzy | POETRY, 40
p. without love | POETS, 7
The p. and the dreamer are distinct | OPPOSITES, 2
The p. gives us his essence | POETRY AND PROSE, 6
To be a p. is a condition | POETS, 14
poetic the laws of p. truth and p. beauty | POETRY, 2
poetical A true poet does not bother to be p. | POETS, 9
that werges on the p. | POETRY, 12
poetry Angling is somewhat like p. | FISHING, 2
As civilization advances, p. . . . declines | CIVILIZATION, 8
Even when p. has a meaning | POETRY, 19; UNDERSTANDING, 5
If p. comes not . . . as leaves to a tree | POETRY, 24
I make p. and give pleasure . . . because of you | INSPIRATION, 4
Mr Shaw . . . has never written any p. | WRITERS, 8
no man ever talked p. | POETRY, 11
no person can . . . enjoy p., without . . . unsoundness of mind | POETRY, 26
One of the purposes of p. | POETRY, 44
P. is a comforting piece of fiction | POETRY, 28
P. is as exact a science as geometry | POETRY, 14
P. is as much a part of the universe | POETRY, 6
P. is baroque | POETRY AND PROSE, 4
p. is . . . more philosophical . . . than history | POETRY, 1
P. is not a turning loose of emotion | POETRY, 13
P. is opposed to science, . . . prose to metre | POETRY AND PROSE, 1
P. is the record of the best and happiest moments | POETRY, 43
P. is the spontaneous overflow of powerful feelings | POETRY, 52
P. is to prose | POETRY AND PROSE, 5
P. is what gets lost in translation | TRANSLATION, 3
p. makes nothing happen | POETRY, 5
p. reminds him of the richness | POETRY, 25
P. . . . set to more or less lascivious music | POETRY, 28

the p. . . . need love, . . . need care, . . . have to be wanted
POVERTY, 28
the p. person . . . thinks money would help   MONEY, 26
The p. . . . their function . . . is to exercise our generosity
POVERTY, 25
Though I be p., I'm honest   HONESTY, 5
To be p. and independent   POVERTY, 4
very p. are unthinkable   POVERTY, 3
What fun it would be to be p.   EXCESS, 2
poorer   for richer for p.   MARRIAGE, 27
poorest   p. man may in his cottage bid defiance to . . . the
Crown   PRIVACY, 3
pop   In England, p. art and fine art   ART, 14
poplars   The p. are felled   TREES, 3
poppies   the p. blow   MEMORIALS, 8
populace   society distributes itself into
Barbarians, Philistines, and P.   AMERICA, 1
the p. cannot exact their demands   HOUSES OF PARLIAMENT, 19
this vast residuum we may . . . give the name of P.   PUBLIC, 2
popular   Nothing can render them p.   CLERGY, 11
The worse I do, the more p. I get   POPULARITY, 5
We're more p. than Jesus Christ   POPULARITY, 6
popularity   P.? . . . glory's small change   POPULARITY, 4
P. is a crime   POPULARITY, 3
population   a starving p.   IRELAND, 4
P., . . . increases in a geometrical ratio   ECONOMICS, 2
populi   Vox p., vox dei   PUBLIC, 1
porcupines   I shall throw two p. under you   THREATS, 2
Porlock   by a person on business from P.   INTERRUPTIONS, 1
pornography   P. is the attempt to insult sex   PORNOGRAPHY, 2
p. . . . it is terribly, terribly boring   PORNOGRAPHY, 1
p. of war   WAR, 7
You don't get any p. . . . on the telly   PORNOGRAPHY, 5
port   Any p. in a storm'   DANGER, 1
'it would be p. if it could'   ALCOHOL, 11
porter   Oh, mister p., what shall I do   TRAVEL, 17
portion   best p. of a good man's life   KINDNESS, 6
portions   P. and parcels of the dreadful Past   TIME, 33
portrait   Every man's work . . . is always a p. of himself
ARTS, 1
Every time I paint a p. I lose a friend   PAINTING, 15
portraits   P. of famous bards and preachers   PAINTING, 16
posh   only two p. papers on a Sunday   NEWSPAPERS, 9
posies   a thousand fragrant p.   FLOWERS, 7
position   only one p. for an artist   WALES, 3
possessing   too dear for my p.   PARTING, 11
possession   P. is nine points   LAW, 4
The p. of a book   OSTENTATION, 2
the p. of it is intolerable   MATERIALISM, 19
possessions   Not the owner of many p. will you be right to call
happy   HAPPINESS, 9
p. for a moment of time   LAST WORDS, 17
possibility   too much of a sceptic to deny the p. of anything
SCEPTICISM, 2
possible   something is p., he is . . . right   SCIENCE, 5
the art of the p.   POLITICS, 11
post   p. of honour is a private station   VICE, 1
post-chaise   I would spend my life in driving briskly in a p.
PLEASURE, 16
posterity   doing something for p.   POSTERITY, 2
The nations which have put mankind and p. most in their debt
NATIONS, 2
Think of your p.   POSTERITY, 1
Thy p. shall sway   ENGLAND, 12
postgraduate   The British p. student is a lonely forlorn soul
EDUCATION, 31
postscript   all the pith is in the p.   LETTER-WRITING, 1
he would put that which was most material in the p.   LETTER-
WRITING, 2
postures   It requires one to assume such indecent p.
CRICKET, 7
pot   greasy Joan doth keel the p.   WINTER, 6
potent   how p. cheap music is   MUSIC, 15
potter   Who is the P.   CREATION, 10
poultry   A p. matter   MONEY, 29; PUNS, 13
pound   the p. . . . in your pocket   ECONOMICS, 14
pounds   My dear fellow, . . . I only ask you for twenty-five p.
BORROWING, 11
the p. will take care of themselves   THRIFT, 9
two hundred p. a year   MONEY, 13
pouvait   si vieillesse p.   AGE, 22
poverty   A hole is the accident . . . a darn is . . . p.   THRIFT, 9
crime so shameful as p.   POVERTY, 7

Do you call p. a crime   POVERTY, 27
from nothing to a state of extreme p.   POVERTY, 23
generations . . . have struggled in p. to build these altars
RELIGION, 46
If p. is the mother of crime, stupidity is its father   CRIME, 4
It is easy enough to say that p. is no crime   POVERTY, 17
Loneliness . . . is the most terrible p.   LONELINESS, 7
Notwithstanding the p. of my . . . experience   CONTENTMENT, 4
P. and oysters   POVERTY, 6
p. . . . is a blunder   POVERTY, 17
P. is a great enemy to human happiness   POVERTY, 18
P. is an anomaly to rich people   HUNGER, 2
P. is not a crime   POVERTY, 2
The misfortunes of p.   POVERTY, 19
three great evils, boredom, vice, and p.   WORK, 23
world p. is primarily a problem of two million villages
POVERTY, 26
powder   keep your p. dry   PRUDENCE, 6
when your p.'s runnin' low   PATRIOTISM, 19
powdered   Stratford, . . . suggests p. history   ENGLAND, 18
power   All that is literature seeks to communicate p.   BOOKS, 1
As we make sex less secretive, we may rob it of its p.
SEX, 46
corridors of p.   POWER, 17
Germany will be . . . a world p.   GERMANY, 4
greater the p.   POWER, 7
He aspired to p.   POWER, 20
If, drunk with sight of p., we loose   BOASTS, 4
its source of p.: ownership   CAPITALISM, 2
Knowledge itself is p.   KNOWLEDGE, 3
love of p. is the love of ourselves   FREEDOM, 15
Men of p. have not time to read   POWER, 9
one of these is the history of political p.   HISTORY, 20
P. . . . and Liberty . . . are seldom upon good Terms   POWER, 10;
FREEDOM, 4
P. corrupts   POWER, 19
p. is apt to corrupt   POWER, 14
P. is the ultimate aphrodisiac   POWER, 11
P. tends to corrupt   POWER, 3
p. without responsibility   JOURNALISM, 2; RESPONSIBILITY, 2;
RESPONSIBILITY, 8
The accursed p. which stands on Privilege   POLITICS, 3
The balance of p.   POWER, 22
the kingdom of God is not in word, but in p.   GOD, 12
they . . . take, who have the p.   POWER, 23
War knows no p.   WAR, 17
When p. narrows the areas of man's concern   POETRY, 4
wrong sort of people are always in p.   POWER, 24
You only have p. over people   POWER, 18
powerful   Guns will make us p.   POWER POLITICS, 1
The rich and p. know   GOD, 2
powerless   Brief and p.   HUMAN CONDITION, 13
p. to be born   LIMBO, 1
powers   a taste for hidden and forbidden p.   SCIENCE, 26
Headmasters have p.   EDUCATION, 12
the p. of a first-rate man and the creed of a second-rate man
POLITICIANS, 2
pox   You will die either on the gallows, or of the p.
REPARTEE, 5
practical   Compassion is . . . an absolutely p. belief   SOCIALISM, 7
meddling with any p. part of life   OBJECTIVITY, 2
P. men, . . . are usually the slaves of some defunct economist
INFLUENCE, 5
practice   a thing may look evil in theory, . . . in p. excellent
THEORY, 1
P. makes perfect   EXPERIENCE, 5
practiced   A genius! For thirty-seven years I've p. . . . and now
they call me a genius   GENIUS, 1
practise   P. what you preach   EXAMPLE, 1
two kinds of morality . . . one which we preach but do not p.
MORALITY, 12
praise   bury Caesar, not to p. him   EVIL, 15
Damn with faint p.   CRITICISM, 38
envy is a kind of p.   ENVY, 2
if we p. ourselves fearlessly, something will always stick
PRAISE, 2
I will p. any man that will p. me   FLATTERY, 7
Let us with a gladsome mind P. the Lord   GOD, 36
My poems are hymns of p.   POETRY, 45
Pavilioned in splendour, and girded with p.   GOD, 22
People . . . only want p.   CRITICISM, 32
P. the Lord and pass the ammunition   WAR, 36
this blest man, let his just p. be given   COMPLIMENTS, 8

To refuse p. PRAISE, 6
we but p. ourselves in other men PRAISE, 5
praises He who p. everybody INSINCERITY, 2
The idiot who p., with enthusiastic tone, All centuries but
this, and every country but his own DISCONTENT, 2
yet he p. those who follow different paths? DISCONTENT, 4
praising advantage of . . . p. . . . . oneself PRAISE, 4
pram sombre enemy of good art than the p. BABIES, 1
pray p. for you at St Paul's PRAYER, 15
P. to God and say the lines ACTING, 3
watch and p. IMPERFECTION, 4
when ye p., use not vain repetitions PRAYER, 4
praye Fare well . . . and p. for me FAMILY, 29
prayed I wish that God had not given me what I p. for!
DISAPPOINTMENT, 7
prayer More things are wrought by p. PRAYER, 14
P. makes the Christian's armour bright PRAYER, 10
storms of p. EXCESS, 14
The people's p. DREAMS, 5
The p. that . . . heals the sick FAITH, 10
prayers better than good men's p. PRAYER, 7
prayeth He p. well PRAYER, 8
prays man p. . . . for a miracle PRAYER, 17
preach two kinds of morality . . . one which we p. but do not
practise MORALITY, 12
preachers Portraits of famous bards and p. PAINTING, 16
P. say, Do as I say, not as I do EXAMPLE, 7
preaching A woman's p. is like a dog's walking on his hinder
legs WOMEN, 38
precedency the point of p. between a louse and a flea
POETS, 18
precedent A p. embalms a principle EXAMPLE, 6
precious Right is more p. RIGHT, 4
so p. that it must be rationed FREEDOM, 26
precisely thinking too p. on th' event COWARDICE, 7
pre-cognitive Love means the p. flow LOVE, 78
predestination Free Will and P. DESTINY, 5
predicament Life . . . is a p. LIFE, 39
predictions Dreams and p. DREAMS, 1
prefabricated a better word than p. WORDS, 6
preferment P.'s door PROMOTION, 1
preferred he . . . coming after me is p. before me
CHRISTIANITY, 11
pregnancy quite lawful for a Catholic woman to avoid p. by . . .
mathematics CONTRACEPTION, 3
prejudge I do not . . . p. the past PREJUDICE, 6
prejudice I am free of all p. HATE, 3
skilled appeals to religious p. EVOLUTION, 9
prejudices collection of p. which is called political philosophy
POLITICS, 58
Common sense is the collection of p. PREJUDICE, 3
freedom to print . . . proprietor's p. JOURNALISM, 25
premise fundamental p. of a revolution REVOLUTION, 8
pre-natal the greatness of Russia is only her p. struggling
RUSSIA, 2
preparation life . . . seems to me p. for something that never
happens LIFE, 51
no p. is thought necessary POLITICS, 67
prepare I go to p. a place for you HEAVEN, 3
I p. for a journey . . . as though for death TRAVEL, 19
prerogative p. of the eunuch RESPONSIBILITY, 13
Presbyter P. is but old Priest writ large RELIGION, 40
presence A certain person may have . . . a wonderful p.
CHARACTER, 19
present an un-birthday p. GIFTS, 3
novelists the story of the p. NOVELS, 6
P. mirth hath present laughter PRESENT, 13
to know nothing but the p., or nothing but the past
CONSERVATISM, 4
preserve p. one last male thing MASCULINITY, 2
president American . . . prepared to run for P. POLITICS, 74
anybody could become P. POLITICIANS, 21
I'd rather be right than p. RIGHT, 3
nobody is strongminded around a P. SERVILITY, 6
one thing about being P. POWER, 8
P. spends . . . time kissing people PERSUASION, 4
the P. is dead, but the Government lives and God Omnipotent
reigns ASSASSINATION, 2
We are all the P.'s men LOYALTY, 7
press a gentleman of the P. JOURNALISM, 12
I'm with you on the free p.. It's the newspapers
JOURNALISM, 24
Never lose your temper with the P. SELF-CONTROL, 7

would not say that our P. is obscene JOURNALISM, 15
presume Dr Livingstone, I p. GREETINGS, 3
Know then thyself, p. not God to scan SELF-KNOWLEDGE, 5
pretending p. to be wicked HYPOCRISY, 17
pretty a p. girl who naked is NAKEDNESS, 3
One girl can be p. BEAUTY, 17
There's only one p. child CHILDREN, 2
Preux Saint P. never kicked the fireirons IMPERFECTION, 5
preventing Politics is the art of p. people from taking part
POLITICS, 73
prevention P. is better than cure PRUDENCE, 4
prevents Nothing p. us from being natural SPONTANEITY, 4
prey lord of all things, yet a p. to all HUMAN CONDITION, 12
price a better p. than old mistresses PAINTING, 1
Courage is the p. . . . for granting peace COURAGE, 10
her p. is far above rubies WOMEN, 17
P. of Herald three cents daily NEWSPAPERS, 3
The p. . . . for pursuing any profession DISILLUSION, 1
the p. of everything and the value of nothing CYNICISM, 4
those men their p. CORRUPTION, 8
Who never knew the p. of happiness HAPPINESS, 29
prick If you p. us, do we not bleed EQUALITY, 18
p. the sides of my intent AMBITION, 16
pride A mother's p. EXPECTATION, 4
Be modest! It is the kind of p. least likely to offend
MODESTY, 5
contempt on all my p. HUMILITY, 12
Is P., the never-failing vice of fools PRIDE, 7
it is p., but understood in a different way PRIDE, 9
P. and Truth, That long to give themselves for . . . youth
AGE, 68
p. goeth before destruction PRIDE, 1
p. that licks the dust SERVILITY, 5
So sleeps the p. of former days IRELAND, 10
There is false modesty, but there is no false p. PRIDE, 8
prides His Royal Highness . . . p. himself upon . . . the excellent
harvest ARROGANCE, 7
priest A p. sees people at their best OCCUPATIONS, 1
For a p. to turn a man when he lies a-dying PERSUASION, 3
p. is a man who is called Father CATHOLICISM, 1
Presbyter is but old P. writ large RELIGION, 40
rid me of this turbulent p. ASSASSINATION, 4
That waked the p. all shaven and shorn NURSERY RHYMES, 57
That whisky p. CLERGY, 6
priest-craft e'r P. did begin RELIGION, 17
priesthood Literary men are . . . a perpetual p. WRITERS, 7
priests All things, oh p., are on fire FIRE, 1
I always like to associate with a lot of p. CLERGY, 1
In old time we had treen chalices and golden p. CLERGY, 7
prima donnas They are for p. or corpses FLOWERS, 11
prime having lost . . . your p., You may for ever tarry
MARRIAGE, 67
One's p. is elusive AGE, 55
prime minister society . . . pays a harlot 25 times as much as it
pays its P. INJUSTICE, 14
that of P. is filled by fluke POLITICIANS, 57
when a British P. sneezed BRITAIN, 11
prime ministers rogue elephant among British p.
POLITICIANS, 51
primitive The classics are only p. literature CLASSICS, 6
primroses smiles, Wan as p. FLOWERS, 5
Prince of Wales who's danced with the P. SNOBBERY, 4
princes mine were p. of the earth JEWS, 2
They say p. learn no art truly, but . . . horsemanship HORSES, 7
principal It is not my interest to pay the p., nor my principle
to pay the interest BORROWING, 10
principle A precedent embalms a p. EXAMPLE, 6
except from some strong p. MOTIVE, 4
the most useful thing about a p. . . . . sacrificed to expediency
EXPEDIENCY, 4
the p. seems the same WATER, 1
you never can tell. That's a p. PRINCIPLES, 4
principles All universal moral p. are idle fancies MORALITY, 13
And wrote 'P. of Political Economy' ECONOMICS, 2
easier to fight for one's p. PRINCIPLES, 1
If one sticks too rigidly to one's p. PRINCIPLES, 2
The p. of a free constitution GOVERNMENT, 10
The p. of logic and metaphysics are true PHILOSOPHY, 1
Whenever two good people argue over p. PRINCIPLES, 3
whether I embrace your lordship's p. or your mistress
REPARTEE, 5
whoever is moved . . . is conscious of a continued miracle . . .
which subverts all the p. of his understanding CHRISTIANITY, 29

print decomposing in the eternity of p. CRITICISM, 53
news that's fit to p. NEWSPAPERS, 8
pleasant, sure, to see one's name in p. BOOKS, 9
The big p. giveth and the fine p. taketh away BUSINESS, 15
printers those books by which the p. have lost BOOKS, 17
printing Gunpowder, P., and the Protestant Religion CIVILIZATION, 3
priorities The language of p. is SOCIALISM, 1
prison an extraordinarily pleasant p. LEXICOGRAPHY, 1
Anyone who has been to . . . public school will . . . feel . . . at home in p. EDUCATION, 59
Stone walls do not a p. make IMPRISONMENT, 4
the true place for a just man is also a p. JUSTICE, 24
The world . . . is but a large p. EXECUTION, 23
prisoner I object to your being taken p. ROYALTY, 20
P., God has given you good abilities THEFT, 3
prisoners If this is the way Queen Victoria treats her p. IMPRISONMENT, 11
p. of addiction and . . . prisoners of envy MATERIALISM, 10
prisons not enough p. . . . in Palestine to hold all the Jews JEWS, 10
P. are built with stones of Law HYPOCRISY, 4
privacy a right to share your p. in a public place PRIVACY, 4
That should assure us of . . . forty-five minutes of undisturbed p. INATTENTION, 2
private He was meddling too much in my p. life PSYCHIATRY, 11
P. Means is dead PUNS, 20
Scientific discovery is a p. event SCIENCE, 24
sex has been a very p., secretive activity SEX, 46
The grave's a fine and p. place DEATH, 77
Travel is the most p. of pleasures TRAVEL, 22
Whatsoever . . . the p. calamity, I hope it will not interfere with the public business of the country FIRE, 3
when religion is allowed to invade . . . p. life RELIGION, 38
privilege a defender of p. PESSIMISM, 2
an Englishman's heaven-born p. of doing as he likes PUBLIC, 2
The accursed power which stands on P. POLITICS, 3
prize Men p. the thing ungain'd DESIRE, 13
Not all that tempts your wand'ring eyes . . . is lawful p. TEMPTATION, 6
prizes just miss the p. at the flower show MEDIOCRITY, 2
The world continues to offer glittering p. RUTHLESSNESS, 6
P.R.O. partly a liaison man and partly P. BUSINESS, 3
problem ineffectual liberal's p. LIBERALISM, 1
Not every p. someone has with his girlfriend is . . . due to . . . capitalist . . . production CAPITALISM, 8
problems Among the many p. . . . the choice of the moment . . . to begin his novel WRITERS, 37
There are two p. in my life POLITICIANS, 23
procession A torchlight p. ALCOHOL, 44
prodigal P. of Ease WORLD-WEARINESS, 1
producing Man . . . consumes without p. CAPITALISM, 10
production Capitalist p. begets . . . its own negation CAPITALISM, 9
profession Politics is . . . the only p. POLITICS, 67
The price . . . for pursuing any p. DISILLUSION, 1
professional A p. is someone whose wife works to enable him to paint ARTISTS, 8
professor A p. is one who talks in someone else's sleep ACADEMICS, 1
professors American p. like their literature clear and cold and pure and very dead LITERATURE, 10
As to religion, I hold it to be the . . . duty of government to protect all . . . p. thereof GOVERNMENT, 22
Culture is an instrument wielded by p. CULTURE, 3
now-a-days p. of philosophy but not philosophers PHILOSOPHERS, 9
profit Drop . . . what tomorrow may bring . . . count as p. every day that Fate allows you PRESENT, 8
No p. grows where is no pleasure EDUCATION, 46
Philosophers never balance between p. and honesty PHILOSOPHERS, 3
profound turbid look the most p. WRITING, 18
progeny A p. of learning MALAPROPISMS, 3
progress All p. is based EXTRAVAGANCE, 2; PROGRESS, 2
Man's 'p.' is but a gradual discovery PROGRESS, 10
Our p. . . . Is trouble and care LIFE, 32
P. . . . depends on retentiveness HISTORY, 21
'p.' is simply a comparative PROGRESS, 3
the things which government does . . . social p. GOVERNMENT, 30
What p. . . . In the Middle Ages PSYCHOLOGY, 1
What we call p. is PROGRESS, 5

progression Without Contraries is no p. CONFLICT, 4
prohibition Communism is like p. COMMUNISM, 6
proletarian you are polite to a p. you . . . bolster up the capitalist system POLITICS, 78
proletariat The dictatorship of the p. MARXISM, 5
the p. will . . . wage a class struggle for Socialism CLASS, 18
prologues P. precede the piece PLAYS, 4
prolonged the War is being deliberately p. WAR, 102
promise A p. made is a debt unpaid PROMISES, 5
rarely . . . one can see in a little boy the p. of a man CHILDREN, 20
promised Only do always in health what you have often p. to do when you are sick ILLNESS, 12
promises P. and pie-crust are made to be broken PROMISES, 7
young man of p. CHURCHILL, 3
promisin' Once you were so p. SHYNESS, 3
promptly He gives twice who gives p. PROMPTNESS, 4
pronounce foreigners . . . spell better than they p. PRONUNCIATION, 3; SPELLING, 2
p. foreign names as he chooses PRONUNCIATION, 1
spell it Vinci and p. it Vinchy PRONUNCIATION, 3; SPELLING, 2
pronouncements Science should leave off making p. SCIENCE, 21
proof feeling p. against it WINTER, 1
propaganda P. . . . consists in nearly deceiving your friends PROPAGANDA, 1
propagated If human beings could be p. . . . aristocracy would be . . . sound ARISTOCRACY, 7
propensities the silk stockings and white bosoms of your actresses excite my amorous p. LUST, 3
proper He never does a p. thing without . . . an improper reason MORALITY, 16
The p. study of Mankind is Man SELF-KNOWLEDGE, 5
property P. has its duties CAPITALISM, 2
P. is organised robbery CAPITALISM, 13
P. is theft CAPITALISM, 12
poor have no right to the p. of the rich POVERTY AND WEALTH, 6
The future is the only kind of p. SLAVERY, 1
the right of governing was not p. but a trust GOVERNMENT, 9
prophecies bring about the verification of his own p. PROPHECY, 10
prophet A historian is a p. in reverse HISTORIANS, 6
a p. is not without honour HONOUR, 1
there arose not a p. . . . like unto Moses PROPHECY, 2
The sons of the p. were brave men and bold COURAGE, 1
proportion strangeness in the p. BEAUTY, 6
Proportional Representation P. . . . fundamentally counter-democratic POLITICS, 37
proposes Man p. GOD, 29
proposition undesirable to believe a p. SCEPTICISM, 4
propriety The p. of . . . having improper thoughts about . . . neighbours MORALITY, 4
prose anything except bad p. PROSE, 2
difference between . . . p. and metrical composition POETRY AND PROSE, 7
I can only write p. today POETRY AND PROSE, 8
I have been talking p. for over forty years PROSE, 3
no one hears his own remarks as p. PROSE, 1
P. . . . can bear a great deal of poetry POETRY AND PROSE, 3
Poetry is opposed to science, . . . p. to metre POETRY AND PROSE, 1
Poetry is to p. POETRY AND PROSE, 5
poetry sinks and swoons under . . . p. POETRY AND PROSE, 3
p. = words in their best order POETRY AND PROSE, 2
the p. for God LANGUAGE, 12
to write good p. is an affair of good manners POETRY AND PROSE, 4
prosper Treason doth never p. TREASON, 3
prosperitee A man to have ben in p. MISFORTUNE, 7
him that stood in greet p. MISFORTUNE, 6
prosperity P. doth best discover vice MISFORTUNE, 3
prostitutes the small nations like p. DIPLOMACY, 13
prostitution P. . . . keeps her out of trouble SEX, 18
P. . . . provides fresh air and wholesome exercise SEX, 18
protect p. the writer BUREAUCRACY, 1
protest lady doth p. too much EXCESS, 8
Protestant A P. with a horse NATIONALITY, 2
Gunpowder, Printing, and the P. Religion CIVILIZATION, 3
I am the P. whore RELIGION, 28
P. women may take the Pill CONTRACEPTION, 6
Too much counterpoint; what is worse, P. counterpoint CRITICISM, 3

Protestantism The chief contribution of P. to human thought
PROTESTANTISM, 1
Protestants God knows how you P. . . . have any sense of
direction CATHOLICISM, 12
P. protesting against Protestantism CATHOLICISM, 7
Proteus P. rising from the sea DISCONTENT, 10
protozoon Organic life . . . has developed . . . from the p. to the
philosopher PROGRESS, 11
proud Death be not p. DEATH, 42
He who does not need to lie is p. LYING, 13
no guarantee . . . you will not be p. of the feat HUMILITY, 4
p. me no prouds GRATITUDE, 3
too p. to fight WAR, 132
Yes; I am p. PRIDE, 6
proudest the moment of greatest humiliation is . . . when the
spirit is p. PRIDE, 5
prove p. anything by figures STATISTICS, 1
proved p. upon our pulses PHILOSOPHY, 8
What is now p. was . . . imagined PROOF, 2
proverb A p. is much matter SAYINGS, 4
no p. to you till your life has illustrated it EXPERIENCE, 17
p. is one man's wit and all men's wisdom SAYINGS, 6
proverbs p. provide them with wisdom STUPIDITY, 7
provided Add: 'p. he is really dead' ADMIRATION, 6
providence a kind of P. will . . . end . . . the acts of God
DISASTER, 2
fathom the inscrutable workings of P. REPARTEE, 4
that P. dictates with the assurance of a sleepwalker
DESTINY, 11
This is the temple of P. LUCK, 7
providential a case of P. interference LUCK, 12
province all knowledge to be my p. KNOWLEDGE, 4
provinces The reluctant obedience of distant p. DIPLOMACY, 16
provincial worse than p. – he was parochial WRITERS, 20
provincialism rather be taken in adultery than . . . p.
FASHION, 4
provocations To great evils we submit; we resent little p.
TRIVIALITY, 9
provoke p. not your children FAMILY, 9
P. The years OLD AGE, 49
provoked an opportunity of being p. PROVOCATION, 1
provokes No one p. me with impunity RETRIBUTION, 2
prude twenty is no age to be a p. PRUDERY, 2
prudence freedom of speech, freedom of conscience, and the
p. never to practise . . . them FREEDOM, 50
Psyche Your mournful P. SOUL, 9
psychiatrist Anybody who goes to see a p. PSYCHIATRY, 4
A p. is a man who goes to the Folies-Bergère PSYCHIATRY, 9
the century of the p.'s couch PSYCHIATRY, 8
psychiatrists P. classify a person as neurotic PSYCHIATRY, 10
psychic p. development of the individual PSYCHIATRY, 3
psychological the profession of historian fits a man for p.
analysis PSYCHOLOGY, 2
There is no such thing as p. CHARACTER, 18
psychology Children . . . have no use for p.. They detest
sociology BOOKS, 36
psychopathologist the p. the unspeakable PSYCHIATRY, 7
psychotic Psychiatrists classify a person as . . . p.
PSYCHIATRY, 10
puberty We are all American at p. NATIONALITY, 10
public a more mean, stupid, . . . ungrateful animal than the p.
PUBLIC, 13
a right to share your privacy in a p. place PRIVACY, 4
false to his friends . . . true to the p. HONESTY, 5
flinging a pot of paint in the p.'s face CRITICISM, 43
give the p. what they want to see and they'll come out for it
FUNERALS, 8
If the British p. falls for this . . . it will be . . . bonkers
POLITICS, 28
Never lose your temper with . . . the p. SELF-CONTROL, 7
not describe holding p. office GOVERNMENT, 1
Not even a p. figure POLITICIANS, 20
strike against p. safety STRIKES, 2
The p. be damned. I am working for my stockholders
CAPITALISM, 15
The p. buys its opinions as it buys its meat PUBLIC, 7
The P. is an old woman PUBLIC, 8
three things . . . the p. will always clamour for NOVELTY, 3
transform this society without a major extension of p.
ownership SOCIALISM, 8
twenty years of marriage make her . . . like a p. building
MARRIAGE, 119

Whatsoever . . . the private calamity, I hope it will not interfere
with the p. business of the country FIRE, 3
public school Anyone who has been to . . . p. will . . . feel . . .
at home in prison EDUCATION, 59
enjoy a p. EDUCATION, 13
Keats's vulgarity with a P. accent CRITICISM, 26
P. are the nurseries of all vice EDUCATION, 16
p., where . . . learning was painfully beaten into him
EDUCATION, 41
the p. system all over EDUCATION, 58
publish I'll p., right or wrong PUBLISHING, 2
P. and be damned PUBLISHING, 9
p. and be sued PUBLISHING, 7
published not so much p. as carried screaming
NEWSPAPERS, 14
you may destroy whatever you haven't p. PUBLISHING, 6
publisher Barabbas was a p. PUBLISHING, 3
publishers those with irrational fear of life become p.
PUBLISHING, 5
Puccini Wagner is the P. of music COMPOSERS, 4
puffeth knowledge p. up, but charity edifieth CHARITY, 6;
KNOWLEDGE, 8
pulse two people with one p. LOVE, 82
pulses proved upon our p. PHILOSOPHY, 8
pumpkin coach has turned into a p. DISILLUSION, 3
pun A man who could make so vile a p. PUNS, 3
punctuality P. is the politeness of kings PROMPTNESS, 2
P. is the virtue of the bored PROMPTNESS, 5
punished Am I not p. enough in not being born an Englishman
NATIONALITY, 9
Men are rewarded and p. not for what they do MOTIVE, 6
Those who offend us are generally p. REVENGE, 14
punishing p. anyone who comes between them MARRIAGE, 100
punishment Corporal p. is . . . humiliating for him who gives it
PUNISHMENT, 12
let the p. fit the crime PUNISHMENT, 9
Virtue is its own p. RIGHTEOUSNESS, 2
punishments In nature there are neither rewards nor p.
NATURE, 11
pupils Time is a great teacher, but . . . kills all its p. TIME, 10
puppy Frogs and snails And p.-dogs' tails NURSERY RHYMES, 65
purchasers a pattern to encourage p. BUSINESS, 18
pure All those who are not racially p. RACISM, 1
Because my heart is p. INTEGRITY, 7
p. as the driven slush PURITY, 2
purgatory the p. of men ENGLAND, 16
puritan A p.'s a person who pours righteous indignation
PURITANISM, 1
The P. hated bear-baiting PURITANISM, 3
To the P. all things are impure PURITANISM, 2
puritanism P. – The haunting fear that someone . . . may be
happy PURITANISM, 4
purity I have laboured to refine our language to grammatical p.
LANGUAGE, 13
purple-stained And p. mouth ALCOHOL, 35
purpose p. of God and the doom assigned DESTINY, 21
the creature hath a p. and its eyes are bright with it
PURPOSE, 5
You seem to have no real p. in life AMBITION, 5
purse consumption of the p. MONEY, 38
Put money in thy p. MONEY, 39
pussy P. cat, p. cat, where have you been NURSERY
RHYMES, 40
P.'s in the well NURSERY RHYMES, 9
put I p. away childish things CHARITY, 5
p. up with bad things TOLERANCE, 7
pygmies wars of the p. will begin WORLD WAR II, 10
pyjamas I in p. for the heat WEATHER, 15
pylons P., those pillars Bare TECHNOLOGY, 9
pyramid bottom of the economic p. POVERTY, 24
pyramids Books are made . . . like p. BOOKS, 16
Pyrenees The fleas that tease in the high P. NONSENSE, 3

Q

quack uses his words as a q. uses his remedies VERBOSITY, 4
Quad I am always about in the Q. EXISTENCE, 1
no one about in the Q. EXISTENCE, 4
quadrupeds Dogs, like horses, are q. ANIMALS, 15
Quakers I was beaten up by Q. SHYNESS, 1
qualities Almost every man . . . attempts to display q. which he
does not possess DECEPTION, 3
q. . . . necessary for success upon the stage ACTING, 8

quantity a prodigious q. of mind INDECISION, 2
Does it contain any abstract reasoning concerning q. or number?
No PHILOSOPHY, 3
quarks Three q. for Muster Mark NONSENSE, 14
quarrel a q. in a far-away country WORLD WAR II, 1
a q. in the streets is . . . to be hated ARGUMENTS, 10
It takes . . . one to make a q. ARGUMENTS, 8
Out of the q. . . . we make rhetoric POETRY, 53
q. at the same time MARRIAGE, 88
q. . . . energies displayed in it are fine ARGUMENTS, 10
The justice of my q. JUSTICE, 16
quarrelled I did not know that we had ever q. ARGUMENTS, 15
I have q. with my wife MARRIAGE, 84
quarrels q. which vivify its barrenness LOVE, 61
Q. would not last ARGUMENTS, 12
quart one cannot put a q. in a pint cup IMPOSSIBILITY, 1
Quebec I would rather have written those lines than take Q.
POETRY, 51
queen 'Fella belong Mrs Q.' LANGUAGE, 19
he . . . happened to marry the Q. ROYALTY, 31
how very different from the home life of our own dear Q.!
ROYALTY, 2
isn't a bad bit of goods, the Q.! COMPLIMENTS, 1
I've been to London to look at the q. NURSERY RHYMES, 40
I would not be a q. For all the world ROYALTY, 30
Move Q. Anne? Most certainly not MEMORIALS, 12
sorrier for my good knights' loss than for . . . my fair q.
LOSS, 3
the British warrior q. BRITAIN, 6
The Q. of Hearts She made some tarts FOOD, 12; NURSERY
RHYMES, 51
The q. was in the parlour, Eating bread and honey NURSERY
RHYMES, 47
queenly She keeps on being Q. AFFECTATION, 2
queens for q. I might have enough LOSS, 3
queer All the world is q. SUBJECTIVITY, 5
girls are so q. WOMEN, 8
the q. old Dean SPOONERISMS, 4
There's nowt so q. DIFFERENCE, 6
thou art a little q. SUBJECTIVITY, 5
queerer the universe is . . . q. than we *can* suppose
UNIVERSE, 7
questing plashy fen passes the q. vole ANIMALS, 21
question a good q. for you to ask DIPLOMACY, 9
A timid q. will . . . receive a confident answer SHYNESS, 1
man who sees both sides of a q. OBJECTIVITY, 5
Nature has never put the fatal q. as to the meaning of their
lives PURPOSE, 4
No q. is ever settled Until ARGUMENTS, 18
not a wise q. for me to answer DIPLOMACY, 9
q. . . . which I have not been able to answer WOMEN, 32
That is the Irish Q. IRELAND, 4
that is the q. SUICIDE, 10
the q. that we do not know KNOWLEDGE, 28
questioning Q. is not the mode of conversation
CONVERSATION, 4
questionings Those obstinate q. DOUBT, 8
questions all q. are open OBJECTIVITY, 3
I do not answer q. like this without being paid MASCULINITY, 1
make two q. grow where only one RESEARCH, 4
queue An Englishman . . . forms an orderly q. of one
ENGLISH, 23
quiet Anythin' for a q. life PEACE, 8
Here, where the world is q. PEACE, 16
quietness unravish'd bride of q. SILENCE, 9
quince dined on mince, and slices of q. FOOD, 29
quintessence this q. of dust MANKIND, 26
quotable It's better to be q. than . . . honest QUOTATIONS, 12
quotation Classical q. is the *parole* of literary men
QUOTATIONS, 4
Every q. contributes something QUOTATIONS, 5
q. is a national vice QUOTATIONS, 13
the great spring of happy q. QUOTATIONS, 6
To say that anything was a q. QUOTATIONS, 10
quotations A book that furnishes no q. is, . . . a plaything
QUOTATIONS, 9
a list of q. QUOTATIONS, 8
good thing . . . to read books of q. QUOTATIONS, 1
It needs no dictionary of q. EYES, 3
quote can q. Shakespeare in an economic crisis
SHAKESPEARE, 14
quotes q. . . . give us a nodding acquaintance with the originator
QUOTATIONS, 14

rabbit The r. has a charming face RABBITS, 1
rabbits a tale of four little r. RABBITS, 2
except to shoot r. and hit his father on the jaw NASTINESS, 5
race A loftier r. KNOWLEDGE, 32
I wish I loved the Human R. MANKIND, 21
my opinion of the human r. MANKIND, 16
Slow and steady wins the r. HASTE, 7
races human species . . . composed of two distinct r.
BORROWING, 5
the r. of Europe are melting AMERICA, 40
Rachmaninov R.'s immortalizing totality was his scowl
COMPOSERS, 5
racially those who are not r. pure RACISM, 1
racing happy state of getting the victor's palm without the dust
of r. VICTORY, 6
rack Leave not a r. behind MORTALITY, 17
radical A r. is a man IDEALISM, 6
I never dared be r. when young YOUTH, 7
The r. invents the views. . . . the conservative adopts them
CONSERVATISM, 7
radicals Few r. have good digestions POLITICS, 12
radio I had the r. on NAKEDNESS, 6
Simply a r. personality CHURCHILL, 7
rage all Heaven in a r. IMPRISONMENT, 1
R., r., against the dying of the light DEATH, 117
rages the weight of r. SPOONERISMS, 1
rags no scandal like r. POVERTY, 7
only men in r. . . . Mistake themselves for carpet bags
ETIQUETTE, 3
railing R. at life, and yet afraid of death OLD AGE, 12
railway when they think they are alone in r. carriages HABIT, 5
raiment they parted his r., and cast lots FORGIVENESS, 4
rain A Hard R.'s A-Gonna Fall PESSIMISM, 5
drop of r. maketh a hole in the stone PERSISTENCE, 7
droppeth as the gentle r. MERCY, 2
falls not hail, or r., or any snow AFTERLIFE, 9
He comes in the terrible R. CHRISTIANITY, 39
R. before seven WEATHER, 2
R., r., go away WEATHER, 3
singing in the r. WEATHER, 11
rainbow Somewhere over the r. DESIRE, 7
the R. gave thee birth BIRDS, 3
raineth it r. on the just JUSTICE, 4
rains It never r. but it pours MISFORTUNE, 1
rainy Keep something for a r. day THRIFT, 2
when it is not r. WEATHER, 8
raise My God shall r. me up FAITH, 17
Now he will r. me to be a martyr MARTYRDOM, 1
rake every woman is at heart a r. WOMEN, 58
lene . . . as is a r. HORSES, 4
rallying-point The party is the r. for the . . . working class
COMMUNISM, 9
Ralph R. wept for the end of innocence INNOCENCE, 5
Randolph the only part of R. that was not malignant
INSULTS, 37
rapidly but not so r. TIME, 8
rapping r. at my chamber door SUPERNATURAL, 11
rapture a r. on the lonely shore NATURE, 3
The first fine careless r. BIRDS, 1
rare as r. things will, it vanished TRANSIENCE, 9
keep it shut up . . . like a r., r. fiddle NAKEDNESS, 5
rascal Get down you dirty r. NURSERY RHYMES, 23
rascals R., would you live for ever WAR, 38
rat Mr Speaker, I smell a r. MIXED METAPHORS, 4
That killed the r. NURSERY RHYMES, 57
ratchet politics of the pendulum, but of the r. POLITICS, 72
rationalized Happiness . . . should never be r. HAPPINESS, 7
rats R.! They fought the dogs ANIMALS, 1
ravages What do the r. of time not injure? AGE, 30
raven Quoth the R., Nevermore EVIL, 9
ravished He . . . r. this fair creature SEX, 15
raw the working-class which, r. and half-developed PUBLIC, 2
razor Satire should, like a polished r. keen SATIRE, 2
razors R. pain you SUICIDE, 5
reach a man's r. should exceed his grasp AMBITION, 3
reactionaries r. are paper tigers POLITICS, 46
read A lonesome man . . . who does not know how to r.
READING, 4
A man ought to r. just as inclination leads him READING, 8
beautiful . . . for someone who could not r. AMERICA, 7

books.... criticized and r. by people who don't understand
them BOOKS, 23
do *you* r. books *through* READING, 7
Education . . . has produced a vast population able to r.
READING, 16
everybody wants to have r. LITERATURE, 17
He writes as fast as they can r. WRITERS, 18
His books were r. BOOKS, 5; PUNS, 5
In my early years I r. very hard KNOWLEDGE, 24
I've just r. that I am dead OBITUARIES, 2
King George will be able to r. that SIGNATURES, 2
Men of power have not time to r. POWER, 9
R., mark, learn and inwardly digest LEARNING, 3
sooner r. a time-table . . . than nothing NOVELS, 10
When I want to r. a novel NOVELS, 3
will bear to be r. twice, . . . was thought twice WRITING, 3
reader A r. seldom peruses a book with pleasure WRITERS, 1
not to inform the r. BUREAUCRACY, 1
send the r. to the dictionary STYLE, 4
the writer . . . is the impregnator, . . . the r. . . . is the
respondent READING, 19
readers his r. are proud to live in it WRITERS, 12
The human race, . . . many of my r. HUMAN CONDITION, 5
to trade a hundred contemporary r. for POSTERITY, 6
Was there ever yet anything written . . . that was wished longer
by its r. LITERATURE, 8
reading as much pleasure in the r. PLEASURE, 25
a substitute for r. it OSTENTATION, 2
a tragedy and therefore not worth r. PLAYS, 2
but I prefer r. READING, 14
half learned the art of r. READING, 2
If a book is worth r. BOOKS, 32
I have led a life of business so long that I have lost my taste
for r. READING, 17
I loitered my life away, r. books DISCONTENT, 3
I shall lose no time in r. it INATTENTION, 1
Peace is poor r. WAR AND PEACE, 4
R. . . . ingenious device for avoiding thought READING, 6
R. isn't an occupation we encourage among police officers
POLICE, 4
R. is to the mind READING, 15
R. maketh a full man READING, 1
There are two motives for r. a book READING, 13
The r. of all good books LITERATURE, 3
When I am not walking, I am r. READING, 9
ready I have but ninepence in r. money CONVERSATION, 2
ready made critics all are r. CRITICS, 2
Why not r. WORDS, 6
Reagan disastrous fire in President R.'s library both books
were destroyed INSULTS, 18
real I could have become a r. painter LAST WORDS, 33
Nothing ever becomes r. till it is experienced EXPERIENCE, 17
whether Zelda and I are r. FICTION, 2
realistic he is going to make 'a r. decision', . . . resolved to do
something bad DECISION, 3
reality art . . . r. which is . . . in our minds ARTS, 6
As far as the laws of mathematics refer to r. MATHEMATICS, 1
by r. I mean shops like Selfridges REALITY, 3
Cannot bear very much r. REALITY, 2
statesmen of the world . . . are far more dangerous, and far
more estranged from r. NUCLEAR WEAPONS, 1
The whole of art is an appeal to a r. ARTS, 6
realize I saw it, but I did not r. it PERCEPTION, 4
realm A worse king never left a r. undone ROYALTY, 6
realms travell'd in the r. of gold TRAVEL, 15
reap sown the wind . . . r. the whirlwind RETRIBUTION, 5
whatsoever a man soweth, that shall he also r. RETRIBUTION, 4
Reaper a R. whose name is Death DEATH, 74
reaping No, r. PUNS, 2
reappear all great events and personalities in . . . history r.
HISTORY, 18
reason A man who does not lose his r. REASON, 4
Faith consists in believing when it is beyond the power of r. to
believe FAITH, 19
happiness is not an ideal of r. HAPPINESS, 13
He never does a proper thing without . . . an improper r.
MORALITY, 16
he who destroys a good book, kills r. BOOKS, 24
Human r. won. Mankind won VICTORY, 7
it was neither rhyme nor r. CRITICISM, 33
man . . . is R.'s slave PASSION, 1
nothing is law that is not r. LAW, 21
not to r. why OBEDIENCE, 4

Once the people begin to r. PUBLIC, 18
Only r. can convince us OBJECTIVITY, 3
right deed for the wrong r. MOTIVE, 2
R. is itself a matter of faith REASON, 2
r. not the need NECESSITY, 5
The madman . . . has lost everything except his r. MADNESS, 3
the r. of the case LAW, 21
The ruling passion conquers r. still PASSION, 6
who turns mad for a r. MADNESS, 2
woman's r. WOMEN, 64
reasonable Act of God . . . *something which no r. man could
have expected* DISASTER, 3
figure of 'The R. Man' LAW, 15
Who kills a man kills a r. creature BOOKS, 24
reasoners most plausible r. THINKING, 3
reasoning *Does it contain any abstract r. concerning quantity or
number?* No PHILOSOPHY, 3
reasons Metaphysics is the finding of bad r. METAPHYSICS, 2
never give your r. JUDGMENT, 11
r. for not printing any list of subscribers FRANKNESS, 2
The heart has its r. MOTIVE, 5
two r. for drinking THIRST, 1
rebel how to r. and conform at the same time YOUTH, 5
What is a r. REBELLION, 2
rebellion A little r. now and then REBELLION, 5
recall The Gods themselves cannot r. their gifts
IRREVOCABILITY, 2
receipts How were the r. today in Madison Square Garden
LAST WORDS, 5
receive whoso shall r. one such little child CHILDREN, 15
received freely ye have r., freely give GENEROSITY, 2; GIFTS, 2
receiver your wife . . . is a r. of stolen goods INSULTS, 19
reception men that . . . hinder the r. of every work CRITICS, 8
recession r. when . . . neighbour loses his job ECONOMICS, 11;
UNEMPLOYMENT, 2
reckon'd beggary in the love that can be r. LOVE, 110
reckoning take you . . . at your own r. SELF-RESPECT, 3
recognize did not r. me by my face PUNISHMENT, 14
recoils Revenge . . . back on itself r. REVENGE, 13
recompense R. injury with justice KINDNESS, 1
reconcile How r. this world . . . with . . . my imagining?
BLINDNESS, 2
It takes a long while for a . . . trustful person to r. himself to
. . . God FAITH, 15
recounting calms one's grief by r. it SORROW, 4
recreation woman accepted cooking . . . but man . . . made of it
a r. FOOD, 40
red Coral is far more r. ANALOGY, 3
it's not even r. brick, but white tile CLASS, 25
leeches have r. blood LAST WORDS, 14
R. Badge of Courage COURAGE, 6
R. lips are not so r. WAR, 81
R. sky at night WEATHER, 4
The people's flag is deepest r. SOCIALISM, 2
The sand of the desert is sodden r. WAR, 75
thin r. line tipped with steel WAR, 94
redemption married past r. MARRIAGE, 50
red-hot The Last of the R. Mamas SINGERS, 3
redundancy hiring taxis . . . handing out r. notices to its own
workers INCOMPETENCE, 2
redwood Nixon . . . would cut down a r. tree POLITICIANS, 67
reeling R. and Writhing EDUCATION, 9
references Always verify your r. RESEARCH, 2
refined One of those r. people CLASS, 6
reflection a r. of the British Museum Reading Room
INTELLECTUALS, 8
reform All r. . . . will prove unavailing CHANGE, 2
Any attempt to r. the university EDUCATION, 25
reformation Every r. must have its victims SUFFERING, 10
refreshed The tree of liberty must be r. FREEDOM, 21
refuge God is the immemorial r. of the incompetent GOD, 34
Idleness . . . the r. of weak minds IDLENESS, 3
Patriotism is the last r. PATRIOTISM, 15
refuse To r. praise PRAISE, 6
refused She r. to begin the 'Beguine' PETULANCE, 1
refute I r. it *thus* PHILOSOPHY, 5
regardless r. of their doom IGNORANCE, 7
regime No r. has ever loved great writers WRITERS, 43
regiment led his r. from behind COWARDICE, 3
register history . . . is . . . the r. of the . . . misfortunes of
mankind HISTORY, 14
I want to r. a complaint COMPLAINTS, 5
regret My r. Becomes an April violet SORROW, 25

remember and r.	REGRET, 6
wild with all r.	NOSTALGIA, 20
regrets the Cup that clears TO-DAY of past R.	PRESENT, 5
The follies which a man r.	REGRET, 11
rehearsing R. a play is making the word flesh	PLAYS, 9
reign Better to r. in Hell	POWER, 12
reigned I have r. with your loves	ROYALTY, 14
reigns king r., but does not govern	MONARCHY, 25
reject If you r. me on account of my religion	PREJUDICE, 1
rejoice new sights of Nature made me r.	NATURE, 7
related A group of closely r. persons	FAMILY, 26
relation If a man's character is to be abused . . . there's nobody	
like a r. to do the business	FAMILY, 41
relations Fate chooses your r.	FAMILY, 13; FRIENDS, 6
great men have their poor r.	FAMILY, 14
relaxation Man . . . can only find r. from one . . . labour by	
taking up another	CHANGE, 7
relief For this r. much thanks	COMFORT, 2
There is a certain r. in change	CHANGE, 11
thou wilt give thyself r.	LIFE, 33
religion a feeling of inward tranquillity which r. is powerless to	
bestow	CLOTHES, 5
Art and r. first; then philosophy	IMPORTANCE, 3
As to r., I hold it to be the . . . duty of government to protect	
all . . . professors thereof	GOVERNMENT, 22
brothels with bricks of R.	HYPOCRISY, 4
Fascism is a r.	FASCISM, 2
If you reject me on account of my r.	PREJUDICE, 1
Love is my r.	LOVE AND DEATH, 3
Men will wrangle for r.	RELIGION, 14
no reason to bring r. into it	RELIGION, 43
Not a r. for gentlemen	RELIGION, 10
Nothing is so fatal to r. as indifference	INDIFFERENCE, 2
One r. is as true as another	RELIGION, 8
One's r. . . . yours is Success	SUCCESS, 4
R. Has made an honest woman of the supernatural	
	RELIGION, 23; SUPERNATURAL, 7
R. is an illusion	RELIGION, 22
R. is by no means a proper subject	RELIGION, 11
R. is love	RELIGION, 60
R. . . . is the opium of the people	RELIGION, 37
r. of feeble minds	SUPERSTITION, 7
r. of Socialism	SOCIALISM, 1
R.'s in the heart	PRAYER, 13
Science without r. is lame	RELIGION, 20; SCIENCE, 12
Sensible men are all of the same r.	RELIGION, 16
talks loudly against r.	RELIGION, 47
that God is interested only . . . in r.	GOD, 47
To become a popular r.	RELIGION, 31
when r. is allowed to invade . . . private life	RELIGION, 38
when r. was strong . . . men mistook magic for medicine	
	MEDICINE, 7
religions a country with thirty-two r. and only one sauce	
	AMERICA, 32
sixty different r., and only one sauce	ENGLAND, 9
The r. we call false were once true	RELIGION, 21
religious a r. animal	RELIGION, 7
first, r. and moral principles	EDUCATION, 1
not r.-good	VIRTUE, 8
r. outlook on life	RELIGION, 33
skilled appeals to r. prejudice	EVOLUTION, 9
To be at all is to be r.	RELIGION, 9
relished the taste by which he is . . . r.	WRITING, 37
reluctant The r. obedience of distant provinces	DIPLOMACY, 16
remarkable nothing left r. Beneath the visiting moon	
	MOURNING, 11
remedies Extreme r. . . . for extreme diseases	REMEDIES, 9
He that will not apply new r.	INNOVATION, 1
Our r. oft in ourselves do lie	SELF-RELIANCE, 7
paralyse it by encumbering it with r.	REMEDIES, 12
r. . . . suggested for a disease	REMEDIES, 7
remedy a r. for everything except death	REMEDIES, 8
Force is not a r.	FORCE, 1
r. is worse than the disease	REMEDIES, 2
Tis a sharp r., but a sure one	EXECUTION, 25
remember I only r. what I've learnt	KNOWLEDGE, 34
I r., I r.	INNOCENCE, 6; NOSTALGIA, 9
Oh! don't you r. sweet Alice, Ben Bolt	MEMORY, 4
one man to r. me	LAST WORDS, 52
r. and regret	REGRET, 6
R. me when I am gone away	MEMORY, 13
she did not r. . . . her jewelry	PRUDENCE, 9
The world will little note, nor long r.	MEMORIALS, 6

we shall be glad to r. even these hardships	ENDURANCE, 22
We will r. them	MEMORIALS, 3
When I meet a man whose name I can't r.	MEMORY, 5
remembered By this may I r. be When I should be forgotten	
	MEMORIALS, 1
I r. my God	GOD, 45
remembrance r. of things past	REGRET, 17
reminiscences the old have r.	AGE, 47
remorse r. for what you have thought about your wife	
	MARRIAGE, 89
remove all faith, so that I could r. mountains	CHARITY, 5
Renaissance the R. was . . . the green end of one of	
civilization's hardest winters	CIVILIZATION, 5
render husband r. unto the wife due benevolence	MARRIAGE, 21
rendezvous a r. with Death	DEATH, 95
renegades Political r. always start their career of treachery	
	POLITICIANS, 41
renewal urban r. in New York City	EDUCATION, 25
rent they r. out my room	EXPEDIENCY, 1
repair the landlord does not intend to r.	LAST WORDS, 2
repartee A majority is always the best r.	MAJORITY, 1
repast A new r., or an untasted spring	PLEASURE, 2
repay whatsoever thou spendest more . . . I will r.	CHARITY, 7
repeal the r. of bad or obnoxious laws	LAW, 14
repeat obliged to imitate himself, and to r.	IMITATION, 5
repeated A platitude is simply a truth r.	SAYINGS, 1
repent Do you, that have nought other to lament, Never . . . r.	
	PARTING, 8
r. at leisure	MARRIAGE, 35
repentance A Christian . . . feels R. on a Sunday	HYPOCRISY, 18
There's no r. in the grave	DEATH, 121
with the morning cool r.	REGRET, 12
repetition constant r. will finally succeed in imprinting an idea	
	PUBLIC, 14
History is an endless r.	HISTORY, 9
replenished His intellect is not r.	IGNORANCE, 13
replied And I r., 'My Lord.'	RELIGION, 29
reporter A r. is a man who has renounced everything	
	JOURNALISM, 20
I am a r.	ATHEISM, 6
reporting Language is not simply a r. device for experience	
	LANGUAGE, 26
reprehend If I r. any thing	MALAPROPISMS, 8
representation Proportional R. . . . is fundamentally counter-	
democratic	POLITICS, 37
Taxation without r.	REPRESENTATION, 1
reproductions accurate r. of Anne Hathaway's cottage	
	HOUSES, 3
I've seen colour r.	PHILISTINISM, 5
republic An aristocracy in a r. is like a chicken	
	ARISTOCRACY, 10
the r. of letters	MANKIND, 1
Republican The R. form of Government	POLITICS, 61
Republicans Please assure me that you are all R.	POLITICS, 53
republics Revolts, r., revolutions	POLITICS, 69
repulsive Roundheads (Right but R.	HISTORY, 24
reputability Conspicuous consumption . . . is a means of r.	
	MATERIALISM, 20
reputation ever written out of r. but by himself	REPUTATION, 2
it is better for the r.	ORTHODOXY, 3
it wrecks a woman's r.	JEWELLERY, 1
O, I have lost my r.	REPUTATION, 5
spotless r.	REPUTATION, 5
Until you've lost your r., you never realize . . . what freedom	
really is	REPUTATION, 4
requests thou wilt grant their r.	PRAYER, 6
requires all the Human Frame r.	FOOD, 7
research R.! A mere excuse for idleness	RESEARCH, 1
The outcome of any serious r.	RESEARCH, 4
resent To great evils we submit; we r. little provocations	
	TRIVIALITY, 9
resentment It is very difficult to get up r.	BITTERNESS, 4
reservoir a gigantic r. of good will	AMERICA, 36
residuum this vast r. we may . . . give the name of Populace	
	PUBLIC, 2
resist r. everything except temptation	TEMPTATION, 10
there is almost nothing to r. at all	ENGLISH, 21
resisting fond of r. temptation	TEMPTATION, 3
resolution In war, r.	WAR AND PEACE, 3
native hue of r.	CONSCIENCE, 5
resources statistics, born to consume r.	STATISTICS, 3
respect A child deserves the maximum r.	CHILDREN, 27
Civilization is . . . equal r. for all men	CIVILIZATION, 1

riding Commuter – one who spends his life In r. to and from
his wife TRAVEL, 27
riff-raff r. apply to what is respectable CLASS, 16
rift the . . . r. between the sexes is . . . widened by . . . teaching
. . . to the girls SEXES, 18
Riga There was a young lady of R. ANIMALS, 1
right All's r. with the world PERFECTION, 2
better to be irresponsible and r. RESPONSIBILITY, 5;
RIGHTEOUSNESS, 6
Every man has a r. to utter what he thinks truth FREEDOM, 22
I am not and never have been, a man of the r. POLITICIANS, 52
I disapprove of what you say, but I will defend to the death
your r. to say it FREEDOM, 51
I'd rather be r. than president RIGHT, 3
It will all come r. in the wash OPTIMISM, 4
Keep r. on to the end of the road PERSISTENCE, 8
Liberty is the r. to do everything FREEDOM, 35
Minorities . . . are almost always in the r. MINORITY, 3
no r. to strike against public safety STRIKES, 2
No, this r. hand shall work it all off WRITING, 30
One of the pleasures of middle age is to *find out* that one WAS
r. AGE, 43
'orthodoxy' . . . no longer means being r. ORTHODOXY, 2
our country, r. or wrong PATRIOTISM, 7
publish, r. or wrong PUBLISHING, 2
R. is more precious RIGHT, 4
r. mindfulness, r. contemplation RELIGION, 6
r. of all, . . . duty of some SEPARATION, 4
settled r. ARGUMENTS, 18
something is possible, he is . . . r. SCIENCE, 5
The customer is always r. BUSINESS, 13
The man who gets angry . . . in the r. way . . . is commended
ANGER, 1
The minority is always r. MAJORITY, 3; MINORITY, 2
The r. divine of kings to govern wrong MONARCHY, 16
The r. people are rude RUDENESS, 1
the r. to be consulted, . . . to encourage, . . . to warn
MONARCHY, 2
the r. to criticize Shakespeare CRITICISM, 45
Those who believe that they are exclusively in the r.
SELF-CONFIDENCE, 1
Ulster will be r. IRELAND, 2
Women would rather be r. than reasonable WOMEN, 51
righteous leave r. ways behind RIGHTEOUSNESS, 4
righteousness He made r. readable EDITORS, 2
The eternal *not ourselves* that makes for r. RIGHTEOUSNESS, 1
the r. of the scribes and Pharisees RETRIBUTION, 6
righter much r. than one knew at say 17 or 23 AGE, 43
rights All human beings are born free and equal in dignity and
r. HUMAN RIGHTS, 1
The Sovereign has, under a constitutional monarchy . . . three r.
MONARCHY, 2
ring Don't carry away that arm till I have . . . my r.
PRACTICALITY, 5
One R. to rule them all POWER, 21
R. down the curtain LAST WORDS, 48
r. is worn away by use PERSISTENCE, 11
The r. so worn . . . So thin, so pale, is yet of gold
APPEARANCE, 10
They now *r.* the bells WAR, 120
rings R. on her fingers and bells on her toes NURSERY
RHYMES, 41
riot A r. is at bottom REBELLION, 6
ripe Cherry r. BUSINESS, 9
we r. and r. LIFE, 42
ripeness R. is all ENDURANCE, 17
ripp'd mother's womb untimely r. BIRTH, 1
rise Early to r. and early to bed BED, 9
Fish die belly-upward and r. . . . their way of falling FISH, 1
in the name of Jesus . . . r. up and walk REMEDIES, 1
nobody who does not r. early BED, 4
Thanks to words, we have been able to r. above the brutes
WORDS, 11
risk a bank that would lend money to such a poor r.
BORROWING, 2
risks what r. you take . . . to find money in a desk THEFT, 4
Ritz like the R. hotel JUSTICE, 17
river build your House of Parliament upon the r. HOUSES OF
PARLIAMENT, 19
can't step into the same r. twice CHANGE, 9
Fame is like a r. FAME, 2
Ol' man r. RIVERS, 1
On either side the r. lie ARTHURIAN LEGEND, 2

On the breast of the r. of Time HUMAN CONDITION, 1
the r. of knowledge has too often turned back on itself
SCIENCE, 21
The vanity of human life is like a r. LIFE, 38
road All I seek, the heaven above And the r. below me
TRAVEL, 24
a r. . . . that does not go through the intellect EMOTION, 1
Does the r. wind up-hill ENDURANCE, 15
free as the r. FREEDOM, 17
Keep right on to the end of the r. PERSISTENCE, 8
On the r. to Mandalay PLACES, 9
tell us of the R. DEATH, 47
the Golden R. to Samarkand KNOWLEDGE, 14
There is a r. from the eye to the heart EMOTION, 1
the rolling English r. TRAVEL, 5
They shut the r. through the woods TIME, 21
roads all r. lead to France WAR, 118
How many r. must a man walk down EXPERIENCE, 13
New r.: new ruts PROGRESS, 4
Two r. diverged CHOICE, 2
roam Mid pleasures and palaces though we may r. HOME, 7
roamin' R. in the gloamin' SCOTLAND, 5
roar luck to give the r. CHURCHILL, 5
roast the learned r. an egg FOOD, 39
rob Why r. one to feed the other? DEATH, 64
robb'd He that is r., not wanting what is stol'n IGNORANCE, 14
robbed We was r. INJUSTICE, 8
when you've r. a man of everything POWER, 18
Robbins President R. was so well adjusted to his environment
ADAPTABILITY, 3
robes R. and furr'd gowns hide all APPEARANCES, 20
Robin R. Gray, he was gudeman to me MARRIAGE, 17
Who killed Cock R. NURSERY RHYMES, 68
robin A r. redbreast in a cage IMPRISONMENT, 1
Our little English r. BIRDS, 13
robot the modern conception of a r. POLITICIANS, 16
rock R. and roll or Christianity POPULARITY, 1
R. of ages, cleft for me RELIGION, 52
upon this r. I will build my church CHURCH, 1
With my little stick of Blackpool r. FOOD, 20
rocked R. in the cradle of the deep SEA, 11
rocks The hand that r. the cradle INFLUENCE, 9
rod he that spareth his r. hateth his son CHILDREN, 16
rule them with a r. of iron LEADERSHIP, 2
spare the r. INDULGENCE, 1; PUNISHMENT, 6
rode and r. madly off in all directions NONSENSE, 15
rodent-like music critics. . . . small and r. with padlocked ears
CRITICS, 15
Roland *Childe R. to the Dark Tower came* SUMMONS, 4
role he saw his r. as being that of Moses LEADERSHIP, 4
roll our soul Had *felt* him like the thunder's r. BYRON, 1
R. up that map PEACE, 14
rolled bottoms of my trousers r. OLD AGE, 16
rolling Like a r. stone TRAVEL, 8
The r. English drunkard TRAVEL, 5
Rolls She has a R. body and a Balham mind STUPIDITY, 9
Roma *R. locuta est* AUTHORITARIANISM, 1
Roman noblest R. of them all NOBILITY, 2
the Holy R. Empire was neither holy, nor R., nor an empire
NATIONS, 3
The Papacy is not other than the Ghost of the deceased R.
Empire CATHOLICISM, 5
the R. people had but one neck RUTHLESSNESS, 1
romance The r. of *Tom Jones* NOVELS, 5
Twenty years of r. makes a woman look like a ruin
MARRIAGE, 119
Romans Friends, R., countrymen, lend me your ears EVIL, 15
The R. and Greeks found everything human
ANTHROPOMORPHISM, 1
which came first, the Greeks or the R. IGNORANCE, 5
Romanticism R. is . . . presenting people with the literary
works . . . affording . . . the greatest . . . pleasure
LITERATURE, 16
Rome I lov'd R. more PATRIOTISM, 26
R. has spoken; the case is concluded AUTHORITARIANISM, 1
R.'s gross yoke Drops off INFLUENCE, 1
R. shall perish REVENGE, 9
R.'s just a city like anywhere else EUROPE, 1
R. was not built PATIENCE, 5
The farther you go from the church of R. PROTESTANTISM, 3
When in R. CONFORMITY, 2
when R. falls – the World EUROPE, 5
Romeo R.! wherefore art thou R. NAMES, 5

S

sailors It is always opening time in the S. Arms PUBLIC HOUSES, 4
S. have a port OCCUPATIONS, 6
saint before we *know* he is a s., there will have to be miracles PROOF, 4
I consider myself superior to the s., the scientist NOVELS, 9
never a s. took pity on My soul SOLITUDE, 2
S. Preux never kicked the fireirons IMPERFECTION, 5
saints All are not s. HYPOCRISY, 1
many bodies of the s. which slept arose LAST WORDS, 8
sake Art for art's s. ART, 6
sakes king . . . men have made for their own s. MONARCHY, 17
salad My s. days YOUTH, 14
salary The s. of the chief executive BUSINESS, 7
this is the week I earn my s. MERIT, 5
Salkeld I am married to Beatrice S., a painter CHILDREN, 7
Sally
There's none like pretty S. LOVE, 35
sally a sudden s. RIVERS, 5
salmon cider and tinned s. FOOD, 44
serve both cod and s. PUNS, 11
the choice between smoked s. and tinned s. FOOD, 47
salt nobody likes having s. rubbed into their wounds AGGRAVATION, 2
speech . . . seasoned with s. SPEECH, 3
S. water and absence LOVE, 9
salvation There is no s. outside the church RELIGION, 2
The s. of mankind RESPONSIBILITY, 12
Sam Play it, S. NOSTALGIA, 1
Samaritan But a certain S. . . . had compassion on him CHARITY, 7
No one would have remembered the Good S. MONEY, 45
ready enough to do the S. CHARITY, 19
Samarkand the Golden Road to S. KNOWLEDGE, 14
same he is much the s. ILLNESS, 1
It will be all the s. WORRY, 3
it would be all the s. a hundred years hence TRIVIALITY, 1
principle seems the s. WATER, 1
we must all say *the* s. UNITY, 11
we're all made the s. SIMILARITY, 4
samite Clothed in white s. ARTHURIAN LEGEND, 3
Samuel When they circumcised Herbert S. INSULTS, 24
sanction Happiness is the only s. of life HAPPINESS, 21
sand and throws . . . s. in their eyes SLEEP, 9
The s. of the desert is sodden red WAR, 75
They wept . . . to see Such quantities of s. SEASIDE, 1
throw the s. against the wind FUTILITY, 4
World in a grain of s. WONDER, 2
sane Show me a s. man and I will cure him for you MADNESS, 5
sans S. teeth, s. eyes, s. taste, s. every thing OLD AGE, 36
Sappho Where burning S. loved EUROPE, 2
sarcasm petulance is not s. IMPERTINENCE, 1; PETULANCE, 2
S. . . . the language of the devil SARCASM, 1
sardines Life is . . . like a tin of s. LIFE, 10
sat The . . . gentleman has s. so long on the fence NONCOMMITMENT, 3
Satan And S. trembles PRAYER, 10
beheld S. as lightning fall from heaven DEVIL, 2
S. exalted sat, by merit raised DEVIL, 10
S. finds . . . mischief . . . For idle hands IDLENESS, 10
S., Nick, or Clootie DEVIL, 6
satire hard not to write s. SATIRE, 1
S. is a sort of glass SATIRE, 3
S. should, like a polished razor keen SATIRE, 2
satirists S. should be heard and not seen CRITICISM, 46
satisfaction complacency and s. . . . in . . . a new-married couple MARRIAGE, 70
the s. of knowing that we are avenged REVENGE, 14
satisfied his soul is s. with what is assigned to him CONTENTMENT, 1
The superior man is s. SUPERIORITY, 2
Saturday betwixt A S. and Monday SUNDAY, 3
Died on S. NURSERY RHYMES, 48
S.'s child works hard for his living NURSERY RHYMES, 33
what he did on S. HYPOCRISY, 18
satyr man is . . . either a stoic or a s. AGE, 42
sauce a country with thirty-two religions and only one s. AMERICA, 32
Art is not a special s. ART, 12
sixty different religions, and only one s. ENGLAND, 9
The best s. in the world HUNGER, 4
savage a time when Britain had a s. culture CIVILIZATION, 2

soothe a s. breast MUSIC, 14
s. place! as holy and enchanted SUPERNATURAL, 6
The young man who has not wept is a s. AGE, 48; WISDOM, 19
savaged s. by a dead sheep INSULTS, 16
savait *Si jeunesse s.* AGE, 22
save S. your breath SPEECH, 1
To s. a man's life against his will is . . . killing him KILLING, 3
saved he that endureth to the end shall be s. PERSISTENCE, 4
they only s. the world HEROISM, 2
saviour But it's 'S. of 'is country' when the guns SOLDIERS, 1
saw I came; I s.; God conquered VICTORY, 15
I came, I s., I conquered VICTORY, 1
I s. it, but I did not realize it PERCEPTION, 4
Saxon The S. is not like us Normans NATIONALITY, 6
say cannot s. what you have to s. in twenty minutes SPEECHES, 1
if we s. that we have no sin, we deceive SIN, 5
I have nothing to s., I am saying it POETRY, 8
Preachers s., Do as I s., not as I do EXAMPLE, 7
S. it with flowers FLOWERS, 10
s. what you have to s., and then sit down SPEECHES, 5
The great consolation . . . is to s. what one thinks FRANKNESS, 3
They are to s. what they please FREEDOM, 11
they do not know what they are going to s. SPEECHES, 6
What have we to s. to India? COMMUNICATION, 4
When you have nothing to s. SILENCE, 4
saying S. is one thing ACTION, 5
when . . . speaking, they do not know what they are s. SPEECHES, 2
sayings Dr Johnson's s. WRITERS, 19
His s. are generally like women's letters LETTER-WRITING, 3
scab The itch of disputing will prove the s. of churches RELIGION, 64
scaffold no middle course between the throne and the s. MONARCHY, 7
scandal In England there is only silence or s. ENGLAND, 26
It is a public s. that gives offence MORALITY, 10
s. by a woman . . . proved liar POLITICS, 29
There's no s. like rags POVERTY, 7
scape who shall s. whipping MERIT, 6
scarce S., sir. Mighty s. WOMEN, 74
scare A good s. is worth more ADVICE, 1
scarecrows Logical consequences are the s. of fools and the beacons of wise men LOGIC, 3
scarlet His sins were s. BOOKS, 5; PUNS, 1
pious bird with the s. breast BIRDS, 13
though your sins be as s. FORGIVENESS, 3
scatter We plough the fields, and s. AGRICULTURE, 1
scenery Mountains . . . the beginning and the end of all natural s. MOUNTAINS, 3
S. is fine HUMAN NATURE, 13
scenes I'll come no more behind your s., David LUST, 3
sceptic too much of a s. to deny the possibility of anything SCEPTICISM, 2
scepticism only her s. kept her from being an atheist SCEPTICISM, 5
sceptred this s. isle ENGLAND, 34
Scheherazade S. . . . a woman saving her head SELF-PRESERVATION, 11
schemes best laid s. o' mice an' men DISAPPOINTMENT, 2
schizophrenia if God talks to you, you have s. MADNESS, 12
S. cannot be understood PSYCHIATRY, 6
schizophrenic S. behaviour . . . a special strategy PSYCHIATRY, 5
scholar the last humiliation of an aged s. OLD AGE, 14
scholars great men have not commonly been great s. GREATNESS, 8
S. and gentlemen HONOUR, 7
S. dispute ARGUMENTS, 6
school enjoy a public s. EDUCATION, 13
Example is the s. of mankind EXAMPLE, 2
fleshly s. of Poetry POETS, 6
If every day in the life of a s. EDUCATION, 30
never gone to s. may steal from a freight car EDUCATION, 43
nothing on earth . . . so horrible as a s. EDUCATION, 48
public s., where . . . learning was painfully beaten into him EDUCATION, 41
The Stealthy S. of Criticism CRITICISM, 41
The world is but a s. of inquiry CURIOSITY, 5
Three little maids from s. CHILDREN, 23
till he's been to a good s. EDUCATION, 44
schoolboy a s.'s barring out POLITICS, 69

secretive As we make sex less s., we may rob it of its power SEX, 46

secrets Conversation . . . elicits s. from us CONVERSATION, 7

sect paradise for a s. FANATICISM, 2

sedate, sober, silent, serious, sad-coloured s. RELIGION, 30

secure only place where a man can feel . . . s. MEN, 4

The past, at least, is s. PAST, 9

security only freedom can make s. secure FREEDOM, 4

Sedan in a flood of tears and a S. chair HUMOUR, 34

sedge s. has wither'd from the lake ILLNESS, 8

seducers evil men and s. EVIL, 4

see change we think we s. NOVELTY, 2

complain we cannot s. COMPLAINTS, 1

I s. none coming out MISTRUST, 2

It is . . . at my age I now begin to s. things as they really are LAST WORDS, 20

My business is to paint . . . what I s. PAINTING, 17

seem to s. things thou dost not POLITICIANS, 61

s. . . . into a hypocrite HYPOCRISY, 8

there shall no man s. me, and live GOD, 11

Why don't you come up sometime and s. me INVITATIONS, 3

seed Fair s.-time had my soul SOUL, 12

I do not want to die . . . until I have . . . cultivated the s. ACHIEVEMENT, 4

In s. time learn, in harvest teach SUITABILITY, 1

seeing S. is believing BELIEF, 2

seek I will undoubtedly have to s. . . . gainful employment GOVERNMENT, 1

To toil and not to s. for rest SELFLESSNESS, 2

We s. him here, we s. him there ABSENCE, 9

We s. it, ere it come to light PERVERSITY, 3

seem Things are not always what they s. APPEARANCES, 1

seen Who has s. the wind WEATHER, 17

sees fool s. not the same tree WISDOM AND FOOLISHNESS, 4

What, when drunk, one s. in other women COMPLIMENTS, 3

Seine Today I spat in the S. WORLD WAR II, 23

seize S. the day PRESENT, 7

seldom s. attribute common sense AGREEMENT, 4

selection Natural S. EVOLUTION, 5

self All censure of a man's s. SELF, 10

nothing, . . . is greater . . . than one's s. SELF, 20

sickness enlarges the dimensions of a man's s. ILLNESS, 9

to thine own s. be true BORROWING, 8; INTEGRITY, 6

self-adjusting No man . . . who has wrestled with a s. card table TECHNOLOGY, 10

self-assertion Self-sufficiency at home, s. abroad NEWSPAPERS, 12

self-denial S. is not a virtue SELF-DENIAL, 1

self-employed I'm s. ROYALTY, 24

self-indulgence her favourite form of s. WOMEN, 47

write an essay on 's.' SELF, 16

self-interest S. speaks all sorts of tongues SELF-INTEREST, 5

selfish all Governments are s. GOVERNMENT, 8

a man becomes slack and s. MARRIAGE, 105

French governments more s. than most GOVERNMENT, 8

I have been a s. being all my life SELFISHNESS, 1

self-love S. is the greatest of all flatterers CONCEIT, 14

S. seems so often unrequited CONCEIT, 13; SELF, 12

true s. and social are the same SELF-KNOWLEDGE, 6

self-made A s. man . . . believes in luck SELF-MADE MEN, 3

a s. man who owed his lack of success to nobody SELF-MADE MEN, 2

self-praise S. is no recommendation PRAISE, 1

Selfridges by reality I mean shops like S. REALITY, 4

self-sufficiency S. at home, self-assertion abroad NEWSPAPERS, 12

self-sufficient know how to be s. SELF-RELIANCE, 6

selling A best-seller . . . because it was s. well FAME, 5

A living is made . . . by s. something that everybody needs ARTISTS, 13

semed he s. bisier than he was APPEARANCES, 10

senators Do you pray for the s., Dr Hale POLITICIANS, 31

green-rob'd s. of mighty woods TREES, 1

senile a sign that they now consider him s. OLD AGE, 14

seniors to hear . . . valuable or even earnest advice from my s. ADVICE, 13

sensations life of s. rather than of thoughts SENSATION, 1

sense because Americans won't listen to s. AMERICANS, 1

between a man of s. and his books BOOKS, 13

Common s. is the collection of prejudices PREJUDICE, 3

drowsy numbness pains my s. MELANCHOLY, 7

Let's talk s. to the American people ENDURANCE, 19

Money is like a sixth s. MONEY, 31

Science is nothing but trained and organized common s. SCIENCE, 18

seldom attribute common s. AGREEMENT, 4

Take care of the s. MEANING, 2

The sound must seem an echo to the s. WRITING, 26

senses If Parson lost his s. ANIMALS, 12

sensible S. men are all of the same religion RELIGION, 16

sensitive more s. one is to great art ART, 3

sensual The only s. pleasure without vice MUSIC, 23

sent If this belief from heaven be s. MANKIND, 36

sentence S. first – verdict afterwards INJUSTICE, 4

structure of the . . . British s. GRAMMAR, 3

sentences The most attractive s. are not perhaps the wisest LANGUAGE, 23

sentiment Sentimentality is only s. SENTIMENTALITY, 4

sentimentality S. is a superstructure covering brutality SENTIMENTALITY, 2

S. is only sentiment SENTIMENTALITY, 4

s. . . . rubs you up the wrong way SENTIMENTALITY, 4

sentiments high s. always win in the end NOBILITY, 3

sentinels men . . . who stand as s. in the avenues of fame CRITICS, 8

separation prepare for a s. SEPARATION, 4

they should declare the causes which impel them to . . . s. INDEPENDENCE, 2

September Clear in the cool S. morn AMERICA, 35

Thirty days hath S. NURSERY RHYMES, 56

Septuagint The S. minus the Apostles NUMBERS, 4

sepulchre To famous men all the earth is a s. FAME, 20

sepulchres whited s. HYPOCRISY, 3

seraphs Mammon wins his way where S. might despair MATERIALISM, 4

serious a damned s. business WAR, 124

A joke's a very s. thing HUMOUR, 6

a noble nature, . . . treats . . . a s. subject POETRY, 3

Mix a little foolishness with your s. plans FOOLISHNESS, 14

they are too s. FRANCE, 14

seriously Everything must be taken s., nothing tragically PERSPECTIVE, 4

sermons Ever since his s. were discontinued SERMONS, 2

He that takes pleasure to hear s. PLEASURE, 26

serpent sharper than a s.'s tooth DULLNESS, 1

that old s. DEVIL, 4

the s. beguiled me SEXES, 2

servant for the last time in my life, Your Humble S. ARGUMENTS, 16

The cracked looking glass of a s. IRELAND, 8

the politician poses as the s. POLITICIANS, 27

thou good and faithful s. SERVICE, 1

servants Few men have been admired by their s. ADMIRATION, 8

good s., but bad masters PASSION, 4

half of them prefer hiring their s. for life SLAVERY, 2

he wouldn't have white s. RACE, 15

part of English middle-class education is devoted to the training of s. EDUCATION, 62

Socialists treat their s. with respect POLITICS, 68

S. should not be ill CLASS, 7

We teachers can only help . . . as s. EDUCATION, 37

serve They also s. who only stand and wait SERVICE, 3

served I must have things daintily s. ETIQUETTE, 1

Youth will be s. SATISFACTION, 1

service I will see you in the vestry after s. CLERGY, 10

Small is true s. SERVICE, 4

serviettes kiddies have crumpled the s. ETIQUETTE, 1

Sesame Open S. SUPERNATURAL, 4

sessions s. of sweet silent thought REGRET, 17

set all, except their sun, is s. EUROPE, 3

best plans is s. VIRTUE, 1

sets on which the sun never s. BRITISH EMPIRE, 4

setting clouds that gather round the s. sun MORTALITY, 21

settled No question is ever s. Until ARGUMENTS, 18

Thank God, that's s. BORROWING, 9

Settlement coach and six horses through the Act of S. IRELAND, 12

seven his acts being s. ages HUMAN CONDITION, 15

S. swans a-swimming NURSERY RHYMES, 55

seventh God . . . rested on the s. day SUNDAY, 1

seventy Being over s. is like being engaged in a war OLD AGE, 41

Being s. is not a sin OLD AGE, 28

Oh, to be s. again LUST, 4; OLD AGE, 13

sever a tie that only death can s. MARRIAGE, 77

severity Summer has set in with its usual s. SUMMER, 4
sewage piped growing volumes of s. into the sea
ENVIRONMENT, 2
sex As we make s. less secretive, we may rob it of its power
SEX, 46
Christian view of s. SEX, 40
Continental people have s. life ENGLISH, 24
farmyard world of s. ANIMALISM, 2
How can I . . . dislike a s. to which Your Majesty belongs
MISOGYNY, 2
if there was a third s. MEN, 9
In the s.-war thoughtlessness is the weapon of the male
SEXES, 6
Is s. dirty SEX, 1
it's s. with someone you love SEX, 3
Literature is mostly about having s. LITERATURE, 11
meant us to have group s. SEX, 6
Money, it turned out, was exactly like s. MONEY, 7; SEX, 5
much more fundamental than s. MONEY, 17
no more weakness than is natural to her s. WOMEN, 70
No s. without responsibility SEX, 25
Personally I know nothing about s. SEX, 17
Pornography is the attempt to insult s. PORNOGRAPHY, 2
professed tyrant to their s. MISOGYNY, 3
s. has been a very private, secretive activity SEX, 46
S. is one of the nine reasons for reincarnation SEX, 29
S. is something I really don't understand SEX, 41
s. . . . must itself be subject . . . to evolution SEXES, 3
the s. novel is now normal NOVELS, 14
we English have s. on the brain ENGLISH, 27
sexes husbands and wives . . . belong to different s. SEXES, 8
more difference within the s. than between them SEXES, 5
several other old ladies of both s. FUSSINESS, 1
the . . . rift between the s. is . . . widened SEXES, 18
sexton went and told the s. PUNS, 5
sexual avowed purpose is to excite s. desire PORNOGRAPHY, 4
Industrial relations are like s. relations INDUSTRIAL
RELATIONS, 2
music throatily . . . s. MUSIC, 22
shabby For tamed and s. tigers ANIMALS, 12
shade a green thought in a green s. OBLIVION, 3
shade inviolable s. HOPE, 4
No s., no shine, no butterflies, no bees MONTHS, 10
Nothing grows well in the s. GREATNESS, 5
the s. Of that which once was great REGRET, 22
shadow be caves . . . in which his s. will be shown GOD, 38
lose the substance by grasping at the s. GREED, 4
unhappy s. SORROW, 3
Who live under the s. of a war WAR, 110
Your s. at morning FEAR, 9
shadows brooding tragedy and its dark s. can be lightened
HISTORY, 12
half sick of s. MARRIAGE, 109
shak'd when degree is s. ORDER, 3
Shakespeare after S. and Milton are forgotten LITERARY
CRITICISM, 1
A strange, horrible business, . . . good enough for S.'s day
CRITICISM, 48
Besides S. and me, who do you think there is? CONCEIT, 15
he had read S. and found him weak in chemistry SCIENTISTS, 12
I despise S. SHAKESPEARE, 15
myriad-minded S. SHAKESPEARE, 2
reading S. by flashes of lightning CRITICISM, 8
S., I come LAST WORDS, 16
S. is . . . really very good SHAKESPEARE, 7
S. never had six lines together without a fault SHAKESPEARE, 8
S. – the nearest thing SHAKESPEARE, 13
S., undoubtedly wanted taste SHAKESPEARE, 17
sweetest S., Fancy's child SHAKESPEARE, 12
the making up of a S. or a Milton SCIENTISTS, 4; WRITERS, 10
the right to criticize S. CRITICISM, 45
tried lately to read S. SHAKESPEARE, 3
We can say of S. SHAKESPEARE, 6
When I read S. I am struck SHAKESPEARE, 11
who speak the tongue That S. spake FREEDOM, 53
Wonderful women! . . . how much we . . . owe to S.
SHAKESPEARE, 16
shaking After s. hands with a Greek MISTRUST, 1
all these great interests entrusted to the s. hand
POLITICIANS, 75
Shalimar Pale hands I loved beside the S. LOVE, 67
shambles Our civilization is founded on the s. DEATH, 60
shame expense of spirit in a waste of s. LUST, 7

Neither s. nor physical pain have any . . . effect PUNISHMENT, 12
shamefaced Perjury . . . is truth that is s. TRUTH, 20
shapely it's . . . more important for a theory to be s., than . . .
true THEORY, 5
share s. in the good fortunes of the mighty INJUSTICE, 2
sharp those who have stout hearts and s. swords
RUTHLESSNESS, 6
shaves man who s. and takes a train TRAVEL, 27
Shaw Bernard S. WRITERS, 25
G. B. S. POPULARITY, 8
George Bernard S. is sadly miscast CRITICISM, 46
Mr S. . . . has never written any poetry WRITERS, 8
S. CRITICISM, 46
she s. is my country still PATRIOTISM, 5
shears marriage . . . resembles a pair of s. MARRIAGE, 100
shedding without s. of blood is no remission EXECUTION, 4
sheep A s. in s.'s clothing WEAKNESS, 3
Baa, baa, black s. NURSERY RHYMES, 4
good shepherd giveth his life for the s. CHRISTIANITY, 15
hungry s. look up, and are not fed CORRUPTION, 3
like lost s. SIN, 8
make a man by standing a s. PUBLIC, 4
not armies . . . but flocks of s. DELUSION, 3
savaged by a dead s. INSULTS, 16
s.'s clothing DECEPTION, 2
The mountain s. are sweeter, But the valley s. are fatter
GREED, 7
The s.'s in the meadow NURSERY RHYMES, 28
the wolf in the s.'s clothing APPEARANCES, 8
useless for the s. to pass resolutions in favour of vegetarianism
ARGUMENTS, 8
shelf The dust and silence of the upper s. NEGLECT, 3
Shelley S. and Keats were . . . up to date in . . . chemical
knowledge POETS, 15; SCIENCE, 15
the right sphere for S.'s genius POETS, 1
shells With silver bells and cockle s. GARDENS, 1
shelter Our s. from the stormy blast RELIGION, 57
shepherd Go, for they call you, S., from the hill SUMMONS, 1
I am the good s. CHRISTIANITY, 15
This is the weather the s. shuns WEATHER, 13
shepherds Governments needs to have both s. and butchers
GOVERNMENT, 29
s. abiding in the field CHRISTMAS, 8
s. watch'd their flocks CHRISTMAS, 17
Sherard S. Blaw, the dramatist who had discovered himself
WRITERS, 39
sherry With first-rate s. flowing into second-rate whores
MEDIOCRITY, 6
shift for coming down let me s. for myself EXECUTION, 18
shilling I'm sorry to hear that, sir, you don't happen to have
the s. about you now, do you? BEQUESTS, 2
shimmy Put thy s. on, Lady Chatterley PARTING, 7
shine s. on, s. on, harvest moon MOON, 6
shining A woman of so s. loveliness BEAUTY, 39
shins long dresses, . . . cover a multitude of s. CLOTHES, 18
ship A whale s. was my Yale College EDUCATION, 34
being in a s. is being in a jail BOATS, 9
Don't give up the s. LAST WORDS, 36
S. me somewheres east of Suez DESIRE, 8
The s. follows Soviet custom CLASS, 33
ships Heart of oak are our s. COURAGE, 11
I spied three s. come sailing by CHRISTMAS, 3
something wrong with our bloody s. BOATS, 1
stately s. go on NOSTALGIA, 21
S. that pass in the night TRANSIENCE, 16
the face that launch'd a thousand s. BEAUTY, 24
the little s. of England brought the Army home BOATS, 8;
WORLD WAR II, 20
We've got the s., we've got the men, we've got the money too
PATRIOTISM, 14
shipwreck husbands and wives make s. of their lives
MARRIAGE, 47
shirt no s. or collar ever comes back twice NEGLECT, 2
shit the sun shining ten days a year and s. in the streets
ENGLAND, 20
when you s.? Singing, it's the same thing SINGING, 1
shock Anybody can s. a baby SIMPLICITY, 7
deliberately set out to s. THEATRE, 9
shocked how to be amused rather than s. AGE, 14
shock-headed S. Peter CHILDREN, 25
shocking little man wears a s. bad hat CLOTHES, 20
shocks s. That flesh is heir to SUICIDE, 10
shoemaker I take my shoes from the s. RELIGION, 26

shoes before you let the sun in, mind it wipes its s.
CLEANNESS, 2
I take my s. from the shoemaker RELIGION, 26
s. and ships and sealing wax NONSENSE, 9
shoot do not s. the pianist EFFORT, 7
except to s. rabbits and hit his father on the jaw NASTINESS, 5
It is not the business of generals to s. one another
OFFICERS, 14
S., if you must, this old gray head PATRIOTISM, 30
they could s. me in my absence JUSTICE, 2
shooting A bit of s. takes your mind off VIOLENCE, 1
war minus the s. SPORT AND GAMES, 15
shop A man must keep a little back s. SOLITUDE, 12
shop-keepers A nation of s. BRITAIN, 2
England is a nation of s. ENGLISH, 28
shopping Today you're unhappy? . . . Go s. MATERIALISM, 15
shore adieu! my native s. DEPARTURE, 3
waves make towards the pebbled s. TIME, 30
Shoreditch When I grow rich, Say the bells of S. LONDON, 2
shores eternal whisperings around Desolate s. SEA, 8
short Good things, when s., are twice as good BREVITY, 1
Is not life . . . too s. . . . to bore ourselves? BOREDOM, 6
it will take a long while to make it s. WRITING, 33
Life is too s. to do anything for oneself WORK, 13
make the beat keep time with s. steps FUNERALS, 1
s. and simple annals of the poor POVERTY, 12
the life of man, solitary, poor, nasty, brutish, and s. HUMAN
CONDITION, 10
We have s. time to stay, as you TRANSIENCE, 14
shortage a s. of coal and fish . . . at the same time
INCOMPETENCE, 1
shorter not had the time to make it s. VERBOSITY, 5
s. by a head ROYALTY, 15
shortest I never realized that I'd end up being the s. knight of
the year PUNS, 19; TITLES, 8
the s. works are always the best BREVITY, 4
shot had them all s. LAST WORDS, 39; RUTHLESSNESS, 4
he once s. a bookseller PUBLISHING, 4
shots God is on the side not of the heavy battalions, but of the
best s. POWER POLITICS, 8
They really are bad s. ASSASSINATION, 3
shoulder-blade I have a left s. CONCEIT, 10
shoulders it is by standing on the s. of giants PROGRESS, 9
shout S. with the largest MAJORITY, 1
show I have that within which passes s. MOURNING, 12
I often wish they would s. off a little more OSTENTATION, 4
showers Sweet April s. MONTHS, 12
shows All my s. are great BOASTS, 3; CONCEIT, 11
shreds A thing of s. and patches SINGERS, 2
Shrewsbury They hang us now in S. jail: The whistles blow
forlorn EXECUTION, 11
shriek That s. and sweat in pigmy wars TRIVIALITY, 14
shrine Melancholy has her . . . s. MELANCHOLY, 8
shrink all the boards did s. WATER, 1
shuffled s. off this mortal coil SUICIDE, 10
the human pack is s. and cut EDUCATION, 31
shut when I was there it seemed to be s. PLACES, 5
shy Why so s., my pretty Thomasina SHYNESS, 3
sick A person seldom falls s. HUMAN NATURE, 8
being s. with other people singing. PARTIES, 7
I am s. at heart COMFORT, 2
Dante makes me s. LAST WORDS, 10
if you don't object if I'm s. SMOKING, 1
Let me remind you what the wary fox said . . . to the s. lion
MISTRUST, 5
make any man s. to hear her INSINCERITY, 3
The prayer that . . . heals the s. FAITH, 10
We have on our hands a s. man DECLINE, 7
sickness in s. and in health MARRIAGE, 27
Love is a s. LOVE, 43
s. enlarges the dimensions of a man's self ILLNESS, 3
S., sin and death . . . do not originate in God RELIGION, 19
Sidcup If only I could get down to S. PROOF, 5
side A door is what a dog is . . . on the wrong s. of DOGS, 10
a s. dish he hadn't ordered CONTEMPT, 3
He who knows only his own s. . . . knows little SUBJECTIVITY, 4
Time is on our s. PROGRESS, 7
sides Do not . . . write on both s. of the paper
EXAMINATIONS, 1
said on both s. OBJECTIVITY, 1
We . . . assume that everything has two s. SUBJECTIVITY, 7
sighed They s. for the dawn and thee LOVE, 128
sighs over the Bridge of S. into eternity DEATH, 70

S. are the natural language of the heart SPEECH, 14
sight a s. to make an old man young BEAUTY, 37
Out of s. ABSENCE, 2
we walk by faith, not by s. FAITH, 5
Who ever loved, that loved not at first s. FIRST IMPRESSIONS, 6
sightless clapped the glass to his s. eye BLINDNESS, 1
sights And see all s. from pole to pole SOUL, 3
few more impressive s. in the world SCOTS, 2
sign Never s. a valentine SIGNATURES, 1
s. of an ill-spent youth SPORT AND GAMES, 18
writing a letter and forgetting to s. his name INSULTS, 4
significant s. form ART, 4
signifying S. nothing LIFE, 41
signing I am s. my death warrant PROPHECY, 3
silence Come to me in the s. of the night NOSTALGIA, 18
foster-child of s. and slow time SILENCE, 9
In England there is only s. or scandal ENGLAND, 26
Make him a bishop, and you will s. him CLERGY, 3
occasional flashes of s. INSULTS, 32
S. is as full of potential wisdom SILENCE, 8
S. is become his mother tongue SILENCE, 6
S. is the best tactic SILENCE, 10
S. is the perfectest herald of joy SILENCE, 12
S. is the . . . perfect expression of scorn SILENCE, 13
Sorrow and s. are strong ENDURANCE, 9
s. sank Like music SILENCE, 3
That man's s. is wonderful to listen to SILENCE, 7
The cruellest lies are . . . told in s. SILENCE, 14
The dust and s. of the upper shelf NEGLECT, 3
the impression that their normal condition is s. SILENCE, 11
the more absolute s. of America ENGLAND, 23
the rest is s. DEATH, 96
With s. and tears SEPARATION, 2
silent burst Into that s. sea EXPLORATION, 1
the great s. majority MAJORITY, 5
the man who can be s. in several languages DIPLOMACY, 11
thereon one must remain s. SILENCE, 15
silicon If s. had been a gas EXAMINATIONS, 3
silk rustling in unpaid-for s. CONTENTMENT, 7
s., too often hides eczema STYLE, 2
the s. stockings and white bosoms of your actresses excite my
amorous propensities LUST, 3
silks Whenas in s. my Julia goes CLOTHES, 3
silly A s. remark can be made in Latin LANGUAGE, 5
it's lovely to be s. at the right moment FOOLISHNESS, 14
some damned s. thing in the Balkans WAR, 9
silver for a handful of s. BETRAYAL, 2
s. and gold have I none REMEDIES, 3
S. buckles on his knee NURSERY RHYMES, 5
Selling the family s. POLITICS, 43
S. threads among the gold OLD AGE, 33
The s. apples of the moon DESIRE, 16
When every . . . thing you hold Is made of s., or of gold
ECONOMICS, 6
silvery the s. adamant walls of life's exclusive city DEATH, 71
Silvia Who is S.? What is she ADMIRATION, 16
Simon Simple S. met a pieman NURSERY RHYMES, 46
simple short and s. annals of the poor POVERTY, 12
Teach us delight in s. things GOOD, 7
simplicity O holy s. SIMPLICITY, 3
simplify ability to s. means SIMPLICITY, 2
S., s. SIMPLICITY, 8
simplifying s. something by destroying nearly everything
CIVILIZATION, 4
sin A branch of the s. of drunkenness DRUNKENNESS, 14
All s. tends to be addictive SIN, 2
a more dreadful record of s. than . . . countryside SIN, 12
A private s. is not so prejudicial SIN, 10
beauty is only s. deep BEAUTY, 3
Being seventy is not a s. OLD AGE, 28
he that is without s. . . . let him first cast a stone SIN, 4
if we say that we have no s., we deceive SIN, 5
it is no s. to s. in secret MORALITY, 10
nicest boy who ever committed the s. of whisky ALCOHOL, 56
no s. but to be rich HYPOCRISY, 14
no s. except stupidity STUPIDITY, 13
S. brought death DEATH, 44; SIN, 14
Sickness, s. and death . . . do not originate in God RELIGION, 19
than that one soul . . . should commit one single venial s.
SIN, 17
The physicists have known s. SCIENTISTS, 7

They are written as if s. were to be taken out . . . by . . . sleep
SERMONS, 1
which taketh away the s. of the world CHRISTIANITY, 12
your s. will find you out SIN, 7
sincere Some of the worst men in the world are s.
SINCERITY, 3
sincerest Imitation . . . s. of flattery IMITATION, 2
sincerity A little s. is a dangerous thing SINCERITY, 6
style, not s., is the vital thing STYLE, 2
sinecure a widow . . . is a kind of s. EXPEDIENCY, 6
sinews Anger is one of the s. of the soul ANGER, 4
sing Did certain persons die before they s. SINGERS, 1
I will s. of the sun WOMEN, 60
The Welsh . . . just s. WELSH, 4
we s. no more COMPOSERS, 2
singed s. the Spanish king's beard WAR, 33
singing s. in the rain WEATHER, 11
when you shit? S., it's the same thing SINGING, 1
single a s. man in possession of a good fortune must be in
want of a wife MARRIAGE, 9
Behold her, s. in the field SOLITUDE, 16
sink The s. is the great symbol of the bloodiness of family life
FAMILY, 28
sinn'd More s. against than sinning INJUSTICE, 12
sinners At such an hour the s. are still in bed SIN, 18
It's your combination s. . . . who dishonour the vices VICE, 10
sinning nothing so artificial as s. nowadays SIN, 15
sins atone for the s. of your fathers INJUSTICE, 7
from Expensive S. refrain SIN, 13
gravest s. it was possible for a gentlewoman to commit
READING, 18
her s., which are many, are forgiven FORGIVENESS, 5; SIN, 6
His s. were scarlet BOOKS, 5; PUNS, 1
One of the unpardonable s., . . . , is . . . to go about unlabelled
CLASSIFICATION, 1
she must not reheat his s. for breakfast FORGIVENESS, 10
though your s. be as scarlet FORGIVENESS, 3
to read a novel before luncheon was one of the gravest s.
READING, 18
Sir I am S. Oracle EGOTISM, 8
sirens Blest pair of S. POETRY, 29
sister I kissed her little s. UNFAITHFULNESS, 2
no friend like a s. FAMILY, 35
sisters And so do his s. FAMILY, 17
little s. to all the world WOMEN, 27
O! men with s. dear WOMEN, 37
sit I will s. down now PROPHECY, 4
men s. and hear each other groan HUMAN CONDITION, 11
nobody can tell you when to s. down POWER, 8
say what you have to say, and then s. down SPEECHES, 5
So I did s. and eat LOVE, 65
sitting Are you s. comfortably? Then I'll begin BEGINNING, 12
by s. down round you HOUSES OF PARLIAMENT, 19
I do most of my work s. down HUMOUR, 31
situation s. excellent. I shall attack WAR, 35
six Candidates should not attempt more than s. BIBLE, 2
S. geese a-laying NURSERY RHYMES, 55
s. of one and half-a-dozen of the other SIMILARITY, 5
two and two do not make s. LAST WORDS, 63
sixpence He found a crooked s. against a crooked stile
NURSERY RHYMES, 52
I love s., jolly little s. NURSERY RHYMES, 22
Sing a song of s. NURSERY RHYMES, 47
sixpences there go two-and-forty s. . . . to one guinea
MERIT, 4
sixth Money is like a s. sense MONEY, 31
sixty at the rate of s. minutes an hour TIME, 22
close-up of a woman past s. APPEARANCE, 4
Men come of age at s. AGE, 57
S. horses wedged in a chimney JOURNALISM, 19
sixty-five I have been drinking it for s. years and I am not dead
yet DRINKS, 9
size I am not this s., really OBESITY, 4
skating s. over thin ice HASTE, 6
skeleton Every family has a s. in the cupboard FAMILY, 2
ski unbecoming for a cardinal to s. badly SPORT AND GAMES, 9
skies looks commercing with the s. SOUL, 9
look up at the s. STARS, 2
skill In arguing too, the parson own'd his s. KNOWLEDGE, 16
S. without imagination is craftsmanship ART, 25
skin I've Got You Under My S. LOVE, 94
never . . . sell the bear's s. ANTICIPATION, 6
There is more than one way to s. a cat DIFFERENCE, 4

skinning When you are s. your customers BUSINESS, 10
skins beauty of their s. SEXES, 19
skipper s. had taken his little daughter BOATS, 11
skirt a woman . . . ought to lay aside . . . modesty with her s.
SEX, 31
skittles Life isn't all beer and s. LIFE, 28
sky a Friend for little children Above the bright blue s.
GOD, 35
inverted Bowl we call The S. DESTINY, 8
Which prisoners call the s. IMPRISONMENT, 7
Skye Over the sea to S. ROYALTY, 5
slack a man becomes s. and selfish MARRIAGE, 105
slamming little girls . . . s. doors CHILDREN, 10
slander it is always said of s. that something always sticks
PRAISE, 2
slang All s. is metaphor LANGUAGE, 8
The one . . . poetry . . . continually flowing is s. LANGUAGE, 7
slapped We had shown that anyone who s. us . . . would get
his head kicked off REVENGE, 12
slave Be not the s. of Words WORDS, 5
man . . . is Reason's s. PASSION, 1
s. for livelihood ENVY, 3
slavery Freedom is S. DOUBLETHINK, 1
slaves In a consumer society there are . . . two kinds of s.
MATERIALISM, 10
love, an . . . intercourse between tyrants and s. LOVE AND
FRIENDSHIP, 2
Practical men, . . . are usually the s. of some defunct economist
INFLUENCE, 5
S. cannot breathe in England SLAVERY, 3
that the masters willingly concede to s. SLAVERY, 1
slaying the s. of a beautiful hypothesis by an ugly fact
SCIENCE, 19
slays moves, and mates, and s. DESTINY, 6
sleave ravell'd s. of care SLEEP, 13
sleek you will come and find me fat and s. PRESENT, 10
sleep A professor is one who talks in someone else's s.
ACADEMICS, 1
Better s. with a sober cannibal than a drunken Christian
DRUNKENNESS, 16
haven't been to s. for over a year SLEEP, 17
How do people go to s. SLEEP, 12
Let me s. the s. of the earth SOLITUDE, 14
Now I lay me down to s. SLEEP, 2
Our birth is but a s. METAPHYSICS, 5
our little life Is rounded with a s. MORTALITY, 17
s. begins for weary mortals SLEEP, 16
s. in your closet rather than ENGLISH, 8
S. is good, death is better PESSIMISM, 6
s.! it is a gentle thing SLEEP, 6
S. . . . knows not Death SLEEP, 14
S. that knits up the ravell'd sleave SLEEP, 13
The past was a s. BEGINNING, 6
They are written as if sin were to be taken out . . . by . . . s.
SERMONS, 1
To s., perchance to dream SUICIDE, 10
we must s. REST, 2
youth would s. out the rest YOUTH, 15
sleepin' Capten, art tha s. there below? WAR, 76
sleeping fuss about s. together . . . sooner go to my dentist
SEX, 51
Let s. dogs lie TACT, 2
S. as quiet as death OLD AGE, 43
There will be s. enough DEATH, 12
we have only awakened a s. giant WORLD WAR II, 31
sleeps eats, s. and watches the television WOMAN'S ROLE, 1
sleepwalker that Providence dictates with the assurance of a s.
DESTINY, 11
sleepy Come, let's to bed Says S.-head NURSERY RHYMES, 7
sleeve let the last man . . . brush the Channel with his s.
WAR, 104
slick I have three phobias which . . . would make my life as s.
as a sonnet OBSESSIONS, 1
slimy thousand thousand s. things GUILT, 4
slings s. and arrows of outrageous fortune SUICIDE, 10
slip he gave us all the s. ABSENCE, 5
There's many a s. ALCOHOL, 3
slippers Same old s. MARRIAGE, 71
slipping Time is s. underneath TIME, 16
slogan democracy is just a s. DEMOCRACY, 4
slogans If you feed people just with revolutionary s.
PROMISES, 4
Slough Come, friendly bombs, and fall on S. ENGLAND, 3

slough the s. was Despond — DESPAIR, 2
slow On a s. boat to China — BOATS, 10
S. and steady wins the race — HASTE, 7
S. but sure — PERSISTENCE, 3
Tarry a while, says S. — NURSERY RHYMES, 7
too swift arrives as tardy as too s. — LOVE, 108
with a s. deliberate carelessness — READING, 10
slug-horn the s. to my lips I set — SUMMONS, 4
slum if you've seen one city s. — POVERTY, 3
slumber A s. did my spirit seal — IMMORTALITY, 7
Love itself shall s. on — MEMORY, 17
Oft in the stilly night, Ere S.'s chain — NOSTALGIA, 14
slumbers Golden s. kiss your eyes — SLEEP, 7
slush pure as the driven s. — PURITY, 2
smack much more indecent . . . than a good s. — PUNISHMENT, 13
small Errors look so very ugly in persons of s. means — POVERTY AND WEALTH, 5
From s. beginnings — BEGINNING, 2
In Western Europe there are now only s. countries — EUROPE, 10
Microbe is so very s. — SMALLNESS, 2
Popularity? . . . glory's s. change — POPULARITY, 4
S. is beautiful — BEAUTY, 4
The best things come in s. parcels — SMALLNESS, 1
virtue's still far too s. — VIRTUE, 6
smaller accepts a s. as a favour — INJUSTICE, 3
someone s. than oneself — PRUDENCE, 8
these have s. fleas to bite 'em — PARASITES, 3
small-talking Where in this s. world — MEANING, 4
smartness the s. of an attorney's clerk — INSULTS, 13
smarts No creature s. . . . as a fool — FOOLISHNESS, 17
smattering A s. of everything — KNOWLEDGE, 12
smell rose . . . would s. as sweet — NAMES, 6
Sweet S. of Success — SUCCESS, 10
smells the only dead thing that s. sweet — PAST, 7
smile a s. I could feel in my hip pocket — SEX, 12
s. at perils past — PAST, 6
S. at us, pay us, pass us — ENGLISH, 12
s., s., s. — OPTIMISM, 13
the vain tribute of a s. — POETS, 22
smiled the soldiers he s. at — WAR, 101
smiles She is Venus when she s. — COMPLIMENTS, 2
s., Wan as primroses — FLOWERS, 5
The s., the tears, Of boyhood's years — NOSTALGIA, 14
smite whosoever shall s. thee on thy right cheek — ENEMIES, 2
Smith Chuck it, S. — RELIGION, 13
smith The s., a mighty man is he — OCCUPATIONS, 9
smoke no woman should marry . . . a man who does not s. — ABSTINENCE, 8
resembling the horrible Stygian s. of the pit — SMOKING, 6
S., my friend — SMOKING, 13
There's no s. without fire — GOSSIP, 4
smoking resolve to give up s., drinking and loving — ABSTINENCE, 4
s. at such a rate — SMOKING, 10
s. cigars . . . before, after, and if need be during all meals — ALCOHOL, 20; SMOKING, 3
What a blessing this s. is — SMOKING, 5
smooth course of true love never did run s. — LOVE, 113
many cities had rubbed him s. — TRAVEL, 11
smyler The s. with the knyf — HYPOCRISY, 7
snail said a whiting to a s. — HASTE, 5
s.'s on the thorn — PERFECTION, 2
snails Frogs and s. And puppy-dogs' tails — NURSERY RHYMES, 65
snake A s. came to my water-trough — WEATHER, 15
There's a s. hidden in the grass — DANGER, 7
snapper-up s. of unconsidered trifles — BUSINESS, 14
snare a s. in which the feet of women have always become readily entangled — WOMEN, 5
Snark For the S. *was* a Boojum — NONSENSE, 6
sneezed Not to be s. at — IMPORTANCE, 1
when a British Prime Minister s. — BRITAIN, 11
snipe well-shot woodcock, partridge, s. — HUNTING, 1
snob He who meanly admires . . . is a S. — SNOBBERY, 7
impossible, in our condition of society, not to be sometimes a S. — SNOBBERY, 8
no s. welcomes another — SNOBBERY, 1
snobbish Don't be s., we seek to abolish — CLASS, 21
snobs His hatred of s. — SNOBBERY, 5
snore s. and you sleep alone — SLEEP, 5
snorer can't hear himself s. — SLEEP, 15
snotgreen The s. sea — SEA, 7
snow both its national products, s. and chocolate, melt — SWITZERLAND, 1

I used to be S. White — PURITY, 6
Like an army defeated The s. hath retreated — SPRING, 9
S. had fallen, s. on s. — WINTER, 5
the s. blind twilight ferries — WINTER, 7
wish a s. in May — SUITABILITY, 4
snows the s. of yesteryear — NOSTALGIA, 22
snub-nose Vile s., flat-nosed ass — APPEARANCE, 30
snuff time for me to enjoy another pinch of s. — EXECUTION, 1
so It is s.. It is not s. — ARGUMENTS, 4
soap S. and education . . . are more deadly — EDUCATION, 53
soar to run, though not to s. — IMAGINATION, 8
sober a s. colouring from an eye — MORTALITY, 21
as s. as a Judge — DRUNKENNESS, 12
Better sleep with a s. cannibal than a drunken Christian — DRUNKENNESS, 16
England should be compulsorily s. — FREEDOM, 30
he that will go to bed s. — ALCOHOL, 26
How do you look when I'm s. — CLOTHES, 11
'My mother, drunk or s..' — PATRIOTISM, 4
one sees in Garbo s. — COMPLIMENTS, 7
sedate, s., silent, serious, sad-coloured sect — RELIGION, 30
Tomorrow we'll be s. — DRUNKENNESS, 3
sociable I am a s. worker — SOCIETY, 1
Society is no comfort to one not s. — SOCIETY, 7
social Man is a s. animal — SOCIETY, 8
our s. spheres have been widely different — SNOBBERY, 11
the things which government does . . . s. progress — GOVERNMENT, 30
the . . . world was stumbling . . . in s. blindness — BLINDNESS, 2
to enter s. life on tiptoe — FOOTBALL, 5
true self-love and s. are the same — SELF-KNOWLEDGE, 6
socialism Marxian S. must always remain a portent — MARXISM, 2
Only s. would put up with it — SOCIALISM, 4
religion of S. — SOCIALISM, 1
restating our s. in terms of the scientific revolution — SOCIALISM, 14
s. . . . alien to the British character — SOCIALISM, 13
S. can only arrive by bicycle — SOCIALISM, 3
the proletariat will . . . wage a class struggle for S. — CLASS, 18
the worst advertisement for S. is its adherents — SOCIALISM, 10
to banish . . . the dark divisive clouds of Marxist s. — MARXISM, 6
To the ordinary working man, . . . S. — SOCIALISM, 11
Under s. *all* will govern — SOCIALISM, 9
socialists S. treat their servants with respect — POLITICS, 68
We are all S. now — SOCIALISM, 6
what are you s. going to do about me — SOCIALISM, 5
societies range of human s. in time, the other in space — MANKIND, 15
society a free s. . . . where it is safe to be unpopular — FREEDOM, 49
a poor s. cannot be too poor — POVERTY AND WEALTH, 8
A s. . . . of individuals . . . capable of original thought would probably be unendurable — IDEAS, 6
Comedy, we may say, is s. — HUMOUR, 22
if it be our clothes alone which fit us for s. — CLOTHES, 4
impossible, in our condition of s., not to be sometimes a Snob — SNOBBERY, 8
In a consumer s. there are . . . two kinds of slaves — MATERIALISM, 10
it proved that I was in a civilized s. — EXECUTION, 21
Mankind is a closed s. — MANKIND, 24
Man was formed for s. — SOCIETY, 2
Never speak disrespectfully of S. — SNOBBERY, 12
no intellectual s. can flourish where a Jew feels . . . uneasy — JEWS, 7
no new baby in the womb of our s. — RUSSIA, 3
nothing to distinguish human s. from the farm-yard — MANKIND, 28
only possible s. is oneself — MISANTHROPY, 4
S., friendship, and love — SOLITUDE, 4
S. goes on and on and on — IDEAS, 4
S. is no comfort To one not sociable — SOCIETY, 7
S. is now one polish'd horde — BORES, 2
so famous, that it would permit me . . . to break wind in s. — FAME, 3
s. . . . pays a harlot 25 times as much as it pays its Prime Minister — INJUSTICE, 14
s., where none intrudes — NATURE, 3
The history of all . . . s. is the history of class struggles — CLASS, 22
There are two classes in good s. — CLASS, 28

the transition from the . . . 'closed s.', . . . to the 'open s.'
SOCIETY, 5
transform this s. without a major extension of public ownership
SOCIALISM, 8
sociology Children . . . have no use for psychology. They detest s.
BOOKS, 36
socks His s. compelled one's attention   CLOTHES, 15
sodium Of having discovered S.   SCIENTISTS, 1
sodom S. and . . . Gomorrah   PUNISHMENT, 3
the men of S. were wicked   HOMOSEXUALITY, 1
sodomy Comedy, like s., is an unnatural act   HUMOUR, 11
rum, s., and the lash   NAVY, 2
sofa rather lie on a s. than sweep beneath it   LAZINESS, 4
soft I'm not hard – I'm frightfully s.   CHARACTER, 22
our love . . . of the mind does not make us s.   RESULTS, 4
solar the whole s. and stellar systems   COMFORT, 1
soldier a chocolate cream s.   SOLDIERS, 5
Ben Battle was a s. bold   PUNS, 8
I never expect a s. to think   SOLDIERS, 6
in the s. is flat blasphemy   INJUSTICE, 11
The summer s. and the sunshine patriot   COWARDICE, 6
Tinker, Tailor, S., Sailor   NURSERY RHYMES, 60
soldiers English s. fight like lions   OFFICERS, 8
Old s. never die   OCCUPATIONS, 4
S. are citizens of death's grey land   SOLDIERS, 4
soliciting supernatural s.   SUPERNATURAL, 13
solitary Man is not a s. animal   SOCIETY, 6
solitude In s. alone can he know true freedom   SOLITUDE, 12
In s. What happiness   SOLITUDE, 10
so companionable as s.   SOLITUDE, 13
s.! where are the charms   SOLITUDE, 5
the bliss of s.   SOLITUDE, 15
Whosoever is delighted in s.   SOLITUDE, 1
Solomon S. Grundy, Born on a Monday   NURSERY RHYMES, 48
solution A difficulty for every s.   BUREAUCRACY, 6
total s. of the Jewish question   NAZISM, 1
some I . . . may be s. time   LAST WORDS, 41
s. more than others   SIMILARITY, 1
You can fool s. of the people all the time   DECEPTION, 4
somebody s. may be looking   CONSCIENCE, 4
someone I wouldn't be . . . talking to s. like you   SNOBBERY, 3
like sleeping with s. else's wife   NEWSPAPERS, 4
somer In a s. season   SUMMER, 6
Somerset corroboration . . . in the records of S. House
HUMILITY, 11
something Everybody was up to s.   INTRIGUE, 2
S. must be done   UNEMPLOYMENT, 3
S. nasty in the woodshed   EVIL, 9
sometime Why don't you come up s. and see me
INVITATIONS, 3
somewhere 'Tis always morning s.   BEGINNING, 9
son An only s., sir, might expect more indulgence   FAMILY, 18
I've examined your s.'s head, Mr Glum   STUPIDITY, 10
the S. of man coming . . . with power   DOOMSDAY, 2
sonatas The s. of Mozart are unique   MUSIC, 39
song I have a s. to sing O   SINGING, 2
the s. that is sung in our hearts   MUSIC, 30
Who loves not wine, woman and s.   PLEASURE, 20
songs Sing no sad s.   DEATH, 92
Where are the s. of Spring   SPRING, 3
sonne when soft was the s.   SUMMER, 6
sonnet I have three phobias which . . . would make my life as slick as a s.   OBSESSIONS, 1
s. is a moment's monument   POETRY, 37
son-of-a-bitch The poor s.   WRITERS, 32
sons I have a wife, I have a   FAMILY, 25
Now we are all s. of bitches   NUCLEAR WEAPONS, 1
S. of Belial had a Glorious Time   TREASON, 2
sophistry Commit it then to the flames: for it can contain nothing but s. and illusion   PHILOSOPHY, 3
Universities incline wits to s. and affectation   EDUCATION, 4
sores Lazarus . . . laid at his gate, full of s.   POVERTY AND WEALTH, 2
sorrow Down, thou climbing s.   SORROW, 22
in s. thou shalt bring forth children   SEXES, 4
Its narrow measure spans Tears of eternity, and s.   SORROW, 10
Much in s., oft in woe   ENDURANCE, 24
One for s.   SUPERSTITION, 3
Parting is such sweet s.   PARTING, 10
Pure and complete s. is as impossible   EMOTION, 6
S. and silence are strong   ENDURANCE, 9
S. is tranquillity remembered in emotion   SORROW, 14
s. makes us wise   SORROW, 24

There is no greater s.   SORROW, 6
Through the night of doubt and s.   ENDURANCE, 5
sorrows When s. come, they come not single spies
MISFORTUNE, 17
sort that like that s. of place   OXFORD, 5
Soudan to you, Fuzzy-Wuzzy, at your 'ome in the S.   RACE, 11
sought Love s. is good   LOVE, 121
Pleasure is . . . seldom found where it is s.   PLEASURE, 14
soul And never once possess our s.   SOUL, 3
Anger is one of the sinews of the s.   ANGER, 4
Artists are not engineers of the s.   ART, 10
a . . . s. like season'd timber   VIRTUE, 10
become a living s.   DEATH, 125
company, . . . have neither a s. to lose nor a body to kick
BUSINESS, 17
education is a leading out of what is . . . in the pupil's s.
EDUCATION, 52
Education is . . . the s. of a society   EDUCATION, 11
Fair seed-time had my s.   SOUL, 12
His s. is marching on   MEMORIALS, 4
his s. is satisfied with what is assigned to him   CONTENTMENT, 1
I am positive I have a s.   SOUL, 11
I am the captain of my s.   RESPONSIBILITY, 7
Impropriety is the s. of wit   HUMOUR, 18
In mystery our s. abides   SOUL, 2
I pray the Lord my s. to keep   SLEEP, 2
Man has no Body distinct from his S.   SOUL, 4
My s. in agony   SOLITUDE, 2
my s. is white   RACE, 4
Never mind about my s. . . . get my tie right   PAINTING, 5
No coward is. is mine   COURAGE, 2
passion in the human s.   MUSIC, 25
Raises from Hell a human s.   HELL, 1
real dark night of the s.   SOUL, 6
seal the hushed casket of my s.   SLEEP, 11
than that one s. . . . should commit one single venial sin   SIN, 17
The British postgraduate student is a lonely forlorn s.
EDUCATION, 31
The dark night of the s.   SOUL, 8
the . . . essence of a human s.   BOOKS, 10
the eyes are the windows of the s.   EYES, 1
the iron enter into his s.!   BITTERNESS, 3
the iron has entered his s.   NONCOMMITMENT, 3
the largest and most comprehensive s.   SHAKESPEARE, 4
The Life and S., the man who will never go home   PARTIES, 9
The s. hath not her generous aspirings implanted in her in vain
SMOKING, 9
the s. is not more than the body   SELF, 20
the s. of a martyr with the intellect of an advocate
POLITICIANS, 3
The s. started at the knee-cap   ANIMALISM, 5
The S. that rises with us, our life's Star   METAPHYSICS, 5
The voice of the sea speaks to the s.   SEA, 3
Thy rapt s. sitting in thine eyes   SOUL, 10
Thy s. was like a star, and dwelt apart   NOBILITY, 7
souls Above the vulgar flight of common s.   SUPERIORITY, 8
damp s. of the housemaids   MELANCHOLY, 5
Our s. have sight of that immortal sea   METAPHYSICS, 6
S. of poets dead and gone   PUBLIC HOUSES, 1
the s. of five hundred . . . Newtons   SCIENTISTS, 4; WRITERS, 10
The s. of women are so small   WOMEN, 19
Two s. dwell, alas! in my breast   CONFLICT, 6
Two s. with but a single thought   LOVE, 81
soul-sides the meanest of his creatures Boasts two s.
HYPOCRISY, 5
sound full of s. and fury   LIFE, 41
s. of a great Amen   MUSIC, 35
The hills are alive with the s. of music   MUSIC, 19
The most persistent s. . . . through men's history   WAR, 57
The s. must seem an echo to the sense   WRITING, 26
The s. of the English county families   ARISTOCRACY, 14
the trumpet shall s.   DEATH, 26
whispering s. of the cool colonnade   TREES, 3
sounding s. brass   CHARITY, 5
sounds Music is the arithmetic of s.   MUSIC, 16
the s. will take care of themselves   MEANING, 2
soup concludes that it will . . . make better s.   IDEALISM, 4
S. of the evening, beautiful S.   FOOD, 13
Take the s. away   FOOD, 23
sour How s. sweet music is   ORDER, 4
I am sure the grapes are s.   ENVY, 4
source her Majesty . . . must not . . . look upon me as a s. of income
TAXATION, 5

s. and fury	PATIENCE, 11
S. through joy	NAZISM, 2
We are not now that s.	DETERMINATION, 14
strenuous doctrine of the s. life	WORK, 19
stretched things which he s.	LYING, 18
strife God and Nature then at s.	NATURE, 15
With phantoms an unprofitable s.	LIFE AND DEATH, 10
strike If you s. a child	VIOLENCE, 6
no right to s. against the public safety	STRIKES, 2
S. while the iron is hot	OPPORTUNITY, 7
themselves must s. the blow	FREEDOM, 6
the twenty-four-hour s.	STRIKES, 3
where ever you meet with a passage . . . s. it out	WRITING, 15
strikes the last four s. we've had, it's pissed down	STRIKES, 4
Strindberg S. when you have a temperature	LITERATURE, 12
string chewing little bits of S.	FOOD, 8
strings 'There are s.', said Mr Tappertit, 'in the human heart . . .'	EMOTION, 2
stripling yon pale s.	EXPECTATION, 4
strive I s. to be brief, and I become obscure	BREVITY, 2
needst not s. . . . to keep alive	KILLING, 2
To s., to seek, to find, and not to yield	DETERMINATION, 14
strives s. to touch the stars	AMBITION, 17
stroke man fears . . . only the s. of death	DEATH, 20
none so fast as s.	BOATS, 2
strong be s. and of a good courage	GOD, 8
disarm the s. and arm the weak	INJUSTICE, 6
how sublime . . . To suffer and be s.	ENDURANCE, 10
S. enough to answer back to desires, to despise distinctions	CHARACTER, 10
s. enough to bear the misfortunes of others	MISFORTUNE, 14
Sorrow and silence are s.	ENDURANCE, 9
the errors of those who think they are s.	MISTAKES, 3
the s. shall thrive	SURVIVAL, 4
the wall is s.	IMPRISONMENT, 10
woe unto them that . . . follow s. drink	ALCOHOL, 12
strongest S. minds . . . the noisy world Hears least	MIND, 10
strongminded nobody is s. around a President	SERVILITY, 6
strove I s. with none	LIFE AND DEATH, 7
struck Certain women should be s. regularly	WOMEN, 24
structure s. of the . . . British sentence	GRAMMAR, 3
struggle each man must s., lest the moral law become . . . separated	MORALITY, 1
manhood a s.	AGE, 17
The perpetual s. for room and food	SURVIVAL, 2
the s. for existence	EVOLUTION, 4
struggles The history of all . . . society is the history of class s.	CLASS, 22
struggling the greatness of Russia is only her pre-natal s.	RUSSIA, 2
strumpet a s.'s fool	LOVE, 109
struts player that s. and frets	LIFE, 41
stubborn s. spear-men	COURAGE, 15
student an over-ambitious essay by a second-year s.	CRITICS, 13
a s. to the end of my days	LEARNING, 5
He was . . . – a s. of history	EXPERIENCE, 18
studies S. serve for delight	EDUCATION, 5
study much s. is a weariness of the flesh	BOOKS, 7
s. what you most affect	EDUCATION, 46
The proper s. of Mankind is Man	SELF-KNOWLEDGE, 5
the result of previous s.	FLATTERY, 2
studying By s. the masters	EXPERTS, 1
stuff Ambition should be made of sterner s.	AMBITION, 15
such s. as dreams are made on	MORTALITY, 17
The future is made of the same s.	FUTURE, 7
to s. a mushroom	HOUSEWORK, 2
stumble they s. that run fast	HASTE, 11
stumbling the . . . world was s. . . . in social blindness	BLINDNESS, 2
stupid anger makes us all s.	ANGER, 6
clever man . . . came of . . . s. people	INTELLIGENCE, 4
he ceased to be mad he became merely s.	REMEDIES, 10
Living in England, . . . must be like being married to a s. . . . wife	ENGLAND, 17
s. are cocksure . . . intelligent full of doubt	DOUBT, 7
The s. neither forgive	FORGIVENESS, 15
To be clever enough to get . . . money, one must be s.	MATERIALISM, 6
stupidity Against s. the gods . . . struggle in vain	STUPIDITY, 12
Human S. consists in having lots of ideas, but stupid ones	STUPIDITY, 8
If poverty is the mother of crime, s. is its father	CRIME, 4

It is a s. . . . to busy oneself with the correction of the world	IMPROVEMENT, 3
no sin except s.	STUPIDITY, 13
Stygian resembling the horrible S. smoke of the pit	SMOKING, 6
ye S. set	LUST, 5
style s. is the man himself	STYLE, 1
s., not sincerity, is the vital thing	STYLE, 7
s. . . . often hides eczema	STYLE, 2
the grand s. arises in poetry	POETRY, 3
The s. is the man	WRITING, 2
styles All s. are good except the tiresome sort	STYLE, 6
subject a noble nature, . . . treats . . . a serious s.	POETRY, 3
Every s.'s duty is the King's	MONARCHY, 18
Her Majesty is not a s.	ROYALTY, 12
the individual s. . . . 'has nothing to do with the laws but to obey them.'	LAW, 16
subjects Although there exist many thousand s.	CONVERSATION, 1
subjunctive S. to the last, he preferred	GRAMMAR, 9
sublime a step from the s. to the ridiculous	DECLINE, 6
Beethoven's Fifth Symphony is the most s. noise	MUSIC, 18
how s. . . . To suffer and be strong	ENDURANCE, 10
The s. and the ridiculous	OPPOSITES, 4
submit To great evils we s.; we resent little provocations	TRIVIALITY, 9
subscribers reasons for not printing any list of s.	FRANKNESS, 6
subsequence It is incident to physicians . . . to mistake s. for consequence	DOCTORS, 5
substance faith is the s. of things hoped for	FAITH, 3
lose the s. by grasping at the shadow	GREED, 4
substantial he that chiefly owes himself . . . is the s. Man	SELF-RELIANCE, 3
substantives be able to tell the s. from the adjectives	POLITICS, 44
substitute a s. for reading it	OSTENTATION, 2
no s. for talent	TALENT, 3
substitutes and finally a single dictator s. himself	COMMUNISM, 11
subtle Time, the s. thief of youth	AGE, 38
suburbia I come from s.	SUBURBIA, 1
subverts a continued miracle in his own person, which s. all the principles of his understanding	CHRISTIANITY, 29
succeed If at first you don't s.	PERSISTENCE, 5
If they s., they fail	HOMOSEXUALITY, 3
I'm . . . ugly enough to s. on my own	INDEPENDENCE, 1
It is not enough to s.	RUTHLESSNESS, 7
Never having been able to s. in the world	ENVY, 8
those who ne'er s.	SUCCESS, 6
to s. unconventionally	ORTHODOXY, 3
succeeds Nothing s.	SUCCESS, 1
Whenever a friend s.	ENVY, 7
success a self-made man who owed his lack of s. to nobody	SELF-MADE MEN, 2
I thought that s. spelled happiness	HAPPINESS, 15
I was never affected by the question of the s.	SELF-CONFIDENCE, 2
no s. like failure	FAILURE, 2
not in mortals to command s.	SUCCESS, 2
no very lively hope of s.	PRAYER, 15
only place where s. comes before work	SUCCESS, 13; WORK, 21
religion . . . yours is S.	SUCCESS, 4
s. and miscarriage are empty sounds	DISILLUSION, 4
s. . . . by dint of hard work	EFFORT, 5; SUCCESS, 11
s. depends . . . upon individual initiative and exertion	EFFORT, 5; SUCCESS, 11
secret of my s.	JEALOUSY, 3
S. is counted sweetest	SUCCESS, 6
Sweet Smell of S.	SUCCESS, 10
The moral flabbiness born of . . . S.	SUCCESS, 7
The penalty of s.	SUCCESS, 3
two to make a marriage a s.	MARRIAGE, 92
successful It was very s.	WEAPONS, 2
we do everything we can to appear s.	SUCCESS, 12
sucker a s. born every minute	GULLIBILITY, 1
suckle To s. fools	TRIVIALITY, 12
sucks s. the nurse asleep	SUICIDE, 9
suddenly No one . . . s. became depraved	DEBAUCHERY, 6
sued publish and be s.	PUBLISHING, 7
Suez Ship me somewheres east of S.	DESIRE, 8
the S. Canal was flowing through my drawing room	POLITICS, 20

suffer courage to love . . . courage to s.　LOVE, 134
how sublime . . . To s. and be strong　ENDURANCE, 10
If s. we must, let's s. on the heights　SUFFERING, 6
Rather s. than die　SUFFERING, 8
s. fools gladly　WISDOM AND FOOLISHNESS, 3
suffered love a place the less for having s.　SUFFERING, 3
suffering A man who fears s.　SUFFERING, 9
pity for the s. of mankind　PHILOSOPHERS, 7
sympathize with everything, except s.　SYMPATHY, 6
we cannot be created for this sort of s.　AFTERLIFE, 5
sufficient s. unto the day is the evil thereof　WORRY, 7
sugar like sulphuric acid and s.　VIRTUE AND VICE, 3
S. and spice And all that's nice　NURSERY RHYMES, 65
suicide committed s. 25 years after his death　DIARIES, 3
Never murder a man who is committing s.　SUICIDE, 12
Not only is s. a sin　SUICIDE, 2
s. in this man's town　SUICIDE, 8
thought of s. is a great . . . comfort　SUICIDE, 4
suit in a light so dim he would not have chosen a s. by it　LOVE, 37
My s. is pale yellow. My nationality is French　NORMALITY, 2
suitable no s. material to work on　OBEDIENCE, 2
Sukey S. take it off again　NURSERY RHYMES, 39
sulphur land of Calvin, oat-cakes, and s.　SCOTLAND, 8
Puffed its s. to the sunset　TRAVEL, 4
sulphuric like s. acid and sugar　VIRTUE AND VICE, 3
sultry common where the climate's s.　ADULTERY, 1
sum Cogito, ergo s.　THINKING, 2
sumer S. is icumen in　SUMMER, 1
summer after many a s. dies the swan　MORTALITY, 19
All on a s. day　FOOD, 12
Beauty sat with me all the s. day　BEAUTY, 10
Before the war . . . it was s. all the year round　NOSTALGIA, 16
Made glorious s.　OPTIMISM, 23
Now the peak of s.'s past　TRANSIENCE, 10
S. afternoon – s. afternoon　SUMMER, 5
S. has set in with its usual severity　SUMMER, 4
Spring and s. did happen in Cambridge　CAMBRIDGE, 3
the last rose of s.　FLOWERS, 9
summit the s. of Everest was hardly the place　PHOTOGRAPHY, 3
summons when Fate s.　MORTALITY, 5
summum S. bonum　GOOD, 3
sun all, except their s. is set　EUROPE, 3
aweary of the s.　WORLD-WEARINESS, 7
before you let the s. in, mind it wipes its shoes　CLEANNESS, 2
better is he . . . who hath not seen the evil work . . . under the s.　EVIL, 3
between me and the s.　REPARTEE, 2
Busy old fool, unruly S.　SUN, 2
Fear no more the heat o' th' s.　MORTALITY, 16
Follow thy fair s.　SORROW, 3
Furnish'd and burnish'd by Aldershot s.　ADMIRATION, 1
If they had said the s. and the moon was gone　BYRON, 2
it were better for s. and moon to drop from heaven　SIN, 17
I will sing for the s.　WOMEN, 60
let not the s. go down upon your wrath　PUNISHMENT, 1; SIN, 3
Light breaks where no s. shines　EMOTION, 5
My s. sets　OPTIMISM, 16
nothing like the s.　ANALOGY, 3
on which the s. never sets　BRITISH EMPIRE, 4
s. came dazzling thro' the leaves　CHIVALRY, 11
s. had risen to hear him crow　ARROGANCE, 3
So sicken waning moons too near the s.　MOON, 4
Thank heavens the s. has gone in　LAST WORDS, 57
The kiss of s. for pardon　GARDENS, 7
The people – could you patent the s.?　DISCOVERY, 7
there is no new thing under the s.　NOVELTY, 1
There rises the s. of Austerlitz　WAR, 73
The S. came up upon the left　SUN, 1
The s. does not set in my dominions　ROYALTY, 26
the s. shining ten days a year and shit in the streets　ENGLAND, 20
this s. of York　OPTIMISM, 23
To have enjoy'd the s.　LIFE, 4
we cannot make our s. Stand still　LOVE, 84
with peaches and women, it's . . . the side next the s. that's tempting　TEMPTATION, 8
sunburn S. is very becoming　APPEARANCE, 9
Sunday A Christian . . . feels Repentance on a S.　HYPOCRISY, 18
Buried on a S.　NURSERY RHYMES, 48
only two posh papers on a S.　NEWSPAPERS, 9
The feeling of S. is the same everywhere　SUNDAY, 5

sung I have s. women in three cities　WOMEN, 60
sunk thanks to words, we have often s. to the level of the demons　WORDS, 11
sunless Down to a s. sea　PLEASURE, 8
sunset a s.-touch　WORRY, 8
Puffed its sulphur to the s.　TRAVEL, 4
S. and evening star　DUTY, 5
s. breezes shiver　BOATS, 14
sunsets I have a horror of s.　SUN, 3
superfluous that controversy is either s. or hopeless　ARGUMENTS, 11
superior I consider myself s. to the saint, the scientist　NOVELS, 9
One is not s. . . . because one sees the world in an odious light　CYNICISM, 1
The French want no-one to be their s.. The English want inferiors　PRIDE, 9
superiority their insolent and unfounded airs of s.　FRANCE, 15
The s. of one man's opinion over another's　OPINIONS, 2
superiors equality . . . with our s.　EQUALITY, 5
In America everybody is of the opinion that he has no social s.　EQUALITY, 16
superlative we have not settled the s.　PROGRESS, 1
Super-Mac Introducing S.　POLITICIANS, 74
superman I teach you the S.　SUPERIORITY, 9
supernatural Religion Has made an honest woman of the s.　RELIGION, 23; SUPERNATURAL, 7
This s. soliciting　SUPERNATURAL, 13
superstition necessary for a s. to enslave a philosophy　RELIGION, 31
S. is the poetry of life　SUPERSTITION, 8
S. is the religion of feeble minds　SUPERSTITION, 7
S. sets the whole world in flames　SUPERSTITION, 11
superstitions new truths . . . end as s.　NOVELTY, 4
s. of the human mind　PURITY, 4
superstructure Sentimentality is a s. covering brutality　SENTIMENTALITY, 2
supp'd I have s. full with horrors　WORLD-WEARINESS, 6
support atheist . . . no invisible means of s.　ATHEISM, 5
s. me when I am . . . wrong　SUPPORT, 4
supreme Our s. governors, the mob　PUBLIC, 20
sups He who s. with the devil　CAUTION, 4
surgeons Human beings, yes, but not s.　MEDICINE, 8
surmise with a wild s.　DISCOVERY, 5
surpassed Man is something that is to be s.　SUPERIORITY, 9
surprised it is I who am s.; you are merely astonished　WORDS, 20
the audience want to be s. . . . by things that they expect　PLAYS, 3
surrender No terms except . . . s.　WAR, 42
we shall never s.　WORLD WAR II, 4
survey When I s. the wondrous Cross　HUMILITY, 12
survival the S. of the Fittest　EVOLUTION, 6
without victory there is no s.　VICTORY, 2
survive as fitted to s. . . . as a tapeworm　EVOLUTION, 4
only the Fit s.　SURVIVAL, 4
Out of their cataclysm but one poor Noah Dare hope to s.　SEX, 22
survived I s.　SELF-PRESERVATION, 9
survives Education is what s.　EDUCATION, 51
suspect I rather s. her of being in love　LOVE AND MARRIAGE, 2
suspected New opinions are always s.　NOVELTY, 5
suspense This s. is terrible　SUSPENSE, 1
suspension willing s. of disbelief　POETRY, 10
suspicion Caesar's wife must be above s.　INTEGRITY, 2
people under s. are better moving　JUDGMENT, 10
suspicions S. amongst thoughts　SUSPICION, 1
swagman Once a jolly s. camped by a billy-bong　PLACES, 14
swains all our s. commend her　ADMIRATION, 16
swallow One s. does not make a summer　PROOF, 1
swallowed death is s. up in victory　DEATH, 26
swallows I hate a man who s. it　FOOD, 27
one master-passion in the breast, Like Aaron's serpent, s. up the rest　PASSION, 5
swan after many a summer dies the s.　MORTALITY, 19
Sweet S. of Avon　SHAKESPEARE, 10
What time is the next s.　MISTAKES, 13
Swanee 'Way down upon de S. Ribber　HOMESICKNESS, 2
swans S. sing before they die　SINGERS, 1
sway A little rule, a little s.　TRANSIENCE, 12
swear not by the moon　UNFAITHFULNESS, 8
swear-word A foreign s. is　LANGUAGE, 22
sweat blood, toil, tears and s.　EFFORT, 3

it is only because miners s. their guts out — SUPERIORITY, 10
That shriek and s. in pigmy wars — TRIVIALITY, 14
sweats Falstaff s. to death — OBESITY, 10
sweet Heard melodies are s. — MUSIC, 24
How s. are looks that ladies bend — WOMEN, 69
if TODAY BE S. — TIME, 16
Is trifle sufficient for s. — FOOD, 9
Pleasures newly found are s. — PLEASURE, 31
Revenge, at first though s. — REVENGE, 13
S. childish days — NOSTALGIA, 24
S. day, so cool, so calm — DAY, 8
so s. as Melancholy — MELANCHOLY, 2
S. Smell of Success — SUCCESS, 10
s. will be the flower — PATIENCE, 9
that bitter beer that tastes s. — IMMORTALITY, 5
sweeter The mountain sheep are s., But the valley sheep are
fatter — GREED, 7
sweetes' S. li'l' feller — BABIES, 5
sweetest s. things turn sourest — CORRUPTION, 7
s. thing that ever grew Beside a human door — ADMIRATION, 18
Success is counted s. — SUCCESS, 6
sweetness Culture is the passion for s. and light — CULTURE, 2
He who works for s. and light — PERFECTION, 1
waste its s. on the desert air — WASTE, 2
sweets Stolen s. are always sweeter, Stolen kisses much
completer — THEFT, 7
Stolen s. are best — THEFT, 5
swift Too s. arrives as tardy as too slow — LOVE, 108
swimming s. under water — WRITING, 7
swine a s. to show you where the truffles are — VULGARITY, 1
Come in, you Anglo-Saxon s. — INSULTS, 6
pearls before s. — FOOLISHNESS, 9
swing S., s. together — BOATS, 4
swings we pulls up on the s. — LOSS, 2
Swiss if the S. had designed these mountains — MOUNTAINS, 4;
SWITZERLAND, 4
The S. . . . are not a people so much as a . . . business
SWITZERLAND, 2
Swithin St. S.'s Day, if thou dost rain — WEATHER, 5
Switzerland Austria is S. . . . with history added — EUROPE, 12
In S. they had brotherly love — SWITZERLAND, 5
S. . . . an inferior sort of Scotland — SWITZERLAND, 3
swollen mere existence is s. to a horror — IDEALISM, 3
sword Islam unashamedly came with a s. — RELIGION, 45
more cruel . . . the pen than the s. — WRITING, 4
nation shall not lift up s. against nation — WAR AND PEACE, 2
pen is mightier than the s. — WRITING, 3
s. sleep in my hand — ENGLAND, 4
the bank was mightier than the s. — LIBERALISM, 3
they that take the s. shall perish with the s. — WAR, 8
swords beat their s. into plowshares — WAR AND PEACE, 2
those who have stout hearts and sharp s. — RUTHLESSNESS, 6
swound Like noises in a s. — SEA, 4
Sydney There was the vast town of S. — PLACES, 10
symmetry S. is tedious — BOREDOM, 4
thy fearful s. — ANIMALS, 4
sympathetic To be s. without discrimination — SYMPATHY, 2
sympathize s. with everything, except suffering — SYMPATHY, 6
sympathy failed to inspire s. in men — WOMEN, 14
machine-gun riddling her hostess with s. — SYMPATHY, 4
S. . . . lay over the gathering like a woolly blanket — SYMPATHY, 1
symptom common s. of immaturity — ORIGINALITY, 6
symptoms One of the s. of approaching nervous breakdown
WORK, 20
syne For auld lang s. — FRIENDSHIP, 13
Syrian The S. stars look down — DEATH, 18
system Christianity accepted . . . a metaphysical s.
CHRISTIANITY, 30
I'm not interested in the bloody s. — CHARITY, 13
systems Our little s. have their day — TRANSIENCE, 18
the whole solar and stellar s. — COMFORT, 1

T

table A man is . . . better pleased when he has a good dinner
upon his t. — WOMAN'S ROLE, 3
crumbs which fell from the rich man's t. — POVERTY AND
WEALTH, 2
patient etherized upon a t. — DEPARTURE, 5
put them at a t. together — FEAR, 5
tableau history is . . . a t. of crimes and misfortunes
HISTORY, 32
tables It is not your trade to make t. — CRITICISM, 18

tact T. consists in knowing — TACT, 4
tactic Silence is the best t. — SILENCE, 10
tae Here's t. us wha's like us — INDIVIDUALITY, 1
tail A case of the t. dogging the wag — HUMOUR, 50
The only man who really needs a t. coat — CLOTHES, 17
tailor I go to a better t. than any of you — CLOTHES, 3
Tinker, T., Soldier, Sailor — NURSERY RHYMES, 60
tails t. you lose — VICTORY, 5
taint That's right. 'Taint yours, and 't. mine — PUNS, 21
tainted the supply is not t. — JOURNALISM, 22
take T. care of the sense — MEANING, 7
They have to t. you in — HOME, 4
they . . . t., who have the power — POWER, 23
T. things as they come — WORRY, 4
You can't t. it with you — WEALTH, 2
takes It t. all sorts — OPPOSITES, 1
taking not winning but t. part — VICTORY, 4
tale A t. never loses — GOSSIP, 1
a t. Told by an idiot — LIFE, 41
Life is as tedious as a twice-told t. — LIFE, 40
thereby hangs a t. — LIFE, 42
t. to tell of the hardihood, endurance, and courage of my
companions — ENDURANCE, 16
talent A best-seller is the gilded tomb of a mediocre t.
BOOKS, 37
a country full of genius, but with absolutely no t. — IRELAND, 9
any man who has no t. — ENGLISH, 4
T. alone cannot make a writer — WRITERS, 13
T. develops in quiet places — CHARACTER, 9; TALENT, 2
T. does what it can — TALENT AND GENIUS, 3
the difference between t. and genius — TALENT AND GENIUS, 1
the meanest . . . deeds require spirit and t. — INSENSITIVITY, 3
the most extraordinary collection of t. — TALENT, 4
There is no substitute for t. — TALENT, 3
There is no such thing as a great t. without great will-power
DETERMINATION, 3
the t. of flattering with delicacy — FLATTERY, 2
t. instantly recognizes genius — MEDIOCRITY, 3; TALENT AND
GENIUS, 2
talents If you have great t., industry will improve them
WORK, 18
the difference between our t. and our expectations
DISAPPOINTMENT, 1
talk If you can t. with crowds and keep your virtue
IDEALISM, 2
my ministers t. – as long as they do what I say
AUTHORITARIANISM, 7
Teas, Where small t. dies — CONVERSATION, 8
the need to t. is a primary impulse — IMPETUOSITY, 1
think too little . . . t. too much — VERBOSITY, 3
Two may t. . . . yet never really meet — FRIENDSHIP, 14
when I hear anyone t. of Culture — PHILISTINISM, 4
When two Englishmen meet, their first t. is of the weather
ENGLISH, 20; WEATHER, 14
When you and I are together we never t. about anything except
me — CONCEIT, 21
women should t. an hour — SEXES, 1
you wished him to t. on for ever — POETS, 16
talked He t. on for ever — POETS, 16
The more you are t. about, the more you . . . wish to be t.
about — FAME, 18
There is only one thing . . . worse than being t. about — FAME, 24
talker A good listener is a good t. with a sore throat
CONVERSATION, 10
a non-stop t. to whom someone has given a typewriter
WRITERS, 4
Nothing is more despicable than a professional t. — VERBOSITY, 4
talkers fluent t. — THINKING, 3
talking for thirty-five years he had not stopped t.
SCIENTISTS, 11
Frenchman must be always t. — FRANCE, 9
good newspaper, . . . is a nation t. to itself — JOURNALISM, 18
if you ain't t. about him, ain't listening — ACTORS, 2
I wouldn't be . . . t. to someone like you — SNOBBERY, 3
People t. without speaking — FUTILITY, 9
T. and eloquence are not the same — SPEECH, 11
T. of Michelangelo — WOMEN, 30
While we're t., time will have meanly run on — PRESENT, 9
tall Let our children grow t. — TALENT, 6
tambourine Hey! Mr T. Man — LEISURE, 2
tame the tongue can no man t. — SPEECH, 6
tamper Who am I to t. with a masterpiece? — CONCEIT, 25
tangerine t. trees and marmalade skies — IMAGINATION, 7

tankard heart which grief hath cankered . . . remedy – the T. ALCOHOL, 17
tanned getting more t. and more tired ROYALTY, 23
tapeworm as fitted to survive . . . as a t. EVOLUTION, 8
Tara through T.'s halls IRELAND, 10
tarnished neither t. nor afraid COURAGE, 5
tarry having lost . . . your prime, You may for ever t. MARRIAGE, 67
Tartar Scratch the Russian and . . . find the T. RUSSIA, 4
tarts He's lost us the t.' vote JOURNALISM, 11; RESPONSIBILITY, 6
she made some t. FOOD, 12
The Queen of Hearts She made some t. NURSERY RHYMES, 51
Tarzan Me? T.? CINEMA, 10
task No t. is a long one but the t. on which one dare not start BEGINNING, 5
The trivial round, the common t. SIMPLICITY, 4
Tasmanians the T., who never committed adultery, are now extinct ADULTERY, 4
taste A different t. in jokes is a . . . strain on the affections HUMOUR, 10
bad t. is better than no t. TASTE, 1
Drink deep, or t. not the Pierian spring KNOWLEDGE, 29
Every one to his t. DIFFERENCE, 9
great common sense and good t. CHARACTER, 21
I suspect his t. in higher matters FOOD, 27
no t. when you married me TASTE, 7
people who always go on about . . . good t. TASTE, 5
Shakespeare, undoubtedly wanted t. SHAKESPEARE, 17
the bouquet is better than the t. ALCOHOL, 47
the t. by which he is . . . relished WRITING, 37
The t. was that of the little crumb of madeleine MEMORY, 11
Things sweet to t. prove . . . sour REGRET, 13
T. is the feminine of genius TASTE, 2
willing to t. any drink once DRINKS, 3
tasted Sir, you have t. two whole worms SPOONERISMS, 5
Some books are to be t. BOOKS, 7
tastes It is like a cigar. . . . it never t. quite the same LOVE, 139
Our t. greatly alter TASTE, 3
There is no accounting for t. DIFFERENCE, 5
taught a woman who knows all . . . that can be t. KNOWLEDGE, 9
I forget what I was t. KNOWLEDGE, 34
tavern A t. chair is the throne PUBLIC HOUSES, 1
he has . . . opened a t. for his friends PARASITES, 1
There is a t. in the town PARTING, 2
There is nothing . . . by which so much happiness is produced as by a good t. PUBLIC HOUSES, 2
tawney that t. weed tobacco SMOKING, 7
tax A hateful t. TAXATION, 4
For God's sake, madam, don't say that in England for . . . they will surely t. it TAXATION, 10
hardest thing . . . to understand is income t. TAXATION, 2
taxation T. without representation REPRESENTATION, 1
taxes collect legal t. from illegal money TAXATION, 1
Death and childbirth INCONVENIENCE, 1
The avoidance of t. . . . still carries . . . reward TAXATION, 6
taxi done almost every human activity inside a t. BOASTS, 1
taxis hiring t. . . . handing out redundancy notices to its own workers INCOMPETENCE, 2
taxpayer The t. is someone who works for the federal government TAXATION, 8
Tay Beautiful Railway Bridge of the Silv'ry T. DISASTER, 4
tea Dinner, Lunch and T. FOOD, 7
honey still for t. NOSTALGIA, 4
it is just like having a cup of t. SEX, 36
sometimes counsel take – and sometimes T. DRINKS, 7
Take some more t. LANGUAGE, 4
T. for Two, and Two for T. DRINKS, 5
we drink too much t. DRINKS, 8
When I makes t. I makes t. HUMOUR, 38
teach Don't t. your grandmother ADVICE, 2
For every person wishing to t. EDUCATION, 45
He who shall t. the child to doubt DOUBT, 3
It is no matter what you t. them first EDUCATION, 26
You can't t. an old dog OLD AGE, 2
teacher Experience is a good t. EXPERIENCE, 6
Time is a great t., but . . . kills all its pupils TIME, 10
teachers We t. can only help . . . as servants EDUCATION, 37
teaches He who cannot, t. EDUCATION, 49
teacup Storm in a T. TRIVIALITY, 2
team Is my t. ploughing AGRICULTURE, 3

team games The British, being brought up on t. HOUSES OF PARLIAMENT, 14
tear Every t. from every eye SORROW, 14
Some stars in sudden fear Fell like a falling t. STARS, 6
tears blood, toil, t. and sweat EFFORT, 3
foolish t. upon my grave HYPOCRISY, 15
He spoke, and loos'd our heart in t. POETS, 2
If you have t., prepare to shed them SORROW, 21
in a flood of t. and a Sedan chair HUMOUR, 34
mine own t. Do scald SUFFERING, 11
No t. in the writer WRITING, 4
our t. Thaw not the frost MOURNING, 14
shed t. when they would devour HYPOCRISY, 2
The bitterest t. . . . are for words . . . unsaid and deeds . . . undone REGRET, 19
the land of t. SORROW, 19
The smiles, the t., Of boyhood's years NOSTALGIA, 14
the women whose eyes have been washed . . . with t. WOMEN, 27
T., idle t. SORROW, 26
T. such as angels weep SORROW, 12
T. were to me SORROW, 5
Violet Elizabeth dried her t. THREATS, 1
With silence and t. SEPARATION, 2
teas T., Where small talk dies CONVERSATION, 8
tease The fleas that t. in the high Pyrenees NONSENSE, 3
tea-stirring t. times PRESENT, 11
teatray Like a t. in the sky NONSENSE, 5
teche gladly wolde he lerne, and gladly t. CHARACTER, 4
technological For t. man it is time TECHNOLOGY, 7
technology t. . . . indistinguishable from magic TECHNOLOGY, 3
tedious People are either charming or t. CHARM, 4
They shorten t. nights SEX, 8
tedium t. is the very basis of mourning BOREDOM, 4
teeth I had braces on my t. and got high marks APPEARANCE, 23
I have let dentists ride roughshod over my t. TEETH, 1
I'll dispose of my t. as I see fit TEETH, 2
natural false t. TEETH, 3
take the bull between the t. MIXED METAPHORS, 3
taking out his false t. and hurling them at his wife MARRIAGE, 48
They will steal the very t. out of your mouth THEFT, 2
to lose one's t. is a catastrophe TEETH, 4
teetotaller a beer t., not a champagne t. ALCOHOL, 52
no woman should marry a t. ABSTINENCE, 8
teetotallers T. lack the sympathy ABSTINENCE, 7
telephone I don't know his t. number NUMBERS, 2
telephone-exchange we are supposing the brain . . . more than a t. MIND, 7
television but to do it on t. TELEVISION, 2
eats, sleeps and watches the t. WOMAN'S ROLE, 2
stay at home and see bad t. for nothing? CINEMA, 5
T. brought the brutality of war TELEVISION, 4; WAR, 64
T. is more interesting than people TELEVISION, 1
T.? No good will come TELEVISION, 5
T. . . . permits you to be entertained in your living room TELEVISION, 3
tell do not t. them so WISDOM, 12
How could they t. POLITICIANS, 54
people who love to t. us what to do ENGLISH, 22
T. the truth TRUTH, 3
you must not kiss and t. SECRECY, 7
you never can t.. That's a principle PRINCIPLES, 2
telly People will cross the road . . . to say 'We saw you on the t.' TELEVISION, 2
You don't get any pornography . . . on the t. PORNOGRAPHY, 5
Téméraire She's the Fighting T. BOATS, 14
temper A tart t. never mellows with age CHARACTER, 11
if I were not king, I should lose my t. ROYALTY, 21
Never lose your t. with the Press SELF-CONTROL, 7
temperament artistic t. is a disease ARTS, 2
temperance I prefer t. hotels ALCOHOL, 61
tempests On whom Thy t. fell all night OLD AGE, 21
That looks on t. LOVE, 117
temple in the very t. of delight MELANCHOLY, 8
The Arab who builds . . . a hut out of . . . a t. . . . is more philosophical MUSEUMS, 1; PRACTICALITY, 3
the veil of the t. was rent in twain LAST WORDS, 8
This is the t. of Providence LUCK, 7
tempora O t.! O mores CUSTOM, 2
temporary force alone is but t. FORCE, 2
temptation blessed is the man that endureth t. TEMPTATION, 4

T. is but the stream I go a-fishing in   TIME, 34
T. is like a river made up of the events which happen
    TRANSIENCE, 2
t. is money   BUSINESS, 6
T. is on our side   PROGRESS, 7
T. is slipping underneath our Feet   TIME, 16
t. is the greatest innovator   INNOVATION, 1
T. is too large   TIME, 26
T. may restore us   POETS, 3
To choose t. is to save t.   TIME, 7
to waste my t. making money   MONEY, 4
T. present and time past   TIME, 14
t. quietly kills them   TIME, 12
T.'s up for Sir John, an' for little Lady Jane   PARTING, 7
T.'s winged chariot   AGE, 35
T., the subtle thief of youth   AGE, 38
T. was away and somewhere else   LOVE, 82
T. whereof the memory of man   MEMORY, 3
T. will tell   TIME, 6
T. wounds all heels   TIME, 25
We have short t. to stay, as you   TRANSIENCE, 14
We take no note of t.   TIME, 38
What do the ravages of t. not injure?   AGE, 30
While we're talking, t. will have meanly run on   PRESENT, 7
Work expands so as to fill the t.   WORK, 15
timeliness the t. of the gift   PROMPTNESS, 1
Times one copy of The T.   NEWSPAPERS, 6
The T. has made many ministries   NEWSPAPERS, 3
The T. is speechless   NEWSPAPERS, 5
times It was the best of t.   FRENCH REVOLUTION, 1
logic of our t.   DECLINE, 3
The good old t.   NOSTALGIA, 5
the true old t. are dead   NOSTALGIA, 19
We live in stirring t.   PRESENT, 11
time-table I would sooner read a t.   NOVELS, 10
tim'rous Wee, . . . t. beastie   ANIMALS, 7
tinker T., Tailor, Soldier, Sailor   NURSERY RHYMES, 60
tinkling a t. cymbal   CHARITY, 5
to set a chime of words t. in . . . a few fastidious people
    PURPOSE, 7
tinned t. food is a deadlier weapon   WEAPONS, 3
tip-and-run watch him play t.   ENGLISH, 13
Tipperary a long, long way to T.   HOMESICKNESS, 4
tipping Do they allow t. on the boat   MONEY, 30
tipster A racing t. who only reached Hitler's level of accuracy
    HITLER, 5
tiptoe T. through the tulips   FLOWERS, 3
tired getting more tanned and more t.   ROYALTY, 23
Give me your t., . . . Your huddled masses   AMERICA, 21
I haven't got time to be t.   WORK, 26
I'm t. of Love   MONEY, 8
Life . . . process of getting t.   LIFE, 15
tiresome All styles are good except the t. sort   STYLE, 6
Titian Nobody cares much at heart about T.   ARTISTS, 7
title Because of my t., I was the first   COURAGE, 7
That t. from a better man I stole   IMITATION, 6
title-page The book written against fame . . . has the author's
name on the t.   HYPOCRISY, 9
titles I've been offered t., . . . get one into disreputable
company   TITLES, 11
Kinquering Congs their t. take   SPOONERISMS, 3
T. distinguish the mediocre   TITLES, 10
toast I had never had a piece of t. . . . But fell . . . on the
buttered side   PERVERSITY, 5
toasted cheese – t., mostly   DREAMS, 12
tobacco leave off t.   SMOKING, 9
that tawney weed t.   SMOKING, 7
what pleasure . . . they have in taking their roguish t.
    SMOKING, 8
who lives without t.   SMOKING, 11
today here t., and gone tomorrow   TRANSIENCE, 3
He who can call t. his own   PRESENT, 5
if T. BE SWEET   TIME, 16
Its history dates from t.   ROYALTY, 35
the Cup that clears T. of past Regrets   PRESENT, 5
they will listen t., they will listen tomorrow   PROMISES, 4
wiser t. than . . . yesterday   MISTAKES, 10
toddle I'd t. safely home   WAR, 100
toe that old enemy the gout Had taken him in t.   ILLNESS, 6;
    PUNS, 6
the light fantastic t.   DANCING, 7
together And the loved one all t.   PERVERSITY, 2

two people living t. for 25 years without having a cross word
    MARRIAGE, 65
We must . . . all hang t.   UNITY, 9
toil as some men t. after virtue   SMOKING, 10
blood, t., tears and sweat   EFFORT, 3
Horny-handed sons of t.   WORK, 11
they t. not   WORRY, 6
To t. and not to seek for rest   SELFLESSNESS, 2
tolerance lead this people into war and they'll forget . . . t.
    WAR, 134
tolerant Eddy was a tremendously t. person   WELSH, 1
tolerate the greater part of the law is learning to t. fools
    LAW, 18
toleration t. produced . . . religious concord   RELIGION, 25
toll'd The sexton t. the bell   PUNS, 5
tolls for whom the bell t.   DEATH, 43
Tolstoy Their teacher had advised them not to read T. novels
    INDOCTRINATION, 1
Tom T., he was a piper's son   NURSERY RHYMES, 61;
    NURSERY RHYMES, 62
tomb A best-seller is the gilded t. of a mediocre talent
    BOOKS, 37
drink a dozen of Claret on my T.   ALCOHOL, 33
Tom Jones The romance of T.   NOVELS, 5
Tommy Little T. Tucker, Sings for his supper   NURSERY
    RHYMES, 31
Oh, it's T. this, an' T. that   SOLDIERS, 2
tomorrow assure him that he'd live t.   DESTINY, 16
Drop . . . what t. may bring . . . count as profit every day that
 Fate allows you   PRESENT, 8
here today and gone t.   TRANSIENCE, 3
jam t.   PROMISES, 3
let us eat and drink; for t. we . . . die   TRANSIENCE, 7
Never put off till t.   PROCRASTINATION, 1
T., and t., and t.   LIFE, 41
t. is another day   HOPE, 7; OPTIMISM, 9
tom-tit little t. sang Willow   BIRDS, 4
tone Take the t. of the company   CONFORMITY, 3
tongue A burning forehead, and a parching t.   PASSION, 3
a sharp t. is the only edged tool   CHARACTER, 11
him whose strenuous t. can burst Joy's grape   MELANCHOLY, 8
hold your t. and let me love   SILENCE, 5
neither eye to see, nor t. to speak   HOUSES OF PARLIAMENT, 11
One t. is sufficient for a woman   EDUCATION, 35; WOMEN, 50
saying right off what comes to my t.   IMPETUOSITY, 1
Silence is become his mother t.   SILENCE, 6
the t. can no man tame   SPEECH, 6
the t. is a little member   SPEECH, 5
the use of my oracular t.   MALAPROPISMS, 8
who speak the t. That Shakspeare spake   FREEDOM, 53
tongues Self-interest speaks all sorts of t.   SELF-INTEREST, 5
Tony T. . . . he immatures with age   INSULTS, 41
too You can have t. much   MODERATION, 2
tool a sharp tongue is the only edged t.   CHARACTER, 11
time as a t., not as a couch   TIME, 20
tools Give us the t.   WORLD WAR II, 9
tool-using Man is a t. animal   TECHNOLOGY, 2
tooth t. for t.   RETRIBUTION, 3
toothache man with t. . . . teeth are sound   ENVY, 6
philosopher that could endure the t.   ENDURANCE, 18
top I shall be like that tree; I shall die from the t.   DECLINE, 10
I started at the t. and worked my way down   DECLINE, 13
looking at the men at the t.   AMBITION, 6
People at the t. of the tree   EDUCATION, 54
There is always room at the t.   AMBITION, 18
top-boots did pleasure me in his t.   SEX, 26
torch like runners hand on the t. of life   MORTALITY, 15
Truth, like a t.   TRUTH, 25
tormentor it is I who am my t.   SELF, 15
torments I cannot help it; . . . infinity t. me   INFINITY, 2
torrent When the t. sweeps a man against a boulder   THEORY, 7
Tory a deep burning hatred for the T. Party   POLITICS, 6
end up in the T. knackery   POLITICIANS, 41
Every Briton is at heart a T.   POLITICS, 4
to what is called the T., . . . called the Conservative, party
    POLITICS, 17
tossed you t. and gored several persons   CONVERSATION, 3
total t. solution of the Jewish question   NAZISM, 1
totter t. towards the tomb   OLD AGE, 35
touch keep the Nelson t.   PATRIOTISM, 20
mere t. of cold philosophy   PHILOSOPHY, 7
only t. the hem of his garment   REMEDIES, 4
sunset t.   WORRY, 8

t. of a vanish'd hand	NOSTALGIA, 21
Wound with a t.	SATIRE, 2
tourist the most vulgar, . . . is the British t.	BRITISH, 7
tourists t. . . . take in the Monarchy . . . with . . . the pigeons	
	LONDON, 8
toves slithy t. did gyre	NONSENSE, 7
towels never darken my t. again	DISMISSAL, 5; HUMOUR, 42
tower Childe Roland to the Dark T.	SUMMONS, 4
towering the height of his own t. style	POETS, 8
towers The cloud-capp'd t.	MORTALITY, 17
town man made the t.	COUNTRYSIDE, 2
toy but a childish t.	IGNORANCE, 11
trade Every man to his t.	OCCUPATIONS, 2
God will pardon me. It is His t.	LAST WORDS, 30
half a t. and half an art	LITERATURE, 6
It is not your t. to make tables	CRITICISM, 18
man must serve his time to every t.	CRITICS, 2
no nation was ever ruined by t.	BUSINESS, 5
Two of a t. can ne'er agree	ARGUMENTS, 5
trades The ugliest of t. have their moments of pleasure	
	OCCUPATIONS, 7
trading t. on the blood of my men	EXPLOITATION, 3
tradition We don't want t.	HISTORY, 11
traffic the t. of Jacob's ladder	HEAVEN, 12
tragedie go litel myn t.	BOOKS, 12
T. is to seyn a certeyn storie	MISFORTUNE, 7
tragedies t. are finish'd by a death	THEATRE, 4
There are two t. in life	DESIRE, 14
tragedy a t. and therefore not worth reading	PLAYS, 2
brooding t. and its dark shadows can be lightened	HISTORY, 12
farce brutalized becomes t.	THEATRE, 7
great t. of Science	SCIENCE, 19
That is their t.	SEXES, 25
the wine was a farce and the food a t.	FOOD, 41
T. is if I cut my finger	THEATRE, 1
We participate in a t.	THEATRE, 8
what t. means	THEATRE, 11
world is a comedy to those who think, a t. to those who feel	
	LIFE, 49
You *may* abuse a t.	CRITICISM, 18
You're a bloody t.	POLITICIANS, 50
tragically Everything must be taken seriously, nothing t.	
	PERSPECTIVE, 4
train man who shaves and takes a t.	TRAVEL, 27
The only way . . . of catching a t.	TRAVEL, 6
trained Science is nothing but t. and organized common sense	
	SCIENCE, 18
trains t. all night groan on the rail To men that die at morn	
	EXECUTION, 11
tramp He began to think the t. a fine . . . fellow	FAMILIARITY, 5
the Lady Is a T.	DECLINE, 1
the t. of the twenty-two men	SPORT AND GAMES, 2
trampling He is t. out the vintage where the grapes of wrath	
	GOD, 25
tranquillity Sorrow is t. remembered in emotion	SORROW, 14
transform t. this society without . . . extension of public	
ownership	SOCIALISM, 8
transformation The universe is t.	LIFE, 8
transit Sic t. gloria mundi	GLORY, 3
transition I expect no very violent t.	HEAVEN, 9
translation original is unfaithful to the t.	TRANSLATION, 1
Poetry is what gets lost in t.	TRANSLATION, 3
translations T. (like wives) are seldom faithful	TRANSLATION, 2
transplanted Many ideas grow better when t. into another	
mind	IDEAS, 3
trapeze daring young man on the flying t.	SPORT AND GAMES, 13
trappings the t. and the suits of woe	MOURNING, 12
trash Who steals my purse steals t.	REPUTATION, 6
travel T. broadens the mind	TRAVEL, 1
t. for t.'s sake	TRAVEL, 25
T., in the younger sort	TRAVEL, 2
T. is the most private of pleasures	TRAVEL, 22
T. light	THEFT, 2
To t. hopefully is . . . better . . . than to arrive	ANTICIPATION, 7
wherever the wind takes me I t. as a visitor	FREEDOM, 19
travelled I t. among unknown men	HOMESICKNESS, 4
traveller a t. from an antique land	MEMORIALS, 11
from whose bourn no t. returns	AFTERLIFE, 8
travelling The grand object of t.	TRAVEL, 14
T. is . . . like talking with men of other centuries	TRAVEL, 7
travels A man t. the world over	HOME, 6
He t. fastest	SELF, 4
too old to go again to my t.	ROYALTY, 10

treachery Political renegades always start their career of t.	
	POLITICIANS, 41
tread fools rush in where angels fear to t.	HASTE, 8
frightful fiend . . . behind him t.	FEAR, 6
Where'er you t.	ADMIRATION, 11
treason If *this* be t., make the most of it	TREASON, 4
T. doth never prosper	TREASON, 3
T. was no Crime	TREASON, 2
treasure Preserve it as your chiefest t.	BOOKS, 6
purest t. mortal times afford	REPUTATION, 7
treasures lay not up . . . t. upon earth	WEALTH, 7
Treasury the Vatican, the T. and the miners	DIPLOMACY, 2
treated Actors should be t. like cattle	ACTORS, 5
treaties T. are like roses and young girls	DIPLOMACY, 10
treaty hand that signed the t. bred a fever	SIGNATURES, 3
tree A billboard lovely as a t.	TREES, 11
A poem lovely as a t.	TREES, 7
as the twig is bent, the t.'s inclined	EDUCATION, 42
If poetry comes not . . . as leaves to a t.	POETRY, 24
I shall be like that t.; I shall die from the top	DECLINE, 10
only God can make a t.	TREES, 3
Rock-a-bye baby on the t. top	SLEEP, 4
same t. that a wise man sees	WISDOM AND FOOLISHNESS, 4
spare the beechen t.	TREES, 2
The difference between a gun and a t.	TREES, 12
the fruit Of that forbidden t.	SIN, 16
The t. of liberty must be refreshed	FREEDOM, 21
the t. of life	GARDENS, 3
the t. of the knowledge of good and evil	GARDENS, 3
t. of life is green	REALITY, 3; THEORY, 4
treen In old time we had t. chalices and golden priests	
	CLERGY, 7
trees Loveliest of t., the cherry	TREES, 5
Trelawny shall T. die	EXECUTION, 10
tremble t. like a guilty thing surprised	DOUBT, 8
trembled And t. with fear at your frown	MEMORY, 7
trembles And Satan t.	PRAYER, 10
trenches digging t. and trying on gas-masks	WORLD WAR II, 1
trial T. by jury . . . a delusion	JUSTICE, 5
triangles if t. invented a god, they would make him three-sided	
	RELIGION, 42
tribe Abou Ben Adhem (may his t. increase!)	DREAMS, 11
Mankind is not a t.	MANKIND, 11
Richer than all his t.	LOVE, 22
tribute the vain t. of a smile	POETS, 22
trick When in doubt, win the t.	SPORT AND GAMES, 7
trifle Is t. sufficient for sweet	FOOD, 8
trifles observance of t.	TRIVIALITY, 5
snapper-up of unconsidered t.	BUSINESS, 14
trigger Whose Finger do you want on the T.	GOVERNMENT, 3
Trinian's Though loaded firearms were strictly forbidden at St	
T.	WEAPONS, 6
Trinity I the T. illustrate	DRINKS, 7
Triton Old T. blow his wreathed horn	DISCONTENT, 10
triumph One more devils'-t. and sorrow for angels	
	DAMNATION, 1
We t. without glory	VICTORY, 3
triumphed So I t. ere my passion	PASSION, 8
trivial mighty contests rise from t. things	RESULTS, 2
The t. round, the common task	SIMPLICITY, 4
triviality you're deluded by t.	DELUSION, 5
Trojan open that Pandora's Box . . . T. 'orses will jump out	
	MIXED METAPHORS, 1
Trojans Do not trust the horse, T.	MISTRUST, 11
troops t. of unrecording friends	LIFE, 46
trot I don't t. it out and about	VIRTUE, 6
trouble a lot of t. in his life	WORRY, 10
A t. shared	WORRY, 1
a woman is on a . . . hunt for t.	MARRIAGE, 47
it saves me the t. of liking them	NASTINESS, 2
man . . . is . . . full of t.	HUMAN CONDITION, 3
One stops being a child when . . . telling one's t. does not make	
it better	DISILLUSION, 5
Our progress . . . Is t. and care	LIFE, 32
Prostitution . . . keeps her out of t.	SEX, 18
troubled let not your heart be t.	PEACE, 1
troubles Don't meet t. half-way	WORRY, 2
I have had t. enough	MISFORTUNE, 5
pack up your t. in your old kit-bag	OPTIMISM, 2
take arms against a sea of t.	SUICIDE, 10
troublesome t. . . . bondage of Rhyming	POETRY, 31
trousers bottoms of my t. rolled	OLD AGE, 16
I shall wear white flannel t.	OLD AGE, 17

man should never put on his best t.   FREEDOM, 20
She is trying to wear the t. of Winston Churchill   POLITICIANS, 7
trout as when you find a t. in the milk   PROOF, 6
trowel laid on with a t.   EXCESS, 9
Troy from the shores of T. came destined an exile
     ENDURANCE, 23
Now there are fields where T. once was   DECLINE, 8
true a great advantage for . . . philosophy to be . . . t.
     PHILOSOPHY, 13
All one's inventions are t.   POETRY, 14
A thing is not necessarily t.   MARTYRDOM, 5
because a novel's invented, it isn't t.   NOVELS, 12
Be so t. to thyself   INTEGRITY, 1
be yourself, imperial, plain and t.   SINCERITY, 1
false to his friends . . . t. to the public   HONESTY, 3
Geometry is not t.   MATHEMATICS, 8
He said t. things   WORDS, 3
if they keep on saying it . . . it will be t.   JOURNALISM, 4
it's . . . more important for a theory to be shapely, than . . . t.
     THEORY, 5
Journalists say a thing that they know isn't t.   JOURNALISM, 4
Many a t. word   TRUTH, 2
Mr. Speaker, I said the honorable member was a liar it is t.
and I am sorry for it   APOLOGIES, 4
No man worth having is t. to his wife   UNFAITHFULNESS, 5
One religion is as t. as another   RELIGION, 8
Small service is t. service   SERVICE, 4
T. and False are attributes of speech, not of things   TRUTH, 26
The religions we call false were once t.   RELIGION, 21
T. love never grows old   LOVE, 11
to thine own self be t.   BORROWING, 8; INTEGRITY, 6
truism is . . . none the less t.   SAYINGS, 7
t. to you, darlin', in my fashion   FAITHFULNESS, 5
whatsoever things are t.   VIRTUE, 4
truffles a swine to show you where the t. are   VULGARITY, 1
truism A t. is on that account none the less true   SAYINGS, 7
truly A t. great man   GREATNESS, 1
trumpet the t. shall sound   DEATH, 26
trunkless Two vast and t. legs of stone   MEMORIALS, 11
trust I don't t. him. We're friends   FRIENDSHIP, 11
Never t. a husband too far   TRUST, 4
never t. a woman   AGE, 64
Never t. the man who . . . hath injured you   TRUST, 2
the one God whose worshippers . . . still t. in Him   LUCK, 7
the right of governing was not property but a t.
     GOVERNMENT, 9
t. ye not in a friend   TRUST, 1
Where large sums of money are concerned, . . . t. nobody
     MONEY, 15
trustful It takes a long while for a . . . t. person to reconcile
himself to . . . God   FAITH, 15
trusting it never extended to t. him   HITLER, 2
truth And seek for t. in the groves of Academe   EDUCATION, 22
any t. but from a clear perception   TRUTH, 29
A platitude is simply a t. repeated   SAYINGS, 1
Appearances are not . . . a clue to the t.   APPEARANCES, 13
a short armistice with t.   TRUTH, 16
A t. that's told with bad intent   TRUTH, 13
a t. universally acknowledged   MARRIAGE, 9
Beauty is t., t. beauty   BEAUTY, 23; TRUTH, 30
before the t. has got its boots on   LYING, 6
cheated into passion, but . . . reasoned into t.   TRUTH, 23
cinema is t. twenty-four times a second   CINEMA, 4
Cynicism is an unpleasant way of saying the t.   CYNICISM, 2
dearer still is t.   TRUTH, 8
economical with the t.   LYING, 3
Every man has a right to utter what he thinks t.   FREEDOM, 22
few enthusiasts . . . speak the t.   ENTHUSIASM, 2
hard to believe . . . a man is telling the t.   LYING, 10
He believes, . . . that there *is* such a thing as t.   POLITICIANS, 3
I am the way, the t., and the life   CHRISTIANITY, 17
if the people . . . can be reached with the t.   DEMOCRACY, 12
If you do not tell the t. about yourself   HONESTY, 13
in the end the t. will conquer   TRUTH, 43
it cannot compel anyone to tell the t.   LAW, 8
It takes two to speak the t.   TRUTH, 39
Let us begin by committing ourselves to the t.   TRUTH, 34
loving Christianity better than T.   CHRISTIANITY, 22
mainly he told the t.   LYING, 18
Much t. is spoken, . . . more . . . concealed   TRUTH, 19
My way of joking is to tell the t.   TRUTH, 37
Nobody speaks the t. when   LYING, 5

No poet ever interpreted nature . . . as a lawyer interprets t.
     LAW, 12
not even Marx is more precious . . . than the t.   TRUTH, 41
Now I may wither into the t.   AGE, 69
Perjury . . . is t. that is shamefaced   TRUTH, 20
Photography is t.   CINEMA, 4
polite by telling the t.   COURTESY, 3
Pride and T., That long to give themselves for wage   AGE, 68
put him in possession of t.   TRUTH, 31
Some men love t. so much   TRUTH, 15
speaking nothing but the t.   HONESTY, 12
T. be veiled   OPTIMISM, 24
T. comes out in wine   ALCOHOL, 45
T. fears no trial   TRUTH, 4
T. has no special time of its own   TRUTH, 35
the laws of poetic t. and poetic beauty   POETRY, 2
the t. is not in us   SIN, 5
the t. of imagination   IMAGINATION, 6; TRUTH, 28
the t. shall make you free   TRUTH, 11
the unclouded face of t. suffer wrong   JOURNALISM, 22
The worst enemy of t. and freedom   MAJORITY, 4
those who live . . . believe . . . to be the t.   HONESTY, 4
t. is always strange   TRUTH, 17
T. is on the march   TRUTH, 44
T. is stranger   TRUTH, 5
T. is . . . the test of experience   TRUTH, 24
T., like a torch   TRUTH, 25
to the dead we owe only t.   RESPECT, 4
T., Sir, is a cow   SCEPTICISM, 3
T. sits upon the lips of dying men   TRUTH, 9
T. telling is not compatible with the defence of the realm
     TRUTH, 36
t. that makes men free   TRUTH, 7
T. will out   TRUTH, 6
Two half-truths do not make a t.   HALF MEASURES, 1
whatever remains, however improbable, must be the t.
     TRUTH, 21
What is t.   TRUTH, 10; TRUTH, 12
When t. is discovered by someone else   TRUTH, 38
whilst the great ocean of t. lay all undiscovered before me
     DISCOVERY, 6
who ever knew T. put to the worse   TRUTH, 32
You can only find t. with logic   LOGIC, 2; TRUTH, 18
truths All great t. begin as blasphemies   NOVELTY, 9
all t. are half-t.   TRUTH, 42
commonplaces the great poetic t.   TRIVIALITY, 13
He was a man of two t.   LYING, 12
new t. . . . begin as heresies   NOVELTY, 4
t. being in and out of favour   NOVELTY, 2
The only t. which are universal   TRUTH, 40
There are no new t.   NOVELTY, 7
those three fundamental t.   OBJECTIVITY, 1
try t. everything once   EXPERIENCE, 7
T., t. again   PERSISTENCE, 5
trying I am t. to be, and you can't help it   RUDENESS, 4
tu *Et t., Brute*   BETRAYAL, 7; LAST WORDS, 9
tub Rub-a-dub-dub, Three men in a t.   NURSERY RHYMES, 44
tubby a t. little chap   OBESITY, 13
Tuesday Christened on T.   NURSERY RHYMES, 48
T.'s child is full of grace   NURSERY RHYMES, 33
tulips Tiptoe through the t.   FLOWERS, 1
tumbler He who drinks a t. of London water   WATER, 8
tune There's many a good t.   AGE, 2
Whistle a Happy T.   WHISTLING, 2
tunes I do not see . . . why the devil should have all the good
t.   MUSIC, 20
tunnel light at the end of the t. . . . of an oncoming train
     PESSIMISM, 8
turbot would give the price of a large t. for it!   BOOKS, 34
turbulent rid me of this t. priest   ASSASSINATION, 4
turf The blue ribbon of the t.   HORSES, 5
turn I wouldn't have left a t. unstoned   CRITICISM, 51
One good t. deserves another   HELP, 3
turning Life is a maze in which we take the wrong t.   LIFE, 18
The lady's not for t.   INFLEXIBILITY, 3
turnip he had rather Have a t. than his father   NONSENSE, 13
turtle the voice of the t. is heard   SPRING, 1
tu-whit T., Tu-who   WINTER, 6
tu-who Tu-whit, T.   WINTER, 6
twain never the t. shall meet   OPPOSITES, 3
twang the triumphant t. of a bedspring   SEX, 37
Tweedledee Tweedledum said T. Had spoiled his nice new
rattle   WAR, 21

Tweedledum T. and Tweedledee Agreed to have a battle
WAR, 21
twelve I was born at the age of t. CINEMA, 2
T. lords a-leaping NURSERY RHYMES, 55
twentieth T. Century Blues MELANCHOLY, 4
the t. century will be . . . the century of Fascism FASCISM, 2
twenty the first t. years YOUTH, 17
The United States, . . . are t. years in advance of this country
AMERICA, 17
twenty-five My dear fellow, . . . I only ask you for t. pounds
BORROWING, 11
twenty-four There are only t. hours in the day TIME, 2
the t. hour day TIME, 9
the t.-hour strike STRIKES, 2
twenty-nine t. distinct damnations BIBLE, 3
twenty-two the tramp of the t. men SPORT AND GAMES, 2
twice can't step into the same river t. CHANGE, 3
desire to be praised t. over PRAISE, 6
Literature . . . something that will be read t. JOURNALISM, 9;
LITERATURE, 1
no shirt or collar ever comes back t. NEGLECT, 2
will bear to be read t., . . . was thought t. WRITING, 32
you shall drink t. while I drink once DRUNKENNESS, 20
twig as the t. is bent, the tree's inclined EDUCATION, 42
twilight T. grey DAY, 11
twinkle T. t. little bat NONSENSE, 5
T., twinkle, little star STARS, 1
twinkling in the t. of an eye DEATH, 26
Twist Oliver T. has asked for more BOLDNESS, 2
twist last t. of the knife LIFE, 22
You cannot hope to bribe or t. . . . the British journalist
JOURNALISM, 28
two Great God grant that twice t. be not four. PRAYER, 17
if we knew one, we knew t. METAPHYSICS, 3
It takes t. ARGUMENTS, 1
It takes t. to speak the truth TRUTH, 39
It takes t. to tango COMPROMISE, 1
make t. questions grow where only one RESEARCH, 4
One step forward, t. steps back PROGRESS, 8
t. and t. do not make six LAST WORDS, 63
Tea for T., and T. for Tea DRINKS, 2
The formula 'T. and t. make five' PHILOSOPHY, 1
T. nations; between whom there is POVERTY AND WEALTH, 4
T. of a trade can ne'er agree ARGUMENTS, 5
T. turtle doves NURSERY RHYMES, 55
what can t. do against so many? AUDIENCES, 6
two-faced 'I grant you that he's not t.,' NASTINESS, 8
twopenny I don't care a t. damn INDIFFERENCE, 6
typewriter a non-stop talker to whom someone has given a t.
WRITERS, 4
tyrannize better that a man should t. over his bank balance
TYRANNY, 4
tyranny Ecclesiastic t.'s the worst CHURCH, 3
They that are discontented under *monarchy*, call it *t.*
GOVERNMENT, 12
Where laws end, t. begins TYRANNY, 5
tyrant professed t. to their sex MISOGYNY, 3
tyrants all men would be t. TYRANNY, 1
love, an . . . intercourse between t. and slaves LOVE AND
FRIENDSHIP, 2
the English seem . . . to act with the barbarity of t. IRELAND, 15
'Twixt kings and t. there's this difference TYRANNY, 2

U

U U and Non-U CLASS, 27
ugliest The u. of trades have their moments of pleasure
OCCUPATIONS, 7
uglification Ambition, Distraction, U., and Derision.
EDUCATION, 9
ugliness the u. of adults, in a child's eyes CHILDREN, 33
ugly an intimate knowledge of its u. side DISILLUSION, 1
better to be first with an u. woman than the hundredth with a
beauty BEAUTY, 11
I'm . . . u. enough to succeed on my own INDEPENDENCE, 1
There are no u. women, only lazy ones BEAUTY, 30
There is nothing u. BEAUTY, 15
Ulster U. will fight; U. will be right IRELAND, 2
umblest I am the 'u. person SERVILITY, 2
umbrella The unjust steals the just's u. JUSTICE, 4
unacceptable u. face of capitalism CAPITALISM, 4
unacted than nurse u. desires DESIRE, 2

unanimity Our agenda is now exhausted. . . . we find ourselves
in such complete u. AGREEMENT, 6
unartificial Surely you don't mean by u. insemination SEX, 49
unassuming u. common-place Of Nature FLOWERS, 13
unavailing All reform . . . will prove u. CHANGE, 2
unawares happened u. to look at her husband MARRIAGE, 11
unbaptized Fraser . . . left his children u. CHRISTIANITY, 46
unbearable in victory u. OFFICERS, 3
unbecoming nothing . . . so u. to a woman WOMEN, 80
u. the character of an officer OFFICERS, 1
un-birthday an u. present GIFTS, 3
unbowed My head is bloody, but u. ENDURANCE, 5
unbribed seeing what the man will do u. JOURNALISM, 28
uncertainty I have known u. UNCERTAINTY, 2
unchartered Me this u. freedom tires FREEDOM, 52
unchivalrous just a bit u. CHIVALRY, 2
unclouded the u. face of truth suffer wrong JOURNALISM, 22
unclubable A very u. man CHARACTER, 14
uncomely Nakedness is u. NAKEDNESS, 1
unconcern Is not a Patron, my Lord, one who looks with u. on
a man struggling for life PATRONAGE, 2
unconfined let joy be u. DANCING, 1
unconquerable the u. hope HOPE, 4
unconscionable most u. time dying DEATH, 36
unconventionally to succeed u. ORTHODOXY, 3
uncreative that ineluctable oblivion which awaits the u. mind
SCIENTISTS, 6
undecorated No part of the walls is left u. EXCESS, 5
undefeated Walter Mitty, the u. EXECUTION, 28
under U. the greenwood tree COUNTRYSIDE, 9
underdogs never find an Englishman among the u.
ENGLAND, 39
underestimated effect of boredom is . . . u. BOREDOM, 5
underground Johnny u. IDEALISM, 5
Just the other day in the U. OBESITY, 2
underprivileged Compassion is not a sloppy, sentimental feeling
for people who are u. SOCIALISM, 7
understand books. . . . criticized and read by people who don't
u. them BOOKS, 23
child of five would u. this SIMPLICITY, 5
if he could make *me* u. . . . it would be clear to all
UNDERSTANDING, 8
I u. only because I love LOVE, 132; UNDERSTANDING, 10
not to weep at them, nor to hate them, but to u. them
UNDERSTANDING, 9
people . . . may not be made to u. UNDERSTANDING, 3
When men u. what each other mean ARGUMENTS, 11
Wot do they u.? DISCONTENT, 3
You suddenly u. something . . . in a new way LEARNING, 6
understanding a candle of u. UNDERSTANDING, 1
a man of u. WISDOM, 2
God grant him peace . . . but never u. MONARCHY, 3
Most men . . . give evidence against their own u. SPEECH, 10
piece of cod passes all u. FOOD, 31
the peace of God, which passeth all u. BLESSING, 5
u. will . . . extinguish pleasure POETRY, 19; UNDERSTANDING, 5
We need more u. of human nature HUMAN NATURE, 11
understood Only one man ever u. me UNDERSTANDING, 4
undertakers I have nothing against u. personally
OCCUPATIONS, 10
undertaking The love of life is necessary to . . . any u.
ENTHUSIASM, 4
undiscovered whilst the great ocean of truth lay all u. before
me DISCOVERY, 6
undone estate o' th' world were now u. WORLD-WEARINESS, 6
left u. those things SIN, 9
Things hitherto u. should be given . . . a wide berth
ORIGINALITY, 1
uneasy U. lies the head that wears a crown MONARCHY, 21
uneatable the unspeakable in full pursuit of the u. HUNTING, 8
uneducated Democracy . . . government by the u.
ARISTOCRACY, 5; DEMOCRACY, 3
unendurable A society . . . of individuals . . . capable of original
thought would probably be u. IDEAS, 6
unequal Men are made by nature u. EQUALITY, 9
unexamined The u. life SELF, 14
unexpected Old age is the most u. of all . . . things OLD
AGE, 44
unfaithful better to be u. FAITHFULNESS, 1
original is u. to the translation TRANSLATION, 1
unfortunates one of those u. to whom death is
EXPLANATIONS, 1
ungain'd Men prize the thing u. more DESIRE, 13

V

vacuum A v. can only exist . . . by the things which enclose it
SCIENCE, 14
vagabond a fugitive and a v. PUNISHMENT, 2
vaguery For V. in the Field INCOMPETENCE, 3
vain The soul hath not her generous aspirings implanted in her
in v. SMOKING, 9
thou shalt not take the name of . . . God in v. GOD, 10
V. are the thousand creeds BELIEF, 3
V. wisdom all, and false philosophy WISDOM, 18
vale *ave atque v.* GREETINGS, 1
vales the cup of the v. WINTER, 7
valet No man is a hero to his v. FAMILIARITY, 2
valiant v. never taste of death but once COWARDICE, 9
valid If . . . 'feeling good' could decide, drunkenness would be
. . . supremely v. DRUNKENNESS, 13
valley One sees great things from the v. PERSPECTIVE, 2
valleys Piping down the v. wild MUSIC, 11
valour The better part of v. is discretion SELF-PRESERVATION, 8
valuable riches to be a v. thing WEALTH, 27
value All knowledge is of itself of some v. KNOWLEDGE, 22
Friendship . . . has no survival v. FRIENDSHIP, 22
the price of everything and the v. of nothing CYNICISM, 4
values ideas are of more importance than v. INTELLECTUALS, 4
Victorian v. . . . were the v. when our country MORALITY, 21
Van Gogh V.'s ear for music INSULTS, 40
vanished as rare things will, it v. TRANSIENCE, 9
vanity all is v. and vexation of spirit TRANSIENCE, 5
The v. of human life is like a river LIFE, 38
v. and love . . . universal characteristics WOMEN, 22
V. dies hard CONCEIT, 17
V. of vanities GREATNESS, 14; WISDOM, 22; TRANSIENCE, 4
V. plays lurid tricks CONCEIT, 6
vanquished redress of the grievances of the v. WAR, 25
variable light-headed, v. men MARRIAGE, 103
varies quality of moral behaviour v. MORALITY, 6
variety a sad v. of woe SORROW, 15
custom stale her infinite v. ADMIRATION, 14
V.'s the very spice of life CHANGE, 4
various man so v., that he seem'd to be HUMAN NATURE, 7
vary money appears to v. MONEY, 23
vast The universe ought to be presumed too v. UNIVERSE, 10
Vatican One of the best warehouses I ever see was the V.
EUROPE, 19
the V., the Treasury and the miners DIPLOMACY, 2
vaulting 'Fan v.' . . . belongs to the 'Last-supper-carved-on-a-
peach-stone' ARCHITECTURE, 5
veal I could eat one of Bellamy's v. pies FOOD, 38;
LAST WORDS, 45
vegetables you must talk to your v. GARDENS, 5
vegetarianism useless for the sheep to pass resolutions in
favour of v. ARGUMENTS, 8
vegetarians V. have wicked, shifty eyes PREJUDICE, 4
vegetate When I am in the country I wish to v.
COUNTRYSIDE, 5
veil Death is the v. DEATH, 106
the v. of the temple was rent in twain LAST WORDS, 8
v. which those who live call life DEATH, 106; LIFE, 43
veils v. of the morning PEACE, 18
Velasquez Why drag in V.? CONCEIT, 20
venerability If you live long enough, the v. factor creeps in
LONGEVITY, 3
vengeance No one delights more in v. than a woman
REVENGE, 11; WOMEN, 39
venial than that one soul . . . should commit one single v. sin
SIN, 17
Venice She only went to V. INSULTS, 22
V. is like eating . . . chocolate liqueurs VENICE, 2
V., the eldest Child of Liberty VENICE, 3
ventured Nothing v. OPPORTUNITY, 5
Venus She is V. when she smiles COMPLIMENTS, 2
verb a v. meaning 'to believe falsely' BELIEF, 8
verbose Revolutions are always v. REVOLUTION, 7
verbosity inebriated with . . . his own v. VERBOSITY, 1
Verdi strains of V. will come back to you tonight HUMOUR, 44
verdict Sentence first – v. afterwards INJUSTICE, 4
verification bring about the v. of his own prophecies
PROPHECY, 10
verify Always v. your references RESEARCH, 2
veritas *In vino v.* ALCOHOL, 1
vermin lower than v. POLITICS, 6
vernal One impulse from a v. wood LEARNING, 10
Versailles a lady at the court of V. LANGUAGE, 24
verse Curst be the v. POETRY, 34

Having v. set to music POETRY, 48
If Galileo had said in v. that the world moved POETRY, 18
no v. can give pleasure for long, nor last, that is written by
drinkers of water WATER, 5
Writing free v. POETRY, 16
verses v. . . . as a literary performance POETRY, 50
versified excellent poets that have never v. POETS, 23
versifiers now swarm many v. POETS, 23
vertical The v. man POSTERITY, 3
vessel the weaker v. MARRIAGE, 25
vestry I will see you in the v. after service CLERGY, 10
vex they die to v. me CLERGY, 9
with no deep researches v. the brain CLARITY, 1
vexation all is vanity and v. of spirit TRANSIENCE, 5
viable I'm v. from ten o'clock till five BUSINESS, 3
vice extremism in the defence of liberty is no v. EXCESS, 4
Hypocrisy is the most . . . nerve-racking v. HYPOCRISY, 11
Is Pride, the never-failing v. of fools PRIDE, 7
no v. but beggary HYPOCRISY, 14
Prosperity doth best discover v. MISFORTUNE, 3
Public schools are the nurseries of all v. EDUCATION, 16
quotation is a national v. QUOTATIONS, 7
The only sensual pleasure without v. MUSIC, 23
there is no distinction between virtue and v. MISTRUST, 6
This v. brings in one hundred million francs . . . every year
SMOKING, 12
three great evils, boredom, v., and poverty WORK, 23
V. and virtues are products VIRTUE AND VICE, 6
V. is its own reward VICE, 6
V. is often clothed APPEARANCES, 6
V. itself lost half its evil VICE, 5
When v. prevails VICE, 1
vices It's your combination sinners . . . who dishonour the v.
VICE, 10
one of the v. of our age ARMY, 4
small v. do appear APPEARANCES, 20
virtues and v. couple with one another VIRTUE AND VICE, 1
virtues are . . . v. in disguise VIRTUE AND VICE, 2
We make ourselves a ladder out of our v. VICE, 2
Vichy There's something V. about the French FRANCE, 12
vicious can't expect a boy to be v. EDUCATION, 44
He was a v. man, but very kind CHARACTER, 13
victim more easily fall v. to a big lie LYING, 8
v. must be found I've got a little list PUNISHMENT, 8
victims Every reformation must have its v. SUFFERING, 10
Man is the only animal . . . on friendly terms with the v. . . . he
eats HYPOCRISY, 6
The little v. play IGNORANCE, 7
There are born v. MURDER, 8
v. who respect their executioners RESPECT, 3
victor happy state of getting the v.'s palm without the dust of
racing VICTORY, 6
Victoria If this is the way Queen V. treats her prisoners
IMPRISONMENT, 11
take a ticket at V. Station FREEDOM, 2
Victorian the most antagonistic to the V. age WRITERS, 48
V. values . . . were the values when our country MORALITY, 21
Victorians The V. had not been anxious to go away
TRAVEL, 28
victories Peace hath her v. WAR AND PEACE, 10
victorious Send him v. BRITAIN, 5
victory Before Alamein we never had a v. WORLD WAR II, 15
death is swallowed up in v. DEATH, 26
every v. turns into a defeat DISILLUSION, 4
in v. unbearable OFFICERS, 3
In . . . war it is not right that matters, but v. WAR, 46
O grave! where is thy v.? DEATH, 87
Such another v. and we are ruined VICTORY, 13
to gain such a v. as this VICTORY, 1
'twas a famous v. VICTORY, 16
V. at all costs VICTORY, 2
V. has a thousand fathers SUCCESS, 9
v. under the belly of a Cossack's horse RUSSIAN REVOLUTION, 2
without v. there is no survival VICTORY, 2
vidders be very careful o' v. CAUTION, 11
vieillesse *si v. pouvait* AGE, 22
Vietnam To win in V. WAR, 111
V. was lost in the living rooms of America TELEVISION, 4;
WAR, 64
vigilance eternal v. FREEDOM, 9
vile every prospect pleases, And only man is v.
MISANTHROPY, 1
orgies are v. DEBAUCHERY, 8

W

With our backs to the w. . . . each . . . must fight on to the end
WAR, 43
wallet a crowd like that . . . brings a lump to my w.
MATERIALISM, 22
Time hath . . . a w. at his back TIME, 31
wallop the cod's w. is always fresh made COMMUNISM, 5
walls by faith the w. of Jericho fell down FAITH, 2
No part of the w. is left undecorated EXCESS, 5
Stone w. do not a prison make IMPRISONMENT, 4
W. have ears GOSSIP, 6
walrus The W. and the Carpenter SEASIDE, 1
waltzing You'll come a-w., Matilda PLACES, 14
wandered I w. lonely as a cloud FLOWERS, 14
wanderer A w. is man from his birth HUMAN CONDITION, 1
wandering Poor w. one RETURN, 1
W. in a vast forest at night GUIDANCE, 2
w. minstrel I SINGERS, 2
want Economy is going without something you do w. THRIFT, 7
evil is wrought by w. of thought EVIL, 10
for w. of a nail NEGLECT, 1; PRUDENCE, 3
freedom from w. HUMAN RIGHTS, 4
give the public what they w. to see and they'll come out for it
FUNERALS, 8
If you w. a thing well done SELF-RELIANCE, 1
The w. of a thing is perplexing enough MATERIALISM, 19
What does a woman w. WOMEN, 32
wanted bought things because she w. 'em WOMEN, 75
Every man is w. HUMAN CONDITION, 7
I have w. only one thing to make me happy DISCONTENT, 3
wants Man w. but little MORTALITY, 24
war Against the beautiful . . . one can wage a pitiless w.
BEAUTY, 18
All diplomacy is a continuation of w. DIPLOMACY, 14
all's fair in love and w. JUSTICE, 8
An empire founded by w. WAR, 69
As long as w. is regarded as wicked WAR, 129
Before the w. . . . it was summer all the year round
NOSTALGIA, 16
Being over seventy is like being engaged in a w. OLD AGE, 41
could lose the w. in an afternoon OFFICERS, 4
defeat without a w. WORLD WAR II, 3
done very well out of the w. HOUSES OF PARLIAMENT, 4
except the British W. Office WAR, 108
him who desires peace, prepare for w. WAR AND PEACE, 12
I could have lost the w. in an afternoon WAR, 51
I'd like to see the government get out of w. altogether
WAR, 45
I don't care for w. WAR, 74
If we lose this w. WAR, 31
I make w. on the living REVENGE, 8
In a civil w., a general must know WAR, 88
In starting and waging a w. it is not right that matters, but
victory WAR, 46
In w. . . . there are no winners WAR, 23
It is well that w. is so terrible WAR, 60
lead this people into w. and they'll forget . . . tolerance
WAR, 134
Lenin was the first to discover that capitalism 'inevitably' caused
w. CAPITALISM, 14
let slip the dogs of w. WAR, 106
life is more interesting in w. than in peace WAR AND PEACE, 9
makes a good w. makes a good peace WAR AND PEACE, 8
My subject is W., and the pity of W. POETRY, 33
never was a good w. WAR AND PEACE, 6
No one can guarantee success in w. WAR, 27
Now w. has a bad conscience WAR, 53
Older men declare w. WAR, 48
on this wall will hang my weapons and my lyre, discharged from
the w. SEX, 20
Stand your ground . . . if they mean to have a w., let it begin
here WAR, 83
Television brought the brutality of w. TELEVISION, 4; WAR, 64
that devil's madness – W. WAR, 105
the . . . barbarity of w. . . . forces men . . . to commit acts
WAR, 54
The first casualty when w. comes WAR, 52
The quickest way of ending a w. WAR, 79
there was w. in heaven DEVIL, 4
the second rule of w. WAR, 70
The W. between Men and Women SEXES, 22
the W. is being deliberately prolonged WAR, 102
the w. of the giants is over WORLD WAR II, 16
The wrong w., at the wrong place WAR, 11

The w. we have just been through, . . . is not to be compared
WAR, 133
they'll give a w. and nobody will come WAR, 96
this liking for w. WAR, 6
this massed multitude of silent witnesses to . . . w. WAR, 40
This w. . . . is a w. to end w. WAR, 61
this w., . . . which did not justify the sacrifice of a single
mother's son WAR, 82
Those who can win a w. well WAR AND PEACE, 4
w. can only be abolished through w. WAR, 63
we are . . . in the midst of a cold w. COLD WAR, 1
We are not at w. with Egypt WAR, 34
We have all lost the w. WAR, 59
W. even to the knife WAR, 20
W. hath no fury like a non-combatant WAR, 68
What they could do with round here is a good w. WAR, 12
when there was w., he went PUBLIC, 3
When the rich wage w. POVERTY AND WEALTH, 7
when they learn how we began this w. WORLD WAR II, 25
When you're at w. you think about a better life WAR AND
PEACE, 13
Who live under the shadow of a w. WAR, 110
W. is, after all, the universal perversion WAR, 87
W. is an organized bore WAR, 47
W. is capitalism WAR, 114
W. is hell WAR, 109
W. is like love WAR, 14
W. is not an adventure WAR, 95
W. is Peace DOUBLETHINK, 1
W. is the continuation of politics WAR, 28; WAR, 62
W. is too important OFFICERS, 5
W. is w. WAR, 77
W. knows no power WAR, 17
W. makes rattling good history WAR AND PEACE, 7
w. minus the shooting SPORT AND GAMES, 15
W. should belong to the tragic past WAR, 84
w. which . . . left nothing to be desired WAR, 13
W. will never cease until babies WAR, 65
wards key deftly in the oiled w. SLEEP, 11
Ware And I should dine at W. MARRIAGE, 39
warehouses One of the best w. I ever see was the Vatican
EUROPE, 19
Waring What's become of W. ABSENCE, 5
warmongers w. who . . . have others pull the chestnuts out of
the fire POLITICS, 62
warmth No w., no cheerfulness, no healthful ease MONTHS, 10
warn the right to be consulted, . . . to encourage, . . . to w.
MONARCHY, 2
warned my Friends, be w. by me FOOD, 7
warning will it come without w. Just as I'm picking my nose
LOVE, 18
warrior the British w. queen BRITAIN, 6
wars All w. are planned by old men WAR, 91
All w. are popular for the first thirty days WAR, 103
end to the beginnings of all w. WAR, 93
Just like an old liberal Between the w. LIBERALISM, 3
military don't start w. WAR, 128
my w. Were global WAR, 89
No kingdom has . . . had as many . . . w. as the kingdom of
Christ CHRISTIANITY, 34
Still w. and lechery SEX, 43
W. are not won by evacuations WORLD WAR II, 14
W., conflict, it's all business WAR, 24
w., horrible w. PROPHECY, 11
warts pimples, w., and everything as you see me REALISM, 1
war-war To jaw-jaw is better than to w. DIPLOMACY, 5
wary Let me remind you what the w. fox said . . . to the sick
lion MISTRUST, 5
wash Don't w. your dirty linen GOSSIP, 2
I do, and I also w. and iron them HOUSEWORK, 5
washed Pilate . . . w. his hands GUILT, 5
washing painting a face and not w. APPEARANCE, 15
wasps w. and hornets break through LAW, 27
waste biggest w. of water in the country CONSERVATION, 5
Far too good to w. on children YOUTH, 16
The years to come seemed w. of breath FLYING, 4
W. not, want not WASTE, 1
wasted most w. of all days LAUGHTER, 6
wasting she did not believe in w. her effects THREATS, 1
watch Either he's dead or my w. has stopped DEATH, 78
keeping w. over their flock by night CHRISTMAS, 8
The W. on the Rhine RIVERS, 3
w. and pray IMPERFECTION, 4

the world's work, . . . is done by men who do not feel . . . w. ILLNESS, 4
We never do anything w. ACHIEVEMENT, 3
worth doing w. EXCELLENCE, 1
well-bred a w. sort of emotional anarchy CLASSIFICATION, 2
well-dressed The sense of being w. CLOTHES, 5
well-knownness The celebrity . . . known for his w. FAME, 4
well-rounded whole man in himself, polished and w. CHARACTER, 10
well-spent as rare as a w. one BIOGRAPHY, 2
well-written A w. Life BIOGRAPHY, 2
Welsh but he wouldn't put up with the W. WELSH, 1
The W. . . . just sing WELSH, 4
wembley W., adj. Suffering from a vague *malaise* HUMOUR, 36
wen the fate of the great w. LONDON, 5
Wenceslas Good King W. looked out CHRISTMAS, 14
wench beside the w. is dead SEX, 27
Wenlock Edge On W. the wood's in trouble . . . the Wrekin heaves TREES, 4
went as cooks go she w. HUMOUR, 51
wept They w. like anything to see SEASIDE, 1
young man who has not w. AGE, 48; WISDOM, 19
west closing time in the gardens of the W. CAPITALISM, 1
East is East, and W. is W. OPPOSITES, 3
Go W., young man EXPLORATION, 2
the safeguard of the w. VENICE, 4
western W. philosophy is, . . . a series of footnotes to Plato's philosophy PHILOSOPHY, 15
wet joly whistle wel y-w. ALCOHOL, 19
out of these w. clothes and into a dry Martini ALCOHOL, 64
whale A w. ship was my Yale College EDUCATION, 34
Very like a w. AGREEMENT, 5
what Aye, and w. then PROOF, 3
W. is truth TRUTH, 10
wheat An editor . . . separates the w. from the chaff EDITORS, 3
wheel bound upon a w. of fire SUFFERING, 11
wheels A cruel story runs on w. CRUELTY, 4
spoke among your w. OBSTRUCTION, 1
when have they fixed the where and w. EXECUTION, 10
w. a man should marry MARRIAGE, 13
where have they fixed the w. and when EXECUTION, 10
to die, and go we know not w. DEATH, 99
W. are you now LOVE, 67
W. were you fellows when the paper was blank EDITORS, 1
where'er W. you tread ADMIRATION, 11
wherefore There is occasions and causes why and w. EXPLANATIONS, 2
w. art thou Romeo NAMES, 5
whey Eating her curds and w. NURSERY RHYMES, 30
Whig Sir, I perceive you are a vile W. POLITICS, 33
Whigs caught the W. bathing POLITICS, 19
whim The strangest w. SUICIDE, 1
whimper not with a bang but a w. ENDING, 3
whipping W. and abuse are like laudanum CRUELTY, 5
who shall scape w. MERIT, 5
whirlwind sown the wind . . . reap the w. RETRIBUTION, 5
whisker can't speak above a w. PUNS, 12
whisky nicest boy who ever committed the sin of w. ALCOHOL, 56
That w. priest CLERGY, 6
with education and w. the price it is CHARACTER, 24
whispered it's w. every where SECRECY, 8
whispering w. sound of the cool colonnade TREES, 3
whisperings It keeps eternal w. around SEA, 8
whistle I heard the bullets w., . . . charming in the sound WAR, 121
So was hir joly w. wel y-wet ALCOHOL, 19
W. a Happy Tune WHISTLING, 2
W. and she'll come to you SUMMONS, 2
whistles They hang us now in Shrewsbury jail: The w. blow forlorn EXECUTION, 11
whistling W. aloud to bear his courage up WHISTLING, 1
white architecture . . . only passers-by who can contemplate it . . . are those . . . with a w. stick and a dog ARCHITECTURE, 6
Britain . . . is going to be forged in the w. heat of this revolution SOCIALISM, 14
'E was w., clear w., inside APPEARANCES, 16
If the w. man *says* he does, he is instantly . . . mistrusted RACISM, 2
it's not even red brick, but w. tile CLASS, 25
I used to be Snow W. PURITY, 6
I want to be the w. man's brother RACE, 9

my soul is w. RACE, 4
One black, and one w., and two khaki RACE, 1
so-called w. races RACE, 7
Take up the W. Man's burden – RACE, 10
the . . . w. bosoms of your actresses excite my amorous propensities LUST, 3
The w. man knows how to make everything, but he does not know how to distribute it CHARITY, 18
When a w. man in Africa RACE, 13
When the w. man came we had the land RACE, 8
White House gathered together at the W. TALENT, 4
Log-cabin to W. ACHIEVEMENT, 6
no whitewash at the W. TRUTH, 33
standing between Nixon and the W. POLITICIANS, 37
whites the w. of their eyes WAR, 86
whitewash no w. at the White House TRUTH, 33
whither w. thou goest, I will go LOYALTY, 5
Whitman Walt W. who laid end to end POETS, 21
who If you have to tell them w. you are, you aren't anybody FAME, 17
W. is Silvia? ADMIRATION, 16
whole a w. is that which has a beginning, a middle, and an end PLAYS, 1
if she knew the w. of it LOVE, 135
the greatest happiness of the w. REPUBLIC, 1
whom for w. the bell tolls DEATH, 43
'W. are you?' said he GRAMMAR, 1
whore a w. in the kitchen and a cook in bed MARRIAGE, 64
I am the Protestant w. RELIGION, 28
the morals of a w., and the manners of a dancing master CRITICISM, 20
the old man does not care for the young man's w. TASTE, 2
The woman's a w. PROMISCUITY, 3
You can lead a w. to culture PUNS, 16
whorehouses virgin territory for w. AMERICA, 6
whores After all, we are not political w. POLITICS, 49
With first-rate sherry flowing into second-rate w. MEDIOCRITY, 6
whoreson w. zed INSULTS, 31
whoso W. would be a man CONFORMITY, 4
why For every w. ARGUMENTS, 3
occasions and causes w. and wherefore EXPLANATIONS, 2
they knew not w. WAR, 19
W. should I go FUNERALS, 7
wicked As long as war is regarded PUNISHMENT, 5
no peace . . . unto the w. PEACE, 2; PUNISHMENT, 5
the men of Sodom were w. HOMOSEXUALITY, 1
There is a w. inclination . . . to suppose an old man decayed in his intellects OLD AGE, 23
to see men w. REGRET, 20
wickedness men alone are quite capable of every w. EVIL, 7
The w. of the world VICE, 4
wide Things hitherto undone should be given . . . a w. berth ORIGINALITY, 1
Widnes men become attached even to W. ENGLAND, 37
widow a w. . . . is a kind of sinecure EXPEDIENCY, 6
better to be the w. of a hero than the wife of a coward COURAGE, 13
Tonight the American flag floats . . . or Molly Stark sleeps a w. WAR, 112
you, my dear, will be my w. JEALOUSY, 2
widows When w. exclaim loudly against second marriages MARRIAGE, 55
wife A loving w. will do anything MARRIAGE, 86
A man should not insult his w. publicly MARRIAGE, 115
A man who's untrue to his w. INTELLECTUALS, 2
A professional is someone whose w. works to enable him to paint ARTISTS, 8
better to be the widow of a hero than the w. of a coward COURAGE, 13
Caesar's w. must be above suspicion INTEGRITY, 2
chose my w. . . . for . . . qualities as would wear well MARRIAGE, 63
Commuter – one who spends his life In riding to and from his w. TRAVEL, 27
Here lies my w. MARRIAGE, 49
He that has no w. ADVICE, 4
he that is married careth . . . how he may please his w. MARRIAGE, 23
He that loves not his w. and children MARRIAGE, 108
His w. could eat no lean NURSERY RHYMES, 25
his w. is beautiful and his children smart TOLERANCE, 4
If a man stays away from his w. MARRIAGE, 42

I have a w., I have sons — FAMILY, 25
I have quarrelled with my w. — MARRIAGE, 84
light w. doth make a heavy husband — MARRIAGE, 94
man . . . shall cleave unto his w. — WOMEN, 15
Mother to dozens, And nobody's w. — BABIES, 3
My w. hath something in her gizzard — PROVOCATION, 1
My w. . . . is troubled with her lonely life — WOMEN, 55
My w. won't let me — MARRIAGE, 72
No man worth having is true to his w. — UNFAITHFULNESS, 5
one w. and hardly any mistresses — MARRIAGE, 91
remorse for what you have thought about your w.
— MARRIAGE, 89
single man . . . must be in want of a w. — MARRIAGE, 9
taking out his false teeth and hurling them at his w.
— MARRIAGE, 48
that a man lay down his w. for a friend — FRIENDSHIP, 21
that monstrous animal a husband and w. — MARRIAGE, 54
The first w. is matrimony — MARRIAGE, 4
The husband frae the w. despises — MARRIAGE, 29
the w. . . . the weaker vessel — MARRIAGE, 25
Whose w. shall it be? — ADULTERY, 6
with a w. to tell him what to do — LAZINESS, 2
Would you allow your w. . . . to read this book — PRUDERY, 1
your w. . . . is a receiver of stolen goods — INSULTS, 19
wifehood w. and motherhood are but incidental relations
— WOMEN, 66
wig man with a w. to keep order — APPEARANCE, 36
wild an old, w., and incomprehensible man — POLITICIANS, 75
mother bore me in the southern w. — RACE, 4
wilderness a little w. — GARDENS, 10
a lodge in some vast w. — SOLITUDE, 3
plants left over from the Edwardian W. — CHANGE, 16
the w. of this world — WORLD, 2
W. is Paradise enow — CONTENTMENT, 3
wild-fowl more fearful w. than your lion — FEAR, 12
will complies against his w. — YIELDING, 2
Do what you w. — FREEDOM, 43
formation of the political w. of the nation — POLITICS, 31
His right was clear, his w. was strong — RIGHT, 1
John Stuart Mill By a mighty effort of w. — ECONOMICS, 2
let my w. replace reasoned judgement — AUTHORITARIANISM, 4
Man has his w. — SEXES, 10
The man who leaves money to charity in his w. — BEQUESTS, 3
We have to believe in free w.. We've got no choice — CHOICE, 4
Where there's a w. — DETERMINATION, 2
W. ye no come back again — RETURN, 3
You w., Oscar, you w. — IMITATION, 7
William You are right, Father W. — OLD AGE, 9; OLD AGE, 40
Williams Shirley W. . . . a member of the upper-middle class
— CLASS, 37
Willie Wee W. Winkie runs through the town — NURSERY
RHYMES, 64
willow a little tom-tit Sang W., titwillow, titwillow — BIRDS, 4
willows W. whiten, aspens quiver — WEATHER, 26
will-power There is no such thing as a great talent without
great w. — DETERMINATION, 3
will-to-live The thing-in-itself, the w., exists . . . in every being
— SURVIVAL, 3
Wilson Mr W. . . . is the 14th Mr W. — TITLES, 1
win Heads I w. — VICTORY, 5
high sentiments always w. in the end — NOBILITY, 3
I am certain that we will w. the election with a good majority
— SELF-CONFIDENCE, 6
The conventional army loses if it does not w. — WAR, 56
Those who can w. a war well — WAR AND PEACE, 4
wind Blow, blow, thou winter w. — INGRATITUDE, 4
gone with the w. — MEMORY, 6
It's an ill w. — OPTIMISM, 3
I will not permit thirty men . . . to agitate a bag of w.
— FOOTBALL, 7
like W. I go — LIFE AND DEATH, 5
of w. and limb — FAITHFULNESS, 2
O Wild West W. — WEATHER, 24
so famous, that it would permit me . . . to break w. in society
— FAME, 3
The answer . . . is blowin' in the w. — FREEDOM, 10
The story is like the w. — SENSATION, 2
throw the sand against the w. — FUTILITY, 4
what w. is to fire — ABSENCE, 6
wherever the w. takes me I travel as a visitor — FREEDOM, 19
Who has seen the w. — WEATHER, 17
words but w. — WORDS, 4
windmills not giants but w. — DELUSION, 2

window Serve up . . . and throw . . . out of the w.
— NONSENSE, 21
wine A Flask of W. — CONTENTMENT, 3
A man may surely be allowed to take a glass of w. by his own
fireside — FIRE, 4
And drink of my Algerian w. — INSULTS, 6
days of w. and roses — TRANSIENCE, 11
drinks his w. 'mid laughter free — PARTING, 2
for its poisonous w. — OBLIVION, 2
Frenchmen drink w. just like — ALCOHOL, 38
full of new w. — DRUNKENNESS, 8
Give me books, fruit, French w. and fine weather — PLEASURE, 17
good w. needs no bush — PLAYS, 10
look not thou upon the w. when it is red — ALCOHOL, 16
no man . . . having drunk old w. straightway desireth new
— AGE, 10; ALCOHOL, 15
the guests must be chosen as carefully as the w. — ALCOHOL, 50
the water that was made w. — ALCOHOL, 14
the w. was a farce and the food a tragedy — FOOD, 41
This w. upon a foreign tree — AGRICULTURE, 5
Truth comes out in w. — ALCOHOL, 45
use a little w. for thy stomach's sake — ALCOHOL, 13
W. comes in at the mouth — AGE, 70
When the w. is in — ALCOHOL, 7; DRUNKENNESS, 7
Who loves not w., woman and song — PLEASURE, 20
w. is a mocker — DRUNKENNESS, 9
wingèd Doth the w. life destroy — PLEASURE, 5
Time's w. chariot — AGE, 35
wings Fear lent w. to his feet — FEAR, 13
the w. of a dove — SOLITUDE, 4
whether pigs have w. — NONSENSE, 9
wink I will w. and hold out mine iron — COWARDICE, 8
never came a w. too soon — NOSTALGIA, 9
winners In war . . . there are no w. — WAR, 23
winning not w. but taking part — VICTORY, 4
W. isn't everything, but wanting to win is — VICTORY, 4
Winston It hasn't taken W. long to get used to American ways
— CHURCHILL, 1
The first time you meet W. — CHURCHILL, 6
W. with his hundred-horse-power mind — CHURCHILL, 2
winter got through the perils of w. till at least the seventh of
May — WINTER, 8
It is a w.'s tale — WINTER, 7
Many . . . say that they enjoy the w. — WINTER, 1
No one thinks of w. — SEASONS, 2
the furious w.'s rages — MORTALITY, 16
The stars grew bright in the w. sky — ANIMALS, 13
W. is icumen in — WINTER, 4
w. of our discontent — OPTIMISM, 23
wintry sailed the w. sea — BOATS, 11
wisdom follies as the special evidences of our w. — PRIDE, 10
in much w. is much grief — KNOWLEDGE, 6; WISDOM, 2
Knowledge can be communicated but not w. — WISDOM, 16
Love is the w. of the fool — LOVE, 71
privilege of w. to listen — KNOWLEDGE, 18; WISDOM, 17
proverb is one man's wit and all men's w. — SAYINGS, 6
proverbs provide them with w. — STUPIDITY, 7
Silence is . . . full of potential w. — SILENCE, 8
The highest w. has but one science — MANKIND, 32
The only infallible criterion of w. — SUCCESS, 5
the palace of W. — EXCESS, 3
the price of w. is above rubies — WISDOM, 6
therefore get w. — WISDOM, 8
Vain w. all, and false philosophy — WISDOM, 18
want of human w. — WAR, 58
W. be put in a silver rod — WISDOM, 10
w. . . . cometh by opportunity of leisure — LEISURE, 1; WISDOM, 4
w. excelleth folly, as . . . light excelleth darkness — WISDOM AND
FOOLISHNESS, 1
W. has taught us to be calm and meek — REVENGE, 10
W. in minds attentive — KNOWLEDGE, 11; WISDOM, 14
with how little w. the world is governed — GOVERNMENT, 20
with the ancient is w. — OLD AGE, 5; WISDOM, 5
w. of the crocodiles — HYPOCRISY, 2
w. . . . sweetly doth . . . order all things — WISDOM, 9
wise A w. man will make more opportunities — OPPORTUNITY, 9
Coffee which makes the politician w. — DRINKS, 6
How very weak the very w. — GREATNESS, 14; WISDOM, 22
Many have been the w. speeches of fools — WISDOM AND
FOOLISHNESS, 5
more of the fool than of the w. — HUMAN NATURE, 3
No man . . . so w. as Thurlow looked — APPEARANCES, 14
sorrow makes us w. — SORROW, 24

The only wretched are the w.	IGNORANCE, 12
the w. forgive	FORGIVENESS, 15
To be w. and love	LOVE, 119
where ignorance is bliss, 'Tis folly to be w.	IGNORANCE, 6
wisely deserves the name of happy who knows how to use the gods' gifts w.	HAPPINESS, 9
lov'd not w., but too well	LOVE, 122
wiser Be w. than other people	WISDOM, 12
foreigner should . . . be w. than ourselves	PRIDE, 10
sadder and a w. man	WISDOM, 13
The French are w. than they seem	APPEARANCES, 9
the old have rubbed it into the young that they are w.	OLD AGE, 27
w. to-day than . . . yesterday	MISTAKES, 10
wisest The most attractive sentences are not perhaps the w.	LANGUAGE, 23
wish Conscience is . . . rejection of a . . . w.	CONSCIENCE, 2
Justice is the . . . perpetual w.	JUSTICE, 14
most . . . w. they were the only one alive	EGOTISM, 2
Someday I'll w. upon a star	DESIRE, 6
The w. to hurt	CRUELTY, 1
The w. to spread those opinions that we hold	ENGLISH, 7
wished consummation devoutly to be w.	SUICIDE, 10
wishful There is w. thinking in Hell as well as on earth	DESIRE, 10
wit An ounce of a man's own w.	WISDOM, 21
Attic w.	HUMOUR, 20
a w. out of two half-wits	FOOLISHNESS, 16
Brevity is the soul of w.	BREVITY, 7
cause that w. is in other men	HUMOUR, 25
fancy w. will come	STUPIDITY, 11
His foe was folly and his weapon w.	HUMOUR, 14
I have neither w., nor words, nor worth	SPEECHES, 4
Impropriety is the soul of w.	HUMOUR, 18
love robs those who have it of their w.	LOVE, 44
Music-hall songs provide the dull with w.	STUPIDITY, 7
proverb is one man's w. and all men's wisdom	SAYINGS, 6
To the Greeks the Muse gave native w.	CLASSICS, 4
True w. is nature to advantage dress'd	HUMOUR, 21
wine is in, the w. is out	DRUNKENNESS, 7
W. that can creep	SERVILITY, 5
witch thou shalt not suffer a w. to live	SUPERNATURAL, 3
witches I have ever believed, . . . that there are w.	SUPERNATURAL, 4
wither Age cannot w. her	ADMIRATION, 14
wither'd w. is the garland of the war	MOURNING, 11
withered lonely of heart is w. away	LONELINESS, 10
within that w. which passes show	MOURNING, 12
when the fight begins w. himself	CONFLICT, 5
without I can do w.	LUXURY, 4
witness thou shalt not bear false w.	GOD, 10
witnesses this massed multitude of silent w. to . . . war	WAR, 40
wits Great W. . . . to Madness near alli'd	GENIUS, 3
homely w.	HOME, 8
their poetry is conceived and composed in their w.	POETRY, 4
This man I thought had been a Lord among w.	CRITICISM, 19
witty a very w. prologue	MARRIAGE, 36
I am not only w. in myself	HUMOUR, 25
stumbling on something w.	MEN, 1
wives Bricklayers kick their w. to death	CLASS, 36
husbands and w. . . . belong to different sexes	SEXES, 1
husbands and w. make shipwreck of their lives	MARRIAGE, 47
husbands, love your w.	MARRIAGE, 20
I met a man with seven w.	NURSERY RHYMES, 3
O! men with mothers and w.	WOMEN, 37
The others were only my w.	JEALOUSY, 2
Translations (like w.) are seldom faithful	TRANSLATION, 2
W. are young men's mistresses	MARRIAGE, 12
you do not make the laws but . . . are the w. . . . of those who do	WOMEN, 35
wiving Hanging and w. goes by destiny	DESTINY, 19
Wodehouse like P. G. W. dropping Jeeves	WRITERS, 45
woe a sad variety of w.	SORROW, 15
Much in sorrow, oft in w.	ENDURANCE, 24
suits of w.	MOURNING, 12
Wednesday's child is full of w.	NURSERY RHYMES, 14
w. to him that is alone when he falleth	FRIENDSHIP, 8
W. to the vanquished	DEFEAT, 4
w. unto them that call evil good	LYING, 4
w. unto them that . . . follow strong drink	ALCOHOL, 12
wolf The boy cried 'W., w.!'	LYING, 2
the w. in the sheep's clothing	APPEARANCES, 8

wolf's-bane neither twist W.	OBLIVION, 2
wolves people being thrown to the w.	POLITICIANS, 42
woman A diplomat . . . always remembers a w.'s birthday	AGE, 26
A man is only as old as the w.	AGE, 36
And a w. is only a w.	WOMEN, 41
Any w. who understands the problems of running a home	POLITICS, 70
a w. is on a . . . hunt for trouble	MARRIAGE, 47
a w. . . . . ought to lay aside . . . modesty with her skirt	SEX, 31
A w.'s place is in the home	WOMEN, 2
a w.'s reason	WOMEN, 64
A w.'s work	WOMEN, 3
A w. will always sacrifice herself	WOMEN, 47
a w. yet think him an angel	LOVE, 131
body of a weak and feeble w.	ROYALTY, 13
Christ-like heroes and w.-worshipping Don Juans	MEN, 6
close-up of a w. past sixty	APPEARANCE, 4
educate a w. you educate a family	EDUCATION, 32
every w. is at heart a rake	WOMEN, 58
Every w. is infallibly to be gained	FLATTERY, 5
Every w. should marry	MARRIAGE, 45
Frailty, thy name is w.	WEAKNESS, 4; WOMEN, 63
God made the w. for the man	WOMEN, 28
good w. if I had five thousand	MONEY, 44
hell a fury like a w. scorned	LOVE AND HATE, 3
I am a . . . w. – nothing more	WOMEN, 72
I am a w.? When I think, I must speak	WOMEN, 62
if a w. have long hair	APPEARANCE, 5
If a w. like Eva Peron with no ideals	IDEALISM, 7; POLITICIANS, 72
I had become a w. of . . . character	CHARACTER, 5
International W.'s Day	RUSSIAN REVOLUTION, 1
It is a great glory in a w.	WOMEN, 70
It's a sort of bloom on a w.	CHARM, 1
I would . . . guess that Anon . . . was often a w.	WOMEN, 81
Man for the field and w. for the hearth	SEXES, 20
Man to command and w. to obey	SEXES, 20
Man with the head and w. with the heart	SEXES, 20
No one delights more in vengeance than a w.	REVENGE, 11; WOMEN, 39
nor w. neither	MANKIND, 26
No w. should ever be quite accurate about her age	AGE, 63
No w. so naked as . . . underneath her clothes	NAKEDNESS, 4
Old age is w.'s hell	OLD AGE, 11
Once a w. has given you her heart	WOMEN, 76
one can . . . see in a little girl the threat of a w.	CHILDREN, 20
One is not born a w.	WOMEN, 13
one of w. born	BIRTH, 7
One tongue is sufficient for a w.	EDUCATION, 35; WOMEN, 50
She makes love just like a w.	WOMEN, 76
She was a w. of mean understanding	INSULTS, 3
such beauty as a w.'s eye	LEARNING, 8
Than to ever let a w. in my life	MISOGYNY, 1
the help and support of the w. I love	LOVE, 141
the most beautiful w. I've ever seen	BEAUTY, 26
The really original w. . . . . imitates a man	WOMEN, 67
There was an old w. Lived under a hill	NURSERY RHYMES, 53
There was an old w. who lived in a shoe	NURSERY RHYMES, 54
the rib . . . made he a w.	WOMEN, 15
the sort of w. now, said Mould, . . . one would almost feel disposed to bury for nothing	WOMEN, 26
the sort of w. who lives for others	CHARITY, 14
The w.'s a whore	PROMISCUITY, 3
The w. that deliberates is lost	WOMEN, 6
the w. who is really kind to dogs	WOMEN, 14
To know the *mind* of a w.	LOVE, 78
Twenty years of romance makes a w. look like a ruin	MARRIAGE, 119
w. alone, can . . . commit them	SEXES, 21
w. as old as she looks	AGE, 16
w. governs America	AMERICA, 24
w. 'has her way	SEXES, 10
What does a w. want	WOMEN, 32
When a w. behaves like a man	WOMEN, 31
When lovely w. stoops to folly	GULLIBILITY, 2
who can find a virtuous w.	WOMEN, 17
Who loves not wine, w. and song	PLEASURE, 20
Why can't a w. be more like a man	MEN, 7
will not stand . . . being called a w. in my own house	WOMEN, 79
W. is always fickle and changing	WOMEN, 77
w. is an animal that	WOMEN, 46

w. is his game	SEXES, 19
w. . . . knowing anything	WOMEN, 10
w. of education	WOMEN, 75
wrecks a w.'s reputation	JEWELLERY, 1
W.'s at best a contradiction	WOMEN, 59
w. seldom asks advice	WOMEN, 7
W.'s virtue is man's greatest invention	SEXES, 17
w.'s weapon is her tongue	WOMEN, 34
w.'s whole existence	SEXES, 4
W. was God's *second* mistake	WOMEN, 52
W. will be the last thing civilized by Man	WOMEN, 49
womanhood W. is the great fact in her life	WOMEN, 66
womb mother's w. Untimely ripp'd	BIRTH, 7
no new baby in the w. of our society	RUSSIA, 3
teeming w. of royal kings	ENGLAND, 34
women A homely face . . . aided many w. heavenward	
	APPEARANCE, 3
all w. do	MARRIAGE, 8
An experience of w.	EXPERIENCE, 12
a snare in which the feet of w. have always become readily	
entangled	WOMEN, 5
Because w. can do nothing except love	LOVE, 86; WOMEN, 48
Few w. care to be laughed at	RIDICULE, 2
great city . . . has the greatest men and w.	GREATNESS, 15
If men knew how w. pass their time	WOMEN, 36
I have sung w. in three cities	WOMEN, 60
Monstrous Regiment of W.	WOMEN, 42
Most good w. are hidden treasures	WOMEN, 54
Most w. have no characters	WOMEN, 55
Most w. set out to try to change a man	CHANGE, 5
Music and w. I cannot but give way to	MUSIC, 33
Older w. are best	SEX, 16
proper function of w.	WOMEN, 29
several young w. . . . would render the Christian life intensely	
difficult	CHRISTIANITY, 31
souls of w. are so small	WOMEN, 19
the only advantage w. have over men – . . . they can cry	
	SEXES, 16
There are two kinds of w.	WOMEN, 56
The War between Men and W.	SEXES, 22
the w. come and go	WOMEN, 30
the w. whose eyes have been washed . . . with tears	
	WOMEN, 27
W. . . . are either better or worse than men	WOMEN, 43
W. are much more like each other	WOMEN, 22
w. become like their mothers	SEXES, 25
W. . . . care fifty times more for a marriage than a ministry	
	WOMEN, 12
w. dislike his books	WRITERS, 31
Were't not for gold and w.	SIN, 19
W. have served . . . as looking-glasses	WOMEN, 82
When w. go wrong	SEX, 52
Why are w. . . . so much more interesting to men	SEXES, 27
Why need . . . w. know so much	WOMEN, 18
w. . . . ill-using them and then confessing it	WOMEN, 73
with peaches and w., it's . . . the side next the sun that's	
tempting	TEMPTATION, 8
W. never have young minds	WOMEN, 25
w. . . . not so young as . . . painted	COSMETICS, 1
Wonderful w.! . . . how much we . . . owe to Shakespeare	
	SHAKESPEARE, 16
W. represent . . . matter over mind	SEXES, 26
w. require both	WOMEN, 20
w. should be struck . . . like gongs	WOMEN, 24
W. who love the same man	LOVE, 20
W. would rather be right than reasonable	WOMEN, 51
womman worthy w. al hir lyve	MARRIAGE, 32
won Human reason w. Mankind w.	VICTORY, 7
wonder knowledge and w. . . . is an impression of pleasure	
	KNOWLEDGE, 5; WONDER, 1
Many a man has been a w. to the world	ADMIRATION, 8
Philosophy is the product of w.	PHILOSOPHY, 14; WONDER, 4
the common w. of all men	INDIVIDUALITY, 3
wonderful It is a w. case of nature imitating art	ACTORS, 10
the ancient cathedrals – grand, w., mysterious	RELIGION, 46
wonders His w. to perform	GOD, 18
wondrous When I survey the w. Cross	HUMILITY, 12
wont seen me as he was w. to see me	PUNISHMENT, 14
wood about the dreadful w. Of conscious evil	GUILT, 2
would rather hew w. than be a king	MONARCHY, 6
woodcock well-shot w., partridge, snipe	HUNTING, 1
woodman W., spare that tree	TREES, 10
w. spare the beechen tree	TREES, 2

woods fresh w., and pastures new	CHANGE, 15
Spring Flow down the w.	SPRING, 5
The w. are lovely	TRAVEL, 10
the w. decay and fall	MORTALITY, 19
They shut the road through the w.	TIME, 21
We'll to the w. no more	ENDING, 4
When the green w. laugh	HAPPINESS, 5
woodshed Something nasty in the w.	EVIL, 9
woodworm the w. obligingly held hands	HUMOUR, 35
word better w. than prefabricated	WORDS, 6
but a w. and a blow	VIOLENCE, 2
Good isn't the w.!	CRITICISM, 14
Greeks had a W. for It	LANGUAGE, 1
in the beginning was the w.	WORDS, 1
in the captain's but a choleric w.	INJUSTICE, 11
Rehearsing a play is making the w. flesh	PLAYS, 9
the kingdom of God is not in w., but in power	GOD, 12
the W. had breath	CHRISTIANITY, 43
The w. is half Greek and half Latin	TELEVISION, 5
What is honour? A w.	HONOUR, 4
when *I* use a w.	MEANING, 3
words Be not the slave of W.	WORDS, 5
best w. in the best order	POETRY AND PROSE, 2
big emotions come from big w.	STYLE, 5
by skilful arrangement of your w.	WRITING, 11
Don't listen to their w. fix your attention on their deeds	
	SCIENTISTS, 5
Fine w. and an insinuating appearance	SERVILITY, 1
fine w. butter no parsnips	WORDS, 18
For w., like Nature, half reveal	WORDS, 19
I always try to get as many w.	VERBOSITY, 1
I put the w. down	WRITING, 35
It wasn't the w. That frightened the birds	INNUENDO, 1
learn the use of living w.	WORDS, 15
Men of few w. are the best	BREVITY, 8
my w. are my own	REPARTEE, 1
neither wit, nor w., nor worth	SPEECHES, 4
Thanks to w., we . . . rise above the brutes . . . sunk to the	
level of the demons	WORDS, 11
the barbarous, gothic times when w. had a meaning	WORDS, 9
The bitterest tears . . . for w. . . . unsaid and deeds . . . undone	
	REGRET, 19
to set a chime of w. tinkling in . . . a few fastidious people	
	PURPOSE, 7
uses his w. as a quack uses his remedies	VERBOSITY, 4
use the most common, . . . w.	LANGUAGE, 25
W. . . . , are great foes of reality	WORDS, 7
W. are like leaves	VERBOSITY, 6
W. are men's daughters	WORDS, 14
w. are the daughters of earth	LANGUAGE, 15
W. are . . . the most powerful drug	WORDS, 13
w. but wind	WORDS, 4
W. may be false and full of art	SPEECH, 14
w. never seen . . . before outside of a dictionary	POETS, 21
w. once spoke . . . never be recall'd	SPEECH, 13
You can stroke people with w.	WORDS, 8
Wordsworth Mr W. is never interrupted	INTERRUPTIONS, 3
W.'s healing power	POETS, 3
wore w. enough for modesty	CLOTHES, 1
work All w. and no play	WORK, 1
dignity in w.	WORK, 5
Every man's w. . . . is always a portrait of himself	ARTS, 1
For men must w., and women must weep	SEXES, 12
How can I take an interest in my w.	ENTHUSIASM, 1
if any would not w., neither should he eat	WORK, 4
I like w.; it fascinates me	IDLENESS, 6
it is poor grub, poor pay, and easy w.	AMERICA, 23;
	ENGLAND, 24
No, this right hand shall w. it all off	WRITING, 30
no w., nor device, nor knowledge . . . in the grave	
	TRANSIENCE, 6; WORK, 3
one must do some w. seriously . . . and not merely amuse	
oneself	WORK, 10
only place where success comes before w.	SUCCESS, 13;
	WORK, 21
prejudice against w.	CHANGE, 3
success . . . by dint of hard w.	EFFORT, 5; SUCCESS, 11
the w. comes out more beautiful	ARTS, 4
the world's w., . . . is done by men who do not feel . . . well	
	ILLNESS, 4
they must hate to w. for a living	MARRIAGE, 90
To sport would be as tedious as to w.	LEISURE, 3
W. banishes those three great evils	WORK, 23

W. . . . by those employees who have not yet reached . . .
incompetence INCOMPETENCE, 4
W. expands so as to fill the time WORK, 15
When w. is a pleasure WORK, 9
W. is much more fun than fun WORK, 7
W. is necessary for man WORK, 16
W. is the curse of the drinking classes WORK, 25
W. is the grand cure WORK, 6
you can't call yourself a great w. of nature INSULTS, 38
worker a sociable w. SOCIETY, 1
workers He is used to dealing with estate w. POLITICIANS, 24
hiring taxis . . . handing out redundancy notices to its own w.
INCOMPETENCE, 2
W. of the world, unite MARXISM, 3
working God as a w. hypothesis GOD, 14
No writer before the . . . 19th century wrote about the w.
classes CLASS, 35
The party is the rallying-point for the . . . w. class
COMMUNISM, 9
the w.-class which, raw and half-developed PUBLIC, 2
To the ordinary w. man, . . . Socialism SOCIALISM, 11
workman A bad w. RESPONSIBILITY, 1
works all his w. RENUNCIATION, 1
faith, if it hath not w., is dead FAITH, 7
more copies of my w. are left behind WRITERS, 3
they were judged every man according to their w. JUDGMENT, 4
W. done least rapidly PERFECTION, 3
workshop England . . . the w. of the world ENGLAND, 15
worktime the bustle of man's w. OPTIMISM, 17
world a citizen of the w. NATIONALITY, 8
A great writer creates a w. of his own WRITERS, 12
All's right with the w. PERFECTION, 2
all the uses of this w. WORLD-WEARINESS, 5
all the w. as my parish RELIGION, 61
All the w. is queer SUBJECTIVITY, 5
All the w. loves a lover LOVE, 2
All the w.'s a stage HUMAN CONDITION, 1
a man for whom the outside w. exists CHARACTER, 8
A man travels the w. over HOME, 6
as good be out of the w. FASHION, 2
a W. in a grain of sand WONDER, 2
brave new w. That has such people in't MANKIND, 27
chess-board is the w.; the pieces . . . the phenomena of the
universe GOD, 27
citizen of the w. COURTESY, 2
Dear W., I am leaving you because I am bored LAST WORDS, 53
dominate the w. INFLUENCE, 10
excellent foppery of the w. MISFORTUNE, 18
Germany will be . . . a w. power GERMANY, 4
glory, jest, and riddle of the w. HUMAN CONDITION, 12
God so loved the w. CHRISTIANITY, 13
good deed in a naughty w. GOOD, 15
Grant me paradise in this w. HEAVEN, 13
Had we but w. enough, and time SHYNESS, 4
he could not avoid making Him set the w. in motion
CREATION, 11
I am the light of the w. CHRISTIANITY, 14
I called the New W. into existence AMERICA, 1
If all the w. were paper NONSENSE, 1
If the w. were good for . . . speculation SPECULATION, 2
If you were the only girl in the w. LOVE, 62
I have . . . been all round the w. TRAVEL, 3
in mourning . . . for the w. MOURNING, 15
in this harsh w. MOURNING, 13
Into the dangerous w. I leapt BIRTH, 3
I . . . pass through this w. but once MORTALITY, 1
it's a jolly strange w. CONFUSION, 1
It's the same the whole w. over POVERTY AND WEALTH, 1
joy that a man is born into the w. BIRTH, 1
little sisters to all the w. WOMEN, 27
Looks the whole w. in the face RIGHTEOUSNESS, 7
Many a man has been a wonder to the w. ADMIRATION, 8
Never having been able to succeed in the w. ENVY, 8
One w. at a time AFTERLIFE, 10
Our country is the w. AMERICA, 14
queen for all the w. ROYALTY, 30
say to all the w. 'This was a man' CHARACTER, 20
Stop the W., I Want to Get Off WORLD-WEARINESS, 4
Superstition sets the whole w. in flames SUPERSTITION, 11
the greatest week in the history of the w. SPACE, 5
the hand that rules the w. INFLUENCE, 9
The wickedness of the w. VICE, 4
The w. is becoming like a lunatic asylum MADNESS, 7

The w. . . . is but a large prison EXECUTION, 23
The w. is but a school of inquiry CURIOSITY, 5
The w. is disgracefully managed COMPLAINTS, 2
The w. is everything that is the case LOGIC, 4
The w. is made of people who MEDIOCRITY, 2
The w. is made up for the most part of fools FOOLISHNESS, 11
The w. is too much with us WASTE, 3
the w. may talk of hereafter WAR, 29
the w. must be made safe for . . . fifty years WAR, 26
the w.'s mine oyster OPPORTUNITY, 15
the w., the flesh, and the devil JOURNALISM, 20; TEMPTATION, 5
the w. would not be the same NUCLEAR WEAPONS, 12
they only saved the w. HEROISM, 2
This is the way the w. ends ENDING, 3
this little w. ENGLAND, 34
This w. is very odd we see CONFUSION, 4
This w. nis but a thurghfare LIFE AND DEATH, 3
though the w. perish JUSTICE, 7
triple pillar of the w. LOVE, 109
turn your back upon the w. PERFECTION, 4
What a fine comedy this w. would be LIFE, 20
When all the w. dissolves DOOMSDAY, 5
When all the w. is young, lad YOUTH, 11
where in this small-talking w. MEANING, 4
which taketh away the sin of the w. CHRISTIANITY, 12
w., I count it . . . but an hospital WORLD, 1
wilderness of this w. WORLD, 2
w. is a comedy to those who think, a tragedy to those who feel
LIFE, 49
w. is charged with the grandeur of God GOD, 24
with how little wisdom the w. is governed GOVERNMENT, 20
w. . . . made safe for democracy DEMOCRACY, 18
w. will make a . . . path to his door FAME, 8
w. without end ETERNITY, 2
w. would go round . . . faster INTERFERING, 1
worldly The W. Hope men set their Hearts upon
TRANSIENCE, 13
worlds best of possible w. OPTIMISM, 27
So many w. ACTION, 12
Wandering between two w. LIMBO, 1
we live in the best of all possible w. OPTIMISM, 19; PESSIMISM, 3
worm a w. at one end and a fool at the other FISHING, 1
Even a w. will turn ENDURANCE, 1
The cut w. FORGIVENESS, 7
To tread by chance upon a w. DEATH, 86
worms Sir, you have tasted two whole w. SPOONERISMS, 5
w. have eaten them, but not for love LOVE AND DEATH, 6
wormwood her end is bitter as w. WOMEN, 16
worrying W. is the most natural and spontaneous of . . .
functions WORRY, 12
worse Defend the bad against the w. DECLINE, 3
Dublin, though . . . much w. than London PLACES, 7
for better for w. MARRIAGE, 27
If my books had been any w. CINEMA, 1
The w. I do, the more popular I get POPULARITY, 5
who ever knew Truth put to the w. TRUTH, 32
worship freedom . . . to w. HUMAN RIGHTS, 4
No one can w. God . . . on an empty stomach BUSINESS, 23
O w. the King GOD, 22
worshippers the one God whose w. . . . still trust in Him
LUCK, 7
worst His w. is better than any other person's best
WRITERS, 17
it was the w. of times FRENCH REVOLUTION, 1
They . . . like to be told the w. BRITISH, 6
we can say 'This is the w.' OPTIMISM, 22
w. kinde of infortune MISFORTUNE, 7
You do your w. WORLD WAR II, 10
worth A man's w. something CONFLICT, 5
If a job's w. doing EFFORT, 1
Paris is w. a mass PARIS, 2
The w. of a State STATE, 4
Whatever is w. doing EXCELLENCE, 1
W. seeing? yes IRELAND, 6
worthless a more w. set than Byron POETS, 25
Our parents' age . . . has produced us, more w. still AGE, 30
worthy is not w. to live SMOKING, 11
would He w., wouldn't he? DENIAL, 4
wound W. with a touch SATIRE, 2
wounds To fight and not to heed the w. SELFLESSNESS, 2
wrapped w. him in swaddling clothes CHRISTMAS, 7
wrapping perceive Christmas through its w. CHRISTMAS, 19

wrath He is trampling out the vintage where the grapes of w.
          GOD, 25
let not the sun go down upon your w.   PUNISHMENT, 1; SIN, 3
wreathe W. iron pokers into true-love knots   POETS, 10
wreckage Literature is strewn with the w. of men   WRITERS, 49
Wrekin His forest fleece the W. heaves   TREES, 4
Wren Sir Christopher W. Said   ARCHITECTURE, 1
wren Four Larks and a W.   APPEARANCE, 19
The w. goes to't   ANIMALISM, 7
wretch a w. who supports with insolence   PATRONAGE, 1
I w. lay wrestling with . . . my God   SOUL, 7
wretched love – all the w. cant of it   LOVE, 61
The only w. are the wise   IGNORANCE, 12
wretches feel what w. feel   HUMILITY, 10
Poor naked w.   WEATHER, 20
w. hang that jury-men may dine   JUSTICE, 19
wring they will soon *w.* their hands   WAR, 120
writ I never w., nor no man ever lov'd   LOVE, 118
write A man may w. at any time   PERSISTENCE, 6
as much as a man ought to w.   WRITING, 34
Better to w. for yourself   WRITING, 6
Do not on any account attempt to w. on both sides
          EXAMINATIONS, 2
he does not w. himself down   WRITERS, 18
I like to w. when I feel spiteful   WRITING, 19
look in thy heart and w.   INSPIRATION, 5
signing his name and forgetting to w. the letter   INSULTS, 4
w. and read comes by nature   LITERACY, 2
w. for children . . . as you do for adults   WRITING, 10
writer A great w. creates a world of his own   WRITERS, 12
Asking a working w. . . . about critics   CRITICS, 6
A w.'s ambition should be   POSTERITY, 6
Every great and original w.   WRITING, 37
it is necessary to go to a university . . . to become a successful
w.   WRITERS, 5
not a w.'s business to hold opinions   WRITERS, 50
No tears in the w.   WRITING, 8
protect the w.   BUREAUCRACY, 1
successful w. . . . is indistinguishable   AMERICA, 22
the w. . . . is the impregnator, . . . the reader . . . is the
respondent   READING, 19
writers American w. want to be . . . great   AMERICANS, 12
As w. become more numerous   READING, 5
Clear w., . . . do not seem so deep as they are   WRITING, 18
Creative w. are . . . greater than the causes . . . they represent
          WRITERS, 14
Irish w. – the ones that *think.*   IRISH, 3
No regime has ever loved great w.   WRITERS, 43
The only way for w. to meet   WRITERS, 11
W., like teeth, are divided into incisors and grinders
          WRITERS, 2
writes He w. as fast as they can read   WRITERS, 18
Moving Finger w.   DESTINY, 7
writhe Uriah, . . . made a ghastly w.   SERVILITY, 3
writhing Reeling and W.   EDUCATION, 9
writing All good w. is swimming under water   WRITING, 7
as I had in the w.   PLEASURE, 25
I wouldn't give up w. about God   WRITERS, 45
the disease of w. books   WRITING, 23
the incurable disease of w.   WRITING, 17
the worst . . . , is w. about w.   CRITICISM, 4
True ease in w. comes from art   WRITING, 26
w. an exact man   READING, 1
When a man is in doubt about . . . his w.   POSTERITY, 4
W. . . . is but a different name for conversation   WRITING, 31
W. is like getting married   MARRIAGE, 81; WRITING, 24
writings historians left blanks in their w.   HISTORIANS, 5
written Books are well w., or badly w.   BOOKS, 5
books . . . w. by people who don't understand them   BOOKS, 23
you would have been very glad if I had w. it   PLAYS, 6
wromantic Cavaliers (Wrong but W.)   HISTORY, 24
wrong A door is what a dog is . . . on the w. side of   DOGS, 10
A man should . . . own he has been in the w.   MISTAKES, 10
anxious to do the w. thing correctly   ETIQUETTE, 5
History is . . . the w. way of living   HISTORY, 9
Of course not . . . I may be w.   UNCERTAINTY, 1
orthodoxy . . . practically means being w.   ORTHODOXY, 2
our country, right or w.   PATRIOTISM, 7
responsible w.   RESPONSIBILITY, 5; RIGHTEOUSNESS, 6
right deed for the w. reason   MOTIVE, 2
sentimentality . . . rubs you up the w. way   SENTIMENTALITY, 4
something is impossible, he is . . . w.   SCIENCE, 5
something w. with our bloody ships   BOATS, 1

support me when I am . . . w.   SUPPORT, 4
their authors could not endure being w.   CRIME, 2
The multitude is always in the w.   PUBLIC, 17
The right divine of kings to govern w.   MONARCHY, 16
the unclouded face of truth suffer w.   JOURNALISM, 22
The w. war, at the w. place   WAR, 11
W. from the start   POETRY, 35
When women go w.   SEX, 52
Yes, once . . . I thought I had made a w. decision.   MISTAKES, 7
wrongdoing W. can only be avoided if those who are not
wronged feel the same indignation   VICE, 8
wronged Not to be w. is to forgo . . . goodness   INJUSTICE, 13
wrongs for one class to appreciate the w. of another   CLASS, 31
Two w. do not make a right   MISTAKES, 1

X

Xanadu In X. did Kubla Khan   PLEASURE, 8
X-ray to replace X. by hearsay   GOSSIP, 9

Y

yacht I had to sink my y. to make my guests go home
          PARTIES, 3
Yale all the young ladies who attended the Y. promenade dance
were laid end to end   SEX, 35
A whale ship was my Y. College   EDUCATION, 34
Yankee Y. Doodle came to town   AMERICA, 3; NURSERY
          RHYMES, 69
yard a y. . . . 3.37 inches longer than other people's   FRANCE, 3
yarn web of our life is of a mingled y.   GOOD AND EVIL, 4
yawn When a book is boring, they y. openly   BOOKS, 36
yawns grave y. for him   BORES, 7
year all the y. were playing holidays   LEISURE, 3
Another y.! – another deadly blow   DEFEAT, 9
each day is like a y.   IMPRISONMENT, 10
I said to the man who stood at the gate of the y.   FAITH, 11
Let it be kept till the ninth y.   PUBLISHING, 6
Not to hope for things to last for ever, is what the y. teaches
          TRANSIENCE, 15
That time of y. thou mayst in me behold   OLD AGE, 38
two months of every y.   WEATHER, 8
y.'s at the spring   PERFECTION, 2
yearning learning, earning and y.   LIFE, 35
years After long y.   SEPARATION, 2
he that cuts off twenty y. of life   DEATH, 97
how many y. can some people exist   FREEDOM, 10
I have been talking prose for over forty y.   PROSE, 3
It will keep for y.   LONGEVITY, 2
One thousand y. more. That's all *Homo sapiens* has
          MANKIND, 33
world must be made safe for . . . fifty y.   WAR, 26
Y. hence, perhaps, may dawn an age   FUTURE, 1
y. of discretion   AGE, 12
yes girls . . . say No when they mean Y.   WOMEN, 8
yesterday wiser to-day than . . . y.   MISTAKES, 10
yesterdays And all our y.   LIFE, 41
yesteryear snows of y.   NOSTALGIA, 22
yet A young man not y.   MARRIAGE, 13
but not y.   PROCRASTINATION, 4
My time has not y. come   POSTERITY, 9
yeti little in civilization to appeal to a Y.   CIVILIZATION, 7
yid put the id back in y.   JEWS, 12
yield To strive, to seek . . . and not to y.   DETERMINATION, 1
yo-ho-ho Y., and a bottle of rum!   ALCOHOL, 57
yoke good . . . that he bear the y. in his youth   YOUTH, 2
Rome's gross y. Drops off   INFLUENCE, 1
the inevitable y.   OLD AGE, 49
Yorick Alas, poor Y.   MOURNING, 10
York Oh! the grand old Duke of Y.   ARMY, 1
you For y. but not for me   DEATH, 15
young aged diplomats . . . bored than for y. men to die
          DIPLOMACY, 1
ale from the Country of the Y.   KNOWLEDGE, 35
All that the y. can do for the old   AGE, 53
a man of about a hundred and fifty who was rather y.   OLD
          AGE, 47
A man that is y. in years   AGE, 6
a sight to make an old man y.   BEAUTY, 37
can't put off being y. until you retire   MONEY, 27
country of y. men   AMERICA, 13
first sign of old age: . . . how y. the policemen look   AGE, 29
Grieve not that I die y.   DEATH, 56

Z

NAME INDEX

Potter, Stephen   ALCOHOL, 46, 47;
INATTENTION, 3; ONE-UPMANSHIP, 2, 3; SPORT
AND GAMES, 16; WORDS, 17
Pound, Ezra   AGE, 43; ARTS, 7; BOOKS, 27;
GENERALIZATIONS, 3; HISTORIANS, 5;
LITERATURE, 14, 15; POETRY, 35; TREES, 12;
WINTER, 4; WOMEN, 60
Powell, Anthony   CONCEIT, 13;
COUNTRYSIDE, 7; FAMILY, 33, 34; FOOD, 41;
NASTINESS, 6; NOVELS, 12; OLD AGE, 32; SELF,
12
Powell, Enoch   DIARIES, 4; POLITICIANS, 56,
57; PROPHECY, 8; RACE, 16
Powell, John   LAW, 21
Prescott, William   WAR, 86
Previn, André   MUSIC, 34
Priestley, J. B.   CHURCH, 4; CRITICS, 13;
DRINKS, 8; FOOTBALL, 5; GOD, 42; HUMOUR, 22;
INSULTS, 30; MARRIAGE, 86; MUSEUMS, 2;
PLAYS, 7; POLITICIANS, 58; WORLD WAR II, 25;
WRITERS, 35
Prior, Matthew   DOCTORS, 7; HOPE, 9;
IGNORANCE, 12
Pritchett, V. S.   NOVELS, 13
Procter, Adelaide Anne   MUSIC, 35
Proudhon, Pierre Joseph   CAPITALISM, 12
Proust, Marcel   ATHEISM, 9; DESIRE, 11;
IMPERFECTION, 10; LOVE, 97, 98; MANKIND, 20;
MEMORY, 11; NEUROSIS, 1, 2; OCCUPATIONS, 12;
PARTING, 9; REGRET, 10; REMEDIES, 10; SEX, 39;
SNOBBERY, 35; SORROW, 17, 18; SUN, 3
Pryce-Jones, David   BOREDOM, 7
Pudney, John Sleigh   IDEALISM, 5;
REALISM, 3
Pyke, Magnus   ECOLOGY, 6
Pyrrhus   VICTORY, 13
Quarles, Francis   PLAYS, 8; PLEASURE, 25
Queensberry, Duke of   RIVERS, 2
Quesnay, François   FREEDOM, 42
Quincy, Josiah   SEPARATION, 4
Rabelais, François   BORROWING, 7; DESIRE,
12; DESTINY, 16; FREEDOM, 43; LAST WORDS, 48,
49, 47; NATURE, 14; THIRST, 2
Rachmaninov, Sergei   MUSICIANS, 5
Racine, Jean   CRIME, 5; INNOCENCE, 2; LOVE
AND HATE, 4; LOVE, 99
Rae, John   WAR, 87
Raglan, Lord   PRACTICALITY, 5
Raleigh, Walter   AMBITION, 14; BOOKS, 28;
EXECUTION, 23, 24, 25; FAITH, 17; LAST WORDS,
50; LOVE, 100; MANKIND, 21
Raleigh, Walter Alexander   ETIQUETTE, 3
Ramanujan, Srinivasa   NUMBERS, 3
Raphael, Frederic   CAMBRIDGE, 4; FOOD, 42;
PHILOSOPHY, 10; SUBURBIA, 1
Rattigan, Terence   AUDIENCES, 4; CLASS,
26; SUICIDE, 4
Reade, Charles   WRITING, 27
Reagan, Ronald   AGE, 44; AMERICANS, 8;
ECONOMICS, 11; POLITICS, 52, 53; TAXATION, 8;
WORK, 27
Reed, Henry   BOOKS, 29; GIFTS, 5; WAR, 88,
89; WEAPONS, 4, 5
Reed, Rex   CINEMA, 7
Reedy, George Edward   SERVILITY, 6
Reich, Wilhelm   ABSTINENCE, 6
Reinhardt, Gottfried   MONEY, 35
Reith, Lord   THINKING, 5
Remarque, Erich Maria   WAR, 90
Renard, Jules   MODESTY, 5; PRIDE, 8;
WRITING, 28
Rendall, Montague John   PEACE, 15
Renoir, Pierre Auguste   ENDURANCE, 14;
PAINTING, 14
Revson, Charles   COSMETICS, 3
Rexford, Eben   OLD AGE, 33
Reynolds, Joshua   ARTISTS, 6; IMITATION, 4,
5; WORK, 18
Reynolds, Malvina   HOUSES, 4
Rhodes, Cecil   ENGLAND, 32; ENGLISH, 31;
LAST WORDS, 51; MISOGYNY, 2

Rhys, Jean   OLD AGE, 34; SEXES, 16; SUICIDE,
7; SUNDAY, 5
Rice, Grantland   SPORT AND GAMES, 17;
VICTORY, 14; WAR, 91
Rice, Stephen   IRELAND, 12
Rice-Davies, Mandy   DENIAL, 4
Richards, Gordon   PUNS, 19; TITLES, 8
Richards, I. A.   POETRY, 36
Richardson, Ralph   ACTING, 6, 7; SPEECH,
12
Richelieu, Cardinal   EXECUTION, 26
Richelieu, Duc de   ADULTERY, 5
Richler, Mordecai   JEWS, 11; POLITICS, 54;
WRITERS, 36
Richter, Jean Paul   EUROPE, 13
Ridge, William Pett   CHANCE, 5;
ETIQUETTE, 4
Rilke, Rainer Maria   CRITICISM, 39; DEATH,
90; IMMORTALITY, 5; SPRING, 4; TECHNOLOGY, 8
Rimsky-Korsakov, Nikolai   MUSIC, 36
Ripley, R. L.   BELIEF, 6
Rivarol, Antoine de   CRITICISM, 40
Rivera, Antonio   WAR, 92
Robbins, Tom   WATER, 7
Robespierre   CORRUPTION, 5
Robin, Leo   MATERIALISM, 17; MEMORY, 12
Robinson, Edwin Arlington   DEATH, 91
Robinson, James Harvey   SUBJECTIVITY, 7
Robinson, John   PORNOGRAPHY, 4; SEX, 40
Robinson, Robert   AMERICA, 27; TEETH, 3
Roche, Boyle   MIXED METAPHORS, 4
Rochefort, Marquis de   WRITING, 29
Rochefoucauld, Duc de la   ADVICE, 9;
AGREEMENT, 4; ARGUMENTS, 12; CONCEIT, 14;
EGOTISM, 7; EMOTION, 4; EVIL, 13; FRIENDS, 12;
HAPPINESS, 17; HOMESICKNESS, 5; HUMAN
NATURE, 16; HYPOCRISY, 13; IMPERFECTION, 11,
12; INTELLIGENCE, 5; JUDGMENT, 12; JUSTICE,
20; LOVE AND HATE, 5; LOVE, 101; LUCK, 11;
MISFORTUNE, 14; PRAISE, 6; SELF-INTEREST,
5; SILENCE, 10; SPONTANEITY, 4; SUCCESS, 2;
VIRTUE AND VICE, 2
Rogers, Samuel   BOOKS, 30; MARRIAGE, 87
Rogers, Will   COMMUNISM, 6; GOVERNMENT,
24; HEROISM, 6; HUMOUR, 23, 24; IRELAND, 13;
LYING, 14; POLITICIANS, 59; POLITICS, 55;
PROGRESS, 10; RESPECTABILITY, 4; SCULPTURE,
2
Roland, Madame   EXECUTION, 27;
FREEDOM, 44
Rolleston, Humphrey   DOCTORS, 8
Rolmaz, James   CLOTHES, 13
Roosevelt, Eleanor   DEMOCRACY, 12;
INFERIORITY, 5; OPPOSITION, 5;
UNDERSTANDING, 8
Roosevelt, Franklin D.   AGE, 45; AMERICA,
28; BOOKS, 31; CHARITY, 15; DEMOCRACY, 13;
EDUCATION, 43; FEAR, 10; HASTE, 9; HUMAN
RIGHTS, 4; IDEALISM, 6; INATTENTION, 4;
POLITICIANS, 60; POVERTY, 24; WAR, 93; WORLD
WAR II, 26, 27
Roosevelt, Theodore   EXPEDIENCY, 5;
JUSTICE, 21; LOYALTY, 8; PATRIOTISM, 24, 23;
POWER POLITICS, 9; ROYALTY, 25; WORK, 19
Rorem, Ned   MEDIOCRITY, 7
Roscommon, Earl of   PUBLIC, 17; SPEECH,
13
Rosebery, Earl of   BRITISH EMPIRE, 5;
BRITISH, 8; IRELAND, 14; POLITICS, 57
Ross, Alan Strode Campbell   CLASS, 27
Ross, Harold W.   CONFUSION, 7;
PHILISTINISM, 8
Rossetti, Christina   DEATH, 92;
ENDURANCE, 15; FAMILY, 35; MEMORY, 13, 14;
NOSTALGIA, 18; REST, 1; WEATHER, 17; WINTER,
5
Rossetti, Dante Gabriel   CRITICISM, 41;
DISAPPOINTMENT, 6; FAMILIARITY, 4; POETRY,
37
Rossini, Gioacchino   CRITICISM, 42; MUSIC,
37
Rostand, Edmond   APPEARANCE, 30

Rostand, Jean   KILLING, 7; MARRIAGE, 88, 89
Roth, Philip   JEWS, 12, 13
Rourke, M. E.   BEAUTY, 29
Rousseau, Jean Jacques   FREEDOM, 45;
MANKIND, 22
Routh, Martin Joseph   RESEARCH, 2
Rowe, Nicholas   INDIFFERENCE, 5
Rowland, Edward   FRANCE, 13
Rowland, Helen   LOVE, 102; MARRIAGE, 90;
MISTAKES, 12; REGRET, 11; TRUST, 4
Rowse, A. L.   ART, 21
Rubens, Paul Alfred   DISMISSAL, 7
Rubinstein, Arthur   MUSICIANS, 6
Rubinstein, Helena   AGE, 46; BEAUTY, 30
Runcie, Robert   TACT, 5
Runciman, Steven   RELIGION, 45
Runyon, Damon   APPEARANCES, 17;
ARISTOCRACY, 11; BEAUTY, 31; EVIL, 14; GREED,
8; INNOVATION, 2; LAST WORDS, 52; MONEY, 36;
PARASITES, 2; SIN, 18; SUICIDE, 8
Ruskin, John   ARCHITECTURE, 8, 9; ART, 22,
23; ARTISTS, 7; BEAUTY, 32; BOOKS, 32, 33, 34;
COMMUNICATION, 4; CRITICISM, 43; FREEDOM,
46; HONESTY, 6; MOUNTAINS, 3; POETRY, 38;
POVERTY AND WEALTH, 6
Russell, Bertrand   ABSTINENCE, 7;
AMERICA, 29; ARGUMENTS, 13; BIBLE, 7;
CLOTHES, 14; DOUBT, 7; DRUNKENNESS, 17;
EQUALITY, 16; FAME, 18; GOSSIP, 8; HAPPINESS,
18, 19; HATE, 7; HUMAN CONDITION, 13; LOVE,
103, 104; MATHEMATICS, 10, 11, 12, 13, 14;
MEMORIALS, 9; MODESTY, 4; MORALITY, 12;
NUCLEAR WEAPONS, 14; PATRIOTISM, 25;
PHILOSOPHERS, 7; PHILOSOPHY, 11; POLITICS,
58; POWER, 15; PROGRESS, 11; PRUDERY, 4;
RACE, 17; READING, 13; SCEPTICISM, 4;
SOCIETY, 5; THINKING, 6, 7; UNCERTAINTY, 3;
WORK, 20
Russell, George William   DRUNKENNESS,
18
Russell, Lord John   FAMILY, 36; SAYINGS, 6
Russell, William Howard   WAR, 94
Rutherford, Ernest   RESEARCH, 3
Ryle, Gilbert   MIND, 6; MYTHS, 2;
PHILOSOPHY, 12
Sackville-West, Vita   CAMPING, 1; HEAVEN,
8; SPRING, 5; TRAVEL, 22; WRITERS, 37
Sade, Marquis de   MORALITY, 13
Sagan, Françoise   LOVE, 105
Sahl, Mort   TRUST, 5
Saint-Exupéry, Antoine de   PROGRESS, 12;
RESPONSIBILITY, 1; SORROW, 19; WAR, 95
Saintsbury, George Edward Bateman
ALCOHOL, 48
Saki   ADDRESSES, 1; AGE, 47; ALCOHOL, 49, 50;
BEAUTY, 33; CHARACTER, 17; CLOTHES, 15;
DECLINE, 9; EDUCATION, 44; ETIQUETTE, 5;
EUROPE, 14; EXCESS, 6; EXTRAVAGANCE, 14;
FISH, 2; HUMOUR, 51; MARRIAGE, 91; PLACES,
15; QUOTATIONS, 10; SELFLESSNESS, 3;
SORROW, 20; SUFFERING, 10; SUPERIORITY, 11;
WRITERS, 38, 39
Salinger, J. D.   ACTORS, 8; SEX, 41
Salisbury, Marquess of   EUROPE, 15;
NEWSPAPERS, 10
Salk, Jonas E.   DISCOVERY, 7
Sallust   FRIENDSHIP, 24
Salvandy, Comte de   REVOLUTION, 5
Sampson, Anthony   TITLES, 9
Samuel, Herbert   BOOKS, 35; BUREAUCRACY,
6; GOVERNMENT, 25; HOUSES OF PARLIAMENT,
15; MARRIAGE, 92; MORALITY, 14; SAYINGS, 7
Sand, George   HAPPINESS, 20; LOVE, 106
Sandburg, Carl   WAR, 96
Sanders, George   LAST WORDS, 53
Santayana, George   AGE, 48; BIBLE, 8;
BREVITY, 6; BUREAUCRACY, 7; ENGLAND, 33;
FASHION, 5; HAPPINESS, 21; HISTORY, 21;
HUMILITY, 8; LIFE AND DEATH, 9; LIFE, 39;
PHILOSOPHERS, 8; PHILOSOPHY, 13; SCIENCE,
31; WISDOM, 19
Sarasate, Pablo   GENIUS, 7

Smollett, Tobias ENGLISH, 33; MEN, 8; PATRIOTISM, 27; WISDOM, 20; WRITERS, 42
Smythe, Tony CENSORSHIP, 2
Snow, C. P. NASTINESS, 8; POWER, 17; PROMISES, 6
Snowden, Philip GOVERNMENT, 27
Socrates GOD, 44; GOOD, 16; LAST WORDS, 58; LUXURY, 4; NATIONALITY, 8; SELF, 14
Solon LAW, 26; VICE, 8
Solzhenitsyn, Alexander COMMUNISM, 7; DEATH, 110; FREEDOM, 48; IMPRISONMENT, 5; INDOCTRINATION, 1, 2; LOVE, 123; LYING, 15; POWER, 18; RESPONSIBILITY, 12; TRUTH, 38; WRITERS, 43
Sondheim, Stephen CLOWNS, 2; PERFECTION, 7
Sontag, Susan ILLNESS, 13; PHOTOGRAPHY, 6
Sophocles SEX, 44; THEATRE, 10
Sousa, John Philip MUSIC, 44
Southey, Robert CURSES, 2; GOD, 45; OLD AGE, 40; VICTORY, 8; YOUTH, 17
Spaak, Paul Henri AGREEMENT, 6
Spark, Muriel AGE, 55; ALCOHOL, 56; APPEARANCE, 33; CHILDREN, 34; COMMUNISM, 8; EDUCATION, 52; EXCELLENCE, 4; FASCISM, 4; IMPORTANCE, 3; IMPRESSIONABILITY, 3; INTELLECTUALS, 8; OLD AGE, 41
Sparrow, John DOGS, 12
Speight, Johnny INSULTS, 33; POLITICS, 60; PORNOGRAPHY, 5; STRIKES, 4
Spencer, Herbert POLITICS, 61; SPORT AND GAMES, 18
Spencer, Stanley LAST WORDS, 59
Spender, Stephen POETS, 24; TECHNOLOGY, 9; WAR, 110
Spenser, Edmund AMBITION, 17; DEATH, 111; RIVERS, 4
Spiel, Hilde NASTINESS, 9
Spinoza, Benedict DESIRE, 15; IMMORTALITY, 6; SOCIETY, 8; UNDERSTANDING, 9
Spock, Dr Benjamin WAR, 111
Spring-Rice, Cecil Arthur ACADEMICS, 5
Spyri, Johanna ANGER, 6; DISAPPOINTMENT, 7
Squire, John Collings APPEARANCE, 34; DRUNKENNESS, 19; SCIENTISTS, 9
Stacpoole, H. de Vere HOMESICKNESS, 7
Stalin, Joseph CATHOLICISM, 10; COMMUNISM, 9; POLITICS, 62; STATE, 5; STATISTICS, 9
Stanley, Henry Morton GREETINGS, 3
Stanton, C. E. GREETINGS, 4
Stanton, Elizabeth CLASS, 31; FEMINISM, 23, 24, 25; RELIGION, 46; WOMEN, 66
Stanton, Frank L. BABIES, 5
Stapledon, Olaf AMERICANS, 10
Stark, John WAR, 112
Stead, Christina SELF-MADE MEN, 3
Steel, David POLITICIANS, 66; POLITICS, 63, 64, 65
Steele, Richard MARRIAGE, 101; READING, 15
Steffens, Lincoln FUTURE, 6
Stein, Gertrude AMERICA, 30; CONCEIT, 15, 16; NORMALITY, 1; WAR, 113
Steinbeck, John ADVICE, 11; INSULTS, 34; MANKIND, 29
Stekel, Wilhelm AGE, 56
Stendhal LITERATURE, 14; NOVELS, 15
Stephens, James AGE, 57; CURIOSITY, 7; PERFECTION, 8
Stern, Richard G. SIMPLICITY, 5
Sterne, Laurence BITTERNESS, 3; FAMILY, 39; FRANCE, 14; RELIGION, 47; SOUL, 11; STUBBORNNESS, 3; TOLERANCE, 6; TRAVEL, 23; WISDOM, 21; WRITING, 31
Stevas, Norman St John SNOBBERY, 6

Stevenson, Adlai COMPLIMENTS, 6; DISAPPOINTMENT, 8; EDITORS, 3; ENDURANCE, 19; FLATTERY, 8; FREEDOM, 49; LYING, 16; NUCLEAR WEAPONS, 15; POLITICIANS, 67, 68; POLITICS, 66; POWER, 19; SUCCESS, 14
Stevenson, Robert Louis ABSTINENCE, 8; ALCOHOL, 57; ANTICIPATION, 7; BOOKS, 39; CONCEIT, 17; DEATH, 112; DREAMS, 12; EXCESS, 13; HAPPINESS, 24; IMITATION, 6; MARRIAGE, 102, 103, 104, 105; MONEY, 43; MORALITY, 20; MORTALITY, 18; POLITICS, 67; SEXES, 18; SILENCE, 14; THEORY, 7; TRAVEL, 24, 25; TRIVIALITY, 13; WISDOM AND FOOLISHNESS, 6
Stocks, Mary HOUSES OF PARLIAMENT, 17
Stockwood, Mervyn PSYCHIATRY, 9
Stoddard, Elizabeth Drew LOVE, 124
Stone, I. F. LONGEVITY, 3
Stone, Samuel J. CHRISTIANITY, 40
Stoppard, Tom ART, 25; ARTISTS, 9; CRITICS, 14; DEMOCRACY, 15; ETERNITY, 4; HOUSES OF PARLIAMENT, 18; JOURNALISM, 23, 24; JUSTICE, 23; LIFE, 44; POLITICS, 68; QUOTATIONS, 12; RESPONSIBILITY, 13; THEATRE, 11; WAR, 114
Stout, Rex Todhunter AMERICA, 31; STATISTICS, 10
Stowe, Harriet Beecher CREATION, 12; CRUELTY, 5; INSPIRATION, 6; REGRET, 19
Strachey, John St Loe CATHOLICISM, 11; FASCISM, 5
Strachey, Lytton GOD, 46; LAST WORDS, 60; PURPOSE, 8; ROYALTY, 31
Stratton, Eugene LOVE, 125
Stravinsky, Igor COMPOSERS, 5, 6; CRITICS, 15; HASTE, 14; MUSIC, 45, 46; MUSICIANS, 9
Streatfield, Geoffrey FACTS, 3; STATISTICS, 11
Strindberg, August DOGS, 13
Sullivan, Annie ADVICE, 12; LANGUAGE, 21; SENTIMENTALITY, 5
Sully, Duc de ENGLAND, 36
Svevo, Italo WOMEN, 67
Swaffer, Hannen JOURNALISM, 25
Swift, Jonathan BUSINESS, 18; CLERGY, 11; COMPOSERS, 7; COURAGE, 17; DECLINE, 10; ENGLISH, 34; FLATTERY, 9; FOOLISHNESS, 19; GENIUS, 8; LAST WORDS, 61; LAW, 27; MARRIAGE, 106, 107; OPINIONS, 4; PARASITES, 3; POLITICIANS, 69; PROMISES, 7; REGRET, 20; SATIRE, 3; TAXATION, 10; WAR, 115; WEALTH, 27
Swinburne, Algernon Charles MANKIND, 30; PEACE, 16; SPRING, 6
Sylvester, Robert BOOKS, 40
Symonds, John Addington KNOWLEDGE, 32
Symons, Arthur MEMORY, 18
Synge, John Millington LOSS, 6
Syrus, Publilius NECESSITY, 7; PROMPTNESS, 4
Szasz, Thomas FORGIVENESS, 15; HAPPINESS, 25; MADNESS, 12; MEDICINE, 7; MOTIVE, 6; PSYCHIATRY, 10; RIGHT, 2; SEX, 45, 46
Szent-Györgyi, Albert DISCOVERY, 8
Taber, Robert WAR, 116
Tabrar, Joseph DOGS, 14
Tacitus FAME, 19; HUMAN NATURE, 18; WAR, 117
Taft, William Howard DEFEAT, 7
Taine, Hippolyte Adolphe VIRTUE AND VICE, 3
Talleyrand AMERICA, 32; CHRISTIANITY, 41; DEFEAT, 8; FIRST IMPRESSIONS, 7; GOVERNMENT, 28; MODERATION, 4; SPEECH, 15
Tarkington, Booth ALCOHOL, 58
Tate, Allen DEATH, 113
Tate, Nahum CHANGE, 17; CHRISTMAS, 17; THIRST, 3
Taupin, Bernie ACTORS, 9
Tawney, R. H. POVERTY AND WEALTH, 8

Taylor, A. J. P. CAPITALISM, 14; COMMUNISM, 10; ENGLAND, 37; EXPERIENCE, 18; HISTORY, 30; HITLER, 5; OLD AGE, 42; POWER, 20
Taylor, Bert Leston BORES, 5
Taylor, Elizabeth PATIENCE, 13
Taylor, Jane STARS, 4
Taylor, Jeremy LIFE, 45; MARRIAGE, 108
Taylor, John CLOTHES, 17
Tebbitt, Norman POLITICIANS, 70; UNEMPLOYMENT, 1
Temple, Frederick CLERGY, 12; LUCK, 12
Temple, William CHRISTIANITY, 42; CHURCH, 5; CRICKET, 6; GOD, 47; HUMAN NATURE, 19; RELIGION, 48; SELF-CONFIDENCE, 5
Templeman, Mr Justice LAWYERS, 8
Tenniel, John DISMISSAL, 9
Tennyson, Alfred, Lord ACTION, 12; AFTERLIFE, 9; ARISTOCRACY, 12; ARTHURIAN LEGEND, 2, 3; BEAUTY, 37, 38; CHANGE, 18; CHIVALRY, 11; CHRISTIANITY, 43; CLERGY, 13; CONSTANCY, 4; COURAGE, 18, 19; CURSES, 3, 4; DEATH, 114; DECLINE, 11; DESTINY, 20, 21; DETERMINATION, 14; DREAMS, 13; DUTY, 5; ENDING, 7; ENEMIES, 8; EXCESS, 14; EXPERIENCE, 19, 20; HUMAN CONDITION, 18; HYPOCRISY, 15; INTEGRITY, 7; INVITATIONS, 2; IRREVOCABILITY, 2; LEARNING, 9; LIFE AND DEATH, 11; LIFE, 46; LOVE, 126, 127, 128, 129, 130; LYING, 17; MARRIAGE, 109; MARTYRDOM, 4; MERRYMAKING, 5; MORTALITY, 19; MOURNING, 16; MUSIC, 47; NATURE, 15; NOSTALGIA, 19, 20, 21; OBEDIENCE, 4; PASSION, 8; POLITICS, 69; PRAYER, 16; PURITY, 3; RESPONSIBILITY, 14; RIVERS, 5; ROYALTY, 32; SEXES, 19, 20; SLEEP, 14; SORROW, 24, 25, 26; SPRING, 7; SUICIDE, 11; SUMMER, 7; TIME, 33; TRANSIENCE, 18; TRIVIALITY, 14; UNFAITHFULNESS, 4; WEATHER, 26; WOMEN, 68, 69; WORDS, 19
Terence COURAGE, 20; MANKIND, 31; OPINIONS, 5; ORIGINALITY, 5
Teresa, Mother CHARITY, 20; FAMILY, 40; LONELINESS, 7; POVERTY, 28
Teresa of Avila, St RELIGION, 49
Terry, Ellen ACTING, 8; DIARIES, 5; FUNERALS, 9; SHAKESPEARE, 16
Tertullian BELIEF, 7; CHRISTIANITY, 44, 45
Thackeray, William Makepeace FAITH, 18; FAMILY, 41; GREATNESS, 14; LOVE, 131; MARRIAGE, 110, 111; MONEY, 44; NEWSPAPERS, 11; SINCERITY, 7; SEXES, 21; SNOBBERY, 7, 8; WISDOM, 22
Thales LIFE AND DEATH, 12
Thatcher, Denis FEMINISM, 40; HOUSEWORK, 5
Thatcher, Margaret ARGUMENTS, 14; AUTHORITARIANISM, 6, 7; CHARACTER, 22; CLASS, 32; COMMITMENT, 5; FEMINISM, 39; IDEALISM, 7; IDLENESS, 8; IMPERFECTION, 13; INFLEXIBILITY, 3; MARXISM, 4; MERIT, 7; MONEY, 45; MORALITY, 21; PEACE, 17; POLITICIANS, 71, 72; POLITICS, 70, 71, 72; SELF-CONFIDENCE, 6; SOCIALISM, 13; TALENT, 6; WORK, 22; YOUTH, 18
Thayer, W. M. ACHIEVEMENT, 6
Themistocles INFLUENCE, 8
Theodoric LOYALTY, 9
Theroux, Paul CLASS, 33; LANGUAGE, 22; MOUNTAINS, 4; PLACES, 19; SWITZERLAND, 4
Thiers, Louis Adolphe MONARCHY, 22; PERSPECTIVE, 4; SNOBBERY, 9
Thomas, Brandon PLACES, 20
Thomas, Dylan AGRICULTURE, 5; APPEARANCE, 35; BORES, 6; CLEANNESS, 2; DEATH, 115, 116, 117; EMOTION, 5; EXPECTATION, 5; INNOCENCE, 9; LIFE, 47; LONELINESS, 8; MARRIAGE, 112; MUSIC, 48; OLD AGE, 43; OPPORTUNITY, 16; PAINTING, 5; POETRY, 47; PUBLIC HOUSES, 4; RELIGION, 50; SEX, 47; SIGNATURES, 3; WALES, 2, 3; WINTER, 7
Thomas, Edward DEATH, 118; ENGLAND, 38; PAST, 7; WALES, 4; WAR, 118